THE
COMPLETE BOOK
OF FOOD AND
NUTRITION

THE
COMPLETE BOOK
OF FOOD AND
NUTRITION

J. I. RODALE
Editor-in-Chief

RUTH ADAMS
Editor

Charles Gerras
Assistant Editor

John Haberern
Assistant Editor

RODALE BOOKS, INC.
Emmaus, Pennsylvania

STANDARD BOOK NUMBER 87596-020-0

COPYRIGHT MCMLXI BY J. I. RODALE

ALL RIGHTS RESERVED

PRINTED IN THE UNITED STATES

NINTH PRINTING — FEBRUARY, 1972

H-160

CONTENTS

BOOK ONE

SECTION 1

Beverages

SECTION 2

Bread

SECTION 3

Cereals

SECTION 4

Dairy Products

[v]

BOOK TWO

SECTION 13

Natural and Organic Foods

[x]

INTRODUCTION

THE HEALTH-CONSCIOUS person of today, seeking information on diet which will guarantee him the best possible health and protect him against nutritional deficiencies, has almost nowhere to turn in the official literature that is available to him. Government publications reflect the thinking of our most conservative food researchers—"eat a good, well-rounded diet and you will be well nourished," they say.

A hundred years ago, such advice was sound. Our grandparents who had access to wholesome meats, eggs, fresh fruits and vegetables the year round, cereals grown on their own farms with organic manures and dairy products fresh from healthy farm animals were probably as well nourished as anyone could be. What little sugar they used, sweetened stewed or canned fruits. Soft drinks, commercially made candy and bakery products were all but unknown. Ice cream was a delicacy to be enjoyed once or twice a year. There was little danger of overeating on sweets and starches. Even in poor families where protein foods were expensive and scarce, the hard manual labor demanded of men, women and children alike assured them that foods would not be stored as fat, but would be worked off in the energetic bodily exercise involved in chopping wood, driving teams of horses, walking miles to schools or stores, hand-laundering clothes, ploughing fields with hand ploughs, threshing grain and the other work which is almost completely unknown to today's Americans.

Most of us eat far more in terms of calories than we should, even if we do take some exercise to "work it off." Most of us never bother with the exercise, but spend our lives sitting or driving in cars and wondering why we put on weight. We eat too much because today's food has been so denatured that we do not know when we are eating too much. The child who has had so many sodas or so much candy during the day that he refuses to eat dinner has had too much to eat—too much of the wrong kind of food. The consumption of white sugar in our country today has risen to considerably more than 100 pounds a year per person. In grandfather's time it was about 48 pounds. White sugar provides empty calories—nothing more. Foods containing it take the place of good, nutritious foods, when one does not know how to eat healthfully.

Meats and dairy products today are loaded with chemicals, drugs, hormones, preservatives—all of them unknown a hundred years ago. Cereals are refined to the point where they bear little resemblance to food. Fresh fruits and vegetables, now available the year round almost everywhere, are contaminated with insecticides, preservatives, waxes, dyes, and scores of other chemicals unknown in former times.

A large percentage of today's fats have also been denatured— treated with bleaches and hydrogenated, so that the valuable fatty acids they originally contained have been changed into quite different chemical compounds, that may be extremely dangerous to human health. Perhaps the worst feature of modern food is its convenience. For, as preparation of foods becomes more and more convenient, the quality of the food decreases and its content of chemicals increases. Prepared mixes, prepared and cooked frozen foods, fruit juice powders, and the thousand and one variations on these themes bring onto American dinner tables such an array of chemicals and synthetic foods that we wonder how anyone survives!

Meanwhile, the figures for heart disease and cancer climb steadily. Diseases unknown a hundred years ago or even 25 years ago are now so prevalent that foundations have been established to study them. There can be no doubt that the food the average American eats is largely responsible for the terrifying rate of degenerative disease. We know that many of the chemicals now being used in or on food may be cancer-causing. We know that denatured fats and the empty calories of white sugar have a certain relation to heart and blood vessel disease.

We know that there are almost a thousand chemicals at present being used in food and many of them have never been tested for possible toxicity. The number of these chemicals increases daily.

So the old-fashioned rule "eat a good, well-rounded diet" is not enough today to guide the average housewife and mother through the glittering aisles of the super market, where brightly-dyed foods compete for her attention with the glistening plastic wraps and the gaudy labels on cans and bottles. Nor is it enough today just to eat the best possible diet, nutritionally speaking.

You must, in addition, make up for the serious deficiencies in our food by taking food supplements. They help, too, to protect you against the many poisons to which you are continually exposed—in water, air, food and other aspects of life.

In this book you can read what PREVENTION magazine stands for so far as food is concerned. We have covered individually as many foods as we had room to cover, devoting more or less space to them depending upon how much there was to say about the particular place of each food in our diets. We have not endeavored to cover every single variety of every food (beans, for instance), but what we say about one variety is, in general, true for others.

You will find some surprising things here, some things which you may challenge. We do not base our conclusions about food on any-one else's theories but our own. Our theories are the result of years of research and observation which we have done for our health magazine PREVENTION. Much of this material appeared in PREVENTION.

In addition to information about food, you will find a wealth of information about nutrition here. We have assembled facts from medical and scientific journals from all over the world to defend our position, which is that America must awaken, before it is too late, to the absolute necessity of returning to unprocessed, unchemicalized food; the necessity for avoiding foods poisoned with insecticides and chemicals, the necessity for fortifying diets with food supplements.

We hope you will agree with us when you finish this book.

J. I. RODALE, *Editor*

Assistant Editors
Ruth C. Adams
Charles Gerras
John Haberern

BOOK ONE

The Complete Book of

FOOD and NUTRITION

SECTION 1.

Beverages

America's favorite drinks, coffee and sodas, are probably the worst things one can drink, nutritionally speaking, except for alcoholic beverages. Milk and citrus juices, though they have their drawbacks, are certainly far better beverages. Best choices are spring or well water and many kinds of herb teas. Most important, supervise the beverages your children drink, for they are urged on every side, by advertising, to drink dangerously.

CHAPTER 1

The History of Coffee

A little tree, about 12 to 20 feet high, garlanded with waxy white blossoms and later with red berries about the size of a small cherry—such is the coffee tree, a profitable and flourishing member of the madder family, botanically speaking. Inside the berries grow two small beans packed tight and pressed together so that one side of each is flat. These are the coffee berries which, when properly processed, give us the fragrant brew as American as hamburgers and apple pie a la mode, the brew served hot and strong as demitasse in drawing rooms, the brew slopped over into the saucer in a greasy spoon restaurant, where it goes by the name of "draw one."

The original coffee tree probably grew in Ethiopia. Culture of the tree spread to Arabia in the seventeenth century or so, from there to India, Ceylon and Java. It was not until the eighteenth century that coffee was introduced into Brazil which today produces approximately more coffee than all the rest of the world together.

Coffee Discovered

The first mention that can be found of coffee in literature was about 99 A.D. when an Arab physician discoursed on it. The berries were first used as food—ground finely and mixed with fat. Later the coffee berries were made into wine. Then they were used as medicine. Their use as a beverage dates back about seven hundred years. Legend has it that a herd of goats first discovered the pleasures of coffee-imbibing. Grazing on a hillside in Arabia, the goats belonging to a Mohammedan monastery ate some berries from the coffee tree and spent the night dancing instead of going to bed. One of the monks brewed up a concoction of the berries with some hot water and himself spent the night without sleeping, although there is no record that he danced.

Coffee as a beverage was introduced into Turkey from Arabia and coffee houses sprang up in Turkey about 1554. The story goes that when the Turks besieged Vienna in the seventeenth century and were driven out, they left behind 500 bags of coffee which became the basis for a whole new business and pastime in Vienna. The first London coffee house was opened in 1652 and coffee was introduced to America in 1668. France, Germany and England took up the new fad rapidly. Coffee houses became almost as great a nuisance as later saloons. Way back in the seventeenth century employers in London were complaining about the amount of time folks spent in coffee houses, "Many a promising gentleman and merchant, who had previously been a trustworthy person . . . will spend 3 or 4 hours in a coffee house to converse with friends. These friends bring other friends,

[5]

and thus many a worthy man is kept away from his occupation for 6 or even 8 hours."

The word coffee comes, it is believed, from the word qahwah, or, in Turkish, *kahveh,* which originally meant "wine" in Arabic. It is believed that the word was first used when coffee became a substitute for the wine which is forbidden by the Koran in Mohammedan countries.

Processing the Coffee Bean

Today the coffee that we drink is roasted. The green berries themselves have little odor and a most unpleasant taste. Roasting coffee was first thought of in the thirteenth century. The bean is gathered and spread in the sun to dry for about 3 weeks. The roasting is done at a very high temperature and different processes are used, according to what kind of coffee you want. There are, in the coffee-roasting trade, about 8 different "roasts"—light, cinnamon, medium, high, city, full city, French and Italian. As you might assume these get progressively darker in shade, "City" coffee is quite dark. "Full City" is even darker, French coffee darker yet and Italian coffee almost burned. Generally, green coffee beans are exported from the country of origin and roasted in the country where they will be sold. In this country coffee is generally roasted for about 16 to 17 minutes. Preference for different "roasts" is indicated in different parts of the country. On the west coast coffee is fairly "light." In the eastern part of the country it is medium, while residents of the south prefer the darkest roasts. When we speak of a coffee "blend," we mean the mixture of coffees from different countries, each of which has its own characteristic taste.

It is known that the roasting of coffee produces very significant chemical changes in the coffee bean. Of course, cooking any food does this, and the higher the temperature the more profound are the changes produced. We do not know as yet all of the chemical ingredients of coffee. We do know that roasting drives off the water and develops the oils which give coffee its characteristic odor and taste. Most important of these oils is caffeol. Caffeol is lost rapidly from coffee once it is ground, so that ground coffee which has stood for any length of time exposed to the air becomes flat and eventually rancid. Grinding your own coffee immediately before you brew it will naturally give the best results. But today's process of vacuum-packing ground coffee preserves most of the flavor. It is best, however, to keep coffee always in airtight containers and to use it rapidly once it has been exposed to air.

What Coffee Contains

One cup of coffee contains about 100 to 120 milligrams of caffeine. This is what is known as an alkaloid. Our medical dictionary defines the word "alkaloid" as a compound containing nitrogen which occurs in plants and has the power of combining with acids to form salts. Alkaloids are usually the most active part of the plant, chemically speaking, and hence are often used as medicine. It is the caffeine in coffee that begins to worry most coffee drinkers about the time they pour out their sixth or seventh cup. But there is another alkaloid in coffee, too. This is tannin, the same

[6]

substance which appears in tea. Apparently tannin should be reckoned with, too, in computing the possible harm to health that may result from too much coffee-drinking. The longer the coffee stands brewing, the more tannin is deposited in the brown fluid you pour into your cup. So boiled coffee which has been standing on the stove—grounds and all—will be likely to do most damage from the point of view of health. Caffeine is tasteless. It is the caffeol not the caffeine which gives the pleasant coffee aroma. So the caffeine can be removed from coffee without spoiling its taste.

Coffee has no food value, with the possible exception of a very small amount of several B vitamins. In a test reported by L. J. Teply, W. A. Krehl and C. A. Elvehjem in the *Archives of Biochemistry*, Vol. 6, p. 139, 1945, roasted coffee was found to contain about 10 milligrams of niacin per hundred grams. When coffee was fed to animals which were already deficient in niacin, a further and more serious condition developed. They were found to be deficient, then, in biotin, another B vitamin. Animals who were fed 5 to 10 per cent finely ground roasted coffee developed an eye condition, which disappeared when they were fed inositol, which is still another B vitamin. Normal animals which were fed 5 to 15 per cent roasted coffee with their meals had stunted growth and, in some cases, loss of hair. The other constituents of coffee from the nutritional angle are:

in one gram— .84 milligrams of sodium
31.0 milligrams of potassium
10. micrograms of thiamin (a B vitamin)
3. micrograms of riboflavin
(another B vitamin)

Decaffeinated coffee has about 95 per cent of the caffeine removed. It tastes good but does not give the stimulating effect of real coffee. Several interesting experiments have been done to decide once and for all whether or not drinking de-caffeinated coffee at night will bring restful sleep to those who believe that real coffee keeps them awake. It was found in general that, regardless of what actually was in the cup, those who *thought* they were drinking real coffee stayed awake. Those who *thought* they had de-caffeinated coffee went blissfully to sleep. However, this does not alter the fact that caffeine has a very definite stimulating effect on the human body. Instant coffee, so far as we can determine, from correspondence with many coffee companies, contains nothing but coffee, very finely pulverized and concentrated. Coffee substitutes, on the other hand, may be made of roasted cereal grains, which, we imagine, do not have a flavor that approaches the coffee flavor.

How to Make Coffee

It is generally agreed by coffee experts that the best way to make coffee is that way by which the coffee is in contact with the hot water for the least possible time. Therefore, drip or vacuum coffee pots appear to be preferable to percolators or the old-fashioned pot in which the coffee boiled. In fact, experts are unanimous in agreeing that coffee boiled is coffee spoiled. Percolated coffee contains slightly more caffeine than drip or vacuum-made

[7]

coffee. And boiled coffee contains the most caffeine of all. However, if you must make coffee by the boiling method, add the coffee after the water has boiled and let it steep for only two or three minutes. Drink immediately. Freshly made coffee is infinitely preferable to warmed-over coffee—and not just because it tastes better. When the coffee stands, the oil, which is irritating to the body, separates in the coffee and cannot be reunited by merely heating the coffee again.

The taste of coffee depends on how much of the soluble solids you dissolve out of the ground bean by whatever way you make your coffee. Many people enjoy the flavor of chicory added to coffee. Chicory is a plant, the wild endive, which grows profusely in most parts of the country. Dried and pulverized, it is a black powder, very much like finely ground coffee. A little chicory added to a pot of coffee appears to strengthen the taste and is not to be sniffed at in these days of high coffee prices.

Statistics on Coffee Consumption

Here are some further facts about coffee consumption which may prove significant later on when we begin to investigate the possible harm it may do to health. At present, Americans use about 17 pounds of coffee annually per person. This is how our consumption of coffee has increased during this century; in 1821 we imported 21 million pounds of coffee beans. By 1836 this had risen to 93 million pounds. In 1941 we imported 2,254,-694,000 pounds. It is estimated that 95 per cent of the families in this country drink coffee daily, eight out of ten adults drink it daily, one out of every four children drinks coffee daily. We are today drinking each year a billion more gallons of coffee than milk, 4 times as much coffee as beer, 3 times more than soft drinks and 50 times more than hard liquor. Again according to estimates, 25 per cent of all American coffee drinkers consume 5 or more cups per day.

Coffee is the American beverage, just as tea is the national beverage of England. Jean Bogert in her book, *Nutrition and Physical Fitness,* tells us that many an Englishman accustomed to drinking several cups of strong tea a day is thrown into a panic at the thought of drinking a cup of coffee. In the same manner many a Frenchman, accustomed to coffee-drinking considers tea as a dangerous beverage to be taken only in emergencies under direct medical supervision! In this world of ours it seems you choose your own poison! Whether or not coffee comes under the heading of poison is for you to judge after reading the evidence we have assembled in the following pages. We have tried to be fair to our national beverage, but we have not pulled our punches.

[8]

CHAPTER 2

Abundant Evidence
Against Coffee

We made a very significant observation in our research on the scientific proof of the harmfulness of coffee-drinking. From 1900 to 1915 medical and scientific journals were full of articles on experiments done. From 1915 to 1925 there were far fewer articles. From 1925 to 1945 the number declined still more. And from 1945 on there has been, practically speaking, little or no investigation of the effect of coffee on human health. We do not know what this may mean. Does it mean, perhaps, that medical men are discounting the facts discovered earlier and hence do not think it worth while to pursue the investigation further? Does it mean that new drugs, chemicals and poisons now demand so much time that we cannot spare time to investigate older substances? Or does it mean simply that physicians and researchers alike have decided that the fragrant brown beverage most of them drink all day long can't possibly need any further investigation?

As far back as 1746 a treatise was published on *Tobacco, Tea and Coffee* by Simon Pauli, an Italian writer. Pauli appears to be a writer of some substance, for his works were accepted widely among the learned of his day. We know there were many misconceptions about physiology in those days and, of course, present-day methods of investigation were not available. Yet it is startling to read that Pauli believes "it (coffee) is esteemed a great cooler (thirst quencher) for which reason it is drank by most, but if it is used to excess, it extinguishes the inclination to venery and induces sterility." He tells us further that in ancient times women of the East used coffee brewed extra strong as a purgative to prevent conception. Perhaps this is the reason why its use was forbidden to women for many centuries by the early caliphs. He advances the theory that coffee induces sterility because it gradually dries up the body's procreative powers on account of the large amount of sulfur it contains.

Dr. Alcott's Contributions

Later in our own country a writer on health, Dr. William Alexander Alcott, wrote that coffee is essentially and properly a medicine—a narcotic. He quotes authorities of that day (his book was published in 1844) as saying that coffee possesses nervine and astringent qualities, is suspected of producing palsies, has a powerful effect on the nervous system, a pernicious effect on the stomach and bowels, exhausts the sensibilities of the part on which it acts, induces weakness, produces debility, alters the gastric juice, disorders digestion and often produces convulsions and vertigo, feverish

[9]

heat, anxiety, palpitations, tremblings, weakness of sight and predispositions to apoplexy.

He quotes Dr. Hahnemann, founder of homeopathic medicine, as saying that "coffee is strictly a medicinal substance. All medicines in strong doses have a disagreeable effect on the feelings of a healthy person." He also quotes Hahnemann as saying that coffee drinking produces the following diseases: nervous or sick headaches, toothache, darting pains in the body, spasms in the chest, stomach and abdomen, costiveness (constipation), erysipelas, disease of the liver, uterus and bones, inflammation of the eyes, difficulty in breathing and bowel affections. He compares the action of caffeine, to that of arsenic, lead or prussic acid, asking "will anyone attempt to say that these substances are not poisonous because they poison slowly?"

Dr. Alcott is a cousin and associate of Amos Bronson Alcott, who was a famous educator and the father of Louisa May of *Little Women* fame.

An Established Fact—Caffeine Is a Poison

Now perhaps these older writers may have jumped to conclusions when they laid down the unqualified statement that coffee was responsible for all the ills mentioned. Undoubtedly they did not use present-day laboratory methods to prove their statements. But they must have questioned their patients as to whether or not they used coffee and based conclusions on the answers. So while it does not follow that coffee-drinking was the sole and only cause of the symptoms their patients described, it does seem quite possible that coffee-drinking may have played a part in them. And it does seem significant that so much was written in times past about the possible harm of coffee-drinking. We do not find treatises attacking the use of apples, potatoes or carrots. So we know, that, from way back, physicians have been concerned with the medicinal and narcotic aspects of coffee. And we cannot discount this concern as an old wives' tale.

We know that caffeine, the substance in coffee which apparently is responsible for its effects on the human body, is a powerful poison. A drop of caffeine injected into the skin of an animal will produce death within a few minutes. An infinitely small amount injected into the brain will bring convulsions. The amount of caffeine in a cup of coffee is quite small. Yet we drink coffee because of the effect of the caffeine, just as we smoke because of the effect of the nicotine. Both are drugs, both are habit-forming. We uncovered some interesting accounts of headaches produced as "withdrawal symptoms" when coffee-drinking was abruptly stopped. We also know that efficiency of work performance decreases when a confirmed coffee-drinker stops taking his daily dose of coffee. These are symptoms typical of addiction. When any drug is taken away from a drug addict, he suffers "withdrawal symptoms."

Habitual Coffee-Drinking and Stomach Ulcers

What do some of the modern researchers have to say about the effect of coffee on the human body? There are two modern disorders that the general public usually associates with coffee-drinking—ulcers and heart trouble. This may be mostly because physicians frequently forbid coffee to their heart and ulcer patients. There seems to be no doubt that coffee is bad for the ulcer patient, although we do not find any researcher who has proved that coffee actually produces ulcers in human beings. J. A. Roth and A. C. Ivy whose animal experiments on coffee are famous, tell us in *Gastroenterology* for November, 1948, that: 1. Caffeine produces gastro-duodenal ulcers in animals to whom the drug is given in a beeswax container so that their stomachs are absorbing caffeine continually. 2. Caffeine moderately stimulates the flow of gastric juices. 3. Caffeine produces very definite changes in the blood vessels of animals which are similar to changes produced by prolonged resentment, hostility and anxiety. 4. As we know, one difficulty involved in ulcers is an excessive flow of hydrochloric acid into the stomach. Most peptic ulcer patients, says Drs. Roth and Ivy, respond to caffeine with a prolonged and sustained stimulation of the output of free hydrochloric acid. In other words, coffee causes more and more hydrochloric acid to pour into the stomach of the ulcer patient for quite a long time after the coffee has been taken. So, say these authors, although they cannot prove that caffeine causes ulcers, still it does seem that taking fairly large amounts of coffee may contribute to the development of ulcers and may aggravate the condition of an ulcer that exists already.

Digestive Juices Stimulated

An investigation carried on at the University of Oklahoma by Vern H. Musick, M.D., Howard C. Hopps, M.D., Harry Avey, M.D., and Arthur A. Hellbaum, M.D., and reported in the *Southern Medical Journal* for August, 1946, involved a total of 39 patients—10 of them with no symptoms of digestive tract trouble of any kind, 25 of them patients with duodenal ulcers and 4 patients with gastric ulcers. The researchers found that the flow of digestive juice is considerably increased in the normal person when caffeine comes into contact with the lining of the stomach. In the patient with duodenal ulcer the flow of digestive juice is "prolonged and excessive." Dr. Musick, in discussing the subject before a meeting of the Southern Medical Association concluded, "I think it is all right for the normal person to drink caffeine-containing beverages but an ulcer patient or a patient who has a high secretory curve (that is, someone with a generally high level of hydrochloric acid in the stomach, which might predispose him to ulcers) should not drink coffee. He should not drink alcohol and by all means he should not drink black coffee the next morning after alcohol."

Now you will notice that, in all of these researches, caffeine was used —not coffee. This might lead someone to say, "Well, of course, straight caffeine is bad for you, but there is so little caffeine in coffee that surely coffee can't hurt me." On the same basis one could say there is so little nicotine in cigarettes, so little preservative in processed foods, so little arsenic on the outside of a sprayed apple, so little fluorine in fluoridated water, that there is no harm in taking any of these either. Once you begin to add up all these "small doses of poison" that you are taking every day, the sum total gets to be quite frightening.

Dr. R. Wood, M.A., B.M., B.Ch., B. Sc., writing in the *British Medical Journal* for August 7, 1948, tells us of experiments with cats in which he found that caffeine in the stomach has a powerful action on histamine, a substance which regulates gastric secretion. He also found that theobromine and theophylline (substances that occur in cocoa and tea) also have a similar action in some animals. "Our results support the Roth and Ivy conclusions," he says, "that ulcer patients should restrict their intake of beverages containing caffeine and also that it is desirable to limit their consumption of foods and drinks containing theobromine and theophylline."

Coffee, Heart Disorders and Blood Pressure

Concerning heart trouble and coffee-drinking, most nutritionists and books on health state that coffee has a definite effect on the heart and blood pressure. According to James S. McLester, M.D., in his book, *Nutrition and Diet in Health and Disease* (W. B. Saunders, 1927), coffee raises the blood pressure slightly, slows and strengthens the heart, stimulates renal activity and prevents fatigue and depression. It also gives mild brain stimulation. He goes on to say that its excessive use is harmful, for stimulation and irritation are closely related. In cases of insomnia, cardiac irritability and rapid heart beat, even one cup a day will cause trouble when the heart is already irritated. More than one cup is especially harmful.

H. M. Marvin, M.D., in his book, *You and Your Heart* (Random House, 1950), states that the effect of alcohol, tobacco and coffee all vary among different individuals. Some find that their heart beats faster after a few drinks of alcohol or cups of coffee. Others find that their hearts beat just a little faster, or not at all faster. He says that no one knows why this should be so. Perhaps some people develop a "tolerance" for coffee and others do not.

That word "tolerance" keeps recurring in all the literature about coffee. Our medical dictionary defines "tolerance" as "the ability of enduring the influence of a drug or poison, particularly when acquired by a continued use of the substance." It seems peculiar that the word should be used in speaking of coffee if indeed coffee has no harmful effects on the body. And, is it possible that those of us who suffer no apparent ill effects from coffee have simply accustomed ourselves to it over a period of time, so that we can throw off the ill effects?

Kathryn Horst, Rex E. Burton and William Dodd Robinson, writing in the *Journal of Pharmacology and Experimental Therapeutics,* Vol. 52, 1934, tell of an experience involving a number of young men whose blood pressure was tested before and after they began to drink coffee habitually. The maximum rise in blood pressure occurred during the first week they were drinking coffee. Later on, the article explains, a "tolerance" was developed, and the blood pressure remained at the same level.

When the coffee was withdrawn, the blood pressure returned to "normal." We don't know how you interpret this experiment, but to us it seems to show definitely that some substance in the coffee does have an unhealthful effect on the blood pressure. For those who can, after a time, build up a "tolerance" to this effect, the blood pressure does not go higher. But what of those who do not build up this tolerance? Might not coffee be a very important factor in continued high blood pressure which, of course, is one of the most widespread disorders in our country today?

Leafing on through our notes on coffee and heart ailments we find that Jean Bogert in *Nutrition and Physical Fitness* (W. B. Saunders, 1949) states that coffee quickens the respiration (that is, makes you breathe faster), strengthens the pulse, raises the blood pressure, stimulates the kidneys, excites the functions of the brain and temporarily relieves fatigue or depression. Max M. Rosenberg, M.D., in *Encyclopedia of Medical Self Help* (Scholastic Book Press, 1950) tells us that coffee should be avoided by individuals who have heart disease, angina, high blood pressure, stomach trouble, skin affections, arthritis, liver trouble. Garfield G. Duncan, M.D., in *Diseases of Metabolism* (W. B. Saunders, 1952) tells us that caffeine causes an increase of 3 to 10 per cent in the basal metabolic rate within the first hour after the coffee is taken. (So, incidentally, does the smoking of one cigarette!) Basal metabolism is the rate at which your body makes use of the food you eat.

Does a Tired Body Need Stimulation or Rest?

We want to elaborate a little on the whole business of coffee stimulating the heart. For someone whose heart needs a momentary stimulation you might use coffee as you would use a hypodermic injection—for that occasion only. But what happens, do you suppose, when the heart, sick or well, is constantly stimulated, day after day, while all the time it is protesting that it is tired and wants to rest? One writer on the subject compares coffee to a whip used on a tired horse. Of course, the horse will move faster when he is whipped, but how long can you keep up this form of stimulation before the horse drops from exhaustion? The main danger, it seems to us, in the use of coffee by people who may have heart trouble (as well as the rest of us) is that instead of resting as they should when they are tired, they whip themselves to more effort by a cup of coffee and eventually—sooner or later—they are going to have to pay for the rest they are not getting.

Many people use the excuse that they drink coffee only in the morning, so it doesn't matter if they over-stimulate their bodies. They are not trying to go to sleep! Instead they have to gird themselves to meet the day's problems, responsibilities and hard work, so they need to be stimulated. There is a serious fallacy in this kind of reasoning. If they are indeed so tired and run-down that each morning they cannot face the day without a cup of stimulation, then certainly there is something wrong somewhere. Either they do not get the right food, enough sleep, enough relaxation or enough freedom from worry. Over-stimulation even at breakfast time, means that an already tired body is "hopped up" to carry on when it should be resting.

How Effective Is the Coffee Break?

A phrase which has crept into American usage in recent years is "coffee break." Manufacturers and office executives were somehow sold on the idea that a mid-morning cup of coffee would greatly increase the efficiency of the staff resulting in more output at less cost. At direct odds with this supposition is an experiment described in the *Journal of Pharmacology and Experimental Therapeutics* (1934). It was found here that coffee exerted a marked influence upon man's performance of an acquired motor skill. When coffee was drunk, all performances suffered and there was a sustained deleterious influence on the subject. A statement of a more general nature, carried by *Chemical Abstracts* (1948, Vol. 42) further demolishes the idea that coffee improves performance. It says, "Maximum performance of healthy, rested subjects cannot be improved by alcohol or drugs (caffeine, etc.)."

It can be safely assumed that any increased efficiency brought on by artificial stimulation will be temporary and will be followed by a reversal that will drag efficiency to a point far below the norm. Doctors maintain that the body must repay by rest added hours of stimulation by any source.

Coffee Tars and Cancer

Does the use of coffee have any relation to cancer incidence? There are some researchers who believe that it does. We know well that certain kinds of tar produce cancer. Coal tar is cancer-producing. The tar from tobacco products produces cancer in laboratory animals. A. H. Roffo in an article published in *Boletin del Instituto de Medicina Experimental,* Vol. 15, 1939, describes obtaining tar from coffee. He found that this tar has the same physical characteristics as that obtained from tobacco. He treated laboratory animals with this tar and 73 per cent of them developed tumors which ended as cancerous growths. In a later experiment he fed coffee tar to rats in nontoxic doses, that is, they did not receive enough of the tar to make them ill at any one time, for he was trying to discover what the long-continued effect of the tar would be. Definite sores in the stomachs and digestive tracts soon became ulcers which eventually developed into cancers.

Roffo believes that it is the roasting of coffee that produces these tars. He also says that they are not soluble in water, so perhaps they are not present in coffee as we drink it. Still, in chemical tests such as spectography and fluorescence, the coffee tars show the same characteristic as coal tar.

Another experiment reported in *Chemical Abstracts* (1939, Vol. 33) used tar obtained from coffee by distillation and condensation. This tar again had the same physical characteristics as that obtained from tobacco. A group of rabbits was treated with this tar for from 7 to 20 months. Seventy per cent of the rabbits developed papillomas which ended as cancerous tumors.

The latest report in this connection is one which appeared in the New York *World Telegram and Sun* for April 12, 1957: "A potent cancer-causing chemical known as 3,4-benzypyrene has been found in coffee root obtained from coffee-roasting plants." Are these the first murmurings that will one day swell into a roar like the close association between cigarettes and cancer?

[14]

Should Pregnant Women and Nursing Mothers Drink Coffee?

A German scientist, Heinz Fischer, has done research on the effect of caffeine on the placenta and embryo of pregnant rabbits. The rabbits were given caffeine daily in water solution. In an article in the German medical publication, *Zeitschrift fur Mikro-Anatomischer Forschungen*, Vol. 47, 1940, Dr. Fischer describes the results.

The growth and development of the embryo were slowed down. In the liver and kidneys of the embryo as well as in the blood vessels, there was obstruction of the passage of blood, resulting in edema or unhealthful swelling. The skin of the embryo was damaged and the cells of its liver showed definite disease. When all these harmful symptoms became serious enough, the embryo died and was re-absorbed, becoming just a crumbled mass in the mother's womb. The placenta (the sac covering the unborn child) became swollen and diseased.

It is interesting to note that these results were reported for rabbits to whom caffeine was given first when they became pregnant. Other rabbits were given small amounts of caffeine over a period of time until they established a tolerance to it. (There's that word "tolerance" again!) Then, when they became pregnant, the placenta and embryo suffered no damage. Once again, we remind you that caffeine (the concentrated poison that exists in coffee) was given to these animals—not coffee. But, even so, does it sound like such a good idea for an expectant mother in these days to drink coffee, taking into account the already considerable amount of various poisons she is getting in food, in air pollution, in chemicalized water and perhaps in cigarettes?

Does Coffee Affect Brain and Nerve Tissue?

The Department of Agriculture published a booklet in 1917 called *The Toxicity of Caffeine*. Their experiments involved animals. They tell us that the reaction of human beings and animals to caffeine may be quite different. Yet most scientific research these days (on chemicals, insecticides, cosmetics and so forth) is done with animals and it is taken for granted that any substance that shows up as poisonous to animals is quite likely to be not very good for men.

The authors tell us, too, that the effect of caffeine on individual animals is different in its intensity and the effect varies with the dose. On the same basis, undoubtedly some human beings are less resistant to poisons than others. William Salant and J. B. Rieger, authors of the booklet, tell us that only one rabbit in ten survived injected doses of caffeine. Those that survived generally succumbed to a second or third dose. The effect of caffeine on guinea pigs was even more drastic, although dogs and cats reacted differently. All showed symptoms of poisoning, which resembled poisoning from strychnine. In relation to its harmful action on tissues (chiefly brain and nerve tissue) caffeine is far more destructive than morphine. They conclude that the continued use of caffeine-containing beverages over a long period of time seems bound to be harmful.

Well, would you consider giving your family—children and old folks included—ever so small a dose of morphine every morning as part of breakfast, no matter how much they might like the taste? Keep in mind that caffeine showed up as being far more destructive than morphine.

This is the bulk of our evidence on the possible harm that may result from habitual, prolonged and excessive coffee drinking. It does not seem to us that someone who drinks one cup of coffee a day should go to a lot of trouble to give it up. But probably he will be the person who could give it up most easily. The person who is in danger from coffee, we believe, is the person who simply can't get along without it and who, if he stops and soberly counts up how many cups of coffee he has in any one day, may find that coffee is indeed a drug to him and that the habit of throwing off weariness and worry with a cup of coffee has brought him nothing but sorrow and ill health. These are the people who should be persuaded to give up coffee entirely.

If this should prove to be impossible, we have one last suggestion. According to our standards, we should eat and drink nothing that does not contribute in some way to nutrition. Any food or drink that contains neither vitamins, minerals, enzymes or protein should automatically be crossed off the list, for it is crowding out in our diets those beneficial protective foods we all need so desperately. If you must continue to drink coffee, then at least make certain that the rest of your diet is as healthful as possible. This means plenty of fresh raw fruits and vegetables every day along with meat, eggs, fish and nuts. This means only completely whole grain cereals. This means no food at all that contains white flour or white sugar in any form, even including chewing gum and soft drinks. This means taking food supplements: fish liver oil for vitamins A and D, brewer's yeast or desiccated liver for the B vitamins, rose hips for vitamin C and wheat germ oil for vitamin E.

CHAPTER 3

Coffee and Blood Sugar

Day by day scientists are coming to an increased appreciation of the importance of proper blood sugar levels to good health. All of us know that the one sure symptom of diabetes is a high blood sugar—that is, the mechanism in the body which controls the use of sugar goes awry and the veins and arteries are flooded with sugar, which eventually shows up in large quantities in the urine. Not so many of us know about low blood sugar—the opposite of diabetes which also involves a defect in the mechanism that controls the use of sugar.

According to E. M. Abrahamson, M.D., and A. W. Pezet writing in

[16]

Body, Mind and Sugar (Henry Holt, 1951) low blood sugar is far more common among Americans than high blood sugar or diabetes. Its symptoms are perhaps not so dramatic, but it, too, can lead to poor health. And because it has just recently come to the foreground as a cause of all kinds of disorders, ranging from asthma and epilepsy to fatigue, gnawing hunger and dizziness, many doctors do not give patients tests to determine whether or not their blood sugar is too low.

The way low blood sugar (hypoglycemia or hyperinsulinism are the scientific names for it) comes about is this. When sugar is eaten, it goes almost immediately to the blood because it does not need to be digested. This raises the blood sugar to an abnormal height. But instead of staying at this height, the blood sugar level plunges almost immediately to far below what it should be. Then the individual feels uncomfortable, tired or hungry and eats something else that is sugary or starchy. His blood sugar level soars again, only to drop far below what it should be a half hour or an hour later. You can see that such a condition produces a vicious cycle, in which the blood sugar level is not continually high, as in diabetes, but instead rises precipitately, then drops just as fast. A graph of the blood sugar level goes up and down in peaks and valleys. The ideal blood sugar level is one which rises a little after a meal, when the body is busy digesting the food just eaten, then falls gradually just a little and levels off in a plateau, falling down just a little again before it is time for the next meal.

Three Causes of Low Blood Sugar

White sugar and products made from it are among the worst offenders in producing low blood sugar. A second criminal in the low blood sugar case is tobacco, for puffing on a cigarette has the same effect of lifting the blood sugar level, only to plunge it to dangerous depths within a half hour or so. The third offender is—you've guessed it—coffee. We do not know whether it is the caffeine in coffee that produces this effect, but we rather imagine it is, for blood sugar responds in this way to any poisonous substance taken in. At any rate we know that this is one reason for the "lift" you get from a cup of coffee.

Quite apart from its effect on heart, breathing, blood pressure and so forth, coffee causes the blood sugar to rise rapidly then fall just as rapidly. So, if you suffer from low blood sugar, the effects of those 3 cups of breakfast coffee will wear off in an hour or so, and you will find your efficiency decreasing. Your head may begin to ache, you may get grumpy and irritable, you may have an "all-gone" feeling in the pit of your stomach, you may be just plain hungry. Obviously it's time for you to have another cup of coffee. You do and the cycle begins all over again.

Folks who take their morning cup of coffee and don't run into any of these difficulties apparently have a sugar-regulating mechanism strong enough to bring up the blood sugar level after the drop occurs. These are the folks who work vigorously and well straight through the morning and feel just pleasantly hungry by lunch time. Nine chances out of ten they won't feel the need for coffee at lunch. With their blood sugar level holding

[17]

steady throughout the afternoon, they won't need a "coffee break" at the office around three o'clock. By dinner time, once again they are just pleasantly hungry and while they may or may not have a cup of coffee with dinner, they don't feel a violent craving for it, as many of the rest of us do.

Coffee Addiction Must Be Broken

What about the coffee-addict, who has 3 or more cups for breakfast, another at 10 A.M., several more for lunch and dinner and tops off the day with a midnight snack and several more cups of coffee? His blood sugar level must be zigging and zagging all day, from depths to heights. The main reason for the low blood sugar is the coffee he drinks and the lower the blood sugar goes, the more coffee he must have to bring it up again! Truly a vicious cycle!

About coffee, Dr. Abrahamson says in *Body, Mind and Sugar*, "Caffeine stimulates the adrenal cortex to produce more of its hormones, which in turn induce the liver to break down glycogen into glucose which flows into the blood stream. This is why a cup of coffee "gives you a lift." Trouble develops because the islands of Langerhans (that part of the pancreas which is disordered in diabetes and in low blood sugar) cannot distinguish between the effects of drinking coffee and eating food. They don't know and don't care whether the sugar has come from the food that is being digested or from previously stored glycogen, broken down by the action of the caffeine's stimulus to the adrenal cortex. To the islands of Langerhans sugar is sugar. They go to work to force the blood sugar to its normal level. In the course of time, because of their repeated stimulation, the islands become so sensitive that they overrespond to a normal stimulus.

"Anyone trying to lose weight who drinks black coffee to still the pangs of hunger is only making matters worse for himself. The repeated stimulus to the islands of Langerhans makes them more sensitive, and the resultant low blood sugar only makes the onerous diet more onerous. Dieting to reduce is much easier if coffee, as well as caffeine in other forms (such as strong tea, chocolate and soft drinks containing that alkaloid) is excluded."

Dr. Abrahamson in his book gives a case history of one patient whose addiction to coffee was nearly her undoing. At the age of 36, she was nervous and irritable. She had trouble taking care of her home and never had enough energy to go out in the evenings. Her test for blood sugar level showed that it was low. She responded very well to the recommended diet and expressed her amazement that she got along without barbiturates which she had been taking, on her doctor's advice, for her "nervousness." But she missed her breakfast coffee— 3 cups! She was advised to omit the coffee and she did and got along nicely. But she kept inquiring how soon she might drink coffee again. She was then told that she would never be able to drink it. "Moderate use of caffeine is perfectly harmless to the average person; once the insulin apparatus has been sensitized by overindulgence, however, coffee must be avoided. In a way this is similar to

[18]

the alcohol problem. Moderate use of alcohol is not only relatively harmless, but actually of help in withstanding the stress of civilized life. If a person has been an alcoholic and conquered his craving, he must not take another drop."

Our patient could not believe that "just one" cup of coffee would hurt her. So she tried it for a few months and her symptoms returned— butterflies in her stomach, indigestion and nervousness. As soon as she returned to the diet once again, the symptoms disappeared. This is but one of the case histories related in Dr. Abrahamson's book. They are all equally revealing. And we believe that every reader should have the book for the wealth of splendid information it contains. You can buy it at your local bookshop or order it from Rodale Books, Incorporated, Emmaus, Pennsylvania.

The Diet for Attaining a Normal Blood Sugar Level

The cure for low blood sugar is a diet high in protein and fat and low in starches, sugars and coffee with as few cigarettes as possible. Dr. Abrahamson lists the following foods as permissible on the diet to raise blood sugar levels: Vegetables: asparagus, avocado, beets, broccoli, Brussels sprouts, cabbage, cauliflower, carrots, celery, corn, cucumbers, eggplant, lima beans, onions, peas, radishes, sauerkraut, squash, string beans, tomatoes, turnips. Meats, fish, cheese, milk and eggs. Apples, apricots, berries, grapefruit, melons, oranges, peaches, pears, pineapple, tangerines. Salads, mushrooms, nuts. Any unsweetened fruit juice except grape juice or prune juice. Weak tea, decaffeinated coffee, coffee substitutes.

These foods are forbidden: sugar, candy and other sweets such as pie, cake, pastries, sweet custards, puddings and ice cream. Caffeine— ordinary coffee, strong brewed tea, beverages containing caffeine, potatoes, rice, grapes, raisins, plums, figs, dates and bananas, spaghetti, noodles, macaroni, wines, cordials, cocktails and beer.

By this second list we mean *that you should not eat any of these foods,* even if it means changing your meal habits entirely, getting up early enough to eat a hearty high protein breakfast, carrying lunch instead of eating at restaurants and declining evening invitations when you know that coffee and forbidden sweets will be involved when refreshment time comes. It should take you only a short time to revise your blood sugar level readings so that you can ease up on the restrictions. But by this time if you have really been concentrating on a high protein diet, you may be surprised at your own reluctance to go back to the diet you were eating before.

You may be delighted to find that you simply don't crave dessert, that a piece of pie or a doughnut looks repulsive at ten in the morning, that the evening meal leaves you feeling satisfied and content without any dessert other than fresh raw fruit. What a happy state of affairs for someone trying to reduce! Quite apart from the beneficial effects on blood sugar levels, such a diet is just about all that one could wish for as a permanent diet. After your blood sugar level has risen to normal and you feel you can begin to add some of the forbidden foods, you should add only the fruits and vegetables, *never* the pastries, cakes, pies, candy and so forth. Those should be on your permanently forbidden list.

Food supplements are another excellent source of protein. Brewer's yeast, meat flour, wheat germ, sunflower seeds, amino acids, desiccated liver and many other health-giving food supplements are rich in high-quality protein and, of course, can be added with great success to Dr. Abrahamson's diet.

CHAPTER 4

Thyroid Trouble or Too Much Coffee?

A recent book (*Kathy,* by Katharine Homer Fryer, published by Dutton) tells the story of a young girl who was near death because of a wrong diagnosis of thyroid disorder. Or rather, no diagnosis at all. From a normal healthy child, Kathy changed very gradually into a shadow of her former self. She lost weight steadily and lost all her good spirits and energy along with it. Day after day she drooped and weakened.

Doctors could find nothing wrong and she was finally taken to psychiatrists who declared she was suffering from a psychosis. They recommended that she be sent to a mental hospital. Almost by accident she happened to be in the office of an M.D. who decided to test the functioning of her thyroid gland. He found it dangerously deficient. She was given a thyroid preparation—to supply the substance her own thyroid gland was not supplying—and improved within a matter of hours. In a few weeks she was back to normal.

The Importance of the Thyroid

It seems to be extremely difficult to diagnose thyroid disorders, possibly because the thyroid is such an important gland that it takes part in many body processes. Any or all of these can go awry when something goes wrong with the thyroid. But, of course, they may be disordered from other causes than thyroid trouble, too.

The thyroid, through its hormone, thyroxine, regulates the way the body uses its food—the rate of metabolism or the rate at which food is broken down and built into cells. It has to do with the way the body uses calcium and other minerals. It influences the growth and the weight, determines personality and emotional behavior, is related in some important ways to reproductive function. The pituitary gland, the sex glands and the parathyroid glands are all closely related in function to the thyroid. So the jobs of all these, too, are influenced by the thyroid. If it is disordered, they are disordered, too.

The heart beat, the body's reaction to heat and cold, the function of memory, the making of red blood corpuscles—all these are influenced by the thyroid gland. The interaction of the thyroid and the adrenal glands has something to do with blood pressure. It seems as if everything you do or are is determined at least in part by the working of your thyroid gland. So we can't possibly emphasize enough the vast importance of this gland to you, from the point of health, personality, happiness, mentality, appearance.

More Evidence of Wrong Diagnosis

An issue of the *Journal of the American Medical Association* (November 23, 1957) tells us of mis-diagnosis of a different kind in relation to thyroid trouble. The author of this article, Arnold S. Jackson, M.D., has discovered that many people are diagnosed as having thyroid trouble when they don't at all! And, since the handiest treatment for thyroid trouble is to take the gland out, many, many people have thyroid operations when there is nothing or perhaps very little wrong with their thyroid glands.

Dr. Jackson says in 1937 he went to a meeting of the American Association for the Study of Goiter where 100 cases were presented. All of these patients had been advised to "have it out." Dr. Jackson found that in no instance was there any evidence of hyperthyroidism. At another meeting he and Dr. Elexious T. Bell, then professor of Pathology at the University of Minnesota Medical School, presented the cases of 200 patients, all advised to have thyroid operations, in all of whom the thyroid gland was either completely normal or just slightly abnormal.

In the *Journal* article Dr. Jackson tells us about 228 patients whose physicians had recommended thyroid operations, and all of the patients were suffering from something else—nervous tension and exhaustion in 112 cases, menopause in 30, physical exhaustion in 27; 11 were normal; 11 had colloid goiters; 3 had rheumatic endocarditis; 8 had psychoneurosis; 6 had hypothyroidism (too little thyroid activity instead of too much) and 20 had assorted other ailments.

None of these patients should have had his thyroid gland removed, of course. But one of them, away from home and in a highly agitated condition was rushed off to a hospital and a large section of his perfectly normal thyroid gland was cut out. Dr. Jackson goes on to tell us what symptoms indicate hyperthyroidism (too much activity of the thyroid gland, for which operations are commonly performed). These are: steady weight loss although the appetite is good, progressive weakness, increased pulse rate, shaking, insomnia, sweating, palpitation of the heart and pulse pressure. A rise in the basal metabolism rate is another symptom.

However, in the case of the 228 patients we are discussing here, although certain of these symptoms were present, there was nothing wrong with most of the thyroid glands involved. In the 167 patients of the first

3 groups, what do you suppose was causing these frightening symptoms— serious enough to result in 167 recommendations to have healthy thyroid glands removed? Says Dr. Jackson, *"The most important single factor responsible was the overindulgence in the use of stimulants—coffee, tea and nicotine."*

Many of the patients smoked from two to 3 packs of cigarettes a day. Many drank from 5 to 30 cups of coffee every 24 hours. An average cup of black coffee contains 2½ grains of caffeine, so anyone who drinks 10 cups daily is getting about 3 medicinal doses of this drug, which doctors give with great caution. Anyone drinking 30 cups of coffee is getting about 10 such doses.

In addition, since the stimulants made them jittery, irritable and nervous, most of our patients were taking large doses of barbiturates, tranquilizers and other drugs, trying to combat the nervousness. Listen to some of the case histories. Do they sound like anyone you know?

Some of the 228 Patients

The first case was a young woman who had come from a farm to get a job in the big city. Under the strain of city life she took more and more coffee, nicotine and soft drinks to keep going. One day she had an accident, and her doctor diagnosed her case as goiter resulting from the accident. It was decided to operate. Through the insurance company's insistence she was examined by Dr. Jackson who took her off all stimulants and sent her home to rest. She recovered rapidly. With no operation.

Another woman, middle-aged, was brought from another state to have the thyroid removed by surgery. Dr. Jackson's examination revealed that her thyroid was normal. She needed rest from too much work and over-stimulation.

A patient from New York City came expecting an operation. Instead, a few months rest in the country, without stimulants, sent him back to work in good health.

Two Lessons To Be Learned

There are two lessons to be learned from this story. First of all (and Dr. Jackson says this in just so many words), if in doubt as to the diagnosis of hyperthyroidism, *don't rush into surgery or any other type of therapy.* First, make certain of the diagnosis. This, of course, is advice for a doctor. It's advice for you, too. Don't decide on operations—any kind of operations —while there is the vaguest chance the diagnosis might be wrong.

Our files are full of information about useless surgery—for gall bladders, for hysterectomies, for appendices, for tonsils, for prostate glands. Prominent surgeons themselves have made strong statements about the prevalence of unnecessary surgery. You need the various parts of your body with which you were born! It's senseless to have them cut out unless you have exhausted every possible chance of attaining good health by other means. And certainly, considering its importance in body function, the thyroid is the last item that should ever be removed without exhausting every other possibility.

The second lesson to be learned is the tragic fact that symptoms so serious as to be almost fatal can result from the use of such harmless-appearing substances as coffee, soft drinks, tea and nicotine. Who knows what proportion of all the ills being treated in all the doctors' offices in this country are the result simply of overindulgence in these everyday drugs!

We said "overindulgence" and there are bound to be some people you talk to who will say, "But I never overindulge! Thirty cups of coffee a day? Three packs of cigarettes! Not me. I'm temperate." Ask them if they've ever kept strict account of the amount of coffee, tea and soft drinks they drink over a period of a week. Ask them exactly how many cigarettes they smoke in a week, by actual count.

And even if they don't "overindulge," the story we have told illustrates the terrible harm that can come from these drugs. Isn't it logical to assume that if one uses a little less than these amounts, he is doing his body just a little less harm—it's still harm! The best precaution to take with drugs is to avoid them entirely whether they come as medicines or in the attractive form of a hot cup of coffee or tea, or a sociable cigarette.

CHAPTER 5

Fruit Drinks and Tooth Erosion

The child with a soda bottle in his hand has become almost as notorious a symbol of modern American civilization as the child with the toy gun. We know, in a general way, that soda is not good for us, for often you hear mothers protesting the second or even third bottle of soda. "It'll spoil your appetite for dinner," they say. And it does spoil your appetite for dinner. Unfortunately this is not all it spoils.

Our hestitancy in giving the children free rein with the soda bottles indicates that we have some inkling of possible harm in this quarter, but rare indeed is the mother who has any appreciation of the fact that fruit juices are likely to harm the teeth. On the contrary, most of us think of fruit juices as the most healthful of beverages.

We were interested to find in the May 6, 1958, issue of the *British Dental Journal* a new piece of research done by 3 famous British scientists incriminating fruit juices—especially fruit juices—as trouble makers. They (P. J. Holloway, May Mellanby and R. J. C. Stewart) tell us that reports of tooth erosion from fruit drinks have been studied for years. In 1907 W. D. Miller reported loss of calcium from tooth structure due to excessive fruit consumption, and Pickerill in 1912 noted that tooth enamel wasted away in persons who sucked lemons.

In recent years there has been considerably more research on the subject, due to the fact that consumption of fruit juices (especially canned ones) has increased along with the tremendous increase in the drinking of soft drinks—cola or soda. Many research projects have shown that tooth erosion produced in laboratory animals by the consumption of fruit juices and acid beverages has its counterpart in man.

What is Erosion?

What do we mean by erosion? It is quite different from tooth decay, although there seems to be considerable evidence that sweetened drinks produce tooth decay, too. But erosion is a loss of tooth substance leaving rounded outlines, increased sensitivity and dental fillings standing up from the general tooth surface.

In the tests performed by the British scientists rats were given different substances as their only source of liquid. All of them were given the same diet. The drinks used were as follows: 20 different kinds of fruit squash (which, we assume, resembles our American fruit drinks like lemonade) cola and other carbonated beverages, canned and fresh fruit juices, iced lollipops (popsicles) and fruit candies.

In addition, another group of rats was given distilled water, another group citric acid and sugar combined and a third group just sugar in water.

All the soft drinks brought about erosion of the teeth. The fruit drinks gave about the same amount of erosion as the mixture of citric acid and sugar. Rats which drank distilled water, whether or not the water contained sugar, did not show tooth erosion. The degree of erosion from cola and other carbonated drinks was not so great as that produced by the fruit-flavored drinks. This fact clearly incriminates the acid fruit in the beverage as the cause of the erosion. It was also found that the type and amount of the sweetening agent in any of the acid solutions made a difference in the amount of erosion. Sucrose, glucose or saccharine increased the erosion, but replacing these by an equivalent amount of fructose reduced the erosion by 20 per cent. Note that saccharine fruit mixtures (widely used in this country in the so-called non-calorie soft drinks) created as much erosion as the sugar-fruit drinks did.

Candies made from acid fruits and sugar, popsicles and freshly-made fruit juice were tested as well as black-currant juice and bottled rose hip syrup. The latter two are outstanding sources of vitamin C in England. The orange juice and the black-currant juice both produced considerable erosion. The rose hip syrup was less destructive. The rose hip syrup is, of course, sweetened to make it palatable. The popsicles caused less destruction of enamel than the candies.

Findings Indicate Saliva Resists Acid

Speculations on why the different concoctions should have the effects they do dwell mostly on the acidity of the foods and drinks tested. It is agreed that extremely acid foods or drinks cause erosion if they are held in the mouth. But there seems to be something in the saliva which protects against the corrosive strength of the acid. So the final amount of destruction depends not only on how much acid there is in the beverage, but also on the resistance of the saliva. It is generally agreed that sweetening the beverage makes it more corrosive, probably because sweetened beverages are held in the mouth longer. In a test on extracted teeth in either sweetened or unsweetened solutions, equally acid, the same amount of calcium was lost from each tooth.

Have the above results any bearing on human tooth disease, ask the authors. "The amounts of acid beverages normally drunk by adult human beings are probably too small to be of any great significance (remember, these authors live in England), but in the young and especially with certain methods of consumption, their influence is without doubt deleterious."

Sucking on anything that contains fruit syrup seems to result in tooth erosion. So eating popsicles which are held in the mouth for long periods of time would seem to be particularly undesirable. The same is true of fruit-and-sugar candy and especially lollipops or all-day suckers.

We are sure that readers will not be surprised at these findings in regard to sweet candies, frozen lollipops and soft drinks. All of us surely know that these things are harmful in other ways as well. The damage done by the sugar content of such foods is not limited to tooth erosion. Sugar in the digestive tract is absorbed much too quickly and goes immediately into the blood, shooting blood sugar level up far too high and then plunging it down to dangerous depths. Sugar destroys the calcium-phosphorus ration in the blood, bringing about another dangerous condition. Sugar depletes the body's store of B vitamins—a rare enough vitamin in these days of refined foods.

Fruit Juice—An Unnatural Food

So we are hardly surprised to read of the harmfulness of soft drinks and candy. But the news that fruit juice can erode teeth must come as a shock to many readers. Yet we must caution against these beverages. In many fruit juices such as the canned varieties and especially in canned fruit nectars there is a great deal of added sugar. As we have seen in the testimony from the *British Dental Journal*, both the sugar and the acid in the juice cause trouble where teeth are concerned.

Freshly made fruit juice seems to be acid enough to erode teeth, too, even though not to the extent of the other foods tested. Does this mean we should avoid all fruit juices? What about freshly squeezed orange juice? What about frozen citrus juices? We say no to all of them.

Any way you look at it, fruit juice is an unnatural food. We were meant to eat fruit, not drink it. Dr. Melvin Page of Florida who is an authority on foods and the effect on the human body has reminded us that we have a thirst center and a hunger center in our brains. When we drink something that was meant to be eaten, we confuse this mechanism. Our hunger center would have told us we wanted only one orange. But it is not consulted when we drink the juice of two or 3 oranges. The thirst center is involved and we may not even be thirsty! So we give our digestive tracts something we don't actually want.

[25]

Finally, the very worst thing of all that we do to orange juice is to strain it. And, of course, all frozen and canned juices have been strained. The bioflavonoids, fully as important as vitamin C in fruit juice, exist in the fibrous parts of the fruit. In citrus fruit they are present chiefly in the white inner lining of the skin and in the white fibers that separate the segments. Juicing fruit means that you throw away all these valuable food elements. And whatever small bit of them might remain is finally lost when you strain the juice.

We strongly recommend eating fruit—not juicing it. And, because of its high content of citric acid which causes difficulty to many people, we believe you should not eat more than several oranges or grapefruit halves a week. Get your vitamin C and bioflavonoids from other fruits and from rose hips.

And, of course, watch your diet and take bone meal for good strong teeth!

CHAPTER 6

Raw Juice Therapy

Many readers frequently inquire about the drinking of vegetable and fruit juices. Should they buy juicers and should they make freshly juiced vegetables and fruits part of their daily diet? If so, why?

A new book, *Raw Juice Therapy*, by John B. Lust, publisher of *Nature's Path*, treats the question in a most satisfactory way. Mr. Lust believes heartily in drinking raw juices, both to cure diseases and to maintain good daily health. We have some points of disagreement with the book. But let us discuss first those aspects with which we are in accord.

Mr. Lust has obviously had a lot of experience in using vegetable and fruit juices and he gives a great deal of practical information on combining the juices of different foods, fruits and vegetables, how to prepare juices, how to decide on a juicer and how to care for it. He also gives several menus indicating how juices may be used in the daily diet of the health-conscious person. Three juice cocktails a day seem to be his recommendations.

You understand, of course, when we talk of "juice therapy" or the use of raw juices, we are not talking about anything you can buy at the grocery store. Canned tomato juice, canned grape juice, frozen citrus juice—things of this kind are not what we mean. Mr. Lust's book deals entirely with the fresh *raw* juice of carrots, parsley, garlic, spinach, apples, celery, cucumber, water cress and so forth, juiced before drinking. This, of course, necessitates having equipment for juicing and there are many juicers available.

He tells us that raw juice is the best way to get minerals and vitamins in quantity. Cooking, of course, destroys much vitamin content, creates grievous loss of minerals and entirely eradicates enzymes. Eating the raw fruits and vegetables rather than juicing them involves the body's handling a great deal of roughage—the cellulose which makes up the largest bulk of foods like carrots, celery and so forth. We need a certain amount of bulk. But by taking some of our fresh foods in the form of juice, we have access to vast quantities of vitamins and minerals that we could not get by eating the foods whole, simply because the stomach could not handle that much food at one time.

So far so good.

We know that juice therapy has been used by many outstanding medical and naturopath practitioners. Dr. Max Gerson cured cancer using chiefly the freshly-made raw juices of fruits and vegetables—high in potassium and other minerals. However, we are inclined to doubt that there can be any such definite prescribing of juices as this book goes into—one combination of juice for asthma, another for bladder disease, another for diabetes, another for gallstones and so forth.

Actually, most vegetables contain quite similar amounts of minerals. Then, too, there is no one mineral or combination of minerals which is important for one organ or one disease. They are all important. Even iron deficiency anemia is not cured by giving iron, unless you give copper at the same time.

So, granted that it is important to get plenty of minerals, can anyone say categorically that a juice providing a large amount of such-and-such a mineral will cure whatever is wrong with as complicated a mechanism as the kidney? Or the lungs? Headaches may result from any number of causes. Can anyone say definitely that the juice of a certain 4 vegetables will cure all headaches no matter what their source?

We are inclined to doubt it. In other words, we believe that Mr. Lust has over-simplified the process of "cure" in his enthusiasm for the general overall benefits one may derive from freshly-made juices.

We have the feeling about this book that we have about many books on diet. So long as they advocate the eating of natural foods and advise against refined foods (which Mr. Lust does) we're with them one hundred per cent. But we think the success readers have in following such diets comes from their avoidance of refined foods, not from whether they take celery juice for sodium or lettuce juice for magnesium. Or, for that matter, whether they take juices at all.

Get Organically Grown Vegetables and Fruits

One other serious doubt in our minds about juice therapy in these days of insecticides is just that—what about the insecticides? The average person might eat in one day a carrot, a couple of salads and 3 or 4 pieces of raw fruit. This would guarantee him getting a certain amount of insecticides. But when you use raw juices, you may use as much as 4 or 5 carrots, a pound of greens, 3 or 4 apples and so on for making just one juice cocktail. If you take 3 of these a day, you are getting a fine amount of minerals and enzymes, but you are also getting a stiff dose of concentrated insecticides, for, remember, they cannot be washed off. Organic gardeners, of course, need have no worries on this score.

In addition to well over a hundred pages of information on juice therapy, this new book contains tables of calories, vitamins, recommended daily requirements of various food elements, information on normal blood pressure, temperature, pulse, pollination schedule for hay fever victims and much more helpful material. We think it fills a definite need, for it answers fully the questions of those who want to know more about and experiment with juice therapy.

CHAPTER 7

What's Wrong With Soft Drinks?

Probably most of us Americans have by now a general idea that soft drinks are not especially to be recommended as part of one's diet. But did you ever get into a discussion of the subject with a friend or neighbor, or, what is worse, at your P.T.A. or club meeting, and find that you can't actually state with clarity and conviction just why soft drinks are harmful? You won't find today many people who will give you an argument when you discuss the harmfulness of alcohol and tobacco. Even the most devoted addicts will admit that they are harming their health when they drink or smoke to excess. But have you ever tried to reason with someone who regularly consumes from one to 5 or 10 bottles of carbonated drinks per day?

Have you ever raised your voice at the meeting of the committee which is planning the Sunday School picnic, or the field day or the club outing to which the kids are invited? Pop, colas, ginger ale, birch beer and sodas are accepted as part of the day's fun and you are nothing but a wet blanket if you enter any protests suggesting that other kinds of drinks might be more healthful, especially for the children.

Here is some ammunition that may be helpful to you in your next discussion over carbonated drinks. Written by George Blumer, M.D., the first article appeared originally in *Annals of Western Medicine and Surgery* for February, 1952. Dr. Blumer reminds us that the American Medical Association through all its outlets of literature for the laymen has for a number of years been calling attention to the possible harm that the habitual consumption of soft drinks can bring about.

This harm falls under 3 heads: 1. some of the drinks contain harmful drugs, 2. most of them have a chemical reaction strong enough to injure certain parts of the body, especially the teeth and 3. their constant use is almost bound to have a deleterious effect on other aspects of diet.

Caffeine in the Cola Drinks

The cola beverages contain caffeine—about ⅔ of a grain of caffeine to 6 ounces of the beverage. That is, 3 bottles of "Coke" contain about as much of the drug as one cup of coffee. We know many parents who will not permit their children to drink coffee but, knowingly or unknowingly, permit them to drink day after day cola drinks whose total caffeine content may far exceed that of a cup or two of coffee. Most medical men today believe that the use of caffeine is harmful, especially for youngsters. We know that it is a drug which has a stimulating effect. There is evidence, says Dr. Blumer, that caffeine increases gastric secretion, making it undesirable for use by individuals with peptic ulcers. Ulcers have been produced in animals and in some human beings by the excessive use of caffeine. Some people, hypersensitive to caffeine, are unable to take it at all. Others develop dizziness from drinks containing caffeine.

The American cola beverage has a pH of approximately 2.6. This means that it is highly acid. Erosion of the enamel and dentine in rats' teeth has been brought about by habitual consumption of cola drinks. Human teeth suspended in a cola beverage gradually lose their calcium over a period of two weeks. The relation of the consumption of carbonated drinks to the high incidence of tooth decay in America is undoubtedly being investigated right now by a number of highly qualified researchers. Meanwhile, does it not seem reasonable that a substance which can in two weeks erode the calcium from human teeth suspended in it cannot help but harm tooth enamel, when this same substance is in contact with the enamel day after day, year after year, summer and winter?

Perhaps their most dangerous aspect, especially for the health of our children, is the effect of carbonated drinks on dietary habits. These drinks contain absolutely no food value, except for calories, which produce quick energy and fat. So there is no way to compare the value of milk, or a fruit or vegetable drink with a cola drink. The former contain in varying amounts proteins and fats, along with many, many vitamins and minerals. The cola drink contains nothing the body uses but the calories of its sugar.

When your children select a soft drink at the school lunch counter, at the drug store on the way home from school or at home in the evening, they are consuming a disproportionate amount of sugar which contributes nothing useful to their health and which satisfies their appetites so that they have no desire for the healthful foods, containing food elements their growing bodies must have. Then, too, it is surprising how rapidly one can get the habit of soft drinks on every occasion rather than milk, fruit or vegetable juices as the natural accompaniment of food. Of course, radio and television programs, billboards and magazine advertising present your favorite screen star or crooner swigging down soft drinks by the gallon— this is bound to have an effect on all of us, too, but especially on the young folks.

Erosive Power of Soft Drinks on Teeth

The experiments to which Dr. Blumer refers are those performed at Cornell University by Dr. Clive McCay and Lois Will. Four sets of rats were used. One group was given tomato juice to drink as their only beverage. The second group drank orange juice, the third distilled water and the fourth phosphoric acid and sucrose in the same percentages in which they are found in the cola drinks.

Distilled water was the only drink that did not erode the rats' teeth. Tomato juice caused the least erosion, phosphoric acid the most. In fact, at the end of 6 months the researchers could no longer estimate erosion of the teeth of those rats who drank the cola mixture, because their teeth had eroded right down to the gum line. Remember, conditions of the experiment were not exaggerated in any way. The rats ate a good diet and all other circumstances of their existence were directed toward good health. But they drank the cola mixture every day. (How many folks in your family do the same?)

As further proof of the violent action of phosphoric acid on tooth enamel, the two Cornell experimenters suspended human teeth in a cola solution, then calculated the quantity of calcium in each tooth at intervals. In 3 hours 1.4 milligrams of calcium per gram of tooth had been dissolved. In 336 hours 14.6 milligrams of calcium had been dissolved. Now this doesn't mean that a human tooth, suspended in a cola solution will disintegrate before your eyes. It does mean, however, that over a period of time (two weeks, for instance) that tooth may lose its calcium which is the most important constituent of tooth enamel.

What relation does this fact have, do you suppose, to the current rate of tooth decay in this country, especially among our young people?

Consumers' Reports became greatly interested in Dr. McCay's experiments and did some investigating of their own which they reported in their July, 1950, issue. Their laboratory purchased 13 common soft drinks and tested them for their acid content. The results follow. To interpret these results, one must understand the chemical term pH, which is the way of indicating acidity or alkalinity. A neutral liquid, like water, has a pH of 7. Numbers less than 7 indicate acidity and the lower the pH number, the greater the acidity. In other words, according to *CR* investigation, the cola drinks are much more acid; club soda less so.

	Brands	Average pH
Colas	6	2.4
Ginger ale	12	2.7
Lime, lemon, and lemon & lime	7	2.9
Grape	6	3.0
Raspberry	4	3.1
Cherry	7	3.1
Orange	11	3.2
Root Beer	4	3.4
Cream soda	11	3.9
Sarsaparilla	5	4.0
Cocoa cream	3	4.3
Club soda	10	4.7

Consumers' Reports counsels: "The safest procedure is to minimize the risk of acid erosion by going easy with the more acid beverages, drinking them in moderation and preferably with food (which dilutes the acid effect)."

They're All Erosive, Regardless of Acidity

Another experiment performed by Carey D. Miller of the Foods and Nutrition Department of the University of Hawaii is reported in the *Journal of the American Dietetic Association* for April, 1952. One hundred and twenty-nine rats were given carbonated drinks with their food— flavored sodas, root beer and other nationally advertised drinks. The lower molars of the rats were observed and rated respectively for the following 5 conditions: 1. high polish of enamel, 2. slight etching, 3. mild destruction, 4. moderate destruction and 5. severe destruction.

Results ranged from .8 for root beer to 3.4 for one kind of orange drink. This researcher discovered the interesting fact that the *p*H, or acidity, of the beverage apparently did not indicate always the amount of erosion that would occur. Some of the less acid drinks were found to be as erosive as the more acid ones. Three cola drinks produced 3 different degrees of enamel erosion; two ginger ales gave entirely different results and one orange soda produced almost twice as much erosion as the other, even though their degree of acidity was very similar.

Miller brings up the use of lithium in soft drinks, indicating that lithium seems to reduce somewhat the erosive quality of the liquids. One lemon soda *without lithium* gave a score of 1.4 erosion. Another of the same brand with *lithium* gave a score of .9. Incidentally, lithium is a substance "regarded unfavorably" by the Food and Drug Administration which recommends that its use be discontinued. However, when the Food and Drug Administration "recommends" that lithium be discontinued in soft drinks, this apparently remains a matter of choice to the manufacturer.

It is interesting to note, in Miller's report, the erosion scores resulting from the use of noncarbonated beverages—drinks made from synthetic beverage powders. Both of these noncarbonated drinks—orange and strawberry—brought about a higher rate of erosion than the carbonated drinks. Miller is careful to point out that no one has proved definitely that enamel erosion brings about cavities in human teeth. But we agree with him when he states that it seems reasonable to assume that overindulgence in such acid beverages as carbonated drinks and powdered fruit drinks must cause defects in the enamel of human teeth.

Nearsightedness and Cola Drinks

Dr. Hunter H. Turner in an article in the *Pennsylvania Medical Journal* for May, 1944, on the subject of prevention of myopia or degenerative nearsightedness suggests that incorrect diet undoubtedly plays an important role in producing myopia. Furthermore he believes that carbonic acid is the eye's worst enemy and he attributes the alarming increase in cases of myopia to "the pernicious guzzling of carbonated beverages by young children today." Carbonated beverages exposed to air break down into their basic ingredients of water and carbon dioxide so that such drinks would be much less harmful if they were allowed to stand until they were "flat." But, of course, their most attractive characteristic is their "fizz." So they are taken into the stomach while they are still actively effervescing. There is no atmospheric pressure in the stomach, so a large amount of the acid is assimilated by the body.

Soft Drinks Worthless as Food

Dr. Michael J. Walsh, Instructor in Clinical Nutrition at the University of California and past president of the American Academy of Applied Nutrition had this to say about soft drinks at a meeting of the California State Dental Association in 1950: "When it comes to the comparison of the fruit juices with some popular soft drinks, this table shows the actual difference in nutritive value:

	Lemon Juice	Orange Juice	Grapefruit Juice	Cola	Ginger Ale
Protein, grams per 100 grams	1.0	.5	.5	—	—
Fat, grams per 100 grams	.7	.1	.1	—	—
Carbohydrates, grams per 100 grams	8.5	11.4	9.8	10.5	9.0
Calories	48.	49.	42.	42.	36.
Calcium, milligrams per 100 grams	28.	26.	19.	—	—
Phosphorus, milligrams per 100 grams	7.	14.	18.	—	—
Iron, milligrams per 100 grams	.2	.1	.2	—	—
Vitamin A, I.U. per 100 grams	50.	270.	14.	—	—
Thiamin, milligrams per 100 grams	.060	.080	.028	—	—
Riboflavin, milligrams per 100 grams	4.	80.	90.	—	—
Niacin, milligrams per 100 grams	.15	0.5	—	—	—
Vitamin C, milligrams per 100 grams	45.	45.	30.	—	—

Now ask yourself, are these beverages comparable?

"Lemon juice, when consumed consistently and regularly is known to be a prominent factor in erosion (of tooth enamel). . . . The cola drinks are well known for their caries-producing effect, not only because of the sugar content, but also because of their known content of free phosphoric acid which is a well-known solvent of tooth enamel. When Dr. Hockett asks 'is the orange juice better than the soft drinks for total health,' I refer him to the table and let the facts speak for themselves." As you know, we are opposed to the excessive use of citrus juice, because of its harmful effects on the teeth. But at least citrus juice, taken in moderation, is *food!*

What Exactly Is In Soft Drinks?

Soft drinks contain carbon dioxide which makes them "fizz." The carbon dioxide used by soft drink manufacturers may be the by-product from some other manufacturing process, such as the brewing or coke industry, or it may be produced by reacting chalk, limestone or bicarbonate of soda with sulfuric acid.

As one of the earnest defenders of soft drinks points out, the only sugar used in making these beverages is "sugar of the highest degree of purity." This means, of course, sugar that has been refined until there is not a chance of even one iota of food value remaining in it. This means, too, that all of the other food factors in the sugar cane, beet or corn from which the sugar was made, are omitted in the refined sugar. These other food factors are important for a proper assimilation and metabolism of sugar in the body. But you don't get them in refined sugar. Sucrose made from cane or beet sugar and dextrose made from corn sugar are the most commonly used sweetening agents in soft drinks. Of course, in many states saccharin or some other synthetic sweetening agent is used. The acids poured into the carbonated beverage may be citric, tartaric or phosphoric, depending on what the flavor of the final product is to be.

The sparkling clear green of a lime drink does not mean that the product has been anywhere near a lime. If the luscious purple of a grape drink bears any resemblance to a grape living or dead, it is purely coincidental, for this drink has probably never been near a grape. The coloring agents for soft drinks are almost without exception certified coal tar colors. This means that they are the coloring matters made from coal tar which the government has certified as safe for human consumption, in spite of the fact that other coal tar colorings are known to produce cancer.

The flavors of soft drinks may come from natural or synthetic sources or compound essences which are a combination of both. In other words, the orange drink reposing in your refrigerator may perhaps actually contain some orange juice, or it may contain merely an approximation of orange flavor produced from coal tar.

When Dr. Clive McCay reported his rat experiments before the Delaney Committee investigating chemicals in foods, one lawmaker present reminded him that the soft drink industry has large proportions. (Indeed it does—it is a billion dollar industry!) He suggested soft-pedaling the facts Dr. McCay had reported because they might disrupt this industry and have a serious effect on the economy as a whole. Dr. McCay agreed that they might, but added that he believed the health of the nation's children might be as important as the welfare of the soft drink industry. However, a conspiracy of silence seems to surround McCay's testimony. At any rate it never made the headlines in our newspaper—did it in yours?

Harmful Chemicals in Processing

Aside from the contents of the soft drinks, there is a relatively new source of danger in the container. In 1953, Walter S. Mack, former president of Pepsi-Cola, and now president of Cantrell & Cochrane Corporation, makers of Super Cola, Super Ginger Ale, Super Grape Soda, Super Club Soda and Super Root Beer announced the revolutionary innovation of the use of the no-deposit, no-return can instead of bottles. Since that time the can business for soda pop has sky-rocketed and many other beverage manufacturers have taken over the idea.

However, a carbonated beverage can present problems. *San Francisco Examiner,* for January 22, 1954, discussing the subject, states that "the pop would eat the liner and attack tinplate alloys of a conventional can. Pacific (Can Company, which started the boom) started with corrosion and acid-resistant steel. Then it developed a special organic coating, rolled on flat steel. Finally, a vinylite plastic lining is sprayed on after the can is fabricated."

All this shows a great deal of industry on the part of the can company, but even with its final product, who can determine the chemicals that have eaten away at the lining of the can and entered the beverage? The damage from this source alone can be considerable.

Difficulties in Combating Sales

With so much positive evidence against soft drinks, why is something not being done to prohibit their sale? First, the public is not fully educated to the facts. School boards continue to allow soda machines in the schools, and offer pop with school lunches; factory officials allow the machines in the factories for a handy "lift" for their workers; and parents innocently allow their children to drink as long as their nickels hold out.

The following astounding figures in the business end of the story give, perhaps, the best reason for the continued sale:

The retail value of the sale of soft drinks increased from $150,939,553 in 1935 to over $700,000,000 in 1949. In 1943 there were over 6,000 bottling companies in this country. In 1950 Pepsi-Cola had 66 plants in foreign lands, Canada Dry had 38 and Coca-Cola, the biggest of them all, had 275 bottling plants—an increase from 65 in 1939. Over 100,000 people are employed in factories in this country. Sugar manufacturers supply over 250,000 tons of sugar to the industry each year. As well as the above, there are the flavoring concerns, the can companies and the newspapers, periodicals, radio and television which are royally supported by their advertising. Even government officials who are looking into the matter are under strong political pressure to "go easy."

When you look at the picture of this mammoth enterprise, its relation to our economy, individual jobs, and its influence on so many unrelated concerns, it becomes frighteningly clear that the fight for our health must be hard and long.

What Can We Do About Soft Drinks?

Dr. Miller's article makes no recommendations for solving the problem of excessive consumption of acid beverages, except to point out that it may play a part in promoting dental decay. Dr. McCay would, we strongly suspect, advise, nay insist upon, the complete elimination of soft drinks from the diet of any health-minded individual. Dr. Blumer has 3 positive suggestions to make.

First, further education of the public, especially parents, in regard to the possible dangers of excessive soft drink consumption. (Through the newspapers and magazines, Dr. Blumer, which also carry millions of dollars worth of soft drink advertising?) 2. Requirement by law that the contents of such beverages be printed on the label and 3. further research and investigation of the effects of carbonated drinks, so that presentations may be made intelligently to parent-teacher associations, medical societies and so forth with far more factual material than is now available.

It seems to us that enough research has already been done to incrimi-

[34]

nate carbonated drinks. We agree whole-heartedly that the contents of soft drinks should be listed on the label, just as the contents of all packaged, canned and bottled foods should be listed on the label. Furthermore we insist that this labeling be made simple enough that it really means something to the average housewife who has not had a course in the higher intricacies of chemistry. Which of us shoppers in the super market would have any idea what was meant by the chemical names of coal tar flavorings and colorings? We believe, too, that all government agencies that deal with general health, state, national and local, should make available to interested persons all the facts reported above on the subject of soft drinks. You might try writing to your congressman, state legislature and local board of health about this.

We hope sincerely that any adult who has read this chapter will be wise enough to shun soft drinks in the future. And for the young folks, we have another suggestion to make. Children nowadays are scientifically-minded. They study and respect science. They are, in general, aware that good health must be earned and learned—it is not just a hit-and-miss proposition. They admire and respect good health. And—when they're teen-agers at any rate—they admire good appearance. We think it's possible to educate the children of America away from carbonated drinks, beginning individually in our homes, if we do it on a scientific basis without resorting to blind unreasonable commandments.

We can say to our children, "We know you like to drink soft drinks. They taste good. Everybody else drinks them. But here are the facts, the scientific facts, mind you, about soft drinks and the harm they may do to your good health and your appearance." Scientifically-minded as they are today, young folks will take heed, we believe, if you point out to them calmly and objectively just where the harm lies in soft drinks.

CHAPTER 8

About Tea

"In order to rightly estimate the advantages of tea, we must not look at its value abstractly, but on the influence it exercises on the country at large. We look at its use as one of the greatest counteracters of intemperance, for the man who enjoys his tea with his family is not a person who seeks the stimulus of the tavern, and in the lower classes the public house and the gin-shop. These are pitfalls purposely placed to entrap the footsteps of the unwary. Few are so heedless as to fall into a pit if exposed to their view; but the warmth of the fire, the brightness of the lights, the temporary excitement of the draught are as flowers strewn over the chasm beneath. We do not go as far as to say that good and cheap tea would in any decided manner remedy this evil. But we do say this, and every man who has bestowed a thought upon the subject will agree with us, that the man who enjoys a good cup of tea and can get it, with its necessary concomitants, fire and comfort, at home, will not be in much danger of turning out after the labors of the day to seek the poisonous excitement of the drinking house."

So said an anonymous writer in London in a little booklet called *The Tea Trade,* published in 1850. It seems that, not only in England but in other countries as well, tea has been introduced and promoted for the express purpose of luring wayward fathers of families away from stronger drinks. A Chinese legend tells us that tea was first used in China in 2737 B.C. However, it is first mentioned in Chinese literature in 350 A.D. Its use spread rapidly through China and Japan under the guidance of the Buddhist priests who were trying to combat intemperance. The United States at present consumes only about seven-tenths of a pound of tea per person annually, where the British use about 10 pounds.

How We Get Tea

The tree which produces tea looks a little like myrtle and blossoms like a wild rose. When the leaves are being picked, the end ones—that is, the newest and tenderest ones—are picked for high-grade tea. The next leaves down on the branch for the next grade of tea and so forth. In all about 3,200 leaves or "shoots" are necessary for one pound of tea. There are over 2,000 possible blends.

In processing black tea the leaves are "withered" with heat, then rolled and allowed to ferment. For the green tea, the leaves are withered in hot pans, then rolled and dried. Oolong tea is partially withered at ordinary temperatures before it is dried. The fermentation of black tea removes some of the tannin, so that a cup of black tea properly made contains less tannin than a cup of green tea.

It appears that the criterion for excellence in tea is the amount of caffeine contained in it, in relation to the amount of tannin. The aim seems to be to achieve a tea high in caffeine and low in tannin. It is suggested that the best way to do this is to infuse the tea only 5 or 6 minutes and then immediately pour it off the leaves. For making tea, the water should be freshly boiled, the water and tea put into a hot teapot, then the brew poured off into another hot teapot. And, of course, teapots should always be of crockery, glass or china, never metal.

Tea contains caffeine, tannin or tannic acid and essential oils. The caffeine is the stimulating element, the tannin gives tea its color and body and the oils give it flavor and aroma. Tea contains 2.5 to 5 per cent of caffeine and 7 to 14 per cent of tannin. The tannin in concentration has an unpleasant effect on the mucous membranes of the mouth and digestive tract, but in the concentration in which it appears in a cup of tea it is not believed to be harmful. It is, of course, the same substance used widely in medicine as an astringent and for skin diseases and burns.

[36]

Whether Or Not You Should Drink Tea

In general, everything we say about caffeine in relation to health applies to tea as well as to coffee, except that the caffeine content of tea is not so high. Then too, it appears that there are fewer people in this country in danger of becoming tea addicts. There are, of course, people who drink tea in quantity, people who simply cannot get along without their tea. These folks are caffeine addicts just as the coffee drinkers are.

There is one aspect of tea which should be mentioned, because of the recent controversy over water fluoridation. Tea, as we drink it, is extremely rich in fluorine. A government booklet tells us that cheap grades of tea may contain as much as 398.8 parts per million of fluorine. Many of our foods contain fluorine in its natural form, in combination with other food minerals. So far as we have been able to determine, this naturally occurring fluorine is not harmful, any more than naturally occurring iodine in foods is harmful, in spite of the fact that a concentration of purified iodine, not combined in a food product, is of course poisonous.

If fluorine is indeed powerful against tooth decay as the "experts" would have us believe, how does it happen that the English people, drinking such quantities of fluorine in their daily tea, do not have wonderful teeth? As a nation, the British people have notoriously bad teeth. So far as we know, the "experts" who are promoting fluoridation, have never explained these curious facts.

We would say, however, if the water in your locality is fluoridated, you would do well to stay away from tea because tea-drinking is bound to add considerably to your fluorine intake. And the fluorine in tea does not appear with other minerals as it does, for instance, in the case of bone meal. Bone meal provides the calcium necessary to neutralize the toxic effects of fluorine, according to W. J. McCormick, M.D., of Toronto, Canada.

So, if your local water supply is fluoridated and you still feel that you cannot get along without your tea, perhaps bone meal as a food supplement would be your best safety bet.

CHAPTER 9

Tea and Stomach Disorders

Is the consumption of tea harmful for individuals who have stomach disorders? This question forms the basis of an article in the *Journal of the American Medical Association* for June 19, 1954. The authors, C. Wilmer Wirts, Martin E. Rehfuss, William J. Snape and Paul C. Swenson, all M.D.'s, did their study on patients of the Jefferson Hospital in Philadelphia.

All of the patients studied had either inactive duodenal ulcers or some other kind of digestive tract disorder. They were tested very scientifically with all kinds of apparatus for determining the emptying time of the stomach, the amount of acid produced and the motility, or activity, of the stomach walls. To further control the results, the same patients or others were given water rather than tea and the same measurements were taken. Both the water and tea were tested hot and cold.

The investigators found that tea seems to increase the rate of time in which the stomach is emptied after a mixed meal of protein, carbohydrates and fats has been taken. They found that iced tea and iced water seemed to have a greater effect on rapid emptying of the stomach than hot beverages.

They also found that tea seems to stimulate motility or movement of the stomach walls. They made this test with a stomach tube, then made it again using a fluoroscope through which they could observe the movements of the stomach. Finally they demonstrated the same fact using a balloon which the patient swallowed.

Tea and water seemed to have about the same effect on stomach acidity. Generally speaking no more and no less of the stomach secretions were produced regardless of which beverage was used. They gave the tea in doses of about two cups, which is the amount commonly taken at one meal. The tea was prepared according to the directions on the tea bag.

CHAPTER 10

Additional Information
on Beverages

Watery Ending for Meals

By J. I. Rodale

Children are just as much slaves to habit as their elders! Where does it stand written that a meal must finish up with a liquid? In the application of the newer knowledge of health, we have come across many commonly accepted fallacies. Is this another one? Habit! What crimes are committed in thy name! Is there some dread penalty to anyone who would dare to terminate a meal without milk, coffee, tea or other liquid?

A well-masticated, balanced meal with a good complement of watery food, such as fruits and raw vegetables, might fare better in the stomach. A good watery fruit like a pear or two could furnish the necessary liquid conclusion. Such a fruit is more than 85 per cent water, and what wonderful water! But extra-good mastication would be essential in such a meal. This, however, applies only to starches. Meats and such do not require much handling in the mouth. Their digestion takes place fully in the stomach.

A good idea, however, for those who want water at the end of meals, would be to follow up the custom of certain European racial groups and have the soup at the end of the meal. Such liquid could stand in place of the usual hot or cold drink. There are many clear hot soups that could serve the purpose very nicely, and in summer cold soups can be taken like the Russian borscht, or beet soup. The Swedes take rose-hip soup at the end of a meal.

For children or adults who absolutely must have a drink at the end of a meal, there are many teas such as alfalfa, mint, etc. There is postum, but it will taste a little peculiar at first without milk or cream. However, a little persistence and one will get used to it. A dish of stewed prunes in their natural syrup, with no sugar added, at the end of the meal, or fresh fruit cup with plenty of liquid portion, could serve as an excellent finale. A drink could be made from carob powder that is rich with minerals and tastes like chocolate. And what is wrong with a nice glass of plain water, without any chlorine or fluorine in it? Vitamins should be taken at the end of every meal, with a little water, of course. It should be a fitting ending to any meal.

The more important thing that should not be overlooked is to take table salt completely out of one's diet. The takers of salt require much more water; the taking of salt makes one overly thirsty. The ones who strongly demand liquids at the end of meals are the salt users. Most foods contain enough salt naturally to serve the body's needs. Remember, the human cell should have no salt (sodium chloride) in it. The salt should remain in the blood stream, but, too, large quantities of it in the blood can force some of it into the cell. And it is not wanted there. Did you know this? When people tell you that you must take salt, explain this simple fact to them.

There is a long-standing controversy that asks, shall we take water with our meals or not? The answer is not a simple one. A meal of refined foods, white breads, sugar, salt and ice cream or other desserts, might need water. But a healthy primitive-type meal with plenty of raw fruit and vegetables might not require it. The test is in the doing of it. Everyone's body is a law unto itself. Your general feeling of good health and buoyant energy will be the judge. But don't think that every meal requires a watery ending.

Coffee And Overweight

Leo B. Janis, M.D., quoted in the *Health Yearbook* (Stanford University Press) believes that reduction of coffee-drinking will be helpful among obese patients. Drinking decaffeinated coffee and cutting down the number of cups to 3 should produce excellent results. He reminds us that the average cup of coffee contains 1.5 grains of caffeine, so the effect on the nervous system of 6 or 7 cups a day is considerable. The caffeine content of regular coffee is roughly 6 to 8 times that of the instant, decaffeinated coffee, he says.

Tea Drinking Linked with Insomnia and Anemia

Those who have taken to using tea as a substitute for the coffee that causes their sleeplessness may find that their insomnia is as bad as ever. A letter in the British medical magazine the *Lancet* (December 7, 1957) gives a doctor's observations on tea-drinking. He noted that 9 of his patients who complained of "causeless" insomnia admitted to drinking 5 to 10 cups of tea (or coffee) each day. Four of these patients found that their problem ceased when they gave up tea. In some persons, says the letter, tea drunk even early in the day might cause sleeplessness. Many persons tend to forget that the stimulant and drug, caffeine, so clearly connected with coffee, is also contained in tea in almost the same amounts.

The writer adds a theory of his which makes tea-drinking responsible for chronic anemia in some cases. By simulating stomach conditions he found evidence that properties contained in tea act on iron the body consumes to make it impossible for the body to absorb it. This could mean that the iron in any meal that is topped off with a cup of tea does the body no good whatsoever.

Ink in Tea

Tea drinkers in several Detroit suburbs may be drinking ink occasionally. Research chemists of the manufacturers of a water softener report that when water rich in iron is used for tea, an ink is formed from the combination of tannic acid and iron. It's harmless, but it may cause a metallic taste.

Wine

In a 223-page report on alcoholism issued by the French government, it is stated that wine is a powerful germ killer and is as good as penicillin. It is said to be a killer of the bacilli of typhoid fever, paratyphoid, staphylococci and many others, destroying them on contact. But how many beneficial bacteria in the intestinal tract does it also kill on contact? These bacteria, called the intestinal flora, are sorely needed as an aid in the process of digestion. Many illnesses can be laid at the door of an improverished intestinal flora. Nature has its own way of inactivating disease-producing germs if given half a chance.

Synthetic Liquor Might Be Next

The distilleries must be places of happy delirium since the announcement by Robert Carroll, working with Connecticut's Perkin-Elmer Corporation, that the hangover might turn out to be only a dim, unpleasant memory for the hard liquor drinker (*Time* magazine, April 20, 1959). It seems that all hard liquor has tiny amounts of substances known as "cogeners," and these are the things that make one swear off on the morning after. Dr. Carroll seems to be convinced that removal of these factors will lead to synthetic liquor some day. It will mean no more hangovers, and drinks made to the exact taste of the buyer.

What will happen if drinkers can drink all they want with no discernible physical reaction, until the insides are too rotted to be helped? Will anything stop them before it's too late? Will a synthetic whiskey be able to duplicate the aged, natural stuff exactly, or will it be like synthetic vitamins, orange juice and other foods—something missing? And will what's missing be an undiscovered element that keeps the alcohol in liquor from killing the drinker outright? Will the manufacturer try to fill in with a couple of B vitamins added?

This announcement may intrigue a few into trying synthetic whiskeys, but we think it will give thinking drinkers pause and they might give up drinking just to avoid an unannounced dose of synthetic liquor.

Cola Drinks

By J. I. Rodale

In a letter to the *Lancet,* in the April, 1959, issue, Ernest George of Johannesburg, South Africa, writes: "I have been associated with the analysis of U.S.A. cola drinks over many years and your correspondent would probably like to know my findings. They contain orthophosphoric and citric acids, extracts of cola and vanilla, added caffeine (about ¼ gr. to the 6 oz. drink), sugar, caramel, salt, CO_2, and commonly used essential oils, seven-eighths of which are citrus oils and the remainder spice oils. The drinks are sterile and contain no artificial preservative. In caffeine content they are equivalent to weak tea and they are undoubtedly safe and wholesome, while being truly thirst-quenching."

I was not aware that cola drinks contained salt, a dangerous item of food for heart cases and those with high blood pressure. Orthophosphoric acid by no stretch of the imagination can be considered wholesome, and CO_2, which is the formula for carbon dioxide, is certainly not healthful. It is suspected as a weakening factor of the eyes, and recently a friend of mine who has the gout was advised by his physician not to drink even unsweetened carbonated beverages on account of their carbon dioxide content. I wonder whether in the cola drinks they use the vanilla actually extracted from the vanilla bean, or the artificial coal tar variety. Then the caffeine . . . about ¼ gram to a 6 ounce drink . . . . that's a lot of caffeine, brother, although they compare it to weak tea. And essential or spice oils . . . I wonder what they are. Nothing is said to indicate that the acidity of the cola drinks is the equivalent of vinegar. And, of course, it's sterile. Not a germ can live in it. Give me foods in which germs can live. When I'm dead I want to be embalmed, not when I'm alive.

No, excuse me, please, this is not a wholesome drink!

Soft Drink Advertising

The soft drink industry has announced an all-out campaign to further cultivate the teenagers market, according to a clipping from the *Milwaukee Journal* for February 11, 1958. It was announced that teenagers make up 15 per cent of the population and drink 41 per cent of the annual output of soft drinks. It is important to aim sales campaigns at them, said the spokesman for the industry, because of their influence on the buying habits of their families.

Need we look any farther than this for the answer to poor scholastic records, juvenile delinquency and a physical condition so under par that the President has appointed a special Youth Fitness committee to investigate the matter? And need we wonder why these conditions will continue so long as vast profits are to be made by aiming propaganda directly at these impressionable young people who are never allowed to read or learn anything derogatory to soft drinks?

The Dangers of Seltzer Water

The possible dangers you may run into drinking seltzer water are reviewed in a French medical journal—*Archives des maladies Professionnelles,* Vol. 15, p. 385. It seems that the metal head of a seltzer bottle may be made of lead. The seltzer water, because of its carbonic acid content, is capable of taking up considerable quantities of lead. In examining water from a number of samples of seltzer bottles it was found that they all contained far, far more lead than is permissible in drinking water in France. Although lead poisoning has never resulted, so far as we know, from using seltzer water in France, it seems that Spain has reported cases arising from this practice.

The authors advise making seltzer water bottle tops from some non-toxic material other than lead. We advise dispensing with the use of seltzer water entirely. Carbonated water and all of its relatives in the field of soft drinks contribute nothing but trouble.

SECTION 2.

Bread

The many valuable ingredients in whole wheat are well-known to nutritionists, and for this reason they have recommended bread made with the whole wheat kernel, rather than the bleached and drained flours used by most commercial bakeries. We agree that, if one is to eat bread at all, whole grain bread is best. However, research has shown that wheat is not a desirable food for everyone and has many unfortunate properties which one would do well to avoid. One can get the best values of wheat, without the undesirable ones, by using wheat germ oil or flakes.

CHAPTER 11

The Story of a Loaf of Bread

by J. I. Rodale

The making of a loaf of bread, from the time the seed of wheat goes into the ground until the wrapped loaf issues from the bakery, lends itself beautifully to demonstrate the extent of chemicalization that goes on in the manufacture of the average food product that the public eats. If you will follow me, step by step, you will be amazed at the recklessness of American manufacturers, at their lack of consideration for the health of the bread-consuming public and at the incredible apathy of that public and its medical advisers in not electing to power, public officials who will see to it that toxic chemicals are banned from use in food products.

The average person eats bread but never stops to look behind the loaf. To him or her, bread is bread. Man has eaten bread since cave-man days, and some think it sacrilegious to utter a word against it. However, I intend to utter quite a few words against it. I will tell you my story of a loaf of bread. Hear me out and then *you* be the judge.

Good Soil is Important For Good Bread

First, we must consider the soil in which the wheat crop is going to grow. Soil erosion has removed some of the finest topsoils of our country. It has been stated that over 61 per cent of the topsoil of American agricultural land has been lost in the last hundred years of farming, most of it probably in the last 20 or 30 years. Consider the fearful loss of topsoil in all midwestern floods, which cost millions of dollars of damage. This is in the wheat-growing section of our country. A great part of the wheat produced in the United States comes from the Dust Bowl. That name itself indicates what can be expected insofar as quality of soil is concerned. It has been stated that people are merely an expression of the soil from which their food is produced. Poor soil, poor people.

Our suicidal agricultural policy of using chemical fertilizers takes from the soil without putting back, kills bacteria and deposits caustic, corrosive chemicals in the soil, which destroy the natural antibiotic organisms such as penicillium. The wheat seed is planted in a soil in which we are spraying poisons, such as 2, 4-D and other insecticides to kill weeds. In many cases previous crops grown on the land have required highly poisonous insecticides, which have killed off many of the necessary bacteria and earthworms. The earthworm is such an important ally of the farmer. He burrows into and aerates the soil, and deposits his own manure in it to enrich it.

All of this is the introduction for the little wheat seed that goes into the ground. He starts life in a dirty, devitalized medium. The cards are stacked against him right from the beginning.

Wheat Seed Must Be Healthy

Secondly, we must see what is done to the seed and what it has become from years of abusive practices in agriculture. Dr. William Albrecht, of the University of Missouri, has said that the protein-content of the grains grown in the Middle West has gone down 10 per cent in the last 10 years. This is due to the commercial type of farming with its over-use of chemical fertilizers, especially potash, which increases the carbohydrate and reduces protein.

In medical literature in the last 20 years, the value of protein has been stressed. It is not only concerned about the diminishing quantity of protein that is left, but of late there have been researches showing that the quality too has been degenerating. Protein, for example, consists of amino acids, of which there are about 20. One of them, as a typical example, is arginine. A medical research has shown that cancerous tumors in animals could be cured by the use of arginine. On the other hand, Dr. William Albrecht himself has also shown that the more fertile the soil, the more arginine would be reflected in the crop. At any rate, we are now placing our little seed into the ground with less protein and with less arginine. But that is not all. In our agriculture in the last 20 or 30 years, disease has been on the increase, and the organisms of such disease are carried in the seeds. The average wheat seed is full of the smut and rust organism. The seed then is subjected to a treatment with a substance called *ceresan,* which is a mercury poison and which kills the smut and rust disease organisms, but unfortunately it has been known that the poison penetrates into the seed and some of it will show up in the seed of the new crop which will be used to make bread. Today, when you purchase wheat seed at the feed dealers, it has probably already been treated with the mercury poison, and the bags are marked "caution," with prohibiting instructions so that the seed will not be fed to chickens or other farm animals. Occasionally, however, a farmer is careless or forgets, and kills animals with such feed. In veterinary laboratories, mercury poisoning is seen each year on specimens of swine and chickens, which have been submitted to them for testing.

The Harm of Chemical Fertilizers

Now we come to the third step, the farmer saturates the soil with a chemical fertilizer. When the plant is growing and at a certain point, if it is infested with weeds, a spray of 2, 4-D will be given from the air. Very little research has been done as to the effect of these weed-killers on the soil and the bacterial life of that soil, as well as on the crops and the health of people consuming such crops. We do know that some of these weed-killers kill other crops. For example, grapevines can be hurt badly if the wind goes the wrong way and brings some of the 2, 4-D to it. The same thing would apply to a crop of soybeans. These weed-killers are chemicals that are used because the farmer is at his wit's end as the result of poor farming practices, and it seems to him to be the simplest thing to do. On our own experimental farm, on the other hand, where the organic method is practiced and where no chemical fertilizers are used, the soil is in such fine shape that at the proper time we can cultivate out the weed seeds and kill them. Our soil's sponge-like quality and the ease with which it can be worked by farm implements are due to the structure that is given to it by the organic matter that we use. Our farm is a wonderful example of the control of weeds by natural biological methods rather than by chemicals.

Must Wheat Be Fumigated?

We now come to the fourth step. The farmer harvests the wheat. In the old days, when there were not the automatic combines which took the wheat in and threshed it at the same time, the farmer shocked the crop and let it season in the field. The heads of the seeds ripen slowly in this manner and give the flour mill a much easier seed to work with. Today, I have been told by a flour mill manufacturer that he has all kinds of trouble because of the fact that the wheat is taken in somewhat green and is not seasoned or ripened in the field. Various treatments are given, therefore, to prevent spoilage or to make it easier to handle, but very little is known about such treatments and what they consist of. The farmer himself takes in the wheat, stores it in his bin in the barn and now treats it with cyanogen gas, which is such a dangerous poison that he has to wear a gas mask while applying it. Cyanogen is used to kill grain weevils. On my own farm we do not spray any gas, and we have very little trouble. It is possible that wheat grown by the organic method, that is, with the use of organic matter and rock fertilizers ground up without the use of acids, has a better keeping ability. At any rate, I would rather have the few grain weevils than saturate the whole mass of a food product with something as violently poisonous as cyanogen.

Stone Grinding Is Best

We now come to the fifth step. The wheat is ground fine in the steel roller process. In the old days, grain was ground in stone mills which revolved slowly and kept the flour at a low temperature. But a new process was discovered by a Hungarian about 80 years ago, in which rapidly revolving steel rollers were used. This heated up the flour and removed a large amount of the valuable nutrients it contained. It is rather strange that the first known cases of polio came about just a little after the steel roller mill process began about 80 years ago. Several physicians have remarked about the coincidence. The flour that came out of the old-fashioned mill, 75 and 100 years ago, contained about 75 per cent of the vitamin B_1 of the wheat. Your white flour of today probably retains only 10 per cent of it. The difference is what is destroyed in our modern milling and refining process.

Since the beginning of steel rolling, many physicians believe that we have more digestive disturbances, poorer teeth, more constipation and more widely spread nervous diseases. It is a known fact that the steel rolling process produces a poorer gluten in the flour, which makes it difficult to work with in the mill. Add to this the fact that the wheat itself is poorer today, because of the deterioration of soil fertility brought about by its over-stimulation with chemical fertilizers.

There's Profit in Removing the Bran

We now come to the sixth step. In the milling process the bran or outer coat is removed. This is a very important part of the wheat seed, and contains large amounts of vitamins and minerals, especially iron which is so necessary to make good red blood, and phosphorus for nerves and bones. The outer bran contains proteins of very good quality. But because the bran is so good, it is set aside and sold to farmers who feed it to pigs. In this way, the flour mill makes more money. What is left is the inner part of the seed kernel containing, outside of the wheat germ which we will discuss in the next step, practically no vitamins or minerals. It is mostly starch and gluten and is good for making paste.

It would certainly be fairer to the public if it was placed at least on the same level with the pig. Actually, the separation of the two elements of the grain creates nothing. The pig gets the bran, and man gets the white stuff. Why not give both the man and the pig their proper share of the whole grain? Let each one get some of the white and some of the brown. Why should pigs become healthy at the expense of the ill-health of man?

The Germ is Removed, Too

We now come to step number seven. The wheat germ is removed from the wheat. In the human being this would be equivalent to removing his heart. The wheat germ is the very heart and life of the seed, rich in vitamins and minerals, and when that is gone, the seed certainly will never grow into a plant. It is one of the richest sources of vitamins B and E and contains valuable proteins and fat. The vitamin E is usually sold to farmers to make their horses more fertile, and some people buy it for themselves. The drug industry makes millions out of this wheat germ. The public, therefore, must take vitamin E to replace the lost wheat germ from the bread that it is eating. It is our suggestion that the public be sure to take wheat germ, brewer's yeast and bone meal to replace the valuable vitamins and minerals that have been lost in the removal of the bran and the germ from the wheat. We are now left with a really dead substance.

Why Bleach Flour?

The eighth step is the bleaching of the flour, which Dr. Carlson of the University of Chicago called "social custom and biological stupidity." In Germany and England I found that all the bread and rolls there are of a grey color, which indicates that the wheat is not bleached. I also noted that the span of life is higher, especially in Germany. In bleaching, various chemicals are used, such as alum, ammonia, gypsum (which is plaster of Paris) and others, which are known to be toxic to human

[48]

beings, in spite of some in high authority who say they are not. All bleaches are poisonous. It cannot be otherwise. The amount, however, is small, but when you consider the cumulative effect of the various preservatives that the public gets in all of its foods and the chlorine in its drinking water, that cumulative amount then becomes a serious factor in the equation of health. Gypsum is used partly for its bleaching effect and also because it absorbs water, thus cutting down more expensive ingredients needed in the bread. Bleaching enables the miller to use inferior flours—flours that are also of undesirable grades. One of the most common bleaches is nitrogen trichloride or agene. A few years ago, Sir Edward Mellanby in England discovered that the use of this chemical gave fits to dogs. The government of England became aroused and began to hold hearings on the question of discontinuing the use of nitrogen trichloride. A controversy raged in this country also between the Food and Drug Administration and the baking industry regarding its use. The bakers say that dogs are not people. Personally, it doesn't make any difference whether it is dogs or even flies, if it will give fits to anything that lives, I want none of it. Nitrogen trichloride ages the flour at once instead of waiting two or three weeks for natural aging to take place. That is why it is called agene. It enables the miller to work without skill. Bleaching increases the acidity of the flour. It is done also to deceive and it takes the strength from the flour. It is a reproach to the milling trade and an insult to the customer. It certainly does not make us think of the miller as the "merry miller of old" with his friendly, jolly face, a man in whom we had the utmost confidence and who was really turning out what is the staff of life. This reminds me of a little jingle that I once heard: "The whiter the bread, the sooner you're dead."

As we have seen in the fifth step, the rolling mill process and the nitrogen trichloride that was used did something to the gluten in the flour which made it difficult to work. Therefore, other things have to be added at a later stage of manufacture in order to make the flour easier to work with.

Is Bleaching Dangerous?

A great deal of work has been done in England to find out whether the use of nitrogen trichloride is dangerous. Dr. Barnet Stross, in the December 1, 1951, issue of the *Lancet,* stated that this chemical had been tried on more than just one species of animals, namely, dogs. It has already been tried on 6 animal species, and in every case it has caused the symptoms that were found originally, which gave running fits to dogs. Sir Edward Mellanby himself stated that the nitrogen trichloride causes part of the wheat protein to be converted into a substance that is poisonous to all species of animals. Actually, this bleaching agent converts the yellow carotenoide pigment to colorless compounds. By taking the color portion out of the flour, vitamins are removed. Sir Edward Mellanby also stated that "some of the increase in the common disorders of the alimentary tract—appendicitis, cholecystitis and peptic ulcer—might possibly be attributed to this large-scale tampering with natural foodstuffs." Dr. H. Pollak, physician in charge of the allergy clinic of the Central Middlesex Hospital of London, stated in the issue of July 5, 1950, of the *Medical Press,* that "Since then in the course of the last 3 to 4 years, we have encountered many food allergic patients whose symptoms were partly or entirely controlled on a restricted diet containing non-agenized, but excluding 'bleached' (agenized) wheat products, in whom symptoms could frequently, or invariably, be reproduced by ingestion of agene-bleached 'white' bread. In numerous subjects such symptoms have followed from as little as a slice of 'white' bread. In a few patients, usually with dyspeptic symptoms, the 'white' bread was better tolerated than the 'brown' (non-agenized) one."

Dr. Anton J. Carlson, professor emeritus of the University of Chicago, and world renowned physiologist, in the United Press dispatch of December 29, 1950, called nitrogen trichloride (agene) a nerve poison and asserted that it might be a contributing cause of alcoholism. Dr. Carlson says that this chemical changes a good protein into a bad one, which causes nervous instability, very frequently, and which instability causes a person to become an alcoholic addict.

Dr. William Brady, M.D., in his newspaper column has stated that "dogs fed mainly on entirely white bread or white flour products, may develop what is mistaken for rabies—shunning food, losing weight, avoiding light, trembling, cringing when patted, climbing walls, falling backwards, howling piteously, falling into their pans if they try to eat and running around madly."

Psychiatrists claim that bleached flour may contribute to mental diseases. Dr. Ethel Mae Shaull, of the Stanford Medical School and former staff psychiatrist at Agnew State Hospital, has suspected that the tremendous increase of mental diseases among Americans is due in part to eating of bread and other foodstuffs made of bleached or agenized flour.

In spite of all this evidence the baking industry still claims that nitrogen trichloride is not dangerous to human beings. However, they have decided not to use it in this country, and now they have gone back to chlorine dioxide which was used a long time ago for this purpose. It is hard to believe that they would rush right in to substitute another chemical which might perhaps be not quite as harmful as nitrogen trichloride, but might still be toxic. But I read in an article that chlorine dioxide is definitely toxic to laboratory animals, although tests on humans so far have shown no injurious effect. However, the tests have not been carried on long enough in the opinion of such distinguished food scientists as Dr. McCay of Cornell and Dr. Carlson.

Here is something, however, that is very incriminating to chlorine dioxide. It is taken from Lockwood's *Flour Milling,* 1948 edition. It says: "Chlorine dioxide is more powerful than nitrogen trichloride; the quantities used are one-third to one-half those of nitrogen trichloride. Chlorine dioxide not only oxidizes the flour pigment, but also has a valuable bleaching effect on the coloring matter of bran, which makes it particularly valuable for bleaching very low grade flours." This has not received any publicity. Everybody just takes for granted that since bakers are changing over, they would naturally change over to something that is not dangerous, but really I believe that something very fast is being pulled on the public and on the government officials and scientists who are passing on this matter. Let's look into this chlorine dioxide.

Trying To Put Back What Has Been Removed

We now come to the ninth step, the enriching of the bread with synthetically manufactured vitamins and some iron. After the heart is removed, the conscience of the miller is disturbed and he rushes to enrich the bread with vitamins made from coal tar. Twenty-eight states have laws that require bread to be thus enriched. It is sad to think of states passing such laws without making the thorough researches that would show up definitely whether this has any harmful effect on the people eating the bread. Yet, some 20 odd natural vitamin and mineral elements are removed from the wheat by an expensive process and then only 4 or 5 are put back, including a little iron. It reminds me of the way orange juice is being sold to the public today. In the Florida factories the water is first removed from the orange juice. The resulting product is sold to the public who then put ordinary sink water that has been treated with chlorine back into the concoction. In this case the orange product is "enriched" with sink water. In the bakery enriching is a very simple process. All the baker does is to add a few cheap vitamin tablets to his batches.

Natural Products vs. Synthetics

There is a question whether substances such as vitamins or medicines made from synthetic chemicals are worse than the same vitamins made from natural substances such as food. There are experiments which have been done on an optical instrument which throws a beam of light, and it seems to show that when a certain element made synthetically is placed in this instrument, the light will be thrown on one side. When the same element made from a natural source is placed in the machine for test, it will usually throw its rays on the opposite side. I do not know what the significance is but evidently there *is* a difference. There are also researches which show that vitamins produced from natural foods are better than those made synthetically. For example, I know of one that was done within the last 15 years in Russia and which was reported in the Russian medical publication called the *Vitamin News.* Two groups of mice were taken and each was given a diet that was supposed to produce scurvy. But one group was given synthetically made vitamin C, while the other was given vitamin C made from a natural food product. The group of mice that got the synthetic vitamin C still had their scurvy after the experiment was completed, but those that obtained the vitamin C from natural food were cured. It would seem, therefore, that when synthetic vitamin tablets are thrown into the flour mix, there is a question in my mind how good it is.

There are also researches that indicate that an excess of vitamin B_1 can produce sterility in humans. I do not think any comparative research was made in these experiments of vitamin B_1 produced from natural sources, as against those produced synthetically, but I *do* know that vitamin

[51]

B_1 by itself cannot be made or isolated from natural food sources. In such a product it must be the whole vitamin B complex, such as is obtained from brewer's yeast, or nothing. It is, therefore, dangerous to take the synthetic vitamin B_1 over long periods of time. I wonder what happens to drunkards who are given tremendous doses of vitamin B_1 in order to cure their alcoholism. They must all become sterile, I imagine, which in itself is not such a bad thing either, in their case. It is a form of poetic justice.

The Baker Embalms the Bread

We now come to step ten, or the disinfecting process. The flour finally goes to the baker, and brother, what he does to it is just plain murder. He looks at the flour. He is not satisfied with it, because it is not completely dead. The success of commercially manufactured bread is to make it completely dead so it does not pose any problems to the baker as he works it and as it goes through the various processes in the bakery. The flour must be completely embalmed. That is the only word I can find that would fit it. The baker takes another look at the flour and scratches his head. It seems to him that the flour still has a little life. Its toes are wiggling so to speak. A bug might want to take a little nibble on it. You know that when something becomes sterile and lacks the spark of life, a bug has sense enough not to want to touch it, but it is different, of course, with man. The baker wants the bread so dead that a bug won't touch it with a 15-foot pole. So he calls in the experts, and whom does he call? The same firm that made the mercury poison that we started off with, way at the beginning when the seed was doused with mercury in order to kill the smut and rust organism. This company obliges the baker with a product which kills fungi and the remaining bacteria. It saturates itself into every atom or molecule of the bread. Naturally, it would have to do that so that no bacteria or fungi would work in the minutest part of the bread. It is more or less of a disinfectant, you might say. The bread is thoroughly disinfected. The baker would not use CN or Lysol, but he does use Mycobahn. Mycobahn is calcium propionate, which was discovered by the Du Pont Company. They had noticed the fact that Swiss cheese did not mold the same as other cheese and found that the presence of calcium propionate retarded mold's growth. Anything that would retard growth of a living thing is dangerous to people and to our intestinal flora. Only a pinch of Mycobahn is put into the bread mixture, mind you, but it is a powerful enough pinch that spreads itself into every atom of the dough mixture. It is a known fact that Mycobahn destroys the enzyme that makes it possible for the body to assimilate the limited amount of calcium left in the flour after all this *Farben-izing* and *ersatzing* to which the staff of life is subjected.

Then More Chemicals Are Added

The next step, eleven, is the conditioning of the dough. This is accomplished by chemicals which are known as emulsifiers, extenders and improvers, and were developed as a result of war conditions when milk, fat and eggs were scarce. By the use of these emulsifiers, some foods such

[52]

as milk, fat and eggs are not put into the bread, and instead chemicals are substituted. Some of these chemicals, I am told, are used in the anti-freeze of auto radiators. The general name of this kind of chemical is surface-active compounds, which are added during the processing of the flour to make the bread retain its freshness longer and to give it a smoother texture and more attractive appearance.

The baker has a problem of staleness of the bread on his hands. He wants to bake a loaf that will stay in the stores for extra days and feel soft to the touch. The chemical accomplishes this by making the flour absorb much more water, in some cases 6 times its weight, which makes it retain its softness and fresh-looking appearance. It is a game of fooling the customer. The lady buyer feels it and thinks it is fresh, but really it is not fresh. The bakery trade has given a name to the way a woman customer feels the bread to see if it is fresh. The way she touches and pinches it is called "playing the piano on the bread." There are doctors who claim that it is healthier to eat stale bread. Probably one of the reasons is that you have to chew stale bread more and thoroughly salivate it, whereas with the soft, chemicalized loaf, the tendency would be to gulp it down.

One of the most common emulsifiers is polyoxyethylene monostearate. Note the ethylene. The bakers use nothing but the best. I have before me an article from the December, 1951, issue of *Industrial Medicine and Surgery*, entitled "Clinical Experiences with Exposures to Ethylene Amines." It seems that workers in factories where ethylene is used develop various kinds of trouble, mostly skin rashes. In one case, asthma was developed. In another, a man stepped into some ethylene amine compound which had been spilled on the concrete and some of the chemical splashed on his leg. Five days later he reported to the medical department with a very bad rash all over his feet. It was found that he always developed a rash after each contact with these liquids or the vapors of this compound. Surely, even though small quantities are placed in the bread, this substance should be looked upon with suspicion. Dr. Pollak, mentioned above, has suggested that these bread "improvers" could be a cause of cumulative adverse effects and cause some persons to easily develop allergies.

Is the Addition of Chemicals Lawful?

On May 20, 1950, Dr. William J. Darby of Vanderbilt University, repre-senting the American Medical Association Council on Food and Nutrition, said the following in the government Food and Drug bread hearings:

"Available knowledge of the possible toxicity of these substances," he said, "is fragmentary. Particularly is evidence lacking as to chronic toxicity. . . . Unless the complete harmlessness of these agents can be demonstrated beyond a reasonable doubt, they should not, in the Council's opinion, be used in basic foods." And, he added, the reduction of natural food products in bread that might be entailed by the use of these extenders "is not desirable from a nutritional standpoint."

Dr. James R. Wilson, of the American Medical Association Council on Nutrition, also made a statement in the *American Medical Journal* of

July 2, 1949, in which he viewed with alarm the use of these surface-active compounds, because he said "little is known about the poisonous effect of these substances that are being added to the food and possibly reducing their nourishing value." But Joseph Callaway, of the Foods Standards Committee of the Food and Drug Administration, said, "It seems pretty clear that these substances are not poisonous in the ordinary sense." Mr. Callaway, can you please tell us in what sense they *are* poisonous? He does say that there is a possibility that over-use of the materials might be injurious, and "the use of these substances may be ruled out later on the possibility that they might be dangerous, but so far there is no evidence that any individual has been injured by eating these agents." This is a very unscientific type of allusion, trying to find one individual instead of conducting experiments on groups of people, possibly persons in jails. What Mr. Callaway overlooks is that perhaps small amounts of chemicals in bread may not be directly toxic to the individual who eats a loaf containing it, but what is the effect of a diet which all day long includes items which have chemicals in them. The total cumulative effect may be highly toxic and highly dangerous. That is the type of testing that must be done in connection with the use of chemicals in foods.

Is Money or Health More Important?

It seems that the use of these surface-active compounds has practically replaced one-third of the soybean crops raised in this country. When the soybean association came to be heard in the Food and Drug Administration, their representatives did not attack the use of these surface-active compounds from the point of view of health. They merely stated that it threatened their industry. They were worrying about economics and not health. This is true of so much in industry today.

Polyoxyethylene monostearate is also being used in the making of peanut butter, ice cream, candy, salad dressings and many other foods. In our opinion, one is safest to eat as much of natural, primitive, earthy sorts of food as possible and to stay away from anything that becomes processed in factories. I do not trust the food processors. Either they are deliberate in their means of going about making a dollar, or "they know not what they do."

And they do all of this in spite of a ruling of the Supreme Court in 1918 that flour must not be tampered with by adding any poisonous substances and that such an inclusion is a violation of the Pure Food law, but evidently this Supreme Court ruling has been forgotten, just as the dangers of chlorine dioxide have been forgotten, when now the bakers are going to substitute it for nitrogen trichloride.

In his book, *A History of a Crime Against the Food Law,* Dr. Harvey A. Wiley, who originated the food and drug legislation in this country wrote, stating what he would do if he could really enforce the Food and Drug Act:

"No food product in our country would have any trace of benzoic acid, sulfurous acid or sulfites or any alum or saccharin, save for medical purposes. No soft drink would contain caffeine or theobromine. No bleached flour would enter interstate commerce. Our foods and drugs would be wholly without any form of adulteration and misbranding. The health of our people would be vastly improved and their life greatly extended. The manufacturers of our food supply, and especially the millers, would devote their energies to improving the public health and promoting happiness in every home by the production of whole ground, unbolted cereal flours and meals."

The Baker Does Other Things

Other things that the baker does may make your hair stand on end. But not all of his doings are known to the public or possibly to government officials who are too busy coping with the high spots, so that the low spots may become very dangerous. For example, the baker uses artificial colorings and flavorings. Some of these are coal tar products which are certified by the government as safe, but which many scientists look upon as cancer-causing. Many fancy breads and cakes have had nitric acid applied to the mixtures, in very small quantities, true. This is done to give the cake a deep yellow coloring as if eggs were used. Only a pinch is used, but a pinch here and a pinch there add up to a handful. Gold and silver decorations on cake icings have been found to be very harmful by the California Bureau of Food and Drug Inspection in reference to the California Pure Food Act. In one case they found a sample of cake icing that contained aluminum and brass. The county health officer banned the use of metallic decorations by county bakers. The amount of copper present in the brass was considered very dangerous for human beings, particularly children. In some cases ammonium bicarbonate is used, in old-fashioned cookies, and God knows what else. All over the country health inspectors are at their wits' end in trying to regulate bakeries, and as soon as they clamp down on them regarding the use of one item, the baker will pop up with something else.

One of the purposes of bread is to furnish the teeth with a hard food to chew upon. Trying to masticate or break down the hard crust in former times gave the teeth much exercise and was probably exceedingly good for their well-being. Today you would have to chew on a piece of wood or leather to get the same prophylactic benefit.

We now come to the last step, twelve, where the bread is pre-sliced, made moisture- and air-proof in a waxed paper jacket and as one writer said, "It is given to you as white as Kleenex." In other words, when the bread has been so disinfected and embalmed that a bug will not go near it with a 15 foot pole, you, the public, get it. And when I say get it, I mean it. Some writers have spoken disparagingly of the taste of such bread. They refer to it as a tasteless mass, probably with the flavor of a brim of a straw hat, but I do not want to tell a fib. These darn bakers are so clever that they have given us a loaf of bread that really does not taste bad at all. The only trouble is that there is an Ethiopian in the woodpile, in the form of the chemicals I have spoken about, which are tasteless, like carbon monoxide gas, but which poison nevertheless.

As you can readily see, that little seed that we started with, way back at the beginning of this story, never had a chance.

Whole Wheat Bread

You would imagine that it would be safer to eat whole wheat bread rather than the white kind, made as described herein. But it has been found by scientific experiment that the average whole wheat bread on the market is even worse than the white bread, for a peculiar reason. I am talking about whole wheat bread that contains the wheat germ. There are many so-called whole wheat breads today which are called whole wheat but which do not have the wheat germ. The whole wheat flour must be treated with the poisonous preservative chemicals in much higher quantities than the white flour which does not have the wheat germ, and it has been found, therefore, that this type of whole wheat bread is terribly deadly to test animals that were fed with it.

A few years ago, the Wellcome Research Laboratories at Tuckahoe, New York, made an experiment in which they fed 50 mice with whole wheat bread diet and 50 with white bread diet. Then all were injected with pneumonia germs. The mice receiving the whole wheat diet died in an average of 1.7 days, while those receiving white bread survived more than twice as long, namely, 3.8 days. Another experiment was done by Riggs and Beaty, which was written up in the *American Journal of Dairy Science,* Vol. 29, pp. 821 to 829, 1946. Six groups of female laboratory mice, each subsisting on one of 6 types of bread, were observed on the same diets until they had produced and weaned their third litters. Where on ordinary non-fat milk white bread, the mice were able to wean 54.8 per cent of their litters into the third generation. In the case of those that were fed whole wheat bread, none were able to live into the third generation.

In other words, in order to put such a type of whole wheat bread on the market without any danger of its turning rancid, the amounts of preservative chemicals that have to be used in it are toxic, sometimes 400 per cent more of such chemicals being used in the whole wheat than in the white. Now it is interesting to see that if ordinary tests are made with a group of mice in one generation, probably nothing would show up. But in this type of scientific test where it was worked into the third generation, the dangers *did* develop. Is it possible that in the case of many chemicals being absorbed into our bodies through our foods, some of the dangers may not show up until a later generation? Is it possible that 4 or 5 generations from now sterility in women will be so common that the race may have difficulty perpetuating itself because of the chemicals that the present generation is eating. This is something that we owe to future generations to study now.

The consideration of the way in which bread is made and the public robbed of important ingredients of the wheat seed is an indication of why the public must take such things as vitamins (made from natural foods and not the synthetic variety) and bone meal containing minerals. Bread is only one of the examples, but for every item of food that we eat, there is always something that is taken out of it. We are usually getting only a fragment. That is why, unless everyone takes the right kind of natural vitamins plus bone meal and such things as brewer's yeast, he is not getting a whole diet. When you consider the way foods are refined, pasteurized, sterilized, homogenized, fortified and enriched with coal tar derivatives, and chemicalized in so many different ways, it is a wonder that disease is not worse than it really is. This is a tribute to the strength of the body that God gave us.

Is Bread Really the Staff of Life?

This whole thing about the importance of bread as the staff of life leaves me cold. I think the average person is better off to entirely restrict the use of bread. About 10 or 11 years ago, our family made an experiment in which we absolutely cut out not only bread, but all the grain food such as rice, corn and such foods as spaghetti, etc., for a whole year. The results were extremely interesting. There were less colds in the family. But one thing we observed was startling. My son Robert used to get poison ivy attacks every summer, even if he never went into the ivy; but the year that we didn't eat bread, he never had a touch of it. The following year when we went back to eating bread, back came the poison ivy. The way we figured it out was that when he did not eat bread, he had to satisfy his hunger by eating more vegetables and fruit. (With children there is always a tendency to give them a few slices of bread and stuff them up. Thus, when it comes to eating the other important foods of the diet, they just won't.) Evidently, my son was suffering from what might be called a sub-clinical case of scurvy in the skin, caused by a lack of the vitamins and minerals contained in vegetables. In other words, contact with the burning poison ivy substance, when the skin is afflicted with a scurvy condition, caused it to burn much easier. By being better nourished the skin probably became more "thick-skinned," and resisted the burning effect of the ivy leaf. Persons who have begun taking bone meal and vitamins have written to me that suddenly they have found themselves immune to poison ivy. In fact, this occurred in my own case, and when I realized what had happened, I went out one day and actually took poison ivy, rubbing it on my skin, and nothing happened, whereas I used to get it any time I had contact with poison ivy.

Interesting Observation With Birds

On our farm we raised wheat for the last two years in an experiment in large cylinders, some of which were fertilized with chemical fertilizers and some by our organic method, using only organic matter, plus mild ground up phosphate and potash rock. To our great surprise one day when the wheat was heading out to ripeness, a flock of birds came to eat the heads, but they went only to the plots containing the wheat raised organically. They would not touch those that were grown with chemical fertilizers. Evidently an animal's taste is more selective than a human being's, and the birds could easily see that the organically produced wheat seed was much tastier, a sign that it contained more vitamins, minerals and general nourishment. It is interesting to note that the public consumption of bread in this country is going down alarmingly and the bread-baking industry is having all kinds of meetings about it. In their frantic frenzy to

[57]

preserve their profits, they think that by enriching their bread they are going to make the public come back into the fold. Actually and eventually, this will mean more reduction in public consumption of bread. Of course, some of the reduction is due to corpulent persons who are trying to reduce their weight, but I really believe that a considerable portion is due to the fact that the public is becoming more health-conscious. The bakers must study this new trend in public thinking. Twenty years ago I read in a report that Americans were eating bread at the annual rate of 713 pounds a person. Now the rate is down to about 140 pounds. This is a terrific reduction.

CHAPTER 12

Bread Again

By J. I. Rodale

I am definitely against any wheat or rye product for human consumption, and am never afraid to express my attitude, which, as a rule, brings down a shower of verbal brick-bats and dressingdowns from the whole-wheat school of health, and especially from those who make their own bread from organically raised wheat. To them it has become a sacred ritual— a symbol. To me it is a matter of searching for the truth. What is the best program for a person who wishes to live to 120? I say, don't eat bread. It is the worst form of starch. I put bananas at the head of the starch list, and somewhat further down . . . potatoes, but bread? I wouldn't even give it any place in the list. It is not edible starch. It is for paste. I eat the wheat germ and perhaps the bran portion . . . but not the paste portion of the wheat.

Bread Positively Cited Common Cause of Colds

What is wrong with wheat? First of all it is one of the most fattening foods. The *Esquire* reducing diet which consists of merely cutting out wheat and rye guarantees a loss of about 20 pounds in two months. Bread is one of the most common causes of colds, a fact proven by medical researches. If you suffer from a stuffed-up nose or head, cut out bread and see what an improvement will come about at once. Bread fills people up, it gives them a false feeling of hunger satisfaction. Thus they eat less of fruit, vegetables and other important foods. Bread is difficult of digestion of the human stomach. Dr. Alvarez, of the Mayo Clinic, showed that bread can pass through the whole of the small intestine without becoming digested at all. Bread requires a large production of digestive juices for its complete solution. The protein of the bread especially is defectively absorbed by the intestine. A medically proven fact is that whole wheat bread interferes with the absorption of other foods. I have found this to be so in my case.

Bread is fine for cows who have 4 stomachs and keep chewing their cud. But in the human digestive system, because it is not completely digested, it ferments or rots.

It is one of the most common causes of constipation. Wheat causes rickets in children where there is an overconsumption of this type of food. It is the underlying factor in a disease of children called celiac disease, which is increasing alarmingly. The abdomen becomes distended, there is fat in the stools. The doctor orders an immediate elimination of all wheat products. Wheat has been found to be one of the causes of tooth cavities. Wheat products are one of the common causes of asthma.

Bread Held Responsible For Several Diseases

One physician discovered that bread was one of the causes of conjunctivitis (an eye involvement) under certain conditions. In a study of two African tribes, the Masai and the Kikuyu, it was found that the latter eat a great deal of grain foods. Deaths from bronchitis and pneumonia in that tribe were 10 times as great as in the Masai. The Kikuyu also had bone deformities, dental caries, lung conditions, anemia and tropical ulcer.

Many persons suffer from gastric irritation due to the large amounts of bran in whole wheat bread. Wheat is the greatest culprit among foods in connection with the causing of allergic effects. Dr. Albert H. Rowe checked on 500 persons with allergies. He found that at least one-third of these allergies were caused by wheat. Bread is a common cause of hives, eczema and migraines. Dr. Alvarez, of the Mayo Clinic, recently said that "according to allergists the commonest cause of migraine is wheat."

I could go on and on . . . and I haven't mentioned the 7 or 8 harmful chemicals used in the milling and baking of bread, nor the recent work that indicts bread and other starches as a cause of heart attacks.

A Controversial Letter

All of this is merely a prelude to a copy of a letter a reader sent to me. That letter states, "While Mr. Rodale in general is doing a pretty good job (thank you), he goes off the beam once in a while (?????) with unwarranted statements. Bread and the grains in general are staple foods, and animals will stay in perfect health on grain and grass (a cow has 4 stomachs). The grass is alkaline and the grain is acid, and they balance each other. (True) All vegetables are alkaline and serve the same purpose in the human diet. . . . People who do not get the acid grains soon develop allergies (this is counter to the medical evidence), calcium deficiency reactions, neuritis and various disorders (just the opposite), whereas they remain in perfect health after they get acid foods to balance the alkaline. . . .

". . . . It is unwarranted statements like this of Mr. Rodale's which cause the health-food-minded to be branded 'crack-pots,' and he is really helping the synthetic food industries when he makes such statements." (I thought it was just the opposite. The people who attack us as food faddists and crack-pots visualize us as worshipping whole wheat bread. The whole wheat loaf is inextricably interwoven with food-faddism, but it has never been proven clinically to be of any value in creating real health.)

Now let us look at the writer's contention that there must be a balance between the acid and alkaline in our diet. True, there must be some kind of balance between them, but one doesn't have to worry about the exact percentages between the two. One textbook says it should be 80 per cent alkaline and 20 per cent acid. Another ups the alkaline to 85 per cent. A third says, "Nonsense! Forget about this acid-alkaline business." But people *do* differ in their requirements and we can't set definite rations. It is best that we should have some of both categories in our diet.

Enough Acid Foods To Fill Dietary Needs

The grain group is not the only acid class of foods. Meats, fish, poultry, eggs, cheese, filberts, walnuts, cranberries, plums and prunes are also acid, so that if one were to eliminate the grain group there remain sufficient acid foods to more than fill one's needs.

One trouble with vegetarianism is the leaning on whole wheat bread to fill the acid gap. But the vegetarians can eat filberts, walnuts, cranberries, plums and prunes. However, there are many vegetarians who eat eggs. George Bernard Shaw did so. This could fill the acid gap quite effectively.

In my own case (I have a heart condition) wheat has an immediate effect, and I am sure this is not an allergy. After a meal that is heavy with bread or cake, I experience severe angina symptoms on my chest. I will eat such food perhaps on my birthday when the pressure from "well-meaning" relatives is too great to resist, but ordinarily I go for months without a slice of bread or a piece of cake.

I want to stress the weight-producing aspect of eating bread. It seems not only to add the weight of the bread consumed but, because it prevents the complete digestion of other foods in the stomach, it adds some of their weight also.

A Wheatless Diet Well Worth Trying

Every once in a while someone will complain of a stomach ache, and would never think it could come from overconsumption of bread, cake or pie at a meal. How could it be? Bread is the staff of life. It can be tolerated by very healthy people . . . by persons who have wide arteries, perfectly operating glands, who lead an active outdoor life, and they will write in and tell me how wrong I am about my attitude on eating bread, not realizing that if they avoided this food they could live to 100 instead of a mere 80 or 90. Some of these oldsters are old, but they suffer from various chronic conditions, including the various phases of senility. Who knows? Without bread they might free themselves of all these things.

If you never have gone on a completely wheatless diet, it is worth a trial, regardless of whether you are over- or underweight. Cut out all bread, cakes, pies, gravies in which there is flour, spaghetti, breaded foods, etc. Try it for a month and see what it does for you. But include wheat germ flakes or wheat germ oil perles, or both, in your diet. And increase your fruit and vegetable intake, especially bananas. It will give you a volume type of food and a type of carbohydrate which will be a delight to your system and a great help to it.

SECTION 3.

Cereals

We believe that most of us eat too much of the cereal foods. We take up the subject of bread in another section. Cold processed cereal (the kind most modern American children eat for breakfast) is the worst possible food, we believe. Ads have convinced mothers that breakfast cereals are loaded with food value. Children eagerly eat their way to the bottom of the box to obtain the toys offered as premiums. These cereals have been so denatured by processing that they contain little of the original nutriment of the cereal, and also may contain much that is harmful in the way of changed forms of protein. Then, too, many of the present-day cereals are loaded with sugar, to which the average child adds still more sugar when he eats them.

CHAPTER 13

Processed Cereals Are Not for You

An article that cheered us more than anything we have read in a long time appeared in the December, 1957 issue of *Pageant* magazine. Entitled "The Unappetizing Truth About Dry Cereals" the article, by Richard Carter, pulled no punches in revealing the sordid and shocking truth about a business which garners some 300,000,000 dollars every year from the American people.

We disagree with some of Mr. Carter's point of view and we only wish he would do a similar story on other refined cereal products like white bread and polished rice. But, considering the fact that most magazines get a handsome income from advertising the cereal products he is attacking, we must congratulate *Pageant* for its courage in publishing such an article and Mr. Carter for his in writing it.

Some of his facts will astonish you. Did you know that roughly 800,000,000 pounds of cold, processed breakfast cereal are consumed in this country every year, in spite of the fact that the average serving of cold cereal weighs less than an ounce! Did you know that an estimated 15,000,000 Americans (almost a tenth of our entire population) eat nothing but cold cereal for breakfast! "A depressingly large number of children" are among these, according to Mr. Carter.

Some of the forms of dry cereal which are most popular are flakes (bran, corn, wheat, rice, etc.), puffs (rice, wheat), shreds and nuts. Here is the process through which flakes are put before they get into the cardboard box with the enticing premium offer that is propped before so many children every morning at breakfast.

Grits (kernels of corn which have been soaked in lye) are cooked in live steam, mixed with a flavoring syrup (refined sugar, of course), dried until hard and then run through rollers which exert 75 tons of pressure. The end product is then toasted and packaged as corn flakes. What you started out with was a grain of corn, fairly rich in protein, phosphorus, vitamin A and the 3 most important B vitamins. What you take out of the attractive cardboard box contains no vitamin A, very little, if any, vitamin B (unless it has been added synthetically) and, what is perhaps most dangerous of all, the protein remaining in the poor, processed kernel has been changed irrevocably, perhaps into something that is definitely harmful to the body.

Why Do People Eat Prepared Cereals?

It's perfectly true, as Mr. Carter says, that the American public has been completely sold on the healthfulness of eating cold cereal for breakfast. "As they put this mixture into their mouths," he says, "many of the feeders

[63]

actually glow with a sense of well-being. Decades of tradition and millions upon millions of dollars in advertising have trained them to regard their ready-to-eat breakfast cereal as the last word in morning nourishment. Any suspicion that the stuff is nutritionally inferior to other breakfast foods is bound to be dispelled by the sales literature printed on the brightly-colored boxes."

How many mothers do you know who actually insist that their children spoon down a bowlful of this woefully inadequate food every morning? And actually the kids don't object. One reason for the great popularity of cold cereals is that the advertising companies have turned the box tops, the premiums and the TV and radio programs into veritable treasure troves for the youngsters. At a cost of practically nothing to the food companies, millions of dollars worth of junk is sent out each year with a come-on that is so attractive to kids that you can't really blame them for putting up an awful squawk if Mom tries to get them to eat something else for breakfast. What difference do calories, food values, minerals and vitamins make to a youngster who is bent on getting a free treasure map, a ray gun, a spaceman's mask, a set of picture cards?

But, you may object, isn't it better for the children to eat cold cereal for breakfast than to eat nothing at all? Possibly. But the only reason we say this is that they may eat milk and fruit on the cereal—even if ever so little—and possibly the small amount of calcium. protein and B vitamins that comes in the milk and fruit is better than nothing.

Good Food Habits Are Important

But look at the harm that's being done. Probably the most important single good health heritage you can give your child is a set of good habits where food is concerned. One of the most important of these is the habit of eating a serviceable breakfast. By this we mean a breakfast high in protein, which "sticks to his ribs," a breakfast in which refined carbo-hydrates are ignored as if they did not exist.

For many people breakfast is the one meal in which they are com-pletely bound by habit. Many people eat the same breakfast menu every day throughout their lives. Every day your child eats cold cereal for breakfast he is making stronger an eating habit that with every passing year becomes harder to break. And many children consume cold cereals not just for breakfast, but for lunch, too, sometimes for dinner and very often for a bedtime snack. What chance does such a child have to eat even a small portion of the nourishing food he must have if he is to grow up healthy, physically and mentally? The worthless refined starch of the cereal has stuffed him until he doesn't want anything more to eat!

But cold cereals are so cheap and so easy to fix! Of course they're cheap. They're mostly air and starch. Why shouldn't they be cheap?

What Should You Do About Breakfast Cereal?

What should be your attitude toward cold cereals? Are there any that are any good? Not so far as we are concerned. We think they should be ignored completely in planning meals. Hardly a month goes by that a great new promotion campaign is not launched to sell you on some new cold cereal, praising its high protein content, its nourishing vitamins and so forth. Bunk. And please don't write us sending in box tops to check on some favorite that you've been using. There are no exceptions, so far as we are concerned. None of the cold, processed, ready-to-eat cereals should be on your grocery shelf. None.

The only cereals that are worth eating are real whole grain cereals. So far as we know they cannot be purchased in grocery stores, with the exception of brown rice which is now pretty widely available. You must make special arrangements with somebody to get real whole grain cereals. Your local health food store has them. Or you can buy whole cereals from farmers quite cheaply and grind your own. Of course, all of these must be cooked.

In some cases the most valuable part of the cereal is available as a separate food. The germ of the cereal contains practically all of the nutriment except starch. The rest of any cereal kernel consists mostly of starch. This makes wheat germ a peculiarly valuable food in which protein, minerals (especially iron), the B vitamins and vitamin E are concentrated. There are 24 grams of protein in one half cup of wheat germ. There are only about 3 grams of protein in more than a cup of a processed cold cereal. Rice polishings (a little harder to find) contain the germ of the rice, so they, too, are crammed with vitamins and minerals and protein.

What if your family absolutely refuses to relinquish their cold cereal? We suggest taking it away from them so gradually that they won't know what happened. Wheat germ is your best ally on an operation like this. Add a little to the bowl of cold cereal tomorrow morning. Nine chances out of 10 no one will notice. In a month or so begin adding a little more. And a little more. This will mean a little less of the cold cereal. In due time, suggest hot cereal for breakfast and make the hot cereal whole grain. If the family is unenthusiastic, serve it with some special treat—real maple syrup, raisins, nuts or dates. Finally, you should be able to wean even the most stubborn of families away from cold cereal. Part of the battle will be won because they will discover for themselves that the right kind of breakfast sticks with you so you don't have to have a coffee break around 10, or 15 minutes for a snack around 3. Improved teeth, skin, nerves, hair and general good health will come gradually as you shift from phony breakfast food to real food.

We have addressed these suggestions to folks who have been confirmed users of cold cereal. Most of us eat too much cereal, you know. Fruit and eggs make the best breakfast by far—high in protein and the natural sugar that doesn't upset your blood sugar level and leave you hungry, inefficient and grumpy by 10 o'clock.

CHAPTER 14

You Need Cereal Germs

It should not surprise us that many diseases unknown to our fore-fathers should be related to the absence of the germ of whole grain in our diets. For thousands of years mankind has eaten whole grains. In many countries it is almost the only food; in many others it is the mainstay of the diet. Until we began to refine our grains, bread was the staff of life—and deserved to be.

But today our food processing companies have persuaded us that we want to eat white bread and refined cereals. Not because we really prefer them, mind you, but because this makes things easier for the processors. They no longer have to deal with the highly perishable germ of the cereal. They just remove it and—lo and behold—flour can be stored for years at any temperature, shipped in any kind of boxcar to all parts of the world with nary a rancid taste to spoil it and deplete the profits of the millers and the bakers. The germ—the live, nourishing part of the grain—is disposed of elsewhere. We feed it to our domestic animals, for any raiser of cattle or other animals knows full well that they cannot live or thrive on a diet such as their owners eat.

What do we remove when we remove this germ from wheat? We don't know. That sounds peculiar, considering all our modern scientific skill. But it's true. We know some of the things in cereal germs, the B vitamins, for instance. Cereal germ is one of our richest sources. Calcium and phosphorus are plentiful in cereal germ. Calcium is the mineral in which we modern Americans are most deficient. Cereal germ is a rich source of iron. Did you know that modern American women are, in general, so anemic that a large percentage of them have been rejected as blood donors by the Red Cross? Could the removal of iron from our cereals have anything to do with this? Finally, vitamin E is plentiful in cereal germ.

Wheat Germ Oil Increases Physical Endurance

Many times we are inclined to think of vitamin E as the only important food element we miss when we do not eat whole grains. But there seems to be no doubt—wheat germ oil contains something else that is a powerful force for good health.

Wheat germ oil was tested in the laboratories of a great university for its effect on physical endurance and heart response. The tests were conducted like this: all subjects ate what they usually did and as much as they wanted. They were brought up to the peak of condition by exercise. They were given various tests to measure their physical condition. Then one-half were given a teaspoon of wheat germ oil daily. The other half were given a teaspoon of another vegetable oil containing as much vitamin E as is found in wheat germ oil. Neither group knew who was getting the wheat germ oil. Both groups continued their exercise for several weeks, then they were tested again.

Everybody being tested improved 24.8 per cent during the 12 weeks of physical training. But those who were given wheat germ oil improved 47.4 per cent during the test. In other words, after they had reached their very best performance, without added supplements, they were given wheat germ oil and improved another 22.6 per cent.

The next year the experiment was repeated, most men on the wheat germ oil being given the other oil instead. The results were the same—those taking the wheat germ oil excelled in physical endurance. Said Dr. T. K. Cureton of the University of Illinois who gave the test: "We've tried vitamins, gelatin, fruit juices, hormones and other foods in the laboratory, but wheat germ oil has consistently shown the best results in enabling men to bear hard stress without deteriorating."

Other Conditions for Which Wheat Germ Oil is a Specific

This powerful substance may prevent sterility, tendency to miscarriage, menopausal flushes and so forth. It seems that the germ of cereals is especially important in this field because of its own function as the tiny portion of seed from which the cereal reproduces itself. This is truly the "live" part of the grain.

Bicknell and Prescott in their book, *Vitamins in Medicine* (Grune and Stratton, 1953) tell us that past research indicates that muscular dystrophy may be caused by the inability of the muscles to use vitamin E. They can produce muscular dystrophy in any animal at any time by simply removing all traces of vitamin E from its diet. However, giving wheat germ or vitamin E does not necessarily bring about a complete and certain cure in human beings. So these authors believe that the muscular dystrophy patients simply cannot use the vitamin E in their food.

However, an article in *Archives of Pediatrics*, Vol. 49, 1949, tells of 25 children with muscular dystrophy treated with fresh wheat germ oil every day, all of whom improved and one of whom recovered completely. These children, incidentally, were given the B vitamins and vitamin C as well as the wheat germ oil. Doesn't this seem to indicate that wheat germ oil, *plus a good diet* may be the answer to the prevention of muscular dystrophy?

Drs. Bicknell and Prescott tell us that children who have improved on the wheat germ oil are, in general, children who have been given excellent, fresh diets including whole wheat and homemade bread. In general, children whose diets remain unchanged except for the wheat germ do not show improvement.

Vitamins and Enzymes in Wheat Germ

An article in the German publication *Kinderartzl. Praxis* for May, 1955, tells us that wheat germ contains the following in addition to the B vitamins, vitamin E, unsaturated fatty acids, amino acids: calcium phosphate

[67]

and magnesium phosphate, diastase, amylase, lipase, phosphatase and tyrosinase. These last items are enzymes, all of them important for the way the body uses various foods like carbohydrates, phosphorus and so forth.

In the German experiment, 71 prematurely-born infants were given ground wheat germ, another 71 were used as controls and did not receive the wheat germ. The wheat germ increased the weight of the infants and, while it had no effect on their resistance to infections or on anemia, it did seem to reduce the incidence of rickets in the prematurely-born infants. In rickets the body does not get enough calcium, phosphorus and/or vitamin D. Do the various enzymes in wheat germ have something to do with the way the body uses these precious minerals and vitamins?

Vitamin E And Oxygenation

A clipping from the *St. Louis Post* for September 29, 1955, tells of a lecture by Dr. William B. Kountz, Assistant Professor of Clinical Medicine at Washington University. Said Dr. Kountz, there is a decline in the body's consumption of oxygen as one grows older, leading to such ailments as hardening of the arteries, heart disease, body wasting and other typical manifestations of old age. He went on to say that the proper understanding of diet and the stimulation of body build-up by food is infinitely important for good health.

Vitamin E, contained in wheat germ, has a peculiar relationship to the body's oxygen. When vitamin E is present, the body can get along on less oxygen. So you are sparing yourself and, perhaps, postponing old age when you add vitamin E to your diet. Remember, the body is able to use less and less oxygen as it grows older. But, with vitamin E present in sufficient quantity, it doesn't need as much oxygen.

Wheat Germ For Neuromuscular Disorders

One final review. In the *Journal of Neurology, Neurosurgery and Psychiatry,* London, for May, 1951, we learn of 151 patients with neuromuscular disorders who were given wheat germ oil, and whose cases were followed for 12 years. About 10 per cent showed definite improvement. These include two cases of a typical muscular atrophy. In 5 (3 children and two adults) out of 25 patients with progressive muscular dystrophy, symptoms were arrested, and moderate to marked improvement occurred. Three out of 5 patients with menopausal muscular dystrophy showed remarkable improvement. Three cases of dermatomyositis (inflammation of both skin and muscles) responded favorably.

These patients were not placed on any particular diet. What excellent further results might there not have been had they been given a diet rich in unprocessed and raw foods, vitamins and minerals!

If you are, like most of us, compelled to do without cereals entirely because you cannot get real whole grain ones, then certainly you should make sure that you take a wheat germ product—either flakes or oil. The flakes make an appetizing addition to many foods or can be eaten as breakfast cereal.

CHAPTER 15

History Teaches Us to Go Easy on Cereals

One of the most powerful indictments of bread and other cereal foods that we have ever read can be found in a book by a famous Arctic explorer whose theories and writings on diet have caused more controversy than anything that has happened in dietetic circles in the past 25 years.

The explorer is Vilhjalmur Stefansson and his writing is so full of worthwhile lessons on diet that we cannot recommend it too highly. Dr. Stefansson is an anthropologist, that is, he studies mankind, past and present. He is chiefly concerned with the daily habits of men, so, of course, comments on food take up a large part of his writings. Because his work has often taken him to the far north for long periods of time, he is able to talk about food habits in the far north from personal experience, not just observation. And because his work has brought him into contact with explorers of different parts of the globe, he can easily compare his findings and experiences with those of men who have travelled in other parts of the world.

Dr. Stefansson is one of the men who lived on meat alone (fat and lean meat) for a year in New York City while every conceivable nutritional test was given and continual observation was made by leading scientists in the field of nutrition. In spite of dire predictions of a fatal outcome to such a project, Dr. Stefansson and his associate came out at the end of the experiment in excellent health. He has written very entertainingly about the experiment in this book, *The Fat of the Land* (Macmillan).

His reasoning about bread and cereals in man's diet comes directly from a study of man in past ages, the food he ate and the approximate time that was involved in changing from one kind of food to another.

During the period before there was any agriculture, he tells us, men who lived in the tropics were "gatherers," that is, they lived on fruits, berries and roots. Over possibly millions of years the digestive tract of man evolved and developed as a processing organism for this kind of food—food that grows on trees or bushes or as roots in the ground. Later in history when he moved farther north, man became a hunter and a herdsman—that is, he lived exclusively on food of animal origin—meat and milk, along with whatever of his former vegetable foods were still available. As he developed his skill as a hunter, man could move farther to the north since he did not have to depend on warm weather to provide his food.

Dr. Stefansson quotes Dr. Ellsworth Huntington's *Mainsprings of Civilization*—the chapter on agriculture, "Disease and Diet." "The ideal diet, it would seem, must be essentially that to which man becomes adjusted during his long, slow evolution. Among most of the ancestors of modern Europeans and Americans, an agricultural diet has prevailed less than two thousand years. There is no reliable evidence that in that brief span any appreciable change has occurred in the inherited dietary requirements which had become established during a preceding period perhaps a thousand times longer." Huntington believes that about two million years elapsed between the time that mankind ate chiefly the foods he could "gather" and the time when he began to establish communities where he could farm. Of course, the backbone of agriculture is cereal.

The reason for this becomes apparent when we remember that while our ancestors were "gathering," hunting or herding, they had to move about, constantly searching for food. Large communities such as we know today could not exist, because there was not food enough for that many people in any given locality. So mankind roamed and lived mostly a lonely life. When, eventually, he found that certain grasses which he could plant and harvest could be stored and eaten during the winter, he arrived for the first time at a condition of life where a permanent home could be established. There was no need to move along as game disappeared or seasons changed. Cereal was the answer. So, in a very real sense, one can say that the discovery of cereal culture was the beginning of civilization.

We Have Not Been Eating Cereals Long Enough!

But this was only about two thousand years ago! So, according to Huntington and Stefansson, mankind owes much of his present-day degeneration, health-wise, to the inclusion of cereals in his diet. His digestive tract has simply not had time to adjust to such a change.

Huntington says, "The most important effect of agriculture on efficiency probably results from malnutrition . . . One of the main reasons for poor nutrition is that agriculture has lowered the quality of man's diet and at the same time made it possible for more people to subsist. Mechanical methods of preparing food have gone still further along this same path until the typical 'modernized' diet has become appallingly poor."

Says Stefansson, "Humanity may have needed most of Huntington's two million years for evolving from the largely vegetarian habit of the anthropoid to where it could make the best use of the diet of a hunter. We should not feel discouraged, then, if in a mere 5 or 10 thousand years of agriculture we have not as yet grown fully reconciled, biologically, to the intrusion of large quantities of sugars, starches, vegetable proteins and vegetable fats, into a regimen which had so long consisted in the main of animal proteins and animal fats."

The difficulties in childbirth experienced by modern women, as well as malformation of teeth and jaws are very possibly results of diets high in cereals, he tells us. Dr. Stefansson points out the difficulty most of us have with wisdom teeth which seem to be completely useless parts of anatomy because our jaws have shrunk to the point where there is no room for these teeth that appear later in life.

[70]

No matter what differences there are in points of view on cereals and health, Dr. Stefansson tells us that when archeologists discover anywhere "a group of several skeletons, of no matter what probable antiquity, they may be sure that if the teeth have cavities in them, signs of dental caries, then those are the skeletons of a people who had lived under a fairly well developed agriculture."

After the "gathering" period in man's history when he lived almost entirely on fruits, berries and roots, came the hunting period and then the "herding" period. Mankind may have existed as a hunter for from one to three million years. So far as we can gather at present, says Stefansson, men who lived entirely on products of the hunt and those who lived partly on vegetable food and partly on game did not suffer from deficiency diseases. When men began to keep flocks and became "herdsmen," they still had made no basic change in their diet.

But when they became agricultural, there was a profound change in the kind of food eaten. Ancient civilizations were founded and a communal way of life began simply because man found that large numbers of individuals could live permanently on small areas by planting crops—chiefly cereals. Ten or even 20,000 years is a very short period of time for adapting to a new kind of diet. Man has not adapted himself as yet, and this is the main reason for the many diseases he suffers. "Most of us conceive of nothing different, take as inevitable, as the common lot of man, the pains and derangements which we suppose to have been universal at all times and in all places," says Stefansson. Most of us (nutritionists and specialists included) do not know that man's diet was ever very different from what it is today. We know what recorded history tells us, *and this kind of history began with agriculture.* Anthropologists and archeologists, concerned as they are with prehistoric man, know differently.

Modern Primitives Who Do Not Eat Bread Are Healthy

The anthropologist in his work gets closely acquainted with peoples of our present time who are still living as our prehistoric ancestors lived. Primitive Eskimos, for instance, are hunters, having access to berries and fruits only occasionally. What happens to their health, their bone structure, their adaptation for childbirth and breastfeeding when they are exposed within a single generation to cereal foods and sugar should be a terrible lesson to us. Dr. Stefansson says, "On the agricultural diets now taken for granted this nation, like most or all other civilized nations, is having a deal of trouble with malnutrition. Except among those who can afford a lot of hunting man's food, like beef steaks and chicken, or a lot of monkey food, like fresh fruit and raw vegetables—except for these fortunates, we suffer on our usual diets with endemic deficiency troubles, among them pellagra, beriberi, scurvy, rickets, contracted lower jaws and poor teeth."

Just as man required many thousands of years to become accustomed to a diet of meat, after living on fruits and roots for so many years, so he will require many thousands of years to become accustomed to diets in which cereals play a large part. Considering that our author is talking about natural cereals—not refined ones—just think for a moment how much more serious the whole picture becomes when you realize that a large part of the diet of the "civilized" part of the world consists of products made from *white sugar and refined and processed grains*—two items of food that have been in general circulation for only about 100 years. If man cannot adapt himself, without serious metabolic disorders, to a completely natural but new item of diet within a period of several thousand years, what is his digestive tract expected to do with large quantities of foods *that have been available for less than a century?*

Surely the one big lesson to be learned from Dr. Stefansson's work is to beware of cereal foods in any shape or form. There are no exceptions. If you think back to what we have said before, you can easily see that there can be no exceptions. We are talking about an entire class of foods—the grains, which were not used as food by man until he settled down into communities, which was only a few thousand years ago. This would include wheat, rye, barley, oats and so forth. And any products made from them.

Editor Rodale believes that wheat and rye are especially harmful and warns all health-seekers to avoid these two cereals especially. Since the gluten in wheat flour is essential for the making of bread, as we are familiar with it in this country, this means avoiding any and all forms of bread.

CHAPTER 16

Cereal Foods: a Prime Suspect in Bronchial Asthma

Bronchial asthma is due, in most cases, to food allergy or in combination with some irritating substance inhaled from the atmosphere. This is the contention of Albert H. Rowe, M.D., who is one of the country's, possibly the world's, leading experts on the treatment of bronchial asthma. In collaboration with his son, Albert Rowe, Jr., M.D., and E. James Young, M.D., Dr. Rowe has set forth his observations and theories in the *Journal of the American Medical Association* (March 11, 1959). The most important foods involved in causing asthma are cereals, says Rowe. When he is confronted with a new asthma patient, he immediately puts him on a trial diet which eliminates all cereal grains (wheat, corn, oats, rye, barley, etc.) in any form, and certain other common allergenic foods such as milk, eggs, chocolate, fish, etc. If these prohibitions do not reveal the cause of the asthma, then Dr. Rowe feels justified in trying other foods or considering objects, climates or infections. Dr. Rowe considers infections the least likely cause of bronchial asthma.

The course of recurrent bronchial asthma follows a pretty regular pattern and can usually be expected to act in the following manner: it acts up about every two to 6 weeks, with moderate to severe symptoms for one to 3 days, then diminishing within the next 5 days and disappearing until the next full scale attack.

What An Attack Is Like

These attacks are not easy to take, and it is no wonder that the prospect of their regular occurrence is enough to make the victim seek relief through injections, diet, change of locale or any other means that offers hope. The inability of the patient to take a good breath of air is one of the most common and alarming characteristics of an asthma attack, but this is accompanied by coughing and wheezing and a fever that hovers between 100 degrees and 104 degrees Fahrenheit, for as long as 4 days. Couple this with loss of appetite, nausea and vomiting and you have some idea of the ordeal imposed by an attack of bronchial asthma.

The physiological reasons behind susceptibility to bronchial asthma are rather hazy. Dr. Rowe and his son, in *California Medicine* (October, 1948), attempted to explain attacks as due to reacting bodies, present in the systems of unlucky asthma victims, which gradually accumulate in the cells of the lungs. When a sufficient number of these bodies are present, they unite with the trigger elements in the food or pollen to which the patient is allergic, and react on the cells of the lungs which control our breathing. The reaction continues until, for some reason, the reacting bodies become exhausted. Then the symptoms disappear, even though the allergenic foods continue to be eaten or the allergenic air continues to be breathed by the patient. During this "quiet" period, the reacting bodies are again building up in the body and after a regular interval the attack can be expected again. Between attacks the patient may be partially or completely free of any hint of his asthma condition.

There is no age limit to consider in cases of asthma. It can occur at any time in life, though bronchial asthma usually makes itself known within the first 3 years. In a study of 411 children plagued by the disease, it was found that boys outnumbered the girls two to one, though this ratio generally tends to even out in later years. It is interesting to note that a disposition to bronchial asthma was shown in 50 per cent of the families of the children in this group. (Remember, families have the same eating habits.)

What of the patch tests that are widely used in cases of allergy for determining the cause of the irritation? Dr. Rowe contends that these tests, in which patches spread with the suspected allergen are taped to the skin for possible reaction, are not conclusive in bronchial asthma conditions. He tells us that many patches of substances which were serious causes of asthma have shown little reaction when put in contact with the skin.

No Limit to Possible Allergens

It is obvious, from several instances quoted in the *Quarterly Review of Allergy* (September, 1954) by Rowe, that the possible causes of bronchial asthma among foods are limited only by the number of foods we know. One of Dr. Rowe's patients was found to be allergic to all foods, with equally intense severity, except beef, sugar, salt, water, and a tolerance for a few vegetables which are rotated every 3 to 7 days. She supplements her enforced diet with vitamins A, B, C and D and remains well and free from the symptoms of her disease.

Another of Dr. Rowe's patients found himself similarly afflicted with allergies which caused him severe discomfort. As a result of tests he found that the only foods he could tolerate were fish, frogs legs, tapioca, rice, potato and cottonseed oil.

The testing period is a complicated and exact one. The patient must exercise great patience, in the initial weeks especially. He must continue with his cereal-free diet without deviation until the doctor is sure. it has been given a fair trial. It takes more than a few days for most food allergens to leave the body, and an even longer time for cellular changes to diminish or disappear. Only then can one expect the normal function of a body that is free from allergens. This whole process is so sensitive that Dr. Rowe does not even permit the patient to smell suspected foods, nor to touch them. He suggests that they be kept out of the house until they have been proven safe.

Difficult to Avoid

One can imagine the difficulty of avoiding certain foods used in the commercial preparation of others, for example wheat and milk in bakery products, citric acid in canned foods. For this reason allergic patients are wise to use foods that are fresh and unprocessed so that they can be assured of what they are eating.

It is noted that the persistence of attacks usually abates in the summer due to the seasonal influences on food allergy. It is not difficult to progress from that fact to the thought that vitamin C-rich foods are largely available in the summer months, and that this vitamin has often been mentioned in connection with allergies.

One of the more unusual types of sensitivity is that of some people to fruit. Dr. Rowe says that if one is allergic to one type of fruit, one is then likely to be allergic to most or all types of fruit, condiments, spices, flavorings and to fresh, though not to cooked, vegetables. When such a patient occurs, Dr. Rowe prescribes a daily supplementary dose of vitamin C. For that matter, whenever a patient is treated by him, Dr. Rowe insists that the patient's nutritional level be maintained during testing.

Drugs to Control Allergies

The use of drugs in treating bronchial asthma is scored by Dr. Rowe and his colleagues in the *Journal of the American Medical Association* (3-11-59) article in these words: "The control of bronchial asthma with corticosteroids (ACTH) and other new and old drugs without the adequate and persistent study of allergenic causes and especially of usually neglected food allergy is unscientific. It unfortunately ignores the responsibility of the profession to recognize and control atopic allergy which is causative in practically every patient." It would indeed be unfortunate to ignore food as a factor if one believes Dr. Rowe's estimate, in *California Medicine* (April, 1950), of food as the sole cause of bronchial asthma in 20 per cent of 970 cases and a major or secondary cause in an additional 53 per cent.

The popular psychosomatic causes of asthma are given short shrift in this same report. The author states that such influence was not recognized as the sole cause in any true case of bronchial asthma. If the disease is already present due to food or inhalants, at times it was shown to be activated or aggravated by excitement or nervousness. This situation did not occur when the allergenic causes were known and controlled.

The undesirable aspects of cereal foods, especially for some individuals, are shown quite plainly in the attitude of Dr. Rowe. He eliminates them immediately, along with milk, eggs and chocolate, as the first and most likely suspects leading to bronchial asthma. Perhaps they are responsible for other diseases whose causes elude us, especially those which seem to affect one individual and pass by another for no apparent reason. Editor Rodale has written of his distrust of wheat and other grains. Could the elimination of these foods from your diet be the one thing you haven't tried in licking a persistent disease?

CHAPTER 17

Oatmeal

In a section of rural Wales there is a legend of a famous giant who attributed his strength to eating oatcakes and buttermilk. In the same county, we are told, there were also two blacksmiths who used to walk 18 miles from Bala to Dolgelley carrying their heavy tools with them, shoe about 25 horses each and then walk back home the same day. As you surely do not need to be told, oats are staple fare in this part of the world, even today.

They are the second leading cereal of this country, corn being the first. The annual per capita consumption of oatmeal in the United States is about 4 pounds. More oats are used in the breakfast cereal business than any other cereal. The part that we eat is called the groat and it is obtained by removing the tough hulls of the oat grains.

Interestingly enough, when oats are milled, the germ and bran remain in the portion used for human food. So actually oatmeal is a whole grain cereal, like brown rice, containing far more of the nutritional value of the original grain than white flour contains, or white rice. In the milling process the fibrous hull is first removed. Then, in making the slow-cooking kind of rolled oats, the whole groats are steamed, which partially cooks them. The quick-cooking oats are chopped with rotary cutters into varying sizes. Afterwards they also are steamed. Then both kinds are rolled to make the "rolled oats" we have for breakfast.

A number of years ago Sir Edward Mellanby, a famous British nutritionist brought down on himself the wrath of the Scottish people by publishing the results of experiments showing that there is a substance in cereals, especially in oatmeal, which robs the body of calcium. The substance is phytate or phytic acid. Mellanby proved in his experiments with puppies that a diet high in oatmeal (or other cereals to varying degrees) would produce rickets. The Scots were enraged that anyone dared to say such things about their national dish, oatmeal, or porridge as they call it. Their newspapers published satiric cartoons in which they made fun of Sir Edward. However, at the time rickets (a disease of calcium and phosphorus deficiency) was widespread in certain parts of Scotland where oatmeal was the staple food.

Many other nutritionists have since challenged Sir Edward's findings, but so far as we know, no one has managed to disprove them. So we must accept the fact that cereals, even cereals whose calcium content is high, such as oatmeal, do have an unhealthful effect on the calcium stores of the body, under certain circumstances. It seems that these circumstances are important, too. Plenty of calcium and vitamin D in the diet appear to counteract the effect of the phytate in the cereals. This, says Sir Edward, is the reason oldtimers always ate plenty of milk with their oatmeal, for milk is rich in calcium. The fisherfolk who did not have milk ate fish livers which gave them vitamin D. And in the presence of plenty of calcium and vitamin D, perhaps the anticalcium effects of oatmeal would do little harm.

However, it is well to keep in mind when you are planning meals that cereal—any kind of cereal—prepared either as breakfast food or bread, should not have too large a place in your plans. Cereals are cheap, filling, easy to prepare and convenient to eat, so we all tend to use more of them than we should, especially in children's diets they tend to replace the healthful fresh fruits and vegetables. So, even though oatmeal contains valuable food elements as we show below, remember that you are losing some calcium from your diet when you serve it. So make up for the calcium in some other way. You can add powdered bone meal to oatmeal. This will add calcium to the meal you are making.

Three-fourths cup of cooked oatmeal (and we are speaking here of rolled oats, either the quick or long-cooking kind—we are not speaking of processed cold cereals made of oats) contains approximately the following vitamins and minerals:

Vitamin B:

Thiamin	.55 milligrams
Riboflavin	.14 milligrams
Niacin	1.1 milligrams
Pantothenic acid	250. micrograms
Choline	150. milligrams
Vitamin E.	2.10 milligrams
Calcium	54 milligrams
Phosphorus	365 milligrams
Iron	5.2 milligrams
Copper	.50 milligrams

CHAPTER 18

Rice

Rice is an extremely important cereal from the point of view of humanity in general, for about one-half of the world's population considers rice as their basic food. In some countries it is eaten at every meal, almost to the exclusion of all other foods. So we must admit that rice has great value as a nourishing food, even though no nutritionist would advise eating it exclusively.

The best possible use that we, in western countries, can make of rice is to use it oftener than we do for the starchy part of a meal. If you're hesitating between rice or potatoes for dinner tonight, for instance, you should take into account what else your family has eaten during the course of the day. If cereal for breakfast and several slices of bread per meal are the rule in your household, then potatoes would be a better choice, for rice is a cereal and has the disadvantages as well as the advantages of other cereals. Like other cereals, it has an acid reaction in the body's metabolism, whereas potatoes, being a vegetable, have an alkaline reaction. On the other hand, if you're hesitating between noodles, macaroni or spaghetti versus rice, your choice should be rice. Products like noodles, macaroni and so on contain little real nourishment if they are made from white flour which all commercially-prepared products are. On the other hand, rice—brown rice, that is—contains all the original nutriments of the grain.

The Milling Process

The chief crimes committed against rice in the name of civilization are those same ones we commit against wheat when we mill it. The original brown rice, as it comes from the rice plant, contains protein, starch, fat, minerals and vitamins, chiefly in its bran, endosperm and germ. As brown rice is milled to make white or polished rice, these important nutriments are changed for the worse. Milling results in a loss of about 10 per cent of the protein, 85 per cent of the fat and 70 per cent of the minerals. What happens to the vitamins is even more drastic. Brown rice contains approximately 2.93 milligrams of thiamin, .67 milligrams of riboflavin and 49.2 milligrams of niacin for every hundred grams. These are the major B vitamins. White rice contains only .60 milligrams of thiamin, .26 milligrams of riboflavin and 18.5 milligrams of niacin.

The milling of rice was the accidental cause of an important discovery in vitamin research more than 50 years ago, when a disease called beriberi first became widespread in oriental countries. Investigations showed in 1884 that milling and polishing the rice caused the disease by removing the B vitamins mentioned above. Since rice is the staple food in these countries, there was no possibility of making up this loss in other foods, and beriberi, a disease which often proves fatal, became common. Reverting to brown rice completely cured and prevented the disease. Since all this has been known for half a century, you might wonder why we still sell white rice in stores. There is no logical answer to this question. Processors tell us that people won't buy brown rice because they've become accustomed to white, and we consider this answer an insult to the intelligence of the average American woman who simply does not know which foods are nutritious, but would gladly buy them if she did know. In the orient and in this country as well, we have resorted to "enrichment" of rice—that is, we first remove most of the vitamins and minerals from the rice to make it white, then we replace only a part of the vitamins and minerals by a synthetic process which leaves the rice still looking white.

This is how this process is accomplished. After the white, gleaming, polished rice has come from the mill it is coated with a "premix" of zein (a protein substance obtained from corn) and alcohol. Then iron pyrophosphate is added (to replace the natural iron just removed from the rice). Then the rice is dipped into the mix again and a synthetic vitamin is added, and so forth. This "mix" has been so cleverly compounded that it is not affected by washing, cooking or storage. How it affects your stomach has probably not been studied. We don't know. However, we do know that "enriched" rice does not contain the original substances put there by nature and we believe it is no improvement over white or polished rice.

Brown and Wild Rice

You can obtain brown rice in most grocery stores these days. If your grocer does not have it, ask him to order it for you. Perhaps we can convince the food processors that we are more than eager to have nutritious food, regardless of color. Incidentally brown rice, after it is cooked, looks only a little darker than white rice. There is so little difference that your family or guests will never suspect that a wholly nutritious food is being served them in place of a dead, starchy mockery of food.

Wild rice is a rare delicacy. It is unrelated botanically to cultivated rice and grows in this country chiefly in Minnesota where it is harvested by the Indians of the Great Lakes region. Only about 350,000 to 500,000 pounds are for sale every year and the amount of labor involved in finding the rice and harvesting it make the price very high. If you can afford wild rice at about a dollar a pound, you can be sure that you are getting the very finest and most nutritious food, for wild rice contains twice as much protein as white polished rice, 4 times as much phosphorus, 8 times as much thiamin and 20 times as much riboflavin. And it has not been tampered with.

CHAPTER 19

The Food Value of Rice Germ

The story of rice bran and rice polish is actually the story of how scientists first came to suspect the existence of the minute substances we now call vitamins. It was in 1883 that a Japanese naval officer, Baron Takaki, discovered something important about the disease that was the scourge of sailing men in the East—beriberi. The Baron declared that the disease was caused by the sailors' diets. He added other foods to their daily fare of polished rice and the disease was soon conquered.

Baron Takaki thought the answer was simply that the diet he prescribed contained more protein. It was up to other investigators to show that, although the protein was important and although polished rice was nearly entirely starch, still something else that existed in *unpolished* rice was necessary for human health.

A Dutch physician, Eijkman of Java, did some experimenting with pigeons. He could give the pigeons beriberi in a short time by feeding them polished rice. He could cure them by giving them unpolished rice. Three workers at the school of Tropical Medicine in Liverpool, England, found that laboratory animals got beriberi when they were fed exclusively on either polished rice or white bread. They recovered when they got whole grain bread or unpolished rice. So it appeared that there was some important substance in the unrefined grains that the refined ones did not contain.

Years later Casimir Funk named the substance a "vitamine"—a food element present in minute quantities which is absolutely necessary for human health. Today we know that the vitamin in rice polishings is thiamin, a B vitamin. It exists there along with the other vitamins of the B complex which are present in considerable amounts in unrefined grains of all kinds. Beriberi as such has been all but wiped out in civilized parts of the world where there is any knowledge of nutrition. But a slight deficiency in thiamin is still widespread, even in America, because most of our grain and cereal products are refined.

Why You Need More Thiamin

As Mark Graubard expresses it in his book, *Man's Food, Its Rhyme or Reason* (Macmillan Company), "Nature apparently saw to it not to make life too easy for us so as to oblige us to keep our wits about us and be on the alert. To begin with, the amount of thiamin needed depends on what the other items of our diet are. Also, the higher the energy expenditure of the body the more thiamin is required. The more sugar we consume or the more starch, the more of that vitamin is needed. Should we feed largely on protein or fat, for example, we would need less thiamin to maintain our system in good shape. Thus, eating polished rice or white, unenriched bread or potatoes cooked in much water which, in addition, is discarded, makes for quite a vicious circle. Not only is the thiamin thrown out or destroyed in the preparation, but because these foods are all starches, the body requires more thiamin than normally."

Thiamin is needed for the body to digest starch. So as soon as you remove that vitamin from a starchy food (like grain) the food becomes a peril, for eating it can produce a dangerous deficiency in thiamin.

Rice is grown chiefly in the Orient and is staple food for more than half the world's population. After the rice is threshed the "rough rice" consists of a kernel contained in a hull. When the hull is removed you find that the rice grain is made of a pericarp (the outer bran) and the seed, which includes the inner bran, the endosperm and the germ. In this state the rice is called "brown rice." When it is milled into polished rice the bran and germ are removed. Nothing but the pure starchy endosperm remains. This is white rice, or polished rice, such as you buy in the grocery store. This is the food that devastated eastern countries for many years before it was discovered that the milling and polishing of the rice had removed the necessary part of the cereal.

What Is Lost When Rice Is Polished?

As we stated in the preceding chapter, when rice is converted to white rice, about 10 per cent of the protein, 85 per cent of the fat and 70 per cent of the minerals are removed. Large amounts of the B vitamins also disappear during the refining process.

The polishing process removes the bran and the germ. These contain the vitamins, minerals and much of the protein. So it is easy to see that the fluffy white starchy grains we serve regularly at dinner contain none or practically none of the real food value of the rice. It has departed into the bran, germ and polishings.

It's very much the same story as what happens when wheat is refined. Here, too, by far the best part of the wheat is left in the wheat germ which was generally sold for cattle and stock food. That's what happens to the rice polishings, too. Except, of course, that some of those food faddists eventually came along and asked a very pertinent question. "Why," they asked "should we keep our cattle and pigs healthy by taking away the best part of the grain and feeding it to them, while our people get only the starch with none of the value left in it?" So they began to package wheat germ and rice germ and polishings and sell them as "health foods." Now actually, as you can see, they are not special "foods"—they are simply what originally was in the grain and then was removed. So they are really far more natural "foods" than white rice and white flour. And you can tell that to anybody who laughs at you as a food faddist for eating wheat germ or rice germ.

According to Marinus C. Kik of the Department of Agricultural Chemistry of the University of Arkansas, the nutritive value of wheat and corn germ has been well investigated. So, in an experiment reported in the November, 1954, issue of *Agricultural and Food Chemistry* he tested rice germ and compared it to the two other foods from the standpoint of nutrition. It rated high. For instance, its thiamin content is about twice as high as that of wheat or corn germ. It contains good protein, including 10 of the amino acids which are essential for human beings to have in their food. We manufacture some of the amino acids (or blocks of protein) ourselves. The rest we must get from food. Rice germ has some of all of these.

Here is a table, according to Professor Kik, showing the vitamin and mineral content of rice germ:

B vitamins

Thiamin	65	micrograms per gram
Riboflavin	5	
Niacin	33	
Pantothenic acid	30	
Pyridoxine	16	
Biotin	.58	
PABA	1	
Inositol	3725	
Folic acid	4.3	
Choline	3000	
Calcium	.275	per cent
Phosphorus	2.10	
Iron	.013	
Protein	14.93	
Fat	11.52	

What should all this mean to you in terms of your own daily meal planning? First of all, we hope you never serve your family white rice. Your grocery store probably sells brown rice. If not, they can surely order it for you. Your health food store probably sells rice germ or rice polishings.

Perhaps your family is already eating wheat germ. You might want to include rice germ or rice polishings along with the wheat germ, or alternate the two. We have demonstrated how vitally important it is for you and all the members of your family to get plenty of the B vitamins the rice products contain. If you are not taking brewer's yeast or desiccated liver, this is doubly important. Don't neglect them, especially if you eat any refined carbohydrates at all. By this we mean products made from white flour or anything that contains sugar, refined cereals (the kind you get at the grocery store) prepared or packaged "mixes" or any other processed food. The more of these you eat, the more B vitamins you need to be healthy.

[81]

CHAPTER 20

Wheat Germ: Wonderful Food

Why all the enthusiasm for wheat germ? Why should we, while cautioning readers against getting too much of cereal foods, recommend wheat germ in the highest possible terms? Here are some of the reasons. We're sure they will make you agree that you should add wheat germ to your daily menus.

What Is Wheat Germ?

Wheat germ is that part of the wheat which is responsible for sprouting and making the new plant. This means that it is very much alive, carrying, as it does, the spark of the new life. In addition, it must provide everything the new plant needs to sustain itself—chiefly protein, vitamins and minerals.

Look at Fig. 1. Notice how the valuable parts of the kernel are concentrated in the bran and in the germ. The endosperm, the large, light-colored section, is mostly starch. Yet, believe it or not, when wheat is milled into white flour, the bran and the germ are discarded and the starchy endosperm is all that is used.

Nutritional Value of Wheat Germ

A half cup of wheat germ contains 24 grams of protein—as much as ¼ pound of turkey, more than ¼ pound of beef, 4 times as much as an egg and 8 times as much as a slice of white bread. A pound of wheat germ supplies about 200 grams of protein and may cost as little as a quarter, whereas an amount of steak yielding that much protein would cost in the neighborhood of 10 dollars.

Only a few foods (liver, parsley and greens of various kinds) are richer in iron than wheat germ. Iron-deficiency anemia is common in America and many a child and woman is condemned to a lifetime of swallowing iron-containing medicines, just because they eat white flour products and

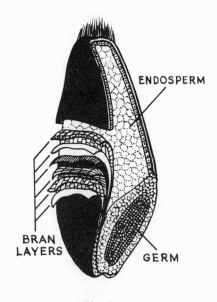

Fig. 1

thus avoid the very best food we have for supplying an abundance of iron.

There is not a great deal of calcium in wheat germ. Cereal products are noted for their lack of calcium. And wheat germ is extremely rich in phosphorus. Here we must caution our readers. Lots of phosphorus demands lots of calcium. The two work together. Large amounts of phosphorus will be excreted if your diet is high in it and calcium will be carried along with the phosphorus. So be sure to get enough calcium from another source if you are eating foods like brewer's yeast, wheat germ and other cereal products rich in phosphorus. Bone meal is your best natural source.

Wheat germ is also rich in many other minerals that are essential for good health—manganese, magnesium, copper, potassium.

Vitamin Content

Perhaps most important of all are the B vitamins—important because there are so few foods rich in the B vitamins and because wheat germ is abundantly endowed with all of them. That half cup of wheat germ gives us far more vitamin B_1—thiamin—than any other food except brewer's yeast—about 2½ milligrams. Riboflavin, perhaps the B vitamin most difficult to get enough of, is plentiful in wheat germ, too. Only 4 foods— yeast, liver, kidneys and milk—contain more riboflavin than wheat germ. About the same is true of niacin. Pyridoxine, pantothenic acid and inositol, other B vitamins, are all present in goodly quantity in wheat germ.

One reason why these B vitamins are so important (apart from their own worth) is that they take part in the processes our bodies use involving other important substances, the unsaturated fatty acids, for example. These, too, are present in wheat germ, along with vitamin E, so necessary for the health of all muscle tissue, especially the heart. As you know, not a single one of all these vitamins remains after wheat has been milled to make white flour.

The so-called "enrichment" of white bread consists of putting into the flour a dab of synthetic thiamin, niacin and iron Don't make the mistake of believing that this remakes the flour into something worth eating. Some 25 known food elements are removed and two or three are substituted, synthetically.

Care Given to Wheat Germ

Like all worthwhile fresh foods, it spoils easily. Once it is removed from the wheat it deteriorates rapidly and the fats it contains become rancid. This destroys vitamin E. So you must treat wheat germ as if it were as perishable as milk. It should be refrigerated at all times and it is best to buy not too large a quantity at a time. Usually, wheat germ is vacuum-packed which means there is no air inside the package to cause any rancidity or spoilage. Once this vaccum seal has been broken, it's into the refrigerator with the wheat germ!

Wheat Germ with Food Supplements?

It's best to, just because this superlatively fine food is so inexpensive and can be used in so many ways. Once you and your family have come to like the taste, you can add wheat germ to almost any dish and bring up its nutritive value like magic.

What is the difference between wheat germ and wheat germ oil? Just the same difference there is between peanuts and peanut oil, or corn and corn oil. Wheat germ oil is pressed out of the germ. It contains all the fat-soluble vitamins that are in the germ. But not the protein or the water-soluble vitamins like the B vitamins. Of course, wheat germ flakes like the kind you buy have not had the oil removed from them. It is still there for your benefit.

By the same token, of course, wheat germ oil is far richer in the fat soluble vitamins than wheat germ flakes could be, for these are concentrated in the oil. So you will get more vitamin E and the unsaturated fatty acids in the oil.

Toasted or Raw Wheat Germ?

Most people prefer the taste of the toasted germ. Raw germ has more in the way of vitamins, for some of the very sensitive B vitamins are destroyed by heat. However, if you buy raw germ and then don't like the taste of it, you can toast it yourself in a very slow oven, spread out on a large pan. You will lose very little vitamin content. If your family will eat more of it willingly, if it is toasted, then toast it.

It goes well with almost anything. It is particularly useful as a substitute for bread or cracker crumbs—in meat loaves, casseroles, cutlets, things of that kind. Many people use it in salads as well or sprinkled over fruits or berries for dessert. It is perfectly acceptable as a breakfast cereal all by itself or with fruit or yogurt. And, of course, you can add it to any kind of bread you are making, with no change in the recipe except that you may need more liquid.

Are Vitamins Lost During Cooking?

Yes, and for this reason we advise eating it as it is, and not cooking it. But if you want to enrich cooked foods, then the wheat germ must be cooked, too. And you do not lose any more vitamins out of wheat germ in cooking than you lose out of liver or eggs when you cook them.

CHAPTER 21

Wheat Germ the Food
of Champions

Evidence continues to mount on the effect of wheat germ oil on human endurance and physical performance. The latest clipping from the Philadelphia *Evening Bulletin* carries these headlines "Wheat Germ Diet Helped Aussies Smash Olympic Swimming Records, Doctor Says." The doctor was Thomas K. Cureton of the University of Illinois.

Dr. Cureton announced that Australian swimmers made "chumps" out of their Olympic opponents partly because they trained on a scientific "power-packed" diet, the main ingredient of which was wheat germ.

Six months before they were to compete in the games, the Australian team was put on a supervised program of physical training, in which heavy emphasis was placed on scientific feeding. The athletes were fed an allotment of wheat germ oil and wheat germ cereal every day and their diet was heavily fortified with vitamins and minerals. This was in addition to their regular meals at which they might eat anything they wanted except fried foods.

American athletes, who got an allotment of wheat germ just before they took off on the Olympic trip, got too late a start to do them much good, according to Dr. Cureton. The 3 American swimmers who had been taking wheat germ for a long time before made the best showing of all the American team in the games.

Here is a brief review of some of the other evidence Dr. Cureton has gathered over a period of years at the University of Illinois. Wheat germ oil was found to be a valuable food supplement which helped the endurance of middle-aged men to run on a treadmill and produced significant results in a matched group which took the same course of exercises for 8 weeks. The physical endurance of the group taking wheat germ was superior, tests showed that their heart, blood pressure and pulse had a better response and they reacted faster to light and sound. No effort was made to regulate their diets except for the addition of the wheat germ oil.

Director of Cortland State Teachers College confirmed these findings of Dr. Cureton's, stating that Cortland track stars showed improved endurance when wheat germ oil was given to them. A swimming star at Springfield, College, Massachusetts, broke the world's record for the 200 meter-race after he took wheat germ oil. A woman swimming champion set a new A.A.U. record for the women's 100 meter free style at Indianapolis in 1955. We are told that when she came out of the pool her first remark was, "Wheat germ oil! I don't get tired at the end of a race anymore!"

Vitamin E Improves Their Game

Some time ago we published the story of the Canadian Maple Leaf baseball team. According to the *Toronto Daily Star* for September 6, 1956, "a vital factor in the overall picture has been the use of vitamin E by the Toronto team this season." Before the season began each player received a bottle of vitamin E capsules and was instructed to begin taking them before training began. They started with 200 milligrams of vitamin E and the dose was later increased. What happened to the batting averages of that ball team when the vitamin E began to take effect reads like a club manager's dream. And vitamin E gets all the credit!

Vitamin E occurs in wheat germ, of course. Wheat germ contains many other substances as well—unsaturated fatty acids and certain other fatty substances which doctors are now claiming prevent hardening of the arteries and accumulation of cholesterol. It is our belief that everyone should take both vitamin E and wheat germ.

Experiments on Race Horses

An interesting study of the effect of vitamin E on race horses appears in *The Summary* for December, 1956, (published by the Shute Foundation for Medical Research, London, Canada). At two racing stables tests were made by giving certain horses vitamin E, increasing the dosage just before the race, "to increase muscular stamina and utilization of oxygen further."

Earnings of the horses were almost doubled, indicating, of course, many more wins. The percentage of wins per horse was 2.7 compared to 2.3 last year when a smaller dose of vitamin E was given and 1.8 the year before when no vitamin was given.

Horses taking vitamin E showed far less nervousness than those which did not, and the stamina of the vitamin E-fed horses was markedly increased. The owners of the horses warn that vitamin E is not a shot-in-the-arm which can make a Derby winner out of a mediocre horse overnight. The horses to which the vitamin was given were all in excellent condition at the beginning of the experiment. But vitamin E brought about a great improvement even in their former excellent performance.

Important for Human Beings, too

The editor, commenting on this experiment, reminds us that the same conditions apply to human beings. "If there is such a thing as optimal health these athletes possessed it during the period of their competition. It is of genuine physiologic interest that one can improve the cardiac efficiency and skeletal muscle power of the superb "normal" animals.

"This further emphasizes the importance of vitamin E for so-called normal men, or men who regard themselves as being in excellent health. Obviously it means even more to men in failing health, people who have less than normally efficient hearts and skeletal muscles. The whole study stresses the importance of improving tissue oxygenation."

Endurance Influenced by Desiccated Liver

We have only two other reminders—the experiments on endurance performed by Dr. Ershoff with desiccated liver in which he found that animals given quite large doses of the liver showed many times the endurance of animals given no supplement. Desiccated liver is rich in B vitamins, vitamin A and many important minerals, as well as certain other factors which apparently exist only in liver, for results like this cannot be achieved using other foods rich in B vitamins, it seems.

Remember, too, that bone meal is important for the health of the sportsman. This is particularly evident in the case of the dangerous sports. How many skiers and hockey players could be spared broken bones if they went to the fray well fortified with bone meal—for years, of course, not just a few hours before the sporting event begins. Since bone meal is so important for good teeth, it should interest young sportsmen even more. For what would-be baseball player or trackman wants to miss practice because he's gone to the dentist?

Often mothers write us asking how they can interest their children in eating healthfully amid the ever-present lure of the candy-coke-ice-cream-parlor world in which they live. Surely experiments like those reported above can be used effectively to convince the young ones. What boy would not like to follow the example of Olympic champion swimmers and Maple Leaf baseball players? Wouldn't he be willing to take almost anything, if it might make him better at sports? Wouldn't stories like the ones above be likely to convince him that there *is* something to this nutrition business after all—it's not just a dull subject dealt with in laboratories—it's the real stuff of which champions are made!

Think of the amount of money spent by high schools, colleges and universities to produce winning teams in athletics—just for the glory of the old alma mater. But think of the rewards if a program of good nutrition, and especially a regular program of taking vitamin E and wheat germ were to be instituted. The glory of the old alma mater would grow brighter with every new victory. But, far more important than that—the team's improved stamina and good health would be reflected in better grades, better citizenship, finer personalities.

Professional athletes and the men who coach and manage them are interested in profits. Winning games means more money, and good nutrition (especially vitamin E and wheat germ) means winning more games. Couldn't we amateurs learn a lesson from the pros?

[87]

CHAPTER 22

Wheat Germ and a Healthy Reproductive System

Wheat germ oil has been used in animal experiments and in human therapy many, many times. Although results have not always been perfect, they are significant enough for us to draw some heartening conclusions about the potency of this oil extracted from the living part of wheat.

Vitamin E was discovered in 1922 in wheat germ oil. Since then research has disclosed this vitamin in different foods, but in rather scanty quantity. In 1939 pure vitamin E was isolated and soon afterwards synthetic vitamin E (tocopherol) was made. Experimenters immediately tried to produce the same effects with the synthetic vitamin E that they had had with wheat germ, and failed. So the general consensus of opinion now is that there is some substance in wheat germ, aside from the vitamin E, which accounts for its very significant benefits.

Since the earliest days of recorded history, men have worshipped wheat. Throughout most of the world wheat is a main foodstuff and the times of planting and harvesting wheat have become the occasion for festivals and ceremonies. Not until some 50 years ago did it occur to civilized man that his wheat should be milled so that his flour would be white. When that time came, mills were revolutionized so that flour might be ground different-ly. Then, too, since milling and baking were no longer local or home industries, flour had to be processed in some way so that it might be preserved to be shipped across whole continents and stored in warehouses until the baker needed it. One part of the wheat interfered with both these processes—the wheat germ—that part of the wheat seed that germinates each season to produce new wheat. If the bran and germ were left in the wheat, the flour was dark rather than white. And if the germ were left in the flour, the flour spoiled, since wheat germ is highly perishable. So millers began to remove the wheat germ. White flour then remained nothing but starch—all the good nourishing part of the wheat was contained in the germ. No one knew what to do with this germ that had been milled out of the wheat and for a time it was thrown away. Then someone discovered that it made good feed for cattle and other farm animals. So the wheat germ was sold for feed.

Meanwhile mankind went on eating white flour, and a host of new degenerative diseases developed for which there was no explanation—heart disease, muscular diseases, nervous diseases, paralysis and, in many people, sterility. Up until quite recently it never occurred to anyone that the new milling processes might have anything to do with these diseases. Then, after vitamins were discovered and vitamin research was proceeding apace, someone discovered the new vitamin—in wheat germ oil.

Vitamin B and Vitamin E in Reproduction

As long ago as 1927 in the *American Journal of Physiology*, H. A. Mattill, M.D., studied the effect of lack of vitamin E and vitamin B in a rat's diet. Rats were placed on a diet in which vitamin B was completely lacking, but there was ample vitamin E. Because of the B vitamin deficiency, the rats rapidly declined in health, finally becoming completely paralyzed. Yet at death, the reproductive organs of these animals had not degenerated, and moving, living sperm were found present in the male organs even after death.

On the other hand, rats fed a diet abundant in vitamin B but lacking in vitamin E remained healthy and grew to normal size. But their reproductive organs were underdeveloped. The experiments showed a relationship between vitamin E and vitamin B. Diets deficient in B created such lassitude and poor health that sex interest was lacking, whereas diets deficient in vitamin E caused definite physical deterioration in the sex organs. However, it is significant to remember that vitamin B and E occur together in the food. Since Nature has sound reasons for the things she does, it does not surprise us that these two vitamins, each in its own way so necessary for proper functioning of the reproductive system, should both occur plentifully in the germ, or live part, of the wheat.

In *Nature* for December 4, 1937, another experiment with rats indicates that lack of vitamin E completely disorganizes sex life. Experimenting with 76 male rats, B. P. Wiesner and A. L. Bacharach fed them a diet adequate in all known vitamins except vitamin E. In some of the animals sex behavior was normal for the first months of the experiment. In others it was disturbed and confused—the activity resembling that of an animal whose pituitary gland has been removed. In a fourth of the animals, no sex activity at all was observed during the experiment. These authors believe that vitamin E deficiency produces this effect by preventing the proper functioning of the pituitary gland.

Vitamin E Therapy For Male Sterility

Dr. Evan Shute of Canada, whose work with vitamin E and heart disease is famous, has also used vitamin E extensively in therapy for reproductive disorders. In the *Urological and Cutaneous Review*, Vol. 48, 1944, he summarizes his conclusions up to that time about the effect of vitamin E on animal fertility. Experiments had shown, he says, that complete lack of vitamin E in the diet of a rat produces gradual atrophy of certain of the generative organs, resulting first in inability to produce sperm and eventually in complete sterility. But before complete atrophy of the male organs takes place, vitamin E therapy can restore some sperm productivity.

In dealing with his own patients, Dr. Shute prescribes vitamin E in cases of barrenness or interrupted pregnancies. He describes in particular his method of treating the husband as well as the wife. When childless couples come to him, he suggests that the husband's semen be examined for the possibility of defective sperm. Very few of his male patients agree to this suggestion. "This illustrates better than anything else one could say, pernaps, men's fixed belief that their wives are at fault when their marriages are barren, and their peculiar vanity in respect to their own potency," says Dr. Shute.

He recounts histories of 27 cases in which complete sterility and habitual abortions or miscarriages were the complaints. In 10 of these cases conception took place within several weeks or months after two weeks of vitamin E therapy. Others of the group of patients might have had similar results except that they became discouraged and dropped the treatment.

Vitamin E and Female Reproductive Disorders

Vitamin E is also extensively used to prevent and cure disorders of the female reproductive organs. Dr. Shute in the *Urological and Cutaneous Review* for April, 1943, describes his use of vitamin E in 153 pregnancies in which there were 122 threatened abortions and 87 threatened miscarriages. (In medical terminology incidentally, an abortion means the loss of the unborn child any time between conception and 16 weeks of pregnancy; miscarriage means loss of the fetus later than 16 weeks.) Dr. Shute tells us that the tendency for these tragedies to repeat themselves in pregnancy after pregnancy indicates that the condition of the parent is to blame rather than the environment. A large percentage of those women having either severe pains or considerable bleeding were saved with the help of vitamin E. Sixty per cent of the abortions and 86 per cent of the miscarriages were handled successfully by vitamin E therapy. This means that the lives of the infants were saved and they had normal births. In addition, very few of the mothers suffered from pregnancy toxemia or poisoning. Vitamin E deficiency seems to be very common in pregnant women, concludes Dr. Shute.

Vitamin E in the metabolism of the pregnant woman protects the safety of the fetus and the health of the placenta, writes Mlle. M. V. Quadras-Bordes in the French journal, *Revue francais de Gynécologie et d'Obstétrigue* for November, 1936. She indicates that some authorities believe vitamin E is necessary for the assimilation of iron by the embryo. She says that possibly all the iron in the mother's system cannot benefit the unborn child unless vitamin E is also present.

In a much later article in the *Ohio State Medical Journal* for June, 1951, Wynne M. Silbernagel, M.D., and James B. Patterson, M.D., pursue the matter further. "Any patient who threatens to abort is a deserving candidate for some form of therapy," say these authors. "Obviously prophylaxis (prevention) if available would be better management. Such an approach has been made possible by the use of a concentrate of wheat germ oil." They remind us that by wheat germ oil they do *not* mean concentrated synthetic vitamin E—*they mean wheat germ oil*, which contains substances that are not present in the pure synthetic vitamin E. Their figures for a series of 1,973 patients untreated and 825 patients treated with wheat germ oil are revealing. No patient was excluded from wheat germ therapy because of toxemia, syphilis, diabetes, tuberculosis, heart trouble, etc.

Eighty-seven per cent of the patients started taking the concentrate between the third and sixteenth week of pregnancy and 5 per cent were taking it before conception.

Of the untreated patients, 15 per cent aborted. Of those taking wheat germ oil, only 3.7 per cent aborted. Premature delivery of the infant took place in 7.1 per cent of the untreated mothers. Among those taking wheat germ oil, 3.7 per cent delivered their babies prematurely. Toxemia was present in 10 per cent of the untreated mothers and in only 2.1 per cent of the treated ones.

"This study indicates that the fetal loss from abortion may be nutritional in origin. While a concentrate of wheat germ oil may be considered a therapeutic agent, it is equally important to emphasize that our modern diet, lacking in natural vegetable oils derived from (whole) grains may be deficient in substances which protect the fetus." We add a heartfelt amen to this statement.

It seems rather strange to us that medical science should be so tardy in recognizing the potency of wheat germ as a preventive of abortion. An article in the *Breeders' Gazette* for May, 1950, relates the long history of the use of wheat germ to prevent abortion in farm animals. "The old desert horsemen who insisted on feeding whole wheat to their mares whether they themselves had any bread or not, may have had a hint for you, modern breeders," says Samuel R. Guard, author of this article.

Treatment For Menopausal Flushes

One article from a medical journal gives us all too briefly and, as the authors themselves point out, too inconclusively, the results of vitamin E therapy for menopausal flushes. Discussing the cases of 4 patients, A. M. Hain, D.Sc., Ph.D, and J. C. B. Sym, M.D., D.P.H., in the *British Medical Journal* for July 3, 1943, describe considerable relief from menopausal discomfort in the case of 3 of the patients. The fourth woman was given a hormone substance, estrogen, and appeared to obtain some relief from this. These two doctors advise that vitamin E therapy may be effective in only some cases of menopausal disorder, but they plead for more work to be done along these lines so that the complete story may be known.

Finally in *Endocrinology* for September, 1951, comes the story of experiments done by Ezra Levin, John F. Burns and V. K. Collins at the Viobin Laboratories, Monticello, Illinois. Using a carefully extracted wheat germ oil these researchers produced 3 kinds of activity in laboratory rats—estrogenic, androgenic and gonadotrophic. Estrogenic refers to female sexual activity or "heat"—the period when female animals are fertile. Androgenic refers to masculine characteristics, which these researchers produced in castrated animals, which, of course, would not otherwise show these characteristics. Gonadotrophic activity refers to fertile conditions of the ovaries and uteri of female rats whose pituitary gland had been removed. The removal of this gland would under ordinary circumstances prevent the growth of the uterus. But when wheat germ oil was administered, these reproductive organs grew normally and displayed the appearance of normal reproductive glands. It is extremely interesting to note that several other

[91]

different vegetable oils, synthetic vitamin E and rancid wheat germ oil administered in exactly the same way did not produce the same results.

Some Cautions About Using Wheat Germ Oil

This last point brings us to another very important aspect of the use of wheat germ oil. Dr. Evan Shute, writing in the *American Journal of Obstetrics and Gynecology* for April, 1938, outlines several cautions in the use of wheat germ oil therapy. Because of its high perishability and the methods used in extracting it, wheat germ oil rapidly becomes rancid. Not only is rancid wheat germ oil completely ineffective in producing the results we have described, but the presence of any rancid oils whatsoever in the digestive tract will counteract the good effects of the wheat germ. Dr. Shute relates a number of instances of therapy in which disappointing results could not be explained until it was discovered that the patients were keeping their wheat germ oil at room temperature in quite warm rooms. It has also been pointed out by other physicians that it is wise to take wheat germ oil between meals, when the stomach is reasonably empty, to make certain that the oil does not come into contact with any rancid fat that one may have eaten at meals. Dr. Shute concludes that wheat germ oil in bulk or in capsules retains reliable potency very little longer than 8 weeks, even when it is refrigerated.

He notes also that there is a seasonal need for wheat germ therapy, depending on what other vitamin E foods are available. We all know that green foods grown in the fall or early spring do not contain all the vitamin substances present in foods grown during the summer when the sun is at its zenith. In addition, those green foods that are available in winter have probably been shipped long distances and stored for considerable periods of time, resulting in further loss of vitamins. Disorders associated with pregnancy occur much more frequently from January to June and infrequently from July to December, says Dr. Shute, indicating that there are high and low periods of vitamin potency in foods such as watercress, celery and even butter and cream. These periods when the vitamin content of food is low are the times when the need for wheat germ oil therapy is greatest.

Another aspect to be carefully watched in administering wheat germ oil is whether or not you are taking any of the commercially prepared iron supplements. These are made of iron salts and when they appear in the digestive tract along with wheat germ oil, they completely nullify its beneficial effects. In the case of iron (which is, of course, especially necessary for pregnant women, to prevent anemia) liver is the perfect solution to the problem. If you do not like liver, desiccated liver is a food containing iron in natural form, which will not destroy the good effects of wheat germ oil.

Wheat Germ Should Be Part of Your Daily Diet

Throughout all our study of the potency of wheat germ oil, we were continually amazed at the general attitude of researchers—an assumption that wheat germ oil is a medicine to be taken at special times in order to prevent or cure certain conditions of the reproductive system. With one exception (Dr. Silbernagel and Dr. Patterson, whom we quoted) it did not seem to occur to anyone to advise a completely different diet in which wheat germ would naturally occur. Besides, if taking this oil prevents or cures disorders, why not advise taking it every day all during one's lifetime, so that there will be no chance for the disorders to get even a start?

We know that until about 50 years ago wheat germ was present in products made from wheat. We know that with the removal of this vitamin-rich part of the wheat seed, people of the western world began to be subject to many different kinds of degenerative diseases, among which are certainly a host of reproductive disorders. Why then, do researchers not suggest—nay, demand—a return to natural whole grains for everyone, so that we need not concern ourselves further with "cures" for various diseases we have had only since the disappearance of the wheat germ from our food? Perhaps this is not part of the job of researchers. Their business is to investigate and report. It's *our* business to demand, once we know all the facts.

Some nutrition books dismiss vitamin E with the statement that it is widespread in foods so no one need worry too much about not getting enough. But is this actually the case? Butter and whole eggs contain about 3 milligrams of vitamin E per 100 grams. But how much butter and how many eggs by weight does each of us eat per week? Green celery (not blanched) contains 2.6 milligrams of vitamin E per 100 grams. Roasted peanuts contain about 30 milligrams, and so on. Would you call this a wide and plentiful distribution in foods? *Wheat germ oil contains as high as 420 milligrams per 100 grams.* And wheat germ is the substance our milling companies sell for cattle feed! Since vitamin E is not the only substance in wheat germ oil which makes it so potent, you might eat all the butter and eggs you can get and still not obtain enough of this unknown substance in the wheat germ which is so important to good health.

Our conclusion is easy to guess. Not all of us are immediately concerned with pregnancy or even fertility. But everyone of us, old or young, must be concerned with the good health of our reproductive systems, whether or not we ever plan to have children. So *avoid refined cereals, white flour and all products made from it.* When you eat any wheat product, make certain it is whole wheat, containing the wheat germ. Keep in mind, too, that the flour used in commercially baked whole wheat products has been treated with a preservative, since the wheat germ is very perishable. Your safest bet is to buy whole wheat flour from an organic farmer and do your own baking. In addition, make wheat germ or wheat germ oil one of your food supplements that you take every single day.

Wheat germ is delicious just by itself; with cream it's a dessert! Used in recipes (you can use it in almost any kind of food) it will daily add nutritive value to every meal. If you want to be perfectly sure and safe and healthy, add wheat germ oil capsules to your food supplements. Keep them in the refrigerator.

One last suggestion: next time you talk or write to your congressman, give him a little lesson in good nutrition by telling him some of these facts and asking him why there are no effective laws to protect our foods, so that we wouldn't have to take food supplements to stay healthy.

SECTION 4.

Dairy Products

Scientific evidence from reliable sources all over the world has shown milk and milk products to be less than the jewels of good health we were formerly led to believe they are. While they do contain many valuable nutrients, they are also possessed of an alarming number of undesirable properties which health-conscious people should take into account. There are excellent substitutes for milk, which will make up for food value lost when milk is removed from the diet—be sure to make some equivalent substitution. The following pages do show several dairy products which are exempt from our general statement—yogurt, lactose, whey and, of course, eggs.

CHAPTER 23

Butter

In seventeenth century England butter was eaten on bread by the working people, but rich folks thought it was an uncouth kind of food and used it only for cooking. Doctors disapproved of its use in the diet generally, saying, "It is also best for children while they are growing and for old men while they are declining, but very unwholesome betwixt these two ages, because through the heat of young stomachs, it is forthwith converted into choler." During the eighteenth century it was still widely regarded as unhealthful for children, for, said the learned doctors of that day, it causes them to grow "weakly, corpulent, big-bellied, very subject to breakings-out and to breed lice."

In our day and age it is hard to imagine how such ideas arose in regard to butter which today is known as a food of surpassing nutritional value. Possibly the disapproving attitude of the medical profession came about because the butter, as served on city tables, was practically always rancid, for there was no means of refrigeration and apparently no one objected to the taste of rancid butter. Today we know that rancid fats destroy the fat soluble vitamins when they encounter them in the digestive tract. So, if all the butter was rancid, perhaps the children did suffer from all these various symptoms, not as a result of eating butter, but as a result of eating *rancid* butter.

Today over one-third of all the milk produced in this country is used for making butter. In general, the milk, or the separated cream is shipped from the dairy regions to creameries located in some centralized spot. Most butter is made from soured cream, although some is made from sweet cream. From 10 to 13 per cent salt is added to the cream to help prevent the growth of yeasts and molds. The salted cream is neutralized at the creamery by the addition of an alkaline salt, such as sodium carbonate, magnesium oxide or calcium carbonate. Then it is pasteurized and inoculated with a starter to sour it. It is left to ripen for several hours, and is then churned. The buttermilk is removed from it, and it is worked for some time longer until it is of exactly the right consistency. Coloring matter may or may not be added, depending on the ideas of the manufacturer. Whipped butter is made by whipping air into the butter, which lightens its consistency and renders it "spreadable" at cold temperatures.

In 1946 Americans were eating only 10.2 pounds of butter per person per year. Undoubtedly the reason for this was the high price of butter and the low price of butter substitutes. Why do we recommend butter rather than margarine? First of all because we need the animal fat and secondly because there are factors in butter that margarine simply does not possess.

Butter is extremely rich in vitamin A and also carotene which can be changed into vitamin A by the body. Winter butter contains about 2,000 International Units per pound. But summer butter from cows that have been fed on fish liver oil may contain as much as 40,000 units per pound. Since the minimum daily requirement for vitamin A has been set at 5,000 units per day, it is easy to see that summer butter would contribute a considerable part of this quota for the average family. In margarine, synthetic vitamin A has been added, for the vegetable oils from which it is made do not contain the vitamin. It is our belief that synthetic vitamins added to a substance are not at all the same thing as the natural vitamins. Undoubtedly there are substances that go along with the vitamin A in butter that we have not as yet discovered. For instance, it is known that summer butter (that is, made from cream given while the cows are on summer pasture) contains something called the "Wulzenfactor" which prevents an arthritis-like disease in animals. Is this perhaps a new undiscovered vitamin? We do not know, nor do we have any proof that eating summer butter will prevent arthritis in human beings, but it illustrates well our point that natural substances are superior to synthetic.

Butter does not contain much vitamin F (unsaturated fatty acids) but margarine has been carefully hydrogenized to destroy *all* these fatty acids. In addition, margarine generally contains many different synthetic substances, including benzoate of soda, a preservative that is anything but healthful. Now, as you saw above, butter, too, goes through considerable processing at the creamery, but it is not "hopped up" with preservatives and it is, in general, a completely natural food, quite apart from its fine vitamin content. Some nutritionists suggest eating storage butter during the winter, if you can be certain you are getting "summer butter" from the storage plant, for this will contain far more vitamin A and other valuable food factors than the fresh winter butter. Be sure to include the salt content of your butter when you are figuring your salt intake for the day, or better still, eat unsalted butter.

The vitamin and mineral content of 100 grams or about 6 tablespoons of butter is listed as follows:

Vitamin A	up to 8,000 International Units
Vitamin B	
Thiamin	up to 120 micrograms
Riboflavin	up to 37 micrograms
Niacin	.1 milligram
Vitamin D	up to 150 units
	(in summer butter)
Vitamin E	2.1 to 3.3 milligrams
Calcium	15 milligrams
Phosphorus	17 milligrams
Iron	.20 milligrams

CHAPTER 24

Cheese

Cheese is one of the most popular dairy products in this country as well as abroad. How are cheeses made and what chemicals go into their manufacture?

In general, cheese is made by coagulating the casein, or protein, of milk, skimmed milk or milk enriched with cream. The coagulation is accomplished by means of rennet or some other suitable enzyme, souring or a combination of the two. Rennet is a digestive fluid from the stomach of a calf. It breaks up the milk protein and reconstitutes it into a different form. Sometimes sour milk is used for cheese.

The curd, or solid, coagulated mass that results is then processed by heat, pressure, molds or other special treatment, depending on what kind and flavor of cheese is wanted.

Hard cheese is made by souring milk and adding rennet. This is then heated, stirred, the solid part (curd) separated from the liquid part (whey). During the process, calcium chloride may be added, salt is added and the rind of the cheese may be coated with paraffin or vegetable oil.

Processed Cheese Is the Most Objectionable

Processed cheese is, as its name implies, a product that has gone through several more processing steps. It involves mixing several kinds of cheese with an emulsifying agent to produce the consistency so much admired for the topping of casseroles or grilled cheese sandwiches. The emulsifying agent is, we are told, any of the following: monosodium phosphate, disodium phosphate, dispotassium phosphate, trisodium phosphate, sodium metaphosphate, sodium acid pyrophosphate, tetrasodium pyrophosphate, sodium citrate, potassium citrate, calcium citrate, sodium tartrate or sodium potassium tartrate. Are these chemicals added in minute quantity so that there is only a remote possibility of their doing you any harm? Quite the contrary. Regulations state that they may be added to make up 3 per cent of the final product. Artificial coloring is added, and an acidifying agent may be added, such as citric acid, acetic acid, phosphoric acid, etc.

The two dyes that are used to color cheese, margarine and other dairy products are two of those suspected by scientists of being cancer-causing. Alginic acid is also used in processed cheese as a stabilizer to give uniformity of color and flavor. Methyl cellulose is used as a thickening agent in processed cheeses. Sugar may be added if the flavor demands it. The smoked flavor some cheeses boast of is prepared by precipitating wood smoke. The hydrocarbons produced by this burning process have also been incriminated as possible cancer-causers.

The wrappers of processed cheese have long been the source of trouble. These wrappers may be coated with preservatives—mold inhibitors and like chemicals. Of course, no company making dairy products wants to lose profits through spoilage. So the processed cheeses, especially, are treated to thorough dosages of preservatives before they reach grocery shelves.

In 1956 the cheese industry decided to use a chemical insecticide on the cheese itself to prevent attacks from the cheese mite. The insecticide is made of pyrethrins and piperonyl butoxide. It is applied to the rind cheeses like cheddar after it has been made into blocks. It is coated with paraffin, then the insecticide is applied. This insecticide is so strong that it guarantees that the cheese will not be attacked by insects during the entire time that it is aging or "ripening," which may be many months. How much of it seeps through the paraffin covering into the cheese? Is it harmful? We do not know. This is probably one of the chemicals which the FDA must decide on shortly, after it has studied tests presented by the manufacturers of the product.

Just as yellow dye is added to many cheeses because the milk from which they are made does not contain enough vitamin A to color the cheese, so other milk must be bleached in order to make swiss cheese, which, the cheese institute says, must be pale-colored, or consumers will not buy it.

Cottage cheese is made from sweet skim milk, making it low in fat. Calcium chloride and salt may be added.

Cream cheese is made from cream or a mixture of cream and milk, skim milk or powdered milk. In preparing cream cheese, various gum products may be used to produce the right texture and body. These are natural products in that they have a vegetable source, but they are surely not "natural" to dairy products.

Other Dairy Products

Buttermilk is made from pasteurized, skimmed or partly skimmed milk to which a bacterial culture is added to sour the milk. Although buttermilk looks as if it contains lots of fat, because of the small specks of fat in it, in reality it is very low in fat.

Whey is the liquid left after the milk curds have been used to make cheese. It consists of water, lactose (milk sugar), milk protein and most of the minerals of the original milk. Whey has been used by doctors as a food for normalizing the intestinal tract in cases of constipation, dysentery and so forth. Apparently it is effective in changing the intestinal flora, so that harmful bacteria are discouraged and helpful ones are encouraged.

Yogurt and acidophilus milk are two fermented milk products which also achieve this purpose.

Dried or powdered milk products are recommended by many nutritionists because they provide in highly concentrated form all the protein, vitamins and minerals found in liquid milk. However, this product is even more highly processed than other dairy products, so, of course, we do not recommend it.

[100]

Our Recommendations on Dairy Products

We do not recommend milk as a food for adults. We believe it has been greatly overrated as food and that the agricultural practices on dairy farms have made the modern cow a milk machine and nothing more. Then, too, milk these days is contaminated with antibotics and other drugs used on sick cows. The antibiotics have been so plentiful in milk at various times and places that cheese could not be made from it, for the antibiotic killed the bacteria necessary for making the cheese. Someone trying to avoid antibiotics because of a sensitivity to them may find that he is getting considerable quantities of them in milk.

The processing through which modern dairy products go is another basis for our complaints against them. Pasteurization, homogenization, emulsifiers, stabilizers, preservatives, dyes, possibly toxic wrapping materials, insecticides—all these must be taken into account these days when the health-seeker considers milk as a food. From the evidence we have produced above, it seems that cheese is an even worse bet than plain milk, since it may contain so many objectionable things.

We recommend deleting milk and dairy products from your grocery list or taking them in extremely small quantities. You can make up the minerals by taking bone meal and the B vitamins with brewer's yeast.

CHAPTER 25

Eggs

Eggs are in truth one of our best foods, especially to satisfy individual needs for protein which are heightened under certain circumstances. Children and infants, for instance, need protein for building new cells during growth. Prospective mothers need protein. Invalids recovering from sickness need protein for rebuilding broken-down tissues. And for those of us who are healthy, the need for protein is also great, since body cells and tissues are constantly breaking down and wearing out and must be replaced.

Eggs are high quality protein—that is, they contain the essential amino acids, or building blocks of protein, in the correct quantity and proportion. This is not surprising when you stop to think that the actual substance of eggs, which we eat, has been carefully supplied by nature to nourish the unborn chick. So naturally just the proper food elements are there in just the right proportion. One egg contains about 6 grams of protein. The white of an egg is almost pure protein even to its jelly-like consistency. Aside from protein, eggs are rich in all the protective and essential vitamins and minerals, with the exception of vitamin C.

Parts of the Egg and Their Nutritive Value

The shell makes up about 10 per cent of the weight of an egg, the white about 60 per cent and the yolk 30 per cent. The shell consists mostly of minerals—calcium, magnesium and phosphorus. The old practice of eating ground egg shells is a sensible one, as we now know, for it is one of the easiest and cheapest ways of securing minerals. If the shells can be ground finely enough, the resulting powder will not be gritty. The egg white of a fresh egg should be a thick opalescent jelly. We sometimes try to judge the freshness of an egg by observing whether the white keeps its shape after the egg is broken rather than "running." But it has been discovered that some hens lay eggs whose whites are naturally "runny" even when they are fresh. The yolk of the egg is inside a protective membrane and we have not as yet discovered all the substances contained in egg yolk—they are many. And all of them apparently are important for human nutrition, as well as chick nutrition.

From the point of view of nutritive value, the fresher the egg, the better it is for you, quite apart from the fact that its taste is better. Some slight amount of value is lost with every day the egg is in storage. Aside from fresh eggs, we can buy frozen or dried eggs. The whole egg does not freeze well, for the yolk becomes leathery, due to the content of the membranes in which it is enclosed. But eggs which have been separated and beaten may be frozen, either as whites, yolks or whole eggs. The resulting product will keep almost indefinitely in a deep freeze and, after thawing, can be used for cooking just as a fresh egg is. Since about half the "lay" for the entire year takes place on poultry farms between March and June, these good quality eggs may be frozen for use during the rest of the year when eggs are scarce and expensive.

Eggs are dried commercially by spraying them into heated air. During World War II the dried egg business grew into a major industry in this country. In the year 1941 alone 42 million pounds of dried eggs were processed. Dried eggs do not keep very well when stored at room temperature, for they have a tendency to develop "off flavors" and to absorb odors from other foods stored about them.

Handling and Storing Eggs

Candling is the process whereby eggs are inspected so that they may be graded as AA, A, B or C quality eggs. The egg is held against a strong light in a darkened room and the experienced egg-candler can thus determine from a glance at the egg what it will look like after it is broken. If the embryo chick has already started to develop blood vessels, the egg is discarded. If the white of the egg is bloody, indicating a possible hemorrhage in the egg-duct of the hen, the egg is discarded. Small flecks of blood in the egg yolk are not considered to be defects important enough for condemning the egg for human food. The government sets specifications for eggs which must be strictly followed by egg dealers. Incidentally, so far as we have been able to determine, there is no difference nutritionally between white and brown eggs. In some localities white eggs are preferred and hence are

[102]

more expensive. But there is no reason for this aside from customer preference.

You might think, looking at eggs, that the shell forms an impermeable coating capable of keeping out all bacteria. But egg shell is covered with microscopic air holes, making the egg liable to infection from germs unless it is handled correctly. Using water to wash eggs makes it even more likely that germs will pass through the air holes into the eggs. And, of course, by washing dirty eggs you will be certain to wash some of the dirt into the inside of the egg. So experts tell us that eggs should not be washed until they are ready for use. If they are to be stored, they should be stored dry. They should always be kept at a cool temperature. Even a few hours at room temperature in the summer may render an egg useless for marketing, for, of course, heat encourages the growth of bacteria which cause spoiled or rotten eggs. So put your eggs into the refrigerator as soon as you bring them into the house—just as you do milk or butter.

Two Cautions About Eggs

In scientific literature we find only two cautions about eggs in human dietaries. It has been discovered that large amounts of raw egg white given every day produce illness. A substance in the raw egg white (called avidin) destroys the B vitamin biotin in the intestinal tract. So if you like raw eggs, in milk or fruit juice, we suggest having them that way not oftener than once or twice a week. Cooking destroys the avidin, so cook your eggs on the other days. Egg yolk contains cholesterol, the substance that has recently come into the limelight as a factor in hardening of the arteries. Some physicians forbid eggs to their high blood pressure patients. It is our belief that the formation of cholesterol on blood vessel walls indicates a disorder of body functioning and does not mean that too much cholesterol is being eaten. In natural foods, such as eggs, we believe that the substances (B vitamins) protect against hardening of the arteries and are present in ample quantity to safeguard health.

Down through the ages eggs have been the symbol of happiness, fertility and rebirth. In almost every culture, eggs are used ceremonially at holiday time, as we use them at Easter. The roundness of the egg indicates wholeness; the fact that it is the forerunner of the chick signifies rebirth, including all the hope and gladness of spring when the earth is renewed and reborn.

Their Vitamin and Mineral Content

Eggs are rich in vitamins and minerals. They assume great importance as infant food because the human baby is naturally very short on iron. Eggs contain lots of iron and, in addition, copper which is necessary for the body to use iron properly. Eggs are one of the very few foods that contain vitamin D. They are rich in vitamin A and all the B vitamins. Here is the vitamin and mineral content of 100 grams of eggs—which is about two medium sized ones:

Vitamin A .... 1140 International Units
Vitamin D .... 50 units

Vitamin E	....	3 milligrams
Vitamin B		
Thiamin	....	120-150 micrograms
Riboflavin	....	340 micrograms
Niacin	....	.1 milligram
Pyridoxine	....	22 micrograms
Pantothenic acid	....	800-4800 micrograms
Biotin	....	9 micrograms
Calcium	....	68 milligrams
Phosphorus	....	224 milligrams
Iron	....	2.52 milligrams
Copper	....	.23 milligrams
Magnesium	....	.03 milligrams
Chlorine	....	106 milligrams

CHAPTER 26

One Good Reason for
Eating Eggs

Is it possible that eating or not eating eggs may have something to do with the occurrence of rheumatic fever? An editorial in the April 17, 1954, issue of the *British Medical Journal* discusses this theory at some length. It seems that one researcher, Wallis, first began to study the question of eggs in the diet of rheumatic fever patients. May G. Wilson, in her book, *Rheumatic Fever* (published by Oxford University Press, 1940), theorizes on the fact that cases of rheumatic fever reach their height in April and then decline during the summer months. Could this be because of the fact that eggs are plentiful during the spring and summer and not so plentiful (hence more expensive) during fall and winter months?

The scientific argument goes like this: Eggs contain choline, a B vitamin, which is essential for the health of the liver. Further facts about choline—it is necessary for all animals, especially the young. It must be present in the diet for the normal nutrition of baby chicks and for egg production in the hen. Choline is necessary for the manufacture of a certain substance in the blood—phospholipid. This substance, phospholipid, is one of the elements in normal blood that fights against streptococcus infection. Rheumatic fever is associated with streptococcal infection. Therefore, the reasoning goes, rheumatic fever might be conditioned partly by egg intake.

The editor of the *Journal* states that this is a long and tenuous chain of reasoning, but it can be tested to a certain extent. Wallis, writing in the *American Journal of Medical Science,* Vol. 227, p. 167, 1954, relates how he did a survey among 184 adult and adolescent patients with rheumatic heart disease and a group of normal subjects. Forty-one per cent of the rheumatic heart patients said they thought they ate few eggs in childhood. Only 16 per cent of the normal people claimed they did not eat eggs. Ten per cent of the rheumatic heart patients declared they did not like eggs, as compared to 5 per cent of the other group.

How dependable can such figures be, since they are based on the patients' memories of their childhoods? Perhaps we cannot call them infallible, but all precautions were taken during the survey to eliminate bias from the answers. Two other researchers, Coburn and Moore, reporting in the *American Journal of the Diseases of Children,* Vol. 65, p. 744, 1943, state that the former diet of rheumatic heart children appeared to be lacking in eggs as well as other valuable nutritional elements. So they supplemented the diet of 30 convalescent children with the equivalent of 4 egg yolks a day. (The yolk of the egg is the part highest in choline.) The rheumatic fever recurred in only 7 per cent of these children compared with a recurrence of 38 per cent in children whose diets were not so supplemented. Later in 1950 Coburn reported in the *Journal of the American Dietetic Association,* Vol. 26, p. 345, that 8 to 10 egg yolks daily given to children who had previously had rheumatic fever prevented relapses when the children were later subjected to streptococcal infection.

What Does This Theory Mean To Us?

The editor of the *British Medical Journal* frankly admits that this whole theory about egg yolks is only a theory, but, says he, "we should welcome theories if they are founded on fact and lead to the discovery of more facts. The egg theory might be described as 'good in parts'."

By telling this story from one of the leading medical journals of our day, we do not mean to imply that stuffing children with egg yolks to the exclusion of other foods will positively prevent or cure rheumatic fever. We think the theory is interesting from an entirely different point of view. What if a close examination of the diet of children who contract rheumatic fever should indicate that, through some quirk of circumstance or appetite, their diets were completely lacking in choline—the B vitamin that is apparently so important for preventing the disease? This would certainly mean that other B vitamins were lacking as well, for they appear in most of the same foods as choline. The lesson to be learned, we believe, is simply that the rules of good diet cannot be disregarded by any conscientious mother. And how and where are mothers expected to learn these vitally important facts about the proper foods for their children?

Every mouthful of candy, soda pop, white bread, cake or dessert robs a child of a mouthful of good wholesome nutritious food which will protect him from many diseases, not just rheumatic fever. Every egg, piece of fruit or meat, every vegetable, every salad, every serving of real honest-to-goodness whole grain cereal means just so much more protection from the menace of poor health. And for the mother whose child refuses to eat foods that contain choline and the other B vitamins, the answer is just as simple as buying a package of powdered brewer's yeast (higher than any other food in most of the B vitamins) and using it liberally in preparing food in the kitchen. For suggestions on using brewer's yeast every day in your kitchen, we recommend our favorite general cook book, *Let's Cook it Right,* by Adelle Davis, published by Harcourt, Brace and Company, New York, New York.

CHAPTER 27

Raw Eggs and
The Hungry Protein

It seems that during the research that went on around the discovery of the vitamin biotin there was renewed interest in the fact that laboratory animals do not do well on diets that include a lot of raw egg white. Now egg white is a protein and proteins are essential for life and health. Other proteins seem to be far more valuable as food when they are eaten raw. So what could be the cause of this peculiar reaction to egg white? Was it some poison in the egg white that disappeared when it was cooked? Or was it something else in the diet that did not get along with the egg white?

Actually in the laboratory experiments, animals on very good, nutritious diets invariably showed symptoms of great distress if the diet contained a high amount of raw egg white. The animals lost their hair, became sluggish and nervous and contracted a dermatitis chiefly around their eyes, noses and paws.

Foods rich in the B vitamins prevented these symptoms. But which of the B vitamins was involved? By feeding carefully controlled diets in which trials were made with each of the known B vitamins, it was finally revealed that the newly discovered vitamin biotin was the victim. Further research showed that there is a substance in egg white, called avidin (the hungry protein) which binds the biotin in our digestive tract so that it cannot be utilized by our bodies. The laboratory animals were consuming an amount of egg white which used up every vestige of biotin, so that they suffered from a severe biotin deficiency.

Experiments Show Harm Done By Raw Egg White

As word got around in the scientific journals, researchers looked further into this strange phenomenon. A group of workers at the University of Wisconsin tried nutritious diets plus egg white on 5 different kinds of animals—chicks, rats, rabbits, monkeys and guinea pigs. Their results are reported by J. G. Lease, H. T. Parsons and E. Kelly in the *Journal of Biochemistry* for March, 1937. They found that the first 4 animals showed similar symptoms of baldness, skin eruptions, swelling, scaliness and redness about the eyes, ears, paws and mouth. In the rat only, there were nervous symptoms as well. The guinea pig showed the least reaction to the egg white. The diets fed were healthful, nutritious diets, containing plenty of all the necessary vitamins. However, about 40 to 50 per cent of the daily ration was dried, uncooked egg white.

In 1939 E. Uroma published an account of the reaction of children to raw egg white. In *Acta Societatis Medicorum Fennicae Duodecim,* Vol. 21, 1939, he described feeding one raw egg daily for from one to 3 weeks to 48 children between the ages of one week and 7 months. It was found that the blood of the children developed antibodies against the egg white—seeming to indicate that some poisonous substance was present and the antibodies were mobilized to fight it. Two of these children also developed a slight eczema on the face and neck. This breaking out disappeared when the eggs were omitted from the diet. It began to appear that raw egg white had indeed a very serious effect on the health of human beings.

Then came the famous experiment that provided final proof of the harmfulness of raw egg white. V. P. Sydenstricker, S. A. Singal, A. P. Briggs and N. M. DeVaughn of the University of Georgia School of Medicine set out to produce the so-called "egg-white injury" in human beings and, if possible, cure it by administering biotin. Their experiment is reported in *Science* for February 13, 1942. Seven human volunteers agreed to the test. This is the diet they were placed on: polished rice, white flour, farina, cane sugar, lard, butter and lean beef. This diet contains practically no biotin. Then the volunteers were given vitamin and mineral supplements to make up for the vitamins and minerals that were missing from their food, so that whatever symptoms they showed could not possibly be the result of some other vitamin deficiency. Then they were given each day enough raw egg white to make up 30 per cent of the total caloric intake.

Only 4 of the volunteers followed through to a satisfactory termination of the experiment. This is what happened: during the third and fourth week all 4 developed scaliness of the skin, without any accompanying itching. In the seventh week one man developed a dermatitis over his neck, hands, arms and legs. During the seventh and eighth week all of the volunteers developed a gray pallor of their skin and mucous membrane and later extreme dryness of the skin, with additional scaliness.

After the fifth week they all developed other kinds of symptoms as well—depression which progressed to extreme lassitude, sleepiness and, in one instance, a mild case of panic. All experienced muscle pains, excessive sensitivity to touch and localized sensations such as numbness, tingling, "pins-and-needles" and so forth. After the tenth week they began to lose their appetites and feel nauseated. Two of the volunteers complained of distress around their hearts and an electrocardiogram revealed that their hearts were not normal. The blood of all showed a decrease in hemoglobin (the red pigment that carries oxygen to the cells) and in red blood corpuscles, even though their diet was planned to prevent anemia. The cholesterol content of their blood was also very high. When biotin was given to them, the symptoms disappeared within several days.

Now the conditions of this experiment are exaggerated, of course, as this kind of test necessitates. In real life, it is hardly possible that anyone eating such a diet as these volunteers were eating would at the same time be taking raw eggs and vitamin supplements. Since the symptoms of the human subjects were so similar to those of animals deprived of biotin, it seems we are safe in assuming that a biotin deficiency can indeed be induced in human beings who eat a great deal of raw egg white.

Possible Relationship Between Biotin and Cancer

Somewhat later, interest was aroused in the possibility of biotin having something to do with cancer formation. It was found that certain kinds of cancer contained more biotin than normal tissue. Biologists reasoned that if an excess of biotin caused the cancer, they might prevent it by feeding raw egg white whose avidin content would neutralize the biotin. Three researchers at the University of Wisconsin experimented with rats, feeding them a diet that included butter-yellow, a cancer-causing substance. Then they fed one group of the rats raw egg white, another group raw egg white plus biotin and a third group cooked egg white, in which the avidin had been destroyed by the heat. Of the rats which ate the cancer-producing diet to which nothing had been added, 77 per cent developed liver tumors. The rats on any or all of the other diets developed from 10 to 18 per cent of liver tumors, which indicated that something in the white of egg protected them against tumor growth. The authors comment on the fact that the egg white exerted this protective effect equally well whether it was fed raw, or with biotin, or cooked to overcome the effect of the avidin. It would seem from this experiment that the peculiar relationship of biotin and avidin has nothing to do with cancer formation, even though signs of severe biotin deficiency appeared in those rats who received raw egg white in their diets, without any extra biotin.

Our study turned up numerous other experiments on biotin-avidin, but nothing that gave us any more of a clue as to just where we should stand on the raw egg white controversy. Our favorite book on animal nutrition, *Nutrition of the Dog,* by C. M. McCay of Cornell University (published by Comstock) tells us that as early as 1898 it was discovered that the feeding of raw eggs was often followed by vomiting and diarrhea in dogs. It was also found that from 30 to 50 per cent of the raw egg white could be recovered from the dog's feces, indicating that he had digested only 50 to 70 per cent of it. On the other hand, tests showed that the same dog digested 90 per cent of cooked egg white. One researcher thought that this might be due to the rapid rate at which raw egg white leaves the stomach —the digestive juices simply do not have time to digest it. Raw egg starts to leave the stomach almost as soon as it reaches it. An hour and a half after it is eaten the egg white is well on its way through the small intestine. Boiled egg white, on the other hand, remains in the stomach two or 3 hours, until well digested. Knowledge of this fact about boiled egg white is·valuable for someone on a reducing diet. If you eat your eggs hard-boiled, they will stay in your stomach longer and ward off those uncomfortable hunger pangs.

Helen T. Parsons and a group of fellow workers showed in an article in *Proceedings of the Society of Biological Chemistry*, Vol. 31, p. 77, that in rats the effects of raw egg white could be prevented by including certain amounts of brewer's yeast or dried liver in the diet.

Dr. McCay is one of the country's outstanding animal nutritionists. In his recommendations for feeding dogs, he advises *that you should not feed raw eggs,* but feed whole, hard-boiled eggs, shell and all. He admits that no one knows why the raw egg white is not digested properly by dogs. He also mentions that it is better digested if it is thoroughly beaten or thoroughly mixed with milk before it is eaten.

Why Should Raw Egg White Be Harmful?

We have only one possible solution for the egg white question. Wild animals do not, of course, cook their food. Many wild animals eat bird's eggs. Nature provides ingenious and extremely successful ways of protecting new young life in various species. Could it be that avidin has been placed in egg white so that animals which prey on eggs will discover that the egg white eventually makes them ill and will be forced to find other kinds of food? Can avidin in egg white be just one of mother nature's ways of maintaining the proper balance among all the different kinds of life? Perhaps, who knows, if there were no such substance as avidin, birds would long ago have become extinct and the valuable functions they perform—scattering seed, pollinating flowers and destroying insects—would have suffered.

However, if it is possible for any animal to perceive the potential harm in raw egg white, you would think that dogs would refuse to eat it; whereas there is nothing they enjoy more than a fresh raw egg, even if they must steal it from the chicken house and break the shell themselves. So far as we know, however, no one has ever done any research on how many whole raw eggs any one dog will eat during a given time, if he is left to his own devices. Maybe he is able to sense just when to stop in order not to do himself harm. But, if this is so, why did the laboratory animals in the experiments above not refuse to eat the raw egg white after it had begun to produce unpleasant symptoms in them?

There is one other possible explanation, too. You will notice that in all of the experiments in which raw egg white produced unhealthy symptoms, *only the egg white was fed.* No one tried to induce "egg-white injury" by feeding whole eggs. So perhaps we were intended to eat raw eggs, and "egg-white injury" is another example of what happens when we eat part of a food and throw away or change another part. We were meant to eat foods whole, undivided, unrefined and untampered with—of this we are certain. We know that egg yolk contains large amounts of biotin. Perhaps egg yolk contains other substances, too, aside from biotin which protect against the hungry protein, avidin.

What do we advise, then, to people who, for instance, eat two raw eggs for breakfast every day? We would not advise them to stop it entirely at once. We would be inclined, however, to advise changing the menu frequently—eating raw eggs perhaps once or twice a week and boiling or poaching them on other days. We do not like to give way an inch on our recommendation of eating as much food raw as possible, for we know that this is sound and sensible from every health point of view. We know that it takes a lot of raw food, every day, every meal, to make up to our bodies for the roasting, frying, boiling, toasting and broiling procedure we put most of our food through before our digestive juices get a chance to work on it. But perhaps we have not as yet developed such a state of nutrition that we can withstand the possible injurious effect of raw egg white.

But maybe those of us who are in excellent health and those of us who are getting ample supplies of B vitamins in our food supplements might be able to eat quantities of raw eggs without any ill effects whatsoever. But, if you have a suspicion that your supply of B vitamins may be deficient, better poach or boil those eggs, and take only an occasional eggnog.

CHAPTER 28

Some Facts on Ice Cream

Ice cream is something like the weather—everybody eats it but nobody does anything about it! In view of the fact that the per capita consumption of ice cream is almost 18 pounds per year in the United States, it is surprising that the federal government has not yet gotten around to insisting on a statement of ingredients on the containers in which ice cream is packed. When you buy ice cream, if you do, you have no legal right to expect that the label tell you what you're letting yourself in for when you eat it. If it has harmful dyes for artificial colorings, if objectionable chemicals are used to harden or hold it together, the manufacturer doesn't have to say so. What he prints in the way of ingredients, on the label, is entirely up to him barring outright technical fraud, of course.

Today's Ice Cream

Regardless of the vitamins and minerals which are present in the milk or cream which is used, the other ingredients found in commercial ice creams make it undesirable from a health standpoint. When the soda fountain clerk dips into a gallon container of ice cream, he is dipping into a stiffened bucket of emulsifiers, artificial sweeteners, artificial flavorings, artificial colorings and dozens of other chemicals which make ice cream (as we know it today) taste and behave as it does. The ice cream that many of our readers remember helping to crank into solidity in a home freezer some years ago was an easy combination of milk, eggs, sugar and perhaps one fresh fruit or another. Now that the machine age has taken over the cranking and icing, the age of chemistry has dug its hand deep into the process, too. There are substitutes for the milk, substitutes for the fruit, substitutes for the eggs and substitutes for the sugar. The ice cream we buy is more often than not, just a substitute for ice cream! And what these substitutes will do to the human body is not yet known.

Not a Treat, But a Dietary Staple

Ice cream, like soda, was not the menace when it was first introduced that it is today. The reason is simple: it was a rarely eaten treat. A small portion of ice cream eaten perhaps once a week, or even less often, and made of fresh and unchemicalized ingredients, was not the source of health problems that we see in it now. Our ice cream eating habits have changed. As Jacobs, in his monumental work, *Food and Food Products* says, "Ice cream was formerly considered more nearly a confection than a staple article of our diet, but for many people, especially children, it is a regular item of their daily fare. Consequently its manufacture and sale should be as rigidly controlled as that of milk." We know that such control is nowhere to be seen.

Who Decides What's in Ice Cream?

The fact is that pronouncements on what is and what is not to be included in ice cream and other so-called frozen desserts, are left entirely to state legislatures and dairy organizations. If the state legislature is not prodded by alert personnel, and the dairy associations are less than enthusiastic for the health and welfare of the citizens they serve, what kind of security have the people who buy ice cream products in the state? Even attributing the best of motives to most of the people involved, is the chance of undue influence not more likely when laws are formulated on such a local level?

For example, an emulsifier is an ingredient used for holding other ingredients together. Eggs are excellent for this purpose—but expensive. The simple solution is a cheap chemical designed to do the same job. One such chemical sometimes used in ice cream is diethyl glucol. And when it isn't used to hold the ice cream you eat together, it's being used as an antifreeze in radiators, and it also removes paint. Sound appetizing? All chemical emulsifiers, including those containing glucols, have been outlawed for use in salad dressings, mayonnaise and bread, but in ice cream, anything goes.

Aside from emulsifiers, your ice cream can be filled with dozens of other chemicals that make it commercially marketable. Among these are: thickeners and stabilizers (agar-agar, carboxymethyl and so forth) which help to maintain the desired smoothness of ice cream; antioxidants (dihydroguaiaretic acid) to prevent spoilage.

Ice Cream Substitutes

An idea of the confusion which reigns over this situation is evident in the manufacture of ice cream substitutes. Two of the best known are ice milk and a product trade-named Mellorine.

Ice milk is sold in 41 states and the District of Columbia and has come to account for more than 8 per cent of the sales of frozen desserts. While it is true that ice milk sells for a few cents less per pint than ice cream, the main selling point has been the fact that it has fewer calories than ice cream, due to a lower fat content. The Connecticut Agricultural Experimental Station of New Haven, Connecticut, in its annual report, analyzed two brands of ice milk advertised as "Low in Calories—High in Proteins." In comparison with two commercial ice creams, the ice milks showed an average of 4.33 per cent fat content as opposed to ice cream's 10.75 per cent. The protein count was, however, lower in ice milk than in ice cream, although the advertising would lead one to expect the opposite. And though the calorie count was lower in ice milk than ice cream the difference per pint (608 to 515) was hardly enough to qualify the ice milk as a "low calorie" food. The buying public needs better protection against this sort of misleading advertising. How many people will there be who will take the time, even if they can, to discover the facts we've presented above before they buy a pint of ice milk. And remember, the label on the package is not required to say anything in many cases.

Mellorine is a step farther in taking ice cream manufacture out of the dairy and putting it into the laboratory. *Science News Letter* (September 18, 1954) characterizes this product as "difficult to distinguish from ice cream, even in a laboratory." Butterfat is replaced here by vegetable oils and other animal fats in this mixture. Only 9 states permit the sale of this product, but even with such limited distribution its sales account for 1.5 per cent of the sales of frozen dessert products in the United States. Again, what other substitutes have been made besides the vegetable and animal oils, we don't know. And again, there is no federal law to make the manufacturer divulge the information.

Because so much of what goes into ice cream is sugar, it's a food that has been forbidden to diabetics. However, the attraction for this sweet is so great that there is an eternal struggle to make eating it possible for diabetics, too. Sugarless ice cream is the result. Sorbitol, a sugar substitute, is used instead. We are still of the opinion that a chemical substitute for sugar is just as harmful as sugar itself. The only way for a diabetic to deal with ice cream is to let it alone.

Of course, this is our suggestion to anyone where ice cream is concerned. The sugar it contains is a killer, and our views on milk as a food that adults and children past weaning can do without, apply with equal or more force to the cream used here. Cream is that part of milk which contains cholesterol. Tie this to the appalling number of chemicals in ice cream and our point is obvious. It is strange though that ice cream is always the first thing a patient will be given to eat in his convalescence. "It slides right down," they say; or "It'll help bring the fever down." But it will shoot the blood sugar down, too. It will eat up some important B vitamins! The milk and eggs it contains might rekindle some long-dormant allergy!

The dangers hidden in ice cream are apparent to all who are willing to look at them realistically. Even with strong federal regulations it is a food that is better left untouched; without such regulations eating it is unthinkable. If the children are persistent about frozen desserts, give them crushed ice in sherbet dishes saturated with fresh fruit juice. Or for more uniform distribution of the flavor, freeze fresh fruit juices in your ice cube tray, then serve them crushed in sherbet glasses. And if you're wondering why we don't have food laws to govern ice cream, write and ask your congressman. It's his job to know the answer or find one.

CHAPTER 29

Lactose, Whey and Your Digestive Tract

Some interesting facts about the friendly intestinal bacteria come to light in a far-from-recent book by a researcher for whom we have the greatest respect, Dr. Boris Sokoloff.

Dr. Sokoloff tells us, in *The Civilized Diseases* (published by Thorsons Publishers, London, no date) that Thomas Parr, who lived to be 152, many years ago in England had a very healthy digestive tract, due mostly to his diet which consisted practically entirely of goat cheese, whey and raw vegetables. Why should whey have played such an important part in the health of this now-famous man and why is his eating of whey important to his longevity?

"Digestion is a delicate biochemical process," says Dr. Sokoloff, "requiring about 30 hours to reach completion. After being evacuated from the stomach, the food enters that part of the intestinal tract called the duodenum, then moving slowly up and down the large intestinal tract until it reaches the colon 24 hours after entering the mouth. It is hard to visualize fully the colossal task that falls to the share of the tiny 'chemical entities,' the millions of microscopic kitchens that line the digestive tract. They transform the wide variety of foods consumed into simple, elementary substances that may be utilized by the organism. . . . The colon, more than any other organ, seems poorly adjusted to civilized life. It is easily affected by anything associated with our modern way of living; improper food, nervous strain, fatigue affect the colon immediately."

In the colon are the intestinal bacteria. Since the days of the famous scientist, Metchnikoff, we have known that the colon houses a particular kind of friendly bacteria, to which he gave the name of *Lactobacillus acidophilus.*

Intestinal Bacteria and Constipation

"Without reservation," says Dr. Sokoloff, "we may call this microbe our friend, since it protects the colon from hostile microbes. It fights them, it destroys them by means of lactic acid which it produces in abundance. A normal, healthy colon houses a number of these benignant (friendly) microbes, which do not allow any hostile or dangerous germ to gain the upper hand. But if for any reason or other, our friend disappears from the colon or is decreased in numbers, the hostile germs immediately infiltrate into the colon and constipation appears."

Then he gives us some examples. Someone who becomes constipated because of the wrong kind of food may take a laxative. A very small number of the friendly bacteria will be left in the colon after the laxative has "cleaned out" the colon. If he continues to take laxatives, the intestinal bacteria will almost disappear and, too, the constipation will become chronic. To increase the number of lactobacillus in the intestine, Dr. Sokoloff advises "drink plenty of acidophilus milk."

The friendly bacteria never disappear completely from the colon. There are always a few still alive ready to come to the aid of the sufferer if he provides the proper environment for them. Dr. Sokoloff tells us that Dr. Torrey, of Duke University, has found that providing lactose will favor the return of the friendly intestinal bacteria. Lactose, which is a milk sugar, is broken down in the intestine into lactic acid, the same substance which acidophilus milk produces which wars on hostile bacteria. So there is no need to drink acidophilus milk as long as somehow we create lactic acid in the colon.

Lactose is completely unique among sugars in several ways. First of all, it is not digested until it reaches the intestines. Absorbtion of lactose takes place in the colon. When the lactose is being absorbed, the presence of certain minerals helps. Whey, which contains the minerals of milk, hastens the absorption of the lactose.

What happens to the intestinal bacteria when lactose reaches the colon? Because lactose is so long in being digested and absorbed, it takes quite a while to pass through the colon. As the partially digested food material moves through the small and large intestines, a carbohydrate is present which enables acid-forming bacteria to thrive and to produce a degree of acidity in the colon in which only they can survive. In other words, the friendly bacteria create from lactose a very acid surrounding. The unfriendly, putrefactive or disease-causing bacteria cannot live in acid. They require alkaline surroundings. So they gradually disappear.

A number of investigators have shown that taking lactose has a laxative effect. It seems that this is largely due to its effect on intestinal bacteria, but, in addition, the fact that the lactose is slowly absorbed may have something to do with it, too.

Lactose Helps in Other Ways

Apart from its value in establishing healthful intestinal bacteria, lactose aids the body indirectly in another way. It helps in the assimilation of several important minerals—chiefly calcium, phosphorus and magnesium. Though they are not sure, researchers believe this is also because of the acid environment that lactose produces. Robinson and his associates, writing in the *Journal of Biological Chemistry*, Vol. 84, p. 257, found that when they gave lactose along with bone meal they doubled the calcium retention from the bone meal. In other words, animals taking lactose along with their bone meal got from the bone meal twice the benefit they would have without the lactose.

Another great advantage of taking lactose is the fact that B vitamins are manufactured in the intestine when lactose is taken; this has been found by several researchers who found that when lactose was being fed, their experimental animals could get along with very little or no vitamin B_6 and vitamin B_2 in their diets, apparently these were being manufactured in the intestines, due to the lactose.

Much of this information on lactose comes from an article in the *Journal of Dairy Science*, September, 1957, pp. 1114-1132: *Lactose in Animal and Human Feeding:* a Review by R. L. Atkinson, F. H. Kratzer and G. F. Stewart.

Lactose appears only in milk. There is no other way to get this natural sugar. Of course, milk contains many other things as well, including a very large amount of water. So we think the best source of lactose is either yogurt or whey. Yogurt is the delicious tart food, of about the consistency of junket, which can be easily made at home using yogurt cultures—that is, small colonies of the bacteria which are necessary to make yogurt out of milk. Yogurt is also available from dairies in many parts of the country.

The second good source of lactose is whey, which is available in powdered form that can be mixed with other foods or taken in tablets. Whey is actually 70 per cent lactose, which proceeds immediately to the colon and is not digested until it has had time to establish an environment friendly to the beneficial intestinal bacteria.

CHAPTER 30

What Have They Done to the Cow?

by J. I. Rodale

The cow that went aboard Noah's Ark was a far different critter from what she is today. Noah's cow did not have heavy milk bags to carry around to plague her. Noah's and Father Abraham's cows had only small teats, like those of a horse. There was no dairy business in those days. Those that wanted milk kept their own sheep, goat or cow. But in the Eastern part of the world, milk even today is generally not drunk.

Now, why does a cow give milk? A cow gives milk for the same reason that a woman does—to provide food with which to nurse a new-born thing. As soon as a woman or a cow becomes pregnant, forces are set in motion in the body to build a milk supply. After a certain period goes by and the calf gets to the age where it can forage for itself, the cow's supply of milk dries up. You can see, therefore, that in order for the cow to give more milk, she must have another calf. Thus, keeping a cow in milk involves maternity.

Most people are of the opinion that the cow has a set of spigots to be turned on and off when one needs milk and that's what most city folks believe. Now, in the old days a family that kept a cow sometimes appropriated some of the milk for their own use, but the wise, all-seeing Creator foresaw this propensity of man's for taking things without asking, and he gave the cow a bountiful extra reserve of milk. But as the centuries rolled on, man saw an opportunity of making money from the cow's milk supply, and with that devilish cunning he shows wherever money is concerned, he found a way to force the cow to give more milk.

He observed that some cows give more milk than others, and by closer study, discovered that such cows had larger teats than others. He found also that this ability to give more milk ran in families. So he mated cows from such families to bulls from similarly endowed families and, that, still further, increased the capacity to give milk.

The Cow Becomes A Machine

The result was that from generation to generation, cows gave more and more milk and their udders thus gradually became larger and larger. Now, by the time of George Washington, the cows' udders were at least 20 times the capacity of a cow in the days of King David. In Revolutionary War times you could already begin to call them milk bags, though they hung down only about 5 inches or so. But today, by further breeding, the cow's milk bags have been enlarged to 10 times the size they were when George Washington was president. Yes, sir! Today the milk bags of some cows are so huge that they pretty near drag the ground, and you will find listed in Sears Roebuck's catalog girdles for cows to hold up their udders so that they won't drag or crack.

Man has made a factory—a milk machine out of the cow. Where, in Noah's time, a cow gave about 200 pounds of milk in a year, today there are cows that give 15,000 pounds or 75 times as much milk. And this overproduction is causing more disease in cows. A lot of cows are getting leukemia today and many other diseases which they never used to get.

Now, getting back to what we moderns call milk—it is very diluted because of the large quantity the cow has to give. Milk is a very delicate thing, interrelated to almost every gland and organ of the cow's body. It is a part of the function of the animal in creating life. All of the best elements in its body must be assembled to make it, so that the calf can have a good start.

Our scientists do not seem to be aware of what they are doing. They are shallow fragmentists. All they are after is to secure increased volume of an opaque white liquid, with a reasonable amount of butter-fat content, but are they worried over the fact that its vitamins and hormones are below a safe level? No! Why, there were more vitamins in a thimbleful of milk at the time of King David than in a whole beer mug of today.

Artificiality

When we force a cow to give 75 times the amount of milk that God intended her to, it must be a kind of milk that is not up to snuff. That is point number one. Now we come to point number two. Artificial Insemination.

The dairymen seem to delight in making the cow a completely artificial animal. Formerly a bull mated with a cow in order to give her a calf, but that is too much trouble for dairymen today, so they have this artificial insemination. The bull is masturbated, and the amount of semen ejaculated is used to inject into 40 or 50 cows or even more. It is nothing but male prostitution. It is an irreligious, impious trick if I ever saw one. First they hang a hundred pound weight under the cow, then they deprive her of her gentleman friend! What next? They are piling artificiality upon artificiality. Poor bossy, with her big sad eyes waiting for the father of her children who never comes. One day she may realize that she has been let down, deceived, tricked, cheated out of the natural biological satisfaction which is her inherent right. Can the milk of such a cow be any good?

And the bull—what of him? There are going to be disasterous effects upon his character. Already bulls are refusing to work and are becoming obstreperous. Recently near Winchester, Indiana, a bull gored the auto of the county's artificial inseminator.

God does everything for a purpose. He makes fruit colorfully attractive and sweet so that the birds will seek it out and scatter the seed. Thus fruit trees spring forth all over creation. He has put glorious colors in the flowers so that the bee will be attracted to pollinate them and that they will grow in profusion on the face of the earth. He has made the cow and the bull for each other but who is man to say, "I will change what God hath intended?"

[117]

When God promised the Land of Canaan to the children of Israel, describing it to Moses as a land flowing with milk and honey, did he mean milk from cows artificially inseminated and with oversized milk bags? According to Leviticus the cow offered up for sacrifice in the temple was supposed to be absolutely pure and without a single blemish anywhere. Would a cow begotten in artificial insemination be an acceptable animal for the temple ritual? Would you consider her bloated milk-bag a blemish? Should a good Christian drink milk produced in such a profane, ungodly way?

Nature's Balance

Now, since the practice of artificial insemination began there is much more disease in cows. They are dropping dead from unknown causes, and there are all kinds of reproductive diseases—mastitis of the udders for one. A cow's life is 20 per cent shorter than it was 30 years ago.

But God has methods of his own. In artificially inseminated births more male calves are being born than ordinarily, and this tendency will keep on increasing even with human artificial insemination births—we call them test-tube babies—60 per cent more boys than girls.

Do you realize what this means? If the percentage of males in birth keeps on increasing, and it will if these dairymen insist on continuing this suicidal insemination practice, God will see to it that eventually no females will be born at all. The species will die out.

Chemicalization

You would think that scientists would be more careful. They should have tested artificial insemination for 50 years before letting it loose on the public. But science is running ahead of human wisdom and the public is not without blame, either. The public is lazy. It shirks its responsibilities. And that's not all about artificial practices and cows. Already there is a new and vicious thing that is being used. Instead of spraying insecticides in the barn and on the outside of the cow's skin, they are now injecting this chemical right into the cow's blood stream, so that if a fly or mosquito bites her anywhere, it will automatically get a dose of the chemical and die.

This chemical that is powerful enough to kill a fly at one bite will be present in every cell of the cow's body, and will get into the milk. How brave these scientists are at the public's expense. Cato the Elder was right when he said, "There is a wide difference between true courage and a mere contempt of life." Nor have I mentioned the formaldehyde preservative that some dairies put into milk. Formaldehyde is a chemical used to embalm people.

There are many other artificial practices that are perpetrated against the cow, but it is all part of the processes of chemicalization and artificialization which have been thrust upon us—people as well as cows. The scientists are in the woods and cannot see the cows. And as far as I am concerned, I am through with milk. I have been through with it for many years now and feel as fit as a fiddle. Of course, I see to it that my diet is well balanced—the bone meal taking care of what was in the milk far more effectively than the milk did.

[118]

CHAPTER 31

Don't Drink Milk

by J. I. Rodale

I don't drink milk, and am not ashamed to admit it. I have been away from milk-drinking now for over 5 years and as yet there have been no signs of any deficiencies or repercussions of any kind. So far my body has taken no reprisals against me. At first there was a feeling of anxious uncertainty. Would lightning and thunder figuratively come and destroy me for such sacrilege? Not only has nothing of the kind happened, but I am going my merry way, thriving healthfully without milk, full of buoyant energy and with the confident feeling that (pardon the grammar) me and the cow, (that is, its liquid white portion) have parted ways forever.

Now, from whence comes my calcium if I do not get it from milk? I have news for you. I now get it from *bone meal!* If there had been no bone meal substitute, there could have been trouble unless in expert fashion the rest of the diet had been tailored to make up for that calcium deficit.

For many years I would come across an item here and another there in health magazines, and in an occasional health book, disputing the value of milk as an item of diet, and I put them down as the unscientific talk of rabid physical-culturists. There were many of them, and I wish I had preserved them all. But one day, about 10 years ago, a man from Boston visited me and related the following story:

He had obtained a position with a mining company in an isolated section of Montana, and in a few months a very bad case of arthritis which had plagued him for over 10 years mysteriously cleared up; but completely! However, when he went back to Boston a few years later, his condition returned in full virulence. At first he put it down as being caused by living again in "civilization," but finally he recalled the fact that in the section of Montana where he had worked there had been no source of milk. For two years he had lived without it.

He decided to eliminate milk again and see what happened. Miracle upon miracles! In a few months his arthritis vanished. Again he began to drink milk and again his malady returned. No wonder he began to shout from the housetops, what he had learned and had to come all the way to Emmaus to tell me, first hand, what he had observed.

This made me think again about all those items I had read in the health literature, attacking milk as an item of our diet. Now arthritis is no mere result of an allergy. It goes deeper than that. I became thoroughly convinced that there were thousands of other persons suffering from this disease merely because they were drinking milk, and I was quite sure that the medics to whom they went were approaching their problem purely through palliation with drugs.

[119]

I found confirmation of this idea in a booklet by C. Ward Crampton, M.D., formerly Associate Professor of Medicine of the New York Post-graduate Medical School and Hospital and Chairman of the Subcommittee on Geriatrics and Gerontology, Public Health Committee, Medical Society of the County of New York. Dr. Crampton says, "The daily need of calcium is about one gram or 15 grains. A quart of milk daily will supply this. It is the natural food of the young. Cream, however, may be bad for the 'gouty and arthritic.' This is not as yet fully established but some arthritics seem to do better without any milk. Calcium is not harmful in arthritis even though there are some calcium deposits in and around the joints."

My Wife's Story

I recalled the case of my own wife who hasn't drunk milk or eaten any cheese since she was weaned from her mother's breast. For some mysterious reason or other she developed a deep-rooted aversion to milk and its whole family of related products. Yet, today, at the age of 50, she is as hard as a rock. Where other women have already had an appendix removed and a hysterectomy performed, friend wife has a perfect record in keeping the surgeon's knife at a respectful distance. And how that woman hates milk and cheese! I have seen her in a restaurant returning a luscious-looking stuffed potato because her sharp nose detected that it had been surfaced with a microscopic amount of cheese. Which reminds me of her keen sense of smell—5 times better developed than my own. Can its sharpness have something to do with her no-milk diet? I would not rule the possibility out, yet I cannot submit this as a scientific affirmation. Oh, I forgot! My wife seems to have gotten along without milk and without having had the benefit of bone meal, until about 5 years ago when we all began to take the latter. During all those former years she must have gotten her calcium somewhere else. But she used to get cavities in her teeth.

It is a strange thing, though, that although she got along so beautifully without milk, yet she tried to stuff it into our 3 children. Somehow or other she felt that it was wrong not to drink milk. She wanted to go along with the herd. On the other hand, for at least 15 years I had heard rumblings against milk and therefore was a considerable force in subduing this over-powering desire of hers to compel the children to drink milk.

Septic Sore Throat

In thinking back about milk I recalled a visit I once made many years ago to a farming school where a herd of cows was kept. This was a school, mind you, not a private farm or dairy. When I went into the place where the cows were being milked, I immediately experienced a suffocating tightness. I will admit that the ventilation in the barn was poor. The next morning I had the most beautiful case of septic sore throat of my entire life.

A few years ago while I was taking a summer course in geology, the students took a field trip to nearby quarries, and we took our lunches along. One of the teachers, after he finished his sandwiches, began a mad search for a grocery store. Soon he returned with a whole quart of milk which he drank down with an avid fervor as if his life depended upon it. I am sure he felt that unless he drank at least two quarts of milk a day he was doomed to get cancer at the earliest possible moment.

I sized him up. I could see that his nose was a little on the stuffed side. When I questioned him, I found that his nose gave him more torment than a human could ever endure—sinus, colds, catarrah and what have you. And when I told him that his overconsumption of milk could be at the bottom of his trouble, he laughed so loud that he must have scared some rabbits a mile away.

Still—Hesitation!

Looking back at all these facts I still hesitated to take up my cudgels in print against milk. For years I thought and thought about it, debating whether or not we should tell our readers what we knew against milk drinking, but it seemed too revolutionary a thing to do. There had been built up such a sacred attitude towards milk that it had become more than a fetish. Down through the ages it had become a powerful symbol. It had grown into a magic belief, a refuge, a sort of sacred fountain from which one drank and imbibed eternal youth. How could we snatch away this source of comfort from our friends?

But my conscience could not remain quiet. When I saw people breaking every rule of health and then resorting to milk as if it would quench out all this error, I became aroused. When I realized how many persons are needlessly suffering through an overconsumption of milk, I came to a decision. I would do it regardless of consequences. I would cast the data I had upon the waters. If it comes as a shock to some, I hope that they will study the matter most thoroughly, possibly experimenting a little before they make up their mind.

I will say one thing most positively—if you think that milk, as it is produced under modern conditions, will be an appreciable factor in giving you health, I must tell you that you are not basing your belief on reality. Today's emasculated product is not fit for human consumption, not to mention the needs of the calf itself for whom the milk was intended. Poor thing! The modern calf is not growing up into a healthy cow.

The Use of Antibiotics

This is proven by the increasing use of the antibiotic drugs given to cows. No one can tell me that this doesn't affect the cow's meat and its milk in some detrimental way. I have before me several strange circulars issued by the Tarkio Molasses Feed Company of Kansas City. In one of them dated March 22, 1955, and addressed to "Dear Cattle Feeder," the company says, regarding the stilbestrol drug that was approved by the United States Food and Drug Administration, that it causes meat to go "soft" and not to age properly, and that their company did not intend to put any stilbestrol into its cattle feed. The other circular is a letter from the Williams Meat Company of Kansas City, one of the outstanding meat provisioners of our country today, who furnishes the best of meat for many large fancy restaurants. Here is what Mr. Williams of that company said

[121]

in a letter to the Tarkio Molasses Feed Company on March 14, 1955: "As you know we specialize in prime quality meats, making Kansas City meats nationally famous. For some reason in recent months, the texture of the meat is exceptionally soft and not responding to proper aging. Are feeders experimenting too much with drugs?"

Much of this sort of wonder drug is "happening" to cows and I wonder what it will do to the milk? At any rate, the whole thing is so unpredictable that one will never know at what moment Bossy will be given another "wonder" treatment, without waiting the necessary time in laboratory checking of dangers.

Propaganda

A great part of milk's popularity is due to the propaganda of the milk interests. They are powerfully organized. They send their tons of literature to the schools, the PTA's and to other places where it will do the most good. I recall an experience I had about 7 or 8 years ago which will throw some light on this activity. When we started the Soil and Health Foundation I had some correspondence with a professor in a dental college who wished to know whether I could run an experiment on our farm, feeding two groups of mice—one with foods raised with chemical fertilizers, the other with foods raised by the organic method. Then he came to the farm for further discussions. He advised that the experiment would be financed by a big milk foundation, but when he said that milk had to be one item of food for each group of mice, and when I expressed a few negative thoughts about milk, he left, never to return. I received no more letters from him.

Much of our opinion regarding the healing quality of milk stems from this endless stream of propaganda—a torrent of advertising costing hundreds of millions of dollars. We are bombarded by it at every turn, through the newspapers, radio and television until milk has become crowned with a halo. But it is a halo purchased with dollars, and therefore I do not feel guilty when I tarnish it a little.

There is no question that milk has a delightful, satisfying taste, but so has strawberry short cake and ice cream. However, one cannot live by taste alone if one wishes to live a long, healthy life, although there is nothing wrong with the taste of apples, carrots and roast beef.

How about those who do not drink coffee? If they also eliminate milk, they might complain of the loss of a hot or cold liquid with which to end the meal. But there are always the various kinds of mint and herb teas that one can come to enjoy highly. I occasionally drink an alfalfa mint tea and rose hip tea and soon expect to experiment with fenugreek seed tea.

My own diet consists of meat, eggs, vegetables (mostly raw, some cooked) and a lot of fruit. I do not eat anything that has gone through a factory, and to me, milk is a highly factoryized thing—not only in the aspect of pasteurization but also in the fact that a high production factory has been made out of the cow's udders. I eat no bread or cakes, and no soups, because I am on a reducing diet. But my diet is a very satisfying one. I take a great many different natural vitamins, plus bone meal.

[122]

I am on a low salt, no sugar diet, and because of this and my general diet, my blood pressure is like that of a newborn babe—120 over 65. Before I began all this I had a very high blood pressure.

Now a few words of advice. What you intend to do is entirely up to you. Read the information that follows. Then make up your own mind. Some will cut milk out entirely. Others will merely reduce the amount they consume. But do not let nostalgia influence you, for nostalgia has filled too many a grave. You can point to some persons who are heavy milk drinkers and yet who are perfectly healthy, but it is possible that it is the way they are built. Perhaps they have wider arteries than the average person and a more tuned up set of glands. It is the way they were born, due to their heritage. Those are the people who smoke and drink and live to over 80. But you and I may not be in that class.

It is too bad about the cow! If there were only a way that we could start to unbreed her—to breed her backwards so to speak, to progressively reduce the size of her udders so that one day again she could become a scrub cow. Then, and only then, would I consider taking a drink of her milk. In such a day, perhaps ways could be found to keep her healthy and clean and by some other method, milder than pasteurization, to preserve her milk's nutritional qualities as well as kill its germs. Man has abused a good thing.

I say to you who are really health-conscious, who want to live to 100 and over without the usual signs of crippling senility—don't drink milk, which means also, don't eat butter or cheese or any other dairy product. If you are satisfied to live to only 70 or 80, or even 85, and if you have been endowed since birth with a body structure that enables you to snap your fingers at the average health-producing procedures, and if you feel that you must drink milk, then drink it! But you will probably pay for it in some way or another. You won't have that elastic step. You will dodder more. Your eyes may grow dimmer, your ears may lose their hearing edge.

There is so much medical evidence against the drinking of milk, that where there is smoke there may be fire. Remember that half the world, the eastern half, does not drink milk. I was talking to a Chinese professor the other day and he confirmed this fact to me and more. He stated that the average Chinese student who comes to this country, and hears about the supposed health-giving qualities of milk, begins to drink it, and as a result, he gets gas on the stomach and many other digestive ills. But he does not get it from eating meat, fruits or vegetables!

What about raw milk? Only the other day I was told of the case of the wife of an advertising executive who visited her uncle's farm where there was a herd of 200 purebred cows. They kept one cow for themselves under unusually sanitary conditions and did not pasteurize its milk. The lady in question, who drank some of this milk on this visit, contracted a severe case of undulant fever which took 3 years to cure. But the people who were drinking this milk all along had become inured to it. Somewhere, years back, they may have experienced some kind of trouble, unless they may have had some natural immunity.

Heart Disease And Milk

I would like to speak about another phase of milk drinking—the heart disease question. In a recent study of this disease, the unusual amount of heart attacks in this country was attributed to the large amount of fat consumed in our diet, namely 40 per cent. The authors found that in Italy the consumption of fat is only 20 per cent of the total food consumed, and heart fatalities there are not one-third of what they are in this country. There can be no question that the total fat consumed is an important factor in bringing on heart attacks to vulnerable cases. This is brought out in hundreds of medical researches which I have gone over.

The usual practice is to tell the heart patient to cut down on eggs, but from what I have seen, as between eggs and dairy products, I would say to the average heart case, cut out all dairy products completely, but by all means eat eggs, for eggs are a seed from which a chick will come out. The egg contains terrific, living, nutritional elements. It is a complete package. There is sufficient food in it to feed the emerging chick for a few days and the poultryman does not have to do it. Anyone who passes up eggs is denying himself one of the finest foods that God made.

Of course, both eggs and dairy products contain fat. And the body needs some fat, to be sure. We cannot eliminate all fat from our diets. Another angle to remember is that most cheeses are quite high in salt— also bad for the heart patient.

And the government encourages the farmer to so feed his cows that more butterfat will be in the milk. That is the government standard as to how the farmer should be paid for his milk. It is based on its butterfat content. Less would be better. Of course, the physician will advise his heart patient to drink skimmed milk. Yet in restaurants he will put regular milk —even cream—in his coffee.

Antibiotics and Antibodies

Another thing that militates against milk, as far as I am concerned, is the fact that practically all milk today contains traces of penicillin, from shots given to the cow to prevent or cure disease. If we keep drinking such milk, the effect of this cumulative penicillin will be to kill all the body's protective bacteria, and already there is evidence that this will cause trouble when a real emergency arises. But now some research scientists are speaking of a new practice that they wish to see inaugurated with respect to milk— a practice which should be killed dead in its track by public outcry. It is based on researches conducted at the University of Minnesota, aided by the American Dairy Association of Chicago, which may set off such a dangerous trend in nutrition that anything that has gone before will pale into insignificance.

What is suggested now is that disease germs be injected into cows. They will then give milk containing large quantities of disease-fighting agents, or antibodies, which would protect people against certain diseases if they drink this milk. Already 10 years have been spent in these researches,

[124]

all with animals, and the idea has worked, according to the research scientists.

Hidden Dangers

However, two questionable thoughts arise in my mind. One—what will be the ultimate effect in the human body of 20 or 30 years ingestion of such antibodies? Will it completely inactivate the body's own mechanism to produce the protective antibodies? Disuse encourages petrification. The day may arise when something will happen to the cow. She may become unable to pass on the antibodies. What will happen then, if the body has become so coddled and weakened that it has "unlearned" its ability to fight for itself? Modern practices tend to continually weaken the ability of the individual to assert the resistive qualities of his body. He has been called a machine, and is being treated purely as a machine in this case. But it is far safer to improve our primitive qualities in regard to the physical operation of our bodies, rather than to reduce them.

Number two—The dangerous trend set off by the fluoridation of drinking waters (namely, the concept of preventing something by doing something to that which we take into our bodies every day) is given another shot-in-the-arm. There is no telling where this idea will end up. What will the Christian Scientists think of such milk? Nothing, I am sure. Such procedure is a threat to the liberty of the individual who has a right to decide for himself whether he wishes to be "medicated" in such unorthodox ways.

Another hidden defect in this milk treatment is (and the same is true of fluoridation to reduce tooth cavities in children) that it lulls us into a false sense of security, it prevents us from searching out the real causes of disease and rooting them out. If it were not for the prejudiced money-tainted commercialism of the large-scale food-producing factories, the public would today know the simple basic causes of cancer, polio, heart disease and the host of other ailments that are bringing prosperity into the doctors' offices. The problem is to get the general public to know these causes and to resist the fancy pseudo-scientific Salk vaccines, the water chemicalizations and the attempt to put a white coat on cows. That's what they are trying to do —to make doctors out of cows. This is really laughable, for if you knew the extent of disease that exists today in cows, you would see how badly *they* need the doctors themselves.

I, therefore, urge you to write to your congressmen, to your senators, both federal and state, and to other interested officials, write to the University of Minnesota and to the American Dairy Association of Chicago, telling them of the dangers involved and that it may cause many persons to stop drinking milk.

Milk looks innocent in its innocuous whiteness, in its wonderful taste, but still waters flow deep. God alone knows what the dairyman already is doing to the cow and to the milk. There are far better, and more certain ways of getting the finest nutrition. And that's what you are entitled to— the finest.

CHAPTER 32

Milk

by Horace W. Soper, M.D., F.A.C.P. St. Louis

A review of the recent literature concerning milk as a food for human beings, reveals many interesting observations. Man appears to be the only mammal which habitually consumes milk after the period of lactation has ceased. Crumbine and Tobey, in their excellent monograph on milk, state that it was used as a food 4,000 years B. C. The Aryans of Central Asia were the first herdsmen, and honey and milk was a prized drink. Goats' milk and mare's milk were consumed by the ancient Greeks. Most authorities on nutrition, particularly McCollum, consider milk a food for which there is no adequate substitute. He advises that one quart of this "protective food" a day should be consumed, but also points out that the inhabitants of the wet regions in southern Asia subsist on a diet of rice, soy beans, sweet potatoes and many other vegetables. Bamboo sprouts and other leafy vegetables are eaten in large quantities. They have no herds and do not consume milk. He states that these people are better developed physically, have more capacity for work and endurance, that they escape the skeletal defects in childhood, and have the finest teeth of any race in the world.

Dental caries, foot infections and pyorrhea form too large a subject to attempt elucidation here. Bunting concludes his study of the subject as follows: "To this end it is highly desirable that group studies be made in which the allied sciences of chemistry, nutrition, bacteriology and dentistry may be correlated in a truly scientific attack on this difficult and important problem in human welfare.

Can milk be implicated as an etiologic factor? Ernst A. Hooton, Professor of Anthropology at Harvard University, in a broad survey of "The Teeth of Apes and Men," a recent article in the *Scientific Monthly,* concludes that "foci of infection in teeth undermine the entire bodily health of the species and that degenerative tendencies in evolution have manifested themselves in modern man to such an extent that our jaws are too small for the teeth which they are supposed to accommodate." "I firmly believe that the health of humanity is at stake and unless steps are taken to discover preventatives of tooth infection and correctives of dental deformities, the course of human evolution will lead downward to extinction." Professor Hooton points out that primitive man was singularly free from tooth infection with the single exception of the Rhodesian man—equipped with the longest face, the largest palate and the worst teeth of antiquity; that examination of the skulls of savage races reveals that they did not suffer from dental caries and apical abscesses. The teeth are usually found to be worn down by attrition. It is notable that such people were not

[126]

consumers of goat's or cow's milk. Professor Hooton is greatly impressed with the fact that 9 out of 10 school children in the United States have decayed teeth.

Bunting, Professor of Oral Pathology in the University of Michigan, came to the following conclusions after 5 years research work: "Dental caries is dependent on the infestation of the mouth by specific types of bacteria capable of producing acids by the fermentation of residual carbohydrate food materials and capable of living in their own products. Lactobacillus acidophilus is the organism always found in dental caries. It is never found in the mouths of persons free from dental caries. It is also found in the intestinal tract of carious persons." Bunting believes that the character of the foods eaten by civilized people is a great factor in the production of dental caries. Primitive people, living on simple foods are free from caries until they come in contact with civilization.

An important report on the milk supply of London was recently made. It appears that the milk is gathered in the country and transported to London in large glass-lined tanks, each holding 3,000 gallons. These tanks contain milk from different herds. The first examination of 10 road and rail tanks showed all contained living virulent tubercle bacilli. The latest figures for tank milk show that out of 41 samples, 34 or 83 per cent contained tubercle bacilli. After pasteurization and examination of 282 samples purchased over the counter, 9 or 32 per cent contained tubercle bacilli. In the cities of Edinburgh, Glasgow, Aberdeen and Dundee, specimens of pasteurized milk as retailed gave a figure of over 5 per cent of samples that contained tubercle bacilli. In England, 45 per cent of tuberculosis of the cervical glands, 47 per cent of lupus, 30 per cent of tuberculosis of the meninges, and 18 per cent of that of bones and joints have been found to be due to the bovine bacillus. In Scotland, the corresponding figures are 73, 53, 12 and 42.

The work of Saunders, et al, in "Infection in Gastric and Duodenal Ulcer," is of extreme importance. Their conclusions are as follows: "The organism studied by us is found in milk from cows suffering with mastitis, and is not identical with any other type of *streptococcus* tested. It will stand the heat of pasteurization, it does not live in bile media of the lowest dilutions, and is not affected by a high acidity. It is the only factor which can explain the epidemic-like occurrence of ulcer in children from one to six months of age as reported by Helmholz. An identical organism has been isolated from 30 resected ulcers of the stomach and duodenum, and has been proved identical with 3 others isolated from cows' milk, and is not identical with any other streptococcus tested."

Place and Sutton have reported an epidemic of arthritic erythemia or Haverhill fever which was traced to the use of raw milk. They have isolated an organism (*Haverhilla multiformis*) found in the blood and fluid of involved joints of patients suffering from the disease. G. M. Fyfe reports a milk-horne Sonne dysentery epidemic affecting 150 persons. Rosenow reports an institutional outbreak of poliomyelitis or infantile paralysis in a midwestern college apparently due to streptococcus in raw milk. The epidemic ceased to spread after discontinuance of the use of unpasteurized milk and cream. Rosenow, Rozendaal and Thorsness have reported the results of their investigation in a Minnesota epidemic of poliomyelitis. They found a streptococcus isolated from raw milk at the time of the epidemic that was identical with that isolated in cases of poliomyelitis in human beings and monkeys. They also found the poliomyelitis streptococcus in several samples of pasteurized milk. Much work has been done on the subject of pathogenic (disease producing) bacteria in milk by Ayres and Johnson who found that pasteurized milk soured due to the development of lactic acid bacteria which had survived pasteurization or due to reinfection.

Recently I submitted to the Gradwohl Laboratory 13 specimens of milk, representing the different St. Louis dairies. These were cultured according to the United States Health Standards. Five of the specimens showed the presence of *streptococcus viridans*. Four showed *acidophilus*. One showed almost a pure culture of pneumococci-like organisms. The cow is essentially an unclean animal. Efforts to sterilize the udder are unavailing. The skin cracks and becomes eczematous and the scabs fall into the milk. Mastitis is a frequent development. Despite all strenuous efforts and precautions, the best milk delivered from the dairies continues to show the presence of pathogenic bacteria. Milk is such a good culture medium that it is easily contaminated. It was largely implicated as a carrier in the great epidemics of typhoid and cholera that occurred in the days before pasteurization was employed.

The tremendous importance of the problems involved is obvious, particularly so in view of the fact that all our municipalities are engaged in strenuous but futile attempts to secure a pure milk supply. The question of immunity to streptococcus infection arises. Perhaps 75 per cent of the population do establish such an immunity. Clinicians, however, are not concerned with them but are concerned about the 25 per cent or more of the individuals who do not establish immunity and fall a prey to its devastations. These questions come before the clinician every day. Where did this case of *streptococcus viridans* originate? Why do such a large percentage of school children develop infected tonsils? Where did this patient acquire septic sore throat? Why is the increase of dental caries in children concomitant with the augmented consumption of milk?

It is easy to exclude milk entirely, and follow a well balanced diet, as recently emphasized by the eminent physiologist, Professor A. J. Carlson. Important minerals, such as calcium and phosphorus are found in gelatine, whole wheat, beans, spinach, broccoli, nuts, etc. Vitamin A is present in all the leafy vegetables, the yellow vegetables, bananas, tomatoes, oysters, and many other foods; therefore, butter and cream can be eliminated.

I conclude the tremendous incriminations of milk as a disseminator of infection as follows:

1. All mammals, excepting the human, cease the use of milk as a food after weaning. The mother's mammary gland remains quiescent until activated by parturition.

2. As a result of his violation of a primary biologic law, man has been severely penalized by the host of infectious diseases that are disseminated by milk.

3. The dairy cow, stimulated and bred to yield milk over a long period of time, develops hypertrophy of the mammary gland. She is frequently found to be infected with a low grade streptococcus mastitis. Efforts to disinfect the udder often cause a chronic eczema; crusts and scales fall into the milk.

4. Milk is such a good culture medium that it is frequently contaminated by infectious agents not originating in the cow. "Bacterial soup" is a good synonym for it.

5. Research into the habits of the people of ancient as well as modern civilizations reveals that they were consumers of milk and all suffered from dental caries. Primitive peoples and savages were free from this disease until they came in contact with civilization.

6. Raw milk is unfit for human consumption.

7. Pasteurized milk as it reaches the consumer usually contains pathogenic bacteria and is not to be relied upon as a safe food.

Reprinted in part from a longer article in "Archives of Pediatrics" for January, 1943.

CHAPTER 33

Is Milk a Curse?

by James A. Goodfellow, M.B.C.M.

Great stuff this milk! There are 1,000,000,000 gallons consumed annually and it requires 2,500,000 cows to produce that quantity. Truly a gigantic business. It is, however, a very modern industry. This great river of milk began to flow in small rivulets about 150 years ago, and has continued to flow in each succeeding year with ever increasing volume until it reached its present huge dimensions, and it may grow still bigger. The British Minister of Agriculture, backed by his medical and other advisers, is urging the farmers to give him another million gallons a day within the next few years.

On the other hand, if the views I am here ventilating obtain even moderate acceptance, it is possible the Minister may not require that extra million gallons. Shall I make many converts? I can hear the modern mother and housewife exclaim: "If you are trying to put us off using milk, you have failed at the outset, because we know its value, not only for the nourishment of our children, but in the kitchen. We use it in our tea, coffee, cocoa, in sauces, puddings and cakes, and in many other ways. Milk is indispensable, and a housewife's life would be intolerable without it. We refuse to read another word." And yet, the housewives of 150 years ago, and later, had to feed themselves and rear large families without its help.

To disarm such hostility this seems to be an appropriate place to make a few reassuring remarks. A poet once said: "There will always be an England," and I feel sure we can say with equal certainty, there will always be a milk. But it will be a far, far better milk than you have ever known. It will be compounded and scientifically prepared from a prescription supplied by Mother Nature herself, and it will be free from bovine influence. Until the modern mother regains the power to feed her baby from the breast—and it can be done—we may have to rely on the cow for milk supplied to babies under 12 months, but such milk should be specially selected and humanized. Do you think you are paying your child a compliment when you feed it on a fluid Nature intended for the nourishment of a calf? The human child, with its marvelous brain, is worthy of the very best. Let us see that he gets it. My appeal is to your common sense. Now please read on.

Of course, before the period I have mentioned, milk as a food had some appreciation. In all ages everyone must have been impressed on observing the remarkable growth of the mammalian young at the beginning of their lives when fed on nothing else but what they sucked from their mothers' teats. Why, it may be asked, was such a remarkable food so long in becoming a commmercial commodity?

The answer is easily found. Before root crops were grown in quantity and concentrates were introduced, farmers found it impossible to keep alive many cattle during the winter. Each year there was a great slaughter of stock in the late autumn, and butcher's meat was cheap. But the chief reason was the absence of a demand for liquid milk. Farmers used it for making butter, and also for cheese. Mothers in those days usually had an abundant supply of milk for their own babies, and when any child had the misfortune to lose its mother at birth, the service of a wet nurse was called for. Doctors kept a list of wet nurses whom they could recommend. Failing a wet nurse, no mother at that time would ever have accepted cow's milk as a substitute. A mother's instinct told her that the milk from the cow was wholly unsuitable for her precious baby, and the mother's instinct was right. Prejudice or instinct was so strong that sooner than see a cow deputize for her, the child would be fed on pap, which is bread moistened with sweetened water, even if it died, which it usually did. But what did it matter; babies were plentiful then.

Eighteenth Century Recommendation

Just before the commencement of the nineteenth century doctors began to recommend the milk from the cow in preference to a wet nurse, who often brought trouble into the home. When mothers saw their neigh-

[130]

bors' children reared on cows' milk grow quicker and taller, weigh more and look healthier than their own babies fed from the breast, their opposition weakened. Above all, when they saw that such children did not develop horns, grow a tail, nor chew a cud, their fear gradually vanished, and thus was born a new industry that was to develop year after year, until it can now be said that the nutrition of Western Civilization is based on the cow's udder!

What is this milk that has played such an important role in recent human history? The young of all mammalian animals are born in an imperfect condition. They will require help from their mother, and this is provided by two or more milk glands supplied with teats from which the youngsters suck and so obtain further nourishment. For all practical purposes milk may be regarded as blood which has been bereft of its red coloring matter. The red blood corpuscles are no longer required to carry oxygen, because the offspring is now able to procure its own oxygen from its lungs by means of its own red blood cells. In all other respects the composition of milk very much resembles the composition of blood. There is an extra amount of fat and carbohydrate, because extra heat is now required to maintain the necessary temperature.

Just as each animal has its own special blood composition, so the milk each produces is different, and one milk is not interchangeable with another.

It is a common practice today to administer blood transfusions. If we were to attempt to put cow's blood into human veins there would be a rough house, possibly with fatal results. Just as with blood, so with milk. We have no right to assume the milk from the cow will suit the human baby. In fact we know it does not, but in this case fatalities do not immediately occur, because Mother Nature is an adept in the art of "making do." Unfortunately "making do" means second best. Make shifts make handicaps.

Whatever the composition, it should be noted this additional help is continued only for a definite limited time, which varies in each species. It is called the period of lactation. As soon as the digestive organs are sufficiently developed to receive, digest, and assimilate an ordinary diet, the milk supply is cut off. There is a brief transition time, during which the two methods overlap. This is called the period of weaning, and is usually of short duration, for two reasons. The mother is anxious to put an end to this drain on her strength, so that she can build up her body in preparation for another pregnancy. And the youngster soon derives more pleasure from the act of eating than from sucking. In the case of the human child the lactation period is about 12 months. That is long enough; for no organs, least of all the digestive organs, can become strong and efficient without exercise—exercise which solid food provides, but which liquid milk fails adequately to supply.

Age-Old Principle

All through the ages since the first mammal appeared this method of supplemental nourishment has prevailed, with its period of lactation definitely and permanently terminated by a short time for weaning. The rule applied to human babies as well as to animals, and it worked very well. About 150 years ago, however, doctors began to have exaggerated ideas about their importance to the community. They said: "This definite and early end to the period of lactation is all humbug, at least where human babies are concerned. We know we cannot continue with mothers' milk much longer than a year, but by selective breeding we can induce cows to yield far more milk than is needed for their calves, and the surplus we can feed to our babies so that the lactation period in effect is prolonged indefinitely, to the great benefit of the children and the race." Now this was a nasty snub for Mother Nature, because it reversed the policy she had been pursuing for a million years. The trouble was that the doctors appeared to be right. Babies fed on cows' milk grew better and bigger and appeared healthier than breast-fed babies, and when the lactation period was prolonged into childhood the same happy results followed the practice. Similar results can still be witnessed today. Most of the leaders of the medical profession and the veterinary profession are never tired of trumpeting from the house tops this warning and advice:

"The people are perishing from lack of milk. Many of the children of the nation are suffering from malnutrition, and the only remedy is—

DRINK MORE MILK."

This article is written to announce in feeble voice, which probably will never be heard, this message: "The people may possibly be suffering from too much milk. The children of the nation are certainly suffering from malnutrition, but malnutrition takes many forms. If you come to believe, as I hope you will, that it is wrong to feed human babies and children on the liquid designed for the nourishment of a calf you will probably come to the conclusion that we should STOP DRINKING MILK."

Colossal Blunder

What caused doctors 150 years ago to make this colossal blunder in child nutrition, and why do the doctors of today persist in the same huge mistake in ever increasing intensity?

I think the answer is that they are so obsessed with the apparently good results produced by excessive cows' milk administration that they fail to perceive the remote harmful effects. Or rather they do perceive these harmful effects but fail to link them up with the use of cows' milk. How do we judge whether a child is well or badly nourished? Simply by its physical appearance, backed by the evidence of the tape measure. Size and weight are the criteria by which we estimate nutrition. If the intention of child nutrition is to produce big, bonny, bouncing babies, cows' milk wins every time. These babies take first prize at baby shows. I hold, however, that Nature's intention in child nutrition is to produce healthy adolescents and perfect adults. And this is where cows' milk miserably fails. Can we take this huge river of cows' milk and pour it down the gullets of the juvenile population for 150 years without some change in the national character and constitution? Is it likely? Why is cows' milk apparently so successful in the rearing of human babies and children? The answer is obvious if we remember that Nature has designed the milk of every species specially for that species only, and that the rate of growth for each species is determined by something attached to the protein molecule. Roughly the percentage of protein in any milk is an index to the rate of growth. A rabbit, for example, doubles its birth weight in 6 days, a kitten in 9 days, a calf in 47 days, and a human baby in 6 months.

In other words, a calf grows at 4 times the rate of a baby. When we supply the baby with lashings of cow's milk we ginger up its growth rate and increase its weight beyond the normal. But is that right? Here are some figures giving protein percentages. Cat's milk has 9.1 per cent, cow's milk 3.5 per cent, human milk 2.3 per cent. Here are the respective figures for fat content—3.3 per cent, 3.7 per cent, and 3.8 per cent. Now let me give the figures for the milk of a porpoise. It contains 11.2 per cent protein—5 times the amount in human milk, and the fat content is 48.5 per cent—13 times the amount in mother's milk.

Porpoise Milk for Bouncing Babies

Here is a suggestion for our specialists in nutrition, who cannot see further than the big, bonny bouncing baby. Let them provide a school of porpoises and keep them in a salt lake. The youngsters as they arrive would be killed and the milk would be used to feed the human baby. It might be too rich to stay in their stomachs, but if that difficulty could be overcome, it would be interesting to watch their growth. Probably they would double their birth weight in 6 weeks instead of 6 months, and with fat so plentiful they would soon resemble balloons. It would be amusing but it would not be wise, and the experts would soon reach the conclusion that the milk of the porpoise is not suitable for human babies. Let the baby porpoises have their mother's milk. They thrive on it. And I hope the lesson would enable the experts to go further and say, "Henceforth also let the calf have its mother's milk."

Cows' Milk Failure

In what respect does cows' milk fail to build up satisfactory human beings? The most important constituent in any milk is the protein, and we judge each protein by the number of amino acids into which it can be split. These are the real bricks from which our bones and organs are constructed. Now cows' milk is deficient in one of these amino acids which is used for making our stomach lining, for making blood, and for making brain.

The number of mentally defective and backward children is increasing at an alarming rate. It will go on increasing. Most children have not sufficient brain power to absorb enough education in 8 years to fit them for life, so the school leaving age is to be raised to 15, then 16, and finally, 18. Will 18 years be enough? Let us see what Lord Moran says of most of the young men aged not less than 18, from the public schools, who have chosen the medical profession as a career. "A great many are incapable of accurate observation, unable to reason correctly from observed facts, and generally deficient in intelligence. As a class they are unfit to make satisfactory doctors." Heaven help us!

This century and a half of cows' milk may have so altered our mentality and physiological functions that the national health has been undermined to such an extent as to necessitate the creation by the government of a wonderful public health service for the treatment of ailments which in a nation properly fed should never occur

Nation Bovinised by Foolish Milk Policy

I dare say every one of my readers will say that my remarks are a gross exaggeration of the facts. Let me put it in another way. Cow's milk is for all practical purposes cow's blood, bereft of the red blood corpuscles and their coloring matter. If Nature had decided to let the red cells through, the milk would then have resembled blood and its administration to your child would have been repulsive. You would have rightly said, "I am not going to let my boy be fed on cow's blood. I do not want him when he grows up to resemble a cow either mentally or physically, and I shall take no risk." But you are now allowing your child to be fed on cow's blood. Should the mere absence of color make so much difference to your attitude? There are substances normal to the blood of a cow which should never be allowed to enter into the blood stream of your boy. If they do you may expect trouble and you will certainly get it. Probably then you will agree that Dryden was right when he said, "God never made His work for man to mend."

Businessman's Milk

When I hear of the businessman in the prime of life ordering a pint of milk to be delivered to his office daily, I feel I would like to say to him, "Don't you think at your age it is time you were weaned? You really don't like this stuff; you are merely taking it because doctors praise it and tell you its protein has high biological value. Do you know this milk contains a growth stimulating principle that enables the young calf to grow at a fast rate? But you have long since stopped growing. On what part of your body are these growth stimulating agents going to expand their energy? Don't you think as you get older and some of your organs get enfeebled that they may respond to this stimulus and start growing on their own?

Cancer has baffled the medical profession, although vast sums have been spent on research, and are still being spent without result. They are seeking for the cause of this scourge in all sorts of out of the way places. It may be a germ or a virus, needing a microscope, culture plates and test tubes for the investigation, but maybe all the time the real cause lies just under their nose?

If our experts used less science and more common sense, greater progress might be made. All I can say is that if a completely grown man

[134]

or woman drinks over a long period of time a nutrient fluid which persistently stimulates cell growth when all normal cell growth has finished, then, if he does not get cancer (which is cell growth without rhyme or reason), he is lucky, for he has been using the means for its production unwittingly.

What Does Nutrition Signify?

Let us try to discover what nutrition in early life signifies. I hate the word "law" in describing Nature's methods, and the word "rule" is not much better. They are too rigid. By extending our studies over a wide range we usually can discover what was Nature's purpose in developing the various physiological processes that occurred in the animal body. These I shall call "Nature's intentions," assuming quite unscientifically that an intelligent mind has been at work.

Nature's Intention No. 1

When Nature designed the mammary gland for the nourishment of the young immediately after birth, she intended the milk only to be used as a temporary measure both in the interest of the mother and of the child.

Nature's Intention No. 2

She fixed the composition of the milk in each species with the intention that it should be used for that species only.

Nature's Intention No. 3

When she forms the milk in the mammary gland it is sterile, and her intention is that it should pass directly from the gland through the teat straight into the stomach of the offspring without contact with the contaminating air, or the destructive action of light.

When we frustrate any one or all these intentions, when we defy or disregard them, Nature usually exacts the appropriate penalty. The trouble is that the punishment may come such a long time after the crime that we fail to link up the two in the relationship of cause and effect, and thus fail to profit by the experience. Consider, for example, the millions of young lives that have been sacrificed in the last century through our persistent disregard of Nature's intention No. 3. All the deaths that have occurred through drinking contaminated milk, all the epidemics that have occurred from milk borne infections, a great many of the cases of scurvy, latent and obvious, would never have occurred if we had kept our milk from contact with air or light.

"The mills of God grind slowly, but they grind exceeding small."

CHAPTER 34

Is Milk the Perfect Food?

by Michael Rabben, D.D.S.

Digest

As a food milk was intended by nature as the secretion to nourish the suckling animal until weaned. When so used by the species for which it was designed and prepared by the mother, it is the perfect food for that animal.

When milk of one species is used as a food for an animal of another species and certain environmental changes are made in it, whether physical or chemical, it loses its character as the perfect food for the animal to which it is given.

Based upon the foregoing premises this article challenges the widely accepted belief that cow's milk is a perfect food for infant and adult human beings. The composition of milk is detailed and the possible harmful results of an intake of this food are explored.

Variation in Composition of Milk

From the first secretion of colostrum, milk as taken from the breasts of any species varies constantly according to the needs of the growing infant until weaned.

Little Known of Hormone Content—Milk contains antibodies, minerals, vitamins, proteins, fat and carbohydrates. Amino acids, enzymes, steroids, and other hormones of which little has been written or investigated are contained in the proteins of milk. The hormone content of milk, however, is rarely mentioned. As often happens when knowledge of a substance is meager, the hormone factor is dismissed with the statement that it is unimportant. It would be more accurate to state that the role of the hormone substance is unknown.

Lack of Uniformity in Composition—The elements contained in milk vary in amount according to 1. species, 2. stage of lactation, 3. the food intake of the mother and her metabolism, 4. the mother's state of health. Milk is never, therefore, a uniformly composed, unvarying product.

While most of the minerals considered essential in human nutrition are present in milk, it is notably poor in iron. It has been stated that the human infant is born with enough iron in its body to last it 6 months. When the baby begins to get teeth it is nature's sign for the child to begin eating other types of food. Before long the child is weaned.

Vitamins Present in Raw Milk—In raw milk nature has incorporated all of the vitamins necessary for the optimum health of the infant. They are present in the amounts best determined by the wisdom of nature without any addition brought about by the incomplete knowledge of man who thinks he can improve upon the achievements of nature. The amounts of vitamins vary from species to species according to the needs of the animal.

Protein Content of Milk—Milk has been described as the perfect food because it contains all of the amino acids, because of its protein content. The proteins of milk are described as casein, lactalbumin, and lactoglobulin. The difference in content and proportion of albumin to casein in cow's milk and human milk may explain why the curds of cow's milk are so much heavier and tougher than those of human milk. It must be borne in mind that the enzymes and hormones are also present as proteins.

Difference in Fat Content—The fat of milk is valuable for the content of fatty acids and the fat soluble vitamins A, E, D, and K. There is a difference in the fat content of human and cow's milk: the fat of human milk more nearly resembles that of body fat and few or none of the fatty acids have chains shorter than 10 carbons.

Lactose Content Higher in Human Milk—The carbohydrate of milk is the milk sugar, lactose. The lactose content of human milk averages about two per cent higher than that of bovine milk. It is thought that this is so because of the larger brain of man, the food for which is galactose.

Role of Enzymes—In unpasteurized milk, the enzymes may be found in an active state. As a matter of fact, their presence in an active state is used as a test of the effectiveness of pasteurization. The enzymes present are a catalase, a peroxidase, and a phosphatase. Their role in human metabolism seems unknown, but the phosphatase is thought to ensure the utilization of calcium.

Consideration of Hormonal Factor in Milk

Milk, as many other foods of animal origin, contains steroids. These are not usually mentioned in biochemistry texts. The hormonal content is not discussed at all. In discussions with food chemists blank stares are the response to questions of hormones in milk.

Initiation of Lactation—It is known that lactation is initiated by one of the hormones of the anterior pituitary body, prolactin. Certainly this hormone is found in the blood when lactation is to begin. Milk is made of blood as are other glandular secretions whose nutrition is furnished by blood. Other hormones must be present because in cases of acromegaly, an endocrine dysfunction, lactation is unduly prolonged after childbirth. Under certain circumstances, such as the use of estrogen in males and testosterone in females, milk may be secreted.

Possible Presence of Growth Hormone—It has been thought that the growth hormone of the anterior pituitary body may be present because the greatest amount of growth of the infant takes place during the first year of life when its food is principally milk. Children who are heavy milk drinkers have been known to exceed their parents noticeably in growth. Indeed, Spies describes experiments in which growth was stimulated by giving children two quarts of milk daily, exceeding the skeletal maturation of the controls by 93 per cent.

Lactation Increased by Growth Hormone—It has been shown that the pure growth hormone of the anterior pituitary increases lactation in cows better than prolactin. The thyroid, posterior pituitary, and adrenal cortex are known to have an influence on lactation. The androgens, including progesterone, are also recognized as exerting an effect upon lactation. These hormones must all be transported by the blood.

Reprinted with permission from Dental Digest for September, 1956.

CHAPTER 35

Chemicals in Milk

The Food and Drug Administration in Washington has forbidden the use of antibiotics as preservatives in food, because "the consumption of food so treated may cause sensitization of the consumer to such antibiotics and may result in the emergence of strains of pathogenic microorganisms resistant to these drugs." No such foods are at present being sold, FDA believes, but they are taking no chance on any food processor using an antibiotic for food preservation.

This statement made us feel good until we began to run across news items like the following:

"A new form of aureomycin . . . (an antibiotic) that can be given orally to small animals and to calves is now being marketed . . . said to be especially effective in treatment of scours and pneumonia." This article appeared in *Chemical Week* for February 27, 1954.

In the *Drug Trade News* for December 7, 1953, came the warning "Antibiotics No Panacea, Animal Men Warned. A caution on overdependence on antibiotics by cattle, sheep and poultry raisers was sounded at a meeting of the Agricultural Research Institute here recently by George H. Hart, dean of the University of California veterinary school." Dr. Hart emphasized that he was not advising farmers to give up the use of antibiotics entirely, either in animal feeds or as drugs, but he warned against placing sole dependence on them. We gather from this that antibiotics are administered to farm animals just about as indiscriminately as they are given to human beings. Dr. Hart seemed to think that lack of attention to nutrition and sanitation may result in trouble.

The *Lancet* (a British medical journal) reported in August 22, 1953, that the American use of antibiotics in animal food had finally resulted in England adopting regulations that permit the use of penicillin and aureomycin in food for quick fattening of pigs and poultry. Mind you, this is not just drugs for sick animals. Antibiotics are now being incorporated into *food* for animals. They get a small amount of antibiotic every day. According to *Nutrition Abstracts and Reviews,* Vol. 23, 1953, no one knows just how soon the intestinal bacteria of the animals will develop resistance to the antibiotics, nor is it known whether the farmer actually saves money on the deal because of the cost of the antibiotics, but "it is reasonable to expect a small margin of profit."

Sensitivity to Penicillin is Increasing

Our file on antibiotics is crammed full and running over with clippings on the dangers of widespread use of antibiotics. The November 9, 1953, issue of *Time* magazine carried the story of a meeting of the world's top authorities on antibiotics where Dr. Harry F. Dowling sounded the keynote by saying, "as each antibiotic is introduced, we hear first of miraculous cures, second of deleterious reactions and third of the appearance of resistant strains (of bacteria)." There was plenty of talk about the increasing number of serious or fatal reactions to antibiotics. Dr. Ethan Allen Brown of Boston called today's use of antibiotics "appalling." He said that it is misleading to speak only of patients who appear to have died instantaneously from reaction to antibiotics. There are more deaths which never make the headlines. Still more numerous are the reactions short of death. And finally, most frequent of all are the allergic reactions which are never reported anywhere because the patient did not die. He continued, "What the medical reports fail to stress is how many had wished themselves dead. Of these exquisitely sensitive-to-penicillin patients, I am one."

From the *Pittsburgh Press* for June 6, 1954, comes the news that antibiotics are now being used on plants—to combat hitherto incurable plant blights which have been destroying millions of dollars worth of crops. Terramycin and streptomycin are being used to cure "fireblight" in apple trees, for instance.

We found another yellowed clipping from the Kansas City *Star* for February 22, 1951, revealing that Dr. Alton Ochsner (whose book on smoking and lung cancer is making history) stated at a meeting that the incidence of blood clotting had doubled in the past 5 years, the chief reason for which was the use of the antibiotics which tend to increase the clotting tendency. "Because of penicillin and other infection-fighting drugs, the medical profession will have to find new methods to save lives from blood clots," said he.

Penicillin dog tags were proposed in all seriousness by the chief of an allergy clinic in New York in a statement released by the American Foundation for Allergic Diseases on December 22, 1953. Said Dr. Horace Baldwin, two out of every hundred patients now suffer penicillin reactions ranging from hives to high fever and severe joint pains that may last several months. Among the million or so Americans who suffer from asthma and the six million allergics the rate is considerably higher and shock and death may result from exposure to antibiotics. He suggested that dog tags be worn by persons known to be penicillin-sensitive.

Does your Milk Contain Penicillin?

This is but a smattering of the material on penicillin and the other antibiotics that we have in our files. Then we have a quote from *Food* for July, 1952, written by the director of the Express Dairy Company, London. Says he: "The general use of penicillin for combatting mastitis (in cows) from about 1945 onwards has resulted in considerable trouble in the cheese industry, due to the antagonistic effect of the residual penicillin in the milk used for starter cultures. Instances have been known where farms and factories have been forced to discontinue cheese-making. The same effect may occur with yogurt manufacture. Ordinary pasteurization has little effect on any penicillin-milk and even autoclaving (heating at high temperature and pressure) will not remove it."

We have not been able to find any investigation that has been done on the possible residues of cleaning fluids in milk. Of course, all the equipment involved in processing milk—from the milking machine right on down to the bottling machine—must be cleaned often and thoroughly. Since milk is a fluid in which bacteria can grow and flourish, the materials used for cleaning must be strong and antiseptic indeed. We suppose that each local dairy has its own cleaning methods. How much of the cleaning fluids remain in the milk? We have no way of knowing, but we think you should take this into account when you are adding up the pluses and the minuses where milk is concerned.

CHAPTER 36

An Unusual Milk Allergy

According to an article in the *British Medical Journal* for June 11, 1955, a woman was brought to a Bombay hospital with a history of rectal bleeding for 7 years. She had been operated on for both internal and external piles a number of years before. She passed blood every day. Her father and her son seemed to have allergic tendencies.

The hospital conducted the usual tests. The patient was apparently normal. All the blood tests, the heart, lung, digestive tract tests, the liver and spleen were normal. The doctors thought she might be inventing at least part of her story, for they knew that she had a most unhappy home life and thought she might simply want to stay on in the hospital to avoid some of her personal problems. However, there was no doubt of it—the bleeding was real.

It was decided that perhaps the patient was allergic to something.

According to Drs. F. P. Antia and S. H. Cooper who wrote the article, milk is the commonest allergen, so they decided to give her a diet free from milk. On November 20 she was put on fruit juice and water only. The bleeding stopped on November 22—for the first time in seven years. Two soft boiled eggs were added on November 25 and crackers on November 27, without any more bleeding resulting. On November 28, in addition to this diet, half a cup of milk with half a cup of tea twice a day was started. On November 30 the bleeding started again and continued until the milk was stopped on December 2. Then only fruit juice, eggs, crackers and mashed potatoes were given for two days, during which there was no bleeding. On December 5 three cups of milk were added to the diet and the next day bleeding recurred and continued until December 8. From then on the patient was given the regular hospital diet, *without milk*, and had no more difficulty.

Because her family was impatient to have her at home, the hospital could not undertake the lengthy task of de-sensitizing this patient to milk. But she was told how to do it at home. And some months later she wrote that she had been taking milk, beginning with one drop a day and gradually increasing the amount until she could safely use a little milk in her tea. The bleeding had not returned.

This story shows, we think, what can be accomplished quite simply in the way of determining which foods may be harming you. In this case, food from your diet. See if the condition clears up within a few days if you have some disorder that won't clear up, you can find out if some given food is causing it by simply doing as this patient did. Eliminate the food from your diet. See if the condition clears up within a few days or a week. Then eat some of the food again and see if the condition returns. If you have a genuine allergy to that particular food, you can determine it quite easily. In this case it was milk.

This does not indicate, certainly, that anyone who uses milk is going to develop bleeding. It does indicate that sometimes the most harmless-appearing food can produce frightening symptoms in susceptible persons. People *are* allergic to milk, we know, just as they are allergic to other foods. We have read some medical opinions that disagree with the statement that *more* people are allergic to milk than to any other food. But it seems that milk is, indeed, high on the list of allergens. So it should be considered as a possible cause of allergic symptoms.

CHAPTER 37

Milk and Alkalis Don't Mix

Ever hear of something called the Milk-Alkali Syndrome? Doctors put that mouth-filling name to a disorder that is often associated with stomach ulcer. Taking it apart, the phrase means just a certain condition that is apparently caused by taking too much milk and something alkaline.

In ulcer cases there is generally too much hydrochloric acid in the stomach. This is one of the digestive juices—absolutely necessary for good digestion. It is, of course, strongly acid. Minerals and water soluble vitamins like vitamin B and C must be mixed with plenty of hydrochloric acid in the stomach or they will not be absorbed. You also need it to digest protein.

However, there can be too much of a good thing. Some doctors think stomach ulcers cause too much hydrochloric acid; others think that too much of the acid is responsible for the ulcers. No one knows for sure. But at any rate, we do know that having ulcers generally means as well having too much hydrochloric acid for your own good. So doctors frequently prescribe alkaline substances to counteract the hydrochloric acid. Many ulcer diets have milk as their base, if not their sole item. You have probably known people who lived on milk and cream for at least several weeks while the doctor was treating their ulcers. And probably they were taking alkaline powders at the same time.

A Dangerous Treatment

Then, too, many patients take alkalies without their doctor's advising it. In the *Southern Medical Journal* for February, 1948, there is the story of a man—an ulcer patient—who took bicarbonate of soda at the rate of a third of a box a day! He did not drink milk, but he ate as much as a fourth to a half of a pound of cheese a day. What exactly took place in this man's digestive tract as he drank down the bicarbonate of soda followed by the cheese? (And remember, any other so-called "alkalizer" would have done just the same thing.)

The cheese is rich in calcium. But the alkalizer neutralizes the acid in the stomach so that the calcium cannot be utilized. Of course, all the B vitamins in the cheese are wasted, too. In the book, *Diseases of Metabolism*, edited by Garfield G. Duncan, M.D. (W. B. Saunders Company, 1952), we are told that calcium absorption is governed by 3 things: 1. Other substances in the diet. 2. Vitamin D and 3. The acidity of the intestine where the food must be digested. The acidity of the normal duodenum (the opening of the intestine) is from 2.3 to 7. That is very acid indeed. And the more acidity, the better the calcium is absorbed.

The higher the phosphorus content of the diet, the less calcium is absorbed. This is one reason why diets high in cereals tend to rob the body of calcium—for cereals contain lots of phosphorus. But so does milk. So what little calcium might be absorbed in these decidedly un-acid surroundings is cancelled out by the high phosphorus content of the milk.

So our poor patient gradually gets into a state where all the fine and necessary calcium which should have dissolved and gone into his blood stream where it could nourish nerves and cells, has not dissolved at all. It is collecting at various spots and what is actually happening to our patient is that he is gradually turning into limestone. He may get calcium deposits in his kidneys. Certainly all of the various minerals and vitamins whose functions are related to those of calcium in the body go out of balance. Magnesium, for instance, gets entirely out of control and much larger quantities of it than normal appear in the blood stream. Now all these various food elements are not just circulating around for lack of a better place to go, you know. Each of them has a number of jobs to perform in the body. And when one is thrown out of balance, it is bound to affect all the rest.

Patients Living on Milk and Alkali

In *Archives of Internal Medicine,* Vol. 95, p. 460, 1955, there is a report on 8 patients who had had ulcer symptoms for from many months to several decades. All but one consumed in excess of a quart of milk a day. Several took as much as 3 or 4 quarts. In addition, each of them took alkaline powders frequently. One patient estimated that he took as much as two and a half pounds of "sippy powders" a week. It was not unusual for the patients to state that for weeks or months they had lived on milk and alkaline powders.

In another article in *Annals of Internal Medicine,* Vol. 42, p. 324, 1955, several patients are discussed who have deposits of calcium in eye tissues, the tissues just underneath the skin, in the lungs and the walls of the arteries. Why do not the kidneys excrete the calcium harmlessly? It is not known why. Perhaps the kidneys have already been damaged. Usually as soon as the diet is stopped and all alkaline medicine is forbidden the kidneys return to normal and no permanent damage is done.

We have another suggestion as to why the part that calcium should be healthfully playing is so distorted under these abnormal circumstances. Vitamin C is destroyed in an alkaline medium. There is practically no vitamin C in a diet of milk to begin with, especially if the milk has been pasteurized or boiled. Whatever small amount happens to remain in the milk is promptly destroyed by the alkaline powders once it arrives in the stomach. We believe that vitamin C has a lot to do with the proper disposition of calcium in the body. We think that lack of vitamin C can cause kidney stones and deposits of calcium in the arteries. So it seems reasonable to suppose that when the diet contains not a bit of vitamin C, the calcium supply is going to get completely out of control in a very short time.

Medical Men Agree

As you have gathered by now we do not approve of milk and alkali diets for ulcer patients. It seems that the medical profession is rapidly coming to that conclusion, too. *Time* magazine for March 21, 1955, reported Dr. Edward Kessler as saying that "ulcer victims who swill milk and assorted alkalies can do themselves more harm than good." He had seen 3 patients, he said, who were petrifying themselves by clogging their kidneys with excess calcium. The danger from the treatment increases with the duration and degree of the self-medication, especially sodium bicarbonate which is, of course, baking soda.

The news that physicians are concerned about what may develop on the usual ulcer diet is encouraging. But we must not forget all those ulcer victims who prescribe for themselves and will continue to take medicines that "alkalize" them, along with enormous amounts of milk.

There is a large amount of research indicating that we human beings cannot have too much calcium in our diets, provided that other elements in the diet are in balance. In other words, you can take as much calcium as you can get, provided that everything is in order to use the calcium properly. You should have the right amount of phophorus in the diet, enough vitamin D and enough fat, too, for proper use of the calcium. Then vitamin C is also extremely important. The milk-bicarbonate diet contains very little vitamin D, plenty of phosphorus and fat. But, after the alkali has counteracted the natural stomach acid, can either the phosphorus or the fat be used by the body? The diet contains no vitamin C. We have read in medical journals of ulcer victims who eventually showed signs of scurvy (the disease of extreme vitamin C deficiency) after they had been on such a diet.

Taking bicarbonate of soda or any other "alkalizer" is extremely hazardous to health. You are bound to get into serious difficulty, for nothing will be properly digested or absorbed into the body unless there is some acid in the stomach. You need to keep a certain "alkaline balance," true. By this we mean that you should eat not only foods, such as meats, which cause an acid reaction in the body, but also plenty of fruits and vegetables which will adjust your alkaline balance.

CHAPTER 38

A Note on Homogenized Milk

Figure 2   Figure 3   Figure 4

Figure 2 shows a specimen of mother's milk which has been retained in the human stomach for 30 minutes, then regurgitated. Figure 3 is cow's milk, homogenized, which has been retained in the human stomach for 30 minutes, then regurgitated. In Figure 4 are the curds (regurgitated) from cow's milk—the standard pasteurized kind, which has not been homogenized.

As you can see, the curd from human mother's milk is soft, fine and dispersed. Produced by a 120-pound mother for her 6-pound baby, it seems apparent that the digestibility of this milk for the infant could not be improved upon. In Figure 4 are the curds of milk from a 1200-pound cow for her 96-pound calf. This milk is quite different from human mother's milk when it has been worked on for one-half hour in a human stomach.

In the second picture (Figure 3) are the curds of homogenized milk which approach more nearly the consistency of human milk. We do not think nearly enough research has been done on homogenization. If indeed it gives us milk whose curds are more nearly like those of human milk (as the pictures above would indicate) are we perfectly sure that nothing in the homogenization process changes the basic constitution of the milk?

CHAPTER 39

Miscellany on Milk

Detergents in milk are the subject of an editorial in the *Lancet* (Britain) for December 10, 1955. It seems that in regulation testing for the bacteria content of milk, inspectors found such an extremely low count that they could not explain it except on the basis of some disinfectant being added. The dairies said they had added nothing. But, of course, the utensils used had been washed with a detergent, so milk cans were tested and 12 per cent were found to have substances which "might have been of this nature."

As many readers know, detergents are practically impossible to remove from any metal or glass surface. This is the reason why glasses washed in detergent shine so—it's the layer of detergent left there that shines! How does it happen that no one has officially done something about checking on the possible contamination of milk with detergents? Says the *Lancet,* "Chemical technology is bounding forward at such a pace that new compounds whose properties are but half known are on the market within a short time of their discovery. Seldom has the buyer or the seller the scientific knowledge to form any estimate of the possible risk from some secondary action."

Is it possible that many of the recent reports of allergies and sensitivity to milk products might be the delayed effect of the traces of detergent they contain?

Antibiotics in Milk

Penicillin in milk is another headache for cheese producers, for doctors, for you and for me. Dr. Henry Welch, of the Food and Drug Administration, antibiotics division, found traces of penicillin in some of the 474 quarts of milk he tested in 1955. According to a press release from the Food and Drug Administration for February 22, 1956, trace amounts of the drug were found in 8 per cent of some 1700 milk samples from all sections of the country. No one could trace any ill effects to the antibiotic. But experts agree that they could create serious complications to milk-drinkers who are already super-sensitive to the drug.

Dr. C. C. Beck of Michigan State University is quoted in an undated newspaper clipping as saying at a dairy field men's conference that the low level of antibiotics in milk is building up a sensitivity to the drug. In other words, we suppose, if you are one of those people who do not have any adverse reactions from a dose of penicillin, you are likely to develop sensitivity to the drug through milk-drinking. Then, if you are given a dose of penicillin later, you might develop serious symptoms. Medical journals are constantly pointing out the ever-present danger of serious or even fatal reactions from all the penicillin being given indiscriminately for slight indispositions. They plead for less hasty use of the drug by doctors.

But what good will it do you to shun penicillin assiduously and avoid it when you have colds or minor infections, if you are then going to get daily doses of it in your food?

The penicillin in milk comes, says the FDA, from farmers using the milk from cows too soon after they have been treated with the drug for mastitis, or inflammation of the udder. The FDA has instituted an educational campaign to enlighten dairymen as to their obligations to protect the public so far as penicillin is concerned.

Some Infants Can't Take Milk At All

A mysterious blood disease came into the news recently when it was discovered that it is caused by a sensitivity to a certain substance in milk. *Galactosemia* attacks babies a few days after birth; they become ill with diarrhea, enlarged liver, loss of appetite and weight and jaundice. About half of them die within two to three weeks; those who live may be blind or imbeciles.

The cause of the disease was revealed by a team of Public Health scientists. It is this—the stricken children lack a certain enzyme in the blood which is necessary for changing galactose to glucose. Galactose is a form of sugar existing in milk. It must be changed into glucose before the body can use it. Normal children have the enzyme that does the job. Children who lack the enzyme can be put on a milkless diet and will come back to good health almost miraculously. Scientists are now working to perfect a simple test for the disease.

Is Milk the Universal Antidote?

Milk as the universal antidote is called a myth in a new German medical journal published in English—*German Medical Monthly*, for February, 1956. In an article on treating poisoning in children, Dr. L. Lendle tells us some physicians still accept the popular lay remedy of milk as a universal antidote for poisoning. He gives an instance of a doctor who gave a child milk to counteract a poison that had been injected into the child's veins!

Milk treatment for poisoning, he says, probably comes from ancient times when every kind of milk including asses' milk, mare's milk, camel's milk or mothers' milk was used as medicine for various illnesses, including poisoning. One can consider using milk if there is local corrosion of the throat or stomach from some corroding poison, he says, but in the case of poisons which should be quickly eliminated from the stomach to save the patient's life, milk may make matters worse, for the protein particles in milk, having absorbed the poison may break down in the process of digestion and release the poison again. Just another superstition about milk going the way of all superstition!

An All-Milk Diet Is Hazardous

The extremely dangerous practice of keeping babies on an all-milk diet for lengthy periods of time is shown by a story which appeared in *Time* for May 21, 1956. A girl two years old who lived on milk and pablum became desperately ill with an ailment no doctor could diagnose. Finally a blood expert was called in who found that the little girl's blood was very low in copper. There is a certain kind of anemia which is cured only by adding copper as well as iron to the diet. Milk is low in both iron and copper—so low that a diet consisting chiefly of milk, or even milk with a few vegetables and "vitamins" added, is likely to bring on this form of anemia.

We mentioned "vitamins" in quotation marks above because we believe most mothers give their children synthetic vitamins these days. And it is noteworthy that synthetic vitamins *could not prevent this child's illness.* Natural food supplements, rich in iron and copper as well as natural vitamins, would probably have prevented the anemia even if the child had been living on milk alone. However, the story aptly illustrates how important it is for all of us, children included, to get a well-rounded diet and not to depend on one food to supply us with everything we need. Certainly any mothers who are raising their infants chiefly on milk should make a point of adding other foods immediately and of giving their children natural food supplements rather than synthetic preparations. Brewer's yeast, wheat germ oil, rose hips, bone meal, kelp and fish liver oil are just as good for your children as they are for you.

Ulcer Patients, Beware!

Another warning against the use of milk and alkalis for ulcer patients comes in the *Archives of Internal Medicine,* Vol. 95, pp. 460-468, 1955. Say the two authors, the prolonged treatment of peptic ulcer with milk and alkalis may cause a hypercalcemic state—that is, a state in which too much calcium is floating around in places where it is not needed. Other features of the milk-alkali disease are kidney trouble, uremia and occasionally alkalosis—that is, a too-alkaline system.

The general idea behind the milk-alkali diet for ulcer patients is, of course, to reduce the amount of acid in the patient's stomach. The alkali is supposed to do this. The milk provides food and also soothes the stomach tissues, since it is a bland and neutral food. What actually happens is that in such a diet the sufferer gets none of the terribly important substances so necessary for digesting and absorbing calcium. And the stomach acid, essential for preservation of B vitamins and vitamin C, is made alkaline so that none of these important vitamins survive the trip through the stomach.

In addition, such a diet contains practically no vitamin C to begin with, so ulcer patients living on the milk diet are quite likely to develop scurvy—a disease that we have known how to cure for hundreds of years—with fresh raw fruits and vegetables! It is our private belief that eventually researchers will discover that the reason calcium accumulates in the system on the milk-alkali diet is that there is no vitamin C present to make certain the calcium is well handled by the body.

Cavities Caused By Milk

Cavities in children's teeth are caused by milk, according to a theory by a Danish dentist. Dr. E. A. Bruun, who practices on the dairy-farming island of Bornholm, has invited further investigation of his observations that farm children have uniformly bad teeth, while children in fishermen's families, who drink less milk, have teeth much freer from cavities.

Dr. Bruun published his theory privately and circulated the paper to fellow dentists and the Danish Dental Association. He first hit on his theory some years ago when he was treating the staff of a large Swedish dairy. He was struck by the extreme decalcification of their teeth, which had gone beyond anything he had ever observed. Investigating further, he found that the dairy employees drank milk in large quantities. He asked some of them to stop drinking milk and claims that after about six months the teeth of the non-milk drinkers showed improvement, while those of the others were as bad as ever. (This information came from the New York *Herald Tribune*.)

A somewhat similar theory is put forth by a French dentist in an article in *Revue francais odontostomat* for June-July, 1956. Says Dr. R. Dubois-Prevost, milk must be pasteurized or boiled before given to children, because it contains microorganisms which are harmful to the teeth. These bacteria are added to those already present in the mouth. Research on the prevention of decay reveals, says our French dentist, that excessive milk consumption parallels an increase in decay. He then suggests something we cannot agree with—that after drinking milk, children should rinse their mouths with fluoridated water which will, he says, counteract the effects of the bacteria.

DDT Contamination

Reports William Longgood in the New York *World Telegram* for June 3, 1957: A DDT spraying plane recently sprayed by mistake the farm of an organic farmer who, of course, uses no insecticides. Previous laboratory tests have shown that milk from this farmer's cows contain absolutely no trace of DDT. But, within 24 hours after the farm was sprayed, milk from his 75-head herd was contaminated with the spray. A wire sent by the farmer to the Secretary of Agriculture said in part: "How can the Department of Agriculture justify its position when it contaminates dairy farms in a wholesale fashion not only in the three million acres under attack (for gypsy moth) but also outside the intended area where they are not even supposed to be sprayed. Since DDT is extremely persistent once deposited on pastures or elsewhere, many years must elapse before the milk from our dairy farm will again be free from contamination." What do you suppose the DDT content of milk is among dairy farmers who regularly use DDT on fields, garden, cattle feed and barns?

Misuse of Calcium

According to the *Lancet,* famous British medical magazine, for February 23, 1957, dried milk, such as the government provides in England for infants and children, is relatively low in the essential fatty acids and rich in vitamin D. This might, according to Dr. Hugh Sinclair of Oxford University, lead to the wrong use of calcium in the bodies of infants. Such a consequence, goes on the *Lancet* editorialist, "might be regarded as a physiological penalty for our persistence in feeding babies with milk designed farm herd, one can easily see that the goiter-causing factor would assume harmful proportions.

Radioactive Substances in Milk

A question to the editor of the *British Medical Journal* for December 28, 1957, asks what ill effects in infants, children and adults might result from the ingestion of milk contaminated by radioactive iodine. We do not know why such a question should be asked, but we suppose almost anything might be contaminated with radioactive substances in these enlightened and advanced times in which we live. And we know that several quite serious accidents at atomic installations in Britain have caused considerable alarm. Whether or not this question applies to such an emergency we do not know. The editor replies with a calculation which indicates that a child drinking about a quart of milk a day might get about 1/10 of the minimal toxic dose. He continues, "However such calculations are far from precise and hence the need for caution." We say amen.

Milk as a Cause of Goiter

An interesting piece from the *Medical Journal of Australia* for November 2, 1957, indicates that in districts where cows may be feeding on certain weeds, their milk can contain a "goiterogenic factor"—that is, something which may produce goiter. The weed is called *chou-moellier* in Australia. We could not find it in our garden encyclopedia. But it seems, according to the *Journal* that several other weeds—all of the *cruciferous* family—are also involved. The *crucifers,* incidentally, include those plants whose flowers have 4 petals placed opposite one another—cabbage, turnips and radishes are all in this family, as well as the weeds, shepherd's purse, swine cress, crowsfoot and longstorkbill.

We know that eating a diet consisting almost exclusively of plants of this family will cause goiter in human beings. Conditions of war and famine have shown this. The Australian cows, during seasons when the weeds of this family are plentiful, eat large quantities of them and it is believed that this is responsible for the goiters which are caused in children who drink the milk.

It seems unlikely that milk from a dairy, coming as it does from many different farms, would be dangerous as a possible carrier of this goiter-causing factor. But on farms where weeds of this family grow and are widely eaten by milk cows, and where all the milk consumed comes from the farm herd, one can easily see that the goiter-causing factor would assume harmful proportions.

A Famous Nutritionist Speaks

Is milk a proper food for healthy adults? According to *Time* magazine for December 30, 1957, a change made in the dining halls at Yale University started a chain reaction that finally got as far as New York City's famous nutritionist, Norman Jolliffe. Instead of one big glass of milk per meal, dining room officials at Yale issued a smaller glass but allowed the

[150]

students as many refills as they wanted. Partly to protest against a fancied inconvenience, but largely out of orneriness (says *Time*) the undergraduates started on milk-drinking binges. Many went back for 4 or 5 glasses; some drank as much as 20.

This brought a warning from the director and assistant director of the university's public health department: "The normal, healthy individual can readily precipitate kidney stone formation by the simple ingestion of excessive mineral salts (in) ice cream, cheese, butter, and milk . . . a good rule of thumb to insure ample dilution: two glasses of water for each glass of milk."

We agree with *Time's* comment that the formation of kidney stones is a complicated procedure involving much more than how much calcium one gets in his diet. However, the final authority on this matter was eventually consulted—Dr. Jolliffe, one of the leading nutritionists in our country today. Said Dr. Jolliffe: "With an adequate diet, milk is not necessary for an adult."

Milk's Value Questioned

Two nutritionists of world-wide fame, R. A. McCance and E. W. Widdowson of Cambridge University, reporting on some feeding experiments that they have conducted recently have something to say about the importance of milk in the diet. These two researchers have written many books and are quoted widely everywhere throughout nutrition literature. Their point of view has generally been that of the conservative nutrition school which usually goes out of its way to praise milk as the perfect food. However, according to the *Lancet* for July 30, 1955, their latest observation led these two professors into a little different path of thinking.

They say: "We have naturally reexamined the papers describing the experiments upon which current opinions about the value of milk had been based. A number of these had been made without any supplement having been given to the control group. In some, basal diet was unknown and uncontrolled, while in others the tests had been sponsored by people interested in the sale of milk. In Corry Mann's (1926) pioneer experiments the important ingredient may have been the calcium in the milk, not the proteins or vitamins. We were forced to conclude that the intrinsic and almost mysterious value of milk had not been demonstrated so conclusively as we had supposed."

Note, please, they do not say milk should not be taken. They do not say that it is an unhealthful food. But they do say that apparently its "intrinsic and almost mysterious" value has not been demonstrated conclusively. And they do point out the fact that experimentation with milk-feeding may turn out in one way or another depending on who is sponsoring (that is, paying for) the experiment. Is it people who are interested in furthering the sale of milk or not?

Allergies to Milk Sugar

We want to mention again the uncommon congenital disease—that is, babies are born with it—called "galactosemia" which means an inability to

[151]

digest properly the galactose, or milk sugar, that occurs in milk. There is apparently nothing that can be done, except to see that the baby gets no milk. Not at all difficult for an adult, but just how are you going to accomplish this with an infant? Soybean milk is, of course, one answer and is the food most commonly prescribed, we believe, in this country for infants who cannot take milk.

In the *Lancet* for July 9, 1955, we found a letter to the editor in which 3 doctors from the University of Manchester, Department of Child Health, advised a diet for children suffering from galactosemia. It consisted of a gruel made of milk-free cereal, water, sugar, egg, salt and "a pinch of bicarbonate of soda." This demonstrates the errors one can fall into when he attempts to make up a substitute for a purely natural product like milk. Why sugar? Why salt? And, most horrifying of all, why bicarbonate of soda? There is sugar in milk, of course, but it is not like the refined white drug you buy at the grocery store. Why not add honey to your gruel, sirs? Bicarbonate of soda can accomplish only one thing—alkalinize the stomach fluids of the poor baby so that no food will digest.

Dermatologist Criticizes Both Bread and Milk

From Fort Worth, Texas, a dermatologist spoke up recently, pointing the finger of suspicion at two favorite foods and asking how much their consumption might have to do with skin disease. Dr. Arthur G. Schoch of Dallas, told Texas family doctors assembled in Forth Worth that he has successfully treated many skin disease patients by removing bread from their diet and others by removing milk. He reported that many of his patients with severe chronic skin disease had improved markedly within a few weeks after they quit eating bread and chemically treated flour. Said he, "On the hypothetical assumption that bread and flour, as consumed in this country, contain one or more noxious products that could be a major or contributing cause of illness, we are continuing our investigations along this line."

Milk is banned for his patients suffering from penicillin reaction, he went on. How does penicillin get into their diets? The veterinarian puts it there, said Dr. Schoch, by injecting it into infected udders of dairy cows. The cows continue to excrete penicillin in their milk for about 14 days after the treatment.

So widespread is this practice, said Dr. Schoch, that much of the milk consumed over the country contains penicillin. He recalled a Wisconsin cheese-maker who purchased a lot of milk which contained so much penicillin that it wouldn't turn sour, hence wouldn't make cheese.

Speaking of bread, Dr. Schoch explained that his patients' trouble comes from the interaction of flour-refining chemicals and the protein of wheat. For 25 years or more prior to 1947, he said, nitrogen trichloride was the primary maturing agent used by millers of white flour. About 1947 it was shown that this chemical produced convulsions and death in dogs. The Food and Drug Administration advised its reduction "to a minimum." In its place we now have chlorine dioxide used for bleaching and "maturing" flour. In England recently, according to Dr. Schoch, in a human case of widespread dermatitis coupled with mental depression, the causative agent was found to be bread made from flour treated with nitrogen trichloride and also bread made from flour treated with chlorine dioxide. *In this patient one chemical was as harmful as the other.*

In Dr. Schoch's own practice, he said, patients with one skin disease in particular have shown improvement when they omit bread from their diets. The disease is *lupus erythematosus.* We add that, although white bread contains more of this particular chemical, it has been shown in one experiment at least that store-bought whole wheat bread is less healthful than white bread, probably because of the many chemicals needed to keep whole wheat flour from spoiling.

An Old Court Decision on Raw Milk

Here is a quote from the decision of the supreme court of Missouri in 1926 relating to a proposed ordinance prohibiting the sale of raw milk. Said the judge: "A great volume of evidence was offered regarding the relative qualities of raw milk and pasteurized milk. A large number of practicing physicians, chemists, bacteriologists and users of milk were sworn. The evidence conclusively shows that pasteurization altered the character of the milk, and the testimony of far the greater number of physicians and bacteriologists who testified was that pasteurization impairs its quality; that it destroys some of the vitamins in the milk and impairs others; that it destroys the lactic acid which causes milk to sour; that souring is a process of self-preservation and lactic acid is an important element in counteracting pernicious bacteria; that pasteurization disintegrates the salts, such as calcium, iron and phosphates, causes them to lose their organic quality and makes them more difficult, if not impossible, to assimilate; that pasteurization caused constipation and indigestion particularly among babies and children; that it breaks down the enzymes, though other physicians said there was sufficient of that element in the digestive organisms of persons who drink milk. It was shown that doctors generally require raw milk for ailing babies and children; that children who could not flourish on pasteurized milk usually improved in health and flourished on raw milk. There was other evidence to show that one reason for the satisfactory healthfulness of raw milk is that it increases the vitality and resistance of a child because it is easier to assimilate; that the destruction of pathogenic germs by pasteurization was more than counterbalanced by the superior quality of raw milk.

"On the other hand, a few physicians of eminence testified that the digestibility of milk was improved by boiling. The evidence was also conflicting as to whether pasteurization, by which milk is raised to 60 degrees centigrade or 140 degrees Fahrenheit and kept at that temperature for 30 minutes impaired the vigor of pathogenic bacteria. A good many bacteriologists testified that, while it impaired, it did not destroy them; that their destruction depended upon their vitality. Some of them are more vigorous individuals than others and would survive more vigorous treatment.

"In addition to the professional evidence offered, the relators offered the testimony of a number of mothers and other raisers of children, and they uniformly testified that children who were not healthful when fed on pasteurized milk were healthful when fed raw milk, and were often cured of ailments when they took to raw milk. The respondents made no attempt to counteract that testimony, but contended it was unimportant coming from nonprofessional source. But it was the opinion of several physicians that actual experience, particularly clinical experience, was more valuable than laboratory tests in determining the effects of milk upon the system." The court decided that the ordinance was in conflict with the law and should be invalidated.

CHAPTER 40

Nutritive Substitutes for Milk

More and more frequently parents are discovering in their children the inability to handle cow's milk. But how, they wonder, will the child ever get along without it? The parents are victims of an eternal campaign waged by dairies and Public Health officials to convince us all that a quart of milk per day is vital and that no child can grow up without drinking his quota. We have shown evidence many times which proves the contrary.

Further testimony occurs in *Modern Nutrition* (February, 1959) in which Dr. Irvine McQuarrie, Head of the Department of Pediatrics at the University of Minnesota points out that many civilizations simply do not have access to milk of any kind, once the child has been weaned, so substitutes must be found. It's only a matter of analyzing the food values of milk and seeing that the child gets them from another source. For example, the main value of milk is as a source of calcium, phosphorus, some B vitamins and protein. The Eskimos, who don't have milk, meet these needs with fresh eggs from wild or domesticated birds, intestines and meat from warm-blooded animals and fish containing small bones. The food values of milk, and then some, are all there.

Protein Alone Is Not Enough

It is important that no single nutrient be missing when we substitute for milk so that feeding a child lean meats, finely chopped, as a milk substitute, would not be enough. Rich as lean beef, lamb or liver might be in protein, iron and B vitamins, they do not offer enough calcium, phosphorus, magnesium, fat or carbohydrate. These, too, are essential. Without the minerals, fats and carbohydrates normal body growth is not supported.

In experiments with young rats bone development could not continue beyond 10 to 15 days on protein and B vitamins alone.

Dr. McQuarrie worked out a formula that will assure mothers of children who do not drink milk, for one or another reason, that they are giving these youngsters proper nourishment. It is as follows: ½ cup strained beef, ½ teaspoon of veal bone ash (bone meal), 1 level table-spoon of soy oil, 2 tablespoons of honey, 1 heaping tablespoon of rice. Enough water should then be beaten into the mixture with a blender or an egg beater to bring the entire mixture to a pint volume, and this is nutritionally equal to one pint of cow's milk. Notice Dr. McQuarrie's use of bone meal in the formula. He characterizes bone meal (veal bone ash) as a "nearly complete mineral supplement because of its content of nutritionally significant trace elements as well as calcium and phosphorus which are present in suitable proportions. The importance of traces of copper, manganese, nickel and fluorine is already fully recognized by nutritionists."

Variations Possible

While the formula suggested by Dr. McQuarrie is a handy device for assuring proper nutrition in an infant, it is obvious that many common variations are possible so long as bone meal is included as a source of calcium and other minerals. The protein, carbohydrates, fats and vitamins are available from many good foods aside from beef, soy oil and honey, but a well-balanced mineral supplement, as complete as bone meal, is hard to find.

We have gone into much detail on our reasons for opposing the use of milk in those past early childhood. Allergies, excessive tallness and antibiotic content are only a few of the reasons for our objections. Dr. McQuarrie mentions the many types of allergy which can make milk intolerable. He also details the symptoms of galactosemia, a congenital disorder which interferes with the body's proper use of carbohydrates and is manifest in the most alarming signs. For example, the baby shows a fine appetite for a regular milk formula, but fails to grow; eye trouble that might result in cataract also occurs. One can also expect galactosemia to lead to anemia, jaundice, enlargement of the liver and arrested mental development. When the child is taken off milk and put on a lactose-free diet, the change is remarkable. If serious physical changes have not already developed any tendency toward them is immediately reversed. The child simply must stop drinking milk in order to recover.

Other nutritive substitutes for milk include soybean milk and Tahini milk which is a milk made from ground sesame seeds. Tahini milk appears to us to be an excellent substitute for milk in the diet because of its extremely high content of calcium.

We mean by these suggestions to emphasize once more the fact that milk is not indispensable. Many people have developed through childhood into healthy, well-nourished adults without its help. Nor are the dangers it presents to be ignored. Get your calcium through bone meal or homogenized whole bone, and eat a high protein vitamin-rich diet. You will be getting the best milk has to offer and not chance its ill effects.

CHAPTER 41

Yogurt

Yogurt is probably the most popular of all so-called health foods. Many people who are not at all health conscious eat it. Supermarkets sell large quantities of it from their dairy section to shoppers who simply like the taste of it, with no consideration as to its nutritional value. And why not? Yogurt is delicious and has an appetizing appearance. It is served cold and has the look and texture of very firm whipped cream. The taste is tangy and smooth, on the order of satiny buttermilk. When served with raw fresh fruit or vegetables, it is a gourmet course. It can also be combined with chopped onions or chives to make an excellent spread or dip. And it is low in calories—about 330 calories per pint.

There's nothing new about yogurt but the bright-colored containers it is packaged in nowadays. In some form or another yogurt has been a familiar food in many parts of the world since Biblical times.

What is Yogurt?

Basically, yogurt is simply soured milk prepared a certain way. This "certain way" was first investigated scientifically by Metchnikoff in the nineteenth Century. In conducting tests and experiments with a Bulgarian drink called *yahourth,* he isolated a number of organisms, but it was soon apparent that the most important one was a strong, lactic acid-producing one, since called lacto-bacillus bulgaris, for its Bulgarian origin.

Very close to yogurt is another soured milk preparation known as acidophilus milk. It looks and acts as yogurt does, but the taste is not nearly so pleasant. For this reason acidophilus milk has not been able to match yogurt's popularity. However, it has been discovered that acidophilus has the power of affixing itself to the wall of the stomach and exerting its good influence on the contents of the stomach for a longer time. In an attempt to combine the desirable qualities of both, a very small amount of acidophilus has been introduced into some yogurts. This blend retains the flavor of yogurt, plus the staying power of acidophilus.

If you are wondering what yogurt can do for you, here are the words of Drs. J. G. Davis and D. Latto as printed in the *Lancet* for February 2, 1957: ". . . there is considerable evidence that for some complaints (e.g. gastro-enteritis, colitis, constipation, biliary disorders, flatulence, migraine, nervous fatigue) cultured milks, and especially acidophilus milk, can be extremely valuable."

Although we believe that milk is a vastly overrated food, yet we feel a responsibility to report on a food like yogurt, even though milk is its prime component. Yogurt has all of the advantages that milk has, and is without several of milk's disadvantages.

The *Lancet* article quoted above tells us that the digestive problem presented by ordinary milk for some babies and older people is absent in yogurt. The curds formed by yogurt and acidophilus milk are much finer than those of ordinary milk. The difference in digestibility is best shown by the fact that milk is only 32 per cent digested after an hour in the digestive tract, while 91 per cent of the yogurt has been digested in the same amount of time!

Another of the less wholesome effects of regular milk is the allergic reaction experienced by many who drink it. A large percentage of the people who show an allergy to milk are able to tolerate yogurt with no ill effect whatsover. Science has blamed allergic reactions on the introduction of foreign protein into a blood stream which for some reason cannot deal with this stranger as easily as it should. The struggle that goes on is, then, the "reaction" a victim of allergies experiences. The yogurt organism destroys protein molecules in milk, thus eliminating the source of the problem.

How Yogurt Functions in the Digestive Tract

One of the stomach's prime tools in digestion is hydrochloric acid. This acid is so powerful it can break down the solids ingested in a normal meal very quickly. Yogurt bacteria convert the lactose in milk into lactic acid and this reaction continues in the stomach for as long as the converting bacteria can be retained there. This acid supplements the action of the hydrochloric acid in the stomach, easing digestion in perfectly natural, drugless fashion. Older people might note this, especially since it is known that the body's production of hydrochloric acid decreases with age. It is in this function of cultured milk that one can appreciate the staying power of acidophilus bacillus. It remains in the stomach, performing this service long after the cultured milk itself has been eaten and digested. Furthermore, this bacillus helps to combat any imbalance that might occur in the intestinal flora of the stomach after prolonged use of antibiotics such as penicillin, by mouth. (*Lancet*, November 24, 1956.)

An article on yogurt in *Food* for July, 1952, by John G. Davis, Ph.D., D.Sc., who is technical director of Express Dairy in London, England, says that yogurt's therapeutic effects lie "in its reducing putrefaction of the bowel, and possibly in other effects in metabolism." In almost every statement we read on the effects of yogurt, its beneficial effect on the intestinal tract and bowel function was mentioned.

In the *Journal of the American Medical Association*, November 11, 1955, there is an interesting history of group therapy with yogurt. One hundred and ninety-four hospital patients suffering with constipation, who were being cared for in wards and had typical geriatric ills (no gravely ill patients were included), were treated with a combination of prune whip and yogurt. The average age of these people was 71.6 years and 46 of them were diabetic.

During the period of the combination yogurt-prune whip, no laxatives were required for 95.8 per cent of the patients. They also showed improvement in skin tone and diabetic ulcers. Further there was a general improvement in morale and there were fewer requests for extra food.

Dr. Raffe, in his piece in the *Lancet* referred to above, tells of 20 consecutive cases of gastro-enteritis in babies under 6 months of age at The Royal Liverpool Babies Hospital. All samples of their stools showed the presence of pathogenic (disease-causing) organisms. Yogurt was administered, after a course of antibiotic treatment. In 3 weeks the pathogenic organisms were gone and had been replaced by lacto-bacilli which showed up in the stool. Babies also respond to the use of yogurt in treating infantile dyspepsia, diarrhea and constipation. The success of treating infants with yogurt might indicate that there is a problem created for them by the use of uncultured cow's milk.

Belching, stomach rumbling and flatulence are also said to be remedied with the use of yogurt. The article in *Food* (July, 1952) definitely states, however, that for cases such as those just mentioned, a prolonged trial is essential. The suggested dosage is at least ½ pint of yogurt per day for a month.

Making Yogurt

The use of yogurt is economical. It can be made at home in this way: Fresh milk is boiled to reduce it, cooled to 72 to 77 degrees Fahrenheit, the bacillus is added, kept at room temperature for about 18 hours and then chilled and ready to serve.

Care must be taken to be sure the mixture is not jarred in any way during curdling, lest the whey and curds separate.

Sometimes yogurt and other lactic acid milks are warmed slightly to cause the separation of the curds from the whey. The separated curds are called pot cheese or cottage cheese. The remaining yellowish liquid is whey. Whey is, therefore, the plasma part of milk—whole milk modified by the lactic acid culture, with, of course, the curds and the butterfat removed.

In dehydrated form whey has all the advantages of yogurt and the other lactic acid milk, without any of the disadvantages of whole milk. Dried whey, when dehydrated without excess heat, contains 20 times the mineral of liquid milk and 50 times as much lactose or milk sugar as yogurt or buttermilk. Lactose is a valuable food element, for it acts more rapidly than any other food to change the intestinal flora to beneficial ones, and to combat any harmful ones which may be present.

Do We Recommend Yogurt?

No, we are not changing our position on milk, we still feel that if one can get one's nutrients in some other food or foods, one should do so, to avoid the unwelcome effects of regular milk. True, yogurt is basically milk, but we are convinced that the changes wrought in its composition by the culture mitigate many of the bad features of milk, such as poor digestibility and allergies in some cases, and offer many excellent ones, such as increased benign intestinal flora and decreased bowel putrefaction. Also, yogurt contains all of the food values that were in the milk from which it was made.

As for making yogurt a part of the daily diet, we are not inclined to think that this is necessary. But should a difficulty arise in the digestive area, yogurt certainly sounds like a better remedy than the seltzers, laxatives and other patent medicines so commonly used these days. At least yogurt is a natural food.

We don't think yogurt is the remedy for everything. We think it might bring with it some of the problems plain milk brings to those who have difficulty with milk. But it is not simply milk. It has unique properties that cannot be ignored. We cannot recommend any milk product without the reservations our research on milk impressed on us, and we do not recommend yogurt unconditionally. We think it is a food which has merit.

Try it. Observe its effect on you over a period of weeks. If it seems to be beneficial to you, keep using it by all means. If you notice any allergic manifestations, stop the yogurt for a while to see if the symptoms persist.

CHAPTER 42

Additional Information
on Dairy Products

Diseased Eggs

Watch out for eggs with blotchy, enlarged yolks, says *Consumers' Research Bulletin* for October, 1957. The cause, according to tests at Cornell University, is a medicinal feed ingredient, nicarbazin, designed to control a certain disease in chickens.

Radioactivity in Milk

The Ohio Dairy Products Association was warned by the Editor of the *American Milk Review* that the biggest challenge to the dairy industry's public relations staff is the admitted presence of radioactivity in today's milk. He urged the dairy industry to fight "scare headlines" with *facts*. Since the facts are that the world's greatest authorities on radiation are appalled and horrified at the amount of radioactivity we are exposed to at present and the prospect of its steady increase, it's a little difficult to know just what weasel-words can be used to lull the public into not worrying about radioactivity in food. The only answer, of course, is an immediate and world-wide cessation of all atomic tests.

[159]

Breast Milk Best for Babies

For those who insist that milk is milk, whether cow's, goat's or human, we suggest their reading a paragraph in *Science News Letter* for October 20, 1956. Under the title, "Mother's Milk Good Because of Enzymes," we are informed that human mother's milk contains protein-digesting enzymes in excess of 4 to 5 times the amount found in cow's milk. These facts came to light while Armour and Company of Chicago were conducting experiments to improve the digestibility of cows' milk for babies. As a result the experimenters found that the low-curd tension of mother's milk could be approximated by adding animal pancreas enzymes to cow's milk. We use the term "approximated" with good reason. We feel that Nature has implanted certain life-giving ingredients in human milk that cannot be duplicated or imitated by scientists, no matter how they rearrange the composition of Old Bossy's output. The differences found in the make-up of the milks of various species only serve to illustrate again and again that the milk of an animal is suited best to the offspring of the same animal, and no other.

SECTION 5.

Fruits

The attractiveness, flavor and food value of fresh fruits should place them high on the preferred list of anybody's daily menu. They are an excellent source of vitamins and minerals and they have in them the natural sweetness that makes an excellent dessert and a healthful, satisfying snack. The variety of fruits available to us in these days of quick transportation and refrigeration makes it possible for almost anyone to have his favorite fruit all year round. So eat all you can.

CHAPTER 43

Apples

Winesap, Delicious, Rome Beauty, Russet—they are names to conjure with! Since the earliest days of history, apples have been one of man's favorite foods and deservedly so. Here is a fruit we can recommend without reservations. Whether you are young or old, sick or well, reducing or trying to gain weight, apples are good for you. The natural sugars in apples are easily digested. And apples do not have such a high sugar content as some fruits such as grapes, figs, dates, and prunes, etc. In green apples there is no sugar, but starch, which is converted to sugar as the fruit ripens. A fully ripe apple contains little or no starch.

Apples have been used as medicine by physicians for many years. In cases of infant diarrhea apple pulp alone given with no other food resulted in remarkable cures. On the other hand, the laxative qualities of the apple are well known and stubborn cases of constipation often yield to this same prescription of apple pulp, or scraped apple. Scientists do not know which ingredient of the apple is responsible—is it the acid that detoxifies the system in cases of diarrhea or is it the pectin of the apple that solidifies watery stools? Any one of the ingredients of the apple tried separately does not have this same good effect, so we must believe that there is something else in these crisp, juicy beauties that is so very beneficial for the digestive tract as a whole.

Apples May Solve the Overweight Problem

Someone on a reducing diet may find that raw apples will solve most of his problems. One small apple contains only 64 calories, in spite of its sweet taste. (An avocado contains well over 500.) The bulk of an apple is hunger-satisfying. Reducers should eat apples between meals instead of pining for chocolate bars they may not have. An apple, or perhaps, two, eaten before dinner does such an excellent job of satisfying hunger that you can easily pass up all those tasty dishes the rest of the family is eating, which are not on your diet. But beware of the treacherous apple pie, or even applesauce or baked apple. You obtain all the splendid vitamins and minerals there are in a raw apple, when you eat it raw. But when you cook it, you lose these food elements. Then, too, you must add sugar and up goes your calorie count! So, taken altogether, apple pie, no matter how good it smells coming out of the oven, is a worthless kind of food compared to a raw apple!

Acid and Vitamin Content of Apples

For some reason, possibly their acid content, apples aid the body in absorbing iron from food, which is an important factor, considering our widespread national anemia. In addition, tests have shown that the de-calcifying effect of apples is less than that of any other food except carrots. In other words, all foods are apparently hard on one's teeth to a certain extent, but apples and carrots to a much less degree than any other foods. So eating an apple after a meal not only cleans one's teeth, but actually helps preserve the body's store of calcium.

The sunny side of an apple (that is, the side next to the sun while the apple is growing) contains more sugar and more vitamin C than the other side. The skin contains more vitamin C than the pulp. Apples lose a certain amount of food value in storage—especially vitamin C. Storage at 40 degrees Fahrenheit results in greater loss than storage at 32 degrees.

Insecticides on Apples

The only unpleasant thing about our delicious apples in present-day America is the very considerable residue of insecticides they may carry. For this reason we must sadly caution you to peel apples before you eat them. Even if you are cooking them, be sure to peel them, for cooking does not destroy the spray residue. Of course, if you possibly can, eat only organic-ally grown apples. If you live in the country, raise your own, of course. If you live in the city, try to find some farmer not too far away who is not using sprays and will sell you apples. Yes, even if you find a worm from time to time, a worm is a lot less of a menace than a couple of grains of lead and arsenic.

And remember, too, that vitamins and minerals protect you against the poisons in these sprays. So if you must buy commercially raised fruit, make doubly sure you take natural food supplements for vitamins and minerals.

Here is the vitamin and mineral content of apples, in terms of 100 grams. One small apple weighs 100 grams.

Calcium	6 milligrams
Phosphorus	10 milligrams
Iron	.3 milligrams
Copper	.10 milligrams
Vitamin A	90 International Units
Thiamin	.04 milligrams
Riboflavin	.02 milligrams
Niacin	.2 milligrams
Vitamin C	5 milligrams

CHAPTER 44

Which Apples for Vitamin C?

by Robert Rodale

Does an apple a day really keep the doctor away?

Yes, in many cases, it does. There is a lot of truth to that statement. Apples are very important to health because they are one of the most readily available sources of vitamin C. Human beings, guinea pigs and monkeys are the only creatures on this earth that do not manufacture their own vitamin C in their bodies, and if we and our monkey friends are to stay healthy we must get our minimum daily requirement of this important vitamin.

Although many people rely on apples to give them vitamin C, it is a fact that varieties of apples vary greatly in the amount of that vitamin they contain. You would have to eat five Delicious apples to get your minimum amount of vitamin C. But you could get the same amount by eating two Winesaps or one Baldwin.

Tomatoes and citrus fruits actually are richer sources of vitamin C than even the better varieties of apples, but vitamin C is so important to nutrition that it is important to have as many good sources in the diet as possible. Some people find the acid in citrus fruits objectionable, and tomatoes are available fresh for only a short time of the year. Canning and storage reduce vitamin C values in a fruit like the tomato.

The minimum daily requirement for vitamin C is 30 milligrams per day. But that amount is just sufficient to prevent scurvy. You can easily see that if you are even *close* to getting scurvy you are in bad shape. So we should all count on getting much more than 30 milligrams of C per day. Some doctors recommend 200 or 300 milligrams per day.

The New York Study

The most comprehensive study of the vitamin C content of different apple varieties was made by the New York Experiment Station in 1946. They found that a French apple, the Calville Blanc, was several times richer in vitamin C than any American apple. But the joker is that the Calville Blanc doesn't grow well at all in this country, and even when grown in Europe it doesn't taste particularly good.

There are several good U.S. apples that are quite a bit higher in vitamin C than the general run of fruit. If you are planning on setting out some trees, you should give careful consideration to these high-vitamin varieties. Best of the American types are Northern Spy, Baldwin, Yellow Newton and Winesap. Apples that are low in vitamin C are McIntosh, Jonathan and York

Imperial. Here is a list showing a selection of apple varieties rated according to their vitamin C content:

VARIETY	Ascorbic Acid (Vitamin C) Milligrams per hundred grams
Calville Blanc	35-40
Sturmer Pippin	29
Yellow Newton	16
Northern Spy	15-20
Baldwin	15-20
Winesap	10
York Imperial	8
McIntosh	4

You can see from that listing that there is a considerable difference in vitamin C values among different apples. However, when selecting varieties for a home planting it pays to consider whether the trees you want will grow well in your area. Yellow Newton, for example, is particularly adapted to the Shenandoah Valley region in Virginia, an important American apple area. It is not grown much commercially in other areas, but you might want to experiment with it in a home planting.

Baldwin is widely grown in the eastern United States. It is sensitive to the climatic extremes existing west of Lake Michigan; however, Northern Spy, another high-C apple, is also adaptable to the mid-continent and eastern region.

Northern Spy is an excellent dessert or eating apple, but is not too useful for cooking. Baldwin is just the reverse. It is good for making pies and apple sauce, but not too good for eating fresh. So by planting both of those trees you will get a good supply of both cooking and eating apples that are rich in vitamin C.

The Vitamin C Content of Apples

Tests have shown that most of the vitamin C in apples is right in or under the skin. The skin can contain 5 times as much of the vitamin as the flesh. It is also interesting that small apples are richer in vitamin C than large apples. Small apples have more area of skin per pound of fruit, and this greater percentage of skin is probably the cause of the higher vitamin C content.

One good thing about apples is that they lose very little of their vitamin C in storage. If stored at 36 degrees, Baldwin apples will lose no vitamin C over a period of 5 or 6 months. However, if the storage temperature gets up to 45 degrees, some of the vitamin will be lost.

Because there is such a considerable difference in the vitamin C content of different varieties of apples, we feel organic gardeners should give serious consideration to these superior varieties. After all, apples are grown for their food value, and we might as well get as much value as we can.

[166]

CHAPTER 45

Bananas

Yes, we have bananas, today. We have them in all kinds of diets, for infants, adults—stout and thin—and old people who have trouble with their digestion. Not so many years ago it was fondly believed that bananas were hard to digest. This was probably because the bananas were eaten before they were fully ripe, and their raw starch caused considerable digestive trouble, just as that of green apples does. Faintly green bananas look attractive and feel firm to the touch. When dark specs begin to appear on their yellow surfaces, we are inclined to turn them down as rotten. But a banana is not fully ripe until its skin shows brown specks. By then its starch has been changed into completely digestible fruit sugar.

They knew about bananas way back in history, for Alexander the Great found the people of India eating bananas in 327 B. C. Within the past few years bananas have been found to be a specific remedy for several infant diseases, such as celiac disease of which the outstanding symptom is diarrhea. It has also been discovered that bananas in the diet of infants result in better growth than is achieved with either apples or cereals. We have learned that people who are allergic to bananas can eat dehydrated bananas with no distress. Banana flour is sold as a substitute for wheat flour, tapioca, oatmeal, arrowroot and so forth. You can make bread from banana flour mixed with 5 per cent wheat flour.

An investigation was made of the suitability of bananas in the diet of elderly people. Even those who had never eaten bananas found that they felt well with a banana or two every day, had no trouble digesting them, enjoyed their flavor and were especially pleased with how easy they are to chew in comparison with other fruits.

The average-sized banana weighs about 100 grams, contains less than 100 calories, has an alkaline reaction in the body, as do most fruits, and, in addition, contains the following quantities of vitamins and minerals:

Calcium	8.	milligrams
Phosphorus	28.	milligrams
Iron	.6	milligrams
Copper	.21	milligrams
Manganese	640.	micrograms
Sodium	.5	milligrams
Vitamin A	430.	International Units
Vitamin B:		
Thiamin	.09	milligrams
Riboflavin	.06	milligrams

Niacin	.6	milligrams
Pyridoxine	300.	micrograms
Inositol	34.	milligrams
Biotin	4.	micrograms
Folic acid	95.	micrograms
Vitamin C	10.	milligrams
Vitamin E	.40	milligrams
Protein	1.2	grams
Fat	.2	grams
Carbohydrates	23.0	grams

You will find recipes in your cook book for baking or frying bananas It seems to us that there is actually less excuse for cooking a banana than for cooking any other fruit. So we would advise eating them raw. We have read a good many stories about gases used in ripening bananas commercially. So we would suggest that you buy them fairly green and ripen them yourself. The best way to do this is to keep them with little or no ventilation until they begin to color rapidly. Then keep them always at room temperature until they show the brown mottling which means they are ready to eat. Like other tropical fruits, bananas should not be kept in the refrigerator.

CHAPTER 46

The Nutritional Treasures
Bananas Hold

How would American industry fare by substituting a banana-break for the time-honored coffee-break allowed in so many plants? A couple of experiments recorded in the *Journal of the American Dietetic Association* give evidence that this would be a worthwhile switch in policy. In one issue (11:239, 1935) we read that when bananas were given as a mid-morning pick-up, reported illnesses decreased among industrial women workers. A later issue (15:435, 1959) described bananas, given to employees as a snack, as a definite factor in improving morale and decreasing absenteeism.

The explanation of this exceptional effect is due to the unique qualities of bananas, both in flavor and nutrition. They are able to satisfy the craving for "something sweet," that often signals the need for new energy. They have a rather high carbohydrate content, with plenty of starch and sugar, but unlike vitamin-destroying foods such as cake, candy, coffee, etc., all of these elements are contained in bananas in such a way that they work to benefit the body. The carbohydrate, for example, is not only highly digestible, but actually aids in the body's protein storage.

Low Calories and Full Ones

For all its bulk and appetite-satisfying quality, the banana has a low calorie count—about 88 calories for the average 6-inch banana. This makes it lower than a serving of cottage cheese, and only 3 calories more than the gelatin desserts whose major claim to fame is their low-calorie appeal to diet-conscious consumers.

More important than the number of calories a banana contains is the food value that comes with them. The banana's calories are not "empty," that is, lacking in any nutrients the way candy or soft drinks are. On the contrary, they are full of well-rounded nutrients, which work toward increased body health while they satisfy the appetite. Few foods can boast of a more varied list of nutrients, whether in the vegetable, fruit or meat category.

The B vitamins, so scarce in our usual diet of processed foods, are well represented in bananas. These are the vitamins upon which we depend for the proper bacterial climate in the intestines, as well as for the health of our nervous system. Pyridoxine, vitamin B_6, is present in values equal to that of calf's liver, and pantothenic acid is contained in amounts as high as in any other vegetables and fruits. Other B vitamins present in respectable amounts are thiamin, riboflavin, niacin and folic acid.

Vitamin C and Surgery

Vitamin C is present in amounts that approximate 1/5 of man's daily requirements in each banana. It is no wonder then that the fruit was considered essential as a nutritional supplement on ocean voyages long ago as a source of scurvy-preventing vitamin C. And today the value of bananas is recognized for surgical patients, both before and after the operations, for the vitamin C they contain which helps to prevent shock and promotes quick wound healing. The anti-constipation action of bananas is helpful for surgical patients who tend to have difficulties with bowel movements due to long confinement in bed.

Vitamin A is present in bananas in uniquely large amounts, and works toward maintaining the health of the mucous membranes, as well as the skin and the eyes.

The protein contained in bananas has been found to be free of allergenic properties, and includes 3 essential amino acids, lysine, tryptophane and methionine, present in what are considered to be significant quantities. Several unfortunate allergy victims have found that their diets must consist exclusively of bananas, for the protein contained in all other foods causes such a violent reaction with their systems that it could result in death.

[169]

Devoid or Undesirable Factors

Aside from being rich in desirable elements, bananas are almost devoid of undesirable ones. They contain minute amounts of sodium (.5 milligrams per 100 grams), which makes them ideal for inclusion in low-salt diets prescribed for kidney and heart cases, as well as those who are trying to lose weight. The fat content is minimal (.2 grams per 100 grams) and consists largely of the beneficial unsaturated fats. This fact qualifies bananas for inclusion in low-fat diets often prescribed for gall bladder cases. Bananas contain absolutely no cholesterol, a factor which will further recommend them to the diets given by many doctors to heart patients.

Bone-building calcium is present in the banana, and so is phosphorus. Iron occurs in quantities double that of the apple, and all of it, unlike the iron in some foods, can be used by the body in forming hemoglobin, the essential element in blood, the shortage of which causes anemia.

Bananas for Seniors

Bananas are really an ideal food for older people who tend to ignore basic dietary principles in favor of soft, mushy foods which are easy to chew, but often of very little nutritional value. In this circumstance bananas are the perfect answer. They offer enough calories to maintain weight, without the risk of obesity, they have good protein value, spare fat content, sufficient starch and carbohydrates to supply needed bulk, and much of the required minerals and vitamins. But best of all, there is no preparation involved with bananas. You simply peel them and eat them.

For some years the impression has persisted, and falsely, that bananas create a problem in digestion. Ross and Gardner, in the *Journal of the American Dietetic Association* (16:208, 1940) told of an experiment in a home for the aged in which 117 residents received one fresh, ripe banana daily for 16 to 30 days. They all said they enjoyed eating the fruit, and not one suffered from digestive disturbance.

A few words should be said about the condition of their ripeness when bananas are eaten. The best time to eat them is when they are yellow and flecked with brown. At this point they are sweetest and properly moist, with just the proper texture. As the banana grows riper, the starches are converted into energy-producing natural sugars, which, unlike refined sugars, are vital to the body. Bananas can be eaten when they are green, but then they are eaten as a starchy vegetable, much like a potato, and should be baked. We are of the opinion that fruit and vegetables should be eaten uncooked, whenever possible, thus preserving water soluble nutrients which might be lost in cooking. In the case of bananas, cooking could hardly improve them in their ripe state, and it is only when they are fully ripe that the greatest food value is present in them.

For a fully detailed analysis of the banana's nutritional properties see the accompanying chart, and compare it with any other fruit or vegetable. You will find few that have the variety and wealth of nutrients offered by the banana.

[170]

Banana Nutrients
1 Medium, 6-inch Banana
(100 grams pulp)

Food Energy	88	calories
Protein	1.2	grams
Fat	0.2	grams
Vitamin A	430	I. U
Thiamin (B_1)	0.04	mg.
Riboflavin (B_2)	0.05	mg.
Niacin	0.7	mg.
Ascorbic Acid (C)	10.0	mg.
Calcium	8.0	mg.
Phosphorus	28.0	mg.
Iron	0.6	mg.
*Sodium	0.5	mg.
*Potassium	378.0	mg.
*Magnesium	31.0	mg.
*Manganese	0.6	mg.
*Copper	0.2	mg.
*Sulfur	12.0	mg.
*Chlorine	125.0	mg.
*Iodine	0.003	mg.

Figures provided by United Fruit Research Department; all other figures quoted from United States Department of Agriculture Handbook No. 8 Composition of Foods.

CHAPTER 47

Bananas as a Prescription
for Disease

Bananas have been taking a quiet but effective place in the treatment of disease in the last half century. Doctors with access to the latest drugs and surgical techniques still find that including bananas in the diet some-times works more effectively than other more complex therapies. The medical journals have yielded a great store of information on stubborn ailments which have responded to banana-eating when other more con-ventional efforts have failed. Perhaps you will come across a problem that has been bothering you, and find evidence that bananas might be the answer.

One could certainly not find a cheaper or more appetizing form of medication than a golden banana.

Bananas are best known as normalizers of colonic functions. They are instrumental in controlling constipation through their bulk-producing properties, as well as through their ability, beneficially, to change bacterial flora in the intestines. The bulk is produced by the water-absorbent pectin contained in bananas and their non-irritating fiber.

Constipation Relieved

In so-called spastic constipation, all irritants must be eliminated from the diet, for they can cause soreness and great pain in the intestinal lining if they are not completely smooth. The problem, then, is to select a food which will provide bulk enough for normal movements, without causing irritation. In the *Medical Times* and *Long Island Medical Journal* (62: 313, 1934) Dr. E. E. Cornwall emphasizes this need, plus the requirement that animal protein be kept low to discourage (intestinal) putrefaction. He restricts starches moderately and feels that any resulting caloric deficiencies should be made up with fruits. Many clinicians believe that bananas deserve first place among the fruits in such a diet.

Dr. L. Weinstein, in *Archives of Intestinal Medicine* (6: 21, 1939), remarks that he noted relief from constipation was often associated with the number of acidophilus bacteria in the intestinal tract. He instituted an experiment in which he observed 9 adults and 15 children, all of whom had suffered from constipation for over 4 weeks with no relief from any other treatment. They began eating a diet which included 3 to 4 ripe bananas each day. Within one or two weeks it was demonstrated that the bananas had produced normal movements in all subjects. The acidophilus in the intestinal tract rose to a count of 60-95 per cent by the end of the second week.

Soothing and Healing of Colitis and Ulcers

A related problem, ulcerative colitis, seems to cry out for the special properties offered by bananas. Once more the difficulty is irritation, whether it be mechanical or chemical, which causes further soreness of the inflamed or ulcerated lining of the colon. Patients are plagued by nausea, lack of appetite and frequent bowel movements. The need is for adequate intake and absorption of foods. Bland bananas, ripe and mashed, are recommended and, if used early enough, can lead to complete remission of the disease, whereas most raw fruits are poorly tolerated.

The special texture and flavoring of the banana make it ideal as a food for the ulcer patient. It buffers or neutralizes the hydrochloric acid in the stomach, the acid which causes much of the ulcer patient's woe. Bananas are believed to coat the lining of the stomach in such a way as to lessen the irritation the ulcer is exposed to, as well as to promote healing and prevent recurrence. The banana feedings, small and frequent, are well tolerated, easily digestible and palatable. When they are mashed and added to a protein preparation, such as soybean milk, the buffer action is even more complete, and certainly the nutritional values are even higher.

Non-Allergenic Properties of Bananas

Bananas are known to contain only benign protein constituents, and therefore they are often used in cases of food allergy which manifest themselves in skin rashes, digestive ailments or asthma. L. W. Hill (*Journal of Pediatrics*, 47: 648, 1955) remarks that he routinely includes bananas in a basic diet for allergic eczema. It is usually one or the other of the amino acids to which the body has a basic intolerance that causes one of these distressing allergy symptoms, which are actually manifestations of the body's defense mechanisms. Bananas can serve as an excellent background food, rich in needed nutrients while food elimination tests are carried out, and, later, should a basic food be found to be the culprit, bananas can be retained in the diet to offset any deficiency.

Anemia is another condition which can be helped by adding bananas to the diet. The *American Journal of Public Health* (23: 129, 1933) carried the opinion of W. H. Eddy which held that iron in bananas is present in sufficient amounts to cause some regeneration of hemoglobin in anemic rats. In the book, *Chemical Composition of Foods,* by McCance and Widdowson (New York Publishing Company, 1940) this conclusion is supported with the added opinion that all of the iron in bananas is in a form that can be used for forming hemoglobin.

Pellagra is a disease due primarily to a shortage of niacin, and secondarily to other factors of the B complex which are missing. The body simply does not make use of the B vitamins it takes in, due to an unfavorable climate in the intestines. Bananas help to make these conditions more suitable, so that the dietary intake of patients is used more profitably.

Kidney Diseases

In cases of uremia presence of toxic urinary constitutents in the blood) bananas are suggested by J. Raiboff, in the *Urological and Cutaneous Review* (40: 850, 1936); as a help in avoiding an overloading of the kidney. His prescription is 9 bananas per day for 3 or 4 days.

In the *Journal of the American Medical Association* (69: 440, 1917) the value of bananas in treating nephritis (inflammation of the kidney) was already being recognized by A. F. Chase and A. R. Rose who suggested bananas with every meal for the patient with this kidney disease. Because gastrointestinal upsets so often accompany this disease, the bland, non-irritating, mildly laxative action of bananas is favored.

More Instances of Banana Versatility

Aside from those above, bananas are considered valuable in the treatment of other diseases such as gout (since they have no purine and are adaptable to the soft diets often prescribed); heart disease (they are very low in salt and fat content and have no cholesterol content); typhoid fever (diarrhea is often a complicating factor and bananas have been shown to bring prompt relief and change the pH of stools from acid to alkaline, as well as to eliminate blood and mucus from the stools).

Hardly any diet for a diabetic can be found which would not recom-

[173]

mend the use of bananas, both for slow absorption rate, high satiety value, taste appeal and easy digestibility. In the Mayo Clinic diet manual bananas are recommended on standard and special diabetic diet menus.

Pre- and post-operative patients were known to benefit from the use of bananas in the diet. One of the main reasons for this is probably the high vitamin C content, which both protects from shock and aids greatly in the healing of wounds.

Bananas are obviously a valuable tool for maintaining good health, as well as for regaining it when it has been lost. The year-round availability of this fruit leaves little excuse for not including it regularly in your diet. It is inexpensive, easy to handle and prepare, and even comes in a natural wrapper that surely protects the edible portion of the fruit from insecticides and sprays better than any other natural food.

CHAPTER 48

Bananas and Babies

It was not very long ago that bananas were considered out of bounds in the diet of infants or young children. They were thought to be too heavy, too difficult to digest for the new and untried gastric mechanism of a baby. In the mid-1920's, Dr. S. V. Haas began experiments with the feeding of bananas to children which have since led to a complete revolution in the thinking on the use of this food. Today bananas are often the first solid food a baby gets, and they are used to combat indigestion, diarrhea, constipation and malnutrition in children as well as adults.

A fairly common, and a most terrifying childhood disease, is celiac disease. Its symptoms include loss of appetite, chronic intestinal indigestion, persistent foul diarrhea and severe malnutrition. Investigators have not yet been able to uncover a clear-cut cause of celiac disease, but it has shown a tendency to appear in succeeding generations of particular families. Victims have also frequently been shown to be sensitive to the gluten of wheat and rye.

Celiac Disease Responds

Dr. S. V. Haas, reported on his treatments of a three-year-old child suffering from symptoms of celiac disease in the *American Journal of the Diseases of Children* (28: 421, 1924). The patient refused all food and threw up any that was forced down. Dr. Haas, on a hunch, offered bananas, which the child accepted. The result was that other food was taken in normal amounts within 48 hours. However, as soon as bananas were withheld, the child relapsed into the same sick condition. Food could be eaten normally only so long as bananas were included in the menu. The situation persisted for what would appear to have been several years, until the child's digestive mechanism was able to take food normally with or without bananas.

Dr. Haas also described 10 other cases of celiac disease which he treated with bananas. Eight of them were cured, and two died. The success of this treatment led to the wide adoption of the banana diet in managing this disease. A fairly reliable pattern has evolved for the course of the disease once a banana diet has been instituted: the number of stools decrease and the consistency becomes firmer. The appetite improves and the child grows less irritable and sleeps better. There is an increase in vitality, anemia begins to disappear and the over-all condition of the patient shows improvement. All of this change occurs within the first week of treatment.

Stimulates Appetite

Apparently Dr. Haas' work broke the ice, for since 1924 there has been much in medical literature describing the effective use of bananas in treating diseases of children. The appetite-stimulating qualities of bananas were described by H. Thursfield in the *Archives of the Diseases of Childhood* (2: 49, 1927). He told of a group of emaciated infants who vomited their food constantly. They were fed the strained pulp of one to four bananas in their milk and whey formulas as a substitute for prepared infant food and decided gains in appetite and weight were observed. It was found that the amount of milk could then be increased, where previous increases had caused indigestion and weight loss. Dr. Thursfield stated that appetite stimulants in the bananas were partly responsible for the improvement in the infants who had not responded to other diets, and the soft consistency of the pulp had reduced the likelihood of vomiting.

Similar results were reported by Dr. J. A. Johnston in the *Journal of the American Dietetic Association* (3: 93, 1927). A group of malnourished infants, between 15 and 25 months of age, with a history of infections and poor feeding records, were fed ripe banana pulp. It was noted that all showed an improvement in appetite and a definite gain in weight.

Predictable Weight Increase

The ability of bananas to stimulate a weight gain in underweight infants became so dependable that Dr. J. D. Craig, on the basis of observing 444 cases, felt able to generalize on what's to be expected. When banana pulp is fed to babies, apart from their milk formula, the more underweight the infant, the more the average weight gain will be. In so-called uncomplicated cases (no recognizable disease), infants more than 15 per cent underweight were found to gain an average of 4.2 ounces weekly. In cases that did hold complications, the average weekly gain was 3.6 ounces. Infants of more normal weight gained 3.6 ounces weekly when the case was not complicated, and 2.8 ounces when complications were present.

Scurvy, that painful and serious disease of vitamin C deficiency, has been showing up increasingly in infants and young children in the past 50 years. The value of bananas in preventing scurvy as well as their ability to protect against degenerative changes in teeth and blood vessels due to ascorbic acid deficiency were shown in experiments with guinea pigs by Dr. J. A. Johnston, as reported in the *Journal of the American Dietetic Association* (3: 93, 1927). Going a bit further into the subject, Dr. L. Von Meysenbug, in the *Southern Medical Journal* (21: 496, 1928), wrote that, in young subjects, one of the most striking symptoms of scurvy is a change in the bones. An X-ray of the bones of one infant Dr. Von Meysenbug examined showed healed scurvy within 4 months after starting the inclusion in the diet of two bananas, mashed and sieved, each day.

Chronic eczema is another common hazard of infancy and childhood. An article in the German medical publication, *Kinderaerztliche Praxis* (10: 219, 1939), told of favorable response observed in a group of infants, suffering from chronic eczema, who ate a diet of rich foods, milk, vegetables and fruits, which included 3 bananas daily. The *Journal of Pediatrics* (47: 647, 1955) agrees in an article by Dr. Z. W. Hill in which he says that the success of bananas in treating eczema is due to their non-allergic nature.

Bananas and Diarrhea

For most mothers, the anti-diarrheal action of bananas is the most important and most reassuring of all of their powers. In the *Journal of Pediatrics* (37: 367, 1950) J. H. Fries attested to the fact that bananas have superceded apples and other raw fruits in anti-diarrheal action. This view is supported by E. W. Brubaker in the *Journal of the Michigan Medical Society* (36: 40, 1937) who tells of his experience with 56 cases of diarrhea in infants and children. It was found that those who were treated with bananas recovered faster than controls who were given other therapy.

International Medical Digest (32: 369, 1938) carried Drs. Bethea and Bethea's article which contained a description of the banana treatment for diarrhea in children. Babies are given ⅓ of a ripe banana as mashed pulp for each pound of body weight every 24 hours. (For example, if the baby weighs 6 pounds, he would receive two mashed bananas in a 24 hour period.) This pulp is, of course, given in small feedings of two or 3 ounces each, 8 or 10 times a day. The fruit may be given with water or incorporated in 1½ ounces of skim milk or buttermilk for each pound of body weight in the first 48 hours. (A 6 pound baby would drink his banana pulp in 9 ounces of liquid.) In the second 48 hour period, just about any accepted infant liquid is able to be used with the banana pulp. Diarrhea generally subsides after 4 days of treatment.

What is the reason for the effectiveness of bananas in conquering diarrhea? Dr. Fries, mentioned above, gives several properties of bananas which have this effect: 1. the pectin contained in bananas swells and causes voluminous, soft, bland stools that clear out the intestines; 2. the number and kind of intestinal organisms are changed favorably because bacteria are absorbed by this pectin, and the growth of beneficial bacteria species is promoted; 3. from the outset of the illness, bananas help to maintain nourishment and weight.

The inclusion of bananas in the diet of small children and infants would appear to be one of the wisest things a mother can do. She has plenty of support from researchers and the more practical word of the New York Foundling Hospital, which regularly gives bananas as the first solid food for all infants who come there, and has done so since 1931. Aside from these points, consider the high nutritional content of bananas, and the flavor appeal they seem to have for all children. Finally, and most important from our point of view, if bananas can be effective in treating allergies, diarrhea, malnutrition and poor appetite, why not prevent the occurrence of such conditions by including bananas in the child's diet regularly?

CHAPTER 49

Bananas—A Healthful Reducing Agent

For the dieter who wants to lose weight without losing his health, bananas are a wonderful help. Here is a food that is bulky and satisfying, takes no preparation, is low in calories and fats and high in nutritive value. If most overweight people would only reach for a piece of fruit when they have that overwhelming desire to eat something between meals, the pounds would probably melt off with little further effort. It is not the nutritious foods in the meals we eat, but the desserts and between-meals snacks of worthless carbohydrates, which add unwanted pounds.

Bananas have some advantages beyond those of other fruits. They are quite low in calories, about 80 to 100 calories to an average-sized banana. They are filling, and tend to decrease the yearning for more food even more easily than other fruits do. Bananas are known to be easily digested by the most finicky stomach. Babies are often given mashed bananas as their first solid food, due to this fact. Older people find the texture of bananas a plus when it comes to chewing with false teeth or no teeth, for it is obvious that the crunchy texture of apples and pears, and the fibrous quality of pineapple can create mechanical problems that one never encounters with a banana. Of equal importance, with all the other advantages, is the fact that bananas are a tasty food which most people enjoy eating. Also, fresh bananas are commonly available all year round, a claim which few other fruits can make.

The Problem of Retained Fluids

One of the main difficulties faced by many overweight persons is the fact they retain fluids. This can be due to any number of reasons, but often it lies in their use of too much salt (sodium chloride) or an inability of the body to use the sodium it gets, even in minute doses. Normally, sodium, as it is contained in natural foods, is excreted by the body. If large quantities are added to foods in the kitchen or at the table, some of this sodium is often retained in the cells of the body. The sodium attracts liquid to the tissues, and overweight is the result. In such cases, the weight is not the tissues themselves, but the moisture being held in the tissues.

The first step in reducing is, or should be, the complete elimination of salt from the kitchen and the dinner table. Doctors then try to map out a diet low in sodium-containing foods. Such foods are hard to come by, because every food has some sodium in it, and in some natural foods it is quite high. In bananas, however, sodium is classed as a trace mineral, less than one microgram per gram.

Bananas for Low Sodium Diet

A group of 4 doctors, whose work was reported upon in the *Journal of the American Medical Association* (February 14, 1959), determined to discover just how effective bananas would be as an adjunct in treating salt-retaining conditions. Congestive heart failure, cirrhosis of the liver and kidney disorders were considered as typical sodium-retaining conditions. Reports on two patients are included in the article. The first showed a rheumatic heart, with insufficiency of 3 heart valves and general dropsy. The second had cirrhosis of the liver due to alcoholism, as well as ascites (a deposit of clear yellow fluid in the abdomen).

Doctors decided to combat the fluid retention problem by instituting a strict, *and carefully supervised* diet of bananas and low sodium milk. Each day the patient received 10 bananas and 1,500 cubic centimeters of low sodium milk. The bananas and milk were served 3 times a day at meal times, with a snack before bed. The feedings could be prepared in any way—the bananas whole, or mashed and blended with the milk. Eating only this diet, the patients received 1,980 calories, 62 grams of protein and only .8 grams of fat per day. The desired result was quickly achieved in the large-scale voiding of urine, containing large amounts of sodium. The diet was retained two and three weeks respectively, for each patient.

Unsupervised Diet Needs More Variety

It is to be emphasized that the diet outlined above was used to combat a particular physical condition, and was administered in a hospital under supervision. We are strongly against the use of such a diet by the layman for the exclusive purpose of losing weight. While bananas are an excellent food, and do contain a great deal of nutriment, they must be supplemented by other foods apart from milk, to maintain the normal person's nutritional balance. The 62 grams of protein and .8 grams of fat each day are not enough to sustain an active person. Then, too, we do not believe that milk is a good food for adults.

The experiment was useful, however, in proving the effectiveness of bananas in a low-salt diet, a diet which all of us should be eating. Eat plenty of protein, as found in lean meats, broiled or roasted. Get the extra B-complex vitamins from wheat germ and brewer's yeast. Fill in your A and C vitamin requirements with fresh, raw or lightly-cooked vegetables, and rose hips. Then use bananas between meals or as dessert, in fact, any-time. There is no doubt that on such a diet one will not only arrive at a weight level that is healthful and attractive, but one's general health is bound to improve as well.

CHAPTER 50

Berries—Poisonous and Edible

by DOUGLAS HENDERSON, B.SC.

Royal Botanic Garden, Edinburgh

The commonest symptom of yew poisoning is sudden death—so writes an authority on poisonous plants, adding emphasis, if any is required, to the need for speedy and accurate identification of plants involved in cases of suspected poisoning. Berries, frequently brilliantly colored and highly attractive, especially to children, are most commonly implicated.

Identification

If a complete plant is available recourse may be made to a standard flora, e.g., 'Flora of the British Isles' (Clapham, Tutin and Warburg, 1952), used in conjunction with 'Illustrations of the British Flora' by Fitch and Smith (1939). Often, however, only the berries or portions of them in stomach contents may be available but even they may be identified within certain limits, especially if the patient can give some details of the plant from which the berries came: where it grew, in hedgerow or moorland, or whether it was a low herb or tall shrub. It may often be a matter of considerable detective work to discover the plant involved and on-the-spot investigation may more quickly give the answer. Fears of poisoning are dispelled if the berries prove to be harmless, whilst the most appropriate remedies may be applied immediately if the plant proves dangerous. The other approach to treatment in cases of plant poisoning, that via diagnosis from patient symptoms, and the particular course of treatment must be left outside a botanist's sphere. Laying aside therefore the question of symptoms of specific poisons, what are the commonly occurring berried fruits of Britain and how may the identity of berries be determined from purely botanical characters? It should be noted at the outset that the term 'berry' must be used in the very widest sense to include any fleshy fruit and not merely the restricted connotation given to it by botanists. With a few

[179]

FIG. 5.—Atropa belladonna.

exceptions the berries commonly occurring in Britain are either red or blackish when ripe; but of course all are greenish when young and in this state even the most edible can cause illness when eaten. Indeed, berry color is certainly the most convenient primary division of berries for their recognition.

Black Poisonous Berries

Among the black-colored berries the most feared—and justifiably so—are those of the *deadly nightshade (Atropa belladonna)* (fig. 5). Three berries are quite sufficient to kill a child. The plant usually grows in semi-shaded sites with annual, branching stems up to 3 feet high. The ovate leaves occur in pairs on one side of the stem; one of the pair usually conspicuously larger than the other. The dingy purple, drooping, bell-shaped flowers with triangular green calyx lobes occur from June onwards. The berries, ripe from July, are dull black, almost spherical, often as large as a small marble, and are surrounded by the persistent withered calyx. Within the rather dry fruit is a number of seeds. The fruits of the potato are very similar in shape and structure but lack the conspicuous calyx lobes. They are equally poisonous, containing the same principle—solanine.

A less common but extremely poisonous plant the *baneberry (Actaea spicata)* grows in woods on limestone in Yorkshire, Lancashire and Westmorland. The green, then black, shining, juicy fruits, nearly a quarter of an inch in diameter, are borne on stems one to two feet long with the remains of the divided leaves at the base. The berries cause severe gastroenteritis if eaten, but the comparative rarity of the plant renders it of minor importance. Somewhat more common is *Herb Paris (Paris quadrifolia)* growing usually in semi-shade. The stems up to two feet high bear single whorls of leaves at the apex surrounding inconspicuous yellow-green flowers which later yield single, slightly lobed, purplish-black, juicy fruits up to a quarter of an inch in diameter which contain 16 to 20 dark-colored seeds.

In woody thickets, usually on peaty soil, grow the *buckthorn (Rhamnus cathartica)* and the *alder buckthorn (Frangula alnus or Rhamnus frangula)* (fig. 6), shrubs up to 20 feet high. The leaves have characteristically curved, sub-parallel veins and both species have clusters of inconspicuous flowers and globose blackberries about the size of black-

FIG. 6.—Rhamnus frangula.

[180]

currants which are reminiscent of those of the birdcherry or the cherry laurel. But whereas the cherry type has only one seed, both buckthorns have four per fruit. Both buckthorns act as violent purgatives and are especially dangerous for children. Cascara sagrada is prepared from the bark of another member of the genus, *Rhamnus purshiana.*

Common throughout the country, but less commonly seen in flower and fruit owing to their use in hedges, are the *privets* (*Ligustrum vulgare* [fig. 7] and *Ligustrum ovalifolium.*) Only on unpruned plants do the masses of white flowers and small black globular berries form in quantity. Each berry is about the size of a pea with two chambers inside, usually with one or two seeds in each. These berries, so easily accessible to children, have caused fatal poisoning.

Fig. 7.—Ligustrum vulgare.

The kernels of many of our most attractive fruits, including cherry, plum, almond and apricot, contain a certain proportion of amygdalin, a cyanogenic glycoside which yields hydrocyanic acid on enzymatic breakdown; but, of course, unless the contents of the kernel are chewed they are not a cause of trouble. In the *cherry laurel* (*Prunus laurocerasus*), however, this substance is present in the leaves and flesh of the fruit and presents a more likely source of poisoning. Cherry laurel is commonly grown in gardens and parks where it develops as a rather coarse shrub with thick, leathery, evergreen leaves. It bears tassels of white, scented flowers and in late summer small, black, spherical berries very like small, black cherries except that the fruit stalk is short and rigid and the fruits, up to about 12 in number, are borne along a common inflorescence stalk 4 inches long. Within the fruit is a single "stone" just as in the related cherry and plum. In woodlands in England the *spurge laurel* (*Daphne laureola*) occurs sparingly. The inconspicuous greenish flowers are borne below clusters of shining evergreen leaves on sparingly branched stems up to 4 feet high. The blue-black berries are egg-shaped and very poisonous.

Fig. 8.—Hedera helix.

The *ivy* (*Hedra helix*) (fig. 8) is curious in that its dingy greenish-white flowers appear in early winter from October to December and the blackish berries, globular and about the size of a pea, are ripe in early spring. Adults are not liable to confuse them with any edible fruit at this season but their potential danger

[181]

to children remains, and although the fruits are not extremely poisonous they act as violent purgatives. Among blackberried fruits, the *elder* (*Sambucus nigra*) holds an intermediate position. It is commonly used in making preserves and wine but there is some evidence that eaten raw it can act as a rather violent purgative, although cases of more serious poisoning are not forthcoming.

Red Poisonous Berries

FIG. 9. Solanum dulcamara.

Whilst black-colored berries may lead to confusion and poisoning, the chance is even greater with red-berried plants as their number is greater and, of course, the color tends to attract children more readily. Particularly along hedgerows and on waste ground is there a number of poisonous, red-berried plants. Several are weak, straggling, plants such as the *woody nightshade or bittersweet* (*Solanum dulcamara*) (fig. 9). With attractive purplish flowers reminiscent in form of those of a potato or tomato, its weak stems scramble over other plants and die down each winter. The lower leaves are dark, glossy green, three-lobed with the center lobe the largest; the upper leaves are heart-shaped and entire. The berries, borne in the clusters 6 to 8 together, are bright-red, translucent—very like redcurrants except that there is no tuft of old flower parts at the upper end of the fruit—and there are numerous seeds within, compared to the 6 or 8 in the redcurrant. The woody nightshade is common in South and Central England becoming more scarce farther North. The berries and all parts of the plant contain the same poison, solanine, as the deadly nightshade.

Two other poisonous scrambling plants of wayside and wasteland deserve mention; both are most frequent in Southern England and almost entirely absent in the North. The *white bryony* (*Bryonia dioica*) is a vigorous, hairy plant with twining tendrils and leaves deeply divided into 5 to 7 segments. The flowers are yellowish-green, rather inconspicuous and the fruits dull scarlet, globular, berries about one centimeter in diameter with 3 to 6 large, flat, yellow-and-black mottled seeds within. The *black bryony* (*Tamus communis*) (fig. 10), although similar in name, habit and poisonous properties, is not closely related to the white. Its long straggling stems are quite smooth, the leaves simple and undivided, and the unisexual flowers greenish and inconspicuous. The bright crimson, translucent berries

FIG. 10.—Tamus communis.

[182]

borne in small bunches are superficially like redcurrants. It could most easily be mistaken for the woody nightshade but can be distinguished by the simple leaves on the lower part of the stem.

In thicket, scrub and woodland grows another group of red-berried poisonous fruits. Most conspicuous perhaps is the *cuckoo-pint* or *lords and ladies* (*Arum maculatum*) (fig. 11). It occurs abundantly in damp woodlands, sometimes in hedgerows, especially on basic soils. In spring and early summer the curious, sheathed flower clusters and the arrowhead-like leaves on long stalks are quite characteristic. The bright-red berries—reminiscent of those of the mountain ash—ripe from August onwards—cluster 8 to 20 together at the upper end of a sturdy, naked, green stem about 6 to

FIG. 11.—Arum maculatum.

9 inches long. By the time the berries are ripe the leaves have withered completely, although a few remains may aid identification. The berries themselves, about the size of a pea, bear 3 small marks at their apex and usually contain 3 brownish, rough-coated seeds.

One plant in the wild state uncommon in Southern English woodlands and absent farther north but commonly cultivated in gardens is the *mezereon* or *dwarf bay tree* (*Daphne mezereum*) (fig. 12). The whole plant, including its red berries, is intensely poisonous as is its near relative the black-berried spurge laurel. Mezereon is prized in gardens for the early appearance of its heavily scented, pink or purplish flowers from January onwards. The flowers are borne in small clusters on the bare branches. The simple spatulate leaves appear in tufts at the ends of the branches; beneath them the red berries are grouped in small clusters and are ripe from August onwards. When they have been responsible for poisoning they have usually been mistaken for redcurrants but can be distinguished by the lack of a tuft of

FIG. 12.—Daphne mezereum

withered flower parts at the upper end of the fruit—so characteristic of all the currants.

Finally among the poisonous red berries, is the *yew* (*Taxus baccata*) (fig. 13) of whose poisonous properties there is probably more general awareness than of any other, but whose temptation to children is great. It is widespread naturally in Southern Britain but is planted widely elsewhere for ornament, particularly as hedges or in churchyards. Indeed it is held

FIG. 13.—Taxus baccata.

that yews commonly occur in churchyards due to the early need to grow them for bow wood and at the same time keep them away from cattle and children—the foliage is also intensely poisonous. On the dark, evergreen branchlets the fruit is ripe from August onwards. The pale, half-inch-long seed is half submerged in a soft, red juicy cup. This fleshy cup is rather sickly sweet and not itself particularly poisonous but the seed is highly toxic due to its content of the alkaloid complex, taxine.

Edible Berries

If commonly grown garden plants are included, the number of berried fruits in Britain is very high and by far the great majority are harmless—at least if eaten in reasonable quantities. It is superfluous to mention the commonly cultivated berried fruits—the currants—except to add a reminder that both *redcurrants* (fig. 14) and *blackcurrants,* especially the former, and the *gooseberry* do grow wild in Britain and are also often semi-wild as escapes from cultivation, and may be confused with the poisonous bryonies, woody nightshade and mezereon. The *wild blackberries* and *raspberries,* also, with their cultivated relatives are, of course, quite harmless.

It is convenient to note that none of the berried fruits of heathlands and mountains is poisonous. This group includes the purplish *whortleberry* or *bilberry (Vaccinium myrtillus)* (fig. 15), the bright-red *cowberry* or *red whortleberry (Vaccinium vitis-idaea),* the black *crowberry (Empetrum nigrum),* the large, purplish-black *bearberry (Arctostaphylos uva-ursi),* the bog-dwelling *cranberry (Oxycoccus palustris)* with brownish mottled fruits, as well as the rarer *cloudberry (Rubus chamaemorus)* and *alpine bearberry* of the North-West Highlands (*Arctous alpinus*).

With this group belongs also the *juniper (Juniperus communis)* with pale bluish-black fruits —an inhabitant of similar habitats to those mentioned above but also occurring on chalk and limestone grasslands.

In hedgerows the *barberry (Berberis vulgaris),* with its very spiny stems, simple obovate leaves and tassels of yellow flowers, bears in autumn, elliptical, waxy, berries, each with a single seed—the whole quite harmless. Indeed, the spread of the plant is probably due to its former more wide-spread use in making preserves. The straggling, twining stems of *honeysuckle (Lonicera periclymenum)* with clusters of shining, red berries might be confused with those of the black or white bryony or the

FIG. 14.—Ribes rubrum.

woody nightshade. However, the oppositely arranged leaves of the honeysuckle, its woody
stems and dense clusters of stalkless berries
should suffice to distinguish it. The fruits are not
poisonous and the similar fruits of the many
cultivated honeysuckles are apparently equally
innocuous.

The harmless fruits of the *lily of the valley* (*Convallaria majalis*) are small, round, red,
berries on short, nodding stalks on a short,
delicate stem. They occur in similar situations
to the poisonous cuckoo-pint and the two
might be confused, but the lily of the valley is
much more delicate and graceful in its fruiting
stage. The *wayfaring tree* (*Viburnum lantana*)
with softly hairy leaves, oppositely arranged

FIG. 15.—Vaccinium
myrtillus.

on the branches, has panicles of laterally compressed berries, red at first,
then turning rapidly black, just on reaching maturity. The related *guelder
rose* (*Viburnum ebulus*) which, unlike its near relative, occurs throughout
Britain and is not restricted to the South of England, has much smoother,
thinner leaves and the berries remain red at maturity. Both species are
innocuous. So too, are the wine-red to blackish fruits of the *hawthorns*
(*Crataegus spp.*) each with a single stone. The orange-red fruits of the

wild *roses*, including the *dog rose* (*Rosa
canina*) (fig. 16), are, of course, edible but
the chaffy appendages of the seeds inside may
cause irritation and inflammation of the throat.

Other orange-red or scarlet fruits which
are harmless are those of the *mountain ash* or
rowan (*Sorbus aucuparia*), the *whitebeam*
(*Sorbus aria*), the commonly planted *Sorbus
intermedia* and the *sea buckthorn* (*Hippophae
rhamnoides*). The mountain ash, whose berries
yield a rather tart jelly, is of widespread occurrence; the other *Sorbus* species are less
common whilst the sea buckthorn is more or
less restricted to coastal districts. One would
expect the fruits of the *blackthorn* or *sloe*
(*Prunus spinosa*), the *wild plum* (*Prunus do-
mestica*) in its various forms, and the *wild
cherry* (*Prunus avium*) to be edible, but the

FIG. 16.—Rosa canina.

black fruits, especially the former, could be confused with those of the
deadly nightshade until attention is paid to the single stone of the *Prunus*
as opposed to numerous minute seeds of the *Atropa*. The blackish-purple,
very astringent, fruits of the *birdcherry* (*Prunus padus*), about a dozen on
a common fruit stalk, might well be mistaken for those of the very poisonous cherry laurel. The birdcherry, however, is deciduous whilst the cherry

laurel is evergreen; also the birdcherry is relatively uncommon except in the Scottish Highlands.

The white fruits of the *snowberry (Symphoricarpus racemosus)* are often the cause of alarm but are quite harmless. The plant occurs either in cultivation or naturalized in hedges, thickets and waste places where it bears its white pulpy berries, about the size of a marble, on slender branches in the late autumn.

Conclusion

Whilst the number of berried fruits in Britain is high enough to make recognition quite difficult, the inclusion of garden "berries" makes reference to an expert imperative, although it is worth noting that many cultivated plants are harmless including the commonly encountered *Cotoneaster, Escallonia, Amelanchier* and *Pyracantha*. Some reference to them is made in "British Poisonous Plants," Bulletin No. 161 of the Ministry of Agriculture and Fisheries, where good accounts of all poisonous plants in Britain, with special reference to livestock, are given. A further aid to identification, Sowerby's "English Botany," in 12 volumes with colored plates, includes descriptions of all the plants and notes on their poisonous properties.

The illustrations are reproduced by courtesy of L. Reeve & Co. Ltd., from "Illustrations of the British Flora," fifth edition, by W. H. Fitch and W. G. Smith.

Reprinted with permission from The Practitioner, *an English journal.*

CHAPTER 51

Cantaloupe

Queen of the midsummer fruits, cantaloupe comes to us with much to recommend it from a nutritional standpoint—quite apart from its wonderful taste.

Fresh from the garden, it is an excellent source of vitamin C and vitamin A, comparing very favorably with the citrus fruits and currants without any of the citric or other acids which cause trouble for some people who find they cannot take these fruits in quantity.

It Should Be Vine-Ripened

The only trouble with cantaloupe is the difficulty most of us have getting vine-ripened ones. And if you have never tasted a cantaloupe ripened on the vine, then you have never tasted cantaloupe. As the melon ripens, its sugar content increases and, of course, it becomes soft and juicy. Immature melons, taken from the vine and ripened artificially, may be soft and juicy but they lack the flavor of the vine-ripened ones because they lack the sugar.

This is why it almost seems a waste of money to buy cantaloupe in winter because, no matter how carefully you choose and ripen them, they are bound to be pretty tasteless. However, their vitamin content is still there. Cantaloupe should be eaten when it is quite soft. You can generally tell by smelling the stem end of the melon when it is ripe enough to eat. You should be able to detect a good, rich, musky melon smell when it is ready to eat.

Vitamin C Content of the Fully Ripe Melon

They have discovered a peculiar thing about growing cantaloupes which we are sure will surprise our gardening readers. Cantaloupes raised in the light shade of a tree are a little higher in vitamin C content than those raised in full sun. The vitamin C content, of course, increases rapidly as the melon ripens. In a green melon it may be 30 milligrams per hundred grams, but will rise to 40 or so in the fully ripened fruit and will decrease rapidly to 20 in the overripened or decomposed melon.

In *The Health Finder* (Rodale Books, Inc., $6.95 and $7.95-indexed) Editor Rodale has the following to say about cantaloupe:

"I am glad to be able to write about cantaloupe which I think is a wonderful food. Not only does it contain large amounts of vitamin C to supplement a diet in which citrus fruits have been cut down somewhat, but it also contains the natural sugars as a substitute for the artificial, and the heavy rind protects the inner portion from the insecticides used.

"I have recently come across an interesting fact, however, about cantaloupe which is worthy of being passed along. It is high in inositol which is one of the vitamin B complex. Inositol is a factor in preventing hardening of the arteries, according to some researchers that we have come across. For older persons who are worried about hardening of the arteries, we would therefore recommend cantaloupe. We would not say that this would be a definite preventative, but certainly along with a diet that contains fruit, vegetables and meat, with a reduction of such things as candies, soft drinks, pies, processed factory foods, etc., there certainly should be a smaller chance of getting hardening of the arteries."

Incidentally, inositol is also plentiful in peanuts, peas, beef brain and beef heart and raisins. Wheat germ and brewer's yeast are its richest sources.

Here are the vitamins and minerals in one hundred grams of cantaloupe which equals about one-half cup of cantaloupe balls or about a third of a small cantaloupe:

Vitamin A	3420	International Units
Vitamin B		
Thiamin	.06	milligrams
Riboflavin	.04	milligrams
Niacin	.8	milligrams
Pyridoxine	36	micrograms

Inositol	120	milligrams
Folic acid	130	micrograms
Vitamin C	30 to	50 milligrams
Calcium	17	milligrams
Phosphorus	15	milligrams
Iron	.51	milligrams
Copper	.06	milligrams
Calories	23	

CHAPTER 52

Cherries for Gout and
Arthritis Sufferers

Gout is a disease characterized by an excess of uric acid in the blood, arthritic attacks and, in advanced stages, the appearance of stones of gravel in the kidneys.

Ludwig W. Blau, M.D., writing in "Cherry Diet Control for Gout and Arthritis" in the *Texas Reports on Biology and Medicine*, Vol. 8, fall, 1950, proposed a large cherry intake as effective in the treatment of these diseases. Though he adds that "apologies are offered for unsatisfactory clinical and laboratory data and control," he feels nonetheless that the discovery merits the "propriety of publishing the information available."

Twelve cases of gout responded so favorably to this food that the blood uric acid of the sufferers dropped to its usual average and "no attacks of gouty arthritis have occurred on a non-restricted diet in all 12 cases, *as a result of eating about one-half pound of fresh or canned cherries per day.*" Supporting his evidence with details concerning 3 of these cases, Dr. Blau demonstrates the relief brought by the eating of either canned cherries, sour, black or Royal Anne, or fresh Black Bing varieties. In one case the juice only was drunk, and this proved to be about equally effective.

Re-evaluation of Cherry Juice

Eight years later, in *Food Field Reporter* for November 10, 1958, appeared an article on canned cherry juice relieving arthritis. Says the *Reporter:* New evidence that canned cherry juice may relieve gout, gouty arthritis and similar ailments is reported by Reynolds Brothers, Incorporated, at Sturgeon Bay, Wisconsin. According to the article, a number of residents of Sturgeon Bay cooperated in testing the cherry juice daily. "Outstanding results were reported," said the president of the firm who sold the cherry juice. He says further that sales of his product have increased considerably in Texas since the article appeared there linking cherry juice to arthritic cure. He also disclosed that several local dentists have been suggesting cherry juice to their patients and one of them found it useful for the treatment of pyorrhea.

"To date," says *Food Field Reporter,* "there is no definite scientific data on just how the juice aids in relieving pain caused by diseases where improper balance of calcium is evident. However, it is believed that it may be the pigment in the cherries that brings relief."

What Do Cherries Contain?

Morris B. Jacobs' book, *Food and Food Products,* tells us that cherries contain several pigments. They also contain quite a concentration of malic acid and a surprising amount of pectin. That is the substance in fruits that is used to make jelly harden and "jell." There are also small amounts of citric acid, oxalic acid, succinic and lactic acid in cherries. The oxalic acid exists in only trace amounts, fortunately, for this is a substance very destructive of one's calcium supply. Surprisingly enough, there is also a small amount of linoleic acid in cherries. That is the unsaturated fatty acid which apparently has such a powerful effect on the body's use of the fatty substance, cholesterol.

In this information there seems to be no clue as to what may be effective against gouty arthritis. It would certainly be a challenging experiment for scientists to work on. And we are sure that any of the thousands of gout sufferers would be more than willing to act as guinea pigs for such an experiment, if there was the slightest possible chance that they might be relieved of their symptoms.

Use Only Organically Grown Cherries

Meanwhile, what can readers who are suffering from gouty arthritis do about this information? Canned cherries are, of course, available in grocery stores everywhere. Most brands are loaded with sugar, probably also artificial coloring matter and other chemicals. The cherries themselves were, of course, sprayed with insecticides and on a small fruit like this which is not peeled, these insecticides can mount up to a frightening total.

We have located a source of organically grown cherries which are bottled rather than canned—of course, without sugar or chemicals. These cherries can be obtained from manufacturers of health food products.

If you have cherry trees or know anyone who does, by all means freeze or can some this spring for your own use. If you get very sour cherries, you can use honey for the processing. Remember that honey has almost twice the sweetening power of sugar, so judge the amount you use accordingly.

CHAPTER 53

Citrus Fruit Issue

By J. I. Rodale

I recently came across some most unusual material which tends to show that oranges and grapefruit are not as healthful foods as we think they are. This will come as a shocking surprise to most of our readers, especially those who are really health-conscious and who have been subjecting their bodies to high gallonage of these juices. It may furnish the answer to many vegetarians as to why their health is not perfect. Vegetarianism, with a severe minimum of the citrus fruits, may have a much better chance of "paying out."

The Antiseptic Power of Fruit Juices

Professor Theophile Bondouy, of the School of Medicine, Tours, France, made an excellent study of this subject which was published in Paris in 1947. Entitled in the original *Les Fruits, Leur Pouvoir Nutritif et Leur Valeur Therapeutique,* it states that most fruits are in general beneficial and wholesome. The author points out, however, that an excess of fruit juices in our diets can cause impaired digestion (dyspepsia), generally a forerunner of stomach ulcers. Citing a certain Professor von Sohlern as his authority, he says, "One of the reasons for the extreme rarity of stomach ulcers among Russians, and also Bavarians in the Alpine regions, is that they live almost exclusively on vegetables."

The essence, or concentrates, of certain fruits are so antiseptic that lemon juice, for example, can kill microbes. M. Bondouy lists the action of certain fruit essences on the following microbes and bacilli:

1. *Meningococcemia*—killed in 15 minutes by the vapors or essence of lemon, orange or bergamot (a small tree of the citrus family).

2. *Typhus bacillus*—killed in less than an hour by the vapors of lemon and orange essence, and in 2 hours by bergamot.

3. *Staphylococcus dore*—killed in 2 hours by lemon vapors and in 5 by orange ones.

4. *Bacillus of Diphtheria*—killed by exposure to the vapors of either orange or lemon or bergamot essence for the shortest time.

The author states that sometimes the typhoid, staphylococcus and diphtheria bacilli can be killed in as little as from 10 to 20 minutes by contact with either lemon or orange essences. One wonders whether, since lemon and orange are astringent enough to kill bacilli, in large and undiluted amounts they might not be corrosive on the human throat and digestive membranes.

M. Bondouy believes that citrus juices, such as orange, grapefruit and lemon should be forbidden to persons suffering from ulcerated or dyspeptic digestive ailments, on the grounds that they speed up the manufacture of gastric secretions which are in turn harmful to the ulcerated tracts. Apple, however, is soothing in such cases, whether it is mashed raw or cooked. Against the citrus juices he states further that they produce surcharges of intestinal gas and flatulence.

Lemon Juice Destroys the Teeth

A study was made by Edward C. Stafne, D.D.S., and Stanley A. Lovestedt, D.D.S., of the effects of lemon juice and other acid beverages on the teeth. They published it in the Proceedings of the Staff Meetings of the Mayo Clinic, Rochester, Minnesota, March 5, 1947. Entitled "Dissolution of Tooth Substance by Lemon Juice, etc.," it was later republished in the *Journal of the American Dental Association* for May of that same year.

The two authors investigated the relationship between the drinking of lemon juice and the dental health of 50 patients at the Clinic. Comprising 39 women and 11 men, the entire group had made it a personal habit to drink a glass of lemon juice and water upon arising in the morning. Showing how universally spread is the drinking of lemon juice, which is popularly misregarded as an essential dietary supplement, these patients originated from 22 of the United States, two Canadian provinces, Mexico and Puerto Rico. Like many other addicts of the habit, they took it for a variety of reasons: some to cure rheumatism, others for constipation, still others to reduce in weight, or treat colds, or just for what they called its "tonic" value. Many of the 50 patients also had the especially bad habit of drinking it daily and at a time when it was not mixed with meals.

All were suffering from varying degrees of dental decalcification; that is, the calcium in their tooth enamel was cracking due to the erosive effect of the ascorbic acid in the lemon juice. Some of the patients had lost most of their front teeth, while others had gaping cavities in the front teeth, side and rear ones. On questioning their patients, the authors learned that some of them had started drinking the juice because it had actually been prescribed by professional persons, whereas others had been taking it on nonprofessional advice. Drs. Stafne and Lovestedt were most astounded, however, to learn that a few of the patients had taken up this extremely bad habit as a result of reading advertisements which strongly recommended the drinking of lemon juice.

The authors conclude: "It is a concern of everyone who deals with diet that there be adequate intake of vitamins, including vitamin C. However, an adequate amount of vitamin C can be had without resorting to improper use of lemon juice. In view of its apparent harmful effects on the teeth, its use as a daily drink in any appreciable concentration should be discouraged."

Erosive Effects of Various Fruit Juices

Worried over the increasing incidence of tooth decay in humans, Winfrey Wynn and John Haldi (Department of Physiology, Emory University, Georgia) related the problem to "the acidic nature of many fruit juices that have an extensive commercial distribution, and inferentially have become fairly common articles of diet." Experimentally testing "The Erosive Action of Various Fruit Juices on the Lower Molar Teeth of the Albino Rat," they published their findings in the *Journal of Nutrition* for April, 1948.

The experiment consisted of two parts, in the first of which they fed young rats on a diet of dog food and fruit juice (the latter being their sole source of liquid intake) for 100 days. Each rat was given only one of the seven fruit juices used in the experiment. At the end of the testing period, the rats were killed and their lower molars graded according to the amount of erosion that had resulted from the particular fruit juice imbibed by each animal. These gradations were 5 in number: classification in grade one meant that the enamel still retained a high degree of polish; grade two, slight etching or scratching of enamel had appeared: grade three, mild destruction; grade four, moderate destruction; grade five, severe destruction.

The table of results showed the erosive effects of the 7 different juices to be as follows: tomato juice, one degree of erosion; prune juice, one degree of erosion; pineapple juice, two degrees; orange juice, three degrees; apple juice, four degrees; grape juice, four degrees; and sweetened grapefruit juice, five degrees.

In part two of the experiment, the animals were not allowed, as in part one, to drink whenever they wanted and however much they wanted daily. Nor were the fruit juices served the only source of liquid for drinking purposes. Instead, the juices were administered at specific intervals 3 times a day and in measured amounts with other fluids. Only 3 fruit juices were used; tomato, orange and grapefruit juice (the latter sweetened to improve its palatability for the rats, which would not otherwise drink it). Results of this test showed that grapefruit juice caused two degrees of erosion, orange juice one degree and tomato juice no erosion at all.

Generalizing the results of the two parts of the experiment, the authors conclude that juices from grapefruit and oranges caused the most erosion because they contain the highest concentrate of citric acid. Although grape juice contains no citric acid and relatively small amounts of malic acid (derived from apples), it caused almost as much erosion as grapefruit juice because of its large content of tartaric acid. The least erosive of the juices proved to be those from tomatoes and prunes. And the erosion caused by all the juices on teeth and enamel was considerably lowered when they were diluted with water.

The Effect of Fruit Juice on Peptic Ulcers

A study was conducted by John D. Yeagley. M.D., and David Cayer, M.D., on "Changes in gastric pH following the administration of fruit juice to patients with peptic ulcers." (Note: the term pH indicates a scale of numbers that tells whether a chemically tested substance is acid or alkali in content.) Publishing the results of their study in the *North Carolina*

[192]

Medical Journal for November, 1948, the authors state that they set out to test the "general belief that fruit juices are 'acid' and that they aggravate the symptoms of peptic ulcers."

For their experiment they selected 51 patients at the North Carolina Baptist Hospital, 19 of whom suffered from active ulcers, 14 from ones in initial stages and 18 from inactive ones. The authors then found that the drinking of orange juice by the 19 actively ulcerated patients increased their discomfort by bringing on pain and burning sensations one hour later. In the 32 less active cases, intake of orange juice brought an increase of gastric acidity without, however, causing pain.

Drs. Yeagley and Cayer conclude that orange or other fruit juices may be added to the diet of patients with peptic ulcers only if given with regular meals or in combination with other foods. Only when they are necessary to supplement a vitamin C deficiency, however, does it seem advisable to drink these juices.

Conclusion on Citrus Fruit

The idea of eating oranges and grapefruit is so ingrained in the popular imagination that it takes a great deal of courage to write against them. But I am enlisted in a crusade to encourage better health and must let nothing deter me from presenting facts which I believe will *do* that, regardless what axioms of health it may shatter. In this case I do not advise the complete elimination from the diet of oranges and grapefruit, but to reduce them drastically. I *do* suggest the elimination entirely of the taking of orange or grapefruit *juices*.

When I first read Dr. Hicks' article in the *Journal of the American Dental Association* (see chapter entitled "Reduction in Citrus Consumption Beneficial") I immediately cut down on orange and grapefruit. I was taking large quantities of their juices and I eliminated that entirely. My gums bled occasionally but after a month it stopped completely. I have noticed that, when I would eat more than a moderate amount of oranges or grapefruit after that, they would bleed again.

While on oranges and grapefruit, I noticed I could start my gums bleeding by using a toothpick, but after a month off of citrus, even a toothpick would not draw blood. I have noticed that shelling sunflower seeds with the teeth acted to reduce or eliminate bleeding gums also.

Again, I must repeat that this is the most unusual health fact I have come across in a lifetime of seeking after health facts. When I think of the amounts of citrus fruit I consumed in a quest for health, I wonder what other health information we accept as gospel which is based on error. Like other people I practically worshipped the citrus fruits. I invariably started lunch and dinner with a half a grapefruit and another half for dessert, as I do not eat pie, cake or ice cream.

Recently I noted a few comments by readers, in my correspondence, about their experience with citrus. Frank Shaw of 135 North Harvey Avenue, Oak Park, Illinois said: "I get cramps following the use of frozen orange juice and frequently from the use of pineapple juice." I regard all canned juices with suspicion.

Here is what another reader said, (name lost): "For some time I've placed squeezed-out oranges in a corner of the sink before disposing of them. The enamel of the sink in this particular place shows ridges which I believe the citric acid of the oranges caused. For some time I had been drinking two glasses of cool tap water in the morning with a half lemon squeezed in each and noticed that the enamel on the front teeth appeared a little rougher, so I gave up the idea."

A third communication will be found interesting from Luther C. Henry of Ellenton, Florida: "I suffered a physical and nervous breakdown in Illinois, 4 years ago; and came here to Florida—just to get enough citrus juice. Soon I became worse, and eventually learned that I was allergic to all citrus. Also there were cavities developing in my teeth. I *quit* using all citrus, and began on eggshell dust and bone meal. The cavities ceased to hurt and are apparently healed, for in over two years they have not as yet hurt me. So I know for *us* anyway, lemon juice especially is too acid— and I am sure grapefruit is also. Orange juice may be the least harmful, but I have rejected them all—and am much better."

Here is another powerful item against the citrus fruits. A few months ago a pharmacist visited me and when I mentioned the medical data I had unearthed against the citrus fruits, he told me a most interesting thing about them. He stated that the eating of them produced in him *Pruritus Ani*, which is itching rectum. He has proven to his own satisfaction any number of times that he could clear up this condition by eliminating the taking of citrus fruits. When I mentioned this to a friend of mine who suffered from the same condition, he also cut out oranges and grapefruit and within a few days was relieved from all itching.

There are hundreds of thousands of persons suffering from *Pruritis Ani* many of whom are among our readers, and it will be interesting to note whether the discontinuance of the citrus fruits always brings a cure. Readers who try it, please keep me informed.

Here is an interesting item taken from the *Democrat and Chronicle* of Rochester, New York, of August 10, 1951: "Tallahassee, Florida— Scurvy is cropping up in Tallahassee, the capital city of citrus-producing Florida.

"The condition is caused by a deficiency of vitamin C which is abundant in citrus fruit.

"Leon County Health Officer Joseph Bistowish said there are indications the severe form of scurvy may be rather common in the county. The disorder isn't infectious and need not be reported directly to the health unit.

"Effects include loosening of teeth, loss of appetite, pain in the arms or legs and such susceptibility to bruising that even the pressure of shoes may bruise the feet.

"And California can't gloat. The health officer said a recent national survey showed 48 per cent of the children on the west coast of the United States also were failing to get enough vitamin C."

There are many possible interpretations to place on this item, but it may be that the people in Florida have seen so many cases of ill effects coming from overdoing orange juice that they shun it. If they do, then they must substitute other foods that contain vitamin C.

It is my opinion that citrus fruits raised by the organic method, that is, without the use of chemical fertilizers, have more vitamin C and less citric acid. They may cost a little more, but they are safer. However, they also should be partaken of in moderation.

Recently 14,400 cans of Orange King frozen orange concentrate were seized by the Food and Drug administration at Seattle, Washington, because they were adulterated with a yellow coal-tar dye. Synthetic citric acid had also been added. Anybody who drinks such a product is extremely brave.

What would happen to the orange groves in Florida and California if we cut down on our citrus fruits? I sent for the statistics of production and after a few computations discovered that if everyone in this country ate two oranges a week, it would take up the entire crop. But there is still a safety factor in the large amount that is exported. Besides, I would recommend that the citrus acreage be somewhat reduced and other crops substituted.

CHAPTER 54

Reduction in Citrus Consumption Is Beneficial

Egon V. Ullmann, M.D., in his book, *Diet in Sinus Infections and Colds* (The Macmillan Company, 1933, out of print), says:

'A word may be said here about the abundant use of citrus fruits in relation to calcium. Like everywhere else, so here, too much may be as harmful as not enough. Year's ago, Von Noorden showed that citric acid precipitates calcium and makes it ineffective. The enforcement of the calcium action against inflammation by natural ways is one of the main principles of our diet. If large amounts of citric acid are taken the effect of this principle will be lessened. It is in my opinion unnecessary to drink huge amounts of orange juice and grapefruit juice in order to provide the organism with vitamin C. For this purpose minute amounts are sufficient. In cases where calcium as a drug is given, citrus fruits should be left out for about 4 to 5 hours after the calcium is given. The second reason for which citrus juices are given is their alkaline effect on metabolism. This alkaline effect can be produced just as well with other fruit or vegetable juices. I, therefore, advise the reduction in the amount of orange and grapefruit juices to some extent. This should be remembered especially in cases suspected of calcium deficiency. The problem is different when quick action against acidosis is needed, as in very acute conditions or before and after an anesthetic."

Editorial Speaks Against Citrus

The following editorial appeared in the *Journal of Home Economics,* June, 1951, commenting on an editorial which appeared in the February 3, 1951, issue of the *Journal of the American Medical Association.*

"Erosion of the teeth by acids was recognized as the fundamental cause of dental caries a half century ago. Experimental evidence has supported this hypothesis repeatedly during the past 50 years, both in small animals and in man. The demonstration of a high acidophilus count in carious mouths suggested a mechanism for the production of acid from food residues in the mouth. In a group of caries-free children, the buffer capacity of the saliva was found to be strikingly higher than it was in those with active caries. That contact of food with the tooth surface is a prerequisite for caries production was demonstrated in an experiment with young rats in which a caries-producing ration was fed through a stomach tube without resulting in caries.

" 'Soft' drinks, which usually contain a considerable concentration of organic acid, and various acid-sugar combinations, as well as acid fruit juices were all found to produce etching of the enamel and dentine in the teeth of laboratory rats, hamsters, and dogs. The buffer action of the saliva tends to counteract the erosive action. Tomato and prune juice were found to have a less pronounced effect than apple, grape, pineapple, orange, and grapefruit juices. The fruits themselves were found to produce much less etching of the tooth substance than the juices from these fruits.

"Although there are doubtless nutritional and metabolic factors favoring the sound development and integrity of the teeth, the presence of acids in the mouth appears to be a prominent factor in dental decay."

Citric Acid and Tooth Damage

Grapefruit juice has now been proven to have an effect many times more erosive on the teeth than grapefruit eaten in sections. An article in the *Journal of Nutrition* for January 10, 1951, describes the experiments of Ross A Gortner, Jr., and Reuben K. Kenigsberg of Wesleyan University, who attempted to discover what it is about the juice that makes it so much more erosive.

They tell us that it has been known for many years that acid fruits and beverages can damage the teeth considerably. In tests done in 1950, it was shown that the juices of acid fruits were 3 to 10 times more erosive than the same amount of fruit eaten in sections. It was believed that the explanation might be some protective substance in the fruit itself which was not present in the juice, or some ingredient created in the juice after it had been removed from the fruit, or, possibly, a difference in the way in which the juice and the whole fruit come into contact with the teeth while the juice, or fruit, is in the mouth.

What Is the Real Cause of Tooth Erosion?

All these possible explanations were taken into account and tested in the experiments described by Gortner and Kenigsberg. First of all, two groups of laboratory animals were tested with the juice and the sections of grapefruit. It was found that the animals receiving juice developed about 3.5 times more erosion than those who ate sectional fruit. Then a simulated fruit was made using grapefruit juice mixed with a gelatin material. The animals eating this "fruit" showed no greater tooth erosion than those who ate the original grapefruit, so it seems that no destructive substance is present in the juice and no protective substance is present in the whole fruit.

Then the experimenters tested to see whether the effect of the salivary glands reacting on the juice or the fruit might make a difference. Rats whose salivary glands had been removed were tested along with normal rats. It was found that there was no noticeable difference in the amount of erosion resulting. Hence, the only possible explanation left, these experimenters believe, is that the difference in the manner of ingesting the juice and the whole fruit is responsible for the erosion.

A Dentist's Evidence on Citrus Fruit Consumption

Dr. Henry Hicks, D.D.S., is convinced that excessive citrus juice consumption is responsible for unpleasant symptoms in the mouth and health generally. The entire article from which this is taken appeared originally in the magazine *Oral Surgery, Oral Medicine and Oral Pathology* for July, 1951.

"My subject," says Dr. Hicks, "one of the most confused and abused of the past two decades, has been of special interest to me for the past 15 years. Excessive citrus juice consumption and its effect on the superficial and deep tissues of the oral cavity has been overlooked by professional and lay groups alike because citrus fruit juice has been oversold to the public. It has become the standard, highly nationalized, and most advertised health food in America, its vitamin C factor a cure-all! Citrus fruit and vitamin C have become synonymous in the minds of most people. While we cannot deny that citrus fruit is one of the best sources rich in vitamin C and that vitamin C is essential for normal connective tissue and bones and for normal metabolism, we overlook the fact that other substances which are also present in citrus fruits may do more harm than the good that is derived from the vitamin C when taken in excess."

It would be uncommon for one to consume 3 or 4 whole oranges at one time, Dr. Hicks believes, but it is common for one to consume the equivalent of this in the form of juice. Those who do this do not stop with that, but eat or drink some other similar fruit containing citric, tartaric, or malic acid during the day. So over a period of time, too much of these substances must be handled by the body and Dr. Hicks believes that this is the reason for the harmful effects his case histories show.

During the last two decades many professional and lay persons have written that large quantities of citrus fruit juices are healthy. For instance, says Dr. Hicks, a leading magazine recommends for prettier skin a large glass of fruit juice for breakfast, stewed fruit, and a large glass of fruit juice for lunch, with a fruit cup and stewed fruit or gelatin dessert for dinner. A standard obstetrical text recommends the daily consumption of about 10 ounces of orange juice daily and the use of one-half grapefruit twice daily, to take the place of rich desserts.

Citrus Juice Overemphasized in Average Diet

"These are only two examples of the numerous diets which contain quantities of citrus fruits and are being followed for other purposes such as weight reducing, treatment of hypertension, and treatment of common colds. These diets may or may not have merits. However, there is the question of whether in an attempt to meet adequately the requirements of vitamin C, citrus fruit juice, as the sole source, is not overemphasized. Many other fruits and vegetables are fairly good sources. Green peppers, for instance, are extremely rich in vitamin C, but no one would think of eating three or four peppers at a time."

I have discussed this aspect of the subject in detail, says Dr. Hicks, because it is not my purpose to disagree with the findings of investigators regarding the beneficial effects of moderate quantities of citrus fruits upon connective tissue, but the words "moderate quantities" should be strongly emphasized. We have learned to recognize the results of an overdose of drugs, food and drink. It is rather shortsighted on our part not to conceive that serious effects might result from this innocent food drink, the citrus juice.

Mouth Tissues Affected by Citrus Juice

After 15 years of the closest kind of observation and record-keeping, Dr. Hicks finds that there is an element of harm for the mouth tissues in the drinking of large quantities of citrus juice. These effects include easy and excessive bleeding, teeth that move about in their sockets and tissues of the mouth that become hypersensitive. Other physical symptoms have included headaches, constant physical exhaustion, stomach pains, dizziness, prolonged colds and joint pains.

Starting in 1932, Dr. Hicks kept careful records of all patients, questioning them closely about their daily intake of citrus juices. All those whose gums bled easily and whose teeth were hypersensitive were instructed either to eliminate or decrease the amount of citrus juices they were taking and to substitute calcium, vitamin B, and ascorbic acid (50 milligrams daily), when it was found that these were deficient in their diets.

Case Histories from Dr. Hicks' File

Case 1. This patient, a school teacher 21 years old, habitually drank large quantities of citrus juices. When she came to Dr. Hicks in 1934 with an aching tooth, he found that she had a number of cavities, but her gums and the tissues of her mouth appeared to be fairly normal. He advised her to reduce the amount of citrus juice she was taking, but she refused to believe that this was wise. By 1937 she had a number of new cavities and by 1939 a great many more. She had also developed a severe case of sinusitis. By 1944 her teeth were loose in their sockets and were sensitive to air and touch. Her gums bled easily. She also suffered from exhaustion, nausea, stomach pains and loss of weight. Finally, convinced of their harmful effects, she stopped taking citrus juices on March 10, 1949, supplementing her diet with brewer's yeast, calcium gluconate and vitamin D. Two months later, her gums showed great improvement with less redness and bleeding. Her teeth were also firmer in their sockets. Up to 1951 the patient, avoiding citrus juices entirely, regained her health, showed no evidence of bleeding gums or loose teeth, had no new cavities and no fillings. Her sinusitis also disappeared.

Case 2. A woman of 28 came to Dr. Hicks in 1931 with many cavities, shrinking gums and redness of the gums. They also bled at the slightest touch. This patient had been drinking 6 to 8 ounces of citrus juice daily for 4 years. During the following 6 years she continued to drink citrus juices against Dr. Hicks' advice. Her cavities increased and her teeth began to loosen in their sockets. She also complained of anemia, stomach pains, acne and physical exhaustion by 1941. She was again advised to give up citrus juices and did so immediately. By August 1, 1942, her mouth appeared almost normal, her teeth were more firmly imbedded and her general health was much improved. Up to 1945 she had only two additional cavities and from 1945 to 1950 no new cavities. Today her teeth are firm, her gums do not bleed. Her acne disappeared along with the complaints of exhaustion and stomach pains. However, these pains recur when acid food is eaten.

Case 3. A woman aged 33 whose teeth and gums were in excellent condition came to Dr. Hicks for examination. She showed no signs of tooth movement or recession of gums. She ate 3 whole oranges per week, alternating them each day with other fruits. From 1925 to 1950 her mouth was completely normal, with no gum symptoms.

Case 4. A man aged 37 came to Dr. Hicks in 1936 with a great many cavities, red gums which bled when touched and symptoms of stomach and digestive disorders. He had been drinking from 6 to 8 ounces of orange juice daily. He was advised to take only 3 whole oranges per week and alternate them with other fruits. By 1938 only one additional cavity had developed. Since then there were no additional cavities, his gums returned to a normal and healthy state and his physical condition improved.

Case 5. A 35-year-old woman who had had diabetes all her life came to Dr. Hicks, believing that she should have all of her teeth extracted. Her gums were blue, bled profusely at the slightest touch and exuded pus. Her teeth were all loose. Her physical condition was poor and she was in a state of exhaustion. Her complexion was yellowish. She was able to do only a minimum of housework and, for this, she found it necessary to consume 5 oranges a day for quick energy. She used only standard diabetic foods and was on a regular schedule of insulin. Oral examination and X-ray revealed pyorrhea of all teeth.

With her physician's cooperation, her diet was changed as follows: rather than 5 oranges daily, she was told to eat only 3 oranges weekly, alternating with other unsweetened fruits. She was given calcium lactate, cod liver oil, vitamin C and brewer's yeast. Later her oranges were reduced to

[199]

two a week. Thorough gum treatment was performed and rigid home care was instituted. In 3 months, from November, 1949, to February, 1950, all bleeding and pus disappeared and all teeth began to tighten. By the beginning of May all her mouth tissue appeared normal and her teeth were quite firm. Her physical condition improved until she was living a completely normal life, "with plenty of energy and vitality to carry on the same as any individual without her affliction. There had been no change in insulin requirement and no necessity for any quick energy food."

Conclusions after Fifteen Years of Observation

Dr. Hicks' conclusions are that during the 15 years in which he kept these records he found that 3 oranges or 3 grapefruit halves, or one orange and two grapefruit halves per week, interspaced with one normal helping daily of other fruits, together with good dental care and adequate diet, will maintain absolutely normal oral health.

He says that the following conditions are traceable to the habitual ingestion of large quantities of citrus fruits regardless of other diet factors: 1. Hyperemia (a condition in which the gums bleed easily). Between one and 3 years are required in the majority of cases with otherwise adequate diet. In occasional cases hyperemia may develop within 6 months. 2. Hypersensitivity of the teeth will usually occur in about 6 months to one year. 3. Mobility of the teeth will be apparent in from 3 to 7 years. 4. Resorption of the bone will begin in from 7 to 10 years.

The general quality of the diet influences the speed of change caused by the ingestion of excessive amounts of citrus juices, says Dr. Hicks. Those taking diets deficient in vitamin B and minerals, together with excessive amounts of citrus juices are more easily susceptible to pyorrhea, while those with good adequate diets and excessive citrus juice intake had less serious symptoms at any given time. Those with poor diets who did not take excessive citrus juices did not develop symptoms. However, with good diets and an elimination of excess citrus juices, all mouth tissues of all patients returned to normal rapidly and remained so. The usual age at which mobility of the teeth and definite resorption of the bone becomes evident is about 32 to 35. Complaints such as exhaustion, headaches, digestive disorders and joint pains may occur from the age of 35 to 45.

Should We Totally Condemn Citrus Fruits?

In commenting on the vitamins B and D prescribed, Dr. Hicks mentions that, for controls, there were many cases in which the improvement was obtained by simply reducing the intake of juices alone, without supplementing the diet with vitamins B and D. However, with the addition of these vitamins, the recovery becomes more rapid.

"Again I wish to emphasize," says Dr. Hicks, "that citrus fruit is an excellent source of vitamin C which is necessary for connective tissue repair, but other substances present in this source seem to be the detrimental factor. In all cases where excessive juice was eliminated and pure vitamin C substituted, the patient improved both generally and orally. When calcium, vitamins D and B were added, the result appeared to be more rapid and the recovery positive. The current popular belief that ingestion of large quantities of citrus fruit juice is healthful should be carefully appraised. Citrus fruit in moderate amounts as a source of vitamin C in the diet is not to be condemned, it would seem that more than 2 or 3 oranges or one grapefruit per week is excessive in view of the fact that vitamin C is obtainable from other sources."

CHAPTER 55

An Allergy to Citric Acid

Allergy to foods manifests itself in different ways and can give rise to a host of clinical manifestations, according to an article in the November, 1956, *Journal of Allergy*. If, for instance, a child is allergic to eggs, he may develop a swelling of the mouth and an attack of asthma, when he eats eggs. The allergist can then give a skin test which will have a positive reaction. He will find, too, that there are "antibodies" circulating in the blood of the child. These are substances which appear in the blood to overcome the toxic effects of the allergenic substance.

Given a set of circumstances like these, it is easy enough for the allergy specialist to locate the offending food and remove it from the diet. But in many instances things are not quite this simple. The skin test does not "take"—that is, there is no reaction in the skin—no swelling, no redness, etc. There is then no way for the specialist to decide what is causing the allergy except to eliminate various foods one at a time, and see which is apparently causing the trouble.

Cause of Canker Sores Unknown

Dr. Louis Tuft and Dr. L. N. Ettelson of Philadelphia, writing on "Canker Sores from Allergy to Weak Organic Acids," in the *Journal of Allergy,* tell us that a patient who had been allergic for years had come to accept his almost continual canker sores as inevitable. Through various tests the doctors found that he was actually allergic only to citric acid and acetic acid. So long as he avoided foods in which these acids occurred, he was well.

The patient, a member of the Air Force, had been tested for allergies and had been found to be allergic to milk and a few other foods, dust, feathers, pyrethrum and ragweed. He was given desensitizing treatments for more than a year because of "migraine" headaches and asthma. After this treatment he had less trouble with asthma, but he still got headaches when he consumed chocolate or milk. The canker sores which he had had most of his life continued.

When the patient was discharged from the Air Force, he went to college in Philadelphia. Skin tests there revealed that he was allergic to house dust, ragweed, timothy and plantain. His reactions to milk and chocolate were negative. While taking a course of desensitizing for these allergens, the patient continued to have canker sores and headaches. Also, frequent spells of lassitude, vague pains, irritability and inability to concentrate.

When he came finally to see Drs. Tuft and Ettelson, he reported that he attributed the canker sores to eating sugar, sweets, "acid foods" or certain alcoholic drinks. He had found that taking alcoholic drinks alone did not bring on canker sores. But if he took them in fruit juice he invariably developed symptoms. The doctors found that the canker sores followed also the eating of grapes or anything made from grapes, chocolates and certain kinds of candy and carbonated beverages.

It seemed that the allergy might be due to citric acid—either the kind that appears in citrus and other fruits, or the kind that is added to many other products in the processing, such as soft drinks. The patient, who was now eating a restricted diet, began having spells of weakness so he took to eating candy. Chocolate bars gave him gas, headache, fatigue and brought on the canker sores. He took to eating Necco wafers.

Citric Acid Is Definitely the Cause

Then he began to notice that after he ate a yellow, green or orange wafer, he would notice a puckering or itching sensation in his mouth and discomfort in the stomach. The cinnamon, white or chocolate wafers gave him no trouble. To eliminate the possibility that sugar was to blame, he then ate pure cane sugar cubes and also rock candy without difficulty. Then he tried pure bitter chocolate that had not been processed into candy or candy bars. This caused no symptoms. But eating one of the regular candy bars brought on symptoms. (Candy bars contain citric acid.)

"This seemed to indicate that the patient was not allergic to chocolate itself but to substances combined with it. As a result of these experiences, the patient became quite adept at determining whether anything he ate or drank contained citric acid. Thus, for example, he found that he could not tolerate certain cough drops or troches (such as the red-colored Smith Brothers), whereas others were all right. This also was true of certain beverages; for example, he could drink unlimited amounts of Hires Root Beer (which, according to the label, does not contain citric acid) without symptoms, whereas one Coca Cola or even club soda (both of which contain citric acid) induced canker sores. As a result of experiences, the patient became label-conscious, inspecting all labels for citric acid and avoiding foods containing it. By strictly avoiding all substances containing citric acid, the patient could remain relatively free of canker sores for long periods and also could induce the sores at will by eating citric acid containing foods."

Proof Against Citric and Acetic Acids

The doctors then tested their patient with samples of citric acid and foods containing it, samples of which were placed on a certain spot within his mouth. Sure enough, every food containing citric acid produced an ulcer at that point. Other substances such as aspirin, bicarbonate of soda and so forth did not. Then other naturally occurring acids were tested in the same way. Tartaric acid, acetic acid, lactic acid, uric acid, ascorbic acid, a B vitamin and benzoic acid were tested. Of these acetic acid, occurring in vinegar, was strongly positive. Tartaric acid and lactic were mildly positive.

The reaction to acetic acid was surprising, but it appeared to explain why the patient got canker sores after eating foods like cole slaw, potato salad or beef cooked in vinegar. Vinegar is, of course, a source of acetic acid. The patient eliminated foods containing these two acids from his diet and suffered no more from canker sores except when he unknowingly ate some food that contained one of these acids.

Does this experience prove that these two acids are responsible for all canker sores? Not at all. Four researchers at Columbia University took up the challenge implied in the article we reported on above and tested 10 of their patients who suffered from chronic canker sores. They placed test swabs containing acetic acid, citric acid and ascorbic acid in the mouths of the patients and made careful checks for a period of a week. Not a single one of the patients showed any sensitivity to the tests. These researchers conclude, therefore, that the patient studied by Drs. Tuft and Ettelson was an isolated case and should be more or less ignored. This article called "Recurrent Ulcerative (Aphthous) Stomatitis: Intradermal Food Test Studies" appeared in the *Journal of Allergy,* September, 1958.

What About Other Food Additives?

Our conclusions are quite different. We are not allergists, of course. We are concerned chiefly with the troubles of the average modern American trying to find his way to good health in the complexity of today's food world. Citric acid is one food additive used in a great many different foods. In the book entitled *The Use of Chemical Additives in Food Processing,* published by National Academy of Science in Washington, D. C., we found listed some of the foods in which citric acid may be added during processing: buttermilk, mayonnaise, salad dressing, French dressing, cheese products, fruit butters, jams and jellies, canned vegetables, canned artichokes, cheese spreads, sherbets, candy, canned figs, dried egg whites, fruit juices, soft drinks, frozen fruits, frozen dairy products, margarine, lard, frozen peaches, wine, canned fish cakes, piecrust mix, prepared breakfast cereal, soup base and wine and beer.

This is one food additive to which an individual was found to be allergic only by the persistent efforts of two cooperative doctors. There are almost a thousand food additives being used in our food today and the number is increasing constantly. Where are you going to start to find out which of these food additives may be the one causing allergic trouble in yourself or some member of your family?

Beware of Citric Acid

Meanwhile, it is helpful, we think, to know that citric acid (even though it occurs quite naturally in many foods) can produce allergic symptoms such as the one patient described above suffered from. Possibly citric acid may be at the heart of trouble you or some member of your family has with certain foods. It won't hurt to experiment. Try leaving the foods out of your meals for several weeks. See if your difficulty is relieved.

The best way, of course, to make certain you don't get any citric acid that has been added to food by processors for one reason or another is to shun like the plague any of the foods listed above. They are all processed, canned or frozen foods. They shouldn't be on your market list anyway. Eat fresh foods and prepare them at home, yourself, so that you know everything that goes into them.

CHAPTER 56

Eat Foods—Drink Water

By Melvin E. Page, D.D.S.

One of the common roadside signs to be seen in Florida is, "All the juice you can drink for a dime." Now the man selling the juice does not want to injure his customer; he wants only to create business and to make a little money for himself. But actually he is doing both and the customer is usually well pleased, especially if he has driven a shrewd bargain and has consumed what he considers to be more than a dime's worth.

To explain, let us look a little more closely at the mechanism involved in the drinking of the juice and the possible effects of so doing.

Man has learned to separate juices from fruits. He then drinks the juices. All because it is a little less messy than peeling the fruit and separating it from the seeds.

The physiological difficulty here is that when he drinks the juice, he uses the thirst center, when if he ate the fruit, he would use the hunger center of the brain.

The thirst center of the brain was made to work only on water. When we drink juices, we will drink until thirst is satisfied, not until hunger is satisfied. In this way we are apt to get more at a time than we should have.

If we eat the fruit we are not apt to get an excess of this type of food. An orange or two will do us, but when drinking the juice, we may take the contents of a dozen oranges to satisfy our thirst.

About 10 per cent of almost any fruit is sugar, the best kind of sugar, it is true, but even *it* can be used to excess. When this is done, it puts undue strain on the mechanism of the body which maintains the correct sugar level of the blood.

Again the acid-base balance of the body is a most important part of body chemistry. The multitude of chemical reactions which take place in the body depend in part on a critical *p*H or acid-base relationship. All fruits and juices affect this valuable relationship. When we eat fruit, the proper boss is in charge. If our *p*H is too high, we may not want the fruit at all. If we can use a little vitamin C and a slightly more alkaline blood, then we are hungry for the fruit. It tastes good to us and we will eat just about enough and no more to do the work.

This is not all theoretical. My work is in the field of body chemistry. We analyze thousands of bloods. The *p*H of the blood should be 7.4. We often find it more alkaline than that. 7.5 is twice as alkaline as 7.4, yet to find the blood two, three or four times more alkaline than it should be is not uncommon. One of the bad results of too alkaline blood is the precipitation of calculus on teeth, yet this is but one of the many chemical processes which a too alkaline blood interferes with.

The moral of this article is, "Let nature work as it was intended to work." The consequences of drinking juices instead of eating the fruit are bad.

CHAPTER 57

Cranberries

The holiday season and a golden brown turkey or chicken on the table almost automatically means cranberry sauce or jelly as a side dish. Cranberries are natives of the western hemisphere. In Europe they are not produced commercially. For some reason or other these bright red berries like dampness while they are growing. They grow in bogs where the weather is cool and moist. New Jersey and Cape Cod are famous on the east coast for their cranberry crops.

Like other fruits cranberries are at their best when they are allowed to ripen on the vine. Indeed their total sugar content does not develop properly until they have ripened on the vine. Furthermore, they lose sugar when they are stored. However, they can be stored fairly well at about 32 degrees Fahrenheit. They should not be kept in airtight boxes with no ventilation whatsoever, for the berries soon die from "smothering." So when you store them, let them breathe.

Three Objections to Cranberries

Cranberries are good food, fairly rich in vitamins and minerals. Our objection to them is that they are generally prepared with sugar. Indeed if you plan to make cranberry jelly, you must add sugar if you want it to "gel." We recommend instead eating the berries raw (you can grind them in your food grinder very successfully). Mixing them with whatever vegetables you enjoy you can make a fine raw cranberry relish which has all the good flavor of cranberries but does not need sugar. If you need to sweeten the relish, you can use raw honey.

We don't advise buying canned cranberry jelly. Part of the reason, of course, is that we don't recommend canned foods at all. Then, too, the cranberry jelly has had sugar added to it. But, in addition, listen to this comment from Jacob's *Food and Food Products* (Interscience Publishers), "The discoloration of canned cranberry sauce was found to be due to the formation of soluble iron from the inner surface of the can and to the reaction of the iron with the coloring matter and to a less extent with the tannin in the fruit."

One other fact to keep in mind about cranberries—they have an acid reaction in the body. All other fruits and vegetables except cranberries, plums and prunes eventually add to the body's alkaline store. But these 3 fruits, for some reason, contribute instead to acidity. When you are planning meals, you should try to balance alkalinity and acidity. Meats and other animal products, cereals, some nuts and the 3 fruits mentioned above are acid in reaction. All the other fruits and vegetables, milk and other nuts are alkaline in reaction. Starches, sugars and fats are neutral. So don't count on cranberries as an alkaline fruit when you are planning meals.

Here is a listing of the vitamin and mineral content of cranberries:

Vitamin A	40 I. U.	in every cup
Vitamin B—		
Thiamin	.30	milligrams
Riboflavin	.02	milligrams
Niacin	.9	milligrams
Vitamin C	15	milligrams
Iron	.6	milligrams
Sodium	1	milligrams
Calcium	14	milligrams
Phosphorus	11	milligrams

CHAPTER 58

The Cranberry Incident of 1959

by J. I. Rodale

Now that the smoke of the Great Cranberry Battle has cleared away, we can look back dispassionately and see what has actually occurred. It was quite a bombshell, and hard to believe by the organic and prevention-minded world. We have been confronted by a hard, negative wall of government and scientific thought that denied that chemicals in the soil or in foods could be harmful in any way. Now came a sincere government official upon the scene who was brave enough to tell the truth. He saw that matters had gone too far and that the time had come for action.

They found that a chemical weed killer, aminotriazole, that was used to kill weeds in cranberry bogs, was capable of producing cancer in mice. The usual practice is for the cranberry growers to wait until their crop is off the fields before applying this chemical. In fact, that is the regulation of the Food and Drug Administration, but this season many of the growers jumped the gun and applied the weed killer before the cranberries were harvested. As a result the berries were contaminated by the aminotriazole, and Arthur S. Flemming, Secretary of Health, Education and Welfare, issued a warning to consumers to suspend cranberry purchases while further investigation went on. He ordered all sales of cranberries to be suspended while it was determined which lots of cranberries were affected. The losses in the cranberry-producing industry ran into the millions of dollars, and the same held true for the American Cyanamid Company, the sole manufacturers of aminotriazole.

Immediately hundreds of letters and telegrams came pouring into our offices suggesting that we jump into the fray and make as much capital out of this incident as possible. But our reaction was to take it all calmly, to rest on our oars for the moment. Our work had been done over a period of almost 20 years, during all of which time we never stopped drawing attention to the health dangers of using various kinds of chemicals in agriculture and in food processing. Now we thought it best for the public, the newspapers and magazines to take up the cudgels. For us to have stepped in at this time would have been like, after having lit the fuse on a bomb, trying by hand to accelerate the action of the fuse. In this case the fuse blazed heartily on of its own momentum. In a few months this incident has accomplished more than the whole of our 20-year crusade. During all of this time the chemical people were getting bolder and bolder and something like this was bound to happen sooner or later. They gave themselves their own rope.

Public Support

It is amazing the way the public jumped on this cranberry thing. It took hold like a fire. People sent hundreds of letters of encouragement to Mr. Flemming, and letters to the editor by the thousands demanding action and protection. It was discussed on radio and television. Many jested about it, but it was good publicity. As George M. Cohan used to say, "I don't care what you say about me, but please spell my name right." A typical item was the following advertisement in a newspaper:

MY WIFE

IS FEEDING ME

CRANBERRIES

BETTER GET YOUR PORTRAIT

APPOINTMENT NOW

PECK'S PHOTOGRAPH STUDIO

I have often said that some day some aspect of food adulteration—that is, some specific happening in connection with it—would capture the public imagination and would be seized upon by it, to be kept to the fore for a long time. The Great Cranberry Crisis of 1959 is one example of what I mean. There probably will be more explosive incidents in the future which will be attended by more violent pyrotechnics. The American public as a public is easily led by columnists and slogans, but once it is aroused there is the devil to pay. This happened when Upton Sinclair wrote *The Jungle,* a novel that graphically drew the popular attention to the sordid conditions in the slaughterhouse industry. As a result such a public outcry arose that laws were quickly enacted that cured the festering sores in this up-till-then unsanitary industry.

Perhaps some day not too far off in the distant future, a great novelist will write a more modernized *Jungle* relating to the whole field of producing our food, from the soil to the food factories, from the seed to the can. It could be a work that will arouse the wrath of the masses. Our statesmen always accede when such massive demonstrations take place. The public grasps a story quicker than it does speeches or articles of news. Books can be powerful instruments of reform, as can be seen in what *Don Quixote* did to knight-errantry.

Important People Aroused

One of the effects of the Cranberry Incident was that many people learned more about the scandal that exists in connection with the use of chemicals. Many well-known writers commented. For example, Ralph McGill, editor of the *Atlanta Constitution,* wrote as follows:

"There are times when some who profit most from the American system seem to be doing all they can to destroy it. It is, for example, utterly fantastic that a lobby should protest laws forbidding the use in food— whether grain, meat, fruit or poultry—of additives which can produce cancer in animals. Yet there is one. It is quite powerful. It is willing to take a chance on human beings because use of such additives fattens beef and poultry quicker, and makes for more profit.

"And, as they argue, it has not been 'proved' harmful to humans. The almost incredible avarice of these groups will do the American free enterprise system more harm than any amount of so-called creeping socialism. They will undermine the system in the minds of the American people who, slow to learn, finally will recognize naked greed."

In other words, from cranberries his attention was drawn to other chemicals used in food processing. The effect will be like pulling at a thread in a garment; it will go on and on, and may establish a trend. There was a black jelly bean crisis in March, 1960, because carbon black, a coal tar product suspected of causing cancer, is used to color this candy. I know a little about carbon black. In our electric wiring devices factory we have a rubber-producing division which uses carbon black to color rubber, but to put this coal tar chemical into a confection that is eaten by children is a crime of the vilest kind. According to the law, there are about a thousand chemical additives put into foods that will have to be justified as safe by the food manufacturers. So watch for further fireworks.

Such things as waxed-paper cartons, wax-lined cartons for frozen foods, lacquer-lined cans used for foods and drinks, cellophane, food coloring and many other chemicals are being questioned. It is all based on a 1958 law sponsored by Congressman James J. Delaney, a New York Democrat, which shifts the burden of proving an additive's safety from the government to the industrial user. According to this law, sometimes a limited use of a chemical is allowed, but when it is a question of cancer, absolutely no amount at all is permitted. Delaney had a little trouble with the chemical industry. But when he showed that his opponents were willing to tolerate "a little cancer," his amendment won out.

Foreign Countries See Danger

It is not only in this country, but on the other side of the ocean as well that attention is being given to the danger of chemicals used on food that is ingested by the public. A few months ago a shipment of Lebanese apples was withdrawn from London shops because the trees had been sprayed so heavily with an arsenic-containing insecticide that the apples were coated with a generous covering of arsenic which, says the *Medical Press* of London (December 9, 1959), "not only repelled insect pests, but ultimately consumers as well." It is a case of biting the hand that is feeding one.

The *Medical Press* has the following to say on the subject:

"If a country with whom, heaven forbid, we were at war were to spray our countryside with a poison which produced such results we should not be slow to denounce them for their savagery and wanton destructiveness. None the less, it is being done every day by our farmers not merely in the interests of national food production but of their own bank balances. The habit is not only already widespread but it is growing rapidly, encouraged, and indeed fomented, by the unbridled publicity of our chemical manufacturers. If we were to say that in pursuit of their pet preoccupations no less than of the profit motive these people had lost all sense of proportion, so much as to approach the point of recklessness, it might well be regarded as an understatement. For what they are doing is to imperil the whole ecology of these islands, on which we have subsisted from time immemorial . . .

"Contemporary historians of the social scene suggest with justice that the one overwhelming motive in human conduct today is economic gain. We can scarcely blame our farmers if they snatch greedily at quick returns regardless of the desert they may in the long run leave behind them."

What the *Medical Press* is referring to as far as ecology is concerned is the destruction of the natural balance in nature . . . the killing of the good insects with the bad . . . the poisoning of insect-destroying birds . . . the killing of fish in the rivers and the bees that pollinate the flowers.

Much research is going on to find ways of controlling insects and plant diseases by natural means. Projects that breed beneficial insect predators are growing in number. These insects are purchased by farmers and gardeners as an attempt to restore the balance of nature. Way back in 470 B.C. Democritus tried to sell a product made from olives which he claimed would prevent plant blights, but his attempt was unsuccessful. Agricultural history must be full of similar attempts. Research in this field with the idea of learning more natural ways of controlling insects and diseases might be very fruitful in results. Let us not be too proud to bend over backwards a little if necessary.

Destruction to Soil and Man

Coming back to the Great Cranberry Scandal, it is a case of man being hit hard by his desire to sit and to work physically as little as possible. In this case he was punished for his laziness. What I mean is that aminotriazole, the weed killer, was put on the market as a substitute for the hoe. But there are those who feel that hand labor in removing weeds would be healthier for soil and man . . .for man because it would give him badly needed exercise . . . for soil because it would not contaminate it year after year. Aminotriazole is a powerful chemical which has a deleterious effect on the soil's flora and fauna, its microscopic life, its digestive apparatus so to speak. It is contributing to an eventual destruction of the soil's fertility. And lack of exercise, generation after generation, may eventually sap man's fertility, his ability to perpetuate his existence upon the earth. Man is becoming more dependent on the machine to do his work for him, and as a result his muscles, tissues and organs are weakening; he falls easy prey to the degenerative diseases.

There may be a lame excuse for applying poisonous insecticides to crops to kill insects, but there is absolutely none for broadcasting cancer-causing substances over the land merely to enable the farmer to avoid much-needed, health-giving manual labor. In this case hand labor is not only desirable for its own sake, but it means more employment. Chemical weed killers should be banned by law.

There is much doubt that weed killers even do the job they set out to do. Ask any gardener who has used weed killers to try to clean out crab grass what he thinks of them.

The Start of a Chain Reaction

Aminotriazole is not the only offender. There are about 25 different chemical compounds used as weed killers and action should be taken against all of them. We must not overlook the fact, also, that aminotriazole is used for crops other than cranberries, although I think I saw an announcement that the American Cyanamid Company is going to cease to make it, for fear that there will be repercussions in other fields. Its loss of income on this product alone will be about a million dollars a year.

As stated above, the cranberry incident may be likened to pulling a thread out of a garment. Once started there is no telling where it will end. Now it has reached into another field. A voluntary ban was announced in December (1959) on the use of the fattening hormone, stilbestrol, in the poultry industry. But this hormone is still used in fattening cattle. In the New York State Legislature a bill will be introduced in the next legislative session requiring that livestock producers list all additives added to the feed of cattle. The Cancer Research Institute recently announced that such hormones used in fattening beef cattle would induce cancer in people who ate such beef.

Our Knowledge May Destroy Us

Where were the doctors all this time? Where was the AMA? Were they and the dentists spending too much time advocating the fluorine be added to our drinking water? (At the Bio-Chemical Institute, University of Texas, experiments recently showed that fluoridated drinking water shortened the life span of mice an average of 9 per cent.) Shouldn't doctors be interested in seeing that their patients get food that is not contaminated by disease-causing chemicals? The doctors are collecting so much money from the public to be used for medical research. Why not spend some of this to police agriculture and industry, to see that the food is as pure as possible?

It is claimed that losses in the cranberry-producing industry amount to $13,000,000 and that it could well reach $30,000,000 if the 4,000,000 cases of cranberries in warehouses at that time were not sold. It is unfortunate that the cranberry people were so hard hit, but it will be justified if this incident will be the means of creating a healthier world. It is like a war. Soldiers have to die. In this case it is only money.

We must come to a realization that with regard to chemicals in foods there is now an emergency situation. Since 1950 the volume of insecticides used in agriculture has increased over 600 per cent. The problem now is, according to Dr. Price, Assistant Surgeon General of the United States, "how to get the genie back into the bottle." Our destruction as a civilization could be brought about by our knowledge and misuse of chemicals.

The old-time vaudeville comedian used to jest about how wonderful chemistry was. "It gave us bleached blondes," he would say. Today chemistry has gone much further than that, and it is time we made an attempt to get the genie back into the bottle.

[211]

CHAPTER 59

Dates

A food of great antiquity, dates are mentioned frequently in ancient writings. One researcher says they must have been utilized as food in the Near East and India before the Bronze Age.

At some time or other back in prehistoric days someone must have noticed that any fruits left on the tree dried in the sun and were thus preserved. They probably tasted good, too, and so we got our idea of drying fruit in the sun.

The date grows on the date palm, a graceful, long-lived tree which may grow to 80 or 100 feet in height. The trees are unisexual—that is, there are male and female trees. The female trees are the only ones that bear fruit. The date-grower must fertilize the fruit artificially, using pollen from the male trees. When harvest time comes, all the fruit does not ripen at once, so that each tree may have to be picked as many as 8 times. The harvesting season in Southern California may last from September into early January. Picking fruit from a tree a hundred feet high presents problems which those of us who have apple and peach orchards are unaware of. Each tree produces from 200 to 350 pounds of dates a year. They require large amounts of water and a warm climate that makes southern California about the only spot in the country where they can be grown.

Why Are Dates Fumigated?

Standards of excellence for dates have been set extremely high. We are told that not a single insect is permitted in any shipment of dates. To make certain that this regulation is kept, dates are fumigated. The only way that the freshly picked dates can reach the room where they are packed is through the fumigation room. Fumigation takes anywhere from 12 to 24 hours.

The fumigant used is methyl bromide. This is a gas that is shot into the closed rooms where the dates lie. In one instance poisoning took place among a group of workers who came into a fumigating room that had not been aired sufficiently. Their symptoms were alarming and in several cases were severe enough that the workers were taken to the hospital.

However, we are told that all dates coming from California must be fumigated, so one has no choice if he buys the California dates. In addition, one of our readers who grows dates wrote and explained a little more about the fumigation. Said she, the fumigant is a gas which is pumped off after the fumigation period, leaving no possible residue in the dates. It's just the same, she told us, as leaving food in a room where there is a leaking gas jet. Human beings in the room could easily be suffocated. But food would be unaffected. And, of course, when the gas jet was turned off and the room aired, the gas would disappear and would no longer be a hazard to anyone.

However we still want to see a chemical analysis of the contents of fumigated dates before we agree to be convinced that no trace of the fumigant remains in the dates.

The Amount of Sugar in Dates

For readers who are looking for a substitute for desserts and sugar, there is no better answer than the date, unless you happen to be reducing, in which case we strongly advise you to avoid dates. Their sugar content is too high, and they taste so good that they tempt one to go on eating after he has eaten one. And the calories mount up.

As the date ripens, the amount of sugar it contains increases steadily until, when fully ripe, its sugar content may be from 35 to 75 per cent of the whole fruit. We are sure that no one could possibly finish off a meal with two or three dates for desert and claim that his sweet tooth was not satisfied. In fact, many people find dates too sweet for their taste. They are fairly rich in calcium, phosphorus, iron and copper and good sources, too, of chlorine, potassium, manganese and magnesium. In addition, they contain some vitamin B and A.

The vitamin and mineral content of 15 medium-sized dates is as follows:

Calcium	72	milligrams
Phosphorus	60	Milligrams
Iron	2.1	milligrams
Sodium	1	milligram
Potassium	790	milligrams
Vitamin A	60	International Units
Vitamin B		
Thiamin	.09	milligrams
Riboflavin	.10	milligrams
Niacin	2.2	milligrams

CHAPTER 60

Figs

Pliny, the Roman naturalist of the first century A.D., wrote:

"Figs are restorative, and the best food that can be taken by those who are brought low by long sickness, and are on the way to recovery. They increase the strength of young people, preserve the elderly in better health, and make them look younger, and with fewer wrinkles. They are so nutritive as to cause corpulency and strength; for this cause, professed wrestlers and champions were in times past fed with figs."

We know from history that figs are indeed a superlatively good food, for there are nations of people who live healthfully and almost exclusively on them. They probably originated in South Arabia; were known in Greece as early as the ninth century B.C. They were probably planted in England by the Romans. An Egyptian papyrus dated 1552 B.C. mentions figs as a tonic. Mithridates, the ancient king who was an expert on poisoning, honored figs as one of the 3 ingredients of his "universal antidote."

There are many accounts in the Bible and various histories of figs being used medicinally, for respiratory illnesses, measles, smallpox, as a poultice on boils and so forth. We even have a record of Aaron Burr once using a fig poultice on a swollen jaw. The swelling was gone by morning. There seems to be nothing about the chemical composition of figs that gives any clue to their reported effectiveness against disease. True, they are rich in minerals, but so are many other fruits which do not have half this reputation. Perhaps the fact that figs have been plentiful and cheap down through the years has accounted for some of their popularity with the early doctors.

A Natural Laxative

Figs are most noted for their effectiveness as a laxative. To this day, in spite of all the research that has been done on figs, we do not know why this should be. Some researchers believe it is simply the bulk fiber and seeds of the fig that give it its laxative properties. Others believe that the acids and minerals in the fruit are responsible. Syrup of Figs, incidentally, contains very little fig juice. It depends for its results on its content of senna.

Preparation and Uses of Figs

Figs are not shipped raw to any great extent because of their extreme perishability. They are dried or canned. They are also made into preserves, syrup, jam, paste, coffee substitute; they are spiced, pickled and candied. In countries around the Mediterranean they are distilled into alcohol and made into wine. The fig newton is a product of America. No one knows exactly why it is called a "newton" except that it was originally manufactured in the town of Newton, Massachusetts. It appeared first on a price list in 1892.

Figs are dried in a drying yard where they are fumigated and stored in gas-tight houses. Then they are dumped and spread on trays for drying in the sun. They can also be dried in a dehydrator in which hot air circulates. They are then washed, cooked in boiling water and packed in bricks or bulk.

Health Giving Properties of Figs

Like papaya and pineapple, figs contain a protein-dissolving enzyme called *ficin* or *cradein*. This enzyme could be used for tenderizing meat. On the island of Majorca housewives prepare curdled milk by beating the milk, then stirring it with split fig branches which cause it to coagulate rapidly. There is apparently so much of the enzyme in the branch of the fig that it brings about the desired reaction.

The total mineral content of figs is two to four times that of most fresh foods. Only cheese and one or two nuts have a higher calcium content. Figs are also richer in iron and copper than most foods. Figs are a fair source of riboflavin, a B vitamin, and a good source of thiamin, another B.

Here is the vitamin and mineral content of 100 grams of dried figs (about 6 small figs).

Vitamin A	80	International Units
B Vitamins		
Thiamin	.16	milligrams
Riboflavin	.12	milligrams
Niacin	1.7	milligrams
Calcium	186	milligrams
Phosphorus	111	milligrams
Iron	3	milligrams
Sodium	34	milligrams
Potassium	780	milligrams

A news story tells us that a French scientist believes that figs contain an anti-cancer factor. Dr. L. F. Bordas says that the anti-cancer factor appears to be related to the infinitesimal radioactive bodies which have been shown to be present in figs both from this country and the Mediterranean. These are also present in some other food products—pollen grains and royal jelly. There have been reports that cancer is rare in regions where lots of figs are eaten. Dr. Bordas thinks they can prevent the formation of precancerous conditions in the body.

CHAPTER 61

Grapes

America produces more grapes than any other fruit except apples and oranges. Flame Tokay, Malaga, Emperor, Cornichon and Thompson Seedless are grown in the western states and Concord, Catawba, Moore Early, Worden, Niagara and Delaware in the eastern part of the country. The state of California heads the list, with 90 per cent of all the country's grape production.

Though grapes have been used by man since earliest days, we rather suspect that their chief popularity was due to their very satisfying taste and their adaptability to wine-making, rather than any wealth of health-giving qualities they might possess. For a number of years the European "Grape Cure" has attracted devotees who claim marvelous benefits from having lived on a diet of grapes alone for several weeks. Undoubtedly the very simplicity of the diet and the invigorating living conditions under which it is carried out do much to correct the effects of heavy diets of rich food.

As in the case of other fruits, sugar develops in grapes as they ripen and they should be eaten only after they are fully ripe, a condition that cannot always be observed just by judging the color of the grapes. Grapes shipped from California are generally fumigated with sulfur dioxide before shipping to reduce the browning of stems and to delay the growth of decay organisms.

Grape juice is prepared in this country by heating the grapes and extracting the juice by hydraulic pressure. In Europe a cold process is used, which is superior to ours. Grapes are easily digested, except for the skins and seeds which cause trouble to some folks. Grape juice then is quite easily digested, and we would recommend it heartily except for the fact that commercially bottled juice contains sugar or some form of synthetic sugar of which we disapprove. Raisins are made by drying grapes. In California they are sun-dried with no pretreatment. Sulfur bleached grapes are prepared by dipping seedless grapes in alkali to check the skin, then sulfuring them, then exposing them to the sun for 3 or 4 hours, then drying them in the shade.

A pound of grapes contains about 400 calories. The minerals and vitamins contained in about 20 Malaga grapes are as follows:

Calcium	17	milligrams
Phosphorus	21	milligrams
Iron	.6	milligrams
Copper	.06	milligrams
Vitamin A	80	International Units

Vitamin B
Thiamin	.05	milligrams
Riboflavin	.03	milligrams
Niacin	.4	milligrams
Vitamin C	4	milligrams

CHAPTER 62

Peaches

So far as we can tell, peaches originated in China about the tenth century, B.C. They were known in Persia by the fourth century B.C., then were introduced into Europe and America. Today they hang, luscious and golden and juicy, on trees all over our country, even in the northern sections. Peaches contain 3 of the fruit acids—malic, tartaric and citric. But, as do other fruits, they have an alkaline reaction in the digestive system of the body. The sugar in peaches increases as they ripen and is least in the early varieties.

Peaches can be stored successfully at 32 degrees Fahrenheit, but they soften rapidly at temperatures higher than this and do not keep well even at optimum temperature for longer than two to four weeks. Commercially grown peaches are ripened by being exposed to gas, and are sometimes stored in this way to preserve them longer. Peaches that are bagged when they are just blossoms do not spoil as rapidly as those which grow in full sunlight. Bagged Elberta peaches developed a higher vitamin A content than those not bagged.

How They Are Preserved

Since they are difficult to store, peaches are preserved in many different ways. Canned peaches are a favorite American dessert. Peach jam and butter is popular. Freezing peaches is the best solution for those who have freezers. Peaches are dried commercially by the use of sulfur dioxide. They are exposed to these fumes for 5 or 6 hours, so that the color will remain and the vitamin A and C will be preserved. Then the peaches are exposed to the sun's rays for two to nine days. Before they are packaged, they are put through a brushing machine that removes the fuzzy part of the skin. Then they are sulfured a second time.

Dried peaches are concentrated food. One pound of dried peaches can be made from 6 or 7 pounds of fresh ones. So the vitamin and mineral content of dried peaches is also greater than that of fresh ones. But, as you know, we prefer not to eat fruit that has been sulfured (or canned), for it seems to us that the concentration of inorganic sulfur remaining in the fruit is most harmful. Fresh peaches contain about 5.7 milligrams of sulfur per hundred grams of fruit. *Dried peaches contain as high as 240 milligrams of sulfur.*

Vitamin And Mineral Content

The skin of a peach contains more vitamins than any other part of it. But we must caution against eating the skins, unless you are sure your fruit is grown organically. Many different kinds of insecticides are sprayed on peaches, for there are many pests that attack this soft and tender fruit. Since the skin is fuzzy, it is almost impossible to wash off the spray and we don't doubt that some of it penetrates into the meat of the peach as well. Just beneath the skin is the next highest concentration of vitamins, and the flesh around the stone has the least. As hard peaches ripen, their vitamin C content increases. It differs according to variety and also according to growing conditions within the different varieties.

Peaches are valuable chiefly for their content of vitamin A and vitamin C. Yellow peaches contain more vitamin A than white ones. Here is the approximate vitamin content of one average-sized peach:

Vitamin A:
  White Peaches—5-10 International Units
  Yellow Peaches—880-2000 International Units

Vitamin B:
  Thiamin—20-40 micrograms
  Riboflavin—50-60 micrograms
  Niacin—.9 milligrams
  Pantothenic Acid—35-45 milligrams
  Inositol—96 milligrams

Vitamih C:—8-10 milligrams
  (An orange contains about 25)

Here is the mineral content of one average-sized peach:

Calcium	10 milligrams
Phosphorus	21 milligrams
Iron	.36 milligrams
Copper	.01 milligrams
Manganese	.11 milligrams
Chlorine	4 milligrams

CHAPTER 63

Pineapple

Did you ever wonder why so many old bedsteads, chairs and desks carry a stylized pineapple as their major decoration? In colonial America this beautiful fruit was carved, painted and embossed on furniture because it was thought of as a symbol of hospitality. So a carved pineapple on the bedstead indicated to the guest that he was welcome. And, of course, its graceful form and handsome tuft of leaves made the pineapple an ideal subject for carving, just as it is a beautiful centerpiece for a table decoration.

But quite apart from its beauty, a pineapple is good food. Possibly its greatest appeal to northerners is that it is available in winter and early spring when the vitamin C content of our food reaches its lowest ebb. True, it is picked when it is green so that it can be transported to our markets from its faraway tropic home. And picking green means with the pineapple, as with other fruits, that vitamins are lost. We are told that there is a very great difference in the vitamin C content of pineapples depending on the variety, the way they are grown and the condition in which they are picked.

Investigators have found in one study of pineapples that some contain as much as 165 milligrams of vitamin C compared to only 24 milligrams in other varieties.

Canning Destroys Food Value

Fresh pineapple contains a protein-digesting enzyme. Enzymes are substances formed in our saliva, stomach and intestines for digesting various food. We are all familiar with the enzyme from the papaya which is sold commercially as a meat tenderizer. The enzyme in pineapple will perform the same job, that is, sprinkling some fresh pineapple juice on your tough steak a little before you cook it will tenderize the steak. Or eating fresh pineapple as the first course of a meal will assure you of good digestion for the meat course.

As readers know, we do not advise eating canned foods. There seems to be little or no reason for eating canned pineapple when it is so widely available in the fresh state. However, the way pineapples are canned in Hawaii seems to guarantee that as much food value as possible remains with the fruit, for they are picked when they are ripe and every effort is made to have them in the cans within 36 hours. But, of course, the very process of canning is bound to destroy water-soluble vitamins—the B and C vitamins that we need so desperately. Canned pineapple shows up with about 10 milligrams of vitamin C to 38 of the fresh pineapple.

One reason why we recommend pineapple so highly is that its thick skin protects the fruit from poisonous insecticides that seep through the thin skins of other fruits. You can't eat the skin of a pineapple; it's too spiny and too tough. You lose vitamins when you peel it, but you can be fairly sure that you are not going to be eating a mixture of pineapple, lead, arsenic, chlordane and DDT, after you have the skin off!

In choosing a pineapple this is what you should look for. It should have a fresh, clean appearance, a dark orange, yellow color and a delicious fragrance. Usually the heavier it is, the better the quality of the fruit, provided that the pineapple is fully mature. The "eyes" should be flat, almost hollow.

Why not put pineapple on the menu for dessert or appetizer at least one day a week? And, for goodness sake, don't spoil it by burying it in sugar or sugar syrup. A normally ripened pineapple is 12.11 per cent sugar already—good, healthful fruit sugar that doesn't need any more sweetening from a sugar bowl.

Here is the approximate vitamin and mineral content of about ⅔-cup of fresh pineapple:

Vitamin A	150	International Units
Vitamin E	.1	milligrams
Vitamin B		
Thiamin	.1	milligrams
Riboflavin	.02	milligrams
Niacin	.2	milligrams
Some pantothenic acid		
Vitamin C	38	milligrams
Calcium	8	milligrams
Phosphorus	26	milligrams
Iron	.32	milligrams
Copper	.07	milligrams
Magnesium	1.07	milligrams

CHAPTER 64

Prunes

Plums (from which prunes are made) were grown originally in the region of the Caucasus and the Caspian Sea. Later they were brought to central Europe and the Balkans. And today they are grown mainly in California. The French prune, with a small pit, is the most sought-after one for drying. Prunes drop from the trees of their own weight when they are ripe, are gathered carefully and dipped in a mild alkaline solution to boil, so that tiny cracks will be formed in the skin. From these the moisture escapes evenly while they are dried. Some prunes are sun-dried, but most of them today are dried in dehydrators in 18 to 24 hours, at an even temperature. Be sure not to buy prunes that have been dried with sulfur.

The prunes are packed according to size. Just before being packed, they are dipped into boiling water to sterilize them. Statements on the labels indicate the size of the prunes inside the packages. Small prunes pack 85 to the pound, medium 67 to the pound, large 53 and extra large 43 or less to the pound. So a label reading 30/40 means that there are 30 to 40 prunes in the package.

Prunes have long been noted for their laxative qualities. There seems to be nothing about prunes to produce this effect except for their cellulose content which is very high. It is well known that foods high in cellulose tend to regulate the bowels. And it is also true that most modern foods are low in cellulose, because of the refining and processing they undergo. So perhaps prunes deserve their wide fame as a laxative.

One further reminder about prunes. When you are considering the acid alkaline content of your diet, keep in mind that prunes (like plums and cranberries) produce an acid reaction in the body, rather than the alkaline reaction resulting from all other fruits. So if you are trying to arrange for a more alkaline diet, prunes are not for you. But if you eat lots of fruits and vegetables, so that you have plenty of alkaline material to work with, prunes will be highly beneficial, for they will contribute to the acid balance.

They should be cooked quickly. And there is no need to soak them these days, for the treatment they are given when they are packed guarantees that they will cook in a very short time without soaking. If you allow them to stand in the cooking liquid before serving them, they are softer and plumper and generally tastier, for they have absorbed some of the cooking water. Of course, you should always eat this cooking water along with the prunes, for it contains much food value.

Prune juice is made by cooking the prunes in water, just as you would at home, then pressing the whole business through a strainer. The pulp may be left in the juice, or strained out. We imagine that juice which contains the pulp would probably be richer in vitamins and minerals.

Prunes are richer in some of the B vitamins than any other fruit. They contain large amounts of vitamin A and minerals, especially iron. And they contain a trace—the merest trace—of vitamin C.

Here is the vitamin and mineral content of 100 grams of prunes which would be about 12 medium-sized ones:

Vitamin A .... 1890 International Units
Vitamin B

Thiamin .... .10 milligrams
Riboflavin .... .16 milligrams
Niacin .... 1.7 milligrams
Pantothenic Acid .... 60 micrograms

Vitamin P	300-400	units
Vitamin C	3	milligrams
Calcium	54	milligrams
Phosphorus	85	milligrams
Iron	3.9	milligrams
Copper	.41	milligrams
Manganese	.18	milligrams

CHAPTER 65

Watermelons

What could be more inviting on a hot summer day than the sight of a crisp, sweet watermelon? Watermelons are naturally included in the long list of familiar signs of summertime activity—and well they should be, for this food is both cooling and refreshing, containing an abundance of pure water distilled by Nature. What child and, for that matter, what grownup would dream of passing an entire summer without once sinking his teeth into a thick chunk of juicy watermelon? Although the watermelon is one of the most popular of all melons, especially with the younger generation, there are 400 other varieties equally capable of providing a most healthful and delicious summertime treat. All are alike in providing a rich store of vitamins, organic minerals, natural sugar, a strongly alkaline balance and, as we mentioned above, pure water distilled by Nature.

History of Watermelon

It is hard to believe, knowing the present day popularity of the watermelon, that several centuries ago the watermelon, in fact all melons, were a lost or forgotten food. If we examine the origin of melons, we find that they date back to the time of the ancient Greeks and Romans. These people knew and enjoyed the nutritional treasures which melons held. However, their successors failed to recognize these health-giving properties and therefore did not include the melon in their dietary regimen. Thus the melon was lost as food for many centuries.

Translators many centuries later came across the word for melon in Greek and Latin texts. They translated this strange word as cucumber and then began investigations into the past history of the cucumber. Their research renewed interest in the melon as a delicacy. People once more began to realize its value and delicious taste. From that time on history carried the melon as food.

It was not until the year 1619, however, that an English slave trader introduced the first watermelon into the United States. From that year on to the present time the watermelon has increased in popularity, reaching during these years a height of such great importance as a summertime food that we can truly say that it, together with the other most common melons, shares the title of King of the Summer Foods—truly a taste delight which cannot be missed.

Watermelon's Appeal

What is it about the watermelon that attracts every member of the family? Well, the youngsters, we are sure, are fascinated by the tempting red or pink edible portion of the melon. Yes, and Mom and Dad, too, for they know that this food, in addition to being appealing to the eye, is both sweet and juicy, easily eaten and nourishing for young and old alike. And how easy for Mom to prepare! All she needs is a good, sharp knife and a plate to serve the melon on (no plate for the youngsters, please! This is one time that etiquette takes a back seat to the enjoyment which children can derive from eating the watermelon Southern style). One slice of the knife into the large, long, smooth-surfaced, solid or striped melon produces a never to be forgotten adventure in summertime food eating. And to add to the pleasure the cook can be assured that she is serving a most healthful food, a truly natural food which has so far by-passed the out-stretched pseudo-beneficial arms of the food processors, a food which is not contaminated with poisonous insecticide sprays because Nature provided it with a thick rind, which does not allow the spray to penetrate into the edible portion of the melon. And that's not all, as far as the watermelon's benefits are concerned.

According to Arthur W. Snyder, Ph.D., food chemist, watermelons contain a rich source of vitamins A and C, some of the B vitamins and at least 9 minerals. He says that he finds them helpful in treating kidney and bladder troubles, obesity, dyspepsia, fever, arthritis and high blood pressure. Below is a chart showing the average vitamin C content of 4 common varieties:

Variety	Vitamin C mg. % heart	Vitamin C mg. % under rind	Shape
Tom Watson, N. C.	9.25	5.64	Long
Tom Watson, S. C.	6.37	4.56	Long
Stone Mountain	10.04	6.49	Round
Thummond Gray	8.05	5.51	Long

Watermelon Seeds

The seeds of the watermelon also are a known nutritional aid. Editor Rodale in the section on seeds has spoken of their medicinal value in helping to cure the kidney disease, nephritis. The oil extracted from the seeds of the Cuban Queen Variety, one of 29 common varieties of the giant of the cucumber family, was found to contain 68.38 per cent linoleic acid, that unsaturated fatty acid so valuable for good health. Because they are "unsaturated" these fats take an active part in the chemical reactions in the body which saturated fats cannot. They are capable of combining with other parts of foods in order that these foods may be carried through the miles of blood vessels in our body. This one process alone has brought these fats into the light of controversy due to the huge scare cholesterol has thrown into the public. Linoleic acid helps to control the cholesterol movement in the blood vessels thus alleviating the possibility of a blood clot by preventing the accumulation of cholesterol in the blood vessels. Considering this one merit alone, would it not be a worthwhile project for someone to take up the production of watermelon seed oil so that all health conscious people would be given the opportunity to add this valuable unsaturated fatty acid to their diet. The chief sources of these important acids are the oils of cereal germs and various seeds. In our estimation, watermelon seeds should be added to this list.

How to Select the Best Melon

In selecting your watermelon to obtain the maximum of these health benefits and at the same time the maximum in flavor and taste, it is best to make an incision into the melon. If the flesh is bright red, firm, crisp and sweet, you can be sure that this melon will meet the above criteria.

Wouldn't it be wonderful if we could test all our food products in a similar way. Only Nature's natural products will permit such a test, while man's tampered with, processed, unnatural foods are so doctored up with preservatives to sustain their shelf-life that such a test would be a meaningless and foolish waste of time. The antibiotics and other additives have destroyed Nature's set of values and in their place man has substituted his own—staying quality and, thus, profit. The watermelon is one of the few foods which has not been subjected to this set of values. We hope it never will be. For this and the other reasons we outlined above, we say, "for real summertime enjoyment, don't pass up the thrill of eating one of Nature's best foods, watermelon."

Here is the vitamin and mineral content of 100 grams of watermelon which is about ⅓ of an average slice:

Vitamin A	590	International Units
Vitamin B		
Thiamin	.05	milligrams
Riboflavin	.05	milligrams
Vitamin C	6	milligrams
Calcium	7	milligrams
Phosphorus	12	milligrams
Iron	.2	milligrams
Sodium	.3	milligrams
Potassium	110	milligrams

CHAPTER 66

Additional Information on Fruits

Some nice news in the *Medical Press* (January 7, 1957) for apple lovers—an apple a day can keep the dentist away, too. Though there was much speculation on the role apples could play in cleansing the teeth of decay-causing nests of refined carbohydrates, no one ever did much to prove it. Two British doctors, Slack and Martin, set about experimenting along those lines and had gratifying results. Two groups of children were selected at random, representing various ages to 15 years. One group ate a thin slice or two of raw apple after each meal or snack, while the others did not.

Apples Inhibit Tooth Decay

It was found that the low acidity of the apples stimulated a large salivary flow. The apple particles sweeping over the teeth with the increased saliva removed debris and stimulated gum tissue. The authors wrote that the gum condition of the children eating apples was significantly better than the other group, and the effect on reducing caries was also encouraging. They felt that a larger, more controlled, study of the effect of apples on the inhibition of dental caries is in order. We agree. Anything which will call attention to the effectiveness of this natural food should be promoted by all who have become disgusted with the false claims of modern toothpastes.

Children Should Eat More Fruit

Cavities in the teeth of American children could be reduced to half what they are now if all children would eat a piece of fruit after each meal or as a between-meal snack, according to one of our country's leading authorities on dental health, Dr. Maury Massler, professor of children's dentistry at the University of Illinois. He says that American children consume an average of 154 pounds of sugar a year compared to 10 pounds a year in such areas as southern Italy and southern India. Because most of our sugar is eaten in the form of candy bars, chewing gum and soda pop between meals, the mouth bacteria can immediately begin to reduce the sugar to acid and start the process of decay. Natural cleansing agents for teeth are pulpy, fresh, raw fruit, nuts or vegetables, Dr. Massler says.

Fruit Juice and Fresh Fruit

The per capita use of frozen fruit and juice increased by 10 times during the past 10 years, while the consumption of fresh, dried and canned fruits decreased. Fresh fruit makes up only 50 per cent of the total at present.

Avoid Seedless Fruits

Nowadays, in accordance with our obsession to change and "improve" all our food, fruits and vegetables are being developed without seeds. Seedless grapes we have had for years. Now seedless tomatoes are being promoted. We have a clipping about a chemical compound which will "cause tomato blossoms to develop seedless fruit." We are not at all sure that this trend is healthful.

Plants naturally produce seeds—even those which reproduce themselves generally by some other method. The seed contains the vital part of the plant—all locked up forces that enable this tiny group of cells to produce, with the aid of warmth and moisture, a sprout that will grow into a plant, a bush or a tree. Is there any reasonable excuse for persuading plants that we use as a food to grow without seed?

The notion that perhaps the valuable food material in the seed goes into other parts of the seedless plant has been disproved. Seedless fruits have been found to contain less of the vitamins and minerals than one of the same family containing seeds. We strongly recommend the avoiding of seedless fruits.

Powdered Citrus Juice Now Being Made

At long last the citrus industry has developed a formula for producing orange and grapefruit juice in the form of soluble crystals, according to a note in *Food Technology* for March, 1955. My, what problems were involved! Drying stripped out the essential oils and flavors. Then when the engineers discovered a way to preserve these oils in the crystals, they had to find a way to make certain they would be released back into the juice mixture again when it was reconstituted.

It is claimed that the continuous drying method retains at least 96 per cent of the original vitamin C of the fruit "along with other important nutritive values of the fresh juice." Commercial production has begun— the processing of 15,000 fresh oranges per hour to make a total of two million pounds of orange crystals.

A New Orange Dye

There's a new suggestion for dyeing Florida oranges. An engineering company has come out with a vegetable dye made from citrus rind itself. Sounds good, so far, but before you apply the dye you have to dunk the oranges in a hot dip which precoats them with "an edible fat." Hmmmm, that might mean anything, because the word "edible" these days means almost anything that isn't lethal in 20 minutes.

Ration Your Intake of Citrus

The large number of people who suffer from *pruritus ani* (itching of the rectum) prompted *Modern Medicine* (July 15, 1957) to write of current findings on the complaint. The author lists several possible causes (fissures, hemorrhoids, diabetes, allergies, etc.), and remedies (management of systemic diseases, elimination of digestive tract irritants, treatment of skin directly), then he states: "Food and drinks that may irritate the involved area include excessive citrus fruits and juices . . ." Remember, the advantageous food values contained in citrus fruits are sometimes tempered by unfortunate accompanying effects such as the erosion of tooth enamel and pruritus ani. We say take your citrus in moderation, and eat the whole fruit, not just the juice. Most of the food values are in the pulp.

[226]

SECTION 6.

Herbs and Spices

Down through history, herbs and spices have come to have almost magical properties where health is concerned. Undoubtedly, in the days when there was no refrigeration, spices were extremely important for preserving foods and masking rancid flavors. Herb teas were powerful against poisoned food, for many are emetics or diuretics. Today we use herbs and spices for their flavor and their wholesomeness. The flavor they add is especially important for low-salt diets. The vitamins and minerals they contain contribute to one's daily health.

CHAPTER 67

Let's Talk about Spices

Spices are making a comeback! Modern cooks have become increasingly aware of spices as an easy and healthful means of adding interest and flavor to the meals they prepare. The transformation a bit of clove or cinnamon can accomplish with an ordinary dish is really quite wonderful. And any spice you can imagine is as close to you as the neighborhood super market and so inexpensive that anyone can afford a complete selection.

Such ease and convenience in obtaining spices stands in strong contrast to their history. They were once so rare that death and financial ruin were quite incidental to obtaining them. Because of the risks involved, the cost was prohibitive, and only kings and noblemen could pay the price for a pound of cinnamon or cloves.

Until the time of the Crusades, the trade routes to the warm lands of Asia, where spices grew, were treacherous and almost impassable. Explorers were kept busy full time trying to find a short cut to the East. Columbus was one of these. He was known in his time not as the man who discovered a New World, but rather a man who got lost while looking for a simple way to get ginger and allspice for Isabella and Spain.

Most Spices Unadulterated—Some Exceptions

Spices are defined in Morris Jacob's three-volume work, *Food and Food Products* (Interscience Publishers), as "aromatic vegetable substances used for the seasoning of food. They are true to name and from them no portion of any volatile oil or other flavoring has been removed." It is interesting to discover that they are sold in a completely unadulterated state, for the most part, because any tampering might release the aromatic essences and oils upon which a spice's quality depends. Notable exceptions to this general rule are the attempts to bleach or preserve certain of them with chemicals. Most commonly abused of all spices in this manner is ginger. *Food and Food Products* tells us that when it is not bleached by the sun, as in former times, sulfur dioxide or chloride of lime is sometimes used to accomplish the bleaching. Lime is also used on ginger to combat insects and to conceal imperfections. Cardamom is another spice that is bleached by the sun or by some chemical agent such as sulfur dioxide.

Probably the rarest and most expensive of today's spices is saffron. It is the stigma of a plant from the iris family and must be picked by hand very carefully. It is used as a dyestuff as well as a flavoring. However, because of its high price, we are warned that it is subject to much adulteration.

The packages in which these products are sold should contain information about any chemical processes they have been exposed to, so shoppers should read the label carefully to be sure that the spices they buy are unadulterated.

Spices Have a Fascinating History

It is generally agreed that cinnamon is the most ancient of all spices, with a history that dates back to 2700 B.C. But the use of other spices must have followed very shortly thereafter, for they are continually mentioned in the Bible, and the Chinese also mention cloves as being used in ancient times, for it was required by law that anyone addressing the emperor hold a clove in his mouth while doing so.

Early in the Christian era, 3000 pounds of precious pepper were a part of the ransom Alaric demanded of Rome during his famous siege of that city. Still quite rare in the Middle Ages, spices were believed to be the source of all kinds of supernatural and curative powers. Their supposed potency as an aphrodisiac was famous, so that every love potion was sure to contain some secret and mysterious mixture of spices and herbs.

The power to prolong life and prevent disease was another of the graces spices were thought to possess. It was reasoned that their sweet smell must rise from some healthful ingredient, just as the putrid stench of disease grew out of some harmful core. When these two elements were brought together, obviously the good and the evil would battle, with the triumph of the just a foregone conclusion.

Ginger was especially prized as a medication. It was a major ingredient of a medicine which was highly valued as a preventive of the plague and a relief for other fever-producing diseases. In *Man's Food, Its Rhyme and Reason* (Macmillan), by Mark Graubard, the theory behind the power of ginger is explored in the light of modern physiological knowledge. We are reminded that ginger is an extremely pungent spice. It acts physiologically to produce a dilation of the superficial blood vessels which causes warmth, followed by perspiration, and this in turn promotes the coolness which is, of course, the outward sign of a fever's breaking and disappearance.

Sixteeenth century Europe used spices quite extensively, but no one depended on them quite so heavily as the meat vendors of the day, who would saturate their fast-spoiling meats in the strongest of spices to disguise their rancid odor and make them reasonably palatable. But there was more to it than that, for spices were also considered to act in retarding spoilage in the meat. Tests recently conducted by the National Chemical Laboratories of India have shown that cumin, caraway, cinnamon, nutmeg, cloves, pepper, tumeric and red chillies actually do have ingredients that act to preserve fats.

Spices in Modern Times

The role of spices today is much less dramatic than it used to be. Love potions are a thing of the past, refrigerators do all of our meat preserving and as for spices as a ransom, it is rather doubtful that 3000 pounds of anything but fissionable material could deter a modern-day besieger of Rome. But spices do have an important role as assigned by the *Journal of the American Medical Association* for May 4, 1957. In this issue spices are suggested as an aid to those who, through some illness, are forced to eat an unpalatable diet. The American Heart Association seconds this suggestion by including many of them in a list of suitable condiments for diets restricted in sodium and calories. Just as herbs do, they make excellent alternates for salt or sugar.

Some Reasons for Caution

There is some hesitation in allowing full freedom in the use of spices to ulcer patients. A test outlined in the aforementioned issue of the *Journal of the American Medical Association* seems to be accepted as a fair indication of what effect spices will have on a peptic ulcer. A group of 50 ulcer patients were observed for any untoward effects resulting from a diet which included uniform doses of various spices. Only 5 of the 50 experienced any unpleasant reactions. Two patients found that they couldn't take black pepper, one suffered after using chili pepper, another from nutmeg and the fifth from eating mustard seed. The disparity between cases would seem to indicate that individual peculiarities account for bad reactions rather than any one spice's action on the ulcer. Apparently those who were affected by one spice were not affected by any of the others that were used. If then an ulcer patient has a bad experience with one spice, he should be able to try another with better success, unless his doctor specifically forbids it.

Some people have a strange reaction to nutmeg, according to a note in *Today's Health* for October, 1955. It makes them drunk! The reaction is due to a volatile oil in the nutmeg called myristicene. The effects, mainly narcotic, appear in one to six hours, but recovery follows in about a day.

Some people are allergic to spices. Take the case reported in the *Ohio State Medical Journal* (July, 1950). A 59 year old lady contracted a very severe skin irritation on her hands and forearms. It would come and go periodically. The occurrence was finally traced to the times the lady did her baking for the holidays. Patch tests revealed a supersensitivity of the skin to cinnamon. The odd part of the case lay in the fact that cinnamon taken internally had no unpleasant effect whatsoever.

Though we have seen no clinical evidence of it, fennel seed is said to be wonderfully effective in helping people who are plagued with undue flatulence and belching. There are also recommendations for its use as an aid in the digestion of legumes (peas, beans, etc.) and members of the cabbage family.

For those who have a sluggish appetite (and don't get tipsy on it) a bit of nutmeg sprinkled on fruit or vegetable juice as a snack might help. This spice is credited with being able to stimulate an interest in eating.

Hot Condiments Are Dangerous To the Stomach Lining

Many health-minded people who eat well and shun drugs for the harm they can do, think nothing of a liberal dose of hot mustard, horseradish or pepper with their food. They point out that these condiments are not chemically altered and should be as safe as any other natural foods. Not so, we're afraid. In a part of the extended debate on the dangers of aspirin carried on in the pages of the *British Medical Journal* (November 15, 1958,

[231]

issue), a correspondent who agreed on the dangers of this drug, pointed out that the gastric effects of mustard and other condiments are even more harmful than those of aspirin. Two or 3 aspirins do cause an increased flow of blood in the stomach and consequently oozing of blood from a section of the gastric mucosa. However, a color photograph of the gastric area after a subject had eaten a single dose of mustard, taken with beefsteak, produced a more generalized and equally intense reaction. Be wary of strong condiments in foods. They might be the cause of stomach trouble you've tried hard to avoid.

Our Opinion

What do we think of spices? With the few reservations concerning their processing, mentioned earlier, we think they are a worthwhile food. They have little food value of their own, it is true, nor are they harmful to the body, and it is not to be denied that their enhancement of foods that do have many nutrients can be a valuable asset. If using spices can coax your family into eating better foods, their use is more than justified.

The experts make a wise suggestion for buying spices: always buy a small package. The longer spices are kept, the less pungency they retain. They lose their essential oils to the atmosphere, and with them go flavor and aroma. But no matter what size you buy, be sure to keep the container as tightly closed as possible.

If spices are new to your cooking, experiment with them. You'll find dozens of tasty improvements on old dishes as a result. Spices will put zip in your meals!

CHAPTER 68

Window Garden Edibles

This year plan for an indoor garden. As you sow lettuce and corn and peas, put in a few seeds of plants which will thrive all winter on your window sills. Seeds sown in the summertime will make nice-sized plants for potting up in early fall.

Herbs are, of course, old standbys for indoor growing, and the culture for nearly all of them is the same. Sow seed thinly in short drills or in pots. As the seedlings develop, thin as necessary. After the plants are a few inches high, pinch out terminal growth to promote bushiness. Pot up the plants in early fall to help them adjust gradually to indoor living by being brought into the house while the weather is still fairly warm.

A good potting mixture consists of 4 parts sandy loam and one part good compost, which gives a light, well-drained soil. It may be made heavier by the addition of humus, if desired. Despite claims that "poor" soil is best for herb growing, bacteria is vital to the life and health of any plant, and too often "poor" soil is actually *dead* soil. Compost will introduce bacteria into the soil, and these will make available to the plant all the nutritional elements necessary for maximum growth. The plant can then pick and choose what it needs, without being sickened by the artificial application of unwanted material. Plants may be repotted each year, or additional compost or humus may be scratched into the surface soil at the rate of 4 tablespoons to a five-inch pot.

Most plants do best in a sunny exposure, but many will do equally well in a fully light place. Large amounts of water will be used by the more succulent varieties, and care should be taken that they never suffer from lack of moisture. Placing the pots on water-covered pebbles will increase humidity and prevent excessive drying; spraying the tops with tepid water once a week will keep them dust-free and healthy.

A List of Valuable Herbs

Parsley is the headliner on anyone's herb list, and one of the loveliest plants that can be grown. It is as green and graceful as a fern, will grow even in poor light and contains more pure chlorophyll than a drugstore display. Chewing a sprig of parsley is a pleasant way to overcome strong food odors on the breath; the next time you are served food with a parsley garnish, be sure to eat it. In addition to its deodorizing qualities, it has many minerals and vitamins concentrated in it.

I believe chives are the next most-widely-grown window herb. Valued for the delicate onion-like flavor which they impart to foods, they are also decorative when chopped fine and sprinkled on salads or other dishes. Despite the low esteem in which society holds the onion family, it furnishes some of the most nutritionally valuable vegetables we have. Produce departments of markets frequently offer pots of chives; these invariably need repotting, as they have been jammed into their containers bare-root, to lessen shipping weight.

Pepper Grass or Garden Cress, as it is sometimes called, is a quick-growing plant much used for salads and as a garnish. Seeds should be sown rather thickly on damp sphagnum, and within 6 to 8 weeks will give plants large enough for cutting. Few of my cress plantings ever reach the desired two-inch height because my sons have the "cress habit," neighbors who stop in for morning coffee have developed it and even dinner guests tweak out bunches of plantlets, eating them root and all. With 4 six-inch bowls seeded in rotation, I have yet to harvest enough cress for one big salad.

Mint is an old favorite of mine, as good for nibbling as it is in cooking or used in fruit drinks. Plain boiled potatoes or carrots rate a gourmet's applause when coated with melted butter and sprinkled with fresh chopped mint. Curlymint, Peppermint and Woolly Apple are my choices, although I would never refuse any of the others.

Sorrel makes a rather attractive plant, and has much the same sour flavor as Pepper Grass. A long-lived perennial, it will stand frequent and severe cutting. Sweet marjoram, sweet basil, rosemary, savory, origanum,

[233]

thyme, bay, lemon verbena and ginger are other good herbs for the window garden. With any of these, there is the probability that you will be able to pick small bouquets, for, in addition to their uses in food seasoning, they bear attractive blossoms. Utility and beauty are effectively combined in these flowering plants.

Tiny Tim tomatoes and long "hot" peppers make grand house plants if sufficient humidity can be provided for them. They will flower and mature fruit throughout the winter, even without sunlight. Ordinarily we think of these as annuals; in reality they are perennials. Fruits persist on the plants in good condition for a long time, and may be "stored" thus until needed.

Scented geraniums may not belong in this discussion, and while hardly edible, their leaves do have culinary uses. With so many varieties now available, a pot or two is almost a must for the window garden. My first choice is the lemon-scented, aromatic, decorative and useful in finger bowls. Many catalogs list 40 and more different scented geraniums, and the problem is not so much which ones to choose as it is which ones can you leave out!

The purchase of a few seed packets, the expenditure of a little time and effort, and your windows will reward you with plants just bursting with vitamins and minerals, yours for the picking and eating. The "fruits" of your labors will be vegetables, nutritious and delicious.

Drink Herb Teas for Health and Enjoyment

Books on herbs, used both medicinally and for meal-time beverages, take us back many centuries to those times when tea, coffee and chocolate were unheard of, or were known only to the wealthy. Of course, before modern medicine brought us the dubious blessings of drugs, the only medications known were those made of herbs. Every home had its herb garden and every housewife was a specialist in the knowledge of just which herbs combined best as a cure for cough, fever, rheumatism, hives, tuberculosis or any other ailment that was bothering you.

We need not be patronizing about these old remedies. Many of our modern drugs, such as digitalis, are made from plants. And there is every reason to believe that the vitamin content of the wild and garden herbs was responsible for near miracles of healing among people who knew nothing of vitamins and did not have access to fresh fruits and vegetables the year 'round, as we have.

The whole subject of herbs in cookery has lately come into the limelight. These days it is smart to know how to use herbs in the kitchen. It is sophisticated to have a pot of basil and a pot of chives growing on the kitchen window sill. Modern women's magazines are including more and more recipes calling for herbs. So it's about time we catch up with these advances and get acquainted with the wealth of pleasure and good health to be found in herb cookery. Your local public library contains books on herbs. Ours yielded 3 entrancing books, giving recipes, cures and folklore background for all the common herbs.

Says M. Grieve, F.R.H.S., in his book, *Culinary Herbs and Condiments* (Harcourt, Brace and Company, 1934), "The study of herbs has been neglected—except by a few people—for many years, but now there are signs that it is being slowly revived. It is not at all an unusual thing to find a portion set aside for herbs in country gardens, cultivated by those who really understand something of their properties.

"Many things which we dislike at first, we afterwards acquire a taste for, and there is no doubt that Herb Teas are an acquired taste. They have a strange smell and a strange flavor, and that is the reason why they are not popular, for many people do not try to get used to them. Yet if the taste for them is cultivated, they certainly improve on acquaintance."

He then gives directions for making tea of balm, camomile, ground ivy, sage, peppermint and a whole list of mixed herbs, combining in one tea, for instance, rose leaves, rosemary and balm, in another aniseed, fennel, caraway and coriander, in another meadowsweet, agrimony, betony and raspberry. In each of these the procedure is about the same as for making our regular tea—boiling water is poured over the leaves. If you have your own herb garden, you can make teas with fresh leaves. And, of course, you can dry and store all manner of leaves every fall to last you through the winter.

Herb Teas You Can Make

Rosetta E. Clarkson in her book, *Herbs, Their Culture and Use* (the Macmillan Company, 1942), tells us that there are some 75 or more herbal teas taken for various ailments, even in these days of antibiotics and antihistamines! She goes on to say, "The aroma will remind you of the past summer days when you pressed these same fragrant herbs in your hot moist hand as you strolled down the garden paths. You will also enjoy these refreshing teas when you feel exhausted from the summer's heat. They will be drunk gratefully when you feel shivery with a cold coming on, or when you are ready to scream from frayed nerves.

"For afternoon tea a few leafy tips or a small handful of herbs may be added to a brew of ordinary tea—herbs such as lemon thyme, lemon balm, peppermint, spearmint, apple mint, lemon verbena, costmary, camomile, wintergreen or any one of these brewed by itself makes a deliciously different tea. The French make a fragrant tea of the leaves and flowers of agrimony to be served with meals. Speedwell tastes similar to Chinese green tea and is commonly used on the Continent under the name of *The de l'Europe*." (European tea.)

For asthma sufferers mullein or sweet marjoram make a good tea. For nervous headache you might try camomile, or catnip, peppermint, aniseed, lemon balm, rosemary, mugwort, sage, sweet marjoram, lemon verbena. For indigestion try beebalm, boneset, sage, aniseed, fennel seed, peppermint or basil. Wintergreen leaves, boneset or celery are well known among herb doctors as remedies for rheumatism. Many readers have reported relief from the symptoms of arthritis after drinking tea made from alfalfa seed (the untreated kind sold for human consumption not the kind bought by farmers for planting). A tea made of coltsfoot is a good spring tonic, says Miss Clarkson, sage, red clover and elderblossoms, celandine, ground ivy and camomile are blood purifiers.

Your Own Herb Garden

Garden of Herbs by Eleanour Sinclair Rohde (Hale, Cushman and Flint, 1936), takes us back for almost four hundred years with recipes for herb dishes served in England, when no dish was a dish worthy to set on the table if it did not contain herbs. She mentions plantain tea, feverfew tea, dandelion tea, chickweed tea, eyebright tea—this latter was named by the Greeks and has the reputation of restoring lost eyesight. How would you like to sit down to dinner with a steaming cup of lavender tea, or tansy tea or violet tea?

A garden of your own is the answer, if you are one for experimenting in the kitchen, for the list of possible combinations of herbs for tea-making is practically endless. We cannot give you the evidence of scientific experiments performed in laboratories to indicate that herb teas have the wonderful healing qualities ascribed to them in the old herbals. But we do not discount these tales. The marvelous and age-old folklore that has grown up around the properties of the various berries, seeds and leaves in the sick-room was not invented out of whole cloth. Undoubtedly there are many healthful benefits to be gained from drinking herb teas.

If you do not have a garden (and once again we urge you to have one, even if it means digging up the back lawn) you will have to buy your herb teas. Don't expect to like them the first time you drink them. You had to learn to like tea and coffee, too. And each herb has its own pungent, unmistakable fragrance—a fragrance which is always fresh, clean-smelling, refreshing. Buy small quantities at first until you decide which flavor is your favorite. Then surprise your friends the next time you have them over for dinner with a healthful cup of your own brewing. It's new, it's different and—these days—it's fashionable!

SECTION 7.

Meat, Fish and Poultry

We believe that meat, fish and poultry with a minimum of processing are necessary to the well-rounded diet, because they are actually the only true source of complete protein that we have aside from eggs. Vegetarians point to various high-protein foods that are not meat or fish, but always the protein in one must be supplemented by the protein in another. A specific combination is necessary for proper nutrition, and too few vegetarians are consistently aware of the need to watch this. We say a diet with plenty of lean meat or fish is the only sure way to be certain of proper protein intake.

CHAPTER 69

Meat in Your Diet

Historians and nutritionists have theorized that the American pioneers who settled our continent were able to endure the many hardships, the cold, the hard work, the loneliness, the fear, because their diet consisted almost entirely of meat. Today we know that they lacked, in wintertime especially, many of the food elements needed for good health—vitamin C, for example. But, in general, their meals were high in the complete protein of meat and it seems fairly obvious that this was one reason, at least, why they survived and triumphed. Of course, we must not forget, too, that none of their food was refined or processed, as we think of processing.

Why exactly is meat such a good food? Or is it, for modern man? Perhaps the outstanding reason for the superiority of meat as food is the fact that it is a complete protein, as are all other animal proteins except gelatin. By "complete protein" we mean that meat contains all the amino acids which we human beings cannot manufacture inside our bodies. These are called the "essential amino acids"—for it is essential that they be present in our food since our bodies do not synthetize them.

Some vegetables contain some of these amino acids; other vegetables contain others. Soybeans have been found to be the only non-animal source of complete proteins. If you are skilled enough in nutrition, it is possible to arrange entirely vegetable meals to include all the essential amino acids —but this requires infinite knowledge, patience and attention to the planning of each meal, for you cannot make up at lunchtime the essential amino acids that were lacking at breakfast. You must eat them all at the same time to achieve best results, nutritionally speaking.

Our bodies are made of protein and to be healthy we must provide them with sufficient protein to keep cells and tissues in good repair. These are constantly breaking down and wearing out. If good complete protein is not available, how can they be repaired? Vegetarians believe that we are able to manufacture protein from vegetables and fruits, as horses and cows do. It is our belief that, since our digestive tracts are not made like those of the vegetarian animals, we need to get our protein from animal sources, rather than from vegetable sources exclusively.

Vitamins in Meat

The second valuable food element in meat is its vitamin content. All meats, but especially the organ meats, are high in B vitamins. The different kinds of meat vary in their B content, but, as you can see in the accompanying chart all rank extremely high. For a country like America where refined carbohydrates make up so much of the diet, meat thus becomes doubly important. The B vitamins that have been removed from these starches (white flour and white sugar) during their processing must be supplied somewhere in the diet, for they are necessary for the proper digestion of the carbohydrates. There is a chemical laboratory in each body cell where certain substances must be put into the test tube before other necessary substances can be manufactured. The B vitamins and carbohydrates are linked. One cannot benefit the body without the other. And the B vitamins that have been removed from refined foods are present in meat in large quantity.

B Vitamins in Poultry and Meat

Milligrams per 100 grams
(In general 100 grams equals an average serving)

	Thiamin	Riboflavin	Niacin	Pyridoxine	Pantothenic acid	Biotin
Chicken ...	.90 - .150	.070-.260	8.6	.100	.550	.005-.009
Goose	.150		3	?	?	?
Turkey ...	.120- .150	.190-.240	7.9	?	?	?
Duck	.360	.230	3	?	?	?
Beef	.100- .220	.120-.270	4.5	.077	.490	.002
Lamb	.80 - .210	.230-.266	5.9	.081	.600	.002
Pork	.90 -1.040	.040-.240	.9-4.4	.086-.270	?	?
Veal	.170- .180	.140-.280	3.1-6.5	.056-.130	.110-.260	.001

We sometimes hear of folks who have broken many of the rules of good health. They drink, they smoke, they eat starchy desserts and soda fountain food. And still they are healthy. Probably no one will ever solve this mystery. It may have to do with the glands, arteries and other physical equipment they were born with. It may be that they are just naturally able to resist much of the nutritional degeneration that should affect them. But we have a strong suspicion that, if you look closely into their diets, you will find they eat lots of meat, fruits and vegetables. And perhaps this alone protects them from the results of their other bad habits.

Meat for Infants and Young Children

Meat is now a recommended food for babies. We uncovered a very revealing article on meat diets for infants in which milk was not given at all. Mildred R. Ziegler, Ph. D., of the University of Minnesota writes in the *Journal of the American Dietetic Association* for July, 1953, of the successful results obtained. She tells us that many infants cannot drink milk for one reason or another. (We rather suspect it may be the quality of the milk these days.) These children must have lots of protein, of course, and meat seems to be the answer. She tells us that the American Indians used to feed their infants on meat—pounded dried meat mixed with pounded dried choke cherries and the fat skinned from boiled bones of the buffalo.

Dr. Ziegler also tells us that animal proteins have a much higher digestibility than vegetable proteins—up to 98 or 100 per cent. Meat, which is very rich in iron (needed after the infant is a year or so old) and the B vitamins, is not rich in calcium. Milk is, of course, very rich in calcium. So in preparing the diet Dr. Ziegler had to add calcium and trace minerals to the meat. She used the ash from veal bones. This contained not only calcium and phosphorus in their proper physiological proportions, but also all the various trace elements whose possible importance to nutrition we do not know as yet. The meat was cooked and strained.

All the children on the enriched meat diet throve. Dr. Ziegler describes the cases of two children—one with an allergy to milk, the other with a disorder called *galactosemia* which is an inability to use properly the galactose—a sugar occurring in milk.

The two-and-a-half-month old boy who was allergic to milk had had diarrhea almost since birth. He was in an extremely serious condition, with a distended abdomen, bad color, feeble cry and no gain in weight. He was put on the enriched meat formula and began to improve almost at once. At the end of 5 months he had gained normally and there was no diarrhea. He continued on the meat formula with added fruits and vegetables as he grew older.

The second infant had jaundice, indicating possibly that some liver disorder had brought on the *galactosemia*. "The child showed marked clinical improvement with an amazing change in her activity and in her disposition, after the mineral-enriched meat formula was substituted for the previous milk diet," says Dr. Ziegler.

In an earlier experiment, reported in *Pediatrics* for October, 1952, we learn that the only illnesses that occurred among the healthy children eating the meat and milk diets were respiratory and digestive disorders. Those on the meat diet had considerably fewer of these and they were much less severe. Drs. Jacobs and George who wrote the article estimate that the disease rate for the meat-fed children was about 40 per cent less than that of the milk-fed children. Dr. Ruth Leverton and associates, writing in *Pediatrics* for June, 1952, tell us of another group of children part of whom were fed milk, the others meat. The hemoglobin and red blood cell count were better in the infants who got the meat. She also says, "The infants receiving a dietary supplement of meat had approximately one-half as many colds as the control subjects and the duration of the colds was reduced. All infants were reported to have slept better and appeared more satisfied when they received the meat supplement."

Today's Meat is Chemicalized

We must consider for a moment all the various things that happen to meat before it reaches our tables to make it unhealthful. Cattle and other meat animals are not always fed the most nutritious diet, just as gardens and farms are not always fertilized properly. However, in general, it is well known among breeders that healthy animals are profitable. So there is much less than there used to be of selling diseased or half-starved animals for meat.

However, scientists have recently discovered that animals grow faster when they are fed antibiotics along with their meals. So many farmers use feeds spiked with antibiotics. For years poultry raisers have used a hormone preparation to fatten poultry. By injecting a pellet of stilbestrol into the neck of the chicken, they produced an artificial castration which made the chicken grow fat and big much earlier than previously. During the Congressional Hearings on Chemicals in Foods, there was a lot of discussion of stilbestrol and the possibility that it might be harmful to individuals eating the poultry. It was felt generally among the experts that carelessly injected pellets could easily be eaten by poultry buyers with resulting harm. In fact, there was one government cancer expert who believed there was serious harm, perhaps even the possibility of cancer, to be feared as a result of the use of stilbestrol.

In December of 1959 the Government officially halted the sale and production of poultry injected with stilbestrol pellets. However, no mention was made concerning the treatment of these animals with stilbestrol in their feed. So you can see that although one method of getting stilbestrol into the meat we will eventually eat was denied the poultry raisers, they still can rely on the feeding process as a way to use stilbestrol in fattening their animals and improving the meat's color and texture.

We know that stilbestrol is being used to fatten cattle. The aim, of course, is to save the cattleman money, by causing the cattle to grow much more rapidly so that they can be taken to market much sooner, hence a lot of feed will be saved. But the question, of course, is—what will be the effect of the stilbestrol on the person who eats the meat? And how much nutrition does one get from meat produced to some extent by the action of stilbestrol?

We do not have the answer to any of these questions as yet. We can only assume that any and all unnatural tinkering with animals meant for food is not good. The only way to avoid chemicalized meat is to buy your meat from someone you know, preferably an organic farmer.

Talk to your butcher about the kind of meat he sells you. If you buy from a large super market, find out where their meat comes from and write to the source. Inquire what treatments their animals are given— do they get antibiotics, do they get stilbestrol and so forth? Indicate that you do not want to buy meat from animals that have been treated with any of these substances. One letter will do little good, of course. You will probably get an answer assuring you that there is no harm in any of these things. But if many people write—if you and your friends and neighbors and relatives and health club members write, perhaps the meat producers of this country will wake up to the fact that doping their animals is not really economical.

We have merely scratched the surface of all the things that are done to meat, for, of course, other processes are involved before the meat reaches your grocery store. You may well ask if it is really healthful to eat meat, considering all these outrages. Don't forget that similar things have been done to plants, too. Vegetables and fruits are subjected to hormone treatments, poison sprays, artificial fertilizers, various methods of breeding and forcing that are just as unnatural as the processes the meat goes through. So do not make the mistake of turning from chemicalized meat in disgust and eating nothing but chemicalized vegetables and fruits, for the meat contains much that will keep your body strong against the un-healthful things in your diet—the proteins and B vitamins of meat are necessary to protect you against the possible harm you may suffer from any or all of our modern chemicalized food.

Glance at the table below, which shows the vitamin and mineral content of the various meats. Note that the organic meats contain far, far more nutriments than the muscle meats. Make certain that you serve an organ meat at least once a week—oftener if possible. Get accustomed to using the less popular ones—kidneys, brains, sweetbreads, heart. There are many appetizing ways in which these can be served. They are economical and nutritious.

MINERAL CONTENT OF ORGAN MEATS
Milligrams per 100 grams

	Calcium	Phosphorus	Iron	Copper
Brains	8	380	2.3	0
Heart	10	236	6.2	0
Kidney	14	262	15.0	.11
Liver, beef	8	373	12.1	2.15
Liver, calf	11	205	5.4	4.41
Sweetbreads	14	596	1.6	0
Tongue	31	229	3.0	0

VITAMIN CONTENT OF ORGAN MEATS
Milligrams per 100 grams

	Vit. A	Thiamin	Ribo-flavin	Niacin	Inositol	Pyri-doxine	Panto-thenic acid
Brains	0	.25	.26	6.0	200	?	
Heart	0	.54	.90	6.8	260	.120	1.8-3.6
Kidney (I.U.)	750	.45	1.95	7.4	0	4.0	2.0
Liver (I.U.)	19,200-53,000	.27	2.80	16.1	55	.170-.730	37.0
Pancreas	0	.320	.590	.584	?	?	4.4-7.6
Sweetbreads	0	.150	.550	3.3			?
Tongue	0	.15	.23	4.0		1.25	10.6
Tripe	0	.006	.12	.003			

	Biotin	Folic acid	Choline	Vit. C	Vit. D
Brains	.0074	.052	?	14	0
Heart	.0049	.130	?	14	0
Kidney (I.U.)	.92				
Liver (I.U.)	.096-.112	3.25-.380	.380	31	15-45
Pancreas					
Sweetbreads				20	
Tongue	.003				

CHAPTER 70

Choosing Your Meats

In the preceding chapter we spoke about the necessity of using plenty of meat in your meals so that you get lots of protein. A survey by the Department of Agriculture showed that 9 out of every 10 Americans suffer from protein deficiencies. Meat is your best source of protein.

You have been warned to avoid animal fats? Then how can you eat meat, of which a certain portion is bound to be fatty? There is, of course, some fat in most meat. It's a good idea, therefore, to study the different kinds of meat and make certain you are not favoring the especially fatty kinds day after day. In fact, it would be best to avoid the very fatty ones.

TABLE 1. PROXIMATE COMPOSITION, MINERAL AND CALORIC
CONTENT OF FRESH MUSCLE CUTS

Muscle Cuts Medium Grade	Protein %	Fat %	mg/100g Calcium	mg/100g Phosphorus	mg/100g Iron	100g Calories
Beef						
Chuck	18.6	16	11	167	2.8	224
Flank	19.0	18	12	186	3.0	247
Loin	16.7	25	10	182	2.5	293
Rib	17.4	23	10	149	2.6	282
Round	19.5	11	11	180	2.9	182
Rump	16.2	28	9	131	2.4	322
Veal						
Cutlet	19.0	5	6	343	10.6	141
Leg	19.1	12	11	206	2.9	186
Shoulder	19.4	10	11	199	2.9	173
Pork						
Ham	15.2	31	9	168	2.3	344
Loin	16.4	25	10	186	2.5	296
Shoulder	13.5	37				387
Spareribs	14.6	32	8	157	2.2	346
Lamb						
Breast	12.8	37				384
Leg	18.0	18	10	213	2.7	235
Loin	18.6	16				217
Rib chop	14.9	32	9	138	2.2	356
Shoulder	15.6	25	9	155	2.3	295
Poultry						
Chicken	20.2	12.6	14	200	1.5	200
Turkey	20.1	20.2	23	320	3.8	268
Duck	16.1	28.6	9	172	2.4	322

How do the different cuts and kinds of meat compare as far as vitamin and mineral content goes—for you want to get as much of these substances as possible while you are consuming the good meat protein. In general, the organ meats are much richer in vitamins, so you should plan to include them often in family meals. In the case of vitamin B_{12}—so necessary, so valuable and so scarce in foods—liver contains from 20 to 50 times as much of this vitamin as the muscle meats. Kidney contains up to 10 times as much. If your family refuses to eat organ meats, it's a near certainty that they're short on vitamin B_{12}.

Table 1 shows the protein, fat and mineral content of the various muscle cuts. Notice the wide variety in fat content. Breast of lamb contains about twice as much fat as leg or loin. You would expect, then, that breast of lamb would contain less protein and sure enough, it does. Notice the quite high content of fat in pork products and the low fat content of veal.

The mineral content of meats is not extremely important in your meal

TABLE 2. PROXIMATE COMPOSITION, MINERAL AND CALORIC
CONTENT OF FRESH ORGAN MEATS

Organ Meats	Protein %	Fat %	mg/100g Calcium	mg/100g Phosphorus	mg/100g Iron	100g Calories
Beef						
Brain	10.5	9	8	380	2.3	127
Heart	16.9	4	9	203	4.6	108
Kidney	15.0	8	9	221	7.9	141
Liver	19.7	3	7	358	6.6	136
Lung	18.3	2				89
Pancreas	13.5	25				279
Spleen	18.1	3			8.9	99
Thymus	11.8	33	14	596	1.6	344
Tongue	16.4	15	9	187	2.8	207
Calf liver	19.0	5	6	343	10.6	141
Calf pancreas	19.2	9				156
Calf thymus	19.6	3				106
Pork						
Brain	10.6	9				126
Heart	16.9	5	35	132	2.7	117
Kidney	16.3	5	11	246	8.0	114
Liver	19.7	5	10	362	18.0	134
Lung	12.9	2				71
Pancreas	14.5	24				272
Spleen	17.1	4				103
Tongue	16.8	16				210
Lamb						
Brain	11.8	8				121
Heart	16.8	10				158
Kidney	16.6	3	13	237	9.2	105
Liver	21.0	4	8	364	12.6	136
Lung	17.9	2				85
Spleen	18.8	4				110
Thymus	14.1	4				91
Tongue	13.9	15				189

planning, except for iron and phosphorus. In this country we get, generally speaking, plenty of phosphorus, since meat and cereals, both rich in this mineral, form quite a large part of our diets. But many of us, especially children, young people and women, are short on iron which tends to make us anemic. Meat is valuable for its iron content. One hundred grams is about ¼ pound, or the average serving.

One more fact of importance in selecting meats. There is considerable difference in the amount of fat and protein any given cut of meat may have. For instance, a chuck roast of beef which contains very little fat may have as much as 19 per cent protein content and 9 per cent fat. A very fatty piece of chuck may have only 15 per cent protein and as much as 32 per cent fat. The same is true generally of other cuts.

Table 2 shows the protein, fat and mineral content of the organ meats. Observe the generally low figures for fat content and the high content of iron. Since there is less fat in organ meats there are, too, fewer calories, which should be of great importance to reducers.

Experience has shown that the B vitamins and mineral contents of muscle meats correlate well with the protein content of the cut. If you have a high-protein cut, chances are the vitamin, mineral and amino acid content will be high, too. If you have a fatty cut of meat, lower in protein, the content of vitamins, minerals and amino acids will almost certainly be lower.

In tables 3 and 4 the vitamin content of meats is listed. As you will notice, meat is valuable chiefly for its vitamin B content. With the exception of liver (rich in vitamins A and C), there is little in the way of other vitamins in meat. However, since vitamin B is one element we Americans are deficient in, meat once again shows itself as one of our most valuable foods. And, of course, the organ meats assume an even greater importance here.

For instance, riboflavin is one of the least plentiful of vitamins. But it is extremely important and hundreds of thousands of us are deficient in it. It occurs in quantity only in eggs, milk and meat and, of course, food supplements like brewer's yeast. If you don't use milk and eat few eggs, you are almost certainly not getting enough riboflavin every day. And it is a water soluble vitamin which must be supplied every day. The smallest possible amount you can get along on, without showing symptoms of deficiency, has been estimated as 1.2 milligrams daily for adults. You surely can't get that much from two servings of ordinary meat a day! An egg contains about 1.06 milligrams. But see how rich liver is in riboflavin!

One final word on cooking meats. Cooking at a low temperature saves vitamins and protein. Extremely high temperatures used in frying or pressure cooking are particularly destructive to the protein. Soaking or cooking meat in liquids (water, vinegar or wine) causes loss of many vitamins if the liquid is discarded, for vitamins and minerals have soaked into this liquid.

Table 3. Vitamin Content of Muscle Cuts

Muscle Cuts Medium Grade	mg/100g Thiamin	mg/100g Riboflavin	mg/100g Niacin	mg/100g B6	mg/100g Pantothenic Acid	mcg/100g Biotin	mg/100g Choline	mcg/100g B12	mg/100g Folic acid
Beef									
Chuck	.08	.17	4.5	.38					.013
Loin	.10	.13	4.6						
Rib	.07	.15	4.2		.41	3.4			.014
Round	.08	.17	4.7	.37	1.0	4.6	68	2.0	.026
Rump	.07	.14	3.9						
Veal									
Leg	.18	.30	7.5	.37			102		.023
Shoulder	.14	.40	6.1	.14			93		.018
Sirloin	.19	.31	7.1	.41			96		.020
Pork									
Ham	.74	.18	4.0	.33	.72	5.3	120	0.9	.009
Loin or Loin Chops	.80	.19	4.3	.50	2.0	77	77		.007
Picnic	.94	.18	4.0						
Spareribs	.92	.18	3.9						
Lamb									
Breast						2.1			
Leg	.16	.22	5.2	.29	.59	5.9	84	2.5	.009
Rib Chop	.13	.18	4.3						
Shoulder	.14	.19	4.5						.007

TABLE 4. VITAMIN CONTENT OF FRESH ORGAN MEATS

Organ Meats	Thiamin mg/100g	Riboflavin mg/100g	Niacin mg/100g	B_6 mg/100g	Pantothenic Acid mg/100g	Biotin mcg/100g	Choline mg/100g	B_{12} mcg/100g	Vit. A IU/100g	Vit. C mg/100g	Folic Acid mg/100g
Beef											
Brain	.12	.22	3.6	.16	2.5	6.1	410	4.7		18	.012
Heart	.24	.84	6.6	.29	2.3	7.3	170	9.7	30	6	.110
Kidney	.28	1.9	5.3	.39	3.4	92.3	262	28.0	1,150	13	.041
Liver	.23	3.3	13.5	.71	7.3	101.3	510	65.0	43,900	31	.081
Lung	.11	.36	4.0	.07	1.0	5.9		3.3			
Pancreas	.14	.34	3.1	.20	3.8	13.7		4.8		11	
Spleen	.13	.28	4.2	.12	1.2	5.7		5.1		6	
Tongue	.16	.28	3.9	.13	2.0	3.3	108				
Calf liver	.21	3.1	16.1	.30							
Veal liver	.52	3.3	16.5	.30	6.0	75.2			22,500	36	.046
Pork											
Brain	.16	.28	4.3		2.8		375	2.8		18	
Heart	.31	.81	7.3	.35	2.5	18.2	231	2.4	30	6	
Kidney	.26	1.9	8.6	.55	3.1	128.8	286	6.6	130	13	
Liver	.25	3.0	13.9	.33	6.6	84.7	552	23.0	14,200	23	.074
Lung	.09	.27	3.4		0.9						
Pancreas	.11	.46	3.5		4.6		329	6.5			
Spleen	.13	.30	4.3		1.1		208	4.1			
Tongue							137				
Lamb											
Brain	.15	.26	3.7		2.6			7.3		18	
Heart	.31	.86	4.6		3.0			5.2			
Kidney	.38	2.2	6.8		4.3		360	26.0	1,150	13	
Liver	.29	3.9	12.1	.37	8.1	127.0		35.0	50,500	33	
Lung	.11	.47	4.7		1.2			5.0			
Pancreas	.13	.50	3.9		3.5			19.0			
Spleen	.09	.27	4.7		1.5			6.7			

CHAPTER 71

Watch That Pork

Pork and pork products, especially uncooked ones like Italian-style salami, are still risky meats to eat unless you are 100 per cent positive that they have been sufficiently cooked. This meat is sometimes the carrier of the *Trichinella spiralis* worms that are the cause of the infectious disease known as trichinosis. Depositing their eggs in the intestinal tract of human consumers of pork, the embryos wind their way into the muscles, especially those of the diaphragm, where they develop. Early symptoms of the disease they produce there include nausea, colic, diarrhea, fever, insomnia and sweating, and if the infection gets a strong enough hold on its victim, death often results. The worms and their larvae are commonly found in garbage-fed hogs.

San Francisco, one of this country's principal centers for the manufacture and distribution of Italian salami, was also a heavy sufferer from trichinosis when J. B. McNaught and E. V. Anderson undertook an investigation of its frequency in 1936. Performing autopsies on 200 human diaphragms selected at random, they found 48 of these to be infected, or an incidence of 24 per cent, with living larvae occupying every specimen. The disease was also found to be most common in the higher age-brackets, 10 of their cases occurring in persons from 1 to 24 years of age, 27 in the 25-39 group, 139 in subjects from 40-74 years old and a drop to 24 from 75 years onward.

Since that discovery, strict legislation affecting the pork-packing industry has been passed in many places. Federal, state and some local regulations were enacted to require the salting and drying, or freezing of uncooked pork products in order to kill the worms. In addition to these measures, a campaign was undertaken to educate the public to the necessity of cooking pork thoroughly. And as a third (though accidental) preventive measure, feeding garbage to hogs was dropped because it became an unprofitable business during war years, owing to scarcity of labor, transportation difficulties, etc. This last defensive barrier against the dangers of acquiring trichinosis from infected hogs is likely, however, to be raised at any time since it is not a legal restriction.

The Disease's Prevalence

Wishing to check on the rate of the disease's prevalence, Rodney R. Beard, M.D., of San Francisco, conducted a checkup and published his findings in an article, "Incidence of Trichinosis Infections in San Francisco," in the *Journal of the American Medical Association* for May 26, 1951. Selecting at random 161 diaphragms collected from autopsy, he found only 13 to be infected, 3 of these with living larvae. A rate of 8 per cent, this suggested that the disease is now ⅔ less prevalent than it was at the time of the 1936 report. The fact that 9 of the 13 infections also were found in the 40-74 year age-bracket agreed with the earlier investigation in finding susceptibility to the disease to be highest in older persons. Thinking the reduction in prevalence since 1936 "quite unlikely to have been observed by chance alone," Dr. Beard maintains that trichinosis has been brought under control because of the 3 factors previously mentioned. He does, however, cite evidence to the effect that the worms causing it can live in human beings for as long as from 19 to 26 years, but concludes: "The high proportion of dead larvae that we have observed suggests that some, perhaps many, of the infections that we discovered were acquired long ago, before the initiation of the trichina control measure and educational programs referred to earlier."

Disagreement Among Doctors

In commenting on his work and its implication that the disease is on the way out, 3 other medical doctors disagree with Dr. Beard. Frank B. Queen, of Portland, Oregon, disputes the reason for his low percentage: "The question arises whether or not this reduction indicates a true reduction in trichinosis infection, or is it simply within the variations of biological studies? . . . I believe that it may well be the latter." Stating that a 1936 investigation of the disease in New Orleans showed only 3.5 per cent infection, while another undertaken 3 years later showed "exactly twice that amount," he maintains that Dr. Beard's random sampling gives a false interpretation to the true state of affairs.

Richard D. Friedlander, a San Francisco medico, thinks that it should not be "the primary interest of the medical profession" to count the number of larvae in the diaphragms of dead people. He calls for continued vigilance against the disease by methods of skin-testing of swine for trichinosis, a positive and specific measure. Elmer W. Smith, another Californian M.D., adds that rats are also carriers of the worm causing the disease, and since they infest the quarters of pigs, often themselves convey the larvae to the latter. Finding some specimens of raw Italian salami to be "teeming with living trichinella," he suggests that the rat population problem should be an important concern for public health departments of our cities, and also that even boiling of garbage, should such a diet be again fed to hogs, will not prevent trichinosis from spreading unless the rat problem is also met.

Cook Pork Thoroughly

Dr. Beard himself is aware of the fact that the disease can again appear at any time in epidemic form if regulations on pork manufacture should be allowed to lapse. "While we have no evidence that garbage-feeding of hogs is again increasing, it would seem to be a good time to establish regulations requiring the cooking of garbage used for this purpose against the day when the practice might be resumed on a wider scale. . . . The possibility of obtaining meat from an occasional heavily infected hog still remains and will remain despite the application of any reasonably practical control measure." Since the risk of disability and even death is consequently still involved in the eating of this meat, he pleads with the public that they insist on the thorough cooking of fresh pork.

[250]

CHAPTER 72

Eat More Fish!

One of the complaints most commonly leveled against our diet suggestions and those of leading nutritionists is that a high-protein diet is too expensive. This is a sample of the very justifiable wail we hear when we mention high protein diet: "It's all right for you to talk about how healthy we and our children would be on a diet high in proteins and low in carbohydrates, but just compare for a minute the price of meat and the price of processed cereal, the price of cheese and the price of baked goods, the price of eggs and the price of macaroni."

We agree that protein foods are inexcusably high in price. We remind our readers why this is so. Carbohydrate foods are harvested, processed and sold with a minimum of difficulty. Protein foods are produced chiefly from animals which are fed on carbohydrate foods. The number of cattle that can be raised on a field is very small compared to the amount of wheat that can be raised on that same field. So, sure, the wheat products can be sold for 16 cents a package with a space cadet uniform thrown in. And meat may be anywhere from 60 cents to a dollar and a half a pound.

However, the fact that carbohydrate foods are cheaper does not mean that they are healthier. You need carbohydrate foods, but, 9 chances out of 10, you need more protein and less carbohydrate foods than you are now getting. That is why we are proud to present an excellent source of protein which is also cheap, and which is a good food from many other points of view as well—fish.

Why Fish Are So Cheap

No one has to plant or harvest fish, or worry over the proper proportion of elements in their diet. There's no loss from contagious diseases. You don't have to buy a farm and a lot of expensive machinery, you don't have to give a hoot for the fluctuations of the grain market or the political fortunes of subsidies; you're not even bothered by the weather—if you're a fisherman. All you need is a boat, and a line or a net and you're in business. These, we suppose are some of the reasons why fish can be inexpensive, even in spite of the fact that they are as good a protein as meat.

Fish weren't always inexpensive. J. C. Drummond and Anne Wilbraham in their book, *The Englishman's Food* (Jonathan Cape, London), tells of days in eighteenth century England when the price of fish was exorbitant. This was because there was no refrigeration, and in order to have the fish edible by the time it reached inland towns the most expensive methods of transportation had to be used. One enterprising gentleman set up a system of speedy "land carriages" for bringing fish to inland markets and even succeeded in having a bill passed to exempt these carriages from the customary road tolls. By 1820 fish was being transported packed in ice, but this was expensive, too.

The Fish Business—Past and Present

Earlier, way back in the sixteenth century, the English church established two "fisshe dayes" per week, to encourage ship building and because meat was so expensive. There was a fine of 3 pounds or 3 months imprisonment for anyone eating meat on the two prescribed "fisshe dayes." Of course, this was long before industrialization had concentrated people in cities, so transportation problems were not so pressing. And even so there were laws to prevent the selling of decomposing fish "lest the air might become infected through the stench arising therefrom." The fishmongers' companies enforced these laws. It was at this time that salt became such an important item of trade, for much of the fish was salted to preserve it.

Today fish is an 11 million dollar business. The Boston pier alone handles 300 million pounds of fish annually. And yet the average American eats only about 15 pounds per year of all fishery products. Compare this to the 100 pounds of white sugar per year per American, and you may arrive at some conclusions as to why many of us are sick much of the time.

Eat Ocean Fish—Not Inland Fish

For, make no mistake about it, fish, especially ocean fish, is good food. First of all there has been no tampering with it. Commercial fertilizers and insecticides play no part in the fish business. Preservatives, artificial flavorings and colorings cannot be used on fish. Ocean fish cannot be doped, chemicalized or processed.

We do want to inject at this point just a hint of some of the things that are happening to inland fish. A clipping from *Chemical Week* (August 1, 1953) tells us that trout breeders have found that brook trout can be more easily transported alive from place to place if they are given sleeping pills before they are placed in their containers. This prevents them from moving about so much. What it may do to people who eat the fish over a long period of time has, of course, not been investigated. We also have in our files a horror story about methods now being used to "clear" lakes before trout are released. The other "inferior" fish are killed off, it seems, by scattering rotenone, says *Chemical Week* for August 29, 1953. Then, too, inland fish are subjected constantly to the tons of poisons dumped each day into our rivers and streams by industrial firms. No one gets very excited about this (even though residents are drinking the water) until fish begin to die by the thousands, as happened in the Buffalo, New York area. Then the newspapers take up the hue and cry, the pollution ceases for a while and everyone forgets the entire incident.

So we would advise against eating fish from inland waters, unless you yourself have caught the fish in a mountain stream or lake which you know is far enough away from "civilization" that no contamination could have reached the waters. But ocean fish—taken from the great fishing banks far out to sea—come to us unpolluted. And most of the fish sold in inland markets comes from either the Atlantic or Pacific.

[252]

Freezing—Best Method For Preserving Fish

For a long time there has been a prejudice in the American mind against eating commercially frozen fish, says Morris B. Jacobs in his book, *Food and Food Products* (Interscience Publishers, New York City). This is apparently because, in the early days, only those fish that seemed too far gone to be marketed were frozen, and, of course, their quality was very low. But today with the quick freezing methods that are available frozen fish is every bit as good, or perhaps even better, than fresh fish for inland folks. The marketing of fish is a race against time, for the whole metabolic system of fish is set up on a very rapid scale, because of the cold temperature in which they live. So deterioration sets in much faster than it does in meat. Actually the meat of a fish begins to deteriorate the moment it is taken from the water. Quick freezing halts this process immediately.

So if you live far inland, the frozen fish, packed in airtight containers very shortly after the fish is caught, has probably more food value than a whole fresh fish which has been frozen or packed in ice for the long trip from the ocean to your market. You cannot determine, says Jacobs, by the brightness of the eye or the color of the gills how fresh a fish actually is. Your only criterion for judging is the keeping quality of the fish after you buy it, its appearance and odor while you are preparing it and its palatability. Small pieces like fillets freeze more quickly than whole fish, so less food value is lost in freezing. In addition, when you buy frozen fillets there is no waste and the waste matter in a whole fish may be as high as 70 per cent, as they are sold. Any housewife who has ever struggled to prepare a trout or bass brought in by her ever-loving provider knows well what a pile of fish trimmings accumulates in the garbage can compared to the tiny morsels that find their way to the table. So it's economical to buy frozen fillets.

Amino Acids In Fish

Now, why do we claim that fish is a healthful food, aside from the fact that it is not tampered with? Fish is chiefly protein, as good a protein as meat. By this we mean that it supplies all the different kinds of protein that are needed for health. Some proteins contain all the known building blocks that are needed for building and repairing tissues, while other proteins lack some of these essential building blocks. The building blocks are called "amino acids." About 10 of these are absolutely essential for health— that is, they are required in the diet of man. Comparing the amino acids of fish with those of chicken and beef, we find that they are as good or better.

Other Valuable Constituents of Fish

Fish contains valuable minerals, too. And here we run headlong into a discussion that is at present occupying many Americans who are arguing about the advisability of artificially fluoridating their water supply. Fish contain fluorine in considerably higher quantities than do most foodstuffs. Says Jacobs, "It might appear that the presence of 5 parts per million of fluorine in sea foods would have a harmful effect. However, Lee and

Nilson have shown that this is not the case (United States Bureau of Fisheries, Investigational Report 44, 1939). Apparently, the fluorine is present in some form such that assimilation is much less than is the case with added inorganic fluorides." This seems to us another overwhelming evidence against water fluoridation. Organic fluorine in food is not harmful. It is only when we begin to concoct fluoride compounds in a laboratory with no regard for what form the compound takes or what may accompany it in the solution we end with, that anyone suffers any difficulties from ingesting fluorine.

Fish contain, too, relatively large amounts of calcium, copper, iron, magnesium, phosphorus, potassium, sodium and strontium. It is the high phosphorus content of fish that has made it famous as a "brain food," for phosphorus is one of the important constituents of brain matter.

What is Fishmeal?

Fishmeal is manufactured from the wastes of fish and is used in animal food. Nutritionally it is one of the richest of foods, for it contains all the vitamins and minerals in concentrated form. This being the case, we "civilized" Americans feed it to our animals, of course, rather than eating it ourselves. In New England fisheries the whole carcass of the fish, including the bones, is ground up, along with the head, fins and other waste material. After it is dried it will keep well without refrigeration and has been found to be an excellent source of the rare vitamin B_{12}, along with the other B vitamins.

Sensitivity To Fish

In our research on fish we ran across several reports of sensitivity to fish among folks inclined to be allergic. However, we believe that a correct diet will protect against allergies. We also believe that those who choose their fish with care and eat it along with other foods should not have difficulty with it. A member of our staff recalls that a neighbor's child broke out with hives whenever she ate fish, but the investigating physician discovered that the child ate *only* fish whenever fish was served, so his instructions were to try eating other foods along with it. And there were no more hives. If you happen to be sensitive to fish, here's a hint. Be sure you never lick the sticky side of labels, for the glue on the back is often made from fish gelatin. As a matter of fact, it's just as well never to lick any adhesive substance. A little gadget from the dime store will do it for you much better.

Shellfish and Canned Fish Are Not For You

We have not discussed canned fish for, as many readers know, we take a very dim view of any canned food. We believe you should eat fresh foods, no matter how convenient it is to open a can. But in the case of canned salmon we're inclined to draw the line not quite so sharply, for salmon is canned with the bones intact and perhaps the health value of eating these softened bones outweighs the negative health angle of the can. Let's put it this way: If, because of circumstances beyond your control, you have to eat protein food for dinner tonight out of a can, let it be canned salmon rather than canned meat. You'll be getting a good start on your daily calcium requirements that way. And you won't be filling up on the preservatives that most canned meats contain.

Only 3 words about shellfish—don't eat 'em. True, they are richer in some food elements than fish. But there is a very sound reason why the "Oysters R in Season" sign does not appear on restaurant windows until September. We believe—and we have ample evidence in our files—that present-day Americans are taking too great a chance on pollution when they eat shellfish. Too many of our shellfish are taken from beds near where rivers empty into the sea and untold poisonous matter is released. You do not know where the shellfish you buy have been caught. You could not possibly track down this information. So, from where we sit, Shellfish R Never In Season.

Iodine Content of Fish

We want to emphasize just one more aspect of the healthfulness of fish menus before we list for you the various vitamins and minerals present in fish. One of the recognized deficiencies in diet occurring in many parts of America is lack of iodine which in many cases is related to disorders of the thyroid, or goiter. Iodized salt is not the answer, we believe, for here again, as in the case of fluoridated water, the mineral has been added by chemists. But ocean fish (not inland fish) contain large amounts of iodine. So it seems likely that at least one fish meal a week would supply enough iodine to prevent any deficiency in your family. And this is important, for iodine is mighty scarce in other foods, in many parts of the country.

Vitamins and Minerals in Fish

Here is how fish stacks up in the vital matter of minerals and vitamins. These figures must be approximate, for the content of fish is extremely variable depending on when and where they were caught. We have chosen halibut as a popular and typical fish.

	Amount in 1 serving (about ¼ pound) of halibut
Calcium	20 milligrams
Phosphorus	200 milligrams
Iron	1 milligram
Copper	.23 milligrams
Magnesium	.01 milligrams
Iodine	250 parts per billion
Vitamin B	
Thiamin	90-120 micrograms
Riboflavin	222 micrograms
Niacin	6 milligrams
Pyridoxine	100 micrograms
Pantothenic acid	150 micrograms
Biotin	8 micrograms
Calories	121

CHAPTER 73

Shellfish

The sea like the land has its select list of foods which the gourmet faction of our population has elevated to such a height of eating perfection that they are known as true delicacies, sought after by those who choose the ultimate in fine eating. When considering the gifts to eating pleasure and enjoyment from the sea, we must mention such delicacies as lobster, clams, oysters, crabs and shrimp. Of course, lobster gets top billing in this group. Yet, who can deny the fact that the fascinating flavor of the class of deep sea inhabitants known as shellfish—clams, oysters, crabs and shrimp —far overshadows the commonness of the regular Friday fillet.

Although we stated that some of these shellfish are delicacies in the way of eating pleasure, we cannot recommend them as delicacies in the way of healthfulness. To be sure, they contain a goodly amount of the necessary nutriments, vitamins, minerals and protein, which would certainly classify them as food meriting full recognition as a healthful food. For example, an average serving of 6 oysters will supply more than the daily requirement of iron and copper, about one-half the iodine and about one-tenth of the needed protein, calcium, magnesium, phosphorus, vitamin A, thiamin, riboflavin and niacin. Yet with all these nutritional advantages, advantages which show Nature's habit of nutritional balance in foods, we cannot recommend shellfish because they have two very serious drawbacks which cancel out Nature's well-meaning intentions.

Contaminated Waters

The first of these is the problem of polluted coastal waters, the very waters from which many of our shellfish are harvested. Manufacturing waste products, sewage, etc., drain into these coastal waters and eventually find their way into the shellfish which inhabit these areas. This is a highly publicized detrimental factor to shellfish eating and therefore we will not go into detail on this point. However, we would like to mention that even though the United States government under the direction of the Public Health Service has worked out a feasible solution to this contamination problem, by making sanitary and bacteriological surveys and setting up poison tolerances for the amount of bacteria coming from shellfish taken from these infested waters, the thought of ingesting any amount of harmful bacteria (germs from sewage, etc.) no matter how large or small, no matter if these bacteria will cause poisoning or not, does not sound very appetizing nor healthful. Nature has planted its seeds of nutrition in many shellfish, but man's progress has destroyed any semblance of benefits which could be derived from eating them.

Poisonous Substances In Foods

Shellfish require special scrutiny on a second count also, one which has not been so widely publicized. Many of them during special seasons of the year contain poisons which, if taken in sufficient amounts, can be deadly. Yes, cases of death from poisoning by shellfish are rare, but the danger exists and points to the fact that we Americans have a perverted set of values so far as our food selection is concerned. We value those foods highest which appeal to our taste buds, regardless of their nutritive value—their ultimate effect on our health. Take for example today's overconsumption of sugar and sugar products which can only mean an underconsumption of those food products which contain the necessary vitamins and minerals for optimum health. Consider, for example, the youngster who fills himself on soda and ice cream. What room is left in his stomach for such essential foodstuffs as meat to provide necessary protein and fruits and vegetables for vitamins and minerals? Essential foods are slighted in preference to those that appeal to our sense of taste.

Because of this slavery to the whims of our taste buds, besides becoming a nation of overfed but undernourished people, we sometimes choose as our most sought-after foods those which contain substances which could be dangerous to our health. This is the case when we refer to the shellfish as being a gourmet dish. Sure they are pleasant to eat, but what about the aftereffects. You say you are willing to risk the dangers involved? Well, here are some of the consequences incurred in eating shellfish.

An Early Experience With Shellfish Poisoning

Perhaps the first recorded encounter with shellfish poisoning occurred during the time of Captain George Vancouver's exploratory voyage of what is now Mathieson Channel on the coast of British Columbia. Mr. Menzies, naturalist and surgeon on this expedition, gives the following account, written on June 17, 1793: "Near the head of this arm they stopped to breakfast on the morning of the 15th where the people finding some good looking mussels about the rocks and shore, boiled a quantity of them . . . these mussels proved to be of a deleterious quality as all those who had ate of them in any quantity were, soon after they embarked, seized with sickness, numbness about the mouth, face and arms, which soon spread over the whole body accompanied with giddiness and general lassitude; this was the case with three of the crew of the Discovery's boat . . . One of them, John Carter, puked a good deal, and found himself so much relieved by it that he kept pulling on his oar till about one o'clock when the whole party stopped to dine; but in attempting to get out of the boat he was so weak and giddy that he fell down and he and the other two were obliged to be carried to shore. On this, Mr. Johnstone instantly directed a fire to be kindled and plenty of warm water to be got ready as soon as possible, that each of them might drink a sufficient quantity of it to operate as an emetic . . . but, before it could be got ready, John Carter became . . . very ill . . . his pulse becoming weaker and weaker, his mouth and lips appearing black and his face and neck becoming much swelled together with faintness, general numbness and tremor. Under these circumstances he gradually sank without much struggle and expired just as soon as they were offering him the first draught of warm water which he was unable to swallow, and this sad affair happened within five hours from the time of his eating the mussels."

The Poisonous Organism

Mussels are members of the shellfish group known as bivalves (two shells hinged together) closely related and resembling such popular shellfish varieties as clams and oysters. In fact, this similarity predisposes all shellfish to the same fate, that is, the poisonous substance which seeks out its quarry among the shellfish chooses no favorite victim. All shellfish are susceptible in the same degree to the poison's whim. Thus we can at no time single out a particular shellfish, say, oyster, and announce that this one alone is free from possible harmful substances. When we say beware of "all" shellfish, especially during certain seasons of the year, we mean "all." N. Sapeika, M.D., writing in the *South African Medical Journal* for May 17, 1958, states: "The poison-containing plankton (which serves as food for mussels, clams, etc.) may reach shellfish beds in various places and in varying amounts from time to time, sometimes even within a day after such beds have provided non-poisonous specimens. Several states have strict regulations for handling shellfish. In Massachusetts, for instance, the digging of clams is supervised by wardens who see that all dead or damaged clams are discarded. But who is to say that this is a foolproof method of eliminating the poisonous ones? A single specimen may contain a fatal dose. The affected area may remain contaminated for weeks or months. The poison is extremely potent in its central neurotoxic and peripheral neuromuscular action (poisonous to the nervous system) and its depressant action on the circulatory system. There is no specific antidote, so that gastric lavage with sodium bicarbonate solution, purgation, artificial respiration and pressor drugs form the main treatment."

Just what marine organism is responsible for the poison which afflicts shellfish usually during the summer and early autumn? In 1945 during the height of the epidemic shellfish poisoning in New Brunswick, Canada, Mrs. Needler of the Fisheries Research Biological Station at St. Andrews, New Brunswick, began research work in the attempt to gather enough information to properly answer the above question. Through her thorough investigations she found that a one-celled flagellated (having a long lashlike appendage) plant appeared in the plankton about the time the summer water temperatures approached their peak and disappeared soon after this. Thus we can see that water temperature presents itself as the all important variable in determining whether or not the shellfish will contain poison. Remember, the shellfish feed on plankton and thus ingest this poisonous flagellate as soon as the water is at the correct temperature to enable the *Gonyaulax tamarensis,* biological name for this one-celled organism, to propagate itself. It is during this growth season that shellfish are usually quarantined for human use. Wouldn't it be a wise decision, then, to simply curtail the harvesting of shellfish when the water temperature reaches a

[258]

certain level? To be sure, this is the ideal solution to the problem, however, we are dealing with a situation—water temperature—which does not permit accurate prediction. Let us see how water temperature plus the government's other means of predicting and controlling the poison season figured in the 1957 epidemic shellfish poisoning in New Brunswick.

The New Brunswick Epidemic

The Bay of Fundy region of New Brunswick is especially noted for its almost annual occurrence of poisoned shellfish. Since 1943, the Department of Fisheries and the Department of National Health and Welfare of Canada have made regular checks on the Fundy shellfish and have come up with stringent regulations regarding their harvesting, such as prohibiting mussel fishing the year round and clam digging during the critical seasons. They have even posted conspicuous warnings to the general public concerning the risk of consuming shellfish. Yet with all this strict regulation, shellfish poisoning in this region reached epidemic heights both in 1945 and 1957. The majority of those affected were picnickers who ate clams which they dug while at the seashore and thus excused the government of Canada from any responsibility as to its policing powers governing clam harvesting. However, several of those poisoned were residents of shore communities who evidently ate clams bought commercially and supposedly inspected for poison content by government officials. These cases are not excusable and go to prove that a foolproof system of control of shellfish poisoning is almost impossible. As we said earlier, one clam may in itself contain enough poison to produce death. Will inspectors examine each and every shellfish for its level of toxicity? And, too, what is to be considered a safe level?

Controlling Shellfish Poisoning

In determining this "safe level," estimates of poison dosages from a significant amount of case histories were used. Dosages are conventionally expressed in terms of mouse units (m.u) determined by the number of fish eaten and the average amount of poison per fish. This, plus information on whether or not the fish was eaten raw or cooked, gives the average dosage or mouse units required to produce mild, severe and extreme symptoms of poisoning. And from these averages the Canadian Department of National Health and Welfare and the United States Department of Health, Education and Welfare concluded that shellfish with scores up to 400 mouse units per 100 grams are safe.

But we must remember that these are only averages and do not apply to every individual. What would be a safe level for one person may be entirely unsafe for another. Some persons are tolerant to certain dosages of the poison, others are not. Where individual differences play such an important role, designation of a mean (average) dosage unit offers little hope for safeguarding each and everyone from the dangers of shellfish poisoning. J. C. Medcof and others, writing in the *Fisheries Research Board of Canada Bulletin*, 75: 1, 1947, say, "From the vast differences in susceptibility (individual differences) it now appears that listings of average dosages have only academic interest. To emphasize this, reference is made to Case 6. In this instance a two-year-old child suffered serious poisoning from a dosage of only 600 m.u. Similarly Cases 16 and 24 involve adults who reported experiencing mild symptoms from dosages of only 1900 and 2150 m.u. respectively." Are we going to trust arithmetical deductions and conclusions and government policing powers to safeguard our health? Remember, they failed both in 1945, when there were 26 poisonings in the Fundy region alone, and 1957 when there were 33 poisonings.

And what about the water temperature as a means of predicting the poison seasons? Only mention of this made is that "unusually warm weather which induced a sudden rise in water temperature preceded both outbreaks." Evidently, this is not a reliable criterion of prediction since it is extremely difficult to predict just when a sudden rise in water temperature will take place.

What We Recommend

Yes, science with its newest of instruments and knowledge can predict, but where human lives are involved, there can only be room for final truths, not predictions. If you want to risk the dangers of ingesting a poison capable of being absorbed through the mouth membranes as well as through the stomach and intestines, producing such symptoms as extreme difficulty in respiration, loosening of teeth, pins and needles sensations, numbness in the mouth area, nausea, vomiting, diarrhea, headaches, dizziness and abdominal cramps, then go ahead and rely on the scientists "comparable safety" policy for eating shellfish. But we believe in the "entire safety" policy. This can only be achieved by avoiding shellfish on your food list as much as possible.

CHAPTER 74

Additional Information on Meat, Fish and Poultry

A New Way to Fatten Cattle

If the price of beef goes down in the near future, we are told by a writer in the Washington *Evening Star* for August 12, 1958, that the reason will be tranquilizers. Yes, believe it or not, the cattle are being given tranquilizers which make them less active—hence 25 per cent more meat with no increase in food costs. Of course, sex hormones and antibiotics are also regularly added to cattle feed. In addition, we are told that food animals are now given an anti-thyroid compound which blocks action of their thyroid glands, thus causing them to put on lots of weight. It seems impossible that cattle-raisers will pass along to the consumer any of their extra profits, but if they do, you can be certain the consumer will spend most of his share trying to get rid of the ill health all these additives in his daily food have brought him.

What About Rare Beef?

Out of the 12 to 15 million head of cattle and 5 to 7½ million calves butchered annually in this country under federal meat inspection, from 16,500 to more than 27,000 were found to be infested with the beef tapeworm. Careful as most of us are to cook our pork thoroughly so as to avoid trichinosis, it seems that we might exercise a little more care in eating rare beef.

Don't Eat Pork

An illuminating, if shocking, opinion caught our eye in the August, 1956, issue of the *Canadian Medical Journal*. We were reading a discussion of the incidence of trichinosis in Canadian Eskimos when we came across these glaring sentences: ". . . incidence among humans has been estimated at 1.5 per cent in Montreal, 1.7 per cent in Toronto and 4 per cent in Vancouver. In the USA, Gould (in the *Bulletin of the New York Academy of Medicine,* 1945) has estimated the incidence to be 25 per cent, the majority of cases being subclinical."

In the most ulcer-conscious, vaccinated, antibiotic'd country in the world, we are helpless victims of an old chestnut of a disease like trichinosis. This situation can be caused by nothing more than carelessness. Thorough cooking of pork products is the simple answer to this problem. Never eat pink pork or pork that you are not certain has been cooked through. Or, better still, never eat pork. Trichinosis can be deadly and the precautions one can take to avoid it are simple enough for everyone to observe.

Irradiated Pork

Irradiation of raw pork may be used to protect us from trichinosis according to a recent note in the *American Journal of Pathology*. Of course, we have known for years that it's perfectly possible to kill the larva of trichinosis by cooking the meat thoroughly but that's too easy for modern food technology!

Chemically Cured Bacon

A new chemical developed by Du Pont now "offers a solution to a familiar breakfast-time crisis" according to an article in a grocery trade magazine. A curing compound is applied to bacon making it easy to cook to a golden brown with no fear of burning it. Just imagine the convenience! Perfect bacon every time and a dose of chemical along with it! The curing compound is 30 times sweeter than sugar so it saves the processor space and hence dollars. As usual, you, the consumer, are then sold a bill of goods to convince you that bacon cured this way is actually superior!

[261]

Cured Bacon and Other Salted Meats

The *New York Times* for June 20, 1951, reported on an "improved" process of curing bacon that will take only 48 hours instead of the usual 3 weeks required by other methods. V. R. Rupp, research director of Kingan and Company told the Institute of Food Technologists how it is done. In a matter of some 40 hours, 200,000 pounds of bacon were cured by being put through a single machine lined with surgical hypodermic needles that injected pickling fluid into the meat.

A preparation that will do this must certainly contain some powerful and dangerous chemicals to accomplish their purpose in so short a time. It would be better to pay a few pennies more and trust the older, slower and more natural process of preparing bacon. As it is, we do not recommend salted meats to persons protective of their health. Saltpeter (nitrate of potassium) is contained in some, but even more dangerous than this chemical are the effects of consuming food items so heavily salted as bacon and similar meats.

Eating Raw Meat Unwise

The dangers of eating raw meat are brought to our attention by a letter printed in the *Medical Journal of Australia,* April 27, 1957. The correspondent states that many people, especially competing sportsmen, feel that eating raw meat will give them added strength and stamina. Aside from this impression's being false, the writer warns that the raw meat is quite likely to contain the infectious organism which leads to tapeworm. The beef tapeworm is characterized as an annoyance, the tapeworm carried in pork can be much more serious.

Cooking meat thoroughly is the only sure way to eliminate harmful organisms, which can cause serious trouble in the intestinal tract, if they are alive when they get there.

Precooked Meats Get More Dangerous by the Minute!

People who ordinarily wouldn't dream of serving a roast more than 5 minutes after it comes from the oven, find themselves pre-cooking a chicken or a piece of beef a full day in advance of a picnic during the summer days. There is a strong admonition against this practice in the *British Medical Journal* for February 1, 1957. If cooking is slow and there is a period of warm storage, precooking of meats and poultry carries a risk of *clostridium welchii* (food poisoning) as well as dangers from the development of bacteria such as *salmonellae* and *staphylococci*. These can all result in serious illness and death to the consumer of such meats.

The article suggests that the danger be minimized in the following way: use smaller joints so that cooking will penetrate to the center of the joint, at a temperature that will kill all contaminating spores; meat should be eaten as soon as possible after it has been cooked; or if the meat must be kept, it should be cooled rapidly (within ½ hour) and refrigerated until required. Be careful, too, if a piece of meat must be reheated. If it is not truly hot through and through, heat which is sublethal to bacteria might only serve to increase the numbers of organisms present.

[262]

How Long to Store Frozen Meats

The American Meat Institute recently announced its findings concerning the length of time it is advisable to store frozen meats. Here are their recommendations:

Beef: 6 to 8 months
Fresh pork and veal: 3 to 4 months
Lamb: 6 to 7 months
Ground beef: 3 to 4 months
Fresh pork sausage: 2 to 3 weeks
Variety meats (liver, heart, tongue, etc.): 3 to 4 months
Smoked hams, picnic hams and slab bacon: not to exceed 60 days
Cooked meat: 2 to 3 months
Combination meat dishes (soups, stews, etc.) 1 month

It is recommended that cured and smoked meats should be stored in a freezer for short periods of time only. We add that you will be a lot better off if you skip cured and smoked meats entirely when you are planning your menus.

Danger of Tainted Meat Emphasized

Unappetizing as it may sound, the taste and quality of some cured meats and the rare cheeses are judged by the degree of mold that can be encouraged to grow on them. However, an answer to an inquiry in the *Journal of the American Medical Association* for July 6, 1957, warns that any fresh meat that has become spotted with mold or fungi should be discarded. Food poisoning from eating meat is almost exclusively from bacteria which occur when meat is exposed to an atmosphere and temperature conducive to their growth.

Contaminated Poultry

The Amalgamated Meat Cutters Union has charged that the consumer each year buys hundreds of millions of pounds of filthy and contaminated poultry. They charged that such poultry was responsible for a large proportion of all cases of food poisoning reported. Unlike red meats, poultry is not subject to federal inspection but the Agriculture Department operates a voluntary service, which covers only 21 per cent of the poultry market. Write your congressman demanding a law to cover proper poultry inspection.

Chemically Treated Fish

Fresh-caught fish will now be treated with the antibiotic aureomycin to preserve it longer. The Canadian government has agreed to let the fishing companies use the drug on fish so that they will stay "fresh" about a week longer than they did before. Anyone who definitely knows he is allergic to aureomycin can therefore not eat fresh fish unless he knows when and where it was caught. So far as we know, frozen fish will not be treated, so perhaps it would be better to buy frozen fillets.

[263]

SECTION 8.

Nuts

Nuts of all kinds are actually seeds and are as rich in food value so that old favorite snack, peanuts (unsalted), is really a wonderful health food. Eat walnuts, cashews, Brazil nuts, pecans and any other nuts you can get, raw and unsalted. They make a fine substitute for sweets and starches as snacks.

CHAPTER 75

Nuts Are Good for You

One pound of nuts is equal in calories to 2.3 pounds of bread, 3.7 pounds of steak, 12.3 pounds of potatoes or 15 pounds of oranges. One pound of oily nuts supplies all the calories needed for the day plus 40 per cent of the protein, 60 per cent of the phosphorus, 30 per cent of the calcium and iron and 4 times the daily requirement of fat.

What do you think of a food that has this kind of nutritive value, grows wild and free for the picking, needs little care while it is growing, is harvested by picking it up from the ground, needs no processing and no cooking and keeps well with no refrigeration or preservatives? Doesn't this sound like the absolutely ideal food that we have been waiting for all these years? Well, it's been here and waiting for us all these years. Why have we been so slow in recognizing nuts as one of our best and most practical foods?

Speaking generally, nuts are defined as hard-shelled seeds enclosing a single edible oily kernel. If you want to be technical about it, you will find that nuts are classified biologically as one-seeded fruits, such as beechnut, chestnut and so forth. But we have come to think of a lot of different products as nuts, including such varied edibles as cashews, peanuts, coconuts and so forth. Most of these are high in protein and fat and low in carbohydrate. Some nuts contain as much as 60 per cent fat. Some kinds of pecans contain as much as 76 per cent fat.

This high fat content would seem to indicate that nuts are an excellent food for those who are trying to gain weight. They are a source of natural fat, delicious to pick up as a snack between meals. They are high in protein as well as fat, which means that they do a good job of helping to regulate blood sugar, which is so important to good health. Pound for pound they contain more calories than most foods.

In general, nuts are high in minerals and have peculiar affinities for certain kinds of minerals. The hickory tree, for instance, accumulates aluminum from the soil. The ash of hickory leaves is high in this trace mineral. Hickory trees also accumulate the rare earths—*scandium, yttrium, lanthanum, dys prosium, holium, erbium* and so forth—names we lay folks seldom hear.

The Brazil nut contains much barium, another trace mineral. In fact, some Brazil nuts have been found to cause distress if they are eaten in quantity because of the large content of barium. There is a deficiency of zinc in the pecan, English walnut and almond and a deficiency of boron in the English walnut. The European beechnut contains a toxic substance in its seed coat. The shell of the cashew contains liquids and oils which are toxic and irritating to the skin, much like poison ivy.

However, we need not concern ourselves with these analyses, for, of course, we do not ever eat those parts of the nuts which contain toxic material. And, since none of us lives exclusively on nuts, we need not worry about getting too much or too little of one of the minerals or trace minerals. Our other foods will balance this. Tannins, which most of us associate with nuts, are found only in the shells, wood and bark of the trees.

Vitamins and Minerals in Nuts

Most nuts contain a good supply of vitamin A and thiamin, one of the B vitamins. Some of them contain vitamin E. Immature English walnuts have been found to contain large amounts of vitamin C, which disappears as the nuts ripen. The walnut hulls are an excellent source of vitamin C, containing as high as 1550-3036 milligrams of this vitamin for every hundred grams. Of course, we can't eat the walnut hulls. In some parts of the world, we understand, efforts are being made to extract the vitamin C from the walnut hulls. The red skin of the peanut contains considerable thiamin, incidentally, so don't throw it away when you eat peanuts.

Nuts are not complete proteins, even though their protein content is high. We mean by this that they do not contain all of the amino acids, or kinds of protein essential for human health. Only foods of animal origin contain all these amino acids—they do not occur in any one vegetable food except soybeans. But, even so, nuts are a most important food if you want to increase your protein intake, and most of us should.

The foods of animal origin that are high in protein such as meats and eggs have an acid reaction in the body whereas most nuts have an alkaline reaction. Filberts, peanuts and walnuts are acid. All others are alkaline in their effect in the body. They are a highly concentrated food.

Nuts have the reputation of being hard to digest. But they were often eaten at the end of a heavy meal by an individual who had stuffed himself on all kinds of indigestible desserts and the nuts took the blame for his overindulgence. Nuts must be chewed carefully. Otherwise they will not be properly digested, for the digestive juices cannot break down the tough kernels.

Rich in protein, they do not present any problem of decay or spoilage such as occurs with meat and other animal products. True, nuts eventually become rancid but there is no question of refrigeration and threat of poisoning from spoilage. Nuts are free from uric acid and other substances produced in the body by eating meat. Do keep in mind, however, that they cannot be used as a complete substitute for meats unless you are highly skilled in balancing menus, for their protein is not complete. And they do not supply the same bulk that meat and other foods supply, which is important for propulsion in the digestive tract.

How Nuts Are Processed

Nuts, like other natural products, should be eaten in as nearly the natural state as possible. But we civilized twentieth century folks must always prove our superiority by processing nuts until we finally almost destroy their food value. The cashew nut is shelled in India from whence it comes. First it is heated in liquid to make the shells brittle and to extract the oily substance inside. The shell of the English walnut is sometimes loosened by exposure to ethylene gas. Almonds are bleached by dipping in chloride of lime. Pecans are sometimes bleached, sometimes dyed.

Blanching the nuts—that is, removing the inner skin, is accomplished by soaking in hot water. But pecans and English walnuts are dipped in hot lye, followed by an acid rinse. Another process is to pass the kernel through a heated solution of glycerin and sodium carbonate, then to remove the skins with a stream of water and dip in a citric acid solution.

Cooking the nuts in oil causes considerable loss of vitamin contents. We are told that in an experiment macadamia nuts were cooked in oil at 135 degrees centigrade for only 12 to 15 minutes and lost 16 per cent of their thiamin. Modern commercial methods of processing nuts bring about destruction of perhaps 70 to 80 per cent of the thiamin.

So what can you do to secure nuts whose food value has not been ruined before you get them? First of all, pass by the fancy, toasty-smelling nut and candy shops as if they weren't there. Never buy nuts that have been shelled or roasted. Buy them in the shells and shell them yourself. And then, whatever you do, don't roast all the goodness out of them before you eat them! If you have ever tasted an almond right out of the shell, you will agree with us that there is absolutely no excuse for roasting them. We do not know where you can get nuts that have not been bleached or dyed, except from organic growers who do not use chemicals of any kind. But the dye or the bleach is only on the outside of the nut which, of course, you do not eat.

Where and How We Get Our Nuts

The Southern European and Mediterranean countries are the world's largest producers of nuts. Brazil nuts are grown in Brazil and Bolivia. Cashews come from India and Mozambique. United States is the largest producer of English (sometimes called Persian) walnuts and almost the sole producer of pecans. Although the total value of edible nuts produced in 1949 was seventy million dollars, the people of this country used only about one and a half pounds of nuts per person that same year. So you see we do not begin to appreciate the value of nuts as food. In spite of the fact that they are generally presented to us commercially in candies, pastries and so forth, we still eat only about a pound and a half per person per year, whereas we consume annually well over a hundred pounds of sugar per person. And sugar has no food value whatsoever except calories.

The peanut, which is, of course, not a nut at all but a plant whose nuts ripen in the ground, has recently come into its own as a food of surpassingly high quality from the standpoint of nutrition. Peanut flour contains over 4 times the amount of protein, 8 times the fat and 9 times the minerals that are in wheat flour. It can be used with great success in recipes. Adelle Davis in her excellent cook book, *Let's Cook it Right* (Harcourt Brace and Company, New York), says she has never had a failure using peanut flour in baking recipes. For those who have difficulty of any kind with cereals and flours made from cereals, peanut flour would seem to be the perfect answer.

[269]

Acorn flour is used extensively in Europe and among the Indians of our Southwest. We are told that, in all probability, over the centuries, more human beings have eaten acorns than have eaten wheat. In Spain and Italy as much as 20 per cent of the food of the poor folks may be acorns. Some of them are edible as they grow. Others can only be eaten by first removing the tannins.

Nuts in their shells keep well. Shelled they become rancid in 3 or 4 months, especially in the summer. They can be kept at refrigerator temperatures for a year. With the exception of black walnuts and hickory nuts, those which are available to us in this country are not so hard to shell, so there seems to be no reason for not keeping them right in the shell until you use them. They are an excellent and unusual dessert.

For those housewives who feel lost somehow now that they no longer serve cakes, pies, puddings or cookies for dessert, why not get yourself a big bowl of the family's favorite nuts, a couple of nutcrackers and picks and bring them to the table after each meal along with fresh fruit as the best and most healthful kind of dessert! We often forget about nuts if we keep them in a bag in the kitchen cupboard. So try to keep a bowl of them handy for everyone to dip into for snacks—on a table in the dining room or living room.

CHAPTER 76

The Food Value of Nuts

Here is the composition of a number of kinds of nuts. Note, please, that some of them are relatively high in starch content while others contain little starch. Some are as high in protein content as meat. Others contain less protein. Remember, too, that, although the protein of nuts is excellent protein, it does not contain all of the essential amino acids that are present in foods of animal origin.

	Percentage of			Calories
	Carbohydrate	Protein	Fat	per pound
Acorn	57.10	6.65	5	1909
Almond	4.3	20.5	16	3030
Beechnut	13.2	21.9	57.4	2846
Brazil Nut	4.1	13.8	61.5	3013
Butternut	3.5	27.9	61.2	3165
Cashew	29.4	21.6	39	2866
Chestnut	36.6	2.3	2.7	1806
Coconut	27.9	5.7	50.6	2760
Filbert	9.3	14.9	65.6	3288
Hickory nuts	11.4	15.4	67.4	3342

	Percentage of Carbohydrate	Protein	Fat	Calories per pound
Lychee	78	2.9	.80	1539
Macadamia nuts	8.2	8.6	73.0	3507
Peanuts	8.6	28.1	49	2645
Pecans	3.9	9.4	73	3539
Pine nuts	6.9	33.9	49.4	3174
Pistachio	16.3	22.3	54.0	2996
Walnut, black	10.20	27.6	56.3	3180
Walnut, English	5.0	12.5	51.5	3326

The percentage of the mineral content of nuts is given in the following chart:

	Phosphorus	Potassium	Calcium	Magnesium	Sodium	Chlorine	Iron	Sulfur	Zinc	Manganese	Copper
Almond	.475	.759	.254	.252	.026	.020	.0044	.150	.0019	.0008	.0015
Brazil	.602	.601	.124	.225	.020	.081	.0028	.198			.0014
Butternut							.0068				.0012
Cashew	.480		.048								
Chestnut	.093	.560	.034	.051	.065	.006	.0070	.068	.0004	.0031	.0078
Coconut	.191	.693	.043	.077	.053	.225	.0036	.076	.0010		
Hazelnut	.354	.618	.287	.140	.019	.067	.0041	.198	.0010		.0012
Hickory nut	.370			.160			.0029				.0014
Macadamia	.240		.053				.0020				
Peanut	.392	.614	.080	.167	.039	.041	.0019	.226	.0016	.0020	.0009
Pecan	.335	.332	.089	.152		.050	.0026	.113		.0043	.0010
Pistachio							.0079			.0007	.0012
Walnut, black	.091	.675	.071	.098			.0060			.0033	.0032
Walnut, English	.038	.332	.089	.134	.023	.036	.0021	.146	.0020	.0018	.0011

Although they are not as rich in vitamins as some other foods, nuts provide some of the vitamins that exist in all natural food products that have not been refined. The B vitamins are scarce in modern American diets, for we have removed them from refined foods during the processing. So nuts, even in the small quantities in which we eat them, compared to other foods, are an excellent source of the B vitamins. Here is the vitamin content of some of the common nuts:

	Vitamin A	Thiamin	Riboflavin	Niacin
Almonds (¾ cup)	0	.25 mg.	.67 mg.	4.6 mg.
Brazil nuts (¾ cup)	trace	.86		
Cashews (¾ cup)		.63	.19	2.1
Chestnuts (40)	0	.108	.24	1.0
Coconut (2 cups)		.30 .60	1.0	
Peanuts (¾ cup)	0	.30	.13	16.2
Peanut butter (6 tbs.)		.12	.13	16.2
Pecans (1 cup)	50 I.U	.72	.11	.9
Walnuts, Eng. (1 cup)	30 I.U	.48	.13	1.2

In addition, peanuts are rich in pyridoxine, pantothenic acid and biotin, 3 other important members of the vitamin B family.

The almond includes both bitter and sweet among its relatives. The sweet almond is the one we eat. Both are closely related to the peach tree. As a matter of fact the almond nut itself is almost identical with the peach stone. The bitter almond contains hydrocyanic acid, a toxic substance. Beechnuts, too, as they are grown in Europe contain a substance that can be harmful in quantity. But the American beechnut has no such ingredient.

We usually eat chestnuts cooked almost like a vegetable, but they are delicious raw, once you get used to them that way. In many parts of the world chestnuts are ground into flour which is used as cereal flour is here.

Peanut butter is made of peanuts that have been roasted and halved. Then their skins are removed and they are ground. Usually oils are added to keep them in a smooth, buttery condition. If you have access to it, we'd suggest buying raw peanut butter or grinding your own from raw peanuts. The famous scientist, Carver, produced 202 different products from peanuts —not all of them food products, of course.

Non-food products are made from other nuts, too. A floor covering is made from nutshell flour mixed with pigment and resin. Loud speakers for radios are made from walnut shell flour. For some peculiar reason this substance seems to filter out vibrations more effectively than any other!

CHAPTER 77

Almonds

Nuts in general seem to be one of our best foods. They come to us enclosed in a thick shell through which neither dirt nor insecticides can penetrate. They contain wonderfully fine food elements—carbohydrates, proteins and fats and a wealth of vitamins and minerals. Not only can they be eaten raw, but they taste better raw than cooked. This means we get valuable enzymes from nuts.

The almond is one of the oldest nuts historically. It came to us originally from western Asia and Morocco. The word "Luz" in Genesis has been translated as "Hazelnut" but is generally thought to mean almond. Almond trees are referred to often in the Bible. The sweet almond tree has pink flowers. The bitter almond has white. Sweet almonds are the ones we eat, and they have been developed into a soft-shelled nut which is easy to crack.

Almonds are high in calories—good news for those of us who are trying to put on weight. One-half ounce of almond nutmeats contains about 100 calories—not starch incidentally, for the calories come in the fats of the nutmeat. As you know, we speak of the quality of different proteins. Vegetable proteins are, in general, not so good as meat proteins, that is, they are not so likely to contain the amino acids that are necessary for proper nourishment. But the protein of the almond compares very favorably with that of meat. So if you are contemplating a high protein diet, put almonds on the list!

Are Nuts Hard to Digest?

There is an idea that nuts are hard to digest. This misconception may arise from the fact that we do not chew them well enough, or from the fact that we eat them generally at the end of a big meal. Since they contain a lot of fat, they remain in the stomach longer than carbohydrates or proteins. And if they are not thoroughly chewed, the digestive juices cannot penetrate their rather dense structure and they may be excreted without being digested. This is the main reason why so many recipes call for chopping or grinding nuts. When we eat them, they should be combined with foods that are not high in fats, so that the total amount of fat eaten at one time will not be too high to be digested. This is an excellent reason for having raw fruits and nuts for a special dessert.

Almonds contain an extremely small amount of a substance that changes to hydrocyanic acid, so they should not be eaten to excess, or to the exclusion of other foods. Almond extract is made from oil of bitter almonds from which the hydrocyanic acid has been removed. Because of its soothing effect almond oil is sometimes used in cough medicines.

Try Almonds For a Real Treat

When the youngsters clamor for sweets, and festive refreshments must be provided for guests, it's well to keep a bowl of nuts handy, especially almonds which, for most people, are a real delicacy. Serve them just as they are, with a nutcracker. Blanching (removing the dark outer skin) can be accomplished by soaking them for a minute or so in hot water. But skip all the roasting, frying and salting processes which do nothing but detract from the nuts' nutritional value. Blanched almonds mixed with raisins or dates are a real treat. Or you can make marzipan. Marzipan is a favorite European delicacy which is made up for the holidays in entrancing shapes of tiny fruits, vegetables and animals. It is simply almond paste, made by grinding up blanched almonds and shaping the paste into desired shapes.

Here are the words of a famous nutrition expert, Dr. J. H. Kellogg, on the subject of nuts: "They supply for a given weight nearly twice the amount of nutriment of any other food."

These are the vitamins and minerals contained in 10 almonds:

Vitamin A .... 7 International Units

B Vitamins

    Thiamin .... 15 micrograms

    Riboflavin .... 10 micrograms

    Niacin .... .5 milligrams

Vitamin C .... 1 milligram

Calcium	25	milligrams
Phosphorus	45	milligrams
Iron	.4	milligrams
Copper	.1	milligram
Magnesium	.2	milligrams
Chlorine	.3	milligrams
Potassium	7	milligrams

CHAPTER 78

Peanuts

Junior is showing good judgment when he insists on peanut butter sandwiches rather than jelly or jam. As a matter of fact, if he must eat sandwiches, peanut butter is better as a filling than anything else except meat. Two tablespoons of peanut butter contain more protein than an egg.

In addition, peanuts contain large amounts of the B vitamins and vitamin E. They are rich in minerals. Peanut flour is a very excellent supplement for wheat flour. It contains 4 times as much protein as wheat flour, 8 times as much fat and 9 times as many minerals. In recipes using wheat flour you may substitute peanut flour for 15 to 20 per cent of the wheat flour without making any special change in the recipe.

As yet we have hardly begun to appreciate the value of peanuts as food. You know, of course, that they are not actually nuts, in that they do not grow as the fruit of trees, as other nuts do. Peanuts are legumes, like soybeans and peas. They grow on a peanut plant. As the plant matures, the ends of the branches bury themselves in the ground and the peanuts are formed underground. When the plant withers it's time to dig the peanuts. They're easy to grow. If you have a garden, by all means plant a few rows. Only be sure to buy peanuts meant for seed—roasted peanuts won't sprout. Peanuts will keep, in their shells, in a covered container at about 35 degrees Fahrenheit for two years, losing only little of their food value.

Peanut flour, peanut butter and peanut oil are as nutritious as the peanuts themselves. We have read somewhere that raw peanuts are far better for you than roasted ones. Personally we don't like the taste of raw peanuts, but if you find that you do, by all means eat them raw! In the figures below, we are talking about roasted peanuts:

Vitamin B content		*per 100 grams*
Thiamin	300-400	micrograms
Riboflavin	160-500	micrograms

Vitamin B content   *per 100 grams*

Niacin	16.2 milligrams
Folic acid	280 micrograms
Biotin	39 micrograms
Choline	145 milligrams
Inositol	180 milligrams
Pantothenic acid	2500 micrograms
	(more than any other food except liver)
Pyridoxine	300 micrograms
Vitamin E content	26-36 milligrams
Calcium	71 milligrams
Phosphorus	399 milligrams
Iron	2.31 milligrams
Copper	.96 milligrams
Chlorine	56 milligrams
Potassium	700 milligrams
Sodium	120 milligrams
Sulfur	226 milligrams
Zinc	2 milligrams

Peanuts are also rich in the essential amino acids—those 8 forms of protein that contribute so much to human health. And 100 grams of peanuts are about 100 peanuts.

CHAPTER 79

Peanuts and Peanut Butter

Vegetable oils are good for you. Peanuts are especially rich in oil which contains the essential unsaturated fatty acids—these are substances, recently investigated, which seem to be able to prevent the harmful deposits of cholesterol in blood vessels, which result in hardening of the arteries, strokes, heart attacks and other serious disorders of the heart and blood vessel system.

For this reason we recommend eating peanuts—raw, if you can eat them that way. If not, roast them lightly. They are good food from many other angles as well, for they are extremely high in protein, and contain lots of iron and the B vitamins. Along with sunflower seeds they make about the best possible snack and dessert you could imagine.

We have gotten many enthusiastic letters from readers who make peanuts a regular and important part of their diet. One reader cured a life-long case of constipation by simply adding a handful or so of peanuts to his diet.

Our only objection to peanuts is, of course, what food processors have done to them. Many people do not know that you can eat peanuts unless they have been shelled, the red coating removed, and then fried in a bath of rancid grease, with an incredible amount of salt added. This is what you get when you ask for peanuts in most stores. Nothing could be worse for you than this.

The continual heating and re-heating of the fat in which salted peanuts are prepared makes it one of the most dangerous of all foods, for it has been shown by competent authorities that reheated fats deteriorate into unhealthful and very probably cancer-causing substances. This is one of the reasons why we protest so sharply against French-fried foods. Judging from their rancid taste, most peanuts are cooked in oils that are never changed or replaced.

If this is the only kind of peanut available in your part of the country, don't eat it. If peanuts are prepared this way in some store in your neighborhood, make a deal with the manager so you can get your peanuts in the shell untouched by any processing. Then shell them and eat them just as they are—no salt, no grease! And that will be the difference between good, wholesome, nourishing food and the degenerate spoiled food the other customers will get.

Now, what about peanut butter? Ideally, peanut butter should be ground raw peanuts with nothing added. You can buy such peanut butter at health food stores. It does not have exactly the same taste as butter made from roasted peanuts. When .the commercial processor makes peanut butter, he grinds roasted peanuts and adds salt. Then, because the peanut butter has a tendency to separate, leaving the oil on top of the jar, he adds hydrogenated oils.

These are oils which have been treated chemically with hydrogen so that they become solid at room temperature even though they are vegetable oils which are, in their natural state, liquid at room temperature. The solid, hydrogenated oils keep the peanut butter from separating. However, by adding hydrogenated oils, the manufacturer makes of the peanut butter something no health-conscious person should eat. Hydrogenated oils contain practically none of the wholesome unsaturated fatty acids. These have been changed into saturated acids. And there is ample scientific evidence that this kind of processed fat is a hazard to heart and blood vessels.

SECTION 9.

Salt

There is some salt in just about every food we eat, more than enough to meet the needs of the normal body. The sodium in salt has been condemned many times as a contributing factor in heart and kidney diseases, as well as other physical problems. We do not approve of adding salt to food either in cooking or at the table. If one insists upon using salt, unrefined sea salt is probably least damaging since it contains large amounts of other minerals which help the body to process the sodium it acquires.

CHAPTER 80

Just a Pinch of Salt—Too Much?

How many diseases could be prevented if our bodies could cry out "Too much salt" as our taste senses can when food is too highly seasoned. With the evidence we have against salt and its effects, how much wiser we would be to break ourselves of the salt "habit"—for it is a habit like tobacco and liquor—than to wait for the sword to strike and then run for the cure.

Enough salt can be obtained from most foods in their natural form. R. Ackerly, M.D., in *Proceedings of the Royal Society of Medicine*, 1910, states that the body requires only from two to three grams of salt a day, and that "western nations eat, on an average, seven to ten times as much salt as is necessary, and frequently more." Dr. Egon V. Ullmann in his book, *Diet, Infections and Colds* (Macmillan, 1933), shows how 5 grams of salt a day may be obtained from food without added table salt, and gives a list of everyday foods and their sodium chloride (salt) content. Dr. L. Duncan Bulkley, editor of the medical journal, *Cancer,* believes that one-quarter of an ounce of added salt per week "is ample to supply the body with the actual needs in the replacing of chloride of sodium lost in modern methods of cooking and the preparation of food."

Why Is Excess Salt Bad?

1. *Excess Salt Causes Hyperacidity.* The formation of hydrochloric acid in the stomach depends on the salt intake. The chlorine of the sodium chloride goes to make up part of this hydrochloric acid. So if too much salt is taken, too much of this acid will be produced (hyperacidity). Too much hydrochloric acid is generally accepted as one predisposing cause of stomach ulcers.

2. *Excess Salt May Prevent Use of Calcium in the Body.* Much of the sodium of the sodium chloride will be held in the tissues and will reduce the effect of calcium, which is so badly needed in the body. Where salt is reduced, calcium action will prevail and will counteract inflammations. These two points are made by Dr. Ullmann in his book mentioned previously.

3. *Excess Salt Stimulates the Body and Nerve Cells.* We know how salt irritates an open wound, or salt-water stings the eyes. In the same way it irritates delicate membranes throughout the body. Dr. Henry C. Sherman in his book, *Chemistry of Food and Nutrition* (published by Macmillan, 1952), states that "through over-stimulating the digestive tract, salt may interfere with the absorption and utilization of the food." He also states that an excess of salt may disturb the osmotic pressure of tissues, involving almost every portion of the body. Although some salt is needed

[279]

to keep the tension of the body fluids at a normal level, we get enough in our foods in their natural content to serve the purpose.

4. *Excess Salt Causes the Retention of Fluid.* Every gram of salt binds and holds 70 grams of water. The bad effects of this accumulated fluid may be seen as the causes of many diseases.

5. *Table Salt Contains Chemicals.* Most of us are wary of ordering just any old chemical from the druggist's shelf without competent advice, but how many of us have looked into the effect of the chemicals that have been added to packaged table salt? One box of salt listed the following added items: .01 per cent potassium iodide, .05 per cent sodium bicarbonate and .90 per cent tri-calcium phosphate. Sometimes hyposulphite of soda is added. Though the individual chemical added may not be harmful in itself, the combination of all of them may well be.

6. *Chemicals Must Be Used To Combat Bad Effects of Salt in the Body.* There are research findings that may eventually prove the prescription of salt-free diets unnecessary. Work along this line was described in *Science News Letter* for September 16, 1950. In brief, the researchers found that certain chemicals called "ion exchange resins" can combat the accumulation of fluid and the inability of the body to get rid of too much sodium, such as is contained in common table salt. These resins, they found, can remove the salt from the body. However, why put something irritating into the body that needs something else to undo the harm? And who knows the effect of these added chemicals over a long period of time?

7. *Salt Contains Bacteria.* "Refined salt from various sources was found to contain up to 8,300 bacteria and 400 mould (spores) . . . and toxic cultures were obtained in some cases. Brines of various sources and ages were badly contaminated," according to the *Analyst,* June, 1926. Commenting on this, Frederick L. Hoffman, M.D., a member of the American Association of Cancer Research, in his book, *Cancer and Diet* (Williams and Wilkins), stated: "If this should be substantiated, it might be a clue to the injurious effects of common salt in introducing irritating bacteria into the human body, directly operating as causative factors in tumor growth."

Diseases and Salt

CANCER. Because cancer is still baffling medical science, we have come to assume that its cause must be tremendously complex and mysterious. But there is evidence that the seemingly harmless substance, common table salt, is held in positive suspicion by medical authorities.

One of the earliest writers on cancer, Dr. James Braithwaite, of Leeds, England, tells of the increase in diameter of a tumor from 2⅜ inches to 3¼ inches when one of his patients resumed daily use of salt, even in small quantities. He says that salt, being an inorganic chemical and not a food, is dangerous in oversupply. It harms the body tissue as it is a powerful stimulant to cell metabolism. This information is from his book, *Excess of Salt in the Diet and Three Other Factors, the Probable Causes of Cancer.*

Frederick T. Marwood, a layman, made the interesting observation that in Denmark, where the consumption of salted fish is the highest in Europe, the cancer rate is also the highest in Europe (*what is the root cause of cancer—is it the excessive consumption of common salt, salted foods and salt compounds? 1910*).

In contrast, Dr. L. Duncan Bulkley tells us of the low incidence of cancer in Mexico and among the Indians, where the use of salt is relatively small. He describes how "chloride of sodium, or common salt, in any excess with the food may disturb the balance of mineral ingredients of the blood, replacing the tissue of the cells when worn out, instead of a potassium salt, thus starting them on their riotous malignant action, in response to local irritation, and ending in fully developed cancer." This statement appeared in the publication, *Cancer*, July, 1927.

As salt has the property of holding fluid about it, a diet rich in water again favors cancer cell growth. The tissue of the tumor contains a larger amount of fluid proportionately than any tissue in the body according to Frederick L. Hoffmann, M.D., in *Cancer and Diet*, quoting Dr. Bernhard Fischer-Wasels, Director of the Pathological Institute of the University of Frankfort.

HIGH BLOOD PRESSURE. Dr. Frederick Allen, who introduced the low-salt diet for this disease into this country in 1922 has had consistently good results from the restriction of salt. He also conducted animal experiments which proved that with the feeding of salt, blood pressure increased causing hypertension. This research is reported in the *Journal of the American Medical Association* for June 4, 1949.

"Twenty-one patients treated with low-salt diet were observed by Svith for one to five months. In all cases the blood pressure was reduced from 20 to 75 mm., usually in two to four weeks, and the patients' other symptoms disappeared, too," according to an article in *Ugeskrift For Laeger*, Copenhagen, March 30, 1950.

DROPSY. Doctors now believe that the cause of dropsy is not too much water, but too much sodium, which prompts the body to hoard water in abnormal amounts, usually as a result of a heart or kidney ailment. Dr. Ferdinand Ripley Schemm's salt-free diet has won wide acceptance and his tireless work on the disease resulted in the establishment in 1947 of the Western Foundation for Clinical Research. Dr. Schemm believed that if the sodium taken in with food were cut down, the body itself could in dropsy cases regulate the sodium already in the body and give the kidneys enough water so that they could work properly and flush out the sodium salts through the urine. The "restriction of water is harmful and a cause of suffering," he said in cases of dropsy.

HEART DISEASE. Though a low-salt diet is not infallible, there is definite evidence of its beneficial results in many cases. Wheeler, Bridges and White in the *Journal of the American Medical Association* for January, 1947, describe the treatment of 50 cases of congested heart failure with a diet low in salt, containing about five-eighths of a gram of sodium per day. Patients were chosen for whom all other treatments had failed. Of the 50, only 35 followed the diet honestly, and out of this number 22 received definite benefit, while 13 did not.

PREGNANCY. Seventy patients, put on a salt-free diet in the latter weeks of pregnancy, showed a definite reduction in the length of labor and, as far as could be measured, in the severity of the pains. It is believed that the decreased sodium and chloride (from salt) resulted in removal of water from the maternal tissues, bringing about a lessening in excitability of the nerve centers and a definite sedative effect, according to an article in *Hospital Topics*, 1940.

DEAFNESS AND SINUSITIS. Here is a beautiful "believe-it-or-not," the more beautiful because it is backed up by scientific, medical knowledge. Dr. Frank Graham Murphy, of Mason City, Iowa, had as a patient a woman who had been deaf for years and according to the specialists was apparently incurable. Questioning her eating habits Dr. Murphy found she was a heavy consumer of salt, and advised that she drop it completely. After 3 weeks she returned—her hearing restored, as good as ever!

Dr. Murphy says that the ears and sinuses are affected when there is an excess of salt in the body tissues. When free perspiration does not help get rid of the excess, the kidneys force the salt into other organs or tissues. As salt collects water about it, a water-logged condition may result in the ears and sinuses. Other fluid-retention foods, with a high number of calories, such as bread and sugar, when eaten in excess, may also play a role, he says in *Clinical Medicine* for August, 1944.

OBESITY. A drastic reduction of salt is advised because of its water-holding properties. Fluid adds to the weight. Salt also excites thirst, making for a greater intake of water, and excites appetite by increasing the flow of saliva.

OTHER DISEASES. Hives, epilepsy, insomnia, nervous tension states and rheumatic swelling also respond to the restriction of salt intake, says the magazine *Good Health*.

Forbidden Food on the Salt-Free Diet

The following is a list of foods commonly forbidden by physicians to patients on a low-salt diet: Processed meats: salted, smoked, canned, spiced, and pickled foods, bacon, ham, sausages, bologna, frankfurters, liverwurst, salami; shell fish: clams, oysters, lobster, shrimp; processed fish; canned vegetables (unless specially packed without salt); beets, celery, endive, spinach, kale, sauerkraut; broths, meat soups; regular commercial bread and rolls, salted crackers, pretzels; peanuts; all salted cheeses, salted butter; commercial ice cream. Also forbidden are olives, raisins, catsup, mayonnaise, pickles, relish, salted meat gravy and salted meat sauce.

This list is for sick people who have to be extremely strict. An ordinary healthy person may use his judgment as to how far he wishes to go. Remember that in their raw state fruits, vegetables, meats and cereals naturally provide all the vital food salts we need for our well-being and preservation.

If a person will go to a little pains to figure out an appetizing diet, the saltless features of it won't be hard to take.

Salt Substitutes

There are two kinds of salt substitutes, if substitute you must. First there are the non-chemical substitutes like Vege-Sal which is sold in health food stores. This contains some sodium chloride (which is what you are trying to avoid) soybean extract, sea salt and vegetable powders. This is far safer than the chemical salt substitutes such as Diasal, Gustamate, Neocurtasal and so forth. But it is our opinion that no salt substitutes should be used. By omitting salt in cooking and not adding any at the table you will find, after a matter of several weeks, that you do not miss the taste of it. As a matter of fact you will begin for the first time to appreciate the actual taste of many foods whose flavors you have up to now been drowning out with salt! Honestly, you'll soon begin to enjoy food more without salt! There are many primitive nations in the world whose people have never tasted salt and many other people, such as the Eskimos, who will not eat food that has been salted!

There are diseases such as Addison's disease where the body mechanism is so badly disordered that salt is necessary. If you are suffering from any of these diseases, of course, follow your doctor's direction about the amount of salt you need. Otherwise you are perfectly safe in cutting down on the salt you add to food in cooking and at the table, for you are already getting all the sodium you need in food.

Heat and Salt Tablets

Many people believe they should take salt tablets during the summer months. Taking salt tablets to prevent heat shock or prostration started with steel workers who stand before searing furnaces all their working day, losing a large amount of salt and water in perspiration. In our usual haste to take up anything new, many employers provided salt tablets even in cool offices where employees were not especially active physically. Recently the tendency has been to swing away from taking salt tablets. The National Research Council, official authority on matters of nutrition and health, has concluded that the average American gets from 10 to 15 grams of salt a day which is easily enough to make up for loss in perspiration. In addition, it has been found that one soon becomes accustomed to hot weather and one's perspiration becomes less salty. So it now appears that, for the average person, exerting himself in an average way, there is no need for extra salt during the summertime.

If you eat a purely vegetarian diet, you may feel the need of a little more salt than those of us who eat meats, fish and eggs, for the fruits and vegetables do not contain as much natural sodium as the animal products. Our final word on salt—and we believe the facts we have presented prove our case—throw away your salt shaker, gradually begin to use less and less salt in cooking and enjoy the increased health and good flavor of natural foods that will be your reward!

CHAPTER 81

Added Salt—Necessary or Not?

The task of making table salt respectable from a health standpoint, has been keeping scientists busy a good number of years. Sad to say, the rewards for all of this effort are slight indeed. Two facts consistently emerge from the piles of data and hours of observation: 1. Salt is damaging to even a healthy system; 2. the body does not need any added salt to maintain health.

An article on the subject of salt appeared in *Nature* magazine (November 24, 1956) by Dr. Hans Kaunitz of the Department of Pathology of Columbia University in New York City. In it are some facts and theories which bear repeating and discussion.

Man's love of salt comes to him through long years of habit and tradition. Humans have been eating salt for 5 to 10 thousand years, so the habit is pretty well ingrained. Even the earliest historical records show that salt was always of great importance. Wars were fought over its sources, and as an item of trade it had no equal, even in precious jewels and metals. In early times men were often paid in the form of salt for the work they did. It was in this way that the word *salary* was born.

As men became more aware of the workings of the human body, they began to suspect, then to know, that the effects of salt on it could be disastrous. However, the taste of salt on food was such a familiar one that even scientific man has always struggled against giving it up. That is the reason for the mountains of research that have been carried on to find some redeeming feature in salt that would make eating it seem less foolish or unwise.

Can You Live Without Salt?

Dr. Kaunitz has made a survey of scientific literature on salt and commented upon those works which he considers representative. In a book by C. G. Lehmann, *Lehrbuch der physiogischen Chemie*, there is an answer for all time to the age old cry that no animal, human or otherwise, can long exist without having salt added to its diet. Dr. Lehmann found that most animals in freedom, and in captivity, do very well on natural foods without the addition of any salt. As for those animals (such as cattle, deer, etc.) who do consume salt when it is offered to them, there is no proof that they need it for health, or that it benefits them in any way.

Another German scientist, G. von Bunge, made the guess that extra salt is necessary to those civilizations which depend upon agricultural products for much of their diet. The excess salt was deemed by von Bunge necessary to help excrete larger volumes of potassium. He assumed that a diet high in plant products would lead to a super-accumulation of potassium, while a diet predominantly of meat would not have this effect. It must be noted, however, that von Bunge neglected to mention certain African tribes who not only have predominantly vegetarian diets, but use certain plant ashes, rich in potassium, as a condiment *instead of salt.*

Dr. von Bunge never proved that there is any advantage of ridding one's self of potassium in the body. To the contrary, Kaunitz suggests that loss of potassium might be a strong disadvantage. It is significant to note here that Dr. Max Gerson attempted to build up the body's potassium content as an important part of his famous treatment for cancer. Since salt is known to increase the body's loss of potassium, it would seem to follow that salt might be an indirect cause of cancer by robbing the body of this vital element.

Many People Live Without Added Salt

In doing further research on von Bunge's theory of agricultural people's need for added salt, Dr. Kaunitz discovered that a tribe of Indians in the Northwest Pacific seemed to offer living proof that the theory was not sound. These people are divided into two regions. The Indians in one region use no salt at all, while those in the other region use salt freely, yet there is no predominance of plant or animal food in either region.

Another group of Indians, the Sirions tribe of Bolivia, are a hunting tribe. Until civilized man introduced them to salt, they were totally ignorant of its existence and thrived beautifully, in spite of its absence from their diet. At first the salt was distasteful to them, but as time went on they developed a craving for it. Can this craving then be interpreted by any stretch of the imagination as an indication of the body's need for added salt? Hardly—unless a child's craving for chocolate bars shows the body's need for chocolate bars, or a man's craving for cigarettes shows a need of the body for tobacco.

Nobody has yet been able to demonstrate the body's need for added salt to perform its functions. Quoting Dr. Kaunitz once again: "When carefully weighing the available evidence, one cannot escape the conclusion that normal metabolic processes are possible without the adding of salt to foodstuffs."

Does the Body Have Any Use for Salt?

This is not to say that the body does not use any salt at all. The need for some salt for humans has been established, but the necessary quantity is in doubt. In any case, it is quite apparent from the foregoing information that the body gets all the salt it needs from natural foods, else the many isolated cultures all over the world who know nothing of the existence of salt could not have survived until now.

Salt and the Kidneys

Some theories on the use of added salt suggest that it interferes with the body's powers of excretion. The reasoning goes like this: sodium chloride is a scarce item in the natural diet of most animals. In order to preserve it, therefore, it is the natural function of the kidneys to constantly re-absorb the sodium chloride that the body throws off. When the body has an excess of salt intake, the kidneys must excrete rather than absorb it, and this added function can lead to overtaxing of the kidneys. This view, says Kaunitz, is supported by the rapid occurrence of adjustments in the tissues of animals on high dietary salt intake. In other words, a normal kidney is not equipped to cope with high salt intake, and in order to take care of salt, the kidney must be changed somehow. It is a reasonably safe assumption that if the body were meant to handle increased amounts of salt, the body's organs would naturally be geared for it.

Salt Fits the Definition of a Drug

The reason for the acceptability of salt to the taste of most persons is possibly that it acts as an emotional stimulant, says Kaunitz. He suggests that this stimulation may be consciously, or subconsciously, pleasurable, and this could be the true reason behind our love of salt. This theory is further backed up by the fact that the use of salt can affect the activity of the adrenal glands, making them more or less active according to the increase or decrease of salt intake. This effect is much the same as the effect the cortical hormones (cortisone, ACTH, etc.) have on the body. In this context salt cannot escape the designation of itself as a drug. It stimulates the gland that pushes the body's performance to its ultimate powers, and it does so without regard for factors which might make this effort undesirable. It is certainly as habit-forming as any drug, and the psychological pleasure it is thought to give only adds to the evidence that makes this definition apply.

Salt-free Diet for Everybody?

Dr. Kaunitz closes his discussion with the question of whether or not a physician should prescribe a certain level of salt intake for his patients. He remarks that there is certainly a sound basis for low salt diets in many diseases, particularly those of a circulatory nature. Dr. Kaunitz hesitates, however, to recommend low salt diets, generally for all normal people as well as those who are ill. He dislikes depriving them of the pleasant psychological stimulation they might get from using salt.

When one is "prevention-minded," as we are, and as we hope our readers are, one does not take his chances with sickness and disease by using a food that could prove dangerous to health. One discards at once any and all food habits that are suspect. If salt can be at the bottom of the circulatory disease, or can cause kidney complications, why wait until the trouble shows itself? Stop using salt at once! You will be amazed to see how easily you get used to food without salt; you will be amazed, too, to see how much different, how much better foods taste, when their flavor has not been masked by salt.

Give yourself a two-week trial of unsalted food. Depend on its content in fresh foods for your supply. You'll never miss salt again.

CHAPTER 82

Salt-Eating and
High Blood Pressure

Lewis K. Dahl, M.D., of Upton, New York, writes on *Salt Intake and Salt Need* in the June 5 and June 12, 1959, issues of the *New England Journal of Medicine.* His studies on salt eating and how it affects people were made in a metabolic ward of the Medical Department of the Brookhaven National Laboratory. There was no possible chance to cheat on diets, for they were weighed and prepared in the diet kitchens and the patients who took part in Dr. Dahl's studies had no opportunity to add extra salt at any time. Exhaustive tests on all the patients were done in the laboratory, all of which showed just one thing—that the reduction of salt in the diet brings only benefit and that, in cases of hypertension, or high blood pressure, reduction of salt produces almost magical reduction of pressure to normal levels.

Dr. Dahl reviews facts about salt-eating that we have pointed out many times in the preceding pages—that many groups of primitive people have remained healthy, generation after generation, without ever eating salt at all; that explorers like Stefansson find it difficult to do without salt for a week or so after they begin such a diet but that they gradually become accustomed to saltless food, prefer it and live in perfect health without salt; that only grass-eating animals ever seek out salt licks—those which eat meat apparently never feel the need for salt—that additional salt in hot weather appears to be not necessary at all, except under conditions such as steelworkers encounter at blast furnaces.

All of these facts have been known to science for many years. It is surprising how often they are ignored by popular medical writers, especially syndicated columns by physicians which appear in our daily papers. These gentlemen frequently take off in long, unscientific and undocumented harangues on salt-eating, insisting that nature demands that we add large quantities of this white mineral substance to our food or we cannot survive, let alone be healthy.

How About Doing Without Salt?

Dr. Dahl tells us that no one really knows very much about the amount of salt modern Americans eat because few studies have been done. By reviewing some of these studies, he shows that "the available evidence suggests that, whereas metabolic balance can be maintained on sodium intakes of only a few hundred milligrams, or less, the average intake in contemporary American society is 20 times as much.

[287]

He tells us, too, that studies made of many groups of primitive people show that they do not suffer from high blood pressure. The studies showed that the amount of salt eaten by these people was extremely low, at a level of one or two grams a day or less. Negroes living in West India, on the other hand, eat a diet high in salt. They have a much higher incidence of high blood pressure than people living around them who do not eat so much salt.

It has been known for some time, Dr. Dahl tells us, that high blood pressure can be produced in animals by injections of certain substances. But, for the high blood pressure to occur, salt (sodium chloride) must also be present up to at least two to four per cent of the daily diet. In addition, studies of animals show that continual, lifetime ingestion of excessive amounts of salt leads to a condition in rats similar to high blood pressure in human beings.

In 1954, Dr. Dahl tells us, he published evidence indicating that high blood pressure is much more frequent among people who eat lots of salt. Among 1,346 adults who were studied, 135 had a low intake of salt, 630 an average intake and 581 a high intake. Sixty-one persons among the high-intake group had high blood pressure, 43 of those who ate an average amount had high blood pressure and only one among those who ate little salt.

Is Low-Salt-Intake Harmful?

Dr. Dahl tells us of a woman patient whom he has observed for a total of 4 years, during which time she has been on a diet extremely low in salt. She had been taking as much as 4,000 milligrams of sodium when she came under Dr. Dahl's care. She was seeking relief from high blood pressure. The salt in her diet was reduced to 100 to 150 milligrams a day. "She remains the same active, intelligent and somewhat aggressive woman that she was before sodium restriction although her blood pressure has been normal for several years. Her numerous daily activities include two walks each of one and three miles in length on the laboratory grounds.

We want to note here that perhaps the walks partly helped in reducing the high blood pressure.

Low-Salt Diet and High Blood Pressure

In a later issue of the *Journal* (June 12, 1958), Dr. Dahl gives us details of an extremely complicated and convincing experiment which he carried out to find out all he could about restricting salt in the diet. He was particularly interested in the relation of salt-restriction and reducing. He reminds us that reducing diets may sharply limit the amount of salt eaten, simply because less food in general is eaten—therefore, less salt is eaten. Hence, it must also be true that the salt-eating overweight person must get lots more salt than the average simply because he eats more of everything.

Studying patients in a hospital ward where food was measured and no other source of food was available, Dr. Dahl found that simply reducing the weight of patients by diet did not produce a fall in their high blood pressure. Restricting salt intake, however, caused a lowering of the blood pressure in both obese persons and those of normal weight.

[288]

Was Such Drastic Salt Reduction Harmful?

Dr. Dahl has performed every imaginable test on patients of his who were on reduced salt intake. He tells us that, over the years, he has found that from ¼ to ⅓ of his patients with high blood pressure showed a significant fall in the level while they were eating less salt. In only one case was there a slight decrease in a normal blood pressure. Improvement in heart size was found among patients who had enlarged hearts. No other physical changes could be found in these patients, no matter how long they remained on the low-salt diet.

Elaborate chemical tests which were carried out also revealed nothing but changes for the better among people whose salt intake was restricted. Dr. Dahl had psychological tests made of his patients, since it has been suggested that eating a lot of salt is what keeps us on our toes, capable of meeting successfully all the complex problems of modern society. He found without fail that there were no undesirable changes in the patients' characters and, in fact, there were some improvements. A number of his patients reported that, after they had become accustomed to their low-salt diet, their friends, relatives and, particularly clerks in stores, seemed less irritating than they had before. He did find that, for the first 10 days on the low-salt diet some patients might complain that they felt depressed or nervous. But this disappeared very quickly.

Dr. Dahl's own answer to the question, "Is there potential harm from a widespread reduction in salt consumption?" is as follows: "The evidence that has been presented here indicates that it is possible for individuals and races to live for years and generations on intakes of only several grams of salt a day." He then takes up the several serious disease conditions in which salt loss is so great that a low-salt diet is not advisable—Addison's disease, severe burns, diabetic acidosis, severe vomiting or diarrhea—but he adds that "if excess dietary sodium (salt) plays the primary part in the etiology (cause) of hypertension (high blood pressure) the possible harm from salt restriction in persons with relatively uncommon ailments must be weighed against the radical decrease in the incidence of the second most common cardiovascular disease in Western society"—that is, of course, high blood pressure.

How Can You Get Used to a Low Salt Diet?

Dr. Dahl has devoted years to studying patients on low-salt diets. He tells us that he has found no evidence of salt craving among his patients on drastically reduced amounts of salt. They complained for a week or so that food tasted flat but after that they became used to the taste and there were no more complaints. This suggests, he says, that the salt appetite was acquired in these people. It is the result of social custom—not an inborn appetite or a basic physiologic need. "This does not mean," he says, "that the custom or appetite will be changed any more easily than that of smoking tobacco or drinking alcohol, but it seems very important to indicate that *salt appetite* is not to be equaled with *salt requirement.*"

We want to add one word to Dr. Dahl's thoughts about getting along without salt. After you have drastically reduced the salt in your diet, you soon begin to find that you never really tasted food before. What you tasted was the salt. You will experience a revival of interest in your meals when for the first time you enjoy an egg, a baked potato or a piece of meat, without salt.

How Much Salt Should You Eat?

Should you try to cut out all salt from your diet, as patients who are on the Rice-Fruit Diet do? (This is an extremely strict diet which can be adhered to only under medical supervision.) No, we don't think so. Such heroic measures are not necessary. Surely the salt you get in natural food will not harm you. It's the salt you *add* that does the harm.

Dr. Dahl says that, in the presence of existing high blood pressure there is seldom a reduction in pressure unless the salt intake is reduced below one or two grams. He suggests a maximum salt intake of about 5 grams per day for an adult without a family history of high blood pressure. This could be done by omitting frankly salty foods and using the salt-shaker sparingly if at all. He reminds us that an intake of 5 grams of salt per day is at least 10 times the amount upon which one can live healthfully in good balance.

For people with a family history of high blood pressure, Dr. Dahl recommends the immediate adoption of a diet low in salt—500 to 1,000 milligrams a day at the maximum. This should not be difficult to do, he says, once you have become convinced that it is the best plan. He reminds us, too, that increasing the potassium content of the diet may help, since potassium seems to cancel some of the bad effects of sodium in the body. Foods high in potassium are fruits, vegetables, nuts and seed foods.

Suppose you are worried about high blood pressure or suppose you merely want to cut down on salt so that you won't ever have to worry about high blood pressure—how do you go about it? How do you know how much salt you are getting every day and how can you reduce it? We include in this discussion a chart giving the salt content of common foods in terms of the average serving. You can check through this and easily note which are the foods high in salt.

You will notice that all the foods listed here are natural foods, except for cheese, some of the cereal products, powdered milk and bacon and eggs. You will see, too, how easy it is to control salt intake at a low level when you are eating only natural, unprocessed foods. Making up menus from these foods you will never get near the limit of 5 grams of salt a day suggested by Dr. Dahl if you avoid the processed foods. They all have added salt. In addition, there are many foods that are little else but carriers of salt—olives, pickles, relishes, luncheon meats, dried beef, cheeses—all those foods whose taste is definitely salty are not for you.

What about salt substitutes? We have never seen any research done on the effects of salt substitutes on health, but we are inclined to counsel against them. In general, the commercially available ones are just a mixture of chemicals and many of them contain quite large amounts of sodium (which is what you are trying to avoid). Besides, using a salt substitute is cheating. What you want to do is to get away from the whole idea of "seasoning" your food. Why not enjoy the taste of the food for a change? If you feel that you must use a salt substitute, we suggest powdered kelp which is a purely natural food. Although it contains salt, it contains, too, all the other minerals that occur in sea water, all of which are valuable for you.

SALT CONTENT OF SOME COMMON FOODS

Meats:		Salt in Grams	Vegetables:		Salt in Grams
Bacon	3 slices	1.200	Artichokes	1 medium	.018
Beef	1 serving	.057	Asparagus	10 stalks	.060
Chicken	1 "	.048	Beets	⅔ cup	.100
Duck	1 "	.040	Brussels Sprouts	⅔ cup	.070
Goose	1 "	.060	Cabbage	⅔ cup	.020
Ham	1 "	1.6 to 2.0	Carrots	¾ cup	.060
Lamb Chop	1 "	.057	Cauliflower	½ cup	.060
Lamb Roast	1 "	.067	Celery	¾ cup	.060
Turkey	1 "	.040	Corn	¼ cup	.020
Veal Roast	1 "	.057	Cucumber	10 slices	.050
Fish:			Egg plant	½ cup	.040
Bass	1 "	.069	Endive	10 stalks	.275
Cod	1 "	.066	Greens, dandelion	½ cup	.168
Haddock	1 "	.057	Lentils	¼ cup	.030
Mackerel	1 "	.076	Lettuce	10 leaves	.120
Oysters	1 "	.050	Lima beans	¼ cup	.030
Salmon (canned)	1 "	.059	Peas	¾ cup	.006
Trout, shad	1 "	.061	Peppers	2 medium	.020
			Potato	1 medium	.160
Dairy Products:			Pumpkin	½ cup	.060
Cheese	1 inch cube	.164	Spinach	½ cup	.120
(American)			Squash, summer	½ cup	.010
Cheese (cottage)	2 tablespoons	.280	String beans	⅔ cup	.040
Cheese (cream)	¼ cake	.250	Tomatoes	1 medium	.060
Eggs	1 whole	.088	Turnips	½ cup	.070
Buttermilk	½ cup	.160	Radishes	5 medium	.024
Milk, whole	½ cup	.175	Watercress	10 pieces	.025
Milk, powdered	2 tablespoons	.080			
Fruits:			Cereals:		
Apple, baked	1	.008	Bread, graham	1 slice	.230
Apricots, fresh	3	.003	Bread, white	1 slice	.130
Banana	1 small	.206	Cornbread		
Cranberries	⅔ cup	.015	(without salt)	1 piece	.001
Figs, fresh	1 large	.005	Farina, cooked	¾ cup	.038
Grapefruit	½ small	.008	Macaroni	½ cup	.024
Grapes	24	.010	Oatmeal	½ cup	.033
Grapejuice	½ cup	.003	Shredded wheat	1 biscuit	.034
Muskmelon	½ cup, cubes	.030	Rice	½ cup	.027
Oranges	1 medium	.010			
Peaches	1 medium	.010	Nuts:		
Pears	1 medium	.020	Almonds	14	.009
Pineapple	1 slice	.080	Peanuts	9	.010
Prunes	6 medium	.019	Pecans	12	.024
Rhubarb	¾ cup	.059	Walnuts	3	.010
Strawberries	¾ cup	.010			
Watermelon	1 serving	.010			

CHAPTER 83

Excessive Table Salt
and Pregnancy

Evidence of the harmfulness of salt during pregnancy comes to us from an article by a Dutch gynecologist, Professor DeSnoo, in the July 10, 1948, issue of the *Netherlands Medical Journal,* a professional magazine corresponding in prestige to the *Journal of the American Medical Association* in this country.

Dr. DeSnoo reminds us again that civilized man has been salting his food for centuries, simply because food tastes better that way, rather than because he needs the salt. He tells us that prehistoric man, living a nomadic life and eating plant and animal foods as he found them in nature did not know there was such a thing as sodium chloride or table salt. There are still many localities in the world where the use of salt is unknown and some people who find the taste of salt extremely unpleasant.

These facts alone prove to us, says Dr. DeSnoo, that the sodium chloride existing in its natural form in the food we eat supplies us with quite enough of this substance, so that there is no need for us to use additional salt. The sodium chloride contained in the average unsalted daily diet would be about ½ to 1 gram, whereas, salting food as we usually do, we consume about 10 to 20 grams, surely an enormous overdose. Among the Dutch people, he says, the average sodium content of the blood is 333 milligrams per hundred grams. In an individual who does not salt his food it may be as low as 320 milligrams. In cases of sickness it may fall as low as 300 milligrams or increase to 370 milligrams.

He grants that some salt may be necessary to replace that lost in food through cooking, but certainly we do not need 20 grams to replace a possible one gram that may be lost. It's astonishing, he marvels, that we can generally eat so much salt, year after year, without noticeable harm. Or is the harm being done, perhaps without our knowing it? Thirty milligrams of salt given to a healthy person will produce edema—a swollen condition in which water collects in the body tissues. This is caused by the fact that salt attracts water, as anyone knows who has tried to use a salt shaker on a damp day. Drops of water are clustered even on the outside of the shaker, let alone all the additional moisture that has caked the salt inside.

During the last months of pregnancy, there is lessened tolerance for salt in the expectant mother's body, as evidenced by frequent cases of edema. When salt is omitted or even decreased in the diet, the edema disappears. For a long time, comments Dr. DeSnoo, this proof of salt as a cause of pregnancy complications was not recognized by physicians, for sometimes women on a "saltless" diet did fall prey to eclampsia, a serious, often fatal, complication of pregnancy. From his own experience Dr. DeSnoo says regretfully, he knows that prescribing a saltless diet to an apparently cooperative patient is not enough. By regular checking of the urine, the physician must find out whether or not this diet has been adhered to.

Effects of Saltless Diet on Miscarriages

There are many women whose unborn children die during successive pregnancies, who have had living children when their diet was saltless during pregnancy. Twelve women from Dr. DeSnoo's own clinic were used as examples in a medical article published back in 1917. These 12 women had had a total of 77 children, of whom 55 were born dead. Ten of the women succeeded in having healthy living children after they had been put on a saltless diet. Some of these 10 women started to use salt again and once again had interrupted pregnancies. Those who continued their saltless diets bore other healthy live children. No other therapy was used, no other conditions of the patients' lives were changed, so it cannot be doubted that the saltless diet produced results little short of miraculous.

During the last war when food was rationed in Holland, living conditions were not of the best and, one would suppose, all conditions making for health were at a low ebb. But later research has revealed that fewer children were born dead during the war years than either before or after the war. The same was true in England and Switzerland. In Holland 1700 fewer children died before or during birth while Holland was in the grip of the war. Other writers have attributed this tremendous decrease in miscarriages and other complications to various war conditions: there was a tendency to get more sleep and more exercise and to eat less food. What about salt consumption? Salt was not rationed and apparently as much salt was eaten as during the previous years. However, we'll have more to say about this later. Figures for miscarriages per 1000 births are given below. Note the drop of almost 7 per 1000 during two of the war years:

Miscarriages per 1000 births in Holland 1931-1946

1931-1935	25.1
1936-1939	24.9
1940	25.08
1941	21.26
1942	19.33
1943	18.47
1944	18.50
1945	19.38
1946	20.29

To arrive at an interpretation of these figures, Dr. DeSnoo studied the mortality figures of his own clinic from 1927 on. During those 21 years about 40,000 expectant mothers were cared for there. As methods of treatment at the clinic did not change, it seems logical that, at least among this representative group of the population, some valid conclusions may be drawn.

Decrease in Mortality Rates During War

The death rate for developmental disturbances (that is complications during pregnancy) is the same for the period before the war, during the war and after the war. The death rate for difficulties during birth decreased during the war. The death rate for diseases of the mother and "unknown causes" remained constant up to 1941, then *showed a decrease of 45 per cent during the war*. Hence the greatest saving of life among the children occurs in that group where the cause of death was either an illness of the mother or an unknown cause. This means that death because of hemorrhaging, venereal disease, diabetes and so forth did not decrease. But death from eclampsia and various unknown kinds of poisoning did.

Of all possible factors involved, says Dr. DeSnoo, food is by far the most important. The fact remains that edematous conditions (waterlogging) decreased decidedly and that healthy women do not become edematous on a low-salt diet. So the only possible conclusion is that less salt was consumed during the war.

How Less Salt Improved Health

According to national health statistics in Holland from 1937 to 1941, there was an average of 21.7 per cent of edematous patients. In 1942 it dropped to 16 per cent. From then on it dropped steadily every year until 1945 when it was 9 per cent. In 1946 it rose again to 20.5 per cent. In pregnancies where serious toxic states developed the same was true. From 28 per cent in 1937-41 the percentage dropped steadily each year until 1945 when it was only 12 per cent. The next year it increased again to 29 per cent.

Dr. DeSnoo is convinced that this decrease is due to a decrease in the amount of salt actually consumed. The sales of salt did not decrease. But, in general, people were consuming less food and hence, in an age when food is as heavily salted as it is in our century, food rationing would produce this evident decrease in the amount of salt consumed. Bread, for instance, is apparently very heavily salted in Holland and bread was rationed by 1941.

Less Salt Is Important for All of Us

We must study much more closely all the pertinent facts concerning the food of expectant mothers, says Dr. DeSnoo, and we must try our best to find the optimum food, which will be food that comes close to the natural food of our ancestors, before it had been changed by cooking or salting or the addition of all sorts of other ingredients. We must battle even more strongly against the salt-habit, not only for the sake of mothers and children, but for the population in general. In Indonesia, he tells us, salt is strictly rationed. No one receives more than 4 grams per person per day. Eclampsia is practically unknown and the number of miscarriages is extremely small. There is, of course, recognition of the unhealthy role of

[294]

salt in high blood pressure, for even in our country low-salt or saltless diets are commonly prescribed by physicians for these patients.

We have noticed among our letters from readers an increasing number who are eating less salt and reporting improvement in health. We also get lots of letters from people marveling on how many of their friends are on salt-free or salt-poor diets. For those of you who feel that a diet lacking in salt would be extremely monotonous and dull, we recommend *The Salt-Free Diet Cook Book* by Emil G. Conason, M.D., and Ella Metz, published by Lear Publishers in New York City, 1949. This includes many recipes and menus for patients whose physicians have placed them on diets as low in sodium as possible. In the book the amount of sodium present in the average portion of every food is given, along with the calories that food contains. So if you do without salt and are afraid you may not be eating a normal amount of sodium, you may easily check your menus against the lists of food given in the book.

Get Sodium Naturally . . . From Foods

Included with this article is a partial list of foods high in sodium. If your doctor has already placed you on a sodium-free diet, probably many of these foods are on the forbidden list for you. But if you should decide, on your own, to eliminate or cut down on your consumption of table salt, which we think is a splendid idea, we'd advise you to glance over this list from time to time, just to make certain you are eating enough foods which naturally contain fairly high amounts of sodium.

The list is inclusive enough, but individual eating habits being what they are, there's a chance that you may be omitting just those very foods which contain the sodium and you might end up with getting too little sodium rather than the great overabundance most of us consume every day.

LIST OF FOODS CONTAINING SODIUM

Food	Usual Portion	Milligrams Per Ounce
Almonds	20—1 ounce	7.4
Apples	1—1⅓ ounces	2.8 to 4.2
Asparagus	6—2½ ounces	.5 to 4.5
Bananas	1—5 ounces	.02 to 12
Barley, pearl	3T—1 ounce	.7 to 16
Beans, butter	¾ cup—2½ ounces	17.4
Beans, green lima	½ cup—2½ ounces	.28 to 25.4
Beans, dried lima	½ cup—2½ ounces	47.7 to 80.5
Beef, lean	½ pound	15 to 24
Beets	⅔ cup—3⅓ ounces	15.1 to 31.4
Bluefish	½ pound	19.4
Cabbage, red	½ cup—2 5/6 ounces	1.4 to 10.8
Cantaloupe	¼—3⅓ ounces	3.4 to 13.7
Carrots, raw	½ cup—2⅔ ounces	8.8 to 27
Celery stalks	2—1⅓ ounces	28.8 to 38.9
Cheese, American Swiss	⅛ inch—1 ounce	120.0
Cheese, Cheddar	5/6 ounce	154.2
Chicken, breast	½ pound	15.4 to 26.0
Chicken, leg	½ pound	15.4 to 31.4
Coconut, fresh	1 inch—⅓ ounce	4.7 to 11.4

Food	Usual Portion	Milligrams Per Ounce
Cream	1 T—½ ounce	8.8 to 11.4
Dandelion greens	½ cup—1⅔ ounce	21.7 to 48
Duck, leg	½ pound	27.4
Eggs	1 average—1⅔ ounce	31.7 to 40
Flounder, steamed	¼ pound	32.6
Goose, roasted	¼ pound	41.2
Haddock, steamed	¼ pound	34.4
Halibut, steamed	¼ pound	31.5
Kale	1¾ cup—6 ounces	14.2 to 31.4
Kidney, beef	5 ounces	60 to 69.5
Kohlrabi	½ cup—1⅔ ounce	14.2
Lamb, without fat	1 chop—3⅛ ounces	14 to 31.4
Lentils	¼ cup—2 ounces	16.2
Liver, beef	½ pound	6 to 24.8
Liver, calf	½ pound	24.8 to 31.4
Mackerel	½ pound	43.7
Milk, fresh whole	1 cup—8 ounces	13.4 to 14.5
Oatmeal	¼ cup—1 ounce	.5 to 20.5
Pork, without fat	½ pound	16.5 to 23.1
Radishes	6 med.—1⅔ ounce	2.3 to 23.7
Spinach, boiled	½ cup—3⅓ ounces	34.9
Trout, steamed	4 ounces	25
Turkey, breast	8 ounces	11.4 to 37.1
Turkey, leg	8 ounces	26.2 to 37.1
Turnips, white	¾ cup—4 ounces	10.5 to 29.7
Turnip greens	1 cup—3⅓ ounces	2.8 to 74.2

CHAPTER 84

Salt and Falling Hair

The dietary culprit that we know as salt has a gift for popping up in the least likely places. Scientists study physiological problems for years, testing the most exotic components of our diets without results, when all of a sudden someone thinks to try testing salt, and finds his answer in that common chemical. This has been the case in heart disease, all types of edema and now salt has shown itself as a contributory cause of baldness.

The concern expressed by people who find they are going bald is often a source of amusement for others. To the true scientist baldness is nothing to laugh at. He is not concerned with the looks of the balding person at all. He is anxious to know if aging, of itself, has anything to do with loss of hair. It is not unreasonable to hope that observations on the nature of baldness might throw some light on other aspects of aging.

Salt in the Scalp Tissues

Eugene Foldes, whose report appeared in *Acta-Dermato-Venereologica* 35: 334, 1955, worked under this hope. He knew that under certain conditions an excess of electrolytes—mainly, sodium chloride (salt)—may accumulate in some tissues and may interfere with the proper function of these tissues. Could it be possible, Foldes wanted to know, that baldness develops when an excess of salt is present in the scalp tissues and actually disturbs or thwarts the function they have of growing hair? Could this function be improved by reducing the amount of sodium chloride in these tissues? He would attempt to do so by administering diuretics which would help the body expel extra fluids and, with them, salt.

Finding a way to scientifically measure this information was truly a challenge. Dr. Foldes decided to consider the number of hairs shed during the experiment as an indication of baldness. Should there be a reduction in the number of hairs falling during the experiment, it would be considered an indication that the therapy was effective. The hairs that fell from the experimental patients were carefully counted, but it was found that the daily hair loss fluctuated regardless of outside influences. This divergence in the numbers of falling hair seemed to even out into a weekly figure that varied less than 10 per cent, and a daily average was then arrived at from the weekly figure.

Shampoo Increases Loss

It was also found that shampooing is accompanied by a larger than average hair loss. This is a factor which balding persons might bear in mind in the interests of preserving what hair they have. We do not approve of the use of soap on any part of the body.

In one case the patient was a woman of 62 years of age who complained of loss of hair. She was given the diuretic in the form of rectal suppositories, and abstained from shampoo during the period of observation. In her first 3 weeks of therapy the woman reduced her average daily hair loss approximately 46 per cent.

A young male patient had similar results. He had noticed an excessive loss of hair during the last two or 3 years. In approximately two months his hair loss was reduced from an average daily count of 188 to 74, a decrease of about 60 per cent.

Drugs Only for Experiment

It was found that a tolerance to the drugs being used was likely to occur, and that the drug would then prove to be ineffective in preventing future hair loss.

Though we carry the report of Dr. Foldes' work, it should be understood that we would be strongly opposed to the common use of drugs to prevent baldness. The drugs employed by Dr. Foldes were used only as a means of controlling the salt supply in the tissues of the scalp for experimental purposes. We are certain that he would be against the use of these drugs as a standard treatment for baldness just as we are. What is interesting is that the reduction of salt in the tissues did affect the loss of hair. And it

[297]

follows that a lower intake of salt would reduce the amount of this chemical in the tissues of the scalp without any drugs at all. Dr. Foldes' theory should then be just as effective concerning a scalp which is kept free of salt in its tissues, as it is where the salt already there has been driven out by the use of drugs.

CHAPTER 85

Is Insomnia Related to Salt-Eating?

A French army doctor believes that the amount of sodium one eats has a lot to do with the soundness of his sleep. We came across this information in a copy of a speech made by Professor Coirault before a conference on mental hygiene.

He bases his theory on the well-known biological fact that sodium and potassium are natural enemies in the body's chemistry. "A cell is in a state of repose" he says, "when it rejects sodium and recovers potassium .... A cell is active when it loses potassium and recovers sodium. This frees the energy accumulated during the preceding phase."

Professor Coirault goes on to say that many insomnia troubles come from overactivity of nerves, due to too much sodium intake. He goes further and says that other disorders of sleep such as sleepwalking are the result of too much sodium in the diet.

He tells us that he has established in some of his patients the rhythm of the elimination of various minerals—among them sodium, potassium, calcium and magnesium. He describes one patient who sleeps soundly and well if she is given no salt in her food and, in addition—for purposes of the experiment, we suppose—takes a hormone which causes her to excrete sodium so that she goes to bed, you might say, deficient in sodium.

On the other hand, if she is given 6 grams of salt (sodium chloride) at her evening meal, she will experience many sleep disorders, including sleep-walking and other strange behavior while she is apparently unconscious in sleep.

Sodium Chloride—A Drug

We are told by a classic book on the subject of nutrition, *Clinical Nutrition,* by Joliffe and Tisdal (Hoeber), that good health can be maintained on as little as one gram of sodium chloride a day. Yet the average intake of sodium chloride from all sources is about 8 to 15 grams a day. And some people get as much as 20 grams!

[298]

Let's say your doctor had prescribed a drug for you, telling you exactly how much of that drug to take, and you took 20 times that much. Can you see the terrible consequences such an action might have for you? Salt, as we use it, is a drug. It is a pure mineral substance—the only thing we eat that is not plant or animal. It is pure sodium chloride—a drug. And most of us are using 8 times as much and some of us are using 20 times as much as we need to stay healthy!

Insomniacs of our times take sleeping pills—drugs which have quite harmful effects on health. Can it be that the reason they cannot sleep is another drug—salt? Again we urge readers who have not already done so to cut down drastically on their salt. You get enough salt in your food—there is no need, absolutely none, to add any either in the kitchen or at the table. Begin by tapering off on the amount of salt you use, if you are sure you are going to object to the taste of unsalted food. By getting along on less and less salt as the weeks go by, you will find that you are, for the first time, actually tasting your food rather than just tasting the salt you used to spread on it.

CHAPTER 86

There Are Natural Substitutes for Salt

Some people find the adjustment to a salt-free diet easy enough once they've made up their minds to stick to it. For others the loss of salt seems to take all of the zest out of the food they eat. They complain that it's flat and uninteresting. Because of this, these salt worshippers will disregard their judgment as well as the advice of their physicians, and continue to salt their food even in the face of a physical condition that can be seriously affected by this practice.

Their problem is taken up in some detail in an article by Milton Plotz, M.D., Clinical Associate Professor of Medicine, State University of New York Medical Center, in the *American Journal of Clinical Nutrition* (November-December, 1957). His main suggestion is that the cook use unusual herbs and spices to create new flavors that will make the dieter forget that he ever used salt to bring out flavor. Some of the lesser-used spices and herbs he suggests to add interest to salt-free dishes are: allspice, caraway, chili powder, coconut, curry, ginger, home-prepared horseradish, lemon or lime juice, mustard seed, peppermint, saffron and tarragon.

Some Interesting Salt-free Dishes

Dr. Plotz offers these tempting suggestions among others: For a new taste in asparagus, sprinkle the stalks and tips with nutmeg before serving. Cucumbers take on a new flavor when sliced very thin and marinated in tarragon vinegar before serving. For an exciting and exotic dish Dr. Plotz suggests eggplant baked with tomatoes, bay leaf and oregano. For other ways of serving vegetables try green beans seasoned with nutmeg or savory; onions boiled with clove and thyme are new-tasting; unsalted peas will taste more interesting if they are sprinkled with chopped or powdered mint. For flavoring meats to avoid salt use these suggestions: to goulash or stew add bay leaf, sweet paprika, rosemary or oregano; rub lamb chops with freshly ground pepper or ginger before broiling; a roast of beef treated the same way before cooking with a large bay leaf in the roasting pan will be a pleasant surprise; when it's veal chops, rub them with saffron and ground pepper before simmering them in oil, to which you've added a little water; as for veal stew, it will take nicely to onion, bay leaf, powdered mace and celery leaves for added flavor.

Guard Against Hidden Salt

Dr. Plotz reveals several check points for those anxious to maintain a diet free of salt. For one thing, both butter and margarine are usually sold with salt added. If one wishes to use these foods, one must ask for the unsalted varieties. Nearly all canned foods contain salt, as do some frozen foods. Of course, garlic, celery and onion salts contain huge amounts of sodium. Also be on the watch for sodium in the list of ingredients on labels of flavor improvers. Special foods designated as salt-poor should be checked for just how much salt they do contain. Often "salt-poor" is still too "salt-rich" for some people. Cheeses are usually plentifully endowed with salt. Two types of cheese—Edam and Port Salut—bought by the author as low-salt cheeses in a large department store, were found to contain substantial amounts of sodium.

CHAPTER 87

What About Iodized Salt?

Years ago when it first became apparent that lack of iodine in diet and water might render inhabitants of certain parts of the world susceptible to thyroid disorders, it was suggested that we solve this nutritional problem by adding iodine (as potassium iodide) to common table salt. In this way, it was argued, we could be sure that everyone got enough iodine to prevent any thyroid difficulties.

So in many sections of the world today iodized salt is available and in some countries its use is mandatory. However, a booklet entitled *Iodine in Drinking Waters, Vegetables* . . . by G. S. Fraps and J. F. Fudge published by the Agricultural and Mechanical College of Texas tells us that potassium iodide added to the rations of various animals "rarely gave any beneficial results and sometimes gave detrimental ones." The surveys and experiments were done in areas where it was known that iodine was low in food and where goiter was prevalent. Nevertheless among sheep fed a daily ration of iodine, reproduction was abnormal; in the case of hogs, no beneficial results were found and there was some indication that the animals' use of calcium was disordered. Calves that had the iodine ate less hay and made considerably less gains in weight than those which did not. The conclusion of researchers Fraps and Fudge is, "The use of iodized table salt for human consumption in Texas is not recommended, except under the supervision of a competent physician. The use of iodized mineral mixtures for live-stock in Texas is not recommended."

Dangers Involved

In a book called *Trace Elements in Food* (published by John Wiley & Sons, New York), G. W. Monier-Williams, formerly of the Ministry of Health in England, has a great deal to say about the results of using iodized table salt. He says that it is pretty well agreed that the thyroid gland is of importance primarily in childhood and that treatment with iodine has not the same effects later on in life, except during pregnancy with the object of preventing goiter in the unborn child. Children tolerate iodine much better than adults, he says, and their iodine requirements are 3 times as great. It is alleged, he says, that adults constantly receiving small doses of iodine are likely to develop toxic symptoms.

One researcher in 1936 for instance found that there was a marked increase in cases of hyperthyroidism (overactivity of the thyroid gland) in adults after iodized salt was introduced, which could be ascribed only to the action of the iodine in the salt. She believes that sensitivity to iodine is apparently quite common among adults, especially in goitrous regions. Other authorities have argued that the dose of iodine from table salt is very small indeed—far less than that given in medical treatment and that any excess of iodine over that required to maintain the thyroid gland in good health is promptly excreted in the urine.

However, Monier-Williams reminds us that iodine belongs to the same chemical family as bromine (and fluorine, too, we might add). Bromides are excreted very slowly indeed from the body. "It may be that occasional massive doses of iodides cannot be considered in the same light as daily small doses continued for many years, and that the habitual use of iodized salt, while beneficial and even essential to children, is not altogether without risk to a certain small proportion of adults," he says. "Hyper-sensitiveness to iodine may be commoner in some districts than in others, but even if it affected only two per cent of the population this would seem to be sufficient reason for objecting to the compulsory iodization of all household, or even

[301]

all table salt." We go along with Dr. Monier-Williams one hundred per cent in this opinion.

There are a number of other reasons why we object to iodized salt. One of them is that the potassium iodide is lost very rapidly from salt in cardboard containers. We are told that salt containing 5 parts per million of potassium iodide may lose as much as one third of that within 6 weeks depending on the atmospheric conditions. So one never knows how much iodine may actually be in the box of salt he purchases. If he depends on the iodine to protect him from iodine deficiency, perhaps he will be cruelly deceived.

If, on the other hand, he is sensitive to iodine, the very small amount that may remain in that salt carton may be just enough to start trouble for him, taken day after day and year after year. Consider for a moment—if two per cent of our population suffer from iodine sensitivity—that is more people than suffer from most of our great chronic diseases, so, of course, it is important to consider the reactions of these two per cent before we arbitrarily decree that everyone everywhere should take iodized salt.

"Doctored" Foods and Iodine Sensitivity

Our principal reason for avoiding iodized salt stems from another reason, however. We do not like "doctored" foods. The potassium iodide placed in table salt was not placed there by nature. So it is not accompanied by all the other substances that go along with iodine in foods. And it is not in what we call "organic combination" with the other ingredients of salt. This makes it a drug, from our point of view.

We know that potassium iodide is used extensively in medicine. In fact, one of the principal ingredients of several very famous cancer treatments is potassium iodide. But this, mark you, is treatment, given under the strict supervision of doctors, to very, very sick people. This is surely no indication that we should all be taking potassium iodide every day of our lives along with food!

Iodine sensitivity is nothing to joke about. We have an article from the *Journal of the American Medical Association* for July 2, 1955, in which two Buffalo, New York, doctors discuss the case of a young patient who was suffering from a horrible dermatitis involving ulcers, eyelids swollen shut and so forth. He had been taking potassium iodide as an expectorant. It was believed that taking iodized table salt had sensitized the patient over a period of years so that when he got medicine that contained potassium iodide he reacted immediately with a serious allergic response. The authors go on to tell us that fatalities have resulted even from the application of iodine *to the skin of sensitive persons.*

Teenagers Beware of Iodized Salt

Have you ever seen a warning to teenagers with acne to avoid iodized salt, telling you the added iodine could aggravate their skin condition? Probably few of us have, for the salt companies are much too busy emphasizing the "new taste" salt brings to foods, and the great part iodized salt plays in preventing goiter. However, a Florida doctor noticed a foot-note in a school health textbook which presented this very fact and wrote to the *Journal of the American Medical Association* (December 27, 1958) for confirmation. Perfectly true says the answer. Iodine excreted through the skin, after ingestion, can irritate certain of the skin's apparatus where acne is present. Acne patients who move to the sea coast even get worse due to the iodine in the atmosphere.

Why have we not seen more warnings on the dangers of iodized salt for acne patients? How many of these cases have been worsened by the victim's unconsciously using salt (bad enough in itself) with added iodine?

Now, of course, this does not mean that we should all stop getting any iodine at all in our diets. We must have iodine—a certain very small amount of it—or we will perish. But doesn't it seem that nature is trying to warn us not to take iodine in the concentrated, non-organic form in which it appears in iodized salt? We have never heard of anyone reacting negatively to iodine in food—seafood or seaweed or mushrooms, because here the iodine is part of the food and combined with it in nature's proper way.

Of course, it may have occurred to many readers to ask why we should mention iodized salt at all, since we do not think any of us should salt food, either in cooking or at the table. A highly pertinent comment to make. Those of us who have stopped using salt or have cut down drastically will not need to worry about iodized salt. Yet, from letters we know that these are the very people who worry most, for they write us in great concern, "Since I am not taking salt I am not getting any iodine—how shall I make up the loss?" Our answer is, "Go right on skipping the salt and get your iodine from some organic source—seafood, kelp or seaweed." In fact, it seems to us that powdered kelp would be the best possible salt substitute for those readers who are trying desperately to cut down on salt but haven't yet conquered that all-American gesture of reaching for the salt shaker before eating anything. Fill the salt shaker with powdered kelp—far, far richer in iodine than iodized salt, and with a pleasant taste, too.

We Shouldn't Salt Our Food, Anyway

We have a new story about salt restriction which we think is extremely important. It is generally widely known these days that doctors prescribe salt-poor diets for heart patients. Now we find, in a lead article in the *Journal of the American Medical Association* for November 26, 1955, that salt restriction helps greatly in cases of cirrhosis of the liver, too. The treatment was given to 30 patients in Bellevue Hospital by Dr. Charles S. Davidson. All of them suffered also from *ascites,* which means an accumulation of fluid in the abdomen. Of the 30 patients, 28 were known alcoholics, but two clearly were not, although the cause of their disease was not known. Four of the patients were considered well nourished. In 16 undernutrition was moderate and 10 of the patients were definitely severely undernourished.

These patients were put on a good nourishing diet rich in vitamins and minerals and their salt intake was restricted to 200 milligrams per day—that is, about one-fifth of a gram. (Many Americans eat as much as 15 grams of salt daily.)

[303]

The results were uniformly excellent. All of the patients improved. It took longer in some cases than in others—as long as 16 months in some cases until the patient was free from the terrible swelling that deformed him and, of course, distorted all his body functions immeasurably. At the same time, the nutritional status of all the patients improved, too, and the liver began to function much more normally. The doctors believe that the livers of the patients were actually regenerated. Improvement in a feeling of well-being, return of appetite and successful readjustment of many body functions went along with the salt-poor diet.

There is no medical or physiological evidence that the human body needs more sodium chloride (table salt) than is contained naturally in foods. Our continual daily overconsumption of salt (the only food we eat which has neither an animal nor vegetable source) may well be the cause of many more troubles than we know. Don't depend on iodized table salt for your iodine. Get it from a natural source like kelp or salt water fish. And cut down on salting your food until you arrive at that happy stage where you will not miss the taste of the salt at all and will, instead of salt, be tasting the food you eat.

CHAPTER 88

Shall We Use Sea Salt?

In the *New England Journal of Medicine* for May 3, 1951, we found a letter from an M.D. of Massachusetts, Dr. S. Hoechstetter, who advocates the use of sea salt rather than refined salt. Says Dr. Hoechstetter, "For many years our agricultural chemists and agronomists have been stressing the fact that our soil is steadily being depleted of its trace elements by the combination of excessive cropping and leaching through broken sod. This loss of minerals from our soil is now being reflected in trace-element-deficient food on our dinner tables.

"Experiments conducted by the Agriculture Departments of the Federal Government and many of our states have led to the prescription of mineral supplements to be added to the soil with the usual P.N.P. (Phosphorus-Nitrogen-Potassium) fertilizers and lime. Stress, however, has been on the replacement of those elements that are essential to plant growth, and no effort has been made to replace trace elements which, although not essential to plant growth, are essential to human health.

"In the past the trace-element deficiencies in our food were not too important because the missing elements were available for the most part in our table salt. In recent years, however, the salt producers have refined their table salt almost to the point of chemical purity in their effort to market a product that will not 'cake' in damp weather. In this process much of the trace element material essential to health is lost. It appears that we still have not profited by past experience with polished rice. (By this Dr. Hoechstetter is referring to the deficiency disease of beriberi which became almost an epidemic in rice-eating countries when brown rice was refined and the vitamin B-containing germ was removed to make it white.)

"Recent studies in electrolyte (mineral) balance have called attention to the striking similarity, both quantitive and qualitative, of the electrolyte content of sea water to that of our total body fluids. It is obvious from this that unrefined sea salt is an excellent source of trace minerals, both those that are now recognized as important and others that are not yet known to be essential but may be found essential to health in the future. In the light of recent discoveries about cobalt it would be arrogant for any of us to deny the possibility of some essential function for even gold in our complex metabolism—and sea water contains this precious metal.

"At the risk of being considered a food faddist (hence queer), I strongly advocate the use of sea salt in the preparation and seasoning of our food. While admittedly, it does not shake well and it 'cakes' even in dry weather, but these inconveniences are minor in view of its value in supplying us with the trace elements now lacking in our diet."

Dr. Crane Writes of Sea Water

Quite recently a syndicated columnist, Dr. George W. Crane, who writes on health matters, took up the question of sea water in a series of articles which seemed to us to make very good sense. He said much the same thing said by Dr. Hoechstetter—that sea water may contain the very trace elements that are missing in our diets and food and that replacing them may have a most beneficial effect on our health—especially those middle-age disorders like diabetes, gray hair, baldness, possibly multiple sclerosis, myasthenia gravis and others which are generally spoken of as being "deficiency" diseases.

Dr. Crane pointed out that the cause of simple goiter was discovered when we found out that the thyroid gland needs a tiny amount of iodine in order to manufacture its hormone, thyroxin. Lack of iodine in food will cause the thyroid gland to enlarge, trying to make up for the lack of this important element. Yet the amount of iodine needed by the healthy body is so small that we call this a "trace" element.

He also retells the story of the sheep in Australia who were dying of a mysterious ailment. Nothing helped until someone discovered that a tiny amount of cobalt (another element) in their diet would completely cure the difficulty. Human beings undoubtedly also need cobalt. All water soluble chemicals on earth are dissolved in sea water, says Dr. Crane, which contains traces of nearly 50 chemicals.

He went on in his column to tell of the wonders worked by a teaspoon of concentrated sea water in the case of his aged father-in-law. This 97 year old gentleman improved almost miraculously after the sea water was added to his morning oatmeal. Since he did not know of its addition, he could not possibly have improved because he was expecting something miraculous to occur.

After Dr. Crane's column appeared we received many letters from readers asking if we could give them more information about concentrated sea water, where it could be obtained and so forth. Since we counsel against using salt, did our prohibition include sea water, too, they asked.

Why Should Sea Water Benefit Us?

There seems to be no doubt that life began in the sea and that sea water is very much like blood in its composition. Blood contains many minerals and "trace" minerals—that is, minerals which occur in such minute quantities that we might say there are only traces of them. Sea water also contains these minerals, including the obscure and little-known ones.

The *Medical Press* for November 28, 1956, tells us that the ancient Romans had some extraordinary ideas on cookery, including "the universal use of a sauce of garum, a fluid consisting apparently of sea water impregnated with the products of decaying fish." In many parts of the world today sea salt is used at all times to salt foods, rather than the white refined salt which we use in the western world.

Of course, if you concentrate sea water by boiling or otherwise evaporating it, you get sea salt, which is a much easier product to store and handle. We did some research on sea salt and found that it is indeed a substance extremely rich in minerals and trace minerals. About 75 per cent of it is sodium chloride, which we know as table salt. The other approximately 25 per cent consists of minerals which we expect to find in relatively large amounts—calcium, magnesium, carbon, sulfur and potassium Then there are more than 30 trace elements which occur in such small quantities that they are listed in parts per million. They include such obscure names as yttrium, cesium, scandium—all of which occur in tiny fractions of a part per million—such infinitely small amounts that one can hardly imagine them. Gold, silver, mercury, nickel are familiar metals which also occur in tiny amounts. There are also arsenic, aluminum and lead, 3 ominous-sounding elements, which seem to be not poisonous when they appear naturally in food or water.

From an article by Clementine Paddleford in the *New York Herald Tribune,* November 7, 1955, we find that "some seas are saltier than others, but the proportion of elements in this sea salt is remarkably constant all over the world. The 'mix' is almost identical with the composition of the blood serum which transports nutrients through the bodies of warm-blooded animals." The salt used by early mankind was crude, lumpy and wet because the calcium and magnesium it contained attracted water. So salt was "refined." The "impurities" were removed. That is, the things that made it inconvenient to use were taken out. What was finally left was almost pure sodium chloride which is what we pour from our salt shakers today. Says Miss Paddleford, "As for the 'impurities' of salt, it was hard to see how such very tiny quantities of extra mineral could make any difference to the human body one way or another."

But health-conscious readers can easily understand why we should wonder whether perhaps much of the damage we suffer from using table salt may not be due to the lack of minerals that should accompany the sodium chloride.

We object to refined sugar and flour because the valuable proteins and minerals that occur in these foods naturally have been removed from them and what remains is little more than a drug. Undoubtedly the same is true of salt. Removing the minerals that accompany sea salt, in order to refine it, may be one of the main reasons why salt, as such, is harmful. Perhaps taking it with all the minerals intact makes salt much more desirable as a part of one's food.

Other Testimony on Sea Salt

An article in the Houston (Texas) *Press* for October 21, 1955, relates the story of a reporter who tried sea salt and found that it eliminated colds for him and his family. He believed, he said, that the trace elements were responsible. Another clipping, from the *New York Times* for January 27, 1958, tells of a 78-year-old British Columbia man who claims he has not been ill since childhood. He takes a daily ocean swim, drinks occasional glasses of ocean water and lets sea water dry on his body as a "safeguard to his health."

A. E. Schaefer of the National Institutes of Health, Bethesda, Maryland, believes that sea salt may be quite beneficial in human nutrition according to an article in *Chemical and Engineering News* for April 30, 1956. He says that the majority of the world's population uses this salt. He tells us that some people of India consume as much as 40 grams of salt a day. This would be about 1½ ounces, which is almost an incredibly large amount of salt, we think. However, he goes on to say that this amount of sea salt (note that we said *sea salt, not refined table salt*) would supply 22 to 32 micrograms of inorganic iodine as well as 100 to 140 micrograms of organic iodine per day. Man's requirement for iodine is about 20 to 75 micrograms per day.

In addition, this much salt would supply 2 milligrams of iron (12 milligrams daily are recommended), .4 milligrams of copper, and .02 milligrams of cobalt.

In undernourished countries, Dr. Schaefer continues, the daily intake of calcium from foods is often 250 milligrams or less. Since these populations are primarily cereal eaters, the balance between calcium and phosphorus is further aggravated by the high phosphorus and low calcium content of cereals. However, there are surprisingly few cases of rickets in such countries, which seems to indicate that there is plenty of calcium in their diets. This may come from the quite large amounts of sea salt they use. Eating 40 grams of sea salt a day would supply them with 680 milligrams of calcium. The recommended daily allowance of calcium is 800 milligrams.

Should Health-Conscious Folks Eat Sea Salt?

If, indeed, this salt contains such a wealth of trace minerals that we are not likely to get in food or in food supplements, might it not be wise to use a little sea salt daily—not for its sodium chloride content but for its trace elements?

First of all, it seems to us that the food supplement kelp, which is simply powdered seaweed, would naturally have much the same content as sea salt. It also is extremely rich in iodine, iron, copper, magnesium. It contains the following trace elements: barium, boron, chromium, lithium, nickel, silicon, silver, strontium, titanium, vanadium and zinc.

We do not know the exact figures on the trace element content of kelp. Its calcium and potassium content are considerably higher than that of sea salt.

The sodium chloride content of kelp is only about 18 per cent compared to the 75 per cent of sea salt. So in every way, it would seem that kelp is much preferable to sea salt, if you take kelp every day, in considerable quantity. It is food, you know, not medicine, so it must be taken in the quantities in which you would take food. If you want to use kelp in place of salt, this is what we recommend.

There are many reasons for not using refined salt on food. Chief among these is its effect on heart and blood vessels. Apparently low-salt diets do much to reduce blood pressure. It is true, too, that overweight often occurs from eating large amounts of salt, for it attracts and holds water in the tissues. Sinus trouble, colds, dropsy, difficult pregnancies—these are just some of the many conditions that seem to result from eating salt.

There are, however, many people who cannot or will not give up the use of salt, in cooking and at the table. These folks should certainly use sea salt rather than refined salt. If you happen to be in this category—if you plan sometime to give up salt but can't right now, if the cook of the family refuses to make meals without salt, if you have one of the rare conditions in which salt is an absolute necessity, then surely you would do well to substitute sea salt for refined salt.

SECTION 10.

Seeds

Seeds are the heart and life of most growing things. They have tremendous amounts of energy hidden in them, in the form of nutrients we can all use. Protein elements, vitamins and minerals can be yours with every snack of sunflower seeds, pumpkin seeds, sesame seeds, etc. Experiments have also shown certain seeds to be effective in the treatment of disease. Start the seed habit, you'll like it.

CHAPTER 89

The Chemistry of Seeds

How do seeds in general stack up against other foods from a nutritive point of view? They compose a very necessary and important part of the diet, but they should be combined with other foods, if they are to offer the best possible advantage. The reason for this is that seeds, in general, lack certain minerals and vitamins that exist in large quantities in other classes of food. So the other foods complement the seed foods in a most satisfactory way.

McCollum, one of the country's outstanding experts on nutrition, has this to say about the way in which leafy foods complement seeds: "The leaf proves to be a very different thing from the seed from the dietary standpoint." The leaf contains from 3 to 5 times as much mineral content as the seed and is always rich in just those minerals in which the seed is poorest—calcium, for instance. The leaf contains a wealth of vitamin A and vitamin C, neither of which is found to any great extent in the seed. The leaf contains protein amino acids, as the seed does. And it seems that those of the leaf complement those of the seed, so that leaves and seeds together result in a meal rich in all the various forms of protein or amino acids.

Phosphorus in Seeds

Phosphorus is the mineral which abounds in seeds. It is an important mineral from the standpoint of nutrition and one should be careful to see that he gets enough phosphorus in his diet. But most of us do. The animals that live on grasses and leaves are the ones which are in danger of lacking phosphorus. This is one reason why proper feed for horses and cattle must be planned to include plenty of phosphorus. But human beings get phosphorus in cereals, legumes, nuts and foods of animal origin like meat and eggs. The animals that graze do not, of course, eat these, with the exception of cereals.

Foods high in vitamins (fresh fruits and salads) do not supply large amounts of phosphorus. We are told, for instance, that one would have to eat nearly a bushel of apples a day or half a bushel of oranges to obtain a liberal supply of phosphorus. Nine and a half pounds of carrots, or 11 pounds of beets would be required to provide as much phosphorus as you find in one pound of lentils or beans, wheat or oats. These last are all, of course, seeds.

Phosphorus is important to body functions. It is present in all body cells. Calcium and phosphorus stand first and second respectively in the quantity of mineral elements in the body. The use of phosphorus in the body is closely interrelated to the use of calcium so that when we are speaking of one we must constantly refer to the other. The exact amount of phosphorus needed by the body is not so important as the relationship between the calcium and the phosphorus. This ratio is two and a half to one—there should be two and a half times as much calcium as phosphorus.

Nations that live chiefly on fruits and vegetables might suffer from a lack of phosphorus. Adding meat, cereals or nuts to their diets would improve them. People living chiefly on cereals are likely to get into much more serious trouble, for they are almost bound to have a wrong balance between calcium and phosphorus. Cereals contain little calcium; refined cereals none at all for all practical purposes. Furthermore, cereals contain phosphorus in a peculiar chemical combination called phytate which grabs off calcium wherever it can. So the inveterate cereal-eater loses even more calcium and his calcium-phosphorus balance goes even farther off, unless he takes care to eat plenty of calcium-rich foods—fruits and vegetables, leafy green things. And so we come back to the fact that seeds need other foods in the diet to complement them.

Phosphorus exists in bones and teeth along with calcium. It is present in fluids and soft tissues, too. You need it for your body to use fat properly. It also combines with protein, so that the protein can be digested. You cannot digest several of the important B vitamins unless phosphorus is present. Phosphorus is an important ingredient of brain tissue.

To properly assimilate and use phosphorus, remember, you must have plenty of calcium in the diet at the same time. Vitamin D is important, too —the sunshine vitamin, which you need in order to use either calcium or phosphorus. Furthermore—and this is perhaps the most important single thing to remember about phosphorus in seeds—your body does not use phosphorus unless there is plenty of calcium present at the same time. So, if you are using lots of seed materials in your diet—cereals, nuts, legumes— remember to check thoroughly on the amount of calcium you are getting. Bone meal as a food supplement is your best assurance that all will be well, for it contains calcium and phosphorus, too, in just the right combination as they appear in healthy young bones.

Other Minerals in Seeds

Iron is another mineral in which seeds are rich. Most American women and many adolescents are suffering from iron-deficiency anemia to a greater or less extent. Probably the most significant reason for this is the refining of flour and sugar, for iron is removed from cereals when the germ is removed and the iron originally found in sugar cane is left in blackstrap molasses after the sugar is refined.

Wheat germ is rich in iron. Other cereal seeds when they are taken whole—that is, unrefined—are also rich in iron. So the refinement of our cereals has deprived us not only of our best source of B vitamins, but also of two of the most important of our minerals, for calcium is removed along with iron. So the iron and calcium deficiencies, already widespread in this country, grow worse as we continue to eat and to feed our children on refined cereals.

Magnesium is another mineral substance that is abundant in seed foods. In fact it is surprising to find that the foods listed as highest in magnesium are generally all seed foods. For instance, those that rate high (from 120 to 250 milligrams per hundred grams) are: almonds, barley, lima beans, Brazil nuts, cashew nuts, corn, whole wheat flour, hazelnuts, oatmeal, peanuts, peas, pecans, brown rice, soy flour, walnuts. Apparently magnesium is used for something very important by the seed as it grows into a mature plant.

It is important for the body, too. We have not made any studies of magnesium deficiency in human beings. But in animals on controlled diets a deficiency in magnesium adds up to dilation of blood vessels, kidney damage, loss of hair, rough, sticky coats, diarrhea and edema (unhealthy swelling).

Remember, please, that magnesium is removed, along with all the other minerals when foods are refined. The magnesium we said above would be found in whole grain flour is not present in white flour. The magnesium in brown rice is not present in white rice. So be sure you get your seed foods unrefined.

Vitamins in Seeds

The most precious food element in seeds is probably their content of B vitamins and vitamin E. Apparently the plants need these vitamins just as we do, so the seeds must be well supplied if they are going to grow. Nuts, legumes and unrefined cereals are all rich in B vitamins. Soybeans and wheat germ provide the largest amounts of this vitamin in this group of foods. The B vitamins are important for the health of the nerves. A population whose supply of thiamin has been destroyed by the miller and baker will be a nervous population and will suffer from mental disorders. Their digestive tracts will not function properly, for the B vitamins are especially important for this function. Constipation, diarrhea and dyspepsia will be rampant. The B vitamins are important for the health of the skin. Removing them from foods practically guarantees many different kinds of skin disorders.

Seeds, nuts and legumes are relatively rich in pyridoxine—another B vitamin, not so thoroughly studied as the others up to now. Spies and Jolliffe have successfully treated *paralysis agitans* (palsy) with massive doses of pyridoxine. This leads us to believe that perhaps muscle and nerve disorders of this kind may result from a life-long deficiency in this vitamin. Adding unrefined seed foods to your diet will add to your store of pyridoxine. Remember, this B vitamin has been removed, along with all the others, from any refined food.

Vitamin E, whose richest source is wheat germ, is an absolute essential for the smooth functioning of all the reproductive processes. Its lack results in miscarriages, sterility and difficult births. It is important for the welfare of every muscle in the body, so lack of it can produce paralysis, heart disease (for the heart is a muscle) dystrophy and the host of other cruel twisting diseases to which the people of America are so peculiarly susceptible. These are due, largely, to the refining of their foods, we believe.

[313]

A Rich Source of Vitamin F

The unsaturated fatty acids, called vitamin F by some researchers, are plentiful in seeds, too. A wide variety of disorders may be caused by a lack of these important fats in the diet—eczema, dry skin, dandruff, brittle nails, falling hair, kidney disease, disorders of the prostate gland. Fats are carried in the diet by a substance called lecithin, which dissolves easily in body fluids, so that the fat may be properly distributed to the various places where it is needed.

Cholesterol, a fatty substance that exists in different kinds of foods and is, in fact manufactured in the body as well, depends on lecithin to keep it in a state of emulsion so that the body can use it. Cholesterol, without lecithin, is likely to collect in the walls of blood vessels, or as "stones" in the gall bladder. Where is this essential lecithin found? Chiefly in the fatty portions of seeds. If you get no seeds in your diet or if you eat only seed foods from which the lecithin has been removed by processing, you are likely to run into serious trouble.

Dr. Francis Pottenger, M.D., a nationally known nutrition expert, tells us that "The effect of processing cereals with the accompanying loss of minerals and the vitamin B complex has received much attention. However, the loss of the important fats in the processing of our vegetable oils and our cereals has not received due consideration. The removal of the fats would appear to be as deleterious as the removal of the water soluble parts of the germ," by which he means the B vitamins.

Summary

To sum it all up—what are the most important elements in seeds as food? First, their mineral content—phosphorus and iron being the two most important of these. Keep in mind that both of these are practically destroyed by refining of cereals, so don't count on refined cereals (that is, processed breakfast cereals and white bread) to give you minerals. Remember, too, that if you eat large amounts of seed foods, rich in phosphorus, you should help to balance the phosphorus by eating plenty of calcium-rich foods, too. Green leafy vegetables and fruits supply calcium. Bone meal, too.

Secondly, the seed foods provide vitamins—the nerve-digestive-tract-skin vitamin B complex and the ever-so-important vitamin E which prevents heart disease and other muscle trouble. Then the seed foods provide the fatty substances that are necessary for the proper use by the body of other vitamins and cholesterol—lecithin and the unsaturated fatty acids, sometimes called vitamin F. The seed foods also supply the body with valuable protein.

Look at the chart below showing the mineral and vitamin content of the most common seed foods. Do you think you can afford, nutritionally speaking, to do without a goodly supply of these foods, in their fresh, unrefined, untampered-with state?

THE NUTRITIVE CONTENT OF SOME SEED FOODS

Columns grouped as: **Minerals** (Calcium, Phosphorus, Iron, Sodium, Potassium) · **Vitamins** (A, Thiamin, Riboflavin, Niacin, C, E, K) · **Average Portions** (Measure)

Seed	Cal-ories	Pro-tein (Grams)	Fat (Grams)	Total Car-bohyd. (Grams)	Cal-cium (Mgs.)	Phos-phorus (Mgs.)	Iron (Mgs.)	Sodium (Mgs.)	Potas-sium (Mgs.)	A (I.U.)	Thia-min (Mgs.)	Ribo-flavin (Mgs.)	Niacin (Mgs.)	C (Mgs.)	E (Mgs.)	K (Mgs.)	Measure
Grains:																	
Barley, pearled	711	17	2	161	33	386	4.1	6.12	326	0	.24	.16	6.3	0	6.5-10.8		1 cup
Buckwheat Flour	341	6.3	1.1	77.9	10.8	86	.98			0	.08	.04	.4	0	3-12		1 cup
Cornmeal, whole	459	18.4	4.3	94.5	7.6	226	2.3	.7		558	.4	.10	2.4	0			1 cup
Millet	332	6.2	1.4	78.2	329	254	5.3		131		.33	.10	1.3		4.8		1 cup
Oatmeal, cooked	150	5.5	2.9	26.1	21.4	160	1.7	18.7		0	.24	.05	.5	0	4.9		1 cup
Rice, brown	748	15.6	3.5	161.6	81	630	4.2	7.5	312	0	.67	.10	9.7	0	.74		1 cup
Rice, converted	677	14.2	.6	148	44.8	254	1.5	11.4	318	0	.37	.07	7.1	0	.76		1 cup
Rice, wild	593	23	1.1	123	30.9	552		.8	358	0	.73	1.03	10.1	0	1.8-2.8		1 cup
Rye flour, dark	254	13	.2	54.5	43.2	429	3.6		108	0	.49	.18	2.2	0			1 cup
Sesame seed	610	19.3	51.1	18.1	1,125	614	9.5				.93	.22	4.5	0	2.2-3.5		100 grams
Sorghum	332	11.0	3.3	73.0	28	287	4.4				.38	.15	3.9				1 cup
Wheat flour	400	11.5	1.1	83.7	17.6	9.6	3.2	1.1	95	0	.48	2.9	3.9	0		2.4	1 cup
Wheat germ	246	17	6.8	33.7	57.1	74.5	5.5	1.4	530	0	1.39	.54	3.12	0		2.5	1 cup
Vegetables:																	
Chickpeas, dry	359	20.8	4.7	60.9	162	344	8.4			90	.49	.18	1.6	Trace		.01	1 cup
Corn, sweet, raw	92	3.7	1.2	20.5	9	120	.5	.3-.4	240-370	390	.15	.12	1.7	12			1 ear
Corn, sweet, cooked	119	3.8	.98	28.2	7	73	.84			546	.15	.14	1.9	11.2			1 ear
Cowpeas	44	3.4	.3	9.2	53	65	1.1	.2	560	1,520	.16	.10	1.1	34			1 cup
Lentils, dry, split	204	14.4	.72	36.2	20	175	4.4		720	342	.34	.14	1.3	3			¼ cup
Lima beans, raw	96	5.6	.6	17.6	47	118	1.7	1.8	510	210	.16	.08	1.05	24			½ cup
Lima beans, cooked	76	4	.32	14.6	23	62	1.4	.75		232	.11	.07	.88	12			½ cup
Mung beans, sprouts	23	2.9	.2	4.1	29	59	.8			10	.07	.09	.5	15			1 cup
Mung beans, dry	339	24.4	1.4	59.7	91	320	6.3			40	.68	.21	2.0	3		.52	½ cup
Peas, green, raw	74	5	.3	13.3	16.5	92	1.4	.75	278	510	.26	.12	2	20	1.6		1 cup
Peas, green, cooked	42	2.9	.24	7.3	13.2	73	1.1			432	.15	.84	1.3	9	3.6	Fair	½ cup
Peas, dry, split	344	24.5	1.0	61.7	33	268	5.1	42	880	370	.77	.28	3.1	2			½ cup
Popcorn	54	1.8	.7	3.1	1.5	39	.38	3	33.6	70	.057	.017	.31	0			1 cup, popped
Pumpkin seed	541	30.9	43.1	17.9	33	1,290	12.7			80	.25	.13	2.0				1 cup
Red Kidney Beans, cooked	230	14.5	1	42	122	316	4.8			0	.13	.13	2	0	3.1		1 cup
Soybean, dry	695	73	38	73	477	1,230	16.8	8.4	3,990	231	2.25	.63	4.8	Trace		.39	1 cup
Soybean sprouts, raw	50	6.6	1.5	5.7	51	72	1.07			192	.25	.21	.85	14			1 cup

CHAPTER 90

The Proteins of Seeds

We hear a lot these days about protein, foods containing it and the importance of protein-high foods in the diet. Vegetarians believe that they get enough protein in fruits, vegetables, nuts and cereals. Those who eat animal products declare that only in these foods can "complete proteins" be found, and so animal products must be included in healthful diets. What do we mean by "complete proteins?" Do any of the seed foods contain them? Can the seed foods be used as the only source of protein in a healthful diet?

Protein is the substance of which we are chiefly made. Blood, tissues, organs, skin, hair, nails, bones and body fluids are protein. Brain and nerves are protein. The proteins of which the body is made can be broken down into what we call "building blocks"—the amino acids. There are probably many more of these than have been discovered, but we know of some 20 or so. These amino acids, or building blocks of protein, are present in foods. When we eat these foods our digestive processes re-arrange the amino acids, combining them in different ways, so that they can be built into body structure.

A grain of wheat or even a whole bushel of wheat grains do not look like a human brain. Yet after the wheat has been eaten, the amino acids it contained will go to form part of the protein of which the brain is made. Or the nerves. Or the blood.

The Essential Amino Acids

Certain of the amino acids are absolutely necessary to health and life. We must have them to survive. So they are called the essential amino acids. There are 10 of these whose names are: arginine, histidine, isoleucine, leucine, lysine, methionine, phenylalanine, threonine, tryptophan and valine. As researchers progress in their study of the proteins, it is quite possible they may discover that one or more of the other amino acids at present listed as "unessential" may also have important functions in the body so that it cannot be replaced. However, it seems that we may be able to manufacture within our bodies some of these unessential ones. We cannot manufacture the essential ones in our bodies, so they must be supplied in food. Animal proteins supply all of the essential amino acids. Of course, the animal was made of protein, too, so it is only natural that the amino acids involved would be the same ones that we human beings find essential.

But in the case of foods of vegetable, seed or fruit origin, we find that most of them lack one or more of the essential amino acids or they contain it in such small quantity that it cannot be used by the body to put together another form of protein.

[316]

Corn contains less than half a gram of tryptophan for every hundred grams of corn. This is not enough to support life. In other words, one cannot live on a diet in which corn is the only protein, without suffering from certain diseases which indicate that there is an important protein missing. Peanut flour seems to rank high in most of the amino acids. But it is far below where it should be in methionine and tryptophan. Soybean flour which comes the nearest to supplying "complete" protein is still a little low in methionine and tryptophan.

So someone who depends on soybean foods for protein should go out of his way to eat some foods rich in methionine and tryptophan *at the same meal*. We stress the fact that the essential amino acids must all be eaten at the same meal. If you eat corn as your only protein at lunch and then use some food rich in tryptophan, such as eggs, at dinnertime, the corn protein was wasted, for it does not tarry in your digestive tract waiting until some other food with just the right arrangement of proteins comes along.

The Arrangement of Amino Acid Is Important

So eating a haphazard diet especially if you are a vegetarian, will not only bring ill health, but will also result in wasting proteins which are the most precious elements in our food. The vegetarian who eats eggs or any other form of animal protein will not, of course, get into this difficulty. The vegetarian who takes brewer's yeast is even less likely to get into trouble, for the proteins of brewer's yeast are remarkably complete.

We sometimes hear of staunchly health-minded people who avoid all the refined foods, eat plenty of fresh raw fruits and vegetables, watch their diets closely and otherwise respect health rules. But they are not healthy. Perhaps, much oftener than we know, the reason is that they are not getting "complete" protein at their meals, that is, they are not getting enough of all the essential amino acids to keep rebuilding the worn-out protein cells of the body.

If you have several nutrition books at home, you may find that the amino acids content of different foods varies in the different charts that are given by different authors. Of course, no two pieces of food contain exactly the same amount of any food element, so naturally each researcher will get somewhat different results in his tests. But, in addition to that, we have word from eminent agricultural authorities that the protein content of our cereals is decreasing due to the fact that our soils are wearing out faster than we can rebuild them with out present methods of agriculture. So take this into account, too, when you are figuring the amount of protein you expect to get from cereals and legumes.

To conclude what we have to say about the proteins of seeds, we repeat what we have said in the preceding chapter—eat seed products along with a wide variety of other foods. They do not provide a healthful diet by themselves. Do not look to them to provide all the protein you need, unless you are a wizard at juggling amino acids and combining just the right ones at each and every meal. Laboratory researchers who have devoted their lives to this kind of juggling find it next to impossible to provide healthful diets using seed proteins as the only source of proteins.

[317]

Add Seeds to Your Diet

On the other hand, most of us get far, far too little protein. The adult man should have about 70 grams of protein every day. The average woman 60. The requirement for children ranges from 40 (for one to three-year olds) to 100 grams a day for boys from 16 to 20. Even in prosperous times, even those of us who can afford to eat the best seldom get this amount of protein. Protein food is the most expensive there is. We crowd it out of the diet with refined carbohydrates, desserts, snacks, candy, sodas and all the other trash we put into our stomachs.

So, add additional protein to your diet using seed foods! Don't use them as a substitute for good meat and egg protein. But substitute them for the worthless foods you and your family may sometimes consume. Seed proteins are fairly inexpensive and while they are not "complete" proteins, still they add to the total protein you get in any one day and, when taken with foods that do contain whole proteins, they are well used by the body.

So substitute nuts or sunflower seeds for candy or soda when you're preparing snacks. Get in the habit of sprinkling ground sesame, sunflower seeds or nuts over salads, vegetable dishes, fruit cups. Have an attractive fruit bowl of nuts with a nutcracker ready on your living room table. Keep a jar of tasty seeds handy to munch on. Get acquainted with soybeans which, more successfully than any other non-animal food, can substitute for meat at a tiny fraction of the cost of meat. Try nibbling on fresh raw wheat grains instead of eating bread. Use seeds as they occur in nature and they will enrich your menus with additional protein.

CHAPTER 91

Seeds as Human Food

By J. I. Rodale

"And God said, Behold, I have given you every herb bearing seed, which is upon the face of the earth, and every tree, in which is the fruit of a tree yielding seed; to you it shall be for meat."

This is Genesis, Chapter 1, verse 29 . . . The seed is life itself. It contains the spark which is extremely vital to the functioning of our bodies. The perpetuation of the species is accomplished through the seed. The seed is the vehicle for storing life's reserves. The seed is the crucible wherein the alchemy of life works its magic. In this tiny place is contained the condensed germinating energy, the life-giving elements, including as yet undiscovered gleams. Science still knows very little of the vast and intricate interplay of life forces that lie within the seed.

Its living substance can be preserved for many years, and during the entire life of the seed, which in the case of certain legumes is more than 50 years, there is a continuous respiratory action, showing that it is a living organism. The seed of the Indian lotus plant buried for over 200 years in peat bogs has been known to germinate successfully. Melon seeds carefully stored, packed between paper, have germinated after 30 years. There must be very important life-giving elements that will resist the passage of such long periods of time and this should make a very healthy food for homo sapiens. All seeds are rich in vitamin B, and the sex and fertility factors. That is why the wheat germ is fed to women who do not seem to be able to bear children.

Everyone knows that vegetables are an essential to a properly balanced diet, but their maximum vitamin content is only found in really fresh produce. Compare a crisp lettuce straight from the garden with the limp faded thing it becomes two days later. Its "living" quality has gone, and with it, most of its food value. This cannot be said of seeds.

Proof of the Food Value of Seeds

To get an idea of what nutrition is packed in the average seed we must bear in mind that nature has placed an extra store of concentrated feed in it to nourish the emerging plant for a few days. There is enough food in the seed to be used by the young plant to form a root, stem and several leaves without having to get food from the soil.

Seed foods are wonderful for city folk who are faced with the necessity of eating so much processed foods. They can protect themselves by making seed foods a liberal part of their diets. They are also a protection in winter when one is eating stored vegetables that have lost much of their potency.

Much data is available to prove that seeds are a food of high nutritional value. Let us take one instance: In the magazine, *Science*, in 1932, Vol. 75, p. 294, Davidson and Chandbliss wrote an article called "Chemical Composition of Rice and its Relation to Soil Fertility in China and Japan." It is an astounding article of far-reaching significance to nutritionists. But it was read and promptly forgotten. Davidson and Chandbliss in experimental work discovered that "variations in the nutrient content of soils have less effect on the seed than on any other part of the plant." The best food elements in the soil will be saved for the seed so that the plant will be sure to reproduce itself. Nature wants to be sure of that. This would indicate that seeds have a higher nutritional value than the leafy parts of the plant.

The Nutritional Content of Seeds

R. C. Collison, writing in the *Journal of Industrial and Engineering Chemistry* (August, 1912), proved the same thing. He showed that the proportion of organic to inorganic minerals in the seed is much higher than in the rest of the plant. This is necessary because the seed must have sufficient potency to carry on into the next generation. Therefore, where there is a given amount of organic minerals available, as much of it as can possibly be spared will go to the seed. Even in an infertile soil, whatever organic minerals the roots of a plant can forage out will be available first for the formation of seed.

[319]

Thomas H. Mather, writing in *Scientific Agriculture,* Vol. 10, 1929, about an experiment in which the effect of a chemical fertilizer, super-phosphate, was measured on a crop of alfalfa, in comparison with a similar crop on which no fertilizer was used, discovered that all of the inorganic phosphorus of the fertilizer went to the stalk and leaves. In this experiment it was proven that the seed actually turned back the inorganic phosphorus. It would have none of it. Nature cannot build a strong race of alfalfa plants with minerals that are inorganic. If there is not a sufficient supply of organic minerals, the plant will either produce seed which is defective, or it will not produce seed at all.

I wrote to Professor William A. Albrecht, Chairman of the Depart-ment of Soils, University of Missouri, about this question and he replied: "It is significant to remember that the chemical composition of seeds does not flocculate as widely as the chemical composition of vegetation. The seed is the means of survival of the species, hence this survival will not be possible unless a minimum of food materials are stored in the seed. We well know that when the fertility of the soil drops to a low level less seed is produced. Seemingly the amount of seed is the variable, while the quality of the seed is more nearly a constant. It is the fertility of the soil as a growth-providing substance that seems to determine the seed production rather than the air, water and sunshine that contribute the starches and the energy materials."

Schrumph-Pierron, in the *Bulletin of the Institute of Egypt,* January 4, 1932, says, "Let us observe, however, that the mineralization of seeds is always more stable and less susceptible to wide digressions than that of the leaves or the roots."

This is an extremely important point to be carefully considered. Those of you who are worried about having to purchase food raised with chemical fertilizers, should see to it that a certain portion of your diet consists of seeds, because the seed is not anywhere nearly as much affected by the use of strong chemicals as the leaves or stalks, and thus contains significant amounts of organic elements.

Include Seeds in Your Diet

Luther Burbank, the great plant wizard, realized the value of the seed as human food, but he merely mentioned it casually and then proceeded to forget all about it. In his book, *Partner of Nature* (Appleton-Century, 1939), he stated, "Fruits ripen, not to make food for us, but to encase and protect the seeds inside—pips or pits or kernels. But we pay no attention to Nature's purpose and revel in the delicate flavors and delicious flesh of apples, pears, peaches, tomatoes, melons and all and throw aside carelessly the seeds that the plant went to so much trouble to build and in which it stored the life-giving germ and a reserve of starch to help it start in life again as a baby plant."

Dr. Henry C. Sherman, Columbia University's outstanding nutritional authority, has said that in studying the nutritional needs of man you cannot deal exclusively in terms of known chemical factors. You have to include "natural articles of food" he says, to "ensure adequate supplies of any possible factors which may not yet have been identified and listed in chemical terms. We must give emphasis to those foods which, as the 'natural wholes' to which our species is nutritionally adjusted by its evolutionary history, will furnish us, along with the known essentials, any unknown factors which may also be essential to our nutrition." Could Dr. Sherman have been referring to seeds? They certainly are "natural wholes."

Two other nutritional experts, Burr and Burr, have shown that a diet may be complete in all essentials, including minerals, vitamins, proteins, etc., but if it lacks the unsaturated fatty acids, which are obtained chiefly from seeds, nutritional deficiency will result. Of course, the average eater is bound to get *some* seeds in his diet such as peas, beans, nuts, wheat, corn, etc., but if he is conscious of their importance he will find ways to add more of them in his total food intake.

CHAPTER 92

Seeds and Mental Power

By J. I. Rodale

Is there such a thing as a brain food? It used to be thought that fish was such a food. Nutritionists in discussing it refer to the phosphorus contained in fish as being a brain stimulant. But this idea has been more or less debunked. Let us, however, consider seeds as a food for the brain. Seeds will also satisfy the requirements for phosphorus. In fact, they contain 10 or 20 times more phosphorus than fish. Seeds are truly a brain food.

It is a known fact that animals that are fed raw grain seeds can perform much more work than those grazing pasture grass exclusively. This, of course, is work, not brain power, but let us look a little further.

I will quote G. A. Sutherland, M.D., in his *A System of Diet and Dietetics*, 1925: "Thus among the rodents, the stupid rabbit, unable to climb and with little prehensile power, has to be content with a bulky diet of comparatively innutritious herbs, while the more intelligent squirrel, a nimble climber and possessed of considerable prehensile power, is able to procure highly nutritious seeds and a considerable amount of animal food as well. The intelligence and nimbleness of rats, again, enable them to procure highly concentrated and palatable foods, and to place under contribution even those that man has stored for his own use."

Again, later on, this author states: "The frugivora, which include animals like the squirrel, the rat, and the monkey, consume vegetable food in its more concentrated forms, such as seeds and nuts. Being generally more intelligent than the herbivora, and gifted also with the inconsiderable prehensile powers, they are able to pick and choose their food more cleverly; and hence securing it in much more concentrated forms, they are provided with a much less bulky digestive system than the herbivora."

Proof From The Past

In the early primitive days of civilization, while man ate plants and fruit, a goodly part of his diet was in the form of seed which was consumed without any cooking, tampering or processing. In this regard Dr. James Empringham in his book, *Intestinal Gardening for the Prolongation of Youth,* gives a remarkable instance of how food can sharpen the faculties of the human body. He says: "In the Pyrenean mountains, that separate France from Spain, there is the most interesting cave the writer has ever explored. At some remote time, masses of rock fell down, completely covering up the entrance to this natural, subterranean chamber, so that this marvelous museum of prehistoric art remained buried, according to geologists, for at least fifty thousand years, until rediscovered by accident some years ago.

"That the cavern had been the resort of human beings in former ages is evident from the rude drawings that still decorate the interior. These sketches consist, for the most part, of outlines of animals, long extinct, which hitherto were known to science solely by the fossilized remains found in the earth's rocky strata. The roof of this cave is embellished with representations of the midnight sky. But among familiar constellations, such as the Great Bear, there appear stars that can be seen by no person now living, except with the aid of a telescope.

"Now, inasmuch as the savages of that distant age had no knowledge of glass, and possessed no instrument for assisting the eye, these pictures seem to prove that the people of that far off time, had much stronger vision than men of today.

"Strange as it may seem, there is much evidence to prove that, not eyesight only, but all of the senses of modern man—hearing, feeling, tasting and smelling—are less acute than the faculties possessed by our remote ancestors."

Seeds Down Through the Centuries

In Biblical times a great deal of seed food was part of the daily dietary. Dill and cumin seeds were considered so important that tithes were paid with them. In his book, *Jewish Magic and Superstition,* Rabbi Trachtenberg says that Baladur (Anacardia) was a memory-strengthener. He advises further for strengthening of the memory, "Eat hazelnuts for 9 days, beginning with 6 and adding 6 more each day; eat pepper seeds for 9 days, beginning with one seed and doubling the dose until it reaches 256 seeds on the ninth day, and each time before you consume them, recite Deuteronomy 33: 8-11 and Psalm 119:9-16; grind cloves, long peppers, dates, ginger, galanga-root, and muscot nuts in equal quantities, beat them with olive oil into a paste, and eat a little every morning before breakfast."

The Romans, at the end of their gluttonous feasts, ate spice cakes flavored with aniseed. Seed cakes charged with a large variety of seeds, were a standby of the Middle Ages. Vernon Quinn in *Seeds—Their Place in Life and Legend* describes an Englishman of Pepys' time commending seeds as "marvelously good for a melancholicke person, excellent fine for such as be of a cholericke nature even to free the sleep from monstrous nocturnal visions."

There seems to be some evidence of a dependence in olden days on eating seed to either strengthen the mind, to free it of conditions brought about by dissipation or to cheer it up generally. Our common sense should tell us that the mind is nourished by the food we eat, and that seed food, containing so much potent, living quality should be an excellent means of maintaining its health.

Today's Mentality

Today there seems to be a noticeable deterioration in mental energies. With so much consumption of cola drinks, white hot dog rolls, ice cream, candies, etc. by our teenagers, is it any wonder that the colleges are complaining that there are not enough applicants for the more difficult courses of science, chemistry, etc.? Will there be enough technicians in the future to man the complicated Frankensteinian system of science that is being set up today? Researches must be set going to reevaluate all the factors of our nutrition insofar as it affects the operation of our minds as well as our bodies.

Is it possible that a body that is strengthened by consuming a certain portion of live seed food will be proof against cancer? Who knows? Nobody has researched it.

We once had an old parrot, about 90 per cent of whose diet was sunflower seed. And was he smart! He could sing a wonderful soprano, trilling in human fashion, without uttering a false note. When a knock came on the door he would always say, "Come in!" That is intelligence! There is many a cola-consuming teenager today who hears a knock on the door and who is too lazy to say, "Come in."

The value of seeds in connection with furnishing human mental energy should be investigated.

CHAPTER 93

How to Add Other Seeds to Your Diet

By J. I. Rodale

In my files I have collected odd bits of data regarding various seeds which I will give here in alphabetical order. I have not gone into detail on well-known cereals, nuts and legumes. (In quoting from old books I have preserved the quaint old spelling.)

Acorn

In *Seeds—Their Place in Life and Legend* by Vernon Quinn (Stokes & Company) appears the following: "That same year, 1608, a colonist in Virginia was writing home to London of the strange uses the 'Salvages' made of seeds they gathered in their fall woods and fields. 'The Acornes, being boyled, at last affordes a sweet oyle, that they keepe in Gourdes to to annoynt their heades and joynts.'

"Acorns, in those days, were a common food throughout all of America, wherever an oak-tree grew. But the eating of acorns was by no means limited to the American Indians. Today in the mountains of Albania, and in other parts of the world, the poorer inhabitants live very largely on acorns. In Chaucer's day even the upper classes in England relished them. 'Thei weren wont lyghtly to slaken hir hunger at euene with acornes of okes'."

In a bulletin published by the Missouri Botanical Garden in 1924 the subject of acorns as food for modern man is discussed. Say the authors: "With modern kitchen equipment, acorn meal can easily be prepared at home. After husking the acorns they should be ground in a hand-grist mill or food-chopper. The meal is then mixed with hot water and poured into a jelly bag. The bitter tannin, being soluble, will be taken out by the water, but sometimes a second or even a third washing may be necessary. After washing, the wet meal is spread out to dry and is then parched in an oven. If it has caked badly, it should be run through the mill again before using.

"In cooking, acorn meal may be used in the same way as cornmeal. Its greatest fault is its color, muffins made from it being a dark chocolate brown; the taste suggests a mixture of cornmeal and peanut butter, and some people relish it at once, but others, it must be confessed, have to be educated to it. Because of the high oil and starch content of the acorn, it is very nutritious and is reported to be easily digested. Only acorns from white oaks should be gathered, as those from the black oaks are too bitter.

Typical Missouri representatives of this group are the white oak, the swamp oak, the bur oak, and the chestnut oak.

"Muffins, ⅔ acorn and ⅓ oatmeal, are reported to be good."

We do not know in what part of the country the white oak family is most abundant. But if you are interested in trying some acorn bread, why not ask your county agricultural agent where you might find some white oaks in your neighborhood? Chances are whoever owns them would be glad to have you gather the acorns.

J. Russell Smith in his excellent book on nut-bearing trees, *Tree Crops* (published by Devin-Adair, New York, New York), tells us that possibly far more human beings have eaten acorns than have eaten wheat, down through the centuries. The acorn was certainly a staple food long before man ever became interested in planting and reaping. One reason for the highly nutritious quality of the acorn as food is its high fat content. As Dr. Smith points out, it is not just bread that you make from the acorns, but bread and butter.

In Europe, chiefly Spain, Portugal and Italy, acorns are as common in the diet as chestnuts are here. Some varieties can be roasted over the fire and eaten as a roast chestnut is. In Spain and Portugal oak trees are cultivated for their acorn crops which sell for high prices in the markets. Dr. Smith mentions that there are 38 references to edible acorns in many parts of the world in the 1927 *Proceedings of the Northern Nut Growers' Association*.

We are told that ground acorns are used as coffee substitutes in some parts of the world. Their tannin content is supposed to make them powerful against chronic diarrhea. Of course, to make them tasty the tannin must be removed.

Aniseeds

Aniseeds can be placed in applesauce, stews, teas. The Romans ate aniseed cakes to aid the digestion. Then there is anisette, a liqueur that is supposed to "warm" the stomach. In Europe, especially in Germany, there are cakes with an aniseed flavoring. Anise is also used in soups.

Apple Seeds

A story in the Toronto *Globe and Mail* in the year 1941 (sorry no further date available) tells of experiments on apple seed oil at the University of Oregon Medical School in which muscular diseases in laboratory animals were cured by the use of the oil. It was assumed that the vitamin E in the oil worked the miracle, for the cures went on even after all other vitamin E had been removed from the diet.

At present, of course, we get vitamin E from wheat germ oil, a richer source. But it is well to keep in mind that all seeds contain vitamin E. And it is extremely difficult to get enough of the vitamin E in any other kind of food.

Bananas

The little dark spots on the inside of the banana are not seeds. The banana is seedless. This fruit has lost its seed through propagation for many generations by division. In its wild state it was almost filled from one end to the other with large seeds that were like stones, with just enough pulp in it to attract birds and wild animals.

Barley

Barley, a cereal popular in some parts of the world for bread-making, is used in this country chiefly for making beer. Fermenting barley results in malt which, in turn, is used in making beer.

We understand that barley used to have a medicinal purpose—being used to make hot poultices to apply to infections. It is perhaps the oldest cereal food. It was cultivated in China 20 centuries before Christ. It was also known in ancient Egypt, Greece and Rome and among the lake dwellers in ancient Switzerland.

Basil

Early herbalists believed that a decoction made from it would alleviate sadness. Basil leaves are flavorful with tomato dishes, salads, meats, sauces and egg dishes.

Beans

Wherever possible, in the summertime, some beans should be eaten raw. Possibly in the winter, beans can be softened by soaking so that they can be eaten without cooking. Columbus ate cakes made of pounded beans and corn. Both are delicious in the raw state.

The iron in beans is in a much more available state than that in leafy vegetables. I quote from *Association of Southern Agricultural Workers Proceedings, 37-38, 1937* pp. 257-258:

"For many years it has been assumed that green leafy vegetables, especially spinach, were particularly valuable in the diet because of the assimilable iron which they contained. More recent investigations have revealed that while green vegetables are important sources of essential minerals, and vitamins, a fairly large proportion of the iron which they contain may not be available for hemoglobin regeneration.

"A number of years ago this department began work on leafy vegetables to determine their actual value for hemoglobin regeneration. Turnip tops, mustard, collards, spinach and two varieties of lettuce have been tested for their anti-anemic potency. Composite samples of the dried ground vegetables were fed at a level of .25 milligrams of iron per rat per day 6 days a week, to groups usually of 8 or more rats. At the end of 16 weeks the average hemoglobin for the different groups of rats was as follows: Those receiving New York lettuce 12.8 grams; Grand Rapids lettuce 11 grams; turnip tops 12.3 grams; spinach 10.4 grams; mustard 9.2 grams and collards 6.5 grams. A second lot of turnip tops from the California Vegetable Concentrate Company was fed to a group of rats whose hemoglobin averaged only 6.3 grams at the end of 16 weeks.

"It was then decided to test cowpeas, a vegetable very commonly eaten in the South, both in the fresh and dried state. Two different composite lots were fed to two groups of anemic rats. By the end of the sixth week the average hemoglobin of both groups was 14.1 grams. A third lot of cowpeas, also soybeans, butterbeans, and pinto beans have been tested for their anti-anemic potency, all hemoglobin reaching a level of between 13 and 14 grams by the sixth or seventh week, and remaining at about this level during the experimental period.

"The ash as well as the unashed vegetable was tested for its anti-anemia potency. The results indicated that a fairly large proportion of the iron in the unashed green vegetable was not available. By ashing the vegetable and feeding the ash in solution, all the iron was made available. Copper was also a limiting factor since the addition of copper increased the anti-anemic potency of both the ash and the unashed vegetable."

Berries

Strawberries are full of seed. They used to be prescribed for diabetics and arteriosclerotics because they are not too rich in sugar. The small seeds exert a mild stimulating action in the bowels. In raspberries the seeds are larger. Other berry seeds are currants, gooseberries and blackberries.

Buckwheat

Buckwheat is a cereal almost totally ignored in America. New York and Pennsylvania are the only two states which produce any significant amount of it. The flower has a distinctive taste which, in general, people either like intensely or dislike just as intensely. Most of the buckwheat grown is used for flour to make hotcakes or pancakes. Unhappily it is generally quite thoroughly refined and plenty of other flours such as wheat are added to the buckwheat flour.

However, for those who like the flavor, there is probably nothing that can compare to a breakfast of buckwheat cakes, made from real, whole buckwheat flour, freshly ground. Raise the batter with yeast, to add B vitamins and flavor. Don't think of betraying a wonderful flour like this with baking powder! If you have a sweet tooth, pour some real genuine maple syrup over the cakes. This is an almost pure carbohydrate breakfast and we don't recommend it for frequent use. But for once in a while, it's a taste treat!

Many farmers plant buckwheat for its honey. The flower comes late after most other flowers are gone. And buckwheat honey has a completely distinctive flavor. After you have once acquired a taste for it, any other kind of honey may seem insipid. Buckwheat honey is dark in color, meaning that it is richer in vitamins and minerals than light-colored honey.

Buckwheat has recently come into prominence for quite another reason —as a source for rutin, the flavonoid which has been performing such marvels for patients with high blood pressure. Though buckwheat flour is a perfectly nourishing food, we would not suggest using it as a source of rutin. The rutin is extracted from the buckwheat by a long chemical process and is highly concentrated. You can get your flavonoids from rose hip preparations and fresh fruits.

Cantaloupe

In this fruit there is a vast amount of seed that is thrown away. I could not find any data on it anywhere. It would be worth while experimenting with it. It enriches the garbage of many of our cities.

Caraway Seed

Caraway was well known to Egyptian priest-physicians before the book of Exodus was written. Culpeper says of it, "Caraway comfits once only dipt in sumgar syrup and a spoonful of them eaten in the morning fasting as many after a meal, is a most admirable remedy for those that are troubled by wind."

"Once the seeds of Caraway were prescribed for bringing bloom to the cheeks of pale-faced maidens . . . you may care to follow the aged custom of Trinity College, Cambridge, where a saucer of these savory seeds invariably accompanies roasted apples." . . . in *Herbs for the Kitchen* by Irma Mazza. In Shakespeare's *Henry IV,* Squire Shallot invites Falstaff to a pippin and a dish of caraways." In Scotland to this day a saucerful of caraway is put down at tea to dip the buttered side of bread into and called 'salt water jelly' . . ." *Culinary Herbs and Condiments* by M. Grieve.

Caraway seeds can be used in baked apples, applesauce, soups, goulashes and served to eat as is after meals. Try them with baked potatoes and in salad dressings.

Cardamom

The seeds of an oriental herb, cardamom, which have a pleasant, aromatic odor and an agreeable spicy taste, are used in curries and as spices in cakes, liquors and so forth. In the East they are chewed, like betel nuts.

Carob Seed Pods

Strictly speaking, we do not eat the seeds of the carob. We eat the seed pods. The seeds themselves are too hard to eat. Carob pods are the fruit of the carob tree, related to the honey locust, also called St. John's bread and probably the food spoken of in the Bible as "locust."

Carob is a splendid food, rich in protein, carbohydrate, vitamins and minerals. It is an excellent substitute for sugar and for chocolate, since it is sweet and has a chocolate-like taste.

Celery Seed

Celery seed peps up soups, stews and salads. This is one of the commonest of our seasonings. We can find nothing indicating the possible nutritive content of celery seeds, but we recommend them highly for their fine flavor, especially desirable for those who are on a salt-poor diet.

Coconut

All of the coconut inside the tough outer shell is a seed—the largest we have. Because they grow on beaches close to the sea, coconuts are bound to be rich in many minerals that may be lacking in land-grown seeds. Many of the most precious of these food elements are concentrated in the brown skin that clings so tightly to the white meat, so you should eat this skin when you eat coconuts.

In older times coconut meat was said to be very effective for ridding the body of intestinal worms. In tropical countries today it has the reputation of being good for disorders of the liver and stomach. But, then, in tropical countries where it grows, it forms the main staple item of diet and it contributes generously to the nutrition of all those folks wherever it is widely eaten.

Coriander Seeds

Coriander (*Coriandrum sativum*) seeds are crushed and used in cakes, bread, sausage, cheeses, baked apples or with game or poultry. They are used in the food industry in making gin and curry powder.

The seeds were considered by the Chinese to confer immortality.

Corn

America's favorite and most famous grain. The history of corn goes back farther than we have any records. Apparently it was known to the very earliest inhabitants of the western hemisphere. Don't forget one thing about it—how delicious it is raw—right from the stalk.

Cucumber Seeds

Cucumber seeds, we are told, had medicinal worth: "To such as are payned with the cough, if so many seedes be taken vp and vsed at a tyme, as may handsomely bee taken vp with three of the fingers, and these after the bruising with Commyne drunke in Wine, doeth in short tyme amend the same."

Cumin Seed

The fruits (or so-called seeds) of the *cuminum cyminum* are hot to the taste. They contain lots of tannin and are one ingredient of curry powder. In olden times they were eaten with bread, wine or water as a remedy for squeamishness! During the middle ages this was one of the commonest of the European spices. A stimulant and carminative (powerful against flatulence and colic) it is used today mostly by veterinarians.

Dill Seed

Dill (*Anethum graveolens*) is a delightfully tasty seed that adds so much to pickles, salads, soups, fish, meat, egg and vegetable dishes. Oil from dill has been used in the manufacture of gin. In the East it is ground and eaten as a condiment. Dill vinegar, made by soaking seeds in vinegar for a few days, is relished by many.

Dill is a very old herb, being well-known to our ancestors, who used to chew the seeds in church. In a medical botany of the nineteenth century dill seeds made into a tea were mentioned as a cure for obesity. Hiccoughs could also be cured, it was said, by boiling the dill seeds in wine, then tying them in a cloth and smelling them.

Elderberry Seed

The fruit of the elderberry bush, used widely today for wine and jelly, used to be prescribed for a reducing diet—"to consume the Fleshe of a corpulent Bodie" is the way the old herb books said it. We do not know how elderberries happened to achieve this fame. We do know that birds eat the elderberries ravenously so that one is lucky to find a bush that has not been completely denuded before he reaches it.

Fennel Seed

Fennel *(Foeniculum vulgare)* is sometimes made into fennel-water which is supposed to be a cure for upset stomachs. The seed is supposed to aid in the digestion of beans and cabbage. The volatile oil that comes from fennel is probably the same as that from aniseed.

In an old herb book we ran across the note that fennel tea (made from the seeds) will relieve colic in children. It is good for an eyewash. In cooking, fennel adds to the flavor of puddings, soups, cakes, sauerkraut and spiced beets.

Fig Seeds

Fig seeds, those tiny, crunchy specks in figs, are said to be curative of constipation. Often they pass through the digestive tract unchanged. One should make an effort to chew fig seeds carefully to get all the possible benefit from them.

Flaxseed

The flax plant *(linum usitatissimum)* was apparently found growing wild in this country by the early American colonists. Flaxseed oil (or linseed oil as it is generally called) is used widely in paints and varnishes, printer's ink and artist's colors. The oil is used in Eastern Europe as a cooking oil.

Old magic lore has it that flaxseeds were the source of special magic, which changed as the moon changed. When they were gathered by the light of the full moon, they were used in brewing love potions. If you gathered them when the moon was dark, on the other hand, they could do harm to an enemy.

So far as diet is concerned, flaxseeds are a good source of the unsaturated fatty acids so essential to human welfare. We sometimes call them collectively vitamin F. They are also reputed to have a laxative effect. Some authorities believe them to be highly nutritious. The Indians of the Andes use them extensively as their favorite food—ground flaxseed with barley.

In ancient Greece and Rome flaxseeds were a great delicacy, munched between courses of a banquet much as we eat toasted nuts. The herb books tell us that tea made from flaxseed is good for respiratory disorders.

Grape Seeds

Some time ago a firm was established to make oil from grape seeds. We have no information on their food content, but it seems likely that they contain valuable elements as do other seeds. It would seem best to eat them along with the grapes. Chew them carefully so that they can be digested. There is no evidence, incidentally, that appendicitis can be caused by eating the seeds of any fruit.

Hempseed

Hempseed is the seed of the hemp plant *(Cannabis sativa)* which is cultivated chiefly as a source of raw material for the manufacture of rope. The seeds are widely used in India and are considered more delicious than sesame seeds. Hashish, the drug, is made from hemp leaves and resins. Hempseed is a fine bird food and the crushed seed is made into cattle food.

Hollyhock Seed

The Hollyhock seed was powerful against respiratory disorders, according to an ancient informant, "boyled either in milke or wine and orderly drunke doe remoue a hot cough, recover the Lunges blistered, and is a singular remedie against the consumption of the Lunges."

Lentils

The word *lens* which we use for a ground glass contrivance, was taken from the humble lentil, the sides of which are shaped about the same as a lens. The lentil is perhaps the oldest vegetable cultivated. Well known to all the ancient peoples, it figures in early mythology and superstition.

One historical note concerns the early Christians who were worshipping in the catacombs during the time they were being persecuted by the Romans. They wished to have flowers growing before the altar, but no flowers would grow without light. They discovered that lentils and wheat would sprout and grow in the dark. So these two seeds were annually planted in earthen pots on Ash Wednesday. By Maundy Thursday they were high enough to be carried to the altar. Italians still observe this ancient rite.

The old herbalists were of two minds concerning the medicinal value of the lentil, some of them claiming it was beneficial as medicine, others condemning it as hurtful. However, we know today that lentils rank high among legumes and that they should form a much important part of the American diet. They can be used to advantage in any recipe that calls for dried beans. They mix well with tomatoes, onions, cabbage, vinegar, mustard, mushrooms.

Lettuce Seed

Lettuce seed was supposedly curative for a number of ills, but only if it was used without the patients being aware of it! "The lettuce seeds brused and mixed with the white of an Egge applyed in plaister forme on the temples or forehead warme at the going to rest dooth marvelously procure sleepe." Lettuce leaves can be used, it seems, in case there are no seeds handy. But the leaves must be pulled up by the root with the left hand, before the sun rises and laid under the invalid's pillow so that the bigger end of the stalk and leaf lie toward the feet!

Lotus Seeds

We were enchanted to find lotus seeds listed in a book on the foods of the Eastern peoples. Imagine eating the seeds of that fabulous and exotic flower which appears so often in Egyptian and Hindu art! The lotus eaters, according to the Odyssey, were languid, dreamy and indolent

[331]

because they ate lotus. Perhaps they ate the flower rather than the seed. We rather believe the seed would produce vigor and stoutheartedness, for it contains plenty of protein and minerals. Calcium, phosphorus and iron are all found in the lotus seed. Before you write in to ask, let us assure you that we know of no one in this country who has lotus seeds for sale!

Mustard Seed

Mustard seed is commonly used today in pickle recipes. The "hotness" of mustard seeds was recognized in the old herbals, for they were used for gargling a sore throat. They "amendeth the blistering of the mouth and asswageth the swelling of the throate. The person which every morning fasting shall swallow down two mustard seedes at a time shall be free that day from the falling sickness (epilepsy). The pouder of the seedes drawne vp by the nosthrills not onely procureth the creature to sneese, but marvellously purgeth and amendeth the braine."

Another herbal counsels using mustard seed against dimness of sight and spots and webs in the eyes. A mixture of mustard and vinegar would also quickly cure the bite of a venomous beast.

Or, for those with palsy: "The Mustard seedes retained under the tongue prevaile against the palsey of the tongue. The seedes do like profit against all kindes of palseys hapning in any parte of the body if a linnen bag filled with the seedes and boyled in wine be applyed on the grieved place."

Even today mustard is highly esteemed for making poultices. We have read recommendations in the most conservative of medical journals for using mustard baths for infants in a state of shock or convulsions. Of course, the "hotness" of the mustard readily brings the blood to the skin when the mustard is applied.

Millet

Millet is a cereal, *Panicum miliaceum,* botanically speaking, although when we speak of it we generally mean any of a number of related cereals. Its origin was probably Egypt. It is used in the form of groats and makes excellent bread especially when it is used in a mixture with wheat.

It is easily grown, even in very dry or cold climates. It is not used much for human food in our country, but is used extensively in the East. An interesting story about millet is told by Mark Graubard in his book, *Man's Food* (Macmillan). Two African tribes, studied by a group of nutritionists, both had millet as their basic food. One tribe, superior in physique and health, was found to have an abundance of calcium in their diet. The other tribe, weak and sickly, was found to have a deficiency of calcium. So the millet was studied. That of one tribe contained 16 times as much calcium as that of the other. Was it the kind of millet, the kind of manure used or the kind of land it was grown on? In our book on the food content of Far Eastern foods we find that one kind of millet is listed as having 20 milligrams of calcium, another as having 329 milligrams!

Nasturtium Seeds

Nasturtium (*Tropaeolum majua*) is sometimes called Indian cress.

Many people use both the seeds and leaves of nasturtium in salads or pickle the seeds, as one would a small cucumber.

Nutmeg

Nutmeg *(Myristica fragrans)*, used widely today as a flavoring ingredient, had some therapeutic value, we are told in the old herbals. It was good against freckles in the face and it quickened the sight. We do not know whether the nutmeg was to be applied or eaten in order to do away with freckles.

Mace is a part of the nutmeg seed. These two spices have been known in Europe only since the twelfth century, making them fairly recent members of the spice family. They were used to fumigate the streets of Rome during the coronation of an emperor. The Dutch, coming into possession of the island of Banda, enjoyed a monopoly on the nutmeg trade by destroying all trees that happened to grow on any other island. Birds, however, swallowed the seeds of the Dutch trees, excreted them elsewhere and thus spread the culture of nutmeg trees to other islands.

Nutmeg was used for its antiseptic properties in the early days. In fact, it made a fine embalming fluid.

Okra Seed

Okra seeds, roasted and ground, have found use as a coffee substitute, supposedly a very tasty one. Oil is also extracted from the seeds.

One researcher has investigated okra thoroughly and bred it for its seeds. He found it not only rich in oil for industrial use, but he also bred a strain that would yield up to 2000 pounds of seed per acre with an oil content of up to 400 pounds. He states also that the okra seed is high in food value.

Parsley Seed

Parsley *(Petrose linum sativum)*, a plant rich and running over with vitamins A and C, was treasured in the old herbals for its power to "fasten loose teeth, brighten dim eyes and relieve a stitch on the side." We do not know the vitamin content of parsley seed. But the plant itself in large enough quantity in the diet could well provide enough of vitamins A and C to cure a case of scurvy (loose teeth) and night blindness (dim eyes).

Pepper

Pepper is the berrylike seed of the pepper plant which grows in hot, humid climates. The method of curing the pepper determines whether you get white or black pepper. For centuries pepper was in such demand as an herb that it commanded a high price and was often specified as a tribute or fine. When the barbarian Alaric, king of the Goths, threatened Rome in 409, he demanded a price of 3000 pounds of pepper, among other tributes.

During the Middle Ages it became immensely precious in Europe. Medical men at that time believed that there were 4 "humors" which operated to produce health or sickness in the body—blood, yellow bile, phlegm and black bile. Blood was hot and moist and phlegm was cold and moist. If any one of the humors was out of order, you could repair it by providing a medicine that would restore its original qualities. Hence pepper, being hot, could cure diseases in which the blood was thought to have become cold. It was used, too, for curing indigestion, mistiness of the eyes and other complaints.

How many spices you could afford in your food became a measure of snobbishness in Medieval Europe. We suppose that a large part of the reason for the craze for spices was that there was no refrigeration and little was known about preserving foods in other ways. Spices could be used as preservatives and also to conceal the taste of rancid or spoiled food. Then, too, the perfumes of spices became valuable in an age when baths and personal hygiene were almost unknown.

At any rate, we are told that to this day poor children in some European countries taunt a richly dressed youngster as a "pepper-licker"— a phrase which undoubtedly goes back to the economics of the Middle Ages when only the rich could afford to have pepper every day.

Peony Seeds

Peony seeds were used as medicinal herbs in Greek and Roman times and later in Anglo-Saxon kitchen gardens. The flowers were used for flavoring and the seeds were carried as a charm against evil spirits.

According to an old herbal: "It is found by sure and evident experience that the fresh roots tied about the necke of children is an effectuall remedie against the falling sickness (epilepsy)." The seeds "to the number of fifteene taken in wine or mead is a speciall remedie for those that are troubled in the night with the disease called night Mare, which is as though a heavy burthen were laid vpon them and they opprest wherewith, as if they were overcome by their enemies or ouerprest with some great weight or burthen. And they are also good against melancholicke dreames."

Gardeners who specialize in plant personalities will tell you that peonies are extremely sensitive. They grow well only for those who appreciate them, say these experts. They do not like to be transplanted; one of our gardener friends tells us they will grow well only if you talk to them as you would to a child. This gardening lore seems to be tied in with their reputation against psychological ills.

Pine Cones

Dr. Smith in his book, *Tree Crops*, quotes Dr. Robert T. Morris as saying that nuts in pine cones are near the head of the list of nut foods for human use. Dr. Morris states that there are about 30 species of nut-bearing pines between Quebec and Florida, that one species at least produces nuts the size of the average English walnut, others may be as small as a grain of buckwheat.

Many of the pine trees produce nuts that are edible either raw or cooked. Some of them are rich enough in starch to provide a staple starchy food for natives of South America, South Africa and Australia. Some of them are oily and may be pressed to yield a thick milky substance which can be kept for a long time and used essentially as a substitute for meat.

The reason why we know so little about these marvels of the conifer world is that, according to Dr. Smith, pitifully few of us are interested in tree crops—an error which Dr. Smith tries valiantly and emphatically to correct in his excellent book, *Tree Crops,* which is published by Devin-Adair, New York.

We are told that pine cones were used freely by the old herb doctors, for almost any disorder. Fir cones were "wholsom and much nourishing whilst they are fresh, and although they be somewhat hard of digestion yet they do not offend; especially if they be steeped three or fower houres in warme water before the taking, to soake out their sharpnesse and oylinesse."

Pinon

The seed of the pinon pine is another pine nut, highly recommended as all pine nuts are, because they grow in the wild and so have not been subjected to any chemical treatment.

Pomegranate

A fruit of ancient times. The flesh clings so tightly to the seeds that it must be sucked off. For this reason we do not generally do anything with pomegranate fruit except juice it.

The old Roman legend of Proserpine and Ceres involves the seeds of the pomegranate. You remember, Proserpine, abducted into the Underworld, refused to eat, mourning for her mother, Ceres, whom she thought she would never see again. Finally she ate 6 pomegranate seeds. When Ceres came to rescue her, it was decreed that Proserpine must stay one month in the Underworld for every pomegranate seed she had eaten. That is why, said the ancient storytellers, we have 6 months of summer (when Proserpine is on earth) and 6 months of winter (when she is in the Underworld).

Poppy Seed

Poppy seed is one of the better-known seeds in this country, since it is in wide use on breads and cookies. The seeds are so small that as many as 30,000 of them can be obtained in a single pod. Opium is not made from the seeds, but from the unopened pods of the poppy. But the tradition of sleepiness and death is continually associated with the poppy.

The poppy's name came from a custom of giving children the seeds mixed with their "pap," for "the Poppie seedes (after bringing to pouder) mixed with new milke as broth and given to children to drinke warme procureth them to sleepe." For adults, too, the poppy means sound sleep— "The Garden Poppie boyled vnto the thickness of honey profiteth vnto many griefs. The Seedes confected with sugar and eaten doe marvelously prevaile in procuring the weake patient to sleepe soundly."

Psyllium Seeds

Psyllium seeds, from the plant fleawort, are sold by the drug houses as a laxative. Their action is chiefly mechanical; the seeds swell to create bulk

[335]

in the intestine (which, of course, occurs quite naturally in the digestive tract of anyone who eats foods in their natural state, rather than refined). The seeds lubricate, too, to a certain extent.

Rapeseed

The rapeseed comes from a plant of the mustard family and the seed has much the same characteristics as mustard seed. It is made into oil—not in wide use in this country.

Rye

Rye seeds have been found in tombs in association with weapons of the Bronze Age period, so we can assume that this is a very old cereal indeed. Bread made from rye flour is apparently less likely to cause allergies than that made from wheat.

One caution about eating rye products exclusively. Ergotism is a quite serious disorder caused by eating rye that has been infected with ergot, a disease. We read quite recently in a medical magazine of a theory that just the tiny amount of ergot that might be present in our carefully tended American rye might be enough to produce symptoms, if you are a heavy consumer of rye bread to the exclusion of other kinds.

Senna Seeds

Senna seeds were used in olden times for medicine. Infused in whey and then boiled they were a "physicke" against melancholy and many kinds of depression and sadness. Used as a laxative in modern times, they are generally combined with some aromatic herb to prevent griping.

Sesame Seed

Sesame seeds *(Sesamum)* used constantly over the centuries in the East, are almost unknown in this country. The Turkish candy, Halvah, available in some large cities, is made from them. Oil from sesame seeds, used in the East as a cooking and salad oil, contains a large percentage of the unsaturated fatty acids (vitamin F).

We think that sesame seeds almost equal sunflower seeds as a between-meal snack. And they can be ground finely and mixed with coconut or any other nut, poppy seed, honey, figs or any other healthful food to make a tasty candy. We have read of one case of allergy to sesame seeds, but we imagine this must be extremely rare, especially in this country.

Sorghum

Sorghum is a grain grown in much the same manner as corn. It is hardier than corn in that it will grow in regions that are consistently too hot and dry for corn. In other countries, in Africa and Asia, sorghum is used as food for both human beings and animals. In this country we feed it to the stock. It is said to have about 90 to 95 per cent the feeding value of corn. It should be supplemented with feeds that provide vitamins A and D, protein and calcium.

During the war when our sources of tapioca were lost to us, some enterprising food chemist discovered that a certain kind of sorghum could be used to replace tapioca. (Tapioca comes from the cassava plant. It is a root product, not a seed.) So a limited amount of the sorghum grown today is used for this purpose. Far more was used during the war to make alcoholic beverages.

Squash Seed

The seeds from all kinds of squash and pumpkins have been known for centuries as good food. We have in our files a story written for us by a researcher who lived among the Maya Indians in Guatemala. The seed of the pepitoria squash has been one of their chief sources of protein and fats for centuries. Combined with corn, beans, fresh vegetables and fruits, the squash seeds round out an excellent diet and undoubtedly are responsible, at least in part, for the good health, fertility and excellent teeth of these people.

A learned doctor from the Connecticut Agriculture Station made the headlines several years ago when he succeeded in breeding a squash whose seeds are "naked"—that is not covered with a tough hull. The gourd-like plant which he developed produced seeds which gave about twice as much oil per pound as the soybean and about one and one-half times as much as the cotton seed. Their protein value is high, too.

At the last report, which we read in 1948, the squash seeds were available in nut stores, toasted, buttered and salted. Health-minded readers should raise their own squashes and save the seeds or buy them unroasted and unsalted from a nut store.

Watermelon Seeds

We have several stories in our files on the potency of watermelon seeds in cases of kidney trouble. One is a story that appeared in our local *Evening Chronicle* on January 1, 1946. A Mrs. Helen Kelly was near death in a hospital, according to this story, when her doctor decided to try watermelon seeds. He boiled 3 tablespoons of them in a quart of water resulting in a tea which stimulated the kidneys and brought this kidney patient back to complete health.

Apparently the same tea has been used in many other instances with success. We do not know why watermelon seeds should have any extraordinary effect on kidneys. But we are certain that they could do no harm and may indeed contain some substance that is a specific for kidney health.

We know that the protein of watermelon seed is worthwhile with a biological value of 73 and a digestibility of 92 per cent.

CHAPTER 94

Raw Wheat Seeds

By J. I. Rodale

Another seed that I would like to suggest is wheat—raw wheat seeds. These could very well be substituted in the raw form instead of bread, for in them you get everything, including the living germ. The defect of whole wheat bread is that baking destroys the living qualities of the germ. Bake a wheat seed and then plant it in the ground. Nothing will grow out of it. A few years ago I had a graphic illustration of the value of wheat used as an item of diet.

If you will refer to page 663 of our *Health Finder,* you will find described a method of screening out foods to which you are allergic by means of your pulse. A few years ago, by this method, I checked all the foods I was eating and found that I was allergic to wheat bran. But, strange to say, I was allergic only to baked wheat bran. Eating whole wheat bread raised my pulse unduly, but eating the wheat seed that contained the same bran, but in a raw state, did not. I could eat white bread without raising my pulse.

Of course, the pulse is not the only measure of whether a food is desirable. I would not eat white bread because of the chemicals it contains and for other reasons. If you wish to eat the raw wheat seed, take a handful into the mouth but keep them there for a few moments before you start to chew them. They will soon become thoroughly softened by ensalivation, and then will make a delightful chew. They must be thoroughly masticated and not swallowed till practically a liquid. You have to be careful not to buy wheat seed destined for the farmer's fields. Such seed has been treated with mercury poisons to kill out the rust and smut disease organisms.

Retention of Food Value

May I quote from *Food, Health, Vitamins,* by R. H. and V. G. Plimmer (Longmans, Green and Company, 1936): "Wellington's soldiers were famous for their fine figures and good looks, yet the food they ate would be scorned nowadays. They received one pound of wheat per day. They ate the whole grain as it was issued, or if time allowed they pounded it up and made a coarse bread."

A popular health writer has written, "A few people have gained notoriety by not cooking or baking starchy foods, thinking they thereby draw closer to nature and enjoy better health. The result of this practice, however, is that such people must suffer with gas collection in their stomach and intestines, and many develop a griping pain. Their uncooked food undergoes fermentation within their system, causing intestinal toxemia. Another result is considerable loss of weight." I wonder.

My suggestion would be to start with a small amount daily of raw wheat seed and watch developments.

Raw wheat is better than baked wheat, for many reasons. When wheat is ground and stored, serious losses of vitamins set in as the air begins its destructive process of oxidation, or burning out. Where the outer coating of the seed is preserved until it is in the stomach, this cannot occur. The whole seed will preserve its living qualities for a long time. According to Drs. Sherman and Lanford in their book, *Essentials of Nutrition* (p. 212), wheat seeds have been known to retain their vitamins after 100 years.

In the *Science News Letter* of March 24, 1955, there is an item that wheat "kept over 20 years, still makes good bread if properly stored, report scientists of the United States Department of Agriculture." In tests made it was found that wheat kept 14 to 22 years in a dry, unheated room still had a high content of vitamin B (thiamin).

Food Elements in Wheat Seeds

Let us compare the whole raw wheat seed as far as its wheat germ is concerned with wheat germ oil. Wheat germ oil is not as complete as the wheat germ in the seed. The latter contains the outer layer of the germ which is full of minerals. Of course, the reproductive capacity lies in the oil, but the minerals are valuable, too, from a dietary point of view. So to receive the full benefit, if you do not care to eat raw wheat seed, take wheat germ oil, plus raw wheat bran.

One writer says, "The entire grain is a complete food and contains within itself the factors of equilibrium. During the process of digestion the starch and the protein part, yielding an acid reaction that becomes immediately neutralized by the mineral factors contained in the outer layer, which has an alkaline reaction."

The wheat seed contains a desirable type of non-soluble fluorine, which is in the mineral-carrying outer layer of the seed. May I quote from the October, 1944, issue of the *News Letter on Compost,* published in England: "The time seems to have come when we should reconsider the present practice of extracting the 'crease dirt,' that is, the minerals, including fluorine, from our flour; and whether fluorine derived from sunflower seeds is what benefits the teeth of the Russians who chew them. The minerals are absorbed from the soil, they pass up the vascular bundles to the seed, and in the case of wheat they enter the 'staff' or leash of vessels at the base of the groove or 'crease' and are there deposited. The miller's 'break rolls' break the staff, the minerals fall out. He sieves them from the flour, and calcium, phosphates, fluorine and all, he throws them away."

A New Raw Seed Treat

In 1951 I spent several weeks at the plant of the Madaus Company, a large drug firm in Cologne, Germany, studying their methods of making drugs. They confined their efforts entirely in making drugs from plants, a great part of which they grew in the fields surrounding the factory. I went there on their invitation because they found out about our movement against the use of chemical fertilizers in growing food crops. Over a period of 20 years they had discovered that organically grown plants were more potent in producing drugs that would cure than plants grown with chemical fertilizers.

My trip there was an enjoyable vacation, as I watched them making compost heaps, and learned many things about growing plants and drug-manufacturing methods. They were a health-conscious bunch. I recall one day, when we were discussing the nutritional value of raw foods, that one of their medical scientists said he would show me something. He lived in a house, German style, that was in the park-like factory grounds. He left and in a few moments returned with a dish of fermented rye seed. As he described it, you fill a plate with seeds, either wheat, rye or millet, or a combination of the 3. You then pour a goodly quantity of fruit juices on it and permit it to ferment for a few days. The seed then becomes quite soft and juice-saturated and makes a delicious dish. He has 3 sets of plates going all the time so that one is ready every day.

May I suggest that health-conscious vegetable gardeners consider growing wheat, rye or millet for personal consumption. Millet is the healthiest of the 3 with rye second. Wheat and rye seeds are sown in the fall and mature sometime around July. It is then still time to put in many vegetable crops.

The Hunzas of India, regarding whom I have written in my book, *The Healthy Hunzas,* make a wheat product called *chapattis.* Like wheat cakes, this is made out of ground wheat, but is permitted to be heated on hot plates for only a matter of seconds. Thus the vitamins are conserved.

An Aid To Digestion

May I mention one more thing about wheat? According to an experiment that I saw performed with white rats, it was found that where bread could be constipating, raw wheat was not. It was done with white rats by Dr. Robert Mick of Laurel Springs, New Jersey. A careful record was kept of the rat droppings in the two groups. Since the droppings of the bread-fed group were less, they became fatter. Those who are on diets to reduce their weights should remember this. Cut out all bread and other cooked or baked grain foods. Eat raw wheat seeds instead.

In concluding on this subject we must bear in mind that the wheat seed has enzymes which are valuable when it comes to its digestion. Cooking kills every one of them. Enzymes die at a temperature of about 130 degrees Fahrenheit or over. Then the body must produce a new set of them to do the work of digestion.

So—I make sure to eat about 50 to 60 sunflower seeds and about 3 or four mouthfuls of raw wheat seed every day, seeds that are grown organically on our farm.

CHAPTER 95

Apple Seeds

By J. I. Rodale

Many years ago I read in a medical journal that a physician was curing a certain disease with an extract made of apple seeds. At the time I was already eating sunflower seeds, and knew their healthgiving properties, so I figured, why not add apple seeds to my diet. Since this doctor was curing diseases with them, I imagined that there might be something in apple seeds more potent even than in sunflower seeds. And there was!

I left instructions with the maid one morning to have ready at supper-time a whole teaspoonful of apple seeds, and that night I had them for dessert. It must have been the seeds of about 12 apples. The next day the whole left side of my face felt terrible, from my head down to my chin. I wouldn't call it a paralysis, but it was the closest thing to it that I ever experienced. And it could have come from nothing else than eating those apple seeds.

I re-read the item in the medical journal about the use of the extract of apple seeds. Ah, an *extract* made from the apple seed! It was not the whole apple seed! I decided to look into this matter, in the meantime eating no more apple seeds. I soon found an article in a German medical journal, *Zeitschrift Für Untersuchung Der Lebensmittel (Journal of Food Study,* issue 70, 1935, pp. 255-258). That solved the mystery. In connection with the search for a war-scarce item—fats, German scientists studied apple and pear seeds as a source. They found that about 20 to 26 per cent of the seeds was oil. The article said, "We could use the fat fruit seeds either as fodder or, because of their pleasant taste, even in human nutrition, that is, as a substitute for almonds." I was beginning to wonder, when the author continued, "In this connection Mach observed that apple seeds could not be directly used for this purpose, because of their content of amygdalin, a crystalline principle existing in bitter almonds, etc. Relative to this, we tested apple seeds and actually found prussic acid and benzaldehyde in them . . . Amygdalin was not to be observed in pear seeds."

Poison In The Seeds

Prussic acid! That is another name for hydrocyanic acid, one of the most violent poisons known to man. It checks the oxidation process in living matter (protoplasm). Herman Göring, one of the big 3 Nazis, cheated the gallows with a little phial of this poison. A heavy dose will kill in two minutes, and antidotes are practically useless. In the case of one who has committed suicide with cyanide, there hovers the faint odor of bitter almonds.

So, the mystery was solved. I had taken a dose of the prussic acid almost sufficient to paralyze the left side of my face!

However, I was in no mood to start eating pear seeds, regardless of the opinion of my esteemed German professor. But I cannot stop you from eating them, especially if you are in pear-growing country where they might be obtained from canning plants or in other commercial places. If you try them, however, don't eat them by the spoonful. At any rate, next time you eat a pear you might chew up and eat the pear seeds also. I have done this frequently with no negative consequences.

Note that the German article said that apple seed contained amygdalin, a crystalline principle existing in bitter almonds. In other words, almonds, another seed, contain some hydrocyanic acid. I recall, in the days when I would get headaches at the slightest provocation, I could easily get one after eating a goodly quantity of almonds. However, hydrocyanic acid is found only in bitter almonds which are not the kind we eat.

We see, therefore, that we cannot rush in and eat seeds indiscriminately. I recall a grocer once telling me of a customer, an old man, who would eat nothing unless it was a seed. He would not eat beets, lettuce, celery, carrots, etc. I think that his nutrition was somewhat off balance. We do need other kinds of foods for various reasons, but I do think that not enough emphasis has been placed on the fact that there is a certain amount of insurance in eating a fair amount of live raw seeds full of enzymes as well as their maximum quota of vitamins. The effect on the intestinal flora must be a very beneficial one.

CHAPTER 96

Sesame Seed—An Ancient and Nutritious Food

Sesame was one of the earliest seed crops cultivated by man. Stories and fairy tales from the East speak as casually of sesame seed as western stories speak of peas or beans. Products made from sesame formed the basis of nutrition for many people. In addition, the tasty seeds were used as flavoring in cakes, candy and other foods.

From our point of view, the outstanding characteristic of sesame seed is its fantastically high content of calcium and the fact that it contains almost twice as much calcium as phosphorus. Usually the seed foods are high in phosphorus and deficient in calcium. This is one reason why diets high in cereals are not advisable, unless there is some good source of calcium also available.

But sesame seed seems to be the exception. We find in the booklet, *Composition of Foods Used in Far Eastern Countries* (Agriculture Handbook No. 34, United States Department of Agriculture), that sesame seed contains 1,125 milligrams of calcium for every 100 grams—or about a fourth of a pound. Compare this to other foods rich in calcium—soybeans contain 227 milligrams, Swiss cheese 1,086; there are 590 milligrams in a pint of milk; 230 milligrams in a fourth of a pound of almonds.

Its protein content, too, is high—from 19 per cent to 28 per cent—more than many meats. One of the chief objections to seed foods as substitutes for foods of animal origin is that they are usually lacking or low in one or more of the essential amino acids or forms of protein that are necessary for good health. Methionine, for instance, is one of the building blocks of protein that is scarce in many foods of vegetable origin. Soybeans contain only half as much methionine as sesame seed. Peanuts, otherwise an excellent food, contain little more than a fourth as much. Compared to beef muscle, sesame seeds are slightly low in only 3 of the amino acids and have abundant stores of several of the other extremely important ones.

We have heard much about lecithin and the unsaturated fatty acids—parts of food which appear to be necessary for keeping the fatty substance cholesterol moving along in the body, and never loitering where it is not wanted. Sesame contains ample amounts of lecithin which in turn contains the unsaturated fatty acids. In general, these valuable acids are contained in the fats of unprocessed vegetables, seeds and cereals—and most of us get far too little of this kind of food.

Sesame Is a Good Source of Vitamins, Too

In conjunction with the unsaturated fatty acids there are several B vitamins that are important for helping food fats to be easily used by the body—inositol and choline are two most important ones. Sesame is rich in these two B vitamins as well as niacin, the vitamin so important for preventing pellagra and for preserving the health of nerves, skin and digestive tract. Inflammation of the inside of the mouth and the tongue is a frequent symptom of not enough niacin.

Finally, sesame is a good source of vitamin E. This important vitamin, so necessary for the good health of heart and blood vessels, does a big job of indirectly oxygenating the tissues of the body. When there is plenty of vitamin E present, the tissues can get along perfectly well on less oxygen. So it is advisable for us to get additional vitamin E whenever we can, for it is very scarce in the average modern diet.

Best of all, possibly, in the list of sesame seed's virtues is the fact that it tastes so delicious that it is frequently used just as a garnish or a flavoring in a food. Most of us have eaten cookies or crackers covered with sesame seed and found the taste delightful. So there is no need to plan drearily for some way to cover up the taste of sesame just so you can benefit from its nutritious content. Instead, enjoy it for its taste and count the nutritive benefits a bonus!

You can buy sesame seeds in many grocery stores these days, and we suggest them heartily for between-meal snacks as well as for mixing with almost anything to make a healthful sweet. Honey, figs, dates, ground coconut and many different fruits complement delightfully the intriguing taste of sesame. Sesame seeds are delicious added to tossed salads, used in a sauce for broiled fish or mixed with almost any other food whose flavor they will improve.

For readers on the lookout for milk substitutes we want to suggest Tahini—a milk made from liquefied sesame seed. This is a rather thin, creamy dressing with a taste something like peanut butter. It can be used in a variety of foods or alone, as a sauce on fish, eggs or vegetables. Mixed with honey, maple syrup and nuts it makes a sweet dessert.

In every other case where we have recommended substitutes for cow's milk, we have cautioned that, in order to approximate the calcium content of cow's milk, one must add bone meal. But in the case of Tahini, the calcium is there—plenty of it.

CHAPTER 97

Poisonous Seeds

Many seeds are provided by nature with very effective protection against loss or destruction. Nature is, above all, interested in propagating everything that grows. So she takes good care of seeds, which carry the germ of the new plant. We are all familiar with the many devices that assure seeds of wide circulation—the dandelion's frothy silk that, swept by the wind, carries the seed and spreads it; the burr that sticks to passing animals and so broadcasts the tiny seed inside, the seeds that float on water, sail in air or scatter when they are brushed by passing animals.

Some seeds are protected by being poisonous. In this way nature saves them from animals which would eat them, for, of course, the animals soon learn which seeds can be eaten with impunity and which cannot. Some seed poisons are lethal to men and some to animals but not to birds or certain other animals. So far as we human beings are concerned, we need not concern ourselves especially about these seed poisons unless we are in the habit of breaking off and munching strange plants and berries as we walk through woods or meadows, or unless we have young children or animals who may play near to where such seeds grow.

Poisonous Seeds Used As Drugs

There have been many cases on record of children being poisoned by the seeds of the poison hemlock. This is not the hemlock tree, incidentally, but an herb which looks somewhat like Queen Anne's lace. The whole plant is poisonous to human beings—so poisonous that even a few seeds nearly always prove fatal. This is the hemlock that Socrates drank.

Water hemlock and spotted hemlock are other members of the same family, equally poisonous. Water hemlock, also called cowbane because of its poisonous effect on cows, looks not unlike celery and has seeds that look like anise seeds. Water dropwort, another poisonous plant, is in the same family.

Monkshood (aconite) is a lovely tall spike of blue flowers in the fall, more graceful and delicate than the delphinium. And deadly poison in all its parts. Now surely this is no reason not to plant monkshood, for it will add charm to any garden. But don't plant it near the playpen and don't keep your flower seeds in the food cabinet. Foxglove or digitalis is another strong poison, especially the seeds. Of course, the essence from them is used as a drug, for heart disease sufferers.

The "deadly nightshade" is the plant from which belladonna is made. All of the plant is poisonous to eat, but especially the seeds. Black nightshade is poisonous, too. The berries of bittersweet—the lovely bright orange and red berry that vines over autumn walls—lily of the valley, wood anemone and laurel seeds are also poisonous.

It's surprising how many seeds we list as poisonous that are being used in drugs today. The seed of the handsome castor oil plant is poisonous. Yes, of course, castor oil is made from the seed. And the same mother who warns her children from picking the seeds off the vine and eating them will probably resort to castor oil when "the children need a laxative" without giving it a second thought. The very fact that the seed of the castor bean is poisonous should make us hesitate a long time before taking castor oil as a laxative.

More Seeds to Beware of!

Pokeweed has poisonous seeds. This bush has purple berries that country children used to make into "ink." The seeds of yew are another deadly morsel for human beings. Birds, however, eat them ravenously and harmlessly, as well as the pokeweed seeds. Henbane is a small, disagreeable weed whose seeds are deadly to hens as well as to human beings. The seeds were formerly made into oil and used as a gargle to cure toothache! Apparently the juice contains some kind of narcotic.

Jimson weed, mandrake, Dog's Mercury, poison sumac, "snow-on-the mountain," "burning bush" or "Spingle tree," poison ivy, mistletoe, holly, laburnum—all these have seeds that are poisonous to human beings. Wild cherries and peaches have a powerful poison *in the kernel inside the seed.*

One of the most unusual poisons is found in the fava bean which is grown widely in Europe for food. Just smelling the blossoms causes illness in some individuals and eating the beans can cause death. There have been about 1200 cases of *favism* in this country recently, mostly caused by eating

[345]

the first young green beans. Some persons are so sensitive to the fava bean that they have attacks of favism each spring when the blossoms or the beans appear. The tendency seems to run in families.

Other individuals may eat the fava beans for years without ever having any trouble. We do not know how doctors interpret this peculiar poisoning that may emanate from the fava bean. It sounds like an allergy to us. And, unless you are in the habit of eating fava beans, don't give the matter a second thought. This is a definite family of bean, and is so listed in seed catalogs. So you needn't fear that you will ever get fava beans when you ordered snap beans.

A book entitled *British Poisonous Plants,* Bulletin No. 161 of the Ministry of Agriculture and Fisheries in England lists hundreds of poisonous plants, including even wheat, rye, onions, barley, clover and scores of others. In fact, by the time we had finished reading this book we had about concluded that almost anything, eaten in excess, can be poisonous. However, the seeds we discussed above are, in general, the ones most likely to be encountered on a walk in the woods or fields. They should be avoided.

CHAPTER 98

Sprouting Seeds

Peoples of other lands and times, less surfeited with good food than we, have learned tricks for improving the nutritional content of their meals—tricks which we would do well to study and emulate. Sprouting seeds is one of these. This practice has been known from earliest times, especially in the far eastern countries where sprouts are used as commonly as we use onions or celery.

Why should we sprout seeds? The sprouted seed contains more vitamins than the dry seed. It's just that simple. When the seed is given water and warmth, whatever it is in seeds that starts them to growing gets busy. The seed puts forth a tiny sprout, green and crisp. And as this sprout grows, vitamins are formed in it, right before your very eyes. A dried seed contains little or no vitamin C. But as sprouted seeds grow, their vitamin C increases. For instance, 100 grams of whole oats contain 11 milligrams of vitamin C. After they have germinated for 96 hours, they contain 20 milligrams. After they have germinated for 120 hours, they contain 42 milligrams. Dry peas increase from a vitamin C content of zero to 86 milligrams of vitamin C after 96 hours of germination.

The story on the other vitamins is even more astonishing. Seven parts of thiamin (a B vitamin) become 9 parts in the sprouted wheat. And as for the rest of the B vitamins, listen to what happens to them: riboflavin increases itself by about 4, niacin, pantothenic acid, pyridoxine and biotin just about double their content. And what about folic acid—that precious B vitamin which prevents pernicious anemia, that vitamin so scarce and rare in food that none of us ever get enough of it? Twenty-eight parts of folic acid in a wheat seed become 106 parts after sprouting! In addition, we are told by Dr. Francis Pottenger, Jr. of Monrovia, California, that the sprouts develop into complete protein capable of sustaining life. While you watch, then, protein is manufactured before your very eyes, along with vitamins.

Sprouting seeds is almost a brand new idea in this country, we suppose, because we have always had such a profusion of good, nutritious food available. So information about sprouting seeds is not easy to come by. However, during the last war when we were fearing further food shortages, Dr. Clive M. McCay of Cornell worked on the possibility of promoting sprouted soybeans as an all-around good nutritious food.

A report of his work occurs in *Science News Letter* for May 22, 1943. Soybean sprouts are rich in protein and fat, minerals, including calcium and usable iron, and vitamins, he says. The Cornell workers developed easy methods of sprouting which involve nothing more complicated than a container from which drainage is possible. Place the beans in the pot and pour water over them. Be sure to let the water drain off and keep the beans moist and warm. Cornell students found that they had to develop a taste for the soy sprouts. But apparently plenty of seasoning would help so far as taste goes.

A Book On Sprouting Seeds

The best book we have found covering seed sprouts and how to sprout them is Catharyn Elwood's book, *Feel Like a Million*, which is an excellent all-around book on other aspects of nutrition as well. (This is published by Better Nutrition Institute, 2025 Park Rd., N.W., Washington 10, D. C.) Miss Elwood suggests several methods for sprouting and gives a number of recipes for using the sprouted seeds in tasty dishes.

Says she: "Sprouts from almost every bean (especially the mung and soya beans) peas, lentils, wheat, alfalfa, rye, corn and millet make delicious and nutritious additions to your vegetable bill-of-fare selection." She then goes on to describe several different methods of sprouting, all of them involving, of course, moisture and warmth. She tells us that "sprouts are ready for use as soon as the sprout is seen. The longer the sprout, the more nourishment. When the green appears, vitamin A and chlorophyl are developing. However, most sprouts are less delicious if too long. Here are my preferences:

"Wheat sprouts are most delicious when the sprout is the length of the seeds.

"Mung bean sprouts are best when 1½ to 3 inches long.

"Alfalfa sprouts are best when 1 to 2 inches long.

"Pea and soybean sprouts are good short or long.

"Lentil sprouts mold quickly so must be used when about one inch long.

[347]

"Sunflower seed sprouts are best when no longer than the seed. If longer they develop a strange objectionable sting in the throat after eating.

"When the sprouts have developed to the desired stage, put them in a closed jar in the refrigerator. They keep like any fresh vegetable for a few days if properly covered."

How to Sprout Seeds and Use the Sprouts

Some of Miss Elwood's recipes for sprout dishes involve: almond-mushroom chop suey, vegetable casserole, sprouts with eggs, chicken a la king with bean sprouts and so forth. We strongly recommend your getting the book, *Feel Like a Million,* for its information on sprouts as well as the other splendid nutrition suggestions it contains.

Some years ago, Dr. Pottenger (to whom we referred earlier) wrote us about his own enthusiasm for sprouting seeds. He said, "Among those seeds which I have found most interesting are, of course, the common ones: wheat, rye, oats, barley, corn, alfalfa, clover and parsley. As you know, the list of seeds that can be used is long. The most tasty of the sprouts I have tried so far is parsley when used as a salad. As a breakfast food I prefer the alfalfa. Such common seeds as navy beans, red beans and so forth, when sprouted, require only 10 to 15 minutes to cook, instead of two to three hours. The mung bean also works up well either as a salad or as a cooked vegetable.

"I have experimented with many ways of sprouting, and have found that the methods commonly described in present-day periodicals have been entirely unsuccessful in my hands. With large quantities of seeds, however, the tray sprouter or Japanese method have worked very well, as has a modification of the Korean method, using a strawberry box. The Chinese way, involving the earthenware pot (or flower pot) was only fairly satis-factory, while milk bottles, Mason jars and similar utilities only tend to enhance the growth of mold. I have had the greatest success by rolling the scattered seed inside a bath towel and dampening this roll from time to time.

"I have found that good seeds that get plenty of oxygen during the act of sprouting do not mold. Seeds of low sprouting capacity, an index of poor soil fertility, often succumb to this."

One final word about sprouting seeds comes from the *New York Times.* We do not have the date but we assume the article appeared during the war. In this article Roberta Ma recommends sprouting beans in a flower pot of two-quart size. Cover the hole in the bottom of the pot with a piece of crockery, she says. Wash thoroughly and soak a quarter of a pound of soy-beans for about 6 hours, until they are plump and the skins burst. Then put the seeds into the flower pot. Sprinkle water on the seeds daily, perhaps twice a day or oftener, to keep them moist. In 3 or 4 days at room tem-perature the sprouts should be ready—just branching, without any show of green.

We hope that many readers will get into the habit of sprouting seeds regularly. It is economical, healthful and, really, not a lot of trouble. It's certainly less trouble than peeling vegetables or making cookies or frying foods in deep fat or any of those other kitchen tasks we used to engage in before we realized that they were not only unnecessary but positively harmful. Sprouting seeds takes no time at all, except for the few minutes of sprinkling them. All the rest they do by themselves with the help of nature. Why not start now to accustom your family to some new recipes, using sprouted seeds?

CHAPTER 99

The American Indians, Seed Eaters

Aside from meat, seeds were perhaps the mainstay of diet among the American Indians. Many of the seed foods with which we are so familiar today originated with the American Indians. We are told that more than half the fruits and vegetables we use today were known only to the American Indians before the time of Columbus. Corn is one of these, or maize as it is called by everyone in the world except North Americans.

Wrote Sir Walter Raleigh of the new land, America, "I tell thee, 'tis a goodlie country, not wanting in victuals. On the banks of those rivers are divers fruits good to eat and game aplenty. Besides, the natives in those parts have a corne, which yields them bread; and this with little labor and in abundance. 'Tis called in the Spanish tongue 'mahiz'."

The Indians had figured out just about every way to eat corn that might be devised. They ate it roasted right from the stalk, as we today eat roasting ears. They picked it green, pressed out some of the milk from the kernels and boiled the corn in this milk. They dried the mature ears and ground the kernels into meal which was the staple food for winter. On long journeys Indians carried with them no provisions except a bag of parched, ground corn which sustained them during the entire journey, along with whatever meat they could find in the forests.

The Plains Indians added cornsilk to their cornmeal. They thought it added sweetness to the taste. Many Indians sucked the juicy stalks of the corn as they gathered the ears. The Hurons had a unique way of preparing the cereal. They soaked young corn ears in water until they were putrid, then boiled this evil-smelling soup and drank it. With what we know today about yeasts and molds we might discover some day that this was a very healthful procedure, after all. Other Indians burned the corncob to ashes and mixed the ashes with their corn dishes—an excellent way to preserve all the minerals, of course.

[349]

As important a food as corn naturally figured largely in the folklore of the Indians. The Naragansetts believed that long ago a crow came to their ancestors bearing a bean and a kernel of corn, which marked the beginning of their farming. As a result they would never drive a crow away from their cornfields. Was he not the father of their agriculture?

Samp was Indian mush which was eaten either hot or cold. Succotash, corn and beans together, was a favorite dish. Placing corn or other grain on the grave to feed the soul of the deceased was a common Indian custom.

Sunflower Seeds

Sunflower seeds were and still are a favorite Indian food. "There is a greate herbe in the forme of a Marigold," wrote an early author, "some take it to bee *Planta Solis:* of the seedes therefore they make both a kinde of bread and broth." Since the sun was worshipped extensively in Indian religions, it is understandable that the sunflower should be held in great esteem, for it follows the sun, turning its head across the sky through all the hours of the day.

Today the sunflower is cultivated by the Hopis. A description of this Hopi sunflower is given in the *Missouri Botanical Garden Bulletin,* Volume 33, No. 8. The seeds were a source of food to the early Hopi Indians, but they were even more than that. The Hopi sunflowers have great purple seeds and the color was extracted to make a dye. In addition to the cultivated sunflower, which they cared for with great concern, the Hopis also used the many wild sunflowers that grew near. The flowers of the wild sunflower plant were supposed to be a medicine for spider bites.

The Importance of Acorns

Acorns, the seed of the oak tree, were one of the major foods of many Indian nations. Says Mark Graubard in his book, *Man's Food* (published by Macmillan, New York, New York), "Our earliest known bread was made from acorns and beechnuts. Some American Indians on the Pacific coast prepared cakes from crushed acorns even in post-Columbian days. This fruit contains a bitter substance which primitive man learned quickly enough to extract and dissolve. The acorn meal was washed in boiling water for several hours, the bitter-tasting substance was thereby dissolved out and thrown away, while the remaining meal was dried in the sun and baked in its warmth or over a hot fire."

Dr. Smith in his book, *Tree Crops* (Devin-Adair, New York, New York), has a lot to say about the acorn in the diet of Indians. The Indians used to extract oil from acorns and use it either as a hairdressing or in food. Another authority tells us that acorns were regularly gathered by squaws and old men among the Californians (Indians) and the invariable sound that salutes the ear as one approaches a village is the monotonous thump-thump of the pestles used by the women in pounding the acorn into flour. The Californians dedicated a special ceremonial dance to the acorn.

Other Nuts

Nuts of all kinds were, of course, important to the Indians. According to an early authority they used to shell black walnuts by breaking them between two stones; then they dried them in the sun and ground them in a mortar. Pouring water over the finely crushed walnuts would cause the tiny pieces of shell to sink to the bottom. The water, taking up substances from the nuts, became walnut milk which was tasty in a variety of dishes.

To the Indians of North, Central or South America we are also indebted for the following seed-foods: squash, peanuts, Brazil nuts, pecans, vanilla, wild rice, kidney and lima beans, mesquite beans, pinon nuts, cashews, watermelon, cactus and all of the cereals. The Indians also made use of the following seeds, which we do not generally use: amarinth, brickeye, chia, goosefoot, islay, jojoba, juniper, chickapins, salt-bush, songwae, tarweed, wild flax, wild sage.

CHAPTER 100

Sunflower Seeds

By J. I. Rodale

Deaf Smith County, Texas, in the latter part of 1941 gained national fame as the county whose inhabitants had teeth superior to anything known anywhere in the world. The people in and around Hereford displayed teeth so remarkably healthy that the incidence of dental caries was almost completely nil. To account for this amazing situation, it was found that the soil in and around Hereford was rich in lime and phosphorus and contained some fluorine. These 3 elements are basic to the formation of tooth and bone and since, through the food grown in this soil, the residents absorbed these elements, they developed this extraordinary incidence of healthy teeth and bones.

Dr. S. G. Harootian of the Worcester State Hospital in Massachusetts, after hearing about Deaf Smith County, immediately began investigations into the possibility of finding a food containing these 3 elements. After much research and experimentation, he found that the bones of beef cattle ground fine as flour would serve the intended purpose, for in an astounding 9-month experiment with 9 mental patients, the formation of cavities was absolutely arrested by the addition of bone meal to their diets.

I Check on the Food Value of Sunflower Seeds

As a spectator I was irresistibly fascinated by these momentous happenings. For several years on our farm we had been growing sunflowers and feeding the seeds of this plant to our chickens. Poultry authorities speak highly of this seed as a conditioner of barnyard fowl. Parrots live on them almost exclusively and seem to lead a contented existence. We had never thought of eating these seeds ourselves but when I heard about Deaf Smith County and Dr. Harootian's ingenious experiment the thought occurred to me to check on the food-value analysis of sunflower seeds. To my amazement the ash of the seed showed a tremendous quantity of phosphorus (35 per cent), calcium (7½ per cent) and a trace of fluorine.

My Health Improves

I started to eat the seeds, a couple of heaping handfuls every day, but did not adjust anything else in my diet. My dentist had found only one tiny tooth cavity in about 3 years so I wasn't thinking in terms of dental improvement. But about 4 days later I noticed something that was truly startling. My gums had stopped bleeding. They say that 4 out of 5 suffer from pink toothbrush (actually the figures are more nearly 1 out of 5). If this condition is not checked, it may eventually lead to something far more serious than mere tooth cavities, namely, the dreaded *pyorrhea* and the loss of all teeth. When I used to eat an apple, I could sometimes see a slight bloody imprint on the white pulp. This embarrassing condition cleared up nicely, so I stuck faithfully to my sunflower seeds.

About a week later a slight intermittent quiver in my left eye went away. I usually suffered from this only in the winter when there was little opportunity for exercise or sunshine. I am glad to report that it has not returned, thanks to the fact that I still eat sunflower seeds practically every day.

My eyes are not my strongest point. In the winter I would have trouble in walking on snow-blanketed roads. Before I became aware of the value of eating sunflower seeds I left the house on the farm one day for a walk but had to return after being out only a moment, as the excessive brightness of the snow interfered with my vision. In fact, it made the snow seem a pink color. After being on the sunflower diet for about a month, I noticed I could walk in the snow without distress. A little while later my car broke down and I had to walk over a mile on a snowed-up highway in bright sunshine with no trouble at all for the first three-quarters of the way. On the last stretch the eyes smarted a little.

The sunflower seed is loaded down with vitamin B. The oil found in sunflower seeds is very rich in valuable food elements. I noticed also that my skin seemed to be getting smoother. This doesn't seem to be unreasonable because calcium and the right kind of oils are specifics for a good strong epidermis.

The Value of Sunflower Seeds for Others

I now decided to see if the eating of sunflower seeds would have the same effect on the bleeding gums of others. I therefore furnished these seeds to 4 girls employed in the shops of an electric manufacturing company of which I am president. Within 10 days two of them reported complete success; no more blood on toothbrushes. One girl claimed 50 per cent improvement. This girl stated her tongue did not seem to be coated anymore. The fourth girl estimated a 75 per cent improvement. I have checked with 3 of these girls a year later and the improvements are holding.

I have gone over many books on nutrition and nowhere have I seen reference made to the value of the sunflower seed in the diet. In lists giving the vitamin content of foods, the sunflower is usually left out. Evidently this is because it has always been a bird and chicken food. Thus it seems to be left completely out of the calculations of the best nutritionists. It is the forgotten food, if there ever was one.

Milk is a food extremely rich in calcium and phosphorus and according to all the rules should produce strong teeth and gums. Some persons drink milk until it comes out at the ears, yet are below par in the gums and teeth. In the first place, by selective breeding and forced feeding, cows are giving enormous amounts of milk daily. Under natural conditions the cow is supposed to give sufficient milk to brink up its calf. What it gives today is a fluid which remarkably resembles milk and is sufficient to bring up a large herd of calves, *very* large. So, today the milk is not milk and the cow is not a cow. The cow is subject to many pestilential diseases which oldtime cows never even dreamt about.

Another reason why modern milk does not seem to have the wished-for effect on the teeth is that the heating action of pasteurization seems to change the chemical nature of its lime or calcium, so that it does not become fully absorbed into the system. The calcium of raw sunflower seeds, on the other hand, is readily assimilated by our bodies.

Their Effect on Rheumatism

In a bulletin on sunflower seeds written by the late well-known nutritionist Harvey D. Wiley (United States Department of Agriculture Bulletin No. 60, published in 1901) he says that there was an old idea that the eating of sunflower seeds would cure rheumatism. However, Mr. Wiley stated further that there was no evidence that it would. Many of the so-called home remedies have proven unusually effective when checked by the medical profession. Digitalis for heart disease, for example, is a drug obtained from the foxglove flower. A physician discovered an old woman using it and on checking found it remarkably successful in his work. It is now a standard medical remedy. There are dozens of other similar cases. In fact there is an entire field of botanical drugs used by many physicians. So perhaps, even as a specific for rheumatism, the sunflower cannot be waved away without some experimental testing. Our folklore is rich in cases of wholesome, simple cures by means of various plants.

Sunflower Seeds Are Valuable Food

There are many reasons why the sunflower seed is a valuable food and should be included in everyone's daily diet. In the first place nature protects it with a casing. It, therefore, stores well and loses very little vitamin value for long periods. When you remove the outer shell you have a concentrated bit of healthy nourishment. It tastes almost as delicious a year after harvesting as on the day it was cut down. I have eaten with relish raw wheat seed on harvest day, but a month later it has already lost some of its palatability.

Secondly, you eat the sunflower seed raw. Nutritionists all agree that cooking, however skillfully done, destroys some of the vitamins. It is not factoryized or processed food. It comes to you in virgin form.

This plant is one of the easiest to grow. You have never heard of anyone spraying poisons on it because it is very hardy and is highly resistant to disease.

Now we come to a very remarkable fact about the sunflower. As soon as the head is formed it always faces the sun. This is a phenomenon called *heliotropism*. In the morning the head faces the east. As the sun swings in its orbit across the heavens, the sunflower head turns with it gradually, until, late in the afternoon, it is facing due west to absorb the few last rays of the dying sun. Sometimes before the sun comes up next morning the head turns completely back to start the process all over again. Every farmer boy knows this. In other words it is just drenched with sun-vitality. Perhaps that is the reason it wards off the diseases which plague other plants. Another possible reason for the potency of this little seed is that from such a small speck, there comes in a few week's time quite a quantity of green material, much greater than that of any other of our food crop plants in proportion to size of seed. Nature, therefore, must pack this tiny kernel full of powerful stuff.

In the United States it is sometimes grown as a border to beautify a garden and the seeds are later thrown away. A friend of mine admitted to this crime. He didn't know whether you eat the seed shelled or with its jackets. I have since discovered many other persons who were guilty of the same uncertainty. You throw away the shell, of course.

The Seeds Found Useful in the Past

The American Indian found copious use for the seed of the sunflower which he employed as food, hair oil and soap. Members of the Lewis and Clark Expedition found much evidence of this. In their journal for July 17, 1805, when they were in Montana there is recorded the following:

"Along the bottoms, which have a covering of high grass, we observe the *sunflower* blooming in great abundance. The Indians of the Missouri, more especially those who do not cultivate maize, make great use of the seed of this plant for bread, or in thickening their soup. They first parch and then pound it between two stones, until it is reduced to a fine meal. Sometimes they add a portion of water, and drink it thus diluted; at other times they add a sufficient proportion of marrow-grease to reduce it to the consistency of common dough, and eat it in that manner. This last composition we preferred to all the rest, and thought it at that time a very palatable dish."

Note the use of marrow-grease, a product made from bones. Columbus also noted how popular the sunflower was with the Indians and was instrumental in introducing it into Europe. Today, while this seed is so popular in many parts of Europe, it is practically unknown in this country as a food for human beings.

[354]

Sunflower Seeds And Bleeding Gums

As I stated before, the eating of sunflower seeds cleared up my case of bleeding gums. But I have a confession to make. A few months later the condition reappeared. I soon began to notice it on my morning toothbrush. That was indeed something to think about. I knew that there must be some reason for its returning and I felt confident that the cause would be discovered. In a few weeks, I had a definite answer.

As a result of this new development I want to state that the eating of sunflower seeds does good in 3 different ways. First and most important is its effect as a nutritious food containing much vitamin value which is absorbed by the body. Second, is the oil which it contains which is beneficial to the oral cavity in general. Many persons have irritations and inflammations of the inner cheeks. This becomes covered with the soothing sunflower oil which acts externally and not through the blood stream in this particular situation, although in time, it would have acted in that way also.

The third advantage is the wonderful exercise the teeth get from eating the sunflower seed, not disregarding the benefit of cracking open the seed with the teeth. It was the way I ate the seeds that gradually brought back my trouble, but in order to give you an understandable picture of this whole situation I must go back about 18 years and describe the history of my teeth.

I have always had a fairly good set of teeth but have suffered somewhat from bleeding gums. I visited a schoolmate chum of mine in New York who had become a very prominent dentist. He was putting into very successful practice a method developed by Dr. R. G. Hutchinson of curing pyorrhea by a most revolutionary treatment.

The Hutchinson Method of The Even Bite

According to Dr. Hutchinson very few people have teeth which occlude properly, that is, they do not come together as they should. In a recent survey it was found that out of 35,000,000 school children, over 5,000,000 had malocclusion of the teeth. When the teeth do not come together properly, there is a congestion in the peridental membrane which surrounds the roots. This affects the alveolar septum which separates one root from another, and eventually sets up a condition where the teeth get out of alignment. Then when the process of mastication begins the tooth will rock in its socket.

Dr. Hutchinson worked out a method by which he ground the teeth so as to produce an even bite and to relieve the strain caused by teeth that were out of position. This seemed to work like a charm. I have seen photographs of patients, before and after the treatment, who showed a sensational improvement in the appearance of their teeth. I submitted to this grinding of my teeth and there was a great improvement effected. That was about 18 years ago. Four or 5 years ago my gums started to bleed again and I have already related how the eating of sunflower seeds about a year ago cleared up the condition.

Don't Favor One Side When Chewing

One day, while eating some seeds, I noticed that I always ate them on the right side of my mouth. Thinking back about the way my "bite" was evened out, by the Hutchinson method, it occurred to me that favoring that side must have thrown my teeth out of alignment and thus created the condition as previously described. I then saw to it, that I chewed only on the left side, in order to even out the bite, and after a week or so the bleeding stopped. After a month it started again. I have finally gotten it under control by seeing to it that I do not favor one side more than the other.

It is interesting to note that at the Baltimore Dental Centenary, recently, a Dr. Clyde H. Schuyler spoke about people who have an imperfect bite and that they may "chew themselves deaf," or get sinus trouble, facial neuralgia and other conditions.

"Impaired hearing, stuffy sensation in the ears, tinnitus, snapping noises while chewing, dull pain within and about the ears, dizziness at times of prostrating severity, alleged sinus symptoms, headaches and burning sensation in the throat, tongue and side of nose," Dr. Schuyler said, "have been relieved by establishing the proper relation of jaws and opposing teeth." This condition can be overcome by grinding the teeth, said Dr. Schuyler.

Favoring One Side of the Body

Just as I favored the right side of my mouth more than the left, so do many people favor different sides of the body in many things that they do. In walking, a person stresses one side of the body more than the other. Usually, I believe the right side is favored. The right foot is put forward with more strength and tenseness, the left foot with a more relaxed feeling. The Indians knew how to take advantage of this principle. When they went on a long journey on foot, they would walk for awhile stressing their right side, and then would change the stress to the other, in alternation. This prevented fatigue.

Carrying weights always on one side may cause a lateral curvature in the spine. For the same reason tennis is worse than rowing because it favors only one side of the body. Canoeing stresses one side more than the other. Many Indians had shoulders much more powerfully developed on one side than the other for this reason. Many coaches forbid swimmers to engage in track or other sports because they tend to favor or develop only one set of muscles, whereas in swimming, the entire body must be used.

This principle is very aptly explained in the following paragraph which appeared in a health magazine, the name of which I have apparently failed to make a record of:

"Using the right hand more than the left produces what is known as typical right handed distortion of the spinal column, which is caused by greater development and pull by the muscles on this side. This causes a distortion of every part of the body in a general way, and is more exaggerated in some people than others, according to the degree of the right handed habit. It is claimed by good authority, that even though one is left handed, whenever any task is before him which requires great strength, he always does more with the right side of the body on account of many generations of ancestors following the general rule of right handedness and all having a tendency to do everything that requires strength more with the right side of the body. Our way of thinking and acting in using these voluntary muscles is greatly influenced by this hereditary tendency."

Good horsemen in trotting a horse know the value of not overstressing one side. They will "post" for a few minutes on the right "diagonal" and then change over to the left. When the horseman comes down in the saddle on a right diagonal, the horse's right foot is hitting the ground at the same time that the horseman is coming down with all his weight. Some "public livery" horses that have an overdeveloped right side due to being handled by poor riders, make poor material for good riders.

Coming back to sunflower seeds, because they are so small, they offer much more exercise to the teeth than most of our modern mushy food and it is this mechanical exercise that, I feel certain, brings about the stoppage of bleeding in gums. It conditions the teeth. These short, choppy, masticatory motions have some effect in creating a healthy gum condition. In eating vitamin pills you get none of this advantage. Observe your regular eating motions in general and see whether you favor one side. If so, try and use both sides.

Food Value of Seed

Just about the same time that I was experimenting with sunflower seeds as human food, two men in the Middle West were engaged in doing the very same thing. One of them was Ezra Levin, president of the VIO-BIN Corporation of Monticello, Illinois. His colleague in this research project was Professor Harry G. Day, of the Department of Chemistry of Indiana University. They discovered that a meal made from sunflower seed is superior in vitamin B to that of wheat germ and we all know that the medical profession depends a great deal on the latter substance for use where there are deficiencies in this vitamin. Wheat germ is a specific for persons whose reproductive powers are below normal.

Regarding this experiment the Associated Press wrote at that time:

"Experiments with the yield from 100 acres of the flowers, grown last summer, were so successful that the company is contracting with farmers for planting 500 acres this year, Levin said. If the next crop comes up to expectations, widespread cultivation will be sought, he indicated.

"Oil extracted from sunflower seeds by a low temperature solvent method which Levin said he developed is being shipped to a manufacturer for use in salad oil. Meal was sold to a processor making combination meat-protein foods. Levin said he believed these would be the first sunflowers used for human food.

"Last summer's experiments by about 12 Piatt farmers showed sunflowers can be raised for about the same production costs as soybeans, reported Levin, whose firm is engaged in various types of grain processing. Yields were slightly under 1,000 pounds of seed an acre, but Levin said

[357]

this was because of late planting and that under normal conditions the flowers would produce 1,500 pounds an acre."

The report of their experiment was written up in *Science* of April 27, 1945. My original article appeared in the April, 1945, issue of *Organic Gardening,* which was in the hands of the public only a few days before that date. I am presenting their report herewith in its entirety because it contains so much valuable information on this subject. In reading it please note the reference that is made to the fact that heat is injurious to the vitamins in the seeds. Many persons like to toast sunflower seeds. This practice is not to be recommended.

As a result of their work it is possible that in the future food products such as cake and bread may be enriched with sunflower seed meal. This is much superior to the use of vitamins for this purpose, produced synthetically.

The Levin-Day Report

The report of the work of Levin and Day follows herewith. It is entitled:

THE NUTRITIONAL VALUE OF SUNFLOWER SEED MEAL

In the search for new new food materials of significant value in human and animal nutrition scarcely any attempt appears to have been made to critically evaluate sunflower seed. This is surprising because the sunflower *(Helianthus annus)* is economically important and well known in many parts of the world including the United States and Canada. The production is increasing rapidly. For example, in the season of 1943-44 Argentina's output of sunflower oil amounted to 1,072,000 tons, placing that country second only to Russia as a producer.[1] In 1939-40 the production in Argentina was only 375,000 tons.

The hull-free residue remaining after removal of the oil has been used for livestock and poultry feeding. It is approximately 53 per cent protein, the biological value of which has been found to be quite low.[2] In all probability this conclusion has been based on analyses of oil-free residue obtained by pressure extraction methods which involved severe heat treatment. Such methods are now known to markedly reduce the biological value of proteins[3] and may be regarded as injurious to certain vitamins. Mitchell *et al.*[3] have recently shown that sunflower seed meal, when produced by a low temperature, solvent extraction process, is in the same class as oats, wheat and barley in regard to the dietary quality of its protein.

Practically nothing can be found in the literature concerning the B complex values of sunflower seed or the product left after removal of the oil. For example the word sunflower does not occur in most standard books on nutrition, including the recent "Handbook of Nutrition" of the American Medical Association,[4] although in the latter, mention is made of such unusual foods as caviar, crayfish and edible hips of the wild rose.

We have undertaken an investigation of the nutritive properties of the meal left after low temperature, solvent extraction of hulled sunflower seed (Sunrise variety). The marked ability of this product to promote growth and reproduction in rats restricted to purified diets containing it as

[358]

the only source of B complex vitamins prompts this preliminary note in order that attention might be focused more promptly on this neglected, but promising food.

The following experiments illustrate the major findings. Weanling rats were divided into different groups with due regard for litter membership, sex and weight. The basal ration was: casein (vitamin-free) 15, glucose 66, salt mixture 4, hydrogenated vegetable oil (Crisco) 8, wheat germ oil (VioBin) 2, percomorph oil (Mead Johnson) two drops, and supplement 5. The supplements were respectively defatted wheat-germ meal (VioBin), defatted corn-germ meal (VioBin), defatted sunflower seed meal (VioBin), defatted soybean meal and dried brewer's yeast. In another series the supplements were given at a 10 per cent level, instead of 5, and the glucose level was decreased accordingly. The growth results are indicated in Table 1.

TABLE 1

Growth Rate of Rats fed limited amounts of low-temperature solvent-extracted Sunflower Seed Meal as the only source of B Complex Vitamins, in comparison with that in Rats fed similar levels of defatted Wheat Germ, Corn Germ, Soybeans and Brewer's Yeast

Supplement	Level of Supplement	Average gains*	
		7 weeks	14 weeks
	per cent	g.	g.
Wheat germ	5	47 (12)	70 (3)
Corn germ	5	46 (14)	70 (3)
Soybeans	5	21 (11)	....
Sunflower seed	5	56 (15)	119 (3)
Brewer's yeast	5	121 (2)	180 (2)
Wheat germ	10	114 (5)	169 (5)
Corn germ	10	109 (5)	177 (5)
Sunflower seed	10	115 (5)	186 (5)
Brewer's yeast	10	180 (4)	229 (4)

The numbers in parentheses refer to numbers of rats used.

The growth, as well as the appearance of the animals, clearly show that sunflower seed meal fed at low levels is appreciably superior even to wheat-germ and corn-germ meals at comparable levels as a source of all the necessary B complex vitamins. It is far superior to defatted soybean meal and decidedly inferior to brewer's yeast in this respect.

In the experiments with other rats fed the basal ration containing 5 per cent of the sunflower seed meal the growth rate was not accelerated by daily supplements of thiamin, riboflavin, calcium pantothenate or pyridoxine. Slight acceleration of growth occurred when both thiamin and riboflavin were fed. Growth was markedly increased by administration of these two vitamins plus calcium pantothenate. In fact, it approximated the rate in rats fed yeast at a 10 per cent level. The growth of rats given all 4 vitamin supplements was no greater than that in animals receiving only thiamin, riboflavin and calcium pantothenate. Detailed analysis of the data shows that pantothenic acid and riboflavin are limiting factors for growth in sunflower seed meal fed at the 5 per cent level.

[359]

The sunflower seed meal is a light gray palatable powder. It can be satisfactorily blended with white flour and corn meal to make appetizing baked foods (as shown by the wife of one of us—H. G. D.).

These results reemphasize the importance of examining some of the ordinary, but neglected food materials available to us. They show that in common with wheat germ and corn germ,[5] sunflower seed may be of much more practical value in nutrition than has been recognized hitherto.

HARRY G. DAY
EZRA LEVIN

Department of Chemistry
Indiana University
Monticello, Illinois

1. *Foreign Commerce Weekly,* 17:37, 1944.
2. G. Ganchev and I. D. Popov, *Ann. univ. Sofia. V. Faculte agron. sylvicult.* 14:209-38, 1936; *Chem Abstr.,* 31:3968, 1937.
3. H. H. Mitchell, T. S. Hamilton and J. R. Beadles, *Jour. Nutr.,* 29:13-25, 1945.
4. Council on Foods and Nutrition. "Handbook of Nutrition." American Medical Association, Chicago. 1943.
5. Council on Foods and Nutrition, *Jour. Am. Med. Assn.,* 125:848-49, 1944.

CHAPTER 101

Questions about Production

By Eric D. Putt, Agronomist

What kind of a crop is sunflowers?

The sunflower crop is a cash crop. It is an intertilled row crop and thus is a cleaning crop and partial summer fallow substitute. The varieties used for seed production are of dwarf type growing 4 to 5 feet high.

What type of land is best for sunflowers?

Sunflowers will do well on almost any type of soil but will do better in comparison with grain crops on lighter type soils. Heavy, low lying or poorly drained soils should be avoided.

Do sunflowers require summerfallow?

No. Sunflowers, like most crops, will probably do best on summerfallow, but as they are an intertilled cleaning crop it is recommended that they be sown on stubble land and the summerfallow used for grain crops.

What crops should sunflowers follow?

Sunflowers are best following a cereal crop such as wheat, oats, or barley.

They should not follow potatoes, beets, sweet clover or alfalfa.

What crops should follow sunflowers?

Farmers' experience indicates that oats is the best crop following sunflowers. Barley, wheat or flax can also be used. Flax is not advised unless arrangements can be made for spraying to control volunteers.

Can I plant sunflowers two years in succession on the same land?

Planting the same crop two years in succession is not good cultural practice. Especially is this true of sunflowers. They should not be sown on the same land more than once in 4 years.

Are sunflowers hard on the land?

No definite information is available on this question. Generally speaking a crop of sunflowers will take more out of the land than a crop of corn but less than one of grain. However, some growers feel that sunflowers will leave the land in as good condition as corn or summerfallow.

Do I need any special machinery for handling the sunflower crop?

The only special machinery needed for handling the sunflower crop is a row crop cultivator. Some farmers have even adapted their ordinary field cultivators to row crops by removing part of the shovels, but a better job of weeding can be done with the standard row crop cultivator.

What variety should I grow?

Advance first generation hybrid is the best variety to grow for seed purposes. Advance second generation is recommended where first generation is not available. The second generation yields 10 to 15 per cent lower than the first generation and is not as uniform. It also shatters more easily than first generation. Sunrise is not recommended because of low yield. Mennonite is not recommended because its seed has low oil content and brings a lower price than other varieties on the market.

Can I grow sunflowers in check rows?

Sunflowers can be grown in check rows, and on dirty fields weed control may be easier when they are grown this way. Yields will not be as high as from seeding in solid rows.

How many plants per hill should there be if check rows are used?

Careful study of samples from check row fields in 1947 shows that 4 or 5 plants per hill will give higher yields than any lower number.

[361]

If I seed in solid rows how wide apart should the rows be?

No figures are available comparing yields from different spacing of the rows. Growers usually seed in 36 inch or 42 inch rows. It is likely that 36 inch rows will yield better than wider spacings.

How many pounds of seed per acre should I plant?

The following rates of seeding are recommended for Advance first generation sized seed. These rates are based on a seed every 5 or 6 inches of row length. All figures are in pounds.

Seed Size	42 in.	36 in.	42 in. check
Small	3¼	3¾	2½
Medium	4	4½	3
Large	4¾	5½	3½

These rates seem too heavy. If the plants are only 5 or 6 inches apart won't the heads be small and give a poor yield?

Careful studies over a 5 year period at Saskatoon, Saskatchewan, and samples from fields in 1947 in the sunflower growing area show that these seeding rates will give better yields than any lighter rate. Some farmers have even reported excellent yields from 6 to 7 pounds per acre of seed. Besides best yields these heavy rates give smaller heads which dry out faster in the fall and are easier to handle at harvest time. They also give smaller seed which does not crack as easily in the combine and which has higher weight per bushel and higher oil content.

Where can I buy this sized seed of Advance first generation hybrid that you mention in answer to above question?

This seed can be purchased from Co-op. Vegetable Oils Limited, Altona, Manitoba, Canada.

What do the different sizes mean?

All seed being handled by the Co-op. Vegetable Oils Limited is first cleaned and then divided into 3 sizes. The different sizes are to give samples which will flow more uniformly in planting machinery than unsized seed. There should be no difference in the quality of different sizes or in their yielding ability.

What planting machinery should I use?

The majority of growers use either corn planters or beet planters. Special plates are required for the best planters. Some of the best fields, however, have come from planting with the ordinary grain drill. By closing off runs the correct spacing between the rows can be secured.

What date should sunflowers be planted?

As a general statement planting about May 15 to May 20 is correct. Date of planting will vary with the season. If possible it is advisable to destroy one crop of small weeds before planting. Early planting should be practiced in areas where the season is short. There is little danger of frost damage on early plantings as the young plants are quite resistant to frost injury. Planting late in May or in June must be avoided. There is a large drop in yield from late planting and an extra danger of damage by fall frosts.

What type of seedbed should be used?

A firm seedbed is best. In areas where soil drifting is a danger a lumpy condition or some trash cover is also desirable.

How deep should sunflowers be planted?

The seed must be planted deep enough to have it in moist soil. It can be planted up to 4 inches deep. Shallower planting, however, will give a more rapid emergence providing the seed is in moisture.

Does the seed require treatment?

Seed treatment is good cultural practice for any crop. Rates up to one and one-half ounces per bushel of Arasan or New Improved Ceresan seem satisfactory for sunflowers.

What cultivation is needed during the growing season?

The amount of cultivation will vary with the weed condition of the field. Common practice is to cross harrow with a light harrow just before emergence and once or twice after emergence to control small weeds. This harrowing should be done on a warm clear day to secure the best weed control and least injury to the sunflower plants. One shallow cultivation between the rows running as close as possible to them, followed by one or two deeper cultivations throwing the soil towards the rows should be sufficient. Deep cultivation should not go close to the rows as there is always danger of cutting off roots and injuring the plants.

Does the crop need to be hand hoed?

If machine cultivation is done at the right time and a heavy rate of seeding used, hand hoeing should not be necessary. Many growers do hand hoe, but some of the cleanest fields seen in 1947 had only been machine cultivated.

What date does the crop mature?

When planted about May 15 the crop is usually safe from frost damage by September 10. The fields are usually dry enough to commence harvesting in mid-October.

What type of combine is needed for harvesting the crop?

The main requirement in a combine is that it have a rub bar type cylinder. The small "straight through" machines do very good work but almost any machine will do a satisfactory job. In the larger machines, the auger type is preferable because there are no canvasses for heads and stalks to catch in.

What special adjustments are necessary for the combine?

Cylinder speed must be reduced to one-half or less of that for grain. Concaves must be opened as wide as possible. The reel must be filled in solid with thin boards. The outermost slat is often set at an angle of about 30 degrees to the others. Some farmers also raise the height of the reel and move it forward. Such adjustment requires a longer reel arm as the reel must sweep close to the cutter bar. The number of slats is also often reduced from 6 to 4.

On auger machines the cutter bar is usually raised 6 to 9 inches and moved forward by the same distance to avoid loss from heads being thrown out by the auger. This change requires an extension of the pitman.

Many farmers have also adopted large guards or "grain savers." These guards are about 3½ feet long and about 4 inches narrower than the row width, made of sheet metal reinforced with angle iron at the edges. They are in the shape of an inverted curve with the crest of the curve slightly ahead of the point where the reel strikes the heads. Seed shattered by the reel drops on these "savers" and flows back to the table. At the same time the low front end catches low hanging heads and raises them to the cutter bar.

Does the seed have to be dry before it can be stored?

The safe moisture level for storage of seed under all weather conditions is 9.5 per cent. During cold weather the seed can be safely stored with 12 per cent moisture.

What yield per acre can I expect?

In areas where the sunflowers have been grown yields range from 500 to 1500 pounds per acre, with an average yield of 800 to 900 pounds.

What is the weight per bushel?

Twenty-five pounds can be taken as a fair average weight per bushel.

How much dockage is there in sunflowers?

Dockage of seed ranges from one to 15 per cent with an average of about 4 per cent. The amount of dockage depends mainly on the skill of the combine operator.

Where can I sell sunflower seed?

So far the Canadian Wheat Board through its agent Co-op. Vegetable Oils Limited, has purchased all sunflower seed grown in Canada. If the Wheat Board ceases to purchase, then Co-op. Vegetable Oils will purchase on its own account.

Can I sell the seed at the time of harvest or must I store it?

Some seed will have to be stored. The Co-op. Vegetable Oils plant has storage space for four million pounds. In 1947, at harvest time a quota of 200 pounds per acre was accepted. This quota was increased to 400 pounds in December and 700 pounds on January 1, 1948.

I have heard that there is too much seed already. Is this true?

No. There is good authority for stating that 3 or 4 times the present production of sunflower seed could be used in Western Canada alone.

What products are made from sunflower seed?

The hull is first removed from the seed. The meats are then processed into oil and seed cake meal.

What is the oil used for?

The oil is a high quality human food. It is being processed mainly into shortening by packing house firms. Small quantities are used locally for domestic deep frying and baking. Commercial bakeries also use limited amounts in their products without any further refining.

What is the meal used for?

The meal is a high quality protein feed concentrate used for blending into livestock feed, particularly poultry mashes. It also shows promise as a human food.

What is the hull used for?

The hull is being ground and used as a base for blending with more concentrated feeds. It is also used as poultry litter and livestock bedding. It shows greatest promise of being used as fuel in the form of a log produced by high pressure.

Co-op. Vegetable Oils Ltd., Altona, Manitoba, Canada, January, 1948.

CHAPTER 102

Sunflower Seeds Are Worthwhile

It is difficult to find a staple of our forefather's diet that is still intact, still unadulterated with additives or by processing procedures. One such product is the sunflower seed. It was a very important part of the Hopi Indian's diet. He depended upon sunflower seeds for flour and oil, and it also served as a sustaining food in its original form. The stalks of the plant made excellent fuel for the fires, and the ashes left by these fires became rich fertilizer for future crops.

One of the most attractive things about sunflowers is that just about anyone with a patch of ground can raise his own. This dish-sized flower will grow almost anywhere, and there's little need for special care. Many gardeners consider it almost a weed, and find it wise to keep an eye on this prolific plant lest it move in on the more ordered parts of the flower-bed. This means, of course, that sunflowers usually don't need the encouragement of fertilizer—artificial or otherwise. They are also resistant to disease and this limits the likelihood of insecticides and other chemical sprays being used on them.

A Handsome and Interesting Plant

Those who are not familiar with the sunflower will find it a handsome, interesting plant. The flower, usually one or two to a stalk, is huge, sometimes 16 inches in diameter, and it resembles the conception of the sun that children often show in their art work—a large flat face with a rim of large petals that are flat and triangular in shape. Each of these flowers keeps busy through the day, following the sun across the sky from east to west, a peculiarity known as helitropism.

The flat face of the sunflower is actually a mosaic of sunflower seeds, and when the flower dries, they are easily dislodged. A cupful is the minimal yield from a big flower. Hulling the seeds by hand takes some time, but one can use a small farm hammer mill for hulling quickly and in quantity. Simply remove the screens of the mill and set it running at 350 R.P.M. Use a technometer so no hulled seeds go up the dust collector. Pour the seeds slowly into the machine (about two gallons), then speed the mill to about 1200 to 1500 R.P.M. This keeps the bottom of the mill clear. Now you have the seeds hulled.

A Kernel of Sun

Just what is it that makes sunflower seeds worth the effort? An article in *Magazine Digest* (September 1951) described them as "a little sunlamp in your digestive system" which is beneficial to eyesight, complexion, fingernails and acts as a curb on high blood pressure and jumpy nerves. The article goes on to say that the United States Department of Agriculture rates the protein content of sunflower seeds nearly as high as steak and higher than all other vegetable seeds. And with the protein come calcium, phosphorus, iron, vitamin A, nitrogen, thiamin, riboflavin, niacin (B vitamins) and vitamin E.

The Valuable Oil Sunflower Seeds Offer

Another valuable property of sunflower seeds is the oil they contain. *Chemurgic Digest* (September, 1948) sets the percentage of oil in the meat of the seeds, after hulling, at 51 per cent. This oil is loaded with the unsaturated fatty acids the body needs so desperately. They are the fats that enrich human mother's milk in much greater quantities than are found in the milk of cows and other animals. They are the same fats which are stored carefully in the heart, liver, kidney, brain, blood and muscles. Many researchers have related shortages of unsaturated fatty acids to skin diseases such as eczema, boils and acne. In *Vitamins and Minerals* by Bicknell and Prescott it is suggested that the fatty acids are an important factor in the absorption of other fats, and hence a shortage can be a cause of diarrhea and underweight, among other problems.

The attraction of sunflower seeds as a source of these valuable unsaturated fatty acids becomes even more apparent when we realize that these fats are becoming less and less available. Many of the foods which contain them are so completely processed that these acids either disappear or are transformed into uselessness. Any hydrogenated vegetable oil has lost most of whatever unsaturated fatty acids it contained. High heat also destroys them. Imagine the shortages endured by families who live on a diet of fried foods, using margarine as a spread and eat little or no salad. Avoid any vegetable shortening that is solid in form, for it has been hydrogenated, and use immense salads with your meals coated with plenty of vegetable oil—any kind: peanut, olive, sunflower seed, corn, etc.

Some Immediate Benefits

The immediate benefits of using sunflower seeds may or may not make themselves felt, but many who use the seeds claim remarkable results. Editor Rodale has found them to be especially good for the eyesight. He is convinced that a daily intake of these seeds acts as an excellent protective against the glare of the summer sun, eliminating any need he might have for sunglasses. Not the least of all, Mr. Rodale credits sunflower seeds with an actual improvement in vision that had been physiologically impaired.

Other readers reported improvement in arthritis, colitis and constipation conditions. It would not be an easy task to name many equally palatable foods so rich in nutrition and so effective in retaining or achieving good health. You should be getting a handful of this delightful snack every day.

CHAPTER 103

What Do Sunflower Seeds Contain?

We have received a report compiled in a laboratory of the content of sunflower seeds so far as vitamins and minerals are concerned. We think this should be of great interest to all readers.

The figures are given in terms of 100 grams, which is about ¼ pound. In cases where a minimum daily requirement has been set for a vitamin or a mineral, we give the percentage of that requirement which is furnished by ¼ pound of sunflower seeds. It is well to remember in this connection that those vitamins and minerals for which minimum requirements have not been set are necessary, too, and may be necessary in quite large amounts. But, officially, the research has not been done which shows exactly how much of each of these must be in the diet.

Then, too, you should keep in mind that getting far more than the recommended minimum generally means increased good health.

MINERALS			Per Cent of Official Daily Minimum
Iron	6.0	milligrams	60%
Phosphorus	860	"	115
Calcium	57	"	7.6
Iodine	.07	"	70
Magnesium	347	"	
Potassium	630	"	
Manganese	25	ppm	
Copper	20	ppm	
Sodium	.4	milligrams	
Fluorine	2.6	ppm	

VITAMINS			Per Cent of Official Daily Minimum
Vitamin B			
Thiamin	2.2	milligrams	220%
Riboflavin	.28	"	24
Niacin	5.6	"	56
Pyridoxine	1.1	"	
Para-amino-benzoic acid	62	"	
Biotin	.067	"	
Choline	216	"	
Folic Acid	.1	"	
Inositol	147.	"	
Pantothenic Acid	2.2	"	

			Per Cent of Official Daily Minimum
Vitamin D	92	International Units	23
Vitamin E	31	International Units	
Protein	25%		
Oil	48%	(90% of this being the valuable unsaturated fatty acids.)	
Carbohydrate	15.15%		

Let's talk about these figures for a moment. How do sunflower seeds compare with other foods in the essential nutrients?

Some foods rich in iron are: wheat germ (8.1 milligrams), almonds (4.4 milligrams), liver (6 to 18 milligrams), egg yolk (7.2 milligrams). Sunflower seed compares very favorably with these. Of course, we would expect the seeds to be rich in phosphorus and low in calcium as this is a characteristic of practically all seed foods.

The iodine content might differ with different locales. Seeds raised in parts of the country where there is plenty of iodine in the soil would probably contain more iodine. The potassium and magnesium content are very high. Compare the 630 milligrams of potassium with 720 milligrams in the same amount of raisins, 780 milligrams in wheat germ, 400 to 700 in various nuts, from 100 to 800 in vegetables of various kinds. These are foods that are, in general, higher in potassium than any others.

The magnesium content is even more abundant. The 347 milligrams of magnesium listed are more than we can find record of in any other food. Even such a nutritious food as soy flour contains only 223 milligrams. Almonds contain 252, Brazil nuts contain 225.

The fluorine content of sunflower seeds is not high. In fact, we were surprised to find that it is so low. Most foods contain fluorine. This is one of the reasons why we cannot understand the arguments for adding fluorides to the water supply. The average diet contains far more fluorine than anyone has suggested putting into the water supply. Potatoes, for instance, contain from .07 to 6.40 parts per million of fluorine. Fish contains 1.60 to 9.00 parts per million. An infusion of tea—that is, tea as you drink it—may contain 60 parts per million.

Vitamins in the Seeds

So far as B vitamins are concerned, it is well to keep in mind that these are among the most important food elements for modern man, living in a world where refined foods are the rule of the day. All of the B vitamins have been removed from refined foods and only small fractions of one or two of them have been replaced, by the use of synthetic vitamins.

Important factors like choline, pyridoxine and inositol are missing from so-called "enriched" foods. These 3 B vitamins are absolutely essential for the health of heart and blood vessels. They are related to the way the body uses fat. Whether or not you are eventually going to get hardening of the arteries may have a great deal to do with how much of these 3 B vitamins you have in your diet today. Sunflower seeds are an important source.

[369]

Vitamin E is the essential vitamin for heart and blood vessel health. It enables the tissues of your body to get along with less oxygen. The vitamin E content of sunflower seed makes this food one of the best foods you can eat. Combined with the vitamin E is the valuable oil which makes up almost half the total volume of the seed. Practically all of this is the unsaturated fat that is so valuable a preventive of cholesterol deposits. This fat has also been mentioned in connection with skin and hair health and the prevention of prostate gland disorders. It is a part of food that can be obtained only in cereal and vegetable oils and unrefined foods like nuts, whole grains and seeds. Everyone needs it. Finally, sunflower seeds are 25 per cent protein—putting them on the same protein level as meat.

And you will find that children who are regularly given sunflower seeds rather than candy will come to prefer them to sweets.

Candy gives them nothing but empty calories. Sunflower seeds give them all the wealth of good, healthful eating listed above!

CHAPTER 104

Sunflower Seeds Are Rich in Zinc

There is evidence to show that there may be a possible relation between zinc in the diet and the health of the prostate gland. The normal gland contains more of this mineral than any other organ in the body. Sperm cells contain more zinc than any other part of the gland. Although no final facts are at hand, it seems evident that a diet seriously lacking in zinc might be at least partly responsible for trouble with the gland—a very common condition among men past middle age.

We are told that sunflower seeds contain 66.5 parts per million of zinc. Compare this to the following foods all of which are higher than most foods in the mineral:

Food	Parts per million of zinc	Food	Parts per million of zinc
Barley	27	Milk, cow	4-30
Beef	20-50	Oatmeal	140
Beets	28	Oysters	1600
Cabbage	2-15	Peanut Butter	20
Carrots	5-36	Peas	30-50
Clams	20	Rice	15
Corn	25	Syrup, maple	52-105
Eggs, dry, whole	55	Spinach	3-9
Egg Yolk	26-40	Wheat Bran	140
Herrings	700-1200	Yeast, brewer's	80
Liver, beef	30-85		

CHAPTER 105

Oil and Protein Content
of Sunflower Seed

By C. O. Clagett, George W. Hoffman and Ingmar Sollin

Sunflower seed has been grown for mercantile purposes for the past 100 years, initially in eastern European areas. Its cultivation has spread to all parts of the world including the United States, although production in this country has been rather limited. Prior to 1947 most of the seed grown in this country has been used for feed for poultry and hogs.

Quite recently Canada has become a major producer, probably because of the need for a domestic source of edible oils. The current dwarf varieties, developed by Canadian research, are more easily harvested and in addition produce a higher yield of better quality seeds than earlier varieties.

In 1947, a Minneapolis commission house encouraged the production of these dwarf varieties in North Dakota by guaranteeing a market for the seeds at a price pegged to the flax seed value, based on oil content. This industry price support was dropped in March 1948, but in the short time it was in effect, considerable interest was developed in the crop as can be seen from Table I below.

North Dakota farmers need an inter-tilled crop in the cash grain area west of the Red River Valley to help control weeds. Sunflowers are a hardy drought resistant crop which may serve this purpose.

Table I—ESTIMATE BY YEARS OF SUNFLOWER SEED PRODUCTION IN NORTH DAKOTA *DATA SOURCE NOTED UNDER CHART—AS PER TABLE III (DATA FROM OFFICE OF AGRICULTURAL STATISTICIAN, FARGO, N. D., BAE, USDA.)

Year	Acres Harvested	Yield Lbs. per acre	Total Production
1947	3,500	800	2,800,000
1948	22,000	800	17,600,000
1949	10,000	750	7,500,000
1950	4,700	800	3,760,000

Whether the sunflower will become an important crop depends to a large extent on the development of markets for the seeds.

The meat of the sunflower seed is surrounded with a tough shell or hull. This hull must be removed before processing the seed both for maximum yields of oil and to make the meal satisfactory for protein supplements.

If hulls are not removed, the meal obtained is excessively high in fiber and cannot be used as a protein supplement to poultry rations. Numerous experiments have shown that the hulls can be used for the production of furfural, a solvent used very extensively in the petroleum and synthetic rubber industry. The hulls have also been pressed into molded fireplace logs. The hulls constitute 36 to 46 per cent of the weight of the seed.

Sunflower Seed Oil

After the hulls are removed the oil can be satisfactorily expressed or extracted in the same type of mills used now for the removal of linseed oil and soybean oil.

The oil has a pale yellow color, a mild taste and a pleasant odor. It is used principally as an edible oil and should be quite desirable as a salad oil because of its stability and flavor retention. We have had samples exposed to laboratory temperatures for a period of 3 years with no apparent development of rancidity or off flavors. Furthermore, there was no detectable change in the chemical composition of the oil. . . .

Table II—COMPARISON OF ANALYSES OF SUNFLOWER SEED OILS FROM VARIOUS PARTS OF THE WORLD (PERCENTAGE OF FATTY ACIDS BY WEIGHT.)

| Habitat | Saturated | | Higher Fatty | |
	Fats	Oleic	Linoleic	Acids
India (1)	9.73	49.41	40.48	....
Congo (1)	5.3	42.0	52.0	0.7
North China (2)	8.3	37.4	53.6	0.4
Russia (1)	9.6	36.2	54.2	....
Missouri (U.S.A.) (3)	6.4	34.1	58.5	1.0
Kenya (4)	14	17	69	....
S. Rhodesia (4)	14	14	72	....
North Dakota (5)	11.7	14.1	72.8	1.4

Sunflower seed oil would be classed as a semi-drying oil. Film formation can be expected if sufficient drying time is permitted. By modification of the oil it should be possible to prepare alkid resins with favorable properties for indoor coatings where yellowing is a factor.

Numerous investigations of the fatty acid content of the oil have been made. As might be expected, the analyses varied considerably with the source of the seed and the variety of seed used. Table II lists analyses of some sunflower seed oils reported in the literature.

From this table it is seen that the analyses of oils from seed (Sunrise variety) grown in North Dakota differ appreciably from values previously reported for this country. The values reported by Jamieson and Baughman (3) were based on Mammoth Russian variety. Milner et al. (6) reported averages for 4 varieties (Mennonite, Sunrise, Greystripe, and Manchurian) grown at 7 stations as far north as Ames, Iowa, which were in agreement with the values of the Missouri seed of Jamieson. The values obtained for the North Dakota crop are quite similar to the values reported for the South Rhodesia crop.

In order to determine whether the values for linoleic acid found in the Sunrise varieties were characteristic of North Dakota grown seeds in general, a number of additional samples were examined for this one component. A detailed analysis of a large number of oils is not feasible because of the time and cost factors involved. However, by use of spectrophotometric methods it is fairly simple to determine the major component, linoleic acid, and at the same time determine the presence or absence of linoleic acid. We examined a number of samples from field grown crops and of seeds obtained from the Fargo experimental plots. Six samples of seeds from field grown crops or oil obtained from commercial sources pressed from seeds grown in this area contained 72 to 75 per cent linoleic acid. Oil from seeds grown in the experimental plots showed a lower content (55 to 68 per cent). Immaturity of the seed at the time of harvest may have been a factor in these low values.

Many vegetable oils show a precipitation or separating out of certain components on long refrigeration. Even highly unsaturated linseed oil shows this property. None of the samples of sunflower seed oil thus far have shown any separation.

Sunflower seed oil should find a ready place in the food trade because of the stability of the oil to development of rancidity. It should also find a market in the protective coatings field, where an oil of uniform composition is desired by paint and varnish manufacturers.

Sunflower Seed Proteins

After the extraction of the oil from the dehulled seeds a protein rich residue or meal remains. This meal has been studied by a number of laboratories both from the standpoint of the use of the meal as a livestock protein supplement and as a source of industrial proteins.

In protein content sunflower seed meal tops the list of vegetable concentrates, having around 52.5 per cent. If the kernels are completely dehulled it is comparatively low in crude fibre and for a concentrate of plant origin it is unusually rich in calcium and phosphorus. It is an excellent source of thiamin or vitamin B_1 and niacin and for a plant concentrate it is comparatively rich in riboflavin. There are some indications that the riboflavin as indicated in chemical analyses is not all available for growth of the animal.

The quality of the protein of the sunflower seed meal has been checked by laboratories using as experiment animals the white rat, poultry, and swine. Experiments indicated that the protein in defatted meal was very digestible. Biological value was 64.5 per cent. This places sunflower seed protein in the same class as wheat and definitely superior to raw soybean protein and corn protein. Experimental work at the University of California showed that sunflower seed meal as a supplement to laying mash was equally as effective as heat treated soybean meal from the standpoint of

[373]

average egg production and mortality in the flock. The Missouri Agricultural Experiment Station found that sunflower seed meal fed with corn replaced tankage in swine production with no loss of effectiveness of the ration. The Illinois Agricultural Experimental Station obtained similar results in paired feeding trials.

Table III—*SUNFLOWER SEED MEAL: COMPOSITION COMPARED WITH OTHER HIGH PROTEIN FEEDS AND WITH FLOUR.

	Crude Protein %	Calcium %	Phosphorus %	Vitamins per Pound (Vit. B₁) Thiamin mg.	Riboflavin mg.	Niacin mg.
Sunflower Seed Meal	52.8	.57	.58	16.5	2.2	136
Cotton Seed Meal	43.7	.33	.77	2.0	6.7	18.
Linseed Meal	40.4	.18	1.15	5.8	2.8	22
Corn Gluten Meal	43.	.10	.47		.4	14
Wheat Flour, Patent	10.8	.02	.09	.07	.03	0.8
Wheat Flour, Whole	13.0	.04	.38	.56	.12	5.6

*Data from University of Illinois, Ag. Exp. Station, Circ. 608. (1947)

The home economics department at the University of Illinois also conducted some interesting experiments on the use of sunflower seed flour for human consumption. They tested sunflower seed flour additions to plain, spice, and chocolate cakes and in griddle cakes, muffins and yeast rolls, in each case replacing a part of the white patent flour with the sunflower seed flour. In their experiments, sunflower seed flour was a finely divided sample of sunflower seed meal prepared from completely dehulled solvent extracted meats or kernels. Many of the products containing 10 per cent of sunflower seed flour were reported as being delicious.

It could not be used successfully in light colored products as the addition of sunflower seed meal developed a gray cast. Dark colored products would completely mask this gray cast. The gray color in these products is known to be due to the oxidation of a rather complex organic component called chlorogenic acid found in the kernel. The use of sunflower seed flour certainly increased the protein and vitamin contents of baked products. The Illinois experimenters report added flavor, increased loaf volume and a richer brown crust color.

Smith and Johnson (7) recently investigated sunflower seed meal from the standpoint of the industrial utilization of the protein fraction. They found that the protein could be dispersed very readily with dilute alkali and precipitated by the addition of acids. The resulting proteins had an objectionable dark color which could not be removed by extraction with alcohol or similar solvents. The color of the proteins is caused by the oxidation of chlorogenic acid, mentioned above. Work in the agricultural chemical laboratory at North Dakota Agricultural College has shown that this color formation can be prevented by the addition of small quantities of sodium sulphite to the dispersing medium. Furthermore the resulting protein could be redispersed following precipitation and drying without formation of color. Apparently sufficient sodium sulphite is absorbed to the precipitated protein to prevent oxidation of chlorogenic acid in the redispersed protein.

Proteins have been used industrially for the preparation of adhesives or glues. Bone, hide and casein glues have been used very extensively since earliest recorded history. Recently plant proteins, particularly soybean proteins, have been used in the preparation of adhesives. Many thousands of tons are used for this purpose yearly.

From time to time proteins have been suggested as components for preparation of plastics. Casein from milk has been used quite extensively. In the middle thirty's soybean proteins were suggested for use and have been used rather successfully in the production of some plastics. An interesting example is the use made by the Ford Motor Company for the preparation of decorative trims during that period. Proteins have also been used quite extensively in the preparation of coatings and facings for paper. Approximately 75 per cent of the casein produced in America is used for this purpose. A number of synthetic fibers have been produced from plant proteins. However, none of these has been generally accepted as a substitute for wool or the other synthetic fibers of the nylon or similar types.

Sunflower seed proteins may have properties which would enable them to compete with other proteins in the preparation of these industrial products.

BIBLIOGRAPHY

(1) Singh and Kumar, Proc. Indian Acad. Sci., 26A, 205 (1947).
(2) Ueno and Wan, J. Agr. Chem. Soc. Japan, 17, 735 (1943), cf. C. A., 43, 882 (1949).
(3) Jamieson and Baughman, J. Am. Chem. Soc., 44, 2952 (1922).
(4) Hilditch, J. Oil and Colour Chemists Assoc., 32, 5 (1949), cf. C. A., 43, 4025 (1949).
(5) Ingmar Sollin, The Component Fatty Acids of the Oil From a North Dakota Sample of *Helianthus annus* L., Master's Thesis, Department of Agricultural Chemistry, Agricultural College, 1949.
(6) Milner, Hubbard and Wiele, Oil and Soap, 22, 304 (1945).
(7) Smith and Johnson, Cereal Chem., 25, 399 (1948).

Bulletin of North Carolina Agricultural Experiment Station

CHAPTER 106

The Story of a Quiver

By J. I. Rodale

About 5 years ago there developed in my left eye a slight quiver, which did not seem to want to go away. That was bad for an editor of a health magazine. I let a few weeks pass, thinking that, like a ship that passes in the night, it would go away. I closed my eyes to it, but it persisted.

I thought back to about 10 years ago when a similar intermittent quiver in my left eye went away. I reported earlier, this condition was relieved thanks to the fact that I ate sunflower seeds practically every day.

Well, I seemed to have gotten careless, and had stopped eating sunflower seeds somewhere along the line. So I began eating them again. But I had none of our own organically-raised ones. The previous year's crop of them had been fed to the chickens. So I began to eat some hulled seeds that we had around the house and that had been purchased some months before. I ate them for several weeks, but nothing happened.

Along about October our new crop ripened and I began to eat our own seeds. Within 3 days my eye quiver vanished, but before I could start crowing, that is about two days after that, it returned in fairly full vigor.

"Hm," said I. "This is more serious than I thought. But I must track this thing down. There must be *some* cause." There always are causes and they can be found if one keeps one's mind at it. It is a matter of a little thinking plus a little of trial and error.

Incriminating My Pillow

The next thing that I tried to incriminate was my pillow. Years ago I had a pain in the neck which evidently was caused solely by sleeping on a pillow. Crooking the head causes a bend in the jugular vein of the neck. The veins become wrinkled at the point of bend, and congestion of the blood circulation occurs there. There is not a free flow of blood to and from the head. Within a few days of learning to sleep flat, the pain completely cleared up—but completely. A few months ago I heard one of the girls in our circulation department complaining of a pain in the neck. I described my own experience to her and in a very short time she completely rid herself of it—solely by sleeping without a pillow.

Here again I had gotten careless, and a few years ago had resorted to the pillow again. Nothing happened by sleeping on a pillow this time; that is, the pain in the neck did not return. But now I began to suspect the pillow in connection with my eye quiver. If there was a congestion in the mechanism that feeds blood to the head, perhaps the eyes weren't

[376]

getting enough blood. So I began to sleep without a pillow. A few weeks went by but the quiver remained—and I was exactly where I started.

I noticed, however, that when I took my glasses off, the quiver was less marked. I don't want to give you a wrong impression. The eye did not quiver constantly—it was an intermittent thing. But with the glasses off it was a little more intermittent. My glasses could have something to do with it, thought I. The next day saw me at the optometrist, my personal friend. "It could be one of two things," he said. "Either it is a calcium deficiency, or your left eye has either improved or gotten worse, that is, the lens for your left eye might need correction."

Vision Improved

Now I knew that it couldn't be a calcium deficiency, with all the bone meal I take, and the doctor knew it, too. I now felt sure that the vision of my left eye had improved. Why? Because on the several previous occasions that I had gone up for routine eye checkups there had been slight improvements in my vision. The doctor began the test, and lo and behold, he found that the vision in my left eye had improved. Within 3 or 4 hours, after wearing the glasses with the new, slightly weakened lens, my eye quiver disappeared. That was on October 24, 1955. Today, December 31, 1955, the cure has held with nary a quiver.

Here are the comparative measurements of my lenses:

September 18, 1951
Right	3.50 SPH	1.75 Cyl. Axis	180
Left	4.00 SPH	1.25 Cyl. Axis	12

October 24, 1955
Right	3.00 SPH	1.50 Cyl. Axis	180
Left	3.50 SPH	0.75 Cyl. Axis	7

It seems to be a progressively improving trend and I can attribute it mainly to my nutritional program. I believe the fact that I take no artificial sugar, that I am on a no-salt diet, that I eat no bread or dairy products, that I drink no carbonated beverages, that I take many vitamins and minerals, are all factors in the improvement of my eyesight. Vitamin A (Halibut liver oil perles) is specific for the eyes. Vitamin E, of which I take huge amounts, is also very important. It oxygenates the tissues everywhere in the body. It, therefore, helps the blood circulation to the eyes. The minerals in bone meal help in the mineralization of the blood, and make it a chemically better food for the eyes; etc., etc., etc.

Soft Drinks and the Eyes

May I pause a moment in regard to soft drinks and quote from our *Health Finder*, page 749: "We report on the point of view of Dr. Hunter H. Turner in an article in the *Pennsylvania Medical Journal* for May, 1944, on the subject of prevention of myopia or degenerative nearsightedness. Lamenting over the large numbers of Americans who are doomed to wear glasses, he suggests that incorrect diet undoubtedly plays an important

[377]

role in producing myopia. Furthermore, he believes that carbonic acid is the eye's worst enemy and he attributes the alarming increase in cases of myopia to the pernicious guzzling of carbonated beverages by young children today. Carbonated beverages exposed to air break down into their basic ingredients of water and carbon dioxide, so that such drinks would be much less harmful if they were allowed to stand until they were 'flat.' But, of course, their most attractive characteristic is their 'fizz.' So they are taken into the stomach while they are still actively effervescing. There is no atmospheric pressure in the stomach, so a large amount of the acid is assimilated by the body."

And yet medical journals regularly accept the advertisements of soft drink manufacturers. Here is one sponsored by The American Bottlers of Carbonated Beverages, which appeared in a medical journal recently. The heading is, "The 'catalyst' of everybody's love of carbonated soft drink is CO_2!" It says further that CO_2 "speeds up the digestive processes . . ." but what does it do to the eyes? And who wants to speed up the digestive processes?

Now let's go back to my eyesight. I have not gone in for eye exercises because I did not wish to confuse the issue. I would like to know whether eyesight can be improved solely through nutrition. I feel certain that, had I added eye exercise to my program, the improvement would have been greater, but then I would never have been sure—was it my nutrition, or was it the eye exercises?

Another fact: Many persons believe that overuse of the eyes in close work will eventually ruin the eyesight. Cases in point are the famous authors Thurber, Tarkington and Milton. That may be so where the nutrition is poor, but given the proper nourishment based on the newer knowledge as we know it, the eyes will be able to stand a terrific amount of abuse. In my own case, I have been terrifically over-using my eyes in close work for the last 10 years, and yet my eyesight is actually improving, and what is of even more importance, my doctor tells me that examination reveals an unusually healthy organic condition of the whole eye organ; that is, there is not the slightest evidence of cataracts or other eye disease.

Sunflower Seeds in the Diet

Now let's go back to sunflower seeds. Although they did not cure my eye quiver, I observed a remarkable effect through eating them. About 10 years ago, a heavy book fell on my left foot, hitting the right half of the big toenail, and blacking that part of it. After about 6 months, as the blackness did not show any signs of going away, I went to an Allentown surgeon who treated it by cutting the right half of the nail right down to the base. I would come to see him each week, and as the nail grew back, he would continue to cut it back. But the blackness remained. After a few months of this unsuccessful treatment, I stopped going.

For 4 years I watched that nail and the right half of it continued to remain black. There was absolutely no pain to it, and I felt a feeling of security due to my excellent nutrition. I knew that my vitamin E was keeping the circulation active in my feet. One day, early in the morning, while I was indulging in my usual one-hour walk on the soft turf of the Allentown Fair Grounds, whom should I meet but my old surgeon friend, riding his horse! He stopped, and we exchanged a few words. I told him that my nail was still black and asked him if there was any danger in it. He said absolutely not. I was resigned to carry a black toenail to the grave.

But then I began to eat sunflower seeds in an attempt to stop my eye quiver. Within about 10 days I noticed a lighter region in the newly grown nail, only about a sixteeth of an inch from its base. I kept watching it. Gradually the lighter section kept going higher and higher until, some days later, it reached to the top. The blackness is completely gone and the color is only slightly darker than that of a natural nail. What do you think of that? I can attribute it to nothing else than the effect of eating sunflower seeds, my own organically-grown ones. There must be something extremely potent about them. They are a seed from which a huge amount of plant tissue will grow. They contain a living element, a germ, which represents life and which you do not get when you eat such foods as lettuce or carrots. In the old Czarist days, Russian soldiers were given what was called an iron ration—sunflower seeds. I do not know whether this custom has carried over into modern times.

What About the Electric Potential of the Seed?

I like another thing about the sunflower seed. The sunflower plant usually turns with the sun as it grows, the head containing the seeds always being exposed to it. It thus becomes sun-drenched. A friend has an electric machine that tests the electric potential of plants. He has found that foods growing in the sun contain a higher electric potential than foods like the potato that grows in the ground. He also has found that apples growing on the outside of the tree, that get the sun, have much more electric potential than those growing in the interior of the tree where it is shady.

I will eat a handful of sunflower seeds every day for the rest of my life, and advise you to do likewise—about 50 or 60 of them a day should be enough. And if you have the tiniest bit of grass, you ought to grow your own sunflower plants organically. The sunflower plant is the easiest thing to grow. If you don't have any compost, use a liberal amount of dried blood and bone meal, which are available at chain stores, nurseries and seed stores. Even with compost, add a liberal amount of dried blood and bone meal. If you can get some kind of seaweed fertilizer, so much the better, or rotted manure. Write to *Organic Gardening,* Emmaus, Pennsylvania for its list of publications on the organic method. Think of eating highly potent sunflower seeds which you can grow yourself! What a wonderful item to add to your diet!

A word of caution. The bone meal that you buy for use as a fertilizer is not for human consumption. It may contain disease organisms that are harmful to a weakened human body. Another word of caution—some people have trouble cracking sunflower seeds with their teeth, either through having false teeth or because it might result in chipping sensitive teeth or separating the two front teeth. I would suggest two things: Either soak the seeds in cold water with their shells on, or open them with a pair of pliers.

In conclusion, I have related 3 things in one package. The cure of the quiver, the improvement of my eyesight and the getting rid of the black toenail. If I continue improving at this rate, I will live a long time. It is my ambition to live to be 102 years and one day. Why the extra day? I was born in 1898. If I live to be 102 years and one day, I will have lived in 3 centuries.

CHAPTER 107

Seeds—Conclusion

By J. I. Rodale

We have been eating some seeds without being aware of what we were doing, or how to handle them to best conserve their life-giving elements. In this day of processed, refined, factoryized food, we have, in the form of seeds, a safety valve so to speak, because seeds are rich storehouses of vitamins and other rare as well as undiscovered substances.

When the eating of sunflower seeds will dissipate the blackness of my toenail, when they will enable me to be out in the snow without seeing pink, there must be a powerful element in them which must strengthen every part of the body. I have noticed that if I eat sunflower seeds every day, I can be at the beach without sunglasses.

To anyone bothered with constipation, the eating of seeds will be a boon. There must be dozens of other beneficial effects produced in the body by eating seeds of various kinds. And those of us who are worried about the effect of chemical fertilizers on our foods will now have an anchor, the secure feeling that seeds are a class of food which feel the effects of chemical fertilizers the least.

But we must not go overboard on the subject. Study it carefully. Eat more seed foods, but don't overlook your vegetables, meats, fish and eggs.

Eggs

I would like to dwell for a moment on eggs, the most wonderful food that God has created. An egg is just one big seed, and in it, as in the average plant seed, there is sufficient food to keep the emerging entity alive for several days. But there is a tremendous difference in the nutritional value of a fertile egg as compared with a non-fertile one. What is the difference? A hen can lay an egg without a rooster being present, but such an egg will not hatch out anything. It is an infertile egg. It lacks the living germ. It is not a seed.

It is a commentary on the short-sighted policy of our Government that it encourages the production of such eggs. Because a fertile egg will spoil quickly in storage, due to the presence of the germ, the United States Department of Agriculture encourages poultrymen to keep roosters out of their flocks. This type of infertile egg has a higher economic value, but what about the nutritional needs of the consumer? The United States Department of Agriculture has nothing to do with that. "That is for doctors," they will no doubt say, if pressed. But I'll wager that the average doctor doesn't even know that a hen can lay an egg without a rooster's having a part in the transaction.

Yes sir. The average doctor does not know agriculture, and the average agriculturist does not know the simplest facts about human nutrition.

The egg is a seed, if it is a fertile one, and everyone should eat at least two of them a day. But try to discover a source where roosters are kept, if you wish to get the utmost nutrition out of your eggs. I have the medically researched evidence that a fertile egg is far more potent nutritionally in its effects on the health of the human body than an infertile one.

According to the latest researches, a heart case should not be told to avoid eating eggs because of their cholesterol content. It is not a matter of cholesterol as such, but the total fat consumption. The average American eats a diet which is 40 per cent fat. That is why we have about the highest mortality rate in the world from heart disease. We must cut this fat consumption down to about 20 per cent. My advice to a heart case is to eliminate milk and all dairy products such as cheese and butter. Eat eggs because they are seeds with certain living qualities that will help the heart case. This will cut down your consumption of fats. Also, cheeses and butter are heavily laden with salt, which is very dangerous to a heart case. To get the full value of the egg as a seed, consume it raw. Make an eggnog of the yolk only. The white of an egg contains avidin, a toxic substance if consumed raw. Cooking neutralizes its toxic properties.

Now, coming back to seeds generally, remember, I don't say to eat seeds exclusively. Be reasonable about it, as in everything else. And continue with your vitamin pills, bone meal, etc.

If you are a city person, study seeds in the country in the summer when you go there for your vacation. Get acquainted with farmers who perhaps will ship you seeds during the winter and other seasons, seeds which you might persuade them to set aside for you without poison spraying.

SECTION 11.

Sweets

We are proud of the material we have assembled over the years showing the harmfulness of white sugar. In the amounts in which Americans consume it, we believe it to be the single most pernicious item in our diets. Many pieces of scientific research involving sugar show it to be harmful. Shun it as you would a true poison and get your sweetening from fresh raw fruits and vegetables. We do not recommend brown sugar or raw sugar or any of the commercial synthetic sweeteners. Honey, real maple syrup and blackstrap molasses are the only sweets we condone—and one should use any of these in extremely small amounts.

CHAPTER 108

The Story of Sugar

The story of sugar seems to be one of the finest examples of man's inability to let well enough alone. Considering all the splendid and worthwhile improvements man has brought to his environment, it seems almost incredible that this same being, man, could also have invented and perpetrated one of the most serious and stupid mistakes in history—a mistake which, as one doctor of our acquaintance prophesies, may very well end our civilization within a few generations.

The story of sugar is a story of stupidity, greed and ignorance. It is the final devastating removal of man from his natural environment. We are talking now of white sugar—the sugar you buy at the grocery store—white, crystal, delicious, "pure." Throughout this discussion this is the sugar we mean when we say sugar. When we are speaking of *natural* sugars—from fruits, vegetables, honey and so forth, we will qualify them as natural sugars.

The chemistry of sugar is complex and we will not trouble you with it. There are many different kinds of sugars, chemically—fructose, glucose, sucrose, dextrose, lactose and so forth. They differ from one another in the chemical structure of their molecules. They are all carbohydrates. In other words, when you read or hear the word carbohydrate, as different from protein and fat, you will know that what is meant is sugars and starches.

The carbohydrates are the energy-giving foods, as separate from the proteins, which are the body building and repairing foods. We are told that 68 per cent of the food we eat is changed by the body into sugars to produce energy. The other 32 per cent is used for building and repairing the body. Not only sugars and starches but also fats and proteins can be changed by the body's marvelous mechanism into the kind of sugar that the body needs to produce energy. So it appears that we need sugar! Why, therefore, did we say that the story of sugar is the story of man's most colossal mistake? We do need sugar, yes, but the important thing is the *kind* of sugar we need.

Why Do We Like Sugar?

We have developed a taste for sweet things. Sweet things are delightful to eat. Melvin Page, D.D.S., in his splendid book, *Degeneration and Regeneration* (published by the Biochemical Research Foundation, 2810 First Street, North, St. Petersburg, Florida), tells us we were given a desire for sweet-tasting foods because, in natural foods, a number of very necessary food elements exist in combination with a sweet taste—vitamins and minerals, to be exact. Now a vitamin in the quantities in which it appears in food has no taste, so wise Mother Nature teams up a sweet taste with a number of vitamins. We need vitamin C if we are to live in good health for even one day. But we cannot pick vitamin C off a vine or tree and no amount of persuasion will get us to eat vitamin C if it has a disagreeable taste.

So vitamin C comes ready-packaged in cantaloupes, strawberries, guavas, oranges and so forth and we eat them actually because we have a need for the vitamins they contain. But we *think* we eat them because of the sweet taste. One-half cup of carrots is a compact little bundle of 4500 units of vitamin A, but nobody would eat them if they tasted bitter. So our taste for sweets is a reliable guide to foods that are good for us. But this guide is reliable only so long as the foods we have to choose from are natural foods that man, in his matchless inability to let well enough alone, has not tampered with.

What We Mean By "Refining"

Most of us are not familiar with sugar cane, so let's take as a sample grapes, which are rich in sugar. What could be more enjoyable than pitching in to a big dish of luscious Concords, purple and dewy and fresh from the vines! And healthy, too, for grapes come equipped with vitamins A, B and C, calcium, phosphorus, iron and many more food elements that are good for you, as well as all the substances your body needs to digest them.

Now suppose somebody—a chemist or scientist with a lot of degrees behind his name—came over to your dewy grape arbor and told you he was going to "improve" your grapes. He was going to put them through a process that would guarantee that they would keep practically forever, so that you could have them, in condensed form, on your table. You could flavor all your foods with their sweet taste, summer and winter. In addition, he would "purify" your grapes. This purification process wouldn't mean much to you, except that you have come to believe that "purified" foods are somehow better, because they have no dirt in them, no germs, nothing extraneous. But, on second thought, what needs to be "purified" about your grapes as they come from the vine? Nevertheless your scientist proceeds with his terribly complicated and expensive process, which somehow, due to our technological genius, results in a product that is much less expensive than grapes, keeps indefinitely, tastes sweet and can be bought at any grocery store the year 'round.

Now we've solved all our problems. But have we? Let's look a little more closely at this very practical, sweet, inexpensive pretty-looking product you can use to your heart's content in cakes, candies, cookies, lemonade and coffee. Any vitamin B in it? Not an atom. Any vitamin A or C, any iron, phosphorus, calcium? Not a sliver. What then is left? Nothing at all is left but the sweet taste and the pure carbohydrate which will give you calories and nothing else. Your clever scientist has stripped the grapes of every vestige of food value and has left you only the sweet taste which, remember, was put there by nature to guide you to the healthful food elements that were in the original grapes. Would you say that the scientist was clever or would you say he had made a colossal mistake?

Nobody has yet discovered how to make a satisfactory, practical table

[386]

sugar out of grapes. But the story above is precisely what happens in the manufacture of table sugar from sugar cane or beets. From the point of view of commerce, the refining of sugar is a stroke of genius, but from the point of view of human welfare, it is one of the world's greatest tragedies.

History of Sugar

"Since we have no satisfactory knowledge of the beginnings of the culture of sugar cane, we can only infer that it was cultivated in northeastern India long before the Christian era. The earliest reference to sugar is contained in the comments made by several officers of Alexander the Great during his Indian campaign in 327 B.C.," says Andrew Van Hook in his book, *Sugar,* published by the Ronald Press, New York City. He goes on to say, "It was still to be almost 1000 years before the consumption and cultivation of sugar began to spread beyond the borders of India. During this time, however, its sweet and honey-like nature became known and was mentioned by such writers as Theophrastus, Herodotus, Discorides and Pliny." So we see that human beings have arrived at eating sugar from sugar cane in recent times, in term of man's life here on earth. The Arabs and ancient Egyptians used sugar. The Chinese were using sugar when Marco Polo visited them in 1270-75. As history moved forward and the medieval crusades brought knowledge of Eastern ways to western Europe, the use of sugar spread and eventually, of course, got to America. Among those early Europeans only the very wealthy could have sugar on their tables, because it was expensive to import. In the Western Hemisphere sugar cane planting and slavery went hand in hand. In North and South America the tall sugar cane with its waving tassels was soon a familiar sight. "The sugar in those days was a highly impure and dark product which was shipped to the refining cities of the motherland countries for further processing," says Van Hook.

What exactly does he mean by that? He means that, to collect and ship the sugar, certain things had to be done to it, but in those days men didn't know how to remove all the dark colored substance (containing the vitamins and minerals). So their sugar was dark and sticky and difficult to handle—but much more nutritious than the white sugar we have today. It doesn't seem far-fetched to guess that none of us in the Western world would be alive today if those old-timers had had the technical skill we have for "refining" foods.

As scientific knowledge developed, ways and means were discovered to refine the sugar still further. As refining processes grew more general, sugar became cheaper and more popular. In America the first refining plant was established in New York in 1689. By the middle of the nineteenth century sugar refining as we know it today had developed. Meanwhile someone had discovered that sugar might be made from beets which will grow in climates where sugar cane will not grow. And gradually the sugar beet refining industry began to grow. By 1940 the United States was producing well over two million tons of sugar per year *and consuming more than seven million tons!* A recent estimated value of the world production of sugar was two billion dollars, only a little less than the value of all the iron and steel produced

[387]

in the United States. (Incidentally it is also interesting to note that the cigar and cigarette industry of this country was valued at one billion, two hundred million dollars in 1939.)

In 1939-1940 the people of the United States consumed 106.5 pounds of sugar per person—that means almost one pound every 3 days, *per person!* Taking into account all the babies and the sick people who dare not eat sugar, what kind of an average does that leave for the rest of us?

The Refining Process

There is no need to follow a piece of sugar cane through all the various complications of the refining process, but here are some of the substances used to produce those sparkling white crystals: lime, phosphoric acid, special clays known as diatomaceous earth, bone char, boneblack or animal charcoal. To powdered or confectioners sugar, corn starch or calcium phosphate is added to keep the sugars from caking. In producing lactose or milk sugar which is used mainly in infant foods, "the whey is first clarified with lime, decolorized with carbon and then concentrated and crystallized," says Mr. Van Hook. In refining beet sugar, lime, carbon dioxide and sulfur dioxide are involved in the "purification" process.

In harvesting sugar beets, the tops are carefully cut off while the beets are still in the field. The sugar beet industry has had some difficulty in disposing of its "wastes" which ferment easily. We put that word in quotations, for, of course, the "wastes" in sugar beet refining consist of everything that is worthwhile as food in the beet and beet top. But just as we finally learned that the germ and bran from refined wheat make good food for cattle, so we discovered that cattle thrive on the "wastes" from beet sugar manufacture. Why shouldn't they thrive? In the wastes are concentrated all of the vitamins and minerals from the beets. Out of the whole procedure, the human beings involved—and this means you and me—get once again only the pure carbohydrate, stripped of all food value except calories.

The Food Value of Sugar

Following through on this whole senseless waste of good, healthful, wholesome food in a two billion dollar industry, do you get some idea what we mean when we use harsh and violent language in speaking of white, refined sugar? In the most sweeping evasion it has ever been our misfortune to meet in modern literature, Mr. Van Hook in his book, *Sugar*, has this to say about the food value of the product he is writing about: "In spite of its prominent place in the diet all over the world, the role of sugar as a food has never been completely ascertained." Obviously, Mr. Van Hook, because it has no role as food. Applying even the most lax and generous interpretation to the words "food" and "nutrition," no one can show that white refined sugar has any place at all in the diet of any living thing. In speaking of the fashions in sugar all over the world, Mr. Van Hook says, "In the United States a hard, white sugar of high purity is usually demanded, but in Europe considerable tolerance is allowed in respect to color. Native sugars (this means the sugars of those backward savages who are not as civilized as we) are soft, dark colored and impure, and the purity (that is, the per cent of sucrose in total dry product) is often as low as 60 or 70 per cent. *Whether or not American standards mean a superior product in nutritional value is questionable.*" We italicized that last sentence to emphasize it, for it seems to us a masterpiece of understatement. Certainly any literate person with any nutrition chart before his eyes can readily see that American white refined sugar has absolutely no nutritional value whatsoever, so why do we need the half-hearted word "questionable?" So the uncivilized world which does not have our technical excellence has to be content with dark sugar which includes at least some (perhaps 30 to 40 per cent) of the original food elements of the beets and cane, while we civilized people deliberately choose to eat the pure, white worthless chemical left after refining.

Or do we "deliberately choose" to eat white sugar? Throughout all our research on sugar we found again and again the suggestion that the American public just won't have a dark sugar. No sir, they tell us, it must be "pure" and white as snow or Mrs. America will reject it scornfully. Mrs. America is a refined and cultured lady, they tell us, and her angel cakes must be white as moonlight, her boiled frosting pearly as Mt. Everest on a clear day, even the sugar she dumps into her morning coffee must glisten with silvery lights in her sugar bowl. Somehow we feel that this assumption is a libel on the good sense and practicability of Americans. We are absolutely certain that, if the gentlemen of the sugar industry would go to Mrs. America through the pages of her favorite magazines and in the commercials of her favorite radio and television programs, and would tell her the full story of sugar cane and beet sugar, would show her exactly what is subtracted from the cane and beet in the process of refining and would explain to her what is left in the pure white sugar she uses every day, Mrs. America would not only change her mind practically overnight about white sugar, but would march in a body to Washington and fight for legislation to make white sugar illegal!

And oh, what changes we'd have at the county fair and the mother's club bake sale! For the darkest angel cake would win the blue ribbon. And the cupcakes with the deep brown icing would sell best. To say nothing to the wonderful new opportunity for home economic experts to dream up new recipes requiring raw sugar, blackstrap molasses and honey!

Blackstrap Molasses As Food

What about blackstrap molasses anyway? Is it really the fountain of youth, guaranteed to banish any and all ailments and put hair on the chest of the scrawniest boy scout? No, we don't think so. But we know—because we read nutrition charts—that blackstrap molasses is a food, and a good food. Sugar is not. See for yourself. Here are the vitamins and minerals in one hundred grams of sugar and one hundred grams of blackstrap:

		Molasses			Sugar
Calories		220			400

(All these are B vitamins)

Thiamin	245	micrograms			0
Riboflavin	240	micrograms			0
Niacin	4	milligrams			0
Pyridoxine	270	micrograms			0
Pantothenic acid	260	micrograms			0
Biotin	16	micrograms			0

(These are minerals)

Calcium	258	milligrams		1	milligram
Phosphorus	30	milligrams			trace
Iron	7.97	milligrams		.04	milligrams
Copper	1.93	milligrams		.02	milligrams
Magnesium	.04	milligrams		0	
Chlorine	317	milligrams			trace
Sodium	90	milligrams		.3	milligrams
Potassium	1500	milligrams		.5	milligrams

Where does molasses get all these vitamins and minerals? Obviously these are what is left when the sugar cane is refined. These are the vitamins and minerals Nature put in the original sugar cane to nourish you after you had discovered that the sweet taste is pleasant. But blackstrap molasses is "impure" scream the writers in the big popular magazines! That's right, folks, it is "impure." And the "impurities" are vitamin B, calcium, phosphorus, iron and other minerals which are completely essential to human nutrition. Blackstrap molasses doesn't taste as good as sugar until you get used to it. It doesn't look pretty in your sugar bowl. And blackstrap molasses that has been prepared for use in cattle food is not for human consumption, of course. But blackstrap molasses for human beings (and most grocery stores carry it these days) is every bit as free from germs and dirt as any other food that must pass Federal inspection.

In the following pages we will show you what harm white sugar does to your body. It's not just something you can go right on eating, you know, so long as you eat good foods, too! Anything you put into your body that does not belong there is harmful, you may be sure. White sugar is a drug to which we Americans have become addicted. You will see in the following pages what devastating inroads on American health have been made by this particular drug. As you read, keep in mind that the average American (adult and child alike) consumes in toto about a pound of this drug every 3 days. Keep in mind, too, that white sugar and white flour (another completely worthless food) make up well over 50 per cent of the average American diet.

After you have read, dump the contents of your sugar bowl and sugar canister into the garbage can and start a new life!

CHAPTER 109

Some Plain Talk about Sugars

What do we mean when we say dextrose, fructose, sucrose, glucose or lactose? Are these names for foods you can buy in cans or bags? Should we seek them out or shun them? If we throw away our sugar bowls and stop eating desserts and sweetened fruits, how can we be sure we are getting enough sugar for the body's needs? What about sweeteners that are advertised as having little caloric value?

Some Answers

Sugar is a carbohydrate, which means that it is made from carbon, hydrogen and oxygen. The way these elements are combined in different formulas makes the chief difference in sugars. There are single sugars, double sugars and multiple sugars—a fact which need not concern you in any way, except that it shows you how complex the subject of sugars is bound to be, when you are dealing with 3 separate groups of substances and many subdivisions in each group.

We should be concerned chiefly with sugars which occur naturally in foods along with all the substances that accompany them, as opposed to white sugar and similar products, which are nothing but pure carbohydrate without a single particle of mineral, vitamin, enzyme or anything else that makes them food.

Glucose, also known as *dextrose,* is grape sugar or blood sugar. It occurs in our blood and it also occurs in almost all fruits and vegetables. It is more than half the entire solid matter of honey and grapes.

Fructose is found in most fruits and many vegetables.

Lactose is a sugar which occurs only in milk. It is less sweet than other sugars, digests less readily and hence is not so fattening. As it is digested in the body it changes into *glucose* and *galactose.* Lactose is food for the intestinal bacteria which change it into lactic acid. This, we believe, is one of the reasons why yogurt is such a valuable food and has such a reputation for restoring valuable intestinal bacteria. It contains lactose, of course.

Sucrose is the chemical name for white sugar. This sugar also occurs in fruits and vegetables. It makes up about half the solid matter of a carrot. During digestion it is changed into *glucose* and *fructose.*

Maltose is a sugar found in malt (germinated grains).

Cellulose is that part of vegetables and fruits that is almost completely indigestible by human beings—the skins of fruits, the "core" of vegetables, the husk of grains. The ruminant animals can digest cellulose. Since we cannot, why bother to eat it? It's good for us because it forms the bulk which is so important for our good digestion. People who do not eat enough foods containing cellulose are bound to suffer from constipation.

Inulin is the other sugar which we only partly digest. This occurs in onions, garlic and Jerusalem artichokes. For this reason there has been lots of rather unwarranted enthusiasm about these artichokes. The mere fact that their sugar is largely undigested and hence is not fattening is surely no reason why anyone should decide that they are a "wonder" food.

Now, how are you going to know which of these sugars you should eat and which you should not eat? As you can see, if you look back over our list, you can get lots and lots of all these different kinds of sugar if you eat plenty of fruits and vegetables. Let's say you have crossed white sugar off your list entirely, never have any of it in the house and never eat anything away from home that contains it. Isn't it possible that you may suffer from lack of sugar? After all, sugar in your food is the main source of energy for your body. True. Sugar does not keep you healthy, does not rebuild broken down tissue, does not take part, as proteins and fats do, in many of the intricate and necessary body processes. But sugar does give you energy. How then can you be sure you are getting enough?

Do you have any idea how much sugar you get in a well-planned diet which does not include a single grain of white sugar? Eating fruits, whole grains, cereals, vegetables, eggs, meat, nuts and milk, you would get close to two cups of sugar as a total for the day! Impossible, you will say. But it's so. Do you think you could possibly need more than two cups a day?

Carbohydrates in Food

Here is a list of fruits and vegetables along with their carbohydrate content. We use the word "carbohydrate" here rather than "sugar" for in some of these foods the carbohydrate is in the form of starch rather than sugar. But the starch is changed into sugar almost as soon as you eat it, so in considering the total of your sugar intake you should count this starch as sugar. *Foods very low in carbohydrate content* (the ones you think of first in connection with a reducing diet).

These contain about 5 per cent carbohydrate: carrots, cauliflower, okra, onions, peppers, pumpkin, radishes, string beans, water cress.

These foods contain about 7 per cent carbohydrate: avocado and olives (quite high in fat) grapefruit, lemons, strawberries, watermelon.

These foods contain about 10 per cent carbohydrate: parsnips, peas, Hubbard squash, turnips, berries, cantaloupe, muskmelon, oranges, peaches, pineapple, raspberries.

These foods contain about 15 per cent carbohydrate: apples, apricots, cherries, currants, grapes, huckleberries, nectarines, pears.

These foods contain about 20 per cent carbohydrate: corn, lima beans, navy beans, sweet and white potatoes, rice, bananas, fresh figs, plums and prunes. Dried fruits may contain as much as 75 per cent carbohydrate.

Since so many of our foods are so rich in sugar why then do we, along with all responsible nutritionists, argue against the use of white sugar? There are two reasons. First of all, the very fact that so many of the foods which we should be eating every day contain so much sugar is certainly the best possible indication that we do not need to add any more sugar to our diets. It seems perfectly obvious that this is the way Nature intended for us to get our sugar, as all her other creatures do—from natural foods.

Secondly, all of the sugar that occurs naturally in fruits and vegetables, no matter which kind of sugar it is—sucrose, fructose, glucose or whatever —occurs in the food combined with all the enzymes, vitamins and minerals that belong with it. Your body needs all of these things if you are going to use the sugar as it is meant to be used. Now, suppose you concentrate the sugar, throwing away everything else. Of course, you manufacture sucrose this way. Or glucose. But you will have only a "pure" substance left—like a drug, just as white sugar is. None of the natural accompanying substances will be left with it. And therein lies the terrible danger from the use of white sugar—its unnatural concentration.

Concentrated, pure sugar is a drug, unrelated to anything that occurs naturally. For this reason it makes terrible demands on your body. First, it throws off the calcium-phosphorus balance and disrupts this entire, important phase of your body machinery. Secondly, because refined sugar has been robbed of the B vitamins that are necessary for its assimilation by the body, it latches on to these wherever it finds them—namely in your digestive tract, so that the person who eats refined sugar is bound to be short on the B vitamins. Result? Nervousness, skin troubles, digestive trouble and a host of other disorders which lead to much more serious trouble later on.

What about honey, real maple syrup and blackstrap molasses? They contain minerals and vitamins that are natural to them, so for this reason they are the only sweets we can approve. But don't forget they, too, are highly concentrated—maple syrup is the boiled-down sap of the tree, molasses is prepared from sugar cane. And honey is, let's face it, not a "natural" food for human beings. We steal it from the bees and when we eat it we should take into account the fact that the metabolism and furious activity of a bee are quite different from those of a human being. Honey is a highly concentrated food. Don't eat too much of it.

You sometimes meet with the words we've defined above on labels of foods. Should you buy foods that contain glucose, or dextrose or sucrose? No, because you can be certain that they are "purified" sugars, hence harmful from our point of view.

Some Other Sugars and What They Do

Pure glucose, for instance, is made from cornstarch and is sold as corn sugar. Health-conscious people shouldn't use it, for it is "pure." Some of the sugars we mentioned are used in foods for various reasons. Lactose is used to preserve many foods. It is a coating agent for olives, preserved fruits and sugared almonds and a flavoring agent for chocolate products.

It is used in many bakery products and confectionery products. It is an ingredient of baking and biscuit mixes, of some cheese, of dry coloring matter for edible fats, of infant and invalid foods and is sometimes used

[393]

as a substitute for other sugars in jams. It is used as a preservative in meat products.

Maltose is used in beer and malt production, in making beverages and soft drinks, in bread doughs, in confectionery products, in jams, in milk and coffee substitutes, in tea extracts, in corn syrup.

This will give you some idea of the many, many ways sugars are hidden in food. Apparently it is almost impossible to eat any processed food that does not contain "hidden" sugars, in addition to all the many chemicals that may be there.

Now we must take into account the fact that starchy foods (also carbohydrates) are changed into sugar during digestion. So when you are figuring how much sugar you get in a day's rations, figure as well on the purely starchy foods that don't even taste sweet. There are 35 to 40 grams of carbohydrate in a serving of macaroni which will be pure sugar within a few minutes from the time you eat it. Wouldn't it be better to eat a piece of meat or an egg instead?

Here is a quote from 3 well-known authorities on what your body does with carbohydrates. Say Jolliffe, Tisdall and Cannon, the authors of *Clinical Nutrition* (B. Hoeber, Incorporated): "Factors which influence the amount of carbohydrate absorbed in a given individual at a particular time are: 1. the normality of the mucous membrane of the small intestine and the length of time during which the carbohydrate is in contact with it; 2. endocrine (gland) function, particularly that of the anterior pituitary, the thyroid and the adrenal cortex and 3. the adequacy of vitamin intake, especially that of the B complex." In other words, your digestive tract must be in good shape (watch your intake of B vitamins and vitamin A), your glands must be in good shape (all the vitamins and minerals are important for this and don't forget iodine for the thyroid) and finally you must get enough of the B vitamins along with the sugar or starch.

You fail entirely to fulfill these 3 essentials every time you eat processed sugar or starches, for they contain no vitamins or minerals. Nowhere in a natural food can you find starch or sugar without some of the vitamins or minerals accompanying them. Fruits, vegetables, whole grain cereals— all are rich in the elements you need to use the carbohydrates properly. But the minute you begin to tamper with the natural food, the whole delicately balanced machinery is thrown out of gear. And therein lies the horrible menace of the refined carbohydrates—chiefly white sugar, with white flour products running a close second. Don't forget, too, all the worthless and dangerous "hidden sugars" lurking in prepared foods—bottled, packaged or canned.

CHAPTER 110

Sugar—A Handy Instrument
for Race Suicide

"You shouldn't eat so much candy, dear. It's not good for you. Well, just one more piece." And Mamma hands Junior another piece of candy. Where did we pick up this idea that sugar is not good for us? Even those folks who stuff themselves on sweet things all day will mention meanwhile that they know it's bad for them. Have you ever talked to anyone who believes that eating sugar is good for him? "Oh I just can't get along without my dessert," he will tell you. But he won't add that the dessert is good for him.

Isaac Schour, D.D.S., Ph.D., and Maury Massler, D.D.S., M.S., of Chicago have a lot to say about sugar and dental decay in an article in the *Journal of the American Dental Association* for July 1, 1947. These two investigators have contributed much to the literature on dental decay including a brilliant article in which they showed that fluoridated water is quite likely to be harmful to the teeth of badly nourished children, although it seems to postpone decay in children who are well nourished.

Refined Sugar and Dental Decay

In this particular article mentioned above, they discuss the situation in post-war Italy when 3,905 children were examined for dental decay and the figures were compared with dental decay in our country. In the Italian age group, 11-15 years, there was an average of 1.05 decayed, missing or filled tooth per child. In the same age group in the United States the average was 4.66 per child. On the other hand in 4 Italian cities examined, 53.4 per cent of the children between 11-15 years had no dental decay. In the United States only 9.5 per cent of the children in this age group had no dental decay. Figures on older age groups showed a similar story.

Discussing the reasons for this astonishing difference in tooth decay between Italy, a country which suffered greatly during the war, and the United States, where deprivation was certainly at a minimum, the authors point out that the amount of refined sugar available for Italian children was very limited. The Italian children were not especially well nourished, so apparently good nutrition is not the only essential for dental health. These Italian children lacked in their diets many of the healthful foods they should have had. But—and this is the crux of the matter—they also lacked refined white sugar, or at any rate did not have it in anything like the quantity in which it was available to American children. During the years 1930-34 the per capita consumption of sugar in Italy was 18 pounds, as compared to 103 pounds in America.

The investigators continue, "Clapp reported a remarkably low incidence of caries in young adult Italians who were born in Italy and who were living in Bridgeport, Connecticut. He pointed out that they had grown up on the Italian diet and he emphasized particularly the low intake of sugar— about one-seventh that of American boys. On the other hand, Day and Sedwick examined the teeth of 500 children 13 years of age and of Italian descent (whose diet, presumably was now Americanized and high in sugar) and found no great difference between the prevalence of caries in this group and that of American children. This might lead to the supposition that dietary habits have a greater effect on the incidence of caries than does the genetic influence, although the latter cannot be discounted."

The authors also remind us that the average Italian diet is high in carbohydrates. Spaghetti, bread and so forth make up a large part of it. Some experimenters have shown that carbohydrates produce the mouth acid that leads to tooth decay. But apparently in the case of the Italian children the carbohydrates made no difference. Even though they were badly nourished and their diet lacked many necessary foods, even though they ate a large proportion of carbohydrates in comparison to the amount of protein they had, still their teeth were infinitely better than those of American children who had been living on good diets—but had been eating large quantities of sugar.

One of the most complete discussions of refined sugar in relation to dental health comes to us in a symposium conducted by the California State Dental Association, April 24, 1950, and printed in the journal of that organization . . . *Sugar and Dental Caries.* In this 95 page booklet the speech most interesting to us was that of Dr. Robert C. Hockett of the Sugar Research Foundation, Incorporated, and the answer to his speech given by Michael H. Walsh, M.Sc., F.R.I.C., Instructor in Clinical Nutrition at the University of California.

Proof That Sugar Is Not Economical

Here are some excerpts from Dr. Walsh's brilliant rebuttal to the arguments that sugar is an economical food. . . . "If, as he (Dr. Hockett) asserts, sugar is the most efficiently produced food, why do not the commercial hog feeders, beef producers and poultry raisers feed their animals sugar in large quantities? . . . Surely if sugar were the most efficiently produced food, these scientists who are experts in animal nutrition would have advocated long ago the consumption of sugar in large quantities for the feeding of farm animals. . . . By efficiency (Dr. Hockett) means the ability to produce calories, and calories are identified as the only index of nutritive needs of man, without any regard for the need for nutrients such as essential amino acids, essential fatty acids, the many minerals and vitamins without which all the calories of sugar in the world are not only utterly useless as food but are physiologically harmful. What does it profit a man to have a million calories a year in the form of sugar if he does not have the essential nutrients to enable the sugars to be utilized?

". . . When it comes to animal metabolism, every type of nutrient must be ingested—prefabricated, so to speak, and in that metabolism of animals —including humans—protein assumes primary importance because it is the essential raw material from which tissues are built. The most favorable development is obtained when proteins, fats, carbohydrates, minerals and vitamins are furnished to the animal organism simultaneously in amounts and proportions which we now know to be desirable; if there are to be limitations on the supply of these necessary foods, sugar cannot substitute for protein, fat cannot substitute for protein, but on the other hand, both fats and sugars can be and are derived from the metabolism of protein.

"Hence when it comes to human diets, there is no object in furnishing sugar unless appropriate amounts of proteins, fats, minerals and vitamins are also furnished. Refined sugar, because of its highly concentrated form, and being completely devoid of essential proteins, vitamins and minerals, is now regarded nutritionally as a diluting agent of the modern diet. It is a displacer of other factors far more essential than sugar. Thus, the more sugar consumed, the less opportunity for getting essential nutrients into the diet. If sugar is furnished as a replacement of proteins, fats, minerals and vitamins, then serious physiological consequences follow. This is the essence and the crux of the physiological problem we have to deal with not only in dentistry but also in medicine.

"At this meeting the emphasis is on sugar and caries. To me there are far more serious disease problems to be dealt with than tooth decay. Far more teeth are lost today through periodontal (gum) disease than from tooth decay. There is growing and accumulating evidence that the patterns of food habits—including excessive sugar consumption—which are associated with dental decay in childhood, adolescence and early adult life are similar in structure to those of periodontal patients in later life. There is also coming to light evidence of a dietary relationship between high sugar consumption and polio, rheumatic fever, arthritis and many degenerative diseases."

The Important Matter of Low Blood Sugar

What is some of this evidence Dr. Walsh refers to? First there is Dr. Sandler's fight against polio in North Carolina several years ago, when he brought to a standstill a polio epidemic that had frightened the residents so badly that many of them were willing to try out the diet he recommended. This diet is in the book, *Diet Prevents Polio,* available from the Lee Foundation for Nutritional Research, 2023 West Wisconsin Avenue, Milwaukee, Wisconsin. The essence of the diet is a reduction of sugar.

Dr. Sandler forbids all forms of refined sugars (desserts, soft drinks, candies and so forth) and even limits sharply the amount of fruit to be eaten. His theory (and we are entirely in agreement with it) is that low blood sugar makes individuals susceptible to polio. Low blood sugar is brought about by eating sugar, paradoxical as this may sound. Eating sugar brings up the blood sugar level for a short time, but then it plunges down far below normal. This makes you feel uncomfortable and you need some-thing sweet again, so you have a soda, a piece of candy or a doughnut, and the blood sugar rockets up again, only to fall much too low a little later. As you can see, the net result is a vicious cycle of eating more and more sweets all the time, just to keep going.

Polio is not the only disease related to low blood sugar. Dr. E. M. Abrahamson in his excellent book, Body, Mind and Sugar (published by Henry Holt and Company, New York), tells us that low blood sugar is far, far more prevalent in this country than its opposite—high blood sugar, which is diabetes. Recommending a diet very similar to that of Dr. Sandler, Dr. Abrahamson relates spectacular cures for asthma, alcoholism, neuroses, fatigue, rheumatic fever, ulcers, epilepsy, depression, and so forth—the list is encouraging.

What About Mosquito Bites?

Insect bites are probably not a very serious menace to health, except in countries where malaria is prevalent. But insect bites can spoil a vacation, cause loss of sleep, ruin one's appearance and otherwise be a pesky nuisance, especially when one is dedicated to avoiding insecticides. Over the years we have accumulated an amazing file of information on the relation of sugar-eating to susceptibility to insect bites. The only possible conclusion we can draw is that insects simply do not bite people who eat no sugar, we suppose because of the excellence of their blood chemistry. Here is a letter that came in the other day from a reader—a sample of many in our files: "A friend of mine was working in northern Canada where there was a settlement of Indians. It was during the black fly season and it was quite evident that the flies were concentrating on jabbing me, while the Indian chief who sat nearby was entirely free of them. My astonished friend asked why. The chief's reply was 'One month before the black fly season all Indians naturally know enough to leave all sugars from their diet'." We civilized Americans, with all our knowledge of chemistry, have not figured out a number of basic facts about nutrition that are well known to primitive people.

Concerning other aspects of sugar consumption, J. W. S. Lindahl, M. Chir, F. R. C. S., writing in the December, 1951, issue of the Practitioner, says, "It has been suggested that one predisposing factor (in tonsilitis) is an unbalanced diet with too much sugar and starch in relation to protein and green vegetables and I believe there is much to be said for this theory."

Dr. Sidney A. Portis of the University of Chicago believes that a diet low in sugar will reduce fatigue, according to the Journal of the American Medical Association, Vol. 142, 1950. Dr. Portis, a nervous and mental disease specialist, says that an excess of emotion stimulates the pancreas, resulting in low blood sugar.

Sugar and Vitamin B Deficiency

We have mentioned before the price we pay in vitamin B for eating white sugar. As we have shown, natural sugars, as they occur in fruits and sugar cane, have with them the full assortment of B vitamins that are necessary for the assimilation of the sugars, and its use by the body. As we have seen, none of these B vitamins is present in white sugar. But, if the sugar is to be used by the body they must be present. So they are drafted—from nerves, muscles, liver, kidneys, stomach, heart, skin, eyes, blood. Needless to say, this leaves these organs of the body deficient in B vitamins. Unless a tremendous amount of vitamin B-rich food is taken, this deficiency will become worse and worse. As more sugar is eaten, more B vitamins are stolen.

Look around you. We are a nation of suffers from "nerves," digestive disorders, tiredness, poor eyesight, anemia, heart trouble, muscular diseases and a hundred assorted skin diseases. How much of this suffering is due to lack of the B vitamins caused by the amount of sugar we eat every year? No one will ever be able to answer that question precisely, but we are willing to hazard a guess that nine-tenths of these troubles would disappear within a year of the time that white sugar was banned from our tables and from our food.

Do you suffer from any of the above complaints? Are you "nervous" and tired, do you have any kind of digestive disorder or skin disease? Are you willing to try an experiment to see just how much the eating of white sugar has to do with your complaints? For 6 months drop sugar from your menu. No halfway measures are permitted. You may eat *nothing* that contains refined sugar. This means no bakery products, no candy, soft drinks or chewing gum, no ice cream, canned fruit (unless it is packed without sugar), no sugar in your beverages or on your cereal. You may and should eat lots of fruit and vegetables, meat, eggs, cheese, nuts and fish. In addition, you should certainly take brewer's yeast or desiccated liver which contain all the B vitamins, for, if you have been in the habit of eating white refined sugar, you are almost bound to have a serious vitamin B shortage.

For the first week or so you'll probably suffer gnawing hunger for sweets. Satisfy your hunger with something else. Eat an apple, a handful of nuts, a raw carrot. When you stop with friends at the soda fountain, order milk, fruit juice or tea (with no sugar). Fresh fruit is a wonderful dessert and once you have become accustomed to ending a meal with fruit you'll wonder why you ever wanted all those gooey pastries and sticky pies and cakes. In another chapter we give you more hints on how to get along happily and healthfully without sugar.

CHAPTER 111

Why All this Fuss about Sugar?

By Donald Shriber, D.D.S., F.I.C.D., F.A.C.D., Los Angeles

Although 8 out of 10 people realize that sugar is harmful to the teeth, they think that it is required for energy, hence is a necessary substance for the diet. All are of the opinion that "sweets" have to be eliminated if one wishes to lose weight.

The work of Jay and Bunting of the University of Michigan and Herman Becks at the University of California was fairly well publicized in dental journals, and I can assure you that little, if any, mention was made in the daily press about their work. There is much concern about the "most prevalent disease of mankind," yet the above investigators found that 80 per cent of tooth decay could be prevented by one simple formula—*stop eating sugar!* There are quite a number of people who say that they do not eat sugar because they like their coffee straight. But when asked if they like or eat ice cream, candy, pie, cake, pastries, jam, jelly, fruit preserves, bottled beverages of all kinds, chewing gum and even tomato catsup, the answer is yes. If you don't eat food to which sugar has been added your compensation will be fewer cavities, and you may put an end to dentists.

In my opinion it was rather unfortunate that Becks and others did not consider the general physical well-being of these patients as well as the incidence of tooth decay in this remarkable study. If they had, I'm sure they would come to this conclusion: that sugar has no place in the human diet because it may be the largest contributing factor if not one of the direct causes of many of our degenerative diseases today. I know in many instances this is not an over-statement.

We hear so much about needing sugar for energy. Of course we need sugar for energy—that which is manufactured by the body processes from good carbohydrates, good fats, and even protein. If the energy requirements of a person are very demanding, proteins can be converted into sugar.

Statistically, over 100 pounds of sugar was consumed by every man, woman and child in the United States last year, so I shall continue with the question, "Why all this fuss about sugar?" I hope that my inference is understood.

The value of correlating the incidence of other diseases with mouth health was brought to my attention about 25 years ago by the mother of an 8 year old boy, whose name was Tommy Smith.

He would return to my office every 3 months with from 3 to 5 new cavities to be filled. This continued over a long period of time, resulting in a filling in every tooth including the permanent ones. At first each appointment with him was the same—kicking, biting and screaming. I could have

[400]

rewarded that child with the Empire State Building and still would be bitten, kicked and screamed at. In desperation, since I had to preserve my hands (which to me are very valuable), my glasses, ear drums and nervous system, I prescribed a sugar-and-white-flour-free diet for the boy, mostly for my own protection. It worked. Six months later there were no new cavities and only one cavity a year later. I was amazed at the child's behavior while on this program. Here was a happy contented child, who 6 months before had been a pint sized tornado. His mother revealed some more facts which were amazing to me at this time. The school authorities had been seriously considering placing the child in the "retarded group" because of his inability to keep up with the class; he was continually quarreling with his sister; later there were only a few occasional spats. Before, he was having one cold after another and sore throats frequently, recently he had only one cold and no sore throats. His mother had had to continually watch his bowels, now they moved normally without laxatives. The correlation between tooth decay, the common cold, sore throats, constipation and lack of interest in his school studies seemed important to me. It was quite obvious that the absence of sugar in this boy's diet apparently was the factor which was contributing to the solution of the above dilemma. Before I leave Tommy and his caries problem, I might add that there are those who seriously consider a mother as quite incapable of diagnosing a common cold or sore throat, but I saw a change in his behavior pattern, and she saw a change in his physical-mental well-being.

There have been many Tommy Smiths in the past years and older Tommy Smiths also.

Biochemical tests which were made at the start and then repeated 6 months later will bear witness that Tommy Smith's improvement in symptoms was a genuine physical improvement. The blood sedimentation rate which was too high returned to normal; serum calcium which again was too high (12.5 milligrams per 100 cubic centimeters) became 10 milligrams; the low phosphorus 2.7 milligrams became 4.3 milligrams; there was improvement in the hematocrit, a rise in the hemoglobin from 70 per cent to 82 per cent, and the blood sugar was reduced from 122 milligrams to 96 milligrams which was more desirable. This was the individual reaction of this boy and is not to be construed as the reaction of all Tommy Smiths.

Chronic fatigue must be a national complaint if the hundreds of millions of dollars spent on vitamin pills is to be any criterion. It has been my experience with patients who complain of chronic fatigue that fully 65 per cent to 75 per cent of them will report a decided improvement of their physical well-being within one or two weeks after they have abstained from eating sugar and white flour products, without using vitamins. Not only do we consider the patient's report, but also the results of the biochemical index, which was referred to more in detail above, as indication of his having shown a definite improvement.

A girl of 19 came to see me about a very distressing condition. Her gums would bleed spontaneously even when talking, which was quite embarrassing for her. She felt so miserable and tired that she wept practically throughout the first interview. She had spells of chronic fatigue and dizziness, and occasionally she had collapsed on the sidewalk. She had been constipated as long as she could remember and had to "take something" for relief. Headaches were quite frequent also, and she remarked that "she loaded up on Aspirin." Upon questioning her about her food habits, I found that 6 weeks before she had been advised to eat 5 candy bars daily to correct her low blood sugar and dizziness. After about a week on this program one more difficulty was added to her misery—this spontaneous bleeding of the gums. In addition to that, the dizzy spells increased in severity. The blood chemistry examination showed a marked deviation from normal, and the blood sugar was *even lower than it had been* 6 *weeks prior.* A diet which contained no sugar or white flour products, was high in protein, was moderately low in fat, and contained approximately 250 grams of good starches was prescribed for her for two weeks. When she returned her gums had stopped bleeding; she was full of pep; her bowels were evacuating at least once daily without laxatives, and she had not had a headache since the third day of her diet. All blood tests were markedly improved, and I must add that her blood sugar which had been low (55 milligrams) had risen to 104 milligrams, which is quite normal.

There are those who feel that the mouth is a separate entity from the rest of the body and the treatment of that mouth can only be done surgically. The cutting of a tooth to receive a filling requires surgical skill which is very exacting. Surgery on the gums to alleviate a pyorrheal condition likewise demands exactness. One must acknowledge the need for this procedure, but what is being done to prevent the recurrence? I do not wish to be too presumptuous, but what about Medicine? Recently I had occasion to visit the great Medico-Dental centers of a large number of our great universities throughout the country. The tour guide pointed with great pride to the magnificent structures which had been built or were in the process of being built in his particular locality. All were hospitals dedicated to the treatment and care of the sick, but nowhere did I find even one little building which could be pointed out as having been erected for the sole purpose of prevention—aimed at keeping people out of the impressive structures. The implication, there, I feel is of tremendous importance. Approximately 50 per cent of the inductees for military service are being rejected for physical reasons and 77 per cent of our so-called "healthy boys" who were killed in Korea, upon autopsy were found to have a degenerative heart condition. Isn't it about time that we start spending money on that little building I referred to above?

As mentioned before, when Tommy Smith's mother related these other "incidentals" other than tooth decay, I began at that time to correlate the general complaints of patients with, for example, pyorrhea or what is properly called periodontitis. It was amazing to me to find that chronic fatigue, headaches, chronic constipation, arthritis, gas after eating, etc. were very commonly associated with this disease. Chronic fatigue was the most frequent complaint with constipation following a close second. And there were those who listed all of the above complaints. This was not as uncommon as one would suppose. Periodontitis is a disease primarily of the bone which supports the tooth. In its advanced stages, this loss of bone can no longer support the tooth and the tooth becomes loosened. Deposits of tartar around and below the gum line of the teeth have been listed as a possible cause of the disease. Yet one must ask the why of these tartar formations! It is commonly known that this bone loss occurs in some people without any tartar formations. Here again is where sugar enters the picture. After patients abstain from sugar and white flour products I have noted many times that this tartar formation does not tend to recur and there is a general tightening of the teeth. In support of that statement, the blood chemistry likewise improves.

A fifty-year-old woman came to my office having a well advanced case of periodontitis. There was considerable bone loss around the teeth, which was very uncomfortable. My first interview revealed that about 3 years previously X-rays had been made of the teeth. By comparing them with the present ones, it was seen that there was considerable bone loss in that period of time. She complained of frequent, severe headaches in the back of her head; chronic sinusitis which had been diagnosed by an Ear, Nose and Throat Specialist; she had to get up two or three times a night to urinate; chronic constipation for years was another complaint, her craving for sweets was insatiable, eating from a pound to two pounds of candy a week; upon awakening in the morning she felt utterly exhausted and this feeling continued throughout the day which necessitated frequent naps; she complained of mental depression and menopausal distress with its attendant hot flushes.

Let us examine what a sugar and white flour free diet had accomplished for her, by the time she returned two weeks later. Her teeth according to her statement felt tighter (examination supported this statement) and were free from pain brought about by sudden changes of temperature in food. She had only one slight headache; the sinus condition was not as annoying (post nasal drip); she could sleep through the night without having to get up; her exhausted feeling had disappeared, and her husband told me that she was much more cheerful; the hot flushes had nearly abated; but her craving for sweets had not decreased. There was such a marked improvement in the biochemical index that no further treatment seemed necessary.

When sugar was eliminated from the diet of a patient whom I saw at the County Hospital, the results were quite dramatic. She had a painful pyorrhoetic condition and a blood pressure of 260/150. She was asked to stop taking Serpasil (the alkaloid salt of Rauwolfia, that famous root known for its tranquilizing properties), for two weeks. She had been taking this drug for a period of two months without any apparent relief from her high blood pressure. A sugar free diet was prescribed; and when she returned two weeks later, a drop of 110 points occurred in her blood pressure, making it 150/100. Also there was quite a dramatic reduction in the blood cholesterol, from 360 milligrams per 100 cubic centimeters of blood to 190 milligrams, which is within normal limits. Needless to say she left granulated sugar completely out of her diet and discontinued taking the tranquilizer.

Her blood pressure continued to improve with slight fluctuations around the 130 mark over the diastolic range of from 80 to 85.

Mother Hubbard's activities had something to do with the next word which is bandied about so frequently, *allergy*. One evening a speaker was asking an audience comprised of professional people, for a "good" definition for the word allergy. I thought that the best definition was, "The word 'allergy' is like a Mother Hubbard—it covers everything and touches nothing." You have been wondering, perhaps, what sugar has to do with allergy when this word covers so many illnesses of mankind and touches nothing.

So many illnesses have been written off as an "allergic manifestation." One may safely re-word that quotation and say "sugar manifestation" in many instances. One individual, after 30 years of abstaining from eggs, which He knew from experience caused his lips and tongue to swell to the point where sometimes it was difficult to breathe, by cutting out sugar from his diet can now eat 6 or 8 eggs a day with pleasure without any ill effects. Perhaps some sort of proof can be established here—if he includes sugar in his diet, his symptoms return, including a dermatitis on the hands. If he does not include sugar, even relatively small amounts, his allergic symptoms disappear. This happened to one person and I hope that it will not be construed that the same will happen to everyone with allergies.

A 22-month old child was brought to my office for the treatment of large ulcers, similar in appearance to the common canker sore, and appearing on both sides of the tongue, on both cheeks and on the tonsilar region. They varied in size from the diameter of a pencil to one the size of a quarter. He was feverish and underweight. The mother felt that he was too thin so she had been feeding the child ice cream, candy, cookies, pie, cake, pastries, in fact everything which she thought would put weight on him. Incidentally, it did not increase his weight. By now you must have guessed what I did. You are right. Owing to the emergency of the case, medication was used in support of the diet and a very dramatic result was obtained. The ulcers disappeared in one week's time, although they had resisted other types of medication for two months prior. I believe that the removal of sugar from his diet aided tremendously in his recovery.

This was a case in which I had to restrain the mother from continually bribing the child to eat "what was good for him," and to show no concern whatsoever at meal time about what he ate or did not eat. In other words to leave the child alone. If he were still dabbling with his food when the others had finished eating, she should remove his plate also. That had to be repeated only once or twice; Johnny soon discovered that mommy meant business. The manner in which he selected foods was like a little animal—from sight, smell and taste with no restrictions placed on how much he ate of any one food or the neglect of others. A well balanced meal was placed before him, and the rest was up to him. One day the mother called me very excitedly and wondered whether or not to call an ambulance and have his stomach pumped. The reason? He had toddled up to the table where she was preparing some ground round steak and had eaten a mouthful. Would it hurt him, and what should she do? I replied by asking her if he liked this raw meat and if so, to serve two patties, raw, to him for dinner that evening. To the exclusion of most every other food that was served to him, he had raw hamburgers for breakfast, lunch and dinner. This hamburger "jag" continued for about 15 days. Naturally the mother was quite concerned about his having no milk, no vegetables and little fruit—just raw hamburger. So she called me. Upon inquiry I found that he was feeling fine and was gaining weight. He stopped this regime just as suddenly as he started it and went on a binge of dried apricots. I was informed about 10 days later that Johnny had just consumed 25 dried apricots that day and that she was concerned over the fact that he had drunk very little milk. I must say that this was unusual, but soon after, the apricots were stopped by him rather suddenly, and he went on a milk binge. This continued for another two or three weeks. It was only after these apparent cravings were satisfied that he returned to what one may term normal eating. Lest we forget—there was no ice cream and cake to reward him if he ate his spinach. Many patients have told me that after removing sugar from their diet, they then ate foods which in the past they thoroughly disliked. All food even tasted different and better. It may be in Johnny's case that the nerves governing the sense of taste and smell had been dulled by sugar.

In correlating the incidence of these complaints with conditions present in the mouth, I find that headaches and constipation are the most frequent. Many cases of so-called migraine headaches have responded very well when sugar products were not eaten. I do not have the actual statistics, but in my practice I can say that fully 50 per cent of my patients who complained of migraine headaches enjoyed a complete recovery.

Reprinted with permission from the September and October, 1958, issues of *Modern Nutrition*.

CHAPTER 112

Personal Experiences with Sugar

By J. I. Rodale

A few years ago I was reading the *New York Times* and came across a news item regarding a round-table discussion at the 20th Annual Meeting of the American Academy of Pediatrics at Toronto, Canada. Among other erudite subjects, they took up the question of fleas and insects. They stated that flea bite is a condition well known on the West Coast, but is now becoming more common in the East. Doctors were advised, they said, to consider it seriously as a possible cause of certain skin troubles. They over-looked the fact that there are certain researches which absolutely indicate that where the body is well nourished, (which means then that the skin is well nourished) fleas will not find such a habitation palatable to them. A flea is an insect that thrives on a skin that is filthy or diseased, and in most cases such diseases cannot be seen with the naked eye. There is a condition known as a sub-clinical form of scurvy with which more than 60 per cent of our population is now afflicted.

This is merely a prelude to the main theme. In a further discussion of insect bites, at this meeting, but not referring to fleas, Dr. Earl D. Osborne of Buffalo, referred to a certain piece of research which indicated that if vitamin B_1 was given to individuals in quantity, by mouth, it seemed to act as an insect repellent. This is where sugar comes in. But first let me give you my story.

Eliminating Artificial Sugars

About 1946, I decided to cut out all artificial sugars from my diet. This was on the advice of Dr. Melvin E. Page of St. Petersburg, Florida. Dr. Page has a laboratory in which he checks the blood of patients. He has found that normally the blood of a person who is healthy and who does not eat artificial sugars, has a certain relationship between its calcium and phosphorus. He has found that it is two and one-half to one, or two and one-half times as much calcium as phosphorus. But in all his experience, when working with the blood of patients who are sugar-consumers, he finds this ratio grossly distorted. When that was explained to me, I immediately realized that I wanted to have my blood as healthy as possible, and began to severely eliminate all these artificial sugars. It meant, however, that I could eat fruits and such things as honey and molasses in moderation.

That summer I noticed that I was practically immune to mosquito bites. When all others were complaining about being bitten, I was not. And when I discussed this matter with an aunt of mine who has diabetes, and who also has to forego artificial sugars, she said she has had the same experience. She does not get bitten by mosquitoes.

Now here is the most interesting thing about this whole subject. The doctor mentioned earlier, who gave vitamin B_1 to individuals to act as an insect repellent, was working within the scope of a program that cuts out sugar. This is how it works:

I have since found out that the artificial sugars use up the vitamin B_1 of the body. This would seem to indicate that those people who are using artificial sugars in their diet are not only distorting their calcium-phosphorus in their blood, but are also destroying vitamin B_1 which can lead to many serious conditions.

I might state that alcohol also uses up the vitamin B_1 in the body. People who drink habitually, that is, take liquor every day, will usually suffer from a severe vitamin B_1 deficiency. That is why in the treatment of alcoholism, tremendous doses of vitamin B_1 are given to these unfortu-nates.

I had a very interesting experience recently in meeting with a former aviation pilot, who was active in World War II. He related to me an experience. He used to suffer from blackouts, which would take only a few seconds. But in a plane that would be a very serious and dangerous thing. The doctors cured him by giving him vitamin B_1. This would seem to indicate that airplane pilots should not eat the sweet foods such as ice creams, pies, pastries and others that contain artificial sugars, including cola drinks, because the chances are, if this pilot whom we were talking about, would have been on a diet that did not take in these artificial sugars, he probably would not have suffered from these blackouts, which were caused by a vitamin B_1 deficiency, and which was cured by taking vitamin B_1.

Mosquito's Power of Detection

It is amazing how a mosquito can detect that the blood is not to its liking. In other words, a mosquito is practically a censor, determining whether there is too much calcium or phosphorus for his taste. Probably, he has a sense of smell that can detect an odor from blood which is not properly constituted for him. But I should not want to go around with my blood out of whack, however slight such a distortion should be. The body should be running like a Swiss watch mechanism. Can you picture a Swiss watch with something only slightly out of whack? That would not do. I would like to quote from an article called "Down the Pike" by E. S. Bayard from the *Pennsylvania Farmer*, May 28, 1949, which throws additional light on the subject of diet and mosquitoes.

"I have had some chance to observe the effects of diet, or at least what I was told were such effects. The people of Peru are the smallest I have ever seen. And in the market at Lima the portions of meat sold are the smallest I have seen anywhere on 3 continents. But these two things don't prove anything—they may be merely coincident facts. Many years ago in western Canada the late Herbert Quick and I went to a church event where ice cream and other good things were served. The air was full of mosquitoes and there was a smudge fire in each corner of the yard where the good things were supplied. Mr. Quick and I ate with two Indian women who admired his books. Not a mosquito was on the arms or face of either lady. I was told that this was because they ate no sugar—but that may not be the real reason. In the black fly season in Canada I knew a man and his sister what ate at the same table in the inn in which I was. The black flies filled up on the brother's neck until blood ran down over his white collar whenever the full fly dropped off. And no fly would touch his rosy sister!"

I think that in the case of white people who are going into the tropics where there is fear of mosquitoes carrying some kind of serious disease, it would be a good idea to go into training first and for a long period preceding the trip, take all the artificial sugars out of the diet and possibly add a little vitamin B_1 besides. Imagine if this fact had been known in the Spanish-American War, what lives could have been saved!

[407]

My Calcium-Phosphorus Level

I want to close with an interesting experience that I recently had. I know a physician in Philadelphia, who is helping people by testing their blood specifically for vitamin deficiency and prescribing the lacking vitamins. I have seen 3 cases in which this physician helped immensely. A few weeks ago I took a friend to see this doctor and went along personally to see how it was done. This patient was suffering from hay fever, and the doctor took some of his blood and tested it right before my eyes on a spectroscope. The blood of this patient showed all kinds of deficiencies. Then the doctor looked at me with a peculiar gleam in his eye and said "Look here, Rodale, you are supposed to be eating food raised organically and you are always talking about your wonderful health. Now I've got you here, let me take some of your blood and test it."

I said, "Sure, go ahead."

When he tested some of my blood, he looked at me and said: "Rodale, this is the best blood I have seen in the year and a half that I have been doing this kind of work, and bear in mind that I have been testing blood of healthy people, as well as sick ones, for many persons come here for routine checkups."

But the one thing he particularly showed me was my calcium-phosphorus relationship. He said he rarely comes across a case where it is as close to the two and one-half to one as mine was. My calcium was 10.00 and my phosphorus was 4.575 milligrams. The patient that I brought along had calcium 8.895 and phosphorus 4.620.

This shows what clean living will do.

CHAPTER 113

Sugar in Primitive Diets

A headline from the *Los Angeles Examiner,* June 11, 1953, caught our eye the other day: *Indian Survey Hints Diet May Be Cancer Study Link.* The article went on to say: "Cancer may be linked to the food you eat, particularly sweet food that produces high blood sugar levels, a doctor who made a survey of phenomenally low cancer rates among Navajo Indians reported yesterday.

"Dr. C. G. Salsbury, director of the Arizona State Health Department and for 23 years Superintendent of the Indian Hospital at Ganado, Arizona, told the Western Branch of the American Health Association at the Biltmore:

'During my recent year on the Navajo reservation, I was struck by the apparently low incidence of cancer.

'In a period of 23 years with nearly 35,000 admissions to the hospital, only 66 malignancies of all types were observed and nothing even faintly resembling a cancer of the breast in a Navajo woman was seen during that period.

'Some outstanding authorities have suggested that diet may have some relation to the low incidence. Navajo blood sugar levels consistently run about 25 per cent below that of white people'."

Dr. Page, in his book, *Degeneration and Regeneration,* has more to say about primitive diets and their effect on health.

"We have shown disease conditions reversed by improved nutrition and we have discussed the harmful elements in the food of civilized people but to make the relationship of health and diet more clear, let us consider primitive tribes.

"In his book, *Uttermost Part of the Earth,* Mr. Bridges, the foremost authority on the Fuegian Indians, states that in the early days in Patagonia he never heard of an Indian having a toothache. He believed that they were unacquainted with the malady. Their health in other respects was equally as good. But with the influx of civilization they lost their teeth and their health as a toll to the white man's food and the white man's diseases. Now there are less than one hundred and fifty pure-blooded Indians and possibly a slightly larger number of half-breeds. Yet within the memory of one man the Indian population has been reduced to this figure from an estimated nine thousand persons.

"An interesting sidelight is that at the present time the Indian and white populations have very nearly reversed in numbers. The white population in Patagonia was 9,560 at the last census.

Natural Foods Among Primitive Peoples

"Dr. Weston Price has made a most notable study of the diets of primitive peoples existing in many parts of the world today. His book, *Nutrition and Physical Degeneration* (available from the Lee Foundation, 2023 West Wisconsin Avenue, Milwaukee, Wisconsin) is a landmark in the advancement of applied nutrition. Where he found primitives uninfluenced by the modern diet, the incidence of dental decay and other degenerative diseases was markedly low as compared with the figures tabulated among so-called civilized peoples. In the secluded areas inhabited by primitive tribes, the diet was found to consist chiefly of whole grains, animal foods and dairy products. The most desired parts of the animals were the liver, the heart, kidneys and blood. These parts by chemical analysis were found to contain more vitamins and minerals than the muscle parts which civilized peoples consider particularly choice.

"When white flour and sugar became part of the daily food intake, for these people, dental decay, tuberculosis, etc., became rampant. Never having been exposed to these ills, no immunity to them had been established. Therefore, once their systems had become weakened through an

[409]

inadequate and rapidly changing diet, they were easy victims to bacterial invasion. Even in two or three generations these people could be reduced to one-tenth their former number merely through the breakdown of their bodily chemical balance due to inadequate diet. The rate of deterioration of these hitherto immune people seems to be directly in proportion to the amount of harmful dietary intake.

"Sugar and white flour were introduced to these people simultaneously and in quantities. Within one generation the effects were devastating. Among us the more gradual acceptance of these items of diet results in a less rapid though still too rapid degeneration. Island tribes in some localities were found existing in health upon an unvaried diet of fish, whole grains and some wild plant life. Thus a few natural foods were found to be more productive of health than the refined, delectably concocted dishes of modern man. The percentage of dental decay among these people was negligible so long as they remained on their native diet. A recognition of the value of fish food was widespread. Even high in the Andes Mountains natives were found carrying small pouches at their waists in which were dried fish eggs and seaweed, products which could be obtained only by making long journeys to the sea.

The Value of Native Diets

"Among primitive people much greater thought is given to the diet of both men and women previous to conception than is the custom in modern civilization. Long trips are made for special foods, crabs, the ashes of water hyacinths and certain cereals, because tradition has taught that these foods have peculiar dietary values that influence the physical and mental well-being of future progeny. Doctor Price had laboratory examinations made of these special foods and found that such food customs were scientifically sound. Unusual amounts of calcium, iodine or carotene, which affect vitamin use within the body, were found to characterize these foods.

"Where modern diet was accepted by the natives, structural changes of the bony formation of the body were observable within even one generation. Narrowed dental arches affected respiration and mastication aiding in the onslaught of disease. Pelvic formations in women were altered and affected the bearing of children. In brief, general deterioration of the body was observed with an inevitable effect upon the mental and moral well-being of these people.

"That this process could be reversed by a return to the native diets was evidenced among the people of one of the Pacific Islands. Temporarily the high price of copra permitted the exchange of this for large quantities of white flour and sugar. The children of the island rapidly developed a high rate of dental decay although previously only a small fraction of the people had been so affected. The day came when the value of copra dropped so low that it was unprofitable for the traders to stop. The old native diet was reinstated and shortly dental decay had stopped. Chemical balance of the body had been reestablished and bacteria were no longer able to penetrate the tooth structures.

"Instead of seeking economic profit through exploitation of these people, it might repay us to adopt their customs regulating health and the production of mentally and physically excellent children. By correlating the findings among all these peoples and using them in our own civilization we should be able not only to equal their standards of health but to exceed them."

Editor Rodale's visit to Dr. Page in Florida brought the following comments: "One thing that impressed me about Dr. Page's work should be of interest to women who wish to be beautiful. He noticed that in both men and women as they eliminated sugar, they not only lost weight if they were overweight to start with, but that the lines of their faces took on a much more handsome appearance. He said that it was most uncanny what the mere cutting out of sugar did to the features of the face. It also helped to accomplish miracles in curing many terribly sick people. Today we are a nation of sugar-drunkards, eating over 100 pounds of sugar per year per capita. We have perverted our natural tastes."

CHAPTER 114

Sugar and the
Calcium-Phosphorus Balance

An entirely different approach to the problem of sugar intake is presented by Melvin Page, D.D.S., of Florida, in his book, *Degeneration and Regeneration,* published by the Biochemical Research Foundation, 2810 First Street, North, St. Petersburg, Florida. Says Dr. Page, "We have had up to now no device whereby which we could test the ability of our body-chemistry to withstand strains and exposure to disease. A measuring stick has now been found." He then discusses the importance of minerals in the diet and says, "much research has led me to the discovery that the secret lay not in the amount of these minerals, but in their proportion to each other." The outstanding important element is the relationship of calcium to phosphorus in the blood stream, which should be two and a half to one. "On the basis of 20,000 tests taken during the past 20 years, we can state that in clinical cases, in the adult, the critical point is reached when the calcium shows 8.75 milligrams per 100 cubic centimeters of blood and when the phosphorus shows 3.5 milligrams per 100 cubic centimeters of blood. Below these amounts for either calcium or phosphorus there is a withdrawal of minerals from the dentin and bone, and above these amounts a reserve is maintained.

". . . There has been a great deal of talk about sugar being a cause of dental decay. Directly it is not, but indirectly it is." Dr. Page then relates the case histories of several patients whose blood chemistry he studied. In several of them he could find no reason for sudden changes in an excellent blood chemistry, until they confessed that just recently they had gotten into the habit of eating candy and sweets. He then tested the blood of other patients and immediately gave them candy to eat. Within two and a half hours there was a difference of 9 points in the usable calcium and phosphorus in their blood streams.

Arthritis, Cancer and Sugar

Pyorrhea, an inflamed condition of the gums, is actually a form of arthritis, says Dr. Page, although it is not called that because of its location in the body. "In a series of several hundred arthritics," he says, "nearly all consumed large quantities of sugar. Sugar disturbs the calcium-phosphorus balance more than any other single factor. It disturbs it in the direction of higher calcium and lower phosphorus. When the effect of the sugar has worn off, there is a rebound in the opposite direction, for action equals reaction.

"Someone might ask, why not use sugar to maintain better equilibrium of calcium and phosphorus levels. . . . First of all, it cannot be done effectively without taking just the right amounts at frequent intervals and secondly the method increases the deficiency already existing—adding fuel to the fire so to speak. Sugar is a drug and at times can be used for the purpose of raising the calcium level and lowering the phosphorus level. But its use would be for temporary effect only." In summing up his thoughts on nutrition, Dr. Page lays down two rules: 1. Our diet must not contain any harmful things; 2. It must contain all things necessary to the human body. If these two rules are obeyed, health can be attained and maintained, for adequate nutrition means calcium-phosphorus balance and good health. Refined sugar is not necessary. Refined sugar is harmful, so a sugar-eater has violated both rules for health.

"What is the result of a total discontinuance of sugar?" asks Dr. Page. Do we fail from loss of energy? Do we become tired and worn? Does our food become tasteless? Sometimes we have all these symptoms but only for a few days. A readjustment must take place in the body. We have to learn all over again to use our built-in resources.

"It is remarkable how soon we do this. How soon we feel better than we ever did. How soon our tastes recover their sensitivity so that we find flavors in food that we never realized were there. . . . You know you cannot hear ordinary conversation in a boiler factory. Neither can you taste ordinary flavors when the strong chemical sugar is making such a din. . . . Recently Dr. Otto Meyerhof of the University of Pennsylvania Medical School and the 1923 Nobel Prize winner in medicine stated that possibly growth of cancerous tissue might be stopped if biochemists could find a safe way to curb the appetite of tumors for sugar." This article, incidentally,

[412]

appears in the magazine, *Drug and Allied Industries,* p. 28, Vol. 35, No. 5, May, 1949.

"We believe that the sugar level of the blood is even more important than Dr. Meyerhof states. We do not remember seeing a single cancer case who had a correct sugar level, yet in most non-cancer cases this is easily obtained by means of a sugar-free diet alone." He then describes a case of skin cancer of the face which cleared up entirely within a few months when the patient gave up drinking daily 12 bottles of a widely distributed soft drink.

Here are some more quotes from Dr. Page's book, which we believe should be on the shelves of every health-conscious person.

Sugar and Civilized Man

"The two greatest changes in nutrition have been from the whole grain flours to white flour, from few sweets and those natural, to refined sugar and that in large quantities. These two things, white flour and sugar, are the most common and the most harmful elements in our diet. They have been in use only one hundred to one hundred and fifty years, which is a long time if you think in terms of your life and mine but not when you think in terms of civilization as a whole. In plant life alterations can be developed or new species brought into being but it is a process of selection and repeated reproduction involving generations of plant life. Changes in man come just as slowly if not more so because though we use scientific methods to produce plants, we are hit-and-miss about the propagation of man. To make radical dietary changes in 100 to 150 years is to court disaster. The human mechanism is not adapted to such rapid changes. Our bodies are capable of adaptation but it must be a slow process covering many generations.

"Sugar, the ultra-refined sweet, has had every element but sweetness removed and is lacking in both minerals and vitamins. It is a popular item of diet, especially in America. As previously noted in the discussion on dental decay, it has a deleterious effect on the calcium-phosphorus levels, the health indices, of our bodies. A brief explanation of the relationship of sugar to our bodily processes may make clear the reason for this harmful effect. Sixty-eight per cent of the food we eat is broken down through bodily chemical processes into sugar. Sugar, water, the amino and fatty acids, and mineral salts in solution are capable of permeating the intestinal wall and directly entering the blood stream. If we take refined sugar, a general requirement of the American table, into our systems, it does not need to be changed greatly in order to permeate the intestinal wall. It is nearly ready to enter the blood stream and it does so in a flood. And as in any flood, some one must come to the rescue to prevent disaster. . . . If there is more than one teaspoon of sugar in the entire blood stream or less than one-half teaspoon, we court disaster. . . . But we are most remarkably built and the liver and the pancreas form a rescue team and turn this suger into glycogen and store it for future use. Now that may be very well in an emergency, but think of the abuse which most of us inflict on our systems daily. It is astonishing that any of us are well. And when you consider that the intake of sugar increases the calcium assimilation and that resistance to degeneration and bacteria are dependent upon the maintenance of a proper ratio between calcium and phosphorus, you can not but be impressed by the necessity to use this drug with care. As mentioned earlier, 9 chocolates can throw the calcium-phosphorus levels out of balance within two and one-half hours and keep them below the margin of safety for immunity to dental decay at least 32 hours. Seventy-five per cent efficiency of the human machine will maintain good teeth but that is too low a degree to prevent the occurrence of other degenerative diseases. It would be laughable if we were to represent machines in the open market as only 75 per cent as good as they could be made.

There Are Exceptions

"You can all point to So-and-So who is healthy and takes sugar by the carload in his coffee or So-and-So who just lives on soda pop—one bottle of pop generally contains 4 teaspoons of sugar—and still keeps well. This is true, firstly, because there are exceptions to all rules and secondly, because many do not begin to pay for their extravagances until late in life. But look at their children and grandchildren. Do they hand down bodies as strong as those which they inherited? Natural sweets such as honey, molasses and maple syrup can be used within reason. They do affect the calcium-phosphorus levels but since they are not pure sweet and do contain essentials of diet, their presence among our foods is not as injurious as refined sugar. In generations past sugar was never found alone. It was always accompanied by other materials that the body needed. Sweet is just the label on the package.

"A scientific experiment with the sea-anemone, a water organism, provides an amusing illustration of the folly of being misled by labels. Sea-anemones live on meat but it is the creatine in the meat which attracts them. That is their one sense of taste. However, if the meat from which the creatine has been extracted is placed in the water, the sea-anemones ignore it, but if blotting paper soaked in creatine is placed within reach, they eat it with relish. They eat the label and leave the substance. Silly isn't it? But how about us?

"When we use free sugar we do so at the expense of the other essentials to the body. Our total caloric intake of food may not be changed, but the proportions of the heat-producing and cell-replacing ingredients are considerably altered. In this respect the use of sugar creates a deficiency in these other materials. In every instance where a patient has habitually used refined sugar, deficiencies have existed in the other factors of an adequate nutrition, particularly as regards the vitamin B complex."

CHAPTER 115

Sugar Is Bad for the Heart

Nutritionists at the Agriculture Department's main research center at Beltsville, Maryland, are quietly adding sugar to the lengthy list of foods suspected of causing trouble in the heart and arteries, according to a story in the *Wall Street Journal* for June 18, 1959.

It seems that a series of experiments has shown that ordinary table sugar may play an important role in the body's production of cholesterol—the fatty substance which becomes deadly when it accumulates in places where it doesn't belong. The *Journal* article reminds us that scientists have been blaming consumption of fatty foods primarily for overproduction of cholesterol.

Dr. Callie Mae Coons and Dr. Madelyn Womack did the experiments. They involved 270 laboratory rats who were fed varying amounts of protein, fats, carbohydrates. For fat the animals ate corn oil, hydrogenated vegetable oil (the solid, white kind) and ordinary lard. For carbohydrates they ate ordinary granulated sugar and cornstarch. After a period which corresponds to 40 or 50 years in the life of a human being, the rats were examined to see what combination of foods did the most harm.

In the group which ate 15 per cent corn oil and 50 per cent cornstarch, the average cholesterol count was low—.172 grams for each portion of blood used as a standard measure. Rats eating the same amount of corn oil and 50 per cent sugar had a cholesterol count of .356—more than double that of the starch eaters. Starch eaten with lard or hydrogenated oil also appeared to produce lower cholesterol levels than sugar.

Furthermore—and this is especially important for readers who are worried about overweight—a sugar-plus-fat combination tended to make the rats store more of their food intake as body fat. The average amount of fat in the bodies of rats eating this diet was 38 per cent of their total weight, compared to 22 per cent in those eating a normal diet.

The researchers tell us they do not know why the experiments turned out as they did. There are several possible explanations. One is that the presence of a lot of sugar in the diet may interfere with the body's ability to burn up its normal requirement of fat. The surplus then shows up where it is not wanted. Starch does not appear to interfere with the body's use of fat.

Another explanation is that corn oil and sugar, both easily and rapidly digested foods, may put too great a strain on the liver to handle them. Starch requires more time to be broken down into the various elements the body can use, thus allowing the digestive organs to handle it much more slowly in easy stages.

Whatever the explanation, researchers have now set up a program for testing the diets on college students. We have no final word on these tests as yet.

Economic Effects of This Discovery

Since the *Wall Street Journal* is a finance newspaper, it goes on to tell its readers what products may be affected soon if the human experiments bear out the rat experiments. Starchy foods, like potatoes, have suffered a decline in popularity in recent years. Consumption of 146 pounds per capita in 1938 was down to 107 pounds per capita in 1958.

Consumption of fats and oils and cane sugar has remained about the same. Consumption of sugar in all forms has been running about 100 pounds per year per person. Will the new findings change the trend and boost the potato back to its old popularity, while sugar sales decline? We certainly hope so.

The editor of the *Wall Street Journal* feels, apparently, that firms who deal in starchy foods and sugar should have this information to guide them in future business dealings, production plans and so forth.

It is worthy of note, we think, that no announcement of the findings was made to the public by the Department of Agriculture under whose direction the experiments were carried out.

We did not find in other newspapers or magazines a single word in print dealing with these experiments, although they were performed at a government institution and even though they brought to light highly significant information which might be instrumental in saving thousands of lives, they were not headlined and cheered. We suppose the reason is that no one wants to offend the sugar industry.

Other Researchers Confirm These Facts

Let us remind readers of the findings of a group of California researchers—John W. Gofman, Ph.D., M.D., Alex V. Nichols, Ph.D. and E. Virginia Dobbin, dietitian. In a book, *Dietary Prevention and Treatment of Heart Disease* (published by G. P. Putnam, 1958) these authors disclose the fact that there are two different kinds of lipoproteins (that is, combinations of fat and protein) which can form dangerous fatty substances. One of these results from overeating fat, chiefly animal fat. The other results from overeating carbohydrates.

The authors say, "As a result of the publication of some of the research findings on dietary fats, much of the lay press has indicated that the entire problem of coronary disease lies in the overeating of fats or the overeating of fats of saturated variety (hydrogenated), or of fats of animal origin. That *part* of the problem lies in this direction is certainly true, but generalizations of this sort overlook other major factors of importance and can lead to incorrect treatment. This chapter is concerned with one such other major factor of importance, namely, the dietary carbohydrate intake. Neglect of this factor can also lead to rather serious consequences, first in the failure to correct the diet in some individuals who are very sensitive to carbohydrate action; and second, by allowing certain individuals sensi-

[416]

tive to the carbohydrate action to take too much carbohydrate as a replacement for some of their animal fats. Thus, attention to the carbohydrate factor is a very real and important part of the effort to prevent and treat arterial thickening (hardening of the arteries) and coronary heart disease by dietary means."

Tests, described by Dr. Gofman and his associates, can be given which will show clearly which kind of blood fat is causing the trouble—that produced by too much fat or that produced by too much carbohydrate. If the tests show that neither kind of blood fat is too high, then, according to Dr. Gofman, no dieting is necessary. We disagree with this point of view. We feel this is the person who can benefit most from their discoveries. He can really do a preventive job. By following the right kind of diet he can see to it that he never needs to go on a restricted, unpleasant, intolerably dull diet to escape hardening of the arteries and heart attacks. Such a diet is, of course, the one we advise for everyone—*low in both carbohydrate and fat*—high in protein and the mineral-and vitamin-rich fruits and vegetables.

Why do starchy foods have the power of raising the fatty content of the blood? Dr. Gofman and his colleagues tell us they do not know, any more than the Beltsville researchers do. It is possible, they say, that when the body is taking in large amounts of carbohydrate and thus making sugar available in fair quantities, the body may use the sugar rather than the fat as a fuel for energy. So the fats, which are not used, may accumulate in the blood.

Another theory concerns the ability of the body to convert carbohydrate into fat. We know that it can. Perhaps the fatty substances in the blood of those who eat carbohydrate-rich diets are the converted carbohydrates which simply circulate through the blood before being deposited somewhere. No one knows what the answer is to the question of "why." But we do know that carbohydrates are just as likely to be responsible as fats for unhealthful cholesterol deposits in the body.

And the Beltsville research seems to pinpoint refined sugar as the carbohydate that is responsible.

Vitamin B Deficiency May Be Involved

As we have shown earlier, the use of refined sugar makes demands on the body's supply of thiamin, a B vitamin. The reason for this is that thiamin is essential for the body's use of carbohydrates. Purely natural carbohydrates (potatoes, beans, fruits) come already supplied with B vitamins, which are used by the body to convert the sugar into a useful substance. Refined sugar—that is, white, granulated sugar that you put in your coffee and sprinkle on cereal—has had all its B vitamins removed in the refining process. So the body mobilizes the necessary B vitamins to process this refined sugar and this robs muscles, nerves and digestive tract of whatever B vitamins are there.

Walter H. Eddy, Ph.D., and Gilbert Dalldorf, M.D., say in their book, *The Avitaminoses* (Williams and Wilkins), "Thiamin deficiency impairs the function of the heart, increases the tendency to extravascular fluid collections and results in terminal cardiac standstill." They go on to describe experiments in which heart disease was produced in pigeons by depriving them of vitamin B. When the B vitamins were fed, the heart disease was cured.

Nutrition and Diet in Health and Disease by James S. McLester, M.D. (W. B. Saunders Company), relates experiments in which pigs who were fed a diet deficient in thiamin showed a scarring of the right side of the heart.

The normal heart beat of rats is 500 to 550 beats per minute. When they are fed a diet low in thiamin, for about 3 weeks, the rate goes down to about 350 per minute. This reduction is so dependable a symptom of lowered thiamin intake that it is used in laboratories to test the thiamin content of various vitamin products. The rate of heart beat can be increased automatically, within 4 hours, by giving thiamin.

Beriberi, the disease of vitamin B deficiency, results in heart damage, decreased circulation time, a rise in blood pressure. Dr. Eddy says in a book, *Vitaminology* (Williams and Wilkins), that the effect of thiamin on the heart and blood vessel system is to "increase arterial tone." Surely a lack of thiamin would be involved in the diet of someone who is overeating on white sugar. Could this B vitamin deficiency have something to do with the findings of the Beltsville researchers and Dr. Gofman?

CHAPTER 116

Sugar and Cancer

By J. I. Rodale

Let us see what various physicians have done and said about sugar. Dr. John A. Shaw-Mackenzie in his book, *The Nature and Treatment of Cancer* (1906) said:

"As long ago as 1845, Macilwain maintained it to be a pure assumption that cancer is incurable by the powers of Nature. This observer referred the causes to errors in diet on non-assimilation of food, sedentary habits, the free use of alcohol, and of greasy, fatty, and saccharin matter. He rigidly dieted his patients, excluding sugar, as some authorities at the present day also do."

Here is a quotation from Hoffman's book, *Cancer and Diet*, dealing with the effect of diet on cancer:

"J. Ellis Barker, a layman, in 1924 published a substantial volume on *Cancer, How it is Caused; How it can be Prevented*, with an introduction

[418]

by Sir W. Arbuthnot Lane, which attracted world wide attention and is often quoted. The book is largely concerned with the dietary aspects of cancer which cannot be abbreviated to advantage. He emphasizes the importance of vitamins and concludes in part:

" 'Modern civilized feeding has two great characteristics. Civilized nations are being starved of vitamins in the form of green vegetables and especially of uncooked vegetables, such as salads. They are starved of vitamins in the form of the outer skin of every kind. They are starved of the vitamins contained in uncooked milk and in fresh meat. While civilized men and women are being starved of all these essentials, they are being supplied with a superabundance of sugar. The increase in the consumption of sugar has been as extraordinarily great and as rapid as has been the diminution in the consumption of vitamins.'

"He calls attention to the enormous increase in the per capita consumption of sugar, quoting Hutchinson to the effect that in strong solution sugar is an irritant to the tissues. In contact with the skin, it is apt to set up superficial inflammation. Furthermore he observes:

" 'The instinctive feeling of hale, old people and of the most experienced old practitioners that immoderate consumption of sugar is very harmful is borne out of observation and by the latest discoveries of science. Everybody knows extravagant sugar-eaters. They are usually chronic dyspeptics. Very bad odors emanate from them, and they have a wretched complexion. As a rule, they are very constipated and are bad-tempered. Overfondness of sweets almost invariably goes together with a dislike of vegetables and of fresh fruit and of fresh meat. Thus overindulgence in sweets seems somehow or other to lead to vitamin starvation with all its very serious consequences'."

Hoffman mentions Dr. Bernhard Fischer-Wasels, Director of the Pathological Institute of the University of Frankfort, who in a monograph on *Methods of Preventing Cancerous Diseases* was emphatic in pointing out the danger and harmfulness of an excessive carbohydrate nutrition, and the danger and harmfulness of excessive sugar intake.

Sugar, the Diluting Food

Hoffman quotes C. V. McCollum, who is one of the world's greatest nutritionists, as saying:

"Nature did not intend that we should eat much sugar, such as glucose and cane sugar, else our natural foods would have contained more of them. Primitive man never had sugar in amounts greater than are afforded by sweet fruits, except when he secured occasionally a temporary supply of honey. Nature provides starches in abundance, and these we digest into simple sugars. This process requires considerable time, so that several hours elapse between the eating of a few ounces of starch and its complete absorption from the intestinal tract. When we take sugars which are soluble and easily absorbable, they tend to enter the blood too fast and to tax the body's capacity to take care of them. If much sugar is eaten at one time, there is a tendency to create a high tide of sugar in the blood. This is a very undesirable condition to establish since it taxes the pancreas . . . We should never lose our appreciation of the bland flavors natural to fruits, vegetables, meats, etc., through masking them with sweetness, spices, pepper, flavors, acids, etc. . . . We are as a nation, eating so much sugar that we are crowding out of the diet a considerable amount of other foods which would be far better for us than is sugar." Hoffman follows this with his comment: "It may be pointed out in this connection that the United States has the highest diabetes death rate in the world and the death rate continues to increase from year to year, regardless of insulin treatment which inhibits the disease but does not cure it."

Plimmer and Plimmer in their treatise, *Food and Health* (1925) said:

"Not so very long ago sugar was a rare luxury kept under lock and key in the tea caddy. At the end of the eighteenth century the manufacture of beet sugar was begun in Germany and the industry developed rapidly and lowered the price of sugar. Its consumption has increased enormously and is still increasing in all civilized countries. The Americans, with their love of candy, are the largest sugar eaters in the world. Incidentally, cancer and diabetes, two scourges of civilization have increased proportionately to the sugar consumption."

Hutchinson and Mottram in their book, *Food and the Principles of Dietetics* (London, 1943), say:

"The second factor which influences the digestibility of a sugar is the degree of concentration of its solution. In strong solution sugar is an irritant to the tissues. In contact with the skin, it is apt to set up superficial inflammation. This is familiar in the form of the eczema which is apt to appear in diabetics from the contact of the sugar-containing urine with the skin, and from the similar condition occurring on the arms of grocers and other persons who have frequently to handle sugar, and it is on account of its irritating properties that sugar cannot be used as a subcutaneous aliment (food), though otherwise well adapted to fulfill that function. All attempts to use it in that fashion have been frustrated by the pain which it sets up. The same is true of the stomach."

In other words these two doctors show that excessive use of sugar irritates the stomach and the intestines. They state further:

"This irritating effect on the mucous membrane is accompanied by the production of much mucous and the pouring out of a highly acid gastric juice. These irritating effects seem to be much more pronounced in the case of cane-sugar than in that of glucose."

Hoffman continues:

"J. Ellis Barker, in an extended discussion on *The Faults of Modern Feeding,* quotes a paper by Dr. Nathan Mutch, concluding that, 'We cannot wonder that heavy consumption of sugar leads to gastrointestinal disorder of every kind, followed by various serious diseases, among them cancer'."

In a French health magazine called *La Vie Claire,* there appeared a series of articles entitled *White Sugar and its Effects on the Body* by Dr.

Victor Lorenc which describes certain conditions caused by consuming white sugar. He states:

"Chronic excess of glucose in the blood is a very serious condition. A few dentists who are at the same time scientists have definitely noted that expulsive gingivitis (loss of teeth) accompanies chronic excess of sugar in the blood. Eye doctors also agree that this excess threatens the soundness of the sight." He states further:

"This sugar is a soluble food of which nothing slows down the delivery. It falls into the intestine as though from a waterspout, transforms itself in the twinkling of an eye into glucose, and overexcites the intestinal villi, which send it in mass to the liver. Now our liver has been conditioned by a thousand years in the past which knew nothing at all of the avalanches of glucose let loose by today's industrial sugar. Thus the liver cannot prevent a temporary excess of sugar in the blood. Each cell of the body will have to suffer for this defeat, including those of the liver itself."

Effect on Nervous System

Dr. Lorenc comments in an interesting manner on the effect of sugar on the nervous system. He says:

"The few doctors who have compared a diet of industrial sugar with a good diet which is free of it, have been able to observe the nervous irritation which sugar causes in children. Because they are more delicate, women and children show more clearly the effects of industrial sugar. With women, sugar causes pains during menstruation. Here is the case of Sophie Zaikowska. An old woman, she has been a vegetarian since 1902, but she used to take a daily consumption of approximately 100 grams of industrial sugar. At the age of 30 her menstruation became extremely painful. This discomfort disappeared completely with the suppression in 1911 of this 'murderous food.'

"Since that time we have been able to observe many analogous cases. This fact ought to be known and spread abroad by workers with women. Sugar abstinence rids a woman of what is known as 'natural weakness,' that is to say, of nervousness and incapacity to work which are often the result of difficult menstruation.

Sugar Brings on Fat Which Is Dangerous

"Sugar brings a brutally copious afflux of glucose to the liver, which stores as much of it as it can. Nevertheless, it cannot hold more than 150 grams of glycogen, so it transforms the excessive glycogen into fat globules, which are distributed a bit here and there throughout the body, especially in regions where the muscles do little work: over the stomach, over the hips and under the chin. Fat is not to man's advantage; it is rather a source of trouble. Young people are generally thin, but with age the body defends itself less well. After 30, the fattening effect of industrial sugar shows up more intensely with many people.

"According to a study undertaken by the collaboration of 43 American life insurance companies on 3 numerically equal groups of people

[421]

over 45, the incidence of diabetes in these groups showed up as follows: in the group of *very thin* people there was one case, in the *normal* group there were 5 cases and in the *fat* group there were 227."

Sugar and Dental Caries

I now would like to discuss or quote from a publication by Paul H. Belding, D.D.S., and L. J. Belding, M.D., entitled *Dental Caries*. I know both of these men personally and am familiar with and have always admired their work and research on the health and welfare of human teeth. Paul Belding is editor of the old established dental journal called *Dental Items of Interest*.

The Beldings attack the use of industrial sugar as being a cause of serious disturbance in the alimentary tract which starts in the mouth. Let me quote:

"Human experience suggests that it is not excessive indulgence in carbohydrate *per se,* but generally the addition of one specific carbohydrate, namely refined sucrose, to any kind of diet, which leads to the production of *caries acuta*. This observation is well supported clinically, experimentally, and by anthropological investigations. The Michigan School, under the dynamic guidance of Bunting, has shown that in institutions over which it had rigid control of diet, the initiation of caries could be caused, or the activity of this disease terminated, simply by the addition or deletion of candy from the diet.

"The Iowa Group, under the no less brilliant leadership of Boyd and Drain, by making use of a diabetic diet, though not subscribing to the Michigan explanation, have confirmed Bunting's observation that caries can be controlled clinically by the use of diets low in sucrose.

"Waugh in his noteworthy studies was perhaps the first one to produce intentionally experimental caries in humans and to establish conclusively that without sucrose *caries acuta* does not occur. In feeding experiments among the primitive Eskimos, Waugh, excluding sucrose, found that they could eat any carbohydrate including white flour and the natural sugars without developing dental decay. He further observed that with no other change in the diet, except in the addition of sucrose, caries almost invariably developed. These observations were so striking that this author coined the phrase, 'An unsweetened tooth cannot decay.'

"Most investigators have erroneously assumed that sugar was harmful, as it could easily be converted into acid. Primitives can eat corn, potatoes, cabbage, bananas, apples, beans, and other easily fermented carbohydrates and remain caries free, yet let them add small amounts of the *hard to ferment sugar* and their teeth undergo rapid destruction. Sucrose is primarily dangerous not as a source of acid, but by reason of its activating influence upon the oral streptococci. Before sugar is added to the diet, these organisms do not have sufficient fermenting power to produce enough acid from any of the carbohydrates to cause smooth surface dental caries. Sucrose specifically stimulates the fermenting ability of the oral streptococci and alters the floral enzyme mechanism to such an extent that after this material has been added to the diet, the organisms can produce sufficient acid from any of the carbohydrates to cause dental caries."

It is important that I give as much as possible to the Beldings' ideas, for their work is of the utmost significance in the consideration of human health. In some cases I will quote word for word and in others I will give you their thoughts in my own, more simplified words, translating the technical and medical terms.

"The saliva of dogs, cats, cows, mice, rats, and other animals, breast fed babies, and all others subsisting upon a primitive diet is not a high acid producing mechanism. Saliva samples obtained from these sources can be incubated with any carbohydrate and the resultant action is weakly acid or alkaline. In contrast to this, the saliva obtained from *any human* subsisting on a modern diet will, on incubation with the carbohydrates, rapidly produce sufficient acid to decalcify the teeth. This observed difference in the fermenting power of the saliva samples from these two groups, civilized and primitive, makes it apparent that they are not alike in their bacterial content. It is this difference in the fermenting power of the saliva which is generally induced by sucrose, (sugar)."

This action is for all practical purposes exclusively initiated by certain bacteria in the mouth, the oral streptococci. Once the streptococci have been converted from low acid production to high acid production under the selectively stimulating action of industrial sugar, they are able to convert practically all carbohydrates, including sucrose (sugar), and perhaps protein, into sufficient acid to cause tooth destruction.

Cavities of the teeth, called dental caries, or more technically, *caries acuta,* are caused by specific, infectious, contagious bacteria initiated by the action of the streptococcic bateria mentioned above.

Caries acuta obeys general bacteriological law in much the same manner as do the other infectious diseases, such as scarlet fever and diphtheria. Following the ingestion of the modern diet, these changes in the bacteria occur not only in the mouth but throughout the intestinal tract. It is for this reason that we have named the syndrome, which results from eating sucrose, *alimentary streptococcicosis.* The manifestations of this disease are multiple and varied and its implications extend far beyond the ramifications of the oral cavity. It is probably this activated streptococcus, as postulated by Ashoff, which causes appendicitis and lymphoid hyperplasia to be practically universal diseases in civilized communities. Modern man lives in a state of perpetual siege with pathogenic organisms! No wonder he is alleged to be delicate.

Sugar and Primitive People

This work of the doctors Belding is of far-reaching implications. Why did not the American Indian get appendicitis, nor the Hunzas and hundreds of other primitive peoples? That there might be a connection between appendicitis and the taking of industrial sugars is a fact worth while of further study by the medical profession. I am sure it can easily be discovered that behind each appendectomy lies a violent liking for sweets.

[423]

But, when the Beldings speak of lymphoid hyperplasia they are coming closer to cancer, for lymphoid hyperplasia means an abnormal multiplication of the cells of the lymph of the blood.

The Beldings state that ordinarily the streptococcic bacteria in the digestive system are harmless, in fact helpful to the extent that they oppose the colonization of harmful bacteria, tending to convert them to an innocuous form. These organisms live in intimate biologic relationship with the mucous membranes, where they are present in enormous numbers. They are the most frequent bacteria found in the saliva of man or animal. They live in a state of uncertainty and under the influence of the environment they are constantly undergoing involuntary and evolutionary change. The chief factor determining the direction of their growth is diet. We may be what we eat, but it may be more apropos to say that we are what we feed our bacteria. Of all the foods consumed by man, sucrose (sugar) is the only one which alters the streptococci rapidly and significantly enough to induce variation.

The streptococcus of the infant, especially if it is breast fed, is low acid producing and it cannot break down the sugar molecule, but gradually, by changes in diet, the taking of sugar especially, special ferments or enzymes are developed in the saliva which can readily break down sugar. The Beldings have discovered that after sugar has changed the streptococcus into an organism called *S. odontolyticus,* the latter begins to convert almost any food into sufficient acid to cause caries (cavities in the teeth). This explains why primitives can eat large amounts of easily fermentable carbohydrates and yet remain caries free. Their saliva does not contain a high acid producing bacterial mechanism. In civilization the alteration in the bacteria of the mouth causes white breads and pastries to ferment and to serve as the chief source of acid for the leaching of the enamel of the teeth. (This is the end of the Beldings thoughts which I have simplified somewhat.)

In my opinion the work of the Beldings is of great importance in the prevention of cancer because it shows that by taking sugar there is a serious interference with the natural functioning of the digestive processes, by changing a beneficial bacteria to a harmful one. The whole body is dependent for its welfare on the performance of the stomach, which in delicate and subtle ways prepares the food distribution for the blood and the organs of the body. The efficient operation of each cell depends on the manner in which its food its broken down in the digestive tract. The slightest change may be a disturbing factor in preventing the cells from functioning efficiently.

In *Life and Health Magazine* for March, 1948, another effect of sugar on bacteria is given which is pertinent to our discussion. It states that the requirements for vitamins vary with the kind of carbohydrate used in the diet. In all studies where cane sugar was the carbohydrate given, the vitamin requirement was the highest. Sugars that are converted from starches and other natural sugars are the carbohydrates that give the most sparing effects upon the vitamins. The reason is this—many vitamins are manufactured in the intestinal tract, but to accomplish this a friendly bacterial condition must be present in the intestine for the growth of the bacteria which are responsible for the synthesis of the vitamins. But the proper bacteria cannot thrive without certain carbohydrate products, and evidently these products result from carbohydrates such as starch that break down and absorb slowly. White sugar is rushed out of the digestive system too fast for the bacteria to work on them.

Antiseptics Used In Sugar Making Process

I went to a sugar refinery in Philadelphia to see the process of making sugar and to learn whether any harmful chemicals are used in it. I have often read that sulphuric acid was used in its manufacture somewhere. I found only one place that I could question but it is a serious question. The sugar goes through the plant in the various parts of the process in liquid form and in one place it goes through filters made of blanketing material. Ever so often these blankets have to be cleaned and a disinfectant is used to kill disease or other organisms. A disinfectant, to kill bacteria, must be a poison, and even though the blankets are then washed out, I believe that some residue of the poison remains to get into the sugar. However slight this may be, it adds to other poisons used in factory processes with other foods so that the sum total, the accumulation of a varied daily intake of foods that are processed in factories, involves real danger. I found no evidence of sulphuric acid used as a bleach or for any other purpose, but that does not mean that it may not be used in refineries in other states.

Cheap Glucose

Many of the sweetened products such as candies, soft drinks, cakes, pies, ice cream, canned fruit, etc., are sweetened by glucose because it is half the cost of cane sugar and it makes a clearer looking candy. Glucose is made by applying sulphuric acid upon starch. As I have said before, the state of Pennsylvania does not permit the use of sulphuric acid in the manufacture of glucose but other states do. Dr. Harvey Wiley, the first head of the Federal Food and Drug Administration, did everything in his power to draw attention to the danger of using glucose, but all he received for his pains was a dismissal from the department. In 1912 Doctors Lukens and Dohan of the University of Pennsylvania discovered that mice fed on glucose became diabetic whereas the same amount of cane sugar did not cause it.

Primitive Races

Medical explorers have noted the wonderful health and teeth of savages who do not have access to sugar, but when they begin to consume the white man's sugar they become susceptible to cavities in the teeth, appendicitis, cancer, etc. Let me quote from the Belding paper above-mentioned:

"Human experience has shown that many races have subsisted upon a diet high in carbohydrates drawn from many sources yet have remained

[425]

caries free. The native Hawaiians subsist upon a diet high in carbohydrates, yet they have excellent teeth. The early Pacific Islanders, before they died off as a result of contact with civilization, secured a large part of their total caloric intake from carbohydrates, yet they had practically no decay. Likewise, it has been established that through a century the European colonists in Tristan da Cunha, and their descendants, subsisting on a high potato diet have remained almost caries free. In Tristan da Cunha, where until recently there was no bread or other cereal and the main food was milk, mutton, fish, eggs and potatoes, there was no rheumatism or arthritis and the teeth were relatively free from caries. In recent years, well meaning people have been sending flour and sugar to the island and as might be expected, the first curse of civilized communities, dental caries, is increasing among their children. Incidentally, their physical status is much better than that of their European brethren and during the last hundred years there has been neither an operation for appendicitis nor a death from peritonitis."

There is a sad picture in the December, 1949, issue of the *National Geographic* magazine, on page 754. It shows a woman missionary handing out candy to 40-odd children in a primitive region of northern Australia. In the remainder of the article you see pictures of natives displaying wonderful teeth and you wonder what is going to happen to them under a diet of candy and white flour. This is a poor form of Christianity. Missionaries should study the facts brought to light by medical explorers such as Dr. Weston A. Price and others which show that it would be best *not* to bring to the natives of these far-off places the devitalized white flours and sugars of civilization.

In my book, *The Healthy Hunzas,* it was demonstrated that this race of people who live in the northern part of India were one of the healthiest people in the world. They get no cancer and live long. They eat no white refined sugar. There is no question that their health is due to their marvelous proficiency in the application of the theory of soil fertility, using, of course, no chemical fertilizers, but seeing to it that every bit of organic matter at their disposal is put back in the soil. They do not burn manure for fuel as is done by neighboring tribes. Dr. John Clark of the Central Asiatic Research Foundation of Pittsburgh visited them and in a newspaper account of his observations he said, "What the Hunzas really need are a few new agricultural methods and a couple of small home industries. They haven't any sugar for instance." I will go no further. Dr. Clark is a geologist but should study the organic method of farming and its use by the Hunzas before he advises the use of chemical fertilizers. However, I have been in correspondence with the ruler of Hunza who assured me that over his dead body would any chemical fertilizer ever be used on their soils.

Sugar and Energy

There is a fallacy current that you must eat sugar to gain energy. If this is so, you can get it from natural forms of sugar such as fruits, carrots, beets, etc. However, Dr. Royal Lee of the Nutritional Foundation of

Milwaukee, Wisconsin, in an address (April 2, 1949) to the members of the American Academy of Applied Nutrition, said:

"While sugar is a relatively pure carbohydrate in its natural forms, it ranks secondary to starchy foods as a source of energy or calories. We customarily look to starch-carrying foods for our sustaining foods, foods necessary in larger amounts by those who use their muscles in manual labor or other exercise, for it is a first principle of nutrition that the only increased requirement in food, by those who burn up more energy, is a greater need for carbohydrate and the carbohydrate metabolizing fats and vitamins, the requirement for other foods being relatively constant.

"There is a very good reason why starches are better than sugars as energy foods. It is because they are assimilated slower than the sugars and thereby fail to overload our pancreatic function of supplying insulin. Sugars are absorbed at varying rates, glucose being the quickest to diffuse through the intestinal wall, levulose the slowest. All sugars are converted into glucose after absorption into the body. That is again apparently because glucose is the most diffusable sugar, as once in the blood stream, it is the quickest to pass through the tissues and arrive at the muscle cell, where it is converted into energy. That same diffusibility, however, is the reason that it is the least desirable of sugars to eat. It is the only sugar that has been definitely found to cause diabetes, by its effect of overloading the pancreas, at least in test animals."

One need not worry about sugar, if it is *the* factor in producing energy, because 68 per cent of the starch which our bodies take in is converted to sugar.

Sugar, a Habit

Sugar taking is a habit which can be developed, and once the habit is controlled there is no longer any craving or need for it. Most of us are sugar drunkards. When a waiter saw me eating buckwheat cakes without syrup, he said if he could not use syrup on his wheat cakes and sugar on his oatmeal he would rather cut his throat. His taste buds need a little talking to. When I eat wheat cakes without syrup, I enjoy the taste of wheat cakes, which is what I am after when I order wheat cakes. If you will even eliminate the butter, when ordering buckwheat cakes, you will get the delicate taste of the buckwheat. I would not think of smothering that taste with syrup.

The habit of eating sweet-things is an acquired one and if children were taught proper control over sugar they would never develop such an artificial habit. Even a young horse has to be taught to like sugar. Before I knew better, I used to offer sugar to young weanling colts and they would invariably spit it out. We would hold them and force it on them, thinking it was good for them.

I was in a sugar factory recently and visited the company cafeteria. The atmosphere in the whole factory is terribly saturated with sugar. When you enter for the first time you can feel it forcing itself down your throat. I watched one worker put 6 spoonfuls of sugar in his coffee. His system was so saturated with sugar that he required 6 teaspoonfuls to make a dent on his taste buds. When you learn to cut out sugar you become more the master of your will and then can more easily master other undesirable habits. By reducing the excitation of the taste buds you can more easily cut out the taking of salt. If you go at these dietary errors, one at a time, you will find it much easier. The other day at a banquet I did not turn down the cake that was put before me for dessert. It practically nauseated me upon eating it, for I am no longer used to such a concentrated sweet taste as the icing afforded.

Doctor's Opinion

Here is part of a letter I received recently from Dr. H. R. Lotz of Bristol, Connecticut:

"This I have known for 20 years that positive cancer sufferers in the final stages, and right up to the point of death, can live free of pain if they will live entirely on natural food and completely eliminate all sugar, which means just the *artificial sugar* and the complete abstinence of all products in which sugar enters, such as bread, cake, etc.

"But I do not think this is because of any harmful ingredient in the sweet but rather that the excessive use causes a complete imbalance in tissue cell. Or exactly similar to what happens when an excess of nitrogen and lack of other nutrients are incorporated in a piece of garden."

In a book called *Truth About Sugar,* by H. V. Knaggs (1913), the author says:

"Brandt, an eminent German chemist, has shown that a 6 to 10 per cent solution of cane sugar causes irritation, with the redness of the mucous lining of a dog's stomach."

Here is what the American Medical Association, through its journal, *Hygeia,* thinks about sugar:

"One pound of sugar provides 1,800 calories and nothing else. It contributes none of the nutritionally important protein foods as whole grains, fruits and vegetables.

"The eating of white sugar, either cane or beet, in large amounts, may place a burden on the pancreas. The pancreas secretes a substance which is necessary to enable the body to use sugar as a fuel food. If the pancreas is impaired or injured, its ability to secrete insulin is also impaired and as a result the body loses its ability to burn sugar.

"There is also evidence that excessive consumption of sugar may weaken the protective power of the liver and thereby cause numerous so-called bilious symptoms. Brown sugar has the same effect as white sugar. Eating sugar in excessive amounts may make one feel dull and bilious because of these reasons."

In my own opinion—I would eliminate brown sugar as well as white and endeavor to get my sweets in a less concentrated form such as fruits, carrots, beets, etc.

Nature Hits Back

Here is an item from *Nature Hits Back,* by Macpherson Lawrie, M.D.:

"The increase in the consumption of sugar is the most outstanding dietetic perversion of the age. Apart from any other consideration, it upsets the whole balance of nutrition. Sugar is a fuel, and today we take into our system this purely fuel food in amounts sufficient to shatter every dietetic principle and law. Our digestive glands and organs may be adaptable, but it is impossible to believe that during the last hundred years our physiological processes have so changed as to enable our bodies to deal normally with an excess of fuel so staggering. Especially is the amount 'consumed in tea and other fluids remarkable. Six cups of tea each day, each containing two lumps of sugar will alone account for over 40 pounds in one year. Further in connection with its use in fluid, we must remember that, with sugar so consumed, salivary digestion is lacking. Saliva is an agent of supreme importance in the digestion of carbohydrate food, and a flow of saliva is normally aroused by mastication. By swallowing, in fluid form, such vast amounts of sugar, the digestive action of saliva is not enlisted and as a result we must throw upon other digestive glands an abnormal strain which may have far-reaching and serious effects."

Let me quote a short item from an article entitled *Case of Dental Caries vs. The Sugar Interests,* which appeared in the *Southern California State Dental Association Journal* (November 1949):

"Here we come up against a great obstacle to the solution of our problem, and that is the mis-education of our people by the hucksters who sell white flour, candy, pastries, soft drinks, especially the sweetened varieties which in addition to the sugar frequently contain a great quantity of phosphoric acid, which helps to destroy our children's teeth."

The Truth About Sugar

I would like to present a most important excerpt from the book, *Truth About Sugar,* by H. V. Knaggs, M.D., mentioned above:

"Acidity, or sour stomach, is a common symptom among those who take cane sugars or sweetmeats to excess. The acids formed as a result of the decomposition of the sugars in the presence of meat and other proteins, create a form of acid intoxication, or self-poisoning, which manifests itself in various types of catarrh or rheumatism.

The chief acid produced in this way is that known as oxalic acid. Dr. Helen Baldwin has proved by a number of experiments that animals fed on meat and sugar, both of which are free from oxalic acid, until a state of extreme fermentation ensued, developed marked oxalic acid poisoning. I have repeatedly seen this condition myself among patients who are suffering from dilated or catarrhal stomachs, due to the abuse of milk and sugar foods, and when the gastric contents were in the same condition as that of the animals cited. This oxalic acid when it reaches the blood converts the soluble lime salts into an insoluble oxalate of lime, and thus induces the condition of the system known as decalcification or lime starvation.

"Since lime builds the teeth and bones, and gives stability to the nerves and tone to the muscles, the consequences must necessarily be serious.

"The abuse of sugar, owing to this action of its acid by-products upon

[429]

the lime in the blood, is the usual cause among the young of rickets and decay of the teeth, of adenoid nasal growth and inflamed tonsils . . ."

Athletes and Sugar

A man who was once an athlete and is now a minister, Reverend Gil Dodds, addressed the children at the school my young daughter attended, and cautioned them against the overconsumption of sweets. He told them that when he was in training, he severely eliminated sugar, because he found that it put his body out of condition. He said he took extremely little sugar at other times. This could be an answer also to those who believe that sugar is needed for energy.

Conclusion

It is not maintained that the eating of sugar is a direct cause of cancer, but it may be a contributing cause to it. There probably is no *one* cause of cancer. There are too many factors involved. For example, not everyone who smokes a pipe gets cancer of the lip. Perhaps it gets only persons who do not have a healthy condition of their body. Thus a person who smokes a pipe, and eats excessive amounts of sugar and salt, may be more easily liable to contract cancer of the lip. Perhaps if one smokes a pipe and eats sugar and salt, but has a 100 per cent diet of organically produced food to protect the body, he may not get cancer of the lip.

Sufficient authorities have been produced to show that the taking of sugar is not a healthy thing for the body, and I believe it is common sense to state that a strong, healthy body can resist that paralysis of its functions which we call cancer. Therefore, I unhesitatingly recommend that every one reduce drastically, or eliminate entirely the use of industrial sugars.

CHAPTER 117

Life without Sugar
Has Its Rewards

In our research on sugar we've come across some suggestions that may make your new Life-Without-Sugar easier. First of all, get used to the idea right now that soda fountains are not for you. If you must stop in with friends, order something like fruit juice, milk or tea. The icy soft drink dispenser is out of bounds for you. If you are on a trip, carry your own drinks in a thermos. If you go to a picnic, take along your own drinks, hot or cold. When refreshment time comes after the meeting, the bridge game or the television program, get used to standing around with a cup and a plate in your hand and talking as entertainingly as you know how. Nine chances out of 10 no one will notice that you've had nothing to eat but some peanuts. If the evening's activity has whetted your appetite unbearably, wait till you get home and carve up a slice of cold meat from the refrigerator, eat some fruit, a handful of nuts or raisins or a cup of hot bouillon if the weather is cold.

One difficulty with sweets these days is that they're so easily accessible —on every city street a soda fountain or a candy stand invites you. So get used to having your own sweet substitutes handy, too. A big bowl of fresh washed fruit in the refrigerator or on the living room table is just as handy as any soda fountain. Make certain that you always have on hand dried fruits (if you like them), nuts and sunflower seeds. You'll be surprised at how pleased your guests will be when you offer them sunflower seeds rather than the usual after-dinner mints or chocolates. Popcorn and raw apples are splendid refreshment for a party, as one of our readers pointed out to us.

Carob Flour For Sweetening

If you are "tapering off" on sugar, you may find carob flour the answer to your problems. Carob flour is a nutritious food, made from the pods of the honey locust tree. A sweet powder, it tastes a lot like chocolate and can be used in any recipe that calls for chocolate or sugar. Since it is a natural food you can use it safely. It's a big help if your children are complaining about doing without sugar, for you can make chocolatey drinks out of it. Popcorn is an exciting treat for children and shelling nuts to eat can be as much fun as making fudge. Sunflower seeds are a novelty. If your youngsters are the first in the neighborhood to have any of this exotic new food to chew on, the added prestige will partly make up for the loss of lollipops and sodas.

Visit your local library and get familiar with the cookbook shelf. You'll find all kinds of suggestions for new and different foods to take your family's mind off the missing chocolate cake and cherry pie. We recommend as the best cookbook we know (even though we do not agree completely with everything in it) *Let's Cook it Right* by Adelle Davis, a talented nutritionist whose aim is economical, tasty, and nutritious meals. This is published by Harcourt Brace and Company in New York and your local book shop or library can order it for you.

Get used to cooking with herbs. Here is a whole new field of taste thrills you may not have investigated. Perhaps you will have to learn to enjoy the flavors of herbs. If at all possible have an herb garden of your own, even if it is only a couple of plants in one corner of the lawn. Your own fresh herbs will be much superior to the ones you buy at the store. Keep parsley and chives growing in a flower pot or a window box during winter.

Finally, learn to use salads—big hearty salads made of greens—to fill up on at meals. If you serve your salad first and then the rest of the dinner, you'll find that often you simply don't have room for dessert. If it is at all possible, your family should eat at least one large salad of fresh greens every day.

We receive many letters from readers asking about what kind of sugar to use. So far as we are concerned, the answer is *"none."* Brown sugar is not quite so harmful as white sugar and raw sugar is better for you than brown. But we still say, if you would be healthy, omit all sugar and just get accustomed to doing without it. Blackstrap molasses, honey and real maple syrup in moderation are the only sweeteners of which we approve.

CHAPTER 118

Getting Along Happily without Sugar

In case you think that doing without sugar is a hardship just listen to the comments of people who have decided to do without sugar and have found it easy and healthful. Emory Trott of Andover, Massachusetts, tells us that most people crave desserts because all the rest of the meal has been so badly cooked and tasteless that they look forward to something which will at least taste good. "I cook my vegetables as much as possible in the Chinese way," says Mr. Trott, "cut up rather small, sautéed quickly in a little hot fat, simmered in a little stock and served crisp, thus preserving flavor and incidentally vitamin and mineral content. At our modest dinner parties we have given up planning desserts because our friends won't eat them. Salad and a little cheese is all they can manage. And I don't recall that any of our 4 children ate desserts at home after the age of 10. When they come home from boarding school or on vacation they don't clamor for the pie that mother used to make. They say, 'Can't we have pork chops a' la Rowley Shore or baked chicken or minute steaks with plenty of that steak sauce'?"

Good Cooking Is One Answer

Mr. Trott's conclusion is "that a person who is determined to give up sugar needs to combine this decision with a re-education of taste and substitution of satisfying, flavorful cooking for the admittedly gratifying taste sensations he is giving up . . . As a practical idea, I would suggest the use of garlic in cooking where appropriate. Not only is it healthful, but it vastly improves the flavor of a great many dishes, either cooked or raw, and, to my palate at least, it leaves a satisfying aftertaste in the mouth which suggests sweetness and therefore might tend, I would think, to reduce the craving for sugar."

Mrs. D. R. Coleman of Menlo Park, California, agrees that good cooking is important, but she also uses "tricks in serving" that help. "I plan very large salads," says she, "with delicious dressings and serve them at the beginning of the meal. By the time the protein food and other vegetables are eaten, there just isn't room for dessert. . . . As the protein level of the diet is increased and the vitamin intake maintained at a high level, one finds that one actually ceases to want sweet foods. Proper nutrition maintains the blood sugar at a high steady level without the abrupt drops which set off the craving for sweets. My husband and I believe that the need for sugar is a conditioned need and that one can physiologically 'decondition' oneself by a properly balanced nutrition. The more good food one serves and the less sugar one eats, the less sugar is demanded until it seems almost spontaneously to have eliminated itself."

Mrs. Leon A. Mason of East Bloomfield, New York, uses whole grain flour, arrowroot starch and honey successfully in any receipe in exact amounts to replace what she calls the "cheating foods"—white flour and sugar, corn starch and corn syrup. She uses whole wheat flour (ground in her own small flour mill) to make cakes, pies, cookies, biscuits, short cake and bread. She uses light-colored honey for meringues, frostings and so forth. Mrs. Mason's ideas cannot really be classified as "getting along without sweets" but they may help someone who is trying to give up sugar gradually.

What about canning and preserving? No difficulty at all, says Miss Susan Hahn of Whitefish Bay, Wisconsin. For 10 years she has been canning all her fruit without sugar. She cans fresh Italian prunes, apricots and peaches without sugar. For the few things she bakes, she uses honey or blackstrap molasses. With fresh fruits, dates and prunes always in the house when she wants to nibble on them, she does not feel the need for any more sweets.

Natural, Unprocessed Foods Reduce Desire For Sugar

Mrs. David Howatt of Coopersburg, Pennsylvania, tells us that she has not eaten white sugar for many years. She suggests that anyone wishing to eliminate it entirely should stick to unprocessed and unrefined foods. "By chewing these foods carefully, one will begin to notice delicate flavors which sugar or honey would destroy. One can obtain the necessary sweet elements from dates, raisins, prunes and very ripe bananas in winter and spring, and from very ripe berries and tree-ripened fruit in summer and fall. I believe the use of sugar is mostly a bad dietetic habit instilled in childhood by adults sugaring almost everything a child eats and drinks. Invariably when I have a craving for artificial sweets, it happens when my meals have not been properly balanced."

Because of a long series of illnesses, Mrs. Russell Hoover of Sterling, Illinois, learned the harmfulness of eating sugar. For the past 3 years she and her family have gotten along wonderfully without it. For sweeten-

[433]

ing they use honey "in its natural state, unheated, untreated, just packed with natural vitamins and minerals." Mrs. Hoover says that they did not find it hard to give up sugar for they no longer have that "hidden hunger." "Our old diet did not meet the requirements of our bodies," she says "and so we ate more and more of the wrong food, but on our new diet it takes so little to satisfy us because we are getting the balanced rations, the necessary, natural proteins and vitamins and minerals."

How to Freeze Fruits Without Sugar

"We eat everything just as near its natural state as possible and we raise the greatest part of our food organically, to use fresh in the summer and to fill a huge freezer for winter. All of our fruit goes into the freezer raw with honey for winter use. I never cook syrups and heat the fruit as the rule book advises. I prepare only a few boxes at a time and pop them into the deep freeze before the fruit can discolor. Sometimes I use a little lemon juice. With berries I lightly fill the boxes and trickle honey down through the fruit so it retains its shape. With firmer fruit, I cut it in slices as I want to serve it and stir the honey through it, then pack and freeze.

"Our favorite dessert is a mixture of all sorts of fresh fruits in a tossed salad with a few tablespoons of honey, sometimes dates, raisins or figs. I chop fresh coconut, fresh pineapple, raw apples and raw carrots together, then add a handful of raisins and honey—a treat fit for a king! We often add sunflower seed meal or sesame seed meal to any of these desserts, giving us natural protein. . . . We must realize that if we eat a great share of our food raw, or very lightly cooked, so that the chemical composition is changed as little as possible, we get a great deal of sugar in its natural state, in varying degrees, from all fruits and vegetables. We never use store-bought salad dressing. We use honey for fruit salads, sesame seed oil, lemon juice and chopped garlic for vegetable salads."

Old and Young Benefit From Sugarless Diets

William Ember of Seattle, Washington, tells us he stopped using sugar at the age of 75. "I used to take two spoonfuls of sugar in a cup of tea, four in a cup of coffee, and I liked candy. Lost my teeth at 47. Always loaded my cereals with sugar. Quit sugar at 75. Quite a task but I beat it. I never miss it any more. Red beets and boiled celery seem to satisfy me. It was not easy, but I did it without saccharin or other substitutes." Charles Bickel of Reading, Pennsylvania, is 67 and has not eaten sugar, salt or condiments for 15 years. Honey, raisins, whole wheat grains and vegetables organically grown are his answer to the problem of nutrition. Lorraine King of Glenview, Illinois is only 16 and does very nicely without any sweetening for long periods of time, eating fruit and such vegetables as carrots and sweet potatoes. She feels that natural sweets (honey and blackstrap molasses) are all she needs when she wants something particularly sweet. The Campbells of Bridgeton, New Jersey, advise honey and maple syrup.

J. Westfall of Chicago believes that it is much more interesting to use honey than sugar because the flavor of honey varies in different parts of the country. J. B. Kaufman of Toledo does without sugar and salt with no difficulty at all. Anne Lobstein of Bloomingburg, New York, sends us a mouth-watering recipe for raisin paste which she uses as a jam substitute in the children's school lunches: "Put raisins through an ordinary small meat grinder, alternately with dates, apples, nuts, bananas and sunflower seeds. The consistency can be stiff or smooth, according to one's taste by the addition of more or less apple or banana. When all the fruit is through the grinder, add wheat germ." Sounds good enough to compete with any chocolate sundae, don't you think?

Blueprint For Increased Vitality

We want to share with you the experience of Mrs. Fred Dunn of New York City whose letter on a sugarless and (almost) starchless diet is a real inspiration. "Two years ago I became interested in good nutrition" writes Mrs. Dunn. "The common cold had been taking a heavy toll of my energy and vitality. It was not unusual for me to have 4 or 5 colds a year; these colds were severe, of long duration and kept me in a run-down condition. I was constantly tired, my eyes were dull and weak, my hair dead and lustreless, and I had lost my zest for living. I did my day's work with no enthusiasm, but only by a tremendous effort of will. My eating habits, I learned, were wrong; I decided to change them and see what good nutrition could do for me. I mapped out a plan which I have rigidly followed, and which has paid great dividends, in health, energy and good looks.

"The first step in my plan was to eliminate the things I had discovered were bad for me: processed starches (spaghetti, macaroni, white bread, etc.), refined sugar (desserts, soft drinks, candy). I cut down on fats (butter, cream and salad oils) and went on a diet heavy in protein (meat, fish, cheese, eggs and milk). My new diet also included plenty of fresh vegetables, fruit and fruit juices, whole grain bread, cereals and flour. I supplemented this diet with vitamins and minerals: brewer's yeast, fish liver oil, sea greens and calcium.

"The second part of my plan has nothing to do with diet, but it is so important that I feel it should be mentioned. I made an effort to stay outdoors as much as possible. I never took a bus or taxi when I had time to walk. I did my housework with all the doors and windows open and avoided crowds and overheated places.

"The very first week I followed my new plan I felt better; by the end of the first month my friends were all telling me they hadn't seen me look so well in years. My hair took on new lustre, my eyes lost their dull look, I lost weight—10 pounds the first month—and—best of all—I felt good!

"Two years have passed and it is now possible to look at some of the long range benefits of good nutrition. The first year, I had one very slight cold, during the hectic Christmas rush. This year I have had none, nor have I had an illness of any kind. This is unusual for me. I can remember no other year in my life in which I have been entirely free of illness. My weight has remained the same: I am 47 years old, 5 feet 7 inches tall and weigh 130 pounds. I have twice as much energy as I used to have and lead an extremely active life for a woman my age. I maintain a house in Vermont as well as an apartment in New York and do a great deal of informal entertaining in both places. I ski, play golf, take care of a very large garden and, in my spare time, have managed to take several courses at Columbia University. Surely age is not making me stronger; I feel sure that I owe my vitality to good nutrition.

How To Eat Is As Important As What To Eat

"Have I found it hard to stay on a sugarless, starchless diet? In general, no. I have discovered ways of making it easy for myself. The secret, I believe, is in learning *how* to eat, as well as *what* to eat. The first thing I learned was not to let myself get overly hungry. I eat between meals, but only non-fattening foods, such as raw celery, carrots or apples. Dieting takes will power and, if you are famished, it is easy to fall into the fallacious thinking (that great pitfall of all would-be dieters) that a rich meal won't hurt—just this once. A meal, let's say of fried chicken, rice and gravy, lima beans, hot rolls and apple pie a la mode will undo the benefits of weeks of abstemiousness. When I am forced, by social obligations, to eat food which is not on my diet, I do so sparingly. If I am going out to dinner and suspect that I am going to be faced with a rich and fattening meal, I take the edge off my hunger before I go: cottage cheese, I find, is a good non-fattening filler. When my hostess proudly presents me with her prize dessert, I eat a few mouthfuls, slowly, tell her it is delicious, and find she seldom notices that I haven't finished it.

"Another trick I have learned is to eat food that 'stays with me.' For example, hard-boiled eggs have more staying power than poached or scrambled eggs, a luncheon of meat and vegetables has more staying power than a mixed green salad, whole grain breads stay with you longer than synthetic white breads. I always make an effort to select foods that will keep me from getting hungry.

"Eating nourishing, healthful food becomes habit, just as bad eating becomes habit. I no longer crave the things I used to like, but like the things that are good for me. Good food is harder to purchase than it should be and requires a little more effort in planning and buying, but it is so worthwhile, so rewarding in good health, vitality and good living that I would never consider going back to my old haphazard eating habits.

"So many people in the world today are totally unaware of the energies slumbering within them; they are only half alive, half awake. To all these people I would like to shout 'Try good nutrition! You have nothing to lose, and perhaps a new and better way of life to gain'!"

No Sugar for Growing Boys

T. A. Lamb of Beaverdam, Virginia, writes us: "We have neither bought nor used any refined sugar since the days of rationing and now we have a family of 6 boys. We use no candy, commercial ice cream or other foods to which we know that refined sugar has been added. When friends send candy to the boys at holiday time we give them a quarter each to buy other toys and give the candy to the dog. Incidentally, the dog has more health sense than most people, for he just licks it a little and leaves it.

"As a result, the boys have had no sign of tooth decay or pain, but pass from baby teeth to second teeth as the trees exchange their old leaves for the new. Also we are almost free from colds the year 'round. Of course we think there are other factors, too, such as raw whole milk, fruit and fruit juices, plenty of vegetables and especially potatoes baked in the jackets. Also, we use no white flour, flesh or flesh products except a weekly meal of fish or seafood, no salt except vegetable salt and of course no tea or coffee.

"Now to offset this loss (?) of sugar we use plenty of natural raw honey on our cereals with whole milk, avoiding those cereals to which sugar has been added. We also keep a box of raisins of the unsulphured variety open before the boys to which they can help themselves at all times. This or other raw fruit is all they ever eat between meals. Occasionally, we make ice cream or other sweets, always with honey as the medium of sweetness."

Mrs. John Lienhard of Glenview, Illinois, writes: "I buy a 60 pound can of honey from an organic farm near us. I make my own bread from freshly ground whole wheat flour. I never make cake or pies or sweet desserts. We use fresh fruits and vegetables or frozen fruits in winter. . . . Eliminating all sugars and most starches from our diet we have no trouble whatsoever about overweight. . . . We get most of our proteins from organically-raised grains, cereals, eggs and so forth. I serve liver once a week and a serving of beef if I can afford it. . . . Our doctor is much interested in our diet for we all are in the best of health—high blood counts, good clean, clear, firm skin, radiant health. Amazing, says the doctor. Yet we are on a salt-free diet, sugarless diet, starch-free as we can make it—a minimum of meat. We try to eat living food, not dead food and we buy direct from organic growers."

Homemade Ice Cream Without Sugar

Here is comforting information from Mrs. Alice M. Green of Cloverdale, California: "Having a terrible sweet tooth, it was hard for me to give up candy and desserts. We used raw sugar in place of white for some time, also honey, but gradually used less and less. (Editor's note: the craving for sweets soon disappears on a good diet.) At present we use no sugar and little honey in any food, and seldom give it a thought. We eat dried fruit such as dates, raisins, figs, etc., to satisfy our desire for desserts.

"In hot weather we often crave ice cream and we worked out two recipes that we enjoy ever so much. One is for pineapple ice cream. We open a can of unsweetened pineapple juice and add about the same amount of rich goat's milk (cow's milk will do), pour into a glass baking dish and put into the freezing compartment. Several times during the day we stir it thoroughly. It makes a most refreshing and wholesome dessert. It is so simply and quickly made that even as busy as we are we can take a few minutes to prepare it. The other recipe is date ice cream. I pit from 12 to 20 dates, depending on the size and how sweet you want your ice cream. These I liquefy in the blender with top goat's milk. When it is completely liquefied, I pour it into the glass dish and it is ready for the freezing compartment. This is sweeter than the pineapple and is indeed delicious."

The following wonderful letter came in with no name or address, but we are certain the writer will not mind our sharing it with you: "We thought we were using much less candy and sweets than most people, but we have always had our share of allergies, colds and sickness. Our doctor is very much for preventive medicine if he can get his patients to try it. When I asked him how to keep from having colds he said 'leave sweets alone.' For over a year I left out all sweets, only occasionally using honey in cookies, pie or dessert. I had better health than I had had for years. Still had an occasional cold, but less severe. . . . When I make bread, I save out a loaf and roll out about one-fourth inch thick. I spread it generously with applesauce, raisins and nuts. Then it is rolled up and cut as are cinnamon rolls. These are sprinkled generously with finely ground coconut and baked after they rise. We sprinkle coconut on our bread pudding or use rice and raisins for a festive appearance and brown in a warm oven. We have a rule in our family that we do not eat between meals, thus eliminating many of the knick-knacks that most children eat."

Sugar-Craving Like Alcoholism

Tom Straub of Port Hueneme, California, says "Prior to my breakdown I was a heavy sugar consumer. Lots of sugar in my coffee, sugar in cereals, rich cakes. As my health improved I suddenly noticed that I did not want sugar. I did notice, however, for many months, under conditions of fatigue, I would find myself reaching for the sugar bowl, not as a conditioned reflex, but from a desire for the sugar. I am inclined to think the same applies to the so-called alcoholics, because I have noticed among my friends that they are more inclined to drink under conditions of what might be called nervous or emotional fatigue.

"I do not use any sugar substitutes, but rely on my system metabolizing blood sugar from my day-to-day food. I have toyed wtih blackstrap molasses and honey but did not notice any perceptible improvement. I feel that sugar consumption and alcoholic consumption are closely related to fatigue of the endocrine glands, and the proper way to kill the desire for sugar is to eat strong wholesome foods and keep on eating them until the body improves to where the glands can metabolize the blood sugars from the various carbohydrates and fat reserves."

From Mrs. L. E. O'Keefe of Springdale, Arkansas, comes this refreshing note: "It is all of 25 years since we became convinced that our family would do better without most of the white-sugar, white-flour products. Our first move was to eliminate store candy and bakeshop products;

also commercially-made ice cream. We found the use of honey the most satisfactory. I learned to can all our fruit unsweetened and then when we open it we add liquid honey and sometimes cream. We even deep-freeze some of our fully ripe fruits without added sweetening and for a change in the way of serving we often run a package of frozen fruit through the food chopper, then add honey, just drizzle it over the fruit ice. This makes a good evening dessert for hot days. In our immediate family we do not use any white sugar at all, but do keep it for the pleasure (?) of our guests, though quite often we find our guests like to eat as we do."

An End to Sinus Trouble

H. C. Edinborough of Banning, California, writes: "We never took sugar into account until my dentist lent me Dr. Weston Price's book, *Nutrition and Physical Degeneration,* available from The American Academy of Applied Nutrition, 6238 Wilshire Boulevard, Los Angeles 48, California.

It really opened our eyes to the relationship of foods and health. But what really changed our eating habits was your stories about sugar in ORGANIC GARDENING and PREVENTION.

"My wife and boy—especially my wife—have suffered from sinus trouble for years. Her sinuses had grown shut and it took a number of operations to open them up. But in spite of all kinds of treatments there was still some infection, congestion and pain. She noticed that milk and cheese made the trouble worse, so dairy products were dropped. Little did we realize that the combination of sugar and milk was causing the trouble. When sugar was completely removed from the diet, there was no trouble at all with dairy products.

"All was well up to this point, but now, how to wean our sweet tooth! (It is remarkable how the two words 'sweet' and 'tooth' got put together). . . . I had little trouble cutting out sweets but not so with my wife. She craved white sugar. As long as she ate at home she planned her meals and avoided granulated sugar and sweetened with natural sugar. She got along quite well until she would eat a cup cake, pie or something at a party, then she would come home and walk the floor, or just give in and go on a sugar binge. (Editor's note: we repeat, sugar is a drug.) She realized for the first time that she had been drunk on sugar for years and was reminded of the alcoholics who can't stay away from the stuff once they get a taste of it. So from then on it was total abstinence for her. She can tell by the reaction in her system and her cravings when she has used anything but natural sugars in her diet.

"I must add that her health is greatly improved. Besides dropping white sugar and bleached flour from our diets, we eat our own organically-grown vegetables and use bone meal, wheat germ and brewer's yeast. (Editor's Note: Another reason why the Edinboroughs can get along without sugar easily now—their bodies are getting enough minerals and vitamins.) We have learned many of these good things from the pages of ORGANIC GARDENING and PREVENTION. Your magazines have helped point

[439]

the way to continued good health. We always pass their message on to others."

Fedor Mausolff of Chicago is a 17-year-old dancer. How often have you heard that sugar is an absolute necessity for any kind of strenuous exercise? But listen: "How do I get along without sugar? I still (after 4 years) find sugar tempting and good tasting. I am a tumbler and do ballet as a hobby. After a workout I have found it bad to take anything sweet. It makes my muscles become sore and lowers my endurance, I think. If I take any before a workout then I feel weak and discouraged. Also I do not sweat as easily as I do when no sugar is taken."

Mrs. A. C. Brookey of San Antonio, Texas, uses honey and brown sugar. She tells us: "I use honey in hot tea and really like it better. When the problem of iced tea came up (which we use a lot during hot weather), I sweeten it while it is hot. This is delicious and makes it more convenient when serving." (Editor's note: A sprig of fresh mint cheers up a glass of iced tea wonderfully, too!)

Mrs. S. N. Smith of Montpelier, Indiana, cans fruits in their own juices without water, or sugar. She bakes apples stuffed with a date, fig or some raisins. "I thought I could never eat pumpkin without sugar," she says, "but found if you mix some raisins or figs or dates with the pumpkin it is very good. Cooked breakfast foods need no sugar if a few of these dried fruits are added. Use a little honey mixed with water, diluted peanut butter, and lemon juice for a good mayonnaise. Sweet potatoes need no sugar—try them as they are. (Editor's note: This comment shows how different food habits grow up with you. We had never heard of using sugar with sweet potatoes until we read Mrs. Smith's letter. We always eat them baked, whole, with butter.) When I am where sweets are served I sometimes eat a small amount if I feel it is necesary. I put treat candy in my purse when no one notices!"

A Cure for Stomach Ailments

A lady from Ontario, Canada, who asks to remain anonymous, says: "I want you to know that by eliminating from my diet white flour, white sugar and all foods containing either of these, I have been cured of a stomach ailment which had made my life miserable for many long years. More than one good doctor treated me and for a short time I would be better, but the trouble always returned."

Here are some brief comments from letters we do not have space to print in full:

From Mrs. Rosa N. Morrill (aged 88) of Venice, California: "I do not think any substitute for sugar is required, if one includes in one's diet figs, dates, prunes, raisins, and so forth. I sometimes eat a little honey or a bit of maple sugar."

From Dr. M. D. Stevens, Coral Gables, Florida: "We discontinued using sugar some 20 years ago without trouble at all. We don't drink cocoa, tea or coffee. However, we use honey whenever we have postum."

From Mrs. D. W. Hopwood of Santa Barbara, California: "I use a lot of herb teas—strawberry, red clover, shave grass and camomile. In these I put honey—not just any honey but a good grade of natural honey form the health food store. . . . Another product that is not well known but a wonderful food, as well as a sweet, is carob meal or St. John's bread in flour form."

Mrs. J. P. Atkins of Muscatine, Iowa, tells us that a serious illness started her hunting for a healthful diet. At present "I need no sugar substitute, but I have black figs, dates, raisins and prunes. I cook with pure sorghum and honey. . . . When I go to birthday dinners where I am confronted by 3 big cakes, I nibble on the lemon sponge." Mrs. C. M. Condron of Homer City, Pennsylvania, has been "off white sugar for two years, *positively*. I use raisins and blackstrap molasses wherever I can in baking and I use honey and maple syrup in some cases."

Mrs. Herbert P. Rogers of Burbank, California, has not eaten sugar for 3 years—"Has this paid off? It certainly has! The past two years neither my husband nor I have had a cold of any kind, even though colds have reached epidemic proportions around us."

If you're a sugar-eater and can't face the thought of doing without it, don't these letters give you courage and hope? It's not so hard, really, to throw the poisonous stuff out of your life entirely, and it needn't ruin your social life or get you labeled as a "crank" if you do as Mrs. Smith does and "put the treat candy in your purse," or do as Mrs. Atkins does, and "nibble at the lemon sponge!"

CHAPTER 119

Blackstrap Molasses

Is blackstrap molasses a wonder food, to be included in the diet every day, capable of curing or preventing almost any ailment? Or is it a filthy product, full of dirt and germs, completely lacking in nourishment and fit only as food for animals? We don't think blackstrap molasses is any of these things. But it has come to be such a controversial subject—should you or should you not eat blackstrap molasses?—that we have done some research to try to find the answers to these questions.

Blackstrap molasses is an end product in the manufacture of refined white sugar. According to Jacobs in his *Food and Food Products* (Interscience Publishers), it is the "lowest grade of molasses from which all possible crystallizable sugar has been removed." Those who object to blackstrap will probably declare that this sentence is enough to condemn it. All sugar has been removed from it, therefore we should not eat it. But for those of us who are health-conscious, the fact that the sugar has been removed is the finest kind of recommendation. Whole, raw sugar cane appears to be an excellent food, rich in vitamins and minerals. White refined sugar, which is made from it, is completely worthless as a food, containing nothing but calories—no vitamins, no minerals. These valuable food elements of the sugar cane are left in the molasses after the sugar has been removed.

A second point in favor of blackstrap is that it is widely used as food for animals. Anyone who reads nutrition books at all cannot but be impressed with the fact that, in general, our animals—especially valuable stock animals—are better fed than we are. The wheat germ removed in the milling of flour is fed to animals. It is the most valuable part of the wheat. Feeds for farm and domestic animals are well fortified with grains, alfalfa, kelp, brewer's yeast, fish liver oil, vitamin E and so forth.

Folks who raise animals for profit demand that their feed be high in nutrition. There is no question of how it looks, smells or tastes; whether the color is good or whether it can be speedily and conveniently served by a busy housewife. The one purpose of animal food is to *nourish*. So when we find that some 300 million gallons of blackstrap are imported into this country annually, of which about a third is used for cattle food, we suspect that there is some very good nutritional reason for this.

Blackstrap is rich in minerals, being especially high in calcium, iron and potassium. Here is a chart showing the mineral content of molasses compared in each case, with a food also high in this particular mineral:

Milligrams per hundred grams
(5 tablespoons)

Calcium—Molasses, 258, Milk, 120; Phosphorus—Molasses, 30, Whole wheat, 374; Iron—Molasses, 7.97, Beef liver, 8.30; Copper—Molasses, 1.93, Beef liver, 2.15; Potassium—Molasses, 1500, Dry apricots, 1700.

Blackstrap is also rich in B vitamins, especially inositol. The B vitamins in 100 grams of blackstrap are:

Inositol—150 milligrams.
Thiamin—245 micrograms.
Riboflavin—240 micrograms.
Niacin—4 milligrams.
Pyridoxine—270 micrograms.
Pantothenic acid—260 micrograms.
Biotin—16 micrograms.

The *Journal of the American Medical Association* for July 14, 1951, answers a query as to the nutritional value of blackstrap, lists the vitamin and mineral content, then says, "Note that in no instance, with the exception of inositol, does the vitamin content reach a value that makes an appreciable contribution to the human diet when compared with other recognized protective foods." We are at a loss to understand this statement, con-

[442]

sidering that blackstrap contains almost twice as much calcium as milk, weight for weight, almost as much iron as liver, almost as much potassium as dry apricots and is also so very rich in B vitamins, compared to the foods most of us get along on, day after day.

Of course, one does not eat as much molasses as cheese or liver by weight. So one would not get as much nourishment from a tablespoon of blackstrap as from a serving of liver. But we think blackstrap molasses should be thought of as food in an entirely different way. We believe that anyone eating a good diet gets enough sugar in fresh fruits and vegetables so that he does not need to use any form of sweetening at mealtime. We do not advise using raw sugar, brown sugar or any of the other forms of sugar that are supposedly "better for you" than white refined sugar. Just let sugar alone, we say. In a very short time you will find that you have no craving at all for a sweet taste. Your fruits and vegetables provide it in abundance.

But if you are "tapering off" on sugar, if you simply feel that you cannot finish a meal without something sweet, then by all means use a little blackstrap molasses or honey instead of sugar. In either one, you will be getting nourishment aplenty as well as a sweet taste and calories. But remember to cut down gradually on the use of even these. And incidentally, put no stock at all in the statement that blackstrap is dirty or unfit for human food. Check with the Food and Drug Administration if you have any doubts. They will assure you that blackstrap molasses, prepared for human consumption, must pass all federal regulations for cleanliness and lack of adulteration, just as all other human foods must.

CHAPTER 120

Carob Flour for Your
Sweet Tooth

". . . . . . there arose a mighty famine in that country; and he began to be in want. And he went and joined himself to one of the citizens of that country and he sent him into the fields to feed swine. And he would fain have filled his belly with the husks the swine did eat." The prodigal son in this parable from the New Testament was longing to eat the pods of the carob tree which he was feeding to the swine. What kind of tree is this and what has become of it in our modern world? Who ever heard of pods from a tree making good food for human beings? And yet, why

[443]

not, when most fruits and nuts are not only edible but very nourishing?

The "husk" from the carob tree is, we are told, the bread that John the Baptist ate in the wilderness. This is the reason why it is also called "St. John's-bread." Mohammed's armies on the march sometimes lived on "Kharub." The ancient Romans, the Spaniards, the British all knew the carob tree and lived on its pods when other food was scarce.

We became interested in the carob tree when we ran across references to it in medical and health books and when we began to see advertisements for carob flour in medical magazines. The ads indicated that carob flour is a most effective medicine for use in "non-specific" diarrheas—that is, diarrheas that are not caused by some definite bacteria or disease. Further research told us that carob flour has a pleasant taste not unlike chocolate. A sweet taste.

Nutritive Value of Carob

We have certain criteria that we apply to all the food we eat. We don't just eat it or recommend it for the pleasant taste. Chocolate eclairs taste good, but we certainly don't advise eating them. We don't recommend eating any special foods just so that you can vary your menus or revel in some new taste sensation, or yet so that you can become known among your gourmet friends for your exotic dishes. No, indeed! We believe that every food you eat should contribute something valuable to the nourishment of your body. If it does not, you shouldn't eat it. If it contributes calories alone, or carbohydrates alone, or protein or fat alone, you shouldn't eat it. Your body must make its own good health out of the food you give it. Unless every bite of food contains vitamins and minerals, it is harmful to burden your body with it. So what we wanted to know about carob was the nutritive content of these brown pods. Perhaps you could make a fine-tasting hot drink from the carob flour mixed with hot water, but if the carob flour contributed nothing, why not just drink the water?

Food Element Content

Here is the analysis, insofar as vitamins, minerals and other food elements are concerned:

Moisture	6.3%	Iron	.05%
Crude Protein	7.75%	Aluminum	.05%
Crude Fat	1.90%	Strontium	.05%
Nitrogen free Extract		Manganese	.01%
(Carbohydrates)	72.85%	Barium	.01%
Ash (mineral matter)	2.45%	Boron	.005%
pH value of ash	10.6	Chromium	.005%
Total sugars (Invert)	46.25%	Copper	.001%
Reducing sugars	9.15%	Nickel	.001%
Sucrose	37.90%	Carotene (mg per 100g)	.03
Starch	6.30%	Equivalent to vitamin A	
Calcium	.22%	(I. U. per pound)	227
Magnesium	.95%	Thiamin, mg per pound	.16
Potassium	.28%	Riboflavin, mg per pound	.25
Phosphates	.1%	Niacin, mg per pound	12.0
Sodium	.1%	Calories, per pound	1595
Silicon	.05%		

Thiamin is that important B vitamin so necessary for proper digestion of carbohydrates—so essential for the good health of our nerves and morale. It has about as much thiamin as asparagus, strawberries, potatoes, dandelion greens or water cress. Niacin, another B vitamin, is responsible for the health of our digestive tracts, as well as a good morale. Niacin also is involved in the assimilation of sugars and starches. Carob flour has about as much niacin as dates, bacon, sausage, lima beans, lentils, peas and so forth. Riboflavin, which guards the health of our skin and eyes, is present in carob flour in about the same proportion in which it exists in brown rice.

Vitamin A, the fat-soluble vitamin that protects us from night-blindness and infections, is most abundant in liver, carrots, greens and so forth. Carob flour does not compare with these foods in vitamin A content, but it does contain more vitamin A than eggplant, asparagus, beets, white potatoes, raisins, radishes, onions or rhubarb. The minerals, of course, appear in "trace" amounts, as they do in all foods—that is, extremely small amounts. But we notice that there is calcium and phosphorus (for healthy teeth and bones) iron and copper (for good red blood) and magnesium— all minerals extremely necessary for good nutrition.

So we have a picture of a very good, well-balanced food that will contribute considerably to good nutrition. Carob is not as valuable a staple food as liver, or fresh greens or a number of the vegetables. It is not a food that we would insist you include on your menu every day or every week. But it very definitely seems to be a food worth eating.

Harmfulness of Using White Sugar

Now, satisfied that carob passes our test as a nutritive food, what are the special reasons why we want you to get to know it better? We are at war with sugar. And just for the record, let's look a little more closely at white granulated sugar and see where it stacks up in this nutrition game. Sugar is 99.5 per cent carbohydrate. One hundred grams of it contain one-tenth of a milligram of iron and two-hundredths of a milligram of copper. No calcium, no phosphorus, no vitamins at all. All the vitamins have been removed from white sugar in the process of refining.

This means that sugar does not nourish you, true. But it means a great deal more than that. In order to burn the sugar in your body's metabolism, certain of the B vitamins must be present. If you do not eat them with the sugar, your digestive processes must steal them from the rest of your body. So anyone who eats considerable amounts of sugar, especially if he is not concerned with getting lots of B vitamins in his food, is bound to suffer from vitamin B deficiency. Yet in this country we are consuming incredibly large amounts of white sugar every day—many, many times more than we did 50 years ago. Our sweet tooth has been so developed that we cannot contemplate a meal without a dessert; and, in addition, we gorge on candy, cakes, soft drinks, chewing gum, jelly bread and so forth between meals, as well as doping our coffee, fruit and cereal with heaping tablespoonfuls of the treacherous white crystals. We believe this is one of the most obvious reasons for our national nervousness, our digestive ailments, our epidemics of colds, our alcoholism, our sleeping pill addiction.

Meal Planning Without Sugar

What can mothers who are trying desperately to preserve their children's health, give them to satisfy the omnivorous sweet tooth? What can they pack for dessert in the children's lunch? Holiday candies are an important part of the average American child's life. How can they make them without sugar? It seems to us that carob flour may be the answer to these questions. For our children particularly, carob flour can be that extra special delicacy the other children don't have. It can replace sugar in many recipes. It can replace chocolate or cocoa in all recipes.

And, while we're about it, let's just glance at chocolate and cocoa—those two prime favorites of American children. Are you in the habit of making cocoa for the youngsters at breakfast or lunch when the adults drink tea or coffee? Do you know that cocoa and chocolate contain considerable amounts of caffeine? Do you know that they contain, in addition, a substance called theobromine—another stimulant probably as harmful as caffeine? Chocolate and cocoa are rich in calcium—a fine mineral children need. But they contain oxalic acid, too, which not only renders this calcium unavailable to the body, but also robs the body of stored calcium. Whether the fat content or some other element in chocolate is responsible, it has been established as one of the positive causes of acne—the skin disease of adolescence. Practically all doctors today forbid chocolate to their acne patients.

Carob Flour and a Healthy Digestive Tract

The carob's chief contribution to your bodily welfare seems to be in relation to the health of the digestive tract. A letter to the Editor of the *Lancet,* British medical magazine, calls attention to the usefulness of carob flour in treating vomiting in infants. Some children seem to vomit naturally, says Dr. Theodore James of the Duchess of York Hospital for Babies in Manchester. But in many cases infants seem not to be able to keep any food in their stomach. Naturally they become dehydrated and soon may become badly undernourished as they continue to lose the food that is so essential. Dr. James first heard of carob flour being used by a physician in Paris who treated vomiting in infants with milk thickened with carob flour. It thickens the milk without lessening its digestibility or changing its nutritive value, says Dr. James. (We suggest that it adds greatly to the nutritive value.) Dr. James used carob flour in treating 9 infants all of whom were cured or remarkably improved within a very short time. If there is no relief from the vomiting after carob flour has been given, he says, it is time to suspect that there is some very serious organic disorder. This cannot be a simple case of "habitual vomiting."

The Nestle Company which distributes carob flour in Europe announced in the *International Record of Medicine* that the potency of carob flour in treating diarrheas results from its high content of pectin and lignin.

[446]

Pectin is the substance found in many fruits which offers protection against diarrhea—the same substance that causes jelly to "jell." We would suggest that the B vitamins in carob may have a lot to do with it, too, for they are well-known protectors of the health of the digestive tract.

Finally, we want to call your attention to the sugar content of carob. These sugars listed in the analysis are natural sugars, such as occur in honey, fruits and vegetables. They satisfy your sweet tooth and give you energy, for they contain calories. As you can see, the total calorie content of carob is 1595 per pound. But—and this is the important thing to remember always about naturally occurring sugars as compared to white refined sugar or synthetic sugars such as are used in candies, canned fruits, bakery products and so forth—the natural, unrefined sugars, such as the carob has, carry their own B vitamins with them for digestive purposes, so that eating this kind of sweet does not rob your body of B vitamins. As is the case with most fruits and vegetables, carob has an alkaline reaction within the body. In fact, as you can see on the chart, its pH value is 10.6, which means that it is extremely alkaline.

Summary

Carob flour is the fruit of the carob tree, finely ground, to take the place of cocoa, chocolate and, to some extent, sugar. It contains ample vitamins and minerals to qualify as a worthwhile food. It will satisfy your sweet tooth and that of your family without doing you any of the harm done by refined and synthetic sugars. It will have an alkaline reaction in your body, as other fruits and vegetables do. You can use as much or as little of it as you like without any hesitation as to possible harmful effect.

CHAPTER 121

Carob for Diarrhea

Summer diarrhea! What mother has not heard the sound of those words with dread. Diarrhea, often a mere nuisance for an adult, can easily prove fatal for an infant. And summer is the time when it is most prevalent.

In infants the danger in diarrhea comes from the rapid loss of fluids which carry vitally important minerals and vitamins. Disrupting the delicate balance between these various elements brings on a state called "acidosis" which greatly lowers the infant's resistance.

Many years of study have not enlightened us as to the cause or treatment of infant diarrhea. And the disease still carries a high mortality. At present antibiotics are widely used to combat any bacteria which may be causing the diarrhea. Even though the "bug" is conquered, the child may die because of the terrible loss of fluid which even mild diarrhea involves.

Foods Which Stop Diarrhea

There is no drug which can stop diarrhea—that is, check the flow of frequent watery stools. Many foods have been tried. Raw apples, bananas, vegetable broth and pectin in different forms have been used. A Connecticut physician gave carrot soup for checking diarrhea. In general, we know that there are foods which contain pectin or some other substance which has a tendency to solidify the stool because of the actual composition of the food itself. Such a food is carob—the fruit of the carob tree, sometimes called also the honey locust tree.

The carob has a long history of use both as food and as medicine. The ancient Romans, the Arabs, the Spaniards, the early Britons all knew the carob tree and sometimes when food was scarce lived on its pods. The tree is plentiful along the Mediterranean and the coast of southern Europe, Africa and Asia. Its fruit is a pod with a heavy, hard and woody covering while the pulp is yellow and quite sweet. Carob flour is made from the pulp.

Discovery of the curative powers of the carob bean is credited to Professor Ramos, a Spanish physician. During the Spanish Civil War (1936-39) he observed that children of the poorer classes who ate large quantities of carob beans were less subject to disturbances of the digestive tract than were children of the wealthy, even though the rich children were better cared for generally. Later researchers found that the carob had indeed a marked effect on the health of the digestive organs.

Some Case Histories Where Carob Was Used

Alan E. Smith, M.D., and Carl C. Fischer, writing in the *Journal of Pediatrics* for October, 1949, tell us of experiments in which 30 infants varying in age from two days to 15 months with acute diarrhea were given carob flour as part of their therapy. In 11 infants the stools became formed after only one day of carob flour; in 12 infants after two days; in 6 infants after 3 days. In only one infant was there no beneficial effect.

The *Texas State Journal of Medicine* for September, 1950, relates trials with 96 patients with diarrhea. These children ranged in age from two weeks to 5 years. In the 69 patients whose diarrhea was due to intestinal organisms and/or virus infections, 47 showed "good" results in that there was an appreciable decrease in the number of and a thickening of stools within 48 hours. In 9 cases the results were "fair." In cases of diarrhea from other causes, the results were in general the same. Carob flour was given in a 5 per cent solution in water or boiled skimmed milk.

Three Canadian physicians used a 5 per cent gruel of carob flour in rice water for treating 253 children during the first 12 to 36 hours of treatment. In only 3 cases did they consider that the carob was ineffective. The length of time required to obtain normal stools averaged 1.8 days. Butter-

[448]

milk was substituted for the carob as the infants responded to treatment. According to the *Canadian Medical Association Journal* for June, 1953, these physicians say, "It is our opinion that carob flour is unexcelled by any other pectin base medication that we have heretofore employed."

Thomas R. Plowright, M.D., of Fresno, California, treated 20 infants with carob flour, reporting his results to *Pediatrics* for July, 1951. The type of diarrhea being treated was not bacterial in origin, he tells us. A "control" group of patients were not given the carob preparation, in order to compare their experience with that of the children receiving the carob. The severity of diarrhea was equally distributed in both groups.

The average number of hours for the first formed stools to be obtained in the infants who did not get carob was 174.3, compared to 47.95 in those who got carob. The average number of hospital days required for treatment of the control group was 14.15 compared to 7.85 for the carob-fed group. During a two-week follow-up period after the children went home, there was no recurrence of diarrhea in either group.

The *Journal of the Kentucky State Medical Association* for July, 1951, printed an account of the treatment of 75 children ranging in age from 7 days to 12 years who were fed carob flour in solutions varying in strength from 5 to 10 per cent. Twenty-five more children received the carob in their homes under the supervision of their mothers. Says Harry S. Andrews, M.D., author of the article, "in no instance was carob flour used unless the diarrhea was present as a major problem in the disease." Saccharin was added to the mixture to sweeten it. We fail to see why this should be necessary, since carob flour itself is quite sweet to anyone eating a diet in which sugar is sharply restricted.

More Evidence of the Value of Carob

Dr. Andrews tells us that all children treated at the hospital had excellent or good results, except for 3. Reports from mothers giving carob at home were enthusiastic. In all cases except two the parents thought there was so much improvement that they discontinued the carob after 5 days.

One final report—perhaps the most convincing of all. Pablo U. Abella, M.D., writing in the *Journal of Pediatrics* for August, 1952, tells us of giving carob flour in 300 cases of acute infant diarrhea and comparing results with 300 other infants who did not get the carob. The group getting the carob flour showed an average of 1.16 days necessary for the formation of formed stools, compared to 6.08 days for the non-carob group. It took an average of only 5.97 days before a "going home formula" was tolerated in the group fed carob flour compared to 9.18 days in the other group. Patients treated without carob stayed an average of 3.33 days longer and had 6 per cent more re-admissions.

Dr. Abella refers in his article to the work of physicians in other countries who have also used carob flour for diarrhea, chiefly in Spain, Switzerland and Italy. He believes that both the pectin and the lignin in the carob are responsible for its "constipating" action.

We used the word "constipating" deliberately, because Dr. Andrews found that giving the high concentration of carob too long caused constipation in the infants. He suggested watching the dosage carefully and cutting down on it before such a result should come about.

We have one further, very important, caution in regard to using carob for this complaint. The diarrhea may be a symptom of some extremely serious disease. In all of the cases related above, carob was given *in addition to regular treatment*—not alone. In diarrhea the terrible loss of fluids brings about a serious condition of depletion—in vitamins and minerals. Unless these are replaced, the child may die in spite of how effective carob flour may be in stopping the diarrhea. Furthermore diarrhea may be a simple uncomplicated case of "loose bowels" or it may be a symptom of some extremely serious disease, which could cause death quite apart from the effects of the diarrhea.

So don't attempt to treat diarrhea yourself. Consult your physician. In mild cases carob flour may relieve the diarrhea in short order and your doctor can then decide on diet and supplements to replace the valuables lost.

CHAPTER 122

Had Your Chocolate Today?

Four centuries ago the Aztecs of Mexico made a delicious chocolate drink by crushing the cocoa bean, beating the fluid to a froth of honey thickness, flavoring it with vanilla and serving it cold. It is said that the emperor Montezuma was so fond of this drink that he had no less than 50 jars of it prepared for his own daily consumption. Two thousand more jars were prepared for his household. There was a soda fountain on an illustrious scale!

After the Spaniards conquered Mexico, they took chocolate back to Spain. Although they supposedly guarded the secret of making the chocolate drink, knowledge of it gradually spread to other parts of Europe. By the middle of the seventeenth century chocolate was known in England and Germany. It was not widely used in this country until well along in the nineteenth century, partly because it was very expensive.

An elegant little booklet, *Golden Harvest,* dealing with the cocoa trade of the African Gold Coast, told us much about how cocoa is grown, processed and sold. It is one of the chief products of this part of Africa which produced 248,000 tons of cocoa beans in the year 1950. In the best season yet recorded the total amount paid to the cocoa farmers in the Gold Coast for the full crop was more than 34 million pounds, or about $95,200,000.00 in American money. So the cocoa business is a flourishing one and, as you might expect, the United States buys about twice as much cocoa as the next country on the list. Cocoa and chocolate have become accepted, almost traditional elements of our daily menus. Chocolate cake, chocolate candy, chocolate sodas, chocolate bars, chocolate milk—would America be America without these items on the menu? Yet the story of cocoa and chocolate leads us finally to the conclusion that we would be far better off had the tasty brown substance never reached our shores.

How Cocoa Is Processed

What is cocoa and how is it related to chocolate? In the Gold Coast which produces many times more chocolate than any other region of the world, cocoa is grown by farmers on small family farms. The cocoa tree needs good, deep soil, a warm moist climate and the shelter of forests 'round about. Seed pods develop on the tree when it is about 5 years old. The pods are about 6 to 8 inches long. When they are fully ripe they are harvested and piled. Then the pods are split open with a cutlass and the beans extracted. The beans are then fermented, which means simply spreading them in heaps to lie for 6 days. Then they are dried in the sun. After the cocoa beans are graded and packed, they are shipped, and further processing takes place in the country which is importing them.

The beans are first roasted, which brings out the characteristic chocolate flavor. Then they are cracked between rollers and ground in mills from which they emerge as a thick brown mass, for the heat of the grinding has melted the fat in the cocoa. Powerful hydraulic presses (up to 6,000 pounds per square inch) are then used to extract much of the fat, which is sold as cocoa butter. The cakes that are left contain about 20 to 30 per cent of cocoa fat or butter. This is bitter chocolate, as we know it, which may then be ground to fine powder, producing cocoa. For sweet chocolate, sugar is added. For milk chocolate, milk and sugar are added. From then on, candy, chocolate bars and chocolate syrup are just a few of the hundreds of products our ingenious food processors turn out.

What Cocoa Contains

Cocoa and chocolate are among the foods highest in calories. In one pound of the original chocolate, after its first processing, there are 2,182 calories in fats, 482 calories in carbohydrates and 221 in proteins. This adds up to about 3,000 calories. In one pound of good plain processed chocolate there are about 2,500 calories. Milk chocolate has over 2,600. What else is there besides calories? Well, cocoa, as we drink it for breakfast, is one to two per cent theobromine. This is, like caffeine, an alkaloid. It is closely related to caffeine and acts like caffeine in the body. In other words, it is a drug, very active chemically and frequently used in medicine. Cocoa (and, of course, chocolate) also contains caffeine. One 10 cent bar of chocolate, as you would buy it at the candy store, contains 78 milligrams of caffeine—about half as much as the average cup of coffee.

It is believed that the cocoa bean may develop some vitamin D while it is being dried in the sun. Cocoa, if we make it with milk, may contain vitamin A, vitamin D and two of the B vitamins, thiamin and riboflavin. But, we assume that this vitamin content comes largely from the milk used.

What else does chocolate contain? Interestingly enough it contains a substance called oxalic acid which is also present in some of the green leafy vegetables that grow in our gardens. Beet greens, rhubarb, spinach and swiss chard are especially rich in oxalic acid. Oxalic acid has one very undesirable quality. It combines with whatever calcium is in the plant and by this combination, renders the calcium useless for assimilation by human bodies. Furthermore, after it gets in the digestive tract it combines with whatever calcium is there, too, and wastes it, so far as human nutrition is concerned.

Not so many years ago spinach was widely promoted as the ideal, if much detested, food for youngsters. Popeye and other comic strip characters beat the drum for spinach as *the* food which would put hair on the chest and strength in the arms of puny kids. Spinach is rich in iron and calcium, vitamins A, B and C. But, its oxalic acid content nullifies the calcium and also destroys a considerable amount of the calcium in any other food eaten at the same time. So gradually we came to be much more cautious about spinach, and the related greens that are also high in oxalic acid. Eat them in moderation, we say now, for they contain much that is nutritious. But do not depend on them for calcium. And, if you eat lots of spinach, make certain that you double or triple the amount of calcium you are getting in other foods, for this precious mineral is essential to most body functions and you dare not be deficient in it.

Oxalic Acid in Cocoa

Where does this leave us, so far as chocolate and cocoa are concerned? In a list of common foods high in oxalic acid, cocoa is eighth, coming right after spinach, swiss chard and rhubarb. Spinach contains .89 per cent of oxalic acid, rhubarb .50 per cent and chocolate .45 to .49 per cent. *Bridges' Dietetics For the Clinician* (Lea and Febiger, 1949) states: "If a food contains enough oxalic acid to combine with all of its calcium to form calcium oxalate, the indication seems to be that the calcium is of little or no use to the body."

Adelle Davis, in *Vitality Through Planned Nutrition* (Macmillan, 1949), says that a recent investigation showed that 90 per cent of the milk sold in school cafeterias is chocolate milk, so studies were made of the amount of milk calcium used by the body when the milk was taken in the form of chocolate milk. Two groups of laboratory animals were given the same diet but one group received plain milk and the other chocolate milk. Those drinking the chocolate milk absorbed less calcium and phosphorus from their food. Their growth was retarded, their bones small and fragile, a result surely to be expected if they were not absorbing calcium and phosphorus from the main source available. Miss Davis concludes, "Both chocolate and cocoa interfere with absorption of calcium to such an extent that it is valueless to attempt to obtain this mineral by taking cocoa or chocolate."

[452]

Now if the American diet were overflowing with calcium so that all of us had more than we could use, eating chocolate or drinking chocolate milk or cocoa would be harmless. But we are, as a nation, notoriously deficient in calcium. *The Englishman's Food* by J. C. Drummond and Anne Wilbraham (Jonathan Cape, 1939) tells us that the average fifteenth century diet contained 1.3 grams of calcium per day. The average middle class diet today contains but .6 grams of calcium. The officially recommended daily minimum for children is from one to 1.4 grams of calcium daily. So we are already far short of what we need of this tremendously important mineral.

Part of the reason for this is that we have removed the minerals from many of our foods in processing them. Part of the reason is that we throw away the bones from our meat, rather than eating them. Earlier civilizations got much of their calcium from bones, and many primitive peoples still do. Part of the reason is that we eat so many unnecessary and harmful foods in the way of desserts, soft drinks, candy and so forth that we simply do not have room for the valuable, protective, mineral-rich foods. For most modern children (those who don't take bone meal) milk is about the only reliable, day by day source of calcium.

But if we are going to insist in doctoring up milk with chocolate it is easy to see that even this absolutely necessary source of calcium is lost to us. For the oxalic acid in chocolate milk or cocoa will destroy the calcium in the milk (so far as our body's use of it is concerned) and, if we drink it at the same time we are eating green vegetables or other foods high in calcium, these other good sources of calcium will also be rendered useless.

Adding to Our Deficiency In Calcium?

As we went further in our research on chocolate and oxalic acid, we became convinced that chocolate products must be held responsible for much of the calcium deficiency so evident today in decayed teeth, bones that break easily, nervousness, heart trouble and all the other symptoms that indiate clearly a serious lack of calcium.

You may argue that the amount of chocolate used in cocoa or chocolate milk is very small. You do not, for instance, eat cocoa in the quantity you eat spinach. But on the other hand *you do not eat spinach every day!* And many, many Americans—especially children—eat considerable quantities of chocolate milk, cocoa, chocolate candy, sodas, milk shakes or desserts *every single day of their lives!* How many lunches go to school that do not contain a chocolate bar? It gives energy. Of course, because it contains so many calories. But it is a temporary form of energy. How many youngsters do not stop for a chocolate drink, a piece of candy or a soda fountain concoction after school or after a basketball or football game? Sit down some day and figure out—if you can get the facts—just how much chocolate your own young ones have had during any given week and we think you will probably be amazed.

To sum up, we have in cocoa and chocolate (in a little less quantity) exactly the same caffeine we have pinned so many crimes on in relation to coffee-drinking. Caffeine stimulates the heart, raises the blood pressure, lowers the blood sugar, creates a false sense of security in that it appears to relax and rest tired nerves. In addition, we have in cocoa and chocolate another substance like caffeine (theobromine) which also produces these same undesirable results in body metabolism. And, as if this were not enough, we also have in cocoa and chocolate oxalic acid which wipes out the body's most valuable mineral, vitally concerned with teeth and bone health, nerves, heart function, resistance to infection and so forth.

Cocoa and Chocolate Are Not For Children!

Perhaps we might find excuses for chocolate if it were exclusively food for adults. In past eras it was considered just that. But in present-day America we use chocolate almost exclusively as a treat for the children—a harmless flavoring substance which induces them to drink milk and eat their pudding. We hope we have convinced you that it is not harmless at all, but may in fact be an important source of one of our most troublesome nation-wide deficiencies.

Your doctor may tell you that chocolate products are harmless for the small fry, unless, of course, he is dealing with a child afflicted with acne, in which case chocolate is generally the first food forbidden, probably because of its high fat content. But the Committee on Foods of the American Medical Association has this to say on the subject: "Special recommendations for children are not permissible for foods consisting largely of chocolate or cocoa; no objection will be taken however to such recommendations in the case of foods that are merely flavored with chocolate or cocoa and which in the quantities likely to be consumed are free from any probable effects due to theobromine or caffeine." As we have shown, the amounts of chocolate being consumed by present day American children cannot by any stretch of the imagination come under the heading of "flavoring."

And still, although all these facts are well known to nutritionists, school lunch counters go right on serving chocolate milk, cocoa, chocolate pudding and candy bars. And we go right on importing enormous quantities of chocolate. The booklet, *Golden Harvest,* tells us that even very inferior grades of cocoa are eagerly sought after *for the present world demand for cocoa far exceeds the supply.*

Chocolate and Pruritus Ani

We uncovered a most interesting article in the *American Journal of Surgery* for November, 1951, in which Laurence G. Bodkin, M.D., of Brooklyn discussed the possible causes of pruritus ani (an itching anus). In the discussion that followed Dr. Bodkin's presentation of his paper, Dr. F. B. Bowman of Hamilton, Ontario, Canada, contributed the following: "Allergy has been mentioned. I have found that 3 or 4 foods are frequently the culprits. . . . The question is always asked 'Are you a Coca Cola drinker?' I think of a doctor who consulted me in such a state (of pruritus ani) that he was considering giving up a practice. On questioning him I found that he was a confirmed chocolate eater. The condition was as bad or worse than any discussed by the speaker. In a very short time he was perfectly well after stopping his chocolate. If he takes an ABS and C coated laxative tablet (we assume this is chocolate-coated) it will throw him into a spasm of pruritus ani. A young lady with pruritus ani was cancelling her arrangements for entering a training school. When she stopped drinking Coca Cola the condition disappeared." Dr. Bodkin, in closing the discussion, said, "Chocolate is one of the greatest offenders in the whole group."

What Can You Do About Giving Up Chocolate?

Our suggestions are, first, that you conduct a real educational program, especially among the children of your family. Children admire good health and good appearance. Explain to them what continued eating of chocolate may do in the way of poor teeth, soft bones, bad hearts and nervousness. Second, keep on hand a plentiful supply of healthful snack-foods: peanuts, popcorn, sunflower seeds, apples, raisins and other dried fruits such as dates and figs, bananas, almonds, radishes, celery, carrots. Third, if your children refuse to drink milk unless it is flavored, either hot or cold, with chocolate, start now to change over to carob flour as a substitute. Carob flour is a nutritious food which tastes very much like chocolate. It goes without saying that any sensible adult will be easily persuaded to drop chocolate items from his menu, once he knows in full the harm they may be doing him.

Finally, until you can cut down on your family's consumption of cocoa and chocolate, or if they have been eating large quantities of it in the past, by all means make certain that they get enough calcium by taking bone meal, the richest and best natural source of this supremely important vitamin.

CHAPTER 123

Honey—Food for a Queen

Since the earliest days of recorded history, men have been using honey, as a food, a preservative, a medicine. A cave stone-painting from the neolithic age shows that about 15,000 years ago men gathered honey-combs for food, even as we do today. In the Egyptian pyramids, some 3000-year-old honey has been found—dry and dark, but still pure honey. In Greek and Roman civilization honey was used for preserving and embalming as well as for the choicest food. It was used as a sacrifice to the gods. It was an important part of the folk ceremonies of all nations.

In some countries the bee was regarded as sacred. In most countries the beehive was considered such an important part of the household, not so many years ago, that special ceremonies were held there on holidays. And should a tragedy or some great blessing befall the family, someone was dispatched immediately to notify the bees!

In 1747 the use of beet sugar for sweetening was introduced by Markgraf. With humanity's usual broad assumption that anything new is necessarily better, we took to using sugar rather than honey for baking and cooking. The full story of the results in terms of health will probably not be known until that happy day when refined white sugar is outlawed in every nation of the world. Then perhaps many of our modern diseases may disappear.

In 1942 according to T. Swann Harding, writing in the *American Journal of Pharmacology* for May, 1942, the average annual American consumption of white refined sugar was from 100 to 104 pounds per person. That is, the average American eats about one pound of sugar every 3 days! Our average consumption of honey is about 1½ pounds per person per year. Yet in 1941 the 4½ million hives in this country produced 206 million pounds of honey. An average bee colony may produce as much as 400 pounds of honey a year for its own use, the surplus of 50 pounds or so being what the beekeeper has for sale or for personal use.

If you want some fascinating reading, get yourself a book on bees and read the incredible story of the lives of these little creatures whose society is organized perfectly and ruthlessly for work and production, with no time for loafing or pleasure. Bees process the nectar and pollen of flowers to make honey. This complex and not-fully-understood procedure involves gathering the nectar and pollen on sunny days, packing it into the bee's pollen basket and honey stomach, then transferring it to the symmetrical wax cells of the hive. Somewhere along the line the flower nectar is changed by enzymes into the sweet, fragrant, nourishing honey that we know, which never spoils, molds or ferments.

How Honey Is Produced and Processed

We are told that bees visit about 10,000 different kinds of flowers, acting, of course, as pollinators to these flowers in the process of gathering the pollen (protein) and nectar (carbohydrate) for their food. One pound of honey requires about 37,000 trips of the honeybees and one bee colony may travel 17 million miles back and forth in one year to provide honey for the population of the hive. In addition, of course, each colony collects 40 to 100 pounds of pollen each year.

We don't often get honey in combs these days. Most honey has been removed from the tiny geometric cells of the comb in which the bees placed it. To extract the honey, the tops of these cells are sliced off and the open comb is placed in a centrifuge which whirls the honey out in liquid form. This is called "extracted" honey. When the comb is crushed and the honey strained from it, this is called "strained" honey. Morris B. Jacobs in *Food and Food Products*, the monumental book on the production of all different kinds of foods, tells us that commercially-bought honey may be adulterated with cane sugar or corn syrup. So check carefully on the source of your honey.

We have heard marvelous stories of its curative powers. Down through the ages, it has been used as a medicine. Pythagoras advocated a honey diet, declaring that honey brings health and long life. Charles Butler in his *History of the Bees,* written in 1623, says, "Hooni cleareth all the obstructions of the body, looseneth the belly, purgeth the foulness of the body and provoketh urine. It cutteth up and casteth out phlegmatic matter and thereby sharpens the stomach of them which by reason have little appetite. It purgeth those things which hurt the clearness of the eyes and nourisheth very much; it storeth up and preserveth natural heat and prolongeth old age." It has been used to treat inflammation, kidney diseases, disorders of the respiratory and digestive tract, bad complexions, liver trouble, infectious diseases, poor circulation and as an ointment for wounds.

Vitamin Content of Honey

What is the food value of honey that has led people for so many thousands of years to believe in it as food and medicine? In modern times the first answer to such a question must be given in terms of vitamins. White sugar contains no vitamins. Does honey? Indeed it does. H. A. Schuette of the Department of Chemistry of the University of Wisconsin, is one of the outstanding investigators of vitamins in honey. In an article in the *Journal of Nutrition* for September, 1943, he, George Kitzes and C. A. Elvehjem describe the determination of B vitamins in honey. Each of the samples varied in its vitamin B content, according to the locality from which it came and the kind of flower the honey was made from.

Here are the results of all honeys examined:

Riboflavin	from	7	to	60	micrograms per 100 grams
Pantothenic acid	from	9	to	110	micrograms per 100 grams
Niacin	from	72	to	590	micrograms per 100 grams
Thiamin	from	1.4	to	12	micrograms per 100 grams
Pyridoxine	from	0	to	27.7	micrograms per 100 grams

A few honeys were tested also for their biotin and folic acid content and traces of these were found.

These researchers turned up some other interesting aspects of vitamins in honey. They found that some of the B vitamins might be destroyed in storage over a period of years. They found that the vitamin content of pollen is much higher than that of honey, suggesting that perhaps the vitamins in honey are contained in the small pollen grains found in it. They also remind us that clarifying honey reduces the vitamin contents up to 35 to 50 per cent of the original values. Clarifying is a process which removes the slight cloudiness that may be present, resulting in crystal-clear, brilliant honey, but less nourishing than unclarified honey.

The vitamin C content of honey varies, too, with the kind of honey and the locality from which it comes. Some researchers have found as much as 311.2 milligrams and as little as 0 milligrams of vitamin C in 100 grams of honey. An orange weighing 100 grams contains from 25 to 50 milligrams of vitamin C. Naturally one cannot eat 100 grams of honey as casually as one might eat an orange because of its concentrated sweetness.

Minerals and Amino Acids in Honey

Honey contains minerals, too. Here, interestingly enough, the mineral content depends largely on the color of the honey, those dark honeys, like buckwheat, being richer in minerals than the lighter ones. H. A. Schuette and D. J. Huenink in *Food Research,* Vol. 2, 1937, tell us that honey contains silica, phosphorus, calcium and magnesium as follows:

	Silica	*Milligrams per kilogram* *Phosphorus*	*Calcium*	*Magnesium*
Light honeys	14 to 36	23 to 50	23 to 68	11 to 56
Dark honeys	13 to 72	27 to 58	5 to 226	7 to 126

In this survey 35 honeys were selected from 9 different states and about 14 different blossoms. These writers point out that other investigators have found even larger concentrations of calcium and of phosphorus.

In *Food Research* for July-August, 1939, Dr. Schuette and Warren W. Woessner report on sodium and potassium components of honey. Here, too, the minerals exist in much larger quantity in the darker honeys.

	Milligrams per kilogram *Sodium*	*Potassium*
Light honeys	average of 18	average of 205
Dark honeys	average of 76	average of 1676

Working again with different colors of honey from a widely selected group, Dr. Schuette and C. L. Baldwin, Jr., reported in *Food Research* for May-June, 1944, that amino acids (forms of protein necessary for life) are also present in honey as "minor components." Once again the darker honeys are richer in amino acids than the light honeys. It is an interesting aspect of our study of foods to note that nature likes color and lavishes her richest abundance of health-giving nourishment on foods in which color is most intense. Keep this in mind when you're shopping for food. Take the bright orange sweet potato in preference to the pale yellow one. Buy the head of cabbage with the greenest leaves. Use the outer, dark green leaves of endive rather than the bleached white ones in the center. Pick the reddest watermelon and the greenest celery. And, if you're buying honey for its mineral content, choose the dark honeys, even though you may not at first care for their stronger flavor.

Honey and Anemia

We uncovered several other interesting facts about honey in its relation to health. For instance, in an experiment with laboratory rats reported in the *Proceedings of the Society of Experimental Biology and Medicine* for May, 1943, M. H. Haydak, L. S. Palmer and M. C. Tanquary of the University of Minnesota discovered that dark honey added to a milk diet will increase the hemoglobin count and hence prevent or cure nutritional anemia in rats, whereas light honey added to milk caused the hemoglobin count to fall, meaning that the rats became even more anemic. Rats fed milk and sucrose also became anemic. Incidentally the iron content of honey ranges from 2.4 milligrams per kilogram in light honeys to 17.5 milligrams in dark honeys. And the copper content of honey ranges from .29 milligrams in light honeys to 1.4 milligrams in dark honeys.

In performing these experiments the researchers found that honey also contains an anti-hemorrhaging factor, suggesting the presence of vitamin K. Using vitamin-K-deficient chicks, they tested alfalfa hay and honey and found that they could indeed increase the chicks' store of vitamin K by the addition of alfalfa and honey to their diets.

Honey and Calcium Retention

Perhaps most valuable of all, from the point of view of human beings, is an experiment in feeding honey to infants as the carbohydrate part of their "formulas." Over the first 6 months of their lives 14 healthy babies received formulas consisting of evaporated or half-skim milk, breast milk or dried protein milk for the protein part of the diet. The carbohydrate part consisted of corn syrup or honey. Vitamin D in cod liver oil was added at varying levels. E. M. Knott, Ph.D., C. F. Shuckers, M.D., and F. W. Schultz, M.D., of Chicago, reporting on this experiment in the *Journal of Pediatrics* for October, 1941, tell us that allowing for all other possible variations in the diets, honey came out well ahead of corn syrup as a preserver of calcium for the infants, which is, of course, good news for honey-lovers.

The infants were tested each day for calcium retention. Naturally the amount of vitamin D used that day affected the retention of calcium, for it is well known that vitamin D is essential for proper retention and use of calcium by the body. But it was found that wherever infants were fed under comparable conditions to make the comparison of these two types of carbohydrates completely valid, the average retention of calcium *was always higher if honey had been included in the formula rather than corn syrup*. The authors conclude that "honey is indeed a type of carbohydrate which is well suited to the infant's needs and therefore probably deserves a wider use in infant dietaries."

What about the question of acidity versus alkalinity? In general, meats, eggs, cereals and nuts are acid in their reaction in the body's metabolism. Vegetables, fruits and milk are alkaline. Starches, sugars and fats are neutral. We should strive to maintain a balance in the kinds of food we eat, for most of us tend to lean too heavily on the acid-producing foods and don't eat enough fruits and vegetables to keep the proper alkaline balance in our blood. So it is cheering to know that honey, like fruits, has an alkaline reaction in the body. Even though it is sweet, it contains, like fruits, certain organic acids which react in the body's chemistry by producing alkalinity. So if you are hesitating over whether sugar or honey should go on the youngsters' breakfast cereal or on the fruit salad for tonight's dessert, don't hesitate for another minute. Sugar—white refined sugar, contains no vitamins, no minerals and no other healthful food elements. It makes enormous demands on your body's store of the elusive B vitamins, for it requires B vitamins for its digestion and they just aren't present in sugar. In addition, sugar is neutral in the acid-alkaline balance. But honey contains all the B vitamins necessary for its proper use by the body, contains minerals and amino acids and, in addition, will have an alkaline effect on the body.

Conclusions On Honey

As you know we cast a disapproving eye on sweets of all kinds, except those natural sugars found in fruits and vegetables. The research we have done does not convince us that you should deliberately add honey to your diet. Honey is a carbohydrate food and most of us get too much carbohydrate food in proportion to our protein. But, if you or your family feel definitely that you must have some sweetening, on fruit salads, for example, by all means use honey instead of sugar. Use it for freezing fruits. Use it in any recipe that calls for white sugar. We can guarantee that the unhealthy aftereffects of sugar-eating will not stalk your footsteps. And, who knows, perhaps the ancients were right. Perhaps honey really does contain as yet undiscovered potentialities for health. At any rate, if it is produced and marketed with careful attention, it is a completely natural food. The bees thrive on it—and bees are mighty smart, hardworking insects!

CHAPTER 124

The Case Against Saccharin

Acute urticaria has been caused by a host of agents including foods, drugs, inhalents and injectants. Here is a case caused by sensitivity to saccharin. Acute urticaria is a disorder of the skin involving whitish or pinkish elevations which develop suddenly on the skin and last usually but a short time. There may be sensations of burning and itching. "A severe rash" is how you and I might describe "acute urticaria."

In this particular case, described in the *New York State Journal of Medicine* for December 1, 1955, a surgeon complained of this kind of rash for several months. He suspected it was caused by saccharin because he had been using saccharin freely for several months; when he had stopped using it about two weeks previously, the rash did not occur.

[460]

He was persuaded to place a very tiny amount of saccharin under his tongue. Within two and a half minutes he complained of skipped heart beats and broke out in a cold sweat. He also noticed a prickling sensation of the face and soon, sure enough, the rash appeared. The cold sweat, rash and skipped heart beats persisted for about 3 hours. The next morning he appeared to be normal again.

The two authors of the article, New York physicians, believe that there is no doubt that saccharin was responsible for the rash in this case. "Saccharin is quite widely used and may conceivably be responsible for some of our intractable cases of chronic urticaria," they say. We are glad to know that at least two members of the medical profession have now seen demonstrated before their eyes what may happen as a result of taking saccharin daily.

Saccharin is a product of coal tar in the manufacture of which sulfuric acid and other chemicals are used. It is related to salicylic acid (used in aspirin) and phenol (or carbolic acid) both of which are also coal-tar products. Because it can be made so cheaply and because of its intensely sweet taste its use is widespread in candies, soft drinks and bakery products. Special "dietetic" foods for diabetics often contain saccharin.

An M.D. giving saccharin in "enormous quantities" to two men over the period of a year noticed during the course of that year no ill effects. All that this proves to us is that no one knows what the long-time effects of small, daily doses of saccharin may be. There is no report as to what the two men eventually died of.

Some of the Dangers Involved

An Indian physician reported in 1935 on a 9-year old boy who ate 200 saccharin tablets at one time and exhibited frightful symptoms. He suffered from delirium, loss of consciousness, hallucinations, difficulty in moving and finally developed enormous blisters all over his body. The same Indian physician, Dr. B. M. Gupta, tried to trace a note he had found on research at the Lister Institute showing that saccharin might cause cancer. The Institute reported that they knew of no such research and did not accept such a theory. Dr. Gupta, after expressing his wonder, goes on to say, "A careful consideration of the above investigation will show that saccharin is not an acute poison. It has no food value and in large doses it may cause headache, gastro-intestinal disturbances and mental depression. If saccharin is freely permitted to be substituted for sugar, it will be taken by old and young in all states of health and for all time. *There is at present no evidence to establish the claim that saccharin even in very small quantities so taken is harmless.*" This statement appears in the *Indian Medical Gazette* for September 1935.

An article in a Czech medical journal shows that children in a certain locality there who used saccharin as their exclusive sweetening agent all suffered from goiter. A writer in a German medical publication reported in 1915 on experiments he had done with peas soaked in various solutions. Ninety-four per cent of the peas soaked in plain water germinated.

[461]

Eighty-seven per cent of those soaked in sugar water germinated; 44 per cent of those soaked in salt water did, too. None of the peas soaked in a saccharin solution sprouted. This investigator came to the conclusion that saccharin is a protoplasmic poison. Protoplasm is living, functioning cells. Plants are made of protoplasm; animals and human beings are made of protoplasm of a little different kind.

Another European researcher tested the toxicity of saccharin solutions on one-celled animal life. He found that saccharin is 12 times as deadly to bacteria as carbolic acid—which is known, of course, as a deadly poison. Watching the movements of the tiny, one-celled animals beneath the microscope, this chemist noted that the saccharin solution caused blisters to form on their bodies—just as they had formed on the body of the little boy who ate too many saccharin tablets—remember?

Why Risk These Dangers?

Perhaps you individually can get by without suffering any ill effects from saccharin. On the other hand, you may develop symptoms as the surgeon at the beginning of this story did. Or your symptoms may be entirely different and so unusual that your doctor will not be able to diagnose them.

Even if you don't develop any disagreeable symptoms that can eventually be traced to saccharin—why go on dosing yourself day after day with a fairly mysterious poison? You are exposed every hour of your life to poisons you can't possibly avoid. Why willingly take on another?

You find that your "sweet tooth" must be satisfied and saccharin will satisfy it? We doubt that statement. You crave sweet things because, in nature, a sweet taste comes in foods that are rich in minerals. The sweet taste is there to attract you to the minerals. Once you plan your diet and diet supplements so that you are getting plenty of minerals, your craving for sweets will disappear. The very fact that you feel you can't give up saccharin proves that it is a drug to which you have now become addicted. Cross saccharin off your list, along with sugar, and concentrate on eating foods that are good for you and satisfy you, too.

CHAPTER 125

Additional Information on Sweets

Things About Food
By J. I. Rodale

Some day schools are going to wake up and find that they can have a great influence over the nutritional habits of their students. There is too much defeatism today, such as illustrated by a little incident which occurred one time when I was talking to a Parent-Teacher Association meeting. In the room in the school where I spoke, there was a refrigerated box full of popsicles, ice cream, etc., and I asked the teacher in charge why they should have such an inferior type of food there. Her answer was that they do it to keep the children quiet. They certainly could try other ways of keeping the children quiet.

I noticed in a little item in a newspaper that at Stanton, Nebraska, raw carrots replaced candy bars at the Stanton High School basketball games. The carrots were offered for sale at 5 cents each, and about 30 pounds of them are consumed at each game. Isn't this terrific? My suggestion is that readers type this item and mail it to the PTA groups in the schools of their city, suggesting that that be discussed at the Parent-Teacher's meeting and see if such an innovation in schools could be adopted. If people would only try, there could be other very interestingly gotten up confections and food products that children would go for, rather than ice cream and popsicles.

The trouble with that teacher who wanted quiet children is that her own nutrition probably leaves a great deal to be desired. If she ate right, and corrected her own nutritional deficiencies by taking the right kind of vitamins, she could probably stand a little innocent jumping about of the children. It is a vicious chain.

Increased Sugar Consumption

According to the United Nations Food and Agriculture Organization, the world ate 2 million tons more sugar in 1956 than in 1955. It credits the world's sweet tooth to higher incomes. Possibly in other countries sugar is a luxury. Not in America. In our country the consumption of sugar has increased because there is profit to be had in selling refined carbohydrate products and no profit to be had in telling the American public that such foods are deadly.

New Uses For Sugar

. . . The *New York Times* for March 18, 1956, tells us that candy is listed as a war essential. The Department of Agriculture scientists are working on a candy whose chief characteristic will be its keeping quality.

[463]

An interesting note at the bottom of the article indicates that the Department of Agriculture is not so much concerned with the sweet tooth of the American soldier as in *finding new uses for sugar and dairy products*. The candy market is important for both. That is what one part of your tax money goes for—finding new uses for sugar and dairy products!

Is Sugar Good for Muscles?

A researcher from the famous Johns Hopkins University has raised his voice against sugar! As *Science News Letter* for October 30, 1954, puts it, Dr. Reuben Andres "doubts the role of sugar as the chief energy source." Now this is heresy. For years and years we have been told that athletes eat chocolate and chew sugar lumps because of the instant energy these foods give to their muscles. The folks in charge of promoting refined sugar as a food keep telling us that we must eat sugar because it is the main source of energy for our muscles.

But Dr. Andres has perfected a technique for measuring blood through the forearm so that he can determine what substances are being carried by the blood to the muscles. It has generally been held, he says, that most of the oxygen consumption of muscles occurs while they are breaking down sugars for their own use. But "the present investigations are interpreted to suggest that the older idea is not true and that sugars may not be the major energy source for muscle." This research was reported incidentally, to the Muscular Dystrophy Association. This group of people *has* to be vitally concerned with everything pertaining to muscles. These horribly crippled sufferers are not going to be fobbed off with some glib advertising which will sell more sugar. They want to know everything that is to be known about muscles. Of course, no nutritionist could possibly put an okay on white refined sugar as a necessary or even a harmless food. Now, perhaps, we will hear more from Dr. Andres showing us what muscle energy does come from.

Sugar Makes Your Teeth Ache For Lots of Reasons

"Why does sugar make teeth ache?" asks a reader of the editor in the *British Medical Journal* for December 25, 1954. Answers the editor: "Sugar is apt to make the teeth ache when there is some loss of the protective covering of enamel and dentine so that the dental pulp is more readily stimulated . . . It is not clear whether sugar acts as a chemical stimulus on the exposed dentine or whether the action is entirely physical in nature." He goes on to say that the actual place where the sugar causes most ache is usually at the base of the tooth where the enamel may not completely cover the dentine. Or perhaps the gums have receded, leaving one of the under layers uncovered. Exposing the dentine near the pulp of the tooth uncovers a particularly sensitive spot.

"Sugar making your teeth ache"—do you remember, those of you who don't eat sugar any longer, how dreadful that ache used to be? Of course, when you stopped eating sugar you not only stopped the possibility of any further "sugar-ache," but you also said goodbye to that amount of tooth decay that is caused by sugar—and we dare say it's considerable. Did you know, incidentally, that if your teeth are especially sensitive to hot and cold foods, it may indicate a lack of B vitamins? We don't believe very hot and very cold foods are especially good for you, but if you insist on eating them that way, at least make certain you won't get pains by getting enough B vitamins in brewer's yeast or desiccated liver.

Sucking Hard Candy Leads to Cavities

A particularly insidious kind of candy, so far as the damage to teeth is concerned, is the kind one holds in one's mouth, such as lozenges, suckers, sour-balls, etc. *Consumer Bulletin* (January, 1958) carried a short piece which described the case of a school teacher who took excellent care of her teeth, but was accustomed to hold a candy mint in her mouth most of the day. The enamel of her teeth showed serious erosion. It has been shown repeatedly in experiments that refined sugar, a natural enemy of the teeth, can cause even more serious damage when held in continued proximity to the teeth. The very nature of the hard lozenges and mint drops, so popular for relieving throat tickle and bad breath, makes long contact with the teeth likely, and this is an invitation to tooth decay.

If you must use something to relieve a throat tickle, try honey, and for bad breath, parsley. Skip the candy products or your teeth will surely suffer.

Sugar to Make Peaches "Peachier?"

"Canners should prepare their canned fruits with about 60 per cent more sugar than at present to gain maximum consumer acceptance," says Dr. Henry B. Hass (*Food Field Reporter*, June 22, 1959). Now who can Dr. Hass be, you wonder? Take a guess, and you're probably right: he's the president and director of research at the Sugar Research Foundation, Incorporated. To reinforce this opinion Dr. Hass trots out plenty of evidence in questionnaires filled in by consumers at the California State Fair. These consumers sampled peaches canned in syrup containing 35, 45 and 55 per cent sugar. (The usual percentage of sugar in canned peach syrup is 30 to 35 per cent.) The tasters lodged a preference for the sweetest sugar concentration—55 per cent. Dr. Hass explained the preference by citing the discovery that more sugar makes canned peaches "peachier."

The testing sponsored by the Foundation progressed to the point at which it was found that adding "too much sugar" and then adding enough citric acid to restore the sweet-sour balance, resulted in "the best canned fruit ever canned." One large West Coast canner is already using this principle in his canned fruits and another is planning to do so.

The absurdity of this situation is apparent if one contemplates carrying it to its logical conclusion. If 50 per cent sugar in the syrup is better than 30 per cent, then a hundred per cent concentration, which would have the fruit caked in sugar crystals, should be even better. Is there any reason for including the fruit at all?

Dr. Hass remarked that, "The same principle is applicable to many foods other than canned fruits." We have no doubt that it will be so

[465]

applied. The Sugar Research Foundation has fantastic financial reserves, and they are devoted almost exclusively to inducing American consumers, through the manufacturers of processed foods, to use more and more refined sugar. Such releases as this one are typical: convince canners that the public will buy more canned fruits if more sugar is used. The canners will use more sugar and the Sugar Research Foundation has done its job.

The consumer? Well, he gets double the amount of sugar he did before, and when arthritis, polio, diabetes, etc., come along, he wonders how it happened. After all, if he eats plenty of canned fruit for dessert, instead of cake or pie, he should be healthy! The papers carry feature articles telling the public again and again what a healthy nation we are, due largely to the success of our food processing industry, which lets us eat fruits and vegetables out of season.

Don't be taken in by such propaganda. The canning processors are ready and willing to resort to any trick in the book to make their product salable. They will add anything or remove anything in order to increase sales, and if it ruins the nutritive value of the food, their concern is not great. The sales charts are the only important consideration.

If you want a "peachier" taste, eat a fresh peach. The same goes for any other fruit. There is always some fresh fruit available in these days of swift transportation. If you insist on out-of-season fruits that are not available, freeze or can your own, using honey if you need a sweetener. But stay away from canned processed foods, and resolve to eat in-season fruits and vegetables whenever you can.

Processed Honey

The Arizona Beekeepers Association learned of ways to increase honey consumption at their annual convention. The *Christian Science Monitor* for April 2, 1957, tells us that a group of researchers at the University of Kansas have discovered a way of incorporating just enough sugar syrup into honey to maintain its liquid state. If or when this practice becomes widespread, readers will have to be alert to the dangers of getting in their honey the very sugar they are trying to avoid by eating honey instead.

A Nutritious and Tasty Dessert

Thyra Samter Winslow, famous short story writer and author of a book on reducing, *Be Slim, Stay Slim,* published by Harpers, sent us a recipe for a "sugarless, flourless, eggless, milkless high protein, high vitamin goodie—something like a brownie. You don't even have to bake it," says Miss Winslow, "so it can be made on the top of the stove in a few minutes. You may not approve of all the ingredients, but it is fine for people who like sweets and want good nourishment which they can't get in cakes or candy. Carob powder could possibly be used instead of the dietetic cocoa and any soy granules could be used."

We didn't approve of some of the ingredients, but we are going to print the recipe as Miss Winslow sent it and then add the changes we would make in it.

[466]

PVM Brownies
(Protein, Vitamin, Mineral)

1 cup soy granules
2 envelopes unflavored gelatin
4 tablespoons dietetic cocoa
  equivalent of 1 cup of sugar (I use Sucaryl)
½ cup wheat germ
½ cup lecithin
½ cup of whole hulled sunflower seeds
4 cups water
1 teaspoon vanilla (real vanilla, of course—not synthetic)
pinch of salt
sprinkle of cinnamon

Let water come to boil. Add sunflower seeds. This will soften them enough so people with dentures will be able to chew them easily. They'll taste like nuts. Add soy granules gradually. Dissolve gelatin in a little cold water. Add. Boil for 10 minutes or a little longer depending on what kind of soy granules you use. Remove from stove; add other ingredients. Beat well. Put into a flat pan and refrigerate when cool. Cut into small, one-inch squares. Serve as between-meal nibbles, at tea or with fruit as dessert.

Miss Winslow agreed that we could suggest changes in the recipe for our readers who are, after all, not the ordinary brand of reducers, but very special people, alert to certain dangers in food that other folks may not be aware of.

We, of course, do not recommend using sucaryl, a synthetic sweetener, like saccharin, made from coal tar. And, of course, not sugar. About ¾ cup of honey would be the equivalent. (And honey contains calories, remember.) We certainly suggest using carob flour rather than cocoa. And, naturally, no salt.

Adding up the wonderful nutritional value of the sunflower seeds, the lecithin, the soy granules, the wheat germ and the carob flour, we agree that this is an outstanding dessert.

SECTION 12.

Vegetables

Plenty of vegetables in your diet means plenty of nutrition. Eat them fresh and as close to raw as possible for full value. If you cook them, use only a little water and steam them lightly. Of course, salads should be an important part of every meal, and they should contain several kinds of greens and other raw vegetables. String beans, cauliflower, spinach, peas— all uncooked—are delicious, and healthful, additions to a salad.

CHAPTER 126

Asparagus

Asparagus, consumed in large amouts as a table vegetable and also as an ingredient in soups, is a native of southern Russia, Poland and Siberia. This fleshy green shoot containing scales which in reality are true leaves has, through the passage of history, traveled from its native European home to the shores of America where the states of California and New Jersey have assumed the major role in its growth and production. In 1958 these states together produced two-thirds of the nation's asparagus crop.

Known as the aristocrat of the vegetable family, being a cousin of the orchid, asparagus imparts to the early spring menu a fine delicate taste which can be detected not only in the simple asparagus preparations such as asparagus sandwiches, but also in such fashionable dishes as asparagus vinaigrette. But perhaps primary to this taste sensation for those who want their foods to provide the most from a health standpoint is nature's implanting of a wealth of vitamins and minerals into these pale-green stalks, the delectable taste, we are sure, acting as nature's lure to the treasure chest of healthfulness that lies within. As with so many other foods which contain a rich abundance of nutritive elements, nature always provides some way of attracting to their benefits those of us who would be healthy.

To get the most, vitamin and mineral-wise, when selecting your asparagus, buy straight, firm stalks with a maximum of 3 inches of white base and with the scales or leaves of the spear closely and firmly united. Although there are some 150 species of asparagus known to the world, these simple instructions will serve as valid criteria in evaluating all in terms of eating pleasure and healthfulness.

One hundred grams or about 9, 6-inch stalks of asparagus contain the following vitamins and minerals:

Vitamin A	1000	International Units
Vitamin B		
Thiamin	.16	milligrams
Riboflavin	.19	milligrams
Niacin	1.4	milligrams
Vitamin C	33	milligrams
Minerals		
Calcium	21	milligrams
Phosphorus	62	milligrams
Iron	.9	milligrams
Sodium	2	milligrams
Potassium	240	milligrams

CHAPTER 127

How to Sprout Beans

As long ago as 2838 B.C., when the Emperor wrote a book about the plants of China the orientals knew not only the food value of mung and soybeans, but also that they were more nutritious when sprouted.

During the last war several experiment stations in this country, under pressure of food emergency, began experiments with bean sprouts, in order to discover what the Chinese knew before our civilization was born.

Even so, soybeans are used, here, chiefly as oil source, livestock feed and for industrial uses. The mung bean is little known, except as the sprouts are used in "Chinese" dishes. These "chow meins" and "chop sueys" have become so popular, however, that it is estimated that about a million pounds of bean sprouts are being eaten each year in this country, mostly of the commercial variety.

The home sprouting of soy or mung beans, although a little fussy, is not difficult, and insures the family a nutritious, high-vitamin content food —particularly valuable in late winter and early spring when vitamin C has ebbed slowly from stored and canned vegetables. According to the United States Department of Agriculture, potatoes may lose ⅔ of their vitamin C content during 6 months storage.

Grandma's "spring tonic" was sulfur and molasses. Her grand-children would find greater health and pleasure in the use of bean sprouts.

The beans, with their sprouts, can be used in a variety of tasty ways— as a vegetable, as a salad, in stews or as a replacement for onions or mushrooms in fried or roasted dishes. Many people who use the fresh sprouts in salad prefer them to any other ingredient used.

It is well to become acquainted with both the mung and the soybean.

The sprouts of the mung are more attractive, and because of the low carbohydrate content and other peculiar dietary qualities, they appeal to people who must watch their weight. Also, they are to be preferred to the soybean sprouts when used in the raw state, as the soybean contains an enzyme which tends to oxidize and destroy the ascorbic acid (vitamin C) when the sprouts are chopped and exposed to air. Boiling for two minutes, however, destroys this enzyme without loss of much vitamin C.

Mung bean sprouts are a fair source of vitamin A in either raw or cooked state and are also rich in vitamin B, either raw or cooked. They are especially rich in vitamin C. The mung bean sprout, however, is not adequate as a sole source of protein.

In the soybean nature has produced an easily-raised and inexpensive food which contains two of the most expensive and indispensable substances—protein and fat. Some oriental people have existed comfortably with soybeans as their only source of protein.

In addition, soybeans help prevent deficiency diseases because they contain iron, calcium and other B vitamins. When sprouted, most of the B vitamins are increased, and that all important substance—vitamin C—so lacking in winter meals, is added.

The genius of the soybean sprout, from the housewife's standpoint, is that the vitamin C content increases with storage in the refrigerator, up to one week, while most vegetables (including the mung sprout) lose vitamin C with each hour of storage. It need only be remembered that the soy sprouts need boiling for two minutes to conserve this vitamin.

Protein makes the very flesh and blood of starving peoples. It must be eaten daily for proper health. The protein content of soybeans varies from 35-40 per cent and contains some of all the necessary amino acids.

Analysis for vitamin C content in soybeans shows that after only 4 hours of soaking, some vitamin C is formed. When ready for eating, the content equals that of tomato juice. But—after 7 days storage in the refrigerator, the amount has doubled! After this, it deteriorates. Exposure to light has no effect on the ascorbic acid (vitamin C) content.

With both soy and mung sprouts, riboflavin increased four-fold, and niacin doubled, experiments showed. There is little change in thiamin content.

The mung bean is more expensive and less common than the soybean. The green or golden "gram" usually is used. The ordinary field varieties of the soybean make better sprouts than the garden varieties which are more suitable used as green beans.

There are various methods recommended by the experiment stations, most of which are highly controlled, for the sprouting of either soy or mung beans. Simplest and most satisfactory for the housewife is the method recommended by Cornell:

How to Sprout Beans

1. Select clean, bright, new-crop beans. Yellow soybeans are less conspicuous than black, but black may be preferred.

2. Discard all except clean, whole beans.

3. Wash beans and place in one or two-quart fruit jar. Remember that sprouts increase about 6 times original volume.

4. Cover seed with 4 times volume of lukewarm water and let stand overnight, until swollen (no longer).

5. Pour off water and rinse thoroughly, pouring off last wash water.

6. Cover jar top with cheesecloth or quarter-inch mesh screening. Tie securely.

7. Invert jar in a pan and place in cupboard or dark place, in a slightly tilted position, so that excess water can drain away.

8. At least 3 times a day or every 4 hours, place jar under water tap or pour on plenty of cool water, to wash away molds or bacteria which

[473]

may have developed. The better the washing, the better the sprouts. Return jar to inverted position.

9. In from 3 to 4 days, at room temperature, the sprouts will be from one to two inches long and ready for use. Pour sprouts into clean cold water and shuck off skins if desired, but this is not necessary.

A flower pot can be used for sprouting, but must have a piece of cloth over bottom drain and also a moist cloth over surface of beans to prevent drying. Otherwise the sprouts will be tough.

It is not wise to attempt sprout production in summer unless temperature can be kept about 70 degrees Fahrenheit.

Refrigerated sprouts should be kept moist in a covered container to prevent wilting. Bean sprouts freeze admirably. They should be blanched for two minutes, cooled in ice water and frozen in moisture-vapor-proof containers.

Cook with beans attached. Soybeans have chewy texture; crisp and waxy as a peanut. Cook only long enough to remove "raw bean" flavor—10 to 20 minutes. Use as little water as possible. As some of the vitamin C will be in the cooking water, it also should be used. The Chinese method of "panning" or sautéeing saves vitamin C. Sprouts can be fried without water—with or without onions.

Here is an analysis of the vitamin and mineral content of about one cup of soybean and mung bean sprouts:

	Soybeans		*Mung beans*	
Calcium	48	mg.	29	mg.
Phosphorus	67	mg.	59	mg.
Iron	1	mg.	.8	mg.
Vitamin A	180	International Units	10	International Units
Vitamin B				
Thiamin	.23	mg.	.07	mg.
Riboflavin	.20	mg.	.09	mg.
Niacin	.8	mg.	.5	mg.
Vitamin C	13	mg.	15	mg.

CHAPTER 128

Beets

There's an interesting story about how beets happened to be introduced into the English bill of fare. In *The Englishman's Food* by J. C. Drummond and Anne Wilbraham (Jonathan Cape, London), we are told that the beet, under the name of *mangoldwurzel* had been grown in Holland and Germany for centuries before it was introduced into England. Its use spread to northern France where, during a near-famine, it was often the only food the peasants could get. "Confusion between the German words *mangold* (beet) and *mangel* (dearth) led to the root being given what was thought to be the French equivalent of the original name, that is *racine de disette*," root of dearth, rather than root of beet.

So during the latter part of the eighteenth century when food was scarce in England, it was suggested that this crop should be grown to provide cheap food. But the name of the vegetable was against it, and for years farmers thought the beetroot could be eaten only by stock and not ever by human beings. Was it not a food that people ate only during the worst famines? But gradually, of course, the beet came to be one of our most popular vegetables. The mangold beet is, however, still generally used as stock food.

Botanically speaking, the beet is a taproot, although, of course, today we think of it as a vegetable. Sugar beets, of which there are several kinds, are grown in order to refine their sucrose content into white sugar. Garden beets are rich in sucrose and 3 other kinds of sugar as well. Of course, in the beet the sugar comes along with all the other things that naturally accompany sugar in fresh foods, so there is nothing harmful in this kind of sugar. We wonder whether people who claim they can't get along without some kind of sweetening, have ever tasted raw beet juice made in a vegetable juicer. There is a food so sweet that it is almost unpalatable unless you are used to it or unless you dilute it with other vegetable juices not quite so sweet. Of course, beet juice is rich in minerals and fairly rich in vitamins.

Beets are best eaten raw. Most vegetables are. Shredded finely, they add to salads. Shredded and then cooked in a little oil just until they are tender, as the Chinese cook their vegetables, they are a delicious treat. If you must boil them, keep the skin intact, leave the root on and as much of the stem as you can. The beet is one vegetable that gives away most dramatically the amount of food value lost in cooking. The red color of the cooking water represents beet juice containing minerals and vitamins. Experiments show that in boiling beets and retaining the cooking water, as much as 5 per cent of the vitamin A. 10 per cent of the vitamin C and 15 per cent of the riboflavin (a B vitamin) are lost. If the cooking water is discarded, 65 per cent of the vitamin C is lost and 35 per cent of the niacin (another B vitamin).

We found one interesting note on beet allergy, which rather surprised us, for vegetables are not usually foods that cause allergies. In these cases, reported in the *Annals of Allergy* for September-October, 1950, patients who ate beets along with some other foods to which they were known to be allergic, found that their urine turned bright red. It seems that, during the allergic reaction to the other food, the red pigment from the beets entered the bloodstream and from there went to the kidneys. Normal persons do not absorb this red pigment from the intestinal tract, which is the reason why it generally appears in the stool after you have eaten beets. Red appearing in the urine, however, may be a sign of allergy to beets!

We have spoken of the food value of the good natural sugar in beets. Above are the vitamins and minerals present in about ¾ cup of cooked beets. Then, because beet greens are an excellent source of vitamins, we have included them, too. Remember, however, that beet greens contain considerable oxalic acid, as does spinach, and oxalic acid connects rapidly with calcium wherever it finds it, forming oxalates which are then excreted. So don't depend on beet greens as your main supply of greens, for you are almost certain to be calcium-short if you do.

	Beets (¾ cup)	Cooked Beet Greens (½ cup)
	units	units
Vitamin A	50	22,000
Vitamin B	mg.	mg.
Thiamin	41	100
Riboflavin	37	500
Niacin	13	.3
Choline	8	0
Inositol	21	0
	mcg.	mcg.
Folic Acid	13.5	20-50
	mg.	mg.
Vitamin C	8	50
Calcium	28	94
Phosphorus	42	40
Iron	2.8	3.2
Copper	.19	
Magnesium	23	
Manganese	.54 to 1.35	
Potassium	350	570
Sodium	110	130
Sulfur	17	
Zinc	.93	
	grams	grams
Protein	2	2
Carbohydrate	6.5	4.2
Fat	.1	.3
Calories	40	28

CHAPTER 129

Brussels Sprouts

Brussels sprouts interest us because they are such a highly satisfactory fall and winter vegetable and because they are higher in vitamin C content per serving than almost any other vegetable. Sprouts belong in the cabbage family which is, as one nutritionist puts it, an "enormous tribe"—developed mostly by Dutch gardeners from the wild *brassica maritime*. Mustard, radishes and watercress belong to the same family.

Leaves of the cabbage family spread wide to absorb energy from the sun by means of the chlorophyll in their green parts. Where there is chlorophyll there is almost always vitamin A. You can expect to find iron, too, in abundance. The vitamin C is present to catalyze (or bring about) the changes in the leaf that permit the formation of carbohydrates or sugars from carbon dioxide and water. This is the purpose of that marvelous chemical factory that hums along busily in every individual piece of plant life. The greener the leaf, the more vitamin A, iron and vitamin C you can expect to find. Brussels sprouts grow very prettily upon the tall stem of their plant, decorating it almost as gladioli blossoms bedeck their stems.

Foods of the cabbage family have the reputation of being "gassy" and "strong." Entering a kitchen where cabbage has been cooking all afternoon one can easily understand why. And trying to eat this grossly overdone cabbage one will understand why many people think food of the cabbage family is indigestible.

Properly cooked cabbage has a pleasant odor, taste and effect on the stomach. Cooking cabbagy foods for a long time or over slow heat breaks down the sulfur compounds in them, releasing the objectionably strong smell. Instead, these foods should be washed and dried quickly as soon as they are brought home. They should be stored in the refrigerator if you must store them before eating. When you cook them, drop them, thoroughly chilled, into rapidly boiling water. Keep the heat high until the water comes to a boil once again, then turn it low and cook only until the sprouts are tender. This should be no longer than 8 or 10 minutes. The sprouts will then have a delicate and most enjoyable flavor. Remember, use as little water as possible.

Here are the food elements in Brussels sprouts. They are low in calories and starch, making them an ideal food for dieters.

One cup or about 100 grams of Brussels sprouts contains:

Protein	4.4	grams
Carbohydrate	8.9	grams
Calcium	34	milligrams
Phosphorus	78	milligrams

Iron	1.3	milligrams
Sodium	11	milligrams
Potassium	450	milligrams
Vitamin A	400	International Units
Vitamin B		
Thiamin	.08	milligrams
Riboflavin	.16	milligrams
Niacin	.7	milligrams
Vitamin C	94	milligrams

CHAPTER 130

Cabbage

Cabbage is a vegetable known from ancient times when the Greeks and Romans used a lot of it because of its health-giving qualities. They ate it at banquets where wine flowed freely, because they believed it would keep them from becoming intoxicated. Whether or not it has any potency against tipsiness we don't know; we do know that it contains large amounts of healthful vitamins and minerals.

One-half a cup of raw cabbage contains:

46 milligrams of calcium compared to 118 in a cup of fresh milk.
31 milligrams of phosphorus. There are 93 in a cup of milk.
½ milligram of iron compared to 1½ milligrams in ½ cup of spinach.
7 to 24 micrograms of cobalt compared to 40 for beet tops.
5 milligrams of sodium. An egg contains 81.
80 units of vitamin A compared to 20 units for a baked white potato.
.07 milligrams of thiamin. Whole wheat contains .56 milligrams.
.06 milligrams of riboflavin. Whole wheat contains .12.
.3 milligrams of niacin compared to 5.6 in whole wheat.
95 milligrams of inositol compared to 51 in beef liver.
250 milligrams of choline. Soybeans contain 300.
290 micrograms of pyridoxine compared to 800 in beef liver.
52 milligrams of vitamin C. A medium orange contains 49.
3.2 milligrams of vitamin K compared to 4.6 for spinach.

Positive And Negative Aspects

Since we have compared cabbage, above, with other foods that are notably high in their particular vitamins, we'd say this adds up to a mighty fine food.

The only negative aspect we have ever uncovered about cabbage is that eating much too much of it, to the great reduction of other foods, is likely to cause goiter in susceptible persons. It would not be wise to decide to live exclusively on cabbage, but we doubt that you will.

In 1950 a Stanford University doctor reported encouraging results in the healing of gastric and duodenal ulcers by the use of cabbage juice. An experiment reported in *Food Research* for September-October, 1952, indicates that a water extract of cabbage contains an antibiotic capable of killing certain germs. The researchers noted that it was not the vitamin C in the cabbage that produced these results.

How to Prepare Cabbage

We would suggest using cabbage freely in your everyday menus. Cooking it destroys much of its vitamin content. Throwing away the water in which it is cooked causes further loss of minerals and vitamins. It's best served straight from the garden, crisp and raw. And when you're shredding it for slaw or salad, postpone the shredding until just before time to serve, for vitamin C oozes out of every cut surface. Store cabbage, whole, in the refrigerator, covered tightly against the air. If you must cook it, drop it, still chilled, into a little boiling water. Reduce the heat, cover the kettle and cook no longer than 8-10 minutes.

Eat lots of cabbage, especially if you are trying to cut down on citrus fruits and still want an abundance of vitamin C.

CHAPTER 131

Carrots

They were cultivated in very early times, but were not held in such great esteem as food until more recently—these crisp, golden roots from the garden. Then in later times they were thought of as antidotes for poisons of one kind or another. During the latter part of the eighteenth century carrots were made into paste and applied as poultices to open sores and wounds and apparently demonstrated great healing powers.

Today we know that these powers were probably the result of the vitamins and minerals in carrots, for they are especially rich in the alkaline minerals and carotene, which is a substance that becomes vitamin A in the body. It is the carotene that gives carrots their yellow color. Experiments have shown that only about 2 to 5 per cent of this carotene is absorbed by the body when raw or cooked carrots are eaten, no matter how well they are chewed. But from 4 to 36 per cent of the carotene is absorbed when the carrots are well-shredded before eating. This suggests that it is a very sound practice to drink fresh carrot juice, for in juicing the carrot the cell walls are broken down so that large amounts of carotene may be absorbed.

Vitamins and Minerals in Carrots

Carrots have a considerable quantity of protein, including 4 of the essential amino acids, which are forms of protein. It is richest in vitamin A, containing 10,000 to 12,000 units of vitamin A in every half-cup of carrots.

Other vitamins in a half-cup of carrots are:

B Vitamins

Thiamin	60-70	micrograms
Riboflavin	60	micrograms
Niacin	5	milligrams
Inositol	48	milligrams
Biotin	2	micrograms
Folic acid	97	micrograms
Choline	95	milligrams
Vitamin E	1.5	milligrams
Vitamin K	.1	milligrams
(Carrot tops are rich in this vitamin)		
Vitamin C	5	milligrams

The minerals in carrots are:

Calcium	46	milligrams
Phosphorus	38	milligrams
Iron	.6	milligrams
Copper	.08	milligrams
Magnesium	.06	milligrams
Chlorine	36	milligrams
Sodium	31	milligrams
Zinc	.5 to 3.6	milligrams
Cobalt	2	micrograms

How to Prepare Them

In preparing carrots, as in preparing other vegetables, you should do the shredding, slicing or dicing immediately before the carrots are to be eaten, for vitamin C losses are high when foods are cut and exposed to air. Shredding carrots results in 20 per cent loss of vitamin C immediately and an additional loss of 20 per cent takes place if they are allowed to stand for an hour. However, since carrots are not as rich in vitamin C as other foods, you should consider first perhaps the vitamin A value when you are preparing carrots. And since shredding or juicing makes this vitamin available for the body to use, it is apparently best to shred or juice carrots—but do it just before serving them.

[480]

You may have the wrong idea about when to pull and eat carrots. Young carrots are more tender, but actually they have less sugar and less carotene than fully mature ones, for they both increase during growth and are at their height in mid-August, if the carrots were planted in the spring. Winter-grown carrots are lower in carotene. Carrots can be stored without serious loss of food elements for 6 months at a temperature of 32 to 40 degrees.

Vitamin A is very valuable in protecting against infection. A diet rich in vitamin A assures the health of body tissues, such as the skin and the lining of the nose and throat. It is also essential for good eye health and protects against "night blindness," which is the inability to see well in a dim light or after dark. So if you find that you have trouble with glare when you are driving your car, if you discover that you begin to bump into things when dusk falls, vitamin A is for you! The old tradition about carrots being good for your eyes is not superstition. They really are!

CHAPTER 132

Carrots for Diarrhea

By Carl L. Thenebe, M.D., West Hartford, Connecticut

You perhaps would not remember the days of the not too distant past when the term "Cholera Infantum" in the urban, or perhaps the expression the "Take Off" in the rural districts, could strike terror into one's very being, but I do, most vividly. Not only was it most alarming to the parents, but it was often much more so to the physician who had no specific approach in treating the condition. In other words, thousands of these infants and children did not survive, nor do they all live today. Before the hydration-electrolyte-transfusion-carrot era, I have, personally, observed over 125 of these pitiable infants and children pass away. Our national figures are most delayed in coming through, but the death rate in the United States, alone, for the year of 1949 revealed that 5,012 infants had died, under the age of one year, with diarrhea (enteritis). *According to the statistics, there still remains an appalling number of needless deaths which could be avoided each year with certainty!*

Two Case Histories

Mrs. Smith brought her infant into my office at the behest of my nurse, who has an intuitive sense for determining the urgency of the many phone calls which are cleared each day.

[481]

Mrs. Smith started the history of his present illness. Wee Jim, we call him, for the reason that he appears so tiny alongside of his big father who is also a James.

Wee Jim was just two weeks old. He had diarrhea since returning from the hospital, 8 days before. His stools were never right and were becoming worse, despite what the doctor had prescribed to remedy the situation. Wee Jim's mother stated that the feedings seemed to go right through him. Now he was having 16 watery, green stools daily; in fact, there were so many that she had lost count of them. For the past 18 hours, Wee Jim had been vomiting all of his formula. He had lost one and one-half pounds during the past 4 days.

Mrs. Smith mentioned that she and her husband had hoped and prayed 7 years for Wee Jim, who was her first born, to arrive. *"We do so want you to save him."*

Wee Jim was truly a very sick child. Even his hunger cry was strained and weak. The skin and the mucous membranes of his mouth and throat were very dry. He was one of those "Must Hospitalize at Once Cases" for emergency measures were in order.

And then there was Little Mary whose age was one year. She had been "out of sorts," as her mother explained, for the past 3 days and she had lost her appetite. She had also become irritable and pale in appearance. But it had only been during the past 12 hours that she had 13 watery, green stools, with cramps in her "stomach." There was a slight temperature rise to 100.4 degrees. There was no vomiting present.

Little Mary did not appear too ill. Her mother was given the carrot soup instructions to be used at home. Within 24 hours the abnormal stool frequency had ceased. These had taken on the usual carrot, non-watery consistency and were yellow in color. Her temperature had fallen to normal. Mary's mother stated that she was like herself and she was even playful. Wee Jim and Little Mary are typical examples of the usual cases that the physician is called upon to treat successfully.

Carrot Soup Used in Europe

In the June issue, *Journal of Pediatrics, 1950,* there appeared an article entitled "Carrot Soup in the Treatment of Infantile Diarrhea" by P. Selander, M.D., of Sweden. He stated that the use of carrots for this purpose had received many very favorable reports from Germany, France, Belgium and his own country, Sweden. Judging from the paucity of medical reports upon the use of carrot soup in our own land, it could be definitely stated that little attention has been given to Dr. Selander's paper.

In order for the pediatricians, the general practitioners and the internists to become aware of the value of carrot soup, some one of this group, in a given community, must take the initiative to prove its worth.

Those who do not care for the flavor of carrots might believe that the carrot soup could be quite horrible. To me, the carrot savor is quite agreeable. The young infant cannot determine the flavor of carrot, for the reason that the sense of taste has not developed as yet. For the older infants and children wherein the sense of taste has been acquired, sucaryl, a foodless sweetener, may be added for a sweet taste, or a beef boullion cube may be added for a tastier dish.

Why not try a harmless, foolproof measure which could even be/ started early by the parents, especially in the rural districts where physicians were not readily available, or at least until their doctor could be contacted? To treat diarrhea (enteritis) as early as possible after its inception, before the rapid loss of weight occurs, could be life saving in itself!

It is most important to know just what does take place when a severe diarrhea (enteritis) strikes. When the circulating body fluids, the blood particularly, become depleted of water, the cells of the body are called upon to make up the deficit. When these cells become dry, a state of dehydration exists. Coincidentally with the water loss, there is an outpouring of the electrolytes,* which are so essential in the sustained life of the cells—potassium, phosphorus, sodium, chlorine, calcium, sulphur and magnesium. Finally, there is an outgoing of the cellular protein. The depletion varies from slight to severe; the latter is manifested in acidosis (the reserve base has been expended) and in shock (the state of collapse caused by acute peripheral circulatory failure). These life-giving elements are poured out actually in the watery stools (bowel movements), into the vomitus should vomiting be present, in the expired air and also in the ever present sweat. (The urinary loss is minimal.)

Now the question arises: "What would carrot soup do that could be indispensable to the emergency welfare of the diarrheal sufferer?"

Why Carrot Soup Is Effective

Carrot soup supplies water to combat dehydration. It replenishes potassium (its potassium content is high), phosphorus, sodium and chlorine especially with the added table salt, also calcium, sulphur and magnesium. † Pectin, a proven antidiarrheal remedy, is provided in abundance. Carrot soup renders the secondary effect of mechanically coating the inflamed small bowel, which not only soothes and enhances healing, but it prevents further extension of the process. It reduces the abnormally increased peristalsis (movements of the intestine) to normalcy. It has a slowing effect upon the increased growth of the undesirable intestinal bacteria which have been favored by the diarrheal state. It prevents vomiting, if this has not already started, by impeding the toxic intestinal products and the detrimental bacteria from entering the duodenum and stomach.

Doctor Selander reported a mortality of two per cent in the 450 cases of infantile diarrhea treated with carrot soup. This would have been less if the 4 moribund diarrheal cases, who lasted only a few hours after hospital admission, had not been included in his statistics.

I have used the carrot soup treatment in the hospitals and the homes

---

*Mineralolytes.

†We do not, in general, recommend using table salt in food. But, in this case, since the patient has lost large quantities of minerals, including sodium, it seems advisable to us to include the sodium chloride (table salt).

of over 600 sufferers of enteritis, without a known mortality. These cases included premature infants, epidemic diarrhea of the new born, infantile diarrhea and diarrhea of older children. Many of these were treated and received follow up treatment via the telephone route. I have also observed adults with acute enteritis and children suffering with acute colitis who were truly benefited with the use of carrot soup.

Fortunately none of the patients treated by me had a fatal ending. It could be tomorrow, however, that I would be less favored.

Ingredients in Dr. Selander's Treatment

The carrot soup ingredients described in Doctor Selander's article are as follows: 500 grams (one pound) of fresh, washed, well scraped and finely chopped carrots were placed in a pressure cooker (which is essential)* with 150 grams (5 ounces) of water for 15 minutes at 15 pounds. The entire pulp was passed through a fine strainer and diluted with sterile, hot water to make 1000 grams (one quart); table salt (sodium chloride) is also added, 3 grams (three-fourths level teaspoon). For the bottle and tube feedings, this may be further diluted with sterile tea or Ringer's lactate solution (a solution of calcium, potassium, phosphorus and so forth) by one-third more of the total quantity.

I have modified the above, frequently, to make the dilution with sterile water to one pint, instead of one quart, in the early hydrated patients. The thicker formulas are more difficult to vomit and give twice the concentration of the needed electrolytes. Sterile tea was offered between feedings. The hospital patients, with an appreciable anemia, were given blood transfusions.

Carrot soup is usually spooned in, but it may be bottled in (the entire top of the nipple may be removed) or it may be tubed in. A small plastic catheter is passed through the nose into the stomach and retained in place by anchoring the nasal end down by taping it to the cheek. The diluted carrot soup is injected at regular intervals through the tube into the stomach. (This method of feeding is used, of course, only in a hospital under expert supervision.)

Other Foods To Take With Carrot Soup

At the beginning of the treatment, usually for the first 24 hours, the carrot soup is given at very frequent intervals, often one-half hourly, in small amounts not to exceed one ounce to start.

There is definite improvement within 24 hours after starting the carrot soup treatment in the average child. I usually start boiled, skimmed milk in small, but in daily increasing amounts, after the first 48 hours of the

---

*We do not advocate pressure cookers in the preparation of foods as a routine measure, because vitamins and enzymes are destroyed by the high heat, nor do we approve of artificial sweeteners, the use of which Dr. Thenebe suggested earlier in this article. But so long as carrot soup is used as an emergency measure and for a short period of time, and since there is no safe alternative at this time, we have permitted the author to recommend them.

carrot regime. The adding of skimmed milk depends entirely upon the character of the stool; in other words, is the patient ready for additional food? Mello-ripe or Kanana dried bananas, or very ripe black skinned bananas, or Appella (dried apple) are added next, in order, when the child is ravenously hungry, because of the pectin content. These are discontinued, if not tolerated, and other foods have to be substituted. The carrot soup is continued for about 8 days, or it may be prolonged indefinitely. When the milk and new foods are increased, the carrot soup is gradually decreased. Occasionally, a child may be allergic to cow's milk and substitutions have to be tried, the most popular, at present, being the soybean preparations. Pertaining to the child's sensitivity to carrot, to date I have not encountered one instance.

Doctor Selander stated that he did not use extra fluids parenterally (outside of the digestive tract), for instance, these fluids administered under the skin or into a vein, nor did he use the preliminary starvation treatment of 24 or more hours. For the average patient, the early hydrated one, I have found that starvation and extra fluids are not necessary. (Little Mary's classification.) But, with the border line or the more severely ill patient, the administering of extra fluids cannot be passed over lightly. The decision becomes an immediate *must. The giving of extra water to relieve the dehydration, the electrolytes to replenish the depleted body cells and the combating of acidosis and shock by administering solutions directly into a vein (intravenously) or under the skin (subcutaneously) will depend upon the status of each individual.*

The person suffering with impending shock or the one who is in actual shock, the truly far gone one, demands immediate emergency measures (Wee Jim's physical status). A solution called Ringer's lactate is started at once followed by blood transfusions. These procedures are necessary for the preservation of life.

In summation, I am gratified in being able to report to you that carrot soup is a tried and proven life-saving measure in the defeat of the number two killer (infectious) of infants and children, which is acute diarrhea (enteritis). It should be used more extensively.

CHAPTER 133

Celery

A delectable and crisp accompaniment for fall meals is celery—so easy to prepare and healthful. The taste of celery seems to be almost universally well liked. Indeed there are few vegetables whose flavor is so outstanding that we make salt, oil, essence and so forth of them just for the sake of the flavor, as we do with celery.

Celery is grown on rich, moist, mucky soil and is not an easy vegetable to grow, we are told, because it needs cool temperatures, lots of moisture and, when produced commercially, a certain amount of labor involved in the blanching process.

There seems to be no reason the least bit sensible for blanching or bleaching celery. Yet large amounts of commercially grown celery are bleached. This may be done by the way it is grown—planting it in a trench and heaping earth around it as it grows, or shielding it from the light by boards while it is growing. We discovered that it is also blanched by ethylene gas, one of the constituents of illuminating gas. We are told that a concentration of one part of gas to 1000 parts of air is used to treat the celery for from 6 to 12 days, after which there is no chance of its turning green again before it is sold.

Valuable Food Elements Destroyed

No one knows exactly how the ethylene gas works to achieve this modern miracle of stupidity and waste, but it is assumed that it stimulates enzymes which are concerned with breaking down various compounds in plants. The chlorophyll is completely destroyed by the use of gas or any other method of blanching celery. In our part of the country it is fashionable to eat deep green celery, so the markets have that kind for sale.

Blanching celery is almost as silly as it would be to blanch parsley. Chlorophyll is, of course, one of the most valuable elements we obtain from food. Why then should we deliberately destroy it before we eat the food? We destroy as well all the vitamin A of the celery, much of the vitamin C and a considerable portion of the B vitamins. A stalk of celery that contains 1000 units of vitamin A, green, contains from 0 to 10 units after blanching. One hundred micrograms of riboflavin in a stalk of green celery are reduced to 35 micrograms after blanching. If you can possibly get green celery in your locality, buy it, rather than blanched.

Much of the celery we buy has been on its way to us for some time. Celery can be stored for from 60 to 100 days before it begins to deteriorate. But the first time you taste your own celery right from the garden you will realize that you've never really tasted celery before. We have a lot of notes in our files about preparations used on celery in commercial growing. It is, of course, sprayed and otherwise treated. In fact, one letter from a grocer told us that he gets a rash on his hands from handling the celery in his store, so he must assume that the preservatives or the insecticides used are very strong indeed. You should, of course, wash celery thoroughly. But, as we have pointed out many times in the past, it's next to impossible to get all of the stuff off. Your own celery from the garden or organically grown celery is the answer.

Celery Products and Their Uses

Celeriac is a celery plant of which the root is eaten. It is used widely in Europe. Its texture, after it is cooked, is much like potatoes. Celery seeds, used in salads, are chiefly imported from France. A letter from a reader tells us that she makes tea from celery seed which is a helpful natural laxative. Celery salt is dehydrated celery which is then pulverized.

Celery is popular among vegetable juice drinkers, mostly we suspect, because it makes such a fine-tasting juice. It is famous as a cure for "nerves," gout, diabetes, "sour stomach" and other disorders. There is no doubt that raw vegetables and their juices are our most healthful foods, chiefly because of the vitamins and minerals they contain, but also because they are raw and fresh and completely edible that way. A glass of (unblanched) celery juice brims over with chlorophyll and provides as well vitamins and minerals in abundance.

Here are the vitamins and minerals in about a cup of diced (unblanched) celery:

Vitamin A	1000 International Units
Vitamin B	
Thiamin	30 micrograms
Riboflavin	100 micrograms
Niacin	.4 milligrams
Vitamin C	5-7 milligrams
Calcium	50-70 milligrams
Phosphorus	40-50 milligrams
Iron	.5-.6 milligrams
Sodium	110 milligrams
Potassium	300 milligrams

CHAPTER 134

Corn

"I tell thee, 'tis a goodlie country, not wanting in victuals. On the banks of those rivers are divers fruits good to eat, and game aplenty. Besides, the natives in those parts have a corne, which yields them bread; and this with little labor and in abundance. 'Tis called in the Spanish tongue 'mahiz'." Sir Walter Raleigh was speaking of corn which, even today throughout the world except America, is called "maize."

Corn is today by far the most valuable annual food crop in the country. Only 6 to 8 per cent of the total crop is used for food and industrial purposes. About one-half of this is used for the "wet milling" process in which corn starch, corn oil and feed by-products are made. Of the rest, about one-third is used for corn meal and breakfast cereal, and the remainder goes for distilled liquors. Of the total world supply of corn, only about 21 per cent is used for human food. The rest becomes food for animals.

Processed Corn—Improvement or Not?

In earlier days corn was "water-ground," meaning that it was ground between stones in a mill powered by water. This produced a meal that had the full value of the original grain—germ and all—with the result that the meal was highly perishable. Today, we have "improved" all that. Nowadays we mill corn as we mill flour, by removing all of the vital, alive food elements in it, so that the meal will keep in storehouses and on grocery shelves practically indefinitely. Then we "enrich" some of the meal by attempting to put back (in synthetic form) some of the natural vitamins and minerals we have removed. Enriching corn products presents a lot of problems, for the vitamins are water-soluble and likely to drain away during the various washing processes through which the corn products go. At present the enriching is done by combining the vitamins with a "harmless" substance which renders them insoluble in water, but supposedly leaves them assimilable to the human stomach. Our advice is to buy corn products ground by the "old process," if you can get them. The commercially processed kind available in grocery stores contains no more of the original food value of the corn than white flour contains of the original value of the wheat.

Protein Deficiency Produced By New Milling Process

The protein of corn is called "zein." In general, it is thought that it is slightly less well digested than the protein of wheat or rice. Most of the vegetable and cereal proteins are not as complete as the animal proteins— that is, they lack some of the essential amino acids or building blocks of protein. In corn the amino acid lysine is lacking entirely and the amino

[488]

acid tryptophane is scarce. When the whole grain is eaten, this lack may not cause any trouble, for the other amino acids tend to make up for this deficiency. But when refined, processed corn forms the basis for most meals, as it does in many parts of the world, we run into trouble, for then the lack of these two amino acids assumes serious proportions.

The history of the disease pellagra is a perfect instance of what can happen when we tamper with foods. Tryptophane, the amino acid, changes into niacin (one of the B vitamins) in the body. When processed corn products are eaten as the main part of the diet, especially among poorer populations where other foods containing niacin are lacking, niacin deficiency is almost certain to result. This produces the disease pellagra which for many years raged unchecked in the southern part of our country, after the new milling process began to be used. Now we know that eating processed corn as the mainstay of the diet produces pellagra—not because of any poison in the corn, but because what we have done to the corn has resulted in niacin deficiency among our corn-eating population. Yet we still go right on milling corn and trying to doctor it up with synthetic vitamins, instead of going back to the old-time milling process.

Corn is about 10 per cent protein, of which the germ contains about one-fifth. Seventy-three per cent of the corn kernel is carbohydrate and 4.5 per cent is fat, of which more than 80 per cent is in the germ—which is, of course, removed in the milling. Corn oil is made from the corn germ, and corn oil is a rich source of the unsaturated fatty acid, linoleic acid—a substance essential to good health. Like other cereals corn is quite poor in calcium and rich in phosphorus. The calcium, phosphorus and all other minerals are contained chiefly in the germ which is removed during milling. Most of the vitamins are also in the germ. So when you consult the following table for vitamin and mineral content of corn, keep in mind that we are talking about whole grain corn that has not had its valuable food elements removed by milling. Don't make the mistake of buying corn products from your local grocery and expecting them to provide you with this quantity of vitamins and minerals.

How to Eat and Prepare Corn

One final word about corn. The best way to eat it is, of course, in the ear, right from the stalks. If you have your own garden or if you can persuade a friend to sell you sweet corn from his garden, keep in mind some basic facts about the best way to prepare fresh corn. Eat it raw if you can. You will enjoy the wonderful sweetness of the natural sugar in the kernels. If you plan to cook your corn, don't waste a minute in getting it from the stalks into the kettle. Someone we know once suggested building a fire right in the corn field and dousing the ears into hot water while they are still attached to the stalks! You needn't be quite that fussy, but do remember that every moment away from the stalk means freshness, sweetness, vitamins and minerals lost from the corn. If you must buy your corn at the market, keep it, husks still on, in the refrigerator until you are ready to cook it. Plunge the ears into rapidly boiling water and cook only until they are heated through—the longer you cook corn the tougher it is likely to become.

Here are the vitamins and minerals in about one-half cup of steamed corn:

Calcium	9	milligrams
Phosphorus	120	milligrams
Iron	5	milligrams
Vitamin A	390	International Units
Vitamin B—		
Thiamin	.15	milligrams
Riboflavin	.14	milligrams
Niacin	1.4	milligrams
Pantothenic acid	310	micrograms
Biotin	32	micrograms
Vitamin C	12	milligrams

CHAPTER 135

Eggplant

The impressive color array characteristic of the berry family certainly asserts itself in their finest display piece—the eggplant. Yes, the eggplant is a member of the berry family, and well it should be if one considers fascinating and luring colors as one distinguishing feature of this group of fruits. What would-be shopper, when first focusing her eyes on the deep, dark, satiny purple of the eggplant among the other fruits on the grocer's shelf, could resist the temptation of placing this fruit in her shopping cart? To most people the visual sense has a predominate sway in turning the tide in favor of certain foods. The simple beauty of the eggplant has coaxed many an unwary food buyer into experimenting with eggplant as the main dish on the dinner menu. And to her amazement the concluding comment after the last forkful of eggplant has reached the mouth is, in most cases, "Well, I never thought eggplant could be so delicious. Why haven't we had it before?"

Why Eggplant Is Unpopular

Perhaps the best answer to the above question of "why" is that the name *eggplant* doesn't in itself provide the necessary incentive for regular inclusion on the food list. The lowly egg, in terms of its relatively subordinate place in the American diet and not in terms of its vitamin, protein and mineral content, casts its humble shadow over the eggplant, placing it on the same plane as the egg even though there isn't the slightest resemblance between the egg and the eggplant. To be sure, eggplant was named after certain tropical varieties which are white and small and, of course, in the shape of an egg.

We Americans are a peculiar sort when it comes to trying new foods for the first time. In most cases we have already made up our minds about a certain dietary item before even tasting it. Strange mental associations revolve about this peculiarity, acting as stimuli which prompt us to say no to many innovations on the menu. The above example of the egg and its resemblance to the eggplant is typical. Perhaps this is why we stick so faithfully to chemically doctored-up foods, foods which we know are harmful to our bodies, even though we know that organically grown foods must be best from a health standpoint. We are a complacent group, too retiring to venture out on new paths of food eating adventure. The outcome is our loss—our loss of foods both rich in eating pleasure and vitamins and minerals. What more could be desired in the way of food selection than the choice of foods, such as eggplant, which are both tasty and healthful?

European peoples are far advanced in this respect, especially in reference to the eggplant. Since the earliest of times, the peoples of southern Asia, the Mediterranean countries and Spain have been honoring and enjoying the rich bounty of the eggplant. The people of the Near East, however, surpass all other European people in their keen appreciation of both eggplant's exterior beauty and its interior nutritive food elements.

Eat More Eggplant

Wouldn't it be a wise thing, then, for us modern Americans to follow in the footsteps of the so-called backward countries of the world and begin to include more and more eggplant in our dietary fare? These same backward countries have shown us many times in the past that modernization (processing, refining, etc.) doesn't always mean healthfulness. In our estimation, the eggplant is one of the few foods which so far has sidestepped the modernization process. Of course, insecticides and other chemicals are sprayed on the plants, but nature has provided the eggplant with a skin thick enough to repel these dangerous chemicals. We say accept nature's attracting force of the almost aesthetic beauty of the eggplant and let it guide you to an almost forgotten dish among Americans, a dish highly superior to our most sought after processed foods.

Here is the vitamin and mineral content of 100 grams of eggplant which is about one slice:

Vitamin A	30	International Units
Vitamin B		
Thiamin	.04	milligrams
Riboflavin	.05	milligrams
Niacin	.6	milligrams
Vitamin C	5	milligrams

Calcium	15	milligrams
Phosphorous	37	milligrams
Iron	.4	milligrams
Sodium	.9	milligrams
Potassium	190	milligrams

CHAPTER 136

Garlic's Healing Powers

Headlines make history in the health field:

1922—Paris: "Blood pressure fall of 10 to 40 mm. after two days dosage with garlic."

1923—China: "Garlic possesses valuable antiseptic properties."

1925—Germany: "Garlic effective in treating intestinal disease."

1926—Germany: "In treating human hypertension garlic helps 19 of 20 cases tested in advanced arterial disease."

1930—Japan: "Rabbit tests show garlic reduces blood pressure."

1931—South America: "In 10 cases drop of blood pressure 30 to 50 mm. by garlic injections."

1932—England: "25 uniformly successful experiments in relieving hypertension with garlic."

1938—Sweden: "Garlic used to prevent polio."

1948—Brazil: "Garlic effects 100 per cent cures of 300 patients with intestinal infections ranging from enterocolitis to amebic dysentery."

None of these modern headlines would have surprised a physician of 2000 years ago. He would merely have nodded his head and said, "Yes, of course, we've known right along that garlic could do all these things." And research shows just that—for more than 5000 years physicians have been working cures with the smooth, odoriferous little bulb that anyone can grow easily in a garden plot. The Babylonians 3000 years B.C. knew of the curative powers of garlic. In the days of the Egyptian empire, King Herod spent the equivalent of nearly two million dollars buying garlic to feed the workers who built the great Cheops pyramid. The Vikings and the Phoenicians, intrepid adventurers, packed garlic in their sea chests when they started on their lengthy sea voyages. The Greek physicians, fathers of present-day medicine, used garlic regularly in their practice and wrote treatises on its effectiveness.

An almost miraculous healing power seems to exist in the garlic bulb. Throughout all these thousands of years it has been used to cure many of the conditions of ill health that are being studied today in our super-scientific laboratories. Garlic, said the Egyptians, the Chinese, the Greeks, the Babylonians, is a cure for the following: intestinal disorders, flatulence, infections of the respiratory system, worms, lice and nits, skin diseases and ulcers and the symptoms of aging. Up until recently the reasons why garlic was potent against these infirmities were not known. In the last 10 or 15 years an enormous new interest in the subject of garlic has resulted in laboratory experiments which almost, but not quite, explain why the evil-smelling little bulb is powerful against so many different disorders. A Russian investigator who concentrated on the healing powers of various plant oils made garlic oil so famous among the medical profession that it is sometimes spoken of as "Russian Penicillin."

Antibiotic Power of Garlic

And indeed, its action is comparable to that of penicillin, except that with garlic there are no bad aftereffects, no limit to the dosage and no dangers of disrupting the delicate relationships among the various bacteria that exist in our bodies, for it is believed that garlic inhibits these bacteria rather than killing them outright. Not so long ago it was customary to use the garlic bulb itself in the treatment of various diseases. In diphtheria, for instance, the patient held the bulb in his mouth and scored it with his teeth from time to time, to release the garlic oil. Within a matter of hours he felt better, his temperature went down and the dread symptoms of diphtheria present in his throat disappeared. Garlic juice mixed with oil or lard was customarily used as a plaster or ointment for external relief of respiratory infections, boils, carbuncles and all manner of suppurating sores. We are told that during the great plagues that swept Europe in the Middle Ages those who ate garlic were immune, and garlic was used successfully to disinfect the crowded burial grounds and prevent the plague from spreading.

No doubt the ancients used either the garlic bulb itself or oil extracted by compressing or pounding the bulb. Perhaps in those days there was no social feeling against the smell of garlic. Or perhaps the general lack of sanitary measures resulted in so many assorted smells that the garlic aroma went unnoticed.

Today, however, most of us have a definite prejudice against that individual who may sit next to us in the movies, and who has obviously just come from a meal in which garlic was undoubtedly an emphatic item. So, partly because of this social disapproval of the smell and partly because many very ill patients are nauseated by the odor of garlic, ways and means have been discovered to remove the offensive odor by dehydrating the garlic and packing it in neat little capsules, sometimes with a mite of charcoal which absorbs the odor, or a bit of some other substance which prevents the capsule from disintegrating until it is safely inside the intestine.

The Garlic Cure for Tuberculosis

Down through the years physicians have been experimenting with garlic. One of the earliest of our modern researchers was Dr. W. C.

[493]

Minchin, an English physician practicing in Ireland, who, at the beginning of this century, caused an enormous stir in medical circles in England with his letters and articles about garlic to the *Lancet* and other conservative British publications. Dr. Minchin was in charge of a large tuberculosis ward in Kells Hospital, Dublin. Most of his patients were sent to him as hopeless cases, doomed to die of this disease which was at the time the number one killer. Dr. Minchin invited several physicians to send some of their patients to his hospital. While they were undergoing cure, their own physicians visited them, noticed the great improvement and marveled at the new method of treatment Dr. Minchin was using. He did not tell them what it was and they did not once suspect it. Dr. Minchin used garlic as an internal medicine, as an inhalant and also as ointment and compresses for tuberculous joints and skin.

In answer to his published letters and articles, letters poured in from physicians all over the world who were intensely interested in the subject and reported their own experiences with garlic medication as well as the way garlic was used by individuals to cure illnesses in their own homes. In general, the tone of the correspondence went like this: "The peasants and farmers hereabouts have always used garlic as a cure for coughs, colds, tuberculosis, intestinal and digestive disorders, boils, poisoning and so forth. Perhaps this is not just superstition. Perhaps they are wiser than they know." Indeed the instinct of the country people was sound, for it has now been established that garlic is a powerful warrior against germs, which can be used in almost any quantity with perfect safety.

The numerous case histories which illustrate Dr. Minchin's writings are startling proof of the effectiveness of garlic in the treatment of tuberculosis. Here are some samples. A boy 10 years old with tuberculosis of the hand, in which all the bones of the hand were involved, was admitted to the hospital to have his hand amputated. Dr. Minchin undertook to treat him with garlic compresses and within 6 weeks the hand was completely cured. A girl of 15 suffered from tuberculosis of the cervical glands. All her glands from ear to ear in the neck and beneath the jaw were involved. It took 6 months of treatment with garlic until the young woman was completely healed.

In treating pulmonary tuberculosis Dr. Minchin allowed his less serious cases to go about their work, while they took garlic internally and used garlic compresses and inhalations only at night. Here, too, his record of complete cures is astounding. He also treated tuberculosis of the skin and larynx.

At almost the same time Dr. Minchin's papers were being published in England, Dr. M. W. McDuffie of the Metropolitan Hospital in New York was experimenting with tuberculosis cures. His ward was the hopeless ward where in his own words "practically every case is a stretcher case and the majority die within a few days or weeks after admittance." Dr. McDuffie's article called "Tuberculosis Treatment" appeared in the *North American Journal of Homeopathy* for May, 1914. In it he describes work with 1082 patients using 56 different kinds of treatment, all the way from hydrochloric acid to chest surgery, to garlic. Of the 56 treatments used, he says in his summary, "Garlic is the best individual treatment found to get rid of germs and we believe same to be a specific for the tubercle bacillus and for tubercular processes no matter what part of the body is affected, whether skin, bones, glands, lungs or special parts. . . . Thus nature by diet, rest, and exercise, baths, climate and garlic, furnishes sufficient and specific treatment for the medical aspects of this disease."

How Does Garlic Act on Germs?

Although physicians 50 years ago did not have access to the laboratory methods that can be used today for determining how and why a certain treatment brings about results, yet they were on the right track with garlic, for experiments in modern laboratories show exactly how garlic works in the presence of germs. The *Medical Record* for June 4, 1941, carries a story by Emil Weiss, M.D., of Chicago, on a series of experiments on 22 subjects all with a known history of intestinal disorders. These were observed for several weeks before the experiment began and careful notes taken of everything relating to their digestive processes. Daily specimens of urine and feces were collected. Garlic was then administered to part of the group while the other part took no medication. Headaches, mild diarrhea and other symptoms of intestinal disorder disappeared during the garlic treatment. But, more significant yet, there was a complete change in the intestinal flora of all the subjects who took garlic. Intestinal flora are the bacteria living in the digestive tract. Some of these are beneficial, helping with the digestion of food. Others are harmful, resulting in conditions of putrefaction and ill health. By the end of the garlic treatment, the beneficial bacteria were increasing in all of the cases and the harmful bacteria were decreasing.

An article by T. D. Yanovitch in the *Comptes Rendus de l'Academie des Sciences de l'USSR,* 1945, Vol. 48, No. 7, describes experiments using garlic juice on actual colonies of bacteria. Introducing the bacteria directly into the juice caused the complete cessation of all movements of the bacteria within 3 minutes. When garlic juice was added to a culture of bacteria, the bacteria were dispersed to the edge of the culture. After two minutes, immobile bacteria began to appear and within 10 minutes all activity had ceased. This author notes that dilution of the garlic juice reduced its efficiency and freshly prepared juice was much more effective than juice which had been preserved for several months.

Garlic Valuable in Treatment of High Blood Pressure

So much research has been done on the subject of garlic and the treatment for hypertension (high blood pressure) that current articles do not present much actual information on the facts involved, with documentation of how many patients were cured. Rather these authorities are now disputing exactly how it is that garlic cures hypertension. In an article in a European publication, *Praxis,* for July 1, 1948, G. Piotrowski, visiting lecturer and member of the faculty of medicine at the University of Geneva writes of his experiences with the use of garlic on "about a hundred patients." It is generally agreed by the medical profession that the administration of garlic reduces high blood pressure, but there are two schools of thought as to just how it brings about this result. One group of researchers contends that since garlic is such an effective germ killer, its antiseptic action on the intestines purifies them of all the poisonous substances and putrefaction, and this results in lowered blood pressure.

Dr. Piotrowski however contends that garlic lowers blood pressure by dilating the blood vessels. Although he does not deny the valuable work done by garlic in cleansing products of putrefaction from the intestines, he claims that this is not productive of a fall in blood pressure. He indicates, too, that it is difficult to conduct experiments with hypertensive patients and equally difficult to interpret the results, for it is generally accepted that hypertension is the result of a wide variety of causes.

Verified Results Are Quite Favorable

This researcher eliminated from his study any patients whose conditions might further confuse the results—that is, patients whose blood pressure dropped when other medicines were administered, those who had kidney trouble and so forth. He tells us that Schlesinger, another investigator, secured a drop in pressure after 15 days of treatment with garlic. Pouillard claimed a decided drop in pressure within an hour after the first administration of garlic. Dr. Piotrowski has no such sensational reports to make and he declares that he believes that intermittent dosage with garlic just for the purpose of obtaining a decided drop in blood pressure is not advisable. He prefers to administer oil of garlic for 3 weeks. He reports that he has obtained a drop of at least two mm. in blood pressure in 40 per cent of the cases—these were all cases in which he knew that the drop was due to the garlic and could not have been caused by anything else. Incidentally, all of his patients were going about their daily work as usual during the treatment, so lack of fatigue or rest in bed did not have a chance to influence the results.

He tells us that apparently neither age nor blood pressure reading of any individual patient enable one to predict results, for it seems that good results do not occur just because the patient is young or because his blood pressure is not especially high. The expected drop of two cm. in blood pressure generally takes place after about a week of treatment. Dr. Piotrowski begins his hypertensive patients with fairly large doses of garlic and gradually decreases the doses over a period of 3 weeks. Then he gives smaller doses during the rest of the treatment. He does not say how long "the rest of the treatment" is, but we assume he means until the patient's blood pressure is normal and he has none of the symptoms of the disease remaining.

Uncomfortable Symptoms Disappear

Doctors generally discuss two kinds of symptoms—the ones the physician can discover (in this case, the actual blood pressure reading) and the "subjective symptoms"—that is, the things that are wrong with him that only the patient can know and describe. The subjective symptoms of hypertension vary with the individual, but most such patients have one or more of the following: headaches, dizziness, angina-like pains and ringing in the ears. Some of these patients also complained of pains in their backs between their shoulder blades. In 80 per cent of the patients dizziness disappeared with the garlic treatment. Headaches also vanished. The pains, which seemed to occur in proportion to the degree of hypertension, were relieved in some cases. The only subjective symptom that was not relieved by the garlic treatment was ringing in the ears. Dr. Piotrowski does not give any reason for this, but it seems to us quite possible that this condition may not have been related to the hypertension, for certainly many people complain of head and ear noises who do not have high blood pressure.

Dr. Piotrowski tells us that the subjective symptoms of his patients began to disappear in 3 to 5 days after they began the garlic treatment. They also found that they could think much more clearly and concentrate better on their jobs. His conclusions are that garlic certainly has useful properties in the treatment of high blood pressure. It usually causes a drop in pressure and, even in cases where it does not, its use is justified by the relief it brings for the uncomfortable symptoms the patient has had. He ends by recommending that many more M.D.'s begin immediately to take advantage of garlic therapy in treating their hypertensive patients.

Garlic Therapy in America

It would appear from what we have said so far that Europeans are far ahead of Americans in gathering information about garlic. Garlic has always been a plant more typical of the rest of the world than of America. It is only within the past 20 years or so that garlic has come to have any place even in American diet, whereas Europeans, especially those in south and central Europe, have used it for centuries. An article in the *New York Physician* for September, 1937, gives the experience of two New York doctors using garlic products in their practice. David Stein, M.D., and Edward H. Kotin, M.D., tell us that because of its therapeutic value, they believe that garlic must contain vitamins A, B and C and its C content is probably quite high. The mineral content of garlic, they say, indicates the presence of aluminum, manganese, copper, zinc, sulfur, iron, calcium and chlorine.

Scores of Benefits

Before describing their own experience, the authors review the findings of other researchers on garlic and tell us that garlic has been found useful for the following purposes in therapeutics: as an aid to feeble digestion, because it stimulates gastric juices. It is a fine carminative, which means that it relieves flatulence, dyspepsia and colic; it is an intestinal antiseptic, stimulating the growth of healthful bacteria in the intestine. "Diarrhea from infectious diseases such as diphtheria, scarlet fever and tuberculosis respond favorably to garlic therapy." It is a harmless but potent preventive of pneumonia, diphtheria, typhus and tuberculosis; it is an expectorant, useful in all respiratory infections, but particularly those characterized

[497]

by a dry, hacking cough—in bronchitis, colds and asthma. It is an excellent nerve tonic, effective in cases of neurasthenia and nervous insufficiency. It is an anthelmintic—a destroyer of round and thread worms. It is a rubefacient and counter-irritant which may be applied in compress form for intercostal neuralgia, pleurisy, tuberculosis of the larynx and catarrhal pneumonia.

Then these two authors give case histories of 12 cases treated by them with garlic. The diagnoses of these patients range from tuberculosis to bronchitis, pharyngitis, shortness of breath, asthma, constipation, flatulence, heartburn, nervousness, diarrhea, cramps, nausea, vomiting, chills and fever—chest and abdominal cases, they call them. In every case they treated there was relief, sometimes within a week, always within a month. "In conclusion," say these authors, "we feel that garlic is an excellent medicament, for employment in a diversity of conditions. We believe that the vitamin and mineral factors do much to cause this to be a drug of noteworthy usage."

What We Recommend

In garlic we have yet another example of the kind of food we love to discover and tell our readers about—a food known for thousands of years to the plain, everyday people of the earth who have had to keep themselves strong and healthy in spite of hard work, poverty, ignorance and bad sanitation. Now at last we sophisticated folks of the twentieth century have "discovered" it. And it looks as though the unassuming little bulb may be the answer to many of our problems.

Garlic is a food, a very necessary and important food which should be eaten every day by all of us. Used as an herb in almost any vegetable, meat or cheese dish, cooked or raw, employed as an essential part of every salad, it will probably still not appear in our diet in anything like the quantity we should have.

Besides, there is still the social hazard connected with eating it. There can be no doubt of it—the volatile and highly flavored essence of garlic does infect one's breath. Even though you may educate all your family and friends to the healthful joys of garlic-eating, so that they won't ever notice your breath, you must also have consideration for the strangers you meet—or the people you sit next to in movies. The answer to this problem, of course, is to take garlic perles. They have been treated so that they do not dissolve until they are safely assimilated far down in your digestive system, so, unless you take enormous quantities, there's no chance of garlic perles tainting your breath.

We urgently suggest that you add garlic perles to your daily food supplements. Whether or not you are suffering from any of the disorders discussed above, there's no need to wait until you are ill, when you can so easily prevent symptoms by including as much fresh garlic as possible in your meals and adding garlic perles to your regular food supplements.

CHAPTER 137

Garlic Therapy in Diseases of the Digestive Tract

By E. E. Marcovici, M.D., New York

In recent years the question of the therapeutic value of garlic and preparations derived from garlic has been the object of repeated discussions in medical and lay literature. The pros and cons have been more or less evenly divided, so that physicians, having no personal experience, encounter difficulties in forming an opinion as to the merits of garlic therapy.

My experiences with garlic medication originated in the year 1915 when, as an army physician on the Eastern Front, I had the opportunity of studying and treating innumerable cases of gastrointestinal infections (acute and chronic bacillary dysentery, cholerine, cholera and various kinds of postinfectious and non-infectious catarrhs). In an attempt to check the spread of these disabling conditions and to find new means for their treatment, investigations were carried out on the effect of various aromatic drugs, spices and etheric oils—that is, volatile oils given off from food substances. It so happened that my interest was directed towards the garlic plant. In spite of its widespread use as a vermifuge, mainly against pinworms, and its recommendation for all kinds of ailments in domestic medicine, nothing authentic was known at that time about the true medicinal properties of the drug.

The initial results of my experiments with gastrointestinal infections of various origins were so encouraging that they called for further investigations, including bacteriological studies. These findings, meanwhile confirmed and complemented by the work of other authors, and 25 years of personal experience, have led me to believe that there can be no doubt about the valuable therapeutic properties of *Allium sativum* (garlic). This conviction, moreover, induces me to urge physicians to make wider use of this harmless and excellent medicament even if, hitherto, crystalline active principles have not been isolated, and the exact mode of action has not been fully elucidated. (That is, garlic has not been completely analyzed in the laboratory and we do not know exactly how it works.)

Preliminary investigations were conducted with the fresh raw plant. One bulb per day was administered to patients suffering from acute and chronic dysentery. Rapid subjective and objective improvement occurred, the number of evacuations decreased, appetite returned and the general state of the patient was markedly improved. One drawback of this procedure, however, was the unpleasant taste and burning sensation resulting from the ingestion of the crude plant. Steps were therefore taken to overcome these difficulties and to bring the medicament into a better tolerated form. (Dr. Marcovici then describes the making of a. tablet from garlic.)

This product represents the active principles of the fresh plant adsorbed to vegetable charcoal, and has the advantage of being devoid of the characteristic odor and taste. On account of the adsorptive properties of charcoal, the release of the active substances occurs gradually during the passage through the gastrointestinal tract. Any irritative effect is thus prevented. The unpleasant odor of the breath resulting from the passage of volatile oils into the respiratory system, occurs only with very large doses.

Garlic For Dysentery and Intestinal Catarrh

The original investigations were carried out in 91 cases of acute dysentery. The therapeutic results were good and in some cases recovery occurred in less than a week. A second series of experiments was conducted on 25 patients suffering from acute nonspecific intestinal catarrh with emesis (vomiting), fever, colicky pains and watery stools. These patients were frequently benefited within two to three days. Further gratifying results were obtained in the chronic postinfectious catarrah following cholera and in the gastrogenous diarrheas (originating in the stomach). This procedure was later introduced as a routine treatment and prophylatic measure in hundreds of cases of digestive disorders.

Encouraged by the clinical results, it was decided to attack the problem from the experimental angle. Since experimental studies on humans brought no enlightenment regarding the mechanism of action of the drug, animal experiments were undertaken. The fact that garlic was widely used in all parts of the world as a prophylactic and food preservative suggested that garlic might possess specific bactericidal properties. A large series of rabbits were, therefore, fed dried garlic-powder. This procedure was maintained as a prophylactic measure for several days, following which increasing amounts of dysentery toxin were administered intravenously. It was found that powdered dry garlic administered to rabbits in quantities of 2.5 grams daily protected the animals against a tenfold lethal dose of dysentery toxin. In the rabbit protection is not limited to the intestinal tract but also includes the typical nervous manifestations of the dysentery toxin. Garlic not only exerts a preventive action, but also seems to have curative properties when administered with the dysentery toxin. The poisoned animals became seriously ill, but if adequate quantities of garlic were administered, the series receiving the drug did not die, while the controls perished in all instances. The mucous membranes of the rabbits which had received 2¼ to 5 grams of the dried powder showed no pathological alterations—that is, no signs of harm from the powerful toxin.

How Garlic Works to Kill Bacteria

Frenkel and Lenitzkaja found that an addition of 3 per cent allium (garlic) to the food inhibited gastric putrefaction and the formation of gastrointestinal toxins. Kolle, Laubenheimer and Vollmar studied the bactericidal action of garlic on staphylococcus cultures (one of the most virulent of germs). They found that the volatile components evaporating from freshly cut garlic exerted a considerable inhibitory action on the growth of this bacterium. The phenomenon occurred even at a distance of 20 cm. and reached its maximum within two hours. Sterile agar plates prepared with solutions of garlic remained free from growth after inoculation with staphylococcus.

Waugh conducted interesting experiments with the blood and serum of patients who had previously taken large quantities of garlic. He found that the blood of these individuals exerted an increased bactericidal action on staphylococcus cultures. The bactericidal properties were found to continue for about 10 hours of normal incubator temperature, after which time free growth commenced.

All these experiments, even if not fully convincing, are interesting in view of the fact that garlic is not only utilized for the treatment of gastrointestinal infections, but has been recommended for the treatment of various other infectious conditions. Thus Cooks and Gabriel obtained gratifying effects with diluted garlic juice in the treatment of purulent wounds. It is also widely recommended for the treatment of infections of the respiratory tract. Huss administered allisatin (garlic) to a large series of Swedish school children during an epidemic of infantile paralysis.

Bacteriological studies of the feces of humans suffering from diarrhea have revealed that garlic brings about a characteristic change in the bacterial growth. This product has also been found to be a valuable prophylactic in veterinary medicine. Nohlen recommends it for the treatment of the well known gastrointestinal catarrhs from which monkeys in captivity are known to suffer, and which are responsible for the loss of many a valuable animal in zoos and experimental laboratories.

Becher and Fussgaenger determined the excretion of indican (a waste product) in the urine which they considered an index for the degree of intestinal putrefaction. They observed that, in pathological cases, the excretion was distinctly diminished during periods of garlic medication.

How Garlic Combats Toxemia

In this connection I should like to give expression to my belief that a large part of the beneficial results observed following the use of garlic in chronic hypertension of the aged are due to the control of intestinal putrefaction and consequent prevention of absorption of toxic substances from the digestive tract. These patients are known to suffer frequently from chronic constipation, cecal stasis (intestinal obstruction) or chronic appendicitis. As a result of these disorders, foodstuffs incompletely predigested in the stomach on account of subacidity or hyperacidity, reach the cecal region where they undergo pathological putrefaction. As a consequence, toxins are absorbed and carried into the blood stream. This toxemia is responsible for the varying symptoms from which these patients suffer: headache (migraine) dizziness, fatigue, capillary spasms, etc. I believe that the favorable effects attributed to garlic therapy in these conditions are not due to any direct vasodilatory effect of the drug, but to the mechanism described above.

Improvement in Digestion with Garlic

Examination of the gastric juice by Bonem showed that a marked increase of secretion follows ingestion of allisatin (garlic). He maintains that a prolonged emptying time is the result of this stimulation of the secretory apparatus and leads to a more thorough sterilization of the chyme (the partly digested food). Varga performed gastric lavages and found an increase of free hydrochloric acid and total acidity. This effect was demonstrable even in previously completely anacid stomachs. The physiological stimulus exerted on the secretory mechanism of the pancreas and bile by the increased production of hydrochloric acid is enhanced by the action of etheric oils of garlic—that is, the oils released when the garlic is pounded or cut. Etheric oils have also been found to increase peristalsis—the movement of the intestines which carries the partly digested food along.

Roos, who has done extensive work with garlic, does not attribute its peculiar effect on the pathological intestinal flora to any direct bactericidal mechanism. He advances the theory that garlic brings about an alteration in the general reaction of the intestinal mucosa, as a result of which, the disturbed physiological symbiosis or relationship between the intestinal organisms is restored by means of a "crowding out" process. The return of normal gastrointestinal activity, brought about by these various factors, changes the environmental conditions for pathological organisms and deprives them of the medium favorable to their growth.

The question as to whether garlic has a direct effect on the liver has been studied by various authors. Kretschmer found that the excretion of bile was markedly increased. Schindel, experimenting on a patient with a biliary fistula (ulcer of the gall bladder) found that both the quantity and the constituents of gall were increased by the ingestion of garlic.

All these theories give no satisfactory explanation for cases of non-infectious diarrhea. Beneficial effects obtained with garlic in "nervous" diarrhea, flatulence, distension, etc. are probably due to a mechanism related to the action of the simple stomachics and carminatives. The marked increase of appetite following the intake of garlic preparations obviously is due to the same mechanism.

Summary

It is thought that the antiputrefactive properties are responsible for the gratifying results with allium (garlic) therapy in gastrointestinal intoxication and the subjective complaints of the aged patient with chronic essential hypertension. A wider use of this harmless and effective drug available in the odorless and tasteless form of the new preparations is recommended.

CHAPTER 138

Garlic Tablets Prevent Polio

Attempting to cure a disease after it has reached epidemic proportions is the usual formula. Trying to prevent a disease before it has reached the proportions of an epidemic is the hard but worthwhile way of doing things.

When he was appointed borough medical officer of the town of Malmo, Sweden, in 1935, Dr. Ragnar Huss decided that he would make some practical experiments with preventive treatment of polio as soon as signs of an impending epidemic would warrant it. In an article in the Swedish medical magazine, *Svenska läkartidningen,* Vol. 35, p. 216, he describes such an experiment.

Dr. Huss tells us he has long been impressed with the fact that an unimpared mucous lining of the intestine might give protection from polio. Much laboratory work has shown that animals in whom the intestinal tract is damaged, irritated or inflamed are far more susceptible to infection by polio. He quotes Dr. Mayerhofer, a German biologist, as saying that an initial digestive "catarrh" is necessary before one can contract polio. Catarrh is a term used generally to signify inflammation from whatever cause.

Mayerhofer tried to prevent polio by protecting children from intestinal catarrh. He kept no records of these trials so we do not know how successful he was. However, says Dr. Huss, "Mayerhofer found in garlic a suitable means for the prevention of intestinal catarrh. This vegetable has a property —well-known from European folk medicine and tropical experience—of preventing intestinal catarrhs as well as therapeutically influencing an already existing ailment of that kind."

Another researcher, Nohlen, in Düsseldorf, used garlic preparations to keep 45 monkeys in the city's zoological gardens free from disease during the fall when inflammations of the intestinal tract are most common.

In September, 1937, then, signs were apparent in Malmo that a polio epidemic might be on the way, Dr. Huss tells us. In July the first case appeared. In August there were 8 more cases and a new one when school began in September. By the time the epidemic ceased in the middle of November, it had caused 67 cases of polio, almost half of them without paralysis.

Dr. Huss arranged to have the children in 3 schools take a garlic preparation at school under supervision of the teachers. They were asked to bring a signed letter from their parents granting permission for the experiment. Only 2.3 per cent of the parents declined to participate. Each day the teacher laid out the garlic tablets on her desk, the children filed past and each took two tablets which he carried back to his desk. Then, at a signal from the teacher, everyone in the room downed his garlic tablets. Altogether 1204 children were given the preventive tablets. There were altogether 13,829 children in the Malmo school district. No case of polio occurred among the children given the garlic pills.

Dr. Huss concludes that no cases among the treated children compared to 67 among those who were not treated is a significant percentage which was probably the result of the treatment rather than mere chance.

Interesting as this experiment is as a polio prevention measure, it assumes an added significance when you consider all the other disorders that are undoubtedly preconditioned by an unhealthful state of the intestinal tract. Might one not assume that taking garlic would tend to prevent these disorders, too?

Other Helpful Work on Polio

There are many different theories on the cause and prevention of polio. In North Carolina Dr. Benjamin Sandler stopped a polio epidemic with a special diet which he broadcast daily on the radio. The diet was low in starches, especially refined carbohydrates and high in protein.

Fred R. Klenner, M.D., also of North Carolina, treats patients who have polio and other virus diseases with massive doses of vitamin C. W. J. McCormick, M.D., of Canada, uses massive doses of the B vitamins. Ralph Scobey, M.D., believes that polio occurs toward the end of the summer season because there are many possibilities of pollution by cyanide at this time of year. Chemical insecticides are the most prevalent source of cyanide; polluted water may be another. Shellfish taken from polluted water may be another. W. M. Brumby, M.D., believes that polio is closely related to loin diseases in cattle which is caused by deficiency in calcium, phosphorus and other minerals.

What about having your children vaccinated with the Salk vaccine? Our answer is that we cannot give any advice generally which will apply to all. If your child is in radiant good health and you can personally guarantee from first-hand information that he eats the best possible diet and does not, either in your home or away from it, eat candy, soft drinks, soda fountain items and the other trashy foods that are everywhere these days, then we say that your child certainly stands a better than average chance of not getting polio if he is not vaccinated. On the other hand, a child as healthy as this would probably suffer little harm from the vaccine. The child whose diet is all wrong, who "doesn't like" the foods that are good for him and eats quantities of the trashy foods will be the one most likely to get polio and, too, the one most likely to suffer from the vaccine.

Important Recommendations

Our advice, then, is to do everything possible to prevent polio the year round—not just at the polio season. A diet high in trashy foods cannot possibly contain enough of the good foods. You must make good foods paramount in your diet and even then you will not be getting enough vitamins and minerals unless you take food supplements. Considering the value of garlic for keeping the intestinal tract in a healthy state, don't you think you should add garlic to your supplements, too, making it part of your everyday meal planning.

Garlic is especially useful in cooking when you have cut down on salt or eliminated it entirely, for the zesty garlic flavor is delicious in almost all meat dishes and vegetable salads. Garlic perles contain the essential valuable oils of garlic in a preparation that will never taint your breath, for the perle does not dissolve until it is well beyond the point in your digestive tract where its fumes might reach your breath.

One more point on the subject of polio which we are sure will interest you. A Portugese researcher, writing in the *Arquivos mineiros de Leprologia,* Vol. 17, p. 110, April, 1957, announces that injections of vitamin E have been found to be powerful against muscle-wasting in lepers. Injections of 30 to 300 milligrams, given at intervals varying between one and three weeks, showed satisfactory results in all patients. It is unusual for an experiment of this kind to react favorably in all cases. We might expect that at least several of the subjects would react less favorably. But we are told that in everyone of the lepers the volume of the muscles increased, the muscle tone and muscular movements of hands improved. Partial or total functional recovery was obtained.

Furthermore, the results were permanent. Patients did not relapse to their former condition when the injections were stopped.

Why not try such injections for polio patients, asks Dr. H. C. deSouza Araujo, author of the article? And indeed, this strikes us as a most sensible suggestion. We know that vitamin E is the muscle vitamin. We know that vitamin E, and plenty of it, is essential for muscle health. Why not shoot this wonder-working vitamin directly into the wasting muscles of polio victims? The Portugese article was reported in the *Journal of the American Medical Association* for February 1, 1958. We hope sincerely that many American researchers and physicians will experiment with vitamin E for polio patients.

CHAPTER 139

Experiments with Garlic
and Cancer

Research on the effectiveness of garlic against disease has not been so popular of late as it has been during the past 50 years or so. This is one reason why we were especially pleased to find in *Science*, Vol. 126, November 29, 1957, p. 1112, an account of research that seems to show that garlic is powerful against tumor-formation. And that means, of course, cancer, too.

Working with laboratory mice, Austin S. Weisberger and Jack Pensky of Western Reserve University found that by injecting cancerous cells into mice they could produce rapid growth of cancer and death within 16 days. They could produce the same result even when they treated the cancerous cells with an enzyme they had isolated from garlic. The enzyme by itself did not protect from cancer. But when they treated the cancerous cells with an equal amount of the garlic enzyme and the substrate which is also present in garlic (that is, the substance with which the enzyme is naturally associated in foods), and then injected mice with the treated cells, no cancer grew and there was no mortality among the animals for a period of 6 months (equal to about a fourth of a lifetime in a human being).

Thus we see that the cancer cells were prevented from doing any damage by treating them with the preparation from garlic. But our researchers went further than that. They inoculated mice with the virulent cancer cells and then gave them injections of the garlic preparation. The garlic delayed the onset of the malignant tumor and in some instances completely prevented its formation and saved the lives of the mice. However, in all cases it was necessary to keep giving the garlic preparation, for tumors developed very rapidly if it was discontinued.

Two Important Facts

Such findings, which link the humble, smelly garlic bulb with the prevention of cancer, the greatest modern plague, are spectacular. But, in addition, note some of the details of this experiment. Scientists have known for a long time that there is a certain enzyme in garlic that is powerful against disease bacteria. But when they used just this enzyme, you will notice the Western Reserve scientists got no results. They had to use both the enzyme and the substrate from garlic to attain success in preventing cancer. The word *substrate* refers to the substance which works with the enzyme to bring about chemical changes. Every enzyme has its substrate; indeed every enzyme takes its name from its substrate. Thus the enzyme named *lipase* reacts chemically with fats or lipids. Proteinases react chemically with proteins. And so forth.

In the case of garlic the enzyme alliinase is liberated when the garlic bulb is crushed. It immediately reacts with its substrate to form a new chemical compound which is the powerful anti-bacterial compound for which garlic is noted.

Using the enzyme alone or using the substrate alone produces no effect. The researchers found that they must use them together. They do not, of course, know why they obtained these results and they suggest in the article several possible ways in which the garlic enzyme and substrate may bring about the desired result.

So we learn two lessons from such an article—first, that the simple garlic bulb is indeed a powerful agent against disease and secondly that wholeness is best where health is concerned. The less we separate, divide and fragmentize where food is involved, the better off we are. Whole foods, containing everything that occurs naturally in them, are best.

CHAPTER 140

Garlic for Intestinal Disorders

"Lack of time and space prevents me from going into more detail on the interesting history of this plant (garlic) as a medical and popular remedy. Its use is age-old. It was used by Hippocrates and Paracelsus and is frequently mentioned in the herbals of the middle ages as a remedy. Its range of uses was extremely varied. In recent times garlic has been highly recommended in France particularly as a remedy in the case of lung diseases attended by copious and ill-smelling expectoration as well as a remedy against hypertension."

We are quoting Professor E. Roos of St. Joseph's Hospital, Freiburg, Germany. These words form the introduction to an article of his telling how he has used a garlic preparation in his own practice, treating patients who suffered from a variety of intestinal disorders, most of them involving diarrheal conditions. We found this article in an old (September 25, 1925) copy of *Munchener Medizinische Wochenschrift,* a medical magazine which is, of course, published in Germany.

Dr. Roos speaks mostly in this article of cases of intestinal complaint arising from the presence of disease-causing bacteria in the intestine. Generally speaking, the more serious forms of diarrheal diseases seem to result from the presence of some such bacteria. At any rate, large numbers of one or more of such bacteria are found in the stool of these sufferers. An overabundance of the harmful bacteria in the intestine can completely crowd out the helpful ones which normally live there and unpleasant consequences may result. One of these may well be diarrhea—acute or chronic. And you may be sure that, if the helpful bacteria are not soon re-established, the diarrhea will continue.

Dr. Roos tells us in the 1925 article that he had, at the time he wrote it, treated 96 patients with a garlic preparation which he made himself.

How to Use Garlic

He gave his patients garlic in dosages of one gram or more and one of his tablets which weighed a gram contained the same amount of raw garlic —one gram. He tells us that he feels garlic is effective against 3 different kinds of digestive or intestinal upsets which could conceivably occur all at the same time in the same patient. "There is in garlic," he says, "special intestine-soothing and diarrhea-allaying effect which occurs in various colonic affections." There is an effect, also, that cleanses the intestinal flora (the bacteria that live in the intestines) of disease-causing bacteria or at least abnormal mixtures of bacteria. Then, too, there is an anti-dyspepsia effect in the taking of garlic. "Probably," he says, "the same healing influence on the intestinal mucous membrane lies at the basis of all 3."

The first effect which soothes the intestine is almost, he says, like the effect of a narcotic. So far as the diarrhea is concerned, it is frequently stopped within a very short time and at the same time the pains, the stomach ache or other difficulties disappear, too. If you give narcotics for diarrhea (and this seems to have been the standard treatment at that time), constipation is likely to follow. It seldom does when garlic is taken.

"Quite to the contrary," he says, "we have even observed, following week-long use on the part of patients who do not have diarrhea, regular daily stool, though sometimes in these cases a mildly inhibitory influence makes itself noticeable. It makes little difference what kind of diarrhea you are dealing with or where it principally has its origin. A favorable result has been obtained in the great majority of cases treated, even in stubbornly chronic cases with recurrence." He reminds us that good results cannot be hoped for if the diarrhea is the symptom of some serious organic disorder—cancer or tuberculosis.

Then, almost as if to contradict the statement he has just made, Dr. Roos goes on to describe the case of a young woman who did have tuberculosis and was suffering from a severe diarrhea. In addition, she was subject to spells of vomiting, severe body swelling and pain on pressure. He prescribed his garlic preparation. "The patient takes the remedy in the same dose for 6 weeks. Appetite quickly becomes very good, the general condition improved, the temperature after 6 weeks still showed only occasional light rises. After 4 weeks the stool is practically normal, for the most part once a day."

[508]

The lung inflammation subsided and the swelling disappeared. Says Dr. Roos, "Even if the probable tuberculosis was not cured by garlic, still one receives the distinct impression that the patient has been relatively quickly tided over the serious stage through the rapid improvements in the intestine and the appetite."

In other cases of serious organic trouble the garlic preparation helped. Dr. Roos tells us of a 41-year-old farmer who had had a case of dysentery for many years complicated by rectal polyps. This unfortunate man also suffered from what Dr. Roos describes as a "constant restlessness of body," abdominal rumblings and colic-like pains. For 3 months he took two grams of the garlic preparation 3 times a day, and finally two grams twice daily. For as long as he remained under the influence of the remedy, his trouble was much improved. His stools became for the most part much more solid and less frequent. He became happier and was able to work. He took a long trip each week to obtain the garlic remedy. Four months after completion of treatment he told Dr. Roos that his condition was still more supportable and his body quieter than before, even though diarrhea and slimy evacuations reappeared from time to time.

More Case Histories

A scholar who was troubled with abdominal pains, stomach trouble, hyperacidity and diarrhea found that he apparently had appendicitis and prepared for an operation. By chance the surgeon was not available and meantime the patient took some of the garlic preparation, two grams, twice daily. After a few days he declared that he was perfectly well and didn't want to hear any more about an operation. A couple of months later he wrote for more of the prescribed medicine and Dr. Roos suggested that he have the operation. He says, "I record this not for the purpose of recommending substitution of garlic medication for an indicated appendectomy, but in order to show its soothing influence even in organically conditioned troubles."

One final case history. This was a laboratory assistant who had by accident infected herself with a bacteria which causes dysentery. Her symptoms were alarming. Loss of appetite, vomiting and diarrhea were followed by bloody stools. The girl was pain-racked and weak. She was given the garlic preparation, two grams, 5 times daily for 6 days. The vomiting stopped almost at once, and she began to take food. It was not until the nineteenth day of illness that the illness began to subside, but quite some time before this, the patient was out of bed cheerful and feeling like herself.

"I could not maintain," says Dr. Roos, "that the length of time of actual illness was considerably shortened, only that convalescence transpired in a surprisingly rapid manner. To everyone experienced with cases of dysentery the contrast must be extremely surprising between the obviously very severe form of the disease and the extremely light discomfort following introduction of treatment, along with only a mildly exhausted condition."

Other Conditions Also Cured

In the second part of his article, Dr. Roos goes on to give case histories of other patients suffering from different conditions who improved when they used garlic. Here are some of them.

1. A churchman, 33 years old, who suffered from chronic colitis which manifested itself in frequent diarrhea, along with pain and other unpleasant sensations. In the beginning he took two grams of garlic twice daily for 14 days, then once daily. Within the first few days he felt better. Three weeks after treatment began he had two normal stools daily.

2. Acute enterocolitis. A 24-year-old woman who suddenly experienced terrific body pains, nausea, chills and fever combined with persistent diarrhea. She took two grams of garlic 3 times a day and by the fifth day her condition was perfectly normal.

3. Subacute colitis. A doctor of 35 years, fell sick with diarrhea and colic pains. He took two grams of garlic 3 times a day and soon became normal.

4. Acute enterocolitis. A 28-year old doctor whose diarrhea occurred every time she took food. A dose of garlic—two grams 3 times a day for 3 days—brought her back to normal.

5. A case of nervous diarrhea. A patient who suffered from this complaint when he became excited. The diarrhea was improved from time to time, by the use of garlic. Dr. Roos notes that the patient came for the remedy quite often.

The second group of patients discussed by Dr. Roos are those whose intestinal contents showed evidence of large numbers of harmful bacteria. For 17 years the first patient, a professor, had suffered from gas, dyspepsia and colitis. At times his diarrhea alternated with spells of constipation. Two grams of the garlic preparation taken 2 to 3 times daily were prescribed. In two and a half months this patient was fully satisfied that his troubles were over.

The second patient was an eccentric who had been starving himself. Examination of the stool showed copious infiltration of harmful bacteria. It took 4 weeks of treatment with garlic to bring this patient back to normal.

Another patient was a woman of 59 who had always been delicate and had formerly been constipated. She had suffered from diarrhea for about 9 months. When she began to take garlic there was at first only a slight improvement, but by the end of 6 weeks she was in good health and her stools were normal. Her appearance was better and she had gained weight. When she came for treatment, examination showed rather copious infiltration of harmful bacteria in her stools. After treatment these had disappeared.

Anti-Dyspeptic Effects

Patients who suffered from "dyspepsia" are next described by Dr. Roos. The first was a 23-year-old student who complained of excessive gas, restlessness, loss of weight, general feeling of ill health and diarrhea. After taking garlic he returned to normal with only one brief relapse.

A master baker of 48 suffered from intense pressure pains in the upper abdomen. This pain had bothered him for more than a year and sometimes it was present for the entire day. He did not suffer from gas. Taking two tablets of garlic 3 times a day, he found that he experienced great improvement within a matter of days and within 6 weeks he declared himself in perfect health.

An inspector of 31 suffered from diarrhea, poor appetite, gas. He had taken many drugs with no relief. By the end of the fourth week on garlic, he was satisfied that he was cured.

Two school teachers—one of 35 and the other 47, both suffered from diarrhea, gas, frequent bloating and belching, also headache and heart palpitations. Six weeks on garlic sufficed to do away with these symptoms.

Therefore, says Dr. Roos, we see that garlic preparations show special anti-dyspeptic effects, no matter whether they cause any great change in the consistency of the stools. "Often, after a very short time, the difficulties improve, the patients feel relieved and look better. One has the impression of a complete alteration in the intestine and of its complete transformation. So far as our patients could later tell, the effect also seems to last."

How does garlic achieve its effects? We do not know exactly, he says, but it appears to have a purifying effect on the bacteria of the intestine, brought about probably by some biological healing of the intestinal wall and its glands. But, he adds, in cases where there is no evidence of any unfavorable or abnormal concentration of harmful bacteria in the intestine —that is, for instance, in cases of "nervous" diarrhea, garlic is also helpful, apparently because of this same healing effect on the mucous membrane.

Naturally, he says, treatment with garlic, as with every other kind of treatment, has as well its unsatisfactory results, its failures and its limitations. He recommends as the best possible daily dose for intestinal complaints two tablets 3 times daily. In severe cases one should take two tablets 5 times daily; in lighter ones two tablets once to twice daily. And most important of all, these tablets can be taken without any fear of disagreeable side effects.

CHAPTER 141

Garlic Triumphs over Indigestion

Judging from the mail we get as well as correspondence columns in other health magazines and newspaper columns, one of the most common annoyances for modern man is still old fashioned indigestion. The symptoms may vary—heaviness after eating, flatulence, gas colic, belching, nausea, etc.—but it is a condition which many recognize as a constant visitor, and some view with serious alarm because of the frequently accompanying sensation of heart palpitations and severe headache.

At the first sign of this condition the regular sufferer reaches for one of dozens of stomach-settlers in the form of minty tablets or fizzing seltzers which are on the market. They all do about the same thing; neutralize the hydrochloric acid in the stomach. It is essential that the climate of the intestine maintain a balance of acid and alkali, it is true, but this balance should be brought about by natural diet; that is, the consumption of foods which are acid, such as meat, and alkaline foods, which include fruits and vegetables. To eliminate entirely the acid of the stomach by the frequent use of these bicarbonate of soda compounds is a very dangerous practice. The stomach acids are essential in breaking down foods so that their component parts may be used to nourish the body. Without these acids, calcium, for example, cannot be fully digested. It either passes through the intestines and is eliminated as though it had not been eaten at all, or it is inefficiently used, not properly absorbed and can result in the formation of calcium deposits (stones) in the kidney or bladder.

Nature's Relief

As any reader who is interested in the study of nutrition should know, nature has a way of taking care of the hyperacidity problem without any danger of over-alkalizing. The natural device which performs this service is our old acquaintance, garlic. The value of garlic in this connection has often been hinted at, and people from ancient times to this have used this herb to relieve gastric distress brought on by the accumulation of gas. It remained for Frederic Damrau, M.D., and Edgar Ferguson, Chemist, writing in the *Review of Gastroenterology* (May, 1949) to arrive at some concrete, scientific basis for this usage.

In their paper these researchers class garlic as a carminative, that is, "aromatic or pungent drugs, used in flatulence and colic, to expel gas from stomach and intestines, and to diminish the griping pains." The theory on how a carminative can do such things follows along this line: the oils of carminatives, upon reaching the mucous membrane, cause a decrease in the movements and tone of the stomach wall. This weakening action probably extends to the sphincters (muscles) and their relaxation may explain the feeling of relief from distention and gas in the stomach after the administration of these oils.

Observation by X-ray

Damrau and Ferguson decided to observe, from a truly scientific point of view, just what action garlic would have in the stomach. They proposed to accomplish this by means of X-ray. They would give the subject barium sulfate (the usual tool for a study of the intestines by X-ray) with and without garlic, and study the speed at which the barium was processed by the stomach in each case. Slower processing would indicate that the needed relaxation of the stomach had been accomplished. Twenty-five patients were included in the study: 12 males and 13 females. The average duration of the complaints which included abdominal pain, abdominal discomfort, belching and nausea, was one year. In each case X-ray comparison was made with and without garlic, after a ten-day period. The so-called medication consisted of 6 garlic tablets, each containing 4¾ grains of dehydrated garlic. Two tablets were given with the barium, 2 two hours later, and 2 after 4 hours. With the use of garlic, the size of the barium residue in the stomach after 6 hours was definitely larger than without it. This meant, of course, that, with the garlic, the stomach operated at a more relaxed, more comfortable pace. The researchers were impressed with the patients' reports of relief of all symptoms.

In another series of studies which included 29 patients complaining from heaviness after eating, belching, flatulence, gas colic and nausea, 2 garlic tablets were given twice daily after lunch and dinner, for a period of two weeks. Again the garlic dosage was 4¾ grains per tablet.

Remarkable Results

The results were gratifying. Heaviness after eating, present in 25 cases, was completely relieved by the treatment in 15 cases, partially relieved in 6, and 4 cases had no relief. Belching was present in 25 cases, and was completely relieved in 13 cases, partially in 9 and not all in 3 cases. Flatulence was present in 25 cases, and 20 cases were completely relieved, one partially, and 4 not at all. Gas colic, present in 24 cases, was completely relieved in 13 cases, partially in 8 and no relief in 3 cases. Nausea, present in 8 cases, was completely relieved in 6, with no relief in 2 cases.

As can be seen, the garlic did not bring only temporary relief, but permanent freedom from these gastric disorders. It is to be presumed that garlic was included in the diets of these patients in some kind of maintenance dose, but since it is a natural food, there need be no fear of dangerous accumulation in the intestines of a harmful substance. There is no fear either of a dangerous habit-forming drug. Quite to the contrary, garlic is really an excellent food in its own right, with many valuable nutrients contained in it, and the added knowledge that its use might beneficially affect other parts of the body.

One other well-known use of garlic has been in the normalizing of blood pressure. Now we have come across a new use for garlic in maintaining good health—the treatment of certain forms of lip precancer.

Cancer of the lip, especially the lower lip, is preceded in almost 10 per cent of cases by precancerous conditions including small, white, thickened patches on the skin, deep cracks and ulceration. Ordinary treatment with poultices, ointments, etc., rarely leads to healing. In the journal, *Problems of Oncology* (March-April, 1958), the work of two Russian scientists, D. M. Sergeev and I. D. Leonov is reported. These men used a poultice of garlic which had been mashed to a gruel-like consistency as the only treatment for 194 cases of the precancerous type of soreness of the lip. The garlic was spread on gauze in a thickness of .2 to .3 centimeters. The gauze was then taped to the lip for from 8 to 12 hours.

Healing Occurred in 93 Per Cent of Cases

Healing occurred in 80 per cent of the patients after a single application. Of the remaining patients, 12.7 per cent were healed after the second application. In 6.8 per cent the treatment was not effective. Four of the patients noted a recurrence of the precancerous symptoms after the garlic treatment. The editor of *Problems of Oncology* suggests that this garlic treatment can only be employed after a diagnosis of actual lip cancer has definitely been excluded.

The powers of garlic in the role of a medication continued to amaze us. No one knows just what it contains that is so effective. Sergeev and Leonov take a guess and attribute garlic's powers, in this instance, to its bactericidal and irritant properties. When applied to the sore part it kills harmful bacteria and causes an inflammation in the immediate region. The course of this inflammation has been found to resemble the process of normal wound healing.

CHAPTER 142

Stop that Cold with Garlic!

Have you ever tried garlic as a treatment for a cold? For centuries it has been a European remedy for many types of infectious disease, including clogged and running nose, cough and sore throat. Nobody who used it then could tell you just why it was effective, but they knew that a good dose of garlic held the cure for many an illness that would respond to few other things.

Now such remedies have long been discarded as products of an old fashioned era. How could those ignorant peasants find a cure for diseases the modern laboratories have not been able to conquer? And how could a common and odorous bulb hold the answer?

Curiosity Led to the Answer

Someone finally got curious enough to find out why garlic could do what antibiotics and sulfa drugs had been unable to do. The man was Dr. J. Klosa, and he reported his findings in the March, 1950, issue of a German magazine entitled *Medical Monthly*.

Dr. Klosa found that garlic oil had that elusive ability to kill dangerous organisms without attacking organisms vital to the body's health. It is this danger to bodily health that rules out (or should rule out) the use of many proposed compounds as medications, even though they are effective germ killers. For example, formaldehyde inactivates all viruses, but it also reacts unfavorably with the body's own protein, and is, therefore, a deadly poison to the body. (Unfortunately, many of the drugs actually being used today have shown themselves to be antagonistic to body processes, but because the reaction is not as immediate nor obviously violent as with formaldehyde, they continue to be used.) Oil of garlic is composed in part of sulfides and disulfides. These unite with virus matter in such a way that the virus organisms are inactivated, so their harmful effects cease and they are prevented from any future activity. All of this is done without any harm to healthful organisms in the body.

Dr. Klosa experimented with a solution of garlic oil (obtained under specially engineered conditions) and water, and he administered this preparation in doses of 10 to 25 drops, every 4 hours. It was found that the desired effect was enhanced by the inclusion of fresh extract of onion juice in the dosage. The vitamin C content of the onion juice was believed responsible for this result.

Excellent Results Obtained

The paper by Dr. Klosa reports results with grippe, sore throat and rhinitis (clogged and running nose) patients. Of 13 cases of grippe treated, fever and catarrhal symptoms were cut short in every case. All patients showed a distinct lessening of the period of convalescence required. No patient suffered from any of the common post-grippe complaints such as chronic inflammation of the lungs, swelling of the lymph glands, jaundice, pains in muscles and joints, etc. Even the cough that often accompanies grippe was considerably suppressed.

In 28 cases of sore throat the oil had a prompt and salutary effect. The burning and tickling abated to the point of disappearance in 24 hours. It was found that, if caught in its first stages, the further development of sore throat could be completely stopped by about 30 drops—or about two doses—of the garlic oil solution.

There were 71 cases of clogged and running nose treated in this manner. The oil was taken partly by mouth and part directly into the nostrils. The congestion of the nostrils was completely cleared up in 13 to 20 minutes in all cases. There were no further complications.

Use Fresh Garlic or Garlic Perles

The oil of garlic spoken of by Dr. Klosa was probably distilled through a complicated technical procedure which would be impossible to duplicate in the average home. Nor have we heard of the availability of such an oil. However, the oil he describes does come from natural garlic cloves and these are certainly available to all of us. We can see no reason why a regular intake of garlic would not give the same protection from the cold symptoms described here as did Dr. Klosa's preparation. If garlic has properties that will inactivate harmful viruses, why not include this tasty bulb in your diet. Good cooks use it in preparing meats to superb effect.

If you do not enjoy the flavor of garlic, or if you do not feel that you can include enough of it in your normal diet to be effective, you will find that there are natural concentrates of garlic available in capsules, or perles, as they are called.

Instead of using the aspirins and nose drops that sell by the thousands during the "cold season," why not give garlic a chance? You will be using a natural remedy whose properties have been proven to affect favorably many unhealthful conditions aside from colds, and a remedy you can be sure will do you no harm. Reinforce garlic's powers with accompanying daily doses of vitamin C and A for even stronger insurance against colds.

CHAPTER 143

Lettuce

If you've ever walked down a garden path on a fresh spring day between rows of green ruffled lettuce, you can never afterwards eat "store" lettuce with any satisfaction. Lettuce, perhaps more than any other vegetable, suffers from being picked, handled, transported and stored before it is eaten. Crispness is the most important quality of lettuce. If it isn't crisp, there doesn't seem to be any point at all to eating it.

Commercially grown lettuce can be stored (if it is in excellent condition) for 3 weeks or longer at a temperature of 32 degrees. It freezes at eight-tenths of a degree lower than that, so the storage temperature must be carefully watched. Usually what you buy at the store has been packed in ice for the trip from the farm. Even so, it's a pretty sorry looking head of lettuce as you select it and put it in your shopping bag, for 5 minutes away from the garden is enough to start the wilting process in lettuce. Some brands hold up longer than others, true. But it should always be your aim to eat lettuce as newly picked as possible, for, of course, wilting means loss of vitamins and minerals.

So even if you can't have a garden, at least make some room somewhere to plant lettuce and the other greens you will need for salad during the spring, summer and fall. Then don't pick them until it's time to make the salad and put it on the table. If you must buy lettuce and other greens at the store, wash them as rapidly as possible and put them in a covered container in the refrigerator. Never, never soak them. True, it does "crisp" them, but it also drains off all the vitamins and minerals into the soaking water.

Dangers Involved

Many readers have inquired about insecticides used on lettuce and other greens. Of course, the commercially grown greens have been doused with insecticides and perhaps preservatives as well to keep them from wilting. Furthermore, it is next to impossible to remove these bug killers, for they lurk in every little wrinkle and crevice in every leaf. In many cases the oily insecticides are not affected in the least by water. This is another excellent reason for growing your own salad greens. You should wash carefully any lettuce you get at the store and wipe it with a dry towel as well. It's up to you to decide whether the benefit you will get from the greens will outweigh the possible harmful effects of whatever insecticides are on them. Personally we believe it does. But growing your own lettuce is the best answer of all. Of course, taking your vitamin supplements regularly will help to protect you against harm from insecticides.

One final word on lettuce in the diet. We don't suppose anyone lives on lettuce. But it might be dangerous to do so especially during the hottest of the summer months. Lettuce grown on soil fertilized with nitrates contains nitrates which the hot sunlight may change into nitrites, a substance which, in sufficient concentration, can be dangerous. It unites with the red pigment in the blood that is supposed to carry oxygen. So don't eat leafy vegetables exclusively during the summer months. Eat plenty of the others as well.

Lettuce is not excessively rich in all of the important nutriments. But it does contain a goodly allotment of the B vitamins and vitamin A, and, of course, it makes the best possible base for salads of all kinds. Its protein content is low—only 1.2 per cent. But, considering the fact that its water content is 94.8 per cent, the protein in the remaining solids is quite high. The carbohydrate in lettuce is only 2.9 per cent—good news for dieters. One hundred grams contain 22 milligrams of calcium, which is a little less available to the body than the calcium of milk, 25 milligrams of phosphorus and .5 milligrams of iron. Loose leaf lettuce is generally thought to be more nutritious than head lettuce because it is generally greener and also has access to much more sunlight. Green leaves are, of course, richer in all the vitamins and minerals than pale white ones.

[517]

The vitamin content of 100 grams of lettuce (about 4 large leaves) is:

Vitamin A
    540 International Units
Vitamin B
    Thiamin .... .06 milligrams
    Riboflavin .... .07 milligrams
    Niacin 2   milligrams
Vitamin C 8   milligrams

CHAPTER 144

Lima Beans

Lima beans are a fine year-'round food, high in protein, vitamins and minerals, inexpensive and highly satisfactory to most people's palate. It is well to remember that legumes, such as beans, are a splendid meat substitute. They do not contain all the various amino acids that make up "complete" protein—no vegetable foods do. But they are sufficiently rich in 4 of these amino acids to qualify as very high grade protein.

Lima beans came to us from South America. The fact that they are shelled out of their pods before they are eaten is a good recommendation for them in these days of ever-present insecticides on food. The actual lima bean kernel probably contains very little of whatever insecticide has been dusted or sprayed on the pods. Served fresh from the garden, there are few vegetables that equal them for flavor. Dried, they retain most of their vitamin and mineral content, with the exception of vitamin C. But they must be prepared correctly if they are to retain all these valuable food elements right up to the dinner table.

Until recently it was good cooking practice to soak dried beans overnight, throw away the water in which they soaked (and the B vitamins along with the water) then parboil the beans in fresh water to which baking soda was added for some obscure reason. The soda removed what was left of the vitamins, the parboiling removed the minerals and the beans were served almost devoid of any food value, except that they filled you up. Nowadays we know that dried beans should be cooked in the water in which they are soaked. No soda should be used in preparing them and they should be cooked at very low heat so that their protein will not toughen. Adelle Davis in her excellent cook book, *Let's Cook It Right* (Harcourt, Brace & Company, 383 Madison Avenue, New York,) suggests not soaking the beans at all, but dropping them very slowly into boiling water, so that the water continues to boil. This will soften them, so that they can be cooked. Soaking them, then freezing them before cooking will subtract from the time necessary for the cooking process. There are endless tasty ways lima beans can be served—baked, boiled with meat, made into loaves and so forth.

Here are the vitamins and minerals found in one-half cup of lima beans, fresh and dried. Eat more of them!

	Fresh Lima Beans		Dried Lima Beans	
Calcium	63	milligrams	72	milligrams
Phosphorus	158	milligrams	386	milligrams
Iron	2.20	milligrams	7	milligrams
Magnesium			1.07	milligrams
Copper			.86	milligrams
		International		International
Vitamin A	900	Units	0-100	Units
Vitamin B				
Thiamin	225	micrograms	300	micrograms
Riboflavin	250	micrograms	250	micrograms
Niacin	1	milligram	2.1	milligrams
Pantothenic acid	95	micrograms		
Pyridoxine			550	micrograms
Biotin			9.8	micrograms
Vitamin C	42	milligrams	2	milligrams

CHAPTER 145

Mushrooms

Mushrooms, as everybody knows, are not plants, as vegetables and grains are. They are fungi—a group of plants that includes also rusts, molds and mildews. They do not reproduce by seeds, but by spores. The spore is the fine black dust that is thrown off when a mature plant is laid on a white surface. The spore gives rise to the "spawn"—stringy white material which penetrates dried manure or similar substances and eventually develops into a mushroom. Mushrooms are grown in beds heavily fertilized with manure. We wonder whether or not this may have something to do with the abundance of the B vitamins in the mushroom. We know that the vitamin is produced in the intestinal tract of the healthy animal. Could it be that the mushroom, growing on dung, takes up some of this precious substance that has been eliminated by the animal?

Did you know, for instance, that mushrooms are very rich in folic acid, the yellow vitamin which, along with vitamin B$_{12}$, is the most potent weapon ever discovered against pernicious anemia? The speed with which infinitely small doses of this vitamin rejuvenate patients of this dread disease has amazed doctors ever since the vitamin was first discovered. Brewer's yeast, raw wheat germ, soybeans, kidney and liver are other rich sources.

Mushrooms are fairly good sources of other B vitamins as well—¾ of a cup containing about as much thiamin as a bran muffin, as much riboflavin as an orange and as much niacin as a serving of halibut. Also, surprisingly enough, we are told that mushrooms grown in the light are rich in vitamin D which does not occur in any other foods from non-animal sources. Vitamin D in mushrooms! This seems especially odd, since we automatically associate mushrooms with dark cellars, whereas vitamin D is the vitamin one manufactures from sunlight!

The other astonishing thing about mushrooms is the fact that they are so nutritious and yet grow without chlorophyll, the green life's blood of all other plants that we eat. The mushroom family apparently does not need chlorophyll.

One of the earliest introductions we as children have to mushrooms is the warning that we may by mistake get a poisonous one. And it is just as well, unless you are an expert in recognizing mushrooms, not to eat any you may find growing in the woods or fields. It is indeed true that there are deadly kinds of mushrooms. The poisonous material in this type of mushroom is a narcotic which induces nausea, drowsiness, stupor and pains in the joints. Mushroom growers sometimes find that spores from other (and perhaps poisonous) mushrooms have invaded their planting beds and must be disposed of.

However, in general, one can feel quite safe in eating mushrooms sold in today's markets, for they are grown carefully.

Here is the vitamin and mineral content of 100 grams of mushrooms which is about ¾ cup:

Vitamin B

Thiamin	160	micrograms
Riboflavin	500	micrograms
Niacin	6	milligrams
Pyridoxine	45	micrograms
Biotin	16	micrograms
Pantothenic acid	1700	micrograms
Folic acid	considerable (no exact figure available)	
Vitamin C	1-8	milligrams
Vitamin D	21	International Units, if grown in dark
	63	International Units, if grown in light
Calcium	14	milligrams
Phosphorus	98	milligrams
Iron	3.14	milligrams
Copper	1.79	milligrams
Manganese	.08	milligrams

CHAPTER 146

A Hazard of Onion-Eating

(More Than the Social One)

Vegetarians who read through the May 12, 1951, issue of *Science News Letter* may now be thinking of taking small quantities of at least one of the carefully selected items included in their comparatively limited diets. So, for that matter, may meat-eating Mr. Average American who likewise has an irresistible relish for snacking on butter bread and scallions, or the even more mouth-watering savors of a Bermuda onion sandwich. According to the news source cited, Dr. M. Kalser, of the University of Illinois College of Medicine, gorged (experimentally) on enough onions to bring himself down with an all-out case of anemia in a single week. The findings, which he related before the Cleveland convention of the Federation of American Societies for Experimental Biology, were confirmed by Dr. Kalser in conjunction with 3 other staff members of the same institution.

The original purpose out of which this side-discovery grew had been slanted toward the invention of a drug to relieve a bodily abnormality in which the patient suffers from a superabundance of red blood cells (a condition opposite to that of anemia, the victim of which is diseased as a consequence of having too few red cells and too many white ones). In the course of preliminary discussion, one of Dr. Kalser's colleagues recalled that someone or other had made dogs anemic by feeding them onions in order to cure them of the canine disease of blacktongue.

Experimenting with the same breed of animals, the Illinois scientists first tried out on them the ordinary onion oil extract that is widely used in restaurants and homes for food-flavoring, and discovered that a daily dose of a mere quarter teaspoonful of this substance produced the disease in marked degree. Found to be too potent to try in a proportionate scale on humans, this extract should even be used in extreme moderation in seasoning, they agreed.

Experiments on Humans

The next stage in the course of their study consisted simply in enlisting volunteer medical students to overeat the plain food, and in this stage Dr. Kalser himself participated. Besides their regular diet, the group consumed over two pounds of cooked onions daily for 5 days. At the end of this time all showed typical anemia symptoms, dragging themselves around in an exhausted state and turning pale to their finger tips. On laboratory examination, the red cell count in their blood exhibited a drop of about a million, and its hemoglobin content was also starkly reduced. But this was only a slight anemia when compared with that of the dogs, which for 15 days had been fed comparable amounts of the pungent bulbs. In the animals both red cell count and hemoglobin had sunk to 50 per cent of normal.

Though all the experimentees successfully convalesced out of their self-induced ailment within a week after stopping their onion-spree, Dr. Kalser suggests that persons the nature of whose occupations in itself affects their normal blood content (aviators working at high altitudes and people engaged in strenuous labor) might do best to avoid the highly aromatic food item entirely. And if you are a home-gardener blessed with too bountiful a crop of the tasty food, better to share its delights with neighbors rather than to surpass moderation in trying to eat up the whole amount yourself. Temperance in all things pays off in the end.

CHAPTER 147

Peas

June peas! Fresh from the vines, sweet and crisp and tender! What city-dweller could possibly know the delights of eating a dish of June peas right from the vines in his own garden! We're sure that farmers and gardeners will agree with us that the first peas of the season are a real event.

In addition to their delectable taste, peas are excellent food. They are, of course, seeds, so they are well equipped with all the nourishment the new plants will need to grow and carry on the next generation. They are a plant with a long history, well known to the Greeks and Romans, the ancient Egyptians and Ethiopians. In fact, we are told that evidence of the pea as human food has been found in that area of Switzerland inhabited by the Lake Dwellers during the Bronze Age.

The kind of pea most generally eaten in this country is the seed, wrinkled or smooth, of the *pisum sativum*. Then, too, there are sugar peas whose pods are eaten right along with the seeds. Peas suffer extensively so far as nutrient value is concerned with every hour they remain on the shelf after picking. Not only do vitamins disappear from them as they grow old, but their sugar is decreased and their starch content increased. As a matter of fact we are told that the sugar content of the pea is greatest when the pea is too immature to be eaten.

How to Prepare and Eat Peas

Peas are an excellent food for freezing. It has been shown in carefully controlled experiments that if they are frozen raw and kept at below zero temperature, they deteriorate within a very short time. This is, we suppose, because of the enzymes they contain. So they should be blanched briefly before freezing. Of course, eat them fresh if you can get them that way. But if you are deciding between frozen or canned peas, the decision should be easy. First of all, you should not eat any canned foods—but least of all canned peas which certainly bear little resemblance, either in taste or nutritive value, to fresh or frozen ones.

When you are cooking fresh peas, cook them just until they are tender (a very short time) and use all the water in which they cooked—as little as possible. If you're cooking frozen ones, by all means leave them frozen until you pop them into the utensil. They lose vitamins if they are allowed to thaw.

Undoubtedly the best way to eat peas is raw. Here is what Editor Rodale has to say on this subject: "One of my first experiences with raw vegetables was with peas. It is ridiculous to cook them. They are so easy to take raw and any child will agree that in cooking, something is lost. When you eat them raw you get everything. Don't overlook the fact that peas are seeds. They are living things and will grow if placed in the soil. When you cook them, that living quality is destroyed. Its germination power is annihilated. You are then eating a dead food."

Canned Peas

Speaking of canned peas, here is how peas are cleaned before being canned. Nightshade, a poisonous weed, often grows near or in the rows of peas at the big canning plants. The seed of the nightshade gets in with the shelled peas and up until recently there was no practical way to remove it. Then somebody invented detergents—yes, the kind we use for washing dishes—and a mix of detergents solved the pea-packers' problems. The peas, soaking in the detergent, sink to the bottom of the sorting racks. The nightshade seeds don't absorb the detergent. They float and can be skimmed off. How much detergent you eat in the can of peas you buy at the store is anybody's guess. We suggest strongly that you make your own garden and grow your own peas if you possibly can. However, if you must eat commercially grown peas, it is comforting to know that, when you remove the pod you also remove much of the insecticide residue, so peas and shelled beans are thus probably safer from this point of view.

Vitamin and Mineral Content

Peas are fairly rich in protein—a characteristic of all the legumes. But, they are deficient in two or three of the essential amino acids, so they cannot be counted on to supply whole protein, such as one gets from animal foods like meat and eggs. Here is the vitamin and mineral content of about a cup of peas:

Vitamin A .... 680 International Units
Vitamin B
    Thiamin .... 340 to 400 micrograms
    Riboflavin .... 160-200 micrograms
    Niacin .... 2.1 to 2.7 milligrams

Pyridoxine	79-190 micrograms
Pantothenic Acid	380-1040 micrograms
Biotin	3.5 micrograms
Vitamin C	26 milligrams
Calcium	14-22 milligrams
Phosphorus	17-122 milligrams
Iron	.46-1.9 milligrams
Copper	.10 milligrams
Sulfur	50 milligrams
Bromine	.21 milligrams
Iodine	9 parts per billion
Sodium	1 milligram
Potassium	370 milligrams
Carbohydrate	7.5 to 17.7 per cent
Protein	4.2 to 6.7 per cent
Fat	.2 to .4 per cent
Calories	40 to 90

CHAPTER 148

Peppers

What do we demand of foods that we prefer to eat raw? They must be crisp or crunchy, have a distinctive flavor, be easily chewed and not too inconvenient in the way of skin or seeds. No vegetable fills all these demands so well as the bell pepper—a food many of us neglect simply because we have never learned to appreciate its value.

Peppers are not actually vegetables. Botanically they fit in the category of berries, because they have numerous seeds. They grow, as any gardener knows, on tidy plants with luscious shiny, dark green foliage. They can be eaten any time after they have attained any size at all, but actually they are not ripe until they are red. Peppers are picked green for marketing, so those of us who shop for vegetables seldom see a red one.

Rich In Vitamin C And P

The chief claim to fame of the pepper is its phenomenally high vitamin C content. The vitamin C increases in the fruit as it ripens, so that in a pepper which is half red and half green, the red side will contain more vitamin C than the green side. One ripe bell pepper may contain as much as 300 milligrams of vitamin C. An average-size orange contains about 50.

We hardly need to add that the vitamin C begins to dwindle almost as soon as the pepper is picked from its bush, so it is best to buy peppers as freshly picked as possible. At its best, a pepper is crisp and firm, thick-fleshed with a good color. The limp, wilted, shriveled pepper has lost most of its food value and probably all of its vitamin C. Of course, your peppers should go in a closed container in the refrigerator as soon as you bring them into the house. They lose vitamin C when they are cut or shredded, so serve them soon after they are prepared.

Vitamin P was first extracted from paprika, peppers and citrus fruits, so we know that this valuable vitamin accompanies the vitamin C in our tasty bell peppers. When vitamin C was first discovered, peppers were used extensively as a source of it. Many natural vitamin C preparations are today made from peppers rather than rose hips or other vitamin C-rich foods.

You can cook peppers if you must, and, of course, there are many cooked dishes which owe their tastiness to peppers. But serve them raw as often as possible. They make a fine addition to any vegetable salad, they add a lot to cole slaw and they are most nutritious and attractive stuffed with cheese or meat filling. Of course, don't forget to add them to the plate when you are slicing "finger salads," for their lovely color contrasts beautifully with raw carrots, radishes and celery.

Pimentos, and hot peppers are related to bell peppers. All of them, and paprika, too, give you an abundance of vitamin C and other vitamins. Here are the vitamins and minerals you will find in an average-sized green pepper, which weighs about 100 grams:

Vitamin A	700-3000	International Units
Vitamin B		
Thiamin	30- 70	milligrams
Riboflavin	40- 100	milligrams
Niacin	.4	milligrams
Vitamin C	120- 180	milligrams
Calcium	12	milligrams
Phosphorus	28	milligrams
Iron	.4	milligrams
Protein	1	gram

Peppers fall in the category of the 5 per cent carbohydrate vegetables and one medium sized pepper contains only 25 calories!

CHAPTER 149

Potatoes

The other day a friend of ours was talking to us about the harmfulness of white bread. She agreed she'd better omit it from her diet from now on. "And potatoes, too, of course," she continued. We stopped her right there. "Why potatoes?" we asked. "Well, everybody knows that white bread and potatoes are just about the worst things you can eat, aren't they?" she asked. For some reason health literature of the past 25 years or so has, without meaning to, given the general public a completely erroneous notion about the food value of potatoes. How else can we explain the prevalent idea that potatoes are almost worthless as food?

Potatoes are about 20 per cent carbohydrate, that's true. Carbohydrate foods should not be used to excess, if it means cutting down on protein foods. But potatoes are about two per cent protein. In addition, they contain so many minerals and vitamins that they are quite capable of sustaining life over a period of time, even if no other food at all is available.

A potato is defined as "a swelling at the end of an underground stem." We generally speak of them as tubers. While most kinds are brown, there are some pink-skinned varieties, one of which was cultivated and eaten centuries ago by the Incas who lived in Chile and Peru. Today, we are sorry to say, there are potato growers bent on making this fine food unfit to eat. We have in our file a label from a potato sack in Florida which indicates that the potatoes have been "protected" with a color wax which dyes them pink. A clipping from *Science News Letter,* October 7, 1950, tells us that 2, 4-D, the highly toxic weed-killer, is being used to "intensify red skin color and increase vitamin C content of Red McClure and Bliss Triumph potatoes." The weed-killer is sprayed on the vines while the potatoes are still in the ground. Of course, the fact that the color of the potatoes changes indicates that the spray penetrates right through the plant and into the delicious spud which we then buy to feed our families. "Growers have been warned to be especially careful in use of plant-killing 2, 4-D" the article goes on. The poison is sprayed on the potatoes to make them more attractive to housewives! We have no idea why a poison spray should increase the vitamin C content of potatoes unless, as seems quite possible, the potato is forced to manufacture more vitamin C to protect itself against the poison. Thanks, we'll take our potatoes with a little less vitamin C, and we don't honestly think a poisonous red dye makes them the least bit more attractive! A number of deadly insecticides are used on potato plants, so we advise that you scrub thoroughly any commercially bought potatoes you eat.

Bread and cereal products produce an acid reaction in the body. Potatoes, along with other vegetables, are an alkaline-reacting food. As a matter

[526]

of fact, they are one of the most alkaline of foods. Their vitamin and mineral content is as follows:

Content in One Medium Boiled Potato

Vitamin A	20	International Units
Vitamin B1	.11	milligrams
Vitamin B2	.04	milligrams
Other B Vitamins:		
Niacin	.1	milligram
Pyridoxine	320	micrograms
Pantothenic Acid	400 to 650	micrograms
Inositol	29	milligrams
Folic Acid	140	micrograms
Choline	20-105	milligrams
Vitamin C	24	milligrams
Vitamin E	.06	milligrams
Calcium	5- 11	milligrams
Phosphorus	33- 56	milligrams
Iron	.46-.70	milligrams
Copper	.15	milligrams
Cobalt	2- 3	micrograms
Fluorine	20	micrograms
Potassium	410	milligrams
Sulfur	24.3	milligrams

Food Value And More

The essential amino acids (forms of protein) are present in potatoes. The quality of the protein in potatoes has been the subject of lively debate. By this we mean, is the potato protein such that it will sustain life? In one experiment a researcher lived for 6 years with potatoes as his only protein and abandoned the diet only because he feared the spray residues were accumulating in his body and might poison him. An article in *Science News Letter* for September 3, 1949, tells us that scientists have discovered some substance in potatoes that may aid the body in using protein. In other words, eating potatoes, as well as meat, cheese and eggs, may help your body to make the best possible use of the meat, cheese and eggs.

Many people like raw potatoes and there seems to be nothing wrong with eating them raw if you like them and if they agree with you. Some people find that raw potato starch is almost indigestible. A Rodale employee who suffered from eczema reported to us that she cleared up a stubborn case by eating raw potatoes. We have no medical authority that indicates what in the potatoes might be responsible for this, but it certainly is worth giving a try, if you suffer from eczema. If you buy potatoes in quantity, they are best stored at a temperature of about 40 degrees in a dry, well-ventilated cellar. They lose some of their vitamin C in storage.

We're sure you've been told many times that potatoes cooked in their skins retain far more vitamins than peeled potatoes. To preserve the largest possible amount of vitamins and minerals, boil potatoes in their jackets.

[527]

Pressure cooking and baking destroys only a little of these food elements. Paring the potatoes, then boiling them, results in a 47 per cent loss of vitamin C. Mashing such potatoes then destroys another 10 per cent. And if, for some special recipe you must pare, slice, grate or cube potatoes, chill them in the refrigerator first, so that some vitamin C will be preserved. And never, never under any circumstances soak them in water, for all the B vitamins as well as vitamin C dissolve immediately in the soaking water.

If you find, toward the end of winter, that your potatoes have sprouted, cut deeply around the sprouts before using the potatoes. A substance called solanine accumulates in potato sprouts which in large amounts can be quite harmful. If you're reducing, you might be wise to avoid too many potatoes, but chances are it's mostly the butter, cream sauce or gravy you put on the potatoes that puts those extra pounds on you.

CHAPTER 150

Pumpkin

More attention should be given to that golden-orange, ribbed and almost spherical vegetable known as the pumpkin. It is more than the symbol of the Halloween season—it is food, food rich in many of the valuable vitamins and minerals. The word *pumpkin* in itself should give some indication of the food value that lies within, for it is taken from the Greek word *pepon,* meaning "cooked in the sun." We can infer from this, then, that pumpkin is a natural food, prepared by nature—a food given a protective rind which will ward off the dangerous chemical sprays, a food which, because of these two advantages alone, should be a well-used item in the American dietary fare. However, this member of the gourd family is relegated to a minor role in our diets, becoming a Thanksgiving and Christmas food eating thrill. And, to be sure, this thrill is mostly in the form of the classic dessert, pumpkin pie, which we, of course, cannot recommend because of the considerable amounts of sugar and white flour used as ingredients. The question of why this vegetable doesn't find its way to the food table all year round is certainly a perplexing one since the pumpkin is a remarkable dietary item in that it can be stored for more than a year without losing its flavor if it is kept in a cool, dark place with the proper ventilation.

The Pumpkin Shunned As Food
More often than not, pumpkins lose their true identity as worthwhile and healthful vegetables and assume the role of decoration pieces and objects of mental associations and recollections. For instance, they call

to mind such items as the Halloween season, the child carving out a jack-o-lantern, *The Legend of Sleepy Hollow* and the smashed pumpkin, the corn field spotted with pumpkins between the rows and grade school days with the task of memorizing James Whitcomb Riley's *When the Frost is on the Punkin.* The thought of pumpkin as food is of secondary importance to most people. It is a strange phenomenon to witness this perfectly valuable nutritive element, especially high in the very important vitamin A, shunned as food in preference to its decorative and symbolic values. Or is this such a strange thing when we think of the ridiculousness of modern methods of food preparation? Modernization, too, shuns the nutritive value of many foods in preference to their keeping quality and outward appearance. The American public isn't content to consume food untampered with by modern methods of processing and refining. They must have their food subjected to the scientist's chemical laboratory where it is given the decorative coat which the American housewife looks for and places uppermost in making her final decision when selecting foodstuffs for the family menu. The words "food value" are placed in the background, overshadowed by the primary incentive of eye appeal.

The Value of Pumpkin Seeds

What is needed is a reform movement not only in regards to the merits of pumpkin, but also in regards to other healthful and appetizing foods which for one reason or another are discarded by modern peoples. Many of these foods contain surprise packages, in the form of medicinal advantages, unexplained nutritive elements and undiscovered vitamins and minerals, which are not known to unwary shoppers. One such find was made by Dr. W. Devrient of Germany when he discovered that pumpkin seeds, the same ones thrown away by many a jack-o'-lantern maker, are loaded with materials which are the building stones for the male hormones. This discovery led him to some important information concerning the treatment of prostate gland disorders. To show how far advanced certain of the foreign peoples are in comparison to our thinking on certain foods which we tend to reject, we quote from Dr. Devrient's article entitled *Androgen-Hormonal Curative Influence of a Neglected Plant:* "Only the plain people knew the open secret of pumpkin seeds, a secret which was handed down from father to son for countless generations without any ado. No matter whether it was the Hungarian gypsy, the mountain-dwelling Bulgarian, the Anatolian Turk, the Ukranian or the Transylvanian German—they all knew that pumpkin seeds preserve the prostate gland and thereby also male potency. In these countries people eat pumpkin seeds the way they eat sunflower seeds in Russia: as an inexhaustible source of vigor offered by Nature."

These people trusted in nature to deliver to them the needed incentive to eat certain foods. Of course, we are not suggesting a return to nature, but we are suggesting that more and more people begin to realize that natural, untampered-with foods are best from a health standpoint and this point alone is what we should strive for when we select our foods.

[529]

Pumpkin In Your Garden

Pumpkin can be counted in this class, that is, whole pumpkin, not canned or frozen pumpkin. If this natural source isn't available to you, plant your own. They are easy to grow, requiring little if any attention. One caution: they can't stand the cold, so bring them in before the frost falls. This little effort will reward you many times over by offering you a natural, unprocessed food which can be enjoyed all year-round.

One serving of mashed pumpkin yields the following vitamins and minerals:

	International Units	Milligrams
Vitamin A	3400	
Vitamin B		
Thiamin		.05
Riboflavin		.08
Niacin		.6
Vitamin C		37
Calcium		21
Phosphorus		44
Iron		.8
Sodium		.6
Potassium		480

CHAPTER 151

Rhubarb

Rhubarb, that long and rather thick, rounded on one side and flat on the other, red or green stem, shares equal space with spinach on our list of foods which we are very hesitant to recommend. Both are what we call controversial foods, controversial in that they both contain a substance which, if taken in excessive amounts, can be dangerous to health. However, spinach presents less of a problem since it has nutritive factors which far outweigh its deleterious elements. Rhubarb, on the other hand, has no such balancing factor, being very low on the side of the scale which would classify it as a healthful and thus worthwhile food—that is, low in vitamins and minerals—and being very high on the opposite end of the measure which would classify it as a food which health-conscious folk should attempt to avoid as much as possible.

Oxalic Acid In Rhubarb

The unfavorable substance to which we refer above is oxalic acid. This acid is widely distributed in foods of vegetable origin. Small amounts are found in potatoes, beans, beets, tomatoes, cauliflower, onions, mushrooms, celery, currants, raspberries, grapes, pears, tea, coffee and cocoa. However, there is an extraordinary amount found in rhubarb and spinach. The harmful effects of the small quantities in the above mentioned foods seem less important in the light of the vitamins and minerals they contain. The rhubarb plant contains no such storehouse and thus oxalic acid assumes the role of the predominant factor in determining the final results of the chemical reaction which takes place when rhubarb is ingested. By this we mean that when rhubarb is eaten, oxalic acid is allowed to enter the digestive system of your body full strength, without the accompanying food elements (as is the case with other foods containing lesser amounts of oxalic acid) to weaken the effects of the acid and to augment the depleted elements which the acid destroys in order that the body's chemical balance may remain intact. Oxalic acid cannot be oxidized in the body, so it combines with the body calcium to form crystals of calcium oxalate which are deposited in the kidneys. The disease—called Oxaluria—is the condition in which large amounts of calcium oxalate crystals are present in the urine. These crystals form a large part of most kidney and gallstones. Thus we can see that oxalic acid destroys some of the calcium which is already present in the body.

Rhubarb's Calcium Content

What about the calcium in the rhubarb plant itself? Well on this count also the villain oxalic acid has the upper hand. According to researchers James C. Andrews and Edward T. Viser, writing in *Food Research* for July-August, 1951, the oxalic acid content of rhubarb is .275 per cent. This acid combines with whatever calcium there is in the plant and by this combination renders the calcium useless for assimilation by human bodies. In addition, the toxic character of this acid can have very harmful effects if rhubarb is eaten with any degree of regularity over a long period of time. The fact that oxalic acid is used as a bleach for straw hats should indicate something of its danger to the human digestive tract.

During the First World War it was suggested that rhubarb greens be substituted for spinach—under the impression that their calcium content would be healthful. Several deaths were reported. Post mortems revealed calcium oxalate in the internal organs and the official report of the cause of death was "coma consequent on poisoning by oxalic acid."

Strangely enough, many people have the impression that rhubarb leaves are "poison" but that the stalks are very healthy food. True, there is more oxalic acid in the leaf than in the stalk. Even in the stalk this acid is not present in such concentrated form that it could be deadly in a couple of doses (a suicide dose of pure oxalic acid is 4 to 5 grams). But the cumulative effect of eating considerable quantities of rhubarb over a long time is extremely dangerous, especially if there is any tendency to diseases of the genitourinary tract.

Why risk the dangers involved with ingesting extraordinary amounts of oxalic acid in attempting to fulfill your calcium need? There are so many other really "safe" sources of calcium that rhubarb, and for that matter all other foods containing huge amounts of oxalic acid, should be crossed off your food list entirely. Choose foods such as dandelion, endive, lettuce, broccoli, Brussels sprouts, loose leaf cabbage, collards, kohlrabi, mustard greens, turnip greens and watercress, for these foods are much, much lower in oxalic acid and just as rich in calcium.

Sugar Must Be Used

One final note. In order to enjoy rhubarb, considerable amounts of sugar must be cooked with it to reduce the tartness and thus make it palatable. This is the final death blow to rhubarb as a food as far as our standards are concerned. As many readers know, we do not approve of the refined, pure, white drug known as sugar in any way, shape or form. (See section of this book on sugar.) If eating rhubarb means eating sugar, we say no to any implication of rhubarb as a worthwhile food. If, however, you must eat rhubarb (and we sincerely hope you will eat it only infrequently) use a very small amount of honey as the sweetening agent and be sure to bolster your calcium foundation by eating a goodly quantity of bone meal—more valuable than any of the other food substances for its calcium content. We believe, though, that your taste buds can be conditioned away from rhubarb after you consider carefully the many dangers involved with its eating.

Here is the vitamin and mineral content of 100 grams of rhubarb which is about three-fourth cup:

Vitamin A	20	International Units
Vitamin B		
Thiamin	.01	milligrams
Vitamin C	6	milligrams
Calcium	41	milligrams
Phosphorus	20	milligrams
Iron	.4	milligrams
Sodium	2	milligrams
Potassium	160	milligrams

CHAPTER 152

Eat More Salad Greens!

Every diet recommendation written these days, even by the most conservative dietitian, urges the use of green, leafy vegetables at least once a day. Many people have gotten the habit of the regular eating of salads with meals, but there are still too many who have the impression that a leaf of lettuce under a canned peach is what we mean by salads.

In almost any community today there is a wide variety of green leafy vegetables available at any time of the year. Iceberg lettuce, which is what most of us think of in terms of salads, is perhaps the least nutritive and appealing of these. In iceberg lettuce, it seems to us that much has been sacrificed for crispness and appearance. It is almost white, and seems to have little taste compared with such richly tasty greens as mustard, watercress, endive, dandelion and so on.

Some Tips On Meal-Planning

Here are some basic rules about the use of leafy greens in meal-planning. You should eat them at both lunch and dinner if at all possible. That's how valuable they are to your general welfare. They should be fresh; wilted greens have lost most of their food value. Wash them as soon as you get them home from the store, or the garden, and place them immediately in a closed container in your refrigerator. Although most greens will stay fresh and crisp for a week or more, it is best to use them as soon as possible.

Prepare them immediately before serving. Every fresh food loses vitamins from the moment it is cut or chopped, from all cut surfaces. So postpone the preparation of your fresh, raw vegetables until the last moment before serving a meal.

Salad dressings increase the nutritional value of your greens, so use them often. Salad oil is your richest food source of unsaturated fatty acids, those oils which, it is believed, help your body to use cholesterol properly, so that it does not collect in arteries, gall bladder and so forth. Make the salad dressing any way you like it—with vinegar, lemon juice, tomato juice. Any good cookbook contains many recipes for salad dressings. Of course, we suggest omitting the salt. If you miss it, then increase the amount of herbs, onion or paprika to make a tasty dressing.

We get many letters asking what kind of salad oil we recommend. All of them—sunflower seed oil, corn oil, cottonseed oil, peanut oil, etc.— contain about the same amount of unsaturated fatty acids. Olive oil is preferable from the point of view of refining, for pure olive oil is simply the pressed oil from the olives, with no further processing. But it seems that olive oil falls far below other vegetable and cereal oils in its content of unsaturated fatty acids.

Which Greens Should You Use?

Which are the most valuable green, leafy vegetables from the nutritional standpoint? In general, the greener the leaf, the more vitamins and minerals it contains. Here is a list of the most familiar ones—giving their vitamin and mineral content.

Note that, in general, leafy vegetables are rich in calcium and low in phosphorus. This means that they are excellent additions to diets that contain lots of cereals and breads, for these are high in phosphorus and low in calcium. The balance of these two minerals is important for health. Most of us need far more calcium in our meals than we are getting. Leafy greens in salads are a fine source.

[533]

VITAMINS AND MINERALS IN ABOUT 1 CUP OF GREENS

Food	Calcium	Phosphorus	Iron	Sodium	Potassium	Vitamin A	Thiamin	Riboflavin	Niacin	Vitamin C
Beet greens	118 mg.	45 mg.	3.2 mg.	130 mg.	570 mg.	6,700 IU	.08 mg.	.18 mg.	.4 mg.	34 mg.
Brussels sprouts	34 mg.	78 mg.	1.3 mg.	11 mg.	450 mg.	400 IU	.08 mg.	.16 mg.	.7 mg.	94 mg.
Cabbage	46 mg.	31 mg.	1.3 mg.	9 mg.	300 mg.	80 IU	.06 mg.	.05 mg.	.3 mg.	50 mg.
Chard	105 mg.	36 mg.	2.5 mg.	84 mg.	380 mg.	8,720 IU	.06 mg.	.18 mg.	.4 mg.	38 mg.
Chicory (French endive)	18 mg.	21 mg.	.7 mg.	.....	.....	10,000 IU	.05 mg.	.20 mg.	.....	15 mg.
Cress, water	195 mg.	46 mg.	2.0 mg.	.....	.....	4,720 IU	.08 mg.	.16 mg.	.8 mg.	77 mg.
Dandelion greens	187 mg.	70 mg.	3.1 mg.	76 mg.	430 mg.	15,170 IU	.13 mg.	.12 mg.	.7 mg.	16 mg.
Endive	79 mg.	56 mg.	1.7 mg.	18 mg.	400 mg.	3,000 IU	.07 mg.	.12 mg.	.4 mg.	11 mg.
Kale	225 mg.	62 mg.	2.2 mg.	110 mg.	410 mg.	7,540 IU	.10 mg.	.26 mg.	2.0 mg.	115 mg.
Lettuce, head	22 mg.	25 mg.	.5 mg.	12 mg.	140 mg.	540 IU	.04 mg.	.08 mg.	.2 mg.	8 mg.
Mustard greens	220 mg.	38 mg.	2.9 mg.	48 mg.	450 mg.	7,180 IU	.06 mg.	.18 mg.	.7 mg.	45 mg.
Parsley	193 mg.	84 mg.	4.3 mg.	28 mg.	880 mg.	8,230 IU	.11 mg.	.28 mg.	1.4 mg.	193 mg.
Spinach	81 mg.	55 mg.	3.0 mg.	82 mg.	780 mg.	9,420 IU	.11 mg.	.20 mg.	.6 mg.	59 mg.
Turnip greens	259 mg.	50 mg.	2.4 mg.	10 mg.	440 mg.	9,540 IU	.09 mg.	.46 mg.	.8 mg.	136 mg.

Iron and Potassium in Greens

Iron and potassium are two other extremely important minerals available in good quantity from leafy vegetables. In general, the darker the green of the leaf, the more iron it contains. Parsley, for instance, is almost fantastically rich in iron, and how easy it is to add a bit of parsley to almost anything, improving the flavor as well as the nutriment. Always garnish meats, vegetables and salads with parsley and encourage your family to eat it rather than treating it just as a piece of decoration.

Potassium is of the utmost importance for good health, especially to folks who have not given up salt, for these two minerals balance one another and the more sodium you eat, the more potassium you need for proper balance. Leafy vegetables are just about our best source of potassium. We are sure that one reason why health conscious drinkers of vegetable juices report such excellent results is the large amount of potassium they get in juice made of greens.

Note, too, the large amounts of vitamin A that are available from greens. The more than 15,000 units of this important vitamin in dandelion greens must be the reason our ancestors relied on these for an early spring tonic. How people who had not tasted anything green or fresh all winter must have relished the delicious, slightly bitter tang of these crisp greens! They are just as good to eat and just as good for you today. And free for the picking! Eat them when they are young and tender before the flowers form.

Eat Certain Greens in Moderation

We have one caution about spinach and leaves of the same plant family, like turnip greens and beet greens. They contain considerable amounts of oxalic acid which is destructive of calcium. The acid forms certain compounds with calcium which make it unavailable to the body. So one should not eat these greens daily, to the exclusion of other greens. They are an excellent addition to the diet occasionally, or mixed with other greens.

Finally, the best thing about salad greens is that they are raw, they taste good raw and they are good for you raw. We all know that raw foods are good for us, but we tend to avoid them and eat instead prepared, processed foods that are easier to serve and to eat. Raw foods are natural, straight from the earth, unharmed by any processing at all. Eat more of them!

CHAPTER 153

Soybeans—The Wonder Food

Imagine a food, grown easily on most soils and in most climates, which contains more first class protein than meat, will keep for years without spoiling, is easily and quickly prepared and can be made into almost any kind of a dish for any course of a meal. Imagine such a food (inexpensive, too) endowed with large amounts of calcium, iron and other important minerals as well as the precious B vitamins and vitamin E. Finally imagine a food rich in unspoiled unsaturated fatty acids which keep cholesterol in its place, so that it will not be found in harmful deposits in gall bladder, kidneys and blood vessels.

Such a food is the soybean—used for thousands of years as a staple in the diet of Far Eastern countries where food is so much less plentiful that not a mouthful can be wasted. We Americans know about soy sauce which appears on the table of every Chinese restaurant. But what do we know about the other ways in which this wonder food can be prepared?

During World War II when protein foods were rationed, a determined effort was made to interest American housewives in eating soybeans. Dr. Clive M. McCay of the Department of Animal Nutrition at Cornell University took on the job of popularizing the soybean. In laboratories and cafeterias at Cornell, Dr. McCay and his associates sprouted soybeans, then experimented with methods of preserving, cooking and serving them.

In addition to the beans themselves, there are many excellent products made from them. Soybean flour is a highly nutritious food, rich in complete proteins, vitamins and minerals. It enriches any food to which it is added. It cannot be used for baking as wheat flour is because it lacks the gluten which is involved in the process of raising wheat bread. But it can be added to any recipe in which flour is used. It can successfully replace up to 10-12 per cent of wheat flour in recipes. McLester in his book, *Nutrition and Diet in Health and Disease* (Saunders), states that it is advisable to use soy flour in smaller amounts in many different dishes, rather than using it in large amounts in just a few products.

We assume the reason for this is that the complete protein contained in the soy flour is valuable when eaten with any other food which contains incomplete protein—so it should be eaten with as many different foods as possible. To be more specific—soybeans contain all of the essential amino acids or forms of protein, in good proportions. So do meat, eggs, fish and other animal proteins. Vegetables, fruits and cereals are likely to be lacking or deficient in one or more of these amino acids. The body needs all of the essential amino acids in order to use any of them to best advantage. So it is best to eat foods that contain all of them at the same time you eat foods that are lacking in one or several. This is the most economical way to eat proteins. And you cannot plan on eating incomplete proteins at one meal, hoping that eating a complete protein at the next meal will make up the deficiency. It doesn't work that way.

Soybeans then are one of the few non-animal proteins which are complete—that is, contain all of the essential amino acids in good proportion. For this reason they can take the place of meat, eggs, fish or milk in the diet.

There are several other things to be considered about protein foods, however. One of these is the "availability" of the protein and minerals in the food. How much of the protein of soybeans is utilized well by the body? The average digestibility of protein in cooked whole soybeans, cooked soybean flour and soybean milk is 90.5 per cent, 94 per cent and 89.6 per cent respectively. These are good percentages.

According to *Bridges' Dietetics for the Clinician* (Lea and Febiger), milk, meat and eggs provide protein which is 98 per cent digestible. Vegetables contain less available proteins than other foods. Only about 80 per cent of the protein in fruits is digestible. The percentage for whole wheat bread is 82, for rye bread only about 65.

How Nutritious Are Soybeans?

What is the record of soybeans so far as other nutrients are concerned? Here are some of the figures:

(½ cup or about 100 grams)

	Soybeans	Sprouted Soybeans
Calories	331	46
Protein	34.9%	6.2%
Fat (vegetable fat) good food for you	18.1%	1.4%
Carbohydrate	34.8%	5.3%
Calcium	227 mg.	48 mg.
Phosphorus	586 mg.	67 mg.
Iron	8 mg.	1 mg.
Potassium	1900 mg.	
Sodium	4 mg.	
Vitamin A	110 International Units	
Vitamin C	trace	13 mg.
B Vitamins		
Thiamin	1.07 mg.	.23 mg.
Riboflavin	.31 mg.	.20 mg.
Niacin	2.3 mg.	.8 mg.
Choline	300-340 mg.	
Pantothenic acid	1800 mcg.	
Vitamin K	190 mcg.	
Mixed tocopherols	140 mg.	
(Vitamin E included in this)		

To interpret a little. Soybeans are richer in potassium than any other food except brewer's yeast which, of course, is eaten in much smaller quantities. They contain more pantothenic acid than any other food except egg yolk, brewer's yeast, liver, rice bran and wheat bran. The iron in soybeans is 96 per cent "available"—that is, digestible and used by the body. This compares favorably with many foods whose iron content, although extremely higher, is not well assimilated by the body.

The oil in soybeans is 51.5 per cent linoleic acid—the fatty acid which at present is believed to be the most effective of all in emulsifying cholesterol in the blood so that it does not form unhealthful deposits. The calcium in soybean milk has been tested and compared to the calcium in cow's milk. It has been found that the response is about the same to each, indicating that the calcium of soybeans is about as well digested as is that of milk.

Soybean sprouts (a good and inexpensive source of vitamin C) can be made at home with little trouble. They can be cooked in a few minutes and used as a dish by themselves or added to salads or other dishes. They contain practically no starch. And, as the beans sprout, their content of vitamin C is increased. They provide a very good source of vitamin C, especially for people who, for one reason or another, lack fresh foods in their diets.

Sprouting Beans for Vitamin C

Here is a good method for sprouting soybeans, as developed at Cornell.

1. Handpick the beans thoroughly, and discard everything except clean, whole beans. 2. Wash the beans and place them in a suitable container for sprouting, such as a one or two-quart glass fruit jar. The bean sprouts increase to about 6 times their original volume. 3. Cover the seeds with at least 4 times their volume of lukewarm water and let them stand for a few hours, or at most, overnight, until they are swollen. 4. Pour off this water, and wash or rinse the swollen beans thoroughly, then pour off the last wash water. 5. Cover the top of the jar with a piece of cheesecloth or other thin cloth, and tie it on securely.

6. Invert the jar and place it in a cupboard or dark place, in a slightly tilted position, so that the excess water can drain away. 7. At least 3 times a day, or better, every 4 hours, place the jar under the water tap or pour on plenty of cool water, thus thoroughly and carefully washing the swelling and sprouting seeds, so that bacteria or molds which may have developed are carried away. The better the washing, the better the sprouts. After washing, place the jar back in its slanting position. The sprouts will be fully grown in 4 to 6 days when they are around 1½ to 2 inches in length. They should be taken out of the vessel before rootlets appear. After the sprouts are washed to free them from loose hulls or seed coats and excess water, they are ready to be used in cooking, stored in the refrigerator or blanched for two minutes and placed in the deep freeze.

It is possible, of course, to eat soybeans without sprouting them. The fresh green beans are cooked much as other fresh beans are cooked. They have a characteristic taste to which your family might need to become accustomed. So, for the first few times you serve them, you should probably make special efforts to serve them attractively in some way you are sure your family will like. Dried soybeans which can be stored just as navy beans are, require a long soaking period and a quite long cooking time. They can be prepared just the way other dried beans are.

Here's one thing to remember about soybeans. They do not have many of the characteristics other beans have. They are not starchy, so you should not serve them in place of potatoes. Serve them in place of meat or eggs. They are a protein food. Then, too, they do not ever produce flatulence as other beans sometimes do.

Soybeans Are Economical

What about cost? Sold in bulk, soybean flour costs approximately 10 cents a pound. It is between 40 and 50 per cent protein. So the actual protein in soy flour costs about 20 cents a pound. In comparison, beefsteak is 20 per cent protein and costs 80 to 90 cents a pound. So the protein of beefsteak costs about $4.50 a pound. Speaking in terms of protein in a crop, soybeans yield more protein per acre than any other crop. We find in *Standard Values in Nutrition and Metabolism* (Saunders) the statement that one acre of soybeans will provide the full official requirement of protein for one person for 2,224 days. The crop closest to this in protein yield is peanuts. One acre of peanuts will provide 1,785 days of minimum protein requirement.

The best—in fact, the only book we know of on the subject of soybeans is one by Philip S. Chen, Ph.D., Professor of Chemistry at Atlantic Union College. It is called *Soybeans for Health, Longevity and Economy,* and is published by The Chemical Elements.

We want to quote from Dr. Chen's chapter entitled "Soybeans and Disease," for he adds considerably to our knowledge about cholesterol deposits and one way to overcome them—with soybean fats (lecithin). "This is clearly indicated in the work of Pottenger, Jr. and Krohn as published in the *American Journal of Digestive Diseases,* April 1952. Contrary to common medical practice of giving the patient a low-fat diet to relieve hypercholesterolemia (high content of cholesterol in the blood) these doctors gave their patients the opposite diet—one high in fat and cholesterol— plus soybean phospholipids, which are used in the food industry under the name of lecithin.

"One hundred and twenty-two patients were put on a high-fat regimen that included internal organs of raw liver and raw brains—foods that are rich in cholesterol. Ninety-nine of the patients took a teaspoon of soybean phospholipids (lecithin) with each meal. The remaining 23 served as controls. (That is, they did *not* take the soybean preparation so that the doctors could observe what happened to them.)

"The blood cholesterol showed a marked decrease in 79 per cent of the patients who took the lecithin, but not in the patients who did not take lecithin." This indicates, says Dr. Chen, that it may be possible to correct the condition of too much cholesterol in the blood with soybean lecithin. Heart disease and hardening of the arteries would also be affected by such an improvement.

One final note—and an interesting one—on soybean lecithin appears in

[539]

the *Journal of the American Medical Association* for December 29, 1951. An M.D. from Connecticut writes to the editor that a patient of his, aged 65, declares he has noticed a definite rejuvenation of his sex life as a result of taking soy lecithin. The doctor wanted to know whether there might be any harmful effects from taking lecithin over a long period of time. The editor answered him that there is no evidence that soy lecithin could have any such effect on sex life. And he doesn't know about possible harmful effects of taking it. Of course, in the years since this article appeared, many folks have taken lecithin in large quantities and used it in cooking, with nothing but excellent results.

Soybean Milk for Infants

Soybean milk has been used successfully as a substitute for cow's milk in the feeding of children who are allergic to cow's milk. We will describe only one of the many articles available on this subject. Dr. Sidney Kane of Philadelphia treated with a liquid soy milk 102 infants who had allergic disorders traceable to cow's milk. Their ages ranged from 1 week to 9 months. Symptoms were: eczema, stomach disorders, irritability, asthma and chronic nasal discharge. Of the 76 infants with eczema, 75 improved markedly. Other symptoms present in 62 of the children were alleviated in 53. The information comes from *Medical Science*, January 10, 1957.

Many readers who do not drink milk or give milk to their children have written us about the use of soybean milk. Dr. Chen devotes a chapter to this subject. He describes how it is made, how it can be used. He also gives a chart comparing it with cow's milk, which shows that, although soy milk is far richer in iron, thiamin and niacin, its calcium and phosphorus content does not equal that of cow's milk.

	Soy Milk	Cow's Milk
Protein	3.4%	3.5%
Fat	1.5%	3.9%
Carbohydrates	2.1%	4.9%
Calcium	21 mg.	118 mg.
Phosphorus	47 mg.	93 mg.
Iron	.7 mg.	.1 mg.
Thiamin	.09 mg.	.04 mg.
Riboflavin	.04 mg.	.17 mg.
Niacin	.3 mg.	.1 mg.

It would seem, then, that readers wishing to replace cow's milk with soy milk should certainly enrich the soy milk with bone meal, for calcium and phosphorus. We are also a bit concerned with the small amount of riboflavin in soy milk. Since this is an important B vitamin, it would be best to add brewer's yeast (high in riboflavin) to the soy milk.

We cannot recommend too highly Dr. Chen's book, for it treats the subject completely and well, giving in an appendix names and addresses of sources of soybean products. We have one reservation about the book, however—the recipe section. While the recipes are the best we have ever seen for soybean products, we must warn our readers against the pitfalls—

[540]

sugar, salt, baking powder, margarine, canned foods, etc. We hope that readers using these recipes will substitute ingredients. Honey can always be used in place of sugar—use a smaller amount of honey. Salt should be omitted. Yeast can always substitute for baking powder (remember to let the yeast bread rise before baking), salad oils can substitute for margarine and fresh foods for canned ones.

CHAPTER 154

Soya Milk and Soya Curds

By Dr. W. Kring, Dusseldorf

In the country where soybeans are most widely produced, East Asia, many different kinds of foods made from soybeans are eaten, few of them well known to us. The simplest method of cooking soybeans, which is like the way we cook our customary field and garden beans, is of little importance among the East Asians, since, with this kind of cooking, results are not achieved from the point of view of flavor.

Fresh Soya Milk for Every Household

Every day in East Africa fresh soya milk is produced in great quantity, from which is also made a white cheese known as "tofu." Thousands of small factories in China and Japan are kept busy with this manufacturing process, the products of which are then sold on the street to the consumer.

The production of soya milk in the home and in the diet kitchen calls for, by way of example, 100 grams (about ¼ pound) of the best, undamaged yellow soybeans. Cover them with water to soak for 8 hours or so, or overnight. They swell, from this soaking, to about 3 times their original weight. After thorough washing, whereby a portion of the membranous skin is washed away, the beans are covered with ¾ liter (about ¾ quart) of water and then ground, wet.

This operation is today made very easy and practical by the use of a mixer or blender, which very rapidly turns the soybeans and water into a milky solution. The milk with the insoluble portions of soybeans is then put into a linen bag and pressed out. The remaining small portion of residue is used by the economical Chinese housewife as an addition to baked goods, puddings and so forth.

The soya milk is now cooked in a pot from 5 to 10 minutes. The pot should be quite large, so that the lecithin in the milk will foam to the top. A harder but better way is to do the cooking before straining the soya milk, as this results in more of the nutrient value of the milk being present in the final product.

Cow's milk is hardly known in China, soya milk being widely used there for the nourishment of children. In Western lands, soya milk is used for feeding children who cannot tolerate cow's milk protein or lactose, which is milk sugar. Nutrition-wise, the soya milk is very much like cow's milk. In formulas for infants, carbohydrate in some form is usually added (as it is in America).

Milk foods of many different sorts can be made from soya milk, adding such things as malt, cocoa, etc. (We caution against the use of cocoa, rich in oxalic acid and, of course, requiring the use of sugar to sweeten it. Try carob flour instead.)

Acidophilic Soya Milk—Soya Curds

With the milk-souring bacteria removed, the soya milk yields a buttermilk product with the characteristic taste which is very pleasant once you are used to it. So far as acidophilus milk is concerned, we are told that this kind of milk product made from soya milk will result in the formation and maintenance of healthy intestinal bacteria, just as the cow's milk product does.

Making Soya Cheese or Tofu

The protein materials can be separated from the rest of the soya milk to form a substance similar to curds or cheese. To the heated soya milk, add a precipitating substance (vinegar is probably the most convenient and practical).

(At this point we wish to depart from our German translation and use directions from an American book which will be much simpler for our readers to follow.) "Complete precipitation is indicated by the change of the milk into a yellowish clear liquid and the separation of the solid precipitate. The precipitate should be allowed to stand a few minutes to enable the small particles to flocculate into a large mass of curd, which gradually sinks to the bottom of the container. The water which accumulates on the top is partly drawn off and thrown away. The curd that remains is transferred into a cheesecloth placed in a colander or strainer to drain off excess water."*

From ¼ pound of soya beans, one can make about ½ pound of curd or "tofu."

Tofu is used in China as an addition to many dishes, soups and vegetables, which thereby gain considerably in nutritional content. We Westerners add to it wholesome appetizers like cut leeks, tomatoes or beets, and, on occasion, some salad oil, making a wonderful salad.

-----

*These directions come from Soybeans for Health, Longevity and Economy, by Philip S. Chen, Ph.D., of Atlantic Union College, South Lancaster, Massachusetts.

Reprinted with permission from the German publication, Ernährungs-Unaschau.

CHAPTER 155

Spinach

Rich in iron, calcium, chlorophyll, vitamin A and vitamin C, spinach is one of those controversial foods that everybody likes to debate about. For a long time we believed that spinach was the answer to a lot of problems. It is rich in iron—so we fed it to the kids to keep their cheeks pink and their legs strong.

How did we feed it to the kids? We soaked it all afternoon in a large pan of water, then threw the water away and put the spinach through dozens of careful washings to remove sand. Then we boiled it in large quantities of water. After the spinach had boiled down to a soggy, slimy mass, we drained off all the water and then began to fuss with sauces and condiments to hide the taste and the appearance, for it was obvious that nobody in his right mind could ever be persuaded to eat a food that looked like this overcooked spinach.

During the soaking and boiling processes we lost most of the food value of the spinach, for the vitamins and minerals departed into the water. What was left was just soggy foliage. But we stuffed it into the kids. And Popeye with his can of spinach did his best to popularize it. But we all failed, for almost everybody agreed that if they had to eat spinach to stay healthy, they'd rather be sick.

Then the laboratory technicians made an interesting discovery about spinach. It contains relatively large amounts of oxalic acid, as do all the leafy vegetables of the same family—beet greens, swiss chard and so forth. The oxalic acid combines with the calcium in the spinach during the digestive process and forms oxalates which are not digested. So the calcium in spinach is generally not to be depended on, for it is probably in the form of an oxalate which will do you no good so far as your calcium supply is concerned. In fact, the oxalic acid in the spinach may well combine with other calcium in your digestive system and take it along, so that it, too, does you no good. So then the scientific magazines were buzzing with the tidings—don't eat spinach. It will rob you of calcium.

The real story on spinach seems to boil down to this: don't rely on spinach for calcium and don't eat spinach to the exclusion of other green vegetables. The fact that you lose a little calcium when you eat it doesn't detract from the fact that all the other minerals and vitamins are still there. If, however, you happen to have a spinach farm and you can't sell the spinach, don't decide you'll eat it all up yourself just to save it, for then you might come to grief.

Somewhere we met with the theory that oxalic acid in spinach is troublesome only if the spinach is cooked. If you eat it raw, this theory went, no calcium is lost and you get the full benefit of all the other minerals and vitamins. We don't know if the theory is scientifically sound or whether it's been tested in a laboratory. But it's an attractive theory, for why indeed should we spoil a fine vegetable like spinach by cooking it, when it's so tender, crisp and tasty eaten raw! Eat raw spinach in salads. If you must cook spinach, don't soak it. Wash it hastily as possible as soon as you bring it in from the garden or the market. Keep it in the refrigerator tightly enclosed in your vegetable container. If you are going to cook it, use the least possible water, or no water at all. Adelle Davis in her excellent cookbook, *Let's Cook It Right* (Harcourt Brace and Company), advises cooking leafy vegetables only in their own juices, after you have carefully whirled them in a cloth bag to remove all water. They must be stirred constantly until the juices of the vegetables change to steam, then you can cover them and let them steam for a short time.

The vitamins and minerals in about 4 ounces of raw spinach or 1 cup of cooked spinach are listed below:

	Raw Spinach	*Cooked Spinach*
Calcium	81 milligrams	124 milligrams
Phosphorus	55 milligrams	33 milligrams
Iron	3 milligrams	2 milligrams
Potassium	780 milligrams	
Copper	.12 milligrams	.26 milligrams
Vitamin A	9420 International Units	11,780 International Units
Vitamin B		
Thiamin	.11 milligrams	.08 milligrams
Riboflavin	.20 milligrams	.20 milligrams
Niacin	.6 milligrams	.6 milligrams
Pyridoxine	83 micrograms	
Pantothenic acid	120-180 micrograms	
Biotin	6.9 micrograms	
Vitamin C	59 milligrams	30 milligrams

(In cases where the vitamin or mineral content of the cooked spinach is greater, this means only that the spinach is concentrated by cooking. A cup of cooked spinach represents a lot of raw spinach.)

CHAPTER 156

Strawberries

Nature has a wise way of providing her creatures, both animal and human, with the food elements they need specifically at any given season. Thus rose hips ripen in the fall—extravagantly rich in vitamin C which, Mother Nature knows, her creatures will need in abundance throughout the winter. And one of the first foods of the early spring is the strawberry, also rich in vitamin C. Strawberries are apparently native to this country, for they were here when the first settlers came—wild strawberries, of course. But we defy anyone to produce a cultivated strawberry that matches in flavor the wild ones you pick after a day of hot sunlight.

Size has little to do with the taste of strawberries, small varieties being just as delicious as large ones. They should be bright red when you eat them, with no spots of white. After they are picked, they spoil much more rapidly than other fruits, so they should be eaten or frozen as soon as possible. If you leave the caps on, not so much vitamin C is lost in storage. But once the caps are removed or the strawberries are sliced, vitamin C oozes away at a wasteful rate. If you cannot eat your berries immediately after they are picked or bought, put them unwashed and unhulled into the refrigerator and keep them there until just before eating time. Wash them as rapidly as possible, so that their temperature will not rise, cap them speedily and serve at once. If you are planning to freeze or can the berries, follow the same procedure of chilling them if you cannot go ahead with your plans at once.

Why Cook Them?

It seems disgraceful even to speak of cooking such a delicacy as the strawberry, for there seems to be not the slightest excuse for it. Cooking, of course, destroys a large amount of the vitamin C of any fruit or vegetable. But jam companies still make strawberry jam and preserves, with, we might add, artificial coloring and probably artificial flavoring as well. If you have access to quantities of strawberries, for your own health's sake, freeze them, even if it means renting space in a locker or a neighbor's freezer. You can freeze them just as they are, or a little honey thinned with water can be added. They are one of the best food products for freezing and they retain all their vitamin C content through many months of frozen storage.

Wild strawberries are free for the picking in almost any meadow or pasture near where you live. And we can't imagine any pleasanter way of spending a fragrant sunny June afternoon than to have a wild-strawberry-picking party. True, they are small and it takes a lot of time to fill a basket. But we imagine (although we have not been able to find scientific evidence

of this) that they must contain far more vitamin C than cultivated strawberries. And their flavor is so exotic and delicate that the French have made
a business of providing wild strawberries (*frias de bois,* they call them)
to gourmet restaurants and food stores in New York. They are flown from
Paris every day during the season and sell for fabulous prices. Now how
can you afford to ignore such delicacies which may be growing practically
in your back yard? If you live in the city, ask your country friends if you
may visit them during the season and pick their wild strawberries.

Here are the vitamins and minerals available from a half cupful of
fresh or frozen strawberries:

Calcium	41	milligrams
Phosphorus	27	milligrams
Iron	.8	milligrams
	(almost as much as raisins)	
Copper	.02	milligrams
Vitamin A	60	International Units
Vitamin B		
Thiamin	.03	milligrams
Riboflavin	.07	milligrams
Niacin	.2	milligrams
Pyridoxine	44	micrograms
Pantothenic acid	260	micrograms
Biotin	4	micrograms
Vitamin C	50 to 90	milligrams
	(the average orange contains about 50)	

CHAPTER 157

Tomatoes

A rosy, ripe, fragrant tomato fresh from the vine on a hot summer
day—what could be more refreshing, or, for that matter, what could be
more packed with healthful vitamins and minerals? We can buy tomatoes
the year 'round these days, but there is a big difference between the pale,
tasteless soggy variety we buy in winter and spring, and the luscious crisp
beauty we picked from the vine in the sentence above! And, as you might
suspect, winter tomatoes and ones grown in hothouses just don't contain
the same food value as summer tomatoes.

Tomatoes picked when they are green, then shipped and ripened on
the way are quite inferior in vitamin content to those that are picked ripe

from the vine. To attain the maximum vitamin content, the tomatoes should be ripened in bright sunlight and not picked until they are completely ripe. Ethylene gas is often used to ripen commercially-grown tomatoes, picked green. This gas speeds up the production of the bright red tomato color.

Preserving Vitamin C

The amount of vitamin A in a tomato differs with the variety and also with the growing method, weather, kind of soil and so forth. Tomatoes may be stored for 10 to 14 days at a temperature of 60-90 degrees Fahrenheit without spoiling, if they are picked when they are mature in size but green in color. However, the vitamin C content is much greater when they are ripened on the vine in full sunlight. Apparently the sun itself increases this vitamin C content. So it is best to harvest tomatoes just after several days of bright sunshine, if possible. Also it is best to stake tomatoes, so that the vines are kept off the ground. Staked tomatoes contain more vitamin C than those which have been allowed to tumble on the ground.

In commercial canning of tomatoes, when vacuum methods are used, very little vitamin C is lost, for the cans or bottles are sealed before they are heated, so no vitamin C can escape. When you can tomatoes or tomato juice at home, you are bound to lose much vitamin content in the steam from your canning kettles. So, actually commercially canned tomatoes generally contain more vitamins than home-canned ones. However, there are other things than vitamins to consider, too. Tomatoes you buy in a can have been fertilized and insecticized with all kinds of chemicals. Your own home-grown ones have been grown organically. In addition, some chemicals are added by commercial firms in the canning process. Calcium chloride may be added to firm the tomatoes, sodium chloride will surely be added and probably quite a few other chemicals have been used in the contents of any can of tomatoes you buy.

If you have a freezer and want to preserve garden tomatoes for winter eating with the very least possible loss of vitamins, we'd suggest freezing them or juicing them and freezing the juice.

One of the finest qualities of the tomato is its versatility. Cooked or raw, juiced or whole, used alone or in any of a myriad of recipes, the tomato pays its way in health, for it is richly endowed with the food elements you need.

Here are the vitamins and minerals in one small tomato:

Vitamin A	1000	International Units
Vitamin B		
Thiamin	75	micrograms
Riboflavin	60	micrograms
Niacin	.6	milligrams
Pyridoxine	60	micrograms
Pantothenic acid	110	micrograms
Biotin	4	micrograms
Inositol	46	milligrams
Folic acid	12-14	micrograms

Vitamin C	13-30	milligrams
Calcium	11	milligrams
Phosphorus	27	milligrams
Iron	.6	milligrams
Copper	.06	milligrams
Sodium	3	milligrams
Cobalt	10	micrograms
Fluorine	3-5	micrograms

CHAPTER 158

Additional Information
on Vegetables

Cabbage versus Fallout

Congratulations are in order for the lowly cabbage. It may turn out to be the means of our salvation in the atomic age. A general of the Army Quartermaster Corps is quoted in the *New York Times* (May 14, 1958) as saying, ". . . . We are right now in the midst of some exciting animal experiments in which we have found that the feeding of cabbage and broccoli may be the means of doubling the capacity of man to withstand rays caused by nuclear fall-out."

We wonder if it has occurred to the Quartermaster Corps to analyze the cabbage or broccoli to find out what property in them makes animals more tolerant of the fall-out?

Could it be vitamin C or vitamin A, or some mineral we could get more of? Whatever it is, why wait for fall-out? We're being hit by radioactive rays every day, and we should be taking whatever protection we can get as soon as possible. If your cabbage and broccoli consumption is down, do what you can to remedy it—they're both excellent foods—and supplement them with daily doses of vitamins C and A.

Cabbage Juice for Digestive Disorders

Harland N. Hannon, M.D., wrote fruitlessly to the *American Medical Association Journal* and his letter was printed in the April 6, 1957, edition. Dr. Hannon wrote to say that several of his patients who were suffering from constant digestive complaints and had tried every medical approach to the problem, from antacids to checkups at famous clinics, with no results, were completely relieved when they began drinking raw cabbage juice. He was convinced that the cures had not been psychological and that they had been permanent. Further, the writer judged the patients to be intelligent and sensible people who tried the cabbage juice as a last resort, without much hope for results. This attitude ruled out a psychosomatic cure. Could the *Journal* offer any explanation?

There are two replies to the letter from consultants chosen by the editors. Both of them are tolerant and patronizing. They are glad to hear about the effectiveness of cabbage juice, they say, but, of course, it can't be anything of consequence to medicine in general. Why not, we want to know? Why not initiate a comprehensive investigation of cabbage juice as related to the treatment of digestive disturbance? Such projects have been embarked upon with a good deal less evidence to back them up. Fresh cabbage is a healthful food with many known nutrients and probably many undiscovered ones. Can there be something in cabbage juice that fills a need in the nutrition of a person with digestive difficulties? We think Science should take the time to find out. Maybe a simple natural food like cabbage has the ingredient that researchers have been unable to discover or duplicate in the many drug preparations they turn out. Why not give Nature credit for knowing a thing or two about what our bodies need?

Cabbage Concentrate Heals Peptic Ulcers

A cabbage-juice concentrate can be used to heal peptic ulcers, Dr. Garnett Cheney of the Stanford School of Medicine reported to the National Gastroenterological Association meeting in Los Angeles.

Thus, instead of drinking a quart of cabbage juice daily, the 100 ulcer patients he treated swallowed only about 3 tablespoons of the concentrate. Yet their pain vanished within 5 days, and ulcer craters in most cases healed in an average of 13 to 14 days, about the same time as required when treatment was with the cabbage juice.

Average healing time for ulcer patients under the standard treatment of bland diet and drugs is close to 50 days.

Using cabbage-juice concentrate, patients were allowed to eat whatever cooked foods they pleased. The concentrate has now been completely dehydrated and put into capsules by Merck and Company, and patients are now being tested with such capsules.

Cabbage juice and the concentrates contain large amounts of an unidentified diet factor called vitamin U, which is believed to fortify the digestive tract against the onslaught of pepsin. Pepsin is a digestive enzyme contained in the stomach juices that can bore into tissues and cause ulcers.

Science News Letter, October 24, 1953

Vitamin C and Tomatoes

Tomatoes supported on poles are a better source of vitamin C than unsupported ones. The vitamin C content of tomatoes has been thoroughly studied by two research workers, A. P. Brown and F. Moser, who report their findings in *Food Research*. Five different experimental plots of tomatoes over a period of 3 seasons were found to be a good source.

Two interesting possibilities were uncovered by the study, although no conclusive proof was found. First, there seemed to be an increase in the vitamin C content of the tomatoes as their growing season advanced. Second, there seemed to be a relationship between the vitamin C content and the size of the tomato—large tomatoes yielding less vitamin C per ounce of weight than small ones.

A gardening hint was supplied by the study which showed that the vitamin C of tomatoes from vines supported by poles was significantly greater than that of unsupported vines. Also, tomatoes grown in a greenhouse were found to contain only one-half the vitamin C value of those grown out of doors.

Journal of Living

BOOK TWO

The Complete Book of

FOOD and NUTRITION

SECTION 13.

Natural and Organic Foods

The terms "organically-grown" and "natural" when accurately applied in description of foods and crops, mean specifically that these have been raised on soil fertilized by the organic methods only and prepared for the consumer without being chemically processed, canned or frozen. (The original fruit or vegetable reaches the eater intact without being stripped of its valuable nutrients by modern processing and refining procedures.) They particularly indicate that no chemical fertilizers, conditioners, insecticides or any such type of spray, pesticide or preservative has been used at any time in the growing or preparation of these products. A soil receiving the full organic treatment is not deficient in any element. Any deficiencies that do occur are corrected by natural fertilizers.

CHAPTER 159

The Health Benefits of Organically Grown Foods

We have a letter from a reader who says, "All of us know that many organically raised products are good for us . . . but how about finding out if there are enough data anywhere in existence coming from legitimate formal professional men, and I am speaking both of medical doctors and scientists, to indicate beyond argument and without conditions that we have reached a stage where we can definitely say and advance conclusive proof that we are making progress in this field and that persons whose diet consists largely of whole, fresh natural foods, organically grown, are in better health than persons whose diets are not."

Before we give you the data we have on this subject, we ask you to consider for a moment the difficulties you encounter when you set out to prove, by experiment, that eating a certain kind of food—organically raised or any other kind—will produce certain results. You might be able to work it out convincingly with rats in a laboratory, but then you'd meet with the objections of people who say that we human beings are not laboratory rats and that the fearful and troubled world we live in can certainly not be compared to the antiseptic calm of a laboratory.

So let's say you start with people. Where are you going to find a group of people to carry on such an experiment—over a period of several generations, of course, for that is what you need, with another group of people willing to act as "controls," that is, willing to live exactly as the first group lives, except that this second group will eat food that has not been organically grown!

Do you see what difficulties immediately arise? People move to other locations; they get married to people whose ideas on diet are quite different; they go on vacations where they eat in hotels; their children go away to school and eat what's served there. How could you possibly keep such an experiment going for long enough to mean anything and observe the "scientific" regulations that absolute scientific accuracy demand? You couldn't, obviously.

All right, you'll say, what about studying a country where organic gardening has been practiced for generations and "civilization" has not penetrated? The Hunzas, people living high in the Himalayas, were studied and written about by Sir William McCarrison, one of the greatest nutritionists of all times. He found them to be practically free from degenerative disease as we know it—cancer, heart trouble, appendicitis, colitis and so forth.

Yet a recent book about Hunza relates the devastating diseases found there several years ago. From correspondence with the ruler of Hunza, a great friend of his, Editor Rodale finds that the Hunzukuts no longer live in their isolated paradise. Foods from the "outside" are common there by now; aluminum cooking utensils are used; "civilization" has come to the country; the inhabitants travel to other lands; they bring back new ideas on food and agriculture. So Hunza can no longer be studied as the proving ground for the organic method.

The Peckham Experiment

An excellent experiment on human health which could have meant much to the organic movement in terms of actual facts and figures on the healthfulness of eating organically grown food was the experiment at Pioneer Health Centre, Peckham, England. In this remarkable undertaking, 875 families—about 3000 individuals—gathered together to help in a study of health. Not disease, mark you, but health. Their doctors examined patients to discover not just what diseases they had, but also what degree of health they had, what minor and seemingly unimportant ailments bothered them and how much right living could do to correct these ailments.

In the initial examination it was found that out of every 10 supposedly healthy and uncomplaining persons, 7 had not even the negative attributes of health—that is, freedom from diagnosable disorder. Still less had the positive attributes—vitality, initiative and a competence and willingness to live. The list of diseases found among the first 500 families examined ranged all the way from one case of claustrophobia and 86 cases of overweight to 284 cases of decayed teeth and 983 cases of iron deficiency.

One of the most important considerations of the directors of Peckham was diet. They decided early in the history of the Centre that they could not depend on the excellence of the milk, meat, fruit, vegetables and so forth purchased at the local market. They must secure as much as possible of their food organically grown, or grow it themselves.

Research at Peckham was disrupted by the war; the Centre was closed and the buildings vacated. After the war it was re-established. Many of the original families returned and hundreds of other families clamored to join. However, the Centre was forced to close because of lack of financial support. Apparently none of the grants or public funds available for scientific projects could go to Peckham because such funds are earmarked for studies of disease and this was a study of health!

The story of this experiment is available, incidentally, in a book called *Biologists in Search of Material,* published by Faber and Faber, London.

Organic Gardening Abroad

Some classic examples of better health through organic gardening are given by Sir Albert Howard in his writings. In his book, *The Soil and Health* (published by the Devin-Adair Company), one chapter is entitled "Soil

Fertility and Human Health." In it he tells of the experience of the Chief Health Officer of Singapore who conducted an experiment in his department, giving out small allotments of land to all employees who would farm them according to organic principles using compost and who would guarantee to use all the produce for their own families.

"At the end of the first year," this officer wrote to Sir Albert, "it was obvious that the most potent stimulus to this endeavour was the surprising improvement in stamina and health acquired by those taking part in this cultivation. Debility and sickness had been swept away and my men were capable of, and gladly responded to the heavier work demanded by the stress of war." Unfortunately war put a stop to the experiment after the first year.

A second example quoted by Sir Albert involves a copper mine in Northern Rhodesia—an area formerly so devastated by tropical diseases that it was uninhabited. Through a program of organic gardening, the personnel who were brought in to mine copper were kept at a high degree of health. "The positive health of these people is based on food . . . They have beaten back disease and turned that part of Northern Rhodesia into what is a health resort."

Reference is made, too, to Prince Edward Island in the Gulf of St. Lawrence which, says Sir Albert, is a small community, cut off from the rest of the world. "There we have a high standard of health, an extraordinarily vigorous, active population and no fall whatever in the birth rate. It is the only social organization composed of western Europeans which has not shown in the past 50 years a really sharp fall in the birth rate." Few chemicals are used in farming. The land is kept fertile by composting with "muck" and seaweed.

A third example is provided by St. Martin's School, Sidmouth, England, where for many years the fruits and vegetables were raised from fertile soil. Says the headmaster in a letter to Sir Albert: "Our exceptional health record has been chiefly due to the school menu. I firmly believe that this would have proved impossible had not the soil been maintained in a superlative state of fertility by means of compost beds and farmyard manure. Epidemics were unknown during the last 15 years. We had many lads who came to us as weaklings and left hearty and robust."

Another example is St. Columba's College, Rathfarnham, near Dublin, Ireland, where the boys who attend the college grow their food on about 50 acres, by means of compost made on the spot from animal and vegetable residues. Superlative health has resulted. A fifth example is the Co-operative Wholesale Society's bacon factory at Winsford in Cheshire. The wasteland around the factory was made into productive land by the use of compost; vegetables grown were used in meals at the factory canteen. "Already the health, efficiency and well-being of the labour force has markedly improved," says Sir Albert. "The output of work has increased; absenteeism has been notably reduced."

In a feeding experiment at Mt. Albert Grammar School in Auckland, New Zealand, garden produce grown by organic methods and fed to the students resulted in great improvement in health: a marked decline in colds and influenza, excellent physical growth and stamina, fewer accidents, resistance to fractures and sprains; constipation and stomach upsets are rare; skins are healthy and clear; dental conditions are greatly improved.

Not long ago Editor Rodale learned about the health and diet ideas being put into dynamic operation at Fairleigh-Dickinson College in New Jersey. Many of his own ideas are being followed. And now the college has purchased a farm where they plan to raise food organically for the students' meals. We should have some revealing evidence within a few years from Fairleigh-Dickinson.

The Haughley Experiment

ORGANIC GARDENING AND FARMING reported in the July, 1957, issue on the Haughley Experiment made by the Soil Association in England. Here 3 separate farms have been farmed for 16 years to test organic methods. One of the farms is operated organically. The other two serve as controls. Chemicals are used on these. Crop yields on the organic farm have been up to or greater than yields on the other farms. Soil tests at the organic farm show that even though the yields are greater, the fertility of the soil is actually increasing, while on the other farms it is decreasing. Tests also show that the organically-raised produce contains more minerals. Vitamin analyses have not shown significant variations, but it appears that the animals on the organic farm are reacting better than those on the other farms. Cows produce more milk and the milk has a higher protein content. You can get full information about the experiment from The Soil Association, Ltd., New Bells Farm, Haughley-Stowmarket, Suffolk, England.

We think you can use facts like these to convince skeptics of the advantage of organically-grown food. What we have reported on are not scientifically controlled experiments in the strict sense of the word. We doubt that such experiments involving human beings can ever be conducted for the reasons we outlined at the beginning of this discussion. And we suggest that the best way to test the organic theory is to put yourself on organically-grown food for a couple of years and see what the difference is in your own health.

CHAPTER 160

Specific Properties of Organic Foods

By W. C. Martin, M.D.

Nutrition should be studied as a whole, although specialized study of its individual parts is necessary for a more complete knowledge; it is not necessary to wait until the scientist investigates the multiple factors of the chemistry of food in order to utilize nutrition in medicine.

Unfortunately there is very little information acceptable to science as to the value of total organic nutrition; there is, however, much evidence available that shows the vital influence that organic foods have on health and resistance to disease.

The "magic bullet" theory of medical therapy is applicable to infectious disease where a specific organism can be isolated as the causative agent, but in degenerative disease there is no specific etiologic factor (cause). Degenerative disease is due to "metabolic error" the basis of which is usually nutritional deficiencies and imbalance, and is therefore multiple in nature. Dr. King has called these metabolic errors "Nutritional Time Bombs" which may explode into a disease entity at any time during the life span. This occurs usually following a period of physical or emotional stress. The treatment of such conditions must, therefore, be based on a multiple nutritional approach.

The human body is a living organism and not a man-made mechanical robot. The body cannot long survive on inorganic and synthetic foods but must have living organic food elements. The chemist has not yet been able to instill into his laboratory products the life forces of nature that are essential for the survival of the human organism—neither can these essential factors be removed from the food or destroyed by processing without damage to health.

This life force can be obtained only from a dynamic living organic soil. Foods from such soil, free of chemicals and refinement, have the power to prevent degenerative diseases and increase body resistance to infectious disease. If organic foods are of better quality and nutritional value, what constitutes these extra factors?

Why Organic Foods Are Best

One of the most important factors in quality food is the protein content. Protein is the food constituent that makes the body grow. It helps combat invading organisms by producing active antibodies for protection and immunity in biochemical ways yet unknown. Numerous studies have

[559]

shown that, unless all the essential amino acids are available at the same time, normal protein synthesis cannot take place in the body. In fact, it has been found that simultaneous feeding of all the amino acids, non-essential as well as the essential, is more effective than feeding the essential amino acids alone.

What part does organic farming play in the protein synthesis in the plant? There is much evidence to show that deficient soils upset the process of building proteins in the plant; whereas in organic soil the proteins are properly synthesized. The proteins are not only increased in amount but contain a more complete supply of amino acids, especially tryptophane and lycine. Analysis reveals that wheat is producing less protein and more starch each year. Our hybrid corn grown on regular soil contains only about 6 per cent-7 per cent protein, while corn grown organically contains from 11 per cent-12 per cent protein. It is believed that the low grade protein is imperfectly formed and thus will reflect in the health of animals and humans.

Research is now being done on water extracts of organic matter in the soil. This extract is being tested on plants for its growth hormone factors. Tests have also shown that pigs grow more rapidly if allowed to root in pastures or if they are fed sod soil. Only recently has the "dung factor" from cow manure been discovered, which is now considered an excellent factor in poultry foods. This factor is associated with the "animal protein factor" (APIL.) or the "antianemia factor." This is now believed to be the cobalt containing vitamin B-12. All this gives a clue that organic soil contains an additional amount of essential unidentified micro-nutrients needed for better plant and animal nutrition. This is then transmitted to the human when this source of food is used for nourishment.

Trace Minerals In the Soil

There are 60 trace elements that are known to be essential for plant nutrition and approximately 24 of these are known to be necessary for human health. Dr. William Albrecht has shown that many plant and animal diseases are caused by a deficiency of these trace minerals in the soil. In a test he varied 6 essential minerals in the soil. Whenever calcium, magnesium, sulfur, phosphorous or nitrogen was varied, the plants varied in the concentration of the amino acids that made up the proteins. The variation was at times as high as 80 per cent—this reveals the difference in the quality of proteins in foods on soils deficient in trace elements. This will reflect on the health of the animals and humans living on this food.

Dr. Albrecht has also cited evidence to show the importance of trace minerals in the soil and plants in the prevention of Brucellosis or Bang's disease in cattle. Dr. Allison was able to repeat these findings in chemical tests in humans. A large percentage of the soil in the United States is deficient in some of these trace minerals, a condition which reflects on our health today.

Maximum of organic matter in the soil has been shown to increase the vitamin content of plants—Sir Albert Howard found that grain produced with organic material contained more vitamins than when grown with regular commercial fertilizer. This was true particularly of the important B complex vitamins. Dr. Pfeiffer found by analytical test that carotene, vitamin A and vitamin C content of organic food was increased from 20-80 per cent.

Protective Factors in Organic Soil

Do we have any evidence that organic soil contains any protective factors against disease? It is known that the organic matter of the soil is the habitat of teeming millions of organic life in the form of fungi, bacteria and macro-and microscopic animal life. Dr. Selman A. Waksman, one of the discoverers of streptomycin, says that it has been found that many disease-producing bacteria do not survive long in the soil. They are destroyed through the action of other organisms. He also gives many examples of antagonism between plant pathogens and other soil organisms such as the Dutch Elm disease, potato scab, turnip rot, etc.

There are also present in organic soil certain ultra-microscopic substances, parasitic upon bacteria. These are called bacteriaphage. Many of the soil fungi have been isolated and cultivated and their antibiotic properties used in medicine to cure diseases. Many plant experiments have shown the value of soil fungi as a protection against disease. Sir Albert Howard stated in *An Agricultural Testament* that the presence of mycorrhiza (root-fungus) in the root of the plants is associated with health, its absence is associated with diminishing resistance to disease.

Is it not possible to assume that small amounts of these antibiotic substances are absorbed by the plants and will retain their protective properties when consumed by the humans?

Earthworms and the Soil

Another important organism in the soil that has not been studied for the beneficial effects on health is the earthworm. It has been estimated by E. J. Russell that the addition of manure to the soil will increase the worm population from 13,000 to 3,000,000 to 5,000,000 per acre.

Dr. E. E. Pfeiffer stated that he has found that the earthworm digestive enzymes will destroy T. B. bacilli. He feels that this possible protective factor needs further investigation, to see if these earthworm enzymes will have the same bactericidal effect on other pathological bacteria. These findings suggest the many possible complicated integrations by which nature maintains a balance in the life cycle.

How does this then affect the argument for and against organic farming? The natural food of fungi and earthworms is the organic matter in the soil. As this is depleted the food supply for these organisms is reduced and their number is reduced. Also the commercial fertilizer as used today is a strong irritant and when applied to the soil will destroy a large proportion of these organisms. This is also true of the chemical sprays used as insecticides today. The sprays are absorbed into the soil and poison the fungi, bacteria, worms and other micro-organisms. When this happens, then, the plants become unhealthy. A recent report reveals that when one application of DDT is made to the soil, 80-90 per cent will remain for 8 years

[561]

and still affect the growth of certain plants. The insecticides not only interfere with the growth of the plants but the residue on the plants is cumulative in the human tissues. The author has shown by biopsy that DDT is present in human fat. Twenty-three out of 25 human tissues analyzed showed DDT, and 28 per cent of the cases had 5 P.P.M. (parts per million) or more which has been shown to be toxic in animal tests. These chemicals produce liver and nerve damage. Organic farming eliminates this health hazard and must be considered as a protective factor.

Organic Foods and Health

Is there chemical evidence that organic foods will improve the health and increase the resistance to infections? There are many such examples in animals and some in humans. Unfortunately these tests have not had scientific controls and therefore must be accepted only on their apparent value. One of the early animal tests was by Sir Albert Howard in India. He showed that his cattle fed on organically-grown foods developed resistance to virus infections such as hoof-and-mouth disease. He allowed his oxen to rub noses with infected cattle and they did not contract the disease.

Another example which covers an overall picture of increased health and vitality is the report from a breeding stable in Kentucky. This stable for decades had produced champion race horses, then in 1930, things changed; fewer horses won races and mares began to drop still-born or deformed colts. By 1941 the owner was advised to sell the horses and start with new ones. This he refused to do. Instead he started a program of soil restoration and an increase in organic matter. Within two years, a marked improvement was apparent, and by 1946 the stable stood third among the winners of the country, and the trouble with still-born colts had disappeared.

Dr. Weston Price in his book, *Nutrition and Physical Degeneration,* cites groups of people all over the world that have nearly perfect health, who live on organically-grown unrefined foods. The best known of this group are the Hunza people in Northern India. Dr. McCarrison stated after a 7-year study of these peoples, that they were "unexcelled in health and physical fitness."

To compare this with the physical fitness of the people of the United States where 47 per cent of the young men of draft age are rejected because of physical or mental defects should make us take a new look at our nutritional status.

There are many other unknown and unidentified accessory food factors that are necessary for good nutrition. Also, these numerous nutritional factors must be in harmonious balance for optimum health. This can only be obtained by encouraging natural ecology of the soil. (The science of vegetable and animal economy and activity.)

Optimum health implies maximum reserve capacity for each and every structure and function of the body. This ideal health should be our ultimate goal. It is the duty of the doctor to apply this new nutritional knowledge, but the burden of production of quality foods is on the American farmer.

CHAPTER 161

A Doctor Looks at the Organic Movement

By Wilfred N. Sisk, M.D., M.P.H.

The question has come many times "Why should you, a physician, be interested in organic gardening or farming?" My answer is a personal narrative of interest in health for many years. Even as a medical student I could not work up much enthusiasm for the type of rare and unusual case that so many doctors and students like to show. These cases are interesting like an exhibit in a museum but are usually hopelessly incurable and are often complete with autopsy findings. My philosophy of medicine has been one of prevention as far as possible. I can not see much advantage in adding a year or two of miserable life to a wreck of a human body. If we can do something which will make what life we have more pleasant and enjoyable, then I feel that we have done something worth while. As a by-product of such a program there is usually the addition of several years of healthful life. With this philosophy it is only natural that I have practiced preventive medicine and public health rather than some other form of medical work.

Medical Advances Mainly Benefit Youth

If one were to take seriously many of the glowing articles which appear in the usual run of newspapers and periodicals, one would think that the job of prevention and cure of disease had been done and that there is little left to be accomplished. It is true, of course, that many wonderful things have been done. As Dr. Dublinl expresses it, "The scientific, social and economic progress made in our country in the past century probably has no counterpart in all human history. Every branch of the medical and sanitary sciences has shared in this advance, with the result that the death rate has been greatly reduced and many diseases which once were rampant are now either under control or well on their way toward control." What does not usually reach the headlines is the fact that all this progress, fine as it is, is chiefly of benefit to the person under 30 years of age and particularly to the child under 10 years of age. I shall not attempt to go into detailed statistics. That is not necessary for our purpose. But I would like to point out some of the high spots in present-day trends.

First of all, I think it is important that we understand the use of the longevity table. The insurance companies calculate from the death rates at various ages a set of life expectancy tables. Now the insurance company keeps life expectancy tables for all ages: for day of birth, for one year of age, 40 years of age, etc. These tables are an arithmetic average of the length of life of all persons of the given age in the United States, provided those people were to die according to the death rate of the particular year in question. The table which we usually see in the newspaper is the table of life expectancy *at birth*. That means that the average length of life for all babies born for example in 1950 in the United States will probably be 68 years. The similar average for 1850 was approximately 35 years. (Exact figures are not available for this period.) In 1900 the average was not much better, about 41 years. Similar tables are usually made up for different groups, as an example for white males, for weekly premium insurance policy holders or for people in a small region of the country. Tables have been made up even for a single city or county. All that is necessary to make such a table is an accurate report of deaths.

If a child one day old dies of a streptococcic septicemia, he takes away from the life table many man-years of time. In order to have an average life expectancy of 35 years as our country did in 1850, it means that some other child must live to be 70 years of age. Now that is exactly what happened many times over in 1850. And it is this table of life expectancy *at birth* which has shown so much improvement. Better medical practice has contributed to the really remarkable improvement in the lot of children and young adults.

Picture Different After Age 40

But what of the individual who has already reached the age of 40 years? Here the picture is not so pleasant. In fact when carefully analyzed the picture is downright discouraging. As I stated above, life insurance companies keep expectancy tables for all ages. Let us see what a representative tables means. A fairly complete table is available for white males in the United States from 1850 to 1947. At birth white males could expect to live, on the average, 38 years in 1850, 48.2 years in 1900 and 65.2 years in 1947. This is a clear and really gratifying increase of 27.2 years. Let us compare that with the life expectancy at age 10. In 1850 a child who reached 10 years of age could expect to live to be 58 years of age, in 1900 the expectancy was for 60.6 years and in 1947 for 68.1 years. For the children who reached 10 years of age there was a gain of only 10 years.

Expectation of Life by Race and Sex in the United States From 1850 to 1947 for the Decennial Ages of Life

White Males

Calendar Period	0	10	Age 40	50	60	70
1850	38.3	48.0	27.9	21.6	15.6	10.2
1900-1902	48.23	50.59	27.74	20.76	14.35	9.03
1947	65.16	58.14	30.57	22.32	15.30	9.71

The above figures mean of course that much has been done in the improvement of the health of small children. Let us contrast that with the expectancy at age 40. In 1850 white men who lived to be 40 years old could expect on the average to live 27.9 years longer or to a total age of 67.9. In 1900 the expectancy had actually decreased to 27.7 (total age of 67.7) while in 1947 it had only increased to 30.6 (total age of 70.6). Thus we can see that for men who lived to be 40 years of age the life expectancy had only increased 2.7 years in virtually 100 years. This is certainly not much to be proud of. At age 50 the life expectancy table is no better. In 1850 a man age 50 could expect to live 21.6 more years (to a total age of 71.6 years) whereas in 1900 he could expect 20.8 years (total age 70.8 years) and in 1947 the expectancy was 22.3 years (total age 72.3 years). In almost 100 years we have improved the picture for age 50 by only 1.3 years. As you will see from the table for age 60 and 70 we have actually lost ground. The death rates in 1850 were better than those today.

Here we have a very neat problem. Why are we able to do so much for infants and small children and so little for people over 40? As you have seen from the table a person who in 1850 was able to live until he reached age 40 had just as good a chance to live to a "ripe old age" as has a person today. As I shall show later there is every reason to believe that the lot of people over 40 is not only no better but is worse today than it was 100 years ago. The answer to this problem is quite complicated and is a challenge which is being accepted by many of the best minds of our generation. In the remainder of this discussion I will outline not only the extent of the problem but what I believe to be the best answer possible today for the individual.

Degenerative Diseases on Increase

Let us examine some of the fine points which illustrate what I mean when I say that in many respects we are not doing as well as our fore-fathers. Let's take cancer for example. Even making allowance for the increased aging of our population, for the better diagnosis of the present day and all other reasonable allowances, there is still more cancer today than there was 75 to 100 years ago. This is particularly true of cancer of the lung.

I presume armies of all eras have depended upon the young men as their mainstay, but it strikes me very forcibly as we see the insistence of the armed forces on the 18 and 19 year old boys for combat duty. Why is it that our 29 and 30 year olds are too senile for army duty? I think that we can answer that as we go along in our discussion with the general health of our population. Even in making allowance for better diagnosis and again for the aging population, such diseases as stomach ulcers, coronary thrombosis, arthritis and high blood pressure are on the increase. That is, these diseases are not only on a numerical increase, but are on an increase out of proportion to the aging of the population. The disease which interests me most, for personal reasons, is the disease of allergy, and specifically, the so-called food allergy. Accurate statistics are virtually impossible on this disease, but it is my belief that the increase in the number of cases is tremendous. Diabetes is also on the increase.

What Causes Premature Cell Breakdown?

All of these diseases are in a group known as metabolic diseases. That is, they are diseases which are caused by the poor function of some organ or system of organs within the body. In other words, they are caused by the premature breakdown of normal cellular function of the body. They are all closely related in their cellular manifestations. Some affect the cells of one organ more drastically than another, but they all eventually affect every cell in the body. It is my belief that many cases of neurosis and insanity in this country are a result of the same forces which are producing an increase in the other diseases mentioned.

We do not have time to go into detail on all of these diseases, so let us take as an example allergy, and particularly food allergy. This disease is characterized by the poor functioning of certain of the enzyme systems of the body. We are all familiar with the digestive enzymes which change our foods from starch to simple sugars such as glucose, from protein to simple amino acids and from fats to simple glycerin and fatty acids. These changes are made so that the foods can proceed from the intestinal wall into the blood stream. Now it is this vast system of enzymes within the blood stream and within the cells of the various organs of the body which take these simple foods out of the blood, store them in various depots around the body and finally take them out of storage and use them to produce energy and repair tissues. This is the most amazingly complex system in the world and is only imperfectly understood. There are certain substances which we call vitamins that are necessary to the proper functioning of this complex enzyme system.

Reason for Interest in Organic Foods

Perhaps it will help to illustrate the marvelous nature of this system if we think about fire for a moment. When we wish to produce energy from any substance, paper, wood, coal, etc., we must raise its temperature several hundred degrees before combustion will take place. Now this enzyme system of the human body is able to burn our food just as effectively as a fire and do it at the remarkably low temperature of 98.6 degrees Fahrenheit, and also do it in the presence of a high concentration of water. Is it any wonder then that substances of the complexity of vitamins are needed as catalysts? Here is the crux of my whole interest in the organic production of food. It is my belief that we have not yet discovered all of the necessary vitamin substances, and that there is as yet an undiscovered vitamin which is present in the normal soil and which is, in all probability, produced by the bacteria or fungi in the soil. I will come back to that a little later.

When this enzyme system is imperfect, we find low blood pressure and a low basal metabolism. This means that the individual is using oxygen and hence burning his food at an abnormally slow rate. The tissues are unable to function normally, and in their attempt to correct themselves, collect added water in the individual cells. The inter-cellular spaces also become waterlogged. Once this has happened, the person is likely to have individual disturbances which are noted more prominently in one organ or another. Not all persons have the same symptoms, although a tiredness is characteristic. The person feels more tired upon arising in the morning, then he did when he went to bed. He frequently has so-called catarrh or sinusitis and he may have any or all of the following troubles: muscle pains, migraine headaches, asthma, digestive disturbances, nervous system disturbances and now recently we have even added a certain number of heart attacks as being of allergic origin. In most people characteristic symptoms are relatively mild and are no more than a nuisance, although I have seen patients with nervous symptoms so severe it was necessary to confine them to a mental hospital, and patients with intestinal disturbances so severe as to threaten their life, and patients with visual disturbances so severe that they were unable to see well enough to drive a car.

These allergic disturbances are very closely related to cancer, stomach ulcers and quite probably certain types of high blood pressure, kidney disease and coronary thrombosis. For example, one of the best of the recent theories for production of cancer is the demonstration that in people with cancer there is an increased amount of glutathione and similar sulfur-containing amino acids. These sulfur-containing amino acids are normal in the body and are very necessary for the transportation of oxygen from one substance to another in the normal energy production of the body (that is, the normal burning of the food to produce energy). When these substances are present in too large a quantity it is thought that they, instead of releasing their oxygen for normal metabolism, hold on to too much oxygen with the result that the food substances are not burned with sufficient rapidity. Being unable to burn up the food substances, the body stores them again. After the cellular storehouses have taken on all of the food they can hold, and are like a warehouse bulging at the seams, they can no longer continue to function in their normal manner and go wild, reproducing themselves in a rapid manner characteristic of embryonic cells. They thus become a cancer and, having once gone wild, use up not only their own share of food but virtually all the food of the victim, thereby causing his early death. It has not been definitely proved yet, for these enzyme reactions are, as I said before, infinitely complicated. But there is definite evidence to show that allergy, diabetes, high blood pressure, etc., constitutes a definite but somewhat similar breakdown of the enzyme system in the body.

Are We Poisoning Ourselves?

Now we come to the evidence supporting our contention that the breakdown in these enzyme systems is due to one of two things, and possibly, partly to both of them. I think the strongest probability is the major defect caused by the lack of an as yet undiscovered substance or vitamin. The second possibility is that we are poisoning ourselves by too many sulfur-containing compounds in the food we eat, as well as by too many poisonous sprays on our fruits and vegetables.

I shall discuss the latter first briefly then conclude by giving as much evidence as possible for the first contention. Recent work with radioactive

[567]

tracer substances has shown how rapidly plants take up substances from their leaves. Materials sprayed on the leaves of tomato plants for example have been shown to reach the farthest reaches of the plant, roots and all, within 6 hours. Even dormant trees take up substances from their roots. Substances placed on the roots were found to travel 18 inches up the trunk in 24 hours, even in zero weather. Thus it can be seen that we cannot eliminate all the poison spray from fruit by washing off the outside. The spray reaches all the cells of the inside of the fruit. Apparently anything which reaches the leaves of a plant will be taken up by the plant and will reach its entire body in a very short time. It is possible that we are slowly poisoning ourselves.

This poisoning is especially easily shown in the smoking of cigarettes. Cigarette smoke contains from 35 to 61 parts per million of arsenic. This is not enough to kill a person rapidly, but is quite probable that it has something to do with the increased cancer of the lung in the United States and England. Kennaway has carefully studied the increase in lung cancer from 1850 to the present time. He has shown very clearly that cancer of the lung has increased exactly in proportion to the increase in cigarette use. There are many causes which go into producing a cancer and I would not imply that chronic arsenic poisoning is the only cause. Cigarette smoking certainly cannot account for the increasing number of children and young adults who are contracting leukemia. (A blood disease quite similar to cancer.)

Vitamins Produced By Soil Organisms

Now back to the first point. We know that even without taking into consideration the organic growth of food that we are eating an extremely abnormal diet. We mill our flour and purify our sugar and salt to the point where no self-respecting bug can live on it so that it keeps well. We throw most of the known vitamins to the hogs and cows and eat the junk ourselves.

I think we need not dwell upon the lack of bacterial growth in soils fertilized heavily with minerals and with little or no humus. Soil bacteria simply cannot live on the diet of minerals alone and go into either a dormant stage or their numbers are greatly reduced. I do not mean to imply that most American soil is sterile, because many of these bacteria and fungi are of the spore-producing type and a few of them will survive even with a very small amount of food supply. In recent years we have had increasing evidence that important substances are produced by the natural organisms of the air, water and soil. In the early twenties there was much interest in bacteriophages. These are natural substances which destroy certain bacteria. Of course, we will be interested in the ones which destroy disease-producing bacteria. For example, in a river such as the Ohio which is highly polluted, these bacteriophages are very prevalent, and are given credit for a great deal in the way of destruction of typhoid organisms for example. A little later came gramacidin and in recent years, penicillin, streptomycin, aureomycin, teramycin, chloromycetin and a number of others.

[568]

The Upjohn Company at one time had 120 different antibotic substances which were being screened for possible usefulness. The ones I have named are mainly the ones which can be used within the human body. There are many more which are active in nature, but which are not suitable for use as a medicine. While any soil, or the air for that matter, may have the organisms producing these substances, such organisms are much more frequent in soil and water which has a high organic content.

Vitamin B12 Essential for Red Blood Cells

Probably all of the presently known vitamins are produced in one form or another by soil organisms but we have not been particularly interested in most of this production since the present known vitamins are easily produced by other means, chiefly synthetically. Recently, however, we have become very interested in a "new" vitamin which is produced by the same organism which produces streptomycin. This vitamin is B12 and is an absolute necessity for the production of red blood cells. I believe it was in 1922 when Minote and Murphy discovered that liver contains a substance which could be injected into individuals suffering from pernicious anemia and which would temporarily kill their anemia. This substance was not identified at the time as a vitamin. As years went on, it was shown that certain animals did not mature well without some animal protein. This substance was called "animal protein factor." Chickens, for example, denied some form of this animal protein factor do not do well, and often die. Cow manure, particularly well-rotted cow manure, was found to contain large amounts of animal protein factor. Just within the last 3 or 4 years it was discovered that there was a substance in the brew which produces streptomycin which was beneficial for these chickens. Later it was found that the anti-anemia substance of the liver, the animal protein factor of the cow manure, and the substance in the streptomycin brew were all the same thing. It was given the name, vitamin B12. It is not the cure-all which the patent medicine people have been advertising it to be, but it is an extremely important substance absolutely essential to life, and it is produced by soil organisms furnished with proper organic material.

The penicillin organism produces some substance or substances which are extremely useful in feeding animals. After the penicillin is extracted, the solid residue is sold to feed manufacturers who dry it and mix it with chicken and hog feed. The chickens grow quite rapidly and in all respects appear very healthy. The same thing is true of aureomycin and the residue from the production of aureomycin. Not only has vitamin B12 been identified in these antibotic brews, but B14 and B16 have also been found. We don't know just what B14 and B16 do in the human body, but they are known to be essential vitamins. Another one of the B vitamin group, biotin, is known to be produced by the organisms which normally inhabit the digestive tract of many animals, and possibly man himself. It is virtually impossible to make a rat, for example, biotin deficient without giving him sulfa-suxodine or some other drug to kill off his normal intestinal bacteria.

A New Approach Is Needed

We have shown the need for some new approach to degenerative diseases and we have shown that at least some important substances are produced by these soil bacteria, possibly the substances needed in these diseases. Is there any evidence that people who are fed with foods organically raised are in better health than others? The evidence is not conclusive as yet, but there are a number of sign posts which point in that direction. Dr. Picton in his book, *Nutrition of the Soil,* gives an experience of an English dentist who was serving a boys' school. Very briefly, the boys had the usual bad teeth of most English and American children. Gradually, over a period of 3 years he began to notice a very marked improvement. He went back to his records to confirm his clinical impression, and his records left no doubt that dental caries were on a marked decline in this group of school children. Upon investigation he found that a new family had been hired to do the housekeeping and cooking. The husband enjoyed gardening and used a plot belonging to the school to raise virtually all the vegetables for the school. This plot happened to be high in organic matter and the caretaker improved it by using more organic matter and no commercial fertilizer.

Food Is Chief Factor in Health

There have been a few cases here and there of asthma which have been reported cured by a change to organically-produced foods. These cases are encouraging but are too fragmentary for a definite conclusion. In India there are a number of different tribes who have various different eating and farming habits. Dr. Picton shows quite conclusively that those Indians who have the best land and who give the best organic care to the land are the most robust and by far the healthiest of the Indian group. He summarizes a number of experiments with rats which are fed on the diets of various localities. The rats quickly show all the changes of the human population fed on that same diet. We are all familiar with the Hunzas which are one of the most isolated and one of the healthiest of the Indian groups. Living right across the valley is another group of Indians whose farming practices and whose lands are not as good as that of the Hunzas. Neither are they the physical equals of the Hunzas. If some of the Hunzas go to live in other parts of India, they become subject to the same ills as the people of that locality. There seems little doubt that the food is the chief factor in the health of this group.

Multiple sclerosis is a disease which causes about the same amount of deaths and crippling in the United States as does poliomyelitis. It is thought to be closely related to the allergic diseases, if it is not actually an allergy itself. Multiple sclerosis, while rather prevalent in the United States and in Europe, is virtually absent in China, India and Japan, where at least until recent years, chemical fertilizers were little if at all used. Dr. Randolph of Chicago tells me that Chinese residents (graduate physicians taking extra training in this country) who see his patients with allergic food reactions are quite amazed. He states that they find no such disease as this in China.

[570]

Assuming that soil bacteria produced complex substances which are needed by the plant and animal, is there any evidence to show that the plant's root is able to take up these complex substances? There is such evidence. It has been shown that the plant can easily take up such things as vitamin B_1 and they can probably take up directly more complex substances than this. Dr. Rayner, an English agricultural chemist, has done a great deal of work with mycorrhiza, a form of soil fungus which grows on and around the roots of plants. She has shown that a small amount of soil containing these fungi can make a great deal of difference in the growth of plants. These fungi seem to grow right into the root of the plant. These fungi produce complex substances needed by the plant and virtually inject them into the root. They in turn receive sustenance from the plants as well as the soil. One of Dr. Rayner's experiments was with Norway spruce. The seedlings were planted in a badly depleted soil, while other seedlings were planted in this same soil plus two teaspoons of a good soil containing at least four of these fungi, and the third group of seedlings were planted in this same soil with not only two teaspoons of good soil, but some compost. The first group of seedlings did grow, although at the end of 17 months they were only about two inches high. The second seedlings with only two teaspoons of good soil grew, in the same length of time, to about 10 inches. The third group of seedlings grew to about 24 inches in the same length of time.

Natural Food Is Most Important

I have shown the great need for some improvement in our attack on the metabolic or degenerative diseases, and I have given you the reasons why I believe the soil and properly produced food is the answer.

From the data presented it can be seen that we are far behind our needs in knowledge of degenerative diseases. These are the diseases which chiefly attack persons over 40 years of age. We do not as yet know the complete answer to the degeneration of age but the evidence at hand strongly suggests that food properly grown and prepared can be of great help, perhaps even is the best possible solution to the problem. Many scientists are working on the problems involved. Until they can give us a more complete answer we as individuals must get "back to nature" as nearly as we can. We need moderate outdoor exercise, wholesome food and as pleasant home life and work as we can achieve. Of these, it would certainly seem that the most important is the natural food. As far as possible, the food should be grown organically and should be the whole natural food.

One parting suggestion: there are many quacks in the business of advising people on diets. Use good judgment in selecting a diet. Accept statements of unknown people only after they have satisfied you that their statements are based on valid experience.

CHAPTER 162

A Concept of Totality

By Joe D. Nichols, M.D.

The following is part of an address delivered before the Sixty-eighth Annual Convention, Texas Bankers Association at Galveston, May 12, 1952. It is reprinted from the Texas Bankers Record.

There are 6 chief causes of disease: 1. Emotional, 2. Nutritional, 3. Poisons, 4. Infections, 5. Accidents, 6. Inherited.

The greatest cause of disease is, without a doubt, emotional. Worry, fear anxiety, hate, envy, jealousy—these are the great killers. When any of these emotions take hold of us, we get a conflict and that conflict leads to tension. If you hate me, then I become a "pain in your neck." The conflict causes tension on the muscles of the neck. First, there is a drawing in the back of the neck and finally if the conflict is intense enough a tension headache is the result. The pain is not in the mind or heart—it is in the back of the neck, right where the muscles join onto the head. You have heard the expression, "I am fed up with that fellow." When you get mad at someone, then you do get a full feeling in the stomach. The conflict causes tension and then the glands in the stomach and intestines that produce the digestive juices just dry up so to speak, and you do get a full feeling in the stomach. If you eat when you are mad, then you get nervous indigestion because there are no digestive juices present. If the conflict is intense enough and goes on long enough, and then some of the other factors of disease are present, especially nutritional and poisons, then you get a peptic ulcer. We say that nervous indigestion is inorganic or functional, but the inorganic diseases are the forerunners of organic disease.

Emotional Causes of Disease

Heart disease is the leading cause of death in America today. How do these adverse emotions affect the heart? Conflict and tension cause the coronary vessels to constrict; the heart muscle itself does not get enough blood, and that heart cries out in pain. We call this symptom angina, which is functional or inorganic. If the conflict persists, and other factors of disease are present, the patient gets coronary thrombosis. All organic disease is made worse by emotional upset. I know a man who has gout. He gets along very well until he gets mad; then he has to go to the hospital.

What does one do about the emotional causes of disease? There are only 3 things that can be done to resolve a conflict. The first possibility is to run away from the conflict. If a husband comes home at three o'clock in the morning with lipstick on his shirt, his good wife is likely to get an emotional upset with headache, backache, indigestion and heart pain. What can she do about it? One of the solutions would be for her to go back home to mama. She could run away from the conflict. But there is another solution. She might change the situation. She might be a better wife and make the fellow want to come home at five o'clock with a clean shirt. All of us have conflicts that we can neither run away from nor change. If there is a death in the family, if the house burns to the ground, then what can be done? These conflicts must be accepted. There is no other alternative. But just saying you accept a situation is not enough. It must be completely accepted in order to stop the conflict and tension. But so few people really know how to accept these conflicts. This is done by knowing and practicing the 3 A's.

The Three A's

The first A is Acceptance—acceptance of the other fellow as an individual with rights and opinions of his own, and also with his imperfections. There have been none perfect since Jesus. If the wife expects the husband to be perfect at all times, she will be disappointed and vice versa. The second A is Approval—a pat on the back is much better than a kick in the pants. It just naturally works that way. And it has been said that most of the conflict that arises between people is caused by the tone of voice in which they speak. The third great A, and by far the most important one, is Adoration or love. This suggests a great natural law, The Law of Love.

No man can ever violate any natural law. This is the central idea of our concept of totality. The law of love is a natural law and no man can violate it. Natural law is simple, self-evident, universal and inviolate. You can jump from a 14-story building, but you do not violate the law of gravity. Your broken body is simply the exemplification of the law. The cure for the emotional cause of disease is very simple. All one has to do is to stop attempting to violate the law of love. The law of love is divided into two parts. First, love God, and second, love they neighbor. You cannot hate your neighbor and get by with it. He will become a pain in your neck. And it makes no difference how much he may have mistreated you, you still cannot afford to hate him. Worry, fear and anxiety violate the first part of the law of love. The Sermon on the Mount teaches us not to worry about what we shall eat or wear. It teaches us to think not of tomorrow. The cure for the emotional cause of disease is to stop attempting to violate the law of love.

The second great cause of disease is nutritional. But first, let me give you something of my own family history. My great-great-grandfather lived in South Carolina. He had 2000 acres of very rich land. He was a successful farmer. He made a lot of money growing cotton and tobacco. He built a big house, raised and educated a large family. But when his sons were grown, they found the land was no longer making good crops and the farm was no longer making money. So my great-grandfather took the advice of Horace Greeley and he "went west." He moved to Tennessee where he found a large fertile farm. He did exactly the same thing that his father had done. He was a big man, 6 foot 6 inches and weighed 350 pounds. He was very industrious, worked hard, made a lot of money, built a big house, raised and educated a big family. When his sons were grown, they found the farm had been literally mined year after year and was no longer making a living for the family. So my grandfather moved to Alabama. He got together 2000 acres of very rich land down on Horse Creek in Maringo County, about 40 miles from Selma, Alabama, and here he did the very same thing that his father and grandfather had done. He had a large family. My father was the baby in a family of 12. My grandfather even built a little town. They called the little settlement, Nicholsville. He owned a sawmill, a grist mill, the general store and one of his daughters was the postmistress. By the time my father was grown, what do you suppose had happened? You guessed it. The farm was worn out and he had to move. He moved to Ashley County, Arkansas, down in the Mississippi delta. He bought a rich farm and the same old thing started all over again. He built a big house in town where we also had a general store. But by the time I was grown, all the profits from the farm were going to pay for fertilizer and poison spray. So I had to move, but there was no place left for me to go. By this time the whole country had been settled and most of the land exploited. So I decided to study medicine. I graduated from the University of Arkansas with an M.D. degree in June, 1932. In November, 1933, I started practicing medicine in Atlanta, Cass County, Texas. This was in the depths of the great depression, and Cass County was one of the poorest places in Texas. The average production of corn was 8 bushels per acre. In 6 months I was making more money than the president of the bank who had been there a lifetime. You see all the land was poor and all the people were *sick!* I did not average 50 cents per office call nor more than one dollar for house calls, but I had *volume.*

Now I have a farm. I bought one thousand acres of the poorest land in America. Most of it only cost 10 dollars an acre. It was as hard as concrete and would hardly grow weeds when I got it. My ambition is to restore the fertility to this worn-out land. I believe I can make this farm worth a hundred thousand dollars and the expense of doing it is a legitimate deduction from income tax. This is the only way that I can create an estate for my own old age and for my boys. I believe that a hundred years from now, there will be a Nichols living in my brick house. With this introduction, now let me talk to you about the nutritional cause of disease.

Nutritional Cause of Disease

We live in a country where we have more good doctors, more great medical schools, and more hospitals, more education, and more great scientists, and more money than any other place on earth. We hear so much about the great scientific advances that have been made in public health and medicine. And it is true that great advances have been made in certain branches of medicine. But despite all this, everybody in the country is sick. I do not know anyone anywhere who does not have some physical disability. My own son at the age of 3 had 3 bad teeth! It is hard to find a child in school anymore without dental caries. Last year we had more cancer than ever before. We had more heart disease. It is the leading cause of death, killing young people before the age of 40 all over the land. We had more high blood pressure, more stomach ulcers, more rheumatism, more diabetes and more mental disease. Fifty per cent of the hospital beds in America are filled with mental patients. They are running out the top windows all over the land and more mental hospitals are being built every day. We had more polio last year than ever before. Perhaps we are not so smart after all. Maybe something is wrong here. There are places in the world where these degenerative diseases do not occur. There is a place in India, called Hunza, where a British physician, Sir Robert McCarrison, stayed 7 years looking without success for a cancer. These people live to be 110 years of age and die with their own teeth in their mouths. Seventy year old men run 20 miles a day and think nothing of it. Sir Robert McCarrison said the reason these people have such excellent health is because they do 3 very simple things that we fail to do. They eat natural food grown on fertile soil, and they eat it fresh. We do none of these things. The first great fundamental reason why all of us are sick, from the standpoint of nutrition, is because the land is worn out. The farmers of America violated another one of God's Natural Laws—Nature's Law of Return. This law states that if you take away from me then you must return something to me. But all the farmers violated this law. We cut down the trees, plowed up the land, planted cotton one year and corn the next, and even burned the stalks. We constantly took out and never put anything back. As a result all the land became poor land. And poor land grows poor food that makes poor people, who are sick. Poor land grows food that is poor in vitamins, poor in minerals, poor in enzymes and proteins of poor quality. All this means sick people. The most common disease in America today is hypoproteinosis, that is, not enough protein, or protein of poor quality. This is of tremendous significance. The vitamins, the enzymes and the antibodies, that give us resistance to disease, are all protein substances.

About the time all the land became worn out, along came Science to the rescue. And in this country, we have been taught to bow down and worship this word, science. In this instance, the scientist through the chemical trust using the United States Department of Agriculture, the A & M Colleges and the County Agents, gave to the farmers commercial fertilizer, N.K.P. (Nitrogen, Potash and Phosphate). They said to the farmer: "If you will put this on your land, we promise it will grow twice as much, and it will put money in the bank," and of course it was true. The land did produce twice as much, and the farmer did put more money in the bank as a result of its use. This was true for a while; but then the farmer found it took more and more fertilizer, and he got less and less in return. Unfortunately, N.K.P. does not make land rich. It merely drives out what remaining fertility is present and finally leaves a piece of dead hard concrete. A hardpan or plow sole develops. A concrete slab would be a better name.

Chemical Farming Leads to Disease

The end result of chemical farming is always disease, first in the land itself, then in the plant, then in the animal and finally in us. Everywhere in the world, where chemical farming is practiced, the people are sick. The use of synthetic chemicals does not make land rich. It makes it poorer than before.

There is one way and only one way to make land rich, and that is just exactly like the good Lord does on the floor of the forest. He puts back into the land 3 parts of dead plant matter and one part of dead animal matter. That is what leaf mold contains. This puts everything back into the soil, the major elements plus the trace elements, plus dead and decaying organic matter—and all in the proper proportions. And when we say dead and decaying matter, that presupposes that at one time the material had life. The leaf at one time was a living thing. This is of tremendous importance. You must have death and decay, if you expect to have life and growth. This is a natural cycle that no chemist can get around, no matter how many degrees he may have behind his name. The end result of the decaying process is amino acids and carbonic acids. The amino acids are the little building blocks that the plant uses to make proteins of high quality. How can a plant produce proteins of high quality when it had no amino acids present in the beginning? The answer is that it cannot. This is the fundamental reason why the proteins produced on the farms of America are of poor quality. So, the first great fundamental reason why all of us are sick, is because the land is worn out.

I have 3 acres of, what I consider, the richest land in America. We made it rich by cleaning out the barns, the hen houses, saving the leaves and planting Austrian winter peas for a winter cover crop. I believe there is a difference in the God given free nitrogen that the Austrian winter peas put back into the soil through the little nodule on its roots and the kind most farmers buy in a sack of synthetic chemical fertilizer. I don't know what the difference is, and, I doubt if any chemist will ever know. Perhaps the "Life Factor," whatever that is, could be the answer.

We have restored a 50-acre field to a fertile state by cleaning the bushes, leveling the land and then planting legumes. We have also added ground limestone and raw rock phosphate. We are still using these natural rock fertilizers, but are not yet completely convinced that even they are necessary. We are now subsoiling our land to break up the hardpan and find that this procedure alone increases the growth of grass. And grass is the great healer. The way to change poor land to rich land is to put the land back in grass, and then, for a year or two, mow the grass and leave it on the ground to rot. If we put back the plant matter, nature herself will furnish the animal matter with birds, rabbits, bugs and earthworms. Fertile soil is usually dark in color. It is soft; when it rains, the water soaks into the ground.

Natural Food

We have tried to answer the question, what is fertile soil? The next reason we are all sick is because we no longer eat natural food. What is natural food? Natural food simply means food that still has in it the natural vitamins, enzymes and minerals that nature put there. But 80 per cent of the food consumed by the average American has had them all taken out.

White sugar is the worst food in the American diet. It is so sorry that not even a worm will eat it. You never saw a worm in white sugar, and you never will. Raw sugar is a natural food. White sugar is just like raw sugar except all the vitamins and minerals have been removed. Refining, they call the process. This is a good word, but it is the wrong word. Dead shot would be more descriptive. They take raw sugar through 14 steps in order to remove all the good part. The good part, blackstrap molasses, we feed to the cattle. The pure sucrose, white sugar, a chemical, we eat. It will make you fat and give you energy, but that is all. Guess why the worm does not get into white sugar? He has sense enough to know better. Why is all the good part removed? It is a selfish commercial reason. It is done so that the sugar will keep. White sugar can be stored in 100 pound cloth sacks for years in dirty warehouses and still be sold for a profit. It is true that the love of money is the root of all evil. It is also the root of most of our disease.

Brown rice is one of the best foods in the world. Many people in the Orient live on it almost alone. It is one of the richest sources of natural vitamin B complex which is essential to good health. White rice is exactly like brown rice except all the vitamins and minerals have been polished away. And for one reason only—so that the rice will keep in 100 pound bags and can be sold for a profit. White rice is raw starch, in my opinion, unfit for human consumption.

Our Daily Bread

Whole wheat flour is perhaps the most important of all foods, because most people eat bread 3 times a day and 7 days a week. White flour is also unfit for human consumption, first of all because all the vitamins, the enzymes and minerals have been removed. The kernel or wheat germ and the outside layers of the grain are removed in the milling of white flour. This means that crackers, spaghetti, macaroni, noodle soup, cake mixes, etc., are no good because the essential nutrients have been removed. The endosperm or starchy part of the grain is made into white flour. This part is necessary for energy, but without the vitamins, enzymes and minerals in proper proportions, we end up with a nation of fat sick people. There is another reason why white flour is unfit for human consumption. For 30 years it was bleached with nitrogen trichloride, the Agene process. This is a central nervous system poison. It does give puppies fits, and it is one of the reasons why 50 per cent of the hospital beds in America are filled with mental patients. On October 1, 1949, most of the millers voluntarily changed to the chlorine process of bleaching. Chlorine is also a poison. Still another reason why white flour is no good is because it has been enriched. This, you are being constantly told over the radio and in the press, is a very scientific achievement which has made your daily bread such a valuable food. What is enriched bread? First they take a perfectly good grain of wheat and remove all the vitamins and minerals. Then they start out with raw starch and put back into it 3 little dead synthetic chemicals: niacin, thiamin and riboflavin plus inorganic iron. These true synthetic vitamins are a part of the vitamin B complex. But natural B complex, and the wheat germ is one of the very best sources, contains 20 known parts besides the still unknown factors. The germ is also the richest source of natural vitamin E, which has been proved to be essential to a normal cardio-vascular system. The germ also, no doubt, contains enzymes and vitamins as yet unnamed. All of these many essential nutrients are removed and only 3 synthetic vitamins plus a little iron is added. This is what we call "frag-mentation," and it violates our concept of totality. It seems to me that any-body with a dime's worth of common sense could see that so-called science cannot forever get by with such a senseless scheme. In Canada it is against the law to enrich bread. In this country in most states it is against the law not to enrich bread. The Canadians are right and we are nuts. We have always thought of vitamin E as the reproductive vitamin, and it is essential to normal reproduction. Veterinarians have known this for 30 years and have fed pure wheat germ oil to the barren heifer, and to the bulls with good results. Rats, if they get pregnant, and if we remove all the vitamin E from their diet, will abort every time on the thirteenth day. One of the reasons why we have so much sterility in our young women is no doubt because 80 per cent of the food they eat has had all the life taken from it.

The store bought corn meal is a worthless food. It has been degermi-nated. This is said to improve the keeping quality. It does, it keeps the weevils out. It also keeps me out. If a sack of meal is not good enough for a weevil, I doubt if it is good enough for a man.

I tell all patients that they should never buy any food that has been enriched or has had a vitamin added. If the food is so sorry to start with, that synthetic chemical vitamins have to be added, then it is not worth their money. This removes about 90 per cent of the breakfast foods. They are no good. If they were, the bugs would get into them in the flimsy paste-board boxes they come in, setting around the dirty warehouses.

Fifty per cent of the calories that the average American eats comes from 3 things: white flour, white sugar and hydrogenated fats; that is, the compound shortenings and oleomargarine. Not one of these then, in my opinion is fit to eat. Oleomargarine has been fortified with 15,000 units of vitamin A. That is one reason I think that it is no good. Butter does not have to be fortified.

Grade A Raw Milk

We drink raw milk at our house. I believe that the pasteurization of milk kills the life of the milk. Actually what pasteurization did was to per-mit the dairyman to be dirty. Of course people who live in cities and towns where Grade A raw milk is not available had better use pasteurized milk. Canned milk is not fit to drink. The only vitamin in it is vitamin D and that is synthetic. Yet this is what we feed the babies in America. Canned milk, cornstarch and synthetic vitamins is the modern diet of our babies, and we have more dental caries and more polio. This, I believe to be one of the reasons for sick children. I doubt if we will ever see much less polio until the day comes when mothers can have natural food grown on fertile soil and then nurse their babies at the breast like nature intended. They cannot nurse their babies now, and it is not because they want to play cards. It is because their milk is no good. And the reason their milk is no good is because what they eat is no good.

The best meats are the internal organs—liver, brains, heart and kidneys. Fish is good. Seafood is the best. The ocean does not violate nature's law of return. More goes into the ocean than comes out. The ocean is getting richer all the time and the land is getting poorer. The very best source of natural vitamin A and D is from the liver of the Cod, a salt water fish. Wild game is extra good because usually he eats natural food grown on fertile soil. We have not started using commercial fertilizer out in the woods yet, for some strange reason. Neither do we have to use poison sprays, like D.D.T., in the woods. I believe when we plant a seed in a piece of poor land and then surround it with N.K.P., we get a plant that is diseased. This plant puts on diseased fruit, and the good Lord in his wisdom, sends the bugs to destroy it. This is nature's law of the survival of the fittest. But one "scientific" application of D.D.T. kills the bug, and then what do we do? We eat the diseased fruit plus the D.D.T. No wonder we are all sick.

Most of the eggs consumed by the American people are infertile. The stores will pay more for them. This is because they keep longer. But, I believe it to be a violation of a natural law to keep the rooster off the yard. Pretty soon you have no eggs or chickens either. The fertile egg has in it "life." It has been proved that the fertile egg has a nutritional value not found in infertile eggs.

Fresh Vegetables

The vegetables that we eat should be fresh. Turnip greens for dinner should be cut after breakfast. Canned goods do not taste like fresh ones. I believe that the flavor of foods is given by the vitamins and enzymes found only in the fresh leaf and in the kernel of the grain. The reason why we have to spend so much money for mustard, pepper, sauces, etc. is because 80 per cent of what we eat is dead, and we have to put this condiment on it to get it down. What is worse than a hot dog bun that is 24 hours old, cold and no mustard or pickle on it. Really, it was no good in the beginning!

The fruit we eat is not too good unless it is tree ripened and in season, but the oranges, grapefruit and bananas are all pulled off the tree before they get ripe. Why? They are pulled green so that they can be shipped and stored and sold for a profit. I believe that America's brain could devise methods to distribute fresh vegetables and fruits to the people profitably. Modern highways and refrigerated trucks could answer the problem.

Of all the sweets, honey is the best. That is, provided it is wild honey. Some of the commercial beekeepers now feed the bees simple syrup made from white sugar and then add synthetic flavoring. Then they boast about how scientific and how smart they are. They can give you honey any flavor you like, but the honey is no good. Wild honey is the best.

Natural food grown on fertile soil, eaten fresh is the answer to the nutritional cause of disease. Science is no longer science when it attempts to violate God's Natural Law.

The restoration of the fertility of the soil would not only go a long way toward solving our health problems, it would also solve many other problems. The problems of floods and water shortages will never be solved until we restore the organic matter to the soil. One hundred pounds of humus holds like a sponge 195 pounds of water. The usual 100 pounds of Cass County soil won't hold 30 pounds of water. The construction of dams on the rivers will never solve the water problem. This only treats the symptoms of the disease. The underground water level in Texas will continue to fall until we restore organic matter to the soil. Just suppose all the land was rich again. Economic, political, social and many other problems could be solved. It is said that war itself is really a search for fertile soil.

What can you as bankers do about all this? May I suggest a few practical points for your consideration? For years past, now, when a farmer came into our bank to borrow money, he was asked. "How many acres do you plan to plant in cotton? The first question he is asked now is, "How many acres of Austrian winter peas and vetch did you plant last year?" He is encouraged in every way to plant winter cover crops. The bank's motto has become "Let's turn Cass County green this winter." The farmer is told that his credit rating at the bank will be improved if he cooperates in this program. Another thing many bankers could do would be to get a farm like I did and restore the fertility to it. The expense is a legitimate income tax deduction. And then it seems to me that bankers are going to have to learn how to make conservation loans to reliable farmers; the loans to be paid back over a period of from two to 5 years. This of course will require the services of an agriculture man in the bank to supervise, in the field, these loans. Many banks are already doing this.

CHAPTER 163

Teeth and the Organic Method

By J. I. Rodale

One of the first dividends our family received from the practicing of the organic method and the eating of foods raised organically was a noticeable improvement in our teeth. There were less and less cavities every time we went to the dentist. In the case of our youngest child, Nina, the condition of her teeth is perfect. She does not have a single cavity in any of her teeth. This was made possible in her case because she was only about 3 years old when we began to eat food raised organically. In my own case I have not had a cavity in 12 years. Hundreds of our readers have also noted a wonderful improvement in their teeth. Typical is the case of a family of 3 that came to see me recently, who told that where they used to have a yearly dental bill of about 100 dollars, it is now reduced to about 10 dollars, and consists only of routine cleaning. Only a few days ago a woman from Rhode Island told me that she stopped having cavities 5 years ago, after she began eating organically grown food. And, the peculiar thing is, far from their entire diet is organically produced. Usually the organic portion consists only of the vegetables that they raise in their own garden. Some purchase organically produced food through the mails. It is amazing what a small amount of organically produced food will do for the health of a person.

Tartar Removed

Permit me to quote an item from the *Field Magazine,* published in England, dated January 6, 1945:

"I was interested in your letter from *Dental Surgeon,* because my 7-year-old son and I have only just paid a routine visit to the dentist. He seemed quite unusually impressed by the excellence of my son's teeth and asked me if he had had any special diet. I told him: No, that he had eaten no meat (including eggs) up to the age of 3 years, but since then had eaten meat and exactly what he liked. I added, however, that we grew as much of our food as possible on composted soil and that for more than his lifetime we have never used an ounce of artificial fertilizers.

" 'You have given me the answer,' said the dentist. 'Now I understand why he has teeth like that.'

"In my own case, my teeth used to collect huge quantities of tartar. Every year it had to be scraped off. We began using compost instead of artificials toward the end of 1936. When I went to my dentist in 1942, after a lapse (I am ashamed to say) of two-and-a-half years, I expected a terrific scraping to occur. There was no tartar to remove. Another two years elapsed before I went again, this last time. There was a very little tartar behind two teeth, and that was all.

"We have used compost for just about 8 years, and for the last 5 of those years my teeth have lost their unpleasant habit of collecting tartar. Is this a coincidence? It might be. But I was telling this story to someone else, and she has had exactly the same experience. Incidentally, I asked the dentist if war-time diet could have anything to do with it. He did not think it had, because he finds now just as much tartar collecting on his other patients' teeth as before the war."

(L. F. EASTERBROOK)

Another item from the *New York Times* of May 29, 1947:

"Traces Bad Teeth to Soil"

"Schenectady, N. Y.—Tooth decay as well as serious illness might be traced to our eating vegetables and other foods that were grown on soil deficient in calcium and other minerals, Dr. George D. Scarseth of Lafayette,

Indiana, director of research of the American Farm Research Association, declared in a General Electric Farm Forum address here.

" 'It is not difficult to see how a deficiency of essential vitamins and minerals may cause weakened teeth with subsequent decay and abscesses,' Dr. Scarseth pointed out. 'Neither is it difficult to suspect that prolonged abscesses, pouring toxins into the blood stream, might well show up eventually in kidney disturbances, high blood pressure, or heart diseases.'

"Dr. Scarseth said that data collected by physicians, biochemists, agronomists and engineers working on the problem of soil deficiencies 'indicate there must be a close relationship between the fertility of the land and well-being of the animals that consume the crops.' "

In the March, 1946, issue of the *Dental Magazine and Oral Topics,* published in England, appears an article that shows the remarkable effect of organically produced food on the teeth of young boys and girls. I am going to quote the entire article. It was written by and represents the experience of E. Brodie Carpenter, a dentist:

"The Effects of Increased Quantities of Healthy Food on the Teeth of the Children of the Royal Commercial Travelers' School.

"This school was founded one hundred years ago for the orphans of commercial travellers. The numbers vary from term to term, but in recent years there have been about 95 girls and 135 boys in two separate establishments in the same buildings. There is a good deal of land attached to the school, and from it in the years before the war the school was getting a certain amount of its vegetables. When war was obviously inevitable, the head gardener ploughed up a further five and a half acres which used to be a paddock for the horses, and brought this under cultivation for vegetables also. Every year since then he has grown more and more vegetables until now the school buys none at all.

"The system of agriculture would meet the approval of the most fastidious of the 'natural manure school.' Every ounce of waste is returned to the soil, and up to a hundred pigs are kept for their manure, which is composted with clippings from the playing fields and with straw. No artificial manure is used at all. The vegetables grown are like the picture on the seed packets.

"It is a curious fact that part of the five-and-a-half-acre field is silt from the River Pin; this is in accordance with agriculture on the banks of the Nile. It is even more extraordinary that a smaller field was used by the L. M. S. for spreading the night earth from Hatch End Station in the days of earth closets; this is the method of the Chinaman, who has cultivated his own bit of land with his own and his animal's wastes for 4,000 years.

"The produce of the school's land has gone up by 33⅓ per cent since the war for *nearly a hundred fewer children,* the number now being 240-250, whereas before the war they numbered as many as 340.

"Now what is the effect on the teeth? I took up the appointment of dental officer at the school in 1939, and at the first examination was very perturbed at the state of affairs. I graded the boys and girls into 'A' for none to two cavities, 'B' for three to five, and 'C' for six and upwards. 'A's' were 50 per cent, 'B's' 32 per cent, and 'C's' 18 per cent, and I found a number of cavities in 'fronts.'

"I settled down to an oral hygiene campaign and started with the 'fronts,' but the trouble was that all the children leaving had to be completed by the end of the Christmas term. I toiled on through that school year and the next, examining them every 9 months.

"In September, 1941, things were no better: 'A's' were 56 per cent, 'B's' 27 per cent, and 'C's' 17 per cent. In 1943 and early 1944 there was a very obvious general improvement—cavities were fewer and the unhealthy, gluey sort of saliva so often seen in the adolescent age was decreasing. By 1945 the examination showed that 'A's' were 97 per cent and 'B's' 3 per cent.

"This was dramatic enough, but in September, 1945, there was an average of a quarter filling per child and the boys were 100 per cent 'A.' Out of 230 girls examined in a period of 9 months, the child (a girl) with the most cavities had 4. (Grading of the girls: 'A's' 97 per cent; 'B's' 3 per cent.)

"This simply astonishing change, I feel quite certain, is to the credit of the Board of Management and of the gardener—not mine. How else could one account for the *absence of incidence?*

"I am well aware that there are other items of diet, but I am convinced that, provided that there are no excesses in the rest of the diet, fresh vegetables provided by a sound system of agriculture are the cornerstone of dental health.

"The bread at the school before the war was not white but a special bread 'Nevill's' loaf. I consider 100 per cent whole-meal to be the ideal. The children have always had enough milk, and sweets (if these make any difference, which is doubtful) have always been regulated. The animal protein is restricted, as are fats. Eggs are new-laid on the premises. The diet, in short, is an ordinary all-round one, except that the 'vegetable protein is properly synthetised' and in abundance."

University Students' Teeth

Now let us compare this with what workers at the School of Dentistry of the University of Minnesota are discovering about the teeth of the students of that institution. There were 3 successive studies which were written up in the April, 1951, issue of the *Journal of the American Dental Association*. I quote a portion:

"The 3,388 freshman students, both men and women, who entered the University of Minnesota in 1929 averaged 9.95 teeth affected by dental caries. The 4,348 students who entered 10 years later, in 1939 had 11.8 teeth so affected. The 4,412 who came to the University in 1949 averaged 13.7 teeth affected by caries. All differences are statistically significant.

"Though started only 20 years ago, these decennial reviews of the dental condition of university freshmen really cover a period of approximately 40 years. The young people who entered the University in 1929

[583]

at an average age of about 19 years were born in 1910 or thereabouts. The period since that time has produced more benefits for dental health than any other period in the world's history. Nutrition, particularly among the American people, has greatly improved. Dental hygiene has become an almost universal practice, at least by the majority of persons in the higher socio-economic levels to which university students belong. Dental health education has been carried on at a constantly accelerating rate since 1910, and its emphasis has been increasingly on the desirability of early and frequent dental care to prevent the deterioration and loss of teeth.

"Nor has all this good advice been disregarded by the public. The teeth of most of these university students had been given good care. These young people keep their teeth clean and they go to their dentists to obtain fillings and other repairs or replacements when these are needed. The point is that they are needed. Despite all the care and attention that has been and is being given to the teeth of university students, these teeth are now decaying to a greater degree than they were 10 years ago and a still greater degree than they were 20 years ago.

"In the 1929 group of university freshmen there were 3,388 individuals, of whom 61, or about 1.8 per cent, had teeth entirely unaffected by caries. In the 1939 group, consisting of 4,348 students, there were only 51 who showed no evidence of caries, about 1.15 per cent. In the 1949 group, consisting of 4,412 students, only 30 had perfect teeth, a percentage of 0.68."

Nutrition at a Low Ebb

It is stated in the above article that nutrition of the public has improved since 1910. *That* positively is not so. The ever increasing amount of chemical fertilizers used in growing our food crops and the greater amounts and increasing potencies of the poison sprays is causing an alarming degeneration in the nutritional quality of our food. This does not take into consideration the increasing amount of tampering with foods in the factories where it is processed. Our foods are becoming more and more devitalized and our teeth and general health will retrograde more and more as this tendency continues. Where will this all lead to? If the present method of food production continues for another 50 years, I see chaos in our mouths and in our bodies. Also, more cancer and polio will result, until there will be complete revolt by our bodies. The figures at the University of Minnesota are only one sign. There are many others.

Two Soils Compared

That the health of the teeth depends on the fertility of the soil in which our foods are grown has been demonstrated in an experiment conducted at Tufts College Dental School of Boston, and the Massachusetts Institute of Technology. It was written in the March 8, 1951, issue of the *New England Journal of Medicine*. The intention in this experiment was to compare the soil fertility of New England with that of Texas. Two groups of hamsters were used. One was fed on milk and corn that originated on a New England soil, the other from a North Texas soil. Both groups also

[584]

received alfalfa that was purchased without regard to the place it was grown. It was found that the Texas-fed hamsters suffered 50 per cent less cavities in the teeth. The article winds up with the statement that "a mechanism operated in the New England foods that aided materially in production of dental decay. Investigations to determine whether this factor is organic or inorganic are contemplated."

This experiment demonstrates that the answer to health will be found in the soil to a great extent. There are other factors, but the condition of the soil in which our food is raised may well be the most prominent one. New England has been farmed the longest. Much of its fertility may be farmed out of its soils. Erosion over long periods has depleted it of its best topsoil. Long-time use of chemical fertilizers has reduced its population of earthworms and beneficial bacteria. In the West the same process is going on, but the soils there are still closer to the virgin state than those of New England. This hints at a test of the organic method versus the chemical one. We have received letters from Tufts College with regard to their intention to do this very thing. To persons who reside in New England I would strongly suggest the taking of bone meal daily. Many medical tests have proven conclusively that it greatly aids in arresting the formation of cavities.

CHAPTER 164

Natural Foods Can Prevent Heart Trouble

A theory of what causes heart disease based on Darwin's theory of evolution may seem a bit far-fetched, but that is exactly what T. L. Cleave, Surgeon Captain in the Royal Navy of Great Britain, has written in his latest book, *Fat Consumption and Coronary Disease: The Evolutionary Answer to this Problem.*

Concentrating foods by the use of machinery is largely responsible for degenerative disease, for when foods have been concentrated and processed, the natural instinct of appetite can no longer guide one in selecting foods or in deciding how much to eat. A bar of chocolate contains as much sugar as a dozen apples. The tongue would know when to stop eating the apples. Since concentrated sugar was unknown to human beings up to several hundred years ago, the human tongue has not learned about chocolate bars what it learned thousands of years ago about apples. So one eats more of the chocolate than he should.

[585]

Fat Consumption and Coronary Disease was published by Philosophical Library, 15 East 40th Street, New York, New York. On the first page of this slight, 38-page book, Dr. Cleave tells us that, according to the Darwinian theory, a human being may rely on the instinct of his own appetite with absolute confidence to tell him what to eat, but only so long as the instinct is being exercised on natural substances—that is on foods occurring in the natural environment of the individual.

So that we get this important point clear at the beginning—apples are natural substances, all fruits and vegetables are natural foods in the environment of human beings. Nuts and meats are natural foods. And Dr. Cleave believes that man has been cooking his food for so many thousands of years that cooked food can be called "natural" to his environment. But processed foods are not natural and hence we do not have any way to gauge how much of these foods we should eat according to our appetite for them.

White sugar and white flour, then, are the two foods which have been so highly concentrated that they are not foods natural to our environment, even though they come from grains and sugar cane.

How Can You Tell What You're Really Hungry For?

So one of our troubles is our inability to determine naturally what foods we should eat, since we are surrounded by processed foods. Then, too, there is another reason why we suffer, nutritionally speaking, from our over-civilization, says Dr. Cleave. A man may not want what is available but would like some other type of food; or he may not want any food at all at that particular time, because, for example, his mind is preoccupied with the matter in hand or simply because he is very tired. But it is mealtime and his wife has prepared food, or he must eat according to the menu in the restaurant where he goes, or he is a guest in someone's house, and, of course, must eat with apparent relish what is put before him. "So he disregards his appetite and eats something he is not hungry for; the natural law of adaptation is broken and the damage is done."

Another form of unnatural interference with the exercise of our appetite instinct lies in what the cook does to food in the kitchen. She makes, says Dr. Cleave, "arbitrary food mixtures." Let's say you are hungry for potatoes. If the potatoes are French fried, you are bound to get a considerable quantity of fat which you did not want, along with the potatoes. Let's say you want a piece of veal. If the cook breads it or flours it, dips it in egg, covers it with parsley or tomato sauce, you are getting a lot of different foods you were not hungry for, so eventually you lose the ability to distinguish among them, so far as appetite is concerned. This might very well be another reason, we believe, why primitive people do not have the food problems we have, for their cooking is so simple that these contradictions would never arise.

Ice cream is the perfect example of a "crazy mixed-up" food, so far as Dr. Cleave is concerned. He says, "In Nature sugar is usually derived from a fruit, occasionally from a vegetable and it is rare to find more than a trace of fat in either. Yet in both chocolate and ice cream the majority of the calories are derived from fat." On a hot summer's day your natural appetite regulator might tell you you want something sweet. A piece of fruit would satisfy you perfectly. But there's no fruit around, so you get a dish of ice cream. You get the sugar but you also get a heavy load of fat which you weren't hungry for.

Dr. Cleave says that, if an overconsumption of fat is related to heart disease, then there is only one cause for this overconsumption, that is, not in the fats themselves but in their consumption in excess of the individual's appetite. "In short the cause is eating fats for which the individual is not hungry."

Of perhaps a little less interest is Dr. Cleave's analysis of the statistics on heart disease as related to the various parts of the world. He takes these statistics apart expertly, showing that the effect of fat in the diet is related to many, many things, all of which must be taken into account if the statistics mean anything at all. Diet among the Eskimos is excessively high in fat. But the Eskimo can get practically no energy from carbohydrate foods; they don't exist where he lives, so he must eat large amounts of fat. But in southern countries where considerable carbohydrate food is eaten there is no need for large amounts of fat in the diet.

Individuals who do hard physical work need more calories in their diets than those who sit around all day. So a difference in occupation may make all the difference in how much fat you should eat, regardless of what part of the world you live in or what kind of fat you eat. People whose families have lived in tropical countries for thousands of years who come north and are suddenly exposed to all the hidden fats in foods which they are not adapted to are likely to suffer greatly from this excessive fat consumption.

Preventing Heart Trouble By Eating Properly

Statistics aside, then, what are Dr. Cleave's recommendations? Here they are. First, the two rules: 1. to eat foods in their natural state (which in the case of civilized man permits simple cooking) and 2. to eat these foods in strict proportion to the appetite, which involves eating mixtures of food only if made in accordance with personal tastes.

"With regard to the first rule," he says, "this leads mainly to avoiding two groups of food—white flour and commercial sugar and all the products made from them. These two groups of food are no longer remotely near their natural state, and those who subscribe to natural principles cannot safely have anything to do with either of them. These persons will also be on guard against such maneuvers as the practice of taking natural flour, removing the bran, adding certain vitamins and salts, and then claiming that the result is virtually as good as the natural product. ("Enriching foods" in other words) . . .

"The first rule leads to the exclusion of very few other classes of food, all meat, poultry, fish, eggs, *fats*, vegetables, fruits and unrefined cereals being freely allowed . . . A not so obvious exception is honey, and certain fruits such as dates which contain 76 per cent and 64 per cent of sugar respectively. Honey under natural conditions would be available only in minute quantities, and dates would, to white races, not be available at all; special care is, therefore, indicated with very concentrated foods like these . . .

"With regard to the second rule, this comes down to avoiding the arbitrary meals and food mixtures described earlier in this monograph. In connection with arbitrary meals, it may be noted that it is essential that a man should decide beforehand what it is that he really wishes to eat . . . If circumstances prevent one from eating what one wishes, it is better to defer the meal until this becomes possible later. Trouble will seldom ensue from taking this step, as in civilized conditions the danger lies nearly always in eating too much, almost never in eating too little.

"Finally, it is clear that the more the first rule is departed from, the more the second rule should be adhered to. For the foods disallowed by the first rule are those that have been greatly altered from their natural state, and this alteration nearly always involves *concentration*. And the more concentrated the food, the more obvious becomes the importance of meticulously matching it with the appetite."

One final word on Dr. Cleave's "rules." We hope we have made them crystal clear. When he says that individuals should eat what they feel hungry for, he does not mean that you should choose the chocolate cake rather than the mince pie for dessert because you feel hungry for chocolate cake. Both of these foods are, of course, out of bounds. He means that if you feel like eating a slab of beef and an apple for lunch, then that's what you should have, and if the only food you can possibly get at lunch is chicken a la king in a patty shell, don't eat anything for that meal. Such a chicken dish contains a welter of foods you were not hungry for and the patty shell is stiff and crisp with "hidden fat" that you do not want.

We can foresee all kinds of protests from readers who decide to follow Dr. Cleave's suggestions. What if every member of a family of 8 decides he is hungry for a different food? What do you prepare for dinner? Simplicity in the preparation of meals is the answer—and that is the other part of Dr. Cleave's program. It shouldn't be too hard to get the family to agree on beef one day, fish another, chicken another and so forth. In the matter of fruit, of course, each member of the family can choose his own if you keep a goodly variety on hand and serve them raw, and the same goes for raw vegetables. Simplifying your meal-preparation is best from every angle.

CHAPTER 165

Cherries and Dizzy Spells

By J. I. Rodale

Sometime in May, 1950, I began to suffer from dizzy spells which occurred only during the night, while I was in bed, and only when I was in the act of turning from one side to the other. At such a point I would feel my head whirl, but the feeling would disappear in a moment, as soon as I settled myself, only to come back again when I turned again. This was something to worry about because most of my diet was raised on our farm on a highly fertile soil without the use of chemical fertilizers or poison sprays. This diet had cured me of asthma, headaches, colds, had practically stopped the formation of cavities in the teeth and given me a wonderful feeling of health. So with the appearance of this condition, I knew that there was a new factor that had entered my life which was its cause.

For the last 10 years I have never permitted any new pain or other negative condition that appeared, to stay with me too long. By concentrating on it and studying everything I did daily I always found something new, which by its elimination always cleared up whatever it was. I felt confident that it would not take me too long to track down the offending item this time, too. It could not be a serious change in one of my organs, I was sure, because of my diet and generally healthy habits. I do not smoke. I may take a drink socially about once in two weeks. I get more than 8 hours of sleep a day. What could it be? I actually enjoyed having the condition, knowing it was going to be a game to track down its cause. I always get a wonderful thrill when the problem is solved.

What is Dizziness?

I referred to a medical encyclopedia: Vertigo, which is the term that the medical profession applies to dizziness, may accompany many diseases and abnormalities. It may be acute indigestion, epilepsy or a dizziness connected with the ears because in the ears are located canals which control the equilibrium of the body. It might be anemia or a lack of oxygen in the brain, or a preliminary symptom of an oncoming disease. It might be due to high blood pressure, a stomach disorder, constipation or a food allergy. It could be a disease of the brain. Very helpfully the encyclopedia said, "Treatment of dizziness obviously depends upon the cause in each case," but I figured I would rather remove the cause than treat it.

"Why don't you go and see a doctor?" asked my wife. "You are probably suffering from overwork and it may lead to something serious."

"It wouldn't hurt to wait a few weeks and see whether I can find the cause of it," I replied. "Besides no one suffers from mental overwork if they enjoy the work as intensely as I do. When a person begins to say, 'This work is killing me,' *then* it is time to cut down on it. I do not have any headaches."

Well, there was my dizziness and my family began to look at their bread-giver with concerned eyes. I was on a low salt diet, which means a low sodium diet. Could that be the cause? I decided in the negative, because a low salt diet actually cures high blood pressure, of which one of the symptoms is dizziness. In fact I know of several cases where persons suffered from dizziness and were cured by eliminating salt. My blood pressure for age 52 tested by my physician was as near perfect as it could be.

Tracking Down the Cause

My dizzy spells appeared a few weeks after moving to the farm. In the winter we lived in the city of Allentown. Every year, along about May we moved to our place in the country which is the experimental farm of ORGANIC GARDENING AND FARMING magazine. Could my dizziness be due to this change in some way? I checked on our oil tank in the basement of the farmhouse and found a leak. The floor was all messed up with oil which might have volatilized and spread through the house. Could this be the cause? Was it the mattress of my bed on the farm? Had something happened to it over the winter to produce a condition to which I was allergic, for my dizziness came only during sleep? Sometimes, the organic materials that are a part of mattresses might decay and give off substances that affect allergic people.

I even looked upon my pajamas with suspicion. They had a peculiar chemical odor every time they came from the laundry. But that was true also of the previous season when I slept in Allentown and did not suffer from dizziness.

Could it be caused by bad habits of breathing, sighing, yawning and swallowing air? Could it come from excess of rubbing the scalp? As I was no longer using soaps or shampoos on my hair, I would rub my scalp more vigorously every day.

"Perhaps it is due to that sensitive tooth of yours?" suggested my wife. "You should have it extracted." "It cannot be," I answered. "I take bone meal every day and it has overcome the sensitivity of that tooth. Were it not for the bone meal, I am sure that by this time I would have lost more than that tooth."

I was completely mystified! I seemed to be living a healthy life and eating healthy food. What could be this new factor that was threatening to undermine some organ of my body? Dizziness was not something that could be sneezed at. For every effect there must be a cause. Things do not just happen for no reason at all. The fun of it began to wear off. I began to worry.

Another Kind of Dizziness

One more thing about my experience with dizziness may be of interest to my readers. Several years ago I placed blackboards on the 4 walls of one of my offices where I spend the afternoon each day. My editorial work is done in the morning in a different place and this black-boarded room is where I look after the business interests of our publishing company. The purpose of these boards is to list upon them every mailing of circulars that we make and each year there are hundreds of them. In order to be able to list as much material as possible we ruled the boards rather close together with up-and-down, heavy, white, cloth-strip lines of shiny white material which were pasted on the board. Looking upon the boards there is a rather disconcerting array of these narrow white cloth lines against the contrasting black of the board. And I mean disconcerting! I can assure you it was not soothing to my mind. Every time I looked up from my work heavy white lines would run up and down before my gaze. In a few weeks I began to feel a dullness in the head. There was no dizziness similar to the general subject of this discussion, but there was a confused, uncomfortable feeling which stayed with me all day long. One day, I came to the conclusion that it was those white lines on the board that were doing it. We substituted light gray thinner ones marked with a pencil, which could hardly be seen unless you walked straight up to the boards and within a few days my condition cleared up. My head became as before—clear and light and comfortable. As I say, it was not a feeling of dizziness that it had caused, but a dullness. However, I think it is so close to a state of dizziness that I thought it worthwhile mentioning here, indicating how a simple thing that we do could affect the head. It is possible with some people, such a condition would send them to the doctor and a course of medication.

But my sleeping dizziness came about a year after this black-board experience and is another matter entirely. About June 10 the entire family went up to Massachusetts to attend the graduation of my daughter Ruth at Wellesley and we were away for about a week. What was my surprise when I noted the complete absence of any dizziness on the third night away from home. My first reaction was that it must be due to the fact that I was sleeping on a different mattress. For that entire week I was free of all symptoms of dizziness. It would be necessary to await my return home to see whether there would be a return of my old condition. I was sure that it would be found to be something that I was doing at home.

The Villain Discovered

When I did return it took 4 days for the old condition to return, and return it did with a vengeance. I was back to where I had started from. But within a few days I discovered the cause. It was a dark horse—nothing that I had previously considered in the list of possible offending items. One day I was eating some cherries when I began to think of the poison spray residues that they contained. Wash them as you might, I know that you cannot remove all of the poison spray residues. This is a vicious practice in our agriculture. On many fruit crops, poisons are sprayed from 5 to 20 times a season in order to kill insects that infest the fruit. Fifty years ago, before much chemical fertilizer was used, very little was heard about poison spraying, but with the increased use of artificial fertilizers, the

[591]

balance of nature has become more and more upset and growing numbers of insects are getting into the hair of the orchardist and his trees. This is an interesting subject. There is much evidence that insects prefer foods that contain deficiencies and such conditions prevail where continued artificial practices produce blown up crops which lack the rare mineral elements. Where natural fertilizers such as manure and residue plant and animal matter are employed, a more healthy condition prevails in the soil and less insects come. We do not yet have our own supply of cherries on our farm. These purchased ones that I was consuming in piggish quantities had surely been sprayed with poisons. Was this at the bottom of my trouble? On my trip to Boston I had eaten no cherries. I decided to refrain for a few days and see if anything would happen.

It did. Within 3 days my dizzy spells stopped. Now in order to be sure, I began to eat cherries again, and within a few days the dizziness returned. I did this several times—refraining and then returning to the eating of cherries and each time the dizzy spells returned a few days after eating the cherries and cleared up a few days after discontinuing the eating of them.

My Tolerance To Poisons

Now, permit me to explain something which makes me different from the average person who eats cherries. Most of the food our family eats is grown by ourselves, organically, without the use of chemical fertilizers or poison sprays. Even in the winter we grow our vegetables in a hothouse on our farm. When I eat out in a restaurant two or three times a week, I am careful not to eat vegetables which I know are sprayed. My body, therefore, has become cleansed of the poisons that come from sprayed foods, and has lost its tolerance to them. The body of the average person develops a tolerance to these poisons, and becomes calloused to them to a certain extent. What the ultimate effect on the body is, science must soon determine, for such diseases as polio and multiple sclerosis may be caused by the poisoning of the nerves. Medical science must become alarmed and begin to question the agriculturist, who does not know that what he is doing may be harmful to the public's health. Many headaches that you get may be due to poison sprays on your food. Grow your own vegetables if you can get near a piece of soil, and reduce the amount of poisons you take into your body.

Regarding the fact that my body is sensitive to the intake of poisons, more than that of the general public, I am reminded of an experience a friend of mine had who lived for years among some Peruvian Indians. They use no chemical fertilizers nor poison sprays and his body gradually had become cleansed of such substances. But when he left them and reached Panama, the first meal there made him deathly ill. The poisons that the food contained were too much of a shock to his unconditioned body. We must thank the Creator for having given us such a wonderful body that it can condition itself. It can withstand abuse. It reacts quickly to new healthful practices even though previously it was subjected to insult.

[592]

The High-Powered Poison Sprays

A question that might be asked is, "Mr. Rodale, how is it that you who eat such a fine diet and are so healthy, will react so quickly the moment you do such a simple thing as eating a few cherries?" In fact cherries are a symbol of simplicity. Does not one say, "Life is a bowl of cherries?" But poison is poison. I would be afraid to drink carbolic acid. And our poison sprays are becoming more lethal each year. Lately DDT has been used on cherry trees. Even as recently as 5 years ago I probably could have eaten this fruit without incurring the dizziness. I was a victim of our new high-powered poison sprays. Insects are becoming more numerous and bolder and the chemist must subdue them with more highly poisonous poisons. And what of tomorrow? What more vicious poison will be used then? Now the entomologists are speaking of applying the poisons directly into the soil, to be absorbed into the roots and into the leaves, so that when an insect takes a bite of a plant, he will instantly curl up his toes. But how about people who may eat such a plant? How reckless can science become?

The lesson you can learn from all this is to peel such fruit as apples and pears. Eliminate entirely such fruit as cherries and grapes which are impractical to peel. In their place eat bone meal every day, for it contains the minerals that you would be deprived of by not eating fruit skins.

CHAPTER 166

Nature-Conforming Nutrition— The Best Cancer Preventive

In a lecture on the principles of oncology (the study of tumors) and the crisis of cancer research, A. Greil, at the first Austrian Cancer Congress, 1919, emphasized that "primitive forest-nomads living from hand to mouth with completely natural habits of eating and propagating are utterly incapable of producing abnormal cancerous tissues." During a 10-year residence in East Asia, J. Pick proved the fact that cancer is a rare disease among natural peoples who also do not eat meat. An English physician confirmed this observation during a 9-year stay in Tibet where he was able to establish the existence of only 3 cancer cases. The disease is also said to be rarer in Russia than in other European countries and statistics show it to be more prevalent in cities rather than in the countryside and to occur in higher economic brackets rather than in poorer sections. These differences seem to rest on the more nature-conforming and simple diet of poorer people and farmers according to P. G. Seeger, M.D., in the medical magazine, *Hippokrates,* 1951, Vol. 13.

In 1932 Schrumpf-Pierron found that malignant cancers were 10 times more common in Europe and America than in Egypt and that the degree of malignancy—when they did occur—was far less among Egyptians. The native peasants of Egypt rarely sicken with cancer. However, as they adopt European customs and collect in cities, abandoning their ancestral ways of diet, just to such an extent does their immunity to cancer disappear. According to statistics from South Africa, cancer is extremely rare among the natural-living African peoples there. However, with the adoption of the white man's way of life, including white bread, white sugar and cooked food, the cancer rate rises proportionately and is highest among those sections of the population who have intermarried with the whites. With truth does A. Waerland state: "Civilized man is the only living creature on the earth who defiles his food before he devours it." In this one sentence he touches on the most basic fact of the entire cancer problem, Dr. Seeger believes.

Oxidation—Enzymes

The separation from nature that begins with city-dwelling, in association with civilization-dictated ways of living, requires that civilized man adopt a diet consisting almost exclusively of cooked, therefore denatured, substances. The cooking results in a deficiency of chlorophyll (the substance that makes plants green) and consequently a deficiency in all the products which chlorophyll assists in manufacturing in the body. All living things require oxygen which, by the process of oxidation, changes food into energy and growth. This process is aided by the presence of chlorophyll. If little or no chlorophyll is present, all the other substances created or influenced by it in this very complex process are also deficient. These substances are called oxidation-enzymes. The result, therefore, is an impoverishment of the organism in the vital oxidation-enzymes and in the vitamins, especially C. Cancer cells always show a complete absence of vitamin C.

After 15 years of research, Dr. Seeger's theory on the origin of cancer is (greatly simplified): the cancer virus passes into the cells of a new born child through the placenta or in mother's milk. Up to a certain age the cells of young organisms contain enough oxidation-enzymes to provide for the oxidation process, so that viruses and bacteria are checked and remain in the cells without producing disease. But when, as a result of age and improper nourishment, a deficiency of these enzymes occurs, the virus grows and propagates, unchecked, along with malignant degeneration of the cells. It has been proved that cancer cells do not contain 3 of the enzymes which are active in the process of oxidation. Cancer cells have also been found to be deficient in cytochromes, another substance important in oxidation. These discoveries suggest that deficiency of these substances in the human body may cause, or partially cause, the growth of cancer.

Enzyme Deficiency Traced to Devitalized Food

A condition of deficient oxygen often exists not only in cancer cells but in precancerous ones and in the total organism as well. As a result of this, the molecules of protein in the cells regroup themselves and become instead giant virus molecules. So even without an actual virus infection, a formation of a virus is possible simply because of a deficiency of the various oxidation-enzymes. There follows in Dr. Seeger's article the description of other very complex changes that take place in the structure of the cells under these circumstances, including the release of several substances found in cancer cells. This entire breaking-down process in the cell appears to be the result of deficiency in the oxidation-enzymes, because of the denatured and devitalized food which forms "civilized" diet.

Vitamins

In addition to the oxidation-enzymes, the vitamins have a great significance in the origin of cancer. Cancer cells lack vitamins C, B and A. Cancerous and even precancerous organisms have a terrific deficiency in them. Through a continued deficiency of vitamin A, an idleness in vitamin C supply occurs and the vitamin C is not replaced quickly enough. Hence a deficiency in vitamin C will always exist. The presence of vitamin C is of utmost importance in the entire oxidation process that takes place in the cells. Vitamin A is also important, for the presence of vitamin A brings about the decomposition of certain fatty acids. Through a deficiency in vitamin A the increase of these fatty acids in cancer cells can be explained.

Greatest attention should be paid to the vitamin B_1 deficiency caused by the use of white flour and white bread. On the other hand, vitamin B_1 along with vitamin C may increase twice and even threefold the oxidation-enzymes in the blood, which are so important to the whole oxidation process.

Contrary to the opinion held by the majority of doctors, the cause of cancer has nevertheless something to do with a natural diet and a healthy way of living. Anyone who for a period of 10 years nourishes himself falsely and has an intake of denatured food (that is, a man who omits the items of raw diet and chlorophyll that are needed as suppliers of oxidation-enzymes and vitamins) is on the best way to kill himself with his diet; he has good reason to be fearful of death by cancer. Complete vegetarianism will not be necessary to prevent this, but there is a need for the liver and muscles, for example, to contain considerable quantities of oxidation-enzymes found only in green, leafy vegetables.

The respiratory system consists of systems for the oxidation of the cells and of the smallest blood vessels, the capillaries. The cells are violently disturbed in a cancerous condition. But the capillaries, too, are damaged by denatured diet, the result of which is impaired blood and oxygen supply. Certainly fruits and vegetables rich in enzymes and vitamins are necessary for a healthy, efficient circulatory system, filled with easily flowing blood. Disturbance of the inner respiratory system is not the only basis for the cause of cancer, but it is the chief factor, claims Dr. Seeger. The basis of the disturbance is unnatural, denatured diet.

[595]

Improper Breathing

In addition, Dr. Seeger believes that most persons breathe superficially, with only about one-fourth to one-third of their lung capacity. He says that the farmer working in fresh air breathes better than the city dweller seated at an office desk. One consequence of improper breathing is, of course, a decreased supply of oxygen which creates the danger of oxygen-deficient disturbances. We suggest that the farmer who certainly gets more oxygen in his fresh-air job also needs more oxygen to carry on his heavy physical work, while the city-dweller does little hard physical work sitting at a desk, hence needs less oxygen.

The Dangers of Salt and Food Dyes

Salt, civilization's poison, dare not be forgotten. Salt causes not only increased cramping of the capillaries, but it has also been shown to be concentrated in body cells becoming increasingly cancerous, in reaction to which its biological opponent, potassium, fails. Under the influence of 10 milligrams of salt the activity of one of the oxidation-enzymes in human blood falls to one-half and even one-third of its normal value. As a result of this, cooking salt has a direct effect in stimulating cancer, says Dr. Seeger.

Also to be mentioned are the cancer-producing artificial coloring matters used in food processing, whose effect is to impair and destroy oxidation enzymes. Although the use of butter-yellow (one of these deadly coloring matters) has been prohibited by law, there are many other coloring matters now being used in candy, ice cream, etc., which are looked at with grave suspicion by many cancer experts.

Our Recommendations

We are not convinced of the value of vegetarianism, for we favor a diet high in protein and feel certain that some portion of this protein must be eaten in meats. Nor do we favor eating all vegetables raw. Waterless cooking at low heat, or cooking with as little water as possible preserves nearly all of the vitamins and minerals. Many vegetables, too, are scarcely palatable when eaten raw, because we have become so accustomed to cooking them.

In spite of these small differences of opinion, however, Dr. Seeger's recommendations of leafy vegetables containing large amounts of chlorophyll have our whole-hearted support, and his theory seems to us to represent most encouraging progress in cancer research.

[596]

CHAPTER 167

Farm Practices Influencing the Incidence of Multiple Sclerosis

By JAMES A. SHIELD, M.D., *Richmond, Virginia*
Assistant Professor of Neuropsychiatry, Medical College of Virginia

Man's kinship with and dependence upon the soil are expressed by Dr. V. G. Simkovitch[1]:

"Go to the ruins of ancient and rich civilization in Asia Minor, Northern Africa, or elsewhere. Look at the unpeopled valleys, at the dead and buried cities, and you can decipher there the promise and the prophecy that the law of soil exhaustion holds in store for all of us . . . Depleted of humus by constant cropping, land could no longer reward labor and support life, so the people abandoned it. Deserted, it became a desert; the light soil was washed by the rain, and blown around by the shifting winds."

In the occurrence of multiple sclerosis in Germany, England, Northern Europe in general, and the United States where large amounts of inorganic, incomplete chemical fertilizers are used by farmers, in contrast to the absence of multiple sclerosis in China, Japan, and India where natural fertilizers or manures are used, nature presents us with a challenging fact.

Farm practices which influence the total quality of the crop and, in turn, the quality of man's food, are the concern of this paper. Thus, the soil as a source of man's food, especially the trace elements, becomes the physician's problem. The doctor must demand that the agriculturist produce a food that will meet the multiple protoplasmic needs for optimal growth, development and function. Prescribing a good diet is not enough. There is very wide variation in the composition of fruits, vegetables, grains and meat, milk and eggs, when produced on different soils, in different sections of the country, on different farms, or even on different fields of the same farm. The Peckham Pioneer Health Service Centre in England discovered that feeding families in the Centre with ordinary, so-called balanced food diet bought from a shop was not enough. They were forced to grow the food themselves and to use not new methods but the ancient method of returning waste to the soil. Man's interference with the perfect balance between the natural processes of growth and decay may be largely responsible for the predicament of our malnutrition, in spite of adequate diet by the present standards.

A fertility that is optimal for the production of nutritional foods depends not only upon various elements, humus, physical structure, tillage, moisture, sunlight, but also upon the fauna of the soil. Microörganisms play an important part in making air nitrogen available to plants and in the decomposition of humus. Mycorrhizal fungi surround rootlets and stimulate metabolism as a living fungus bridge which connects soil and sap.[2]

In this discussion our interest centers in deficiency of the trace elements, (iron, cobalt, copper, zinc, chlorine, sodium, magnesium, manganese, sulphur, silver, boron, nickel, aluminum, arsenic, fluorine, iodine) and all protoplasmic needs known and unknown that are influenced by farm practices. The soil is being depleted of its fertility by large urban populations and industries. The maintenance of fertility is a farmer's problem, but the food that the American people consume is everyone's problem. Farm practices must protect and maintain this fertility in order that we may be able to buy quality foods that have the capacity to give optimal nutriment to our bodies.

The soil of England was being depleted in 1836 when Carswell[3] first noted a multiple sclerotic pons and cord, as an interesting neurological specimen. The soils of France were being depleted in 1839 when Cruveilhier[4] described the neuropathology of multiple sclerosis and gave two case histories. A few years later in France, Charcot[5] gave us a description of the clinical and pathological pictures of multiple sclerosis.

The soil of Germany was being depleted in 1840 when a chemist roughly "analyzed a human body."[6] He found calcium, nitrogen, phosphorous and potassium in addition to water. His crude methods showed the same elements to be present qualitatively in plants and animals, and he concluded that as long as these elements were replaced in the soil in generous quantities, neither plants nor people would suffer from malnutrition.

Thus, we see that multiple sclerosis, depletion of soil, and the utilization of inorganic chemicals, as a treatment for the soil were all introduced to man between the years 1836 and 1840.

A century ago, the prevailing practice in agriculture was to take from the soil without adequate replacement of its store of minerals and humus. Cropping had become so intense in Germany, France and England that nature could not replenish the soil. The natural process of laying down topsoils was too slow. The introduction of inorganic chemicals resulted in quantity production of food. The incompleteness of the chemicals used, and their tendency to accentuate incipient deficiencies of certain other elements in the soil, is now being recognized by agricultural research.[7]

There have been many suggested causes for multiple sclerosis, but there has been no proven etiological factor to explain its incidence. Pathologically, it is a demyelinating disease (affecting the nervous system), and there is some agreement that the acute lesions are characterized by perivascular (about a vessel) infiltration, edema and local glial proliferation[8], producing the coming and going of symptoms, exacerbation (increasing) of the old and appearance of the new, resulting in a chronic degeneration of the nerve parenchyma.

My observation has been in agreement with other neurologists in regard to the conditions that precipitate and influence exacerbation of this illness, namely, pregnancy, infections, inorganic chemicals, trauma, strains and stresses, exposure, vaccines, marriage, emotional upsets, lumbar punctures, and gross dietary restrictions. There is one common feature in all of the various things which precipitate the attack, increased demand on the body.

It follows that these factors can only precipitate the illness in individuals who are vulnerable. The geographic distribution of the incidence points out those who are relatively protected and those who are candidates for multiple sclerosis when hit with sufficient force by a precipitating factor.

Who Are the Vulnerable?

Multiple sclerosis, though thought by many physicians to be rare, and almost unheard of by the public, caused 1,301 deaths in the United States in 1944 as compared with 1,361 deaths from infantile paralysis and 2,045 deaths from pernicious anemia.[9] Multiple sclerosis is both less recognized by the physician and more crippling to the patient than infantile paralysis. In the New York City area in the first 46,875 selectees examined, 29 were found to have multiple sclerosis while 734 had tuberculosis, 170 had diabetes, and 8 had pernicious anemia. During 1933 a study of chronic illnesses in 113 New York hospitals revealed 1,050 cases of multiple sclerosis, and 551 cases of pernicious anemia among a total of 573,623 cases. A survey in Switzerland disclosed 36 multiple sclerosis cases per 100,000. In one locality there were 70 per 100,000. A survey in England and Wales showed 16 per 100,000.[10]

In order that we might have a better concept of the incidence of multiple sclerosis in the United States, I obtained, through the courtesy of the U. S. Department of Health, the statistics on the number of deaths that occurred in each state during the year of 1944. I also obtained this data on infantile paralysis and pernicious anemia during the same year for comparison.

TABLE 1

MULTIPLE SCLEROSIS

Year	Country	No. Deaths	Rate
1942	U.S.	1,388	1 per 100,000 population
1943	U.S.	1,399	1 per 100,000 population
1944	U.S.	1,301	1 per 100,000 population

TABLE 2

MULTIPLE SCLEROSIS

Year	City	Incidence
1918	Philadelphia	23 per 100,000 registrants examined
1918	Boston	10 per 100,000 registrants examined
1918	New York	13 per 100,000 registrants examined
1918	Chicago	10 per 100,000 registrants examined

TABLE 3

MULTIPLE SCLEROSIS

In World War I registrants for the draft, there was an incidence of 10 per 100,000 cases examined.

In 1918 there was an urban rate of 12 per 100,000 and rural rate of 8 per 100,000 registrants examined.

TABLE 4

INCIDENCE OF DEATH PER 100,000 POPULATION OF THE
NEW ENGLAND STATES

	Multiple Sclerosis	Poliomyelitis	Pernicious Anemia
Maine	1.5	0.0367	2.7
New Hampshire	3.3	2.2	3.1
Vermont	1.6	0.645	2.58
Massachusetts	1.4	0.42	1.8
Rhode Island	1.8	0.014	1.3
Connecticut	1.21	0.57	0.999

TABLE 5

INCIDENCE OF DEATH PER 100,000 POPULATION OF THE
MIDDLE ATLANTIC STATES

	Multiple Sclerosis	Poliomyelitis	Pernicious Anemia
New York	1.29	2.8	1.4
New Jersey	1.07	1.39	1.1
Pennsylvania	1.18	1.26	1.8

TABLE 6

INCIDENCE OF DEATH PER 100,000 POPULATION OF THE
NORTH EAST STATES

	Multiple Sclerosis	Poliomyelitis	Pernicious Anemia
New England	1.557	.5355	1.78
Middle Atlantic	1.2025	2.021	1.512

TABLE 7

INCIDENCE OF DEATH PER 100,000 POPULATION OF THE
EAST NORTH CENTRAL STATES

	Multiple Sclerosis	Poliomyelitis	Pernicious Anemia
Ohio	1.3	1.29	2.0
Indiana	1.8	0.89	2.29
Illinois	1.053	0.52	2.24
Michigan	1.43	0.87	2.09
Wisconsin	1.69	1.09	2.89

[600]

TABLE 8

INCIDENCE OF DEATH PER 100,000 POPULATION OF THE
WEST NORTH CENTRAL STATES

	Multiple Sclerosis	Poliomyelitis	Pernicious Anemia
Minnesota	1.64	1.48	2.24
Iowa	2.27	0.76	3.17
Missouri	1.005	0.373	2.15
North Dakota	1.92	0.38	1.73
South Dakota	1.7	0.56	2.6
Nebraska	1.54	0.85	2.56
Kansas	0.96	0.602	3.97

TABLE 9

INCIDENCE OF DEATH PER 100,000 POPULATION OF THE
NORTH CENTRAL STATES

	Multiple Sclerosis	Poliomyelitis	Pernicious Anemia
East North Central	1.325	0.9056	2.267
West North Central	1.487	0.76	2.66

TABLE 10

INCIDENCE OF DEATH PER 100,000 POPULATION OF THE
SOUTH ATLANTIC STATES

	Multiple Sclerosis	Poliomyelitis	Pernicious Anemia
Delaware	0.806	2.152	2.152
Maryland	1.005	1.256	0.603
District of Columbia	1.085	1.447	0.036
Virginia	0.65	2.086	0.93
West Virginia	0.475	1.41	1.35
North Carolina	0.484	1.212	0.484
South Carolina	0.333	0.79	0.508
Georgia	0.27	0.473	0.765
Florida	0.85	0.45	1.25

TABLE 11

INCIDENCE OF DEATH PER 100,000 POPULATION OF THE
EAST SOUTH CENTRAL STATES

	Multiple Sclerosis	Poliomyelitis	Pernicious Anemia
Kentucky	0.52	1.92	2.56
Tennessee	0.25	0.57	1.5
Alabama	0.296	0.445	0.519
Mississippi	0.254	0.406	0.914

TABLE 12

INCIDENCE OF DEATH PER 100,000 POPULATION OF THE WEST SOUTH CENTRAL STATES

	Multiple Sclerosis	Poliomyelitis	Pernicious Anemia
Arkansas	0.294	0.294	1.0
Louisiana	0.391	0.522	0.522
Oklahoma	0.872	0.41	1.538
Texas	0.336	0.8157	0.929

TABLE 13

INCIDENCE OF DEATH PER 100,000 POPULATION OF THE SOUTH

	Multiple Sclerosis	Poliomyelitis	Pernicious Anemia
South Atlantic	0.589	1.145	0.793
East South Central	0.3306	0.8417	1.38
West South Central	0.426	0.623	0.96

TABLE 14

INCIDENCE OF DEATH PER 100,000 POPULATION OF THE MOUNTAIN STATES

	Multiple Sclerosis	Poliomyelitis	Pernicious Anemia
Montana	1.304	1.956	1.304
Idaho	0.43	1.72	0.215
Wyoming	1.28	0.427	0
Colorado	2.36	2.19	1.05
New Mexico	0.206	0.823	0.823
Arizona	0.52	0.174	1.22
Utah	0.689	0	0
Nevada	0	0.767	0

TABLE 15

INCIDENCE OF DEATH PER 100,000 POPULATION OF THE PACIFIC STATES

	Multiple Sclerosis	Poliomyelitis	Pernicious Anemia
Washington	1.718	1.61	0.99
Oregon	1.44	1.78	2.37
California	0.741	1.294	0.49

TABLE 16

INCIDENCE OF DEATH PER 100,000 POPULATION OF THE WEST

	Multiple Sclerosis	Poliomyelitis	Pernicious Anemia
Mountain	1.153	1.178	0.727
Pacific	0.991	1.41	0.78

TABLE 17

MULTIPLE SCLEROSIS

China	Incidence
Estimated population 450,000.. 0 per 100,000 population	
Rural population 90 per cent.	
Urban population 10 per cent.	

There is the high urban and low rural incidence of the disease. Contrary to the general impression, it is shown that multiple sclerosis is not rare in the Southern states. I believe there is a tendency for the prevalence of multiple sclerosis to be in direct ratio with the number of neurologists in the respective states. I have seen patients from every Southern state east of the Mississippi. These figures are on the low side due to diagnostic error and intercurrent infections being recorded as the cause of death in patients with multiple sclerosis.

Multiple sclerosis could not well be a deficiency disease in the usual concept. The Chinese caloric intake is from 2,000 to 2,500 per day. The Chinese diet is deficient in calcium, in vitamins, proteins and fats. Yet the Chinese do not have sclerosis of their nerves, their blood vessels, blockage of their veins or hypertension. They do not have kidney or gallstones. They have a limited food supply, but this food is better suited to meet man's body needs as evidenced by the absence of degenerative diseases, in spite of the high incidence of infectious diseases. Their limited supply of food is grown by farmers who do not use inorganic chemicals which, in the light of present knowledge, tend to disturb the chemical balance of the soil and, in turn, to disturb the mineral and chemical content of the crops and, thus, affect the health of the animals that feed on the crops. The Chinese do not have multiple sclerosis.

What evidence is there that absence or insufficiency of trace elements affects plants and animals?

Beeson[11] writes:

"The recent increase of interest in the distribution of nutritional trouble in plants and animals is a natural sequence to the earlier work of diagnosing and classifying these troubles and their symptoms."

He gives 3 United States maps: first of the occurrence of boron and manganese deficiencies in plants; second, of the occurrence of copper, iron, magnesium, and zinc deficiencies in plants; and third, of the occurrence of mineral nutritional diseases in animals, namely, cobalt, copper and iron, causing nutritional anemias, calcium and phosphorus causing bone diseases, selenium toxicity and grass tetany.

The 1943 report of the Administrator of Agricultural Research[7] discussed the soil-plant nutritional relationship.

"Cattle in areas where cobalt is deficient in native plants become gaunt owing to loss of appetite, become listless and anemic; the hair coat becomes rough and the skin is scaly. After extended exposure to the deficiency, muscular atrophy develops and death occurs. In North Carolina cobalt deficiency is accompanied by a low manganese content of the forage,

[603]

while in Massachusetts the iron content is low. These multiple deficiencies have prevented a normal development of dairy and beef cattle. Trouble with sheep and dogs also occurs in North Carolina in those areas where the soil is depleted of certain trace elements."

A survey was made of pastures and hay lands in the Northeast where an ailment in cattle, called grass tetany, has been reported to be associated with intensive fertilization with nitrogen, potash and phosphate.

What is the relationship of mineral imbalance in soil, plants, and animals to multiple sclerosis? Ferraro[12] with repeated administration of potassium cyanide rather regularly produced pathologic changes characteristic of multiple sclerosis. Other chemicals such as injection of sulfanilamide have been followed by encephalomyelitis.[13] Carbon monoxide poisoning has precipitated a progressive multiple sclerosis.[14]

The chemical substances such as sulfanilamide, potassium cyanide, lead, arsenic, arsphenamine, carbon monoxide and nitrous oxide have been found to disturb the structure of the central nervous system and produce pathology closely resembling post-infectious encephalomyelitis. In animals that live on food from soils depleted of some elements such as cobalt, manganese, iron, et cetera, or from soil overfertilized with nitrates, potassium and phosphates, evidence of central nervous disease is found.

"The fertilization may possibly have accentuated incipient deficiencies of certain other elements in the soil. Preliminary results with new technics developed by the laboratory to study the effects of fertilizer and soil treatments on the mineral content of food and forage plants indicated that the amounts present in minute quantities in both hay and green vegetables are affected by liming and fertilization practices. On the basis of these results it seems possible that modifications of liming and fertilization practices may result in an increased content of some of the essential elements in soils and in the foods."[7]

Thus, circumstantial evidence points to the fact that unbalanced chemical fertilizers, either too much or too little, or in the wrong combination of minerals, interfere with the soil's ability to supply the necessary chemical elements for healthy plants and animals.

"The plant needs varying amounts of different elements, much of one, little of another; for example, cotton as a general rule needs at least 36 pounds of nitrogen, equivalent to 225 pounds of natural nitrate per acre. Natural nitrate contains a large amount of nitrate nitrogen, 16 pounds per 100, but application of 100 pounds per acre would not be adequate to correct the nitrogen deficiency of the soil as measured by the requirements of the cotton plant. On the other hand, "saltsick" (an anemia) of cattle feeding on certain pasture land in Florida is prevented by addition of a trace of cobalt to the fertilizer treatment. Application of a little zinc oxide per tree, or driving one small zinc-covered nail in the orange tree, controls the mottle-leaf disease for a period of several years."[15]

Composts of vegetable matters and animal manure contain all of the known elements contained in the human cell that are as yet unknown to the biochemist. Thus, natural manures have the potential capacity to give to the depleting soils a complete fertilizer, while the chemical fertilizer is an incomplete food supply for the plant and will continue to be until we perfect and advance our knowledge of microbiochemistry. Therefore, full quality food can be raised only on virgin soil and on soil that has been replenished by the refuse from all of its produce, both plant refuse and animal refuse.

The natural phenomenon that nature has presented for us of multiple sclerosis occurring here and not there, of its occurrence only in places where incomplete, commercial fertilizers are used in farm practices, presents for our consideration an experiment that has been carried on for over a hundred years. The subjects and potential subjects run into the millions. In order that we may have a limit to our geographic research, let us again take China, which has an estimated population of 450,000,000 people and is 90 per cent rural, and Germany, which, as greater Germany, had an estimated population of 79,000,000 people, with a rural percentage much smaller than China but which cannot be ascertained exactly. The time element in this experiment goes back a century. I do not think statisticians could question the number nor the time of this experiment. The Chinese farmer uses natural manure to produce his food; the German farmer uses inorganic chemical fertilizer to produce his food.

In 1840, von Liebig introduced the practice of applying inorganic material to the lands as fertilizer to replenish the depleted soils of Germany. This practice spread rapidly, and it became customary to apply mainly nitrates, potassium, phosphorus and lime. This incomplete fertilizer provided the major needs of the soil but overlooked the minor needs, minor though equally vital to the soil. On the other hand, in China the agricultural practice of intensified farming demanded that the depletion of these soils be prevented. For centuries the Chinese have returned to the land the refuse of the products of the soil and the manures of animals, including man. In Germany, before the war, multiple sclerosis was second only to syphilis in causing pathology of the nervous system. In China multiple sclerosis is such a rarity that authorities, such as Snapper and others, state that it is non-existent.

Where soils are depleted of certain minerals, biologists tell us of deficiency disease in plants, and they have found that very small amounts of the proper minerals added to the soil will eliminate the deficiency disease. For instance, in New Zealand, there was a soil-deficiency of cobalt in the grasses that made the pasture, which in turn caused the sheep to become paralyzed. The application of 3 or 4 pounds of cobalt per acre prevented the deficiency of the grass and eliminated the bush paralysis in the sheep.

In spite of our present knowledge of chemistry and of chemical fertilizer, we have not developed a technic to determine the minute traces of iron, cobalt, copper, boron, zinc, chlorine, sodium, magnesium, manganese, sulfur and perhaps many other chemical substances that are needed by plants. It is true that plants can grow without these trace elements, but in order for them to give a complete optimal diet to the animals that feed on them, they must be grown on a soil that is completely fertile. Until we develop further knowledge of soil and plant chemistry, reliance can be placed only in the natural manures that give a more complete and balanced fertilization.

Summary

We have a story of depleted soil. Man has attempted in a Western world to correct this by the use of a few chemicals, inadequate to meet the full needs of plants and animals as they represent only a few of protoplasm's mineral needs. These chemicals have the capacity to disturb the mineral balance and the natural fauna of the soil. People whose food comes from soils fertilized with chemicals appear to have more vascular diseases and more degenerative diseases. Multiple sclerosis is a degenerative disease. Its clinical characteristic of acute or subacute onset, with symptoms that improve or disappear, points to involvement of the circulation.

People who have fed on food produced by incomplete, inorganic fertilizers appear to be more liable to circulatory disease, more liable to central nervous system circulatory disease, more liable to vascular constrictions and dilatations, more liable to perivascular infiltration and to edema in the nervous system and to local glial proliferation due to disturbed mineral balance in their bodies and their blood streams. Therefore, when greater demands (the precipitating factors of multiple sclerosis) are put on their vulnerable bodies, these people develop the syndrome of multiple sclerosis.

The conclusion, thus, is indicated that the incomplete fertilization program carried on in Germany, England, Europe and the United States is contributing largely to the inadequacy of the quality of the diet, with deficiency of trace elements and unknown factors, contributing to and being largely responsible for the presence of multiple sclerosis in what appears to be ever-increasing incidence in the occidental world. It is also indicated that the use of complete and natural manures in the oriental world may be the factor in producing a more adequate diet, thus, explaining the Orient's freedom from multiple sclerosis and some of the other degenerative diseases.

(Reprinted in the *Congressional Record* of January 15, 1947)

REFERENCES

1. Simkovitch, Vladimir A.: *Hay and History, Rome's Fall.* Reconsidered from an Understanding of Jesus and Other Historical Studies. p. 161. New York: The Macmillan Company, 1921.
2. Howard, Sir Albert: *An Agricultural Testament,* Oxford University Press, 1940.
3. Carswell, Robert: *Pathological Anatomy.* Illustrations of the Elementary Forms of Disease. London: Longman (et al.) 1838.
4. Cruveilhier, J.: *Anatomie Pathologique du Corps Humain,* ou Descriptions Avec Figures Lithographiees et Caloriees des Diverse Alterations Morbides dont le Corps Humain est Susceptible, v. 2. Paris: J. B. Bailliere, 1942.
5. Charcot, J. M.: *Histologie de la Sclerose en Plagues.* Gaz. d. Hop., 41:554, 557, 566, 1868.
6. Yerkes, A. P.: *Soil—A Foundation of Health.* International Harvester Company, Chicago, 1946.

7. Auchter, E. C.: Report of the Administrator of Agricultural Research 1943, pp. 2-3. United States Department of Agriculture.
8. Putman, Tracy J.: A Multiple Sclerosis and Encephalomyelitis. Bulletin of the New York Academy of Medicine, 19:310 (May) 1943.
9. Statistics obtained through courtesy of the U. S. Department of Public Health.
10. Statistics obtained from the Association for Advancement of Research of Multiple Sclerosis.
11. Beeson, Kenneth C.: The Occurrence of Mineral Nutritional Disease of Plants and Animals in the United States. *Soil Science*, 60: No. 1 (July) 1945.
12. Ferraro, A.: *Experimental Toxic Encephalomyelopathy* Psychiat. Quart., 7:267, 1943.
13. Fisher, J. H.: *Encephalomyelitis Following Administration of Sulphanilamide*. Lancet, 2:301, 1939.
14. Hilpert, P.: *Kohlenoxydvergyting und Multiple Sklerose*. Arch. F. Psychiat., 89:117, 1929-30.
15. *If They Could Speak!* pp. 6-7. New York: Chilean Nitrate Educational Bureau, Inc., 1941.

Reprinted from the *Southern Medical Journal*, January, 1947.

CHAPTER 168

Environmental Errors
and Their Influence on Health

By B. Cooke, L.D.S., F.R.H.S., F.R.I.P.H.H.

Some 40,000 years ago True Man was nomadic. Those herds of animals which formed a valuable source of his food were followed by him during their movements after pasture, and their seasonal migrations.

The vegetable part of his diet grew in the wild state and was searched out during these wanderings. It consisted of the wild forms of most of the fruits and nuts we know today, together with water cress, fungi, the juicy rhizomes of certain plants, and the larger and softer leaf buds.

In addition to these foods, birds' eggs, young birds, newts, frogs, snails, fish, crayfish, grubs, insects, caterpillars and bones smashed up and reduced to a stiff, coarse paste were common sources of nutrition.[15]

It would appear that grain foods had little or no place in the diet of man at this period; and cooking, if practiced at all, must have been rare or primitive as no cooking implements have been discovered which can be attributed to the Azilian Age.

One of the surviving sketches of these early savages depicts two men smoking out a bees' nest, and it seems probable that honey, while being available in such small quantities as to have little influence on the general diet, was much prized as a luxury from which the "sweet tooth" of modern man has evolved.

Shelter from the elements was such as could be found in caves, rocks and other natural barriers, while "clothing" was limited to the use of animal skins loosely fashioned.

Such a mode of existence laid these early men open to sudden environmental changes—changes which frequently brought with them new diseases and pestilences.

Dental Disease

Dental disease would be essentially of a traumatic nature, limited to loss of teeth by violence, to exposure of the pulp due to excessive attrition, and to inflammation of the soft supporting structures either by trauma or as a symptom of systemic disease.

Any food, whether of plant or animal origin, that was procured by man before the beginnings of agriculture, had in its living state to survive a struggle for existence unsubsidized by him. Its successful survival was proof of its being better suited to those conditions of tilth, pH, humus, and mineral make-up of the soil, and to the other factors completing its environment, including exposure to sun, wind and rain.

Such food would be rich in vitamins, inorganic salts and other probable accessory food factors, the discovery of which has yet to be made, and whose importance remains to be assessed. It would be ideally suited to a people sharing the same general environment. What a contrast to the agricultural products of today, most of which would fail but for the vigilance of the grower in removing competition by weeding, and by carrying out other farming procedures!

The absence of cooking would almost certainly assure adequate vitamin and mineral intake, while probably allowing of a greater incidence of parasitic disease than is the case today.

On the other hand, many of the deficiency and degenerative conditions of modern man would be unknown to these early men.

Primitive Man Better Off

In many aspects of physical and nutritive fulfillment primitive man was immeasurably better off than his counterpart of today. The circumstances of his exposure to the rigors of the seasons, the uncertainty of his food supply, the strenuous effort needed to procure food and shelter, the ever-present dangers from wild animals and other men, and the degree of self-discipline he had to make in order to exist, developed his physiological mechanism to an extent scarcely approached by civilized man.

We at the present day regard the exercise of our physiological mechanisms and adaptive functions as requiring an expenditure of energy and effort that would be better reduced to the minimum, so we design our civilized environment to give the individual comfort, security, deficiency diets, mental dullness and loss of virility;[2] and while medicine has brought about a reduction in the number of deaths from infective disease, the more obvious results of a civilized mode of life are increases in length of life and in the degenerative diseases.

Farming, with its settled communities, appears to have become established some 7,000 years ago, and as it increased so nomadism decreased. There was division of labor in the community, and crafts and trades sprang up now that it was no longer essential that each primitive family should hunt for food.

Villages came into being amongst the cultivated fields, and these, together with the small walled cities that were built heralded the dawn of civilization as we know it today.[15]

Crop Production Problems

With cultivation came many problems of crop production, and animal domestication. It presumably did not take long to discover that the sowing of crops on the same piece of land year after year led to a fall in yield, so that after two or three years it was allowed to lie fallow while neighboring land was tilled; a practice which being carried out on a small scale, would have considerable merit if it were possible to spare land in large amounts to such wholesome "idleness."

Yield Primary Object

The importance of adding animal excreta and humus to the soil to keep up a high crop yield was not appreciated for a long time, and although our knowledge of increasing yield by the application of organic manures and mineral fertilizers, by weed control, and by other methods of farming has undoubtedly progressed, research has been directed primarily to crop yield, keeping qualities, and other commercial considerations, rather than to suitability as a food—an aspect of the problem of which our knowledge is scanty.

The growing of the same crop, or of a limited rotation of crops, on the same land year after year leads to a drain from the soil of certain trace and other elements of nutrient value, while further elements may become concentrated in quantities that are toxic to the chosen plants.[14]

In addition, certain mineral ratios of the soil which are of importance to some crops are upset, and in this country where the atmospheric pollution from town and village, and present methods of sewage disposal have such adverse effects on agriculture, the application of farmyard manure and lime—while being admirable in many respects—may not alleviate such mineral shortcomings, and under the conditions of industrialization the addition of certain artificial fertilizers is necessary if crop yield is to be abundant enough to meet requirements.

Stapledon and Howard

Present-day agriculture stands to benefit considerably from the study and furtherance of the work of Stapledon, and that of Howard.[1]

Stapledon introduced certain weeds with his crops, some of which were of value because of the increased aeration and drainage of the soil facilitated by their long roots, while others were of value because of their richness in trace elements.

It has been observed for many years that a little weed known as "eyebright" is beneficial to wheat production in Scotland, where it is known as "mother o' wheat."

For centuries, country folk have been using parsley, chervil, lettuce, purslane, winter-rock, strawberries and many other plants, as well as the extracts of certain berries such as rose hip, for the treatment of scurvy, to fasten loose teeth, to heal spongy foul gums, and for other ailments. We know that the assimilation of such plant food would, among other things, alleviate vitamin C deficiency.

Plants vary in the variety and quantity of trace and other elements they require and contain, and such differences make it appear certain that in addition to the possible vitamin content mentioned above, these plants would provide the body with essential mineral food factors if they were regularly introduced into the diet, and there can be little doubt that some of the beneficial effects attributed to certain forms of herbal treatment may be due to these vitamin and mineral constituents.

Howard's work is important in that he rendered his land fertile by methods of humus treatment, and by so doing attained a high measure of immunity from infective, parasitic and degenerative diseases both for his crops and his livestock.

Object of Soil Treatment

By his physical treatment of the soil, and the addition of organic manures and fertilizers to it, the agriculturist intends to replace those plant nutrients removed by his crop, and to render the pH, tilth and, indeed, the general conditions of the soil suited to the successful propagation of his future crop.

The allotment holder and the gardener frequently place reliance on what are popularly described as "complete mineral fertilizers." Such a mixture is made up of nitrogen, phosphorus and potassium, together with certain nutrient elements as impurities. Wallace[14] points out that the use of such comparative concentrations of these elements probably does more harm than good to plants whose nutritional needs are not met by these substances, and that there can be little doubt that the mineral impurities of such a mixture are to some crops of more nutritional value than the main constituents.

The use of fertilizers in crop production, while undoubtedly increasing yield, frequently does so at the expense of vitamin, mineral and general quality. It is of interest to note that when such crops are fed to animals they are neglected if crops grown on natural compost are available.[1]

Trace Elements

The subtleties of the living processes are of such intricate nature as to be little understood at the present time, but the importance of trace elements to both plant and animal life is beyond dispute. A diminution of the amount of boron normally present in the soil, for example, leads to the appearance of brown patches in such plants as cauliflower and turnip, and it is found that the boron as a beneficial element has more influence on the economics of these plants than have the microbes which bring about the decomposition and rotting revealed by the brown patches.[4]

The artificial selection of crops and the manurial and fertilizer methods employed in their propagation are primarily designed for high yield—very frequently at the expense of quality.

Frequently Destroyed

Even with the products of present-day farming, the vitamin and mineral content of crops is such that their consumption by the human population would lead to a higher standard of health but for the fact that a high proportion of these accessory food factors is frequently destroyed in the case of vitamins, or rendered unassimilable in the case of trace and other elements during their transport, storage, preservation and cooking.

In this connection it is interesting to note that in a large group of children recently selected for their freedom from dental caries, all were found to have a preponderance of raw fruits and vegetables in their diet.[12]

Present methods of sewage and refuse disposal are designed to render inoffensive the organic waste of the population, and while this is achieved, the processes employed are exceedingly wasteful and constitute a serious loss to cultivation.[7]

Lost To Agriculture

Phosphates, for example, are essential to most crops grown in this country, yet half the phosphate content of sewage is permanently lost to agriculture.

Urine is an extremely valuable sources of plant growth-regulating substances, and the number isolated from it is very large, including as it does hormones, auxins and vitamins; while urea is a rich form of nitrogen available to plants in solute form, and from the point of view of plant economy it may be the mammals' greatest contribution to the nitrogenous needs of plants. Under the present methods of sewage disposal, the percentage of human urine available to agriculture is negligible.

Disease and Environment

Disease may be defined as being a disordered state, a disturbance of the delicate physio-chemical reactions which constantly take place in the metabolism of an organism in an endeavor to keep its internal environment in harmony within its own structure, and in concert with its ever-fluctuating external environment.[6]

When considering any particular disease it is impossible to place causation on any single environmental error, although such a factor may be the predominant one.

No microörganisms have been discovered in association with the great majority of known diseases, and it is beginning to be realized that factors other than microbes play their part in disease.[4]

[611]

If a living organism is unable to adapt itself harmoniously to its environment, a condition of physio-chemical strain is set up within it, and if such disharmony cannot be reduced by adaptation by the organism, a state of disease arises which may bring about either the death of the organism, or may adversely affect but a part of it without seriously interfering with its existence as a whole.[4]

Living organisms have a natural power to resist infection, and all that is necessary to make this power operative is to see that the inherited propensities of the individual get the proper nutrition and full functioning essential to the development of the characters on which this power depends.[6]

Eradication of Disease

It will be seen that a valuable contribution towards the eradication of disease, be it of animal or plant, is the removal or modification of those factors of the environment with which the organism under consideration cannot adapt itself.

In humans, in the case of tuberculosis, for example, it is found expedient to move the patient into an environment more favorable to his well-being.

The agriculturist, with the artificial methods of crop production he uses today, finds his crops vulnerable to the ravages of various forms of aphids, blight and fungal disease, besides the very many plant indispositions which are unaccompanied by microörganic invasion of the plant tissues.

Plants frequently become liable to attack by such diseases and pests because the degree of disharmony from which they suffer prevents them from maintaining their tissue integrity, in face of microbic and other competition.

As our understanding of the living processes is so meager, we often adopt drastic measures in our efforts to "cure"—measures which, by their very nature, are a confession of our ignorance of such processes.

It is common practice for the agriculturist to use poisonous sprays on the pest attacking his plan, it having been found by experiment that such sprays properly directed at chosen intervals will be fatal to the parasite, and but of temporary inconvenience to the plant, thus preventing the latter from succumbing to the parasite. By the use of antiseptics, X-ray and radium therapy, the physician adopts methods not unlike these in the treatment of his patients.

State of Disease Persists

Plants treated in this way may survive, and to all outward appearances may reach full maturity and maximum size. Yet notwithstanding this each plant is in a constant state of disharmony with its environment and therefore in a state of disease, and will again be unable to preserve its tissue integrity against further such parasitic attacks when the life cycle of the parasite reaches the stage again when feeding on the plant is necessary to its existence.

The dentist attempts to preserve the dental tissues from microbic destruction by the insertion of fillings into the teeth which are not attacked by the microbes associated with decay, and which in the large majority of instances are tolerated by living tooth structure without obvious symptoms of disharmony, although it is inevitable that a certain degree of physio-chemical strain is set up in the tissues, by the filling, which modifies the original disharmony revealed by the caries lesion.[5]

Wallace[14] states that natural manures are insufficient in quantity to supply the needs of the human population, and as an example he cites the ideally managed allotment, the waste from which would be sufficient to sup-ply but a third of the area annually.

Much of the acidity of British soils can be traced to pollution of the atmosphere by the smoke of industry and that of the domestic hearth. Some 3,000,000 tons of solid matter are belched into the atmosphere of Great Britain every year. In addition, some 5,000,000 tons of sulphur dioxide—the equivalent of approximately 8,000,000 tons of sulphuric acid—are ejected into the air.[10]

The influence of this pollution on our lives is considerable, apart from the amount of damage done to buildings and fabrics.

The part played by the actinic properties of sunlight on vitamin D for-mation in the skin and on calcium and phosphorus assimilation is generally accepted.

Fog and Mortality

Dense fog is a frequent occurrence in industrial areas and large towns, and its formation is accompanied by high mortality from bronchitis and pneumonia in children under 5, and in the aged, due to the exceptionally high concentrations of impurities in the atmosphere on such occasions.[10] The importance of fresh air and sunshine to the tuberculous needs no stressing.

While some of the direct effects of atmospheric pollution are obvious, the indirect effects are not so widely known.

Smoke reduces sunlight, and the rate of conversion of carbon-dioxide into carbohydrate by vegetation is also reduced and still further minimized by the choking of the stomata by the tarry constituents of soot—constituents which damage the plant cells and bring about breakdown of chlorophyll.[3]

A concentration of 0.8 per million of sulphur-dioxide was found by Thomas and Hill to reduce photosynthetic activity by 44 per cent and plant respiration by 38 per cent, although no visible effects on the plant were detected.[3]

A concentration of 5 parts per million of sulphur-dioxide for an hour brings about complete stoppage of photosynthesis, and results in almost complete defoliation.

Oat seeds sown on the outskirts of Leeds showed 98 per cent germina-tion as compared with 68 per cent in the city and 17 per cent in the heavily polluted areas.[3] The smoke pall from the Midlands and the London area is so great that it drifts over Devon and Cornwall, and smoke from the Ruhr is found over Southern England when the wind is favorable to such move-ment.[10]

The amount of acid removed from the atmosphere by rain over large towns is such as to render it unfit for drinking.

Acidity and Soil Organisms

Cohen and Ruston[3] draw attention to the reduction in the total dry yield of vegetable matter brought about by this acidity, to the reduction in nitrogen, and to the increase in crude fibre in plants. They have also shown that soil microörganisms diminish rapidly in numbers as acidity increases, a diminution that is reflected in decreased ammonia production, and reduced nitrogen fixation and nitrification.

We are not content with the deterioration in the quality of food by the unfavorable conditions under which it is grown, but we needs must make things considerably worse by the methods we employ in its storage, preservation, transport and preparation for consumption. The consideration, for one moment, of our daily bread will provide an enlightening example.

Varieties of wheat are chosen for cultivation primarily for the amount of their yield and for their keeping qualities and freedom from disease, while comparative suitability as food for humans would appear to have received little serious consideration. The wheat is then milled so that the husk, germ, and most of the mineral and vitamin content are removed to improve keeping qualities and enhance commercial value, and agene is added to further these ends.

Agenized Flour

Nitrogen-trichloride, or "Agene" as it is commercially known, bleaches white flour still further, has a deleterious effect on proteins, lowers resistance to disease, brings about constipation, and is responsible for a partial loss of reproductive powers; besides being a cause of canine hysteria when flour so treated forms part of the diet of dogs.[8]

The case against the use of agene is a strong one, and more and more use is being made of chlorine-dioxide—especially in the U.S.A., although there is much to be learned concerning the effects on health of this chemical.

White flour will take some 6 per cent of water and will remain free from mould for a comparatively long time. Microbes and fungi have the power to decompose any organic matter that has not the property of being alive and in reasonable health, provided that the condition of moisture, temperature, and the facilities for gas interchange are not extreme. Yet this source of carbohydrate is so chemically treated by preservative, and is so deficient in vitamin, protein, fat and mineral matter as the result of milling, that these organisms cannot readily take advantage of it—it is just as much a deficiency food for them as it is for the human population for whom it is intended.

Refined Sugar

Sugar is a commodity of everyday life which is extracted from plants and rendered chemically pure. It is a refined deficiency food of commercial and domestic convenience, and provided it is kept free from such "contamination" as might provide fat, protein and accessory food factors it will remain unaffected by fungal and microörganic decomposition for a very long time, hence its excellent keeping qualities—qualities which are taken advantage of in the preparation of jam and other "preserves."

[614]

Before the war sugar was consumed at the rate of approximately 4 ounces per head of the population each day. If, in conjunction with this, we take into consideration the white bread eaten, some idea will be gained of the poor quality of our carbohydrate intake.

Sugar and Dental Caries

Recent experiments carried out by the Swedish Medical Board[11] revealed that extra sugar consumed at mealtimes did not obviously increase the existing dental caries rate, but should this extra sugar be consumed in the form of sweets between meals a greater incidence of dental caries occurred in two-thirds of the individuals eating it.

The value of sugar in the treatment of certain forms of illness is not disputed, but it is frequently stated, quite wrongly, that it is an essential item of our diet. As far as the writer is aware, no one who believes this statement has even attempted to explain how man has evolved from the sub-men during the past 500,000 years almost entirely without sugar, while the comparatively small amounts he obtained during this period in fruit, vegetation, and as wild honey were in natural states of organic combination with essential food factors and quite a different proposition from the devitalized product we consume today.

Chemically pure and chemically adulterated foodstuffs are widely accepted and used today because it is agreeable and convenient to do so. It is common practice for food manufacturers to label their products "pure," and while the term is intended to imply, and frequently does, that such foods are free from injurious adulteration, it very often denotes a deficiency food.

As long ago as 1756-1800 Parliament subsidized the wholemeal loaf as its value was appreciated, but it was not popular with the general public as the appearance and keeping qualities of white flour were more attractive.

Toverud[13] informs us that during the German occupation of Norway, when sugar consumption was nil, and raw fruit and vegetables were eaten in increased quantities, there was a sharp decline in the dental caries incidence in Norwegian children.

In this country the incidence of caries fell as the war progressed, and there would seem to be little doubt that this fall was due to a rationing of easily fermentable deficiency carbohydrate food such as sweets, jams and cheap confectionery; and to an increase in the consumption of "protective foods" as provided by orange juice and cod liver oil.

Not Enough "Live" Foods

There are good grounds for believing that we eat too many manufactured "deficiency" foods, not enough "live" uncooked fruits and vegetables, too much cheap refined carbohydrate, insufficient first-class protein and not enough fat.

Recent experiments on mice showed that these animals obtained roughly two-thirds of their calories from fatty food mixtures, and that the amount of protein and fat eaten remained approximately constant under all conditions of summer and winter, and that starch was used as a buffer to make up the balance of their calorific requirements.

In this country protein, fat and carbohydrate were consumed before the war in the approximate ratio of 1:1:4. Wide variations are possible without obvious harm, although it is advisable that 10-15 per cent of the total carlories should be obtained as protein, 20-35 per cent from fat and 50-66 per cent from carbohydrate. The last-named should not account for more than the amount stated but often does.[12]

Cereals are under suspicion as interfering with calcification, some 50 per cent of their contained phosphorus being present in the non-utilizable form of Phytin, and with our knowledge in its very incomplete state it is advisable not to rely on any one source for carbohydrate.

There is, unfortunately, much truth in Carrel's[2] statement that we prefer to study systems that can be easily isolated and approached by simple methods, and we are shy of the more complicated factors, especially if they have become accepted as part of our mode of life.

Huxley on Success

Huxley[9] draws our attention to the fact that most competition in civilized societies is between individuals, success, being social, consisting of one's ability to accumulate worldly wealth—biological and social success frequently being "inversely correlated."

To view the well-being of humanity from every possible angle should be the role of medical research, but to convince the population of the necessity for this would in itself be a formidable task since to remedy many of the environmental errors attendant on our mode of life would change factors familiar to our everyday existence that are almost traditional, while the financial interests associated with our present mode of life would certainly resist any such change.

The health of crops and livestock leaves much to be desired, and we have yet to appreciate that for far too long there has been a divorce between the study of our health and that of our livestock, and between the well-being of animals and plants generally.

We cannot successfully remedy the disharmonies of one artifically classified species of living creature without considering life in all its forms. The generally accepted biological truths show them to be inextricably interrelated.

Appalling Disease Rate

Vast sums of money are spent each year in world-wide medical research. We are appalled by the rising cancer rate; tuberculosis is an anxiety to us; we are puzzled by the high incidence of dental caries; the rheumatic diseases are matters of great concern; while disorganizations of the alimentary system are so prevalent as to be accepted as commonplace. We sadly deplore the pathological conditions with which we are faced, while almost completely ignoring the unfavorable environment we have created for ourselves.

But a few of the more obvious environmental errors have been touched on in this paper. Their existence is well known but their significance is not perceived, and the magnitude of the problem is such that we prefer to close our eyes to it.

What Improvement Entails

Any worthwhile improvement in our environment would necessitate drastic changes in our smoke abatement laws; in our control over stream and river pollution; in our methods of sewage and refuse disposal; and in our selection of crops grown as food, and the methods employed in their cultivation, storage, preservation and transportation, and in the methods employed in their preparation for consumption, and on our dietetic habits generally.

Although the errors of environment enumerated above have been set down as more or less distinct entities, they are, in fact, so interrelated that they are one and the same problem, and for this reason it is impossible to single out any one environmental factor as being responsible for any one condition of health or disease, and in each situation every environmental factor must be taken into consideration as it is their summation with which we have to deal.

When considering our well-being it is an obvious duty to see that the general environment is such that the degree of physio-chemical strain imposed by it on our adaptive mechanisms is such as to be within the limits of biological health.

To spend millions of pounds on medical research while ignoring the environmental perversities attendant on our civilized mode of life is both illogical and wasteful, and while the discovery of new drugs and of new methods of applying them may lead to increased control over disease, usually by changing its nature, pathological conditions will not necessarily be eradicated by such procedures nor their incidence reduced.

Unless the delicate physio-chemical reactions which constantly take place in the metabolism of a living organism in an endeavor to keep its internal environment in harmony within its own structure, and in concert with its everfluctuating external environment, are successful there will be disease.[5]

References:

1. Balfour, E. B.: The Living Soil.
2. Carrell, A.: Man, the Unknown.
3. Cohen, J. B., and Ruston, A. G.: Smoke: A Study of Town Air.
4. Cooke, B.: Disease and Decay. The *Dental Magazine and Oral Topics.*
5. Cooke, B.: Some Factors in the Aetiology of Dental Disease. The *Dental Magazine and Oral Topics.*
6. Cooke, B.: Oral Hygiene. The *Dental Magazine and Oral Topics.*
7. Cooke, B.: The Biological Changes Underlying Organic Decomposition and Their Relation to Dental Disease. The *Dental Magazine and Oral Topics.*
8. Howard, Sir Albert: Nutrition and Dental Health. *British Dental Journal,* 18/7/47.
9. Huxley, J.: Evolution. The Modern Synthesis.
10. Marsh, A.: Smoke. The Problem of Coal and the Atmosphere.
11. Swedish Medical Board: Experiments with Sugar at Meals. The *Dental Magazine and Oral Topics.* December, 1950.

12. Thorpe, W. V.: Biochemistry for Medical Students.
13. Toverud, G.: The Influences of General Health Supervision on the Frequency of Dental Caries in Groups of Norwegian Children. *British Dental Journal.* April, 1949.
14. Wallace, T.: Nutritional Problems of Horticultural Plants with Special Reference to Trace Elements. *Journal of the Royal Horticultural Society.* November, 1948.
15. Wells, H. G.: An Outline of History.

Reprinted from the *Journal of the Royal Institute of Public Health and Hygiene,* in England, June, 1951, by special permission.

CHAPTER 169

Are Chemical Fertilizers Harming Our Food?

Part of a statement made by J. I. Rodale on December 15, 1950, to a Congressional Committee formed to investigate chemical fertilizers

The purpose of this statement is to present data to show that there is a need for a scientific re-evaluation of the use of chemical fertilizers and poisonous insecticides in agriculture. In my opinion sufficient scientific data already exist to show that the extended organic method is far superior to the present general practice with respect to fertilizer usage, not only from the human health standpoint but from the point of view of preventing soil erosion and giving higher yields at a lower cost. It is therefore herewith formally suggested that a series of tests be instituted at every one of the Agricultural Experiment Stations of this country. Only in that way can the truth be arrived at. It will be the purpose of this statement to show the urgent need of such unbiased investigations.

History of the Organic Method

There is a tendency to say that the organic method is as old as history and was practiced by the oldest civilizations. This is not true as evidenced by the downfall of those civilizations. It is possible that with the practice of the extended organic method on a widespread scale in any civilization, that civilization will be able to persevere indefinitely and not go the way of Babylonia and Rome. These old civilizations countenanced the burning of manure as a fuel and stood idly by while the most rudimentary principles of basic agriculture were violated. The world has never seen, except in a few isolated cases, the practice of a thorough organic method, and with such a practice there is hope of building a civilization such as has never before been seen, for not only does physical health come from our food through the fertility of the soil in which it grows, but also our minds and characters are nourished and nurtured through that very soil. The people can only be a reflection of the soil which they culture. Poor soil—poor people. Mediocre soil—mediocre mentality of the people. Science can quickly prove this. And if this is true, the people should find out about it as soon as possible. The members of Congress should find out about it.

The founder of the Organic farming movement is Sir Albert Howard, who in 1940 wrote *An Agricultural Testament,* which was published by the Oxford University Press and has since gone into many printings. This book states in no uncertain terms that the use of chemical fertilizers are dangerous to the health of people, animals and the soil. It describes how oxen in India that were fed on organically-produced food could rub noses with oxen that were eating ordinary food and that had hoof-and-mouth disease and did not contract the disease even though they were not inoculated against it. Sir Albert was a British Government agricultural scientist of the highest standing. He was knighted for his contributions to agriculture.

In this country I introduced the organic method of Sir Albert Howard in 1942 by publishing ORGANIC GARDENING magazine, of which Sir Albert Howard was the Associate Editor until the day of his death in 1948. This magazine had about 90,000 paid subscribers at that time and at present, under its new title, ORGANIC GARDENING AND FARMING, has reached the 250,000 mark. In June 1949, we started to publish PREVENTION magazine, the purpose of which is to reach that part of the public that neither farms nor gardens, so as to teach them the importance of securing food that is organically raised. (Circulation now about 270,000.)

The Organic Method

The organic method is still in a process of improvement and evolution. Originally, it consisted merely of the making of compost from organic matter such as manure, leaves, weeds, etc. Then a source of phosphate was added in the form of phosphate rock ground up fine. Recently we have added the use of potash rocks of various kinds, usually granites. Potash is also used in the form of greensand. These give their nutrients to the soil without the acids or the high solubilities of the chemical forms of these elements. In the organic method we also use lime and slag from steel-furnace processes. There is already available manufactured fertilizers which contain organic matter and ground rocks mixed to give controlled combinations. A striving new industry is gradually being built up to serve the organic farmer and gardener, which has shown interesting growth in the last two years. The chemical fertilizer industry should not disdain this market for it may eventually be like the story of the tortoise and the hare or the railroad and the stage-coach. Once a person has started with the organic method it is rare to find him change back to chemicals.

Originally when the farmer was dependent only on the making of

[619]

compost it was quite difficult to practice the organic method, but now with the various rock fertilizers the need for organic matter is lessened and the method is becoming quite practical. Another thing to bear in mind in regard to the practicality of the method is that originally all the organic matter had to be composed first before being applied to the land. We now apply the raw organic matter direct to the land in places where crops will be planted later. This is not only labor-saving but conserves more of the nutrients of the organic matter.

What Is a Chemical Fertilizer?

The principle underlying the classifying of fertilizer into the two groups—that is, acceptable and unacceptable—organic and chemical, falls into 3 classes. One—those that are caustic or poisonous like ammonia. Two—those that leave undesirable residues in the soil. Three—those that are too soluble and which unbalance the nutrition of the plant.

The Health Aspect

Before I go any further I should like to discuss the effect of the use of chemical fertilizers on the health of man and animal and convey the opinions of physicians on this subject. The first bit of evidence that I should like to present is a piece of research that was done by Dr. Ehrenfried E. Pfeiffer at his laboratory at Threefold Farms, Spring Valley, New York, in 1948-49, which was financed by the Soil and Health Foundation, of which I am president. Dr. Pfeiffer was granted the honorary M.D. degree by Hahnemann College of Philadelphia for his work in diagnosing disease by means of crystallization of the blood. In this experiment two groups of mice were fed—the one on food raised with chemical fertilizers and the other with organic fertilizers—which proved that the group of mice that was fed with organically produced food was much healthier than that which was fed with food raised with chemical fertilizers. The results were recorded in Bulletin 2 dated November, 1949, of the Soil and Health Foundation. It showed, for example, that in a strain of mice that was chosen for its susceptibility to cancer, the survival rate was 64 per cent in the case of the organically-fed mice and only 35 per cent in the case of the mice fed with chemically fertilized food. In connection with deaths from fighting, the organically-fed group suffered 15 per cent of deaths while the chemically-fed mice killed each other off at the rate of 21 per cent.

In examining the mice themselves, an interesting thing could be observed. There were quite a few hundred mice in the experiment and they were housed 6 to a box. Each box was divided by a partition with a small doorway cut in it so that the mice could move freely from one "room" to the other. Mice are strange creatures and thrive best when they have one room to eat in and one in which to sleep. When we would remove one of the boxes in wihch were housed chemically-fed mice and take off the top, the little animals would become extremely nervous and run frantically from one room to the other, invariably two or 3 of them getting caught in a squeeze and not being able to move, squealing as if their lives were being threatened. But when we did the same to the boxes in which were organically-fed mice, they would be extremely calm and not permit it to affect them at all. They would walk nonchalantly through the little opening, one at a time, as if nothing unusual was taking place. It was a remarkable proof that the use of chemical fertilizers had a significant bearing on the health of a living animal organism, an animal which has been accepted in medical research as a good means of making comparisons with man. It should be borne in mind also that this experiment was performed with hundreds of mice.

After the first stage of this experiment was completed, the mice were subjected to an interesting test. A carcinogenic or cancer-causing chemical was painted on the skins of all the mice in both groups. In the chemically-fed group, 71 per cent of them became cancerous. In the organically-fed group, only 45 per cent came down with disease. The mice are continuing to be fed in the same manner. As they go from generation to generation and the organically-fed mice develop more inborn health, it is expected that the disparity between the two figures will widen more and more.

That chemical fertilizers could be detrimental to human health was shown by a professor at Cornell University, a noted soil scientist, the late Dr. J. K. Wilson. In an article in the January, 1949, issue of the *Agronomy Journal,* entitled "Nitrate in Foods and its relation to Health," Dr. Wilson said: "Leafy vegetables, frozen foods and prepared baby foods were analyzed for their content of nitrate. From the findings it is suggested that the nitrate in such foods may contribute to hemoglobinemia found in infants and may produce certain toxic, if not lethal conditions in adults. The high content of nitrate in the foods may be attributed in many instances to the application of nitrogenous fertilizers, especially nitrate of soda, to the growing of crops." Nothing could have been more clearly and forthrightly put than this statement by a government scientist. There is a building up of scientific literature on the effect on the health, of the use of nitrate of soda, based on work in Agricultural Experiment Stations. It is given in Dr. Wilson's article.

More Vitamins in "Organic" Food

An experiment was carried out by M. J. Rowlands and Barbara Wilkinson, two university research workers, who reported their findings in the *Biochemical Journal,* Vol. 24, No. 1, 1930. In it they said: "It was decided to try the effect of artificial manure (chemical fertilizers) versus dung. A crop of clover and grass was grown, one-half fertilized with dung, the other half with chemical fertilizers including basic slag, kainit and sulphate of ammonia. Then rats were tested by feeding them the product of these fields. . . . The rats were divided into two lots: one lot was put on a deficiency diet to which was added 20 per cent of the 'dung' seed, the other on a deficiency diet with 20 per cent of the 'artificial' seed. . . . The rats on the 'dung' seed showed good growth or a slightly subnormal growth. . . . The rats on the artificial seeds all grew very poorly, not one giving normal growth. . . . It can be seen that the former have gained nearly twice as much as the latter. . . . The rats on the 'artificial' seed were in poor condition; in some the hair was falling out."

Sir Robert McCarrison, the great English research physician, in 1926, in experiments with grains at Madras, India, discovered the same thing. He found that grain, if grown organically, contained more vitamins. For more details see the *Journal of Indian Medical Research*, Vol. 14:351, 1926.

In April, 1941, Professor Glen Wakeham of the University of Colorado, before a meeting of the American Chemical Society at St. Louis, described an experiment which he had made, which showed that garden peas grown in poor soil had a greater mineral content than those grown in soil enriched with chemical fertilizers. This is a typical example which shows that the effect of chemical fertilizers is to lock in the trace mineral elements which are in the soil.

Experiments on Turkeys and Chickens

In chapter 12 of *Bio-Dynamic Farming and Gardening* (Anthroposophic Press) the author, Dr. Ehrenfried Pfeiffer, describes an experiment with chickens. The organically-fed chickens were stronger, laid more eggs and produced a more hatchable egg. In the chemically-fed group, only 35 per cent of the eggs hatched. In the group where the chickens were fed on feeds grown organically, hatchability was 68 per cent.

In the same book Dr. Pfeiffer gives in great detail, pages 185 to 190, a description of experiments carried out with turkeys in feeding with chemically-fertilized feed as against feed produced with stable manure. The article summarizing his results was entitled "The Biological Value of the Products of Soil Fertilized with Chemical Fertilizer" and was published in the *Proceedings of the R. Accademia Nazionale Dei Lincei*, Mathematical, natural scientific division, Vol. 13, series 6, 1, Rome, February, 1931. The results were spectacular. The turkeys fed with food grown with stable manure showed a smaller number of cases of sickness, a shorter duration of it and a far smaller number of deaths. He summarizes: "This means that the seeds and still more the leaves of plants fertilized with stable manure have the peculiarity, when used as food for these animals, of increasing their capacity for resisting disease to greater degree than the corresponding seeds and leaves of minerally-fertilized plants. The former have thus a higher biological value than the latter." The stable manure also produced higher yields in the plants.

Organic Cures

In Dr. Pfeiffer's book mentioned above, pages 190-191, the author mentions 3 German physicians, Schulz, Reinhardt and Kalkhof, who wrote articles in German medical magazines giving their experiences in effecting cures of patients with the use of organically-produced bread and other products. They cured a series of metabolical disturbances. They found it to be especially effective with weak and backward children and to have a definite influence on the functioning of the stomach and intestines. They have thus cured without medication cases with marked stomach troubles and sluggish intestinal activity.

"The *Lancet,* English medical journal, reported a case in New Zealand similar to that of the English school. 'In 1936, Dr. G. B. Chapman, of the Physical and Mental Welfare Society of New Zealand, persuaded the authorities of a boys' school hostel to grow their fruit and vegetables on soils treated with humus. This has since been done, and a striking improvement is reported in general health and physique, particularly as regards freedom from infections, alimentary upsets and dental caries.' "

"The *New York Times* on June 30, 1940, also discussed this case, identifying it as the Mount Albert Grammar School. According to the *Times:* 'Dr. Chapman advised that a change should be made from vegetables and fruits grown in soil fertilized by chemicals, to produce raised on soil treated only with humus. The results were startling. Catarrh, colds and influenza were greatly reduced and in the 1938 epidemic of measles, the boys had only mild attacks whereas new admissions succumbed readily.' "

Another case is that of the workers of the Winsford Bacon Factory in Cheshire, described on page 141 of my book, PAY DIRT (Rodale Books, Incorporated, Emmaus, Pennsylvania). The company provided 150 workers with two meals a day, the food coming from soil treated only with humus and no chemical fertilizers. The results were startling; the general health of the worker has improved; there is less absenteeism; the *esprit de corps* is excellent and work is going with a swing.

Another experiment worth while recording is that of Dr. J. W. Scharff, Chief Health Officer of Singapore, who fed 500 Tamil coolies on organically-produced food. A surprising improvement in stamina and health of the coolies was noted.

In the summer of 1948 we took same oranges raised organically by Mr. John E. Volkert of Orlando, Florida, and the same variety of oranges raised by a neighbor of his with chemical fertilizers. The two batches were sent to the Pease Laboratories, New York City. Mr. Volkert's oranges had 30 per cent more vitamin C than the chemical ones. Mr. Edward L. Douglass of Tampa, Florida, had organically grown oranges tested and they showed 70 per cent more vitamin C than others of the same brand grown with chemical fertilizers. This test was made by Thornton and Company of Tampa, Florida. The report of the work of the Biochemical Research Laboratory, Threefold Farm, Spring Valley, New York, for the year 1949, has the following to say regarding the nutritional content of vegetables raised there without chemical fertilizers: "Vitamin testing was begun during the last year. So far, we have made tests for vitamin A, B complex, thiamin and riboflavin. It has been shown that vegetables grown on biodynamic soils have 50 to 80 per cent more vitamin A than vegetables grown on soil treated with mineral fertilizer."

There is a host of scientific information available in the literature to prove that the use of organic matter in the soil makes for healthy plants. I shall quote a statement by Dr. Selman A. Waksman, the discoverer of streptomycin, from his book, *Humus* (p. 409): "Plant deficiency diseases are usually less severe in soils well supplied with organic matter not only because of the increased vigor of the plants but also because of antagonistic effects of the various soil microörganisms which become more active in the presence of an abundance of organic matter." At the Connecticut Agricultural Experiment Station this was confirmed in experiments with fusarium rot of squash seeds (Bulletin 500, November, 1946, Physiology of Fusarium Foot Rot of Squash).

Physicians Praise the Organic Method

If space permitted, I could give data from 10 or more physicians who have written upon the effects of chemical fertilizers and human health. I shall mention one—James Asa Shields, M.D., Professor of Neuropsychiatry of the Medical College of Virginia, who at a meeting of over 1,000 physicians at Miami, Florida, on November 4, 1946, said, "Thus we see that multiple sclerosis, depletion of soil and the introduction of inorganic chemicals as a treatment for the soil were all introduced to man between the years 1836 and 1840."

Hundreds of physicians have written me their belief that chemical fertilizers are responsible for a lowering of the health of the nation and that if the tendency is not curbed serious consequences may be expected. Dr. Weston A. Price, who wrote the famous classic, *Nutrition and Physical Degeneration,* which has a pertinent chapter on this subject entitled "Soil Depletion and Animal Deterioration," felt very strongly about the effect of chemical fertilizers on human health. Dr. Lionel J. Picton, a famous physician of England, in his book, *Thoughts on Feeding,* gives a tremendous amount of proof that chemical fertilizers are a serious threat to human health. Dr. Alexis Carrell in his famous book, *Man the Unknown,* said: "Chemical fertilizers, by increasing the abundance of crops without replacing the exhausted elements of the soils, have contributed indirectly to change the nutritive value of our cereal grains and our vegetables." Read the chapter in my book, PAY DIRT, entitled "Is Our Health Related to the Soil." It is full of many other medical references which limited space here prevents me from using.

Rejection by Our Government

In spite of all this evidence, much of which has been available for many years, many agricultural scientists who are at the head of departments in large American agricultural institutions have pronounced in speeches and in articles that there is no evidence that the organic method of producing food gives people better health. On the basis of evidence which exists we do not ask the United States Department of Agriculture to turn about in their attitude. We merely ask for a series of experiments to be done from two points of view. The first—from a purely agricultural slant, to see whether the organic method will give greater yields and better conserve the soil; and two—from the human and animal health viewpoint. They have closed their minds to any experimenting in this field considering the organiculturists as a bunch of misguided crackpots, and that anything that comes from their camp is not worthy of their acknowledgement or notice.

CHAPTER 170

Fruits and Vegetables

By J. I. Rodale

I would just like to briefly discuss the question of fruits and vegetables from the point of view of the poison sprays that are used in the orchards and on the truck farms in order to keep down insects and disease, in the growing of the respective products. Wherever possible, we would urge readers to grow their own fruit and vegetables by the organic method, namely, without chemical fertilizers and without poison sprays. But where this is not possible, try and purchase these products from organic growers. We have available *The Organic Food Directory* which lists people in various parts of the country who have such food for sale. This is available for 10 cents.

In the event that you do not have your own source of supply that is safe, just a few words of caution about fruits and vegetables. With regard to such fruits as apples, pears, peaches, etc., the way they are sprayed is just plain murder. Every year the big chemical companies are producing more potent poisons, and these are absorbed into the fruit under the skin, and it is therefore necessary, in order to be safe, to cut off the skin. Do not worry about the minerals that you are losing by not eating this skin. You can make up for it by taking bone meal which is a far better source of the minerals. We do not recommend drinking ordinary commercial cider, as this has the spray residues in it, and also benzoate of soda, which is a poisonous preservative. I would not eat cherries because they are sprayed heavily and I once traced back dizzy spells to eating them.

Pineapple would be a good source of fruit because of its heavy skin protection. Very little poison could penetrate beyond that. For the same reason, bananas are a good source, but we would suggest that you buy bananas green and let them turn yellow in your own home because in some of the fruit markets, that is, at the source in the wholesale concerns, they use a gas to turn the bananas yellow. Oranges should be taken only in the whole form and not in the juice, and the same goes for grapefruit. It has recently been discovered that the orange contains a certain amount of critic acid which might harm the teeth of some susceptible people. Others might get away with it. Also, certain susceptible individuals may have stomach trouble on account of this citric acid. We recommend about two oranges and about one and one-half grapefruit a week, unless your teeth are made of steel.

Grapes are pretty badly sprayed and we therefore are awfully sorry that we cannot recommend them unless obtained from an organic source. Coconuts would be a good fruit, and of course, all kinds of nuts in moderation, because they are fattening for those who are inclined toward obesity. If eaten before going to bed, they may cause insomnia. Nuts should always be very well chewed.

I believe that within this range there is sufficient fruit to satisfy a person's sweet tooth and also his or her needs for vitamins and minerals.

Vegetables

Here is a more difficult situation. The extent of chemicalization and poison spraying is unbelievable. If at all possible, get yourself a small piece of ground and grow your own vegetables. You would be surprised how much you can turn out for an average-sized family from a small plot. And there is a wonderful feeling of creation, as, year by year, you set into action the process of raising your own food. It is not difficult at all and many folks who just have a small patch in their back yard usually in lawn have dug it up and grown the finest vegetables by the organic method. It is very simple. Chemical fertilizers should not be used nor any kind of sprays. The use of compost or other organic matter will not only make your soil a pleasure to work with, but will cause the breakdown of minerals which will be absorbed into the plant.

I would recommend peas because the spray goes on the pod and the pod is not eaten. String beans, however, would not be in the same class because the spray goes right up against the string beans. Potatoes are not too bad, because, although the plants are sprayed, and some of the spray seeps into the ground, the potatoes, growing underground, do not have the amount that the average vegetable growing above ground would have. I would suggest, for the same reason as in the case of apples, that the potatoes be peeled, because the contact of the spray in the ground might go up against the skin but probably not penetrate too much into the interior. Here again your bone meal will be the protector as far as minerals are concerned.

Corn is a good vegetable in the summer because it is usually not sprayed, and you also have the protection of the husk.

In growing a vegetable garden, don't forget a little parsley bed. This plant is unusually rich in vitamin C and is very easy to grow. You can even grow it on a window box if you are an apartment dweller.

CHAPTER 171

Food: What Is It Doing to Us?

By Robert J. H. Mick, D.D.S.

After I had been practicing dentistry for about 12 years I came to the conclusion that I was a failure. I reached this conclusion by the simple process of observation; the condition of the teeth of my patients was, year by year, retrogressing.

I could not understand why this should be true. I was a graduate of a dental college of high standing. I was good at the various phases of my job. My fillings did not fall out. I could make a well fitting plate, extract cleanly and without too much pain. I had changed many a malformed child's face into a natural and beautiful one. I had even worked out a simple, effective mechanical hygiene routine for my patients which would, when applied diligently, cut down on the necessary number of visits to my office.

And, I may add, my income grew. But the teeth of my patients, instead of becoming sounder, were deteriorating. I was succeeding as a mechanic and as a businessman, but I was failing as a dentist. At least as the kind of dentist I thought I ought to be. I began asking myself why.

After about two years when I floundered around in a slough of despondency and doubt about my work, some of my patients began to give me what seemed to be a clue to the answer I was after.

South Jersey is populated by a large number of Italian-American families. A large per cent of my patients is made up from this group. Some are farmers, some tradesmen and some are professional men. These are first, second and third generations, with a few of the fourth coming along. The first generation—that is, those who were born in Italy—have the best teeth of any. Many of them, although approaching and past their three score years and ten, have all their teeth in perfect condition.

The second generation, most of whom were born in this country, have had to resort to dental care while quite young. But by doing their repair work early before too much damage has been done, I have been able to save most of their teeth, have kept them functioning and kept them cosmetically acceptable. It was when I began to work on the teeth of the third generation in increasing numbers that the picture of what was happening began to come into focus.

Even the deciduous teeth of this group show extensive damage. The second or permanent teeth always decay early. There are malformed jaw bones, and crooked teeth are the rule. Often I am compelled to remove teeth before a child is 4 years old.

This appalling condition was going on in my younger generation patients in spite of the fact that their parents brought them to me while still young. They are conscientious parents and they have money to pay for the best they can get. Most of them are successful financially. In addition to their cooperation I was applying all the know-how I had gained in my 4 years of training and 15 years of practice. After a while it became evident that whatever was causing this dental degeneracy had something to do with conditions under which the second and third generation Italian-Americans were living in this country and to which the first had not been subjected in the old country.

Getting the Answer to Tooth Decay

I began to take time out from my practice to read. I haunted libraries. I read books. I read the current journals of dentistry and journals on nutrition. I dug into bound volumes of the same publications. (It might be thought that all dentists would keep in constant touch with these but the busy ones have little time for reading.)

Finally I came across a book published by Doctor Weston A. Price, called *Physical Degeneration*. It dealt with a comparison of foods eaten by people in America today with those eaten by people in Europe a generation ago. Practically the whole difference, according to this author, lies in the condition of the freshness and natural state of the food consumed.

Immediately I applied Doctor Price's yardstick to my own patients. My first generation Italian-Americans ate food fresh from the garden or field, the pen, the goat or the cow. None of it was processed or refined, held in bins, bags or cartons for months before it was cooked and fed to the family. Their children and grandchildren, on the other hand, born in this country, are fed food which has been produced, processed and preserved by the great technical advancement of scientific know-how. Could it be, I asked myself, that the difference in the development and preservation of the teeth in these different generations is due to this one fact?

My patients who were not of Italian descent were also having more and more trouble with their teeth. None of them, during the time I had been practicing, had had teeth comparable in soundness to the first generation Italians. But, bad as they were, even they were showing signs of getting worse. This was true of all ages.

The final straw that made me try to remedy the situation I was facing was the dental health of my own relatives and family. They were showing an alarming increase in dental cavities and other malformations. My own two children, in spite of the very best care I could give them, were developing cavities early.

I started first by eliminating refined sugar from the diet of my family, and all foods sweetened with refined sugar. That meant eliminating candy, syrups and pastries made with this source of sweet. For sugar we substituted honey. A curious thing happened. My wife and I had expected difficulty in disciplining the children in regard to this substitution. But we soon learned that when honey is used instead of refined sugar, not only is the desire for sweets satisfied with less amount, but there is practically no desire for

[628]

candy and other sweets of this nature. About the only time the children feel inclined to break the ban is at parties where the refusal of a cookie, candy or ice cream marks them too pointedly as different. But that is working itself out, too, as more and more parents are taking up the same substitution as ours.

After making a start in my own family I began talking to my patients, especially mothers of young children. A few promised to try the experiment. I have proof that several of them carried out the honey substitution faithfully as I shall point out later.

Our next step was to use bread made only from unrefined, unadulterated whole wheat flour. The story of my attempt to find bread of this nature is too long to tell here. But I was never able to find any that I was sure did not have a preservative or had not in some way been treated to make it "keep." The quest ended by my purchasing a small electric flour mill which, after being used for my own family, relatives and friends, finally burned out.

After two years I still was not sure I was on the right track, although I felt I was headed in the right direction. There was so much I did not know. I still felt inadequate as a dentist.

In July, 1949, I decided to shut up my office and get away for a while. I went to Florida, combining a vacation with some special interest I had in the state. While there I met Bill Odom (William P. Odom, D.M.D., of San Diego, California) and it wasn't long before we learned that we had been thinking along similar lines. The vacation turned out to consist of a series of long discussions between Doctor Odom and me as to how we could prove to our own satisfaction whether or not the diet of people in the United States was causing the increase in tooth deterioration.

Our final decision was that we go to some section of the world and examine the teeth of people who live isolated from civilization and refined foods. We chose central Africa.

An Expedition in Search of Dental Health

Accordingly, after about 3 months—October 10—I boarded a plane at Philadelphia International Airport and 32 hours later landed in Cairo, Egypt. There I met Doctor Odom and we flew to Nairobi, 7000 miles from my patients in New Jersey but only 45 hours flying time away. Such is the breath-taking highly developed technical advancement of our means of travel today. This was nothing unusual. It occurs all over the globe every day.

We stayed in Nairobi 4 days settling customs questions and making preparations for our inland trek. We borrowed a few books on African tribes from the medical headquarters of the interterritorial government, hired a station wagon and bought supplies. With the wagon went Kosky, a Nandi, and former cook for the British Army. The wagon, Kosky and gas cost 20 cents a mile. Kosky was not only our driver, guide and interpreter but he became our good friend as well.

We visited the countries of Kenya, Tanganyika, Uganda and the

Belgian Congo. We traveled approximately 3500 miles and examined the teeth of over 3000 natives.

There are fairly large towns and cities in this part of Africa. But as soon as we left the borders of a municipality, we found regions which had been unchanged for centuries. The means of transportation for most of the natives we studied is still by foot. Their location of living becomes fixed. The type of food and water that feeds one generation is, for the most part, the same as that which fed the generation before. The food is affected by the local terrain and water conditions over a long period of time.

The first tribe we visited was the Masai (pronounced *masigh*) of Kenya. Politically they are a British protectorate but after that their relation with any outsider ends. The people are very independent and proud. They are self-sufficient as to food, clothing (what there is of it) and houses. They refuse to work for anyone. Their men are fearless warriors. They have excellent health, are tall, some reaching 7 feet. They are usually thin. We never say a protruding abdomen in the entire tribe. Their muscles and flesh are firm. They had the best teeth of any group which we examined on our entire trip.

Through our interpreter, Kosky, we were directed to the tribe's only school, called the Ylbisil School for Children. Here we examined the teeth of 67 boys, three girls and two teachers. The ages of the pupils ranged from 7 to 14 years. Among these we found not a single cavity, no stains, no fluorosis and not a crooked tooth. All jaw developments were excellent.

Kosky's fluent "Swahili," the international language of Africa, also enabled us to learn about the food which the Masai eat. The children are given about 3 pints of milk each day. They are allowed small amounts of blood, added to the milk, and meat two or three times a week. Because of the severe drought the year we were there, they were securing millet and corn from Nairobi. This was made into a coarse bread. The children were also given some of this.

When the boys reach their eighteenth birthday they become what they call Maronis. (A Maroni is a warrior.) They remain warriors until they are 30 years old, then they are known as Elders. While Maronis, their diet consists chiefly of raw blood, raw milk and meat with emphasis on the meat and blood. A Maroni is not allowed to marry, smoke, drink or use snuff. When he becomes an Elder his diet becomes that of the women and girls which is about the same as that of the children—with the privilege of smoking and drinking. The latter are, for the most part, carried on in moderation.

For sweets the Masai use only honey. They use both the wild and the cultivated. Homemade beehives are made by hollowing out about 3 feet of a log and hanging it from the branches of a tree.

The land on which the Masai live is very arid. Sometimes it is 18 months to 3 years between rains. For this reason the cultivation of vegetables at times is impossible. The juice of the mimosa and other trees is used when available. The tribe moves about, within a restricted area, to secure grazing land for their cattle so their diet is of a very concentrated protein nature. Tartar accumulates on the teeth of the older people. This causes pyorrhea, because of its mechanical irritation, resulting in the loss of some teeth. Even then, there are no cavities. The average length of life of the Masai is 60 years.

The intelligence of the Masai is high. Their knowledge of veterinary science is very good and they understand a great deal about the infectious diseases that plague their people. They know that malaria is caused by the bite of the mosquito and were aware that contracting malaria would cure syphilis a hundred years before it was discovered by civilized man.

Although the food of this tribe is limited in variety and consists very largely of concentrated proteins, the outstanding fact is that it is eaten in its natural state, at least during the period of tooth formation. Milk is consumed raw, blood is eaten in a raw, fresh state and honey is a natural, unrefined sweet. The Masai eat no candies, foods preserved with chemicals or fruits that have been gathered green, then colored to make them look ripe. They eat no bread made from white flour. There is a story told how a hunter once induced some Masai to eat bread made from bleached flour. They tried it once but declined to eat it again because it made "lumps in their stomachs."

The Pygmy tribes which we examined presented a situation in almost complete opposition to that of the Masai. They are small in stature, being from three and a half to four feet tall. They are slaves of other tribes, usually supplying them with meat and in turn receiving protection and bananas which are their chief source of food. Their teeth were among the worst we saw on our trip.

Our first opportunity to examine these little people in any number came when we visited the Putnam's Pygmy Camp located in the Belgian Congo near Mombasa, 50 miles on the road to Stanleyville. We had caught glimpses of little fellows peering out at us from behind thick foliage as we passed along the road and we had caught sight of fleeting forms vanishing in the distance. It was not until we came to the Putnam's Camp that we were able to see them at close range and to examine their teeth with our instruments.

Patrick Putnam, a Harvard graduate, had come to Africa about 20 years before. He found the little natives interesting, set up a home there and soon settled into a comfortable reciprocal working order with them. He and his wife, Ann, supply the natives with medicines (when their own medicine men fail them), they settle marital troubles and sit in at disputes over ownerships. The pygmies supply the Putnams with labor and meat. Patrick is their king and great protector.

In the Putnam Camp itself we examined 13 Pygmies. Their ages ranged from 7 to 45 years. In these we found 13 cavities and 32 teeth missing. Acute pyorrhea was the rule with the older people. Two miles from the Putnam Camp was another Pygmy settlement where we examined 12 people ranging in ages from 20 to 45. All of these had defective teeth in one form or another. There were 8 cavities and 38 teeth missing. At a third settlement we examined 6 adults. One of these had no cavities at all.

There were 17 teeth missing. Most of this group had yaws. (A systemic tropical disease involving serious skin disorders.) At still a fourth settlement we examined the teeth of 20 more Pygmies. Among these we found one child with a perfect mouth—the first in this tribe. One adult had all teeth missing. Twelve others had teeth missing.

The physical condition of practically all the Pygmies we saw was poor. Protrusion of the abdomen was common. Soft flabby flesh and obesity in the adults was the rule. Yaws and other infections were common.

The diet of the Pygmies is almost wholly bananas. They pull this fruit while quite green and hard, mash or chop it up and cook it to a pulp. Other food which they eat is mixed with bananas and also cooked a long time. Millet and sesame plus some meat is eaten in varying amounts. They eat honey for sweets but mix it with water and boil it first. As far as we could determine they eat nothing in the raw state.

One observation which the Putnams made was significant. When Pygmies first arrive at their camp from the interior, they usually have better teeth than they have after living at the camp for some time.

While one of the outstanding characteristics of the Pygmies is shyness, once they are assured that strangers mean them no harm, they are very friendly. They like games and have great fun playing them. They played some for our enjoyment. They are an intelligent people. It was sad seeing them coming to the white man for protection and, while finding a measure of this, securing it at the cost of physical fitness.

Evidence Gathered from Other Parts of Africa

In addition to the Masai and the Pygmy tribes, we examined the teeth and food of over two thousand other inhabitants of central Africa. Some of these were single individuals we met on the road, some were in groups which we came across in work camps. The majority were in schools and in villages to which missionaries, hunters and tradesmen directed us. Acting as interpreters, these in-between people were untiring in their efforts to make it possible for us to carry out our plans. With few exceptions the natives gave us complete coöperation. They were excellent patients and submitted to our examinations and questionings without fear or hesitation.

We found many people with perfect mouths. They were usually in the younger age brackets but not always. The most striking observation we made was the lack of tooth defects comparable to those we find in our patients at home. The average per cent of defects in the intermediary group —that is, between the Masai and the Pygmies—including fluorosis, was .24.

The food of this intermediary group varied considerably, but a large part of it is produced in the immediate environs of the village, school or camp where the people lived. Also, due to lack of refrigeration or other means of preservation, the food is consumed comparatively soon after it is picked, harvested or killed. It is almost universally true that honey is used as a sweet. Where it was boiled before eaten, we always found a corresponding deterioration in the teeth. Also in schools where refined sugar was used instead of honey we saw a corresponding increase in tooth decay.

Some of the more common foods used by this group are bananas, yams, cassavas, millet, maize, peanuts and other nuts. There are also mangos, oranges, lemons, pawpaws, European potatoes, sweet potatoes, beans, squash, fish, chicken but very little meat.

We made one observation when studying this intermediary group which we believe is highly significant. It concerned our findings when examining the teeth of pupils of the Government Indian High School at Kisumu, Kenya, as compared with the findings when examining the teeth of natives in another school in the same town.

Out of 114 Government Indian High School pupils, ages 6 to 16, we found 476 cavities, 61 with fluorosis and 37 with irregularities of teeth and jaw bones.

In the same town we examined the teeth of the pupils of the African Anglican Church Primary School. They were all of the Luo tribe. Out of 276, ages 8 to 16, we found only 78 cavities, occurring in the mouths of 30 pupils. There were 72 cases of fluorosis and 9 irregularities of teeth and jaw bones. We found only one really bad tooth in a boy who said he used a large amount of sugar in his tea. The other cavities were generally grooves with heavy fluorosis which only the sharpest dental explorer could detect.

On comparing the food used by these two groups an interesting fact was brought to light. The Indian children were given typical European food —that is, bread and pastries made from white flour, refined sugar, candies, cookies and no honey. They also ate foods that had been canned or otherwise preserved according to Western custom.

The native children in the Anglican Church School, on the other hand, did not have access to foods brought in from European sources but were compelled to eat that which had been produced nearby.

Water for both schools came from the same source. But the amount of fluorosis in the Indian School was 53 + per cent and only 38 + per cent in the Anglican Church School. Yet this high amount of fluorosis did not protect the Indian pupils from tooth cavities *in the presence of refined food*.

The Answer to Tooth Decay

At the end of 5 weeks, when we had examined the teeth of the last native and returned to Nairobi, I had the answer I had come to Africa to find. What was causing the rapid tooth deterioration in my New Jersey patients? Although I had come with an open mind, I was not surprised at what I found. The answer was refined, processed and preserved food. Whether this effect is due to nutritional disturbances in the body as a whole or due to the direct effect of some food on the teeth in the mouth I am not sure. It could be due to both.

No doubt a third factor plays an important part. This is the chemical nature of the soil in which food is grown or the chemical nature of foods fed to animals which are in turn consumed by humans.

None of these African findings are new. Not a few people before and after Doctor H. W. Wiley was administrator of the Food and Drug Administration at Washington, D.C., have warned about the dangers involved in preserving food, especially by the use of chemicals. Still fewer have ventured to point out what is happening to human health through growing food in soil depleted of its essential growth and health producing chemicals. The effect of refined sugar on tooth cavity formation is widely known. In fact, some state health departments are beginning to suggest that reduction of refined sugar in the diet of children will help reduce cavity formation.

However, the alarming fact is that most of this known information goes unheeded by the great commercial interests of the country in the growing, storing, transportation and distribution of food which is supplied to the 174 million consumers every day.

I had to get my proof first hand. Having secured that without a doubt I could then return to New Jersey and practice my profession in a way I thought it should be done. This assured state of mind cost me around $4000.00 (in addition to loss of income from practice while away) but I do not regret spending one cent of it.

How To Work Out This Lesson

As I write, it has now been over two years since some of my patients started substituting honey for refined sugar in the diets of their children. The change in the rate of cavity formation in the teeth of these children is very marked. It has dropped from 8 to 10 cavities a year to zero to two. Because of this one substitution I have estimated that I have lost 300 office hours of visits from these patients and yet their teeth are in better shape than at any time since I've been attending them. Since my return I include the substitution of honey for all sweets as a regular part of my patients' dental hygiene, especially for the very young.

About 6 months ago I purchased a large 60 to 70 pound per hour capacity stone grinding flour mill and had it installed in the bakery of a man who is coöperating with me in making fresh unadulterated whole wheat bread. I buy wheat from Deaf Smith County, Texas, where the soil is high in mineral content which makes for wholesome, nutritious content of the flour. It is rich in both phosphorus and calcium. The bread is made from this flour ground in my mill. There is no bleach, preservative or conditioner added. Only pure olive oil, honey, yeast, salt and water are used with the whole wheat flour. This bread is sold to my patients and friends at cost. It is delivered to my office twice a week and is available at the bakery daily. It is baked within 24 hours after the flour is ground. Recipes for using the whole wheat are furnished when desired.

The insistence on substitution of honey for refined sugar and the use of pure whole wheat flour in making bread so far constitute the major efforts I am making to give my family and patients food which will help keep them healthy and prevent tooth decay. Other efforts consist of all the educational work I can find time to carry on in the way of talks before interested groups. I make liberal use of charts, lantern slides, dentures made from casts of patients' teeth and jaws, photographs of first, second and third generation patients' teeth and faces showing malformations. We even pass around slices of whole wheat bread for tasting!

As a long view goal I am trying to enable a few people to see the picture as a whole with the hope that eventually a small beginning may snowball into a movement which will make it possible for the consumer to buy unadulterated, wholesome food at every corner grocery store in the land. As a short view goal, if I can, during my lifetime, enable 100 children to finish the grammar grades with perfect dentition, I shall not have practiced dentistry in vain.

I fully realize the difficulties people are up against in trying to secure pure fresh food for themselves and families. The whole economic and social order is geared to make this all but impossible. Most housewives are forced to market for food at one of the neighborhood chain grocery stores. They are forced because of lack of time, lack of transportation and because of the wider variety which these stores offer. These markets are attractively laid out, and the goods are displayed conveniently. More and more types of foods are being made available in them. They should be the perfect place to buy food for the family.

But let the buyer try to find a half dozen foods in these stores which have not been processed, preserved, aged in transit or in some other way changed from their natural state. It seldom can be done. Even the honey is likely to have been heated or otherwise treated to preserve its semi-viscid state. Only by securing this food direct from the beehives can one be sure it has not been tampered with. It is alarming when one realizes that most children in large cities have never tasted milk fresh from the cow, peanut butter in its natural state, whole grain cereal with nothing added, a fresh piece of meat, unadulterated dried fruit, real butter or a slice of bread made from fresh-ground whole wheat flour.

Home grown vegetables and fruits in season which reach the family table via the grocery store, have, perhaps, lost least of their nutritive values, but those picked green and allowed to ripen in storehouses or treated with chemicals to make them appear ripe are defeating the purpose of food.

Solving the Problem of Fresh Foods

The law allows a certain amount of preservatives to be added to some foods if they are stated on the label. If the amount added is below a certain per cent, the fact that it has been added need not be stated at all. We are told that the small amount allowed is not harmful to man. This does not satisfy me. Has anyone fed a group of human beings on commercial bread, canned vegetables, canned orange juice, oleomargarine and a dozen other foods which contain sodium benzoate, for example, from the time these people began to eat solid food until they are 45 or 50 years old? At the same time fed a second group (for controls) on foods which are fresh, unchanged in any way and have had no preservatives added and then compared the state of the teeth and general health of the two groups? Until this is done I shall not be convinced that chemicals in food as preservatives do no harm to the human body.

There is no doubt that foods can be provided to the people of the United States which are pure, fresh and unaltered—foods that will produce sound teeth, strong bodies and healthy minds. However, in order to do this the whole system of trade and transportation of food must be radically changed. Research minds must be put to work on the problems involved. Engineers must draw up new means of transportation of food. Growers of food must learn to think in terms of the effect of their products on the human body instead of profits. Economists must work out ways by which those who deal in growing, transporting, distributing and selling food can make a living at their businesses and at the same time not do so at the cost of health of the consumer.

All this would mean a tremendously big undertaking. But so was the undertaking which made it possible for me to board a plane at Philadelphia and be in Cairo, Egypt, 32 hours later. So was the undertaking which made it possible to split the atom. Our scientists have brains. Our engineers have know-how. But our country has a habit of putting all its eggs in one basket—at a given time.

Today we hear a great deal about the danger of selling our freedom for security. When I hear and read about the rise in vaso-cardiac diseases, in cancer and in certain nervous ailments, I think about the Pygmies of Africa. They are always seeking security and will make themselves slaves to another tribe to secure it. Their food is practically all processed and their state of health among the lowest we saw. On the other hand the food of the Masai is natural, pure and unprocessed. They have strong bodies, are fearless and independent. Perhaps there is a lesson here to be learned by all "civilized" countries.

CHAPTER 172

Primitive People and Health

By J. I. Rodale

There is overwhelming evidence that there exists some relationship between the food intake of the body and its welfare and health. This stands to reason. The body is dependent basically for its functioning and subsistence on the nourishment that is furnished to it. If we do not eat, we die. If the sustenance is inferior, or lacking in necessary elements, malfunctioning must result and does—as is shown in the archives of medicine. Such diseases as pellagra, beriberi, scurvy and others have been traced to dietary deficiencies. When the deficit is mended, spectacular cures have been accomplished.

In the last few generations there has been a grievous and accelerating tendency to tamper with the food supply—to preserve, to refine, to extend, to adulterate, to dehydrate, to fragmentize, that is, to eliminate portions of the food which carry important vitamin and living elements because of processing and storage difficulties, sometimes as with white bread, producing a product of mere starch and fibre, fearfully chemicalized and not fit to be eaten by human beings. We can learn a great deal by studying primitive peoples who eat a primitive, simple diet, untouched by the avaricious hand of the factory. Let us consider one of these, the American Indian of old times.

Dr. Fred L. Hoffman in his book, *Cancer From the Statistical Standpoint*, says, "It was ascertained that in the experience of practicing physicians on Indian reservations, cancer in any and all its forms had been extremely rare. The American Indian possibly knew more about nutritional value of foods in general than the average person gives him credit for, or is it merely that he is a child of nature, worshipping her, and thus living within her jurisdiction, to the benefit and well-being of his body."

Dr. Fred L. Hoffman in an article in *Metron*, Vol. 10—No. 1-2; 15—9—1932 entitled *Causes of Death in Primitive Races,* says:

"Primitive races offer extraordinary opportunities for strictly scientific studies of mortality problems. Until such races come in close contact with civilized men they generally present a healthy, robust and vigorous appearance. That, at least, seems to be the consensus of qualified observers who studied the native Indians in America soon after the early settlement by Europeans. Thus, for illustration, in the work on *The Rise and Fall of Disease in Illinois* it is said:

" 'The Indian constitution was the result of many influences. Because of his lack of thrift, foresight and energy he was subjected to periodic lean years. In consequence of his life he had a capacity for great and sustained effort and an ability to withstand hunger. He had a fine stature on the average and great physical vigor. To those diseases which threatened him in the wild state he had a fine resistance and yet he was short lived. He died at an average early age and there were few children in the average Indian family. It is not easy to understand why so fine a constitution went hand in hand with a short life span and small families with children spaced far apart. History would indicate that wars and famines furnished the explanation.'

Some Anthropological Facts About the Indians

"From the same source I quote a statement by Hrdlicka, the well known physical anthropologist, who observes:

" 'The traditions of the Indians, the existence among them of elaborate healing rites of undoubtedly ancient origin, their plant lore, in which curative agents' properties are attributed to many vegetable substances and the presence among them of a numerous class of professed healers, honored, feared and usually well paid would seem to indicate that diseases were not rare, but actual knowledge and even tradition as to their nature were wanting. The condition of the skeletal remains, the testimony of early observers and the present state of some of the tribes in this regard warrant the conclusion that on the whole the Indian race was a comparatively healthy one. It was probably spared at least some of the epidemics and diseases of the old world such as smallpox, rachitis, while scourges such as tuberculosis, syphilis (pre-Columbian), typhus, cholera, scarlet fever, cancer, etc., were rare if occurring at all.' "

A famous English surgeon, Dr. Tipper, wrote a book in which he described the life of the Bene tribe of West African Negroes which he studied over a period of 20 years. These people were completely free from cancer, appendicitis and most of the other diseases of civilization. The Bene Negro, says Dr. Tipper, pays particular attention to the proper growth of his food. While they eat some meat, they attach great value to the eating of vegetables. Their foods are not canned, nor put through factory processes that devitalize them. They use no poisonous preservatives such as we freely employ. He mentions cases of some of the Benes who went to the coast to be educated or to work on jobs, and who ate the white man's food. Soon their health degenerated and appendicitis, gastritis, stomach ulcer and cancer put in their appearance.

Weston A. Price, a medical scientist of wide renown, spent many years among primitive peoples all over the world studying the connection between nutrition and caries. The results of this valuable work are contained in a remarkable book called *Nutrition and Physical Degeneration,* published by Hoeber. His findings coincided with those of Dr. Tipper. Where people ate natural, unadulterated foods raised on fertile soils, there was a notable absence of all the diseases of civilization, including cancer.

Primitive Diet in a Swiss Valley

He mentions the case of the 2,000 inhabitants of the Loetschental Valley in Switzerland. Price says they have no physicians nor policemen and not even a jail. The famous Vatican guards include many natives of this valley. Says Dr. Price, "Notwithstanding the fact that tuberculosis is the most serious disease in Switzerland, according to a statement given me by a government official, a recent report of inspection of this valley did not reveal a single case." Price studied their foods which he tested for their mineral and vitamin contents. He found them to be high in vitamins, "much higher than the average samples of commercial dairy products in America and Europe, and in the lower areas of Switzerland." Switzerland has a much higher cancer rate than we have, but the figures of chemical fertilizer usage show that Switzerland is far ahead of us in this respect. However, the chances are that this modern product has not yet penetrated into the isolated Loetschental Valley because of its isolation and inaccessibility.

The Navajos

In February, 1949, the following United Press dispatch was printed in many newspapers:

"An American Medical Association study team suggested today that federal officials find out why there are so few cases of cancer, diabetes, scarlet fever and some heart diseases among the Hopi-Navajo Indians.

"The doctors want to know if the Indians' apparently inadequate diet gives them a resistance to the diseases.

"Members of the team who made their suggestion in the *AMA Journal,* are Doctors Samuel Ayres, Jr., and Harold E. Crowe, Los Angeles; A. A. Thurlow, Santa Rosa; Louis Ruschin, Oakland, and Lewis J. Moorman, Oklahoma City.

"They said the Indians provide unusual opportunities for sustained and controlled research in important phases of medicine now posing serious questions.

"The Indians' diet seems to be low in quality and quantity and wanting in variety and the doctors wondered if this had anything to do with the fact that only 36 cases of malignant cancer were found out of 30,000 admissions to the Ganado, Arizona, Mission Hospital.

" 'In the same number of white persons,' the doctors said, 'there should have been about 1800.'

"Diabetes also apparently is rare among the Indians. In 25,000 patients studied at Ganado, only 5 cases were found. Of that many white patients, there would have been about 75 times more cases, they said.

"The Indians also apparently lack susceptibility to scarlet fever, the doctors said, and there is a low incidence of degenerative cardiovascular conditions."

Health From Mother Earth

The dispatch speaks of an apparently low quality or inadequate diet. What these physicians consider inferior may be the very thing that is giving these Indians practical immunity to cancer. In their report in the *American Medical Association Journal* of February 5, 1949, these 5 doctors come close to something that might have given them a clue for further research. They say:

"Among the innate psychologic and spiritual obstacles are the profound attachments of the Navajos to their mother earth, which in their opinion gave birth and ultimate haven to not only their gods but to them and their children as well."

This philosophy the worthy, but unknowing doctors call an obstacle. If all farmers would only consider their soil *Mother Earth,* and treat her with more reverence, would they turn out crops more healthful to the eaters thereof? The Navajo, it is a known fact, uses practically no chemical fertilizers.

Let me quote from the doctors' report in the *American Medical Association Journal:*

". . . the government planted the Navajos on the present reservation without reckoning with the exigencies of the forbidden terrain. The dependence on their herds and the sparsity of herbage inevitably made nomads of the Navajos and kept them on the move, threading ancient arroyas, wading sand dunes, scaling bluffs and unobtrusively blending with sage and sheep on lonely mesas . . . only 20 per cent of the Navajos speak English."

This is scarcely a setup for the prospering of chemical fertilizer dealers. The distances are great, the money supply inadequate and the Navajo loves his mother earth, who is one of his gods. A reader of Organic Gardening who studied this question advised us that the Navajos use no chemical fertilizers. Chemical fertilizers cause an oversupply of carbohydrate in the crop and a reduction in the protein. They encourage formation of cellulose which crowds out the minerals.

Their Living Conditions

The report in the *American Medical Association Journal* draws attention to the poor health generally of the Navajos. They say:

"The diseases afflicting the Navajo-Hopi Indians with few exceptions differ from those found in the white population only in degree, and this difference is due to environmental conditions, want of education and adequate medical care rather than to innate racial factors and influence. For example, the meager statistical data regarding tuberculosis indicate that the mortality from this disease is approximately 10 times that in the general population.

"Yet its course in the Indian closely parallels that in the white man. This being true, we must conclude that the difference must be due to provocative factors in the environment, including faulty nutrition, physical hardships, overcrowding in the hogan and inadequate medical care, which implies the lack of effective case finding, the failure to break the contacts, imperfect methods of management and the lack of sanatorium care with all the modern phases of collapse therapy and eternal vigilance through adequate follow-up service."

For a long time the Navajos had only one doctor for 15,000 to 20,000 persons and their condition is not much better today. Their general lack of knowledge of elementary principles of hygiene takes its toll in the contagious diseases, it can be seen, but they do not seem to be susceptible to the degenerative type of maladies such as cancer, heart disease or diabetes, which are not contagious. They live under difficult conditions. "Few persons know," say these doctors, "that often the Indians are dependent on temporary water holes for drinking water, which is sometimes thick enough because of yellow mud to make good topsoil."

The physicians refer to their apparently inadequate diet, but there is something in their way of life that gives them immunity to the degenerative diseases. Could it be that very inadequate diet? The doctors say:

"They seem to do very well on a rather simple limited diet. Compared to our general population they are virtually free from cancer and diabetes and they have a very low incidence of heart and blood vessel disease (arteriosclerosis). Among our people these 3 conditions are on the increase and contending for first place in mortality statistical columns. Perhaps the limited diet, the slow pace and the desert poise have much to do with this interesting disease discrepancy."

Pace And Cancer Incidence

They bring in another factor, "desert poise," intimating no doubt that the faster tempo of city life induces to cancer. I doubt whether this is so. For the years 1940 to 1944 inclusive in the United States, cancer cases per 100,000 of population in rural sections were about 70 per cent of those in bigger city areas. But with the Navajos there were 36 cases of cancer where there should have been 1800, or only 2 per cent. Another complicating factor is the fact that the lower cancer rate in rural areas generally may be more allied to the closeness of a fresh food supply, and the growing and eating of more vegetables from people's own gardens. I have been led to this line of thought from the fact that there are more mental cases and insanity in rural communities than among city folks, strange as this may seem. One would imagine that the poise and quiet of the country towns would tend toward greater mental health, but this does not seem to be the case. We should attempt to penetrate the mystery of why there is less cancer and more mental disease in rural communities.

Navajos' Cancer Weapon

Another investigator of the Navajos' secret weapon against cancer is Dr. Clarence G. Salsbury, Arizona's commissioner of public health. When he was the head of the Sage Memorial Hospital at Ganado, Arizona, most of his patients were Navajos and regarding their incidence of cancer he found that of 60,000 admissions to the hospital there were only 208 cancer cases. Of the 45,000 Navajos who live on Arizona reservations, 63 should have died of cancer in 1953 if they went according to the cancer mortality of the rest of the country, but there were only 11 deaths or about one-sixth of the general rate. In an interview Dr. Salsbury said:

"The typical primitive Navajo diet does not include highly refined foods. It consists mainly of meat, corn, squash, some fruits and nuts, herb native tea and 'squaw bread'—a type of crisp panbread. That simple diet may be the key to the comparative lack of cancer. Just why or how we don't yet know."

He stated further, "When I was in China, I noticed that when we served highly polished rice to the natives, attacks of beriberi followed almost immediately. Poorly polished or unpolished rice solved the problem. The lack of highly refined foods and sugar in typical Navajo diets may bear a similar relationship to the unusually low cancer rate. Tests have shown, for example, a lower blood-sugar rate among Navajos than is common among others."

Dr. Salsbury said: "For many years they have suffered from malnutrition and a score or more of diseases to which they are particularly vulnerable. Yet they enjoy a freedom from cancer which is little short of amazing. The reason for that freedom—once discovered and identified—could benefit all mankind."

Natural Diet The Answer

I don't see how anyone can fail to realize that at the bottom of this low cancer rate is the naturalness of their mineral-rich food, for it is the food that is the fuel of each body cell that makes each cell healthy, that prevents it from going haywire. The Navajo gathers acorns. He eats pine-nuts (in New York City sold on pushcarts and called *Indian nuts*), hazel nuts and chick peas. He hulls the acorns, dries them and grinds them with chick peas in a rock mortar and pestle, and makes a mush out of them. He gathers mesquite and wild beans which he makes into a kind of bread. The mesquite pod grows quite long, perhaps up to 12 inches, and contains a dry, moist brownish sugar. Here may be a clue to the "inadequate" diet of the Navajo that might be making him immune to cancer. He eats foods that are not grown with chemical fertilizers and that are not sprayed. Note that acorns, pine-nuts, chick peas, wild beans and the bean in the mesquite pod are all seeds. From them will grow huge amounts of plant tissue and trees. They contain living elements which nature has implanted there for the perpetuation of the species.

The Navajos, in using a mortar and pestle or other crude device for mashing or grinding up food, retain practically all the nutritional elements. They do not use anything like the huge steel rolling mills of our flour mills, the heat of which devitalizes the little that is left after the wheat germ is extracted. It is rather strange that the first reported outbreak of poliomyelitis in 1840 in Germany was only one year after the steel roller method of milling white flour was adopted in Vienna. By 1890, poliomyelitis grew to epidemic proportions. The Navajos are immune to infantile paralysis or multiple sclerosis.

The lesson of the Navajos should be taught in our schools and in our churches, and brought home to the general public in powerful publicity campaigns. It holds a word of courage to mothers who are concerned about their children's ability to forestall polio and other serious diseases. It must be the subject of further investigations.

CHAPTER 173

Investigating Primitive Diet

In spite of (or perhaps because of) toothpaste and fluorides and gum massages and dental floss, the teeth of the American people are getting worse. Once we needed dentists to help us keep our teeth, now we find it necessary to have orthodontists to help us keep what teeth we salvage in the proper place! This is progress? Oh for a period of regression to the strength that primitive conditions bred in our ancestors' teeth!

Weston A. Price, D.D.S., is a scientist who became alarmed enough about the deplorable change, not only in the teeth of modern man, but in the shape of the dental arch (the face really) to strike out in a new direction to find out why. It was his idea to stop wasting his efforts in trying to find the reason our teeth are so poor; rather he decided to analyze primitive people—their food, their habits, climate and any other objective factors—to find out why their teeth are so good. Sounds simple, doesn't it? It was so simple that apparently no one ever thought of it before.

In order to gather the material for his research, Dr. Price travelled many thousands of miles to the least visited, most inaccessible places in the world. He describes his travels and his methods in detail in his book, *Nutrition and Physical Degeneration* (a comparison of primitive and modern diets and their effects), available from Lee Foundation for Nutritional Research, 2023 West Wisconsin Avenue, Milwaukee, Wisconsin. The book forms an interesting travelogue, quite apart from the clinical observations, for Dr. Price writes pleasantly of the beauties of the country and the customs of the people.

Our Modern Diet

It is Dr. Price's theory, of course, that modern diet is the only explanation for our dental and skeletal degeneration. He points out that 3 centuries of "progress" in the United States have shown marked physical changes for the worse in Americans, while thousands of years of primitive civilization have left the inhabitants of isolated communities as healthy as they were in the dim past of their founding. The results of Dr. Price's work seem to prove his contention that store food is soon followed by store teeth.

In the process of his investigations, Dr. Price further concluded that moral values and intelligence are transmitted by inheritance in direct relation to the parents' diet. That is to say that children of well-nourished parents are likely to be intelligent and decent, while children whose parents do not eat nutritionally will tend to be mentally dull and morally indifferent. He offers as proof of this last statement the fact that the children of the communities he studied are mentally alert and have a more highly developed moral sense than those in so-called modernized civilization.

The Diet of the Loetenschals

The Loetenschal Valley, high in the Swiss Alps and nearly impossible to approach in any way but on foot, is a case in point. The two thousand or so inhabitants are virtually unaware of the "refinements" of modern civilization because nature has locked them out. This miracle place is lacking in many important adjuncts to our way of life: there are no jails, no police, no doctors or dentists. And why? Because there is no crime, no sickness and almost a total lack of dental caries. The people are perfect physical specimens, and many of the elite Swiss Guard, who by tradition guard the person of the Pope, and who are always of the highest physical and moral caliber, are chosen from the Loetenschals.

The diet and the way of life are simple here. The people raise their own food and make their own clothes. The food staples are cheese, hand-ground rye bread and fresh goat's and cow's milk. (On analysis these foods were found to be much higher in vitamin content than their counterparts in either America or the rest of Europe.) Though the valley has a high altitude, the people are inexhaustible, in spite of the rarified air, and old and young do heavy work without a sign of premature fatigue. Grachen, another town high in the Alps and equally isolated, can tell almost the same story.

Now we don't think that bread and milk are the best possible foods, as old-time readers know. Milk is apparently a food meant for children only. Bread-eating to excess may bring on many complications in health. A diet of bread and milk lacks vitamin C almost completely. Yet in these two Swiss locales the mere fact that no food is refined or changed by processing seems to work magic. Even though their diet seems to be unbalanced and incomplete, the people are healthy in spite of it, because they are completely untouched by refined foods.

Comparing Town and Country

Two other villages, close together in the Swiss Alps, offer excellent basis for comparison. One, Ayer, is geographically difficult to reach; its neighbor, Vissoie, has a new road and has been made into a market for processed foods. Though these towns are less than an hour's walk apart (undoubtedly less than 5 miles) the difference in the incidence of dental cavities is staggering: Vissoie has 10 times as many decayed teeth as Ayer.

It is further noted that the youths who leave their remote homes for a time to go to school or for some other commercial reason, find themselves suffering from dental problems the minute they subject themselves to the metropolitan diet. And the problem is erased immediately upon returning to the simple diet at home.

The large Swiss cities such as St. Moritz show a dietary contrast. There are probably few European cities with the cosmopolitan advantages of St. Moritz. If there is a processed food, it is reasonably certain that it is available in St. Moritz. For this advantage the people suffer. Dental caries is 15 times what it is in the villages just discussed. Logically, the children examined who were found to be relatively free of tooth decay proved to be children whose families resisted the influx of processed foods and maintained the healthful diet of their less progressive days. But it is significant that this city, known as a health spot, a spa, whose climate and altitude are purported to be among the best in Europe, has inhabitants who are only as healthy as the diet they select can make them.

While in Switzerland, Dr. Price carried his investigation to the famous TB sanatoria, perched high on the snowy sides of the Alps, whose crystal air and wonderful sun have proven the salvation of many a patient. The records at one of the largest of these hospitals showed that not one of the 3500 current patients was from any of the isolated villages, but all were from the towns on the plains below. To go a step further, Swiss doctors definitely agreed on a strong relation between the incidence of dental caries and TB.

Absence of Refined Foods

The many photographs which accompany the text show most force-fully the deterioration of the dental arch which accompanies bad diet. The children of St. Moritz have narrowed jaws, with teeth which seem to be stampeding for a proper place on the gum line. The teeth come crookedly, or through the upper gum; they overlap one another, and the bite is grotesquely out of alignment. With the Loetenschal children the opposite is true, the jaw is wide, the teeth evenly spaced and the biting surfaces meet beautifully.

As we shall see, this general situation is repeated again and again when comparison is made between the rugged diet of more primitive peoples and the diet of modern city dwellers.

What is interesting is the fact that people seem to thrive on the native diet, no matter what apparent deficiencies it might seem to have, so long as it is not augmented by the processed foods of the outside world. This point is nicely illustrated in Dr. Price's visit to the Hebrides Islands. The natives of Taransay Island consume almost no dairy products at all—no milk, no cheese, no eggs, etc.—just opposite to the healthy Swiss, yet they exhibit a high immunity to tooth decay and disease. Actually, they seem to have the same commendable moral characteristics as the Swiss, too. Their diet is dominated by high protein foods. Fish is a very important dietary staple, lobster and flat fish being most common and these are augmented by oats and barley, with small amounts of vegetable foods. Here again you will notice the absence of fresh fruits and vegetables in quantity—something that we know should be the biggest part of the diet when refined foods are eaten. But, even without these important foods, the mere fact that refined foods are absent is responsible for good health and good teeth.

Diets Compared

An interesting sidelight to the doctor's visit to the Isle of Lewis is the description of the preservation of the thatch from the roofs of the cottages for use as fertilizer. Peat is the exclusive fuel on the islands, and as it burns, the smoke, unconducted by a chimney, is absorbed into the thatched roof. At the year's end, when a new roof is put on, the smoke-blackened thatch is carefully preserved to be used in the fields. Tests prove that the precious gases trapped by the thatch are tremendously effective in producing the fine crops of the island.

The Island of Lewis produced a boon to Dr. Price's research in the person of two young men, brothers, who showed amazing differences in dental health. The actual pictures show a superb dental arch, filled in with perfect teeth on one boy, while the second exhibits a pitiful example of rampant dental breakdown. The interesting point here is that the brothers live in the same house, perform the same activities and literally live the same lives but for one all-important difference—the one whose teeth were decayed, had been unable to resist the change in diet offered by the new foods being imported to the island; the second, whose teeth were unscathed by disease, had deliberately eaten the diet of the locale, steadfastly refusing to expose himself to the dangers of processed foods. The obvious results would indicate that his was an inspired choice.

The Diet of the Eskimos

Possibly the cruelest and most demanding living conditions anywhere in the world are those imposed on man by numbing cold and fruitless wastes of the Arctic country. Most of us have difficulty imagining how the Eskimos manage to survive, especially since the diet is necessarily devoid of such seeming staples as greens and dairy products. However, their survival is not nearly the struggle we think it to be, they actually thrive on the rugged life they lead and the limited variety of foods available to them. They are much healthier and less troubled than their partially civilized brothers. They have almost no tooth decay (.3 per cent), and do not suffer from any of modern man's contagious or degenerative diseases.

Their foods are of the simplest. A big staple is salmon, which they catch and freeze at the height of the season, and which is eaten dipped in seal oil, known to be rich in vitamin A. Caribou, nuts and kelp round out the diet of these hardy people. But let a tribe be near a trading post, let a government boat bring civilization to a group of these people, and the health and stamina are sure to break down. Dental caries flourish, tuberculosis becomes a major problem and the infant mortality rate skyrockets.

Again and again the sad plight of the native with painfully decayed teeth is mentioned by Dr. Price. Because, for most of us, a dentist is only a bus ride away, we can hardly imagine the desperation inflicted by the torture of decayed teeth on those who have nowhere to turn for relief. The story of a mining engineer who was isolated in the Arctic wastes is a case in point. This man developed a toothache which pained him so much that he was willing to—did in fact!—spend $2,000 to hire a plane that would take him to a dentist for treatment. In the South Seas, toothache is the only known cause of suicide. It is such instances that point up the tragedy of introducing contented natives to modernity, without introducing, too, the refinements necessarily devised to combat its effects. If we must give a native a candy bar, it would behoove us, in the name of simple humanity to see that he has a dentist at hand.

The Effect of Civilization on the Indian

The Indians of Northern Canada were found to be akin to the Eskimos in their rugged good health. They easily withstand temperatures of —70 degrees, while their American counterparts do equally well in the boiling desert temperatures of South Western United States. In Northern Canada the cold eliminates the practicality of dairy animals, as well as the growth of cereals and fruits. These Indians subsist almost exclusively on wild animals. All the necessary vitamins are found in this diet. They have discovered that certain organs in the animals they kill are valuable sources of vitamins unobtainable in any other way. For example, the balls of fat found just above the kidney of a moose have been found to be extremely high in vitamin C.

Kindness and hospitality are a part of the tradition of the primitive Indians. There are no locks required; because of the high moral tone of the people, consideration and honesty are a part of the culture. They have no arthritis or tuberculosis, and their teeth and facial structure are enviable. At point of contact with civilization, however, all of these assets are adversely affected. Arthritis and tuberculosis prevail where modern foods are introduced into the diet. Dr. Price's pictures of these people are pitiful and revealing. At a reservation hospital in Ontario, a doctor tells of the many maternity cases which require surgical aid at the time of delivery. This state of affairs, in a tribe whose grandmothers would retire alone behind a bush, to emerge in a short while with a new addition to the tribe, would make one wonder if progress is everything it is cracked up to be. Certainly the move from the animal ease of childbearing to the agonized labor and forceps technique the reservation Indian undergoes is not a desirable evolution.

The Indians near Sitka are in as bad straits as those on the reservations. Less than half the babies survive to the sixth year, and tuberculosis is chiefly responsible. What kind of prenatal nutrition could breed such a high incidence of this disease? Bear in mind that isolated Indians of the same tribes, even the same families as those in Sitka, are notably free of these diseases. It is a fact that doctors often send tuberculosis patients back to their primitive environment, where, oftentimes, they recover completely. Acute surgical problems such as appendicitis, kidney stones and gall bladder operations are common to Sitka Indians, while the primitives are not even aware that such afflictions exist—again irrefutable evidence that refined foods and physical degeneration have a common denominator.

Sustenance in the Tropics

Dr. Price's survey carried him next from the ice of the Arctic and Canada to the tropical islands of the South Pacific. The Melanesians and Polynesians are essentially the happy brown people of the travelogues—or at least they are natured that way. They live with the climate, wearing no clothes, coating themselves, instead, with coconut oil to avoid severe sunburn and to protect themselves from the torrential rains, which are not able to penetrate the greased skin. Seafood is the mainstay of their diet, and this food is considered so important that, even in war, the fishermen are allowed through the enemy lines to gather the daily quota. This need for fish as a dietary staple necessarily makes these people superb fishermen and navigators.

The physical breakdown which characterizes the intrusion of white man's food on native diet is not missing here. The magnificent dental arch and the low incidence of dental decay has been tragically reversed. On heavily touristed islands, the degree of diseases matches the degree of modernization. It is apparent that had the white man not found his paradise in the South Seas, it might still be a paradise for the natives.

Journeys Into Africa

The most exotic of all the places Dr. Price describes is Africa. The hazards of life on this continent are so formidable that only the strongest survive. Experience has taught the natives that this is so, and their entire culture has been built around this theme—survival of the individual and survival of the tribe. To spend a day in the jungles is to know the basic truth that only the fittest will live to see another sun.

The brute animals have born into them an awareness that they must fight the enemies they can't run from, and run from those they can't fight. This knowledge filters from the mother to the baby and is translated into a strength and agility that is marvelously precocious. The wobbly calf dropped by one of our domesticated cows can seldom stand at all much before he is a day old. The African calf can run swiftly before his mother has had a chance to lick him clean! Even in a rushing herd he can maintain the pace—he must, or he will be left behind, unprotected and easy prey for the hungry jungle animals.

The people, too, are endowed with this innate awareness. To sidestep the everyday hazards of jungle life such as chiggers, lice, tsetse flies, typhus, etc., requires a physical endurance and natural immunity far greater than the stranger to Africa possesses. To live the life of a native without taking the precautions civilization has taught would be suicidal for us; yet to the African such folderol is white man's nonsense. Dr. Price is convinced that such immunity is more than a racial trait, for modernized natives are quick to lose it. A change in diet is the apparent answer. If the food were primitive, the consumers were healthy and vigorous; if it were processed, the consumers showed ill health and lacked ability to withstand living extremes. In the youngest of these, progressively worse physical formation and no disease resistance were common.

The inquiries into native foods were startling and revealing. Though most of the native diets are based on tradition, they all show a keen knowledge of what the body needs to stand up against life in this rugged land. And the diet, limited as it is, still shows more than sufficient nutritional values, due probably to the fact that all foods are eaten intact, with none of the ingrown nutrients disturbed. The Nilatic tribes depend strongly on the blood of their cattle for nutrition. The steers are bled at regular intervals by a unique process which is both painless and harmless. The jugular vein is pierced by an arrow with such skill that the animal does not even flinch, and about a gallon of blood taken, in a gourd. The flow is then halted, a styptic of ashes is applied and the animal is released as good as new. The blood is then shaken in the gourd until it is defibrinated. The fibrin is cooked, like bacon, and the defibrinated remainder is drunk raw, as is milk. The blood is carefully distributed according to the supply. At one time it was the food of warriors exclusively; now each growing child receives a daily ration, as does each pregnant and lactating woman. Blood, milk and meat complete the main diet, supplemented by some fruits and vegetables. Naturally, dental problems and abnormal jaw formations are so rare among these people as to be almost non-existent.

It is common to find tribes who devote much attention to the diet of child-bearing women. Some tribes put the girls on a special diet for 6 months before marriage, and again, each pregnancy is a time for carefully selected foods. The advantages and benefits are so obvious that it is appalling to see modern doctors who do little more than suggest that the mother-to-be ". . . take it easy and try not to gain any more than 25 pounds."

The African tribesman has learned to take full advantage of his environment, so that some of the foods are odd-sounding to our ears. However, when analyzed, even the weirdest foods are found to be extremely nutritious. Many pygmy tribes have found the eggs of certain flies to be most healthful, both fresh and dried for storage. The elephant is also a favorite food of the pygmies. Even ants are more apt to become an integral part of a picnic in Africa than they are here.

The teeth of these people are just about perfect, as low as 0.2 per cent decay in many tribes. But in the hospitals and institutions erected in the same country, but using modernized foods, the incidence of dental caries is up to 12 per cent.

The Aborigines of Australia

In Australia the Aborigines, probably the oldest living race, received special attention from Dr. Price. These people exhibit the most primitive skeletal development along with superb physiques. There is little baldness in even the very old, and full good health in aged people is the norm.

These people are superb hunters. They have the keenest senses and are so used to the habits of the wild life around them that they have an uncanny talent for predicting the movements of their quarry. A hunt, for them, is never unsuccessful, and a fishing trip means literally picking the fish out of the water as they swim by. They can see an animal in the brush a mile away, and can tell a type of fish by the movement it imparts to the water.

It is traditional that a boy may not kill a slow-moving animal. Rather, at such an opportunity, the boy is expected to defer to any older man in the party. The fast animals on the outer edges of the herd are the targets for the youngsters—and they get them! This nobleness is carried into other areas of the behavior of the Aborigines. Their high morals are familiar to all who know them, and they serve as an apt illustration of Dr. Price's corollary which states that well-nourished parents will produce mentally and physically healthy children.

The diet here is rudimentary, and makes full use of low-growing vegetation like berries, leaves, roots and stems, also kangaroos, wallabies, rodents, insects and fish eggs. It is evident from this list that the primitive people are conditioned to take full advantage of all available sustenance. It might well be that the very need to eat whatever is available insures the full nutrition that characterizes these natives.

Where modern diet has crept in, there is the usual breakdown and oral malformation. Caries incidence rushes up from almost none in the primitives to 100 per cent in the latest generation of those eating modern food. What else but treated food can be the answer to such a collapse in a people whose teeth and facial characteristics were perfect for the hundreds of years of existence until the recent introduction of processed foods?

Archeological Studies

In the preceding field studies, Dr. Price's main concern was with living groups. However, the West Coast of South America has been the home of several ancient cultures, and it was felt that the visible remains of these people of long ago might be an excellent basis for the study of modern physical degeneration.

Fortunately, the burial customs of these ancients were careful and efficient. The mummies found are quite intact. Also, the customs called for the body to be surrounded with relics relating to the trade of the deceased while on earth: the fisherman with his nets, the stone mason with his cutting tools, etc. These tombs and the pottery found, which was decorated with scenes depicting the times, offer a rich set of clues to life in that area. Archeologists found, too, that individual tribes had unique burial customs, so that boundaries were easily discerned by the decorations of the graves.

The Benefits of Isolation

They were a very happy and prosperous people, with wise laws and deep intelligence. Gold and silver were easily come by, and it was the white man's insane quest of these that led to the decline of the Peruvian Indians. Even to this day, the descendants of the ancient people are wary of strangers and will seldom leave their mountain homes.

The skeletal remains show evidence of a remarkable surgical skill among these people. Many of the skulls show the effects of delicate operations which called for the removal of portions of the skull which were thought to be depressing the brain—a surgery which even now requires a very advanced technique. It is further seen upon examination of the skulls that many of the patients recovered and lived long enough for the bone to completely regenerate. In amputations the same skill was apparent. The stumps were carefully cut to leave an overlap of flesh over the end of the remaining part of the limb, a method used universally today.

Dr. Price's purpose in studying these remains was to make a comparison between the dental arches encountered in ancient times and those of today. The results, in the light of what has gone before, are not surprising, though they are impressive. In a study of almost 1300 Peruvian skulls there was not found a single sign of deformity; in comparison with these findings, a study of the United States general population showed that 25-75 per cent of the people have definite irregularity in the development of dental arches and facial form. If nothing else these results prove that irregularities of facial bones and dental arches do not have to occur as a part of the law of averages. The Natural Law, if left unmolested, actually dictates physical perfection.

Today the Peruvian Indians cling to their primitive isolation and eat foods which are coarse and simple. Much of the food is consumed cold and dry, such as parched beans and corn. It must be concluded that diet is in some measure responsible for the marvelous physical condition these people display, and which allows them to live and work with any efficiency in the high Andes.

The Story of Guano

In connection with his report on the Peruvians, Dr. Price discusses the Humboldt Current, a swath of water coming down the coast of Peru from the Antarctic, which carries with it spectacular numbers of all kinds of fish. It is apparently full of the chemical elements which produce large quantities of fish. Millions of pelicans and other birds and animals who thrive on fish swarm across the islands off the Peruvian coast. They eat unbelievable numbers of fish (as high as 75 fish have been found in the craw of a single bird) and the supply seems undiminished.

The birds and their appetite for fish has inadvertently proved a boon to the government and economy of Peru. The droppings of these birds, consisting of partially digested marine life, have accumulated on the islands to a depth of 100 feet in some places. Guano, as it is called, is known as the finest fertilizer in the world. It is said to be 33 times more effective than barnyard manure. Not aware of the treasure it had, the government for many years, sold the guano by the shipload to other nations. Now it is kept for home use and a careful method for conservation has been worked out.

We Need Dietary Intelligence

The last quarter of Dr. Price's valuable book on the effects of diet brings his findings closer to home. What have we learned from the native Eskimo and the South Sea Islander? What keeps them so enviably healthy, while we are kept busy dodging diseases as though they were so many raindrops? Why are the Eskimos so happy and free from psychological tensions? How do they avoid the scourge of congenital malformations? Dr. Price translates the secrets these people have discovered into dietary intelligence. It would seem evident that once our diet is corrected, our health problems will greatly diminish or disappear completely.

Modern researchers and laboratory methods have traced the needs of the body so that we know pretty well what elements we require to stay healthy. It is up to us to see that these needs are met in the foods we eat. We are not able to manufacture our own vitamins and minerals as some animals can. (A rat's system makes its own vitamin C, dogs can make vitamin C, etc.) We humans must positively eat what we need, for we can get it in no other way. And apparently, the best way to be sure of including all of our needs is to pattern what we eat after the foods eaten by the primitives whose health we envy so.

A strong characteristic of the American diet is high calorie foods. We like the quick-energy food that picks us up—the candy bar, the soda, the ice cream cone. It is eaten in a twinkling and satisfies our hunger pangs. But there is no sustaining power in this type of eating. Instead, the blood sugar shoots up to a temporary level that induces a spurt of activity in us, and this activity burns the reserves of vitamins and minerals which our body might have stored, but can ill-afford to lose. The primitives, on the other hand, have habits of diet geared to low calorie foods. The low calorie content makes it necessary to eat more of the food to be satisfied, and, incidentally, acquire more of the valuable food elements contained in the good foods. So, eating a variety of low calorie foods is a reasonably certain way of getting enough of the vitamins and minerals we need for good health.

The Proper Food For Our Animals

Another health trick of the primitives is to feed their animals carefully, so that the meat and dairy products offer the dietary advantages they were meant to offer. The cows are grazed in new, young grass whose nutritional content is at its height, and the butter they produce is found to be several times higher than ours in fat soluble activators, including vitamins A and D. The same excellence exists in the quality of eggs from hens which are fed natural foods and are free to roam the barnyard to acquire the healthful germs they instinctively know are good for them. There is not the measured dosage hanky-panky our animals are exposed to, but instead there is the inborn prompting of nature which is far more infallible in producing healthy stock.

This discussion leads Dr. Price to a chapter on the availability of pasture land rich in the necessary minerals. The United States is very poor in grazing area. The natural problems of erosion and dust storms rob us of much good soil. But more alarming than these is the rate at which the soil is being robbed of its treasures by a far-flung economy which grows a crop in one place and consumes it 3000 miles away. How can the ground be reconditioned when what should be returned to it has been exported to, relatively, another world? Science has tried to replace these chemicals, but when the chemicals are not in their natural combination with other, perhaps unknown, elements, the synthetic offerings of Science show very little promise as an efficient substitute. Editor Rodale has more to say along these lines in his book, PAY DIRT.

Genetic Determination of Health

With Dr. Price, good health has its roots in previous generations. On the health of the parents depends the health of the child. Prenatal care consists in more than mile long walks and weight control. It is important that the mother's diet give her the nutrients that the unborn child will demand as it matures within her. For example: To produce good bones the baby will need calcium; when the urogenital tract is formed, vitamin A will be demanded. The mother must be ready to meet these demands, for she holds an absolute monopoly on the supply. If the brain of the unborn child is forming and the stuff which produces a healthy brain is not available, the brain must be formed without it. Mongolism is directly related to underdevelopment of the pituitary gland, so that mothers deficient in vitamin A, which is necessary to the pituitary gland, run the risk of having mongoloid children. Something will be missing. The omission of a dietary need might produce a person with a simple unimportant personality quirk,

[652]

it might produce a killer or an idiot. And the cause will be prenatal diet deficiency—not too much anesthetic, nor plus and minus Rh factors, nor inept delivery—just bad diet.

Dietary Influences On Pregnancy

The effects of bad diet, long considered a responsibility of the mother alone, are extended to include the paternal influence. Experiments by Dr. Price showed that the health of the father is quite a vital factor in the production of a well-formed baby. A litter of dachshunds, for example, showed cleft palate in several of the pups. And the identical deformity showed up in 3 litters of different mothers sired by the same father. The question of the father's dietary responsibility is raised in a history of an Eskimo woman married to a white man. At her husband's insistence, she cooked separate meals for him, using modern foods, while she maintained a personal diet of native foods. In 26 pregnancies she had no tooth decay or other signs of nutritional deficiency. Her husband had rampant tooth decay and some facial deformity. Several of the children had markedly incomplete development of the face and dental arches. One of the daughters—mind you, the daughter of a mother 26 times over!—had such a severe ordeal with the birth of her first child that she determined never to take the risk of having another. Is it likely that a healthy mother could be completely responsible for this condition in her children, when they show such patent similarities to the father's defects?

Many native tribes have charming customs woven into their culture which are meant to insure the nutrition of the mother-to-be. One African tribe actually has a huge feast for her as soon as she knows she is to be a mother. During the festivities, the chief appoints two youths who are sworn to the duty of supplying the lady, daily, with fresh seafood. Here, as in Alaska and other primitive locations, fish is considered a most vital food in reproduction. In Alaska a certain fish is eaten daily by both prospective parents. The man eats a certain part of it to maintain his virility, the wife eats a certain part to increase her fertility, or, if she is pregnant, to nourish the child she carries.

Studies among the natives have convinced Dr. Price that an interval of 3 to 4 years between children is an ideal period for the body of the mother to replenish the nutritional losses normally incurred in pregnancy. To insure this policy, customs in many places forbid the wife to share a hut with her husband before the youngest child is 3 years old. In other tribes it is a matter of public disgrace to give birth to children less than 3 years apart. In many cases this is a deliberate means to develop a healthy self-control for the married couple, in others, polygamy is the answer to preventing a new mother's untimely conception.

Dr. Price's studies tend to show that the reproductive capacity of the mother is depleted with each successive birth and so the quality of health in the later children is not so good as that of the first ones. The interpretation of these figures would appear to be highly arbitrary and grossly dependent on many indefinable factors.

[653]

Personality and Congenital Defects

The child with a congenital defect is the child who will get into trouble, says Dr. Price. The "why" of this conclusion can take two forms: one, a visible congenital defect may be an outward manifestation of a defectively formed brain which could well cause irresponsibility and lawlessness; second, the physical malformation alone might convert a mentally normal person into a criminal by reason of the psychological changes being "different" might give rise to. The first is the theory supported by Dr. Price, the second is one classically cited by a famous plastic surgeon who devoted his life to proving that a criminal was often a criminal by virtue of a facial malformation, and proved his point by reducing the number of repeat offenders by careful surgery which reshaped the faces to remove any oddity in appearance.

In *Nutrition and Physical Degeneration,* these statistics are offered in support of Dr. Price's theory: though they occur in normal population, too, of course, deformed palates are present in 33 per cent of all insane, in 55 per cent of all criminals and in 61 per cent of all idiots. And in examinations of the inmates at prisons and reformatories and asylums, facial deformities are almost invariably evident.

Primitive Diet Best

Whether one is willing to agree completely with Dr. Price's conclusions, it must be admitted that the poor uncultured savages are not the ones with health problems and social problems. We are. If our civilization could display the humility and good grace we expect of the natives, perhaps, instead of forcing our ways on them, we might learn some worthwhile lessons on improving our health and the health of our unborn generations.

This brings us to the end of our discussion on Dr. Price's brilliant and enlightening book. We heartily recommend the reading of it by everyone interested in the return of dietary sanity to the eating habits of the modern world.

[654]

CHAPTER 174

When Having a Baby Was Part of a Busy Day

Any mother will tell you that giving birth to a child is a gratifying experience. Most mothers will tell you, too, that it is a painful and exhausting experience. (This conclusion forms the basis for the famous Read Method of Natural Childbirth.) In the plan of nature this misery was clearly not meant to be. The reproduction of one's own kind takes place in every animal except for civilized man, with relative ease and speed. No wild animal tarries longer than a few hours to deliver herself of often not one, but several babies, after which she is soon up and about, searching for nourishment for herself so that she can properly nurse her young.

Childbirth—Indian Style

That this is the normal course of things, for the human animal as well, is evidenced by the many accounts of childbirth among the primitive natives of North America. Explorers, missionaries and hunters were astounded at the ease with which these native women gave birth. They contrasted the elaborate lying-in period of the European women with the matter-of-fact attitude of the Indian women who thought childbirth hardly worth a pause in the day's occupations. Indeed many of these women did no more than to pause, have their babies and proceed immediately to the next chore of the day. Illustrative of this custom is this account from the book, *New Voyages to North America*, written in 1703 by Baron de Lahontan: "If the women should be in labor in the night they deliver themselves upon their mats without crying out, or making a noise. The next morning they rise, and go about their ordinary duties within doors and without as though nothing had happened." And from Father Sagard's book, *Long Journey to the Country of the Hurons* (1824), we get this picture: "I have seen them (Huron women) come in from the woods laden with a big bundle of wood, and give birth to a child as soon as they arrive; then immediately they are on their feet in ordinary employment." Another writer tells of a group traveling on horseback; included in the party was an Indian woman whose time had come. She simply pulled to the side of the road while the rest rode on. She had her baby, wrapped him against the weather and caught up with the party within an hour.

The journals of the Europeans who explored North America after its discovery, and had a chance to observe the natives in their unspoiled environment are all full of similar accounts. Some say that the Indian woman would go alone from the village to a place in the woods when the baby was due. She would emerge a short time later with the child neatly wrapped and clean, and herself ready to resume housework. All agree that the Indian woman would never cry out in childbirth, and while some writers say that custom forbade their crying out, others are of the opinion that the women didn't cry out simply because there was no great pain, hence no reason for doing so.

What Natural Nourishment Gave to the Indians

How these women arrived at this enviable state of nonchalance in childbirth is open to speculation. Most probably it was their reward for natural living. They ate the most primitive fare, but Dr. Weston Price says the diet of the Indians of the Far North provided 5.8 times as much calcium, 5.8 times as much phosphorus, 2.7 times the iron, 4.3 times the magnesium, 1.5 times the copper, 8.8 times the iodine and 10 times the fat-soluble activators of modern diet. Kaare Rodahl, M.D., in his book, *North—The Nature and Drama of the Polar World*, remarks that ". . . all internal organs and plants which have the highest vitamin content, especially vitamin C, are considered particular delicacies by the Eskimo and that though he knows nothing about vitamins, some of his methods of preparing stored foods offer the best possible preservation of vitamins." Similar statements could be made on the native diets of most primitive people, though further south the problems of preserving food became acute. These natives were trained by necessity to eat the whole animal as soon as it was killed, and it was not unusual for 6 or 8 Indians to eat an entire buffalo at a single sitting, without the slightest discomfort. Then, of course, there were many days of absolute starvation, when no animal food was to be found.

Reason for Ease of Labor Suggested

The theory is offered that the constant activity of the busy, hard-working Indian woman, even in the most advanced stages of pregnancy, serves to place the child in the most advantageous position for effortless passage through the birth canal. Though this might be true, it is more logical to assume that the proper position of the baby was only one of a number of factors. Not the least of these was the superb physical condition of the mothers. They had to be in excellent health to withstand the rigors of the life they led. They slept under the stars in temperatures of 40 degrees below zero, we're told; the women were required to do all of the heavy work, for the men were busy hunting; they were constantly on the move traveling to exhaustion just to keep up with migrating wildlife. These women got plenty of exercise. Their muscles were full of tone and developed to a fine degree. With such physical equipment it is no wonder that child-bearing was, for them, almost as effortless as eating.

As soon as the child was born, it was washed in the snow until it began to cry from the shock. The mother would wash herself in the same way. Her couch was usually a few boughs of fir in a trough of snow, dug for protection against the cold winds. If there were no snow, the mother and child went for a dip in the coldest streams or in the ocean. Some of our North Pacific Coast Indians made a daily ocean bath, winter or summer, an unbreakable ritual from their earliest days till the day they died.

Healthy Children the Result

And what kind of children resulted from these easy births and rigorous conditions of early life? Quoting Baron de Lahontan once more: " 'Tis a great rarity to find any among them (the Indians) that are lame, hunchbacked, one-eyed, blind or dumb." For another impression of native children listen to Captain F. W. Beechey in his book, *Narratives of a Voyage to the Pacific and Bering Strait,* ". . . children are reared to a healthier state than in other countries, and are free from fevers and other complaints peculiar to the greater portion of the world . . . nothing is more extraordinary in the history of the island than the uniform good health of the children; the teething is easily gotten over, they have no bowel complaints, and are exempt from those contagious diseases which affect children in large communities." These opinions are almost universal among those who write of any primitive peoples. There is virtually no congenital disease, and perfect development as the children mature is a foregone conclusion.

Sickness Introduced With Modern Refinements

Sad to say, this condition persists only so long as the people are permitted their proper environment. Once they deviate from the native diet and improve on native discomforts and hardships, their ruggedness and resistance to disease is no more. Dr. A. E. Marden, Surgeon to the United States Indian Service, summed up the situation in these words: "That the robust condition and easy mode of childbearing are rapidly disappearing from even the full-blooded Indian women there can be no doubt. The bed has taken the place of the blanket or the pallet or straw, and the 'puerperal state' (time of recovery) that of the ready condition for renewed toil immediately after childbirth. The daughters and granddaughters of these sturdy aboriginal matrons consult the pale-face doctor, and are rapidly acquiring the methods of pale-face women. . . . From an out-of-door life of activity with plenty of fresh game and wholesome food and clear water, with healthful teepees for homes, the change has been made to log cabins, with overheated close air. Poor food, with flour and salted meat of inferior quality, is mostly what is found in the modern Indian home. In exchange for an active life there is much of idleness and indoor confinement. . . . Partly on this account the naturally robust constitution is deteriorating, and miscarriages and diseases peculiar to women are noticeably increasing."

Should the Modern Woman Go "Primitive"

To many of the women who read this, the "modern" conditions described in that paragraph would seem primitive still. The "overheated log cabins" would seem unbearably chilly and draughty, the "white flour and salted meats" would never compare to our super-market foods in the fine degree of processing we are used to. In short, the women of our society have been living for several generations on this type of debilitating existence that is ruining the Indians—and with refinements that the Indians never dreamed of!

It is, of course, out of the question for our women to do an about-face and expose themselves to the rigors that were commonplace with primitive Indians. These people had been conditioned by centuries of custom and habit to live with the elements and to master them. But there is a lesson—and a clear one—that can be learned rfom all primitive peoples: eating unadulterated, unprocessed, natural foods is a strong factor in their resistance to disease, as well as the resistance to disease displayed by their offspring. When they are introduced to refined food, they are introduced to bad health, susceptibility to disease, difficulty in childbirth and serious contagion.

One Major Concern

For women who are pregnant or in the age of childbearing, a careful diet is a most valuable asset. Good food, coupled with moderate, regular exercise, will help to nourish the child developing in the womb, and to assemble all of the mother's resources that make for ease of delivery and quick renewal of strength. The modern woman should make every effort to fortify herself against the inroads that today's easy living impose on her natural vitality. She should walk in the air whenever she can, and do simple daily exercises that will give tone to the muscles she'll need when she has her child. She should eat fresh, organically-raised fruits and vegetables as well as properly prepared meats. Processed foods, artificial sweets, cigarettes, salt, coffee—all these should be taboo to her. Her only concern should be the baby she is carrying and she should eat nothing without first assuring herself that it will be of value to the health of the expected child or her own health. The primitive Indians didn't have such problems, for the only foods available to them were rich in the food elements they needed. The closer we can come to having that type of diet, the closer we, and our children, will come to the perfect health the primitive Indians enjoyed.

CHAPTER 175

Old Age in Japan

By Ruth Rodale Spira

On the hearth sputter some doughy fritters, browning in deep fat. A Japanese family waits eagerly for their noon-day meal of crisp "yaki-mochi."

At first glance, this morsel seems to have been devised to kill off the human race prematurely. Starchy dough and plenty of fat don't inspire thoughts of a long and healthy life. But just the opposite is true. This is the village of Hizato, where old people are more commonplace than almost anywhere else in Japan, and yakimochis are not at all just doughy fritters.

Diet and Longevity

Hizato, in the Nagano prefecture, has stirred up a great deal of attention among scientists: at least 6.65 per cent of the village inhabitants are over 70 years old. The plain fact is that there are 250 per cent more 70-year-olds living in Hizato than in the average Japanese village. (The United States does not compare too well, with only about 80 per cent the ratio of 70-year-olds there are in Hizato.)

Another non-typical village lies scarcely a few miles away in the deep snow belt of Japan. Kashiwabara is woefully negligent in preserving its elders. Hizato outstrips it by more than 391 per cent, a remarkable figure, considering that the two villages seem identical in almost every way. The peasants work equally long hours in the fields tilling the soil. Everyone is poor by our standards.

Why, then, should statistics show such an amazing difference in longevity? The answer is to be found in their diets, scientists believe. A team of nutritionists, sent to both villages, turned up some curious evidence.

Foods Eaten in Each Village

Fresh vegetables and a great variety of whole grains are eaten regularly in Hizato, reports Ei Yamamoto of the Nagano Health Center. Since the climate is considerably milder than in Kashiwabara, the growing season extends well over most of the year. While the Kashiwabarans have already dug into their winter supply of pickled vegetables, fresh carrots and green onions are still on the menu in Hizato. Their favorite dish, yakimochi, compounds finely diced carrots, radishes and green onions, with wheat and buckwheat flour and a "bean paste." Actually a flavoring, the paste is prepared by fermenting mashed soybeans with a malt and salt solution. The mixture is then rolled together and fried, generally in sesame seed oil.

The concoction, according to the visiting food experts, is exceedingly delightful and nutritious, well supplied with vitamins A, B_1, and the unsaturated fatty acids, so necessary to good health. Few of the hydrogenated oils, suspect as agents in producing heart disease, have become available to them yet.

Caught in the rice paddy zone, the village of Kashiwabara exists mainly on bulky white rice stripped of its valuable germ and hull. Hizato, at a higher elevation, readily grows wheat, buckwheat, millet, Italian millet and barley. All of these cereals no doubt are eaten whole, adding plenty of vitamins B_1 and E, iron, phosphorus and enzymes to the diet. Rice forms only a small percentage of their food. Kashiwabara in removing the germ and hull of the rice, does a great injustice to the food value of this cereal. Complete, as brown rice, it contains quantities of the vitamin B complex and other useful ingredients. A Japanese scientist, Dr. Kuratsune, discovered in 1951 that a diet of whole brown rice and raw vegetables was enough to sustain normal life. Consuming only 931 calories of the rice and vegetables, he was able to perform all his medical duties.

In Hizato, dried seaweed is always on hand, either as "tangle," "wakame" (lobe-leaved undaria) or "hijiki" (spindle-shaped bladder leaf). A special variety, called "tengusa," is prepared almost as gelatin. After boiling and cooling, the congealed seaweed is usually cut into slices and served with vinegar and soy sauce. Even small amounts of seaweed furnish useful minerals, especially iodine, and vitamin A.

Pickling vegetables in Kashiwabara is a major affair. Pickles, or "tsukemono" in Japan can include anything from greens to the unlikely eggplant. Usually radishes and lettuce are most popular, being heavily salted at the end of summer, and lasting until the spring crops are harvested. Lettuce is first treated with a bleaching solution, surely no blessing, healthwise. Late in February, the flavor of the pickles sharpens the appetite, causing the Kashiwabarans to overeat the white rice.

Meats and fish are extremely scarce all year round in both villages. Dried herring or other small fish sometimes is eaten, but far from regularly. Soybeans and the grains provide most of the protein these people consume, and not a great deal at that. Being mainly Buddhists, and therefore vegetarian in principle, the Japanese do not consider a restricted animal diet the sacrifice it would be to many Americans. Nor has it been a sacrifice to the Hizatans, who prove their fine nutrition by the numbers of citizens reaching a venerable old age.

Vitamin and Mineral Comparison

From the vitamin and mineral point of view, the village of Hizato stands considerably above Kashiwabara. The following chart illustrates striking differences:

The comparison is spectacular, indeed—over 4 times more vitamin A, almost twice as much vitamin B_1 over twice the amount of vitamin C and at least 58 per cent more iron consumed in Hizato than its neighboring village.

[660]

Diet Analysis: Hizato & Kashiwabara

Vitamin A		Vitamin B₁	
Min. Daily Requirement	5000 I.U.	Min. Daily requirement	1.8 mg.
Hizato	3140	Hizato	2.86
Kashiwabara	750	Kashiwabara	1.62

Vitamin B₂		Vitamin C	
Min. Daily Requirement	2.7 mg.	Min. Daily Requirement	75 mg.
Hizato	0.74	Hizato	118
Kashiwabara	0.67	Kashiwabara	52

Calcium		Iron	
Min. Daily Requirement	0.75 gr.	Min. Daily Requirement	10 mg.
Hizato	0.378	Hizato	73
Kashiwabara	0.374	Kashiwabara	43

But comparing these figures to the minimum daily requirements set for men in America, even Hizato lags in vitamin A, vitamin B₂, as well as calcium intake. Just the same, the results seem to vindicate the diets of the Hizatans. No one can deny that a diet supporting a number of aged people is a healthy one. Without question, here is an open field for medical research demanding a thorough investigation of the interrelation of foods. Is it possible that the proper combination of vitamins or minerals means better use of them? Or can a person eating a more natural diet better absorb the food he eats?

Mukojima

Although Hizato is celebrated for its many elders, the village of Mukojima in Japan has an even higher percentage of 70-year-olds. Over 8.4 per cent of the people fall into this category.

These people are accustomed to a diet of mainly sweet potatoes, wheat beans, azuki, beans, carrots, pumpkins, seaweed and occasionally fish. The sweet potatoes, carrots and pumpkins no doubt provide a suitable amount of vitamin A, which is somewhat lacking in the food of the Hizatans. Figures are not yet available of the exact amounts of vitamin A in their diet. The beans and fish make up most of the protein consumed, which is rather sparing. The people eat very little fat and only moderate amounts of carbohydrate; rice is not even grown in Mukojima.

CHAPTER 176

Good Health Was Their Habit

The 500 years since the white man came to North America have shown a change in the lives of the natives which can teach us many valuable lessons in preserving human health. The leaders of the early expeditions to North America were fascinated by everything about the Indians, so they made copious notes on all they saw for inclusion in their reports to their homelands.

This fascination with the primitive people of this continent has never abated. Even today books are being written about them, and the chain of information is unbroken through all 5 centuries. What better opportunity to study the effects of our civilization on a primitive people could the world offer?

Hard Life Bred Healthy People

Almost without exception the early writers characterize the life these people led as one long test of physical endurance. Their general opinion also describes the natives as superb physical specimens who were subject to very few of our chronic diseases, and who kept their hair and teeth until they died, either of old age or battle wounds. Even serious wounds did not necessarily lead to death. The Indians had developed many excellent herb remedies, and even used techniques of surgery which seem advanced today. Early writers tell of vital wounds which were quickly healed, leaving the victim with no physical deformity or crippling effect. Whether this resulted from the natives' talent with medicinal herbs or from their amazing powers of recovery is difficult to determine. However, it is known that their physical condition gave them a strong resistance to infection, and gangrene never occurred among them. As for broken bones, they were counted as a rarity and recovery never took more than a week, should such an accident happen.

To offer a more authoritative statement, let us quote the conclusion arrived at by a Seminar Conference between the Universities of Yale and Toronto on the North American Indian: "In this anthropologists agree . . . that before the discovery of America, it was one of the most, if not the most, healthful of continents. There was a richness of population, there were no areas depopulated by diseases, there seemed to be no epidemics that had been reported by early white settlers. Skeletal remains of unquestionable pre-Columbian date, barring few exceptions, are remarkably free from disease. There was no rachitis (rickets), little tuberculosis, no smallpox, cancer was rare (and it still is), and even fractures were infrequent." After reading that, one can hardly be blamed for looking around him, puzzled, and asking what happened to this healthy land and people. America now vies for just about every world record in death rates from chronic diseases, and almost all her people have hospital records.

Eye-witness accounts bolster the seminar's conclusions on the vigor of primitive people. George Wharton James in his book, *California,* says this of the early California Indians: "There were no poorhouses, no hospitals, no asylums for blind, deaf, dumb, incurable or insane, for thank God, there were none so poor as to be separated from the rest, and so few sick, blind, dumb, deaf or insane that hospitals were not needed. The simple primitive inhabitants lived . . . too naturally, too healthfully to often become seriously sick." W. C. Boteler, M.D., of the United States Indian Service, describes the Indians as the "picture of health and development." They were, he says, not susceptible to any epidemic influences; smallpox was almost unknown and diphtheria rare, as were uterine diseases among the women.

Natives of the Far North

We could continue for many pages, quoting experts on anthropology, history and medicine, as well as explorers and adventurers, who willingly vouch for the enviable physical condition of the American Indians. Equally enthusiastic are those who traveled through the polar regions, observing the Northern Indians and Eskimos in their primitive way of life. This description of the Polar Eskimos in the book, *Green Seas and White Ice,* by Miriam MacMillan, is typical. "A meat-eating people with such perfect teeth! . . . casts of their teeth . . . are so nearly perfect that even dentists are amazed. . . . I judged them (Polar Eskimos) to be one of the healthiest races in the world. . . . Deformity, imperfection and imbecility are practically unknown."

How Do They Get All The Necessary Vitamins?

Many of the writers are puzzled by the fact that these natives thrive on a diet of such limited variety. Some of those tribes in the Far North eat almost no vegetables, some rarely eat anything but fish, while in the Southwest, meat is sometimes unobtainable and the natives do without it for long periods. Where do the meat-eaters get their vitamin C? How do the others get their protein? The questions have a simple answer. It lies in the fact that the people eat whatever food is at hand in its natural state. Every nutrient contained in the food is transmitted intact to the consumer. Even a limited diet eaten in this way seems to contain whatever nutrition is necessary. Proof of this is seen in Dr. Weston Price's observation that the native foods of the Far North of Canada provide from two to ten times more calcium, phosphorus, iron, magnesium, copper, iodine and fat soluble vitamins than our modern diets. Another author Kaare Rodahl, tells us that all internal organs and plants which have the highest vitamin content, especially vitamin C, are considered delicacies by the Eskimo. His methods of preparing and storing foods formulated by the habit and custom of centuries, have been found to be best for retaining food values. Balls of fat found above the kidney of the moose are known to be especially high in vitamin C, and these are relished by the people of the Far North.

Vitamin Thieves in Modern Diets

Not only do the natives get sufficient quantities of the vital elements of nutrition from their food, but they are also free from the problem of maintaining a storehouse of vitamins and minerals against the ravages of refined foods. For example, when one eats refined sugar, the sugar cannot move through the body on its own. B vitamins are needed to digest sugar. When sugar is eaten as part of a natural food, such as an apple, the necessary vitamins for digestion are contained in the food, and no demands are made on the body's reserves. When refined sugar is eaten, it comes unattended by these factors and the body must do the job with reserve vitamins, usually with no concern as to how the body's supply of vitamins is to be restored. The same happens with white flour and synthetics. The poisonous additives, the exhaust-ridden atmosphere and the clinging insecticides that we eat or inhale each day make huge demands on our vitamin C supply. Modern life's demands on others of our nutrients leave us always on the rim of malnutrition, with food supplements as the only way to keep abreast of our needs. Knowing this, it is a bit less difficult to understand how the primitive native maintains his nutritional advantage in spite of his limited sources of food. His food is used and stored for maximum good effect.

Race Not Responsible

Many persons, reading of the good health of the primitive Indians and Eskimos, tell themselves dejectedly that these people are healthy by the chance which brought them into the world as members of a superior race. These people are convinced that Eskimos and Indians would be healthy no matter what they ate or how they lived. This, sadly, is not the case. When brought face to face with modern civilization, the North American native quickly loses his effortless resistance to disease. If even a few of the processed foods, so dear to modern hearts, are added to his diet, the Indian or Eskimo finds that he is soon the victim of a Pandora's Box of pestilence and chronic disorders.

S. K. Hutton, in his book, *Among the Eskimos of Labrador,* witnessed this grim fact: "I have seen how the natives degenerate when they take to European food. They lose their natural coating of fat to a great extent and need more clothing to withstand the cold; they become less robust, less able to endure fatigue, and their children are puny."

Among the uncultured Eskimos it is estimated that less than one per cent suffer from any illness. One writer tells us that their one problem is their eyes. The constant glare of the sun on the snow and ice makes snow blindness a threat to all who live in such places. But it seems to be the only major threat to good health. Even tuberculosis is not known among the primitive people, nor are appendicitis, kidney stones or gall bladder disorders. Once they have access to a trading post, all of this immunity changes to complete lack of resistance. It is as though the diseases have been waiting for a chance at these people, and they strike with a devastating effect—smallpox, measles, whooping cough, tuberculosis, scarlet fever and venereal diseases, and anything else that might be around.

Polio and Canned Food Linked

So closely connected with the good health of the primitive Eskimos is his native food, that the first polio epidemic of the Northlands was blamed on canned goods given to the Hudson Bay Eskimos during a shortage of caribou meat. It was the only such epidemic ever experienced by these people, and it coincided with the only year they ate canned food, dropped to save them from starvation. True this case does not constitute positive proof that they wouldn't have gotten polio anyway, but it is strange that polio came only in that year. Consider the case of the Sitka Indians, known to be wholly free from disease when isolated. Those Sitkas who move close to trading posts have an astonishingly high rate of tuberculosis. What cure do doctors use? They try to send the patients to relatives still living the primitive life, and they have remarkably favorable results.

Changes Brought With Refined Diet

Everything changes for these people when they adopt so-called white man's ways. The women are no longer able to have a child unassisted, with little pain and short labor. The children are born instead with the mother under an anesthetic, forceps might be used, Caesarian technique is often necessary. The children are not strong. They are quick to get disease and slow to recover. Their eyes are weak, their teeth quick to decay, some have congenital malformations, many don't live out their first month.

The same holds true of the Indians of the Western United States. When they surrender their diet and customs to ours, these paragons of physical perfection become liable to tuberculosis, heart trouble, rheumatism, digestive diseases, blindness and insanity—in short, just about all of the diseases of modern man.

Who's Backward?

There are still many tribes in North America who have maintained their primitive culture, in spite of efforts of well-meaning persons who have tried to introduce them to a new way of life. In our narrow concept of life, we usually label those who do not accept our version of progress as "backward people." Perhaps it is we who are backward. In spite of the evidence for primitive life as a key to good health, we go on year after year, eliminating whatever we can of the rugged life our forefathers led. We don't walk if we can avoid it; we do all we can to add the worst and subtract the best in treating our foods; we don't get any physical exercise, and therefore have not built up any muscular reserves to fall back on; we cook away what life is left in the foods we eat. As a result, we get sick, while the primitive natives do not. Yet we expect these people to change their way of living to conform to ours!

Let's try it their way for a change. Eat foods that are not processed, not sprayed, not chemically grown for quantity without quality, and not

[665]

loaded down with additives. Get some physical exercise each day—walk, chop wood, do some calisthenics, anything to bring unused muscles into play. Use food supplements to make up for the hazards of modern life you can't avoid. Replace the vitamins and minerals you lose just by breathing foul city air, inhaling somebody else's cigarette smoke, eating meat treated, unknown to you, with antibiotics, and a thousand other things that make your body vitamin-poor without your being aware of it.

SECTION 14.

Food Components

The components of food are the components of you. We need fats, carbohydrates, enzymes, etc., to keep functioning, but in some cases our appetites have been educated toward an excess of one of these at the expense of others. Carbohydrates and fats are particular offenders for excessive use in this country, while we process our foods so thoroughly that enzymes, for example, are almost completely annihilated. We need a balance of all food components, and we should adjust our diet to make sure we are getting a proper amount of each.

CHAPTER 177

Amino Acids,
Building Blocks of Protein

A contractor builds houses out of many different materials, but if he is a man who deals mostly in brick houses, we might say that the most important single material necessary for his houses is bricks. If the design of each of his houses is different, the arrangement of the bricks will be different. Some houses will have brick chimneys, others brick porches, in still other houses the bricks will be arranged in designs to form railings or terraces. Some houses have brick floors, brick fireplaces or brick walls in the garden. There is a wide variety of color and kinds of bricks for the contractor to choose from.

If you buy the house and do not like the design, you can take apart the bricks and put them together again to form an entirely different house, out of the same bricks. If you were to number each brick in the house and then rebuild the house, putting each brick in a different place, you would be able to continue for thousands of years, combining and recombining the different bricks and never getting quite the same house as the original one, for each time you would make some slight change in the arrangement of the bricks.

As your house grows older some bricks would have to be replaced, and after a certain length of time you would probably have replaced all of the original bricks at one time or another. Now regardless of what plumbing, insulation, roofing, wallpaper you use in the house the bricks are still the most important part, for you must have them or there simply will be no house.

Just like a house, the human body is made up of building blocks or bricks, if you want to call them that. These bricks are the amino acids which go to make up the protein of which the human house is made. Although they can be arranged and re-arranged in thousands and thousands of different combinations, they are still protein and they are still the essential part of your human house. Without them life could not go on. No living thing survives without protein. When it comes to building a fire to keep your house warm, you use materials that are largely carbohydrate. But the house itself must be made largely of protein.

What exactly does this mean in terms of body physiology. Your blood is protein, your tissues, organs, skin, hair, nails are protein. Your bones are made of protein which supports all the various minerals that give them strength. The fluids your body secretes are protein—hormones, and enzymes. Your nerves and brain are made of protein. Obviously when you were an infant, then later through childhood and adolescence, you needed large amounts of protein, for then you were building the house and every day you needed more and more bricks for the bricklayers to use. But as a house grows older, bricks crumble and must be replaced. Human protein—marvelous substance that it is—does not have the hardness and durability of bricks. It is subject to terrific stress and strain, and some of it wears out a little each day. So there is no reason to believe that, as you grow older, you require less protein. Quite the opposite is true.

Now taking a look at your human body it is difficult to believe that fingernails are made of the same substance as blood or nerves. They don't look the same. Well, neither does a brick chimney look like a brick floor, but both are made of bricks. The difference in your body lies in the various combinations in which the amino acids, or bricks, are put together. And if you can have many different designs of houses, all made of brick, just think for a moment of all the different kinds of protein you can have by re-arranging the various amino acids. Of course, you can't actually imagine such a number, for it is bound to be astronomical.

What Is Protein?

In 1839 a chemist first isolated a substance containing nitrogen, which he announced was the basis of life. He named it protein, meaning "primary substance." It was not until 1906 that other chemists first demonstrated an essential amino acid—a building block of the substance protein. The carbohydrates that we eat are made of carbon, hydrogen and oxygen. Proteins are made of carbon, hydrogen, oxygen and nitrogen. It is this nitrogen apparently that makes all the difference between proteins and carbohydrates —building blocks and fuel. After the first amino acid was discovered, a great deal of research was devoted to this branch of biological chemistry and many more amino acids have been discovered. We do not have any idea of how many there may be. We have so far discovered about 21 in protein food products.

The study of protein is extremely complex, as you can imagine, for it deals with all the different combinations of these amino acids, which may be put together by Nature in different quantities and different arrangements to make up any given kind of food product. Then, of course, in most foods the protein amino acids are combined with fat and carbohydrates, as well. When we speak of protein, we are not talking about something like vitamins which exists in infinitesimally small quantities and which are necessary just to cause certain processes to take place inside the body. *You can see protein.* The white of an egg is almost pure protein, composed of a series of different amino acids. So the *bulk* of protein food you eat is quite important—for this is the substance from which the body makes or replaces actual body structure.

After you have eaten protein, the digestive juices of the stomach and intestines go to work on it and break it down into its amino acids. This is because the actual cells of a human body are put together differently from the white of an egg, for instance. So the digestive juices, the enzymes and the body hormones are all involved in putting these amino acids together once again in a different combination so that they can form part of the body. One re-constituted protein substance will go to make up red blood cells. Another will be rushed to the fingernails which are constantly growing so that they need new protein constantly. Another will be sent to the brain where a lot of thinking has worn out a number of cells. Still another protein will be transferred to a gland where it helps to form a gland secretion or hormone. You can easily see why we must have protein every day, and must have it in quantity.

The Quality of Protein Is Important

But it appears, from later research work, that the most important thing about protein is not quantity, but quality. What do we mean by "high quality" protein? We mean protein containing all the essential amino acids in the proper proportion. If one of them is missing, the protein will not sustain life in laboratory animals. If one of the essential amino acids is present in too small a quantity, this protein will not maintain health. It is as if you were building your brick wall and trying to use a brick that is smaller than the other bricks. In a wall, you might fill up the gaping space with mortar, but there is no mortar that will replace protein in body structure. So your wall, with several bricks too small, will sag and be out of line.

Practically, in selecting food, how does this amino acid set-up work out? You should try to eat as much "complete" or "high quality" protein as you need. Foods containing an incomplete quantity or proportion of one or another of the essential amino acids will not sustain health. Complete proteins appear in foods from animal sources—meat, fish and eggs are complete proteins. In the vegetable kingdom these are the protein foods that most nearly approach completeness: nuts, soybeans, wheat germ. You can see that a completely vegetarian diet presents hazards. In order to maintain good health a vegetarian must know the amino acid content of all the vegetables and fruits. If he is going to eat a vegetable that is short or completely lacking in one of the essential amino acids, he must also eat another vegetable that contains this amino acid, even though it may be short on another. So a constant vigilance is necessary and a great deal of knowledge about the quality of the protein in the various vegetables and fruits.

The names of the essential amino acids are complicated and not especially meaningful to those of us who are not chemists. But it is well to be familiar with them, for you often run across them in articles dealing with food or health, and if you do not know what they are, you may become confused and think they are vitamins or enzymes or something else. The essential amino acids are those that have been found to be absolutely necessary in the diet of human beings. Nothing can substitute for them. They are: arginine, histidine, isoleucine, leucine, lysine, methionine, phenylalanine, threonine, tryptophan, valine. The amino acids that at present are listed as unessential are: alanine, aspartic acid, cirrulline, cystine, glutamic

[671]

acid, glycine, hydroxyproline, hydroxyglutamic acid, norleucine, proline, serine and tyrosine.

As researchers progress in their study of the proteins, it is quite possible that they may discover that one or more of the unessential amino acids also have important functions in the body and should be considered essential. However, it seems that we may be able to manufacture within our bodies some of these unessential ones. We cannot manufacture the essential ones, so they must be supplied in food. However, just as in the case of the vitamins, the amino acids work together and, if you are getting a lot of the unessential ones, it seems that this makes up somewhat for a slight deficiency in the essential ones. But keep in mind that you can get amino acids—essential or unessential—only from protein. They do not exist in carbohydrate foods. White sugar is the one outstanding example of a so-called food that is pure carbohydrate, without any protein whatsoever. This is one of the main reasons why white sugar is worthless as food. Your body cannot use it to build or replace any cells. And the more sugar you eat, the less you can eat of the protein foods that have so much value for your good health. Vegetables and fruits contain in general far more carbohydrate than protein.

You can make a quick check on all the foods you eat, so far as protein content is concerned, by sending to the Superintendent of Documents in Washington, D. C., for a copy of the *Agricultural Handbook, No. 8* which lists all the common foods, along with their protein, carbohydrate and fat content.

What Results From Protein Deficiency?

The list of diseases resulting from protein deficiency is almost endless. Just stop and think for a moment of all the things that would go wrong with the house you tried to build of bricks if there were few or no bricks available. The hemoglobin of blood is 95 per cent protein. Lack of protein will produce anemia. The antibodies your blood manufactures to fight germs are made of protein. Lack of protein leaves one an easy prey to all kinds of infections. Proteins protect the liver against poisonous chemicals to which we are all exposed all the time. Protein regulates the amount of water in body tissues. The unhealthy swelling or dropsy that accompanies so many diseases (especially of the heart or kidneys) may be simply an indication of too little high quality protein in the food. And speaking of kidney disease, researchers used to think that people with kidney disease should not eat protein. The kidneys were already excreting a great deal of nitrogen (one of the main constituents of protein). Therefore, reasoned these physicians, the nitrogen is irritating the kidneys, so we will eliminate nitrogen (protein) from the diet. But patients died, for, of course, all the diseased tissues of their bodies needed the nitrogen desperately to rebuild themselves. Nowadays kidney disease patients are placed on a high protein diet. And the protein replaces the nitrogen lost through the kidneys.

If you have a wound, cut or burn, protein is lost in the fluid and blood that escape. Furthermore, to remake healthy tissue over the site of the injury the body must have protein, for this is what the cells are made of. So ample protein in the diet helps hasten the healing process. Muscles are made of protein. Lack of protein breaks down these muscles faster than they can be replaced, resulting in fatigue and lack of stamina. The poor posture of adolescents may often be the result of lack of protein, for flabby muscles simply cannot hold the body erect. The health of your skin, hair and nails depends on protein supply—they are made of protein and cannot grow or replace dead tissues unless they are supplied with the necessary substance, protein. Constipation may be the result of flabby muscles in the stomach and intestines that cannot contract and expand as they should to move the food along our digestive tracts. Protein in the diet will firm and strengthen these muscles. Finally, we know that vitamins and minerals will not be used in the body unless the proper hormones and enzymes are there to combine with them. Hormones and enzymes are made of protein. So all the vitamin and mineral preparations in the world will not make you healthy unless you also provide protein so that these substances can be used.

Absorption of Protein

The subject of absorption of proteins is an important topic in itself. People who suffer from diarrheal conditions do not absorb protein properly, so whatever protein they eat may be partly wasted. Bacteria in the intestines can make the amino acids of protein unabsorbable. Protein must be digested in an acid medium, so if hydrochloric acid is lacking in the stomach, protein food will be wasted. Then, too, those folks who follow every meal with a dose of bicarbonate of soda, or one of the other so-called "alkalizers" will produce a condition in the stomach where the protein simply will not be digested. It has been found that the proteins of some foods are more thoroughly digested than those of others. Ninety-seven per cent of the meat you eat is completely digested (in a healthy person), only 85 per cent of the protein of cereal is digested, only 83 per cent of vegetable protein, 78 per cent of legume protein and only 85 per cent of the protein that appears in fruits.

How To Get High Quality Protein

How are you going to know how much protein you need every day and which proteins contain the essential amino acids? And, perhaps just as important, how are you going to pay your grocery bill once you start living on T-bone steak? First of all, there is no necessity for living on T-bone steak, pleasant though the prospect sounds. In general, all meats contain the same amounts of the essential amino acids. Liver, heart, kidneys and brain actually are a little higher in amino acid content. And hamburger may be even more acceptable to the youngsters and oldsters in your family because it is easier to chew. Can you substitute beans or soybeans for meat? Sometimes, but remember no vegetable food is as rich in all the essential amino acids as food of animal origin, so don't depend on beans day after day for protein. Can you substitute macaroni or spaghetti for meat? No, you cannot, despite all the attractive recipes offered in the

[673]

women's magazines during Lent. Cereal foods (especially refined ones) are largely carbohydrate foods and cannot be used as building blocks for a healthy body. Fish is cheap and an excellent source of high quality protein.

What about gelatin as a source of protein? Often we hear recommendations for taking one or two packets of gelatin every day for a good supply of protein. It's cheap, certainly, but we must report that gelatin is the one animal protein that is not complete. In other words, it does not contain all of the essential amino acids. It will not sustain life in laboratory animals when it is used as the sole source of protein. Now, of course, if you were living under extraordinary circumstances where you could not obtain any protein except gelatin, it would be best to eat the gelatin, because it will sustain life longer than a diet completely lacking in protein. And, of course, if you are hesitating between a dessert made of white sugar, corn starch or corn syrup, and another dessert made of gelatin, you should choose the gelatin dessert for it does have protein value and the others do not. But don't depend on gelatin, cheap as it is, for protein, for it simply cannot fill the bill.

How Much and What Kind of Protein?

How much protein do you need? As you know our pioneer ancestors lived chiefly on high quality protein in the days when they hunted game, before they had gardens or farms. Many people believe this is the reason they were able to endure such hardship and perform such prodigious feats of work. Arctic explorers have lived healthfully for as long as two years on meat, lean and fat. Nothing else. No carbohydrates at all. So there is no chance of your getting too much protein. There is every chance of your getting too little. Recent surveys have indicated that as many as 60 to 80 per cent of Americans get far too little protein in their diets. The official recommendation of the National Research Council is 40-100 grams of protein every day for children, depending on age, and 60-70 grams of protein for adults. It is generally agreed among nutritionists that these allowances are far too low and actually may only be enough to keep one from suffering some kind of deficiency disease.

One final word about amino acids. Scientists have learned how to synthetize them. We say it with regret. Our information comes from an article in the *Herald Tribune* for December 27, 1952, in which it was announced: "Four cheap factory-made chemicals can double the protein value of the world's food supply, a chemist said here today." The synthetic amino acids, made from coal tar, are to be added to foods like wheat, corn and so forth to double their protein value. However, the scientific journals are full of warnings about the possible harmful effects of tampering with proteins. Says *Borden's Review of Nutritional Research,* "Recent investigations, however, indicate that indiscriminate supplementation with amino acids may precipitate a dietary imbalance having dangerous consequences." The article goes on to tell of an experiment where, by adding synthetic amino acids, the proper balance of the protein was thrown completely out of line and the experimental rats developed a serious nervous condition very shortly. Protein is the fabric from which living tissue is made. Isn't it obvious to even the most unenlightened of us that you cannot make something out of coal tar and substitute it for living tissue? Be on your guard against any food to which synthetic amino acids have been added. Shun it as you would shun synthetic vitamins.

However, do not confuse synthetic amino acids with natural amino acid preparations made from food. Food supplements exceptionally rich in all the essential amino acids have been made from food substances such as meat, yeast and so forth. These are no more artificial than are dried milk or powdered eggs. And the amino acids are so concentrated in them as to provide a wealth of these valuable food elements in the proper proportions as they occur in nature. If you are in doubt about the source of any amino acid preparation or any individual amino acid, such as methionine, that your doctor may have prescribed for you, check on whether the amino acids came from a food source or whether they are synthetic. The synthetics are not for you.

CHAPTER 178

Eggs, Meat and Soybeans

Here is a comparison, nutritionwise, of 3 of our highest protein foods, foods that can well serve as the main course for any meal from breakfast through dinner, from snack to dinner party.

All of us know the importance of protein. Our body cells are made of protein and, if we are going to repair and replace damaged cells, we must have a sufficient supply of protein in our daily meals.

One of the most important aspects of the problem of getting enough protein is: what kind and quality of protein are you getting? Proteins are formed out of chemical substances called amino acids. Certain of these amino acids are called the "essential" amino acids. Of course, all of them are essential, but certain ones are essential in diet, because they cannot be manufactured inside our bodies.

As we study nutrition, we find time and again that the proportions of things in food are important. Calcium is important for good health, but just as important is the proper balance between calcium and phosphorus. Each of the B vitamins is important, but just as important is the balance among them. Just so, the important thing about the essential amino acids is the balance or proportion of them in your diet.

This is one of the hazards of a purely vegetarian diet which includes no animal products at all. Certain of the amino acids occur in better proportions in animal products and it is extremely difficult to plan a vegetarian diet in which the essential amino acids will all be represented in their proper proportion.

A new book issued by the department of Agriculture in Washington brings us information about the amino acids in various foods. It furnishes as complete information as is at present available, and, while the book in general was prepared for researchers, nutritionists and scientists, there is much that we can learn about foods by studying it. The name of the book is *Amino Acid Content of Food,* Home Economics Research Report No. 4.

Here is a comparison of the essential amino acids in a serving of meat, one of eggs and one of soybeans:

Amino Acids	Meat %	Eggs %	Soybeans %
Tryptophan	.228	.211	.526
Threonine	.661	.637	1.504
Isoleucine	1.020	.850	2.054
Leucine	1.597	1.126	2.946
Lysine	1.704	.819	2.414
Methionine	.484	.401	.513
Cystine	.246	.299	1.191
Phenylalanine	.802	.739	1.889
Valine	1.083	.950	2.005

From this chart you can see what an excellent source of protein soybeans are. Their content of essential amino acids is, in every case, higher than that of meat or eggs—in some cases, much higher. Methionine, which tends to be low in vegetable foods, is plentiful in soybeans. In addition, the balance among the various amino acids is good. There are no gross deficiencies.

Comparison of Minerals

How do these 3 foods compare in other ways? Here is the mineral content of the 3.

	Meat	Eggs	Soybeans
Calcium	11 mg.	54 mg.	104 mg.
Phosphorus	224 mg.	210 mg.	300 mg.
Iron	3.4 mg.	2.7 mg.	4 mg.

Once again soybeans come out ahead. We do not rely on meat as a good source of calcium. Soybeans, being vegetable in nature, would be expected to contain more calcium. They contain almost 10 times as much as meat and almost twice as much as eggs. Although we depend on meat for its iron content, soybeans contain more.

Here is a comparison of the vitamins in the 3 foods:

	Meats	Eggs	Soybeans
B Vitamins:			
Thiamin	.08 mg.	.10 mg.	.52 mg.
Riboflavin	.22 mg.	.29 mg.	.30 mg.
Niacin	5.5 mg.	.1 mg.	1 mg.
Vitamin A	20 I.U.	1140 I.U.	10 I.U.
Vitamin C	0	0	0
Vitamin E	Fair Amt.	3 mg.	3.75 mg.

Meat is a fairly good source of the B vitamins. But soybeans contain considerably more of two of the important ones for which daily minimum requirements have been set—thiamin and riboflavin. Eggs are our richest everyday source of riboflavin (except for milk) and soybeans contain just about the same amount. Eggs surpass both the others in vitamin A, of course. Egg yolk is a very plentiful source of this fat-soluble vitamin. In vitamin E the content of the 3 foods totals about the same.

Meat Substitutes

Soybeans should be part of your diet as a substitute for meat. The "meat substitutes" promoted by the women's magazines and cookbooks in general are not, of course, substitutes at all, nutritionally speaking. Noodles, macaroni, spaghetti and things of this kind cannot substitute for meat. They contain practically no protein, vitamins or minerals. They are largely starch. Don't serve them. They cheat you by filling you up so that you think you've had a good nourishing meal. But they do not nourish. They provide calories which add pounds and not much else. Even though you include plenty of meat in your diet, make use of soybean protein, too.

If your family does not know soybeans, get some and begin to introduce them to a wonder food. The taste is unusual and you may have to disguise it at first with sauces and herbs. Tomato sauces are delicious with soybeans. Buy soybean flour to add taste and nutritional riches to almost any food.

CHAPTER 179

Use Vegetable Protein Wisely

The mystery of the life force that is stored in seeds is impossible to ignore from a nutritional viewpoint. One can't resist the impulse to find out why or how a tiny seed can give life to a giant tree, or be the start of a luscious and nutritious piece of fruit. We wonder if, in eating seeds, we can appropriate some of that energy and power to our own bodies. The answer is yes. Seeds contain a valuable ingredient which we all need for good health—protein.

The value of protein in the body cannot be overestimated. Just about everything in the body is made up of protein. It is the exclusive building material of the body. Protein is arranged in one way to form bones, in another to make the brain, still another to become blood, or an enzyme or skin. We consist of protein in the way an automobile consists of metal. The metal is formed in one way, to make fenders, in another to form the engine, the axle or the generator. When we eat protein food, the body breaks it down to its component parts, the amino acids. These blocks then are dispatched to reinforce the blood cells, the kidney or skin cells, or, perhaps, the cells which make up our fingernails.

No Substitute for Amino Acids

It is obvious that the amino acids are extremely versatile. By the same token, a steady supply of this element in the foods we eat is vital. There is no other substitute for the job they will do. Without protein in the necessary amounts the job remains undone.

The primary source of protein is meat and meat products. Since all animals are made of tissue similar to our own, eating the flesh of these animals is the best and surest way to replenish our supply of essential amino acids. Fortunately, the type of meat does not matter in the degree of protein-richness. If one eats 8 ounces of hamburger one gets as much protein as from an 8 ounce filet mignon. The organ meats (heart, liver, kidneys), however, are believed to be a little higher in protein than the others.

The "Essential" Amino Acids

Other foods contain protein; for example, egg and milk are complete protein foods. The white of an egg (more healthful when cooked) is entirely protein. These animal-derived foods contain all of the essential amino acids. This is not true of vegetable foods. The amino acids called essential are so named because without an outside source for them (and there are about 10), life cannot be sustained. The other 11 amino acids can be manufactured by the body, or so present knowledge leads us to believe, and we need not, therefore, be so concerned about acquiring them through our diets.

Now vegetable proteins (seeds, legumes, nuts) contain some of the essential amino acids, and, in some cases, all of them. Soybeans are especially well-known as a source for protein. Technically soybeans are a complete protein food, as they actually do contain all of the essential amino acids, and they are high in two of them, methionine (an amino acid lacking in just about all vegetables) and tryptophan.

Working Out Proper Combinations

If one were to depend entirely upon vegetable protein as many vegetarians do, one would have to be especially careful to include seeds which would complement the amino acid content of one or the other. To do this properly one should have a large variety of seeds available and keep careful track of the amount and type eaten. For example, corn is deficient in lysine, but contains a rather good amount of methionine. Combining corn and vegetables rich in lysine at a single meal would complete the essential amino acids one needs. One can acquire a complete listing of the protein values in various vegetables from the *United States Department of Agriculture Handbook No. 8* from which to make these calculations with other vegetable protein foods. The "Amino Acid Content of Foods" is available in another government publication.

It is a wiser policy to use seeds, nuts and legumes as a sort of supplement to the protein we receive from meat and meat products. Since seeds, nuts, etc., do have an appreciable and valuable amount of protein contained in them, they can add to the body's total daily intake of protein, and certainly can do no harm. Aside from the essential amino acids, these foods contain many of the non-essential ones, which might be welcomed by individual systems which are not capable of efficiently producing their own.

We All Can Use More Protein

Surveys have shown that, 60 to 70 per cent of the American people get too little protein. The teenager needs about 100 grams per day, while adults require between 60 and 70 grams, at a minimum. Nuts, legumes and seeds are an excellent means of helping to achieve a high protein intake. They are so much more healthful than candy or soda as a snack, and crushed nuts make an excellent garnish for vegetables and salads. When there is a choice between beans and macaroni as a starch for a meal, choose the beans (which are actually seeds) every time. They offer protein and vitamins far in excess of anything offered by processed starches of any kind.

CHAPTER 180

Protein Deficiency Found Prevalent in Children

Dogs, cats and farm animals are sometimes unintentionally fed better than many children. As a result, many youngsters suffer from hypoproteinosis, a deficiency disease caused by insufficient proteins in the daily diet, according to the *Journal of the American Medical Association,* September 8, 1951.

Parents must learn "that it is not how much the child eats but what he eats that is essential to his nutritional well-being," according to the authors of the article, Drs. Harold D. Lynch and William D. Snively, Jr., of Evansville, Indiana.

A child should not be permitted to consume large quantities of any one food, including milk, whenever he so desires, the doctors said. Rather, he should be allowed to become hungry enough to consume a balanced diet at mealtime.

"Typically, (in hypoproteinosis) there is a history that the child is a good milk drinker but that 'he does not eat' at mealtime. It is usually admitted somewhat reluctantly that the child does eat as he pleases between meals, usually such foods as 'cookies, crackers, soft drinks and candy,' all highly refined carbohydrate foods," they stated.

"Animals could not survive a diet of the highly refined carbohydrate food permitted children. Parents are appalled to learn that their dogs and cats and farm animals are given better diets than their children."

Hypoproteinosis may result in loss of appetite, failure to gain weight, vomiting, constipation, increased susceptibility to infections, dental caries, anemia and irritability.

Parents To Blame

"The basic reason (for hypoproteinosis)," the doctors said, "is a general lack of understanding by parents of the fundamentals of nutrition. There is a tendency to overemphasize certain articles of diet, particularly milk because of its calcium content.

The doctors pointed out that even a quart of milk a day will not provide sufficient protein for adequate growth and development, and added: "The consumption of this much milk at certain ages is likely to spoil the child's appetite for the solid foods, such as meat, eggs and cheese, that make a much greater protein contribution in proportion to their bulk."

Psychological factors are also prominent in the causes of cases of hypoproteinosis, the report added. Mothers are determined to see that their children get what they believe are the proper quantities of the right foods. This is often in conflict with the child's growth needs.

"As the mother's anxiety and determination increases," the article pointed out, "the assertive child's persistence in refusal likewise increases. It then becomes a matter of 'getting something into him.' This something is usually the wrong kind of food and is almost invariably lacking in protein. The sweet, starchy foods taste better, subsequently, hypoproteinosis becomes manifest.

"The treatment of hypoproteinosis is sometimes not simply that of prescribing a diet adequate in protein. When hypoproteinosis is due to improper parental attitudes and feeding techniques, education is required."

Parents must learn the proper foods children require at each meal, it was stated. Each meal should contain sufficient quantities of such protein foods as meat, eggs or nuts. Children should not be forced to eat. A pleasant atmosphere at mealtime should prevail.

CHAPTER 181

The Carbohydrate Content of Some Popular Foods

How can you tell which foods to include and which to omit, if you are planning to go on a low carbohydrate diet? There is an excellent book available from the government which will give you the carbohydrate content of every common food, as well as the protein, fat, vitamin and mineral content. It is *Agriculture Handbook No. 8, Composition of Foods,* available from Superintendent of Documents, Washington, D.C. Price 65 cents.

Here is the approximate carbohydrate content of some fresh fruits and vegetables. Note, please, that these are not canned, sugared or cooked in any kind of sweet syrup. They are natural foods with nothing added in the way of starch or sugar.

Some 5 per cent carbohydrate foods (that is, the least starchy of all): cantaloupe, honeydew, watermelon, avocado, olives, tomato juice, radishes, asparagus, beet greens, cabbage, celery, chard, chicory, water cress, endive, lettuce, mustard greens, spinach, turnip greens, green beans, broccoli, cauliflower, cucumbers, eggplant, mushrooms, green peppers, soybean sprouts, summer squash, tomatoes.

Some 10 per cent carbohydrate foods: strawberries, blackberries, cranberries, currants, gooseberries, red raspberries, grapefruit, limes, oranges, tangerines, apples, apricots, cherries, peaches, plums, beets, carrots, parsnips, Brussels sprouts, onions, artichokes, peas, pumpkin, winter squash.

Some 15 per cent carbohydrate foods: loganberries, black raspberries, grapes, guavas, pears, white potatoes.

Some 25 per cent carbohydrate foods: bananas, sweet potatoes, lima beans, sweet corn.

Other starchy foods contain more carbohydrate than 25 per cent. And just to show you how shockingly high is the carbohydrate content of some of our common foods—look at the list below.

How many of these foods does your family eat every day?

Food	Carbohydrate Content
Corn flakes	85%
Puffed rice	87%
Tapioca	86%
White bread	52%
Whole wheat bread (commercial)	49%
Graham crackers	75%
Fudge	81%
Butterscotch candy	85%
Hard candy (lollipops for instance)	99%

[681]

As a sharp contrast to this, here is the breakdown of some of our best and most nutritious foods. In some of these you can easily see the carbohydrate content is rather high. But so, also, is the protein content. So, comparatively speaking, these are not "high-carbohydrate" foods. They are "high-protein" foods.

Food	Carbohydrate Content Per cent	Protein Content Per cent
Sunflower seed meal	7.5	52
Nuts	11 (Brazil to	9 (Pecans to
	27 Cashew)	27 Peanuts)
Sesame seed	18	19
Brewer's yeast	37	36
Wheat germ	49	25
Soybeans	35	35
Pumpkin seed	18	31

See section on *Sweets* for more information.

CHAPTER 182

When You Use Fats and Oils

What kind of fats shall we use? How about lard—isn't it as natural a fat as you can get? When vegetable fats are refined, isn't their food value largely destroyed just as the food value of other refined foods suffers? How does olive oil compare to corn oil from the nutritional point of view? These are some of the questions health-minded readers have asked us. We will try to answer them all in the following discussion.

First, let's talk about what we mean by "fats" in the diet. There are two kinds of fats—those that are solid at room temperature and those that are liquid. The liquid ones are generally spoken of as oil; the solid ones as fats. Of course, all of them will become liquids at some high temperature (different in every case) and all liquid oils will become solids at low temperatures.

Fats and oils make up about 2 to 5 per cent of the average diet by weight. In many recent articles about fats we hear of the fat content of the American diet being as high as 40 per cent. We should keep in mind that this means that 40 per cent of the *calories* of the diet are from fat—not 40 per cent of the actual food eaten. Fat is high in calories, of course, so just a little fat adds considerably to this percentage.

Fats are a vital necessity in the diet. They perform such functions as providing the fat soluble vitamins, and playing a vital part in the body's use of vitamins and minerals.

Animal vs. Vegetable Fats

Animal fats—all of them, including milk, butter, fat meats, lard and so forth—contain cholesterol, the substance that apparently constitutes a grave danger to us since it appears to be responsible for hardening of the arteries, heart disease, gallstones and so forth. Vegetable fats contain no cholesterol. To take its place they have sitosterols, which do not act the same way.

Vegetable fat contains, too, what we call unsaturated fatty acids, as opposed to the saturated fatty acids that are contained in greater quantity in foods of animal origin. Although there is still considerable debate over the digestibility of fatty foods, we know for certain that the vegetable fats are more easily digested than the animal fats.

Some of the Common Fats

Lard, of course, comes from hog fat, hence contains cholesterol and lacks the useful fatty acids. We believe one should not eat pork products. But apart from our objection to lard as a pork product, we find that processors have, in recent years, been doing a lot of things to lard that make it even more objectionable as food. In an attempt to produce lard that compares with the vegetable shortening, they have added chemicals to prevent the lard from becoming rancid; they have hydrogenated and deodorized it.

Margarine is made from vegetable fats which have been hydrogenated—that is, hydrogen has been forced through them to produce a chemical change that makes the liquid oils solid, as margarine is. Such oils as cottonseed, soybean and, in Europe, whale oil, are used. Most margarine in this country is "fortified" with synthetic vitamin A. The reason is that the oils themselves contain very little vitamin A in comparison with butter. If margarine is to be used as a butter substitute, the additional vitamin A is supplied.

As you know, we do not recommend using margarine, mostly because of the many chemical substances used in it, of which the synthetic vitamin A is only one. Artificial coloring, preservatives and so forth are also used. But, in addition, hydrogenating the oils to make them solid destroys most of the essential fatty acids which are the chief reason for eating vegetable oils. So margarine is no better than butter as a spread, in spite of the fact that it is made from substances that do not contain cholesterol.

Linseed oil (made from flaxseed), sardine and other fish oils are generally considered to be inferior for eating purposes, because of taste, even though they contain large amounts of unsaturated fatty acids.

Soybean oil is another popular vegetable oil. We are told that it presents some difficulties since it is subject to some slight "flavor reversion." We assume this means that its taste may suffer with age. Crude soybean oil is our best source of lecithin at present. Lecithin is the substance rich in unsaturated fatty acids which occurs in vegetable fats.

Sunflower seed oil, corn oil and poppyseed oil are all quite similar. Corn oil is a little darker in color than the others.

[683]

Cottonseed oil is the "standard American all-purpose edible oil," according to Jacobs in his book, *Food and Food Products,* published by Interscience, 1951.

Peanut oil is suitable for all purposes for which cottonseed oil is used, except that it tends to cloud and thicken at low temperatures.

Rapeseed oil (we have never heard of this being used in this country) is difficult to deodorize and has an unpleasant reversion of flavor.

Olive oil is the most popular edible oil of Southern Europe and the Mediterranean. Its content of unsaturated fatty acids is not high, however. And we must watch out for the unsaturated fatty acid content of oils. It is important.

Now what about the salad oils you find on the grocery shelves? These are called "refined oils," and right away we can picture many readers shying away from them because of that word "refined." However, it seems that most of the crude oils must be refined if they are to be edible. Cottonseed oil, for instance, is so strongly flavored that we are told we could not possibly enjoy eating it in the crude state. Peanut oil, sunflower seed oil, soybean and sesame oil are refined—which means deodorizing them so that they have practically no odor or taste.

Olive oil is not treated to remove its taste and odor. For this reason some folks feel that olive oil is far superior to other oils, "because it has such a marvelous taste" they say. Others, used to the bland salad oils that have been deodorized, cannot stand the taste or smell of olive oil. It is well to remember, when you are deciding among vegetable and seed oils, that olive oil is low in the unsaturated fatty acids—those extremely valuable substances so powerful for good in the way your body uses fat. On the other hand, it is unrefined which is a recommendation for it, we believe. We have been unable to discover any known disadvantages brought about by refining oils, but we are certain there must be some which simply haven't been discovered yet. We know that the unsaturated fatty acids are not destroyed in the refining process. Isn't it possible that other valuable nutriments may be, however? We think you should make up your own mind as to whether you want to eat olive oil.

Corn Oil Used in Experiments

Corn oil has been used for extensive laboratory experiments. Much of what we know about the relation of cholesterol, lecithin, unsaturated fatty acids, vegetable and animal fats has been discovered in laboratories using corn oil as the source of unsaturated fatty acids in the diet of the laboratory animals.

An excellent book has been written by Dorothy M. Rathmann, Ph.D., entitled *Vegetable Oils in Nutrition, with special reference to unsaturated fatty acids.* The booklet is published by Corn Products Refining Company, 17 Battery Place, New York, New York. It is a technical book written for professional men—doctors, nutritionists and therapists. We advise all readers who are in this category to send for a copy. You will find a great deal of helpful information on fats in general and corn oil in particular.

[684]

Dr. Rathmann tells us, "The opinion is becoming more and more widespread that unsaturated vegetable oils, such as Mazola brand corn oil, possess distinct nutritional advantages. For example, the fact that diets containing corn oil result in lower serum cholesterol levels than do those containing more highly saturated fats has led to the hope that the incidence and course of atherosclerosis may be influenced favorably, in part at least, by dietary means.

"This favorable effect of corn oil has been attributed to the presence of two different types of compounds capable of lowering serum cholesterol levels, namely sitosterols and essential fatty acids. In addition to a relationship to cholesterol metabolism, the essential fatty acids also appear to have important functions in the development of new cells and the maintenance of healthy body tissues, particularly the skin, liver and kidneys. Requirements for the essential fatty acids seem to be increased when food yields large amounts of saturated or isomeric fatty acids, as may be the case in American diets rich in animal and hydrogenated vegetable fats."

The book contains a great deal of detailed information about experiments involving corn oil in relation to cholesterol deposits. The further information is given that corn oil contains: 53 per cent linoleic acid (the most important of the unsaturated fatty acids), 1.5 per cent of sitosterols and, of course, no cholesterol. Compare this to other fats containing unsaturated fatty acids:

Linoleic acid	Per Cent
Linseed oil	20
Sardine	15
Safflower	70
Poppyseed	62
Soybean	53
Sunflower	57
Sesame	41
Cottonseed	50
Rice bran	34
Peanut oil	25
Olive	8
Wheat germ	50
Corn	53

(and 48 per cent of linolenic acid, another unsaturated fatty acid)

Stick to the Vegetable Oils

Our final suggestions to you, then, are these: Judging from the amount of information we have up to now (and remember much more research will be done on fats in nutrition—the subject is new) we would counsel readers to avoid animal fats as much as possible, with the exception of eggs.

One cannot help getting some fat in meat, of course. But eliminate gravies and fatty sauces! Avoid butter and milk. Shun like poison the hydrogenated fats in which the important fatty acids have been destroyed. This means don't buy the white solid shortenings. And don't buy prepared, processed foods, for you can be sure hydrogenated shortenings were used in them.

Do take wheat germ oil every day, because of its essential fatty acid content, vitamin E and the many other factors that it contains. For fats in your meals use salad oils—olive oil if you like the taste (but remember it's low in the important fatty acids), corn oil, cottonseed oil—any of the salad oils you find at your grocery store.

Although many of the experiments quoted in the newspapers and in this discussion concern corn oil, this is simply because that happened to be the oil used by the researchers. It does not mean that other vegetable and cereal oils would be less effective in these same experiments.

The Importance of Sunflower Seed Oil

We especially want to commend to readers our old friend, sunflower seed oil. As you see in the chart above, it is higher in linoleic acid than corn oil. And linoleic acid is generally credited as being the Good Fairy among the fatty acids which puts unwanted cholesterol to flight. We are told that in unsaturated fatty acids as a whole, sunflower seed oil is higher than any other. Its vitamin E content, too, is extremely high—222 milligrams per hundred grams, compared to only 5 milligrams in sesame oil and 22 to 48 in peanut oil.

One of the articles which sparked the whole recent investigation of fats and oils in the diet was published in the *Lancet* for April 28, 1956. In this article a now classic experiment was described by Dr. Bronte-Stewart and his associates in which sunflower seed oil was one of those used to bring about a rapid decrease in blood cholesterol.

And remember, it seems to be true that the more of the processed fats you eat and the more animal fats you eat, the more you need of the vegetable fats, whose unsaturated fatty acids will counteract any cholesterol-forming tendency of the processed and animal fats, low in unsaturated fatty acids.

CHAPTER 183

Heated Fats Can Cause Cancer

Have you ever passed the exhaust fan from the kitchen of a restaurant? When you do, it is easy to detect the dominating odor of frying fats. These fats bubble and spit in deep fryers for days on end, without even a slight decrease in temperatures, which are held at 350 to 400 degrees. When a customer orders fried chicken or fried shrimp or French-fried potatoes, with them he receives a free sample of the fat in which they were fried. This highly heated fat has been shown by some of our most prominent researchers to be a likely cause of cancer.

Are All Fats Dangerous?

The distinction between highly processed or heated fats and natural ones is important. It would be wrong and dangerous to eliminate all fats from our diet. Our bodies need fats, and we number them among our most important foods. They are one of our best energy sources, offering 9 times as much energy per gram as sugar does. Fats carry the vitamin B, pyridoxine and the fat soluble vitamins A, D, E, and K, which make fats vital to cell formation especially cells of the brain and nerve tissues. Finally, the body absolutely needs the unsaturated fatty acids contained in fats. These are indispensable in some processes of metabolism and cell structure. In high heats the vitamins A, E and K are utterly destroyed. This vitamin destruction is illustrated by an experiment conducted by Dr. Lane and reported in the publication, *Cancer*, Vol. 3, 1950. A group of rats were mated for 3 years into 7 generations. They were on a milk and white bread diet. After the second generation, a ration of lard heated to 350 degrees, then cooled, was included in the rats' diet. From then on it was found necessary to feed the rats wheat germ oil and fresh vegetables prior to mating, because of the deficiencies in vitamins A and E caused by the preheated fats.

Use of Heated Fats Common

The use of heated fats by Americans is an insidious habit, so automatic that many health-conscious housewives include them in their menus without even being aware of it. For example, the lady who is so concerned for the health of her family that she wouldn't dream of serving deep-fried foods, can be found making a sauce from the drippings of a roast, quite unconscious that half of this liquor is fat that has been heated to 350 or more degrees for several hours! Such fat has been made as hot as that used in the deep fryer—and it can be just as damaging.

Some Experiments with Heated Fats

In the periodical, *Cancer*, Vol. 3, No. 6, November, 1950, gastric (i.e., stomach) cancer is noted to be the leading cause of all cancer deaths, according to statistics. Further, Dr. Geoffrey Hadfield, Dean of the Institute of Basic Medical Sciences, Royal College of Surgeons, has stated that cancer of the gastro-intestinal tract appears to be associated with a high fat diet. If this is the case, and if the body needs unprocessed fats as seen before, it is entirely logical that the processed, heated fats are the culprits in the case.

It is especially so when one reads that experiments with local applications of heated fats have shown tumors to develop at the site of the application. The *British Journal of Experimental Pathology* (Vol. 22, 1941) published data on experiments that resulted in cancerous lesions at the site of the injection in two out of 12 mice injected subcutaneously with cottonseed oil which had been preheated to temperatures of 340-360 degrees centigrade. When highly heated fats are brought into close connection with part of the body, apparently a weakness and predisposition toward cancer is introduced to that same part. It should be noted, too, that in the same experiment cottonseed oil heated to a lesser degree (200-220 degrees centigrade) did not produce any cancerous tumors in any of the experimental mice when injected in the same manner, leading to the conclusion that the dangers in fats vary in proportion to the heat applied.

In searching for clues to this highly heated fat and cancer relationship, a theory has been advanced by Dr. A. C. Ivy in *Gastroenterology* (March, 1955) which holds that hot fats reheated again and again undoubtedly increase the chance of producing carcinogenic substances. Obviously Dr. Ivy feels that there is a dangerous change in the make-up of the fat each time it cools and is fired again, with the intensity of the heat of less importance. This should be a warning to housewives who save cooking fats for re-use.

A similar point of view shows up in the *Journal of Nutrition* (Vol. 55, 1955) in an article which discusses fats heated to relatively low temperatures (95 degrees centigrade) and maintained at that heat for 200-300 hours. Refined cottonseed oil, heated thusly was included to make up 15 to 20 per cent of the diet of experimental rats. It was observed that rats on such a diet rapidly lost weight and died within 3 weeks. The loss of weight was accompanied by diarrhea and the occurrence of enlarged livers, kidneys, and adrenals and by shrunken spleens and thalamuses.

In spite of varying theories the strongest suspicion for cancerous action of fats still seems to lie with fats that are preheated to a high degree, as witnessed by Lane and associates and reported in the *Journal of the American Medical Association,* February 17, 1951. In an experiment, 54 rats were given regular rations of brown lard heated for 30 minutes at 350 degrees centigrade. Papillomas (tumors) of the forestomach and malignant tumors of the glandular stomach occurred in 37 per cent of the rats, while similar symptoms were observed in only 5.7 per cent of a control group which was fed unheated lard (though the fat was, of course, heated to make the lard in the first place).

For further data Dr. Lane injected 31 experimental rats with heated lard or vegetable oil. Three cancers developed in these rats, while none developed in a control group of 150.

A definite relationship between preheated fats and cancer showed up in a test discussed in *Modern Nutrition* for August, 1953, the official publication of the American Nutrition Society. A healthful, normal diet was fed to a group of rats. Then the rats were separated into two groups, and the normal diet continued, but for one addition: one of the groups was fed a daily ration of heated, hydrogenated fats, while the other group received a like amount of unprocessed fats.

After the eating pattern of this diet had been well established, a known cancer-producing substance, butter-yellow, was introduced into the diet of all the rats. Every one of the rats on the diet which included the preheated, hydrogenated fats developed tumorous growths, some of which proved to be malignant. The rats eating the unprocessed fats developed no tumors of any kind.

What Are Hydrogenated Fats?

Hydrogenated fats are everywhere. They come in cans and jars and cartons, looking as white and creamy as cold cream or yellow as the sun.

They are guaranteed not to spoil, for there is nothing left in them that could spoil. And how did they get that way? They have been through about 18 different processes, including boiling, cooling and boiling again, agitation, straining, catalytic action, bleaching, coloring, etc. Every life-removing process imaginable is applied to these fats. Margarines are hydrogenated, too, and the false security bred by the idea that the margarines are not made from animal fats but from vegetable oils is banished in an instant by this fact. Hydrogenation is what makes them spreadable and unmelting in summer temperatures, etc. They are as damaging to health as the frying and baking shortenings that are white and lardy-looking. Nor does the yellow color they are given, and the merchandising technique of presenting margarines in brick-shaped cartons make them as safe for you as "that other spread."

As seen by the various experiments noted here, it is still not generally agreed upon which heated fats do the most damage. Some say the danger lies only in fats heated to very high temperatures, others say it lies in fats heated and reheated, still another impression has it that fats heated for very long periods, even at relatively low temperatures, are the ones to watch out for. But one thing on which all of the experts agree—preheated fats can and may cause cancer! The investigation of treated fats in this connection is still a largely unexplored area. The explanation as to why these fats are antagonistic to our system has yet to be discovered, but the evidence of danger is clear enough to act as a warning.

We are convinced that the body welcomes the vegetable fats much more readily than the fats from animals. If there were no other reason, it is undeniable that most animal fats go through some processing before we get them. This may consist of cooking them at high temperatures in a roasting pan or broiler.

Of course, the vegetable oils (especially those in unheated nuts, sunflower seeds and so forth) have not been thus exposed and they are able to give the body what it needs without the risk of cancer that is lurking in heated fats. But even vegetable and cereal fats, once they are heated, may be cancer-causing.

Some Practical Suggestions

How can you use this information practically in your kitchen? Does it mean that you should stop using fats altogether? Not at all. Here are some rules to follow if you would be absolutely certain you are not exposing your family to this particular risk so far as cancer is concerned.

First, never buy anything that has been fried. This means no potato chips, no roasted nuts, no frozen foods that have been fried or breaded and fried. Steer clear of anything fried in restaurants—fried clams, fish fillets, French-fried potatoes, fried eggplant, etc. Check closely with the waitress on any food where there is the slightest doubt.

By the same token, don't fry foods at home. This means don't do any frying at all, either in deep fat or in a frying pan. Any meat you would fry can be broiled just as successfully. And we advise removing the fat be-

[689]

fore cooking the meat, if you broil it and also discarding the fat from roasts. Let's say you want to sauté liver. A little vegetable oil—just enough to keep the meat from sticking to the pan—probably couldn't do harm if you keep the heat low at all times.

Finally, don't buy hydrogenated shortenings (the solid kind) and don't ever, ever use drippings or oils over and over again. There is the risk of such fats being rancid, and, of course, there is the additional risk that they may be cancer-causing.

CHAPTER 184

Unsaturated Fatty Acids Are Essential

In determining what food factors constitute a vitamin, certain general principles have been laid down by researchers. If the food factor is essential to good health and if a deficiency in this factor causes a deficiency disease, then the factor is a vitamin. This, in general, is the criterion by which we designate or do not designate certain substances as vitamins.

When a new substance is discovered which seems to have the properties of a vitamin, much research is done with animals. The animals are put on carefully prepared diets which include all necessary elements except the one being tested. If some disorder results, the substance in question is then administered to see whether it will cure the disorder. If it does, then we are fairly sure that such-and-such a food element is necessary for health— at least in the case of animals. With some substances, it seems that animal tests do not prove out in the case of human beings. We then assume that such-and-such an animal needs such-and-such a substance, but human beings do not. This has always seemed to us like a most unsatisfactory way of doing things. Animal physiology is very much like our own. If it were not, there would be no reason at all for using animals in diet experiments.

It has always seemed to us that the very strict controls employed in animal experimentation may be the reason why some of these experiments do not prove out in regard to human beings. When a diet is decided upon for an animal experiment, nothing can be left to chance. There is no possibility for this rat or guinea pig to get out of his cage and go on a binge of eating forbidden foods. Temperature, rest, bedding, possible psychological irritants, family life, emotions, water, air, light—all these factors are most rigorously controlled, so that the animals' health cannot possibly be influenced either negatively or positively by any of these things. In planning diets for the experiments, the utmost care is taken to feed only those foods which have been shown to produce the ultimate in good health; vitamins and minerals, proteins and enzymes are supplied in ample quantities. Only the substance being tested is left out of the food for the first part of the experiment, then put back into the food for the latter part. And it is perfectly true that we know a lot more about what constitutes a healthful diet for a laboratory animal than for a human being. So, safe to say, these animals get the very best of everything that can be had.

Human beings do not live this way. No single human being lives this way. On this troubled planet, it is impossible to conceive of a human being who can live in the safe, unhurried, unstressful, relaxed, healthful atmosphere of one of these animals. Our human diets are full of all kinds of errors, no matter how careful we may be. The air we breathe is full of pollution from industry. Our water is loaded with chemicals. Our lives are subject to stress, insecurity, frustrations, hurry, lack of proper rest, lack of exercise or possibly work that is too heavy and exacting. We try to keep up with the Joneses. Early in life we are endowed with a set of ideals that glimmers before us constantly from then on, inspiring us to try to achieve many things that may be far beyond our reach. Surely we need much more of the important food elements to carry us through this kind of life than a laboratory rat needs to live healthfully in his hygienically controlled environment.

What we are leading up to in the above discussion is a set of food factors that were once spoken of as a vitamin. Animal experiments show that they are essential to the good health of animals. But we still do not classify them as vitamins in speaking of human nutrition. These food factors are the unsaturated fatty acids, once called vitamin F. Specifically they are linolenic acid, linoleic acid and arachidonic acid. The names need not frighten you. The chemical names of most of our familiar vitamins are equally long and unpronounceable.

Unsaturated Fatty Acids in Animal Health

There is a disease which occurs in laboratory rats called "fat deficiency disease." By breaking down the different fatty elements of the diet, researchers have found that the disease occurs not from lack of fat—any kind of fat. It results only from lack of the unsaturated fatty acids. The rats show arrested or retarded growth, a raised metabolic rate (that is, they burn their food up very rapidly), changes in skin and hair, kidney disorders and impairment of reproductive function. Rats who received no unsaturated fatty acids in their food ate just as much as the control rats, but they did not grow or put on weight, so apparently the food was simply burning rapidly without contributing anything to building the body. First over the paws, then over the face and gradually over the rest of the body a dryness and scurfiness (dandruff) spread. Cold weather—the kind that chaps hands—accentuated this condition. The rats developed kidney stones and many difficulties in reproducing. In the case of the female rats there was disturbance of the whole reproductive cycle. In many cases litters were not born but were re-absorbed. Or, if the mother rat finally had the litter, she had prolonged labor and hemorrhage and the litters were underweight and sickly. Male rats deprived of unsaturated fatty acids refused to mate and were sterile. It was found, too, that there was some relationship between deficiency of unsaturated fatty acids and pyridoxine and pantothenic acid, two of the B vitamins. A deficiency of any two of these factors caused a much worse condition than a deficiency of just one.

Now in regard to human beings, there are two extremely important aspects to this problem. First of all, human milk is rich in unsaturated fatty acids—far, far richer than cow's milk. If these acids are not vitally important to human nutrition, how could Mother Nature have made the mistake of including them in such quantity in mother's milk where every drop must count towards the nourishment of the child? Furthermore, it has been found that stores of fatty acids are built up in the heart, liver, kidney, brain, blood and muscle and the body holds on to them tenaciously. In rats who were deprived of fatty acids for a long time, it was found that there was still some remaining when 76 per cent of the body fat of the rat had been used up. As soon as the unsaturated fatty acids were completely gone, the animal became very seriously ill. The body stores food factors it will need. And in cases of deficiency or starvation, it relinquishes first those factors which are not so important and until the very end hangs on to those things that are essential to life. So on this basis, too, we believe we are justified in assuming that the unsaturated fatty acids are important enough to be called a vitamin.

We are told that nothing is known about human requirements for the unsaturated fatty acids. Yet the National Research Council which sets the standards and makes the decisions on matters of this kind in this country, says "in spite of the paucity of information . . . it is desirable that the fat intake include essential unsaturated fatty acids to the extent of at least one per cent of the total calories." Bicknell and Prescott, writing in *Vitamins in Medicine* (Grune and Stratton, 1953), tell us that only about one half this amount has been available in England since 1945. In this country there is no shortage of foods that contain unsaturated fatty acids, but do we realize how important they are and do we make every effort to include them in every day's menu?

Human Diseases May Be Related to Deficiency

A number of human disorders appear to be related to deficiency of unsaturated fatty acids. Medical literature contains many instances of infant eczema that has been cured by including the unsaturated fatty acids in the infants' food. As a matter of fact we found an ad in the *Practitioner,* a British medical publication, for a substance called F99 to be used in the treatment of eczema. It consists of unsaturated fatty acids to be used, says the ad, "in cases of infantile eczema, adult eczema, furunculosis (boils) and other skin disorders associated with a deficiency of essential fatty acids. It is also successful in cases of varicose leg ulcers of long standing." So the physicians are already using these food elements to cure disease. But we

[692]

are not allowed to speak of them as a vitamin. And apparently the amount of research that has been done on them in recent years is sparse indeed, for we could find very few references to them in medical literature throughout the past 15 years.

Bicknell and Prescott (in *Vitamins in Medicine*) suggest that the acids may be very important in any disease where fat absorption is impaired. This includes diarrheal conditions of many kinds. It may include many cases of underweight. Much of the research we did some time ago on acne seemed to show that acne patients are unable to use fat properly. Could a deficiency of unsaturated fatty acids be one of the causes of acne? Could it be one cause of the dandruff that appears almost universally on American scalps? Bicknell and Prescott tell us that the fact that the unsaturated fatty acids are so carefully stored and husbanded by the body may be why symptoms of deficiency are not more marked and severe. In other words, many of us may be suffering from a sub-clinical deficiency—not enough to make us definitely ill, but enough to prevent our being completely healthy.

The Lee Foundation for Nutritional Research, 2023 West Wisconsin Avenue, Milwaukee 3, Wisconsin, has contributed perhaps the most to the study of unsaturated fatty acids in this country. They have booklets available on the subject: *A Survey of Vitamin F* and *Vitamin F in the Treatment of Prostatic Hypertrophy* which present startling evidence of the importance of these substances in human nutrition. Harold H. Perlenfein, who wrote the first booklet, tells us that the unsaturated fatty acids reduce the incidence and duration of colds. He says that deficiency may be responsible for dry skin, brittle, lusterless, falling hair, dandruff, brittle nails and kidney disease. He states that the acids function in the body by co-operating with vitamin D in making calcium available to the tissues, assist in assimilation of organic phosphorus, aid in the reproductive process, nourish the skin and appear to be related to the proper functioning of the thyroid gland.

James Pirie Hart and William DeGrande Cooper, writing on prostate treatment (Lee Report No. 1) describe 19 cases of prostate gland disorder which were treated with unsaturated fatty acids. In all cases there was a lessening of the residual urine—that is, the urine which cannot be released from the bladder due to pressure from the enlarged prostate gland. In 12 of the cases there was no residual urine at the end of the treatment. There was a decrease in leg pains, fatigue, kidney disorders and nocturia (excessive urination at night). In all cases the size of the prostate rapidly decreased. Chemical blood tests which were made showed a great improvement in mineral content of the blood at the end of the treatment. We have been able to find no further work that has been done along these lines, but we believe that these findings are significant.

Processed Foods Cause the Deficiency

Why should any of us be deficient in the unsaturated fatty acids? For the same reason we are deficient in so many other necessary food elements

—food processing. Bicknell and Prescott tell us that in processed and stale foods, these acids have deliberately been destroyed to improve the keeping qualities of the food. Unsaturated fatty acids occur in vegetable and seed fats—such as corn oil, cottonseed oil, wheat germ oil, peanut oil and so forth. They may occur in animal fats, such as butter, depending on what the animal has been fed. They are destroyed very easily by exposure to air, and they then become rancid. This rancidity can be responsible for destroying other vitamins as well—vitamins A, D and K are destroyed in the presence of rancid fat. When fats are hydrogenated, much of the unsaturated fatty acid is changed into saturated fatty acids. This means that certain chemical actions take place which completely change the character of the fat and render it almost useless for the various conditions we have described. Hydrogenizing gives the fat a solid form, rather than a liquid form.

At present, much of the fat we use has been hydrogenized. Shortening such as we use for making pastry or for frying has been hydrogenized, margarine has been hydrogenized—little or no unsaturated fatty acids are left. In a family where the meal-planner depends on fried foods and pastries for fats and where margarine is consistently used in place of butter, there is every possibility that such a family will be deficient in unsaturated fatty acids, unless a lot of salad oil is used, unheated, in salads. This is one reason why we feel certain that Americans in general may have a serious subclinical deficiency along these lines.

Here is the unsaturated fatty acid (or vitamin F) content of some of the common fats:

	Per cent of essential unsaturated fatty acids
Butter	4.0 to 6.0
Beef fat	1.1 to 5.0
Lard	5.0 to 11.1
Mutton fat	3.0 to 5.0
Liver fat	3.0 to 7.0
Milk	.15 to .23
Fish oils	Traces
Margarine	2.0 to 5.0
Barley germ oil	63

CHAPTER 185

The Fat Content of Food

Which are the foods that contain valuable fats and which are the harmful ones? If you want to concentrate on nuts as a source of the valuable fats, which nuts contain the most of this kind of fat? What salad oils should one use? Where do cereals and dairy products stand so far as their fat content is concerned?

The answers to these questions are not simple. We do not know, as yet, enough about fats in general and their relation to health to be able to state categorically exactly how much of which kinds of fats each of us should have every day.

However, there seems to be a definite pattern emerging from all the research being done. It appears that animal fats and processed fats (that is, hydrogenated ones) contain so much of the saturated fatty acids and so little of the unsaturated fatty acids that they should be cut down to the smallest possible level in one's diet. Fats from vegetable origins seem to contain so much of the natural unsaturated fatty acids and so little of saturated acids that we should undoubtedly include in our diets more of these healthful foods.

Briefly, research seems to show that the vegetable fats are more healthful because they do not contribute a fatty substance called cholesterol to the body, and they do contribute some substance that helps the body to use cholesterol properly, so that it does not collect in gall bladders, arteries, etc., making deposits that mean trouble.

It is agreed among nutritionists that the substance in question (plentiful in vegetable fat and not so plentiful in animal fat) is some part of what is called the unsaturated fatty acids. (Some people refer to this substance as vitamin F, although it is not officially designed as such.)

The Department of Agriculture has recently compiled a listing of the various fats in foods. We are reprinting here some information from this list. A brief word of explanation is in order. In the first column we present the total amount of the saturated fatty acids in 100 grams (or an average serving) of each food. These are the fats generally agreed to be harmful if too much of them is consumed.

Unsaturated Fatty Acids Held Good for Health

In the second column we present the total amount of the unsaturated fatty acids in each food. These are the fats generally agreed to be the healthful ones. One of these, linoleic acid, is believed by many researchers to be the most valuable of all—the helpful substance that is the best preventive of fatty deposits that may cause hardening of the arteries, strokes, heart attacks, gall bladder stones and so forth. We give in the third column the amount of this fatty acid in each food.

CHARTS OF SATURATED AND UNSATURATED FATTY ACIDS
INCLUDING LINOLEIC ACID

Food Fat Or Oil	Total Grams Saturated Fatty Acids	Total Grams Unsaturated Fatty Acids	Grams Linoleic Acid
Meats:			
Beef	48	47	2
Buffalo	66	30	1
Deer	63	32	3
Goat	57	37	2
Horse	30	60	6
Lamb	56	40	3
Luncheon meats	36	59	7
Pork			
Back, outer layer	38	58	6
Bacon	32	63	9
Liver	34	61	5
Other cuts	36	59	9
Rabbit, domesticated	38	58	11
Milk Fat:			
Buffalo, Indian	62	33	1
Cow	55	39	3
Goat	62	33	5
Human	46	48	7
Poultry and Eggs:			
Chicken	32	64	20
Turkey	29	67	21
Chicken eggs	32	61	7
Fish and Shellfish:			
Eel, body	23	73	36
Herring, body	19	77	19
Menhaden, body	24	71	3
Salmon, body	15	79	26
Tuna, body	25	70	25
Turtle	44	51	31
Separated Fats and Oils:			
Butter	55	39	3
Lard	38	57	10
Codfish liver	15	81	25
Halibut liver	17	72	
Whale blubber	15	41	21
Cereals and Grains:			
Cornmeal, white	11	82	44
Millet, (Foxtail)	31	61	35
Oats, rolled	22	74	41
Rice	17	74	35
Sorghum	12	81	44
Wheat flour, white	14	76	42
Wheat germ	15	77	48

Food Fat Or Oil	Total Grams Saturated Fatty Acids	Total Grams Unsaturated Fatty Acids	Grams Linoleic Acid
Fruits and Vegetables including seeds:			
Avocado pulp	20	69	13
Cantaloupe seed	15	79	53
Chickpea	9	87	36
Chocolate	56	39	2
Olives	11	84	7
Pigeon pea	33	57	46
Pumpkin seed	17	78	41
Rape seed	6	89	14
Sesame seed	14	80	42
Soybeans	20	75	52
Squash seed	18	77	42
Watermelon seed	17	78	59
Nuts and Peanuts:			
Almond	8	87	20
Beechnut	8	87	31
Brazil nut	20	76	26
Cashew	17	78	7
Coconut	86	8	Trace
Filbert (Hazelnut)	5	91	16
Hickory	8	87	18
Peanut	22	72	29
Peanut Butter	26	70	25
Pecan	7	84	63
Pistachio	10	85	19
Walnut, black	6	90	48
Walnut, English	7	89	62
Separated Fats and Oils:			
Cacao butter	56	39	2
Corn oil	10	84	53
Cottonseed oil	25	71	50
Margarine (varies widely depending on fats used)	26	70	9
Olive oil	11	84	7
Palm oil	45	49	9
Peanut oil	18	76	29
Safflower oil	8	87	42
Sesame oil	14	80	42
Shortening, animal	43	53	11
Shortening, vegetable (varies widely according to fats used)	23	72	7
Soybean oil	15	80	52
Sunflower oil	12	83	63

How can one best interpret the chart and use it in planning meals? First of all, look at the first column and you will see that, in general, the foods at the top of the list contain considerably more of the saturated fatty acids than the foods at the bottom of the list.

Notice, as you go down the second column that almost the opposite is true. Those at the bottom contain more of the healthful unsaturated fats than those at the top. This suggests at once that one should be very careful to balance one's meals so that plenty of the seed, nut and oil foods are included in every day's meals. Remember, too, that one cannot use very much of the salad oils compared to the amount of a solid food one might use. The measurements given are for 100 grams. Now, 100 grams of avocado pulp or soybeans would be an average serving. One hundred grams of salad oil is about 7 tablespoons—lots more than one would need for salads during the day. This suggests using liquid vegetable oils or salad oils for all cooking rather than using butter, so that you get as much of the unsaturated fatty acids as possible, indirectly.

Some Surprising Aspects Of Linoleic Acid

As you study the chart further, you will find some rather surprising things relating to linoleic acid—supposedly the most valuable of the unsaturated fatty acids. There is little of it in animal fats except for poultry, suggesting that it would be a good idea to serve poultry frequently. More surprising facts: coconut contains very little of the unsaturated fatty acids and only a trace of linoleic acid. This suggests that coconut should not be depended upon as the only nut your family eats. While the unsaturated fatty acid content of olive oil is high, it, too, does not contain very much linoleic acid. But it is very low in the harmful saturated fats. Perhaps this might mean that, if you are very fond of olive oil and use it always, you should change off and use sometimes others of the salad oils that have more linoleic acid—safflower or sunflower, for instance.

We are sure that readers will find many uses for the chart in preparing and planning meals. And once again let us repeat the caution we can't state too often—shun the processed shortenings—the white solid ones, and margarine. These fats have been hydrogenated to solidify them. This process destroys unsaturated fatty acids. We are convinced that it also brings about other undesirable characteristics in the food which will undoubtedly be discovered later. The less any food is processed, the better it is for you.

CHAPTER 186

Sunflower Seeds Are the Answer

Our file on fats in food and their relation to hardening of the arteries and heart trouble is about 6 inches thick at this point. No single item in it is dated earlier than 1956, for it was just around that time that researchers began to become concerned about the matter.

There are 7 headings under which the material is filed:

1. Vegetable fats are better for you than animal fats.
2. The amount of fat in the diet is important rather than the kind of fat.
3. The amount of fat in the diet is of no significance at all.
4. Hydrogenated fats are the only ones that cause trouble.
5. Whether you eat much or little, fats have no effect whatsoever on hardening of the arteries or heart trouble.
6. Vegetable fats cause a decrease in cholesterol content of blood with or without any other change in diet.
7. Fats—conflicting opinions of nutritionists.

There are a number of items in each folder. But the last folder is as thick as all others put together.

We have not been able to find any two researchers who agree with one another completely on the subject of what happens when you eat fat—any kind of fat. The reason is, of course, that no one knows. And they don't know because it is only within the last two or three years that they have done any intensive work on this subject in laboratories, so there is bound to be lack of agreement for many years to come until a lot more information is available.

To complicate things still further, vast amounts of money are involved in the sales of fats of all kinds. An expert somewhere makes a statement that margarine is not the best kind of fat for human consumption, showing figures of arteriosclerosis and heart disease in countries where it is the chief source of fat and pointing out that hydrogenation of fat (as in margarine) destroys largely the valuable elements in the fat. Immediately all the makers of margarine are up in arms. So would you be if you had millions of dollars tied up in margarine manufacture.

So the margarine public-relations expert gets busy and hands out to the press a statement from another expert who says, nonsense, margarine is a good food. Why, margarine is made of vegetable fat, he says, and it's a well-known scientific fact that fat of *animal* origin is what causes the trouble. Milk and butter are to blame, says he.

Whereupon the Dairy Council public-relations expert announces a series of meetings to be addressed by prominent nutrition researchers from large universities who will prove that milk and butter are the best foods in the world for all mankind. There is no proof at all that they cause any harm in the body. And all the home economics editors flock to the meetings where they get a free meal and their pictures taken. And the next day your newspaper carries an article quoting this latest "expert" and regaling you with the excellence of the free meal where there was lots of butter and ice cream.

Oh, How the Experts Differ!

Now along comes still another researcher who makes everybody mad by announcing that it doesn't matter what kind of fat you eat. All fat is bad if you eat too much of it. What we have to do is cut down on our overall consumption of fat, he says. And presto—the margarine companies and the dairy companies both rush into print with statements from researchers of equal importance who solemnly declare that there is no more fat in the American diet than there was two hundred years ago when hardening of the arteries and heart trouble were all but unknown.

Meanwhile the folks who make salad oils jump in any time there is a statement made by anybody which is favorable to their side and your newspaper carries headlines proclaiming corn oil as the saviour of mankind, followed in rapid succession by similar announcements about peanut oil, cottonseed oil, safflower oil and several rather vague statements from other companies who feel certain they are going to turn up some new oil that will be better than all the others—any moment now.

Researchers in laboratories and hospitals who have been working quietly, feeding different kinds of fats to animals and heart sufferers come up from time to time with mild statements about the effect of the preparation they happened to be feeding for the past 6 months. And, because any news about heart trouble is big news, the newspapers snatch this mild statement and blow it into headlines 3 inches high. This is it, they shout. No more heart trouble, no more hardening of the arteries! One teaspoonful of this magic mixture every day and you're saved!

Any meaning attached to the mild statement of the researcher disappears overnight in a welter of new companies that spring up to manufacture the magic new substance, whatever it is.

Cholesterol is the word we bandy about so freely these days. Everybody has heard of cholesterol and everybody knows it's a bad word. Whatever you do, don't eat anything that has cholesterol in it, doctors by the thousands are saying to their patients all over the country. So Dr. William Halden, one of Europe's foremost authorities on the subject of fats in nutrition, sent us an article telling us that cholesterol is one of the most valuable substances in our bodies. We can't get along without it and our bodies will stubbornly manufacture it internally if we don't provide enough of it in our diet, proving that it is indeed an essential substance.

In the midst of all this readers write us plaintively and reproachfully, "Why don't you tell us simply but thoroughly just what the truth is about fats in the diet?" Ladies and gentlemen, where are we to find out what the truth is?

The Fats in Natural Foods Are Healthful

Out of all the tumult and the shouting, only one fact emerges which no one has challenged. Indeed no one can challenge this fact. T. L. Cleave, Surgeon Captain in the Royal Navy of Great Britain, has written a book on the subject. The title of it is *Fat Consumption and Coronary Disease.*

The theme of the book is very simple and it gives the only final answer now possible on the subject of fats and oils in the diet. During the course of evolution human beings have developed the ability to select the right food, the healthful food, in every instance—*so long as they are choosing only among completely natural substances.*

So if you would be perfectly, blissfully safe in this matter of fats in the diet, eat only those foods which are in a completely natural state and unchanged by anything, except cooking in your own kitchen which, Dr. Cleave believes, is a practice that the human being has, over thousands of years, adapted himself to, to a certain extent.

What does this leave you to eat? All vegetable substances, for there is some fat in all of them. There is considerable fat in nuts, avocados and sunflower seeds. Peanuts and soybeans are two more completely natural foods rich in good fats. Whole grain, wheat germ and brown rice contain a considerable amount of natural fat, unchanged except for cooking.

Animal Fats

As soon as you begin to consider fats from animal origin, you run into difficulties, for we have done something to almost all of them to render them "unnatural" in the sense in which Dr. Cleave speaks of them. Butter is nothing but fat and water. We have concentrated this food so highly that we cannot say that our taste for "natural" foods will guide us in knowing how much or how little butter to eat. Is cow's milk a "natural" food for an adult human being? Not in the sense in which we are speaking.

So far as meat and fish are concerned, these are certainly natural foods for human beings when they are eaten in their entirety. Carved into steaks, chops, filets and variety meats, as we eat them, they are no longer "natural" in the sense we mean. And it seems to us that you are quite likely to get an unnaturally large amount of fat if you just buy whatever you feel like buying in the way of meat, day after day. Fatty meats like bacon and ham should definitely be omitted. Lard is another concentrated fat like butter. It seems to us that eggs are a completely natural food for human beings. And we believe the fat contained in eggs is not harmful to those who fear cholesterol deposits.

So far as the hydrogenated shortenings are concerned—the white solid pastry shortenings and margarine—these are certainly the least natural of all, so these should be the first to be crossed off your grocery list.

And, finally, we come to the so-called salad oils. All the cooking oils you can buy, including sunflower seed oil, have been refined, that is, they have been subjected to a series of processes which certainly render them "unnatural" foods. Is solvent-extracted oil better for you than "cold-pressed" oil? We are told by one of the world's experts on the subject that the term "cold-pressed" is simply a trade term meaningless to us in that it does not have anything to do with the amount of heat used in the processing. Apparently either high heat or a solvent must be used to extract oils from vegetables and cereal substances. Crude, unrefined oils are completely inedible from the point of view of taste.

There are relatively small differences among all these oils so far as their content of lecithin and unsaturated fatty acids is concerned. These are the two substances mentioned most often in regard to hardening of the arteries. We don't think these differences matter enough to concern us. In fact, we are strongly inclined to believe that a far more important matter is whether or not you get, along with these unsaturated fatty acids, the essential B vitamins which you must have for your body to use the fatty acids properly.

This is why we insist that you take brewer's yeast and/or desiccated liver and/or wheat germ. This is why we insist that you make unheated, unprocessed sunflower seeds the *main* and the best source of healthful fats in your diet. If you have doubts about salad oils, just skip them entirely. Use sunflower seeds as your source of fat. They are rich in B vitamins, high in protein and minerals. And, best of all, they are completely natural foods.

CHAPTER 187

Safflower Oil
a Nutritional Treasure

Have you ever heard of the safflower? Most people on our side of the world haven't, but you can bet your rocking chair that we'll be hearing a lot more about this plant from now on. It has been nominated by some of our country's most distinguished nutritionists as the most effective agent to date against accumulation of cholesterol in the blood stream. Cholesterol, you know, is the fatty substance that sometimes collects where it does not belong, in the walls of arteries and in gall bladders. It is believed by many scientists to be a contributing cause of hardening of the arteries.

Grown in North Africa, India and the Middle East since ancient times (and lately in California), the safflower is a thistle-like plant. When the flower dies, it leaves behind small seeds and these are pressed to yield a pale yellow, oily liquid, which is almost odorless and bland in flavor. But beneath this deceptively uninteresting appearance there lies a nutritional treasure which goes under the name of linoleic acid. Linoleic acid is the most important of the unsaturated fatty acids. This element is found, too, in other oils which contain the unsaturated fatty acids, but none is so high in linoleic acid as safflower. The percentage of linoleic acid in safflower oil is estimated by various sources to be between 70 and 94, plus other unsaturated fatty acids. The closest rival is poppyseed with 62 per cent, and that is followed by a reading of 57 per cent for sunflower seeds. As you can see, safflower oil is far above anything we know as a source of this vital unsaturated fatty acid.

The Function of Linoleic Acid

The function of linoleic acid is an exceedingly complex one. It does not eliminate cholesterol from the body, but rather combines with it, and possibly with vitamin D, to form a useful material which takes part in the formation of cell membranes and connective tissue. That is the explanation offered by Dr. Hugh Sinclair of the Laboratory of Human Nutrition, University of Oxford, Oxford, England, in *Drug News* of July 17, 1957.

The complexity of the body's nutritional functions is emphasized by Dr. Sinclair's statement that in order for the body to use linoleic acid correctly we must also have the assistance of one of the B vitamins, pyridoxine.

The presence of vitamin E is also required to protect the fatty acids from oxidation while they are in the body. We must be certain, therefore, that our diet contains these nutritional assistants which help us make the most of other foods.

This interaction of one food element with another is the basis of our policy in regard to synthetic vitamins and processed foods whose vitamins have been lost in the processing and then synthetically replaced. We consider that it is impossible for man to gauge the subtle dependence of one food element on another and to replace all of the ingredients the body needs for utilizing a food after they've been taken from it. In addition, of course, we begin to tear foods apart in processing, it is quite impossible to replace all the elements that may have been lost in the process, for we do not even know what many of them are.

Researchers' Claims for Safflower Oil

The powers that Dr. Sinclair, as well as the researchers at Armour and Company, claim for safflower are hopeful and exciting. First of all, it holds down the blood level of cholesterol by using it constructively instead of allowing it to accumulate in the body and block the avenues of nutrition. Patients suffering from hardening of the arteries, heart conditions, diabetes, bronchial asthma, nephrosis, rheumatoid arthritis and certain skin disease are likely to find help in this food. Those who are free from these discomforts will find in safflower oil a source of added insurance against them.

One final thought: though there have been no conclusive experiments with humans, animals have been found to be more easily susceptible to duodenal ulcers when their diet was made deficient in unsaturated fatty acids, like linoleic acid, the one that is so abundant in safflower oil. Don't let your diet be deficient in this important element. Choose an unhydrogenated vegetable oil to supplement your diet. Corn oil, soybean oil, wheat germ oil, sunflower seed oil, cottonseed oil and poppyseed oil—all are high in essential unsaturated fatty acids and will supply you with all your body needs if used generously. Put them on your salads, use them wherever you can in your cooking or added to vegetable juices, or just treat yourself to a spoonful now and then. Dr. Sinclair and his associates achieved their results by giving patients about two tablespoons per day. And remember, for a new high in the benefits of linoleic acid, try safflower oil.

CHAPTER 188

About Enzymes

Physiology teaches us that man lives by the process of converting some of his food into building blocks of protein which replace his cells as they wear out, and by burning other food as energy which enables him to play, work and enjoy life. We all learned in school that the various substances of which food is made (carbohydrates, proteins and fat) are "changed" by the digestive process and in this "change" they become useful to our bodies. Now obviously considerable change must take place. Look at a plate of steak, potatoes, vegetables, salad and fruit. It certainly does not look like the flesh of a human being. Yet that is what a large part of it becomes. It certainly does not seem possible that by burning that plateful of food in a fire, one could obtain enough energy to carry a working man through a day of strenuous ditch-digging or hard mental work. Yet the energy re leased by that plate of food does just that, once it has been exposed to the chemical magic of digestion and assimilation.

We know in a general sort of way that our body is equipped with digestive juices. We know that, during a meal, the saliva pours out a substance that partly digests starchy foods; the stomach pours out another substance that digest protein; the pancreas and the intestine exude some substance that finishes up the digestion of protein and starch. So right here— during and immediately after a meal—this process of "changing" food into human substance begins. But what is it in the digestive juices that works this magic? Finding the answer to this question leads us into the complex and largely unexplored, but very fascinating story of enzymes.

Enzymes Are Discovered

Scientists have known for many years that there are substances present in tiny quantities in every living cell that possess marvelous properties. It all began with a study of yeasts and fungi. The active living organism that causes fruit juices to ferment and bread to rise is yeast. As the tiny yeast plant grows, changes take place in the medium in which it is growing. The fruit juice becomes alcoholic; the bread dough rapidly expands to many times its former volume. But early scientists discovered that after the yeast plants had been killed, something remained that was not a living plant as the yeast is. This something was called a "ferment" because it brought about a state of fermentation. Not until many years later was it named an "enzyme."

What are enzymes and where do they exist? Are they alive? Are they necessary to life? How can they best be preserved and how are they destroyed? What do they do in the body? What do they do in plants? Can we make them synthetically in a laboratory? These are some of the questions that have occupied researchers in the intriguing study of enzymes. Out of all this study have come many observations that have greatly increased our knowledge of how human beings live and also what and how human beings should eat. We will try to answer these questions, so that you can understand the immense importance of enzymes. Some of the answers are not completely understood as yet even by the most learned scientists, for enzymes still involve much that cannot be answered with our present means of exploration. Perhaps in the enzyme we have the secret of life itself.

Enzymes Cause Chemical Changes

As you know, many physical things take place in this world because of chemical changes. If you drop some sugar into a teacup of water, the sugar changes. It dissolves. During this process many chemical changes take place in the mixture you have in your teacup. If you let the teacup stand for several weeks, other changes will take place gradually and slowly. But if you heat the mixture, changes begin to take place right away. The sugar and water turn into syrup. Now imagine that you have in your kitchen some substance which, if you dropped it into the cold cup of sugar-water, would immediately change it into syrup, without any cooking. Such a substance is called in chemistry a "catalyst." It brings about a chemical change immediately, without heat.

A catalyst is further defined as a substance which will perform this job of bringing about a chemical change without itself becoming involved in the change. In other words, you could, with proper chemical procedure, remove all the catalyst from your syrup and it would still be syrup. The catalyst needs to be present in extremely small amounts—one part of a catalyst can act chemically to change substances whose volume is millions of times greater than its own. For instance, one part of catalyst to millions of parts of sugar-water would still produce the same effect. And the catalyst would remain unchanged in the middle of all this chemical activity.

An enzyme is a catalyst. So enzymes are present wherever chemical changes take place rapidly without the added stimulus of heat. Since everything that takes place in physiology involves chemical change, enzymes must be present everywhere. They are. They are present in great abundance in every living cell—plant and animal. Are they alive? James S. McLester, M.D., in his book, *Nutrition and Diet in Health and Disease* (W. B. Saunders, 1949), says, "As crystalline organic compounds these materials are lifeless; as substances which have the property of increasing in the presence of living cells, they assume a property characteristic of living things."

How Enzymes Are Destroyed

The antiseptics that kill living organisms like germs and yeasts do not inactivate enzymes. You could drop formaldehyde or iodine or lysol into your teacup, destroying all germs that might be there, but the chemical process brought about by the enzyme you have in the cup would go right on, proving that the disinfectant has not disturbed it.

However, there are two circumstances that disturb the activity of enzymes very much—cold and heat. Cold inactivates them, that is, if you put your teacup into the refrigerator, no chemical change would take place. The enzyme would stay there in the cup, but the sugar would remain sugar and the water would remain water. You would have no syrup. But when you take the cup out into the warm air again and the temperature of the mixture goes up to room temperature, the enzymes would become active again and would make syrup. So they haven't been destroyed. They have only ceased activity for a short time.

A small increase in heat causes the enzymes to work more rapidly. But more heat destroys them entirely and, even after the mixture has cooled down, they will not become active again. Between 32 degrees and 104 degrees Fahrenheit—that is, anywhere from freezing up to the temperature of a hot summer day—enzymes are very active. But when you heat them to a point above 122 degrees Fahrenheit, enzymes are permanently destroyed. The boiling point of water is 212 degrees Fahrenheit. So when you boil vegetables or fruit, all enzymes in the food are destroyed. When you roast meat at a temperature of 200 or 300 degrees, of course, all enzymes in the meat are destroyed.

What does this mean so far as preparing food and cooking are concerned? Well, it means first that refrigeration is one of the greatest inventions of modern times, for foods can be kept with their enzymes intact but inactive so long as you keep them in the refrigerator or freezer. While a plant is growing and ripening, the enzymes are busy inside forming vitamins and bringing about other changes that make the fruit or vegetable tasty and nutritious. But as soon as the food is picked it should be refrigerated, for otherwise the enzymes go right on working and this time their activity is destructive. Lettuce and radishes wilt and fruit skins wither when they are kept at room temperature, for the enzymes go on working. On the other hand, when you cook food at high temperatures, you destroy immediately all enzymes. Is this good or bad? Healthful or unhealthful? To have the answer we must know what enzymes do in the body.

How Enzymes Act in the Body

Actually they must be present (in very small amounts) for any process that takes place in the body. They are present in every cell (and don't

[706]

forget that your body contains many billions of cells) and they are the cell's only connection with the outer world. That steak on your plate is some day going to form part of a certain number of cells of your body, but it can't possibly do that unless there are the correct enzymes in the right places at every single moment during that transformation.

The salivary glands, the pancreas, the wall of the stomach and of the intestines contain the chief digestive enzymes (there are 9 of them). But even after the food has been changed by these enzymes into a form that can be transported to all the cells of the body, there must be other enzymes in those cells that continue the process of changing this substance even more, according to what use the body will make of it.

We talk a lot about vitamins and we know that vitamins are essential for good health. But vitamins can do their work only in the presence of enzymes, for they form part of complicated "enzyme systems." For instance, thiamin, a B vitamin, is necessary to good health. Thiamin forms part of an enzyme system that digests sugar and starches. The thiamin must be present if these carbohydrates are to be converted into energy, but the enzymes must be present, too. Every vitamin whose use in the body is known has been discovered to be a part of an enzyme system. There are (so far discovered) 5 enzymes which contain riboflavin, a B vitamin. "It has been claimed for some time that vitamin C is also an essential constituent in enzymatic reactions in the cell," says Morris Jacobs in his book, *Food and Food Products* (Interscience Publishers, 1951).

Enzymes are named in accordance with the food substance they "work on" chemically. So an enzyme that brings about a chemical change in the presence of phosphorus is called phosphatase, an enzyme that works to break down sugar (sucrose) is called sucrase and so forth.

The Effect of Acidity and Alkalinity on Enzymes

Now, of course, the temperature of the body will never rise high enough to destroy the body's enzymes. But there is another characteristic of enzymes that makes them subject to destruction in the body. They are fussy about the acidity of substances in which they are working. Some enzymes can work only in a quite acid medium. Others need to have more alkalinity. Pepsin, for instance, which is the enzyme that breaks down protein in the stomach, functions at a pH (or acidity) of about 1.2 to 1.8. Trypsin, the enzyme in pancreatic juice, must have much more alkaline surroundings—about 8.2. Now if, because of some condition of ill health, there is not enough hydrochloric acid in your stomach to keep the pepsin working properly, you will not be able to digest proteins. As people grow older, the hydrochloric acid in their stomachs tends to decrease, so they may have trouble digesting proteins because their supply of the enzyme pepsin simply cannot function in an alkaline stomach. Taking bicarbonate of soda also makes your stomach alkaline and stops the activity of pepsin.

How does it happen, then, if the stomach is acid enough, and there is plenty of pepsin that the walls of the stomach are not digested? They are made of protein. There is disagreement among scientists as to why we do not digest our own stomachs. One school believes that there may be anti-enzymes secreted by the cells of the stomach wall which prevent the digestive enzymes from working on them. Others say that the thick mucous coating on the lining of the stomach protects it from coming into contact with the digestive enzymes. How does it happen that tapeworms can live in a human intestine? Apparently, say the scientists, there is something present in living cells that prevents the enzymes from breaking them down and digesting them.

Can We Obtain Enzymes From Food?

Where does the body get the material from which it manufactures enzymes? Just stop and think for a moment of the enormity of this chemical factory that is humming away inside you day and night. Think of all the complicated processes in which these enzymes take part. While you are eating, all the digestive organs are pouring out juices rich in enzymes. In every tiny cell, from your brain right down to your little toe, enzymes are fermenting furiously, combining and recombining into the thousands of different enzyme systems that move your muscles, stimulate your nerves, keep you breathing, thinking and feeling. The body manufactures enzymes out of food, water and air—those are the only ingredients available. So what you eat becomes many times more important when you consider it from the point of view of manufacturing enzymes.

In the days before fire was invented, man ate his food raw, just as wild animals do. Raw food contains enzymes, as we know. Aside from other chemical changes that take place, cooking food destroys enzymes. It seems logical that enzymes from raw food could be transformed into useful enzymes for one body system or another, after they have been eaten. They consist of the same chemical substance—that is, a plant enzyme contains the same elements in the same proportions as the enzyme of a human body contains. Is it possible that the raw food our ancestors ate, far back in history, contributed vast stores of enzymes to their bodies, so that they themselves did not have to manufacture so many enzymes? Might not such an arrangement have a very beneficial effect on the body? After all, manufacturing enzymes is a difficult job, especially when the only materials available are present-day denatured, diluted, processed foods.

A Continuous Process of Manufacturing Enzymes

Yet our bodies must go on manufacturing enzymes in enormous quantity every day if we are to go on living. After an enzyme has completed its work, the next process that takes place generally destroys the enzyme so we must be replenishing the supply all the time. For instance, salivary enzymes function only in an alkaline medium. When we swallow our food, all the salivary enzymes which are busy breaking down starch and sugar are thrown into the stomach where the high acidity destroys them within a half hour or so. So our salivary glands must immediately manufacture more.

Might it not be that this continual loss from the body of enzymes that

[708]

are not replaced in our food is one of the main causes of aging and disease? In the Bible we read of men who lived many times longer than we do today. The mythology of other religions also contains stories of men who lived to a great age. In those early days men lived on fruits, nuts, berries, raw meat and unheated milk. What cooking was done was very primitive and the heat could not penetrate to the very interior to destroy enzymes. Perhaps this kind of nourishment was so full of enzymes that bodies were not worn out so soon by the incessant need for producing more.

Evidence That Raw Food Is Best

Wild animals, who have no contact with man, do not become diseased in their wild state, unless, of course, they must exist under conditions of starvation or drouth. Wild animals brought to the zoos of civilized cities used to show a high mortality from the diseases to which man is subject—pneumonia, tuberculosis, cancer and so forth. Because these animals were so very valuable, zoo keepers experimented and found that diets of completely raw food kept the zoo animals healthy. Morbidity rates have dropped almost to zero in zoos where all animals are fed only raw food. We know, of course, that many of the chemical changes brought about by cooking destroy vitamins and otherwise decrease the nutritional value of the food. *But perhaps the destruction of enzymes is much the most disastrous result of cooking.*

We know that those primitive Eskimos who eat practically all their food raw do not suffer from the diseases of modern man; in fact they have so little sickness that there is no tradition of medicinal remedies or medicine men among them. On the other hand, the American Indians, who cooked their food, have an enormous array of medicines and remedies and their medicine men were the most important persons in the tribe.

Another interesting observation is that an herbiverous animal who lives entirely on uncooked plants, has a pancreas which is extremely small compared to man's. Apparently its pancreas does not need to produce nearly so many enzymes as a human pancreas, because a large part of the necessary enzymes are already present in its uncooked food. It is true, too, that Oriental peoples whose diet consists largely of cooked starch have pancreas glands much heavier than Americans. This seems to indicate that the amount of enzymes needed to deal with this cooked starch necessitates an overworked pancreas which continually increases in size trying to become more efficient. Herbiverous animals have inactive salivary glands. The salivary glands do a big part of the job of digesting starches. But even so, the cow can get along with the small amount of starch-splitting enzymes turned out by a tiny pancreas, while man, with his efficient salivary glands, must have a large pancreas, and the more cooked starch he eats, the larger his pancreas becomes.

It does not seem possible that at our present stage of civilization, we could obtain almost all the necessary enzymes from our food as the cow apparently does. But we do believe that eating raw food day after day, in as great a quantity as possible will, over the years, greatly increase one's body store of enzymes and so will greatly benefit health, for there will be much less strain on enzyme producing organs if they do not have to work overtime supplying enzymes which should logically be supplied by food.

Synthetic Enzymes

What about the possibility of taking synthetic enzymes? We know enough about the structure of enzymes that we can make them synthetically. Quite a number have been synthesized. Jacobs, in *Food and Food Products,* says that our synthesis of enzymes has not contributed greatly to our knowledge of them. We know only that they are proteins and we still have to solve the problem of protein structure. Jacobs also says, "The fact that purification of enzymes appears at times to inactivate them rather than to make them have greater activity may be explained. In their normal environment, enzymes are partially protected against inactivation attributable to heat or other energy factors and to inhibition by metals. As they are progressively purified, these protective factors such as proteins, carbohydrates and the like are removed, leaving the enzymes open to attack by chemical and physical agents which inactivate them."

We do not recommend taking synthetic vitamins. It seems to us that a synthetic "Pure" enzyme would be an even worse gamble, because there is not a chance that any of the natural substances protecting the activity of the enzyme would be present. And Dr. Jacobs substantiates this theory of ours. How then can you add to your enzyme supply, if you are interested in what we have said above and if you agree with us that we moderns probably age earlier than we should and contract needless diseases simply from lack of enzymes?

How To Get Enough Enzymes

First of all, make it your business to eat as much raw food as possible and by this we mean that if half your diet is raw, that certainly won't be too much! Never cook fruits. There is no excuse nutritionally for destroying most of the food value of this excellent food, especially when fruits taste so much better raw! If your family and friends insist on serving stewed, baked or broiled fruits, simply refuse to eat them and ask for your portion raw. In the winter when fresh fruits are scarce, eat frozen rather than canned fruits. Having your own freezer is by far the best idea, for you can hurry the luscious beauties straight from the trees and bushes right into the freezer with a very minimum food value wasted. And remember, frozen food retains its enzymes! They disappear rapidly as the fruit thaws, however, so eat frozen fruit just as soon as it has thawed.

If you must eat often in restaurants, you probably suffer more than the rest of us from lack of enzymes, for the preparation and the wait before serving take just about all the food value from any restaurant food. But even here you can get fresh raw food, if you insist on it. A piece of fruit or a raw fruit or vegetable drink at the beginning of a meal, celery, salad, radishes during the meal and some other fresh fruit for dessert—

these raw foods are available in most restaurants. And if you patronize one establishment, they will be glad to have raw foods on hand for you.

Eat as many vegetables raw as possible. Never cook carrots, cabbage, Swiss chard, spinach, broccoli stalks, onions, celery, turnips. Sure, it's rabbit food, but did you ever know a rabbit who died of heart disease or cancer?

Become an expert in fixing delicious raw vegetable dishes. Use a grater, a food mill, a blender, a chopping board. Use salad dressings for garnish if your family objects to plain raw vegetables. Try raisins, dates and nuts as "fixings." And remember, keep all raw foods chilled all the time.

Buy and Eat Organically-Grown Food

Then, too, it seems quite possible that organically-raised fruits and vegetables are richer in enzymes than commercially-raised produce. It has been shown time and time again that animals raised on organic food do not contract the diseases to which other animals are subject. Sir Albert Howard in his splendid book, *An Agricultural Testament* (Oxford University Press, 1949), recounts the story of his cattle raised on organic food who were pastured alongside cattle with hoof and mouth disease. Even rubbing noses with these diseased animals, Sir Albert's cattle remained completely free from the epidemic malady. Now undoubtedly there is much more food value in food that has been raised organically—that is, without the use of chemical fertilizer and insecticide. Perhaps the most important of these food elements may turn out to be enzymes.

So our second recommendation is to buy and eat organically-raised food if you possibly can. Unless you live in an apartment there is probably a small plot of ground somewhere near the house where you can put in a garden of your own, even if it means spading up lawn to do it. Or you can find through our *Organic Food Directory* (available from Rodale Press, for 10 cents) a list of farmers throughout the country who sell organically-raised produce. Perhaps there are some organic farmers who live near you. Or you can persuade some farmer (or gardener) friend or relative who lives nearby to begin gardening organically so that you can buy produce from him. It isn't really too difficult or expensive to make certain that at least a part of your food is organically-grown. Perhaps a large measure of the increased good health you will experience will be due to the supply of enzymes in this most healthful kind of food.

CHAPTER 189

We Live in a World of Enzymes

By Joseph J. Martin, D.D.S. and Albert Schatz, Ph.D.

You may be surprised to learn that without enzymes plants would not grow, seeds would not germinate, organic matter would remain unchanged on a compost pile, microbes would not function, and there would be no soil. Enzymes are therefore among the most important things in our world, and so it would pay us to learn about them. You already know a lot about enzymes since you've lived with them all your life. You could not have been born without enzymes. They help you grow and keep healthy.

If they stopped functioning for one single minute, the chances are that you would stop living. As a matter of fact, you are already quite familiar with many things that enzymes do. When hydrogen peroxide is poured in an open wound to kill germs, it froths and hisses. This is caused by an enzyme, in our cells, that changes hydrogen peroxide to water and oxygen gas. Other enzymes are involved when blood clots, and when milk sours. It is by means of enzyme action that yeast can raise dough. For the same reason, the freshly cut surface of raw apples, bananas, pears, and potatoes turns brown in the air. Digestion, which is one of the processes that keeps us going, could not occur without enzymes.

Let's do some simple experiments to understand this important process. We know some foods contain starch. Which ones are they? To find out, just add a drop of tincture of iodine from your medicine cabinet to different foods. Try bread, cream, butter, rice, raw egg white and yolk, olive oil, sugar, cake, tapioca, the inside flesh of fresh fruits and vegetables, milk, meat, gelatin, nuts, honey, cornmeal, buckwheat, and other cereals. Do the same thing with corn starch or potato starch. Notice that iodine colors certain foods blue or violet. This is a chemical test for starch. Foods that contain starch turn blue or purple when stained with iodine. If starch is not present, the color will not form.

Would you like to make starch disappear? Don't be surprised to learn how easy this is. You've already done it thousands of times without realizing what was happening. There's no trick involved. Suspend just enough corn starch in half a glass of cold water to get a slight cloudiness. Then make absolutely sure that starch is there to begin with by testing a few drops separately with iodine as you did in the food tests.

Now mix a teaspoonful of the starch suspension with the same amount of saliva. Stir with a toothpick for 10 to 15 minutes. By this time the original cloudiness will have disappeared and the solution will be perfectly clear. Examine it closely and see for yourself. Now try the iodine test for starch once again. This time you will get no blue or purple color because starch is not there any more. Where did it go? What happened is that something in the saliva changed the starch chemically into sugar. The sugar dissolves in water but does not give a color with iodine. Test some sugar with iodine and prove this for yourself.

Enzymes in Digestion

Whenever you eat starchy foods, the starch disappears in this way. It begins to change to sugar in your mouth as soon as you chew food and mix it with saliva. In the stomach and intestine, a similar change takes place with meat, cheese, fat, oil, and other foods that do not dissolve in water. The body changes them chemically into forms that do dissolve in water. To do this, the body digests these foods. Digestion is therefore a way of changing foods so that they can dissolve in water.

Now you may ask, "Why does the body do this?" or "Does the body have to do this?" The answer is that all foods must first be dissolved in water before they can pass through the wall of the intestine. After they are absorbed in this way, digested foods are taken up by the blood and carried to all parts of the body. Unless foods are first digested and dissolved they cannot get from the intestine into our bodies and reach the tissues and cells where they are used. In plants, too, starch and other foods must be digested so they can be transported from one part of a plant to another.

You can see how this works by pouring salt over dry soil. Imagine that the soil is our body and the hard, dry, crusted surface is the wall of the intestine. The dry salt obviously does not pass through the surface and go down into the soil. Now pour a little water over the salt. As it dissolves, see how it is washed into the soil. In living organisms, digestion does the same thing to foods. In our bodies, for example, it dissolves foods so they pass through the wall of the intestine into the body.

You may say, "Very well, I understand that now, but exactly how do animals, plants, and microbes actually carry out the digestive process? What is that mysterious something in saliva that changed the starch to sugar?"

Well, it's all very simple, as you will see. There is absolutely nothing mysterious about digestion or about anything else, as far as that's concerned. To understand how we digest food, we must learn a little about enzymes. Saliva, plant juices, and many microbes contain an enzyme called amylase. This name comes from the Latin words meaning "starch-splitting." The enzyme amylase splits starch or changes it chemically into sugar. This splitting or changing is the digestion of starch. The end product is sugar which easily dissolves in water but does not give the iodine test that starch does. Now you understand how the starch disappears.

Enzymes Need Proper Environment

Enzymes are the chemical tools with which living cells work. We use hammers, saws, and pliers over and over again. Living cells also use their enzyme tools repeatedly. For example, after some enzyme has been used to bring about a chemical change such as the digestion of a microscopic starch granule, it is then freed to digest more starch. From this, you can see how a small amount of enzyme "goes a long way." This is like our doing a lot of work with a few tools, *provided they are the right ones*. This raises another very important point about enzymes. We cannot saw with a hammer, nor do we drive nails with a paintbrush. In a similar manner, each enzyme is a specific chemical tool and has a particular function of its own. A starch-digesting enzyme will not digest protein. Nor will a protein-digesting enzyme produce a chemical change in fat.

Many of our tools are made of metal. A good many enzymes also contain metals. Iron, calcium, magnesium, zinc, cobalt, copper, manganese and other metals are necessary for the normal functioning and the very life of living cells. Some of these metals are part of enzymes. This is one reason why we require iron in our diet and why plants require trace elements.

Tools are ruined, if heated because the metal loses its temper. Likewise enzyme tools cannot stand heating. All enzymes consist of protein in part or entirely. Because of their protein nature, they are easily destroyed by heat since proteins are changed when heated. For example, the common protein egg white coagulates when fried or boiled and cannot be changed back to its original form. It is easy to show how heat affects enzymes. If you carry out the starch experiment with saliva that has been boiled it will not work because the protein enzyme amylase has been destroyed by heating. The amylase has been chemically changed to another form of protein which does not act as an enzyme.

We use wall-papering tools inside our homes and gardening implements outdoors. In a similar manner, there are enzyme tools for use inside and outside of cells. The enzymes that digest insoluble food are secreted or given off by living cells into the environment outside the cells where the undissolved foods are present. These enzymes digest the foods or change them to products that dissolve in water. In this form, the digested foods diffuse or pass into the cells where they are then handled by different enzymes that are present only inside cells.

Enzymes Have Other Uses, Too

This is what happens in our own bodies. Like a hose, our intestine is a long folded tube with open ends. The intestinal contents are as much "outside" of the body as is a coin in a clenched fist or food in one's mouth. Digestive enzymes pass out into the intestine and there digest the food. This takes place completely "outside" of the body cells in which these enzymes were formed. After digestion, the changed and soluble food passes through the wall of the intestine. Then the blood carries it to all parts of the body. Inside of our body cells, it is handled in different ways by many enzymes that never function outside the cells.

Living cells use their enzyme tools for many purposes besides digestion. After food is digested, some of it is oxidized in the body by certain enzymes in order to provide the energy which all living things must have. Oxidation is a process of combustion or burning that goes on within our cells and elsewhere. It is similar to the burning of leaves in the fall, the burning of coal, oil, and wood in a furnace, and the burning of gasoline in an automobile engine.

When we breathe we take up oxygen from the air and give off carbon dioxide. With enzymes as chemical tools, the cells in our bodies are able to use oxygen to burn sugar and other digested food. In this process, they produce the energy required by our bodies and the waste product carbon dioxide. This gas is given off in the air we exhale.

Oxidation by a burning fire and biological oxidation in living cells both yield energy. But there is one very important difference between the two. A fire is an uncontrolled combustion. In a short period of time it releases most of the chemical energy of the fuel in the form of heat. Biological burning, inside of living cells, is controlled so that the energy is liberated slowly and at a rate regulated to satisfy the needs of the body. Certain hormones in our bodies are the thermostats that regulate our temperature. It is believed that these hormones may do this by speeding up or slowing down enzyme action. Plants also have hormones which control their growth and function.

This temperature control in animals is very important. Can you imagine the explosion that would occur if a tank full of gasoline in an automobile were to burn up all at once within a fraction of a second! Just about the same thing would happen in our bodies if a stomach full of food were to be oxidized all at once. We would really burn up in the full sense of the word. That is why it is so important that oxidation inside our bodies be regulated so that the energy is liberated as slowly as it can be handled.

This story about enzymes began with such things as sour milk and bananas. It ended up with the energy all living things need to remain alive, Only a very few enzymes have been mentioned. Many other enzymes are important in the production of antibiotics, and to remove dead tissue in the treatment of wounds. They are also used in the textile, leather, and food industries. Enzymes therefore affect our lives in many ways which we do not usually realize.

CHAPTER 190

The Importance of Trace Minerals

For thousands of years we have been eating trace minerals without ever being aware of them, without knowing that they are in the soil, in our food and in our bodies. Within very recent times equipment has been perfected for detecting and measuring trace minerals. And for the first time there is tremendous scientific interest in the whole subject. In many universities and colleges across the land careful studies are being made of the importance of each of the trace minerals, where it is found, what part it plays in the life of plants or animals, how it may be related to health and disease, with what other food elements it works and how it can be used to promote health for soil, plants and living things.

And high time it is that such studies should be undertaken. For among many top-ranking scientists there is absolute conviction that one of the main causes of today's degenerative diseases is the lack of trace elements or minerals in the soil and in the food. This decrease or complete lack of certain trace minerals has not come about suddenly. And in some cases it is not the result of man's carelessness. For instance, there are parts of the world where sheep cannot be successfully raised. The lambs will, for no apparent reason, develop diseases of the nervous system. The reason turned out quite recently to be the fact that there is not enough copper in the soil and the lambs are suffering from a copper deficiency.

Now who would ever imagine such a thing as this! Copper is a bright, shiny, reddish metal that makes very pretty living room accessories. And copper is used to make pipes which some people have installed in their homes for water pipes, with a resulting greenish tinge to the water indicating that the folks in that house are probably getting a most unhealthy dose of copper along with their water. Now how could lack of such a metal have anything to do with the nervous disease of lambs? But it does. And copper is extremely important for human health. It helps the body to use iron. It's perfectly possible for you to develop iron-deficiency anemia if you aren't getting enough copper in your food, even though you are getting enough iron.

Cobalt is a trace mineral that nobody heard anything about until the past few years. Then, through the lengthy, patient work of a group of scientists, it was discovered that cobalt is necessary in cattle food or the cattle will develop anemia. But the dictionary defines cobalt as "a tough, lustrous, silver-white, somewhat magnetic metal related to and occurring with, iron and nickel." What could such a metal have to do with anemia? As more and more scientists and nutritionists delved deeper into the problem, it finally developed that cobalt is one of the important elements in vitamin B_{12}—the miracle vitamin which prevents and cures anemia. Is it the cobalt alone that does the trick? No, the other parts of the vitamin must be present, too.

How Much Do You Need?

Perhaps the first and most important thing to understand about the trace minerals is that they are necessary in infinitely small quantities. That is one reason we have been so long in studying them. Calcium and phosphorous occur in food and in our bodies in relatively large amounts. A bone or a tooth looks as if it were made of calcium or lime and it is to a large extent. When you boil a bone, adding a little vinegar to the water, you finally come out with a bone that is honeycombed with small holes—the holes where the calcium was. The calcium has passed into the soup you are making. So it's fairly easy to understand that calcium is essential—we can see it with our own eyes.

But the trace minerals that go to make up that bone are just as important as the calcium, even though they leave no visible holes when you take them away. Without these trace minerals the calcium could not have combined with the phosphorus and you would not have a bone at all.

A couple of years ago two doctors at Cornell Medical College announced that they had given strontium to patients whose bones were too porous. And the strontium aided greatly in healing the bones. The patients were relieved of pain and went back to work. Strontium? Who ever heard of strontium as something desirable to eat? This is just an instance of the discoveries that are being made every day, now that, at last, we have begun to investigate the trace minerals.

Some of the trace minerals like iodine, for instance, occur in such extremely small quantities in food and water that we cannot measure them in terms of "parts per million," but can only speak of "parts per thousand million." Of course, you could not see this small an amount of iodine in a teaspoon of bone meal let's say. You could not even imagine how infinitely small such an amount would be. But it is there and the fact that it is there probably has a great deal to do with your good health, if you are taking bone meal, for you need iodine only in infinitely small quantities. But you must have it for good health.

Correct Amount Important

Another important thing to remember about trace minerals is that they are all beneficial to you when they are present in the right amounts in relation to all the other trace minerals and the vitamins. All of them are important, even though the amount needed may vary greatly in every case. Together with carbohydrates, proteins, fats and vitamins they make up everything necessary for the health of plants and animals. How they do this is still largely a mystery.

In the case of some of the trace minerals like iodine and iron we have a pretty good idea of what they do in the body. Iodine helps to manufacture thyroxine, the substance necessary for the thyroid gland. Iron helps in the manufacture of hemoglobin, the red substance in the blood that carries oxygen to the cells. In the case of many of the trace minerals we know that they combine with other minerals and with vitamins to form enzyme systems which carry on most of the physiological work that goes on inside our bodies. Without the trace minerals, these enzyme systems simply won't function normally. So it seems that the trace minerals are very important indeed so far as health is concerned.

But never forget that trace minerals in too large a quantity are dangerous. We all know how unhealthy it is to drink even a couple of tablespoons of iodine. Yet iodine in "trace" amounts is an absolute necessity for health. In just the same way, getting even a tiny bit too much of the other trace minerals is dangerous. Nature has very carefully doled them out in infinitely small amounts. Meddling, by way of using larger amounts, is likely to result in trouble.

Treatment and Prevention of Disease

Doctor William A. Albrecht of the University of Missouri has been using trace minerals in treating cows for Bang's disease. He had already determined that the sick cows had deficiencies of some of the trace minerals. Dr. Ira Allison of Springfield, Missouri, has been working with Albrecht and has treated human patients for brucellosis (milk fever). An article in the *Chicago Daily News* for March 13, 1950, tells us that of 1800 brucellosis patients a high percentage have been cured on a high protein, low sugar diet with trace minerals added. In some cases the cure took only 12 weeks. In almost every case, Dr. Allison said, there was indication of very bad habits of nutrition long before the disease appeared, seeming to indicate that the lack of these essential nutriments was responsible for the appearance of the disease.

Dr. Henry Trautmann of Madison, Wisconsin, said in the same article, "Chemical farming overstimulates the soils to produce bountiful crops. Strange to say, however, disease continues apace. So it is evident that there are some vital elements lacking in the soil and the food it produces naturally lacks the same vital elements.

"Little is known of the effect of the various chemical fertilizers on the plant protein molecule. Since the protein molecule is the basis of life, its change of structure might well be the basis of ill health.

"The problems of malignancies may, sooner or later, be found in such chemical changes. It certainly is true that man's interference with nature processes has much to do with poor health."

Some time ago a reader sent us a copy of a beautiful Finnish magazine which contained the story of a little country town in Finland where a group of people were curing cancer with the ashes of the bark of a certain kind of birch tree that grew there. Now certainly there is nothing about ashes that has any curative property, except that when the bark is burned whatever minerals exist in it remain in the ashes, in concentrated form, for, of course, all the burnable part of the wood is gone. We had the article translated and made many efforts to get in touch with the folks whose names were given in the article, but without success.

Where Can You Get Your Trace Minerals?

Such foods as white bread, noodles, white rice, sugar, soft drinks, hot dogs, ice cream and so forth contain no trace minerals, for all the minerals have been refined out of such foods. So obviously people who live on this kind of food cannot be healthy for they lack any trace minerals at all.

But what about the health conscious folks who are careful not to eat refined and processed foods, who eat lots of fresh fruits and vegetables, no cereals but whole cereals, meats, eggs and the other foods that *do* contain trace minerals? Well and good, if the food they are eating comes from a farmer, or even a field of one farm where the trace minerals exist in the soil in a well balanced harmony. But what if, buying commercially grown food in their part of the country, they get the tomatoes with only one part per million of iron rather than those with 1938 parts per million? What if they have been eating, over the years, the cabbage that contains no cobalt, rather than cabbage that contains the infinitely small amount of .15 parts per million that may mean the difference between health and disease?

Do you see now why we urge readers to eat organically grown food, even if it means digging up the lawn or traveling out into the country to garden over week ends? We'd like to be able to tell you very definitely just why you need a certain amount of manganese, copper, potassium, magnesium, and so forth in your food. We'd like to be able to tell you how much of each of these you need. We'd like to be able to tell you just how much of each of them exists in every piece of food you prepare in your kitchen. But for the answers to the first two questions we must wait probably for years until the answers have been found in the laboratories. For an answer to the last question, we would have to place a battery of scientists and a laboratory of equipment in your kitchen to work night and day.

What is the answer, then? Must you do without these vitally important trace minerals? Must you take a chance on contracting a disease that results from a deficiency? No. The thing for you to do is first of all, get organically grown food if possible. If you can't possibly have your own garden, try to persuade a friend to garden organically.

In addition, eat only foods that *may* contain trace minerals. Soft drinks don't. White bread doesn't. White sugar and all the nuisance foods that spring from it are devoid of trace minerals. Eat vegetables, fruits, meats, eggs, fish, nuts. And finally take minerals with your food supplements. Bone meal contains trace minerals. Kelp contains trace minerals. In fact, if you live in a "goiter area," kelp tablets and ocean fish are essentials in your diet program. The sea contains many minerals which are absorbed by the sea-weed, kelp.

It isn't hard to take bone meal or kelp. And it isn't expensive. It will cost you less than your weekly chocolate sundae which we urge you to relinquish anyway. You can buy these two mineral-rich foods in tablet or powder form. If you're squeamish about taste or if you have little time to

[719]

fuss with foods, buy the tablets and swallow them down. If you don't mind going out of your way to do little extras in the kitchen, get used to including the powdered form (much less expensive) in all kinds of foods. Beat it into health drinks. Bake it in your whole grain bread. Sprinkle it over cereal or fruits. No matter how you may decide to take them, do get your trace minerals. There is nothing else in food that can substitute for them.

CHAPTER 191

Variations in Food Minerals in Five Vegetables

Not all tomatoes are rich in iron, nor all lettuce rich in calcium. The mineral content depends on the soil where the vegetable was grown.

To demonstrate the difference in minerals and trace minerals available in food, we reproduce here a chart showing the highest and lowest quantity found in 5 vegetables tested at Rutgers University. This material was originally part of the Firman E. Bear Report:

	Percentage of Dry Weight			Milliequivalents per 100 Grams Dry Weight			Trace Elements parts per Million Dry Matter				
	Total Mineral Matter	Phos- phorus	Calcium	Mag- nesium	Potassium	Sodium	Boron	Man- ganese	Iron	Cop- per	Cobalt
SNAP BEANS											
Highest ..	10.45	0.36	40.5	60.00	99.7	8.6	73	60	227	69	0.26
Lowest ..	4.04	0.22	15.5	14.8	29.1	0.0	10	2	10	3	0.00
CABBAGE											
Highest ..	10.38	0.38	60.0	43.6	148.3	20.4	42	13	94	48	0.15
Lowest ..	6.12	0.18	17.5	15.6	53.7	0.8	7	2	20	0.4	0.00
LETTUCE											
Highest ..	24.48	0.43	71.0	49.3	176.5	12.2	37	169	516	60	0.19
Lowest ..	7.01	0.22	16.0	13.1	53.7	0.0	6	1	9	3	0.00
TOMATOES											
Highest ..	14.20	0.35	23.0	59.2	148.3	6.5	36	68	1938	53	0.63
Lowest ..	6.07	0.16	4.5	4.5	58.8	0.0	5	1	1	0	0.00
SPINACH											
Highest ..	28.56	0.52	96.0	203.9	257.0	69.5	88	117	1584	32	0.25
Lowest ..	12.38	0.27	47.5	46.9	84.6	0.8	12	1	19	0.5	0.20

CHAPTER 192

Additional Information on Food Components

Our Protein-Starved Children

Well at last we come across a statement by a member of the American Medical Association to members of that august body which admits that our children could stand an improvement in their diets. Dr. Harold D. Lynch, as reported in the *Lafayette* (Minnesota) *Journal and Courier* (December 6, 1958), told the annual clinical conference of doctors that "the chubby, half-starved glutton"—the American child—has become one of our nation's major health problems. He said that the children are growing flabby on foods they don't need while they starve for protein-rich foods that are vital to proper health and growth.

He noted that a low protein diet in young children can cause extreme susceptibility to infection, moderate degrees of anemia, irritability, constipation, flabby muscles, lethargy and tooth decay. Dr. Lynch's list reads like the general symptoms described by most mothers who bring Johnny or Mary to the doctor for a tonic. The best tonic is a good diet, and Dr. Lynch's remarks certainly bear that statement out.

Our children are conditioned to desserts and sweets at meals, and soon they begin to expect cookies and candies between meals. They eat such sweets easily and the result is a rebellion by the child against protein foods which do not have such an appeal. They have no source of tissue and muscle-building nourishment.

It is to be hoped that the medical association took careful note of Dr. Lynch's speech, and will be moved to modify their ostrich-head-in-the-sand point of view about "the wonderful American diet" that needs no help from supplementary nutrients.

Vegetable Oils for Acne

The distressing teenage problem of acne may have met its match in unhydrogenated vegetable oils. In the *Archives of Dermatology* (June, 1959), Dr. W. R. Hubler said that even patients who suffered from acne in its worst form "improved with remarkable rapidity" with oral use of corn oil.

It is common practice for doctors treating acne to prescribe a low fat diet; however, such a diet often results in unintended weight loss and fatigue. The unsaturated fats in the vegetable oil help to maintain weight and vigor in the patient. The oil also relieves the unpalatable dryness of a low-fat diet.

We think Dr. Hubler's treatment is an excellent one, for it provides an excellent means of acquiring the unsaturated fatty acids so vital to the body's well-being and helps to create the habit of using non-hydrogenated oils instead of the common and unhealthful hydrogenated ones. Though Dr. Hubler used corn oil in treating his patients, other vegetable oils are equally acceptable. Among them are peanut, safflower, sunflower, wheat germ and others. Even if you have no skin problem, unhydrogenated vegetable oils should be included in your daily diet—at least several tablespoonfuls with your regular green salad.

Carbohydrates Can Cause Tooth and Gum Disorders

The *Journal of Nutrition* (November 10, 1957) carries the description of an elaborate experiment which points quite strongly to a relationship between carbohydrates and periodontal (gum) diseases. Four hundred and eighty rats were used and were fed on various diets. Periodontal disease was strongest when food was fed in the form of hard pellets, and was greatly reduced when powdered food was used. Complete elimination of carbohydrates from the diet caused major reductions in the disorders of soft gum tissues. There was also a suggestion that high levels of B complex supplementation cause reductions in periodontal disease.

Is your family having tooth or gum trouble? Could it be that carbohydrates are the reason? Substitute fresh green vegetables and fruits wherever you can. Be sure you're getting plenty of the B vitamins—rich in foods like liver, wheat germ, brewer's yeast. Gum troubles will fade fast.

Premature Births, and Starches in the Diet

Today's Health for February, 1954, reports that a survey by Dr. Genevieve Stearns and the late Dr. Philip Jeans showed that more premature births and abnormalities among children occur in families which depend mainly on starches and carbohydrates in their diets. This seems to be the main diet difficulty among Americans—and not only among those in the lower income brackets who cannot afford the higher priced proteins, fresh fruits and vegetables. Take a look through the women's magazines for an idea of how enthusiastically they are promoting menus featuring refined cereals, white sugar and gooey desserts.

SECTION 15.

Nutrition

Nutrition is the process by which food material is converted into living tissue. For this to take place, all the necessary parts of the food must be present in exactly the right proportions. Protein, starch, fat, vitamins, enzymes, minerals, trace minerals and many other components of food are essential for the smooth chemical change which must take place to convert food into tissue. We do not know what other, as yet undiscovered, food elements may also be necessary. We know only that natural food, unchanged by processing, contains all the essential elements. Every form of processing removes some of them.

CHAPTER 193

What Do American Families Eat?

Newspapers all over the country are still carrying articles taken from the press releases of the AMA and the Food and Drug Administration attacking as food faddists those who advocate the taking of vitamin and mineral supplements because of the serious deficiencies in diet to which the average American is exposed. The official point of view is that the American diet is richly nutritious and the average housewife has no trouble presenting her family with meals that satisfy every need.

Just for the record, let's examine some of the surveys that have been done by various groups on how well nourished we are and why.

Here are some headlines from our files:

"Panelists Decry Teenage Food Habits"

"Nutritionist Told of Diet Lags"

"Cows Eat Better Than People, Doctor Says"

"Nation's Nutrition Lacks Cited"

"Eating Habits Leave Much to Be Desired"

"Family Diets Slipping Off: Experts Told to Sell Nutrition"

"U.S. Is Found Spending More Money For Gum Than Medical Study"

"Seventy-five per cent of Children Get Wrong Food, Says Scientist."

What did some of the stories say? In 1950 a study conducted by Dr. Pauline Berry Mack of Pennsylvania State College showed that, of 2564 children studied, 75 per cent did not get enough vital nutrients from food. The children represented every economic group and averaged higher in economic status than the general population. Yet, only one-fourth were getting enough energy from their food or enough calcium, protein, iron, phosphorus or vitamins A, C and B. By "enough" is meant the quantity recommended officially by the National Research Council. It is known, incidentally, that far more than these minimum recommendations will result in increasing good health. Most of those children examined showed signs of healed sores of tongue and gums and excessive tooth decay. More than half had some nervous habit such as restlessness and nail-biting. Two-thirds showed signs of undue fatigue and more than 80 per cent had poor reflexes in some part of the body. Our information comes from an article in the *Detroit News,* December 31, 1950.

An article in the *Rockford Register* for June 3, 1957, tells us that a conclave of nutritionists meeting in Washington discussed a Department of Agriculture survey which showed that 10 per cent of American family diets are actually "substandard" and many more are well below desired levels in some basic food nutrient. Amounts of calcium, vitamin A and vitamin C were found to be smaller in family menus than they were at the last survey.

The *New Brunswick* (New Jersey) *Sunday Home News* for November 2, 1958, published the results of a survey indicating that "4 our of 5 New Jersey teenagers do not have adequate diets." Nine thousand students were surveyed by the New Jersey Nutrition Council and the Department of Home Economics of Douglass College. One-third of the girls and more than one-fourth of the boys had eaten no vitamin C-rich food on the day of the survey. Three out of 5 of the girls and almost half of the boys had eaten no eggs. More than a quarter of the girls and a seventh of the boys had eaten no breakfast. From the *New York Times* for February 25, 1958, we find that "although we are the best fed and most overfed nation on earth, our dietary lacks are appalling. There are vitamin deficiencies at every income level and 20 per cent of the population is overweight." At the meeting described in the article, Dr. Margaret Mead, Professor of Anthropology at Columbia University, commented on the fact that adult eating habits are formed in infancy and early childhood. The food eaten and the way it is eaten by the young will determine what and how they will eat for the rest of their lives. So it appears that our nation is faced with an extremely serious problem.

What Does the Average Family Eat?

Parade magazine printed an article on what the average husband or wife buys in a supermarket. They featured an Allentown family. The husband, worker at Bethlehem Steel, bought the following at the supermarket, for, we assume, a week's diet for his family: olives, mayonnaise, potatoes, chicken, shoulder roast, eye-round roast, pork chops, milk, mozzarella cheese, longhorn cheese, grated parmesan, canned mushrooms, canned mushroom sauce, whole figs (jar), canned peas, canned salmon, salted crackers, frozen pineapple-orange juice, frozen grapefruit juice, TV dinners, frozen vegetables, canned tomato juice and cooking oil.

His wife, on an entirely separate excursion, bought the following: packaged bologna slices, bacon, meat loaf slices, hamburger, packaged beef stew meat, sirloin steak, string beans, lettuce, watermelon, cantaloupe, lobster tails, scallops, jars of junior foods, hamburger rolls, eggs, canned applesauce, canned lasagne, canned evaporated milk, canned dessert topping, candy crackers, frozen tuna noodle casserole, canned soft drinks, gelatin desserts, tea bags and cake mix.

They both bought: mustard, spaghetti, peanut butter, ready to serve cereals, assorted cookies, fruit punch, frozen orange juice, canned soup, canned pineapple chunks, bread, coffee, butter.

The article in *Parade* was concerned with whether or not they were getting the "best buys" in terms of selection, brands, varieties and so forth. We find the list interesting for quite another reason.

Desserts constitute a large percentage of it: canned figs, canned applesauce, dessert topping, candy crackers, gelatin desserts, cake mix, canned pineapple.

Fresh foods constitute such a small proportion of the whole that they are almost non-existent. One small watermelon, a head of lettuce, some beans, a cantaloupe. That is all. That is all the fresh food this family will get for (we assume) a week or more.

This is how we would revise these two grocery lists: Out of the first list we would leave only the meat, poultry, potatoes and cooking oil. Out of the second list we would leave only the meat, fresh foods and eggs. Out of the list of things both husband and wife bought, we would omit everything.

A Few Substitutes Call for Fresh Foods

What would we substitute? Obviously, fresh foods. We would buy probably three dozen rather than one dozen eggs, fresh apples rather than canned applesauce, fresh pineapple rather than canned pineapple, dried figs rather than canned ones, fresh grapes, bananas, pears, plums, strawberries, peaches and whatever other fruit was in season. We would also include fresh vegetables rather than frozen and canned ones.

Why buy canned salmon when fresh fish is everywhere available? Why buy frozen and canned fruit juice when fresh juicy fruits are available for eating—not for drinking!

And one head of lettuce as the only raw salad greens for an entire family for an entire week! Where's the parsley, the spinach, the endive, the celery, the crisp green pepper and cabbage both so rich in vitamin C, the radishes, the fresh tomatoes? These are the foods that are the most essential part of a nutritious diet, aside from its protein content. They were almost entirely ignored by this typical family.

One final word. It is extremely difficult to change food habits once they are firmly established. If you grow up liking nothing but cold cereals, meat, potatoes and gravy and desserts, that's the way your pattern of eating will remain throughout your life, unless something or somebody jolts you out of it. And then it may be too late.

The nutrition surveys we described above show more clearly than anything else could that our boys and girls are growing up to like the wrong kind of food. The grocery lists of our typical family show exactly why.

CHAPTER 194

Some Nutritious
Central American Foods

Some of the foods not commonly used in this country have almost astronomical amounts of several of the important vitamins, compared with the amounts found in foods we use daily. For instance, mangoes from Cuba contain as high as 458 milligrams of vitamin C. Compare this to 45 milligrams for our average orange. Cuban pineapple contains as high as 90 milligrams, compared with an average of 38 in pineapple found in our markets.

There is an incredibly high content of calcium and other minerals in sesame seed of Cuba—as high as 1167 milligrams of calcium per hundred grams. Compare this to 282 milligrams of calcium in the yolk of eggs. Even allowing for the fact that one would be more likely to eat eggs in considerable bulk, still you can see that sesame seeds form an amazingly good source of calcium. They are somewhat richer in iron than egg yolks, too. Yet in this country they are used only by "food faddists."

Some Guatemalan Foods

Coming to the Guatemalan foods, we find that yucca flowers are an excellent source of vitamin C. The botanical name of this plant is *Yucca elephantipes Regel* and it boasts well over 400 milligrams of vitamin C per hundred grams. Something called the cashew apple (*Anacardium occidentale L.*) is also high in vitamin C. A vegetable called malva (*Malva parviflora L.*), a mallow, is phenomenally rich in vitamin A, vitamin C, calcium and phosphorus. Its iron content is almost 6 times that of egg yolk, which is just about our richest source. The flower of a palm tree (*chamaedorea Tepejilote Liebm*) is also rich in calcium.

Yierbabuena (our bergamot mint) is used with other foods as flavoring and sometimes used as a green. It, like malva, is said to have medicinal properties. It is reasonably rich in calcium, iron, vitamin A and riboflavin, a B vitamin.

Macuy, a weed widely distributed, is said to have medicinal value. It is very rich in calcium, iron and fairly rich in riboflavin and vitamin C. Two samples of field mustard (*Brassica campestris L.* is the botanical name) were analyzed and found to be high in calcium, riboflavin, iron and vitamin A. The leaves and tender points of squash and pumpkin plants are used extensively as food in Central America. They are high in calcium, iron, vitamin A, several important B vitamins and vitamin C.

Roselle (*Hibiscus Sabadariffa L.*) is extraordinarily high in calcium, a hundred grams containing more than 1200 milligrams! The content of iron and B vitamins is also high. "Their value as a source of these constituents depends of course upon the amounts extracted in the 'tea' prepared from them." It is easy to see, however, that tea made from plants as nutritious as this might well mean the difference between life and death to an invalid, especially one whose daily diet, low in vitamins and minerals, is responsible for his condition.

Leaves of the laurel tree are an outstanding source of calcium, iron, vitamin A and the B vitamins. This is not our laurel tree, however, but goes under the botanical name of *litsea guatemalensis Mex.* The leaves of our laurel tree contain prussic acid and are certainly not recommended for daily fare in any quantity.

A plant called *Pacaya* (botanical name *Chamaedorea Tepejilote Liebm.*) has quite a high content of calcium. A vegetable called *Guisquil* (*Chayote*) is extremely high in vitamin A.

These Foods Should Be Included in Our Diet

In these "backward" countries, denied the benefit of our scientific knowlege about nutrition, all these various foods are being used *in addition* to the foods we know and use daily. So we, with our fabulous modern supermarkets, our system of transportation so widespread and so efficient that we can import all kinds of delicacies from all over the world, just to tickle our palates, we, with our "high standard of living" are somehow getting along and haphazardly nourishing ourselves without any knowledge of all of the many other exotic and nourishing foods that are available to the poorest resident of one of these "backward" nations.

It is a fact well known to all nutritionists that a wide, varied menu is the one most likely to be adequate in all respects. It is well known that confining oneself to a limited selection of foods is almost bound to lead to deficiencies.

Would it not be sensible for the nutrition experts in our universities and the big food companies to get together on a program of making these foods available to us in this country?

Please don't write in to inquire where you may buy these foods. With the exception of things like sesame seed and the other well-known plants we have mentioned, we don't know where you can buy the various foods. That is the gist of our complaint. *We wish there were some place where you could buy them!*

CHAPTER 195

How Healthy Are We?

Our files contain lots of clippings in which some noted M.D. states that we in America have the best nutrition in the world; that it's nonsense for any of us to take nutritional supplements; that our degenerative diseases cannot be the result of nutritional deficiencies, for we are, generally speaking, not deficient, so far as food is concerned. Many of these comments are from the popular M.D.'s who write newspaper columns. Some of them are from medical journals. The columnists generally sound off in answer to a letter from a reader who inquires whether she or her children should be taking food supplements. Of course not, say these savants, "a good diet" will take care of all your food needs. Then they generally go on to say that food supplements are nothing but the bait which food faddists use to bring hard-earned dollars out of perfectly healthy folks who may worry about their health.

We've collected a few statistics on the diets generally eaten in this country. We want to tell you about them and then we want to ask you whether you believe that we are all as well fed as the above medicos would like you to believe. Let's begin with a survey made by the Louisiana State Department of Health. In 1942 about 1000 children were carefully studied by the Board of Health pediatrician. Of the total group, 44 per cent were considered malnourished. In 1944 a similar survey of 643 school children in the Baton Rouge and Shreveport area reported on the physical or outward signs of malnutrition—such things as flared ribs indicating rickets, or scars at the corners of the mouth indicating a lack of B vitamins. As few as 6 per cent of the children suffered from one symptom. But as many as 69 per cent suffered from another. In 1945 over 100 high school girls were examined in one parish of Louisiana. The report says, "Numerous minor abnormalities often associated with malnutrition were encountered." Sixty-three per cent of the girls suffered from a skin disorder with a long medical name which indicates a deficiency in vitamin A. Twenty-five per cent of the children had red and swollen gums, which is an indication of malnutrition. And so forth.

In another parish a group of 144 children showed from one to twenty-one symptoms of malnutrition per child, with an average of 7.4 symptoms. To break down the diet of some of these children and discover just what they were or were not eating that brought about such conditions was not easy. But we have a report dated June, 1950, which gives some of this information. In 1947-1948 nearly a thousand children in south Louisiana kept a week's dietary history. Of all the children, 6 per cent were rated as having "Good" dietary habits. Fifty-six per cent were rated as having

"Fair" dietary habits and 38 per cent were rated as "Poor." In a study of the weekly diet of 144 children who ate regularly in a school lunch room, it was found that 60 per cent of the children ate no butter. Twenty-four per cent of them ate no eggs. Thirty per cent of them ate no whole grain products. Thirty-five per cent of them ate no fruits or raw vegetables.

Prevalent Vitamin C Deficiencies

The *Bulletin of the Johns Hopkins Hospital,* Vol. 87, p. 569, 1950, gives the results of a series of autopsies on infants showing that 6 per cent of them suffered from subclinical scurvy. By this we mean that they had a case of scurvy (a vitamin C deficiency disease) not bad enough to kill them, but bad enough to show the early symptoms of the disease. The *Journal of the American Dietetic Association,* Vol. 28, p. 718, 1952, showed that, of a group of school children studied, 47 per cent had a low intake of vitamin C, 53 per cent had a low blood level of vitamin C. In the same journal, Vol. 24, p. 957, 1948, we read of college students eating at dining halls. *Sixty-two per cent of the meals analyzed were deficient in vitamin C.* The *Journal of Periodontology,* Vol. 23, p. 228, 1952, describes patients suffering from one form or another of gum disease, in which 44 per cent showed signs of vitamin C deficiency. *California Medicine,* Vol. 74, p. 105, 1951, tells us that of institutional inmates over the age of 50, 87 per cent are deficient in vitamin C. W. J. McCormick, M.D., of Toronto, Canada, tells us in an article in the *Archives of Pediatrics* for January, 1954, that he has examined more than 5000 patients and has found that less than 10 per cent of them had the optimum amount of vitamin C in their blood at any given time.

And remember, please, in the case of this vitamin especially, the Minimum Daily Requirement as it is set officially by the National Research Council is only 70 to 75 milligrams, which is far, far below what you need for buoyant good health and resistance to infections. Yet the folks described above did not have even this insignificantly small amount of this important vitamin. Is it because they are poor and ignorant? Is it because they cannot afford to buy fresh fruits and vegetables or do not know that they should eat them? In the case of the institutional inmates, perhaps these factors may enter in. But what of the college students? Dr. McCormick's patients had enough money and enough education to go to a doctor when they were sick. Is it possible that they did not have enough money or knowledge to eat the proper diet?

Deficiencies in Factory Workers

The *New York Times* for July 11, 1954, gave the results of a two-year study done by Rutgers University scientists, who interviewed 600 men in industrial plants in that area. Forty-four per cent of the men were overweight. One-quarter of the men were deficient in calcium, so necessary for sound bones and teeth and healthy nerves. Nearly one-third of the men were low in vitamin C. Others were deficient in other vitamins, especially thiamin and riboflavin. Since these are both B vitamins, the only conclusion to draw is that they were also deficient in the other B vitamins, since these deficiencies are never single. The *Times* stated that "the coffee-sweet-roll diet, plus a bottle of soda pop or a candy bar in mid-morning not only resulted in overweight, but cut down the appetite for foods rich in minerals and vitamins." Amen to that statement and we think we are safe in assuming that such a diet was also largely responsible for the other shocking statistics we have given above.

When you stop to consider these statistics carefully, just reflect on how shocking they are! Forty-four per cent of a group of school children malnourished! Fifty-three per cent of another group low in vitamin C! Sixty-two per cent of the meals of college students deficient in vitamin C! One quarter of the men in typical industrial plants short on calcium! How can any columnist write smugly that "a good diet" is all you need, and let it go at that, with these figures staring him in the face? All these people think they are eating a good diet, if they think of it at all. And if they don't, why don't we arrange to have the elements of a good diet printed in every daily newspaper, on the front page and learned by every school child just as thoroughly as he learns how to add and subtract.

More Statistics on Malnutrition

Here are just a few more statistics, all of which show plainly the vast extent of malnutrition in this great, rich land of ours.

From the *New York Journal of Dentistry* for April, 1945: "If we take all the American children between 6 and 18 and give them the fillings they need now to restore their mouths to healthy conditions, dentists would have to insert a total of 244,000,000 fillings." For adults—285,000,000 fillings. "If somehow that work was accomplished, dentists would have to place an additional 79,000,000 fillings every year to keep up with the new cavities that form in the mouths of adults each year." (Adding up the cost of this colossal amount of dental work, do you really think it would cost that much money to provide, instead, a proper diet so that all those children and adults need not suffer from tooth decay?)

From a survey made by the United States Public Health Service described in *Time,* Vol. 31, p. 22, 1938, we find that every day, one out of 20 people is too sick to go to school or work. Every man, woman and child on the average in the nation suffers 10 days of incapacity annually. The average youngster is sick in bed 7 days of the year, the average oldster 35 days a year. Two million, five hundred thousand people suffer from chronic disease—heart disease, rheumatism and so forth.

And here is a report from the Albert and May Lasker Foundation, New York, on the 1948 figures for funds raised by several health agencies:

National Foundation of Infantile Paralysis	$18,669,299
National Tuberculosis Association	18,665,524
American Cancer Society	13,221,176
American Heart Association	2,502,176

Now one final set of figures, which is perhaps the most staggering of all, from the Bankers Life and Casualty Company. "More than 8,000,000 families went into debt last year, because of big medical bills—and 500,000 families (not individuals, *but families*) had medical costs *as large as or larger than their entire year's income.*"

We think we have made our point. We think that from now on, when one of your friends (or perhaps your doctor) laughs at you or says you are being extravagant, because you will buy only the best food from a nutritional point of view, and because you take food supplements regularly, you will be able to give them a few facts and figures to back up your point of view.

What Kind of Food Do We Eat in General?

And, here, finally, are some facts and figures from a dietary survey made by *Parents'* magazine in 1953, involving the 2000 families with children who are members of *Parents'* magazine Consumer Adviser Panel which is representative of their readership. Now surely readers of *Parents'* magazine are neither poor nor ignorant. They are, in general, mothers who have access to all the knowledge nutrition books contain, they go to good pediatricians, they attend PTA's and other community organizations where good nutrition is or should be discussed. One thousand of these answers were collected for the survey which we read.

And some of the answers show perhaps more clearly than anything else the misconceptions that are abroad in regard to nutrition. For instance, of the 1,000 mothers who answered, 435 use *only margarine*—never butter. Cold cereal is served an average of 4.4 times per week. By this is meant the processed, degerminated, heat-treated, puffed, sugared and flaked product which has been "enriched" as they say, with a few measly vitamins which cannot possibly make up for all the vitamins that have been removed from the original cereal. Almost a third of these families serve this kind of cereal every day.

Only 233 families "sometimes" bake their own bread, which means that they might have occasion to put in it a few ingredients more nourishing than the air and chemical-filled substance that goes by the name of "bread" at the baker's. But 849 out of the 1000 families bake cakes at home, 733 bake pies, 588 bake cookies. And what kind of shortening do they use for their baking? Six hundred and seventy-two out of the 801 mothers who use one kind of shortening only, use solid vegetable shortening—that is, the white, creamy substance which has been hydrogenated and homogenized and treated with chemicals until very little of the original value of the vegetable oil remains. This same shortening is used by 690 mothers out of 1000 for all the frying they do. Eight-hundred and seventy-two out of the 1000 mothers use packaged pudding dessert at home (in addition, that is, to the cakes, pies, cookies and so forth)! Packaged pudding contains sugar, of course, as well as artificial flavoring and coloring.

For beverages 25 per cent serve their children a concoction called "Kool-aid," 23 per cent serve them soda pop, 8.2 per cent serve them cola drinks.

This survey represents very well, we think, what is mainly wrong with nutrition in this country today. Mothers who ought to know better, who have every opportunity to learn better, are feeding their children on watered down, diluted foods almost completely lacking in the food elements necessary for health. The cereal they use is the processed kind. The shortening is hydrogenated. Margarine they think will do as well as butter (but it won't, you know, if you want to be healthy!) Cakes, pies and cookies fill every nook and cranny of children's stomachs so that there is no room for health-giving fruits and vegetables. And yet every one of these parents undoubtedly prides herself on her devotion to her family's needs. And what good cooks they all are!

Show these facts and figures to some of your friends, won't you?—or the members of your club or PTA. Ask them if a little serious thought given to the matter won't easily divulge the subtle and terribly insidious way in which the figures on disease, vitamin and mineral deficiency and doctor bills are related to the kind of meal being served on the average American table.

CHAPTER 196

How Different Are We?

Cousin Joe eats the worst diet you ever saw and he's never been sick in his life. Uncle Fred has only one peculiarity—he can't take even one little glass of wine without going on an alcoholic spree. Aunt Jessie works like a horse, gets only 5 hours of sleep a night and can eat anything without trouble. Sister Anne has a terrible thyroid condition although no other member of her family has this difficulty.

How do these things happen? Do they disprove all our theories about good nutrition and good health? Actually how extensive are the differences in physiology and anatomy among human beings, which might account for the wide variations in reactions to everything from heat and cold to a new vitamin pill?

The answers to questions like these—sound, reasonable and well-researched answers—are found in a book called *Biochemical Individuality* by Roger J. Williams, Professor of Chemistry and Director of the Biochemical Institute of the University of Texas. The jaw-breaker title of this book means just one thing—when we speak of the chemistry of living things (biochemistry), we must realize that every living thing is different. This is the theme of the book.

Physiological Variations

Take arteries, for instance—those tubes that carry red blood to every cell in our bodies—surely such an essential and basic part of us must be pretty much the same, from person to person. Dr. Williams shows us wide variation in the way *only one artery* (the heart artery) is curved and branched as it leaves the heart. Arteries may be wide or narrow. The chambers of the heart show an infinite variation in size and shape. In a group of 182 perfectly normal young men it was found that the heart beat ranged from 45 to 105 beats per minute. One heart may pump 3.16 liters of blood per minute, another heart in just as good condition may pump 10.81 liters.

Variations in the size, shape and position of organs like the stomach, liver and colon are endless, and each variation contributes to making every human being different from his neighbor, physiologically speaking. Such differences may partly explain why one man is constipated, another has gall bladder trouble, a third has liver disease. "It is a fact," says Dr. Williams, "that some individuals can swallow with ease large capsules or stomach tubes in a doctor's office or hospital, while others have great difficulty." The size of the individual's esophagus may be responsible.

What about nerves? The very number and arrangement of these vary with every individual. Children, all taught to write by the same teacher using the same methods, will have different handwriting partly because their hands, including the nerve connections in them, are different. Ability to feel pain is an individual thing. Some people are completely or almost indifferent to the same degree of pain which drives other people into screaming convulsions.

It seems very possible, says Dr. Williams, that people with large arteries supplying the brain would have little tendency to faint and, in later years, less tendency to become senile. On the other hand, perhaps people who have small arteries "should follow very special precautions in their eating so as to keep the blood vessels as free from internal deposits as possible." Could wide arteries be one reason why Cousin Joe can eat all kinds of rich food and escape hardening of the arteries?

Persons who are exceedingly susceptible to bone fractures have been found to be unable to retain calcium, phosphorus and magnesium properly. This would seem to explain the fragile bones. "It is interesting as well as complicating," says Dr. Williams, "that some individuals whose bones fracture with great ease also exhibit unusual rapidity of bone healing." As hair becomes gray, it contains fewer minerals, indicating apparently a change in the way the body handles minerals as we grow older.

Calcium Requirements

What about nutrition? How different are we in this field of physiology? In the realm of nutrition there are perhaps wider differences among us than in any other aspect of our physical make-up. Take calcium, for instance. It has been found that, all environmental conditions being equal, our requirements for calcium may vary by a factor of 5. In Oriental countries, Dr.

Williams tells us, far less calcium is available in diets, yet the population does not appear to suffer from calcium deficiency, so whole communities of people appear to need less calcium than we Westerners do. It is commonly supposed, he goes on to say, that such peoples have become adapted to living with less calcium.

Individuals who have a need for lots of calcium who are placed in an environment where they cannot get enough will not survive. So the second generation will be children of those whose calcium requirements are lower. And in this generation, too, those who cannot get enough calcium will not survive, so that, after many generations, you will have a group of people capable of living healthfully on far less calcium than might be needed by another group living where calcium is plentiful in food.

Need for Vitamins Varies

It is well recognized, says Dr. Williams, that in experiments with laboratory rats, using vitamin A in diets, there are wide variations in the reaction to various amounts of the vitamin. So usually as many as 10 to 15 carefully selected animals are used and the results are averaged. So far as human beings are concerned, a survey done on 92 people disclosed that there was a ten-fold difference in the amount of vitamin A in the blood of individuals tested. This might be because the individuals simply had different requirements from the day of their birth, which would indicate that this kind of peculiarity may be inherited, or it might be because of a difficulty in absorbing the vitamin which could be the result of things in the individual's environment—the kind of drugs he has taken, the illnesses he has had and so forth.

A favorite question of many readers is, "How much vitamin C do I need?" In the days of sailing vessels when scurvy (the disease of vitamin C deficiency) was a frequent cause of death, long sea voyages provided perfect instances of well-controlled experiments, since all members of the crew ate the same diet exactly, for many months. How did it happen, then, that one man might die of scurvy while the rest of the crew were free from symptoms of vitamin C deficiency? How did it happen that at the end of a voyage some 10 or 15 men might have died of scurvy while the rest of the crew were afflicted only slightly? Obviously, the men who had died had a far greater requirement for vitamin C than those who survived.

The B vitamins present an even more interesting picture, because we know that many of these are manufactured in the human intestine. So one's ability to make his own B vitamins will influence to a great extent his ability to withstand shortages in his diet. Take two people in the same family, eating the same meals day after day. Suppose one of them has taken sulfa drugs earlier in his lifetime and these drugs have destroyed the intestinal bacteria responsible for making B vitamins. This member of the family will never catch up with the others. Even though all diets are the same, this member of the family is quite likely to suffer from a severe shortage of B vitamins on a diet which adequately nourishes others in the family.

Dr. Williams says that cases of burning feet, faltering memory, constipation (all symptoms of pantothenic acid deficiency—one of the B vitamins) might appear in someone who was eating a diet on which everybody else was perfectly healthy. The unfortunate victim simply had a need for more pantothenic acid than the rest, so he developed symptoms on the good diet. Sex may have something to do with it, too, for we are told that females in general have need for less choline (another B vitamin) than males do.

Then, of course, there are diseases which make requirements for vitamins higher. For instance, tubercular patients have far greater demands for vitamin A and vitamin C than healthy people.

Solving Your Own Health Problems

How can we use the fascinating facts Dr. Williams has presented to improve health? Obviously there is no sense in becoming discouraged and deciding that we might as well give up since, according to his findings, we have no way of knowing whether our own or any member of our family's needs for various food factors may be greater or less than average.

There are, of course, certain signs that you cannot mistake. If you are taking what you believe to be plenty of vitamin C, but you notice you still get unexplained bruises, this is a certain indication that your individual need for vitamin C is greater than you thought. Increase the amount you get in meals and supplements. If you are taking brewer's yeast and you still have a mouth that is sore at the corners, if you're still constipated and nervous and tormented with indigestion, perhaps you need far more vitamin B than you are getting. Or the trouble may be that your intestinal bacteria are not doing their job of providing part of the B vitamins you need. Taking yogurt or whey every day may help to re-establish these bacteria so that your requirement for B vitamins would decrease. Some other member of your family who has perfectly healthy intestinal bacteria may not need the yogurt or the whey.

Alcoholism And Nutrition

Dr. Williams, whose book we have been discussing, is one of the country's authorities on the relation between poor nutrition and alcoholism. He says, "It appears that the uncontrolled craving for alcohol in certain individuals is a nutritional deficiency disease. I have had intimate contact with several individuals (and less intimate contact with many more) who initially had this craving to an extreme degree, but who, by eating more wisely and taking nutritional supplements, have had their craving completely abolished so that now they behave as individuals who never were alcoholics; they drink little or none as they wish. The fact that we have not yet devised a supplement which will be effective for all individuals is true, but it does not cancel out the fact that some have had their difficulty removed."

In view of this last statement, please don't assume that either we or Dr. Williams have the complete answer for alcoholics. In spite of his success, Dr. Williams still says he has not yet found the combination of vitamins and minerals which will be effective for all individuals, so please don't write to him or to us asking what it is. We don't know. But it does seem that alcoholism, one of man's oldest afflictions, may some day be conquered when we come to know enough about individual variations in nutritional needs. And surely eating the best possible diet and taking vitamin supplements would be wise for alcoholics or indeed for anyone else interested in good health.

We believe that members of the healing profession will want to get Dr. Williams' book, published by John Wiley and Sons, 440 Fourth Avenue, New York City, New York. The average reader who is not trained in reading scientific literature would find the book to be not very helpful, for it is written for other scientists; it is full of scientific words and references that would mean nothing to the average reader.

One final word. Keep in mind what we've been saying about individual differences, in your relations with others. Don't get impatient with someone whose capacity for work is less than yours. Don't make fun of someone who takes piles of vitamins and minerals with every meal. Maybe you don't need them as desperately as he does. Don't decide that some friend or relative is a little crazy because he suffers from symptoms that you consider imaginary, just because you've never felt them yourself. And if you're one of the unlucky ones with narrow arteries and the excessive need for vitamins, or the impossibly small liver, don't be dismayed. Your recognition of these weaknesses may, by persuading you to cherish your health, lengthen your life and bring you the well-being and happiness you want.

CHAPTER 197

How Would Your Child Fare in a Nutrition Test?

Think of the typical American kid on your block. What does he look like—braces or bucked teeth, glasses, jumpy and unable to sit still a moment? Most likely you will have to answer yes to one of those qualifications, or a similar one. Yet we Americans pride ourselves on the health of our children. None are better fed or happier, we think. But let's be realistic about it. If good feeding means giving them all they can eat of whatever strikes their fancy, then they are well fed. If it means giving them enough of the foods they need for good health, foods rich in body-building vitamins and minerals, then they are starving.

Whether due to a sense of misplaced generosity or ignorance on the part of many parents, children are guided largely by television and newspaper ads in their choice of foods, not by sound parental knowledge and

[738]

authority. The ads tell the kids to eat candy for quick energy, to eat ice cream for milk value and dried cereals for B vitamins. No advertiser mentions the danger of the sugar in these things, or the way the processing has taken any practical value out of the cereal. The parents should be aware of the fake aspects of this publicity. But they don't know any more about it than the children do, nor do they ask any questions. We're all conditioned to believe whatever the ads say, no matter how impossible the claims might be.

Our smug attitude on the superior health of American children got quite a jolt from the findings of a group of researchers which were published in September, 1957, by the Ohio Agricultural Experiment Station in Wooster, Ohio. The work is entitled "Nutritional Status of 9-, 10- and 11-year-old Public School Children in Iowa, Kansas and Ohio." It was the result of blood samples taken from school children in that age bracket in country schools, village and city schools in each of the states. Just a few drops of blood from each child's finger tip were enough to tell the story of how good a child's diet is.

Blood Tested for Four Essentials

Each blood sample was tested for four things: hemoglobin, vitamin C, vitamin A and carotene.

Hemoglobin is the red coloring matter in the blood. About 75 per cent of the body's iron is concentrated in the hemoglobin. Without the minimum of 11.5 grams per 100 milliliters of blood, a child was considered anemic. Sixty-three per cent of the children of Kansas were below the minimum of 11.5 and only 9 per cent had above the satisfactory hemoglobin level.

Vitamin C, or ascorbic acid, is considered a good test for current nutrition, since the body cannot store any of this vitamin for long periods. As we know, this vitamin functions everywhere in the body, rebuilding tissues, helping in formation of teeth and bones, healing of wounds and resistance to infection. There is no single vitamin which the body uses more eagerly than vitamin C. The minimum set for satisfactory ascorbic acid in the blood stream was .6 milligrams per 100 milliliters of blood. Here the findings were appalling. A quite considerable percentage of the children had less than half of the minimal .6 milligrams per 100 milliliters. As for those who simply fell below the minimum requirements for satisfactory vitamin C, Kansas had 56 per cent of its children tested in this category. Iowa had 37 per cent below, and Ohio had 36 per cent who had unsatisfactory levels of vitamin C in the blood. In all, more than ⅓ of the children tested showed a vitamin C deficiency.

Vitamin A is one of the easiest vitamins to come by. It is contained in many vegetables, fruits and meat. The body can store vitamin A for a fairly long period of time, and anyone with a reasonably good diet should be able to show a healthy supply of vitamin A in the system. This vitamin is needed for general growth and development of the body, for healthy looking skin and normal functioning of the eyes, especially the ability to see after dark. Again the children showed an alarming deficiency. One-fourth of them had less than the minimum of 20 to 30 milligrams per 100 milliliters of vitamin A in the blood stream.

The story of carotene (which becomes vitamin A in the body) was even more disheartening. The minimum normal amount of carotene was set of 100 micrograms per 100 milliliters of blood serum. In spite of the availability of this nutritive element, 44 per cent of the Iowa children fell below the minimum; in Kansas the count was 55 per cent, and Ohio had 31 per cent below the minimum of 100.

Alarming as these figures are, one can't help wondering how the children would have fared had they been tested for the vital but scarce B vitamins. The B vitamins are almost strained out of most foods the average American child eats. His white bread and cereals are bled practically free of them, and few children can be found who eat eggs instead of processed cereal in the morning. As for the B-rich organ meats, do you know many children who eat them with any kind of regularity?

Children Tested Are Not Underprivileged

The children whose results are shown in these pages are average, normally privileged youngsters who live in 3 agriculturally rich states of our country. The problem is not one of crowding or lack of available foods. It is likely that the parents of most of these children consider them well-fed. Without this actual evidence, they would no doubt be shocked at the suggestion that their children are not well nourished. And the attitude probably prevails all over the country.

Obviously such exhaustive tests are not likely to be conducted in every one of the 48 states. Nor should such measures be necessary to alert parents to the nutritional dangers their children face. If such inadequacies exist in Kansas, Iowa and Ohio, why shouldn't they be presumed to exist in Georgia, Oregon, Maine and Florida as well? Unless parents are aware of the dangers of processed foods, of white sugar and white flour products, of the hundreds of nutritionless foods which ruin appetites when good food is presented, and forbid these useless foods to their children, the condition will continue and worsen. Guard the health of your family. Face the fact that your nutrition might not be all it should be, and do something about it. Use fresh fruits and vegetables whenever they are available, plus fresh meats that have not been treated with objectionable chemicals. Assure yourself that all nutritional needs are being met by providing your family with natural food supplements, especially wheat germ and desiccated liver for vitamin B and rose hips for vitamin C. Educate them to eat nuts, sunflower seeds and fruits for snacks. The level of the average child's nutrition is dangerously low. Make sure your child is way above average.

CHAPTER 198

Who Pays for Nutrition Research?

"Dr. Stare's Nutrition Department (at Harvard University) received from Food Industries and Foundations representative of their interests between and including the fiscal year 1950 to 1956 gifts totaling approximately $378,000, half of which was from the Sugar Research Foundation, supported by the sugar interests, and the Nutrition Foundation, supported largely by commercial food processors. A large portion of the other half was from the chemical and drug interests."

This challenging statement sets the tone for a series of Open Letters from the Boston Nutrition Society, Incorporated, to Dr. Nathan M. Pusey, President of Harvard University. We think readers will find in these letters the answer to their puzzled query—"Why?" Why must we eat doctored up, chemicalized, refined, cheapened food and above all, why must some of our top food scientists, men like Dr. Stare of Harvard, call everyone a faddist and a crackpot who points out that the modern American food is not everything it should be?

The Open Letters hit at the very heart of the problem. Much university research on nutrition is being financed by the very folks who profit from selling this worthless food. Of course, the scientist whose work is paid for by a grant from the Sugar Foundation is not going to admit in print that white sugar in the quantities in which we consume it today is not only not harmless but actually is as harmful as any other drug. Now is he?

Here are some of the facts from the Open Letters which would make wonderful material for "Letters to the Editor."

Dr. Stare's Aim

"In an article in *McCall's* magazine for July, 1955, among other things, Dr. Stare wrote, 'Refined and processed foods are a favorite target of the "food specialist," who would have us believe these foods are not nutritious. Actually, we get as much food value from refined foods which have been enriched as from natural foods, and sometimes more. This is not to say that white bread is better than brown bread or vice versa. For all practical purposes, in typical American diets they are identical in food values. Choose whichever tastes better to you. . . .'

"Are these *statements* arrived at from unbiased *scientific research?* Or, are they an effort on Dr. Stare's part to satisfy the commercial processors who devitalize American foods and who so lavishly donate to Dr. Stare's

Department funds earmarked to be used under his personal direction? Are his conclusions arrived at in a truly scientific manner or do they represent innuendos and mis-statements, in lieu of facts, designed to lull the public into a false sense of security?

"Here are just a few donations to Dr. Stare's department or to be spent under his direction made between 1950 and 1956. Such gifts would cause anyone's statements to be prejudiced in favor of the donors. But what of the nutritional and psychological effects of such mis-statements upon the public?

"DONATIONS

"Kellogg's Company	$ 45,000
National Biscuit Co.	12,500
Wheat Flour Institute	5,000
*Nutrition Foundation	113,000
Sugar Research Foundation	67,750

$243,250

Deficiency Widespread

"Again, contrary to Dr. Stare's statement, already quoted, to the effect that . . . 'We are a nation of healthy people blessed with the best food supply in the world . . .', the National Research Council's 1945 *Bulletin* (No. 109) *of the Food and Nutrition Board,* in which 189 research reports and surveys from coast to coast are correlated, summarized them by saying that . . . All evidence is in agreement that deficiency states are common among the population of the United States. . .'

"From the book *Diseases of Metabolism* containing articles by 20 of the most famous medical men in America we quote from an article by the late Dr. Tom D. Spies, M.D., chairman of the Department of Nutrition and Metabolism, Northwestern University Medical School; Professor of Nutrition and Metabolism, Hillman Hospital, Birmingham, Alabama: 'Investigation of the diets of large groups of people correlated with laboratory studies and direct examination led to the startling observation that the margin of safety against deficiency diseases is narrow rather than broad, that the presence of nutritional inadequacy is widespread and not limited to the lower economic group. As information is increasing, it is found that relatively few people in the United States consistently eat diets that are adequate in all respects.' (Page 555).

" 'A noteworthy paper by Baker, Wright and Drummond traces the increasing use of white flour to the introduction of silk bolting cloth in 1840 and of roller mills in 1870 to satisfy greater demand. They estimate that "the best fed members of the population today are getting twice as much vitamin B_1 as people on a low income level, yet consume less vitamin B_1 than the parish poor of the eighteenth and early nineteenth centuries." We are realizing more and more that decortification of grain is dangerous,

"*Whose board of Trustees consists of officials of over 40 leading Food Processing Companies.

[742]

that there must be some change in milling methods. Greater care in guarding against loss of vitamins and minerals through processing, marketing and storing of foods would undoubtedly improve the quality of many diets.' (Page 557).

"Yet Dr. Stare writes for public consumption: 'Actually we get as much food value from refined foods which have been "enriched" as from natural foods and sometimes more.'

Other Scientists Speak

"What do scientists who are *not* controlled by or donated to by the Food Processors and Refiners or the Chemical and Drug interests have to say on 'enrichment' with synthetic vitamins? In the *British Medical Journal* for March 31, 1945, in an article entitled, 'Imbalance of Vitamin B Factors,' Marion B. Richards, M.D., D. Sc., of the Rowell Research Institute, Aberdeen, Scotland, writes:

" 'Recent experiments on rats in this institute have produced clear cut evidence of the adverse effects that may be caused by a disturbance of the balance of the vitamin B factors in the diet, and have shown that overloading with one component B_1 can produce a definite deficiency of another component, B_6. It is becoming increasingly recognized that in the treatment of pellagrins with nicotinic acid it is essential to provide other members of the B complex and to prescribe a liberal and well-balanced diet. Our experiments would suggest the necessity for adopting a similar procedure for other B factors, and in particular, when B_1 therapy is indicated, for supplying the whole B complex instead of the single vitamin. . . . The present results emphasize the need for caution in any attempt to improve the diet of these populations by indiscriminate addition of large supplements of single synthetic B vitamins.'

"These experiments have been backed up in this country by Dr. Tom Spies and associates (see above), by Agnes Fay Morgan of Southern California University and recently by Dr. Estelle Hawley, Associate Professor of Pediatrics and Nutrition at Rochester University. Dr. Hawley carried out a series of experiments in which so-called 'enriched' commercial white bread was fed to one group of rats and another group fed on bread made according to Dr. Clive McCay's Cornell formula. The rats on the McCay-Cornell bread thrived, as did their offspring and descendants through the fourth generation. The rats on the 'enriched' white bread became sickly and starved looking and produced stunted offspring. All died off and the strain became extinct before the fourth generation.

Dr. Stare's Backing

"Thus, we find Dr. Stare's Nutrition Department 'abundantly' backed by the Chemical and Drug Interests and the National Food Processors who donated from 1950 to 1956:

"(a) Chemical concerns DuPont, Merck and Upjohn ....$ 50,250
"(b) The Sugar Foundation composed of the large sugar interests (the second largest contributor) 67,750

[743]

"(c) The Nutrition Foundation (the largest contributor) Dr. Stare's article in *McCall's* magazine, January, 1956, in bold type called attention to the statement, 'Approved by Committee on Nutritional Education of the NUTRITION FOUNDATION' 113,000
"(d) Other contributions largely from food processors 147,000

"Total $378,000

"Just what is this NUTRITION FOUNDATION whose so-called Educational Department 'approves' Dr. Stare's writings. It consists of about 45 of the leading FOOD PROCESSORS, CHEMICAL, and DRUG COMPANIES represented officially by the Chairman of the Board or other leading Executive of each. Some members of this NUTRITION FOUNDATION are: Armour & Co., Abbott, Inc., American Sugar Refining Co., Baker Laboratories, Campbell Soup Co., Gelatine Co., Coca-Cola Co., Continental Baking Co., Corn Products Refining, Curtis Candy Co., General Foods Corp., General Mills Co., Gerber Products Co., H. J. Heinz Co., Kellogg Co., Libby, McNeil & Libby, Knox Gelatine, Merck & Co., National Biscuit Co., National Dairy Prod., Nestles Co., Inc., Pepsi-Cola Co., Pet Milk Co. . . ."

CHAPTER 199

A British Nutritionist
Takes Stock

By J. I. Rodale

There is an article in the *British Medical Journal* for December 14, 1957, entitled "Food and Health" that I must discuss, because it represents an attitude closer to our program than any I've seen in a medical journal in a long time. It is by Dr. H. M. Sinclair, Vice-President of Magdalen College, Oxford. It is really not an article, but an address delivered at London University on April 6, 1957, to celebrate World Health Day. I can see no better way to celebrate such a day than by bringing to the light really effective nutritional means of preventing disease.

Dr. Sinclair's is a big name in medicine. He has done a great deal of research in the controversial subject of cholesterol and fats in the causation of arteriosclerosis and heart disease. When Sinclair speaks, the medical world listens and is usually impressed.

In his introduction, Dr. Sinclair states that nutrition stands as the most important single environmental factor affecting health. Then he shows how the infant-mortality rate in England is only one-seventh what it was a hundred years ago, and half of what it was in the 1930's, due to an improved conception of nutrition.

Danger in Cow's Milk

Dr. Sinclair believes that there are serious defects in cow's milk as a food for infants. By experiment he has found that such milk is inferior to human milk in the type of fat it contains. He refers to the present school meals and milk services in England, saying that they are good but that caution must be observed. For years he has "carried on a lonely campaign against the overfeeding of children. In every animal in which the experiment has been made it has been shown that overfeeding during the period of growth and development shortens this period, so that adult size is reached earlier, and also shortens life. I believe this is a real danger in the U.S.A. and I believe we also must be careful lest by overfeeding children we hasten chronic degenerative diseases. Cow's milk it not a perfect food for man, mainly because of the composition of its fat, and I think we most seriously need research into the optimum diet for producing the optimum rate of growth of children."

This is as close to my theory, that milk creates undesirable tallness, as I've ever seen in a medical journal. When he speaks of optimum diet, and he is referring especially to milk, he does not mean a diet with the largest amount of milk in it. The word *optimum* does not mean the most or highest; it means the most desirable kind of. Dr. Sinclair is diplomatically stating that drinking too much cow's milk is not desirable.

Referring again to milk, Dr. Sinclair says, "It has been known for 20 years that the fat of cows and sheep contains very little of the essential fatty acids and a large amount of an isomer that may be antagonistic; milk, butter, dripping, and the fat of the meat of these animals are seriously deficient, therefore, and the time may well come when we shall have to abolish the cow unless we undertake research to overcome this defect by alteration of the fat of milk or of the balance of the diet. The advice given in Leviticus vii, 22-23 may be sound if divorced from its context: 'And the Lord spake unto Moses, saying "Speak unto the children of Israel, saying, Ye shall eat no manner of fat, of ox, or of sheep, or of goat." ' "

But Sinclair does not mention eggs. Eggs are a most desirable form of fat, rich in the essential fatty acids.

In the January, 1958 issue of *McCall's* magazine, there appears a sensational view against too much milk drinking written by Dr. Milton J. E. Senn, Director of the Yale University Child Study Center. Here is what he says:

"Children's diets are under new scrutiny by pediatricians and nutritionists today because of new discoveries about the relationship between diet and adult diseases like arteriosclerosis and heart disease. It's now thought in some circles that *overnutrition* of babies and children may become

[745]

as much of a national problem as *malnutrition* once was, and that the larger children we're turning out now in adult life may have to pay the price in heart and blood-vessel diseases. One of the main objectives of nutrition research is to find out what really *are* the best possible amounts of milk, solids and vitamins for the long-term development and good health of our babies as well as for their immediate nourishment."

Note Dr. Senn's reference to the larger children we're turning out, and that he singles out milk as one of the factors. There seems to be a rash of pronouncements in the current public prints against milk. For example, in the December 30, 1957, issue of *Time,* Dr. Norman Jolliffe, Manhattan's famous textbook-writing nutritionist, is credited with saying, "With an adequate diet, milk is not necessary for an adult." In a December, 1957, issue of the *Yale Daily News,* students were warned "that excessive milk drinking may lead to the formation of kidney stones." The assistant director of University health in the same paper said, "You will rarely catch urologists (specialists in treating kidney stones and kindred disorders) drinking milk."

Citrus Juice Attacked

Coming back to Dr. Sinclair, the next subject he dealt with in his talk was orange juice, upon which subject he said, "Orange juice may not be the ideal vehicle for vitamin C because of the citral it contains (though almost no research has as yet been done on this) . . . the government has accepted a recommendation of a committee under the chairmanship of Lord Cohen of Birkenhead that welfare orange juice is not required by children over 2 years of age, to whom it has unnecessarily been administered for 15 years at a cost of about ½ million pounds yearly. A little research costing a few thousand pounds could have established that, and so saved 7½ million pounds." The pound today represents $2.80.

Time and time again we have stated that there is something about citric acid in oranges that practically nullifies the effect of vitamin C content. But more than that, citric acid is an extremely active chemical and when ingested with orange juice can cause cavities in the teeth, itching rectum, stomach trouble and a host of other serious conditions. Orange juice should never be taken. We recommend the whole orange, used sparingly—about 2 or 3 a week. It could be that the reason sufficient research is not being done on the subject is the power of the citrus industry. But some researches have been performed.

The Causes of Degenerative Diseases

Dr. Sinclair continues, "I had become convinced that what was and is perhaps the most serious problem in medicine arose from alterations in our diet from the processing and sophistication of foods. My clinical teachers could not answer why the expectation of life in this country of the middle-aged man is hardly different from what it was at the beginning of this century or even a century ago. That means that despite the great advances in medicine—pneumonia almost abolished, tuberculosis comparatively rare, the magnificent advances in surgery, endocrinology, and public health—a middle-aged man cannot expect to live more than 4 years longer than he could a century ago—and indeed in Scotland the expectation of life is now actually decreasing. This is because of the dramatic increase in this country, and in the more privileged countries of the world, of certain chronic degenerative diseases. Degenerative diseases found predominantly in the more highly civilized countries include coronary thrombosis, pulmonary infarction, cancer of the lung, peptic ulcer, gall-bladder disease, appendicitis, and the so-called collagen or mesenchymal diseases (which include such widely diverse conditions as certain allergies—for instance, asthma, nephrosis, disseminated lupus erythematosus, ulcerative colitis, and rheumatoid arthritis)."

Dr. Sinclair speaks of a middle-aged man living 4 years longer. In the United States from figures I have checked, a man of 50 has less than two years of extra life to look forward to. But when you get to age 60 or 70 we have actually lost ground when comparing it with the length of life back in 1850. A 70 year old man in 1850 had 10.2 more years of life to look forward to. In 1947 it was only 9.71. For a man of 60 the figures are 15.6 and 15.3, respectively. When we check the average length of life tables, not the life expectancy tables, we find the figures terribly confused by the fearful infant mortality that used to weigh down the mortality statistics. But when you leave the babies out, you get a truer picture of the actual life expectancy of older persons.

Dr. Sinclair goes on to say that the diseases of civilization may have their origin in a relative deficiency of essential (unsaturated) fatty acids, which he calls vitamins. These are unofficially called vitamin F in this country. He remarks that, "These highly unstable vitamins are found mainly in vegetable oils, and they are stabilized in nature by the presence of vitamin E. In the body, conversion into the even more unstable vitamin, arachidonic acid, is achieved by vitamin B_6, pyridoxine, and again vitamin E is required for protection. We, therefore, have this trinity of vitamins required: essential fatty acids, vitamin E and vitamin B_6. Absence of one or another, or all, can produce deficiency."

The Role of Cholesterol and Vitamin C

In lower animals Dr. Sinclair speaks of 3 main structural defects. First, cholesterol and related substances are not transported properly and become deposited in the arteries. Secondly, because certain building stones (nutrition) are absent, cell membranes are not formed properly, with consequent faulty metabolism in the cells. Thirdly, the connective tissue that binds cells together is defective. It is too bad that he did not mention the part vitamin C plays in the connective tissue, or collagen, that binds the cells together, although I am positive he knows all about it.

There is quite a bit of evidence that a lack of vitamin C might be one of the causes of cancer. W. J. McCormick, M.D., of Toronto, Canada, has written considerably on the subject (See THE HEALTH BUILDER). Dr. McCormick refers to the connection between vitamin C and the cement that glues the cells together, sometimes called the "cement of life." According to an editorial in the *Journal of the American Medical Association* (Vol. 117, p. 937, 1941), the breakdown of this cement is brought about through the failure of a certain substance that builds protein with which to repair the tissues. This substance, according to the journal, is "normally furnished by vitamin C."

In his discussion of cholesterol, Dr. Sinclair describes 4 ways in which it can cause trouble. First, in the artery walls, as arteriosclerosis; second, in the skin, causing xanthoma, a condition characterized by the presence of small, flat plaques of a yellowish color; third, in the cornea of the eye, producing a degenerated condition called *arcus senilis;* and fourth, in the lens of the eye, as cataracts; all of which indicate the importance of a low fat diet (no ice cream, butter, milk, cheese). One must have some fat and I suggest eggs as the ideal from every point of view.

Quoting from Sinclair: "It is perhaps of interest that when early in the war I examined Canadian Indians living on a primitive diet in Northern Canada. I found *arcus senilis* almost absent even from elderly ones, whereas in young English and New Zealand pilots being trained there—carefully selected for full health and carefully fed according to accepted rules—10 per cent had this cholesterol deposition in the cornea. I was, therefore, not surprised at the very high incidence of atheroma found in young United States soldiers killed in the Korean War."

Result of Vitamin Deficiencies

The 3 main structural defects, says Dr. Sinclair, namely, that cholesterol is not transported properly, thus getting into wrong places, cell metabolism being faulty due to certain building stones of nutrition being absent, and defective connective tissue that does not bind the cells together properly, give rise in lower animals to a weak state of the body, so that an emergency produces a violent reaction in it. "Several years ago Professor Ramalingswami, now of the All-India Institute of Medical Sciences, showed with me that follicular hyperkeratosis, a common skin condition in India, was probably caused by this deficiency; and more recently I have suggested it also causes the alarmingly frequent bladder stone of malnourished children in the Far East.

"We believe this deficiency of this trinity of vitamins is a basis of certain diseases of connective tissue, of certain nervous diseases, of duodenal ulcer, of certain diseases of bone and teeth, of degenerative diseases of the circulation such as coronary thrombosis and dissecting aneurysm of the aorta, and that it even plays a part in carcinoma (cancer) of the lung, since the defective structure of the cell makes it more susceptible to a chemical carcinogen (cancer causer). In this connection it is worth recalling, as Sir Ernest Kennaway has recently done, that cholesterol is carcinogenic."

Dr. Sinclair mentions that there is "evidence indicating that essential fatty acids in the diet protect man against the virus that causes the common cold."

How We Destroy Vitamins

Going further, Dr. Sinclair says, "Our present practice of producing prime beef and mutton by feeding stable concentrates decreases the unsaturated fatty acid content further. We do the same with pigs, and we stabilize lard to make it keep better. Then we fry it, which not only tends to destroy essential fatty acids but can produce substances that will cause cancer in rats and mice. We feed hens on concentrates that are deficient in the unstable fatty acids, and the eggs in consequence are deficient. We hydrogenate fats to make margarine, though some margarine contains important amounts of essential fatty acids. We now remove from bread and flour much of the vitamin B_6 they contain, and they were our most important source of this vitamin; and we add the flour 'improvers'—agene (now forbidden) and chlorine dioxide—which oxidize most of the vitamin E and destroy at least some of the essential fatty acids as well and even chlorinate part of these with production of what may be a powerful antagonist."

Dr. Sinclair is very much in favor of spices being used in the diet, saying, "Spices were added primarily to conceal off-flavors, but it is interesting that we have lately learned that they contain powerful anti-oxidants that protect essential fatty acids and vitamin E."

Sinclair and his associates have done considerable research with rats, and the following remark, therefore, shows that he is able to take a joke upon himself. He says, "When, after some ration trials I attended in Canada during the war, it was found that a soup prepared by a U.S.A. scientist made ill those troops who managed to drink it, he plaintively remarked: 'That's odd! Rats grew all right on it.' We know a great deal about animal nutrition, and millions of pounds are spent in its study, yet only a negligible sum is spent upon research into human nutrition."

The Fluoridation Question

To me one of the most important parts of this talk is Dr. Sinclair's attitude on the fluoridation of drinking water. He says: "I must add a special word about teeth, for they are connective tissue, and caries—the most prevalent disease of man—is a disease of civilized countries. Yet, as in all these other conditions, almost no research is done into its cause. The annual cost of the National Dental Service is of the order of 40 million pounds, and since the prevention of caries would enormously decrease that expenditure, research into the cause might seem desirable on financial considerations alone. Research has indeed proved that deficiency of vitamin B_6 in lower animals can produce caries, but instead of seeking the cause in man we embark upon a policy of adding fluoride to drinking water without, in my opinion, fully adequate investigation by research into the chronic effects of that, particularly in old people. I am not alone in that view. Two days ago I received a letter from one of the leading nutritional experts in the U.S.A. in which he mentions his recent experimental results that cause him to question the value of fluoridation and to deplore 'the regimentation of the American physicians and dentists (who) know nothing about fluoridation and say what they are ordered to say.' I believe this is one of many examples where a little learning is a dangerous thing, and where health may be injured and science brought to disrepute by the incautious and premature application to public health of insufficiently investigated procedures. Enthusiasm to apply the fruits of research is laudable, but eagerness must be tempered with wisdom, which includes having all the relevant facts available."

The article concludes with a plea for more research into questions pertaining to nutrition.

CHAPTER 200

When and How Much to Eat

Although in times past it was considered healthful to gorge oneself at meals, we know well today that leaving the table still just a little hungry is beneficial, especially for those of us who are overweight. Of course, how much you should eat depends a great deal on what you are eating. There is probably no such thing as eating too much of assorted fresh raw fruits and vegetables. But even a few tablespoons of rich desserts or starchy concoctions made of white sugar or white flour are "too much." And, of course, even one piece of candy is always "too much."

One point, first of all, is pretty well agreed on, that breakfast is essential to good work. However, it has been found that a light breakfast, supplying 25 per cent of the daily caloric needs, is more helpful than a heavier one supplying 40 per cent.

As to the mid-day meals, the aftereffects of a heavy lunch don't need description or scientific proof—we all crave those 30 winks. Here again, light eating appears to be the best formula for good work. R. C. Hutchinson, writing in *Nutrition Abstracts and Reviews,* Vol. 22, 283 (1952), found a definite decrease in production during the first hour after lunch when a full meal had been eaten.

D. A. Laird, D. Deland, H. Drexel, and K. Riemer, in the *Journal of the American Dietetic Association,* Vol. 11 p. 411 (1936), found that a heavy mid-day meal is also harmful to certain kinds of mental work. Over a period of 6 days, the effects of light and heavy meals were compared. Tests for memory of new addresses, speed and accuracy of addition, etc., as well as feelings of fatigue after the light lunch showed that there were 70 per cent fewer lapses of attention and that there was about a 25 per cent increase in mental quickness.

Another point in the discussion against heavy noon meals relates to those engaged in hard physical labor, such as coal miners, who also must be in a crouched position a good deal of the time. Bulky meals are considered unwise, as they hamper movement and do not provide the high energy requirements.

Unfortunately, there are no reports on exactly how "small" these meals should be. It is assumed that each person can find out through experience what is best for himself and how much he requires.

Additional Vitamins for Energy

Though not too much experimentation has been done on the value of additional vitamins to the well-balanced diet, it has been stated by G. Bourne, in the *British Journal of Nutrition,* Vol. 2, p. 261 (1948-49), that an athlete, requiring 15 times the average amount of thiamin, a B vitamin, would probably be unable to obtain this amount from natural foods. He would have to eat over 14 pounds of whole meal bread or nearly twice this amount of lean meat. The same may apply to other vitamins, such as riboflavin, niacin and vitamin C.

We think this statement invites comment. We are told that an athlete requires 15 times as much thiamin as someone who is not an athlete. And let us assume that this applies to other important vitamins as well—riboflavin, niacin and vitamin C. Perhaps someone doing very difficult mental work may require 15 times the average amount of thiamin, too. Someone who has great official responsibility, someone who makes many public appearances, a housewife beset with a thousand tasks and the care of a family of children—do not all of these individuals use up as much energy during an average day as an athlete may use only during training and performance periods? So is it not evident that we all need food supplements in addition to our meals—just for energy, if for no other reason!

From the amazing findings of B. H. Ershoff, M.D., writing in the medical publication called *Proceedings of the Society of Experimental Biology and Medicine,* for July, 1951, there would seem to be little question about the value of adding another substance to the diet of those doing strenuous work. This substance Dr. Ershoff found to be desiccated liver. In his experiments he found that a group of rats which were given 10 per cent desiccated liver, in addition to a basic diet, grew 15 per cent more than the group given none. He also found that when placed in a drum of water the group given desiccated liver was still able to swim at the end of two hours, while those without the liver gave up after an average of 13.3 minutes. This evidence would certainly seem to bear some weight in the discussion of the merits of the addition of energy-giving products to the diet.

Then, too, a teaspoon of wheat germ oil taken in conjunction with exercise has been shown to increase men's physical capacity and endurance by as much as 51.5 per cent, according to experiments performed in the University of Illinois Physical Fitness Laboratory. Wheat germ oil proved consistently effective in all the experiments done in the laboratory where men run on a treadmill until they drop, and undergo other tests of physical capacity while doctors measure heart action, oxygen consumption, blood pressure and other body functions.

Time Between Meals

We all know what it feels like to be hungry, and, if you watch yourself closely, you'll probably be able to see that you don't accomplish as much as late noon approaches, and—if you're the type you may become "cranky" about this time. The connection between your state of mind and these hunger pangs isn't just imaginary.

A number of experiments have been made on the effect of hunger contractions on concentration and efficiency. Hutchinson made two experiments in this line, the results of which indicated clearly that food is definitely an aid to good work when the stomach is empty. In one experiment he used 69 government officials doing various kinds of office work. He divided them into four groups, two for the experiment in the late morning hours, two in the late afternoon hours. The first had not eaten for at least 4 hours, and therefore their stomachs could be assumed to be empty. Half of this group, on one day, was given two sandwiches and hot tea and then given a paper and pencil test. The other half took the test on empty stomachs. The next day the groups were reversed. The tests, which were marked statistically, showed that the food produced a one per cent increase in scores of the tests. However, the tests given in the afternoon, when the time since lunch was less than 3 hours, showed no significant differences, thus showing that food does not appear to have any effect when the stomach is not empty.

There have been other significant experiments showing the relation of food and hunger contractions to nervousness. Laird, Leviton and Wilson, in the *Medical Journal Record,* Volume 134, p. 494 (1913), wrote of using 53 nervous children in an experiment to see the relationship of long periods between meals and lack of calcium, and nervousness. The children were divided into 3 groups: one played with toys, the second was given a half pint of milk to delay hunger contractions and the third was given a half pint of milk containing a food concentrate to provide added calcium. After two weeks, it was found that all 3 groups had improved: the first a little because of the extra attention it received, the second improved much more and the last group showed even twice the improvement of that of the group given the milk alone. Their conclusion is obvious: nervousness can be reduced by avoiding extreme hunger between breakfast and lunch. Of course, the experiment also shows the very beneficial activity of calcium in preventing nervousness.

A similar experiment is described by M. E. Keister in the *Journal of the American Dietetic Association,* Vol. 26, p. 25 (1950), in which pineapple juice and water were given to children, with the result that those receiving the juice showed less irritability and tension during the late hours of the morning. It was not proved whether it was the nourishment or the delay of hunger that produced the good effects.

From these experiments, as well as a number of others, it became clear that long periods between meals may result in lack of concentration, irritability and tension.

[752]

CHAPTER 201

How Food Affects Your Work

We all have some pet notion about what makes us work well; be it the mid-morning pick-me-up of coffee and doughnuts, a chocolate bar or a good heavy meal. But, according to tests and experiments made on the relation of food to work accomplishment, the merit in most of these theories comes more from habit or psychological reasons than the actual relation of nutrition to energy. Of course, we all do vary to some extent in our food requirements, according to our weight and type of activity and other factors, and it is impossible to say point-blank the exact amount and type of nourishment any one of us requires. It is also impossible to conduct controlled laboratory-type experiments with human beings in their work conditions, as can be done with animals, which give clear-cut, unquestionable conclusions applying to everyone. However, general over-all standards can be found which take into account the variation between people.

Calorie Requirements

First of all, and probably most easily determined, is the number of calories needed daily for men and women in different types of activity. A chart prepared by the Food and Nutrition Board of the National Research Council in 1948 recommends the following calorie and protein intake for men and women.

	Calories	Protein
Man (154 lbs.)		
Sedentary	2400	70 gms.
Physically active	3000	70 gms.
With heavy work	4500	70 gms.
Woman (123 lbs.)		
Sedentary	2000	60 gms.
Moderately active	2400	60 gms.
Very active	3000	60 gms.

When deciding the activity group to which a person belongs, employment is not the only factor to be considered. A worker's total number of hours in which he is employed is only about 20 per cent of the total number of hours in a week. The rest of the time is spent in sleep (about 30 per cent), and leisure activities (about 50 per cent). The leisure time may often consist of more and longer strenuous activity than the hours at work. For example, a desk worker may spend much "after-hours" time doing heavy gardening or wood chopping or home repairs, which may add up to greater expense of energy than that of the worker employed in heavy manual labor. The latter often tends to spend his leisure time in some quiet, inactive occupation, such as listening to the radio, watching television, reading, etc. So actually he may spend more time in quiet or sedentary activity than the office worker.

The activity of a housewife is more easily gauged, as her duties are pretty much the same 7 days a week. Contrary to the views of some husbands, the energy required for her daily work is often greater and more consistent than that of many factory workers even, so her calorie requirements must be geared accordingly.

Protein Requirements

The table above shows that the protein requirements for all activity groups are the same. Backing up this statement, Darling, Johnson, Pitts, Consolazio and Robinson, who wrote of their findings in the *Journal of Nutrition*, Vol. 28, p. 273 (1944), made an investigation of the effect of various protein diets on 24 young men employed in work ranging from truck driving, road mending and forestry, to kitchen, laundry and office work. After a period of two weeks on normal diets, the men were divided into 3 groups, one receiving a low protein diet, the second a high protein diet and the third remaining on the original diet as the control. They were tested at regular periods, but at the end of the experiment there was no significant difference in their physical fitness.

However, Kraut and Lehman, writing in *Biochemische Zeitschrift*, Vol. 319, p. 428 (1949), in their investigation of the protein requirements of 3 Hungarian coal miners, whose work conditions were more severe, did find that, though the amounts of protein required for heavy and light work were about the same, when the protein was reduced below the required amount there was a definite reaction in the form of falling off in work capacity, depression and lack of cooperation. When the amount of protein was again raised, these conditions disappeared. It has also been found that a diet must provide the sufficient number of calories for the protein to be of value.

Fat and Carbohydrate Requirements

Though the amount of fat needed in the diet has not been calculated definitely, the Food and Nutrition Board of the National Research Council advises that 20 to 25 per cent of the total calories for a person of average activity should be fat, and that for a very active person requiring the highest number of calories it should be from 30 to 35 per cent fat. However, there tend to be problems of digestion if the amount of fat in the diet is too great.

As to the relative merits of a normal diet, a high carbohydrate diet or a high fat diet, in relation to muscular efficiency, it was found by E. Simonson (writing in *Proceedings of the Nutrition Symposium* of the National Vitamin Foundation, New York, 1951) that the high carbohydrate diet produced better results. Other experiments have added to this that men were able to work two to three times longer on a high carbohydrate diet than on a high fat diet. It was also found that by taking sugar, either before or during work, men were able to work longer, though the experimenters, E. H. Christensen and O. Hansen, writing in *Skandinavisches Archiv fur Physiologie*, Vol. 81, p. 172 (1939) could give no reason.

Contradicting this latter theory of the benefit of sugar, however, are the findings in 1931 of T. M. Carpenter and E. L. Fox, writing in *Arbeits-*

physiologie, Vol. 4, p. 570 (1931). They came to the conclusion that the intake of 50 grams of sugar, glucose or fructose, or sucrose and galactose, resulted in no significant difference in work efficiency.

Many readers are well aware of the fact that taking sugar may give a sudden spurt of energy, because it raises the blood sugar almost at once. But it also causes the blood sugar to drop later on far below what it should be, which would, of course, have a bad effect on efficiency of work. Recent findings about low blood sugar indicate without any doubt the advisability of a high protein diet with as few starchy and sweet foods as possible.

CHAPTER 202

A Revolution in Nutrition?

By J. I. Rodale

About the middle of December, 1956, I paid a visit to Dr. Peter Sammartino, President of Fairleigh-Dickinson University, with campuses at Rutherford and Teaneck, New Jersey. I wanted to meet this man who was so courageously pioneering new ideas in nutrition at this fast growing institution. It was organized in 1941 with 153 students. Today (1957) it numbers 7,821 students, and has a campus of 64 acres valued at $5,000,000. Although I had wanted to see Dr. Sammartino for a long time, what sparked the visit was the acquisition by the university of a farm of 256 acres in Chester, New Jersey, where food is to be raised for the college by the organic method; that is, with organic matter and rock minerals as the fertilizers, instead of the usual chemicals. In fact, title to the farm, by coincidence, was taken on the day of the visit.

I had known for a long time that Dr. Sammartino was slowly introducing new health ideas in his university. No candy or carbonated beverages are permitted to be sold on the campus, in spite of lamentations from the students, and complaint letters, sometimes insulting, from candy and soft drink dealers.

Periodic campaigns are conducted for full breakfasts. In one dormitory where heavier breakfasts were introduced, illness was greatly reduced. Dormitory students can have, without charge, brewer's yeast in their orange juice and milk. Incidentally, Dr. Sammartino does not know about our campaign against citrus foods and dairy products. We had quite a discussion about these two kinds of foods, and Dr. Sammartino, who seems to have an open mind, promised to investigate them thoroughly.

Food Supplements For Students And Faculty

It is planned to make available free cod liver oil mixed in orange juice one evening a week. "This candle will probably burn very low," remarked Dr. Sammartino. Instead, why not give them halibut liver oil perles? They are so easy to take. They should be taken every day. Fruit and yogurt desserts are stressed.

The university has also introduced a health candy that is prepared in such a manner that the harmful effects of ordinary candy are eliminated. So that the faculty can properly lead the students, Dr. Sammartino has stressed good nutrition for the faculty. But some of the latter feel that they are too healthy to bother with any new-fangled ideas. Some do things merely to make Sammartino happy and to alleviate his administrative woes. A good percentage, however, has really taken good nutrition seriously. They have already had actual cases of people who were practically ill with exhaustion who are now abounding in good health.

The university supplies vitamin supplements (multiple vitamins, B complex, and multiple minerals) at the cost of one dollar a month, but these are the synthetic type of vitamins. After Dr. Sammartino becomes exposed to our system of natural food-type vitamins, I am sure that he will adopt them as the only type of vitamin for Fairleigh-Dickinson.

Organic Method Used

As much organically grown food as possible is purchased for the university. They even advertised for chickens and eggs from hens raised on the ground, and not produced in factories. Wheat germ is used everywhere —in cereals, in meat loaf, in veal cutlets and in many other foods. And as far as possible, cooking methods are used which prevent vitamin losses.

Naturally, there are many other things that could be done, but this is a wonderful beginning. The difficulty is that they are running contrary to established habits of poor nutrition and patterns ingrained by billion dollar advertising. These are Dr. Sammartino's own words. But they *are* beginning to see gains. The high schools in the area are encouraged to prohibit school sales of candy and soda pop. Each individual case of better health encourages a score of others to follow the path of nutritional righteousness.

At Fairleigh-Dickinson a new candle has been lit. However, most of their students commute to classes and it is more difficult to control their eating habits. Those students who live at the university, however, come a little more actively under the nutrition program.

What interests me a great deal is the farm that the university has acquired to grow foods organically. Dr. Sammartino feels that they will do as much research on organic farming as his limited budget would allow, but when you consider that the farm will furnish healthy food to a few hundred students, whose gradually improving health will be the proof of its superiority, we can be sure that this new experiment in collegiate nutrition will come graphically to the attention of the entire country.

The dental school of this university should be the means of sending out thousands of dentists armed with the knowledge of the newer nutrition, to teach it to their patients and thus to raise the general health level of the community.

It was an inspired meeting and a great privilege to meet Dr. Sammartino. You rarely see a man these days so full of passionate fervor and possessed of so much energy to fight for good against great obstacles. The world will hear of the man and his university.

CHAPTER 203

Less Food—More Health

Could you get along on less than you eat each day? Chances are that you could, and that you'd be much healthier and live longer for the reduction. Imagine your daily diet short of all the extras and see how the remainder compares with the minimal allotment of food a human needs for survival. This minimum was set after much experiment by a League of Nations group called The Technical Committee on Nutrition. When World War II was becoming a reality in the late 1930's, the specter of food shortages and starvation was close behind. It was important for the world to be told what its people must have to exist with reasonable health and without slowly starving to death. The report stated that one could healthfully survive on less than 20 ounces of nutritious food per day.

Now we are not advocating that everyone embark on a Spartan diet that will barely sustain life, for eating good food is one of the pleasures of life, and in a land of plenty there is no need for us to live on the verge of starvation. Still, it is obvious that those of us who put away several times the daily minimum are forcing our bodies to take much more food than they need! When we do this the body is made to handle more than was originally intended, and a strain is bound to result in some quarter.

This truth was apparent to that wonderful wise man of the fifteenth century, Louis Cornaro. This man turned from a life of every kind of excess to an austere regime which regained his health for him and enabled him to live to a ripe old age, vigorous and alert to the end. One very important part of Cornaro's code was his limited intake of foods. He allowed himself 28 ounces of food per day, 14 of which were wine. The remainder was eaten in the course of 4 meals throughout the day, thereby lowering the amount of food the stomach must deal with at any one time. He was fond of saying, "What we leave after making a hearty meal does us more good than what we have eat." Cornaro lived to the age of 98.

Proof of Cornaro's Ideas

The experiments of Dr. Clive McCay of Cornell University show results which concur with the theories of Cornaro regarding proper amounts of food. In tests detailed in *Newsweek* for October 16, 1940, he found that the life span of rats could be nearly doubled by feeding them only half the regular ration of calories until they reach maturity, when they are switched to a full diet. Rats who were fed in this way lived for an average of 1068 days, while their fellow rats who were on a full diet averaged only 600 days in this world. Aside from increased longevity, the lightly fed rats also showed healthier teeth, with less cavities and breakage than the rats on a normal diet. In later experiments Dr. McCay proved that diseases of the lungs and middle ear were remarkably reduced in rats placed on restricted diets. Even our friend the worm shows a response to a restricted diet that is phenomenal. Charles M. Child in *Senescence and Rejuvenescence* tells us that worms living on plentiful food rations pass through all of their normal life cycles in 3 weeks, while worms kept on smaller diets remain young and prolong this time to 3 years!

Many of us can remember when a ration book was as important as money. In some European countries a ration book was as important as life itself. According to Professor Axel Strom of the Norwegian Health Association, severe rationing did show its beneficial effects. In Norwegian towns in which rationing was severe during the German occupation, mortality from arteriosclerosis and inflammation of the muscular walls of the heart was found to be appreciably lower than in towns in which rationing measures were more haphazard and supplementary food was more available.

Cancer, Colds And Epilepsy

Boris Sokoloff, M.D., Ph.D., a famous cancer researcher, in his book, *Cancer, New Approaches, New Hope,* showed much concern over the relationship between cancer and heavy eating. One of his most revealing tests was made with mice who had been specially bred for their predisposition to breast cancer. These mice were divided into two separate groups, with one group allowed to eat as much as it wanted (about 3 grams per day), the second group limited to two grams per day. Both, however, ate the same kind of food. The breast cancer tendency which was bred into the mice showed itself in more than 50 per cent of the mice on unrestricted diets. In those mice limited to two grams of food per day there was not a single cancerous growth, even though these mice had been chosen because of their tendency toward developing the disease. The same results were recorded time and time again with mice prone to skin cancer, liver cancer, lung cancer, etc. In each case of diet restriction no tumor ever appeared.

An important aspect of this series of experiments is the fact that the tendency toward cancer seemed to disappear if diet restrictions were made during youth and middle age. Middle age is the time when a cancer is most likely to appear. If the diet is especially restricted then, the subject can look forward to a cancer-free old age. Sounds like good advice, does it

[758]

not? Why shouldn't humans profit by this demonstration? If cutting down will help us avoid cancer, by all means, let's cut down!

If a cold should ever penetrate your guard of vitamin C it might be well to recall the results obtained by Drs. Andrew Kuna and Benjamin Battenberg in their experiments with colds as they are affected by a lower food intake. Fifty well-fed rats were studied after they had been injected with cold germs. Twenty-one of the 50 got nothing to eat for 36 hours, while the rest were fed a regular diet. Blood samples taken at the end of 36 hours showed twice as many leucocytes (bacteria-destroying white blood cells) in the starved group as in the well-fed group, and they killed 3 times as many cold bacteria. It was noted that the ravenous appetite the leucocytes have for germs lasts only for the first 36 to 49 hours, with the action dwindling to nothing in 5 or 6 days.

Where the problem of epilepsy exists, the report of the *Journal of the American Medical Association* (July 10, 1948) will be of interest. This report showed that fasting reduces the incidence of epileptic seizures in those who face this problem. This effect is attributed to the acidosis attendant to fasting.

Getting the Most from Food

Strangely enough, scientists agree that the less food one eats the greater the nutriment the body extracts from it. When it is given superfluous amounts of food, the body is so busy juggling the extras that its efficiency in handling the necessary foods is impaired. It is certainly foolish to overeat when we know that the body cannot use the food and that it might do us harm.

The question arises, why do we feel the need to eat more than our body needs? The answer lies in what we eat. Stuffing ourselves with a large quota of sweets and white flour products will not still the body's cry for food. The body interprets "food" as nourishment, nutrients, vital minerals and vitamins. If the food you eat does not contain these, the hungry feeling will be with you shortly after a meal. However, in smaller amounts of healthful food the needs of the body are met through these nutritional tools for growth and repair and the pangs of hunger will be banished. You will eat less and be less hungry. You won't feel the need of the pound-adding, between-meal snack, nor will you stuff yourself at mealtime. You will be eating as nature intended you to eat—with satisfaction and discretion, and without overindulgence.

Are you due for a cut in food consumption? Are you sure that a little less food, with the accompanying reduction in calories wouldn't bring you a little more health and a lot more years?

CHAPTER 204

Good Nutrition Is Even More
Essential if You Are Ill

A highly significant contribution to our thinking about health in relation to diet was made by Dr. Tom Spies of Birmingham, Alabama, in the June 7, 1958, issue of the *Journal of the American Medical Association.* Dr. Spies was one of our country's outstanding authorities on nutrition, a man who worked tirelessly, patiently and understandingly with patients who came to his clinic.

He believed that good nutrition was the best preventive of disease. He believed that, while there are few "classic" cases of malnutrition walking around in America today, "the so-called typical or mild case is the usual one." His aim was to help these patients back to good health and he accomplished wonders by giving them vitamin and mineral supplements. But he also knew that vitamins and minerals by themselves do not constitute a good diet and he spent a great deal of time talking to his patients about their diets and helping them to plan meals, so that they would form good food habits and would not, as soon as his treatment was over, slip right back into the same mistakes that originally made them sick.

"In a series of 914 consecutive patients admitted to the Nutrition Clinic of the Hillman Hospital, Birmingham, the presenting symptom in 329 of these patients was soreness of the mouth and tongue," he told us. Although this symptom would seem to indicate vitamin deficiency, it was not possible, he said, simply to prescribe a vitamin and let it go at that. He said, "Working many years in direct contact with the problem has taught us that dietary deficiency disorders arising from a lack of the vitamin B complex do not occur singly but as mixed deficiency diseases. The pattern of these disorders is different from person to person and even among individual members of the same family who may eat at the same table." Nothing will succeed in curing these patients unless the damaged tissues receive the essential nutrients needed to restore them.

Dr. Spies for 20 years studied the effect of "hidden hunger," or substandard nutrition, on the growth of infants and children. He believed that what happened to an individual during this period may determine to a considerable extent his health later in life.

The things that go on in one's body are so integrated and so dependent upon an adequate supply of food essentials, he said, that an absence or a deficiency in any one food factor may impair the efficiency of a whole chain of reactions, each of which affects the health of a child.

[760]

Diet and Mental Health

As an example, he related the case history of a young girl who was brought to the clinic at the age of 7 because she was nervous, had little appetite, didn't play with other children. She was given the prescription of the usual good diet and food supplements as well. Researchers at the clinic were meanwhile studying her growth with various tests, including X-ray. A year later the child had typhoid fever from which she recovered without much difficulty. During her illness she continued to take a good diet and all her food supplements. However, so great apparently were the demands made on her metabolism by her illness that an interruption of the whole nutritional process could be seen in X-rays of her bones. A defect appeared in the bone showing clearly just when the illness began and how seriously it affected the little girl.

After a number of years of good nutrition and supplements, another X-ray showed that the defect had healed completely. Would it have healed had the good nutrition been lacking? Obviously not. And who knows what dread disease, acute or chronic, might have attacked this patient much later in life as an indirect result of the typhoid fever incident! You could not say that the typhoid fever had caused the disease directly. But the interruption of normal bodily processes which occurs during disease can apparently lead to much more serious disorders later in life, especially if the quality of nutrition is not sustained at a high level.

So, according to these findings, the person who is sick should pay far more attention to diet and diet supplements than the well person, for the drain on the patient's body, the stress and strain of fighting the disease and finally pulling through apparently create the demand for far more in the way of nutrients.

"The study of minor aches and pains is a difficult task," said Dr. Spies. "The breadth of the field, the lack of clearly defined disease manifestations and mechanisms, the almost complete lack of leads makes the medical approach difficult. We find that many persons with minor aches and pains sum up their problem by saying that they have not had any fun in years and that they can barely drag themselves around. They have vague pains, and perhaps even more difficult to endure is their great fatigue. Because of the vague nature of their complaints, such as 'nervousness,' 'forgetfulness,' 'I'm all worn out,' 'aching in my joints and muscles,' they often are called neurotics and usually considered nuisances."

How many of us does that sentence describe! And how much of this unhappiness and ill health would respond to good nutrition!

Mental Health and Good Nutrition

Dr. Spies was particularly concerned with mental health and its relation to nutrition. Bizarre mental disorders are sometimes symptoms of pellagra which is a disease of vitamin B deficiency. Dr. Spies told us how he and his colleagues treated the mental symptoms of pellagra patients. Then they began to wonder about patients who had similar symptoms but did not have fully-developed cases of pellagra. These patients suffered from things like

[761]

hysteria, anxiety, nervousness, depression. They disliked bright lights, bright colors, noises, odors and foods they had once liked. They were jittery, restless, tense. They constantly expected something terrible to happen. Do you know people like that?

"I could not accept the concept that their brains were irreparably damaged; it seemed that the cells were waiting listlessly and would function again at full efficiency when we gave them the required nutrients," said Dr. Spies. He discovered that there was an alteration in the content of lactose and lactic acid in the blood leaving and entering the brains of these patients. He discovered that in patients who lacked B vitamins there was a *60 per cent decrease in the metabolism of the brain*—that is, the rate at which the brain could build foods into cells and energy.

Dr. Spies told us that his group of researchers learned long ago that the emotional disorders of older persons can sometimes be overcome or relieved through good nutrition. He was talking about such troubles as these: Older people come to feel useless; they resist changes and their habits become fixed. Their personalities may become disorganized and their judgment poor. They may develop insomnia and may become disoriented as to time and place. A diagnosis of hardening of the arteries of the brain is not much help to patients like these for this implies that little can be done to improve their condition. Proper nutrition can help, said Dr. Spies.

Among young and old alike, symptoms arise from damaged tissues, he continued. Protecting or repairing tissues will be held up if the tissues are not properly nourished. "Give them what they need and they will muster strength and come back. We do not have enough information, of course, to know all they need. The science of nutrition has only scratched the surface, but it has made some progress toward a real solution of mental illnesses."

Speaking of the tranquilizer drugs, he said that he felt they have helped greatly in the treatment of mental illness. But, he said, we must realize that there is, under certain conditions, a loss of nutrients in a patient who is being given tranquilizers. The best way to use them is to make sure there is a sound pattern of adequate nutrition present at the same time to protect the nervous system of the patient. Vitamin therapy does not replace tranquilizers and tranquilizers should not replace vitamin therapy. They should always be used together when there seems to be a need for tranquilizers.

When to Take Medicine

One final point which Dr. Spies made seems to us important because it throws light on the knotty problem of when one can justify the taking of medicine. Dr. Spies told us that many times the sufferer from chronic diseases is in such a condition that he cannot eat a good diet. The arthritis patient, for example, may be in such pain that he has lost his appetite completely. He may be so incapacitated by stiffness that he cannot earn money to buy food. He may be so depressed by the long years of suffering that he may not care whether he eats. He may not be able to eat because of stiff jaws. He may have nausea and vomiting and hence be unable to eat.

In cases like these certainly it seems to be wise to take drugs which will give temporary relief—even drugs like aspirin and cortisone. But just as soon as the patient is able to eat, every effort should be made to give him a highly nourishing diet and an abundance of food supplements. Otherwise, as soon as he stops taking the drugs he will be right back where he started. But if he steadily builds his body tissues with nourishment *while he is taking the drugs,* he has a good chance to improve steadily and to need less and less of the drugs to control the disease.

In his summary Dr. Spies said, ". . . that excellent nutrition is basic, that disease is chemical in its origin, that the body cells can fight back to an amazing degree, and that our tissues when properly replenished, can come into their own again." An encouraging word for us all.

CHAPTER 205

The Nourishment a Baby Needs

New parents are always concerned about the amount and kinds of food to give a baby in his first year. How does one know if the baby is getting enough to eat? Is what he eats rich enough in vitamins and minerals to give his bones, nerves and muscles the good start you know is necessary? All of these qualms are increased when parents compare notes with others to find that one doctor has recommended puréed fruits and vegetables at 3 months or earlier, while their own doctor is against solid foods for the first 6 months. Without any previous experience, first-time parents become convinced that either their child is being deprived of foods he desperately needs, or the other child is being grossly overfed.

Babies Survive Some Experimentation

Actually, the answer to this dilemma lies in the wonderful machinery for living with which every normally healthy baby is equipped. He stands up remarkably under the most devastating kinds of experimentation. In the *South African Medical Journal* (February, 1959), S. Levin, M.D., gives a slight history of the customs followed in feeding infants since the earliest days. Until the time of the Renaissance, many infants were breast-fed until the age of two or three years, often without any other form of nourishment. Some Greek writers talked of bread crumbs soaked in bone broth or vegetable broth. Generally, however, 6 months seems to be the age at which the babies of most civilizations had their diet augmented with some form of solid food, usually a gruel made of bread crumbs, barley, rice or oatmeal soaked in various fluids such as milk, water, broth, beer or wine.

Solid Food at Six Months

It is interesting to find that the instincts which prompted the addition of solid foods at the age of 6 months have been shown by later scientific observations to have a basis in filling the actual needs of the child. The iron content of breast milk is practically nil. When a child is born he comes into the world with a supply of iron in his system which will last about 6 months. After that time the baby should have some source for this mineral, outside of the milk he gets from his mother. Such a source is provided by the solids he begins to eat. Without this iron, anemia is a possible result in the second 6 months of the new baby's life.

Try a Banana First

To get back to the question of how soon a modern baby can and should be fed solids, we find that the trend is toward introducing such foods earlier and earlier. Doctor Levin writes that he allows his patients to introduce their babies to solid foods as early as 10 days after birth. Some babies seem to wolf down these new foods and others do not like them at all. If the latter situation should prevail, Dr. Levin tells the mothers to wait for 3 months or so, and try again. He advises that the mother try bananas first. They are seldom refused by the baby and are easy to digest, and easy to mash and give by spoon. If the baby takes to this food, Dr. Levin feels that the mother will have the confidence to try other foods such as soups, juices, puréed peaches, pears, prunes, peas, squash and avocado. By the age of 4 to 6 weeks Dr. Levin's babies are eating whole eggs and strained liver.

In defense of this policy of introducing solids to these tiny babies at such an early age, Dr. Levin remarks that milk is actually a solid disguised as a liquid. He tells us that gastric enzymes turn milk into solid clots before digestion, as can be seen if vomiting occurs sometime after feeding. Since this is the case, babies are really eating solids right from birth, so why not solids other than milk?

Are the babies any healthier for this early introduction to solids? *Northwest Medicine* (October, 1953) carries an article by F. H. Douglass that insists there is no advantage to the addition of solids to a baby's diet in the first 3 months of life. In the first place, he says, there are no enzymes to handle starches. Pancreatic amylase and phyatin (a saliva enzyme) are present in small or deficient amounts in the first two months of life. In the stomach free and total acids are not high until after one month. The article goes on to say that the addition to breast or formula milk of cereals, fruits, meats, vegetables and other substances in no way improves the health or well-being of the baby. It may traumatize the intestinal mucosa or even sensitize the infant to some protein products. Many believe that early feeding of complex foods is responsible for many of the allergies of today. . . . There is no reason to hurry; the infant's gastrointestinal tract must be trained and used within its limitations, if it is to act efficiently."

We are inclined to agree with Dr. Douglass. Often the introduction of solid foods to the infant's diet is prompted, not so much by a deep concern over whether or not the child is in need of such nourishment, but by a kind of a contest in which mothers unwittingly engage, to see which child starts doing what first. We believe this is a poor reason for chancing damage to intestinal walls or future allergy problems. Since most authorities are agreed that solids are not necessary for 6 months, and might not even be well tolerated before 3 months, it would seem to be wise to wait at least 3 months before introducing solid foods.

Mother's Milk Is "Just Right"

Of course, the liquid food of these first 3 months should be mother's milk, if at all possible. As has been said and proven by many doctors and scientists, it is the food that is most "right" for a baby. It is pure, always the right temperature, exactly the right formula, easy to digest and has the least chance of being exposed to infection. A breast-fed baby is almost never constipated.

All of the nutrients necessary to a full term, healthy infant under 6 months are contained in mother's milk. If the mother eats properly (salads, fresh fruit, vegetables, rose hips) her milk will be rich in vitamin C. She can also be sure of an adequate concentration of other vitamins in her milk, except for the vitamin D requirement, which will come from the sunshine her child should have.

Food Supplements? Yes Indeed!

What about mothers who cannot nurse their children for one reason or another? Do these babies need supplements? They do indeed. Whether or not the parents act on the suggestions for using soybean milk, instead of cow's or goat's milk, every opportunity should be taken to make the formula as rich in nutritional ingredients as possible. There are many ways of accomplishing this. For example, many formulas require that water be used. Why not save the water from cooked vegetables and use that, instead of water from the tap? Such water is rich in minerals and vitamins that have escaped from the food in cooking.

Another logical addition to the baby's formula is brewer's yeast. About a teaspoon put into the day's formula as it is being mixed adds mightily to the baby's vitamin B intake, and will help in keeping him generally contented and free of gastric disorders. Even if a residue of brewer's yeast is left in the bottle, most of the vitamins will still have been absorbed by the milk. For vitamin C, rose hips tablets can easily be crushed and added to the formula.

Once the formula is no longer necessary, these nutritive elements can be added to the juices or other liquids the child takes. Sometimes the mother finds it easier to put them in cereal or puréed fruits and vegetables. The important thing is to make sure supplements are included somehow.

Manufacturers Don't Hesitate, Why Should You?

Parents are often hesitant about adding nutrients to their baby's food, yet the manufacturers of foods prepared especially for babies add all sorts of synthetic vitamins, preservatives, salt and sugar without a qualm. Synthetic vitamin preparations are recommended by some doctors for use in the first week after birth. Why hesitate, then, to include natural food supplements rich in nutritional values we all need? Adelle Davis' book, *Let's Have Healthy Children,* carries several valuable and convincing chapters on this very subject. Reading them will make any parent wonder why he hesitated at all in giving his baby food supplements. The well-fortified baby will avoid many of the fevers, colds and other common illnesses of infancy; those he does contact will be taken in easy stride. He will sleep better, digest better and be happier. In short, he will be the baby you've hoped he would be.

CHAPTER 206

When Your Baby Begins to Feed Himself

A good many babies begin to want to feed themselves before they are a year old. If your baby wants to get hold of the spoon when you are feeding him, let him have a small spoon so he can "help." Of course his efforts will be a bother at first, but it pays to encourage a baby's desire to do things for himself. To refuse to let him try to use a spoon might make him turn away from what you are feeding him.

It will take him a long time to learn to get the spoon to his mouth right side up. At first, even though you pick out something for him to begin on that will cling to the spoon, like mashed potato, he'll get only a dab of food into his mouth. But learn to shut your eyes to the mess he makes. He will gradually make a go of it. If he wants to use his fingers instead of the spoon—and he will—all right.

Bananas, peas, diced cooked carrots, and chopped meat, for example, can all be eaten with his fingers. But if he gets to playing with his food, just squeezing it in his fingers or daubing it on his chair, it's time to put it out of reach. You may find he'll take a few more bites of what you've been feeding him, but his playing may mean he's had enough.

It will seem so much easier to keep on feeding him yourself that you may be tempted not to let him help. But if you don't let him help when he's eager to learn, he may lose that eagerness, and end up depending on you long after he could feed himself. (Having your mother feed you is a sure way of getting a lot of attention.) *The more concerned a mother is about "getting food into" a baby, the more finicky he often gets about what he'll eat.*

Toward the end of your baby's first year, you may notice a slowing down of his appetite. Don't let it disturb you. Remember, his rate of growth is slowing down, and he may not need as large amounts, in proportion, as he did when he was growing faster. Also, he may not need such frequent feedings as before. Urging food on a baby who eats less than you think he should is much more likely to start a problem than to make him eat more.

Variations in Appetite

Some babies are big eaters, some have small appetites. Some babies eat a big breakfast in proportion to other meals. Don't expect your baby to eat about the same amount at all 3 meals. Remember, he's an individual. The chances are you don't eat the same amount at each meal, either.

You will find, as well, that on some days your baby doesn't want as much to eat as usual. Babies are no different from grownups about being hungrier at one time than at another. If you remember that your baby isn't a little machine, you'll be less inclined to try to stuff into him the amount of food *you* have decided he should have. And if suddenly he begins to turn down a food he's liked before, lay off it for a few days. You may have over-done giving it to him, just because it was a food he took so readily.

The only way a baby can tell us he's tired of a food is by refusing it. Don't be afraid, when you offer him a different food, that you're spoiling him by giving in to his whim. His whim might get to be of the cast-iron kind if you tried to force the unwanted food on him. It's not "appeasing" a baby to offer him a change; it's only common sense.

Vegetables and cereals are the things babies get tiredest of. But there are so many kinds of both that it is easy to offer different ones often.

Your baby may not be able to feed himself entirely until he is 18 or 20 months old, or even older. But he can manage a good many things by the end of his first year. You may be able to leave him to eat part of the meal by himself, and go about your work nearby. If he eats in a high chair, be sure he has on a safety belt when you leave him alone. Otherwise, a baby can stand up and tip over almost before you've turned your back.

While he is learning to feed himself, your baby's meal may go pretty slowly, so a deep plate that fits over a container of warm water is a con-venience in keeping his food warm. Plastic dishes and cups help to prevent breakage. You can get rubber suction cups that hold a plate to the table.

Babies and young children often prefer to eat all of one thing before they start on another. You may find that when the baby is hungriest, serv-ing foods separately, and starting with the ones that aren't favorites works well. Trying to get babies to eat something they aren't fond of by mixing it with a well-liked food may work. But it may make the baby turn against the food he especially liked before. Alternating bites of less well-liked with other foods is another trick to try. Babies usually prefer foods served separately rather than mixtures.

Sometimes a baby's failure to eat as much as usual is the first sign he gives of coming down with a cold or other illness. If a baby's appetite sud-denly lessens, he should not be urged to eat. Offer him water or fruit juice while you wait to see if he gets over his loss of appetite, or if he shows signs of feeling miserable. By the second or third meal you can usually tell whether his lack of hunger was only temporary or whether he is sick, and needs to be seen by your doctor.

Some babies have very strong feelings about foods that are not smooth (like bits of skin in prune sauce), others shudder at slippery things like baked custard. If your baby shows some oddity of this sort you may as well avoid that type of food for awhile. You may make his objection stronger if you don't give him a chance to forget it. A little later he will probably take it more readily.

Babies turn away from certain foods sometimes because they see an older person refuse them. *Parents often have to learn to eat what they want their baby to like.*

A baby's food needs to be attractive. He has a right to object to cereal that's lumpy, or to a vegetable that is strong tasting from being cooked too long.

A baby can get into a habit of gagging or seeming to choke on certain foods if he happens to find that his mother gets excited when he does it. To keep him from resorting to this sort of thing to gain attention, take pains to act pleased about the things he does that you hope he'll repeat, and ignore any antics that may be put on for display.

Feeding Arrangements

When a baby becomes able to sit up well by himself, it is easier to have him sit on a chair than in your lap during his meals.

It takes less stooping on your part to feed him in a high chair, but he will use a low chair and little table much longer.

If you get a little table and chair, be sure that they are strong, as they will get hard wear. If at first the baby's feet don't reach the floor when he sits on his chair, let him rest them on a box or stool. A chair without arms pushes up to a table snugly. The height of the chair should be such that the baby may use his arms easily on the table when he feeds himself.

Tables are on the market that have a built-in chair with a foot rest. They can be used for play, as well as for eating. If the table is made so that it can be raised when the mother feeds the baby, it is a great convenience.

If you use a high chair, be sure to get one that has legs spread wide enough apart at the bottom so that it will not tip over. It should have a footrest, and a safety belt to keep the baby from falling.

One advantage of a high chair is that a baby can feel he is one of the family, once he is old enough to have some of his meals when they do. Even though he may not be eating quite the same variety of foods that the others are, he likes being with them at some meals.

Reprinted from the book, *Infant Care*, Children's Bureau Publication No. 8, 1951, published by the United States Department of Health, Education and Welfare.

[768]

CHAPTER 207

Essential Nutrition in Geriatrics

By W. Coda Martin, M.D.

It is in geriatrics that physicians are mostly brought face to face with medicine's greatest unsolved problem, that of the degenerative diseases in elderly patients. While infectious diseases may be said to have been basically conquered and while as a result the average life expectancy has been raised to 65 years, two painful facts remain: 1. To judge by such figures as those of rejections for military service in World War II (50 per cent unfit for armed services), the average health of the population is becoming worse rather than better. 2. The incidence of degenerative diseases is increasing by leaps and bounds.

Are we prolonging men's lives only to leave them at the mercy of cancer, arteriosclerosis, liver disease, arthritis, and heart disease? Can these and similar diseases be averted by preventive treatment, or even relieved after they have developed?

While the average physician today regards diet as a secondary factor in the treatment and prevention of these degenerative diseases, the author believes that a study of the findings of biochemists will show that a large share of this type of disease is the end result of prolonged malnutrition and can be averted by early adoption of an adequate diet.

Is our present diet so defective that the wealthiest and most bountifully fed people in the world are actually starving in the midst of plenty? The United States Plant, Soil, and Nutrition Laboratory at Cornell has pointed out that some of the principal truck-and-fruit-growing regions of our eastern seaboard are so deficient in essential minerals that the actual nutritive content of the "protective" foods which they supply to our great cities may be questionable.

In 1840, one ounce of genuine whole bread made of stone-ground wheat contained 20 units of vitamin B_1. In 1950, one ounce of white bread contained only 5 units of B_1 before the addition of synthetic thiamin. The Food and Nutrition Board of the National Research Council considers an intake of 1.5 to 2 milligrams (445-660 International Units) of B_1 per day as necessary for maintenance of good health.

The refinement of white bread has removed not only vitamin B_1 but other known and unknown dietary factors such as proteins, other parts of the B-complex, vitamin E and essential minerals. There has been added to what is called "enriched" bread only synthetic B_1, riboflavin, niacin, and iron. This is replacing only a part of the whole and cannot be expected to give the complete nutritional protection as the natural whole grain bread. Other grain food and cereals including polished rice are subjected to similar drastic processing.

Doctors Williams and Spies, who studied diets in various parts of the United States, state in their book, *Vitamin B₁*, published in 1938, that there is much sameness in diets all over the country. This sameness is largely in the enormous consumption of nonvitamin, nonmineral foods composed of white flour and white sugar. The average diet furnishes a vitamin B_1 intake of from 200-300 International Units, which is just enough to prevent beriberi and pellagra. To have the optimum benefit from vitamin B_1, a person of 150 pounds weight should have a daily intake of 750-1000 International Units.

The presence of mouth, teeth, and gum diseases in school children and adults needs no confirmation by laboratory test of the fact that nutritional deficiency is universal in civilized countries. It is also obvious that this condition does not improve with age. Doctor Alice Bernheim has shown that the average person's usual diet, being composed of refined foods, does not contain the needed amount of calcium. This deficiency is universal in all civilized countries. The figures from the *Food and Drug Journal*, which keeps an accurate record of the export and import of food products into New York City, showed that the food intake of the population measured only 25 per cent for the vitamin- and mineral-containing protective foods as against 75 per cent of devitaminized foods composed of white flour and white sugar.

If such depleted diets continue over a period of years the body will develop tissue changes that will inevitably lead to degenerative diseases.

What good nutrition can accomplish is shown in a report by Dr. Robert McCarrison. In 1918, speaking of the Hunza people in India, he writes: "My own personal experience provides an example of a race unsurpassed in perfection of physique and in freedom from diseases in general. Amongst these people the span of life is extraordinarily long; and such services as I was able to render them during the 7 years I spent in their midst were confined chiefly to the treatment of accidental lesions, the removal of senile cataract, plastic operations for granular eyelids, or the treatment of maladies wholly unconnected with food supply. These people are long-lived, vigorous in youth and age, capable of great endurance and enjoy a remarkable freedom from disease in general. . . . During the period of my association with these people, I never saw a case of asthenic dyspepsia, or gastric or duodenal ulcer, appendicitis, mucous colitis, or of cancer."

Later, McCarrison made experiments in which rats were given the type of diet eaten by the Hunza people. This consisted of chapatties, or flat bread, made of whole meal flour lightly smeared with butter, sprouted pulses or legumes, fresh, raw carrots and fresh, raw cabbage *ad libitum* (as much as wanted), unpasteurized whole milk and soured milk, a small ration of meat with bones once a week, and an abundance of water. This food was grown on special soil prepared with organic fertilizers. No chemical fertilizers, insecticides or pesticide sprays have ever been used on the soil.

In this experiment 1,189 rats were watched from birth to the twenty-seventh month, an age in the rat which corresponds to that of about 55 years in man. His report states: "During the past two and a quarter years there has been no case of illness in this 'universe' of albino rats, no deaths from natural causes in the adult stock, and but for a few accidental deaths, no infantile mortality. Both clinically and at post mortem examination this stock has been shown to be remarkably free from disease."

McCarrison then took the customary inadequate diet of the poorer peoples of Bengal and Madras, consisting of polished rice, pulses or legumes, vegetables, condiments, and a little milk. He fed 2,243 rats on this diet and they developed all the diseases suffered by these people. They got diseases of every organ of the body, eyes, nose, ears, lungs, heart, stomach, intestines, kidneys, bladder, reproductive organs, blood, special glands, and nerves.

Later, McCarrison gave a set of rats the diet of the poorer classes in England, consisting of white bread, margarine, sweetened tea, boiled vegetables, white sugar, tinned meats and jams. He reports: "On this diet, not only did the rats grow badly but they developed what one might call rat-neurasthenia. They were nervous and apt to bite their attendants, they lived unhappily together and by the sixteenth day, they began to kill each other and eat the weaker ones amongst them." Because of this cannibalism in the rats, the experiment was discontinued.

This report shows the effect of various diets on experimental animals and humans. It reveals that foods grown on properly prepared soil, so that they contain adequate vitamins and minerals as well as complete proteins, will prevent degenerative diseases. The question then arises whether we can do anything to correct the pathological disease changes once they have developed. Recent experimental and clinical work shows that it is possible to control and retard some of these conditions and to prolong the life of the patient. This is true of liver dysfunction and its associated arteriosclerosis, hypercholesterolemia (excess of cholesterol in blood), and coronary disease. These conditions and many allied diseases of the human organism are recognized as being due to dietary deficiency, especially of the lipotropic factors (those that deal with fat), B-complex, and an excess intake of fat.

Morrison reviewed evidence that arteriosclerosis is a metabolic error and not the inevitable accompaniment of advancing age, and that it may be preventable. He maintained that arteriosclerosis develops through a triad based on 1. high cholesterol-high fat diet; 2. malfunction of the liver, involving disturbances in lipid (fatty substances) and lipoprotein metabolism, and 3. deficiencies and imbalances in endocrine function implicating the thyroid and sex hormones. He advised a program of low fat, low cholesterol diet and lipotropic therapy, choline, inositol combination and where indicated, estrogen and androgen hormones for coronary artery disease. Under this treatment mortality was reduced to one-third, angina pains decreased or disappeared, and patients returned to work or normal activities with a feeling of well-being, optimism, and better morale.

Doctor Boris Sokoloff states that not long ago it was believed that longevity of an animal or man is determined chiefly by heredity, but now scientists are placing greater emphasis on nutrition as a paramount factor in the prolongation of life in man and animal alike. The results of Mc-

Carrison's experiments showing that diet influenced the life span of man and rats have been dramatically confirmed recently by C. McCay and M. Crowell of Cornell University. They were able to double the normal span of life in rats by keeping them from birth on a low calory diet rich in vitamins. In other words diets high in protective foods and low in refined foods, depleted of their nutrient factors, improve the health and prolong the life span.

Henry C. Sherman believes that "old age can be deferred and man's life span lengthened." He further states: "The indicated improvement of the adult life expectation from 70 to 77 years is apparently well within the scientific probabilities for those who use the newer knowledge of nutrition in their daily food habits, beginning early enough in life. It is not merely a longer lease of life that is offered, but a life cycle both longer and lived on a higher plane of positive health, efficiency, and happiness throughout." Sherman stated many times that the larger the percentage of total calories in the form of protective foods, the smaller was the percentage of failure in the preservation of the characteristics of youth.

It is then apparent that when we learn to eat day after day, month after month, year after year, all the essential nutrients, a higher degree of health will result and there will be a marked decrease in the degenerative diseases, and a prolonged, healthy life span will follow. Progress of the science of nutrition and growing knowledge of vitamins, minerals, and enzymes places the physician in possession of facts that enable him to prevent and control the ever-increasing danger of degenerative diseases in geriatric patients.

Food intake should be based on what materials the body needs for its health and efficient function rather than on present-day perverted taste habits. The diet should be low in carbohydrate, low in fat, high in proteins, and high in foods that contain natural vitamins and minerals, such as whole grain products in the form of bread* and cereal, fruit and fresh vegetables, and the intake of refined foods and sugars must be restricted or eliminated. Albrecht states: "We are constantly in danger of deficiencies of proteins and minerals relative to carbohydrates and fats." This he believes results in lowered powers of growth and lowered capacity for reproduction. He also states: "Life is not passed from one fat globule to another, nor from one starch grain to another, but only from one protein molecule to another protein molecule. Proteins are the foods that rebuild the body, carry life and guarantee reproduction."

There is need for a better understanding of how to choose a diet which will contain the factors essential to good health.

1. Delete from the diet any food which has the basic chemistry altered by the removal of those elements essential to human nutrition.

2. Do not depend on "enriched" or fortified foods. These foods replace only a small fraction of the vitamins and minerals removed in the process of refining.

3. The diet should be high in protective food. These include fresh fruits, vegetables, and dairy products,* whole grain bread,* and cereals.

A large portion of the fruits and vegetables should be eaten in the fresh raw state to assure an adequate intake of the important heat labile enzymes.

4. Daily intake of lean meat, fish, fowl and eggs.

5. Daily intake of milk and dairy products. Whole unpasteurized milk is preferable.*

6. Adequate intake of fresh fruits.

7. For adequate intake of important B-complex factors, the diets of geriatric patients should be supplemented with a good natural source of these elements, such as (1) desiccated whole liver. This substance contains not only all the known and identified fractions of the B-complex but a number of unidentified substances that are at least as important to nutrition as those already known. It also contains the antifatigue factor which is so important in elderly people. (2) Brewer's yeast, which is probably the cheapest source of the natural B-complex and is also high in complete proteins. (3) Wheat germ is another excellent source of the whole natural B-complex and also rich in vitamin E.

8. The above diet should supply sufficient vitamin A and D, but if there is a doubt supplement it with a preparation of aqueous natural A and D for better absorption.

9. Organically-grown foods are advisable when available for consumption. Organic foods have 20-40 per cent greater vitamin and trace mineral content than those grown in depleted soils. They are also free from chemical insecticides and pesticides which accumulate in human fat and produce liver damage. For optimum health this type of food is essential. Organically-grown foods contain many unknown protective elements that have not yet been identified. Many feeding tests in humans and animals have proved this fact. If this type of food is not available, a vitamin and mineral supplement is recommended.

In conclusion the diet must be optimum in its protein, vitamin, mineral, enzyme content to assure optimum health, protect against degenerative diseases, and prolong the life span.

---

*Of course, we do not recommend milk and other dairy foods nor whole grain bread for reasons which we take up elsewhere in this book.

Reprinted from the *International Record of Medicine and General Practice Clinics,* September, 1953.

CHAPTER 208

Health and Vigor Depend on the Soil

By P. H. DeHart, M.S., and R. M. DeHart, M.D.

The people of this world are gradually starving themselves into one of the greatest wholesale disappearing acts ever recorded in history unless the doctors, chemists and agronomists wake up to the basic cause of a great increase in so-called mental, physiological and physical diseases. We have definite evidence that deficiency diseases are increasing in both plants and man; but, for some reason unknown in the most scientific nation of the earth, there has not been a general recognition of the cause and source of these deficiencies.

We know when a gas tank on an automobile is empty we can keep the motor running by supplying gasoline in the carburetor with a squirt can, but the common-sense thing to do is replenish the supply of gas in the tank so the motor can feed itself. The deficiency diseases in animals and man are being treated by supplying minerals and vitamins in capsules which is just as ridiculous as the squirt can method of keeping the gas engine running. Doctors and chemists must recognize the basic fact in nutrition that the source of all vitamins, minerals and food is in the soil. When the soil is depleted of these minerals the plants grown on the soil will also be deficient, thereby causing a deficiency to develop in man and animals who live on the soil. There should be a close-working relation between medical science, chemists, agronomists and soil scientists in order to find out more about treatments needed to apply to the soil in order to eliminate the squirt can method of keeping the human engine running smoothly.

The people of this nation have recently become conscious of the great losses of the soil from erosion in terms of material or monetary values. We have also become more conscious of the malnutrition which is so widespread in a nation of plenty. We have not, as yet, recognized the relation of the health and vigor of the people to soil fertility. It will probably require a national disaster to shock us into the realization that poor soils lacking in the basic elements necessary to sustain life have a definite and direct relation to the health and vigor of the people who live on the soil. It has not been recognized that a nation or civilization may be well fed on the basis of quantity of food consumed but at the same time be gradually starving for the lack of certain minerals.

The records of patients in hospitals show an alarming increase, in certain sections of deficiencies in thyroid and certain vitamins, nervous disorders, sterility and many other so-called diseases. Is there any proof that these abnormal conditions are not due to deficiencies in certain minerals? Medical science has recognized goiter as being a deficiency of iodine and certain other abnormal conditions are treated by the administration of calcium, phosphates, iron, copper and other minerals. It has not been generally recognized that these deficiencies may be due to a gradual depletion of the soil, and the failure to recognize this is subjecting the people to a process of gradual starvation and results in loss of vigor and poor health.

Calcium-Phosphorus Ratio

Since there is ordinarily a sufficient abundance of potassium and magnesium and other plant foods, dietitians and cattle feeders limit their attention to calcium and phosphorus. Of the 8 major soil minerals, phosphorus is by far the least abundant. A deficiency of calcium, the most abundant mineral element in the animal body, is associated with the lack of phosphorus. The importance of having an abundant supply of these minerals in the soil is at once apparent when we consider that 95 per cent of the inorganic bone material of animals is composed of calcium phosphate.

Eckles, Gullionson and Palmer[1] in their studies of phosphorus deficiencies in rations of cattle have demonstrated with unmistakable clearness that there is a definite correlation of bone weakness, bone chewing and low phosphate content of the blood plasma, with low phosphate content of the forage upon which the animals feed and with low phosphorus content of soils upon which the crops are grown. Evidences of phosphorus deficiency on forage manifest themselves not only in the most striking symptoms of bone weakness and depraved appetite but also in stunted growth, lessened milk production and lowered capacity for reproduction. Dr. William A. Albrecht, Chairman, Soils Department, University of Missouri,[2] found that male rabbits lost their capacity to become fathers when fed on forage grown on calcium deficient soils. Their litter mates, fed on forage grown on soils with abundant calcium, retained their potency. When feeds of these two lots were interchanged, the situation was reversed. Albrecht states, "Hidden hungers by way of decreasing fertility of the soil may be the quiet force by which species of animal life have become extinct. Nature's warnings allow time for us to heed them against our own extinction if we will look to the soil and conserve its fertility against forces of exhaustion as well as its body against the forces of erosion." He further found that rabbits fed on forage grown on soils low in calcium and phosphorus had enlarged parathyroid glands. This deficiency is recorded in about the same manner as iodine deficiency is recorded in enlarged thyroid glands.

Effects on Plant and Animal Growth

There are many abnormal conditions of plant growth that are due to deficiencies. A few are: sand drown of tobacco and chlorosis of tomatoes due to a deficiency of magnesium; pecan rosette may be prevented by application of relatively infinitesimal quantities of zinc; internal cork of apples, top rot of tobacco, cracked stems of celery and heart rot of sugar beet can be controlled by the application of boron. The yield of alfalfa will

[775]

in most all cases be increased and in some cases doubled by the application of 8 to 20 pounds of borax per acre. Every few years a new chemical element is added to the list of those necessary for plant growth. Magnesium, boron and zinc were found to be necessary for plant growth for over 20 years before they were generally recognized.

In some cases soil deficiencies are not revealed by any effect on plant growth, yet the plant does not contain sufficient quantity of certain elements for normal growth of animals. For example: "Soils and Men"[3] refers to a failure of cattle to develop normally when feeding on plants grown on soils which do not supply sufficient iron, copper or possibly cobalt. The lack of cobalt causes bush sickness of sheep in New Zealand.

We know that copper and iron are necessary to form hemoglobin of the blood. There is ample evidence that anemia, which is due to the lack of hemoglobin, is rather prevalent and can usually be corrected by supplying iron and copper. What is nature's source of these elements? There is only one answer—The Soil. The deficiencies in man may or may not be due to a lack of these elements in the soil or food, but to a deficiency of some other element necessary for proper assimilation of copper and iron by the body.

The birth of hairless pigs has been caused experimentally by feeding brood sows diets low in iodine. Rations carefully freed from manganese produce abnormal lactation. Bone deformities resulting in a condition known as "slip tendon" have been produced in chickens by eliminating manganese from the feed. For more than 75 years the cause of a disease in cattle with symptoms of loss of hair, lameness, liver lesions and edema was not recognized. It has now been found to be due to excess selenium.

Any Value in Increased Yields?

Smith and Albrecht[4] found that the increased yield per acre due to the use of fertilizer is not always a true measure of the value in terms of feeding value. It was found that 4.6 pounds of grain were required for each pound of gain for animals fed on lespedeza hay from soil receiving phosphate alone, while those fed on lespedeza hay from soils receiving both phosphate and lime required only 3.34 pounds of grain for each pound of gain. They state that when deficiencies in soils exist, it is possible that some organic compound essential to animal growth might not be produced within the plant and thus result in food of lower nutrition value. The addition of calcium and phosphorus to the diet of animals will not offset the deficiency in the plant. These elements must be synthesized by the plant into compounds which can be utilized by the animal.

Smith and Albrecht[4] make the following statement on the effect of the use of limestone on the quality of wool: "Analysis of wool showed that fleece from the sheep receiving the limed hay contained two per cent more fat than those receiving the phosphated hay. When the wools were scoured with a one per cent solution of potassium hydroxide, that from the lambs receiving only phosphated hay was attacked and lost 34 per cent of its weight, while the wools from the lambs receiving limed and phosphated hay remained fluffy and lost only 24 per cent. Regardless of the chemical or physical differences in the wools, it is significant that a simple treatment applied to the soil has not only been reflected in increased yield of forage, but when fed to sheep has brought about differences in rate of gain and altered the physiology of the animals sufficiently to be observed in the appearance and quality of the wool."

Vitamins in the Soil

Referring to the increase in nervous disorders, Shield[5] says, "His capacities to withstand trauma—to avoid susceptibility to infection—to survive infection—to evolve through situations—are dependent on his perfection of development. This perfection of development of man is primarily sustained by his food. The quality and quantity of nutriment either help or hinder his developments. The maintenance of man's capacity to function is dependent upon several factors, but one that is absolutely indispensable is nourishment. The health of man and consequently, his efficiency, is dependent on his state of nutrition."

The following is a quotation from the speech of The Earl of Portsmouth in a debate in the House of Lords on February 2, 1944: "Positive health, in my opinion, and I believe in that of most of those who have thought deeply upon this question, must begin in the womb and indeed in the womb before conception starts, with the health and vitality of the mother. In that connection, the doctors working in the Peckham Health Center discovered that feeding the families in the center with the ordinary so-called balanced food diet bought from the shop was not enough. The vitamins and so forth in the ordinary analysis of such vegetables as spinach and in such food as milk were not there; the vitality was not there; and they were forced to turn then to their own farms. They were forced to grow the food themselves, so as to get the beginning of positive health in the unborn child . . . . *They were forced to use not the new methods, but the ancient method of returning waste to the soil and creating humus.*"

In referring to studies on the relation of vitamins in the soil with organic matter in the soil, Shield[5] states, "These findings point to the fact that riboflavin and minerals in the plants may depend upon the humus and mineral content of the soil. Such observations suggest that the quality of the plant is dependent upon the fertility of the soil; thus optimum soil fertility predetermines that the plant will have the potential source from which it can possess optimal food value." He further states, "We in medicine are interested in optimal health and in psychiatry; we are vitally concerned with malnutrition as it affects psychobiology. It is for this reason that we find ourselves today interested in the source of malnutrition—soil, an impoverished soil, as a cause of an impoverished people with psychopathological complaints."

What Can Be Grown on Infertile Soil?

The soil fertility on a farm can be depleted enough in one generation to change it from a profitable farming enterprise and a place of good health to one of low standard of living and poor health. Farms that once provided good crops of red clover and alfalfa 50 years ago have been so depleted of the phosphorus, calcium, potash and boron that today timothy, herds grass and other low mineral requirement crops are grown. Soils that at one time produced good growth of crimson clover as winter grazing for hogs and other livestock in Eastern Virginia are now growing rye, lespedeza and crab grass. Many of our one time blue grass sods are now composed largely of wire grass, herds grass and other low mineral requirement crops. The reason is very evident after comparing the mineral content of these crops as given by Morrison.[6]

	Calcium	Phosphorus	Potash	Total
Alfalfa	1.43	0.21	2.02	3.66
Red clover	1.21	0.18	1.89	3.28
Crimson clover	1.31	0.20	1.86	3.37
Blue grass	0.30	0.22	1.26	1.78
Lespedeza	0.99	0.19	0.84	2.02
Herds grass	—	0.19	1.56	1.75
Rye	Trace	Trace	Trace	Trace
Timothy	0.14	0.06	0.56	0.75
Crab grass	—	—	—	—

It has been a tendency to shift to crops with lower mineral requirement instead of replacing the minerals in the soil. In most of the experiments conducted by our Experiment Station, the main emphasis is placed on increased bushels per acre or tons per acre without considering the possibility that the new high yielding varieties may be actually lower in total mineral content. According to results given in "Soils and Men," the mineral content of different varieties of wheat, corn and potatoes and other crops grown on the same soil may show as much variation as plants of entirely unrelated species. There were also many results of experiments given which definitely show that the mineral content of the plant can be definitely increased by application of minerals in the soil.

Larger crops are being grown on soils with the application of pure salts of nitrogen, phosphorus and potash which tends to cause plants to use up more and more of the other elements in the soil. Early in the development of agricultural science, pure salts were not as widely used which helped to replace some of these minor elements. For example: In early colonial days a fish was placed in each hill of corn, large quantities of fish and guano or bird manure, cotton seed meal, all of which contain many of the minor elements, were used as fertilizer. A majority of the phosphorus was obtained from compounds containing sulphur and the sources of potash contained magnesium. *Today the tendency is toward pure salts as a source of nitrogen phosphorus and potash. Is it not natural that more and more deficiencies will be found? They are being found in both plants and animals.*

The fact that animals will gain more weight on the same quantity of feed grown on soils supplied with limestone and phosphate than with feed grown on soils poor in these elements, even though the difference in the chemical analysis may not be significant, indicates that these two elements must cause the formation of some other compound that is necessary for proper health. It has been shown that wool is of much better quality when produced on good soil, rabbits lose their reproductive power, and many other abnormal conditions in animals are caused or related to deficiencies in lime, phosphate, and in some cases other minor elements.

Nutrition from the Soil

It has been shown also that the health of man is directly related to nutrition. The fertility of the soil from which he obtains his food will determine the quality of the food or type of nutrition. We also know that many abnormal conditions, both mental and physical, respond to the administration of certain vitamins and minerals. It is also generally recognized that the effectiveness of vitamins may be increased by the use of minerals. There is also evidence which indicates that the vitamin and mineral content of the food are related to the humus content of the soil.

This problem of nutrition is a vital one. It has a direct bearing on our own health, both mental and physical, as well as the children of present and future generations. When our forefathers landed on the shores of Virginia, they found a fertile soil. The food produced from this soil and the sea foods gave them an abundant supply of minerals, vitamins and other things which are needed for proper nutrition. They were bold, courageous, strong both mentally and physically. When the soils of the East were depleted of the basic fertility, "Go West Young Man" became the word of the day. At that time it was thought that the supply of virgin soil was unlimited and there was no need to conserve it. That was true at that time, but changes have taken place that make the conservation of our soils necessary to conserve our own existence. There are no more virgin soils. It has been estimated that there are about 600 million acres of tillable land in the United States. Of this, Bennett[7] estimates that 50,000,000 acres have been entirely ruined; another 50,000,000 acres are almost as serious; 100 million acres still in cultivation have been seriously impoverished, and about 100 million acres more of cultivated land are being depleted of productive soil at an alarming rate.

An Enormous Job to be Done

Morris L. Cook, engineer of the National Resource Board, in a statement before the Senate Committee in 1936, stated, "We have been trying to get water off the land into the big rivers and out of the way. We have got to hold it on the fields, or wherever it falls, and do it quickly, if disastrous floods, dust storms, and other calamities are to be stopped . . . .

"Our country is afflicted with *earth disease* . . . as the matter now stands, and with continuance of the manner in which the soil is now being squandered, this country of ours has less than 100 years of virile national existence. If that represents a reasonably accurate statement, it is vastly more significant that we have probably less than 20 years in which to build up the technique, to recruit the fighting personnel, and most difficult of all, to change the attitude of millions of people who hold that ownership of land carries with it the right to mistreat and even destroy their land, regardless of the effect on the total national state."

There is a great need for an awakening on the part of all citizens as to the need for a much more rapid replacement of these life giving elements to our soil as a means of better living. There is a need for a close-working relation among soil scientists, agronomists, doctors and chemists. The first step would be a research laboratory, composed of doctors, chemists, agronomists and soil scientists with the main objective to find out the relation between the large increase in deficiency diseases of man and the soil on which the food is produced. The agronomist and soil scientists and the medical profession have made remarkable progress in their respective field; but their work must be correlated and both work to a much higher ideal, that of producing quality foods rather than quantity, and to prevent many of the deficiency diseases through proper diet instead of treating the deficiency after it occurs which is often too late to be effective.

Bibliography

1. Eckles, C. H., Gullionson, .T. W., and Palmer, L. S.: Minnesota Agricultural Experiment Station Bulletin 91, "Phosphorus Deficiency in the Rations of Cattle."

2. Albrecht, William A., Chairman, Soils Department, College of Agriculture, University of Missouri, "Soil Fertility in Its Broader Implication."

3. Soils and Men—1938 Yearbook of Agriculture.

4. Smith, G. E., and Albrecht, William A.: "Feed Efficiency in Terms of Biological Assays of Soil Treatment, Soil Science," Society of American Proceedings, 1942—Vol. 7.

5. Shield, J. A., Assistant Professor of Neuropsychiatry, Medical College Of Virginia: "The Relationship of Soil Fertility and Psychic Reactions." *Virginia Medical Monthly,* March, 1945.

6. Morrison, F. B., Professor of Animal Husbandry and Animal Feeding, and Head of the Animal Husbandry Department, Cornell University, "Feeds and Feeding"—20th Edition.

7. Bennett, H. H.: Soil Conservation Service. "To Hold This Soil." Miscellaneous Publication No. 321, United States Department of Agriculture.

CHAPTER 209

Nutrition, Soil Deficiency
and Health

The book, *The Work of Sir Robert McCarrison,* is a "must" for the library of anyone vitally interested in nutrition and the organic method of farming. The chapter headings are indicative of the wealth of splendid material to be found in the book: *Researches on Fever, Researches on Goitre and Cretinism, Researches on Deficiency Diseases, Researches on Beriberi, Researches on "Stone," Researches on Human Diet in Relation to Health and Disease.*

Sir Robert McCarrison was one of the greatest nutritionists of our time. He carried on his studies in India, discovering hitherto unsuspected aspects of the problems of food and nutrition in their relation to disease. Perhaps his most famous experiment is the one in which he fed laboratory rats a diet common in England—white bread, margarine, tea, sugar, jam, preserved meats and overcooked vegetables, and produced in the rats the diseases also common to modern Britishers. Another group of rats was meanwhile kept free from these diseases by feeding them a diet that contained all the necessary food elements in the proper proportion.

The chapter on "stone" in this book is particularly significant. Kidney stone is very prevalent in India. In 1926-28 there were more than 34,000 persons who came to Indian hospitals complaining of kidney stone. And undoubtedly there were many more who did not come to the hospitals. There are geographical areas in India where stone is more common than in other areas. But no connection could ever be traced to pin the causes of "stone" on geological, climatic or racial influences, nor on the fact that some areas where stone is prevalent are in the hills and others are in the plains.

However, Sir Robert noticed that in the areas where stone was common the principal cereal crop was wheat, corn or millet, while the other areas grew rice. He began a series of experiments using the various cereals to produce stone in laboratory animals. He found that stone is produced by a diet high in these cereals, in the following order: whole wheat flour, oatmeal, North Indian millet, white flour, rice, South Indian millet. It seemed from the experiments, that the stone was produced probably from an excess of calcium or a deficiency of phosphorus in relation to calcium. Also a lack of vitamin A was evident.

Adding a very small amount of whole milk each day to the diet of every rat prevented the formation of stone. Butter and cod liver oil (both animal fats) had the same effect. But vegetable fats did not. It is not to be assumed from this, said Sir Robert, that milk alone is a protection against kidney stone or any other disease. No single food is a perfect food. Even whole wheat must be taken with other foods. Sir Robert clarified this further as follows: "The truth is that no single food material is in itself a 'complete food'—even milk is not; if it be not faulty in one regard it is faulty in another. The best are those whose faults are least; and in the latter category both whole wheat flour and oatmeal are to be included. Milk, as an exclusive food will cause anemia in rats; onions, anemia in dogs; cabbage, goitre in rabbits and oatmeal or *atta* will cause stone in rats; yet what better food can there be for mankind than a judicious mixture of all four?

"I claim for this experiment (on rats) that it proves conclusively that one-sided diets which are disproportionately rich in cereals and poor in animal fats, milk and fresh vegetables are capable of inducing in albino rats a large proportion of the diseases included in our calendar of human ailments. I may add that of all the faulty diets I have used, that composed of white bread, margarine, tea, sugar, jam, preserved meat and scanty, overcooked vegetables—a diet in common use by many people in this country—proved to be one of the worst, and most likely to be associated in rats with many of the morbid (disease) states I have mentioned, especially diseases of the lungs and of the gastro-intestinal tract.

"I lay stress on the food materials themselves (raw milk, butter, cod liver oil, carrots and fresh green vegetables used in nutritional experiments on animals) rather than on any particular ingredient of them, or any particular quality possessed by them, believing, as I do, that in nature's laboratory all elements and complexes needed for normal nutrition are combined in a way which we cannot wholly achieve, and that the health-giving properties of food are largely dependent on this combination. For my own part, I have been able to devise no synthetic diet which can equal in these properties a mixture of natural food materials such as that on which I feed my stock rats and on which some of the finest physical specimens of mankind are reared."

Nutrition Related to Methods of Agriculture

The kind of soil that food is grown on is important, too, in assessing its nutritive value. The next time you are challenged to produce proof that the organic method produces food that is superior so far as nutrition goes, you can quote the following statements of Sir Robert McCarrison's—"Considerations of this kind led me, in the course of the inquiry on which I am engaged, to attempt, in a way as wide as my limited circumstances permitted, a study of the soil conditions which influence the nutritive value of the commoner food grains of India. Millions of people in this country rely from generation to generation on a single cereal as the main staple of their dietary. It seemed necessary, therefore, to be aware not only of those soil conditions which influence the yield of grains but of those which influence their nutritive quality. . . . The soil conditions which it was thought would be likely to influence the nutritive quality of food grains were 1. the chemical composition of the soil itself, 2. the manurial treatment to which it is subjected,

[782]

and 3. irrigation as compared with normal rainfall. . . . The results already arrived at are of interest. It has been found in regard to millet—a common food grain in south India—that soil on which it is repeatedly grown, but which has received no manure for many years, yields a grain the nutritive value of which is so low that it may actually be harmful to the users of it; suggesting the acquirement by the grain of toxic qualities. It has been shown, moreover, that the nutritive and vitamin values of the millet grown on soil treated with cattle or farm-yard manure are markedly superior to those of millet grown on the same soil when treated with a complete chemical manure. In regard to wheat, it has been found that when it is grown on soil treated with farm-yard manure, its nutritive value is approximately 17 per cent higher than when grown on soil treated with complete chemical manure. The deficiencies of the wheat grown under the latter conditions are due in the main to an inferior content of vitamin A, that substance which is so essential in maintaining the resistance of man and his domestic animals to infectious diseases."

A Sad Cycle of Inefficiency

And, on the same subject: "Human and animal inefficiency is reflected in the soil; in its imperfect cultivation; in inadequate manuring; and in crops scanty as to quantity and deficient as to quality. Too few animals are kept by the cultivator (in India) as the scanty vegetation cannot support them; and so there is returned to the land too little of that organic matter, in the form of barn-yard manure, on which the continued fertility of the soil is so dependent. It has been shown in regard to plants, as in regard to animals, that they cannot thrive, nor their seed attain to the fullest 'reproductive quality' unless they be provided, in addition to the mineral constituents of their food, with certain organic substances known as 'auximones.' These substances, which are akin to vitamins, are as essential to the normal metabolism of plants as vitamins are to the normal metabolism of man and animals. They not only enable the plant to build up from the simple ingredients derived from the soil those organic complexes required as food by men and animals, but they enable it to elaborate vitamins without which these organic complexes cannot be properly utilized by the animal organism. . . . So it is that such disabilities of mankind as are due to faulty nutrition are sometimes traceable to the soil itself, which has become exhausted and unproductive of the best kind of food through improper attention and cultivation. Malnutrition, thus, pursues its harmful course in an ever-widening vicious circle; the cultivator is too often ill-nourished and ravaged by disease which is commonly the result of his ill-nourishment; his beasts are alike ill-nourished, while both toil wearily in a heartless effort to extract from the ill-nourished earth enough to keep them from starvation. The solution of the problem of malnutrition, is thus, to a great extent, one of improvement in methods of agriculture."

Sir Robert's book is not all as easy reading as these portions we have quoted. His observations on his experiments and the diseases he studied in India are couched for the most part in scientific terms. If you have a medical dictionary handy you can become one of the best-informed individuals in your neighborhood by reading the book, *The Work of Sir Robert Mc-Carrison*. We'd suggest that it would make an excellent gift for your family doctor, or some young medical student you know who will probably get nothing but a smattering of nutrition study in his medical courses. You can order the book from your local bookshop. It is published by Faber and Faber, Ltd., London, England. This book is also available from Rodale Books, Inc., Emmaus, Pa.

Editor's note: As readers know, we do not agree with McCarrison's ideas on milk and whole wheat flour. See sections in this book on milk and cereal foods for our views on these subjects.

CHAPTER 210

What Has Happened
to the Hunzas?

By J. I. Rodale

In 1942 I first learned about the Hunzas, from reading *An Agricultural Testament* by Sir Albert Howard (Oxford University Press). The Hunzas, who around 1947 numbered about 22,000 souls, lived at the northernmost tip of India, near outer Mongolia and Tibet, and were considered by explorers who visited them as one of the most healthy races in the world.

Sir Albert Howard in his book referred to the work of Sir Robert McCarrison who had lived with the Hunzas for over 10 years and who spoke so eloquently about their health in his Mellon Lecture delivered in Pittsburgh in 1921. He said at that time: "They (the Hunzas) are unusually fertile and long-lived, and endowed with nervous systems of notable stability. Their longevity and fertility were, in the case of one of them, matters of such concern to the ruling chief that he took me to task for what he considered to be my ridiculous eagerness to prolong the lives of the ancients of his people, among whom were many of my patients. The operation for senile cataract appeared to him a waste of my economic opportunities, and he tentatively suggested instead the introduction of some form of lethal chamber, designed to remove from his realms those who by reason of their age and infirmity were no longer of use to the community."

So vibrant was the health of those Hunzas with whom McCarrison came into contact that he reported never having seen a case of asthenic dyspepsia, or gastric or duodenal ulcer, of appendicitis, mucous colitis or cancer. Cases of oversensitivity of the abdomen to nerve impressions, fatigue, anxiety or cold were completely unknown. The prime physiological purpose of the abdomen, as related to the sensation of hunger, constituted their only consciousness of this part of their anatomy. McCarrison concluded this part of his lecture by stating, "Indeed, their buoyant abdominal health has, since my return to the West, provided a remarkable contrast with the dyspeptic and colonic lamentations of our highly civilized communities."

My Book On The Hunzas

I became so interested in learning more about these Hunzas that I searched for every bit of material that had ever been written about them, for in a way the Hunzas represented an experiment in following the organic method of farming and living. They used no chemical fertilizers or insecticides, fertilizing their soil only with manure. I wrote a book called *The Healthy Hunzas* and at the end of it there is reproduced the bibliography of the 20 books I had unearthed that had material in them about the Hunzas. I never went to Hunza myself, but was in communication with their ruler, the Mir, and with Mrs. and Colonel Lorimer, who had spent several years there and who had written of the wonderful state of health of the Hunzas.

Through my book, the story about the health of the Hunzas spread, and was quoted in many sources. Then in 1956 there appeared a book called, *Hunza, Lost Kingdom of the Himalayas,* written by John Clark, a geologist, who had spent 20 months in Hunza, and who spoke disparagingly of the vaunted health of these people. His book received extensive reviews and furnished material for gloating to many of the opponents of the organic method. For example, the *Herald Tribune* Book Review, (July 15, 1956) said it: "Exploding a legend dear to the heart of nutritionists, Mr. Clark reports that the 'healthy Hunzas' suffer from malaria, dysentery, ringworm, bronchitis, beriberi, goiter and pneumonia. There are no doctors in the area, few schools, a booming population and no more arable land."

There probably is a great difference between the Hunzas of McCarrison's time in 1910 and Mr. Clark's Hunzas 45 years later. Note the mention of the booming population. This is a problem I shall take up later. Note also that the diseases mentioned are of a contagious nature—Clark did not come across one case of cancer or heart disease, although he himself had a heart attack while he was in Hunza. Also, if you will refer to the statement attributed to McCarrison in his Pittsburgh speech, he did speak of having patients, but they evidently were in the contagious category.

McCarrison's Letter

As soon as I finished reading Clark's book, I despatched a letter to McCarrison at Oxford, England, telling him briefly of what Clark had written and here is the reply I received:

Dear Mr. Rodale:

I find your letter of July 5, 1956, awaiting me here on my return from holiday and I hasten to thank you for it.

I have not seen the book by John Clark on the Hunzas in which, as you tell me, he draws attention to "a very sorry state" of these people; and until I do, I reserve judgment. It is now 45 years since I last saw the Hunzas, to whose health I referred in my Mellon lecture at Pittsburgh in 1921. Two World Wars have intervened since then, and I'm told that during the second one, many young men left Hunza for India, Pakistan and elsewhere in search of work. It would be surprising if, on their return to Hunza, they did not bring back with them infections of various kinds. However this may be, I cannot remember that in my time, 1904-1911, there was any notable prevalence of malaria and dysentery.

I am now nearing 80 years of age and have retired from active work.

With best wishes, I am

Yours, sincerely,

R. McCarrison

Reasons for the Changes

From the evidence I accumulated in my book I feel certain that in McCarrison's time the Hunzas were a very healthful lot, but that something has happened since then that has brought about more contagious diseases among them. In 1910 Hunza was a more or less isolated place. There was practically no traffic. Then came radio and aviation. There was more communication and traveling. More curious explorers and travelers came prying, many of them bringing in the devitalized foods of civilization, as you will soon see in the case of Mr. Clark.

A definite change came about when Hunza became a political part of Pakistan. Money began to flow a little more freely in Hunza. The Aga Khan started a few schools. But the increase of the population set off forces that militated against perfect health. On page 215 of Clark's book he said: "The population is increasing at a terrific pace; Hunzas are emigrating to all the neighboring states and still the overcrowding grows worse every year." The Hunzas who emigrate come back on visits and bring with them their newly-learned unhealthy nutritional habits.

On page 145 Clark says: "Unfortunately, every Hunza man 17 to 21 years old was down-country, either in the Pakistan army or working, earning money for his family." In 1910 money in Hunza was practically unknown, and no young men left the country to serve in any outside army, where they ate sugar, salt, ice cream, cookies, etc.

Here is another Clark excerpt, page 105: " 'My old men are good,' the Mir continued, 'and always consult my wishes, just like my children. But my young men all go down-country and learn bad habits from those Punjabis. Why aren't they satisfied with my own traditional ways?' "

The Mir's Explanation

In correspondence with me the Mir has covered this point. In a letter to me dated August 6, 1951, he said, "As regards the health of Hunza as

[786]

in the time of McCarrison, in my opinion they who live in Hunza are still in better health, but owing to the increasing population and the modern requirements, so many of the Hunza youths are spread all over Pakistan and India, and so many of them are in various Pakistan forces as well as in private services, that when they return they bring disease in with them. But, thank God, there is not a single case of syphilis, only sore eyes and stomach trouble which is not rare in Hunza owing to eating so much fruit. Otherwise, Hunza is still enjoying the same good health of old times. In McCarrison's times there were no roads but now there is daily air service to Pakistan. Where it previously took months, it now takes hours. Within a year a jeep road will be ready."

On April 9, 1950, he had written, "As regards goiter in a few persons, the population of Hunza is increasing, and we must earn our living from the outside. That is why more than a thousand Hunza families settled in the Gilgit area in Danyor, which is the center of goiter, and some of these people come to Hunza in the hot season to stay with their relatives, which is the real cause of goiter. As regards dysentery, Hunza is a place of fruit, and in the fruit season children as well as adults eat too much of it, which causes dysentery. Otherwise, what you have written in your book is a real picture of the Hunza State."

There have also been changes in the diet. Due to overpopulation there isn't as much meat available as there used to be. On page 177 Clark says: "They are used to having meat only once a year."

Dangerous Concepts of Nutrition

But let us look into Clark's poor conception of nutrition. That is the trouble with so many explorers who bring sugar, white flour and canned goods to many healthy primitive civilizations, like the Eskimos, and who have caused them, as a result, to contract many of the diseases of civilization. On page 56 Clark says: "I had brought several pounds of tea from Karadis (this is outside of Hunza), and a maund (19 to 163 pounds) of sugar from Gilgit" (also outside of Hunza). On page 57 he says: "We divided the Mir's contribution and the chapatties (wheat cakes), and for a special celebration we opened a can of chocolate syrup."

In prescribing vitamins for a sick man, Clark advised (page 64): "One pill every day and a spoonful of this sugar 5 times a day." Then he states that the man had never tasted sugar before. Any novice in the study of modern dietetics should know that white sugar is one of the greatest dangers in our nutrition. It uses up calcium and vitamin B in the body. It causes cavities in the teeth. So, imagine a man who has come to help a people, introducing them to such a habit as eating sugar and chocolate syrup instead.

Here is another quotation, page 70: "We had finished tea and cookies . . ."

Page 73: "At Nuri Hayat's command, one of the relatives brought a dish of walnuts and apricot nuts, then two soft-boiled eggs and a cup of tea with milk and sugar. These were well-to-do people by Hunza standards . . ." Well-to-do Hunzas did not use sugar in 1910 or 1920.

On page 76 he again refers to a breakfast including chocolate syrup. On page 79 he describes a meal that included soft custard. On page 91 he sends a man ahead to Hunza with a donkey-load of sugar, rice, etc. Probably it is polished rice, without the vitamin B-rich coating. On page 116 he describes a visit to Lahore where they went shopping for American-style milk shakes.

On page 159: "They sat in a close circle around the fireplace, savoring every bit of their sweet custard, while I fried the first batch of potato chips and gave two, fresh and salty, to each boy. Then I couldn't fry them fast enough for the eager hands that snatched them as quickly as I dipped them out of the fat." Salt is another dangerous item in human nutrition. But to encourage fried foods and fat! Is it any wonder that Clark had a heart attack while he was in Hunza! One of the reasons why heart disease is practically nonexistent in Hunza is the low fat content of their diet. But if Clark were their nutritional director, there would soon be a big increase in the fat consumption and in heart cases.

On page 178 he speaks of a candy shipment from America, two boxes of chocolate syrup from the Glen Ellyn Methodist Church of Illinois and a box of cookies from relatives in Illinois. He speaks of his staff becoming "stuffed to the gills with sweets." Anyone who is aware of the newer facts of nutrition can easily see that Clark was giving the Hunzas poor advice about eating. He could not, therefore, be aware of the damage he was doing to these fine people.

Clark's Health

Nor did he stop to consider the injury he was doing to himself. Page 72: "Oh well, perhaps a good climb was just what I needed to cure my chronic dysentery." Page 76: "Hayot scrambled over the boulders like a young ibex while I panted disgracefully behind him, sitting down frequently to rest." Page 84: "Second was my own health, which was slowly deteriorating." Page 234: ". . . the doctor discovered a pararectal abscess (in Clark) which required immediate operation." Page 243: "Say, you look even worse than you did in Karachi. Are you sure you can last out until November?" (Someone else speaking of Clark.)

Page 257: "My own health was degenerating rapidly. Twenty months of worry and dysentery plus my draining abscess has weakened me, and now my heart gave me constant trouble. I had to sit down for breath every few minutes on my walks to treat Hidayat, which wasted a lot of time. I also caught a case of boils from one of my own patients." And a heart attack to boot (page 89). Is it any wonder that these things happened when it is considered that Clark was violating so many basic rules of nutrition?

On the other hand, he refers to the strength and physical development of the Hunzas. Page 56: "The porters (Hunzas) wrapped each locker with black horsehair rope in a complicated hitch, shouldered the 80-pound load without a grunt, and walked off easily." Page 67: "What magnificent patients these people were! Never a coward, never a neurotic among them." Page 129: "Shah had brought only one blanket ('Hunzas don't feel the cold, Sahib!')." Page 180: "The boys played soccer barefoot, which should have

[788]

broken their toes, but didn't." Page 192: "Burhan regarded all this as good fun, laughing at my chattering teeth. Apparently he was impervious to cold." Page 214: "There are not the frequent wife-beatings in Hunza that one sees in China, nor is there much infidelity."

At the same time there are frequent references to the weaknesses of other nearby races. On page 83 he speaks of boxing with his young Hunza helpers and describes exchanges of heavy blows. "Hindu boys would have cried at the first blow." On pages 104 and 129 he talks about Nagir cretins. He did not discover one cretin among the Hunzas. There are other references showing that the Hunzas stood head and shoulders, physically and mentally, over the peoples who surrounded them.

The Mir's Health

Clark speaks here and there of the Mir's ill health. Page 69: " 'Well, John, (the Mir speaking), I have considerable pain shortly after each meal, especially after curries, which I love. Have you something for that, please?' I gave him 100 milk-of-magnesia pills for regular use, as mild alkalizers, and 26 mixed-carbonate pills in case of a violent stomach ache. The Mir was a good trencherman who did not exercise." On page 84 Clark says: "He (the Mir) and his family were using medicine at a rate which almost alarmed me."

I knew that the Mir was not in the best of health in 1953 when he wrote asking me to send him some digestive tablets. He also asked for one-a-day vitamins. But I knew also that the Mir traveled extensively outside of Hunza, eating the refined foods of civilization. In fact about a year before he had written for the digestive pills he had accompanied the Aga Khan all over Europe.

On September 28, 1954, the Mir wrote me that he was in Pakistan for the operation on his wife which took place on August 26, 1954. "I cannot understand what happened," he wrote, "She never was ill in the last 21 years. . . . As regards her habits . . . she likes hot things like green and red chilies." She also traveled outside of Hunza. The operation was on her appendix, a condition that Sir Robert McCarrison stated he didn't see once in his 11 years in Hunza.

In one of the books about the Hunzas, there is mentioned the case of a family that moved out of Hunza. Within a short time they fell ill. It is possible that the food produced on the soil outside of Hunza did not have as much minerals and vitamins as did that grown on Hunza soil. The Hunzas were wonderful farmers who never burned manure for fuel as other surrounding races did. They saw to it that every bit of it went back into the soil, which made it extremely rich and fertile.

But times change. The mistake that Clark made was that he looked at only one part of the picture. If he had studied all of the available literature, he could have turned out a more valuable piece of work.

CHAPTER 211

Foods that Encourage Tooth Decay

Dental decay is the result of loss of calcium from the teeth. This calcium loss is caused by acids formed in the mouth because of bacterial fermentation of carbohydrate foodstuffs that come into contact with tooth surfaces. Theoretically, if you were to cut out sugar and other fermentable carbohydrates from your diet, you should suffer no tooth decay whatsoever. Furthermore, restriction of such carbohydrate intake in the diet should check the further development of all existing decay. Thinking that "a useful step would be taken if carbohydrate foodstuffs were listed according to their relative decay-producing activity," B. G. Bibby, H. J. Goldberg and E. Chen, dental doctors from Rochester, New York, took that step. Their article, "Evaluation of Caries-Producing Potentialities of Various Foodstuffs" (*Journal of the American Dental Association*, May, 1951), attempts to make suggestive recommendations along the lines of withdrawing the more destructive foods from the diet and substituting less harmful ones in the interest of prevention of tooth decay.

The authors devised a method for calculating the potential calcium-cracking rate of various carbohydrate foods. In order to do this, it was necessary to measure: 1. how much of each particular food sticks to the teeth and is retained in the mouth after eating; and 2. how much acid is formed by these foods in the saliva. The results obtained from these two measurements were called the "decalcification potential" (calcium-destroying possibility) of the particular food studied, and 96 such common carbohydrate foods were included in their investigation. As a preliminary step toward measuring the amount of carbohydrate adhering to the teeth, it was, of course, necessary first to determine the total percentage of carbohydrate contained in each of these foods. After this was done, the amount collected in residues clinging to the teeth made it possible to calculate the total food retained on them.

Tests on Humans

The authors then conducted a series of tests in which the subjects chewed each food in the normal way, but instead of swallowing it, expectorated the mass into a container. Into this same container went such fragments as they could readily dislodge from their teeth by methods of tongue-cleansing and tooth-sucking ordinarily used by persons as habitual last acts at a meal. (This total represented the amount of food that would be actually swallowed.) After this, the teeth were carefully brushed and all the washings were collected in another receptacle. (This figure represented the amount of food usually retained on the teeth and not swallowed.) "Determinations of the amount of carbohydrate and thereby the amount of food represented in each fraction were made separately and the result compared with the known quantity of food taken into the mouth for chewing." In all cases the total amount of food expectorated plus the amount recovered by tooth-brushing approximated the total quantity of food taken into the mouth so closely that the method used to brush the teeth could be assumed to represent a reliable equivalent of the amounts of food that will stick to the teeth after eating.

Types of Food Used

Dental doctors Bibby, Goldberg and Chen then ran their actual tests with a variety of commercially distributed products, since they wished to determine the decay-favoring rate of foods in the form in which they are really eaten. Eight classes of such carbohydrate foods were tested: these included breads and bread products, cereal products, crackers, cookies, desserts, candies and soda, fruits and vegetables. The authors then drew up tables for each of these food types, listing in these statistics the total amount of carbohydrate contained in each food (in percentages), the amount of food retained in the mouth after eating (in milligrams), the acid formed by bacterial action on the carbohydrate at the end of 4 and of 24 hour periods (in milliliters) and finally the "decalcification potential." To illustrate the thoroughness of their work the table of "Bread and Bread Products" is reproduced in part below:

Food	Total Carbohydrate per cent	Food retained mg.	Acid formed ml. of 0.1 N. 4 hr.	24 hr.	Decal- cification potential
Egg noodle	71.3	16	1.1	2.0	18
Zwieback	71.3	29	1.2	2.8	35
Swedish bread	70.2	41	1.6	2.3	66
Bread and margarine	43.9	35	2.0	2.3	70
Whole wheat bread	47.3	76	1.5	2.2	114
Rye bread	50.6	67	1.9	3.0	127
Toast and margarine	55.0	73	1.8	3.1	131
Cinnamon melba toast	45.0	94	1.5	1.6	141
White bread	51.6	91	1.8	1.9	164
Potato bread	52.5	120	1.5	1.7	180
Bread, margarine and jam	56.3	99	2.1	2.8	208
Doughnut	61.9	184	1.7	3.1	313
Danish pastry	53.8	181	1.9	2.7	434
Bread and peanut butter	26.2	338	1.6	2.3	541

It is evident at first glance at the table above that there is great variety in the possible calcium-harming properties of the different kinds of breads and bread products, ranging from a low of 18 for egg noodles to a high of 541 for bread and peanut butter. It is also of interest to note that white bread (with a potential of 164) is more destructive of calcium than is either whole wheat (114) or rye (127). Knowing the tooth-destroying qualities

[791]

of sugary foods in general, many readers will not be surprised to observe that the addition of jam to bread runs its rate of damage to the teeth to a high potential (208). It may be news, however, to learn of the buffer role which margarine plays in reducing the damage done by bread to a low of 70. This is because the authors go on to prove in some of their later tables that the fat content of foods lessens to a considerable degree their potential for damage. We do not recommend margarine, however, as it contains benzoate of soda. Remarking on the overall lessons to be gleaned from a study of the Table on Breads, they conclude that its significant feature demonstrates that it is the amount of the food retained on the teeth after eating, rather than the acid-production caused by these particular foods, that runs up the "decalcification potentials" in this table. This is proven by the wider variations in reading the amounts retained, when compared with the figures for acid formed.

Food	Total Carbohydrate per cent	Food retained mg.	Acid formed 4 hr.	24 hr.	Decal- cification potential
Corn flakes	84.6	21	0.7	2.4	15
Popcorn	74.1	32	1.5	2.9	48
Corn chips	54.5	41	1.2	2.4	49
Rice flakes	83.0	60	0.9	2.4	54
Cheese popcorn	62.2	26	2.1	2.6	55
Puffed Rice	83.3	63	1.1	2.6	69
Fried rice	25.1	65	1.6	1.8	104
Boiled rice	23.9	81	1.7	2.3	138
Wheat flakes	74.7	77	2.0	2.3	154
Cream of Wheat and milk	19.3	130	1.5	1.6	195
Shredded Wheat and milk	25.4	181	1.3	2.4	235
Bran cereal and milk	25.3	160	1.6	1.4	256

Cereal Products

The table on "Cereal Products," printed in part above, shows that the low degree of harm done by corn products is due to their low-tooth-retention figures. On the other hand, cheese popcorn is more destructive than ordinary popcorn because of its high capacity for acid-production. The fact that smaller amounts of fried rice are retained in the mouth after eating it than after eating boiled rice, is due to the reduction in food retention brought about by fats.

In their studies of "Crackers" the authors discovered that salted ones were eliminated from the mouth much more completely than unsalted ones, suggesting that "the saltiness of a food may tend to reduce its retention on the teeth." We do not recommend any salty foods, however, for other reasons. Oil-sprayed cheese crackers, though having a lower retention rate than plain crackers, proved to be more destructive of tooth calcium because of a higher degree of acid-forming ability. Pretzel sticks have a high potential for calcium-damage (124), while oyster crackers are the worst of all varieties of this type of food, with a decay-promoting potential of 173.

"Cookies" also have quite high tooth-destroying potentialities, which

[792]

are rather the result of the large amounts of them retained in the mouth than they are of their acid-producing characteristics. The authors suggest that an investigation be undertaken to determine whether this high retention rate is due to their content of sugar or to the method of manufacture which alters the consistency of their ingredients in such a way that they cling to the teeth to a dangerous degree. In this connection, Drs. Bibby, Goldberg and Chen believe that the low figures given for sandwich-style cookies are the result of the sugar's being separated into several layers, an advantage over the style of cooky in which the sugar is uniformly distributed throughout the whole mass. The harm that cookies will do to tooth calcium runs from low to high degree in the following order: lowest in potential are animal crackers (65), then come arrow root biscuits (72), sweet tea biscuits (108), assorted filled sandwich cookies (108), macaroons (115), ginger snaps (126), toll house (210), black walnut (219), graham cracker (226) and milk cracker (250). If you are intent on avoiding dental decay, remember, too, that fig bars are the worst of all styles of cookies to eat (with a potential of 505).

Desserts

Among "Desserts," the dental research authorities warn against fruit cake because of its "outstandingly high acid-production figure." Desserts of a creamy consistency, such as chocolate pudding and ice cream, on the other hand, encourage an unusual amount of dental decay because of the high degree at which these foods are retained in the mouth. The whole subject of cookies and desserts is, of course, a dangerous one on account of the general nutritional damage brought by these "popular" types of foods. Health-minded people should avoid indulgence in these items on a score of other health counts, in addition to the tooth-decay one. "Candies" likewise show a high decay-producing range in their table. The figures cited for hard candies prove this type of confection to be particularly bad for the teeth, because their degree of harmfulness "records only the conditions which were obtained after completion of eating and not those which operated during a lengthy eating or sucking period."

Fruits

Since "Fruits" constitute a healthful and highly beneficial part of our daily diet, it will be of interest to study them in more detail from the point of view of their individual effects on the calcium content of teeth. The table reveals a much greater degree of variation in the amounts of fruit that are retained in the mouth by clinging to the teeth than it does in the acid-producing capacities of the individual fruits. The range in their ability to destroy calcium progresses from a low of 4 for apples to an all-time high of 665 for dried figs which, as the authors point out, were blamed by Aristotle some 2300 years ago for causing dental decay through sticking to the teeth (remember the similarly high figure for fig bars under "Cookies"). Drs. Bibby, Goldberg and Chen also state: "The high figure for dried fruits is noteworthy because it raises serious doubt as to the soundness of some of the dental educational material which recommends such fruits for uses in supposedly caries (decay)—reducing diets."

Food	Total Carbohydrate per cent	Food retained mg.	Acid formed 4 hr.	Decal- cification 24 hr. potential
Apple	13.2	3	1.4	2.5	4
Pineapple (canned)	37.3	31	0.7	2.2	22
Peach (canned)	12.3	30	1.6	3.3	48
Pear	11.0	65	2.0	2.3	130
Grape	19.6	85	1.7	1.6	145
Plum	20.5	93	1.8	1.9	167
Banana	20.2	100	1.8	2.6	180
Dry Prune	70.0	265	1.9	2.6	504
Date	77.5	297	1.7	3.5	505
Fig	73.0	350	1.9	3.7	665

Vegetables

Results of the tests made on "Vegetables," one of the most important parts of our diets, and their effect on tooth-decay ranged from an extremely low rate of destruction for cooked and raw carrots (2 and 4, respectively) to the highest rate for starchy or sweet vegetables like potatoes, squash (314) and parsnips (314). The harm done by these latter vegetables is as high as that done by desserts and cookies. The high degree to which potato chips (61), mashed potatoes (74) and boiled potatoes (128) are retained in the mouth in the form of particles clinging to the teeth, is the result of both the consistency or texture of these foods as well as of their processing or fat content. Acid-producing differences may also be involved in some of the same factors, say the authors. "For instance, the 4 hour acid-production figure for potato chips, mashed potato and boiled potato were 1.9, 3.3 and 2.4, respectively." Part of their table on foods that encourage tooth decay from vegetables is printed below to enable readers to select these foods wisely, if they are confronted by problems of tooth-decay:

Food	Total Carbohydrate per cent	Food retained mg.	Acid formed 4 hr.	Decal- cification 24 hr. potential
Carrot (cooked)	8.3	2	1.0	1.5	2
Carrot	8.0	3	1.4	1.2	4
Lettuce	2.1	13	1.2	1.1	16
Cucumber	2.3	23	1.1	1.0	25
Cabbage	4.3	33	1.3	1.2	43
Potato (chip)	48.2	61	1.9	2.9	116
Potato (mashed)	22.4	74	3.3	3.3	244
Turnip (mashed)	6.8	180	1.7	1.6	306
Potato (boiled)	18.2	128	2.4	2.5	307
Squash (mashed)	8.8	196	1.6	1.6	314
Parsnip (mashed)	10.6	157	2.0	2.4	314

Drs. Bibby, Goldberg and Chen believe that their calculations concerning the potential calcium damage wrought by the foods just discussed are "extremely complex and that it would be an error to oversimplify them in any way." There is only one sure method of ascertaining whether these calculations are exactly proportional to their importance in bringing about tooth decay, and that is through long range dietary studies in humans. Such a study being both "time consuming and expensive," however, they experimented in this connection with white rats and hamsters, which are highly susceptible to dental decay. This resulted in the positive finding that the calcium-destructive rates of certain foods provide an accurate index of the actual amount of tooth decay that they will cause.

Returning to the subject of dental decay in humans, the authors repeat that differences in retention in the mouth of various carbohydrate foods and in the amounts of acid they form are related to the fat and salt contents of these foods as well as to their texture. Both of these factors—retention in the mouth and acid-production—are independent of the total carbohydrate content of foods. The significant points, therefore, hinge on the effects of fat and of salt. Foods with a high fat content cling to the teeth less than those with a low content, animal fats being retained less than ones of vegetable origin. Texture, too, the authors emphasize, is important in deciding the extent to which different foods linger in the mouth after eating. Also, although the differences are somewhat slight, cold foods are seemingly retained less than hot foods.

More important than even the food retention factor in creating the calcium-destroying effects of carbohydrate foods, are differences in the salivas of individual people. The acid-producing capacity of each person's saliva will in a measure either exaggerate or reduce the calcium-crumbling effects of these foods. However, the comparative concentration of foods and saliva taking part in the process of forming acid are still insufficiently understood.

Their Conclusions

In concluding their important article, Drs. Bibby, Goldberg and Chen state that the way in which foods are prepared (for example, the difference between mashed and boiled potatoes) has some influence on their decay-producing potentialities. "In other words, it becomes apparent that there are many factors operating to influence food retention on the teeth, its rate of fermentation in the mouth and its probable capacity to produce dental decay." Consequently, though the carbohydrate content of a particular food is not the sole issue that conditions these factors, the authors do believe that they are justified, in "recommending the substitution of foods which the studies indicate have a low decalcification potential for others which have high ratings." The figures in their tables, therefore, should in their opinion provide a "safe guide for the selection of foods which should prove to be less productive of dental decay." Persons with dental problems ought to observe their suggestions.

CHAPTER 212

A Simple Diet for Reducing

Many readers have written to us about their problems of overweight and have asked us to suggest reducing diets. We are reluctant to recommend any one of the many diets that have received so much publicity, for we have not tried them and we do not know whether they actually do what they are supposed to do without depleting the body's store of energy, vitamins and minerals.

Now we have discovered in the *British Medical Journal* of July 2, 1949, a reducing diet so simple, so practical and so sensible that we are reprinting it here with a few alterations in terms, so that it will apply to American food rather than British and a few—just a few—of our own ideas added. H. L. Marriott, C.B.E., MD., F.R.C.P., who wrote the article believes that most diets are too complicated for people to follow faithfully week after week. In his diet unrestricted consumption of low and moderate calorie foods is allowed, with measurement of only two foods—bread and milk. He believes that potatoes may be eaten 3 times a day, if they are boiled, steamed or baked and eaten without the addition of any fat.

We counsel you to go easy on potatoes and other starchy vegetables such as peas, lima and navy beans and corn. We are completely in agreement with Dr. Marriott's commandment that no fried foods be eaten. Our first reason for this is, of course, that fried foods are fattening. Our second is that experiments have shown many fats and oils, harmless when eaten cold, to be cancer-producing in laboratory animals when these fats are heated to a high temperature as in frying.

Dr. Marriott tells us that weight lost by patients who adhere faithfully to the diet varies from 15 to 35 pounds in 12 weeks. More can be lost by continuing with the diet. Any patient with simple overweight who does not lose weight on this diet is eating or drinking other things outside the permitted articles of food, says Dr. Marriott.

We suggest that if you must eat in restaurants some of the time, you inquire whether or not butter or cooking oils are used in the preparation of vegetables, fish and salads. We have found that most restaurant chefs douse their vegetables, including baked potatoes, in butter. If you can, patronize one restaurant regularly and insist that they prepare your entire meal without the use of fats or oils.

Dr. Marriott Suggests the Following Foods

Now for the diet.

You may eat or drink as much as you like, Dr. Marriott says, of any of the following:

Lean Meat, Poultry, Game, Liver, Kidney, Heart, Sweetbreads—
(Cooked in any way, but without the addition of bread crumbs, flour, sauces or gravy.)

Fish—(Not canned. Boiled, steamed, broiled or baked only. No fats or sauces.)

Eggs—(Boiled or poached only.)

Potatoes—(Boiled, steamed, baked in skins, but not fried, roasted, sautéed or chips.)

Vegetables—(Any you wish—fresh, frozen, canned or dried. No fat or butter to be used in the preparation.)

Salads—(Any kind of salad greens or tomatoes, without oil or mayonnaise.)

Fruits—(Any kind, fresh or frozen, including bananas. Also fruit canned without sugar. Not dried fruits or fruit canned with sugar.)

Sour Pickles—(Not sweet pickles or any relishes made with sugar.)

Clear Soup, Broth or Bouillon.

Water or Non-sweetened Mineral Water.

Tea and Coffee.

Milk—(Up to half a pint daily. No canned milk. No cream.)

Bread—(Three very small pieces per day, either one at each meal or all 3 at one meal.)

You may have nothing else whatsoever. Particularly note that this means:

No Butter.
No Margarine.
No Cooking Fats or Oils.
No Sugar, Jam, Marmalade, Honey.
No Candy, Cake, Pie, Pastry.
No Chocolate, Cocoa, Soft Drinks or Chewing Gum.
No Puddings, Ice Cream.
No Dried Fruits or Nuts.
No Bread (Except as noted above.)
No Biscuits, Toast, Patent Reducing Breads.
No Cereals or Oatmeal.
No Barley, Rice, Macaroni, Spaghetti.
No Salami, Corned Beef, Sausage.
No Luncheon Meats, Cold Cuts, Bacon.
No Cheese.
No Cocktails, Whiskey, Gin.
No Beer, Cider, Wine.
No Salt—(Unless you are suffering from Addison's Disease or some other condition for which your physician prescribes salt.)

This is surely a diet varied enough for the most epicurean taste, practical and simple enough to be completely workable. We suggest that if you want to lose even more weight, eliminate bread, canned vegetables and fruits, all pickles, soups, tea, coffee and milk entirely and, rarely eat potatoes, never eat "as much as you want" at any meal. Substitute wheat germ and brewer's yeast for bread. In addition, taking bone meal (for minerals) and fish liver oil (for vitamins A and B) will assure you of no deficiency of any vital food element. Keep with you at all times the lists of foods permitted and forbidden. And never disobey the rules.

CHAPTER 213

Additional Information on Nutrition

High Calorie Diets

The American diet is low in "protective foods" according to a study conducted by the Department of Agriculture and reported in *Scope* for December 26, 1956. The persons studied were from 30 to 90 years old and represented a good cross section of the public, economically and educationally. The study left no doubt about the popularity of high calorie diets. The interviews with more than a thousand Iowa women showed that they have a consistent preference for fats and desserts, bread, meat and potatoes as their main foods. Women in South Dakota showed a preference for sweets, desserts, cereal products and table fats which accounted for more than 60 per cent of the day's calories. Less than one-fifth of these women got the .8 grams of calcium recommended for good health. Intake of vitamin C was 10 per cent below that recommended as the lowest minimum for good health.

Eisenhower's Diet

The *New York Times,* of June 9, 1956, described the President's dinner as prepared by the Sheraton-Park Hotel chef at Washington at a public affair:

Supreme of Melon Balls
(*good*)

Clear Consommé
(*He would be better off to cut out all soups. Many of them contain fat. Commercial brands of consommés are made with salt.*)

Filet Mignon without sauce
(*good*)

Peas
(*He should eat them raw, unless his recent operation would prohibit it. They could be puréed in some way, raw.*)

[798]

Baked Potato

(good, but with no butter)

Tossed Salad with special lemon dressing

(Depends on what's in it. Probably pretty good.)

Strawberries and sugar

(Sugar? Murder!)

Decaffeinized coffee

(There is still a little caffeine in it.)

According to the newspaper item, "Persons at the head table saw General Eisenhower salt his food rather heavily and put a synthetic sweetener in his coffee." Before the dinner some of the guests reported that the former President ate some hors d'oeuvres (no doubt highly salted and containing fats).

What Our Children Eat

Hot dogs, potato chips and pop for lunch, with candy bars and soft drinks after school fill children full of "empty calories," according to a county health survey in Hillsdale, Michigan. Investigators found that out of 133 fifth-graders queried *only one* had a perfectly balanced diet. All but 6 were found deficient in one of 8 so-called necessary categories.

Good Nutrition for Personality Disorders

There is ample clinical evidence to indicate that deficiencies in some foods may contribute to or be responsible for many psychic symptoms and so may become important factors in what is known as psychosomatic disease. It is possible, too, according to an article in the September, 1954, *Journal of Digestive Diseases* that these deficiencies may even be responsible for organic changes that result from painful incidents.

Experience has shown that patients must have completely satisfactory diets before their medical treatment will be effective. Losing your appetite is one very common reason for going to a doctor. The article suggests that a full examination should be made of the patient's diet and the state of his digestion and nutrition before any diagnosis or prescription is made in cases of so-called psychosomatic illness.

We rather believe that if you'd put everybody in the country on a really nourishing diet, with all refined foods forbidden and organically grown fruits and vegetables served fresh and raw at every meal, psychosomatic illness would disappear within a few months. We know that serious deficiencies in many of the B vitamins can create dementia, depression and other purely mental disorders. Why could not a lesser deficiency in many of the vitamins bring about the anxious, worried, dissatisfied frame of mind that many of us are toting around with us day after day?

Unhealthful Practices in High School Sports

The forms of insanity in which we moderns indulge seem to have no limit. In a recent news release by the American Medical Association it was remarked that the *AMA News* of January 26, 1959, had carried a statement condemning the crash diets and "drying out" techniques used by high school wrestlers and boxers to reduce their weight to make a certain weight class.

It is the practice in these sports to match boys of similar weight to insure fairness in competition, so a 200-pound wrestler isn't pitted against a boy who weighs only 160 pounds. This is the sensible sportsmanlike way of doing such things. However, coaches greedy to win sometimes encourage boys who weigh too much for a particular class to reduce a few pounds and thus come within the bounds of a more advantageous weight class. They compete against smaller boys and stand a better chance of winning the event.

The boys go on crash diets "sometimes approaching the starvation level." We assume that "drying-out" means a reduction of normal fluid intake to keep weight even lower. Such practices certainly are serious hazards to health, especially at this youthful stage in the body's development. What we don't understand is the attitude of those in charge who are presumed, after all, to be trying to instill ethics and good sportsmanship in these boys through competitive athletics. Certainly they could not help but know of a boy's effort at drastic weight reductions to fit into a more advantageous weight class. Aside from the danger to their health, these boys are being exposed to a bad moral principle if such practices are even allowed, much less encouraged. It is simply a form of cheating.

We think that the suggestion of the National Federation of State High School Athletic Association is a sensible solution to the problem. It calls for an unannounced "weighing-in" at the beginning of the season, and stresses the opinion that a boy should remain throughout the season in the class established for him at the "weighing-in." At least this would eliminate the advantage of losing weight during the season and so discourage dangerous dieting.

What are our high schools coming to when such a situation becomes so common as to require the attention and condemnation of organized medicine? If your son participates in any sports in which weight is a factor, make certain that he is not endangering his health by foolish dieting. If such practices are tolerated at his school, let it be known that you object and bring the case to the attention of school authorities who should certainly be willing to put a stop to them.

SECTION 16.

Chemicals in Food

Almost every food we take into our bodies these days contains preservatives, coloring matter, acidifiers and alkalizers, emulsifiers, softeners or some other chemical included in the list of more than 700 similar substances which are being used in foods regularly. The common cry among many of the country's scientists and research authorities is that the minute amounts of these chemicals placed in foods can in no way be harmful to the human body. However, did these experts ever stop to think of the cumulative effect of these additives? These infinitestimal quantities mount up to dangerous and toxic dosages when we consider the total number of foods, each containing its own tiny dosage of poison, one eats each day. We say stick to unadulterated, natural foods whenever possible, and keep your body well fortified with food supplements to ward off any dangers incurred when eating chemicalized food.

CHAPTER 214

Do You Know
What You're Eating?

Once upon a time . . . a glass of orange juice was simply juice from an orange; butter was churned milk, nothing more, a piece of meat had nothing in it but the spices *you* added in cooking it. If you wanted to take your chances on a piece of chocolate cake, a look at the recipe would tell you the whole story of how much sugar and white flour your body would have to contend with—there would be no unknown ingredient in the flour or the chocolate. Even with ice cream or candy you knew what you were up against, and if you wanted to eat such things . . . well, the risk was yours. Today, if you want to eat these things the risk is still yours, but with this difference: to understand just what you're up against, you'd have to be a chemical engineer!

There's Something in Everything!

Food additives have become a mighty part of the food industry in the past 30 years. It is almost impossible to purchase a commercially produced food product that has not been treated in some way to give it a characteristic the producer wants it to have, or one he's educated the consumer to want and expect. There are hardeners and softeners, foaming agents and anti-foaming agents, acidifiers and alkalizers, bleaches, coloring agents, thickeners and on and on—ad nauseum. These chemicals are dumped into the vat, one on top of the other, to create the perfect product that won't spoil, harden, change color, stick together nor fall apart. There are often 5, 10 or even more additives in a single food product. This food, in turn, is often combined with several other food products, each equally "enriched" with additives, to make a single dish.

The casual consumer usually has neither the training nor the interest that would prompt him to attempt an interpretation of the numerous ingredients listed on the label of the average food package. He buys a jar of olives and expects olives; he buys a pound of cold cuts and it never occurs to him to ask about the casing in which the meat is wrapped, nor about the stuff that's used to hold it together or to make it pink. He's thinking of a sandwich, not a course in chemical preservatives.

How Does the Body Cope With It All?

The question that presents itself to one who is concerned by profession, as we are, with what goes into foods is this: how can the body cope with the sheer volume of chemical substances which trickle into it from a hundred different food sources each day? How much of a strain is it on the body's organs to process and rid itself of so many useless and harmful substances which it cannot use? Do all of them leave the body? How do these chemicals react on one another while they are in the body? There are many related questions that come to mind and should have been asked by the food processors long before they incorporated these chemicals into the products they sell. If we find out later that the body can't handle them, it will be too late for a lot of us.

In 30 years the aspects of this question have become so complex that the Federal Food and Drug Administration, which is required to answer only a part of it (are the chemicals poisonous of themselves?), has thrown up its hands and admitted that it can never tell if all of the chemicals in food, even when used one at a time, are poisons or not. An estimate of the effect on the body of the ones being used, over long periods or in combination with other chemicals, has hardly even been attempted.

How Could Such Small Amounts Hurt You?

Rather than tell the public that conclusive tests have never been made on the safety of the additives they use, the food processors pooh-pooh the suggestion that those teensy amounts of chemicals they add could possibly affect American consumers who have been told that they are among the healthiest people in the world. To impress us with the ridiculousness of the suggestion, they quote the additive in parts per million, or the microscopic micrograms per pound and dare us to imagine how we could be poisoned by such infinitesimal amounts. What they don't say is that these infinitesimal amounts accumulate in the body; that we ingest such infinitesimal amounts of chemicals dozens of times a day, for years on end.

A Menu Many Eat Throughout the Country

To dramatize a bit more graphically the menace of food additives that confronts us every day, we have made up a day's menu generally familiar to most persons in our country. As you will see, it is not a menu we would recommend, but we have included foods that many people eat every day and have been told are perfectly safe, even wonderful, for them. With each food item mentioned we have included the intentional additives used in its manufacture, as listed by the National Academy of Sciences, National Research Council, Washington 25, D.C., in their publication 398, *The Use of Chemical Additives in Food Processing,* February, 1956. (Price $2.00.) These do not, of course, include any spray or other insecticides, nor any gases to which most fruits and vegetables are subjected before they are even eligible for additives. Nor are we mentioning more than one additive per food for each specific job; for example, in bread there can be several anti-oxidants (perhaps even in the same loaf), but we will list only one; in sodas there are many additives possible for each soda flavor, but again we will list only one. It should be understood, however, that the consumer who eats a slice from two different loaves of commercially baked bread is likely to get a different set of additives with each slice. The person who eats

[804]

two kinds of processed cheese might well be eating two separate groups of preservatives. Recalling the number of different types of food one eats each day, and the different varieties and flavors in which they come should give one an idea of the complex problem of additives in food which can only be hinted at in the menu below.

Are You Eating a Salt-Free Diet?

For the person on a salt-free diet who thinks he is avoiding salt simply by not adding it to his foods in cooking or at the table, the menu will be a sobering revelation. The sodium and chloride compounds he should avoid are present in almost every food he eats. It would be well for anyone restricted against a specific element commonly employed in foods to study the list of additives given below and carried in labels to be sure that such an element is not contained.

Even if you are careful in selecting the foods you eat, it is practically impossible to live in our civilization without unknowingly eating some food additives. For those who never read a label and try each new work-saving food product that is offered, the chemical intake must be staggering! The only protection you have is to eat as many fresh foods as possible whose origin you know and to fortify yourself with natural food supplements.

Non-Nutritive Sweeteners Not Included

The additives mentioned below do not include non-nutritive sweeteners which are used, as suggested by the National Academy of Sciences booklet, in: beverages, canned fruit products, canned vegetables, flavoring extracts, frozen desserts, gelatin, jellies, jams, marmalades, baked goods, salad dressings and frozen fruits. But remember, they could be added to the list of any or all of these foods' additives. The use of glycerols in each food is also not included, but they can be assumed to be present with any flavoring or coloring, for they act as solvents for these items. Isopropanol is another additive we've omitted, but it is contained as a solvent in foods which require synthetic flavoring agents.

When we came to colorings and flavoring agents, we included only a few representative ones, since items such as cake, pie, sodas or candy can have dozens of variations on these additives.

How many of these foods do you eat? How many can you be sure of?

Even Water Needs Careful Investigation

Of course, no day's estimate of the foods one eats would be complete without the inclusion of water. Many persons drink 8 or more glasses of it each day, and it is the main ingredient of coffee, tea, soda and many other beverages consumed by humans. Those who can get and drink fresh well and spring water, untampered with by engineers who add one chemical after the other to purify metropolitan water supplies, are indeed fortunate. Just for the record, here is a list of the 47 chemicals which are being used by municipal water systems throughout the country to prepare water for us to drink. While it is not likely that all of them would be contained in a

[805]

single supply, you can be sure that a number of them are in any treated water you might drink. You can add these to the estimate of the chemicals you get every day.

Activated Carbon
Activated Silica
Aluminum Ammonium Sulfate
Aluminum Chloride Solution
Aluminum Potassium Sulfate
Aluminum Sulfate
Aluminum Liquid
Ammonia, Anhydrous
Ammonia, Aqua
Ammonium Silicofluoride
Ammonium Sulfate
Bentonite
Bromine
Calcium Carbonate
Calcium Hydroxide
Calcium Hypochlorite
Calcium Oxide
Carbon Dioxide
Chlorinated Copperas
Chlorinated Lime
Chlorine
Chlorine Dioxide
Copper Sulfate
Disodium Phosphate

Dolomitic Hydrated Lime
Dolomitic Lime
Ferric Chloride
Ferric Sulfate
Fluosilicic Acid
Hydrofluoric Acid
Ozone
Sodium Aluminate
Sodium Bicarbonate
Sodium Bisulfite
Sodium Carbonate
Sodium Chloride
Sodium Fluoride
Sodium Hexametaphosphate
Sodium Hydroxide
Sodium Hypochlorite
Sodium Silicate
Sodium Sulfite
Sodium Thiosulfate
Sulfur Dioxide
Sulfuric Acid
Tetra-Sodium Pyrophosphate
Tri-Sodium Phosphate

The same chart gives a list of purposes for which these chemicals are used. They are:

Algae Control
Boiler Water Treatment
Color Removal
Corrosion and Scale Control
Dechlorination
Disinfection
Fluoridation
Iron & Manganese Removal
Softening
Taste and Odor Control
Miscellaneous

B. O. D. Removal
Coagulation
Condition-Dewater Sludge
Chlorination
Flotation
Neutralization—Acid
Neutralization—Alkali
Oxidation
pH Control
Reduction

CHAPTER 215

Chemical Additives
in the Average American Diet

BREAKFAST:

Juice—Benzoic Acid (preservative), Dimethyl polysiloxane (anti-foaming agent).

Cereal—Butylated hydroxyanisole (antioxidant), Sodium acetate (buffer), FD & C Red #2 (dye), F D & C Yellow #5 (dye), Aluminum ammonium sulfate (acid).

Meat—(Sausage, spiced ham, hash), Ascorbate, (antioxidant), Calcium phosphate (anti-caking agent), Sodium or potassium nitrate (color fixative), Sodium chloride (preservative), guar gum (binder).

Toast or Bread—Sodium diacetate (mold inhibitor), monoglyceride (emulsifier), Potassium bromate (maturing agent), Aluminum phosphate (improver), Calcium phosphate monobasic (dough conditioner), Chloromine T (flour bleach), Aluminum Potassium sulfate (acid-baking powder ingredient).

Buns or

Coffee Cake—Calcium propionate (mold inhibitor), Di-glycerides (emulsifier), Sodium alginate (stabilizer), Potassium bromate (maturing agent), Aluminum phosphate (improver), Butyric acid (butter flavor), Cinnamaldehyde (cinnamon flavor), Aluminum Chloride (dough conditioner), Chloramine T (flour bleach), Aluminum potassium sulfate (acid—in baking powder).

Margarine—Sodium benzoate (preservative), Butylated hydroxyanisole (antioxidant), monoisopropyl citrate (sequestrant), F D & C yellow #3 (coloring), Diacetyl (butter flavoring), Stearyl citrate (metal scavenger), Synthetic vitamin A and D.

Butter—Hydrogen peroxide (bleach), F D & C yellow #3 (coloring), Nordihydroguaiaretic acid (antioxidant).

Milk—Hydrogen peroxide (bactericide), Oat gum (antioxidant).

Jelly or

Jam—Sodium benzoate (preservative), Dimethyl polysiloxane (anti-foaming agent), Methyl cellulose (thickening agent), Malic acid (acid), Sodium potassium tartrate (buffer), F D & C green #3 (coloring for mint flavors), F D & C yellow #2 (coloring for mint flavors), F D & C yellow #5 (coloring for imitation strawberry flavor), Gum tragacanth (stabilizer).

LUNCH:

Soup—Butylated hydroxyanisole (antioxidant), Dimethyl polysiloxane (anti-foaming agent), Sodium phosphate dibasic (emulsion for tomato soup), Citric acid (dispersant in soup base).

Crackers—Butylated hydroxyanisole (antioxidant), Aluminum bicarbonate (leavening agent), Sodium bicarbonate (alkali), di-glyceride (emulsifing agent), Methylcellulose (bulking agent in low calorie crackers), Potassium bromate (maturing agent), Chloramine T (flour bleach).

Sandwich—Sodium diacetate (mold inhibitor), monoglyceride (emulsifier), Potassium bromate (maturing agent), Aluminum phosphate (improver), Calcium phosphate monobasic (dough conditioner), Chloromine T (flour bleach), Aluminum Potassium sulfate (acid-baking powder ingredient), Ascorbate (antioxidant), Sodium or potassium nitrate (color fixative), Sodium chloride (preservative), guar gum (binder), Hydrogen peroxide (bleach), F D & C Yellow #3 (coloring), Caffeine (stimulant added to cola drinks), Butylated hydroxy-

Candy—Sorbic acid (fungistat), Butylated hydroxyanisole (antioxidant), Mono- and Di-glycerides (emulsifying agents), Polyoxyethylene (20) Sorbitan monolaurate (flavor dispersant), Sodium Alginate (stabilizer), Calcium carbonate (neutralizer), Cinnamaldehyde (cinnamon flavoring), Titanimoxide (white pigment), Mannitol (antisticking agent), Petrolatum (candy polish), Propyleneglycol (mold inhibitor), Calcium oxide (alkali), Sodium citrate (buffer), Sodium benzoate (preservative).

Soda—Sorbic acid (fungistat), Sodium benzoate (preservative), Polyoxyethylene (20) sorbitan monolaurate (flavor dispersant), Sodium alginate (stabilizer), F D & C blue #1 (brilliant blue coloring), F D & C yellow #5 (coloring), Cinnamaldehyde (cinnamon flavoring), Caffeine (stimulant added to cola drinks), Butylated hydroxyanisole (antioxidant).

Ice Cream—Mono- and Di-glycerides (emulsifier), Agar-agar (thickening agent), Calcium carbonate (neutralizer), Sodium citrate (buffer), Amylacetate (banana flavoring), Vanilldene Kectone (imitation vanilla flavoring), Hydrogen peroxide (bactericide), Oat gum (antioxidant).

DINNER:

Fruit Cup—Calcium hypochlorite (germacide wash), Sodium chloride (prevent browning), Sodium hydroxide (peeling agent), Calcium hydroxide (firming agent), Sodium metasalicate (peeling solution for peaches), Sorbic acid (fungistat), Sulfur dioxide (preservative), F D & C red #3 (coloring for cherries).

Meat—Alkanate (dye), Methylviolet (marking ink), Asofoetida (onion flavoring), Sodium nitrate (color fixative), Sodium chloride (preservative), Sodium ascorbate (antioxidant), guar gum (binder), Sodium phosphate (buffer), Magnesium carbonate (drying agent).

Canned Peas—Magnesium carbonate (alkali), Magnesium chloride (color-retention and firming agent), Sodium chloride (preservative).

Fruit Pie—Sodium diacetate (mold inhibitor), Sorbic acid (fungistat), Butylated hydroxyanisole (antioxidant), Sodium sulfite (anti-browning), Mono- and Di-glycerides, (emulsifier), Aluminum ammonium sulfate (acid), F D & C red #3 (cherry coloring), Calcium chloride (apple pie mix firming agent), Sodium benzoate (mince meat preservative), Potassium bromate (maturing agent), Chloromine T (flour bleach).

(Pie will also contain additives found in shortening and white flour used in making the crust.)

Cottage Cheese—Annatto (vegetable dye), cochineal (dye), Diacetyl (butter flavoring), Sodium hypochlorite (curd washing), Hydrogen peroxide (preservative).

Cheese (Processed)—Calcium propionate (preservative), Calcium citrate (plasticiser), Sodium citrate (emulsifier), Sodium phosphate (texturizer), Sodium alginate (stabilizer), Chloromine T (deodorant), Acetic acid (acid), F D & C yellow #3 (coloring), Aluminum potassium sulfate (firming agent), Hydrogen peroxide (bactericide), Pyroligneous acid (smoke flavor).

Beer—Potassium bi-sulfite (preservative), Dextrim (foam stabilizer), Hydrochloric acid (Adjustment of pH), Calcium sulfate (yeast food), Magnesium sulfate (water corrective), Polymixin B (antibiotic).

CHAPTER 216

Pesticides in Our Milk and Meat

We have closets full of reassurance that the insecticides, antibiotics and hormones being used on our livestock will not affect the quality of the meat or milk we get from these animals. Releases from the Food and Drug Administration announce that no ill effects to the consumer can follow the use of hormones to make fowl grow meatier, the use of massive doses of antibiotics to cure disease or the use of powerful insecticides sprayed on the animals to kill bothersome insects.

The lack of coordination between the FDA and the scientists who run experiments on the safety of such procedures becomes apparent when one reads publications such as the one put out by the American Chemical Society and its Division of Agricultural and Food Chemistry. In it is a series of short summaries covering experiments done to determine just how much of the drugs and insecticides remain in the tissue and milk we consume.

The residue is not negligible. For example, in studies conducted at Utah State University, Logan, Utah, under Joseph C. Street, 36 ewes were given feed containing dieldrin, a powerful insecticide, over a period of many months. The retention was estimated by analyzing the feces and milk which came from these animals. Results showed that the ewes retained from 80 to 90 per cent of the dieldrin they received, less during lactation. After a period of 9 months, samples of tissue were taken from the animals for analysis. Dieldrin storage in all of the samples was found to be roughly proportionate to the intake. This means, of course, that anyone eating the meat from these animals would be ingesting 90 per cent of many months' rations of this deadly pesticide quite unaware.

Similarities Between Insects and Us

C. W. Kearns of the University of Illinois made mention of one of the most important points in the entire controversy over the safety of using deadly pesticides on animals intended to be used as food. He says that present information points to a striking similarity between the biochemical mechanism of insects and other animals—that includes humans. This does not necessarily mean that all of the reactions of insects and other animals are the same, for there are definite differences in metabolism. However, there is a basic sameness in many of the functions of insects and other animals. What is dangerous to a fly must, in some measure, be dangerous to us. It is all another warning to us that the all-out use of pesticides is bound to have an unforeseen, unhealthful effect on animals and man.

Is there a difference in the effect of insecticides sprayed or painted on the animals, rather than included in their feed? Not too much. George Decker, Secretary of Economic Entomology for the Illinois Natural History Survey says most mammals may acquire many pesticides through one or more avenues and such materials may be stored in fat or excreted in milk. For further agreement we have the findings of H. V. Claborn and his colleagues at the Agricultural Research Service. They tell us that chlorinated hydrocarbon, and some of the phosphorus in insecticides, are fat soluble. This means when they are sprayed on livestock (cattle and sheep) for the control of pests they may be absorbed through the skin and stored in the fatty tissues. Often they will make their appearance in cows' milk.

Cream Shows a High Level of Pesticide

The affinity for fats displayed by some pesticides is apparent in the findings of George G. Gyrisco and colleagues at Cornell University. Sevin, a pesticide, was added to the grain of 5 cows at the rate of 50, 150 and 450 parts per million. It was recovered from the cream highest in fat content of these cows in excess of 84 per cent of the total dosage, while the amount in the milk was negligible.

There were several other experiments described in the report which added up to the same conclusion: pesticles used on animals, or in their food, do accumulate in tissue and milk. And, as an answer to those who demand proof that shows a consumer dropping dead from a single taste of meat or milk tainted in this way before they will concede the danger, we offer the opinion of Mitchell R. Zavon, of the Kittering Laboratory of Cincinnati University. He says that despite the absence of positive findings, there is no reason to believe that the possibility of the deleterious effects of pesticide residues in milk does not exist. On the contrary he warns that constant appraisal of the situation is necessary.

We are drinking this milk and eating this meat. And the additives are not removed in cooking! If these pesticides can accumulate in the fatty tissue of other animals, they can accumulate in ours. Our only defense is to purchase meats which have not been so treated (practically impossible) or to petition our representatives in Washington again and again to promote legislation which will tighten the restrictions on the selling of milk and meat from animals who have been treated with drugs, pesticides or hormones.

CHAPTER 217

Now—They're Waxing
Our Produce

After they've soaked up their quota of chemical fertilizer, been sprayed with insecticide a few times and gassed to retard spoilage, you'd think what's left of our fruits and vegetables would be delivered without further ado. But no, there's one more step awaiting the lowly vegetable before release into the custody of the buying public—waxing. This is still another technique in a long line of efforts to make perishable produce last longer enroute to retailers, and for as long as possible once it gets there. You will be told that such measures are only for the consumer's benefit, to give you more attractive produce. Actually, it's the wholesaler and retailer who benefit, by being able to sell older fruits and vegetables as new and fresh. The consumer merely ends up with older goods than she would normally buy if the lack of freshness were not disguised. So please, Madison Avenue, stop telling us that you're doing *us* a favor by adding preservatives to our produce!

We Eat the Wax

Regardless of the dubious benefits, there is no avoiding the fact that the consumer is stuck with the preserved food, and when he eats it, he eats the preservative. With some produce, grown commercially, you can get DDT, a gaseous chemical, a dye and 2 or 3 waxes in a hydrocarbon solution. The waxes don't wash off, and since they are the last to be applied, they cover the residue sprays, dyes and gases so that these can't be washed off either.

"Waxing Vegetables," *Cornell Extension Bulletin No. 965,* by J. D. Hartman and F. M. Isenberg, gives the technical story of the use of wax on perishable produce. The stated purpose of waxing is to improve luster and control shriveling through better retention of the natural moisture. There was a time when luster could be improved by washing fruit in plain water and wiping the dust from it when it was put on display. Don't these methods work anymore? As for retaining moisture and preventing shriveling, these are the two criteria the purchaser has for the freshness of the produce he buys. Shriveled or dried-out fruit is old fruit which we just don't want, yet the waxing tricks us into buying these.

There are all sorts of mixtures for fruit and vegetable waxing. The wax itself is only one of the objectionable contents. For example, *Bulletin 965* tells us that they may include coloring materials intended to add to the appearance of waxed vegetables, and some waxes contain sprout-prevention materials such as borax. Mineral oil is often included in the wax mixture to reduce brittleness. Some waxing methods consist of dipping the fruit or vegetable in a solution of wax and water. When removed the water evaporates, leaving the wax coating on the fruit. There are drawbacks to this system, since the waxes tend to become contaminated with decay organisms and dirt which adheres to the produce.

Fungicide in the Wax

A new wax mixture has been perfected for citrus fruits. It's a self-polishing fungicidal water wax that is entirely synthetic, says the *Bulletin.* It contains something called Dowicide, which is probably the fungicide, and the *Bulletin* observes that this will have to be cut down about one-half if the mixture is to be used for tender vegetables. Will it? Will even half-strength of this strong chemical be tolerated by the body when it is eaten with a tomato or a baked potato jacket? How much of this have our children eaten already in sucking oranges as children do? The rest of the synthetic formula may contain even worse elements which we will eventually be eating with our lustrous, moisture-retaining produce.

Some processors dip their fruits and vegetables in pure melted paraffin, and this material is usually present in most wax mixtures. Certain paraffins are known to be dangerous when taken internally, due to their cancer-causing properties. These dangers were pointed out by a symposium of the International Union Against Cancer held in Rome, Italy, in August, 1956 (*New York Times,* August 21, 1956). It was stated that they had produced cancer in man and experimental animals.

Danger in Waxed Cartons for Milk

These waxes or paraffins are sometimes used in the leak-proof lining for milk cartons, and the danger to which milk-drinkers are exposed by this usage has been pointed out by two Chicago researchers, Philip Schuik and W. Lijinsky (*New York Herald Tribune,* June 13, 1959). These doctors reported that small amounts of cancer-causing agents have been found in

[812]

4 of 40 waxes taken from samples all over the United States. The research was requested by Dr. William Hueper, head of the environmental cancer section of the National Institutes of Health, in order to determine whether the presence of these agents poses a major health threat. Reports had first been published indicating that certain waxes caused cancer in mice when injected into their bladders.

There is no word in the article which would lead us to believe that the use of such waxes in milk cartons has been discontinued or outlawed. The likelihood of our ingesting these waxes is very good. Particles of wax are often seen floating on the surface of a glass of milk poured from a waxed cardboard container. Be careful to remove such particles from any milk you use. If your family uses milk, patronize a dairy that will deliver it in glass bottles. The small effort involved in washing and returning the bottles is well worth the peace of mind you will have for having avoided another of today's cancer hazards.

It may be easy to avoid milk cartons, you say, but what of the dozens of other uses waxed containers are used for? What can one use to pack home grown vegetables, fruits, etc., in the freezer, if not such cartons? Glass might do for a few items, but proves impractical for freezing large supplies of seasonal foods. Consider, too, the waxed paper plates and cups one finds at every picnic. Apparently, waxed containers have quietly become an item hard to avoid in modern life, even when one makes the effort.

The effort must be made, however, so long as this danger exists in the wax preparations used to line the containers. Further, we must petition the Congress, through our senators and representatives, to pass laws prohibiting the use of such materials. If the tests by Drs. Schuik and Lijinsky showed that not all waxes contain carcinogenic chemicals, why shouldn't manufacturers be forced to use the safe ones? In writing to your congressman and the Food and Drug Administration about the matter, ask that simple question and demand the protection to which you or your family are entitled as citizens.

Which Are Waxed?

Avoiding waxed fruits and vegetables, whose coatings might also contain cancer-causing ingredients is not so simple. It is not always possible to know which produce has been waxed and which has not. It is best to buy locally grown fruits and vegetables when possible. Chances are that they will be free of wax since the need for protecting the produce through long days of transportation is not present, and the average individual farmer hasn't the facilities for giving his product the wax treatment.

Peel your fruits and vegetables before eating. Though the peels are often rich in vitamins and minerals, the poisons one gets with them are too strong to make eating them worthwhile. The *Cornell Extension Bulletin* mentions some vegetables that are most likely to be waxed. They are: cantaloupes, rutabagas, carrots, parsnips, eggplants, small summer squash, cucumbers, potatoes, tomatoes. Several others to watch out for are: apples, pears, citrus, melons, plums and peppers.

[813]

CHAPTER 218

Potatoes with "Eye Appeal"

According to *Science News Letter* for October 7, 1950, potatoes are now being given a red-skin color treatment to add to their "eye appeal." The method used to promote the beauty of the lowly potato consists of washing the vines, while the tubers are still in the ground, with a spray called 2,4D. This chemical, which is well known for its weed-killing strength, is so dangerous that potato growers have been cautioned to be especially careful in its use. In fact, Dr. Jess L. Fults, botanist member of the staff of the Experiment Station at Colorado's A and M College (Fort Collins, Colorado), and Dr. Lawrence Schaal, plant pathologist of the United States Department of Agriculture, prepared special instructions for its application.

The scientists make the claim that these artificially colored potatoes show an increase of as much as 12.5 per cent in vitamin C content over their fellow spuds with plainer complexions. Since potatoes are the cheapest source of vitamin C and since this starchy food runs high in popularity on the nation's dinner tables, this is presumed to be a recommendable advantage. But what else may have happened to the colored potatoes as a result of their reaction to the chemical spray? A substance that is capable of killing off ragweed and other nuisance plants, 2,4D must surely be able to penetrate the potato skins in such a way as to cause changes in content other than merely this increase in vitamin C. In accidentally altering the plant beneficially in one respect, it may also seriously damage it in a number of others that will prove detrimental to consumer health.

Supposed to Toughen the Skins

The only serious additional argument in support of this highly dangerour practice is contained in the claim that 2,4D has a "tendency" to toughen the skins of potatoes, an advantage at digging time. This is too slight a benefit to justify the really serious state into which our large-scale commercial agriculturists are progressively falling. With a seemingly dogged determination to discover ever deadlier killer-chemicals, agricultural scientists are daily subjecting our food products to fatally poisonous doses of newly invented pesticides and just plain "stunts," such as this lamentable fad for colored potatoes.

"Health appeal" is a much more important and permanent matter than the current fashion for dressing up plain essential commodities so that they will acquire the lure of extra "eye appeal." If we stay closer to nature in growing and processing our foods, we will at the same time stay closer to the perfect health which nature intended us, like the humble potato, to share in along with all the rest of her creations.

CHAPTER 219

The Threat of Sodium Nitrite

Botulism is food poisoning caused by the presence of bacteria called *clostridium parabotulinum*. These spores which cause the spoilage of food are widespread, but they do not cause foods to become poisonous unless the foods are kept too long or not refrigerated properly. Home-canned foods that have not been properly heated and packed, or that are kept too long, may develop the spores of this bacteria. It cannot be detected by taste, so if the improperly canned food is eaten without being heated to kill the bacteria, the result may be food poisoning or botulism.

In Europe preserved meats have been responsible for most of the outbreaks of botulism. In this country the same is not true. Of the 37 outbreaks of botulism in the past 50 years, sausage has been the villain in 11 cases. These days a lot of sausage is packed in synthetic casings, called by trade names such as Visking and Saran, rather than the natural casings formerly used. The new casings keep the meat tasty and moist, even when it is stored at higher temperatures than ordinarily used. We'll have more to say about the casings later.

Testing Sausage Spoilage

There has been some concern over the possibility of meat dealers becoming careless in their handling of sausage so that cases of botulism might result. Two researchers at the University of Wisconsin have done a series of tests, reported in *Food Research* for November-December, 1951, to determine how long it takes for the usual sausage to become toxic under certain conditions, what effect the new synthetic casings have on this process and to what extent the preservatives, spices and salt used in sausage retard the spoilage.

The authors, P. K. W. Steinke and E. M. Foster, tell us that commercially prepared liver sausage containing sodium nitrate was inoculated with the spores of the bacteria and kept at 98.6 degrees Fahrenheit (body temperature) for 11 days without toxin formation. The same mixture was then tested 1. without salt and nitrate, 2. without salt, 3. without nitrate. Within 9 days all these mixtures were toxic. Then, keeping the sodium nitrate content of the sausage constant, various amounts of salt were tested. The more salt added, the longer time it took for the sausage to become poisonous. The presence or absence of spices seemed to have no effect.

In testing the effect of the sodium nitrate and nitrite, it was found that when both were added, the mixture remained non-toxic longer than when either was added alone. When sodium nitrate alone was added, without salt or nitrite, the sausage spoiled in 4 days.

All these tests were made using synthetic sausage casings. Now the original sausage mixture was stuffed into a natural casing and stored at 86 degrees Fahrenheit. Another portion was stuffed in Saran casings. The meat in the Saran casings became toxic in 16 days, while that in the natural casing was not toxic when the last test was made at 23 days. This can be explained, say the authors, by the fact that the natural casings let the sausage dry out and the bacteria do not grow as fast in dry environment as in a moist one.

There is no way (taste, smell, appearance) to detect the presence of the bacteria. As evidence the authors presented some of the sample sausages to various individuals with the question, "Which, if any, of these would you eat?" Sausages packed in natural casings were rejected most often, because they looked dry and wrinkled. Strangely enough, the one sausage that was acceptable for eating by the greatest number of people *contained botulinum poison.*

Sodium Nitrate and Sodium Nitrite

What does the experiment show? First, to keep sausage looking fresh and appetizing, synthetic casings are used, in spite of the fact that they encourage the growth of bacteria. Then, to discourage the bacteria and make certain the meat will not spoil, no matter how long it remains on the grocer's counter, sodium nitrate and sodium nitrite are added. These are two chemicals which are known to be poisonous in large amounts. They are made of sodium, nitrogen and oxygen. As is the case with all of the chemicals bandied about so freely by our food processors, no one knows what effect small amounts of these poisons may have if they accumulate within the human body. Sodium nitrite, according to *Materia Medica* "has a persistent action. It is absorbed and eliminated slowly; thus its action is prolonged." Vertigo, stumbling, roaring in the ears, hurried and deep or occasionally irregular respiration, increase in the force and rapidity of the heart, decrease in blood pressure and temperature—these are some of the symptoms of nitrite poisoning.

Fertilizers that contain nitrates (especially nitrate of soda) are in common use among growers of vegetables. Apparently the more nitrate fertilizer the farmer uses, the more nitrate substance there will be in the leaves of the plants he raises, for nitrates are stored in the leaves of plants. This means that the vitamin-full leaves of foods like lettuce, beets, spinach, celery and cabbage may contain as much as 1000 to 3000 parts per million of nitrates. Some of these nitrates are changed into nitrites (by the loss of one atom of oxygen) within the body. Nitrites are likely to combine with the hemoglobin of the blood and result in poisoning. If nitrate fertilizer is not used on the plants and they are grown organically, this nitrate content is, of course, greatly decreased.

Nitrate Poisoning of Infants

A number of articles appearing in medical journals over the past few years have discussed cases of methemoglobinemia (blue baby disease) which may result in serious illness or death from lack of oxygen in the blood. In Minnesota, for instance, there were 146 cases and 14 deaths of infants from this disease between 1947 and 1950. Apparently in most of these cases the cause of the poisoning could be traced to well water containing nitrates. The water was used in preparing the babies' formulas. Investigations that followed resulted in the recommendation that no more than 10 parts of nitrate per million parts of water should be considered as safe in preparing formulas.

But, on the other hand, in a survey reported in the *Agronomy Journal* for January, 1949, J. K. Wilson, M.D., of the Department of Agronomy of the New York State College of Agriculture revealed that canned baby foods (depending on where and how they were grown) may contain as much as 833 parts of nitrate per million. Therefore, says Dr. Wilson, "it may be suggested that in some cases the nitrate in the vegetable foods may be solely responsible for this ailment of babies and may cause other disturbances not now properly diagnosed, for the nitrate may be 200 times stronger in such foods than that which was set as the safe standard for the drinking water."

How Much Poison Do You Eat?

Well, what's the answer? Must we stop eating green leafy vegetables, the very ones whose succulent foliage is brimful of so many vitamins and minerals? No, of course not. But these facts about sodium nitrate are another potent argument for buying only organically grown food, if it is at all possible. They are arguments for you to use in persuading farmer-friends of yours to abandon their use of chemical fertilizer and begin to garden organically. Then you can buy produce from them. As for canned baby foods—it's up to you to decide whether or not to use them. Remember the nitrate content of these canned foods will not be indicated on the label, for it is contained in the food itself; it has not been added during the canning.

Finally, in regard to sodium nitrate and sodium nitrite—next time you go to the grocery store, read the labels of the canned and potted meat products on the shelf. You will probably not find more than one or two which do not contain these two chemicals. Then figure out how many times a week your family eats canned meats or commercially prepared sausages and lunch meats of all kinds. (The chemicals are mixed with the meat products not only to preserve them but to give them a fresh, appetizing color.) Now, figure out how much sodium nitrate and sodium nitrite you are getting per week. It may surprise you.

(Incidentally, no separate standards for the regulation of food preservatives are provided by our federal government. Preservatives which are poison are prohibited and the presence of any preservative must be indicated on the label. Obviously the Food and Drug Administration does not consider sodium nitrate and sodium nitrite as poisons.)

If, in addition, you are regularly eating vegetables that contain nitrates

[817]

from commercial fertilizers, the sum total will go up even more. No, probably you won't immediately develop symptoms of vertigo and so forth. But remember that sodium nitrate "is absorbed and eliminated slowly, thus its action is prolonged."

Synthetic Sausage Casings

Now we come to the appalling anticlimax of the story of sausage—the casings in which it is packed. We wrote to the United States Department of Agriculture to discover what synthetic sausage casings like Saran, Visking and Pliofilm might be made of. Their reply tells us that Saran is made of synthetic resins, "modified by the addition of a small amount of harmless chemicals." Visking casings are made of "regenerated cellulose" consisting of "wood pulp and cotton linters, and plasticized by treatment with alkali." Pliofilm casings (you won't believe this, we're sure, but it's there in black and white) are made of "synthetic rubber modified by the addition of a small amount of harmless chemicals." All these casings, the Department of Agriculture tells us, "have been thoroughly tested for possible toxicity and found to be free of harmful materials."

As we read this letter, we could feel the roots of our hair slowly rising with horror. That day last week when we rushed through a hurried lunch of liver sausage—what had we been eating along with it? Synthetic rubber, resin or cellulose, treated with chemicals? Our butcher assured us that sausage which is intended to be broiled or fried in the casings is not packed in synthetic casings. But the sleek, glistening covers of all the cold meats and lunch meats in his refrigerator are synthetic. True, we don't eat these casings; we peel them off as we slice the meat. But the meat has been packed in them for weeks (or perhaps months) before we buy it. How much of the synthetic rubber, resin, cellulose and "harmless chemicals" have been absorbed by that meat before we make it into a sandwich? We do not know what tests have been made on the synthetic casings to prove that they are not toxic. We do know that the casings have appeared only in the past few years, so that no one can possibly know what their effect may be on individual cells of the human body over a period of 10 to 20 years.

Conclusion

If you would keep your family safe from the chemicals used by meat processors, do not eat canned meats or sausages or lunch meats prepared with sodium nitrate or sodium nitrite and packed in synthetic casings. If, because of circumstances, you must eat some foods of this kind, as well as vegetables grown with nitrate fertilizer, protect yourself with food supplements containing vitamins and minerals which make your body stronger in its resistance to these poisons. Take, every day, brewer's yeast (for vitamin B), fish liver oil capsules (for vitamins A and D) and bone meal for minerals.

Apparently in Europe people prefer to take a chance on botulism than to eat foods treated with chemical preservatives. Botulism is not a pleasant thing and we would not like to contemplate it every time we purchase a bit of meat. But are the chemical preservatives less harmful, in the long run, over a span of years? And does it not seem possible that our marvelously complex and efficient system of transportation, distribution and refrigeration might permit the meat processors to sell us fresh meat that has not been embalmed and impregnated with preservative poisons?

CHAPTER 220

Poisons in Your Food

"Last year more than two billion pounds of insecticide were manufactured in the United States. Some 30,000 registered formulas, containing some 100 pesticidal chemicals, have become virtual necessities to American agriculture. These are poisons, yet small quantities of them inevitably get into food." With these words Ralph G. Martin introduces his excellent article "How Much Poison Are We Eating?" in the April, 1955, issue of *Harper's* magazine.

He tells us that, beginning in 1955, a new law made it necessary for the producer of a new insecticide to ask the Food and Drug Administration to "set a tolerance" for his product. This means the FDA must decide how much residue of this insecticide may be left on fruits and vegetables in interstate commerce. The FDA has 90 days to study the evidence. And the manufacturer must abide by their decision. We suppose this also means that, if the FDA should decide that the substance is so poisonous that no residue dare remain on foods, the insecticide would be withdrawn.

The interesting thing is that we have never had any law of this kind before. Up to 1955, any manufacturer might put an insecticide on the market with no proof at all of its possible safety for human consumption. The government had to prove that the insecticide was harmful by showing in court cases that individuals had been harmed (perhaps fatally) by the substance, or that animal experiments demonstrated considerable toxicity. As you can see, such procedures were extremely expensive in time and money and, of course, no one knows how much damage had been done before the poisonous product was withdrawn.

The Toxicological Question

One example is given by Mr. Martin. At the testimony before the Delaney Congressional Committee from whose hearings the bill evolved, Dr. W. C. Hueper of the National Cancer Institute revealed that the discovery that a certain insecticide was cancer-causing was made quite accidentally. So its use was forbidden. But had this accident not happened, the insecticide in question might now be used on food without anyone being any the wiser. How many cases of cancer might it have caused?

Against the pressure of the agricultural forces for more and better and hence more poisonous insecticides are pitted the efforts of many food companies who are trying to keep insecticides out of their products. Beechnut alone spent $100,000 a year trying to buy foods free from insecticides for their baby foods. Other big food companies such as A & P, Quaker Oats and so forth, maintain large laboratories. An article in *Fortune* magazine described the new two million dollar Du Pont laboratory—the largest industrial center for toxicological research in the nation.

Said *Fortune:* "There is, unfortunately, no simple yes-and-no answer to a toxicological question since there is no such thing as a completely safe or non-toxic material. Thus ordinary water, a chemical in its own right, will ruin the kidneys if too much is drunk day after day. For many individuals, the 'natural' chemicals in a strawberry shortcake are enough to make it an allergic poison. The task of industrial toxicology is to find, quickly and harmlessly, the tolerable extent to which any new material should be introduced into mankind's complicated environment."

The Long Term Effects Are Important

Mr. Martin in *Harper's* goes on to tell us that "the reason for all this anxiety is not the microscopic bit of insecticide residue on any one apple you eat. It is fear of the unknown cumulative effect, the long-range build-up inside your body of the vast variety of toxic materials that may crop up in every meal. In his testimony, Dr. Francis E. Ray, director of the Cancer Research Laboratory of the University of Florida, explained why in his field this problem is particularly difficult to solve. 'Long continued application of small doses,' he said, 'is more effective in producing tumors than are large doses frequently applied. . . . Cancer of the internal organs may pass unnoticed until it has progressed to the fatal stage. In human cancer therefore it might be very difficult to prove that a tumorous growth was initiated by the long-continued ingestion of small amounts of chemicals in food'."

How can you judge what the poisonous effect of any chemical will be over a period of years? How much of it is retained by the body? Does it change into any other substance inside the body that may be even more dangerous? Can we assume that tests with experimental animals will give the same results as tests with human beings?

And, in this respect, how is it possible to know in a laboratory experiment how much poison any one individual may be getting from his environment—all of it cumulative? Laboratory animals are raised in safe air-conditioned cages, with a carefully prepared diet and distilled water, protected against any possible poison. Then they are given only one chemical as a test. But the unfortunate human inhabitant of the twentieth century has met with a score of poisons (and may have begun to store them in his body) before he is even born! Every hour of the day and night from then on he is constantly bombarded with one poisonous substance after another. Who is going to test his ability to withstand *all these poisons at the same time* especially if they are all accumulating inside his body?

The Effect of DDT

About DDT Mr. Martin says: "Here is an insecticide that has been almost wholly integrated into our way of life, as familiar as orange juice. Last year we used at least a hundred million pounds of it and sprayed it on everything from hotel beds to whole cities. We eat DDT all the time, all of us. An investigation reported at a recent meeting of the American Public Health Association revealed that no meal had been found on which some trace of DDT did not appear, and that the daily menu for the average American contained 181 micrograms of it. . . .

"What particularly concerns the doctors is the tendency of DDT to store up in the fatty tissues of all animals, humans included. Dr. Francis Pottenger, Jr., secretary for the Los Angeles County Medical Commission for the Study of Environmental Contaminants, made a random sample in his community. 'If people after 4 or 5 years,' he reported, 'who have no reason to suspect that they have DDT in their bodies are found to have from zero to 33 parts per million of DDT in their fat, what is going to happen after we have been using DDT from 10 to 15 years'?"

Staying Power of the New Insecticides

"With chlordane—as with other poisons in common use, like toxaphene, aldrin, dieldrin and heptachlor—the residues are powerfully difficult to remove; you cannot wash them off most foods even with a hot detergent bath. Worse still are the poisons that have staying power in the soil. Even if they are banned for use on edible food, crop rotation may bring them out in foods grown years later on the same ground."

It was found, for instance, that benzenehexachloride (BHC) caused cancer-like growths in test animals. The Department of Agriculture urged all growers not to use it on edible foods. Mark you—this is all the government could do—"urge." It could not *forbid* the use of BHC. But as long as 3 years later BHC in the soil maintained up to half of its original concentration. BHC is still used on cotton. If peanuts are planted in rotation between cotton crops, the BHC shows up in the peanuts, causing an off-flavor and, of course, adding a little bit of deadly poison to be stored in the tissues of the people who eat the peanuts.

Systemic insecticides are so horrible that the mind wavers in an attempt to contemplate them with equanimity. "A systemic poison is absorbed into the plant itself, not merely sprayed on the outside, so that insects sucking the sap from the foliage get it into their own systems and are killed. . . . Only two and a half parts per million of the poison kills an insect who feeds on the leaf so grown. . . . Under the new law, approval for thousands of new systemics will be sought," says Mr. Martin.

Sir Edward Mellanby, the world-renowned nutritionist, speaking before a medical school in London in 1951, said, "Phenyl mercury compounds are used as fungicides on fruit and vegetable crops. It has been pointed out that as little as 2½ parts of chlordane per million in the diet produces pathological (disease) changes in the liver in rats, that 3 parts of the selenium compounds per million in the diet will produce cirrhosis of the liver and, if continued, cancer of the liver in animals; and that in the case of phenyl mercury compounds as little as .5 parts of mercury per million in the liver in the form of phenylmercuric acetate leads to measurable storage in the kidney with damage to that organ in animals."

The Dangers of Chemicalization

Mr. Martin continues: "Nonetheless there is a growing group of agricultural experts who feel that too heavy a use of insecticides may lead us into a downward spiral toward disaster. Many of them belong to what is generally known as the Organic Farming school, which holds that healthy plants in naturally fertilized soil can resist insects and disease without the aid of chemicals. There is often much mystical philosophy in this view; its claims cannot all be supported; and for large-scale farming the composting method would be prohibitively expensive. (Editor's note: We suggest you ask some of the large-scale organic farmers about that, Mr. Martin!) But despite the violence of the discussion Organic Farmers have aroused, there may be much to be learned from the questions they raise. . . .

"For example, Dr. William Albrecht, the nationally-known nutrition expert of the University of Missouri, points out that you can kill insects and get more pounds of corn per acre, but the total amount of protein taken from that acre remains the same. And author-farmer Louis Bromfield, with much-publicized success, has operated farms in France, Ohio and Texas without using insecticides at all. Other 'organicists' have warned that insecticides could backfire (as they may already have done) by creating super-insects, bred from those that are immune, and thus increasing the ultimate pest population."

In spite of the seriousness of the situation, in spite of the fact that the chemical and insecticide manufacturers themselves know what a tough problem they have on their hands, you will find people all over the country rising to announce in loud tones that there is little if any danger and that more and more poisons must be made and spread around on our soil and food, as fast as we can manufacture them. An editorial in the Shreveport (Louisiana) *Journal* for February 15, 1955, praises the chemical industry, saying (believe it or not!), "Chemical fertilizers are putting back into our soils increasing amounts of the plant food removed by crops and erosion. Chemical pesticides are now dramatically reducing the losses caused by pests. . . . Chemicals likewise enhance food values . . . retard molding . . . keep foods soft and moist . . . give better texture." The editorial ends with a strong denunciation of any law which would "require prior government approval of every new ingredient going into food" for it would "hamper new research and drastically limit the nation's hopes for progressing toward its goal of greater abundance."

For this editorial writer we have only one suggestion—that he offer to be the human guinea pig for the new insecticides. The rest of us will wait for half a lifetime or so and see how he makes out.

What Can We Do?

What can readers do in the face of this kind of thinking? First of all, protect yourself and your family if you possibly can. Have your own garden and grow as much of your food as possible, organically. If this is impractical, buy as much organically grown food as you can afford. Make certain your diet is rich in the B vitamins, calcium and vitamin C—3 things that will help to protect you against the doses of poison you get every day.

We do not know of any definite set of experiments proving that vitamin C protects against the evil effects of DDT. But we do know that it is necessary in the fight against any poison. That is one of its main functions in the body—detoxification. So one of your best guards against the possible devastating effects of DDT over a long period of time is plenty of vitamin C in your diet. Fresh raw fruits and vegetables are the best source—and, of course, rose hip and other completely natural food supplements.

Finally, we agree with Mr. Martin when he says that the law for testing toxicity *first* before allowing insecticides on food "will be effective only if public pressure makes it effective. So far, the chemical companies and the food processors have been much more conscious of the need for the law than the average consumer, for the press gave the hearings almost no coverage. . . . The hope of this law is severe enforcement. . . . And it is the hope most of all that public awareness will maintain constant pressure to keep this law strict and strong, so that never again will the American people be 160 million guinea pigs."

Letters to your congressman, your senator, the Food and Drug Administration, your newspaper, your favorite magazines (especially the women's magazines which should be deeply concerned with the wholesomeness of our food) should help to put on pressure. Write to the people from whom you buy your produce. Tell them you would rather have a wormhole now and then, you would rather have beans and peas not quite so full-podded, if you could only be certain they did not contain deadly insecticides. Finally, remember that a federal law protects only food that crosses state lines. Local produce may be loaded with poisons unless you have an equally effective state law forbidding it. Talk to your state representative about it.

[823]

CHAPTER 221

The New Food Additives Law

Often it's easy to make up your mind about something controversial by finding out who its friends and enemies are. Any anticipation we felt over the food additives legislation passed by Congress (1958-1959) was quickly dispelled when we began to read the reactions of food industry leaders to the new bill. *Food Field Reporter, Food Engineering* and *Food Processing,* 3 of the magazines of the food trade, are gleefully predicting that *now* for the first time food processors can really cut loose and go to town so far as chemicals are concerned.

Right away, the Food and Drug Administration announced the names of 118 food additives which are exempt from any testing for safety by food processors. These 118 are completely safe, according to the FDA. The list is amazing. It includes 39 substances listed as "buffers and neutralizing agents." These substances are nothing that you or I have to put in fresh food when we prepare it for the table. But food processors declare that they cannot possibly make food that is acceptable to the American public without the 39 chemicals. They include such items as sulfuric acid, aluminum ammonium sulfate, sodium aluminum phosphate—and so forth. Listed as "preservatives and sequestrants" are some 61 chemicals including several familiar ones like sodium propionate (used as a preservative in bread). Listed as "Miscellaneous" are certain waxes, butane (an anesthetic substance made from coal tar) and another petroleum product called propane. So you can expect at least these 118 chemicals in most things you buy from now on. Nobody plans to do anything at all about removing any of them.

New Names For Food Chemicals

In the same issue of *Food Field Reporter* (December 8, 1958) there is an interesting article on a proposed scheme for giving food chemicals new names. "There is great need for the adoption of simple, easily remembered names which can have informative value to the consumer in place of the incomprehensible chemical names used in food labels which, rather than educate, tend to cause doubts and fears," said a committee of the Food and Drug Administration. As soon as we have set the best minds in the department to work on this knotty problem, the troubles of the consumer will be over. The "butylated hydroxyanisole, propyl gallate and propylene glycol" which now appears as the alarming chemical preservative on your cereal box will now be stated something like this, we suppose: "Crunchy crispets added to preserve freshness." Nothing there to alarm you surely, unless you should write to Washington to find out what this new name means.

There's no doubt of it, the alarm so many Americans feel over the chemicals we are forced to eat every day *has* made an impression in Washington, or officials would not be planning fancy names for chemicals to allay doubts and fears. The more letters you, your family, friends and neighbors write to the Food and Drug Administration, protesting the use of *any* chemicals in food, the more chance there is of removing *all* of them.

Some of the Complications We Face

One astounding paragraph from *Food Processing* (October, 1958) states: "If an additive is poisonous per se, that is, is toxic when consumed without limitation as to amount or frequency, its use in food could (under the old law) not be permitted unless shown to be necessary or unavoidable in production. In this case a tolerance would have to be established. (In other words, in such cases FDA would decide how much of such a poisonous substance might be used in food.)

"This provision of the old law was unworkable," the article goes on, "first, because it has not been possible to demonstrate the necessity of ingredients in question, and secondly, because practically any food ingredient can be shown to be toxic depending on the conditions of testing." Now there's an honest viewpoint for you. What the editor of this magazine is saying in just so many words is (of course, only for the ears of other food processors) that there is no necessity for any chemicals to be used in food and that all of them are poisonous depending on how and in what quantity they are used.

Under the new law, he goes on, "It is not the additive itself which must be shown to be safe under every foreseeable condition of use. It is a particular use of an additive in a particular food at a particular level . . . . The conclusion that the use of an additive is safe does not require absolute certainty that no injury can result; it requires only a practical certainty."

So who's cheering over the new law? You or the makers of food additives or the officials of the Food and Drug Administration whose job has been greatly simplified, we think, at what cost in health and longevity among consumers?

An Incredible Theory

Finally, this same issue of *Food Processing* contains one of the most astounding pieces of writing we have ever seen anywhere. Entitled *Health Hazard or Safeguard?* it propounds the philosophy that the best way to stay healthy is to be constantly subjected to poisons and actually the food industry is not truly serving the public interest by trying to prevent the ingestion of poisons (as if they ever did).

No, the author of this incredible theory is not an escaped lunatic. It is Dr. Henry F. Smyth, Jr., who is in charge of the Chemical Hygiene Fellowship of Mellon Institute, engaged in toxicological investigation for the Union Carbide Company who make—you guessed it—chemicals, many of which find their way into our food.

Showing the fact that human beings, over millions of years, have had to survive many unpleasant and "challenging" misfortunes, Dr. Smyth says that "life seems to thrive upon frequent operation of its regulatory protective mechanisms so long as the challenge is not great enough to overwhelm the defenses."

Dr. Smyth does not take up the, to us, very important question of just who is going to be appointed to stand beside every individual human being and decide at what moment he has had a "challenge great enough to overwhelm his defenses." Naturally no two human beings are exposed to the same amount of poisons over a lifetime.

Nor does he explain that mankind has adapted himself to the "challenge" of adverse environment of one kind or another over a period of probably millions of years, but Dr. Smyth and his fellow poisoners stand ready to overwhelm him with poisons in the brief space of the 20 or 30 years since we began this pernicious chemical poisoning of food.

So the answer is that the more poison you get (so long as it doesn't kill you) the healthier you'll be, according to the Union Carbide Corporation. We think you should be as alarmed as we were by this theory. It is bound to influence the thinking of many people in future years, particularly people involved in the highly profitable manufacture of food chemicals.

To be on the safe side, shun factoryized food. Stick to meat, eggs, fruit, nuts, fish and vegetables. You'll get plenty of chemicals in these, too, but at least you won't be subjecting yourself to the possible poisoning by the additional chemicals added when any of these foods is processed in a factory.

CHAPTER 222

Complications Created by The New Law

There is a monthly magazine devoted to the problems that arise in administering the laws that have to do with chemicals in food and cosmetics. Called the *Food Drug Cosmetic Law Journal,* this publication presents many interesting sidelights on what goes on among food processors, chemical manufacturers and the Food and Drug Administration.

The January, 1959, issue consists of questions and answers about the new food additives law that was passed by Congress in 1958. As with any new law, the actual business of interpreting the law is complicated in the extreme. Hidden in the questions and answers are facts that dismay even the most hardened enemy of chemicals in foods—facts about chemicals in foods that did not occur even to us during these past years.

Most concerned of all those asking questions were the people involved in packaging food. Question after question is listed and all of them involved in packaging materials that eventually get into food—plastic, adhesives, coating agents and so forth. It is taken for granted by everybody concerned that this kind of exchange takes place. In other words, for many years we have been eating many of the chemicals that occur in plastic, in waxes, in adhesives, in coating agents. They have been in our food and nobody has ever tested any of them for toxicity. The very urgency of the questions asked by the manufacturers of such products is certainly an indication of the knowledge they must have about the probable toxicity of these substances. Who knew better than they?

Their questions involve even such things as paper cups used in soft drink or coffee dispensers, plastic or paper plates and eating utensils intended for picnics, cooking utensils, refrigerator bowl covers, plastic tableware, wax paper, foil and so forth. No one volunteers the information that his product may be forbidden by law after the FDA has all the facts about possible toxicity, but plainly everybody who asked questions had possible toxicity in mind.

The FDA is Uninformed

How do you feel about this question, asked, we suppose, by some meat packing or poultry packing company. "Will the law cover arsenic compounds which are now being increased, such as in chicken and pork, as a result of feeding arsenicals to animals?" The answer given by the FDA is, "We are not aware that the quantity of arsenic in chicken and pork is is being increased." The man who asked the question is aware of it, but the FDA is not.

Another question was "How will the control differentiate between compounds such as those related to stilbestrol (a hormone product) that may find their way into infant foods through plant products such as alfalfa, and stilbestrol compounds which are added directly to foods or indirectly from feeding chickens and cattle?" The answer of the FDA is, "We are not aware that stilbestrol is finding its way into infants' food through plant products such as alfalfa." The people who sell the stilbestrol and the people who sell the baby foods are aware of it, but the FDA is not.

We have been assured through all these years in which stilbestrol has been used that none of it ever remains in the flesh of the animal who has received it. Now we are told that it not only remains there, but that it is "finding its way" into baby foods! And this is news to the Food and Drug Administration.

Another question: "Will the law cover the potential accumulation of compounds, such as Megasul, that may accumulate in the giblets of poultry as a result of feeding this compound to chickens and turkeys?" We do not know what this particular chemical is. But there is a good chance that it is toxic or whoever asked the question would not have been concerned.

The Power of the "Food Faddists" Is Well-Known

Here's an interesting question. "In Germany at the present time there is much difficulty concerning the establishment and enforcement of progressive good food laws because of the voice of the food faddists encouraged by those whose selfish interests would be served in this way. The FDA claims to discourage food faddism in the United States. The FDA claims, however, that consumers in the United States want to know through label declaration all the chemicals present in their food, regardless of function and regardless of established safety in the subtolerance levels present. It is believed by much of industry that it is only the food faddist consumer who wants declaration of all chemical substances."

We are glad to say that the FDA answered this one thus: "We believe that responsible consumers want to know what is in their food . . . Further, we believe consumers have a right to know what is in their food. The food industry cannot hope to generate public confidence in its product by trying to conceal what is present in them."

Another question brings to light the fact that some packaging material contains traces of asphalt. Another question brings to light the fact that "many food additives are not single pure compounds and may vary somewhat in composition when made by different chemical manufacturers." We suppose one of these may be toxic and another not toxic. On the deceptive use of an additive, a question was asked concerning the "use of copper in canned peas to make them appear less mature and the use of sulfites to redden stale meat."

The FDA tells us that the new regulations will apply henceforth "in evaluating the safety of residues in meat, milk and eggs which result from use of a new veterinary preparation." We assume this means that up to now we have been eating the residues of whatever new drug has been given to the cow, sheep or the chicken.

The FDA's Impossible Task

How is the FDA going to decide what is and is not toxic? It's right here that the whole idea of legislating this kind of matter breaks down, we believe. We are told that before the FDA permits an additive it will consider:

"1. The probable consumption of the additive on all foods on which it is permitted.

"2. The probable consumption of any other chemicals in the diet that might have the same effect on the body or might make the first additive harmful in smaller amounts.

"3. Bearing both of these factors in mind, FDA will only allow quantities of the additive in food which will be safe, even though the consumer eats a number of foods that contain the maximum amount of additive or additives allowed." The completely impossible nature of such decisions becomes apparent as soon as you stop to think of the wide variety of foods eaten in this country and the peculiar food habits which characterize most of us. We know people who eat catsup every day of their lives. We know people who eat maraschino cherries every day. Just how is the FDA going to decide how much of each chemical in just these two foods is going to be consumed by every individual American? And how is the FDA going to know which of these individuals, getting the most of any given chemical, may be the very one most likely to suffer from it?

Water Fluoridation Gets Into the Picture

Here is an interesting question: "Are tolerances going to be set on incidental fluoride contamination of foods? Fluorides may be picked up from process water or packaging materials, or may be concentrated from naturally occurring fluorides in the raw materials." We believe such a question is of utmost importance to those Americans who must drink fluoridated water. The FDA answers that tolerances will be set on fluorides if someone asks that they be set and if this someone proves that the amount of fluorides in his product is "safe." Safe for whom? For laboratory rats eating the best possible diet and drinking distilled water? Or for Citizen A in a town with fluoridated water who drinks two glasses of water a day? Or Citizen B, resident of the same town, who drinks 12 glasses of water? The rat is getting no fluoride except what occurs in the food being tested. Citizen B is getting a certain amount in his water and—who knows—perhaps 20 times as much in his food as Citizen A.

Who is capable of deciding whether Citizen B is going to be poisoned eventually by the total amount of fluorides he is getting—in food and water?

Coal Tar Dyes

On the subject of coal tar dyes the questions—and the answers, too—are fantastic. We are dealing with a substance known to be completely useless in food, suspected of being highly toxic and very probably cancer-causing (many coal-tar dyes are).

"*Question:* What certifiable coal-tar colors has FDA tested and found to be harmless?"

"*Answer:* We have not completed our toxicity testing on any of the certifiable coal-tar colors and thus we are not in a position to list any of them as clearly harmless . . ."

"*Question:* Mr. Rankin made a statement to the effect that it will require about 20 years to complete the pharmacological testing of 'coal-tar colors.' Is it not true that this estimated period includes not only the 16 food colors, but also the 68 drug and cosmetic and the 32 external drug and cosmetic colors?"

"*Answer:* Yes."

"*Question:* How much time will be required to complete this work on the 16 food colors only?"

"*Answer:* Approximately 8 years."

After only this small sampling of the matters that concern food processors, food chemical manufacturers and the FDA, we are sure you will agree with us that the new law, far from protecting us from harm, will probably result in only more chicanery, more confusion and more chemicals in food.

We urge readers to continue the protests they have so courageously and steadfastly made in the past. Tell your grocer, the editor of your local newspaper, your local and state health departments, and state legislators, your Federal health department and your congressmen and senators. Let them know that we "food faddists" are not interested just in knowing what chemicals are in our foods. We are interested in getting them out of there and we will settle for nothing less than food entirely free from chemicals.

CHAPTER 223

Good Legislation on Chemicals in Food

Recently introduced into Congress was a bill and a joint resolution which should have the support of every reader.

The bill is numbered HR 9150. It proposes a law for establishing a commission to conduct an impartial and scientific study and investigation to determine the effects on the public health of the practice of adding various chemicals to water supplies and food products.

The Joint Resolution, H. J. Res. 523, is to prohibit officers and employees of the United States from treating communal water supplies with fluoride compounds until a report from the Commission on Food and Water Contamination shall have been submitted to the Congress of the United States.

These important pieces of legislation were presented by Representative David S. King of Utah, who made an excellent speech in the House on the day after he presented the bill. He said, among other things, "When the American housewife wheels her cart around the super market, she is only dimly aware, if at all, that it is almost impossible for her to purchase any article of food that has not had chemicals, bleaches, preservatives, additives, dyes, adulteratives and other foreign substances added to it. Until last year, the law was so worded that any new chemical compound which was not a known poison could be added to any food for consumption and the burden then fell on the Food and Drug Administration to prove that these foreign substances were deleterious to human health. This proof was difficult to adduce, from a legal point of view, even when immediate toxicity could be demonstrated. But it was almost impossible to do when the toxicity of the chemical compound was of such a nature that it could not be detected until after the expiration of many years. Because of the outstanding work of the Delaney Commission, the food additive amendment was passed last year which requires food processors to submit to the FDA the results of their tests on new chemical compounds. But the law is still filled with loopholes.

"It seems to me that it takes only a slight leap of the imagination on the part of the American housewife to grasp the proposition that where the incidence of degenerative diseases such as cancer, arteriosclerosis and degenerative heart disease suddenly increases, and apparently for no known reason, and where it is shown that contemporaneously with such increase there occurs a phenomenal increase in the total amount of chemical compounds consumed, then there may well exist a casual connection between these two phenomena. I am quite aware of the fallacy of oversimplification, and I fully recognize the probability of a multiplicity of causes in any phenomenon as complex as disease. What I do say, however, is that the ever-increasing scientific evidence renders it highly probable that the invariable concurrence of disease and body contamination by the consumption of toxic chemicals is more than coincidental.

"It is apparent that this entire subject requires a thorough investigation. The health, and maybe even the survival, of the American nation is at stake. Our laws on nutrition are loose and inadequately drawn. Public knowledge is fragmentary, and riddled with misinformation and discarded dogmas. The means of disseminating information on this subject are inadequate."

We think this is one of the finest statements we have ever seen on the perils we all face from chemicals in food and water. It is well hidden in the Congressional Record. How many of the folks in your town or city will ever know of its existence? How many will ever know that such a law has been proposed?

Work for the Passage of this Good Legislation

There is one sure way that you can help them find out about it. Very few people read the Congressional Record, but almost everybody reads the daily paper. And most people take time to read the "Letters to the Editor" column. If you feel strongly that you want to be better protected against chemicals in food and water by stronger and more easily enforced federal legislation, write a letter to the editor of your local newspaper. Say anything you want to say, so long as you state only facts that you know to be true. We think it would be good policy to quote some or all of the words of Representative King as we have quoted them above.

Ask your townspeople to write to their congressman urging him to support Representative King's proposed law. Give the number of the bill—H.R. 9150 and the Joint Resolution H. J. Res. 523.

Give the name of your representative so that everyone will know where to write. (Your newspaper can tell you his name if you do not know it.) His address is House Office Building, Washington, D.C. He wants to hear from the folks back home. How else can he know what you want him to do in Washington?

Let's have a letter, at least one letter, to the editor on the page of every newspaper in the United States! Now is our chance to be heard—and to be *in favor of something rather than always being against!* We are one hundred per cent in favor of this legislation!

CHAPTER 224

Chemicals and Food Supplies

The following is an address delivered before The House of Lords in the English Parliament on July 4, 1951, by Lord Douglas of Barloch. With a few exceptions as noted by Lord Douglas, the situation in this country is the same as it is in England, so far as chemicals in foods are concerned.

My Lords, only two or three generations ago mankind existed upon naturally occurring foods, either eaten raw or prepared by such simple means as roasting or boiling and, in some cases, preserved for further use by smoking or salting. All that is now changed. It is becoming increasingly difficult to find any natural article of food which has not been treated with chemicals, had some part extracted, been exposed to high temperatures or preserved for long periods in cold storage, or otherwise processed or tampered with. I do not say that science can never find means of improving foodstuffs, but I do say that the addition of extraneous matters, and especially of synthetic chemicals, should be looked upon with the gravest suspicion and should not be permitted except under the most strenuous conditions. This subject has hitherto received too little attention in this country, and the steps taken to protect the public have been hesitating, partial and inadequate.

The gravity of the situation has been revealed in the United States by the well-organized and continuing work of the Federal Food and Drug Administration, which has listed no fewer than 842 chemicals used or proposed to be used in food. Some are no longer used because they were definitely found to be poisonous. The majority are still in use, some very extensively; and in many cases it is not clearly established whether they are poisonous or not. The absolute determination of the toxicity of a chemical added to food requires long and very complex investigations. The chemical may not be toxic in itself, but may combine with substances naturally presented in the body to form toxic compounds. It may be very slow acting but cumulative in its effects. It may be one of those which are stored in the body, and the ill effects of which become evident only after a certain concentration has been passed. It may be a racial poison which interferes with reproduction or injures the next generation. Last year a Select Committee of the House of Representatives of the Congress of the United States was set up, with very wide terms of reference, to investigate the use of chemicals in the growing, preparation and handling of food. It has taken a large volume of important evidence, but so far as I know has not yet reported. Since this Motion was placed on the Order Paper, Sir Edward Mellanby, who was for some time the distinguished Secretary of the Medical Research Council, has, in a lecture on the chemical manipulation of food, drawn attention to the far-reaching implications of this practice and the need for action.

There are two principal ways in which chemicals are added to food. One is as an incident of effecting another purpose. This happens when insecticides, fungicides and weed-killers are used in agriculture, and, in some cases, where fumigants or disinfectants are used during process of manufacture, or where detergents are used for washing food or for washing crockery and food containers. The other is where chemicals are introduced with the express intention of altering the nature of the food or of preserving it beyond its normal life. Besides these there are the cases in which the quality of the food is altered by exposure to very high temperatures, causing chemical reactions in its constituents.

I do not propose to deal with the use of artificial fertilizers in agriculture, beyond saying that it is now admitted, even by ardent advocates of them, that unbalanced use of such fertilizers may easily produce a luxuriant plant growth which is also unbalanced; there may be too little protein, and the human being or the animal fed upon this green stuff suffers injury to health or lowered resistance to disease. It is also of interest to note that lack of proper fertilization renders the plants themselves more liable to fungus diseases and to attacks by insects or other pests, leading to increased use of insecticides and fungicides. It has long been common to use sprays or washes on fruit trees in order to discourage the attacks of mites or insects. A number of these sprays are probably harmless, although, in this whole matter, we should take nothing for granted. Some are definitely toxic; for example, lead arsenate, which, like other compounds of lead, is accumulated in the body with the possibility of its ultimately reaching a dangerous level.

I shall say no more about the older insecticides. It is the newer ones, and the enormous extent of their use, which give most cause for alarm. The most famous of these is DDT which, since the war, has been applied all over the world without any adequate investigation of its effects upon health. It is highly toxic. Test animals—rats, for example—fed with one part per million of DDT perished—and one part per million is equivalent to one teaspoonful in 10 tons of food. Not only is DDT highly toxic but it is fat soluble. Consequently, it may accumulate in the body fats, through repeated small doses, until a toxic concentration is reached. Or, if this concentration has been approached and, owing to illness or for other reasons, the body is consuming its store of fat, the concentration then becomes toxic and the patient is attacked at the very time when his resistance is lowered. Not only is DDT exceptionally toxic, but there is no known antidote. It is absorbed by plants and cannot be removed. Hence, all fruits and vegetables which have been exposed to DDT are carriers of it to the consumers. Animals fed on hay or other food exposed to it are affected. Owing to its solubility in fat, milk is especially affected by it. The spraying of DDT in cowsheds has been found

[833]

sufficient to affect the milk, and in the United States dairy farmers have been officially advised not to do this. Butter sold on the New York market has been found with as much as 13 parts per million of this dangerous drug. The fact that DDT has such an affinity for milk constitutes a serious danger for infants, and for young children who are encouraged to drink large quantities of milk. Even breast-fed infants are not safe, for mothers' milk has been found containing appreciable quantities of DDT.

The New Introductions

Other extremely toxic substances are now being used as insecticides, such as H.E.T.P., T.E.P.C. and parathion. They were invented by the Germans as war gases but not actually used as such. They are so dangerous that those who use them must be covered from head to foot with protective clothing. Already a number of fatal accidents have occurred to farm workers spraying with insecticides. This has engaged the attention of the Ministry of Agriculture, and a working party under the chairmanship of Professor Zuckerman has recently reported on this aspect of their use. Unfortunately, little is known of the effect of these chemicals on the foodstuffs to which they are applied or upon the health of the men and women who consume the foodstuffs. There are on record, however, at least two cases in which people have developed illness which appeared to be due to flour containing one part per million of parathion. The illness ceased upon another flour being used in which none of this poison was found.

I may also remind your Lordships that when fruit trees are sprayed about 95 per cent of the spray falls on the ground; and if this ground should be used for growing other crops, those crops will receive a far higher concentration of the poison than the fruit trees. In the United States in the year 1947 no less than 150,000,000 pounds of insecticides were produced. This is practically one pound per head of the population; and if only a very small fraction of that finds its way into the human body the cumulative results may be catastrophic.

Before I leave the agricultural side of this matter I should like to mention the use of antibiotics and hormones. As a result of treating an inflammation of the udder of one cow with penicillin, the milk was affected to such an extent that it destroyed the organisms essential for cheese-making when mixed with that of 200 other cows. An indirect result of consuming milk thus infected with penicillin or other antibiotics is that the consumer might perhaps become resistant to this remedy in such fashion that, if it were prescribed for some illness, he would receive no benefit. Another example is the use of a hormone powder called tuberite for the purpose of suppressing the sprouts of potatoes. I do not know whether it is for this or other reasons that in recent years it has become almost impossible to purchase potatoes of good quality in London. Other hormones are used as weed-killers, but it does not follow that, because they have a selective action on weeds, they do not affect other plants and the persons who consume them. It is well known that hormones are extremely potent in very small quantities and may have most dangerous effects.

Imported food is as liable to be affected as home-grown food. I have heard of oranges being sprayed with DDT, the fruit when picked being dyed and then waxed. I should not like to eat marmalade made from fruit so treated. Recently, I noticed that a proposal is under consideration for preventing the spread of swollen shoot disease among the cocoa trees of the Gold Coast. The principle of it is that the sap of the tree should be induced to imbibe a poison that will kill the mealy bug by which the disease is transmitted from tree to tree. The idea is ingenious, but what effect will the poison have upon the cocoa bean, upon the cocoa derived from it and upon the health of the consumers of cocoa and chocolate in this country and elsewhere? The effects of poisons used in agriculture received some attention at the Second International Conference on Crop Protection held in London in 1949 and presided over by Viscount Bledisloe. He has authorized me to say that, but for an important and longstanding engagement, he would have been here today and that he considers that this matter deserves the serious attention of the Government.

Flour Bleachers and "Improvers"

Let us now deal with the use of chemicals in the processing of food-stuffs. Various chemicals are used to bleach flour, because it is said that the public insists upon having an absolutely white bread. It is somewhat strange that they do not insist upon having many other articles of food bleached also. Some chemicals are used for "maturing" flour in the space of a few hours, whereas nature takes weeks to effect this, and also for giving to inferior flour the characteristics of better flour. Others are used for the purpose of inducing flour to rise more, in order to produce a loaf which contains more air and water, which may be rather dearly bought in this way.

The most widely used of these so-called "improvers" of flour is nitrogen trichloride, commercially known as agene. After this chemical had been in use for about a quarter of a century, its toxic effects were discovered by Sir Edward Mellanby. The remarkable thing is that this discovery, like many other notable scientific discoveries, was made almost by accident. Professor Mellanby noticed that dogs which were being kept for another experiment were developing nervous disorders, which became progressively more grave and ended in epileptic seizures and death. In a research which is a classic of its kind, he traced the cause of the illness to food made from flour which had been treated with agene. His results were published in December, 1946. They were taken notice of immediately by the Food and Drug Administration of the United States, which caused independent investigation to be undertaken.

The results, which confirmed Mellanby's findings, were published on November 22, 1947, in the *Journal of the American Medical Association,* together with a letter from the Chairman of the Food and Nutrition Board of the National Research Council to the Commissioner of Food and Drugs advising him that the treatment of flour with agene should be discontinued.

The use of agene has been discontinued in the United States. It took several years longer for a decision in principle to be reached in this country, and only a few weeks ago the Parliamentary Secretary of the Ministry of Food stated that about 90 per cent of the flour consumed in this country was agenized. By way of excuse, I suppose, for this delay, it has frequently been stated that there is no evidence of injury to human beings arising from the use of agenised flour. There is abundant evidence that it is toxic to dogs and other mammals. Some people may be able to believe that nature by some queer chance has given human beings a special immunity from a poison which, until some 30 years ago, their bodies had never encountered. That notion flatly contradicts the whole principle of evolution and the adaptation of man to his environment.

It is true that in this particular case nobody has identified anybody as having died because of eating agenized flour, but the cumulative effects over many years may reveal themselves in quite unexpected forms. It has now been discovered that the toxic factor in agenised flour is a compound formed between the agene and the protein in the wheat. This illustrates the important fact that, even if a chemical used in the treatment of food is in itself relatively harmless, it may combine with some of the numerous substances of which food is composed to form a new and extremely toxic product.

I have dealt with this question of agene in some detail because it exemplifies the subtle nature of the perils arising from chemicals in foodstuffs, and because authoritative warnings about its possible danger seem to have been completely disregarded. In 1927 the Departmental Committee on the Treatment of Flour with Chemical Substances reported on the use of chlorine as a bleaching agent. They pointed out that it reacted with various constituents of the flour to form additional products, and that no harm to the body was likely to result from the chlorine itself but that the compounds formed might "act injuriously." They also pointed out that it might "irremediably impair the nutritive qualities of the flour" by affecting the vitamins which are present in small quantities and are very susceptible to mere traces of chemical reagents. The Committee went on to say that these observations applied also to the use of nitrogen trichloride, or agene, which is very highly reactive and on which they had evidence that its action on the protein of flour was probably similar. That was 24 years ago.

"Softeners"

In addition to the bleaching agents and improvers, there is a large class of substances euphemistically known by trade names as emulsifiers, softeners and fat-extenders, which are used in baking bread and cakes or in the preparation of patent flours and cake mixtures. Let me take but one example. Certain chemicals called polyoxyethyline stearates are used and sold under the name of bread softeners, upon the plea that they produce a larger loaf and that they displace part of the lard used for shortening. They are known commercially under various trade names, such as S-541, "Sta-soft" and so on. One manufacturer alone in the United States during a period of a little over 3 years sold more than 7,000,000 pounds of one of these products. But another manufacturer, after experimenting upon rats, hamsters and rabbits, discovered that this substance was highly toxic. It affected the

[836]

kidneys and caused testicular and gastric troubles. I will only add that the use of bread softeners has been banned in the mental hospitals of New York State. But the health of those outside mental hospitals is also important. The very nomenclature of these things is deceptive. "Fat extenders" are substitutes for fat and reduce the nutritive value. "Anti-staling agents" are food preservatives enabling bread and cakes to be kept longer by the manufacturer or vendor before reaching the consumer, but nevertheless it has not been proved that the food does not deteriorate by keeping.

Then in addition to the kinds of chemicals I have mentioned there are whole classes of sweetening agents used as substitutes for sugar, flavoring agents, coloring matter or dyes. Of the sweeteners I may mention P 4000 and dulcin. These have been found to be definitely toxic, although dulcin at least was in common use for many years. Among the substances which have been used as coloring matter were a class of AZO dyes which are known now to be toxic and to be a cause of liver tumors in test animals. One of these dyes was long used under the pleasant name of "butter-yellow," but is now known to be carcinogenic (cancer causing). Mineral oils have been used in the preparation of foodstuffs. Not only do they have no nutritive value, but because of their capacity for absorbing and immobilizing certain vitamins they actually deprive the body of essential elements in the diet.

Let me give one illustration of a drink, as distinguished from a foodstuff. Drinks are perhaps not expected to be very nutritious, but we do not expect them to be poisonous. Among the most popular drinks in the United States (and I notice that they are beginning to gain a market here), are the cola drinks. They are composed of phosphoric acid, sugar, caffeine, coloring and flavoring matter. Although the amount of phosphoric acid may appear to the uninitiated to be small, this acid is so powerful that it rapidly affects the teeth and dissolves the enamel. At the United States Naval Medical Research Institute human teeth were put into a cola beverage, and within a very short time they softened and started to dissolve. They became very soft in 48 hours.

How "Additives" Can Add Up

One article of food may at different stages have chemicals injected into it for various purposes. The wheat or flour may have been affected by DDT used as an insecticide; it has probably been treated with agene or other bleaching agents or improvers. The baker may add to it fat-extenders, emulsifiers or anti-staling agents. A cake-mix may also have added to it, in addition, flavoring or coloring matter. The sum total becomes rather alarming. Moreover, other articles of food consumed by the same person may contain still more chemicals. The manufacturers of these chemicals will say, and, no doubt, honestly, that they have no evidence that the things they are selling are harmful to human beings. We know now that this is not true in the case of many chemical additives to food which have been used for many years, and we have no right to assume, without the most stringent proof, that it is true of the others.

The fact is that man, having a much longer life than animals used in medical research, may in the end suffer serious injury by the continued ingestion of relatively small quantities of these alien substances; and such effects are very difficult to detect. It is, however, significant that there has been an increase in recent years in the incidence of diseases having a neurological (having to do with the nerves) component, such as duodenal ulcers, schizophrenia and disseminated sclerosis. It will be remembered that agene, for example, has a neurological effect upon test animals. Some may believe that men have become less able to cope with strain and worry, but it seems to me reasonable to assume that there are more definite and specific reasons for the increase in such disease. Another significant fact is that the number of yearly deaths from cancer in this country is more than 3 times as great as it was 50 years ago. It has been definitely established that certain chemicals which have been widely used in food give rise to cancer of the liver and other organs in animals. In human beings it is very difficult to establish the actual cause of cancer, but the rise in the number of deaths from this disease in a period in which the use of chemicals in food has increased so rapidly gives ground for reflection, if not for anxiety about the future trend of events.

Three Reforms Needed

Let me proceed to draw some conclusions. The first is that the law relating to the sale of food is defective in that, as a general rule, the onus of proving that something injurious has been added is thrown on to the consumer or on to the authorities responsible for food inspection. I have pointed out to your Lordships the difficulties of proving this, and the long time which may elapse before such proof is forthcoming: in the interval the poisonous article is put on the market with impunity. I would go further, and say that with few, if any, exceptions the use of chemicals in the preparation of foodstuffs should be prohibited. This principle is well stated in the Report of the Departmental Committee on the Treatment of Flour with Chemical Substances, published in 1927. The Committee said:

"The object of maintaining inviolate the purity of the flour supply we regard as inspired by sound instinct, and we think that the responsibility for relaxing the principle is a very grave one, particularly at a time when research is beginning to throw new light upon the existence and properties of the more subtle constituents of foodstuffs."

They also said:

"Our view is that flour should be the product of milling wheat without the addition of any foreign substance."

These seem to me to be wise words, and applicable to all foodstuffs.

As a corollary, it should be made an offense—if it is not so already by Statute or by Common Law—to use any kind of chemical (such for example as fat-extenders) as a substitute for a natural foodstuff. Secondly, all food should be labelled with a precise and clear statement of what it contains, and stating the quantity or proportions of each constituent. This is doubly important if the addition of any chemicals is permitted. The third conclusion to be drawn is that this matter should be under the supervision of one strong well-staffed and well-equipped central department, free from association with any trade influences. It should not be left to the unco-ordinated efforts of sanitary inspectors, medical officers of health and public analysts to try to detect the use of chemicals and their potential dangers. Local authorities have insufficient resources for discharging such complicated and difficult functions. Even if they had adequate resources, to leave such matters to their unaided efforts would result in a wasteful multiplication of effort.

The toxicity or otherwise of these articles can be discovered only by prolonged and expensive experiments, because among the questions to be answered are these. What is the cumulative effect over years, or over a lifetime? Does the chemical affect reproductive capacity? Is it a racial poison? It is beyond the wit of any private organization or of local health departments to keep pace with the ingenuity of the chemist and the food manufacturer. Many associations of food producers have research organizations, often assisted by government grants, constantly engaged upon devising new methods of treating foodstuffs for the purpose of increasing the sales and the profits therefrom. What is needed is a central department free from all dependence upon commercial research bodies. The proper Ministry appears to me to be the Ministry of Health. The Ministries of Food and Agriculture are in a sense concerned, but neither of them deals with the whole field, and both of them have associations which could conceivably be a handicap in undertaking this new task. I am therefore suggesting that the government should take energetic and immediate steps to set up such an organization, and to pass legislation prohibiting, or at least severely restricting, the use of chemicals in the preparation, and as ingredients, of food, and requiring a full and accurate disclosure of the substances contained in all articles sold as food which do not literally and completely conform to the description by which they are sold.

CHAPTER 225

Chemicals-in-Food Laws
Here and Abroad

Discouraging though the news is about current food legislation in our country, it appears that things are not a bit better in any other land. An article in *Food Drug Cosmetic Law Journal* for March, 1959, tells us why. The article is entitled "Progress of Foreign Food Laws." It is written by Julius G. Zimmerman, editor of Foreign Law for this journal. We thought when we saw it that it might reveal to us many startling facts about prohibitions against various chemicals in foods in other countries, an example from which we in this country could profit. Alas, such is not the case. Things are just about as bad in foreign countries.

In order to have an effective law, one must define the things one is legislating about. Mr. Zimmerman tells us that no one has yet arrived at a suitable definition of the words "food additives." It is still, he says, "A puzzle for scientists and legislators alike." He says that there is no civilized country left in the world which does not have in its basic food law a *general* prohibition against the sale of food that is harmful to health because of the presence of toxic ingredients, un-hygienic manufacturing methods or storage facilities, spoilage or other reason."

Four Provisions

He tells us that the joint conference on Food Additives of the World Health Organization, which met in 1955, laid the ground work for the study of the entire subject. This committee decided that "use of food additives to the advantage of the consumer may be technologically justified when it serves any of the following purposes: 1. maintaining the nutritional quality of food, 2. enhancing the keeping quality or stability with resulting reduction in food wastage, 3. making foods attractive to the consumer in a manner which does not lead to deception, or 4. providing essential aid in food processing.

How would you analyze these 4 provisions? We would analyze them about like this. By "maintaining the nutritional quality of the food," the manufacturer generally means adding a few synthetic vitamins to some food from which he has carefully removed practically all the natural vitamins. By "enhancing the keeping quality or stability," he means that he is going to add something to the product so that *he* can keep it on his shelves for months (years maybe) and it will not spoil. This is universally represented as being an "advantage to the consumer." Never is it suggested by anyone who has anything to do with food laws that such additives are *for the advantage of the processor alone*. His profit is safe; he has few problems with spoilage. And he calls this "protecting the consumer."

"Making foods attractive" is another slogan of the food people who deal with chemical additive legislation. Take the case of the dye that has been used on most Florida oranges and which was recently found to be poisonous and ordered discontinued. The chips were down. There was no longer any reason to pretend that the oranges were dyed to "make them more attractive" to consumers. They were dyed because they are sold in competition with California oranges which are naturally orange. The consumer's interest means nothing. The Florida citrus grower's profits are at stake.

Later, an amendment was signed by the President allowing oranges to be colored by these same dyes which have been proven to be poisonous for another couple of months to allow for the transition from the old dye to another temporary one. And the temporary one is to be allowed up to September 1, 1961, if nothing better is found before that time. What is the reason given for this permit to continue poisoning Americans? Says the *Journal*, "This emergency legislation is designed to meet the immediate needs of the citrus industry . . ."

The final justification for the use of food additives comes in the last provision of the WHO Committee—"providing essential aid in food processing." At home you cook without the aid of chemical additives and your family enjoys your meals. Yet food processors who are at present adding close to a thousand chemicals to American food declare that these are "essential aids" and foods cannot be prepared without them. How have we been doing it at home all these thousands of years? Yet we are told the chemicals are added for the "advantage" of the consuming public.

The Way the Law is Phrased

Mr. Zimmerman then takes up the recently passed German food law and shows us that it is an improvement over the old law because it forbids the use of any food additive that is not specifically authorized by law. This sounds encouraging, but as we got deeper into the law we found that there are so many ifs, ands and buts, so many loopholes and interpretations that the law as a whole seems even less successful than our own.

Here are 4 provisions of the new German law which, on the surface, sound fine. In each case we have underlined the "loophole clause" which renders this noble-sounding provision meaningless. It is forbidden to administer antibiotics to cattle *before slaughtering* to influence the durability of the meat. (Nothing is said about *dousing the meat with antibiotics after it goes on sale.*) It is forbidden to *inject* animals with hormone substances to influence the quality of the meat. (*Nothing is said about giving the hormones in feed which we do in America.*) It is forbidden to sell foods that contain chemical additives *"which are technically avoidable or exceed the established maximum amount."* It is forbidden to sell foods which contain preservatives, anti-sprouting agents and so forth *if these exceed the permissible maximum amounts.* It is forbidden to use refrigerants in such a way that part of them passes into food *except for portions that are harmless from the point of view of health . . . or that are technically unavoidable.* Food may be treated with ionizing rays or ultraviolet rays *only insofar as this is expressly permitted.* And so forth.

In Japan the government has recently taken a clear stand in support of the use of harmless additives, particularly of food colors and preservatives, without voicing any basic objection against the use of food additives as such, Mr. Zimmerman tells us. The chief of the food sanitation section of the Ministry of Health had this to say about food colors: "Good appearance of food satisfies the human instinct which is always in pursuit of beautiful things, and good appearance sometimes improves the appetite. It is my belief that the use of colors in foods is justified *provided the colors used are non-poisonous.*"

Again we have italicized the trick phrase. On the subject of preservatives in food the same gentleman stated that they were necessary in countries short of food, like Japan. "For preserving foods, the use of electric refrigerators or canning would be effective but in such poor countries as Japan, it would be hopeless to try to introduce them widely. For this reason, we have to consider the proper use of preservatives *which are not dangerous.*"

In America, of course, practically everyone has electric refrigerators and a large section of our public has electric freezers; there is such a surplus of food that a large chunk of tax money goes for nothing but providing storage facilities for this surplus. So here we must think up some other excuse for stuffing everything we eat with preservatives.

The gist of all the italicized sentences above is that, of course, none of us wants any poisons in our food.

Individual Differences

Now for the final punch line (from the World Health Organization Committee on Food Additives): It is "impossible to establish positive proof of the non-toxicity of a specified use of an additive for all human beings under all conditions."

That's the answer, in a single sentence. We can no longer continue to allow certain additives or certain amounts of other additives on the basis of their being harmless. It is impossible to establish the harmlessness of any chemical additive, "for all human beings under all conditions." When you consider the deadly ring of those last 7 words, you are faced with the fact that chemical additives mean murder for someone. Who?

Perhaps a sickly child whose despairing mother tries to please it with some dainties from the bakery. Who knows if the dye and preservatives may be the triggering factor that costs that child's life? Perhaps an elderly person, living alone without adequate means for preparation of foods, may depend mostly on processed foods and hence have his health completely destroyed by the evil effects of these additives. Perhaps next week *you* will be the human being under that certain condition of life which renders these chemicals harmful. Do you think the Food and Drug Administration or any other body of people in this country or any other country has the right to decide that certain chemicals may be used in food even though their harmlessness cannot be established for "all human beings under all conditions."

Mr. Zimmerman gives the answer in his *Journal* article. He says, "There is one school of thought which favors the completely 'natural' food and is basically opposed to the use of any chemical 'additives' unless absolutely required for technical reasons and which recommends a general prohibition of the use of all such additives except those specifically approved by law or regulation."

We are of this school of thought. In France we are told no chemical preservatives are allowed in bread. No disaster has befallen that nation as a result of this ruling. Instead everyone buys his bread fresh every day. And the bread is freshly made every day. Certainly the same kind of agreement could be worked out for every food, if there were a will to do it.

Let us continue to press for "no chemical additives at all in any food."

CHAPTER 226

Cancer-Causing Chemicals
in Food

The Conference and Symposium on Cancer held at Rome in August, 1956, was the chance many of the world's scientists had been waiting for, a chance to wave a warning flag in front of the fast-moving modern man who looks neither to the right nor to the left as he concentrates on his do-it-yourself destruction. One of the individual reports which was delivered at the Conference has come to us and made several points which seemed important enough to pass on to our readers.

The author of the report is Douw G. Steyn, Professor of Pharmacology, Medical Faculty of University of Praetoria, Union of South Africa. Although he is speaking of conditions as they exist in the food industry of Praetoria, South Africa, it is alarming to note that huge numbers of additives are finding their way into foods there just as they are in America, Europe and everywhere else in the world. It is precisely because of the widespread acceptance of these additives that a watchful attitude should be adopted against possible harm from them. Continued ingestion of a commonly used cancer-causing agent will cripple not only a single nation, but quite probably the whole world!

The fault lies somewhere between the food manufacturers and governmental agencies. The manufacturers are often unscrupulous enough to employ ingredients in the processing, to retard spoilage or improve appearance, which are known to be harmful to the human body, disregarding entirely their obligation to the consumer of their product. The governmental agencies, whose job it is to protect the consumer from harmful goods, are responsible in that considerations of expenditure, personnel, time involved, economic pressure—all these have their effect. But still the government permits many dangerous practices to go on, unchecked, because of a policy which considers an ingredient safe so long as it is not positively shown to be the immediate cause of serious illness or death.

Dr. Steyn repeatedly expresses his concern over the children of the world, for it is they who are most susceptible to the effects of carcinogens. It is a sad fact to note that it is these little ones who most often consume the foods such as bread, cakes, sodas, so saturated with dangerous additives. For some reason, it has been shown, the immature subjects in experiments show more pronounced harmful effects than older animals when they are fed foods which contain suspected or known carcinogens, that is, substances which cause cancer. Possibly fully developed organs are more capable of resisting the attacks of harmful elements, or perhaps the time during which the maturity takes place is used by the body to build an immunity against

[843]

invading dangers. Whatever the reason, the indications which grew from Dr. Steyn's experiments should fortify the determination of the American consumer to guard the health of his children as well as himself by protesting the use of additives whose safety has not been proven.

Testing For Toxicity

In the course of his work, Dr. Steyn made a discovery that may be the key to many seeming contradictions in the research which is dedicated to labeling food additives as safe or unsafe. He concluded that many of the additives used in foods do not act quickly enough for their effect to be apparent in some experimental animals because their life span is too short. Arsenic is one such carcinogen. Its latent period is longer than the life span of rats and mice, so that although arsenic cancer is seen often in human beings, it can seldom be induced in animals. It is not unreasonable to suspect that many ingredients common to our processed foods have eluded our researchers for the same reason. It is apparent that the results of experiments in which animals—especially small animals—are used cannot be considered final. As suspected additives are found to be harmless in one animal, their effect should be ascertained on progressively larger and more complex animals, until, after monkey, man can be given doses of the additive, with frequent examinations, over a reasonably long period of time. This would eliminate the dangerous assumption that what is safe for one species is safe for another.

Professor Steyn enumerates several other ideal procedures for proper results when testing for harmful ingredients in food: 1. Large numbers of animals should be used in each test to allow for maximum variance in individuals; 2. the diets fed to experimental animals should approximate the deficiencies in man's diet where possible (diets with high concentrations of carbohydrates would more realistically imitate the diets of many underprivileged people); 3. the period of experimentation should run over several generations of experimental animals—a period of years, if necessary. There should be time to determine the effects of small and repeated doses of the harmful factors in food on growth, weight, fertility, pregnancy, lactation, unborn children and lifespan; 4. the chemicals should be fed to the animals in the combinations in which they are most often found and used by humans. Only cooked food should be eaten, for chemical changes often take place in the cooking process; 5. a thorough examination should be made of every organ and gland of each experimental animal that dies during the experiment, then the survivors should be killed and examined to note any changes and ascertain just why these changes were not fatal.

We would rest assured if we knew that all experimenters are scrupulous enough in their research to follow the pattern suggested by Dr. Steyn.

More Additives Condemned

As a result of Dr. Steyn's work, two dyes, benzopurpurine and nigrosine, have been taken from the approved list of dyes in the Union of South Africa, after many years of unrestricted use. Both were found to cause loss of weight, retarded growth and general weakness. In addition, after 15 weeks of exposure to benzopurpurine experimental rats showed pronounced susceptibility to lung infections, cirrhosis of the liver and gastric ulceration.

The Union of South Africa's vigilance in matters of food additives is further evidenced by its flat condemnation of stilbestrol in 1954. This hormone mixture was definitely found to be cancer-causing. In America these hormone products are in use for caponizing cockerels, and are often included in cosmetics for women. The use of stilbestrol in cattle food is too well known to need added comment.

The use of antibiotics to preserve food is warned against by Dr. Steyn. He sees in them an invitation to coronary thrombosis because they have been shown to increase the coagulability of the blood, which can lead to clots in the blood stream. Also, continued ingestion of antibiotics can create a tolerance for them that will neutralize the effect of any antibiotic medication which might be needed in an emergency. Antibiotics in food kill organisms in the body which are there to combat minor infections as well as certain flora and fauna in the intestines which are necessary for health.

The report contains a few words on aluminum cookware, which substantiates our position on this point. Dr. Joseph Gillman, Professor of Physiology, University of Witwatersand, Johannesburg, states that he found the gall bladders of many corpses, which he examined in autopsy, contaminated with aluminum. The gall bladders showed a pronounced corrosion caused by an alkaline media. How would this aluminum enter the system? Dr. Gillman points to aluminum cooking utensils as a likely source. Again we repeat, why take a chance? Don't use aluminum cookware!

Cancer and Vitamin Deficiencies

A very interesting conclusion is drawn by Dr. Steyn concerning cancer and vitamin deficiencies. He states that deficiencies of vitamin A and vitamin B complex cause disorders on mucous membranes (mouth, vagina, anus), which are prone to become cancerous. He points out that it is commonly taught that cancer of the oral cavity is preceded by degenerative changes (ulcers, blisters, etc.) in the oral mucous membrane. Since vitamin A deficiency and lack of riboflavin and niacin (two B vitamins) have just such symptoms, the sores thus produced may become malignant in the presence of some cancer-causing substance. We can't imagine a more emphatic reason for making certain that one's diet is rich in the foods which contain these two vitamins. As we have seen, we are unsuspecting prey to all sorts of potential cancer-causers, so that it would be wise to respect the warning of Dr. Steyn by avoiding foods which are suspect.

Over and over again Dr. Steyn's experiments showed that animals were more likely to be affected by cancer-causing elements if they were undernourished. Protein and vitamin deficiencies caused pronounced susceptibility to harmful effects, especially in experiments with soft drinks. It would not be difficult for any of our readers to think of dozens of children they've met over the years whose diet could not possibly be adequate, due to poor appetite or careless nutritional practices of the parents, yet who can be seen

[845]

at almost any hour of a summer's day with a bottle of soda in their hands. These are the people who are most easily affected by harmful food additives —the children, whose health and energy our future is dependent upon.

There is no doubt that Dr. Steyn has rendered the world a valuable service in making this report. He has made statements which with the weight of his influence and authority can reach and convince those who are powerful in the food industry. Dr. Steyn's evidence must be reinforced by public support of his recommendations. Write to your congressman urging his support of legislation which will curb the freedom food and drug manufacturers have in marketing compounds which contain questionable ingredients. If an element can't be proven safe, it should be condemned as a food until such proof is shown. We must be on our guard as it is, but we are entitled to protection from our government by the enactment of just food laws.

CHAPTER 227

Testing of
Cancer-Causing Chemicals

The question of cancer-causing substances in food was one of the most significant topics taken up at the Seventh International Cancer Congress held in London in July, 1958.

William E. Smith, M.D., Director of Nutrition Research at Fairleigh-Dickinson University, brought the matter squarely to a head when he said, in his prepared address before the Congress: "Increasing knowledge of the ability of many different chemicals to incite cancer has, however, pointed to the need for tests extending over much longer periods of time, preferably over the full life-spans of test animals. It is, of course, now well known that a few doses, or even a single dose, of a carcinogenic (cancer-causing) chemical administered to a young animal can lead to development of cancer in middle life or in old age."

Does it surprise you to know that just one exposure to a cancer-causing substance early in life can produce cancer 20 or 30 years later?

Dr. Smith goes on to say that the peculiar long-delayed effect of these substances sets them apart from other chemicals which are just ordinary poisons. In the case of the latter substances, symptoms of poisoning appear rapidly and, if the person lives, he recovers from the experience with few ill effects. But with cancer-causing substances, there are usually no warning symptoms, yet the changes that occur in cells are irreversible and lead to cancer possibly many years later.

In 1939, Dr. Smith tells us, the International Union Against Cancer suggested that governments revise legislation regulating the toxicity of chemical food additives in the light of the fact that they might be cancer-causing. Later this Union established a committee on cancer prevention which, meeting in 1954, stated again that cancer-causing substances must be considered in a different category from other poisons. For substances that poison temporarily we can set "tolerances"—that is, we can allow small amounts of these substances in food, assuming that, in such small quantity, they will be harmless. But, said the statement of the Cancer Congress, "No substance which in tests at any dose level induces any type of malignant tumor in any species of animal can be considered innocuous (harmless) to human health."

Another symposium of the International Union was held in Rome in 1956. At this meeting Dr. W. C. Hueper of our National Cancer Institute made some very strong statements on the subject of chemicals in food and their possible relation to the increasing incidence of cancer in our country. The *New York Times* published a story about Dr. Hueper's speech in which he listed 20 groups of suspect food additives and 17 groups of suspect food contaminants. A condensation of Dr. Hueper's speech appears in the following chapter.

Such a frightening report did not go unnoticed by the American people and such was the clamor that the Food and Drug Administration was forced to make a statement. They said that the people of this country are "well protected" against possible harm from food additives and that Dr. Hueper had been an alarmist. Dr. Hueper was, we assume, officially silenced, for we heard nothing from him since then.

Meanwhile, the congressional committee to investigate chemicals in food held some hearings. Astonishing revelations were made before this committee as to the possible harm chemicals in food might be doing our people especially in relation to cancer. Congressman Delaney, chairman of the committee, introduced a bill in congress which includes provisions to 1. require testing of chemical food additives for their cancer-causing potential, and 2. forbid for use in food any additives that are found to be cancer-causing.

This seems to be a simple solution to the problem, doesn't it? And surely one on which everyone would agree! There cannot be an American food processor alive today so unfeeling as to knowingly cause cancer in any of his customers. Why then has the legislation been shelved? Why then do the years drag on with no regulations on cancer-causing chemicals in food, while at the same time the number of food chemicals is increasing every day? And the number of cancer deaths.

Complications Are Ever Present

Dr. Smith gives part of the answer in his statement before the Cancer Congress. Tests for possible cancer-causers are complex in the extreme. Certain substances may cause cancer under certain circumstances and may be highly beneficial foods under other circumstances. For instance, sesame oil which had been heated to 350 degrees centigrade caused cancer in laboratory animals. Unheated oil did not.

Other aspects of the tests must be considered. Injecting certain substances may cause cancer, while giving them by mouth may not. Substances which occur naturally may cause cancer when they are used out of context— that is, in other than natural ways.

Dr. Smith tells us that estrogen, a female sex hormone, is a powerful cancer-causer. Now obviously estrogen exists naturally in all females and does not cause cancer when it is performing its perfectly natural function of stimulating and regulating the various sex processes. But when estrogenic material from an animal is injected or given to a human being or another animal, it becomes cancer-causing. "The fact that some carcinogenic (cancer-causing) substances appear in nature is hardly a justification for extracting them and adding them to food," says Dr. Smith.

Finally—just what is a "safe" dose of anything which can produce cancer? Several years ago an insecticide was tested and it was found that laboratory rats got tumors when they ate this substance in relatively high doses. So a ruling went out that such and such a residue of this insecticide might appear legally in food. Later, further tests revealed that cancer might be caused *at much lower levels* than the first experiment had shown. So the ruling was changed and no residue of that substance is now permitted in food.

How many people died of cancer because of that earlier erroneous ruling, do you suppose?

Dr. Smith tells us that Congressman Delaney, under whose direction the hearings on chemicals were held several years ago, recently made a speech in Congress in which he drew attention to the irreversible actions of cancer-causing substances on cells. He stated that, when such substances are used in food, their later withdrawal affords no assurance that cancer will not develop years later in persons who ate them during the period when they were in use. Mr. Delaney's bill submitted to Congress specifically requires that all food additives must be tested as possible cancer-causers *before* they are used in food.

In closing, Dr. Smith tells us the unhappy news that what may cause cancer in one kind of animal may not do so in another kind. So tests with animals may show possible hazards for man, but cannot afford complete assurance of safety.

What Can We Do?

What is the answer for those of us who want to avoid cancer—and surely this means every one of us? Dr. Smith believes that, "In legislation to assure safety of chemicals in food, a conservative position would therefore be to limit artificial food additives to as small a list as possible sufficing to meet actual needs for production and distribution of foods." This is a very general statement, of course, and we wonder who is going to be the judge of what will "suffice to meet actual needs for production and distribution of food."

In a recent decision a certain dye was forbidden on Florida oranges because it had been found to be cancer-causing. But the citrus growers convinced the authorities that this dye was necessary "for production and distribution" of their product. It would be the ruin of the citrus industry if they could not dye their oranges, they said, so the dye is still being used. If this is the kind of decision such legislation will produce, then it will be meaningless indeed.

We believe that legislation should be passed *outlawing all chemicals in food*. Certainly with today's provisions for refrigeration preservatives are never necessary. Dyes, thickeners, emulsifiers, bleaches, flavorings—all of these should be outlawed for good. Processed food will look and taste a little different, true. Will the food companies lose money? Of course not, for the millions of dollars they are spending now promoting all these fantastic chemicals in foods they could spend in a grand, concerted publicity campaign to explain to the public just why and how such changes were made and what they will mean in increased health.

Don't you think everyone in this country would be delighted with such a prospect?

When you write to your congressman, senator, state health department and state legislature, ask for legislation outlawing all chemicals in food. Only then can we talk meaningfully of safety from cancer-causing substances.

CHAPTER 228

Cancer Hazards from Food Additives

By Dr. W. C. Hueper

A rapidly growing number and variety of non-nutritive substances have been introduced during recent decades into foodstuffs intended for general human consumption through the use of modern methods of food production and processing. Some of these chemicals are intentionally added to foods for various reasons, while others are employed for different purposes in the production of foodstuffs and remain unintentionally in them as residues. A disturbing aspect of this development is that there exists no mandatory provision for assuring, *a priori*, that biologic properties of each of these additives and contaminants, particularly long-term or delayed effects, have adequately been studied. The circumstances suggest the virtual certainty that many have not.

It is especially important in this respect that observations made during recent years in men and experimental animals have demonstrated a not inconsiderable number of chemicals similar to, or identical with, those introduced into foodstuffs which possess carcinogenic (cancer-provoking) properties. The actual or possible existence of cancer hazards related to carinogens in foodstuffs therefore poses a serious public-health problem. The daily and life-long exposure to such agents would represent one of the most important of the various potential sources of contact with environmental carcinogens for the population at large.

The main groups of food additives and contaminants . . . include . . . natural and synthetic dyes, antioxidants of fats and lipoids and vegetable matter, thickeners, sweeteners, flavoring agents, surfactants (detergents, foaming agents), humectants (smoke agents), preservatives and chemical sterilizing agents, water conditioners (iodine, fluorides), antifoaming agents, salt substitutes, shortening, softeners, bleaches, modifiers and improvers (meat tenderizers, etc.), oil and fat substitutes, organic solvents, emulsifiers and solidifiers, pesticide residues, antisprouting and antimaturition agents of fruits and vegetables, insect repellents, hormonal fattening agents, antibiotics (fed to food animals and added to foodstuffs), enzymes, antienzymatics, panglazes (silicones), pan-greases (mineral oils), water pollutants, chemical sterilizing agents, wrapping and coating materials (paraffin, waxes, resins, plastics), soot adherent to smoked foodstuffs and roasted and toasted products, household detergents and their coloring agents, non-ionizing radiation (ultraviolet) products, ionizing radiation (radioactive) products and radioactive substances taken up by plants and food animals from air, soil or water contaminated by radioactive fall-out.

The bulk of the still rather restricted pertinent information on potential cancer hazards from these additives and contaminants is of relatively recent date. Knowledge of such observations is often limited to parties mainly interested in scientific aspects of carcinogenesis and is sometimes not fully appreciated by those parties concerned with the practical aspects of potential human cancer hazards inferable from these experimental findings.

There is no necessary relation between toxicity (poisoning now effectively prevented by food and drug laws) and carcinogenicity of chemical agents. As a rule, the minimal carcinogenic dose is distinctly lower than the minimal chronic toxic dose. It is for this reason that not infrequently carcinogenic reactions may develop upon exposure to carcinogenic chemicals without a preceding or simultaneous appearance of any toxic symptoms.

In a graduated scale of the relative significance of potential environmental carcinogenic agents from a public health viewpoint, the highest priority for carcinogenic screening should be extended to those agents with which large parts of the general population have frequent and prolonged contact, whose possible carcinogenic effects on man can least readily be ascertained and which for this reason are most difficult to control by preventive methods. Chemicals included in this group are those which enter in general human environment of every home in the form of consumer goods, or as environmental contaminants. Agents of this type are the large group of chemical additives and contaminants of foodstuffs in addition to many environmental poisons, pollutants of water, air, and soil, household drugs, sanitary supplies, cleaning agents, polishes, paints and cosmetics.

If one adopts the principle that the protection of the health of the general public deserves foremost attention, the following considerations may profitably be used as guide lines in arriving at intelligent and rational decisions.

1. Carcinogens vary greatly in their relative potency. Coal tars of different derivations, for instance, vary greatly in their relative carcinogenic potency in man and experimental animals. Coal tars are in turn usually more potent than wood tars or vegetable tars or tars obtained in the fractionation of petroleum.

2. Dose observations made in experimental animals are not directly applicable to man. There exist marked differences in potency of a particular chemical for various species.

3. Repeated exposures to carcinogens produce a cumulative carcinogenic effect in the exposed tissues. Cells once exposed to a carcinogen seem to retain the entire or a considerable portion of the initial effect exerted by individual exposures, even if these by themselves may be insufficient for eliciting a neoplastic (malignant) response. Subeffectively exposed cells can be challenged into carcinogenic activity either by additional subminimal carcinogenic exposures or by contact with specific promoting chemicals.

4. Actual exposure to a dietary carcinogen does not always stop with the cessation of environmental contact. Some chemicals are not metabolically destroyed or excreted but are retained in active form in certain tissues from which they may gradually be mobilized long after the environmental exposure has ceased.

5. Exposure to a dietary carcinogen may be complicated by occupational, medicinal, cosmetic, sanitary or environmental contact with the same chemical or some other chemical.

6. It is perhaps possible to enforce, to a reasonable degree, laws concerning the maximal content and adequate purity of food additives and contaminants in foodstuffs merchandized by relatively large trade organizations dealing in large quantities of nationwide and interstate commerce and using standardized and well controlled methods of processing, handling and shipping. Considerable difficulties in this respect may be encountered, on the other hand, regarding the proper supervision of foodstuffs produced and sold on a local level. The mere passage of laws establishing standards in such matters without providing adequate means to enforce them might produce in the population a deceptive impression of safety. The most effective method of control of health hazards of this type doubtlessly is found under such circumstances in a complete elimination of the dangerous agents from the human environment, wherever such a procedure is possible.

7. Since many foodstuffs containing artificial food additives and contaminants are not adequately labeled as to the amount and type of chemicals added to the natural food products, the general consumer is relatively rarely able to make any intelligent selection between different products of the same type, particularly between "natural" foodstuffs and "artificially modified and

contaminated" ones. Indeed, in many instances, he may have little choice in such matters, because all or nearly all foodstuffs of certain types which he is able to purchase are of the contaminated or modified variety. The consumer under such circumstances is a member of a "captive" population which may be subjected to potential, long delayed health hazards which he has neither consented to nor is able to avoid. For these reasons the general public is entitled to expect that all chemical additives and contaminants are subjected to comprehensive and thorough studies for toxic, carcinogenic and cocarcinogenic properties before they are used or introduced in human foodstuffs.

It is unlikely from an application of our present knowledge of environmental carcinogens that many of the presently used additives and contaminants of foodstuffs introduce any carcinogenic hazard into the general food supply and, therefore, deserve any immediate attention. The large number of additives as well as the complexity and costliness of the biologic testing for carcinogenic properties of any one of them, moreover, precludes for merely practical reasons any large-scale attack of the problem on the entire front at the present time. It is quite obvious that under the existing conditions a step-by-step procedure will have to be adopted and that investigative efforts would best be expended for the time being on those circumscribed groups of chemicals which from the already available information have furnished carcinogenic or cocarcinogenic agents, i.e., synthetic dyes, chlorinated pesticides, animal and plant hormones and detergents.

Among the various formerly and presently used synthetic food dyes, carcinogenic properties were discovered during recent years in a surprisingly large number when tested in rats and mice. Rodent cancers have also been produced by chemical compounds of the same stilbene family which has recently been introduced as coloring matter in many household detergents used for the cleaning of kitchen utensils, dishes and cooking equipment of homes and commercial eating places.

Potential carcinogenic contaminants also may be introduced into foodstuffs if vegetables, fruits, fish, oysters and livestock are grown on soil or in water polluted with known carcinogens, such as radioactive matter, arsenicals, selenium and polycyclic hydrocarbons contained in ship fuel oils. Consideration, moreover, must be given to the possibility that carcinogenic chemicals may be formed from non-carcinogenic ones under the influence of heat. Possible examples are 1. charred or tarry carbonaceous matter formed when bread or biscuits are excessively toasted or meats are grilled or roasted or 2. hydrocarbon constitutents of mineral oils freed by cracking of the oil when it is used as a fat substitute and subjected to heat during grilling or baking.

There exists also the possibility that originally noncarcinogenic additives and contaminants may interreact with each other or with food constituents and form new compounds possessing carcinogenic properties in the foodstuffs. They may be produced under the influence of processing procedures or during the preparation of food in the kitchen. Plastics used as wrapping material, sausage skins and coating material of fruits, cheese, meat, butter and can linings may carry a similar hazard.

[852]

Mention may finally be made of several experimental observations indicating that a dietary intake of certain spices or alkaloids which contaminate foodstuffs (chilies, alkaloids of senecio plants, crude ergot) may result in the development of liver tumors when given to rats.

The use of various types of radiating energy in the processing of foodstuffs also deserves consideration from a carcinogenic viewpoint, since these agents (ultraviolet radiation, ionizing radiation) produce in the constituents of food, such as sterols and nucleo-proteins, definite chemical changes. No reliable information exists and no adequate experimental studies have been made for establishing the non-carcinogenic nature of the radiation products, although both types of radiation are eminently carcinogenic when acting on living tissues of both man and various species of animals.

The great majority of the different cancerous reactions mentioned here were produced either by the administration of excessively high doses or followed upon their introduction through routes distinct from those encountered under ordinary alimentation. The cancers developed in animals differed in various metabolic respects from man. But the mere fact of the existence of such responses presents a definite warning deserving serious attention if possible endemic and epidemic cancerous manifestations among exposed population groups are to be avoided.

Reprinted with permission of the *Saturday Review Research Section: Science and Humanity.*

CHAPTER 229

Coal Tar Colors in Food

Some years ago it was discovered that a coal tar dye (butter yellow) then being used to color butter, margarine and other yellow foods caused cancer in laboratory animals in every case in which it was given. The dye was forbidden for use in food in interstate commerce. Quite recently 3 dyes were declared unsafe for use in foods by the Food and Drug Administration. These 3 yellow and orange dyes had been used for years to color citrus fruit, candy, puddings, hot dogs, cakes, cookies, soft drinks. They had been tested many years ago by the methods then employed. They were on the "certified" list. But the Food and Drug chemists took it into their heads to test them again with methods now available, and promptly recommended that they be withdrawn from use in food.

According to the *New York Times,* reporting on a meeting of cancer specialists that took place in Brazil, in July 1954, Dr. William E. Smith of New York University Bellevue Medical Center, announced that in the

United States alone during 1953, 100,000 pounds of dyestuffs known to cause cancer in animals were approved by the FDA for use in foods to be consumed by human beings. At the same meeting, Dr. Hermann Druckery of Germany observed that there was no recovery factor where substances causing cancer were concerned. "A person absorbing even infinitesimal amounts will still have the cumulative effect and when a certain level is reached and a period of latency has passed, the effect will become evident in the form of a tumor.

A German Scientist Speaks

In 1949 the Science Editor of the *Times* reviewed the speech of a German scientist, Professor K. H. Bauer of Heidelberg, speaking before a congress of surgeons, who said that there are at present some 600,000 compounds made from carbon which were unknown a hundred years ago. Of these, we know that several hundred can cause cancer in animals and in human beings. The many cases of bladder cancer among workers in aniline dye plants finally resulted in the establishment of precautions which cut the incidence down to almost zero. But at present, said Dr. Bauer, what of the general public?

The spot most favorable for cancer growth is the digestive tract. In all of the so-called civilized countries, cancers of the mouth, throat, stomach and intestines are the commonest. The connection with food and drink is obvious. In the "backward" countries such as China where food is not doctored up with coal tar products, the incidence of digestive tract cancer is much lower. Dr. Bauer demanded (and this was 11 years ago) that any and all substances which are known cancer-producers should not be sold in foods, over the counter or in restaurants. As we can see, nothing has been done along these lines in this country and we suppose that European countries also have made little or no progress.

The government's own top-ranking cancer expert, Dr. W. C. Hueper of the National Cancer Institute, United States Public Health Service, testified before the Delaney Committee in 1950 that several dyes are being used in food constantly which are known to produce cancer in animals. He mentioned a green dye used in canned peas and green maraschino cherries. A second, called yellow A. B., is used in popcorn, butter, margarine, cheese, candy and cake icings. It has been repeatedly linked to cancer of the bladder. As late as 1932 the Du Pont Company discovered 23 dye workers with cancer of the bladder. They were working with the dye which we are now using to dye popcorn, butter and other foods.

James Clarke of the Food and Drug Administration declared in 1951 that there are about 18 coal tar dyes that have been listed as "certifiable"— that is, they are permitted in foods. The 3 orange colorings tested in 1954 are 3 of these. What may be the risk in the use of the other 15, in the light of our newer methods of testing? No one knows. And we will not know until someone dies or becomes desperately ill from eating food that contains these dyes, or until the Food and Drug Administration may happen to decide to test them again for possible harm.

[854]

Dyes in Vitamin Preparations

So much for foods. What about vitamin preparations that contain artificial coloring? We know that many readers buy vitamins. Some of them take synthetic vitamins, although ample evidence points to the fact that natural vitamin products are infinitely preferable. But, natural or synthetic, vitamin preparations can and often are artificially colored.

But surely, you might say, nothing sold for health purposes will be harmful! Surely anyone who makes vitamin and mineral preparations can be relied upon to check carefully the healthfulness of everything that goes into his product! Some of these preparations are colored and we want to explain this color to our readers.

It is possible, of course, to color food (or food supplements) attractively without using coal tar colors. You have probably seen in your grocery the little kits of vegetable coloring used by many housewives to color icing, candy and so forth. Vegetable dyes consist of such things as a red dye made from beets, an orange dye made from carotene, which is the coloring matter of carrots, green dye made from parsley or chlorophyll and so forth. Why do not commercial food processing companies use these vegetable dyes in their foods? We are told that they are impractical for quantity production, for there are too few colors, they do not have enough intensity for commercial use and they tend to fade.

It will never cease to surprise us that the color of anything relating to food could attain such importance. We suppose if one manufacturer would agree to give up coloring his products, he would have to have the assurance that all the others would, too. Almost overnight what a difference there would be in the appearance of shelves of processed food in the super market. And what a change there would be on the shelves of your corner drug store where the vitamin preparations are sold. Do you really take one vitamin or another because of the color? Don't you instead read the label carefully and make up your mind that this brand contains exactly what you want? This certainly seems to be the sensible way to do things. And furthermore, it seems eminently sensible, too, to write to the folks who produce your particular brand of food supplements and tell them that you don't want and won't buy any food supplements that contain coal tar dyes, or any other coal tar substance.

In general, makers of the natural products do not color their products at all. If they do, they use vegetable coloring. We learned from one manufacturer that he uses beet juice to color one of his products, carotene to color another and caramel (burnt sugar) to color another. We had word from another that the capsules he sells are made from clear transparent gelatin, the fillers used in his tablets—that is, the base material that holds the tablets together—are made of wheat germ powder. The very few tablets of his that are coated are coated with a vegetable product.

CHAPTER 230

The Risks in Food Dyes

What could be more alarming than the situation we mentioned in the previous chapter concerning the July, 1954, meeting of cancer specialists in Brazil in which Dr. William E. Smith announced that in the United States alone 100,000 pounds of dyestuffs known to cause cancer in animals were approved by the United States Food and Drug Administration, for use in foodstuffs to be consumed by human beings during one year.

Are you as horrified by this revelation as we are?

The American Cancer Society tells us that every day of the year 620 Americans die of cancer, the most dreaded of modern diseases. Cancer, we are told, is mysterious. No one knows how it selects its victims. Formerly thought of as a disease of old age, it is at present one of the leading causes of death among children below the age of 12.

Yet our Food and Drug Administration, charged with protecting the health of the American people, releases for human consumption 100,000 pounds of dyestuffs known to cause cancer in animals. Animal experimentation is the method used for determining whether or not a substance is dangerous to human beings. It is true that different species of animals react in different ways to various poisons and it is possible that some substances that cause cancer in some animals may not cause cancer in human beings. But it is well known that other substances *do* cause cancer in animals and in human beings, as well. Of what use is it to experiment with animals, if we are then going to release for human consumption chemicals that we know perfectly well will cause cancer in animals?

Perhaps the most shocking aspect of this whole revelation is that the substances under discussion are dyes. In respect to other chemicals, the food processors may claim that they serve some supposedly useful purpose in foods. Fats would become rancid without preservatives. Bread would become stale without softeners they tell us. But what possible excuse can there be for dyeing food? It serves no purpose whatsoever except to give the food a supposedly attractive color. Undoubtedly, it is thus possible to pass off old, tired-out vegetables, fruits and meats as fresh, wholesome foods. (Just see what a beautiful color they have!) And, of course, the dye in gum drops and all the other cheap candy is there to trap the eyes of the youngsters—the colors are so bright!

We wonder how long the American people are going to stand for this sort of thing. And we wonder how long they are going to contribute to cancer funds with this sort of thing going on under their noses. We are glad to see that physicians are becoming more alert and more vocal about the dangers of chemicals in foods.

[856]

For instance, an address before the Australian and New Zealand Association for the Advancement of Science appears in the May 29, 1954, issue of the *Medical Journal of Australia*. In it, R. W. W. Cunningham, Ph.C., of the Department of Health of Canberra, Australia, pleads for a better understanding of the risks we are taking and the development of other food dyes that are not dangerous to health. Cunningham is outspoken in relating chemicals in foods to cancer. He begins his address with reminding his litseners that the increase in incidence of certain diseases has gone right along with the increase in the use of processed food in which certain chemicals are used.

Can Cells Deal with These Poisons?

Living cells, he says, can deal with many, many different kinds of poisonous substances, but they may be vulnerable to new substances which differ only very slightly from things that are not poisonous at all. Aniline, from which dyes are made, and many of the chemicals made from it have been shown to cause kidney disease and to destroy red and white blood cells. Many of the substances made from aniline have been shown to cause cancer. Naphthol dyes, thought to be harmless, were recently shown to produce cancer in animal experiments. He speaks of two dyes—trypan blue and trypan red, the first of which causes cancer, the second of which does not. The only difference in the two dyes is just one chemical step that takes place in the body after ingesting the trypan blue.

All of these colors, he tells us, are authorized for use in the United States. Researchers have no way of knowing, he says, from the chemical structure of any substance whether or not it may cause cancer. Furthermore, what is cancer-causing for one kind of animal may not cause cancer in another kind. And we use these same derivatives of aniline in medicines! To be sure, says Cunningham, and physicians know perfectly well how dangerous they are and use them only for very short periods of time. But dyes in food are used possibly every day over the entire lifespan of an individual.

In Australia the death rate from leukemia has risen from 1.8 per 100,000 in 1930 to 4.4 per 100,000 in 1950. More than twice as high in a matter of 20 years! And this is what the *British Encyclopedia of Medical Practice* has to say about the relation of leukemia to chemicals: "It is well known that individuals who have been exposed to chronic benzene intoxications and many other chemical substances frequently develop leukemia. Further it has been noted that there is definite evidence that the sulphonamide group of drugs in some patients has been responsible for the onset of acute leukemia." He goes on to tell of 10 cases of leukemia he has seen who had been treated with sulfa drugs, for colds or infections, just previously. He also points out that sulfanilamide, the parent substance, is widely used in the dye industry.

Cunningham gives the death rate for cancer in the United Kingdom—29.01 per 100,000 in 1851 and 188.09 per 100,000 in 1950. He believes that more people are becoming victims of cancer because of the increased

[857]

period of exposure to the cancer-causing agents, whatever they may be. We know, he says, that among workers dealing with one cancer-causing chemical, the length of time it may take for the cancer to develop ranges from 7 to 22 years. Do not forget, he says, that long-continued exposure to even small quantities of toxic substances ultimately produces recognizable cancer.

What Can We Do About It?

To sum up, he says, "It has been demonstrated by a number of investigators that cancer and the leukemias follow the application or ingestion of various chemical substances. As a number of additives used in food processing are derived from or contain these proven toxic chemicals, it behooves us to take steps to remove these from our foods."

Amen, Mr. Cunningham. But what steps can we take? First of all, insure your own safety by buying nothing that has had dyes added to it, if you can possibly help it. We understand that dyes are being added even to frozen foods these days; canned foods have contained them for years. Practically anything that comes already boxed, canned, bottled or packaged may contain food dyes. Yes, we mean even spaghetti, even bread, ketchup, canned peas, canned fruit, potato chips, pickles, candies, icings, baked goods—the list is endless. BUY ONLY FRESH FRUITS, VEGETABLES, MEATS AND DAIRY PRODUCTS. These are far less likely to have been dyed.

But even things like butter and cheese are dyed these days. We do not know what kind of dye is used—perhaps safe vegetable dyes, perhaps the dyes we have been describing. Do you see any necessity at all for dyeing any of these foods? Do you really care whether your cheese is pale or deep yellow in color? Write to the people who produce the cheese. Ask them whether any dyes are used. Quote the statement by Dr. Smith that occurs at the beginning of this chapter. Tell them that you prefer *not to eat dyes of any kind,* you prefer your food just as it is, without dyes. You will receive an answer to your letter. The processors will write and assure you that the dye they use is completely harmless. Is it? After the statement made by Dr. Smith can you ever take their word for it again? Don't become discouraged. Keep writing. Get your friends and neighbors to write. Who knows? Perhaps long before the Food and Drug Administration or Congress gets around to passing and enforcing really safe laws with respect to food dyes, we can have persuaded the food processors to give up dyes entirely! Let's try!

CHAPTER 231

Additional Information on Chemicals in Food

Fruit can be ripened 10 days faster than normal through an atomic radiation process now in the developmental stage, according to scientists of an international research and engineering outfit. The *New York Times* (November 17, 1959) reported this piece of information. We can't think of any reason why fruit should be ripened faster than it normally is, except that somebody's profits may be increased.

Parathion Poisoning

The Hong Kong (China) *Tiger Standard* for December 6, 1959, announced that the government there has assured the public that the danger of parathion poisoning from vegetables was over. "The deadly parathion insecticides were no longer being used in the New Territories, said a government spokesman." The paper goes on to say that dealers were prosecuted for mere possessions of such insecticides. Vegetables which might have been contaminated were confiscated with a daily loss of $30,000 to the farmer. The parathion group of insecticides was banned completely from this locality in 1955. We think Americans should be interested in knowing that the people of Hong Kong are far better protected from this particular insecticide than we are. Parathion is still a perfectly legal insecticide in our country and there is no possible way of knowing what fruit or vegetable you buy at your local store is contaminated with this poison so deadly that a drop of it on the skin can do serious damage.

The Power of Big Business

A recent column by Drew Pearson points out what happens to scientific men of great integrity when they make use of their scientific knowledge to try to warn the public against hazards. He names 5 prominent men who were fired when they warned insistently that public health was endangered by cancer-causing chemicals being used in industry. Some were fired from universities, obviously because of complaints from the big companies whose products were involved; some were fired from big research jobs with such companies. In addition, the testimony of one of the researchers indicated that all field studies were cancelled by the National Cancer Institute on a program which had turned up facts objectionable from the point of view of the chemical industries. The National Cancer Institute is a government bureau, supported by your money. When facts that its research uncovers turn out to be disadvantageous to big business in-

[859]

terests apparently such research is immediately terminated. Don't you think such practices have a great deal to do with the frightening increase of cancer in our country?

A news release which came to us from a chemical company tells us that the manager of one of their branches in charge of the Analine Division, has been invited to serve on the Expert Committee on Food Additives established jointly by the United Nations Food and Agriculture Organization and the World Health Organization. "Analine" refers chiefly to dyes—many of which are used in food and cosmetics and many of which are the very ones suspected of being cancer-causing. Do you think there is much chance that this gentleman can make any helpful contributions to getting these suspected dyes out of the world's food—and still keep his job at the chemical company?

The Safety Factor

"Many prominent people in the field, however, failed to understand that every use (of chemicals in food) involved some hazard and *that there is no such thing as absolute safety*. Others failed to comprehend the importance of the criteria of safety for intended use—largely, I believe, because they were loath from a public relations viewpoint to admit that ingestion of massive amounts of many common food ingredients could be harmful.

"In the fall of 1954, the food protection committee issued a publication entitled *Principles and Procedures for Estimating the Safety of Intentional Additives in Foods,* which hit hard on the point that it is impossible to establish absolute assurance of safety. It defined the term 'safety' as 'the practical certainty that injury will not result from the use of the substance in a proposed quantity and manner.'" (*Food, Drug, Cosmetic Law Journal,* September, 1959.)

So the very people who are most concerned with proving the safety of chemical additives in food have announced in an official publication that it cannot be done. *There will always be some risk with any food additive.*

The Stilbestrol Controversy

The announcement of our secretary of Health, Education and Welfare that the implanting of stilbestrol hormone pellets in poultry is now illegal should cheer us. It's an indication that at last some steps will be taken, at last some of the protest letters health-seekers have been writing to their government officials have borne fruit. We wonder how people feel who have been eating hormonized chickens all these years that the stilbestrol treatment has been allowed. And how do you feel now about being told every day by the "experts" that chemicals in food can't harm you, *when they said that about stilbestrol only last week*—and *today they announce that it's a potent cause of cancer!*

And, we suppose, the American Medical Association is still saying that there's no harm in stilbestrol. We have in our file a report issued in August, 1957, by the Council on Foods and Nutrition of the AMA declaring that the use of hormones in beef cattle and poultry creates no hazard to

[860]

people eating the meat. So, if your doctor tells you that all the hubbub about stilbestrol is nonsense, he's still quoting the official position of the AMA two years ago—and they are two years out of date. Wouldn't you think that an organization sincerely interested in health would hold an extraordinary emergency meeting the day after such an alarming announcement was made by a government official, to alert all their members to the dangers of chemicals in food and to urge their immediate participation in a program of protest on behalf of their patients?

One final note—stilbestrol, the cancer-causing hormone, is still lawfully being given to cattle, poultry and, so far as we know, all other animals used for food—so long as it is included in their feed, not injected.

Action by the Food Processors

"Give an overzealous bureaucrat a ridiculous legal excuse to scream 'Wolf' and he will do so—at a press conference." This is the lead sentence in an editorial on the cranberry-weed-killer scare that appears in the December, 1959, issue of *Food Engineering*. Reading the rest of the editorial makes you very aware of what we health-seekers are up against in the future. The food processing industry has decided, chiefly on the basis of the cranberry and stilbestrol affairs, that the Delaney amendment to the new Food and Drug Act must go.

The editorial in this leading journal of the food industry goes on to say, "The cancer clause was added at the last minute as the additive amendment was rushed through Congress. . . . Expert food scientists and toxicologists were not given a fair chance to expose its unworkable and damaging aspects. . . . We believe that this case will force modification of the Delaney cancer clause to make it reasonable and workable on a safe, practical basis. . . . Food and additives manufacturers will have to get Congress to take them off their present hot seat—and to keep Delaney out of color legislation (that is, laws to protect us from cancer-causing dyes in foods). . . . the food industry must set up an organization to speak for it in the technical terms of additive toxicology."

The Delaney provision which this editorial attacks states that no additive known to cause cancer in laboratory animals may be used in food. It seems a harmless enough provision, doesn't it, concerning the fact that cancer is increasing by leaps and bounds and the world's greatest cancer experts believe that chemicals in foods are one of the main reasons.

But the food processors are determined to destroy this part of the new law on chemicals in food. In spite of the fact that it seems the cranberry industry is going to be paid handsomely by the taxpayers for money they lost over the weed killer scare, the food industry is determined to use cancer-causing chemicals in food and they are not going to stand for any interference. They have many millions of dollars to spend to influence the minds and votes of congressmen and senators. They can hire the best publicity men in the country to "plant" articles in leading magazines which will state reasonably and calmly that there is no danger in such chemicals. Such articles are already beginning to appear. Why, how many

[861]

cranberries do you think you would have to eat to get cancer, ask the articles prepared by the food industry's publicity men. And, at first glance, the question sounds reasonable. The laboratory rats who got cancer from the weed killer ate far more of it than we are likely to get from cranberry jelly at our Thanksgiving dinner.

But this is not the whole story. We human beings are subjected every single day to hundreds of cancer-causing substances. No one will ever be able to measure which of these, and in what quantity, *was the final one* that brought the fatal cancer—that *has* brought the fatal cancer to so many thousands of Americans.

The horrible thing is that the food industry could even contemplate such brutal disregard for their fellow Americans—just to safeguard their own profits. Scores of substances now being used in food are regarded by experts as being possible cancer-causers. Not one of them benefits the consumer in any way. All of them are used only because they allow the food grower or processor to make bigger profits. As the food industry redoubles its efforts and puts its dollars to work to throw out the small measure of protection we now have in the Delaney amendment, we must redouble our efforts to see that the Delaney amendment stays. Write to Secretary Ribicoff, Department of Health, Welfare and Education in Washington, D.C. strongly reminding him of the cranberry and the stilbestrol affairs. Urge him to press for even stronger legislation. At the same time it wouldn't hurt to remind him that there is strong evidence that fluoridated water brings earlier death from cancer as well as other degenerative diseases.

Write to your congressmen and senators. Urge them to fight any attempt to revise or withdraw the Delaney amendment. Ask them rather to demand even stronger laws for protection from chemicals.

A List of Chemicals Still Used

The Food and Drug Administration has decided on a list of chemical additives which are, they believe, so safe that no objection has been made to their use in foods and no tests were made as to their possible toxicity. Thirty-seven chemicals are listed in *Food Field Reporter* for December 21, 1959. Some of these are calcium silicate which can make up 5 per cent of baking powder, aluminum calcium silicate which can make up to 2 per cent of table salt. Benzoic acid may be used as a preservative. Caffeine may still be used in cola beverages. Ethyl formate may still be used to fumigate cashew nuts, magnesium stearate will be allowed in foods where it appears *as a contaminant from packaging materials.*

Sodium benzoate, sodium bisulfite, sodium metabisulfite, sulfur dioxide, dilauryl thiopropionate, butylated hydroxytoluene will still be used as preservatives. Caprylic acid will still be used in cheese wraps to prevent mold.

The list goes on and on. By March 6, 1960, proof had to be shown that other chemicals in foods are harmless. Up to the end of December only 19 such petitions had been submitted asking to use chemicals in food.

What about mineral oil present in frozen meats as a contaminant from the packaging material on which it is wrapped; zoalene—a drug used to

[862]

combat a poultry disease—presumably this drug is present in every mouthful of poultry you eat; a sprout inhibitor being used on raw potatoes and onions—some of it may be present in potato chips, as well.

The toxicity of these last named chemicals, among others, must be decided upon by the FDA.

Peeling Fruits with Caustic Soda

Magazines of the chemical industry recently carried an ad in full color of a piece of fruit being miraculously stripped of its skin by some marvelous substance which is identified in the ad as caustic soda. "The best way to skin a potato, tomato, peach or pepper is vitally important," says the ad, "versatile caustic soda provides the answer." Our medical dictionary describes caustic soda as "an extremely corrosive substance." If you buy canned vegetables or fruits, they have probably been given this treatment.

Restoring Natural Taste

The food processors have made a great discovery. According to *Food Field Reporter* for June 25, 1956, they have found out, no doubt at great cost, that they can restore the natural flavor to processed foods by restoring to them the enzymes which were removed in the processing! Now we can have a whole new industry busy manufacturing enzymes from other kinds of food. At great cost we'll put the enzymes back in the food and, presto, we'll have just what we started out with—except that, of course, only the taste will be the same. Processed food cannot be restored to its natural state, nutritionally speaking.

It would never occur to anyone, least of all anyone in the food industry, to leave the food unprocessed to begin with. There's no profit in doing things that way.

Soda Vending Machines Dispense Copper Poisoning

One of the first hints of our machine age came a long time ago, when vending machines made an appearance. One of the most popular and fascinating of these, especially to children, is the soda vending machine. The California State Department of Public Health *Bulletin* (October 15, 1957) warns that the machines can be a health menace, aside from the obvious hazards of the sugar and flavoring contained in the product that comes from them. Two outbreaks of copper poisoning were attributed to a backup of the carbonated water used in the drinks. This backup, due to a mechanical failure, resulted in prolonged contact of the carbonated water with the copper pipes. The California State Department of Public Health recommends that the copper tubing be replaced with stainless steel or other material in these machines. We would like to know why the Public Health Department doesn't suggest a replacement for the sugar and other harmful ingredients contained in soft drinks? The harm they do may not be so apparent as the symptoms of copper poisoning, but it can be as dangerous in the long run. We say, stay away from soft drinks, whether they come in a bottle or a vending machine!

[863]

More Chemicals—More Profit

If there's any doubt in your mind as to why we are exposed to so many different possibly toxic materials in food, here's a clipping that gives the most important answer. *Food Field Reporter* for July 21, 1958, reported that grapes raised with the new "gibberellines" brought top prices for their growers in the New York market. A dozen bunches of the larger grapes so raised filled a box which it took 22 bunches of ordinary grapes to fill. More profit for the grower.

A New "Food Saver"

A new "food-saver," so-called, has been introduced. It is potassium sorbate, a fungistatic agent. It is more soluble in water than the ones used up to now. *Chemical Week* for July 12, 1958, tells us it will be used in pickles, soft-drink concentrates, pancake syrups, fountain syrups, baked foods, fruit juices, jams, cheeses and "fresh foods."

Prediction: More Food Additives

"Dispelling food additive confusion" is the headline over a story about Dr. Bernard L. Oser who received an award for his services to nutrition. Dr. Oser, you will be sorry to hear, predicts more and more additives in food and is looking forward confidently and hopefully to the day when synthetic proteins, fats and carbohydrates will "augment the cruder products of nature." He also states that "minor risks can be afforded to win the greater benefits that await man and his descendants." He doesn't mention that the risks are taken by the customer and the benefits are gathered by the processor.

Chemicals in Cattle and Poultry Food

In the *New York Daily News,* an article datelined Washington, D. C., June 23, 1959, announces that chemicals put into about 80 per cent of the cattle and poultry feed in the United States produce cancer. The additives, mainly used to speed growth, were given to laboratory animals in large quantities. They produced cancer in these animals and can be assumed to have the same effect in humans.

It is pointed out that such small quantities are used that their use should be continued since they certainly couldn't do any harm. Who knows that to be true? Who can say what harm these minute amounts will cause in a year, or 5 or 10 years? Who knows how much of these meats each of us eats? Who can say how long these chemicals will stay in the body, or how long it takes for a deadly dose to accumulate? Who knows how they react with other chemicals we eat every day? Who knows, too, how many unexplained cancer cases have already resulted from this set of chemicals in 80 per cent of the feed eaten by United States beef and poultry? Can you imagine how hard it would be to avoid buying some of that meat? How could you know which is not carcinogen-fed?

Avoid processed foods when you can. There are so many that it's harder and harder to do each day, but when you skip processed foods, you might be missing a cancer-causing chemical.

Bees Are Poisoned and So Is Their Honey

It is true that the list of foods one can eat without fear of ingesting preservatives, insecticides, waxes, colors, hormones, etc. is decreasing by leaps and bounds. One of the items sellers always proudly advertised as pure has succumbed—honey. In this case, however, the adulteration is not deliberate. The *Seattle* (Washington) *Times* (June 16, 1959) reports on large scale losses of bees in the Yakima Valley, which has about 65 per cent of the state's bees. A spokesman said that more than 70 per cent of the bees had died, and the cause was believed to be a new type of insecticide being used in the area. There was also a suspicion on the part of the bee-keepers that honey already in the combs might be tainted.

It is impossible to know if the bees whose honey we eat gathered their nectar from contaminated blossoms or not. Perhaps the poison they got was not enough to kill them, but, added to the other poisons we take into our systems daily, it could well take its toll on us.

A ban on the use of insecticides seems to be the only answer. We must persuade our lawmakers that we are sacrificing much more than we are saving, by spraying our trees and other vegetation. We are killing the birds and insects which help with cross-pollination, and make our orchards and farms possible in the first place.

Blueberries without Blueberries

The Pillsbury Company and Duff's Baking Mix Corporation of Newark, New Jersey, put on the market a blueberry mix that does not contain any blueberries. The Pillsbury Company used a product which it called "stabilized blueberries," but when The Food and Drug Administration tested it, they found that the blueberries were made of "purple pellets consisting chiefly of sugar, nonfat dry milk, starch, coconut pulp, artificial coal tar color, artificial flavor, and a very small amount of blueberry pulp."

Needless to say the product is temporarily off the market. How far will the food processors go to reduce costs?

Food Whiteners

There is on the market a product sold in restaurant supply houses called vegetable and fruit whitener. It contains benzoate of soda and sodium bisulfate—two deadly poisons. It is used especially with potatoes, both French-fried and boiled. A tablespoonful is used with each gallon of water in which the potatoes are soaked. Then the potatoes can be stored for days without fear of turning brown or black. They have become embalmed.

This chemicalization is part of the process of automation which is entering into every phase of our lives. The restaurant can peel and trim a large quantity of a food at one time, then store it for future use, and it will appear as fresh as when first prepared. It has gotten to such a point that some restaurants purchase their potatoes already cut to size for French-

[865]

fried potatoes, and pretreated with benzoates and bisulfides at the factory. The restaurateur is taking as much work as possible out of his kitchen, regardless of the way it might affect the health of his patrons.

And in the average restaurant even the raw material for mashed potatoes is purchased in powdered form . . . a product called "Instant Whipped Potatoes." The container of one of these products showed ,the following: "Contains anhydrated potatoes and emulsifier (glycerol monostearate). Preservatives added: sodium sulfate and less than 1/10 of 1 per cent antioxidant (butylated hydroxyanisole, butylated hydroxytoluene, propyl gallate, citric acid, vegetable oil, and propylene glycol." It looks as if they are throwing the whole chemical book at the consumer.

We are especially worried about the amounts of sodium-containing chemicals that are used. This is the part of table salt, sodium chloride, that is dangerous for a heart patient. It would seem to me that the medium and lower class restaurants would be a deadly trap for the heart patient, who should studiously avoid them. Regarding the highest class restaurants . . . who knows? Perhaps they, too, believe that these chemicals help them to keep up the "quality" and color of the foods they serve.

In the meantime, health departments keep on issuing "A" credits to restaurants who use these poisons. The wholesale dealers and the restaurateurs have not been educated to give a thought to the dangers inherent in these chemicals. Where are the doctors in our health departments? Perhaps they are too busy spending their time attacking food faddists who know better than to eat foods containing these chemicals.

Perhaps the time has come for groups of public-spirited vigilantes to inspect the kitchens of restaurants and to draw public attention to their harmful practices. Perhaps organizations like Duncan-Hines should investigate this situation and not include in their approved listing any restaurants which resort to such hazardous chemicalization.

In the meantime, stay away from restaurants as much as possible . . . . and if you *do* have to go to one, the only kind of potatoes to order are those baked in their skins.

Poisonous Fumes from Tomato Preservative

A group of ladies from Modesto, California, won a moral victory in their suit against the Shell Oil Company and the Food Machinery and Chemical Company. They settled out of court for an undisclosed sum. These women instituted a suit for $200,000 against their employers, claiming that the fumes from the preservatives used in a tomato-packing plant in which they worked, had created physical disorders for them, as well as robbing the 6 married women of their sexual desires.

Though we are pleased to see that these women were compensated in some degree, we can only wish that the trial and its resultant publicity had been allowed to run its course. It would be good for the public to know that even the fumes from a preservative the rest of us will actually be eating can cause such serious consequences.

[866]

Chemicals in Rice

A reader writes to J. G. Molner, M.D., who runs a health column in the *New York Journal American,* and asks about a printed notation on a package of rice, which says, "BHT added as a preservative." He says that he thought rice did not have any preservatives, and asks what is BHT? The good doctor replies that BHT is butylated hydroxytoluene and that it is an anti-oxidant, which means that it keeps the food from absorbing oxygen, thus preventing it from becoming rancid. The doctor then adds that he believes that all these approved preservatives are good for the health of his own family and of his own body. He says, "I don't worry, I don't think you should."

Of course, the doctor is entitled to his own opinion, but I wonder whether he has done sufficient reading on the subject to make the statement that one should not worry about eating butylated hydroxytoluene. The heading to this item in the *Journal American* refers to BHT as a food "watchdog." It may be a food watchdog, but it certainly is not a watchdog of the consumer's health. BHT is a poison; that is, if used in sufficient quantities. And along with the dozens of other poisons consumed in our foods each day, it adds up to a frightening amount, an amount that should give pause to Dr. Molner—that should make him worry. Dr. Molner, please take some time off from your practice to go to some medical library and study about this chemical Frankenstein that is throwing its shadow on our confused world. Maybe you might come and visit us out here in the wilds of Pennsylvania and we can have a nice little chat?

Chemicals Go Natural?

We rejoice when we can report a new substance hailed by food processors which is made out of a purely natural food product. "For a long time now," says *Chemical Week* for October 3, 1953, "synthetics have hogged the industrial research limelight." But now someone has introduced a new natural colloid made from the seed of the guar plant.

After this seed has been cracked, milled and refined, we have a product, they tell us, that can be used for such things as tablet-disintegrating agents, bulk-former in laxative and appetite depressants and possibly the manufacture of jellies and toothpaste. Of course, there isn't any reason for dancing in the streets for we honestly don't know why we should get excited over a product to be used in appetite depressants, laxatives and jellies. But at any rate, the folks who use such things may now have a little better chance of survival since they'll be getting a natural substance rather than a synthetic one. Every little helps and we are overjoyed to know that the chemical industry has brought itself to admit that a natural product *can* be used in place of a synthetic one!

Poisons in Poultry Food

Casual mention in *Science* for May, 1955, is made of feeding arsonic acid along with antibiotics to poultry. It seems that adding the arsonic acids and the antibiotics increased the growth of poultry for a while at Michigan

[867]

State College where the experiments were carried out. Then it seems that the chicks went back to the old method of growing slowly and the researchers had to face the fact that these two highly-touted substances may not work out so well in chicken feed, after all.

We don't know how news of this kind affects you. But we do know that antibiotics have been shown to have devastating aftereffects, not only on animals but also on human beings. And we know that arsonic acid means arsenic—a deadly poison. Why do you suppose anyone would dream of feeding two such substances to any animal? And are you as alarmed as we are over the fact that some of the antibiotics and the arsenic as well may still be in the poultry when it reaches the meat market! We don't know anything you can do about such a situation except protest to your board of health and your congressman. And take your vitamin and mineral supplements—they protect you against all kinds of poisons.

Antibiotics in Baby Food

Now we've seen everything! *Chemical Week* for March 20, 1954, announced that baby food manufacturers were experimenting with antibiotics and that we could soon expect to be able to buy baby food that contains them—so that the infants can grow faster, of course! With medical journals brimfull and running over with evidence of the great harm that has already been done by the indiscriminate use of antibiotics in medicine, we are going right ahead and dump the stuff into baby food, so that not a youngster in the land will be able to escape this peril. How can it possibly benefit an infant to grow faster if, in the process we destroy the precious intestinal bacteria that help to synthetize vitamins? How can we hope to overcome any infectious threats in the future, if our children have been so saturated with antibiotics that no dose, however massive, will have any effect on them? And quite apart from all this, what about all the recent reports of extreme sensitivity and even deaths caused by antibotics? Have we taken leave of our senses to believe that "faster growth" is worth taking such a chance as this?

SECTION 17.

Processing

No matter how appetizing and eye appealing processed foods may look, no matter if their shelf life and staying power can be counted in years, these foods have been definitely robbed of the valuable vitamins and minerals which Nature has implanted in them for the nourishment of mankind. We know that it is a difficult task to maintain a diet completely free from processed foods, in these days of modernization, but the time and effort expended in the attainment of this goal will pay for itself many times in the form of good health, both physical and mental.

CHAPTER 232

The Story of the Carrot

By J. I. Rodale

In our search for the guilty factor that is causing the heavy increase in heart disease, we must give most of our attention to nutrition, or, I should say, to malnutrition. The overconsumption of fats and the under-consumption of calcium are of tremendous significance in causing this disease; also the overconsumption of food in general which leads to obesity. Now let us look at the general nutritional picture and see how it stacks up, for or against the heart.

From what I see, after going into the matter most thoroughly, heart disease is nothing more than a symptom of a nutritional deficiency. It is not exactly a starving to death, but it is starving for an adequate supply of minerals and vitamins. Man's body is degenerating. All types of chronic illnesses are on the increase, due to a lack of conception of what is good nutrition. Man is becoming like a hothouse flower, lacking in the old-time primitive ruggedness, and the common denominator is a weakening of the body, a reducing of the ability to resist disease due to a lack of intake of the necessary minerals and vitamins. It is a startlingly simple cause which, if remedied, could cut deaths from heart disease to the vanishing point, but which, if not, is a threat to the continued existence of our civilization.

The average physician will tell you that the way to get your vitamins is with a knife and fork—in other words, by consuming a well-balanced diet. But sad to relate this is impossible under our highly commercialized system of food processing by which our food is bleached, colored, de-hydrated, desiccated, homogenized, pasteurized, gassed, canned, chemicalized and fragmentized in a dozen other ways; a system by which our water is chlorinated, fluoridated, aluminized and sulphated; a system which teaches the housewife to destroy food values in the kitchen. We are not eating wholeness. The parts we lose or throw away are causes of death.

When an animal consumes something, it eats the whole thing—bones and all. Many primitive races do the same thing, and as a result they do not suffer from heart disease. The Chinese eat a dish made of lamb's eyes which they say is delectable, and which must contain a rich supply of vitamins and minerals. How about stewed calf's ear, or lungs, or pig feet jelly? We eat unfertilized, sterile eggs—eggs laid by hens without the inter-vention of a rooster. Research shows that such eggs are of lower nutritional quality than eggs from which chicks can hatch.

Our food raised with chemical fertilizers lacks an adequate supply of mineral elements, and is imbalanced, containing excesses of carbohy-drates and insufficiencies of protein. Modern technology on the farm has been developed to put money in the farmers' pocket, without regard to the fact that it is weakening the consumers' body. Take the old method of growing wheat. At harvest time the plants were placed in stacks in the field and permitted to ripen there. The wheat seed continued to "grow." Many old-fashioned farmers placed the complete plants in their barns, threshing the seed out of them in small batches as needed. A sort of continuing beneficial fermentation took place which improved the nutritional properties of the wheat seed. But today, with the labor-saving combines, the wheat is cut and threshed in the field in one mechanized operation and rushed off to the flour and feed mills while still green, giving the miller much trouble and requiring chemical treatment to prevent it from spoiling.

Let me give you an example—a typical one—the handling of the carrot, showing the monstrous and stupid blundering with which the public, aided and abetted by its nutritional advisers, approaches the problem of eating, and you will see why modern conceptions of nutrition result in a failure to provide the human organism with the means of resisting disease.

1. The Top Greens

GREENS
DESTROYED

Fig. 1

The first thing that is done is that the green top is cut off and thrown away. (Fig. 1.) It goes into the garbage pail, and eventually is burned up in the city incinerator, is fed to pigs or is dumped out at sea. What a terrible blunder this is! Nutritionally the green top has far greater value than the pulpy bottom part which grows underground. The greens contain vitamin K, for example, a vitamin which is completely lacking in the carrot itself. Recently, a friend of ours who suffered a heart attack was given injections of vitamin K. If he had been eating raw carrot greens regularly, is it possible that its abundant vitamins and minerals would have protected his heart? The greens are also rich in magnesium, a lack of which is suspected as a possible cause of cancer.

Dr. George A. Wilson of Denver, Colorado, has developed a method of making electric tests of food and other substances. All life is electro-chemical, we know. Every cell of our bodies has a positive and negative charge of electricity. Dr. Wilson has found that any plant that grows in the sun registers a much higher electric potential on his machine than those that grow underground, and has used this fact in developing diets for sick persons that may completely revolutionize our ideas of nutrition. We can, therefore, realize what an error it is to throw the carrot greens away.

2. Storage

Now we come to step number two. In our system of producing food and getting it to the public, a little time usually elapses—more or less. Sometimes this is quite a considerable period. Research indicates that there are substantial losses in vitamins caused not only by mere passage of time, but also by the method of storing such as refrigeration, etc. On occasion a batch of carrots may come to market in which there have been abnormal vitamin losses because of the great length of time they were in storage under poor keeping conditions. Exposure to light will, for example, cause a loss of riboflavin which is one of the B vitamins.

Now, let us look at our carrot. (Fig. 2.) The shaded portion shows the estimated nutritional loss on account of storage which amounts to about 5 per cent.

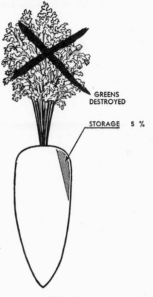

GREENS DESTROYED

STORAGE 5 %

Fig. 2

3. The Skin

Many housewives are not aware of the fact that by far the largest portion of the minerals resides in the skin and in the area immediately under it. They, therefore, scrape the skin off thinking that it is better for their health if they do so. They are afraid of a little dirt. A good washing is all that is necessary, but the skin itself should be saved. The skins of all vegetables and fruits are the most valuable parts, and account for at least 10 per cent of their total nutritional content. Many years ago in a certain part of Nova Scotia there was famine, and Sir Wilfred Grenfell, a famous nutritionist, came to make an investigation as to how it had affected the health of the people. He came to one family and found the parents practically dead because of lack of food, but a child of a few years seemed to be running around full of energy and vigor. When he probed into the matter, he discovered that the family had a few chickens that had the run of the house. The parents ate mashed potatoes, throwing the skins to the chickens, and the child would eat some of these skins. The concentrated minerals and vitamins in them kept the child healthy.

Now let us look at the picture of our carrot: (Fig. 3.)

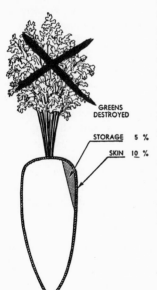

GREENS DESTROYED

STORAGE 5 %

SKIN 10 %

Fig. 3

4. Soaking

In many cases the carrots are soaked in cold

water so that they may become more crisp as an appetizer, a procedure regularly recommended by most cookbooks and women's magazines. This causes a loss of its natural sugar, all the B vitamins, vitamin C and P and all the minerals except calcium.

5. Shredding

Shredding carrots for salads causes a loss of 20 per cent of the vitamin C and an additional 20 per cent if the salad stands for an hour before eating.

6. Cooking

The next step is the unpardonable crime of cooking the carrot. Whole boiled carrots will retain 90 per cent of vitamin C and much of the minerals, but slicing before cooking results in destruction of the vitamin C and the niacin portion of the vitamin B complex. Salt in the cooking water lowers the vitamin C retention in sliced or quartered carrots. It also causes mineral loss in the water. Copper utensils will destroy vitamin C. Soda in the water destroys both thiamin (of the vitamin B) and also vitamin C. Boiling carrots can cause loss of 20 to 25 per cent of their thiamin (vitamin B). If carrots are frozen and you thaw them slowly, you lose vitamin C. If you sieve carrots hot, you lose 15 per cent of their vitamin C. If you sieve them cold, the vitamin C loss is 5 per cent. The poor absorption from cooked carrots is attributed to the fact that the greater part of the cell walls is not destroyed in cooking so the carotene enclosed in the cell walls cannot be absorbed.

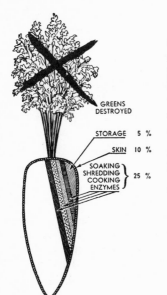

GREENS DESTROYED

STORAGE 5 %

SKIN 10 %

SOAKING
SHREDDING } 25 %
COOKING
ENZYMES

Fig. 4

7. Enzyme Loss

Something regarding which very little is spoken or known are the enzymes which are contained in all living matter. They are important in digestion and in the body's metabolistic processes generally. Nature put them there for a purpose. They are a substance excreted by bacteria or manufactured within the cells. In cooking, all the enzymes are destroyed 100 per cent. In the picture showing the losses within the carrot by what we do to it before eating, we have bunched the effects of 4 items together—shredding, soaking, cooking vitamin and mineral loss and enzyme destruction, which together account for about 25 per cent of the nutritional content of the carrot: (Fig. 4.)

Everything that is shaded is the equivalent of paper or sawdust as far as food value is concerned. It is a total loss.

8. Loss of Cooking Water

In many kitchens the cooking methods are so careless that the water that has drained out of the carrots, a precious essence full of minerals, is recklessly thrown down the sink drain. It is a fact that practically all the potassium is lost in this manner. Now let us see what we have, after losing 20 per cent: (Fig. 5.)

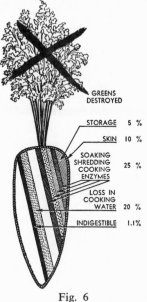

GREENS DESTROYED
STORAGE 5 %
SKIN 10 %
SOAKING SHREDDING COOKING ENZYMES 25 %
LOSS IN COOKING WATER 20 %
INDIGESTIBLE 1.1%

Fig. 6

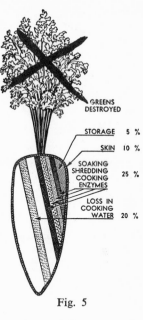

GREENS DESTROYED
STORAGE 5 %
SKIN 10 %
SOAKING SHREDDING COOKING ENZYMES 25 %
LOSS IN COOKING WATER 20 %

Fig. 5

9. Indigestibility

It so happens that the carrot is somewhat fibrous. Some of it resists mastication, and no matter how much you chew it, that portion can do nothing for the human body. So we must chalk up another loss, and we do it as follows, to the amount of 1.1 per cent: (Fig. 6.)

10. Effect of Chemical Fertilizer

We must not overlook the nutritional effect on the carrot of the large amount of chemical fertilizers used in growing them under the artificial conditions of present day agriculture. A carrot grown in 1870, for example, was a far different article than the average one grown today. The present day carrot has less vitamins and minerals, and you can prove this in no time by feeding two groups of rabbits—one with carrots grown with chemical fertilizers—the other with carrots grown with organic matter such as manure, leaves, weeds, etc. To this extent, therefore, there was that much less need in 1870 to take vitamins. We must, therefore, slice off another narrow segment in the carrot amounting to 10 per cent as follows: (Fig. 7.)

11. Use of Added Sugar

Many housewives douse practically everything they cook or handle in the kitchen with

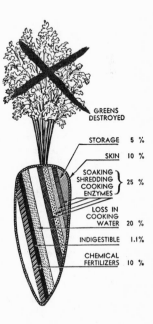

GREENS DESTROYED
STORAGE 5 %
SKIN 10 %
SOAKING SHREDDING COOKING ENZYMES 25 %
LOSS IN COOKING WATER 20 %
INDIGESTIBLE 1.1%
CHEMICAL FERTILIZERS 10 %

Fig. 7

[875]

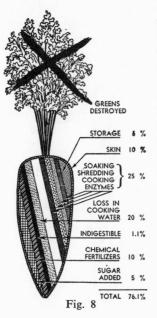

GREENS
DESTROYED

STORAGE   5 %

SKIN   10 %

SOAKING
SHREDDING
COOKING } 25 %
ENZYMES

LOSS IN
COOKING
WATER   20 %

INDIGESTIBLE   1.1%

CHEMICAL
FERTILIZERS   10 %

SUGAR
ADDED   5 %

TOTAL   76.1%

Fig. 8

sugar, and the carrot does not escape. In such cases one does not taste carrot, but sugar. However, sugar, besides other bad habits, neutralizes the calcium with which it comes in contact, and when one considers that the government found in a recent survey that 85 per cent of the public is calcium deficient, one can see in the addition of so much sugar to our foods, one of the reasons for that deficiency.

The addition of sugar causes a 5 per cent loss. The score now stands as follows: (Fig. 8.)

Fig. 9

12. The Garbage Pail

It is not enough that man destroys so much of the nutritional percentage of the carrot but he is not yet satisfied. At the last moment he decides not to eat it all and leaves a small portion, sometimes not so small, to find its way into the garbage pail and to the city incinerator where it is burned up. The next drawing shows how much of the carrot is used up by this practice: (Fig. 9.)

Conclusion

What is left is a painfully pitiful portion of what the carrot had to offer to start with. Yet when we eat a dish of cooked carrots we usually do it with a glow of satisfaction—with a feeling that we are eating something that will fortify us against come what may in the battle for health. Is it any wonder then that the executives of the large companies are dropping dead every day from heart disease? But it is sad to note that the nutritionists have eyes but cannot see that *they* are the ones who could set things right by recognizing conditions for what they are and coming out in a tremendous campaign, recommending the taking of vitamins and minerals by every man, woman and child.

It is not the so-called fast pace that is killing people, but a degenerating and weakening of the body due to an emasculation of its food. It is not only the carrot, but when one sees what is being done to our bread, milk and other foods, a case is built for the increasing deaths not only from heart disease but from cancer, polio and the host of other degenerative diseases which are multiplying at such an alarming rate.

The next time some doctor or friend tells you that you should eat your vitamins with a knife and a fork, tell him the story of the carrot and see what he says then. We *must* take vitamins if we wish to be healthy and the nation as a whole must do it, or God alone knows what will happen to the second or third generation coming up—generations inheriting weaknesses passed on to them by us, generations which few of us will live to see unless we augment our diet with vitamins and minerals. And, as parting advice, don't take coal tar vitamins. Examine every bottle. Be sure that the vitamins you take are extracted from food. Scientific research proves that this is best.

CHAPTER 233

Our Methods of Processing Corn, and the Mexicans' Method

How nutritious are the corn products we buy at the store, the corn meal, corn cereals, hominy grits and so forth? To learn more about the nutritive value of corn, experimenters have made studies in several regions of the world where corn is the main (and sometimes almost the only) item of diet. In southern United States, for instance, among lower income families where corn products make up most of a diet sadly lacking in fresh fruits and vegetables and animal protein, pellagra is a common disease. Pellagra is the result of insufficient niacin (part of the vitamin B complex) in the diet. How then does it happen, ask the scientists, that in large sections of Mexico, where corn also is used almost exclusively for food, there is very little pellagra?

Experiments on Mexican Corn

The Mexicans eat their corn in tortillas, a flat cake of corn meal baked on a hot griddle. The first stage in preparing tortillas is to cook the whole corn in lime water. Does this have something to do with its food value? J. Laguna, M.D., and K. J. Carpenter, M.D., have made tests with laboratory animals to determine just what the story is on corn and niacin. Reporting in the *Journal of Nutrition* for September 10, 1951, they describe 3 diets fed to 3 groups of rats. One group ate raw corn daily; the second group ate corn cooked in lime water as the Mexicans do it; the third group ate raw corn to which niacin had been added. The results showed that the animals fed raw corn grew only 40 grams in 28 days, whereas those fed on the lime-cooked corn grew twice as much. Raw corn with niacin added resulted in growth almost as great as with the lime-cooked corn.

In another experiment Drs. Laguna and Carpenter fed rats with corn that had been "wet-milled" in the process used to produce the commercial corn products, such as cornstarch, feed meal and so forth. This is the process in which the germ and gluten are removed from the corn. The authors describe it as a "fairly severe treatment . . . which includes steeping for 48 hours in a weak sulfurous acid solution." The experimenters found that wet-milled corn had practically no nutritive value, as compared with the lime-cooked corn.

Refining Processes To Blame

The authors say that their findings are not extensive enough to warrant scientific conclusions about human diet, yet it seems to us the experiments prove once again that our modern refining processes remove most of the nourishment from our foods. Hundreds of years ago, the forefathers of Mexican peasants, eating a diet of practically nothing but corn, worked out a way which their descendants still use to make the corn more nourishing and prevent pellagra. In modern corn products, however, almost all of the nutrition is taken from the corn in a process where sulfurous acid is used. And we wonder why evidences of pellagra and diseases similar to it are continually cropping up!

Editor Rodale suggests that the best way to eat corn is the way he likes to eat it: cut the ear from the stalk. Eat it within a few hours. Eat it raw. If you eat corn this way, the sweet corn-milk has not had time to sink into the cob and you will benefit from all the nutritive values of the corn, which might be lost in cooking. And it tastes good!

CHAPTER 234

Shall We Em-Bomb Our Food?

What would you—or anybody—do with the thousands of tons of radioactive trash that has been and will be accumulating from the atomic experiments being made by our government? It's too hot to handle—can't dump it anywhere for there are few, if any, places so remote in this world that a pile of radioactive rubbish would not reach out to contaminate the atmosphere in which human beings live. In the ocean maybe? No, there are fish, you know. Those that wouldn't die outright would swim into the nets of commercial fishermen and be full to the gills with radioactive isotopes. A few fish dinners like this and Americans would be so thoroughly radiated they might begin to glow. The moon has been thought of as a refuse dump (we don't know if anyone up there would mind) but that's out because we don't know how to get it there!

So we've been storing atomic waste in specially constructed tanks, which seems to work pretty well—except that one day soon we won't be able to build tanks fast enough to keep up with the accumulation. But science has been working on this problem for some time and has come up with a dazzlingly simple solution: if we can't sprinkle the radioactive garbage on some remote plain, and we can't sink it deep in the ocean or shoot it to the moon, we'll get the American citizens to eat it! And that, dear reader, is where we stand now.

Why Irradiate Food?

Researchers are working hard and long to find a way to irradiate your food because a. they don't know how else to get rid of the radioactive waste, and b. if atomic power is to be competitive with the power sources we already have, it must begin to pay for itself and eventually show a profit. Selling a by-product to the food industry as a preservative is certainly a way of setting a foot on the path to solvency and profits.

The steady push to more processing of foods finds its logical conclusion in ionizing radiation. Once the food industry was satisfied to simply boil the life and vitamins out of our foods before canning them; then they added waxes and drugs that would paralyze or kill any living organism that our food might contain or acquire from without, with the added danger of possible harm to us from the additive. But now all doubt and possibility will be eliminated—we *know* that radiation can and will kill us. So the misled, uninformed housewife rushes wildly into the local super market clamoring for the irradiated potatoes that she has been told she can store for two years without their sprouting, or the atomic steak that will sit on an unrefrigerated pantry shelf for 3 months without losing its red color.

Advantages and Disadvantages of Food Radiation

Whoa, Madame! Why does she want her potatoes to last for two years? And why does she want a steak she can leave on the window sill for a month? No refrigerator? Too far from a store? Well, she'll need a refrigerator for the meat anyway. And where can she store a two-year supply of potatoes—or why should she want to? Oh, she's been told irradiated foods are better for her. She was probably told that when she was told that less nutrition is lost by radiation than by cooking. But remember, after the food is radiated, it will have to be cooked at home, too! So the consumer will lose not only the 63 per cent thiamin which radiation destroys, or the 8 per cent riboflavin, the 3 per cent niacin, or the 10-30 per cent of valuable and rare vitamin E, which Dr. H. F. Kraybill of the Medical Nutritional Laboratory of Denver, tells us radiations will eliminate, but the cooking done to the food at home will probably destroy what's left. Can it be this loss of vitamin E which makes the effects of radiation so apparent in problems of heredity and fertility?

[879]

Nor has anyone told the consumer of the deadly gamma rays lurking in the food, and what harm they can do to the human body. After all, the object of advertising is to tell the consumer things that will make him buy the product, not disadvantages that will turn him against it.

There is no doubt that the growers will benefit from preserving foods by radiation—they can make fruit stay on the trees until the market is ready for it, or they can pick fruit green and ship it, giving it a quick shot of the rays to ripen it almost immediately at its destination. The shipper will be delighted with these foods, too, for he need never worry about delays in route that might result in spoiling ordinary foods.

The retailer will be in clover. No more sales to move things off his shelves—instead he might advertise the length of time they've been there as though staleness were a virtue! And the consumer's dividend from all this? He will pay for the process (1/25-1/10 of a cent per pound); he will get old produce and meats drained of most of their nutritive value; they will probably taste funny and will be loaded with dangerous radioactive elements that can shorten his life and burden him with disease. The preservative factor? Frozen food keeps just as long, with no change in taste and no loss of nutrients. Radiating food is not a step for progress, so much as a step to profits. The consumer will pay the bill and be convinced that he is getting something he's always wanted, while in reality he was better off before he got it.

What is Food Radiation

The theory behind radiation is quite simple: atomic rays are deadly, so exposure to them should certainly kill any living thing in food—germs, enzymes, vitamins, minerals, etc.—anything in short that makes food food! One of the methods used to accomplish this is by immersion of the food in a large tank of water, where, at the bottom, lies a container of radioactive substance. (The water is necessary to protect personnel against rays.) With the two tanks close together, the radiation passes into the food, burning out every spark of life it might have had. This is how the sprouting powers of potatoes are extinguished for two years or for good, how the enzyme action in meats is stilled for weeks on end, and the natural tendency towards spoilage in vegetables is inhibited or completely annihilated.

There are further refinements in the processes of radiating food. It can be pasteurized or sterilized. When it is pasteurized, the germs present are killed by using a relatively low intensity so that the enzymes and certain microörganisms are inactivated or stunned. The food will keep a bit longer than other foods, but must be refrigerated if it is to keep for any length of time. However, as *Popular Science* for April, 1956, says, "The spectacular sort of thing, making perishables keep outside an icebox, calls for total sterilization—killing every last microörganism in the food. That takes a whammy of a couple of million Roentgens (a unit of radiation, used in the sense that watts are used to describe the strength of light bulbs) of radiation. Since 400 or 500 Roentgens can kill the average man, you can see how tough those babies are."

[880]

Three Deterrents to Radiation of Foods

There are a few snags that have been hampering the movement to radiate all foods. First of all, no one wants to admit what irradiated foods can do to the consumer. Second, all foods do not take to irradiation with equal results. Third, the nutritional value of the food is almost completely eradicated by radiation.

The latter two points are most easily discussed, so we will go into them first. The taste and smell, as well as the texture and color of certain foods are unhappily altered by the radiation process. Milk takes on a burnt flavor; soft fruits like peaches and pears are made softer yet, and the appetizing color is bleached right out of them. Off-odors in cheese, orange and lemon juice also make them unsuitable for consumption.

One noted authority, Professor Brownell, puts it this way: "Sterilized meat smells like a dog when it comes in out of the rain. And it tastes about like it smells."

Don't underestimate our food processors; these difficulties will be surmounted. Several solutions, so-called are advanced now. Freezing the food first, to stabilize the enzymes and other alterable constituents before radiation is one experiment being tried. Another idea has been to exclude oxygen during radiation, presumably thereby eliminating the possibility of the burn ing that creates some of the off-tastes. (Of course, what is left of food made to resist a force that would ordinarily burn it is another question.) Of all these dodges, the one which uses added chemical preservatives to help ward off the radiation effects is most incongruous. If radiation is being used to preserve the food artificially, it is doing what chemical additives have been employed to do for many years now. Why do the same job twice? What point can there be in adding a preservative to food so it will keep while you add another preservative? *Alice in Wonderland* does not contain a more fantastic proposition than this!

Radiation in Botanical Experiments

Besides directly influencing the food prepared for you to buy, radiation has been in use in botanical experiments. The shocks given by doses of radiation so stimulate the growth cells of the plants that they skitter in all directions, rearranging the basic characteristics of the plants to create new entities in the seedlings to come. The results can mean giant peas, or red peas, seedless watermelons or watermelons with seeds so large that the pink flesh is all but eliminated. But not for human consumption—at least not 'till a few generations have held the radioactivity down a good bit, for luckily it diminishes with each new generation of plants.

The ingredients of commercial fertilizers have been injected with radioactive isotopes so that their progress through various plants could be traced with Geiger counters. This has proven to be an excellent way to find out what happens to fertilizer components in plants which absorb them. It shows also how easily radiation can be transferred and how powerfully active it must be to be discernible from such a minute dose as a plant can absorb.

Radioactive materials have had even more peculiar journeys. Isotopes in cattle fodder have been followed into the cow who ate it, into the milk the cow gave, and probably the person who drank it is so full of isotopes he's ticking like grandfather's railroad watch. An article in the *New York Times* for September 19, 1956, tells of cows in Germany giving radioactive milk after eating clover that showed signs of radioactivity, blamed on fallout from bomb tests. Quite possibly much of the food we eat today is already radioactive—and not on purpose at that!

Governmental Promotion

The major force behind this whole movement for irradiating food is the Quartermaster Corps of the U. S. Army. Should another war break out, they say, food perishability in shipping would cease to be a problem. It would simply be irradiated into a mummy-state and could be on a beach or in a ship's hold forever, if need be. The Quartermaster Corps is so interested in this project that 10 million dollars have already been gambled on research. Does this sound as though the government were approaching this project gingerly and with an attitude of revocable experiment?

Anent the government's attitude toward irradiating foods, we have a very pious statement which tells us that the findings of the Food and Drug Administration are awaited and that the government must be completely and absolutely satisfied that *no hazard*, known or unknown, lurks in irradiated food. Words like that tend to make us sit back and relax, were it not for previous experience. This statement has a familiar ring to it because one like it has been made to cover every new type of food processing for years. Yet the proven hazards of using certain cancer-causing food additives have not made the FDA rescind the blessing it gave them. Rather, some of them have been deliberately excluded from the jurisdiction of that Department by the department itself, so that it would not be required to pass judgment.

Radiation Authorities Speak

If the FDA is as intensely interested in protecting us from this dangerous new scheme as they let on, then let them recognize the opinions of authorities in the field of radiation who discuss the *known hazards* of radiation acquired in *any* way whatsoever, before they further pursue an investigation of their own which can only prove the same thing at heavy cost.

For example: A basic resolution of The First International Congress on Heredity at Copenhagen states: "Damage produced by ionizing radiation on the hereditary material is real and should be taken seriously into consideration." And Professor Raymond Turpin of Laboratoise de Genetique, Hopital St. Louis said at the same conference, ". . . every possible precaution should be taken while giving radiation—unnecessary radiation should be eliminated."

N. J. Berrill, Professor of Zoology at McGill University writes in *Harper's* magazine that "there is no threshold below which man-made radiation can be considered safe. All radioactivity above the natural (i.e. atmospheric) level is dangerous if continued indefinitely."

X-Rays and Radiation Compared

Those arguing for the ionized irradiation of foods are quick to tell you that the rays they would use pass through the food just as x-rays do. This sounds reassuring until one discovers that x-rays don't simply pass through the body and disappear! They lounge around for quite a time, and continued exposure to them can be as dangerous as camping out in an atomic devastation area on a test day. As for the staying powers of radioactive materials, note the procedure followed by a patient after receiving radiation treatments for thyroid cancer. The iodized isotope being given him is so "hot" that the patient must wash his own face and neck for days after treatment, because a nurse would receive one full day's allowable treatment by putting her hands within 3 inches of the patient's neck for a single minute. And the radiation swoops in and out of the system so fast that for 7 weeks the patient's urine must be stored in lead containers to control the radiation it carries! How can food radiation be expected to disappear from food any more rapidly than it would from a living body? And if it leaves the food, will it leave entirely? Can we be sure there will not be a residue? We think not.

It has been shown by experiment that any radiation is cumulative in anything that has been treated. Too frequent x-rays are warned against by the National Committee on Genetics because they pile up in the body, and especially in the reproductive system. The maximum number of Roentgens suggested for persons in the first 30 years of life is only 50 and about 8 of these are acquired unavoidably, simply by living in the atmosphere which surrounds us and having our periodic chest x-ray or tooth check-up. Add to this the intense bombardment of x-rays one might need for a picture of a broken bone or a look at a stomach ulcer and we are dangerously close to our maximum.

Dangers of Radiation Are All About Us

It is obvious that there is no room in us for further ionizing radioactivity —least of all the ingestion of uncontrolled amounts of it in food.

If the promoters of this movement are so sure that the danger of radioactive contamination is indefinite, let them explain the longevity statistics published by the National Research Council concerning radiologists, which showed them to be dying 5 years earlier (60 years) than the average citizen (65.6). This bears out another statement of the Council: "One of the effects (of radiation) is a shortening of life. This seems to involve some generalized action. Irradiated individuals may age faster than normally, even if they do not develop *specific radiation-induced diseases like leukemia*." Cell replacement rates are lowered and the body just gives up a lot sooner in its struggle to replace them at all. This, coming from another agency of the government, National Academy of Science, should convince the Food and Drug Administration that the consumption of even a single Roentgen more than is absolutely necessary is dangerous to life. Many experts are on record concerning this fact.

One asserts that "local radiation in almost any part of the body may

[883]

produce cancer." (National Academy of Sciences—"Biological Effects of Radiation," 1956). The nuclear particles either act directly to kill a living cell or they jar the chemical balance, stirring peaceful cells into uncharacteristic activity. Again quoting Professor Berrill, "No matter how small the missiles thrown into the machinery, or how gentle the trickle of electrolyzing energy entering the cells, if activity is kept up long enough, something vital will be damaged. For this reason there is no threshold below which man-made radiation can be considered safe."

In the light of these intimations that the poison of radiation works slowly, the Quartermaster Corps' system of checking for deadly effects of radiated food by observing volunteers who eat it for a year or two seems futile. Indications are that these men will not drop dead for quite a while. Even if radiation took 20 years off a person's life, the Army would be waiting around until these soldiers are 40 before they could see that ionized radiation of foods is a killer. Apparently it will take a dramatic epidemic of leukemia or other cancers to impress them. Certainly if these soldiers walk away from two years of a radiated food diet without eyes that light up or fingernails that glow in the dark, they should not be used as proof that such a diet can't do a human being any harm.

The Effect of Radiation on Reproductive Cells

The reproductive cells show an alarming susceptibility to radioactive particles. It is here that the strong powers of rampant isotopes are most evident. Laboratory rats fed on radiated foods as early as 1948 showed an impairment in fertility of the male and increased mortality in the litters. Tiny doses at long intervals might sterilize a man for a short time—perhaps a week—by stunning the sperm cells, or even killing the current supply. Enough radiation can kill the manufacturing source of these cells, thereby incurring complete and permanent sterility.

Besides sterility, there is the problem of the rearranged chromosomes and genes, and the offspring they influence. "Any radiation which reaches the reproductive cells causes mutations that are passed on to succeeding generations," the National Research Council speaking. These mutations in human beings might be just as incongruous as those in plants. What can happen in a human being if things like two colors of carnations can be made to grow on the same stem, or apples can be forced to ripen in minutes by radiation? And this problem extends itself into many generations to come. It will be multiplied indefinitely, depending on how much radiation each generation is exposed to. If radiated foods become common, then the future generation will be born with mutations which modify what we consider a normal body.

And if they absorb more radiation, then their changes, plus more changes, will be passed on to their children. The mutations will multiply and vary until in perhaps a hundred or a thousand years, humanity will be a grotesque burlesque of itself, and the pictures of the moon-men cartoonists draw will seem quite normal, or enviably attractive.

Radiation is a serious problem of our modern world. It is beginning to permeate every phase of human contact and daily extends its horizons.

[884]

Atomic energy has graduated from bombs to transportation and heating and power plants, and finally is now proposed as a food preservative. Heaven only knows how much excess radiation is being released to the atmosphere by these other activities—we dare not deliberately take more radioactivity into our bodies by eating food that it contaminates. This is one idea America must refuse to buy.

Bibliography:

The Biological Effects of Atomic Radiation: Summary Report to the Public from the National Academy of Sciences.

CHAPTER 235

100% Pure What?

We've come to expect all sorts of "extras" in the processed foods offered for sale. We know that in a can of peaches, for example, the peaches are very likely to be accompanied by a sweetening agent, a firming agent, a coloring agent and some type of preservative. The same holds true with appropriate changes for vegetables, meats, pies, cakes, ice cream and just about everything else we can buy off the shelf. We've objected to the use of these substances many times, and our objections have been met with pronouncements from the food industry on how vital additives are. We couldn't exist without them, they tell us. When a food has been processed, we're told, one can be sure it's been freed from germs and sealed from danger until it's opened in the home. These, and other arguments like them, have created a number of super market customers who wouldn't use a single food that hasn't been "purified" and sealed safely in a container with plenty of "extras."

A Look At Bulletin 617

We think that a look through *Bulletin 617* published in October, 1958, by The Connecticut Agricultural Experiment Station, might cause such persons to revise their thinking. The *Bulletin* is a report on the examinations of 1,464 samples of foods, drugs, cosmetics and other miscellaneous materials that were submitted for testing, most of which were manufactured or processed popular brand-name items. Of the number tested, 44 per cent were found to be adulterated, misbranded or otherwise objectionable. That is not to say that each item was found to be dangerous to the consumer. In cases of misbranding, the product was refused only because the content did not agree accurately with the label:—too little protein compared with what was promised, too many calories for a low-calorie-advertised product, etc. Nothing deadly about these; dishonest, unfair, misrepresentative perhaps, but not deadly. It merely means that when you buy a can or box of processed food you can't be sure of getting what you pay for. When you buy fresh foods there is no question of this, for you can see exactly what you're buying.

In cases of adulterated foods it is a different story. These foods can be dangerous to the point of fatality. They contain foreign matter which is completely alien to the product, and is there due to lack of sanitation or because of carelessness. Here are a few of the adulterants listed in the Connecticut report. Bear in mind, as you read these, that most of the brand-names would be familiar to you. You or your friends have probably bought these exact items dozens of times. They are from the type of manufacturers you "trust."

Flies, Mold, Shoestrings and Hair

A can of condensed beef noodle soup was opened to reveal two lead shot reposing therein. An unopened bottle of pale dry gingerale, from a bottler whose name is practically synonymous with the product, contained a 20-inch-long shoestring. In a sponge cake the surprise bonus was a house-fly which had been baked with the batter, plus an infestation of adult and pupal saw-toothed grain weevils. A can of chow mein with mushrooms delivered this prize: a portion of a woman's belt made of elastic woven fabric with a snakeskin pattern. A spectographic examination of the contents of the same can further showed the presence of considerable titanium, iron and aluminum. A bottle of the world's most famous soft drink contained a trace of kerosene, a few particles of black dirt; another bottle of the same drink showed a white powder that turned out to be aspirin; and a third bottle contained a clump of mold. Then there was a box of "pure" egg noodles that disclosed "a large quantity of human hair clippings present."

The list goes on to include some birch beer in a bottle containing a clump of mold surrounding a housefly, and strawberry soda whose bottle contained "a small, dried-up animal which was either a mouse or a young rat." Some orange soda was the cause of profuse vomiting immediately after drinking—it contained a residue of brown flakes "which appear to be undissolved orange dye."

A 100% Pure Maraschino Cherry

An interesting paragraph of the report concerns the question that arose over passing a brand of green maraschino cherries labeled "100% pure." The true maraschino cherry was so named for having been preserved in Maraschino, a European liqueur prepared from a special variety of European wild cherry. According to the Food and Drug Administration's definition, a 100 per cent pure maraschino cherry is one that "has been dyed red, impregnated with sugar and packed in sugar syrup flavored with oil of bitter almonds or a similar flavor." Under this definition the cherries in question were not 100 per cent pure because they had been dyed green, not red, so they didn't pass inspection. This should be a lesson to one and all to check into any food marked "100 per cent pure" and determine "pure" what?

People on salt-free diets cling to the chemical salt substitutes that have become plentiful in recent years. They figure that they can use all they want safely because, as one label signified, "This delicious salt substitute contains

... less than 1/10 milligram sodium per 100 grams. Milligrams per teaspoon —none." An analysis of the product showed some variance with the label's claim—almost 300 times as much sodium as declared! Again reliance on a chemical substitute proves to be misplaced trust that could be a major cause of death. In doing without salt, herbs make a dependable, natural alternate for flavoring foods.

A physician who suspected that one of his patients might be suffering from symptoms of lead poisoning submitted to the Experimental Station a number of substances, used by the patient, for lead analysis. Among these was a sample of pipe tobacco which contained 20 ppm. (parts per million) of lead and 6 ppm. of arsenic. The government agencies limit lead to 7 ppm. and arsenic to 3.5 ppm. Further tests of 26 samples of pipe tobacco showed an average lead arsenate content of 27 ppm. plus 23 ppm. of lead in some other form. Is there any wonder that smokers have excessive difficulties with their health?

One of the brighter spots in this booklet concerns the testing of a rutin and ascorbic acid tablet. The declared value of ascorbic acid (vitamin C) in the tablet was 300 milligrams. The testers found it to contain 329 milligrams, a safety margin that producers of all foods might do well to emulate.

In a current pamphlet, *The Merchants of Menace*, released by the American Medical Association as part of their campaign against what they call food faddists and food-supplement salesmen, we see this statement. "Herbs, unprocessed cereals and blackstrap molasses do contain nutrients— plus an unexpected bonus of stems, rust and husks!" We are certain that this quotation, even if it were true, would have the author blushing with embarrassment, if he were to read it with a copy of *Bulletin 617* which describes far worse findings among the pamphlet's recommended "standard combinations of more palatable, common foods."

CHAPTER 236

Leviticus

By J. I. Rodale

A few weeks ago I received a letter from a reader which concerned the dietary prohibitions contained in Leviticus. The lady had been purchasing a whole wheat bread made from stone ground flour and the family had been enjoying it immensely. But, she says, "the topic I am writing you about is this: I was suspicious of their declaration of fats used when they spoke of 'animal fats' and wondered if they would use LARD! Yesterday I phoned the distributors and was referred to the bakery itself, and was informed they used 'half and half,' that is, I understand, half lard and half vegetable shortening. This information has given me quite a let-down, as I was so happy to think I had really found a bakery using all good wholesome products with no chemicals, preservatives, dough softeners, etc. I have not touched pork in any form for a number of years now—over 5 anyway. I am not Jewish, but feel the Scriptures are authentic and warn people not to even touch pork, to say nothing about consuming the filthy stuff."

I am not in favor of eating any swine products for the reason that not only is the pig in bad repute for his unsanitary habits, but also in many communities he is fed garbage and as a result carries the deadly trichina worm which has played havoc with consumers of his flesh. Perhaps there are some pig raisers among our readers who will say that if given half a chance, the pig will maintain a surprising cleanliness. But is he usually given that chance? My attitude is, why take a chance when there is so much other meat available? Where there is smoke there may be fire.

Health Rules in the Bible

But this lady sent me scurrying to my Bible. I went to the portion of Leviticus which deals with the food restrictions God gave Moses. *Thou shalt not eat any animal unless it has split hoofs and chews its cud.* This makes such animals as swine, camels and rabbits unclean. *Of fish, only those that have fins and scales may be eaten*—which makes lobsters and oysters taboo. Of birds, certain kinds are mentioned which may not be eaten. These *are the eagle, the ossifrage, the osprey, the vulture and the kite after its kind, the raven and his kind, the owl, the nighthawk, the cuckoo and the hawk after his kind, the little owl, the cormorant and the great owl, the swan, the pelican and the gier eagle, the stork, the heron after her kind, the lapwing, the weasel, the mouse and the tortoise after his kind, the ferret, the chameleon, the lizard, the snail, the mole and whatever goes on its belly.* Quite a list! It is rather strange, however, that Leviticus *does* permit specifically the locust, the beetle and the grasshopper. I should imagine that some of us today would be healthier if we ate grasshopper and locusts rather than frankfurters made with sodium nitrate and sodium nitrite.

To digress a little, I would like to say that there is one thing that bothers me about these Hebrew prescriptions. The chicken and duck are not mentioned because they were unknown to the Hebrews at the time of Moses. They may perhaps have been introduced into Palestine a thousand or so years later by the conquering Greeks who had domesticated these birds. I wonder in what category they would have been placed had they been known to the Hebrews? But we do know that the Hebrews did eat birds for they have a delightful old proverb which says that he who leases a garden eats birds but that he who leases gardens shall be eaten by birds.

Although the earthworm is not explicitly mentioned in Leviticus, the sense of the prescription would definitely prohibit its eating because it moves on its belly. However, there are many races which do eat them and, furthermore, consider them rare delicacies. Dr. G. E. Gates in his talk on the earthworm on the General Electric Science Forum of Station WGY November, 1951, said that earthworms have been used as medicines in every part of the world, and that even today, they are still used in many places. He recounted further the story of a medieval banquet where, as he tells it, roasted earthworms were served as one of the courses and, according to one witness, "the guests arose as one man and cried for more." Down under in New Zealand, some of the earthworms are so delicious that they are reserved for chiefs—or as the last food for a dying man.

Earthworms and Paralysis

Please don't misunderstand me, I am not asking the civilized world to eat earthworms, although as far as its present eating habits are concerned, what could be more repulsive-looking than the slimy oyster? Still, I had an interesting experience with earthworms once which is truly food for thought.

In about the second year of our farming by the organic method, several of our chickens became paralyzed and would not eat anything. In such a case the common practice for farmers is to destroy the paralyzed chickens as there is no known cure for them. I did not, however, destroy my chickens. But I recalled that one of my readers had written that he had cured some of his paralyzed chickens by feeding them earthworms. We determined to do the same thing. The results were truly amazing. The chickens would not touch the mash, but how they gobbled up the earthworms! In about a week, those chickens were running around as healthy and clear of eye as any of the others in the flock.

Now the reason I have gone into such detail is this. Polio is a paralysis. I am of the opinion that the feeding of earthworms to polio patients might help to cure them; that, further, the eating of a preparation which contains earthworms could be an effective preventative. It is incontestable that polio is a serious menace, and one which is growing in proportions. On the other hand, there is nothing dangerous about eating an earthworm. In fact, there used to be an extremely old lady in our town of Emmaus who ate them. Perhaps that is why she attained a ripe old age. In any case, medical science should not overlook this possibility.

Good Diet Kept Ancient Jews Healthy

But to get back to the Hebrews and to Leviticus. Other restrictions in diet and in their method of living developed out of their basic ones in relation to eating of various species of animals. For example, they were not to eat a meat and a dairy product at the same meal. Nor could they eat the rear part of any animal. Furthermore, they had to wash their hands before eating and had to bathe at least once a week. It has been said with some justice that Moses was the greatest hygienist of all time. The result of all these restrictions was that during the Middle Ages the Jews were so little affected by the plagues that the Christians suspected them of having brought about the disastrous epidemics by magic, and persecuted them mercilessly.

Times have changed from the days of Moses, however, and today many Jews are not following the ways of their forefathers in matters of diet. They are eating ham and putting butter on their steaks. It is interesting to speculate on what would happen today if another plague should come. Jew and Gentile would undoubtedly suffer alike.

[889]

Throughout the Orient, food restrictions seem to be common—especially among the Mohammedans. In a book I read recently, a missionary related an incident about a visit to a family in Turkey. He had partaken of a meal with them, but after he left he discovered that he had left something behind in their home. Returning to get it, he surprised the whole family busy at work breaking the earthenware dishes from which he had eaten. According to the Mohammedan religion, the touch of an infidel makes a utensil ritually unclean.

Sometime ago I was reading a bulletin of the Smithsonian Institute and came across a precious item. It was written by a woman who was an expert on kelp. It seems that not too long ago the New York City rabbis had suddenly discovered that the big ice cream companies were making their product with a gelatine filler; the filler being used to give it body. Now, since gelatine comes from animal bones, the finished ice cream was a combination of dairy and meat product and thus not *kosher* according to Mosaic dietary law. The rabbis therefore issued a ban. The matter, however, was not allowed to rest there. The problem was apparently submitted to scientists, and what was my surprise when I was reading a later issue of this same Smithsonian bulletin to see just how the whole affair was consummated. It was discovered that a certain kelp product made from seaweed was even better than gelatine and made an even better ice cream. Thus the rabbis were satisfied, the ban was removed and the ice cream companies continued to make money.

Chemicals . . . The Modern Health Plague

But when I read all of this I perceived something much more subtle in the meat-milk controversy than simply the gelatine-seaweed solution. What occurred to me was that the rabbis were completely oblivious to the dangers of the *chemicals* which were being used in the manufacture of ice cream. They were completely unaware that the poly-oxy-ethylene-monostearate used in its manufacture was far more dangerous than the possibility of harm which might result from the mixing of a meat with a milk product. They had overlooked the alum used in their kosher pickles, the benzoate of soda in cider, the nitrogen trichloride in their matzohs, and the sodium nitrate in their kosher "hot dogs," simply because Moses did not foresee the chemical age.

Had the Great Lawgiver known that the Jews of the twentieth century A.D. were going to drink water with chlorine in it, and eat pretzels whose satin sheen would be obtained by going through a bath of caustic soda, he would have undoubtedly issued prohibitions against them. Had he foreseen the day when Jews were to eat canned foods in which the steel was treated with dangerous chemicals in order to make the food slide out easier, he might have said: "Thou shalt not eat out of tin cans."

It is the theory of many scholars that the reason for the Jew's ability to survive has been his adherence to the Mosaic health rules. Will the Jew's present day chemicalized diet and his renunciation of other portions of Leviticus be the means of causing his assimilation with other races? Chem-

[890]

icals are the great levelers. We cannot blame the rabbis for not knowing about these hidden dangers. Their time and attention are devoted to spiritual affairs. However, we *can* blame those who have been educated at the public's expense, the advisors of government and industry, who should be seriously concerned about such matters.

To the lady who asked me about the lard I would say, stick to your beliefs. The Bible is a wonderful document and is based on natural ways of living. Either write, or go to see that baker. Explain to him your reason for not wishing to eat his product which otherwise is so good. You will be surprised how people will sometimes be guided by the wishes of their customers.

CHAPTER 237

Additional Information
on Processing

Ready-Mixed Food

According to the *Wall Street Journal,* everything today is being ready-mixed. There are pancake mixes, instant coffee, cake mixes, frozen French fried potatoes, frozen Chinese food and frozen meats being served in all kinds of restaurants, from the lowly diner to the swanky ones. It all comes from the trend of not wanting to work. This is a lazy age. These are not tense times. Everything is push-button and ready-mixes. We would do better to get out and walk and to get up and do, and Mrs. America would be wise to do some work in her kitchen, then perhaps she wouldn't need any hysterectomies.

Primitive Processing Means More Minerals, Not Less

A brief note in *Nutrition Reviews* for January, 1955, gives another instance of a primitive people whose food habits have protected them from nutritional deficiency. It was believed, says Dr. Herbert Pollack, that a certain group of people living on Formosa was getting far too little calcium for good health. During a recent extensive survey of their state of nutrition, it was discovered that none of them was suffering from calcium deficiency. So a thorough investigation was made as to the source of the calcium. It was found that the millers in this community added a "stone powder" to the rice during the milling process so that it would flow more easily through the mill and also to whiten the undermilled rice. The "stone powder" was calcium carbonate which worked its way into the rice kernel and resulted in each kilogram of rice containing from 500 to 1000 milligrams of calcium. In our country we polish rice, removing all the minerals and vitamins from it in the process. In Formosa everyone knows apparently that eating white rice is fashionable, but they have no way of polishing the rice. So they add something in the milling that will make it look whiter than it is. And this "something" happens to be the most important mineral of all the minerals. So these Formosans are not deficient in calcium. A large segment of the American public is. Yet our food processors consider that they have reached new heights of skill and knowledge of food processing and they scoff at "primitive" people who eat their rice unpolished and milled by hand.

The Humble Pickle Gets Around

Pickles outsell all other canned fruits and vegetables, according to an article in *Food Technology* for March, 1955. In 1954 an estimated 30 million cases (not quarts, but cases) of dills, sweets, sours, relish and 32 other varieties of green pickled cucumbers were consumed by the American public.

There is little or no food value in a pickle. We wonder why they are an ever-present accompaniment to meals in many homes. Could it be that modern refined food is so tasteless and without texture that we must rely on something to pick up our jaded appetites? Or could it be that the popularity of the pickle indicates that America is a land of snacks rather than complete wholesome meals?

Don't Eat Processed Foods, Frozen or Not

Our view of commercially frozen foods has always been tolerant, if not enthusiastic, for we feel that freezing is the least artificial method of preserving foods. However, the *Journal of the American Medical Association* (June 30, 1956) carries a warning against precooked frozen fish of all kinds. In experiments in which a bacteria (which is eliminated at a low heat) was deliberately introduced to the fish, it was shown that when the fish was fully prepared, the experimental bacteria was very much alive. What then of bacteria in the fish which can stand much higher degrees of heat and survive? It is the same old story of processed foods. Make sure your frozen fish is just that—not cooked, or cured or treated, just simply frozen. But when at all possible, use fresh fish. With today's shipping and refrigeration advances, it is a food available fresh to almost everyone.

The Maraschino Cherry

Don't eat the beautiful maraschino cherry you find in the center of your grapefruit at a restaurant. In the first place it is dyed red with artificial coal tar colors which might be cancer-causing. Secondly, it is soaked in sugar and sugar syrup. Thirdly, it contains a poisonous preservative to make it sterile, so that a germ can't live in it. It is embalmed.

This fact was brought out by a woman who wrote a letter to our sister publication, ORGANIC GARDENING AND FARMING. She had made compost of all her garbage, and allowed it to decompose over a two-year period. At the end of that time the garbage had decayed into a beautiful soil-like compost, all but some maraschino cherries. There they were with their entire structure intact. Not a germ had been able to break down one fiber of their tissues. Like Egyptian mummies.

What more proof do you need? What happens to such a cherry in the human stomach?

Margarine Seen as Cause of Mouth Ulcers

It is suggested in the *British Dental Journal* for November 5, 1957, that margarine used in cooking might cause those painful little ulcers in the mouth that one sometimes experiences. The author tells of two patients who were bothered by these mouth ulcers and were cured simply by giving up margarine and using butter for cooking.

In another case, a mother used butter at table and in cooking until the time her child reached the age of 8 years. She then changed to margarine in the interests of economy. The child developed a number of these ulcers and they subsided only when the margarine was replaced by butter.

Other cases are related and all have a similar outcome. Our readers are well aware of the fact that we do not wish to promote the use of dairy products. We feel that one should use neither butter nor margarine. Margarine is a product that is so crammed with synthetics, additives and artificial coloring that ulcers in the mouth can be only a mild indication of its results when constantly used. And the vegetable oil of which it is made is hydrogenated—a process which makes for an unhealthful food.

For cooking purposes, we recommend the use of liquid vegetable oils such as corn, safflower or peanut oil.

Synthetic Nuts

Another inventor has come up with a marvelous new food—imitation nut meats. These are made from soybeans, casein and corn gluten, of course, artificially flavored with coal tar. And they taste just like real nuts, we are told. It is not immediately apparent what is wrong with eating real nuts—healthful, delicious and inexpensive. But safe to say, our ever-ready food processors will soon be spending millions to persuade us that artificial nuts taste more like nuts than real ones.

SECTION 18.

Cooking

We recommend eating raw as many foods as are palatable raw. Certainly you should never cook fruit. Almost any vegetable, except for the starchy ones like beans and potatoes, can be enjoyed far more in the fresh, uncooked state. We believe that meat should be cooked according to definite rules, for both taste and nutrition benefit. In general, simplify your meal preparation as much as possible—the less you do to food the better it is for you.

CHAPTER 238

Raw Foods

By J. I. Rodale

It is an elementary fact in nutrition that cooking destroys some of the valuable ingredients of foods. But it is not necessary to become a raw food faddist. If you will experiment, you will be delighted at the treat that is in store in the delicious taste of certain vegetables that you never conceived of eating in anything but a cooked state.

No animal eats cooked food. Man is the only creature that does, and he lives only to between two and three times his span of maturity. In general, animals live to between six to ten times such a period. It is a known fact that cats thrive much better when fed on raw rather than cooked meat. Man, of course, is not an animal, fortunately, but he can benefit materially from observing and interpreting some of the ways of these outdoor creatures.

Eating Raw Vegetables

One of my first experiences with raw vegetables was with peas. It is ridiculous to cook them. They are so easy to take raw, and any one will agree that in cooking, something is lost. When you eat them raw you get everything. Don't overlook the fact that peas are seeds. They are living things and will grow if placed in the soil. When you cook them, that living quality is destroyed. Their germinating power is annihilated. You are then eating a dead food. It is ironic to see people eating cooked peas, followed by the taking of vitamin pills. The vitamins are in the peas. Cooking destroys part of them.

The *Journal of Nutrition*, Vol. 44, pp. 205-16, 1951, describes experiments to determine the protein content and the growth factors contained in canned peas and raw ones. Laboratory animals on diets of canned peas gained less weight than those eating raw peas. Supplementing the raw peas with methionine (an amino acid) raised the protein efficiency of the peas. Lysine (another amino acid) added to raw peas also increased their protein value, but, added to canned peas, decreased it. A study of digestibility indicated that raw peas are more digestible than the canned ones. One more argument for avoiding processed foods and for eating some raw fruit or vegetable with every meal.

Another terrible blunder is to cook carrots. It is absolutely unforgivable. Cooking not only dissipates valuable nutritional qualities, but it vitiates the taste of this wonderful vegetable. Then sugar is added to give it flavor. My next encounter was with cauliflower and when you raise it without chemical fertilizers and eat it raw, you get a glimpse into a new world of taste. When you cook it, you then usually add a cream sauce of some kind to bring back the taste which you sold down the river. And so on it goes—

cabbage, beets, kohlrabi, turnips. These vegetables lend themselves wonderfully to being eaten raw.

I would say that my greatest surprise came a few years ago when I experimentally tasted some raw sweet corn just off the stalk. It was so sweet and full of milk that it was a most delightful gustatory experience. That is the way I have been eating corn since. Why waste the time cooking it, when you can get it fresh off the plant? Older corn usually loses its taste when eaten raw.

Another thing about eating corn, whether raw or cooked, is that it exercises the front teeth. Most foods are usually eaten on the right or left side of the mouth. The exercise of the teeth is an extremely important factor in maintaining their health.

While on this subject let us wander a bit from the field of vegetables. Let us consider eggs. This product of the hen in reality is a seed. It is alive and will produce a living thing. When you boil or fry it you destroy its living powers. By eating it raw (the yolks only) you get the most out of the egg from a nutritional standpoint. Remember, as we state in another chapter, we do not recommend eating the whites of eggs raw.

Raw Foods and a Healthy Body

Some time ago I met a man who related a case of an old country woman who advised the eating of raw potatoes for the curing of eczema and other skin eruptions. He said that it worked miraculously in one case he knew of. I related this to one of the girls on our office force who had a severe case of eczema since a child. After a few weeks on the raw potato diet she obtained considerable relief. It did not effect a complete cure but her face showed a remarkable change. She ate one raw potato a day. But I believe she eventually tired of the diet.

In reading a health magazine recently I noticed a statement by an M.D. that "some so-called excellent foods pass through the entire alimentary canal unassailed. Cooked beets is one of these." After eating cooked beets, the red color will invariably show up in the stool, indicating that it was not absorbed in the digestive system. You will find that eating the beets raw will eliminate this red, or show it up in a reduced amount. There is no question that cooking has a powerful effect on the food quality. Take the case of wine. Cook it and you then cannot get drunk on it. It has killed its potency.

It is known that cooking destroys some of the vitamins. In the case of vitamin B, it may be up to about 35 per cent of loss. With reference to vitamin C the loss may range from 10 to about 90 per cent. The addition of soda to the cooking of vegetables is an extremely foolish practice. It practically doubles the rate of loss of vitamin B. Soda is usually added to preserve the green color of peas and beans in cooking.

Pros and Cons of Cooked Foods

It is interesting to note the conflicting theories held regarding the pros and cons of cooked foods. G. A. Sutherland, M.D., in "A System of Diet and Dietetics" (1925) says:

"The chief effect of cooking on vegetable food is to cause the starch granules to swell up and rupture the nondigestible cellulose chambers in which they, as well as the protein and fats, are contained. It is for this reason, and also because starch is more digestible cooked than raw, that cooking greatly adds to the digestibility of all vegetable substances containing an abundance of cellulose, while at the same time it relieves the organs of mastication of much of their work."

On the other side of the fence is the famous Dr. John H. Kellog who in "The New Dietetics" (1927) says:

"Another advantage of the raw food diet which may, perhaps, be one of its chief merits is the fact that it supplies to the colon a considerable amount of raw starch which, being digested and converted into dextrin and sugar by the unused ferments always present in the feces, furnishes the kind of nutriment necessary to encourage the growth in the colon of acid-forming or fermentative bacteria, thus combating putrefaction and encouraging normal bowel action . . . The art of cookery has been used not only to render food more digestible, but more often to lessen its digestibility and to transform the simple, wholesome products of nature into noxious, disease-producing mixtures."

Other Advantages

Some persons cook practically everything they eat, including apples, pears and even bananas. Perhaps some who have delicate stomachs may have to do so, and in individual cases it is advisable to get the benefit of your physician's advice. It is no doubt good to have some warm stuff at every meal. We do not advise the adaption of a 100 per cent raw food diet. Sheep, horses and cows are better adapted to it.

An advantage of raw food is graphically described by the famous Dr. Henry Sherman of Columbia University who says, in *Food and Health* (1941):

"Fruits and many vegetables also have an important relation to the maintenance of good conditions in the intestine. This is largely because of the bulk which they impart to the residues, thus giving the muscular mechanism of the intestine a chance to be effective in keeping the residual mass moving and ensuring its elimination without undue delay, the fiber of these foods also serving to give the digestive apparatus *its daily scrubbing.*"

Raw foods are much more effective than cooked in acting as a cleansing agent of the digestive tract. It is a question as to what our modern diet will eventually do to our bodies, in the evolutionary process extending over the next few thousand years. Eventually we may lose our teeth and become second-rate thinking entities.

In conclusion let me say that the gardener who has spent so much time producing food is entitled to use it to its best advantage and the evidence seems to weigh in favor of its consumption in a raw state.

CHAPTER 239

One Scientific Reason for
Eating Raw Food

Dr. Paul Kouchakoff, who conducted experiments at the Institute of Clinical Chemistry in Lausanne, Switzerland, showing the desirability of eating raw foods, developed his startling theory when he began to study what had always been considered a natural physiological process—an increasing number of leucocytes (white blood corpuscles) in the blood immediately after eating. Biologists called this "digestive leucocytosis" and assumed that it just naturally took place after eating as part of the digestive process. But, reasoned Dr. Kouchakoff, leucocytes appear in increased numbers in the blood only when there are disease germs or other menaces to be combated. They are the body's warriors, which appear immediately when danger must be fought. Why then, should they appear after a meal?

"The living organism is very sensitive to all harmful influences and reacts against them immediately," says Dr. Kouchakoff. "We see this when we make an analysis of our blood during simple and infectious illnesses, when extraneous substances are introduced into our system and so forth. In such cases the number of white corpuscles changes and the correlation of percentage between them is disturbed." That is, the percentages of the different kinds of white blood corpuscles change. This is one sure indication that some kind of disease process is going on in our bodies.

We use for our food, continues Dr. Kouchakoff, 3 kinds of foodstuffs: raw food as it is found in nature, cooked food which has been altered by high temperature and processed or manufactured food. How does each of these act on our blood formula? After we have eaten raw foods, the number of white blood corpuscles does not change and the percentage of the different kinds does not change. Ordinary unboiled drinking water, raw greens, raw cereals, nuts, honey, raw meat, raw fish—all of these have no effect on the number or kinds of white corpuscles.

Changes In Blood Formula From Cooked Food

After we have eaten some of these same foods altered by means of high temperatures—that is, cooked—Dr. Kouchakoff tells us that the number of white blood corpuscles increases but the relation of the different kinds to one another remains the same. After consumption of manufactured and processed foods, both the number and the kinds of white corpuscles change.

The amount of food we have taken is not important, for extremely small portions produce the same reaction as large amounts. Dr. Kouchakoff's experiments also show that the reaction in our blood takes place at the

[900]

moment the food enters the stomach, while the preliminary process of chewing the food well in the mouth softens the reaction.

To how high a temperature, then, may you heat foods without causing them to produce this reaction? Now don't throw up your hands in despair, you valorous housewives who are bent on feeding your family healthfully! What Dr. Kouchakoff actually says is that each single food has a specific temperature which must not be surpassed in cooking, if you would avoid the white corpuscle reaction in the blood. He calls this the "critical temperature." Ordinary drinking water, heated for half an hour to 189 degrees Fahrenheit does not change our blood formula. But this same water, heated to 191 degrees does change it. The lowest critical temperature for cereals, tomatoes, cabbage and bananas is 192 degrees Fahrenheit, for butter 196 degrees Fahrenheit, for apples and oranges 197 degrees Fahrenheit, for potatoes 200 degrees Fahrenheit, for carrots, strawberries and figs 206 degrees Fahrenheit. "Our experiments show," says Dr. Kouchakoff, "that it is possible to paralyze the action of a foodstuff once its critical temperature is surpassed. There exist strictly definite laws for this, and the critical temperature plays the first role here."

Probably at this point you are groaning with frustration. Not only must you buy special, hard-to-get foods, fresh and dewy from the field, not only must you eliminate many kinds of foods you've always eaten, not only must you prepare foods in special ways using special cooking utensils, but now, adding insult to injury, we come along and tell you you have to cook every single food at its own individual critical temperature if you would be healthy! It's enough to try the patience of a saint, isn't it—let alone a harassed housewife who has a thousand things to do every day besides her cooking!

Eating Some Raw Food At Every Meal Is the Answer

However, it's really not as hard as it sounds. Scientists have a way of making things sound difficult, but scientists as practical as Dr. Kouchakoff also suggest ways and means of getting around these difficulties with the least trouble. If a cooked foodstuff is eaten along with the same product in a raw state, there is no unfavorable reaction in our blood, says Dr. Kouchakoff, for the raw product has then neutralized the unfavorable reaction which the overheated food would have called forth. Sounds simple, doesn't it? But, of course, things get complicated again. The critical temperature of the raw food must be the same or higher than the critical temperature of the cooked food. If several cooked foods are eaten, each with a different critical temperature, along with raw food, reaction takes place in the blood. When we eat a processed food, two raw foodstuffs are necessary along with it, if we would avoid the white blood corpuscle reaction in our blood. Even one raw product has a beneficial reaction on this third group, depriving them of one of their properties—the power of altering the relation of the percentage of the corpuscles.

Dr. Kouchakoff performed 300 experiments on 10 individuals of different age and sex in order to arrive at his conclusions, and we believe they are important conclusions. Obviously we cannot test all foods to discover their critical temperatures, nor can we find in medical literature any mention of such tests ever having been performed. In addition, it would surely be completely impossible to complicate meal preparation with critical temperatures of food, as well as vitamin content, proteins, minerals and all the other things we must constantly keep in mind for good nutrition.

Why then do we feel that Dr. Kouchakoff's experiments are significant? Apparently he was on the trail of something very important in relation to food, cooking and human digestion. Perhaps the final answer is that all food should be eaten raw, since man's digestive tract was designed long before fire and cooking were discovered. Perhaps the white blood corpuscles of Dr. Kouchakoff's experiments are simply the body's way of protesting our habit of taking good, natural food and spoiling it by subjecting it to high heat.

A Practical Solution

How are we to work out a practical answer to the problem presented by his research? Our suggestion is just this: get your family accustomed to eating raw all foods that are palatable this way. When you are marketing, glance through your purchases and try always to have at least half of your shopping bag full of foods that can be eaten raw. When you plan meals, begin to include more and more salads, fruits and raw vegetables. Never cook carrots, celery, onions, spinach, cabbage, fruits and so forth. Aside from the vitamins you will save, you will also be doing a lot toward preventing the blood change described by Dr. Kouchakoff. Even if you don't manage to arrive at the perfect balance of cooked and uncooked foods that he holds out as the ideal, at least you can be certain your family is getting plenty of raw food and every bit of it is better for them than the cooked food.

CHAPTER 240

The Best Way
to Cook Vegetables

Many foods are richest in a particular nutritional factor when eaten raw, being seriously depleted of it when cooked. Expert tests to determine the comparative mineral and vitamin retention of vegetables when prepared by various methods of cooking have produced additional statistics, all furthering the thesis that the water in which we simmer our vegetables is far more healthful than are the waterlogged husks we serve on our tables. Truly an ironical state of affairs—when we would do better in drinking the cooking water and throwing away the soggy solids—this has been proved by Willard A. Krehl and R. W. Winters, of the Nutrition Laboratory of Yale University's Department of Physiological Chemistry (School of Medicine), who scientifically measured the exact extent of mineral and vitamin losses in 12 vegetables when their nutrients are leached out of them by the water in which the so-called edible residues are drowned.

Though these vegetables may taste as good without their mineral content of calcium-iron-phosphorus, and savor as appetizingly without their vitamins, deficiency diseases are heading your way and will make a sure-hit if you do not sharply restrict the amount of liquid you may be accustomed to use in the preparation of foods, or eat much of your vegetables raw. Employing 4 different methods of cooking, researchers Krehl and Winters advanced housewives' knowledge of the nutritional value of 12 common vegetables beyond that acquired from the charts and tables appearing in dietetic literature, which generally cites data referring to fresh raw food and overlooks possible losses from cooking. Publishing the results of their experiments in the *Journal of the American Dietetic Association* (December, 1950), they supply concrete information on the values of home-prepared foods served in family-size quantities.

Methods Employed And Results

The methods of cooking used were: 1. with ½ cup of added water; 2. with just enough water added to cover the vegetable being prepared; 3. pressure cooked with ½ cupful of added water; and 4. cooked in the "waterless" procedure (with no added water). For the pressure cooking, an ordinary 4-quart vessel with a 15-pound regulating valve was used, whereas durable sheet aluminum utensils especially made for the new and improved technique of waterless cooking were used for the 3 other techniques. In methods 1, 3, and 4, each cooking utensil was kept securely covered during cooking; in method 2. only was it kept slightly open to allow for the unrestricted passage of steam. The vegetables chosen for the comparative studies were: asparagus, broccoli, carrots, beets, cauliflower, cabbage, sweet yellow corn, potatoes, spinach, green beans, squash and peas. Best qualities of each were selected.

The criterion used to determine the proper amount of cooking in each case consisted in puncturing the vegetables from time to time to establish their exact degree of tenderness. Pressure-cooked vegetables were brought to a desired degree of "doneness" by being placed first on high heat until the steam gauge began to jiggle, the heat then being slackened off in order to keep the weight steady. At 15-pound pressure, the various vegetables prepared in this method required the following number of minutes for thorough cooking: potatoes, 13; beets, 10; corn, 4; asparagus, squash and carrots, 3; green beans, 2.5; cabbage, 2; broccoli and cauliflower, 1.5; spinach, 1; and peas, 0.5.

Vegetables prepared with water to cover or with just ½ cupful of added water were brought to a quick boil at high heat and then kept at a slow boil until done. Distilled water was used in all methods except, naturally,

[903]

the waterless one. The vegetables were kept at only medium heat for the waterless method over a period of about 5 minutes (when the cover became hot to the touch), then put on very low heat until they were done. Seasonings, including salt, were avoided in all cases.

A table was prepared of the mineral retention of the vegetables varying according to the method in which they were prepared. This disclosed the following facts in percentages:

TABLE I—MINERAL RETENTION

Vegetable	Cooking Style	Calcium	Iron	Phosphorus
ASPARAGUS	Pressure	93.5	89.6	91.4
	Water cover	88.4	78.7	70.3
	½ cup water	93.8	90.1	90.6
	Waterless	100.4	97.4	97.1
BEETS	Pressure	95.7	94.2	85.0
	Water cover	84.0	86.1	75.3
	½ cup water	90.2	90.9	83.7
	Waterless	98.7	97.4	93.8
BROCCOLI	Pressure	93.0	89.2	91.5
	Water cover	83.5	76.5	72.6
	½ cup water	87.8	91.4	90.7
	Waterless	96.0	96.1	97.5
CABBAGE	Pressure	91.3	89.2	90.5
	Water cover	79.3	76.5	72.6
	½ cup water	87.8	94.1	90.7
	Waterless	96.0	96.1	95.7
CARROTS	Pressure	88.9	86.2	83.4
	Water cover	80.3	82.6	79.8
	½ cup water	90.8	88.2	87.7
	Waterless	94.5	91.4	94.4
CAULIFLOWER	Pressure	88.1	81.5	84.8
	Water cover	82.7	73.0	72.6
	½ cup water	86.4	82.2	81.7
	Waterless	92.2	88.4	93.4
CORN	Pressure	84.1	79.5	78.8
	Water cover	80.2	72.7	62.6
	½ cup water	89.8	86.4	76.4
	Waterless	91.5	90.9	87.5
GREEN BEANS	Pressure	96.1	93.3	93.5
	Water cover	88.4	85.8	73.7
	½ cup water	92.7	91.0	89.9
	Waterless	100.4	95.5	101.5
PEAS	Pressure	86.7	81.2	76.4
	Water cover	78.9	78.7	72.6
	½ cup water	86.1	84.3	76.5
	Waterless	94.3	89.1	84.3
POTATOES	Pressure	78.9	74.0	78.3
	Water cover	56.1	61.6	70.6
	½ cup water	76.1	71.6	77.3
	Waterless	89.8	85.3	86.1

Vegetable	Cooking Style	Calcium	Iron	Phosphorus
SQUASH	Pressure	75.2	82.6	81.0
	Water cover	58.1	70.0	74.9
	½ cup water	79.7	81.2	83.8
	Waterless	91.0	88.7	87.3
SPINACH	Pressure	83.5	86.7	84.7
	Water cover	73.5	78.0	67.2
	½ cup water	81.1	85.5	80.5
	Waterless	88.4	89.0	89.5

Vitamin-richness of the raw, uncooked vegetables likewise being evaluated at 100 per cent, a table was then prepared of the vitamin-retention per vegetable, dependent on the style of cooking employed. This reveals the following interesting percentile figures:

TABLE II—VITAMIN RETENTION

Code for Table II: A—Thiamin; B—Riboflavin; C—Niacin; D—Ascorbic Acid; E—Carotene

Vegetable	Cooking Style	A	B	C	D	E
ASPARAGUS	Pressure	80.1	0.97	86.9	67.6	78.5
	Water cover	54.1	0.50	59.2	42.5	64.6
	½ cup	78.4	0.91	82.8	66.4	92.3
	Waterless	90.2	1.08	89.3	69.4	101.5
BEETS	Pressure	79.8	87.2	89.7	93.8	81.4
	Water cover	62.3	70.4	70.7	74.0	72.4
	½ cup	70.4	85.1	84.6	87.3	82.8
	Waterless	91.4	92.1	96.3	81.1	96.2
BROCCOLI	Pressure	81.2	88.8	73.2	68.0	88.6
	Water cover	70.1	66.4	45.7	50.6	76.0
	½ cup	74.6	77.2	86.3	68.7	84.3
	Waterless	94.5	83.1	94.1	70.2	97.7
CABBAGE	Pressure	69.1	84.9	74.9	77.5	96.8
	Water cover	62.4	48.3	48.3	44.3	73.3
	½ cup	70.2	70.4	70.4	57.4	89.7
	Waterless	80.2	84.1	86.1	68.4	95.6
CARROTS	Pressure	86.6	89.8	90.4	79.1	88.4
	Water cover	70.6	74.7	73.3	63.1	84.5
	½ cup	83.9	84.2	89.5	75.1	86.3
	Waterless	93.5	96.7	98.1	72.5	98.9
CAULIFLOWER	Pressure	74.6	76.9	76.9	75.5	89.8
	Water cover	51.4	60.8	60.8	47.3	80.7
	½ cup	70.2	76.2	76.2	54.0	83.7
	Waterless	87.4	84.9	89.4	70.7	97.4
CORN	Pressure	80.2	79.6	77.7	74.9	88.2
	Water cover	71.9	50.9	50.9	60.2	86.4
	½ cup	81.4	84.7	84.7	65.1	87.3
	Waterless	92.3	89.5	89.5	69.6	93.1
GREEN BEANS	Pressure	71.8	91.6	91.6	76.1	94.4
	Water cover	66.2	65.6	65.6	58.5	85.6
	½ cup	70.4	79.2	79.2	64.0	90.3
	Waterless	92.4	85.8	89.8	74.8	96.3

[905]

Vegetable	Cooking Style	A	B	C	D	E
PEAS	Pressure	80.7	82.4	91.8	73.7	89.7
	Water cover	59.7	74.2	67.3	51.3	83.2
	½ cup	78.4	88.9	81.3	70.0	89.4
	Waterless	94.3	94.3	94.3	78.8	91.2
POTATOES	Pressure	84.2	81.8	77.4	57.3	86.3
	Water cover	72.1	64.6	64.6	41.0	78.9
	½ cup	80.0	79.2	75.1	48.4	80.5
	Waterless	91.2	91.7	91.4	79.4	85.8
SQUASH	Pressure	31.7	80.7	79.1	65.3	92.3
	Water cover	60.3	63.6	63.7	50.5	82.4
	½ cup	78.6	81.0	79.4	66.5	84.2
	Waterless	88.4	90.2	89.2	74.8	91.9
SPINACH	Pressure	76.9	74.6	69.6	61.7	94.8
	Water cover	50.1	56.7	40.5	49.1	80.7
	½ cup	70.4	71.4	76.8	51.7	87.2
	Waterless	87.2	85.5	88.4	70.0	91.3

After cautioning that improper cooking techniques, involving over-cooking or the use of baking soda to add color will still further amplify vitamin and mineral losses through cooking, the authors conclude that, since the percentage retention after any one cooking method exhibited lively variation among the 12 vegetables tested, it would be more instructive to muster the individual data gathered in Tables I and II under another Table (III) showing average percentile retention of all 12 vegetables contingent on the method of cooking. This table brings to the fore the overwhelming superiority of the waterless method:

TABLE III—AVERAGE RETENTION OF VITAMINS AND MINERALS

Code for Table III: A—Calcium; B—Iron; C—Phosphorus; D—Thiamin; E—Riboflavin; F—Niacin; G—Ascorbic Acid; H—Carotene.

Cooking Method	A	B	C	D	E	F	G	H
Pressure	87.9	85.6	84.9	78.9	82.6	81.6	72.5	89.1
Water cover	77.8	76.7	72.1	62.6	63.1	59.2	52.7	79.1
½ cup	87.9	86.4	84.1	75.6	78.3	80.5	64.5	86.5
Waterless	94.4	90.4	92.3	91.0	87.9	91.3	73.3	94.7

From this table researchers Krehl and Winters deduce the following obvious lessons. Maximum per cent losses in both minerals and vitamins resulted from the old-fashioned style of cooking with water to cover—on the other extreme, maximum retention was guaranteed by use of the "new" fashion of waterless cooking. Vacillating midway between these two, were the techniques of cooking with one-half cup of added water and the pressure method. Though in the instance of carotene and ascorbic acid retention the pressure method afforded results that were somewhat sur-prisingly near to those of the waterless one, this is to be explained on the basis of the shorter cooking time required, thus permitting less chance of losses due to oxidation.

Attention is called to the fact that ascorbic acid (vitamin C) losses proved to be "the most significant by all methods of cooking, although again greatest losses resulted from cooking with added water." Remember, most vegetables and fruits are highest in this important food factor when eaten raw. Precious vitamins and minerals looted from vegetables in the process of cooking disappear from them because of two factors: the influence of oxidation and the leaching effect of cooking water, the latter being deemed productive of the highest losses.

In these experiments it became evident that minerals, which like vegetables suffer major losses when cooked in water as against the relatively light ones promoted by waterless cooking, generally showed higher retention figures than did vitamins. However, in spite of the demonstrated superiority of the waterless method, pressure cooking bids fair today to take over control of the majority of American kitchens because of its economy of time required for the preparation of a meal in a busy household. We therefore, consider it doubly urgent to warn readers against this method of cooking. Dr. Hector W. Jordan ("Mother Earth," *Journal of the Soil Association,* England) stated: "Findings show that foods cooked under pressure tend to increase the white blood cells. I feel that the last word has not yet been said on the subject of pressure cooking. . . . Some years ago, Dr. P. Kouchakoff found that after a meal of cooked food (heated above 83-87 degrees centigrade) the blood showed a temporary leucocytosis or increase of white cells. This is a protective response on the part of the body, and probably means that toxic substances are produced when food is heated above this temperature. After a meal of raw food, he found that leucocytosis does not take place. Also, addition of raw food to a cooked meal prevents the leucocytosis from occurring, but if food is heated above 100 degrees centigrade, as in the case of canned food or of pressure cooking, no amount of added raw food is capable of preventing the leucocytosis."

Beyond the shadow of a doubt, the best way to insure your health with a daily dosage of vitalizing minerals and vitamins is to see to it that you eat a good part of your vegetables raw. If you do have to cook them, do not use water.

CHAPTER 241

Cooking Proteins

Protein is the substance of which living cells are largely made. It consists of carbon, hydrogen, nitrogen, oxygen and sulfur, thus differing from the carbohydrates which contain only carbon, hydrogen and oxygen. Since the chemical composition of protein is different, the method of cooking it is different, too. Only one piece of advice remains the same as for vegetables—the lower the heat, the better.

Many of us have been accustomed to cooking proteins with high heat. We "sear" our meat, to "hold in the juices." We fry eggs in very hot fat; we broil cheese, we bake fish to a state of leathery toughness. If you stop for just a moment and think of your own experiences with protein substances, you will realize the necessity of using low heat at all times when you are cooking protein.

Have you ever tried to wash out a bloodstain with hot water? Can't be done. The heat coagulates and toughens the blood. Ever try soaking an egg dish in hot water before you wash it? All you manage to do is make the egg stick more tightly to the dish. If you would wash milk easily from a container, use cold water, never warm! Milk is largely protein.

Meat Juices Lost

Why is it, then that so many of us ruin our protein foods by over-cooking them and cooking them at high heat? Steaks sizzled to a crisp under a blazing broiler are tough and leathery. Roasts seared and then baked in a hot oven are not only tough but have no flavor, for most of the meat juices have been lost. If you would cook economically, and if you would keep your family healthy and if you would be known as a good cook, keep one cardinal precept in mind—cook proteins with low heat.

Meats—roasts, steaks and so forth—are made of muscle fibers. These fibers are held together by what we call connective tissue, the substance from which gelatine is made. The juices of the meat, which contain the flavor as well as all the vitamins and minerals, are held in these connective tissues. When you cook meat at a low temperature, the proteins of the muscle itself gradually become firm. The connective tissue gradually softens. Tender cuts of meat contain little connective tissue, hence they need a shorter cooking time. The less-tender cuts like stew meat contain a great deal of connective tissue—you can see it sometimes in thick layers which you call gristle. So the less tender cuts must be cooked longer, to soften all this connective tissue. This does not mean, however, that you should subject the tougher meats to high heat!

When you cook meat at high temperatures, the protein substances of which it is made shrink and shrivel, so that you end with only a small part of the meat you started with. In addition, the connective fibers break down completely. Instead of merely softening they may dissolve completely into gelatin and leave long strings of fiber not held together by anything and impossible to slice. You have seen chunks of boiled meat that look like this. You know, too, that such a piece of meat has little or no flavor. All the juices have been cooked out of it.

Now doesn't it seem silly to spend money buying meat, which is the most expensive food we buy, and then ruin it by improper cooking? What about searing meat to "hold in the juices?" As the high heat is applied to the meat, proteins break down and juices spill out. When you sear meat you hear the fat sputtering violently in the pot. Fat sputters when it comes into contact with water. The sputtering of your seared meat represents meat juices lost.

Salting meat while it is cooking or before it is cooked is another crime against a good food. Of course we hope readers don't salt meat, either in the kitchen or at the table. But if you must use any salt, for goodness sake use it just before you eat the meat. Salt attracts water as we all know. When you apply salt to uncooked or partly cooked meat, you can expect the salt to draw unto itself most of the meat juices. Where do they go? Out into the pan to evaporate. Actually, the best way to keep the juices in the meat is to brush the meat carefully with fat before roasting or broiling it.

Always Use Low Heat for Proteins

Cooking proteins—not just meat but other protein foods as well—at low temperatures does not harm the amino acids—the protein building blocks that are absolutely essential for good health. But high heat breaks down some of these amino acids and makes them unfit for use by the body. It also, of course, destroys vitamins. The B vitamins are especially sensitive to high heat. Low heat does not destroy them to any great extent. But what sense is there to buying liver once a week, for its B vitamin content, and then heating it to such a temperature that most of the B vitamins are lost?

How, then, should you cook meat most economically and most healthfully? A friend of ours used to notice that the Sunday roast beef was always more tender and tasty on Sundays when she went to church. Sundays when she stayed home, the roast was tough and tasteless. What was the reason? Days when she went to church she put the roast on early, turned the heat low and let it roast slowly until church time. Then, just before she left the house, she turned the oven fire off and left the roast cooking by its own heat until she returned, when she lighted the oven fire once again. When she stayed home from church, the roast cooked at oven heat for the whole time. And was tough.

The best method for cooking meat is to use a meat thermometer and cook the meat only until the thermometer indicates that the internal temperature is right for eating. Broiling and roasting are preferable to other ways of cooking meat. Boiling meat results in tough tasteless meat out of

[909]

which all juices and valuable elements have been driven. Frying meat involves cooking it in the very high temperature of hot fat. If you must ever fry meat, coat it with flour or crumbs so that *they* will be browned and fried and the meat itself can have slower cooking inside the protective jacket.

Our Modern Stoves

One of the reasons why, it seems to us, so much excellent and nourishing protein is lost today which we would have benefited from 50 years ago, is the efficiency of our modern stoves. The high gas flame, the bright searing hot electric grill spell destruction to valuable proteins. The same is true of pressure cookers where the heat generated is extremely high. If you are planning to buy a new stove, do not be concerned about getting enough heat from the burners. Try instead to get a stove that has a real "simmer" burner, so that you can cook protein foods for long periods of time at a temperature considerably below boiling. And, if you can, get a stove whose oven can be regulated exactly to a very low heat which it will maintain hour after hour.

We think the best discussion of cooking meat that we have run across in a modern cookbook is found in Adelle Davis' *Let's Cook it Right,* published by Harcourt Brace and Company. Miss Davis is the world's champion for the low-heat-for-protein school. She tells in this cookbook of once cooking a turkey for 24 hours over a pilot light. And she claims it was the best turkey she ever ate.

What we have said about meats applies to other protein foods as well. Fish is very tender and delicate and needs little cooking at very low heat. What about eggs? Every cook knows what happens to a souffle put into a hot oven or an omelet left for even a moment over a high flame. You might as well try to eat leather. Keep the flame turned low. Let little heat over a long period of time be the watchword when you are cooking proteins!

CHAPTER 242

The Value of Herbs in Cooking

By Ruth Rodale Spira

Eating properly, our style, can be as exciting as dining in a fine French or Italian restaurant. In fact many of the fine points of gourmet cooking had their origin in time-honored medicinal advice.

Food Prepared With Garlic

Take garlic, for example. Cultivated for thousands of years, it was known as a food and medicine by every ancient race. Today we recognize that garlic is an important anti-bacterial agent, which can work wonders in controlling stomach upsets. In France to this very day, minced garlic is served in a mayonnaise sauce as a tonic.

My husband and I adore the flavor of garlic, perhaps to the dismay of our friends. We find that nearly every meat, many vegetables, and of course, salads, are vastly improved by a subtle suggestion of garlic. Several hours before roasting or broiling a chicken, I always rub crushed cloves of garlic both on the inside and outside flesh. The chicken then is left at room temperature for at least a half hour to allow the flavor to penetrate thoroughly. In this way garlic can be a delightful substitute for salt.

A roast leg of lamb is never complete without a generous rubbing with cut garlic cloves before cooking. Its pungency blends extremely well with the mild yet distinct flavor of lamb. When roasting beef, I suggest plenty of garlic with the less tender cuts. Really fine prime rib roasts, however, need very little seasoning—a sprinkling of paprika and a trace of garlic, if wanted.

A long-standing rule in making appetizing salads is to rub your wooden salad bowl with garlic. For a more penetrating flavor, I suspend two halves of a cut clove in my salad dressing—a 3 to 1 mixture of olive oil (the finest I can get) and red wine vinegar. It is easy to make up a good-sized batch of dressing to have on hand at all times. Those who want to cut down on their oil consumption might try mixing up a half-and-half portion of olive oil and wine vinegar.

Sometimes, the housewife finds it tempting to by-pass fresh garlic by adding a dash of garlic powder. Not only are you cheating yourself of food value lost in the drying process, but also the full, rich garlic flavor. It simply is not the same.

Help yourself to use fresh garlic by: 1. keeping it in a convenient place near the stove, 2. investing in an inexpensive garlic crusher, which saves you time and tears in mincing the cloves.

The Usefulness of Parsley

Another herb which has been greatly neglected by American house-wives is that symbol of luxury—parsley. Of all the greens we use, our treatment of parsley is scandalous, indeed. Let's knock it off its pedestal as a deluxe vegetable. Let's take parsley to heart and make it a staple in our diet.

In the Middle Ages writers of herbals believed that parsley had the power to "fasten loose teeth, brighten dim eyes and relieve a stitch on the side." Today we know that parsley is extremely rich in vitamins A and C. Night blindness is cured with doses of vitamin A; the gums depend on vitamin C for perfect functioning as a seat for the teeth. The Ancients were not very far off this time.

"But parsley chokes in your throat," you say? Who can swallow enough sprigs to make a whit of difference in vitamin intake? Even one large sprig provides you with some part of your daily need of vitamin A.

Chopped parsley, however, can be put to any number of uses by an enterprising cook. Popping ½ cup of parsley into a 4 pound stew will mean 10,000 units of vitamin A on the credit side. Broiled hamburgers, meat balls or a meat loaf are naturals for chopped parsley. Mix with raw ground meat before shaping, for an extra-special, spring-like flavor.

Parsley is unequalled in bringing out the true flavor of mild fish, like haddock or bluefish. Nothing can spark up a seafood dinner so well as a liberal sprinkling of this herb, in combination with chives and tarragon.

For most soups, parsley is indispensable. When the broth is partially cooked, add a parsley bouquet, tied with white thread. Do not allow parsley to fall apart in clear soups: rather remove it and serve with fresh-chopped parsley. A handy parsley chopper now on the market will make short work of it.

If you can't grow your own parsley, buy only very crisp, fresh bunches. Wash thoroughly and quickly, drain and refrigerate in a closed glass jar.

Fruits and Nuts For Dessert

For dessert, take a hint from the French. Serve a fruit-and-nut course for a refreshing treat, especially during the summer. For those who have to coax their family to eat fruit, serve it the continental way with a fine glass bowl for washing. My husband enjoys a bit of huckstering, too. I place the fruit and nuts in a large glass underliner, around an oversized brandy snifter, 12 inches high, which is one-third filled with water. The fruit is washed directly at the table by the eater, making a charming and healthy dessert ceremony. Since washed fruit spoils quickly, it is much better to save the washing for the dinner table. The remaining fruit will last days longer.

An assortment of almonds, Brazil nuts, peanuts and black walnuts are especially nutritious for a dessert course, high in minerals and protein content. Be sure to have the nut cracker handy.

Another pleasant ceremony for the family group is "the giving of the vitamins." An easy method is to keep the vitamin bottles on a good tray (even a silver tray) in the refrigerator. At mealtimes, place the tray at the head of the table if Father likes to officiate, along with a row of small cups. Egg cups work out very nicely. Children, especially, enjoy taking their vitamins with a bit of pageantry, along with the adults of the family. This has been a patriarchal tradition for years in the Rodale family.

Why not be healthy and still serve up meals fit for a gourmet. The extra effort is much more than repaid when every member of the family greets you with "more!"

CHAPTER 243

There's Danger in Hot Foods

If a hot drink will burn your hand when it's spilled, imagine what drinking scalding liquids can do to your insides! We know it must be harmful, yet there are few of us who do not sip a cup of tea or coffee gingerly until the first possible moment when the fiery pain is bearable enough to allow for fast swallowing. The tender flesh of our inner organs is bound to be seared by the hot stuff.

A study on this very subject is published in the *Lancet* for September, 1956, revealing some interesting conclusions. The writers of this piece set out to prove that "the intake of drink at high temperatures is positively associated with mucosal abnormalities in the stomach." An opportunity to experiment suggested itself when 155 patients who had had successful gastric biopsies were being interviewed. At the end of the interview, each was offered a fresh cup of boiling tea made separately each time, containing milk or sugar if preferred. When the patient began to drink it, (not merely sipping) the temperature of the tea was taken. In persons under the age of 50, it was found that only two out of 13 who drank tea below 122.5 degrees Fahrenheit showed any gastric abnormalities; while those who drank above 137.5 degrees Fahrenheit, 14 out of 18 exhibited disorders.

It is also stated that many studies have postulated an association between hot foods and ulcers or cancer.

Argentinians are known to take their foods at temperatures approaching 176 degrees Fahrenheit. They show a high incidence of cancer of the esophagus. A higher incidence of gastric cancer in Holland than in England led a research team in 1936 to conclude that a possible explanation lay in the fact that 21 per cent more Dutch people took their food at over 140 degrees Fahrenheit than did English. In another survey reviewing the dietary habits of patients with and without gastric carcinoma, it was shown that 48 per cent of the cases with gastric cancer admitted taking their food hotter than the rest of their families, as compared with 20 per cent of the controls who showed other abdominal disorders.

Though even the experimenters admit that this evidence is not conclusive, it is a warning sign worth heeding. Overly hot foods are easily avoided and should be. A few minutes wait is all it takes. Besides, the excessive heat of very hot foods paralyzes the tongue's taste sensations, cutting down on the enjoyment of the foods you eat. If a dish of soup is steaming or you can't touch the tea cup because of the heat, bide your time; stir the fluid with a spoon and the metal and the air you stir into the drink will soon carry off some of the heat. This tip may save internal complications—ulcers, cancer or some other disorder of the mouth, the throat or the stomach. We are already exposed to so many possible causes of cancer! Why deliberately add another?

CHAPTER 244

An Open Letter to a Restaurant Owner

We know that pleasing the public is the primary aim of a restaurant owner. The more people you please, the more business you will have, and the greater the success you enjoy. It might be an exaggeration to say that everyone is conscious of his health and concerned about the food he eats, but certainly a great many of your customers, and potential customers are. Perhaps you are not aware of the ease with which you might change your policy, to appeal to health-minded people and increase the service you offer to the customers you already have. In our opinion the management of a good restaurant is eager to do what it reasonably can to preserve the health of its clients through the type of food offered and the means used to prepare and serve it. May we draw your attention to a few of the unhealthful conditions which can easily be corrected by an interested restaurant operator?

The Question of Plastic Dishes

Plastic dishes have found a good market among restaurant owners. The temptation to use them instead of any kind of china or earthenware must be very great. They are cheaper, and they are almost impossible to break. But many a purchaser has found that these dishes stain easily and can't always be washed clean; the cutting edge of a knife often leaves scratches; and they sometimes affect the flavor of the food served upon them. Above all of these objections is the fact that most people just don't like to eat or drink from plastic dishes.

These problems have an immediate effect on your business, but there is a health angle involved with plastic dishes that we hope you will consider. One of the basic compounds used in making plastics is formaldehyde. This is a poison whose danger limit has never even been determined for man. The United States Public Health Service describes formaldehyde as a "protoplasmic poison"—a poison to the living cells of which our entire body is made.

Does this come off the dishes? Indeed it does. One plastics manufacturer admits that a water solution in which plastic dishes were soaked contained traces of formaldehyde. How much would be released in hot coffee, in steaming soup or with a sizzling steak's juices? Can you imagine any one of your customers who would not prefer to keep formaldehyde out of his diet? Staying with china dishes will pay off in eye appeal as well as in the health of your customers.

Getting the Most From Grapefruit

No doubt a great many of your customers begin their meals with a half of fresh grapefruit. You are probably pleased at the popularity of this fruit, commercially speaking, since it is always available, keeps well and is rather inexpensive. From a health viewpoint, it's wonderful to know that so many people enjoy a fresh fruit appetizer.

It is up to you to see that your customer gets all of the benefits grapefruit has to offer. It should never be cut until immediately before serving, for as soon as the skin is broken, valuable nutrients, as well as flavor qualities, begin to escape in the air. A dried-out piece of grapefruit has as much appeal as a wilted leaf of lettuce.

To add to the ease and pleasure of their customers, many restaurants section the grapefruit before serving it. If this is your practice, be sure to include as much of the membrane that lies between the sections as possible. These membranes hold a great supply of vitamin C and the bioflavonoids, nutrients which augment the effectiveness of vitamin C.

Please Let the Customers Do the Salting

The problem of pre-salted foods plagues many health-conscious people in restaurants. Why is it that salt-free food is almost impossible to acquire in a restaurant? Every table has a salt shaker which the customers are free to use to suit their taste, yet the chef insists on adding salt to almost everything while he's cooking it.

We've investigated the question of the harmfulness of salt at great length, and our findings have convinced us that any possible avoidance of extra salt can mean extra years of health. Heart cases are commonly advised

[915]

to do without salt, and experiments, detailed in many medical journals, including the *Journal of the American Medical Association,* have shown remarkable results in curing patients with this simple therapy. People who are overweight find that a low-salt diet is standard procedure in reducing. Salt in the body helps it to retain water which adds to body weight, and eating salty foods creates a thirst for more water, the added water intake again adds weight. Kidney disease, dropsy, diseases of the liver, pregnancy, arthritic swelling, migraine headaches—all of these, and many more, are conditions which have shown unfavorable reaction to salt in the diet.

You can be of great assistance to persons who fight this problem by discontinuing the use of salt in the kitchen. If a customer wants salty food, let him use the shaker on the table. Don't forget that the very popular flavor enhancer, monosodium glutamate, contains that dangerous salt element, sodium. It is as effective in upsetting things in this form as it is in a salt shaker.

A Variety of Healthful Potatoes

Almost everyone who eats in a restaurant orders some type of potato with his meal. The ways of preparing potatoes are tremendously varied. We would suggest that you include, in the choice you offer, potatoes that have been healthfully prepared. By this we mean baked, roasted or boiled in the jacket especially. Fried potatoes are a menace to health, whether fried in deep fat (French fries) or in a shallow pan as are home-fried or pan-fried potatoes. They can be responsible for high cholesterol count in the blood, for ulcers and even cancer, since fats heated several times have shown cancer-causing properties.

A new development, instant mashed potatoes, has caught the fancy of some of the less careful restaurateurs. Because of the ease of preparation many have come to use it regularly. It is rife with preservatives, including sodium nitrate, the chemical responsible for the poisoned fish episode in New Jersey some time ago, in which one person died and several others were made seriously ill, and leaves much to be desired in flavor.

One of the problems raw potatoes present to the restaurant owner is the fact that they turn black once they have been peeled, if they are kept for any length of time. Of course, the wise and healthful thing to do is to serve the potatoes cooked in the jackets. However, the demand for French-fried potatoes has led to peeling the potatoes and cutting them in advance of the rush hours. To keep these cut potatoes white, the cook stores them in containers filled with a solution of benzoate of soda, a preservative chemical to be found in almost every perishable item that is commercially prepared. Here again we have sodium slipping unnoticed into a restaurant-prepared food.

Potato Salad Is Always Popular

While on the subject of potatoes, we should not forget potato salad, probably one of your most popular summer dishes. Do you ever notice that there is a foreign, unpleasant taste to yours? If you are using aluminum pans for storing it, look no further for the cause of the off-taste.

The acidic action of the vinegar used by most chefs in making the salad can react easily with the aluminum. They combine and the result is that metallic taste one finds so offensive in food.

Aside from the taste factor, the danger of poisoning is also present. Potato salad is so often a part of the menu when food poisoning occurs that coincidence cannot be accepted as the complete answer. Consider these facts: aluminum utensils have been proven dangerous by many medical authorities; potato salad is often stored in such containers for considerable periods of time, and the ingredients used in making this dish are likely to act upon aluminum chemically. The danger is obvious. Don't take a chance; store your potato salad and other foods as well, in glass and earthenware containers.

The Aluminum Utensil Controversy

Of course, the use of aluminum cooking and storing containers is equally undesirable for other foods, too. True, the American Medical Association and the United States Better Business Bureau and the United States Public Health Service say that aluminum utensils are not harmful, but let us quote to you a few of the articles we've seen that convinced us otherwise.

In the *Canadian Journal of Research* (Vol. 21, Section C) an experiment was described in which it was shown that there is a greater loss of vitamin C in foods cooked in aluminum containers than in glass or enamel ones. In the book, *Practice of Allergy*, by Vaughn, on page 831, the author tells of "the cure of cases of longstanding refractory colitis following change from aluminum cooking utensils to enamel or glass vessels." Consider the experiment at the University of Colorado, reported in *Food Technology* (December, 1951), in which it was found that cold orange juice would dissolve an average of 37 parts per million of the aluminum in the pot containing it. Aluminum is a toxic substance taken internally, and it obviously is released into food stored or cooked in aluminum containers.

Foreign Reports on Aluminum

Let us go on by quoting the bizarre case reported in the German publication, *Deutsche Aertze Leitung* (pp. 223, 231, 242). Dr. O. Putensen, the author, tells of a dog suffering with rash, sores and intense itching, who was cured only when the aluminum pans from which he was fed were discarded. Dr. Putensen also described human patients cured of gastric and skin disturbances which he traced to cooking with aluminum utensils.

In the *British Medical Journal* (April, 1932), Dr. Corum James said he refused to believe that mere coincidence could account for the cure of several cases of gastric disturbance which cleared up soon after enamel and iron pots were substituted by the patients for aluminum ones. Nor did he believe that these people were unusually sensitive to aluminum. In the following issue of the same publication (April 16, 1932), Dr. Alexander Francis reported that he cured 6 cases of abdominal pain by ordering the disuse of aluminum cooking utensils.

[917]

So you see, the problem isn't all in our minds; the case against aluminum has some pretty authoritative evidence, too. Why not use glass or stainless steel? They wear better and look better—and cook better.

Why Butter Everything?

Many restaurants advertise that they use butter in preparing all of their vegetables. This generous use of butter is impressive and welcome to many diners, but there are some diners who would rather not use butter. Why not consider them, too?

Aside from those people who simply don't like the taste of butter in food, there are those who are on diets which strongly prohibit the use of fats due to digestive or weight problems. What are they to do? One can't pick butter off a portion of string beans the way one can pick the onions out of a salad. The only way to avoid eating the butter in a restaurant is for the chef to leave it out in the kitchen. If you are reluctant to leave it out of all the vegetables, why not keep some of them separate and leave them unbuttered? The rest can be served as always. Make a note on your menu, calling attention to the availability of unbuttered foods for the accommodation of those diners who, for dietary or other reasons, prefer them that way.

There Are Healthful Desserts

No doubt you pride yourself on the large choice of desserts you offer—pies, cakes, parfaits, puddings. But chances are that you don't have a single item listed that a diabetic can eat without worrying, or that a fat man can order while keeping within his new diet. Why not? These are your customers, too. Could you offer a fresh fruit bowl to choose from, a dish of fresh-made, unsugared apple sauce or rice pudding sweetened with honey? Would it be impossible to serve just the strawberries instead of strawberry shortcake, or fresh pineapple instead of pineapple upside-down cake?

If you could only encourage a few customers to form the habit of choosing an apple instead of apple pie, any fresh fruit instead of sugared pastry, you might be saving them from a great deal of trouble in future years.

The File on Refined Sugar

May we remind you of some of the dangers of refined sugar?

1. Tooth decay—even the most conservative dental authorities blame sugar as a major cause.

2. The calcium content of the blood is pulled away down by sugar and this condition is strongly suspected as a cause of cancer, arthritis and other diseases.

3. The body's supply of B vitamins is lowered by white sugar because they are very necessary to help the body use any sugar it receives. When sugar occurs naturally in a food, for example, in a sweet apple, the B vitamins come built into the apple, and process the sugar with which they

occur. When refined sugar is eaten, added as a sweetener, the B vitamins for processing must be robbed from another source—usually the nerves. It is not hard to trace the current "nerves" epidemic along this line.

4. The high and low blood sugar level that pests diabetics and others is an up and down see-saw that can be caused only by refined carbohydrates, of which sugar is the most commonly used.

We realize that you must list pies and cakes on your menu for those who refuse to be careful, but please give those of us who care about our health a break, too.

Herb Teas Make An Interesting Choice

Have you ever tried to find a restaurant where herb teas are available for customers who might prefer them? Order tea just about anywhere and you get a cup of slowly-coloring hot water with a famous-name tea bag hanging over the side. And they all taste the same! An Oriental restaurant is an exception. The flavor of the tea is delicate and it is obviously brewed with care.

Unfortunately, most of the nutritional disadvantages associated with coffee are contained in most commonly used teas, too. Tea is loaded with caffeine. It can make your heart work harder, keep you awake at night, interfere with digestion, help cause ulcers, etc. As a precaution, therefore, doctors often forbid caffeine-containing drinks to their patients. The answer to the beverage problem thus created is herb teas. Herb teas can't cause any of those consequences of caffeine, for they contain none. Is it any wonder, then, that many people prefer—even insist on—them?

You can make herb teas a feature of your menu. They are easily obtained in bags or loose, and in a wide selection of flavors: peppermint, chamomile, rosemint, just to mention a few. We think they will make an interesting choice for even those of your customers who are not concerned with their value as a health food. Ask your wholesaler to give you several addresses you can use as sources of supply.

Perhaps you are a restaurant owner who just doesn't care what your customers eat, how much salt, sugar or pastry they eat, so long as they eat it at your restaurant. Well then, look at the healthful foods idea from a strictly business point of view. Healthful foods available from your kitchen might mean more customers.

Don't change the menu at all, if you don't want to. Let the dessert list stretch to two columns, and the French fryer can work overtime. Just clip a small card to the menu. On the card print something like this: "For the accommodation of our customers who are dieting to lose weight, or for other health reasons, we offer the Diet Luncheon (or Dinner) below. All of these foods are completely salt-free and sugar-free, and as fresh as possible." Then offer a simple platter of, say, lean meat (chicken, turkey, lamb, roast beef), a fresh green salad with optional oil dressing, a fresh vegetable and fresh fruit for dessert—no bread, no butter, no beverage.

We believe that such a specialty will meet with approval and gratitude among even those of your customers who don't take advantage of it. We think, too, that you'll be surprised at how fast this special will move, and at the new faces you'll see, persons who have heard about the diet special and come to see for themselves.

Do something for the diet-conscious customer. He will thank you for it by telling his friends of your consideration.

CHAPTER 245

Additional Information on Cooking

Stomach Ulcers and Raw Food

In *Agricultural and Food Chemistry* for June 23, 1954, mention is made of the new mysterious factor or possibly vitamin that is contained in raw foods which will cure or prevent ulcers in laboratory animals. It has been found to be especially abundant in raw cabbage, the juice of which is used for the cure.

We would suggest that the most important word in this report is the word "raw" and that perhaps the reason for such a seemingly miraculous cure is a return to eating raw foods containing all the enzymes, vitamins and minerals that are a necessity for health. We Americans seem to think that a "good" meal is a cooked one, entirely neglecting the wealth of good nutrition in raw foods, fruits, nuts and vegetables. Oh, to be sure, we sometimes eat a salad but how many of us really concentrate on making sure that a large portion of all our meals is served raw? Not only do raw foods give us precious elements that cooking destroys, but the bulk and the fiber of the raw foods goes a long way toward preventing constipation, appendicitis and allied disorders. If you must eat cooked meals, at least get as much raw fruit and vegetables as you can between meals.

Some Food Superstitions

"White bread is the only good bread," "Fresh cucumbers are indigestible unless you first take the 'poison' out of them with salt," "Soak leafy vegetables all afternoon so they'll be crisp by dinnertime."

Do folks around you quote sentences like these (which are pure superstition and ignorance) to prove that they know a lot about food? Perhaps we aren't so badly off at that. Here are some of the superstitions about food that exist in other parts of the world, according to the World Health Organization Newsletter for October, 1953.

[920]

West Africans have an aversion to food in its raw state as fit only for cattle. The older people think it is undignified to eat oranges and discourage children from eating them. Oranges will make them "soft," say the oldsters.

Greeks can eat many vegetables raw, but some must be cooked or they are not edible. Cucumbers can be eaten only raw, but zucchini squash must be cooked. Green beans and peas must always be cooked. Cabbage may be eaten raw, but cauliflower never! Puerto Ricans, who live on a scanty diet at best, often will not eat fruit that grows wild. It may be poisonous, or dangerous or indigestible.

When we taught New Mexican school children to eat white bread instead of cold corn tortillas we did them a great disservice, for most of their daily calcium came from the limewater in which the tortilla corn was soaked. Their mothers used to give them wild greens, too. We persuaded them to substitute canned spinach. When there was no money to buy spinach, the children had no greens at all, for they could not go back to eating something we had taught them was inferior.

In China a public health nurse met with resistance when she tried to persuade expectant mothers to eat vegetables rather than a diet of fried chicken. These women had been eating mostly vegetables all their lives and they had looked forward to their pregnancy as a time when they could be privileged to have a special diet.

How the Eskimos Eat

Speaking of exotic foods, we recently ran across some Eskimo recipes for foods that are apparently great favorites among the Eskimo gourmets. Ice cream is made from reindeer tallow, seal oil and lard, with a little water added to make it white and fluffy.

You may add berries in season if you want a fruit flavor. The recipe for soured seal liver was so exotic that it left us gasping, not to say a little nauseated. The liver is placed in an enamel pot and covered with blubber. Then it is placed in a warm spot for several days (!) until sour.

Knowing what liver smells like when it has been unrefrigerated for even several hours, it is happily impossible for us temperate-clime residents to imagine the possible fragrance of the "soured" seal liver.

Boiled owl is another favorite Eskimo dish, and the small intestines of ptarmigan are said to be great delicacies when they have been cooked for several seconds in boiling water.

Now will you eat your delicious, crisp vegetables and fresh fruits and thank your lucky stars you live where they are available!

Restaurant Food

According to a recent survey, an average of 70 million meals are served to Americans every day in restaurants, a grim reminder of vegetables whose vitamins have disappeared on the steam table, of salads drained of every mineral and vitamin by soaking and standing, of meats cooked and then left to wait the diner's order while their nutritional value disappears. Food service, says the survey, is the fourth largest industry in the country —larger than petroleum or public utilities.

SECTION 19.

Food Combinations

Even though many authorities on food combining claim victories for their theories in the way of general healthfulness and improvements ranging from slight disorders to major diseases, we say, don't worry about special combinations, just maintain a sensible food balance, avoid refined foods . . . and keep up with your supplements.

CHAPTER 246

Mixed Meals or Food Combinations

One of the favorite ideas in the field of health and diet is the idea that one should use only certain "kinds" of food at certain times. Foods consist largely of proteins, carbohydrates and fats, so the general idea is to separate foods according to these categories and eat only one kind of food at a time, or a combination of two such kinds of food at a time.

Some authorities tell us, "Don't eat starch and protein at the same time. This means no meat balls and spaghetti. No meat and potatoes. No eggs and toast." Other advocates of food combining warn, "Don't eat fats and starches together. No bread and butter, etc." Other specialists in this field go so far as to advise eating individual foods alone and never combining them with any other food at all.

Suggestions From Three Authorities

Daniel C. Munro, M.D., has written a series of books whose chief burden is the proper combining of foods. *Man Alive, You're Half Dead* (Bartholomew House, 205 East 42nd Street, New York, New York) is the latest of these. Dr. Munro believes that man, a definitely carnivorous animal, he says, should eat little in the way of starches and sugars. These foods, which need an alkaline environment for proper digestion, do grave harm when they are placed in the stomach along with protein foods which must be digested in an acid medium, he says. Fats, all of which produce acids while they are being digested, should be eaten with protein foods. Carbohydrates, if eaten at all, should be eaten alone—and never with acid foods such as a fruit juice, vinegar and so forth.

Dr. Herbert M. Shelton, head of the Shelton Health School and Editor of *Hygienic Review,* has ideas on food combining, too—fairly elaborate ones. They go like this: Eat acids and starches at separate meals; eat proteins and carbohydrates at different meals; eat only one concentrated protein food at any one meal; eat proteins at separate meals from fats or acids; eat melons alone; drink milk alone if you take it at all.

Dr. William Howard Hay, M.D., prolific writer on health whose books on the Hay diet have been best sellers during the past 30 years, has still other ideas on food combining. Don't eat starches and acid at the same meal, he says. Don't combine starches with either acids or proteins, with two exceptions—tupelo honey (honey made from the flowers of a certain gum tree) and raisins, which may be eaten with any kind of food.

It seems that people have had great success in following suggestions like these for food combining. Authors of books on the subject can quote one case history after another showing very rapid improvement in disorders ranging from slight to serious. Is this remarkable record due, do you think, to the way in which foods were combined, or is it due to the fact that all of these diets are basically good diets, high in fresh fruits and vegetables and completely devoid of refined starches and sugars? We think that this last aspect of the matter is partly responsible for the good results.

Nature Does Not Segregate Foods

Doesn't it seem somewhat unnatural to segregate foods at meals according to their starch, protein or fat content when nature herself does not do this? No food occurs in nature that does not have at least traces of carbohydrate and protein or fat and protein.

For instance, if you are never going to eat fats and protein at the same time, how can you eat eggs which consist of 6.7 per cent protein and 5.2 per cent fat? Would you list eggs as a fat or a protein food when you are doing your combining? What would you do with soybeans—one of the very best foods, we believe. Soybeans contain 13.2 per cent protein, 13.6 per cent starch and 6.3 per cent fat. Are they a carbohydrate or a protein food? Or would you designate them as a food high in fat? Certainly they contain far more fat than vegetables or fruits! Beef is about 19.2 per cent protein and 15.4 per cent fat. A fatty or a protein food?

How are you going to classify brewer's yeast which is 48 per cent protein, 39 per cent carbohydrate and 2 per cent fat? Or yogurt which is 7.4 per cent protein, 9.4 per cent carbohydrate and 7.2 per cent fat? Almonds, which should be included along with other raw nuts in any good diet, contain 20.5 per cent protein, 53.5 per cent fat and 4.3 per cent carbohydrate. Are they a protein food? No, surely they must qualify as a fatty food. But even so, they contain more carbohydrate than many foods we usually think of as carbohydrate foods, like carrots for instance.

Baker's bread is certainly carbohydrate food—for the white flour of which it is made is almost pure starch. So are you going to classify bread as a starchy food? Perhaps, but what if you make your own bread from organically grown whole wheat flour (high in protein) with added soybean flour and sunflower seed meal? In all probability your bread will be higher in protein than many meats. Do you classify it then as a protein food? And what about this business of never spreading butter on bread because this will involve mixing fats with carbohydrates? It's impossible to make a good bread without using fats of some kind. So bread itself is bound to be a combination of fats, carbohydrates and a good deal of protein if the flour is good.

Rice polishings, another fine food supplement, consist of 11.6 per cent protein, 64 per cent starch and 10.1 per cent fat. Can you consider them as a starch food when actually they contain more protein than some meats? And what about sunflower seeds whose protein content is usually higher than most meats?

It's not hard to decide about the content of concentrated foods like white sugar—99.9 per cent carbohydrate, or butter—85 per cent fat, or egg white—practically nothing but protein and water. Such foods are easily iden-

[926]

tified as to content. Does this make them good foods? Quite the contrary. The very fact that sugar is a pure carbohydrate and nothing more is the most important single argument against eating sugar. Butter is a concentrated fat, containing none of the protein and carbohydrate which accompanies it in milk. Isn't that the chief reason why butter can be dangerous to health?

Then, too, of the foods we mentioned above, the best ones from the point of view of nutrition—yeast, sunflower seeds, almonds and other nuts, soybeans, whole eggs, liver—these foods, packed with vitamins and minerals and other valuable food elements, are foods which have been proven over the years to carry the most nutritive value. In all of them the proportion of fats, carbohydrates and proteins is remarkably even. These foods are high in all 3. Did nature make a mistake in designing them? Isn't the very composition of these foods ample proof that you need starches, proteins and fats all together at the same time in your digestive tract for the best possible use of all 3?

The Best Solution—Natural Foods

Proteins need an acid environment for digestion, granted. They are, therefore, digested in the stomach where there is, or should be, exactly the right amount of acid to do the job. Carbohydrates are chiefly digested in the mouth in the alkaline environment of the saliva. Refined carbohydrates, like white flour products and white sugar products, need scarcely any chewing, because all cellulose has been removed from them. Therefore, they may pass into the stomach practically undigested, true. The answer to this problem is not to seek out a new food combination but to stop eating refined foods.

Natural raw carbohydrates, fruits and vegetables, must be chewed before you can swallow them and in the chewing process they are digested in the saliva which is alkaline.

We think that our arguments against special food combining are sound. But we know we will never convince those readers who are dedicated to the idea of food combining. And we say to them—if you have found that following one or another of the current theories on food combining has improved your health and you enjoy eating this way, then by all means go right on doing so.

To others for whom food combining is a new idea entirely, we say forget about it. The only thing you need to know about food combining is that your diet should be a combination of all foods *in as near their natural state as possible*. So long as you exclude the refined foods and so long as you maintain a sensible balance between protein, starchy and fat foods, you won't run into any difficulty.

One final word. We are certain that taking vitamins and minerals with your meals is an important aid to good digestion and absorption. Their chief function, you know, is to bring about the necessary changes in food substances so that the body can use them well. Some time ago Editor Rodale told of his experiences with his pulse on days when he deliberately omitted taking his food supplements at meal time. The unhappy effect was an accelerated pulse rate after such meals.

CHAPTER 247

How to Take Your Starch

By Herbert M. Shelton

(Editor's Note: Dr. Shelton, head of the Shelton Health School and Editor of "Hygienic Review," has written many books covering the Hygienic System. Among other things, he believes that the proper combining of foods is essential for good health. This article is reprinted by permission from his book, "Food Combinations Made Easy," published by Dr. Shelton's Health School, Box 1277, San Antonio, Texas. The article covers only the subject of starch. Here are Dr. Shelton's other ideas on food combining:

> *Eat acids and starches at separate meals.*
> *Eat protein foods and carbohydrate foods at separate meals.*
> *Eat but one concentrated protein food at a meal.*
> *Eat proteins and acids at separate meals.*
> *Eat fats and proteins at separate meals.*
> *Eat sugars and proteins at separate meals.*
> *Eat starches and sugars at separate meals.*
> *Eat melons alone.*
> *Take milk alone, or let it alone.*

Actually, as you will see below, these suggestions are not so difficult to follow as you might think. And they will most certainly result in your eating far more of the healthful raw fruits and vegetables than you otherwise would.)

One author says: "Don't serve more than two foods rich in sugar or starch at the same meal. When you serve bread and potatoes, your starch-license has run out. A meal that includes peas, bread, potatoes, sugar, cake and after dinner mints should also include a vitamin B complex capsule, some bicarbonate of soda (other than that used on the vegetables), and the address of the nearest specialist in arthritis and other degenerative diseases."

For more than 50 years it has been the rule in *Hygienic* circles to take but one starch at a meal and to consume no sweet foods with the starch meal. Sugars, syrups, honeys, cakes, pies, mints, etc., have been tabu with starches. We do not say to those who come to us for advice: If you eat these with your starches, take a dose of baking soda with them. We tell them to avoid the fermentation that is almost inevitable. In *Hygienic* circles it is considered the height of folly to take a poison and then take an antidote with it. We think it best not to take the poison.

Sugar with starch means fermentation. It means a sour stomach. It means discomfort. Those who are addicted to the honey-eating practice and who are laboring under the popular fallacy that honey is a "natural sweet" and may be eaten indiscriminately, should know that this rule not to take sweets with starches applied to honey as well. Honey or syrup, it makes no difference which, with your hot cakes; honey or sugar, it matters not which, with your cereals, honey or sugar to sweeten your cakes—these combinations spell fermentation. White sugar, brown sugar, "raw" sugar, imitation brown sugar (that is, white sugar that has been colored), black strap molasses, or other syrup, with starches means fermentation. Soda will neutralize the resulting acids, it will not stop the fermentation.

For more than 50 years it has been the practice in *Hygienic* circles to take a large raw vegetable salad (leaving out tomatoes or other acid foods) with the starch meal. The salad has been a very large one, measured by ordinary standards, and made up of fresh uncooked vegetables. This salad carries an abundance of vitamins and minerals. The vitamins in these vegetables are the genuine articles and no chemist's imitations of the real thing. No just-as-good substitutes for vitamins have ever satisfied the *Hygienists*. We take the real article or nothing. Capsule-eating is a commercial program and belongs to the drug fetish.

Vitamins complement each other. We need, not just the vitamin B complex, but all vitamins. A large raw vegetable salad supplies several known vitamins and those that may exist but have not yet been detected. Vitamins not only cooperate with each other in the nutritive process, but they also cooperate with the minerals in the body. These are supplied by the vegetable salad. To take vitamin preparations that are combined with calcium or iron or other minerals will not answer the purpose. These minerals are in non-usable forms. There is no better source of food substances than the plant-kingdom—the laboratory and the chemist have not yet been able to concoct acceptable foods.

Hygienists advise but one starch at a meal, not because there is any conflict in the digestion of these foods, but because taking two or more starches at a meal is practically certain to lead to overeating of this substance. We find it best, and this is doubly true in feeding the sick, to limit the starch intake to one starch at a meal. People with unusual powers of self-control may be permitted two starches, but these individuals are so rare, the rule should be: *one starch at a meal.*

The same author says: "Whether you eat hamburgers at the Greasy Spoon—or filet mignon at the Plaza—you're eating protein. Whether it's griddle cakes at the diner—or crepe suzette at the Astorbilt—you're eating carbohydrates. And whether it's oleomargarine from a relief agency, or butter balls at the Cafe de Lux—you're eating fat. These are the big three; the fourth part of food is roughage. All food will predominate in one of these substances or another. Some highly refined foods—like sugar—will contain only one of these, but—generally speaking, most foods contain all three—which is what makes the Hay Diet somewhat elusive."

It is not true that the fourth part of food is roughage, for roughage is not food, and it is not true that all foods predominate in one or the other of these four "parts of foods." Young, tender, growing plants have very little roughage, their cellulose being practically all digestible. They are valuable largely for their minerals and vitamins. His "big four" does not take into account the minerals that are in foods, and which are very abundant in many foods, while relatively scarce in others.

One may easily get the idea, from reading the foregoing quotation, that one protein is as good as any other, and that foods may be prepared in any manner desired. Its author is not actually guilty of holding any such views, but this statement of his could easily lead his readers to believe that just any old diet is good enough.

The remark that I wish to discuss is that, generally speaking, most foods contain carbohydrates, fats, proteins and roughage and that, this makes the prohibition of protein-starch combinations "somewhat elusive." I want to differentiate between natural food combinations and the haphazard combinations commonly eaten. The human digestive tract is adapted to the digestion of natural combinations, but it is certainly not adapted to the digestion of the haphazard and indiscriminate combinations that are eaten in civilized life today. Natural combinations offer but little difficulty to the digestive system; but, it is one thing to eat two foods of "opposite character." The digestive juices may be readily adapted to one food, such as cereals, that is a protein-starch combination; they cannot be well adapted to two foods, such as bread and cheese. Tilden frequently said that nature never produced a sandwich.

It should be axiomatic that our digestive system is adapted to the digestion of natural combinations and can handle the unnatural ones only with difficulty. Modern civilized eating habits are so far removed from anything seen anywhere in nature or among so-called primitive peoples that it is impossible to think of them as being normal eating habits.

The prohibition is "somewhat elusive" to him simply because he has not given enough attention to the process of digestion. It is true that nature puts up such combinations. It is true that these natural combinations offer but little difficulty to digestion. But, and here is the fact to digestion that all orthodox dietitians miss, the body is capable of so adapting its digestive secretions, both as to strength of acid, concentration of enzymes and timing of secretions, to the digestive requirements of a particular food, while such precise adaptation of juices to foods is not possible when two different foods are eaten. Cannon demonstrated that if starch is well mixed with saliva, it will continue to digest in the stomach for as much as two hours. This certainly cannot be true if proteins are eaten with the starch, for, in this case, the glands of the stomach will deluge the food with an acid gastric juice, thus rapidly ending gastric salivary digestion.

He says that the purpose of saliva is to begin the process of digestion of starches. "That is why," he adds, "you should chew bread, cereals, and other starchy foods very thoroughly; that is why you must not drink water through a mouthful of food. Though water at meal time is not condemned— it is needed to help the body in the chemistry of digestion—it must not be permitted to weaken the action of saliva on starches in the mouth."

The digestion of starches begins in the mouth, or should, but they remain in the mouth for such a short time that very litle digestion takes place. Salivary digestion of starches can and will continue in the stomach for a long period if they are eaten under proper conditions. Eating acids and proteins with them will inhibit or completely suspend their digestion. Drinking water with the meal will weaken the action of saliva upon starches in the stomach as much as it will in the mouth, and it is not true that you need to drink at meal time to have water to aid in the digestion of your food. It will be best to drink your water 10 to 15 minutes before meals. If taken with meals it dilutes the digestive juices and then passes out of the stomach in short order carrying the digestive juices and their enzymes along with it.

The following menus constitute properly combined starch meals. It is suggested that the starch meal be eaten at noon time. Starches should be eaten dry and should be thoroughly chewed and insalivated before swallowing. Acids should not be eaten on the salad with the starch meal. We suggest a larger salad in the evening with the protein and a smaller one at noon with the starch. These menus may be eaten in amounts required by the individual.

Vegetable Salad	Vegetable Salad	Vegetable Salad
Turnip Greens	Spinach	Beet Greens
Yellow Squash	Red Cabbage	Okra
Chestnuts	Baked Caladium Roots	Brown Rice
Vegetable Salad	Vegetable Salad	Vegetable Salad
Spinach	String Beans	Turnip Greens
String Beans	Baked Eggplant	Asparagus
Coconut	Steamed Caladium Roots	Brown Rice
Vegetable Salad	Vegetable Salad	Vegetable Salad
String Beans	Turnip Greens	Collards
Mashed Rutabaga	Okra	Fresh Corn
Irish Potatoes	Jerusalem Artichoke	Brown Rice
Vegetable Salad	Vegetable Salad	Vegetable Salad
Chard	Kale	Beet Greens
Carrots	Okra	Cauliflower
Potatoes	Jerusalem Artichoke	Baked Hubbard Squash
Vegetable Salad	Vegetable Salad	Vegetable Salad
String Beans	Chard	Kale
Turnips	Yellow Squash	String Beans
Sweet Potatoes	Jerusalem Artichoke	Baked Hubbard Squash
Vegetable Salad	Vegetable Salad	Vegetable Salad
Asparagus	Spinach	Green Squash
White Squash	Turnips	Okra
Yams	Jerusalem Artichoke	Baked Hubbard Squash
Vegetable Salad	Vegetable Salad	Vegetable Salad
Beet Greens	Okra	Turnip Greens
Cauliflower	String Beans	Broccoli
Sweet Potatoes	Jerusalem Artichoke	Peanuts

Vegetable Salad	Vegetable Salad	Vegetable Salad
Asparagus	Swiss Chard	Chard
Okra	Peas	String Beans
Peanuts	Hubbard Squash	Peanuts
Vegetable Salad	Vegetable Salad	Vegetable Salad
Okra	String Beans	Spinach
Beet Greens	Broccoli	Green String Beans
Whole Grain Bread	Hubbard Squash	Brown Rice
Vegetable Salad	Vegetable Salad	Vegetable Salad
Yellow Wax Beans	Spinach	Chard
Kale	Cabbage	Okra
Irish Potatoes	Baked Hubbard Squash	Brown Rice
Vegetable Salad	Vegetable Salad	Vegetable Salad
Okra	Beet Greens	Chard
Brussel Sprouts	Yellow Squash	Asparagus
Irish Potatoes	Irish Potatoes	Baked Beans
Vegetable Salad	Vegetable Salad	Vegetable Salad
String Beans	Kale	Swiss Chard
Cabbage	Okra	Yellow Squash
Sweet Potatoes	Brown Rice	Baked Caladium Roots
Vegetable Salad	Vegetable Salad	Vegetable Salad
Chard	Spinach	Okra
Broccoli	String Beans	Beet Greens
Yams	Peanuts	Steamed Caladium Roots
Vegetable Salad	Vegetable Salad	Vegetable Salad
Spinach	Okra	Yellow Squash
Cabbage	Cauliflower	Chard
Chestnuts	Carrots	Potatoes

CHAPTER 248

Food Combinations in
the Hay Diet

William Howard Hay, M.D., became an almost legendary figure in the world of diet, even during his lifetime. Writer of best-selling books on diet, operator of Pocono Haven, a health resort, philosopher, physician and follower of the natural way, Dr. Hay became almost synonymous with the whole idea of diet. For about two decades in American history, just the mention of the word "diet" brought the comment, "Oh I suppose you believe in what Dr. Hay says." So countless people knew of Dr. Hay, even though only those who studied his ideas knew exactly what his philosophy of eating was.

Basically, food combinations are the most important aspect of his system of dieting. "Incompatible" foods should not be eaten at the same meal. According to Dr. Hay, the starchy and sweet foods are partly digested in the mouth, by the saliva. They must have an alkaline medium in order to be properly digested. Animal proteins must be digested in an acid medium, so they are not affected by the saliva, but they do call out hydrochloric acid in the stomach and in this purely acid medium they are digested by the various digestive juices.

So if you eat starchy bread or potatoes with an acid fruit, you have taken away the necessary alkaline conditions which the ptyalin in the saliva must have, to digest the starch. The starchy food then proceeds into the stomach undigested. There is no mechanism for digesting starch there, so it passes (still undigested) into the intestine where it will probably ferment in the presence of heat and moisture.

Eating Protein Foods

Protein foods, such as meats, eggs or fish depend on the pepsin of the gastric juice for their first step in digestion. Pepsin will act only in surroundings that are positively acid. So if you have eaten starchy foods and the starchy-alkaline mass has progressed into your stomach, then eating protein foods will immediately bring about an acid condition of the stomach. As Dr. Hay puts it, "So the gastric juice begins to contain acid for the digestion of the protein, as it must, and away go the alkaline conditions necessary for the digestion of the starchy food, and fermentation sets in, with its formation and release of the fermentation acids."

This, of course, results not only in upset digestion, but also in waste of food, for undigested food does us no good. According to Dr. Hay in *What Price Health,* another result of wrong food combinations is excess acidity. He does not mean in the stomach, necessarily. He means excess acidity in all the body fluids. "Acid end-products" is the name he gives to the debris that accumulates as a result of: 1. wrong kind of foods, and 2. wrong combinations of foods. When we eat so much more than we need, says he, what becomes of the unneeded part? Unless we are extremely active, burning up all our wastes completely, the protein we eat does not reach its final form, urea, but stops in the form of uric acid.

"Another cause for this departure from health is no doubt the very free use of the refined and thoroughly denatured things, such as white flour preparations, white sugar, refined starches or sugars of any kind," says Dr. Hay. We agree one hundred per cent. According to him, these refined carbohydrates are acid-forming to a high degree, for, says he, their oxidation releases carbonic acid in the system. They do not leave behind in the system enough of the natural alkalies, so they predispose one to acidity.

Why We Have Ill Health

The acid-alkaline balance is another extremely important aspect of health, according to Dr. Hay. The body has what is called the "alkaline reserve"—a storehouse of alkaline substances on which it can call when there is too much acid present. Wrong eating uses up some of the alkaline store and creates acidity in its place. The foods that are acid-forming are the animal proteins, such as meat, eggs, fish, milk, cheese and so forth and the cereals—anything made from any of the grains. The alkaline-forming foods in general are fruits and vegetables.

So Dr. Hay's idea as to how ill health is created can be summarized as follows. First, the use of entirely too much protein food in the form of meats, eggs or fish. Second, the use of refined, denatured, starchy or sweet foods. Third, the wrong combinations of foods, such as combining starchy or sweet foods with either acid fruits or proteins. (We disagree with Dr. Hay's opinion that we are eating too much protein. It is our opinion most of us eat far too little. By omitting entirely the refined starches and sugars, we leave plenty of room on our menus for lots of protein and fresh fruits and vegetables—the ideal way to eat, we believe.)

When you are separating sweets from proteins in meal-planning, Dr. Hay has two exceptions to make. There are two sweets, he says, raisins and tupelo honey, which do not require the initial stages of digestion necessary for the more complex kinds of sugars, so these two foods may be eaten with any kind of food—carbohydrates or proteins.

Dr. Hay's theories found many opponents, of course. His answer to criticism was: "It would seem that no further argument is necessary to indicate the incompatibility of the digestion of starches and proteins at one and the same time, but if further argument seems necessary, then try it out for yourself and on yourself, and note the results. Two weeks should be enough to convince anyone, but if longer time is required or seems to be desirable, then extend the period to four weeks to make doubly sure."

Now, how do you go about planning meals according to the Hay diet? Here are some suggestions: Breakfast for the sedentary worker should not contain any bread, so acid fruits can be eaten if you wish. He suggests a cup of coffee unsweetened for those who feel they must have it, a glass of orange juice and a glass or two of milk. For those who do heavier physical work, breakfast should include bread with butter and honey, if desired; a cup of coffee, with a dish of soaked dates, figs, or raisins, better not cooked, but with cream. Lunch for both kinds of workers should be vegetables, raw vegetable salads, fresh fruits and milk or buttermilk. Dinner should contain a serving of meat, eggs, fish or cheese as the main dish, with vegetables, raw salads, fresh fruits. No carbohydrate food in concentrated form should be eaten at this meal—hence no bread or potatoes and, of course, no sweet dessert.

How to Plan Meals According to The Hay Diet

Here are suggested menus:

BREAKFAST

Sedentary

Glass or more of orange juice, or sliced acid fruit, with one or more glasses of milk. Fruit juice or fresh acid fruits are always to be unsweetened.

Active

Coffee if desired or very habitual, sweetened and creamed; three or four slices of toasted or stale whole wheat, rye or graham bread, well buttered and with honey, if desired; sliced fat bacon, broiled; a dish of soaked dates, figs or raisins.

LUNCH

Sedentary

Vegetable soup without meat stock or thickening; cooked vegetables; raw salads, not dressed with vinegar; all the fresh fruit desired, except banana; a glass or two of milk or buttermilk; dessert of fruit ice, or sliced fruit, the latter unsweetened.

Active

Vegetable soup without stock or thickening; raw vegetable salads, dressed without vinegar or other acid dressing, but plain oil or sour cream; cooked vegetables of all kinds; baked potatoes or toasted whole wheat bread if very active; sweet fruits, dates, figs or raisins, with honey and cream, or a dish of ice cream; if coffee must be used, this also may contain both sugar and cream, but it is better not to form the coffee habit.

DINNER

Sedentary

Vegetable soup if desired, but without stock or thickening; raw vegetable salads of all available vegetables, roots or greens, dressed with oil and lemon juice, or with plain sour cream, but no vinegar; all the cooked vegetables desired, with oil or lemon dressing, or butter if used moderately; one moderate serving of meat, eggs, fish, or cheese; sliced fruit dessert, or fruited gelatine; if coffee must be used, then always unsweetened.

Active

Any soup without meat stock or thickening; as many cooked vegetables as desired, no starchy tubers, as potato; large raw vegetable salads of anything available, even cabbage, if nothing more can be readily obtained, dressed with lemon juice and oil or with plain sour cream; one fair serving of meat, eggs, fish, or cheese; sliced fruits or fruited gelatine, always unsweetened; if coffee must be used be sure this is unsweetened.

Children over the age of 6 years come under the active group and may have the same foods as the active adult, for their much greater activity calls for more fuel foods than are good for the sedentary adult.

What Price Health also contains menus for one week and recipes for a number of different dishes suggested in the menus. We were rather surprised to find in these menus such dishes as broiled grapefruit, chocolate clusters, canned blueberries, chocolate custard, butterscotch cream and so forth. We assume that Dr. Hay did not know that eating brown or raw sugar is almost the same thing as eating white refined sugar. We would certainly suggest that readers omit the recipes that use any sugar at all. Then, too, Dr. Hay was writing before we knew all that we know today about vitamins and how perishable they are. We know today that there is no sense to broiling a grapefruit, for the precious vitamin C is very sensitive to heat. And, of course, why should one use canned blueberries, rather than some fruit that can be had fresh?

[935]

SECTION 20.

Food Supplements

Food is important. What you eat at every meal, every day, is probably the most important single aspect of life so far as health is concerned. But, as we have shown in this book, today's food, as it reaches the tables of most of us, simply does not maintain robust health, no matter how carefully you plan menus. Today's soil has been depleted of valuable trace minerals. Much of the fresh food you eat has lost most of its vitamins before it reaches you. This is the reason why you should take food supplements, even though your grandparents didn't have to. Natural food supplements are food. Take them with your meals.

CHAPTER 249

The Vitamin Story

We are presenting here a study of all the known vitamins, the reason why we need each for good health and a list of foods and food supplements in which each is most plentiful. We hope it will help you as a quick reference in planning menus, buying foods and food supplements.

VITAMIN A

Vitamin A is a fat soluble vitamin, that is, it dissolves in fat and it can be stored in the body, so you do not need to eat vitamin A every day. But if you happen to have gotten little vitamin A recently, it may take a long time for you to build up your body store of it again. People who have had serious illnesses or infections are almost certain to be short of vitamin A; anyone who suffers from any stomach, liver or intestinal disorder probably lacks vitamin A; the continual taking of mineral oil destroys vitamin A and the other fat soluble vitamins in the body.

In a recent survey in New York schools it was found that a slight vitamin A shortage is the most common diet deficiency. Experiments at Columbia University showed that animals who receive far more than the recommended daily requirement of vitamin A live longer and are freer from the symptoms of old age.

Why You Need Vitamin A for Good Health

A lack of the vitamin causes: night blindness, sensitivity to glare, difficulty reading in dim light, inability to store fat. It is necessary for skin health, fighting colds and infections, preventing kidney stones, good growth and dental health in children. The official recommendation is that we get a minimum of 5000 International Units of vitamin A every day. Experiments indicate that far more than this is the ideal amount. There is no danger of getting too much in natural foods unless one should take enormous amounts of fish liver oil over a long period of time. We do not recommend taking any form of synthetic vitamin A. Fish liver oil, which we recommend as a food supplement for everyone, young and old, is a natural food taken from the livers of halibut, cod, etc. In the form of perles it is odorless and tasteless.

Foods in Which Vitamin A is Most Plentiful:

Apricots, carrots, collards, dandelion greens, beef liver, mustard greens, sweet potatoes, turnip greens, watercress, butter, egg yolk and fish liver oils. Carotene appears in foods that are yellow or green and carotene is the substance which changes to vitamin A in your body. If your liver is not functioning well, this vegetable form of carotene may be wasted, so we advise again —make certain by taking fish liver oils in capsule form.

VITAMIN B

There are a lot of B vitamins, including some which scientists know are present in certain foods, but have not succeeded in isolating and identifying yet. All the B vitamins are of great importance to Americans because more than half our national diet consists of foods made of white sugar or white flour. These two carbohydrate foods (from which all the B vitamins have been removed during the refining process) must be accompanied by B vitamins or our bodies cannot use them properly. So the more refined foods you eat, the more B vitamins you need.

"Enriched" flour contains only 3 of the many B vitamins removed during refining. Don't depend on it for B vitamins. Smoking, drinking or eating sweets robs you of B vitamins. Many of the new drugs (the sulfas are one example) as well as sleeping pills, estrogen, insecticides and so forth create a condition in your digestive tract that is destructive of B vitamins. It may take years to overcome deficiencies caused by such substances.

B vitamins are soluble in water. They are lost when you throw away water in which meats or vegetables have been cooked. They are harmed, too, by light and heat. Most of the riboflavin (one of the B vitamins) is destroyed in a bottle of milk left on the doorstep in the sunlight for an hour or so. Baking soda or baking powder destroy B vitamins.

The most important thing to remember about the B vitamins is that they should be taken all together and may do serious harm if they are taken separately in massive doses. Synthetic vitamin B preparations cannot supply you with the same effective vitamin B "complex" you get from foods which are rich in all these vitamins. Brewer's yeast and desiccated liver, which we recommend as food supplements for everyone, are natural products. The yeast plant, storing B vitamins for its own use, is dried so that the B vitamins become available to us. Desiccated liver is made from fresh liver with the fat removed, carefully dried at low heat to conserve all the B vitamins. These two food supplements have been found, in experiments, to protect laboratory animals from cancer and many other diseases. Liver has been found to be protective against poisons to which we are exposed today, such as DDT.

The names of the B vitamins are: thiamin, riboflavin, niacin, pantothenic acid, pyridoxine, choline, inositol, vitamin B_{12}, biotin, para-aminobenzoic acid. Do not try to take them separately. Take them all together in foods and natural food supplements.

Why You Need the B Vitamins for Good Health

Among them the B vitamins are chiefly responsible for the health of: the digestive tract, the skin, the mouth and the tongue, the eyes, the nerves, the arteries, the liver. They have been found to: prevent constipation, beriberi and pellagra, prevent burning feet, burning and dryness of the eyes, tender gums, feelings of depression, nausea, indigestion, lack of appetite, fatigue, skin disorders, cracks at the corners of the mouth, certain kinds of anemia, fatty liver and so forth.

There are official recommendations for daily requirement of only 3 of the B vitamins: thiamin—1 to 1.2 milligrams a day; riboflavin—1.5 to 3 milligrams a day; and niacin—10 to 18 milligrams a day. Even though no official minimum requirement has been set for the other B vitamins, they are needed every day, too.

Foods in Which Vitamin B is Most Plentiful:

Legumes, organ meats (heart, liver, kidneys), wheat germ, whey, chicken, peanuts, egg yolk, whole grains, soybeans, milk, fresh raw fruits and vegetables. Brewer's yeast and desiccated liver are the two richest sources.

VITAMIN C

This is also a water soluble vitamin, the most perishable of all. Fruits and vegetables left unrefrigerated for several days may lose most of their vitamin C. Home canning destroys vitamin C, for it is sensitive to air and heat. Soaking foods or discarding the cooking water destroys vitamin C. Cutting, slicing, grating or chopping fruits or vegetables should be done just before they are eaten, for every cut surface exposed to air releases vitamin C. All fruits and vegetables should be refrigerated at all times until they are eaten. Fresh ones are, of course, preferable—eat them as soon as possible after they are picked. Frozen foods contain more vitamin C generally than canned ones. Baking soda or copper utensils in contact with fresh food destroy vitamin C.

There are physicians today who cure polio, pneumonia, influenza, the common cold and many other diseases with massive doses of vitamin C. It is not apparently possible to get too much of the natural vitamin C and it is believed that most of us are deficient in it. Smoking, stress and exposure to poisons use up vitamin C and it must be replaced every day—it cannot be stored.

The official recommendation is for 75 milligrams to 150 milligrams of vitamin C a day.

Why You Need Vitamin C for Good Health

Vitamin C prevents scurvy, protects the health of all body tissues, including teeth, gums, bones, blood vessels, eyes, etc. It is necessary for the body to manufacture the cement that holds cells together—all cells. It protects against infections and colds. It causes wounds to heal quickly. Sure signs that you are deficient in vitamin C are easy bruising, bleeding gums or loose teeth.

Foods in Which Vitamin C is Most Plentiful:

Green peppers, broccoli, cauliflower, watercress, kohlrabi, raw cabbage, strawberries, collards, cantaloupe, turnip greens, tomatoes, fresh peas and citrus fruit. It must be remembered that citrus fruit also contains citric acid which some people are extremely sensitive to. For this reason we advise eating citrus fruit in moderation, and always eating it, never juicing it, as the action of the citric acid is much stronger in the juice.

The richest source of vitamin C is rose hips—the fruit of the rose tree left after the flowers fade. These can be made into puree for winter use.

VITAMIN D

This is a fat soluble vitamin which is absolutely necessary for body health, since it must be present for us to use calcium and phosphorus properly. It appears only in foods of animal origin. It is also available from the sun's rays. A substance in the bare skin manufactures vitamin D from the ultraviolet light.

Fish liver oil, which we recommend to everyone as a food supplement, is the richest source of vitamin D. We believe that children and adults alike should take fresh fish liver oil the year round, for vitamins A and D. It can be had in capsules. The official recommendation is 400 International Units of vitamin D per day for infants and young people up to the age of 20.

Why You Need Vitamin D for Good Health

Vitamin D protects the thyroid gland, prevents some kinds of arthritis, is necessary for strong bones and teeth, helps normal heart action and clotting of blood, may prevent nearsightedness in children, is active in every body function involving calcium and phosphorus—two most important minerals.

Foods in Which Vitamin D is Most Plentiful:

Butter, eggs, herring, liver, mackerel, milk, salmon, tuna fish, fish liver oil.

VITAMIN E

This fat soluble vitamin is removed from wheat when flour is milled. When flour is bleached, any vitamin E that might be left in the flour is destroyed by the bleach. Vitamin E protects the body's store of two other vitamins—A and C, so you will need less of these two vitamins if you are getting enough vitamin E. It has been used extensively in therapy for reproductive disorders, including sterility, miscarriage, menopause disorders and so forth. Many physicians are at present using it in the treatment of heart and blood vessel diseases. It has also produced some spectacular results in cases of diabetes. It has been used successfully in treating muscular dystrophy.

Vitamin E is destroyed in the presence of rancid fats or oils. Mineral oil also destroys it. Medicines that contain ferric chloride or other ferric salts inactivate vitamin E in the body. Our chief sources of vitamin E today are vegetable and cereal oils and whole grain cereals.

Wheat germ and wheat germ oil which we recommend to everyone as food supplements are made from that part of the wheat that is discarded when the grain is milled. We recommend taking both a wheat germ product and vitamin E.

Why You Need Vitamin E for Good Health

It protects the health of the heart, blood vessels, muscles and reproductive system; a lack of it may be a cause of muscular dystrophy; it is a natural anti-coagulant, thus preventing the possibility of a stroke.

Foods in Which Vitamin E is Most Plentiful:

Corn oil, cottonseed oil, peanut oil, soybean oil, wheat germ, wheat germ oil, sunflower seed oil.

VITAMIN K

This is a newly discovered vitamin so we do not know a great deal about it as yet. However, we do know that it protects against hemorrhaging, that it appears to prevent abortions, that it protects the body against some cancer-producing substances.

Taking aspirin, mineral oil or sulfa drugs destroys vitamin K in the body. A liver or intestinal disorder or a lack of bile prevents absorption of vitamin K and may result in a deficiency. Alfalfa or some other food supplement made from green leafy vegetables rich in this vitamin should be taken if you suspect a deficiency.

Why You Need Vitamin K for Good Health

It helps blood to clot, cures high blood pressure in animals, may help prevent miscarriages, protects against cancer-causing substances.

Foods in Which Vitamin K is Most Plentiful:

Alfalfa, spinach, kale, carrot tops, all green leafy vegetables.

VITAMIN P

Vitamin P has recently made the headlines as a traveling companion to vitamin C. They occur together in foods, and it has been found that both of them together work far, far better than either works separately. Rutin and bioflavonoids are two other names for vitamin P.

Why Your Body Needs Vitamin P for Good Health

It has been used in the treatment of bleeding gums, eczema, glaucoma, cirrhosis of the liver and psoriasis. It prevents hemorrhaging, lessens the possibility of "stroke" in high blood pressure cases and is useful in protecting against the harmful effects of X-ray.

Foods in Which Vitamin P is Most Plentiful:

Green peppers, citrus fruit (it is in the white segments—another good reason for not juicing and straining citrus—you lose all the vitamin P), grapes, prunes, plums and black currants, rose hips.

VITAMIN F

We mention this vitamin last because it has not been officially designated as a vitamin yet. It is the term used for the essential unsaturated fatty acids—essential because your body cannot manufacture them as it does other fatty acids. They must be taken in foods. These substances are contained chiefly in vegetable, cereal and fish oils. Animal fats are deficient in them. They are almost completely absent from hydrogenated fats—the solid ones, like margarine.

Why You Need Vitamin F for Good Health

In animals lack of this vitamin results in retarded growth, scaliness of feet and tail, kidney damage, fatty kidney, impaired functions of reproduction and excessive water consumption. Eczema in children has been found to be the result of lack of vitamin F. We have found medical evidence showing that vitamin F is useful in preventing prostate trouble, many skin diseases, mongolism, asthma, psoriasis, arthritis and many other diseases. It is also credited with rendering cholesterol harmless, thus reducing the danger from this fatty substance.

Foods in Which Vitamin F is Most Plentiful:

Vegetable and cereal oils, such as salad oils, sunflower seeds and other unprocessed seeds like peanuts, whole grains and so forth. Fish liver oils are a rich source.

MINERALS

Minerals are actual constituents of body tissue. They also take part in many important processes, along with vitamins and enzymes. Some minerals like calcium and phosphorus we need in fairly large amounts. Others, called "trace minerals," we need in extremely small amounts but, nevertheless, we need them every day. This includes such minerals as zinc, cobalt, iodine and so forth.

Food as it is raised today is likely to be short in minerals, especially the trace minerals which are not present in commercial fertilizer. For this reason we feel that any health-conscious person should take food supplements for additional minerals. Bone meal (the powdered bones of young cattle) contains large amounts of calcium and phosphorus, along with all the trace minerals in exactly the proportions in which they occur in nature. Kelp, made from dried seaweed, is especially rich in iodine, along with all the other ocean minerals which are valuable for good health.

Finally, then, our recommendations for getting plenty of the vitamins and minerals are: eat a diet high in protein (fish, meat, eggs, poultry), nuts, seeds and fresh raw fruits and vegetables. These foods are richest in all the vitamins and minerals. Shun the refined and processed foods, like those made from white sugar and white flour. They dilute your diet to such an extent that eating them is bound to result in deficiencies. Take the following food supplements every day, regardless of how good your diet may be: fish liver oil in capsules for vitamins A, D and F, brewer's yeast and/or desiccated liver for the B vitamins, rose hips for vitamin C and vitamin P, wheat germ oil for vitamin E, bone meal and kelp for minerals.

CHAPTER 250

Alfalfa

Alfalfa has long been thought of as food for herbivorous farm animals, but more recently it has assumed considerable importance as food for human beings. It is a legume, as beans and peas are. But we eat the leaves, stems and seeds, rather than just the seeds. Alfalfa is one of the oldest of the legume family, its history going back for thousands of years. It seems likely that one of the main reasons for its richness in food value is the fact that its roots burrow deep into the earth, seeking out minerals that are buried in the soil. The average alfalfa seed has roots 10 to 20 feet long and reports have been found of phenomenally long roots—even as long as 128 feet.

It is a perennial plant, by which we mean that it need not be resowed every year, as corn must be, for example. It grows readily in almost any land and climate and is produced most abundantly in the southern and western parts of our country. For cattle it is used as hay, pasture, silage and alfalfa meal.

We have long believed that foods that are valuable for stock feed are likely to be good for human beings, too. And such is indeed the case with alfalfa. Frank W. Bower of Sierra Madre, California, has done a great deal to popularize alfalfa for human consumption, according to an article in *Physical Culture* magazine for February, 1948. Mr. Bower who has devoted most of his life to research on alfalfa, makes bread, muffins, flapjacks and tea from alfalfa, to name but a few of the ways he advocates eating it. It is available, too, from many other health food producers in tablet form, as a food supplement, and as seeds or leaves from which to make tea.

Vitamin Content

Alfalfa is perhaps most valuable for its vitamin A content. Vitamin A is a fat soluble vitamin, so it is not lost to any great extent when the alfalfa is dried. Alfalfa contains about 8000 International Units of vitamin A for every hundred grams. This compares favorably with apricots (7500 units per hundred grams) and with beef liver (9000 units per hundred grams). In addition, alfalfa is a good source of pyridoxine, one of the B vitamins, and vitamin E, whose great importance for the health of muscles and heart is well known. Alfalfa is regarded as the most reliable source of vitamin E for herbivorous animals. In addition, it is extremely rich in vitamin K, ranking along with spinach, kale and carrot tops as a good source of this vitamin which protects against hemorrhaging and helps the blood to clot properly. In animals vitamin K prevents and cures high blood pressure, so it may be far more important for the health of human beings than we know. Alfalfa contains from 20,000 to 40,000 units of vitamin K for every hundred grams.

Here are some further interesting nutritional facts: We are accustomed to thinking of foods from animal sources as being richest in protein, so it is surprising to find that the protein content of alfalfa is extremely high—18.9 per cent as compared to 3.3 per cent in milk, 13.8 per cent in whole wheat, 13.1 per cent in eggs and 16.5 per cent in beef.

In mineral content, too, alfalfa shows up well, with the following ash analysis (burning each product until all that remains is an ash which contains the mineral components)in comparison with other products:

	Calcium	Per Cent Phosphorus	Iron
Alfalfa	34.9	7.35	1.30
Soy flour	3.45	17.50	.28
Kelp	1.20	.27	.16
Whole wheat flour	.75	10.90	.30
Corn meal	.36	8.44	.15
Rolled oats	1.10	8.10	.05

It is, of course, perfectly possible to go out into an alfalfa field, pick yourself some stalks and leaves and chew them for dinner. But since we do not, generally speaking, have the same gastronomical preferences as cows, it is possible that the taste may not appeal. So we would suggest getting your alfalfa in meal which you can use in the kitchen, in tablets which you can take as food supplements or as seeds or leaves, which you can make into tea. It was our search for healthful beverages that led us to our research on alfalfa. One further bit of advice—be certain that the seeds you buy have been prepared for human consumption. Seeds prepared for planting may have been treated with chemicals which would not be the best thing for one's digestive tract.

CHAPTER 251

Bone Meal

By J. I. Rodale

What is bone meal? It is the bones of selected cattle ground as fine as flour and taken with water and milk or in soups. Let me tell you what aroused my interest in this subject.

In the latter part of 1941 an amazing situation in Deaf Smith County, Texas, was brought to the attention of the American public. It was discovered that inhabitants of that county, living mainly in and around Hereford, had remarkably healthy teeth with the almost complete absence of dental caries. Authorities who investigated found that the Deaf Smith Countians had teeth superior to anything known anywhere in the world.

Even the horses, dogs and cats in that region of Texas had perfect teeth. When strangers moved into this section their dental troubles vanished. New cavities did not form.

A study of the locality revealed the fact that underlying the soil was a rich deposit of lime (calcium) and phosphorus with a trace of fluorine. Since all soils have been formed from their underlying rock structure in a weathering process extending over eons of time, it was found that the soil in and around Hereford was rich in lime and phosphorus and contained some fluorine. These 3 elements are extremely important in connection with the formation of tooth and bone, and since the food raised in Deaf Smith County soil absorbs sizable amounts of these substances, it gives the residents of this county healthy tooth and bone structure. Farmers of this section bring in spindly cows and steers from across the border in Mexico and after pasturing and feeding them with local produce, build them up into fine big-boned animals.

A New Food is Found

A New England dentist avidly read the reports about the teeth in this celebrated county and his imagination ran completely away from the daily grind of drills, forceps and bicuspids. He cleverly reasoned that if he could find some food that was plentiful and which contained those 3 elements, namely calcium, phosphorus and fluorine in sufficient quantities, he might be able to accomplish the same purpose without causing a gold-rush on Deaf Smith County. That man was Dr. S. G. Harootian, connected with the Worcester State Hospital, in Massachusetts.

He found such a food—the bones of beef cattle ground as fine as flour. In an astounding 9-month experiment with 9 mental patients at his hospital he absolutely arrested the formation of cavities. Only one new cavity was formed in all that time. (The details of this experiment are explained in the following chapter.)

In the case of one of the patients, a filling was removed so as to expose the cavity to the ravages of the elements. It was continually packed with food debris, naturally. This would have been suicide for that particular tooth under ordinary conditions, but this wasn't an ordinary condition. Under the bone flour regimen that tooth did not decay. This experiment received a great deal of publicity and was written up in many journals.

An Experiment On Myself

When I read about all this I decided to experiment upon myself. I had a tooth that was extremely sensitive to cold. When I drank cold water it would act up. After two weeks of taking 3 capsules of bone meal a day, this condition miraculously cleared up. I could drink the coldest water without experiencing pain in that tooth. I had a friend who I knew suffered from the same condition. I gave him some of the bone meal capsules and the same thing happened to him. No more pain on drinking cold water. At this writing my family has been taking bone meal for about 15 years without noticeable harm to our system and we believe it is a factor in the reduction of our cavities in the teeth. Some of the family forget to take it from time to time and suffer more from cavities than the others.

The attitude of the dental profession has been that bone meal is not a factor in reducing caries (cavities in teeth). Many dentists have told me that once the tooth is formed the fluorine that we take in cannot become a part of it. But the evidence that I have assembled seems to indicate that it can—both in children and adults. The dentists prefer to paint the fluorine on the outside of the teeth. But I am sure that after you read the material herein presented, you will be convinced that the best way to get fluorine is through bone meal.

CHAPTER 252

Bone Meal and Dental Caries

Conclusive proof that supplementation of the average American diet with bone meal capsules will bring tooth decay to a virtual standstill is to be found in the testimony of S. G. Harootian, D.M.D., visiting oral surgeon of the Worcester City Hospital, Worcester, Massachusetts. In March of 1943 he read before the Dental Society of that city a paper on "The Influence of Administration of Bone Flour on Dental Caries" (published in the *Journal of the American Dental Association* in September of that same year). Revelation of the results achieved in Dr. Harootian's experiment is so sensational as to merit in full the plea contained in the end of his report: "If by so simple an expedient as the addition of bone flour to the dietary, significant increase in the resistance to dental caries can be secured, the boon should be withheld with the general population no longer than is necessary."

"How long is necessary?" is a logical question to ask at this time. For Dr. Harootian's charitable and humane words were spoken as long ago as 1943 and still the epoch-making success of his work has brought no "boon" to caries-riddled American mouths. We consequently feel that, whether further intervening experimentation has convinced the experts of the efficacy of bone meal in the prevention of tooth decay or has failed to do so, prescription of it is at least worth the try in the attainment of such a bright goal. Readers cannot fail to be convinced by the remarkable results effected by Dr. Harootian's simple approach to the problem.

Dazzled by Dr. Edward Taylor's account of the extraordinary dental health of residents of Deaf Smith County, Texas, he pondered over the possibility of supplementing the diet of Americans less favored geographically with the wonder-working ingredients responsible for the miraculous state of affairs there. After learning that meal from the bones of beef animals is rich in the Texas-prescribed calcium, phosphorus and fluorine, and that this

[948]

readily procurable product exists in unlimited supply, he needed only to be assured that its fluorine content was not too high, in order to embark on his simple test.

Dr. Harootian's Test

Nine patients were chosen from the Research Service of the Worcester State Hospital to be the beneficiaries of his project. All of them suffering major mental disorders of a psychotic type, the resultant slovenliness in personal hygiene, listless psychological torpor and dietary indifference that characterizes patients of this sort might have been expected to take a heavy toll in their general health records including teeth. This was indeed the case, for all had a higher-than-average rate of tooth decay. According to the authoritative work of C. F. Bodecker, "Modified Dental Caries Index" (*Journal of the American Dental Association,* September, 1939), which tabulates the caries incidence of the American people by means of actual statistics taken from the dental records, arranges them in age-brackets and secures from them the expectancy or likelihood of future decay for each group from the extensiveness of the caries noted in the records, these Worcester patients, averaging 34 years of age, should have exhibited approximately the caries average of 41.32 cited by Bodecker for the age-group of 30 to 34. A staggering total, this estimate of normal American dental health underlines the stark fact that, in Dr. Harootian's words, "Our population (to judge from this sample) is considerably more than normally subject to caries."

But in the case of his patients he found an even grimmer picture of dental disease and a sad commentary on the state of American knowledge of dental nutrition. All of them displaying a frightful amount of missing teeth, fillings and new carious surfaces, their decay-average had climbed to the ominously altitudinous peak of 54! And whereas dental statistics compiled by Bodecker estimate average future decay susceptibility at this age to be 9.01, theirs—without Dr. Harootian's proposed preventive treatment —would surely have soared to even more astronomical heights, had they continued untreated in their higher-than-average tempo.

Commencing with January 29, 1942, and extending over a period of 9 months, each patient was given 3 daily five-grain capsules of bone meal with an individual content of about 320 milligrams, 89 milligrams of which were composed of calcium, 45 of phosphorus and 0.31 of fluorine. No other change or vitamin supplementation was made in the normal hospital diet served throughout the study period, so that if any improvement were to be noted, it could not be ascribed to any factor other than the bone meal capsules. The dental condition of all 9 patients was carefully watched and meticulous notes were taken in each case once every month, in order to record the appearance of any new cavities or alterations in the state of existing ones since administration of the bone meal to their diets had been begun.

The Results—"Gratifying"

At the termination of the test period nine months later, Dr. Harootian tabulated results which he calls "gratifying," a very mild word indeed with which to describe them. In all 9 cases there had occurred no progress in caries deterioration at all, a fact which the experimenting dentist believes necessary to explain on the basis of a complete cessation of all decay that must have started practically as soon as the first bone meal capsules made their effects felt on the patients' systems. Treatment with them had reduced the index of susceptibility to future caries from Bodecker's 9.01 plus to an absolute zero in the cases of 8 patients and to a possibility of only one more cavity in the case of the ninth. As another piece of incontrovertible evidence in support of the prodigious efficacy of bone meal, Dr. Harootian cites the case of a gum cavity in one of the patients. This had been drilled to be fitted with a filling but then had been left in a dangerously exposed condition by never being protected with one. Though at each of the 8 monthly check-ups accumulated food debris had to be excavated from it, those deposits that would have given encouraging hospitality to bacterial microbes in even a healthy mouth had in no way at all undermined the dentin or enamel enclosing the hole in the tooth. Both had grown strong and impervious to any further action of decay, and this incredible regeneration of health in the sick tooth could be assigned to only one cause—feeding of that tooth with the vitalizing ingredients found in bone meal.

The Important Constituent

In accounting for the miracle he and the bone meal had wrought, Dr. Harootian inclines to attribute it not so much to the slight additional supplements of calcium and phosphorus contributed to his patients' total diet (already containing enough of these elements to have made their beneficial effects felt to some degree), but rather to the fluorine present in the bone meal. In support of this now idly debated contention as to whether fluorine does any real dietary benefit to a tooth that is already erupted and mature, he cites the work with dogs by F. J. McClure ("Fluorides Acquired by Mature Dogs' Teeth," *Science,* March 6, 1942), who was also successful in increasing the fluorine content of enamel and dentin in his subjects by adding sodium fluoride to their daily digestive intakes, despite the fact that other experts queried on the subject were emphatic in saying—without putting the matter to a test, however—that a fully grown tooth cannot be fed fluorine through dietary channels. Putting them to the right about, McClure produced dog enamel that contained 0.011 per cent of fluorine as contrasted with the 0.006 per cent content of the enamel in control dogs he had not fed fluoride. This ratio corresponds to and is compatible with the 0.0069 content of fluorine found in the enamel of carious human teeth as versus the 0.0111 per cent in healthy noncarious ones.

Though Dr. Harootian envisages the possibility that the most important share of the credit for caries-prevention should be ascribed to neither the calcium, the phosphorus nor the fluorine as found individually or in combination in the bone meal, but to "some (other) unidentified and unrecognized constituent," to the layman it is surely not important to haggle over the particular ingredient on which to pin the medal. Suffice it to recall that McClure's experiments with dogs and Dr. Harootian's treatment of 9 seemingly hopeless cases of pernicious advanced caries were both eminently successful by reason of one or more of the constituents. Consequently, if bone meal does the job (and it does!), it is better prevention to take it internally than to take it apart analytically.

CHAPTER 253

Powdered Beef Bone

A chapter from *Fifty Years A Country Doctor*
By *William N. Macartney, M.D.*
Copyright, 1938, by E. P. Dutton & Co., Inc.

Much has been written of late years regarding deficiency in calcium salts. A review of the literature on this subject is not necessary here since I think that we are all prepared to admit that our present-day dietary is deficient in the mineral intake. It seems self-evident. Our dentist bills are enormous. Rickets, osteomalacia, bowlegs, knock-knees, delayed closure of fontanelles, retarded dentition and imperfect teeth, the dental neuralgia of pregnancy, dental caries, pyorrhea, crockery teeth on vulcanite plates, caries, necrosis and delayed union of fractures and many other affections attest this, the almost universal use of calcium lactate, calcium chloride and other lime salts, the syrups of hypophosphites of calcium and magnesium for various conditions from rickets to hemophilia, is added evidence. Of late, a large number of diseases the origin of which had been a puzzle, have been proved to be due to calcium deficiency.

Take another slant at this question. How often do you see a dog with decayed teeth, or for that matter any other domestic animal? The primitive and savage races are largely exempt from dental caries. If we filed our teeth to sharp points, as many of these do, how long would we have them? (Though I did once dig up a human skull from an ancient burial mound in the Florida Everglades, and found a well-marked cavity in the second lower molar.) Why are they so practically free from dental decay? It is largely a matter of diet.

Take the matter of dental caries and pyorrhea. The dentist tells us that only by the most careful hygiene of the mouth can these things be prevented; that they are due to invasion of various germs; that once the enamel is destroyed, it is never regenerated; that we must never crack nuts, or be otherwise rude to our teeth, lest bridge-work or a dental plate befall us; that we must never use a gritty tooth powder.

What about the dog who never uses any of the much radioed dental creams, who rolls his bone in the grit of a macadam road and crunches it down? Who supplies him with gold crowns? Does he brush his teeth thrice daily with Glisterine? Or Get-hep-so-dent? His excrement, when exposed to the weather, turns white from the excess lime which it contains. What of the horse? When his teeth are gone, he is usually scrapped, sometimes to make one brand of beef extract, as I happen to know. But when his teeth are worn out, and he is fit only for the tannery and the glue factory, he is showing many other evidences of a ripe old age. A man is as old as his arteries, and a horse is as old as his teeth.

Just as long as we de-mineralize our wheat, giving the bran to our domestic animals, just so long as we eat the meat and throw the bone to Fido, just so long, I believe, we and our children will go to the dentist. "When the enamel is gone, the case is hopeless." When the blacksmith wears out the skin on his palms, do they remain forever raw and bleeding? Are cows subject to pyorrhea?

There is no greater heresy than a half-truth. It seems to me that the cause lies far deeper than the prevalent view; that it is more a matter of defective nutrition coupled with a faulty metabolism. If you keep your chickens confined all winter in our cold climate, without plaster, bone meal, or oyster shell, they lay soft-shelled eggs. Feed our women on sugar, candies, white bread, from which most of the phosphates have been removed, on marshmallow creams, on decorticated rice, and they will lay soft-shelled eggs in the way of children who cut teeth with difficulty, whose teeth are discolored and blackened when they first appear, children whose fontanelles fail to close on time, whose legs crook under them, who develop lateral curvature.

The pregnant mother is prone to dental neuralgia and caries. She tells us that she had good teeth until she raised her family. A mother will sacrifice much for her children, some of it unconsciously. She gives of her teeth frequently to supply mineral elements for the child unborn. She suffers from dental neuralgia, from lumbago-like pains in the back, from sacro-iliac trouble. If I recall aright my Sunday School lessons, the Israelites were given the task of making bricks without straw. Is this horse sense, cow sense, or non-sense?

What is the remedy for calcium starvation? Or, is it wholly a calcium starvation. Chemists tell us that bone, aside from its organic constituents, is chiefly composed of calcium phosphate in the form of tricalcium phosphate. Next in order comes calcium carbonate with a moderate amount of calcium fluoride. Then magnesium phosphate, and a host of other mineral ingredients which it is not necessary to mention, others as yet undetermined. Some of the latter, like the iodine in the thyroid, though small in amount, may be indispensable. Are we quite sure that the administration of a calcium salt with or without violet rays, with or without magnesium, the vitamins, is all that is required? We have not yet succeeded in producing a synthetic egg, a good milk from coal tar, a juicy sirloin from sawdust, by any cracking process as we produce gasoline. The time has not yet arrived when calcium gluconate will supply all deficiencies. We make vanillin from coal tar, but we are as yet unable to make a synthetic vanilla bean, or even the ordinary bean of the Boston addict. The synthetic breakfast, the chemical dinner, the coal-tar supper is still in the misty future.

We still lack knowledge of the exact composition of bone and dentine. A slight difference in the proportions of the atoms in the molecule makes the difference between drinking water and peroxide of hydrogen, between calomel and corrosive sublimate. The difference between bone, dentine and enamel is largely a difference in proportion of mineral and animal matter, a difference in density and other physical qualities, likewise, no doubt, a difference in the combinations of the atom in the molecule. Until these essential differences are more fully determined, we will do well to depend on natural foods rather than chemical compounds. We will get more consistent returns, better dividends on the whole, by giving bone flour rather than calcium salts made in the chemical laboratory.

Bone meal, bone flour, prepared from fresh clean bones, contains all the necessary salts in proper proportion for assimilation. It is a natural food, physiological, harmless, can be given safely in any dose, in capsule, in tablet, in meat gravy, in cod-liver oil emulsion, in various foods. When given in a liquid mixture, some preservative must be added if it is not to be used at once, since decomposition may occur. It is, of course, incompatible with acids.

In certain conditions, it is as near a specific cure as anything we are likely to meet within this vale of tears. In the dental neuralgia of pregnancy, I give one oo size (very small) capsule of it once a day. It has been my frequent experience that the patient told me the neuralgia disappeared after taking the first capsule. In no case, so far, has it failed to furnish much relief. I have been testing it out in the morning sickness of pregnancy of late. I can only recommend it as worthy of further trial. One swallow, in capsule form, does not make a proper summary, and I have not yet collected sufficient data to care to put myself on record as to its efficacy in pyorrhea. I know what it will do in defective dentition. I have treated many cases of delayed union in fracture cases. In no case where the bones were in reasonable apposition have I failed to get sufficient callus formation and an eventual good union. I do not refer to cases where muscle or other tissue was interposed between the fragments. Such instances are not properly cases of delayed union. Here, bone meal would be useless.

In 1899, I had a case of acute osteomyelitis involving the entire shaft of the femur in which I cut from the great trochanter down the outer aspect of the thigh to the knee, channeling the bone through the length of the shaft. I put him on bone flour and got a complete involucrum through which I chiseled later, removing the necrosed shaft. He made an excellent recovery without shortening, deformity, or any loss of function. He became a baseball player.

Another typical case. A young girl on the St. Regis Indian Reservation had a neglected case quite similar in every way. Spontaneous fracture of the femur occurred while she was very ill in bed. I was called. I drained the abscess, put the leg under extention, fed her bone meal. Later, the shaft was removed piecemeal, since it was badly disorganized. She was married this year. Her leg is straight; she is free from any lameness or disability. Beyond the scars of the operation, there is no deformity.

Bone flour of good quality is procurable from some of our large meat-packing houses. It is inexpensive. It is safe to use under almost any conceivable condition where such treatment is indicated. It has proven itself of great service in my practice. I can recommend it with the utmost confidence as above indicated, and it is deserving of a more thorough trial than at the hands of a few general practitioners. In this way, and in this way only, can its utility be either confirmed or disproved, its use extended, and its proper scope and limitations defined.

I have purposely omitted any general discussion of the therapeutic action of the calcium salts, the action of the parathyroids, etc., for obvious reasons. I only hope that someone with better facilities will investigate bone flour in conjunction with violet ray and the action of the glands referred to.

CHAPTER 254

Report on the Clinical
Use of Bone Meal

By Elizabeth M. Martin, M.D.

Because of the recent popular and professional interest in bone meal as a therapeutic agent we have considered that the records of our past 4 years' experience with it may be of interest and value to the profession.

The case for which this agent was first used extensively was that of the six-year-old son of one of our nurses. The child had a cleft palate and hare lip, both of which had been repaired before the age of two years. There was, however, a grave defect in his dentition, his primary teeth being very poor and having almost no covering enamel. He had gained only two pounds in the previous year. In consultation with our dentist, Dr. William J. Siebert, we decided to have these poor upper teeth removed. There was considerable question as to how sound the secondary teeth would be, but it was felt this would give them a better chance.

There were no further physical defects in the child, excepting his undernutrition. He complained bitterly of pains in his legs—the so-called "growing pains" of children. He was given a brand of dicalcium phosphate with vitamin D in 10-grain doses twice a day with some improvement in his symptoms but no weight gain and he had much restlessness with night terrors. His mother noticed that the little chamber he used at night was becoming encrusted with calcium deposit. We supposed from this that he was getting very little absorption of the calcium which he took.

It occurred to us that if we gave bone meal to calves and young pigs and puppies to promote proper growth, why should not nature's own combination of bone minerals be completely utilized by any animal body? Accordingly, we sifted and pulverized the available bone meal and filled 10-grain capsules by hand. In one week the child was playing as hard as any of his schoolmates. There was no more excess calcium deposit, although he was getting three 10-grain capsules daily. He began to grow and gain weight, until he caught up to the normal average for his age. His teeth were very slow to appear, it being about a year before his central incisors came through, but they were sound when they did arrive. He then made steady progress in the 3 years in which we had him under observation.

The results in this case were so striking and so immediate that we decided to run a series of cases. Any child complaining of "growing pains" or whose parents stated that he or she kicked and screamed in the night was put on calcium gr. xx daily, and alternate patients, on bone meal capsules gr. xx daily, with the minimum requirement of A and D as a supplement in each case. Records kept over a two-year period on 112 children showed complete remission of symptoms in all children on bone meal (57) and of 22 on dicalcium phosphate; with some complaints still, though not so marked, in the remaining 34 children. Just as a matter of curiosity these 34 were changed to bone meal and in all cases the symptoms disappeared.

We also had a small group of pregnant women who were very much interested in preserving their teeth during pregnancy, and in some cases the multiparae dreaded the dental neuralgia they had had to endure during previous pregnancies. All of these women agreed to have their teeth checked and all cavities repaired at 3 months' gestation, with a final check-up at the 6 weeks' examination. Dr. William J. Siebert, our dentist, kindly did all the dental work and kept dental charts for us. Twenty-five women were given 10-grain bone meal capsules 3 times a day (two of the women who would have been on dicalcium phosphate, thought it gave them heartburn, so they were changed over in the first week) and 20 women were given 15-grain dicalcium phosphate wafers twice daily during the last 6 months of pregnancy and the first 6 weeks of lactation. None of the women had dental neuralgia. Those who had suffered from this previously had never had supplementary medication during their former pregnancies. Each one of these women also received A and D; 7,500 units "A" and 750 "D" daily to ensure proper mineral metabolism. None of the women had aching legs or cramps in the legs at night nor cramps in the legs on delivery. All of the babies were healthy at birth, but those whose mothers had been given bone meal had such long silky hair and such long nails that the phenomenon was remarked upon by the nurses.

At the 6 weeks' examination all of the babies were doing very well and the mothers were healthy. About one-quarter of the babies were still breast-fed. The dental check-up revealed that not one woman on bone meal had a new dental cavity and the cavities for the other women averaged one and two-tenths per patient. The dentist stated that even this was well below the expected number following an unprotected pregnancy.

We use bone meal in place of any other form of calcium for all evidences of calcium deficiency in our patients, including muscular pains and cramps in the legs in both sedentary workers and laborers. The condition exists very widely because of the habit of most Canadians in ingesting a diet very low in calcium. All of these symptoms clear up promptly on 10 to 15 grains of bone meal daily. This is now supplied to us in a soft gelatin capsule containing finely pulverized meal from selected bones, combined with sufficient A and D to ensure absorption.

If vitamin D is to be effective as an aid to calcium metabolism, the calcium ingested must be at least the minimum requirement* and must be available for absorption. The availability appears to be greatly enhanced by using natural bone minerals without trying to make any alteration in nature's formula.

*Reference: 1. Jeans, P. C. and Stearns, G.: Physiol. Rev. 1939. 19:415. 67 King St. East.

Reprinted from the *Canadian Medical Association Journal,* June, 1944.

CHAPTER 255

Bone Meal for Minerals

In order to understand what you are getting when you take bone meal, let us review broadly a few simple facts of nutrition. In the constitution and functioning of the human body, proteins, carbohydrates, minerals and fats take part. Let us express it in a different manner. Our foods consist of two groups—organic and inorganic. The inorganic is water and mineral matter. The organic is proteins, fats and carbohydrates.

The proteins build the tissue of the body. The carbohydrates are mainly for the purpose of furnishing energy. Naturally we must have both of these, although the latest medical researches indicate that a high protein diet is best for optimum health. But an exceedingly important part of the diet is the mineral group and often there are serious deficiencies in this classification. Minerals are needed to carry out the physiological processes of the body. The rigidity of our skeleton depends on them. A lack can produce nervous irritability. They take part in digestion and are needed in the metabolic processes of the body. For example, iron is so important to the oxygen-carrying function of the blood. A lack of it causes one to fear and worry about things. Iodine is needed to prevent goiter. A lack of potassium will cause painful menstruation, and a shortage of magnesium will induce a lack of sex control. If there is too little sulfur there may be intestinal stasis, that is, a reducing of the peristaltic contractions of the stomach that are so important to good digestion.

We are supposed to get our minerals in our food—in the vegetables, fruits and meats that we eat. But with the modern methods of farming and the use of chemical fertilizers there is a progressive depletion in the mineral content of our foods and we must take it in the form of mineral supplements. Bone meal is ideally suited for this purpose. In the book, *Nutrition and Physical Fitness*, by L. Jean Bogert, M.D. (published by Saunders), there appears the statement: "The bulk of the mineral substances in the body is concentrated in the skeleton or bony framework." In the case of calcium 99 per cent is found in the skeletal framework, which includes the teeth. In the case of phosphorus 70 per cent is in the bone structure.

Dr. Henry C. Sherman of Columbia University expressed the same fact as follows in his book, *The Nutritional Improvement of Life* (Columbia University Press, 1950): "The body's framework or skeletal system of bones and teeth owes its strength and normal form to the fact of its being well mineralized. Smaller amounts of much more soluble mineral salts are constantly present in the soft tissues and fluids of the body." He refers to the minerals as "putting life into" the proteins of the body tissues and fluids.

Here is a statement from another source, *Dietary of Health and Disease*, by Gertrude I. Thomas, assistant professor of Dietetics, University of Minnesota (Lea and Febiger): "From 4 to 5 per cent of the body weight is mineral matter. It is found in all tissues and fluids, but especially in the bones, teeth and cartilage."

Bone Meal Analysis

Here is a typical analysis of raw bone meal as furnished in a letter from the United States Department of Agriculture dated September 1, 1950. This is an average figure from a number of samples:

	Per Cent		Per Cent
Sodium oxide (Na_2O)	0.46	Chlorine (Cl)	0.22
Potassium oxide (K_2O)	0.20	Carbon dioxide (CO_2)	1.59
Calcium oxide (CaO)	30.52	Phosphoric oxide (P_2O_5)	22.52
Magnesium oxide (MgO)	0.73	Boron oxide (B_2O_3)	TRACE
Barium oxide (BaO)	0.001	Fluorine (F)	0.043
Copper oxide (CuO)	0.0005	Iodine (I)	0.00002
Iron oxide (Fe_2O_3)	0.004	Sulfur (S)	0.25
Manganese oxide (MnO)	0.0014	Organic matter	34.88
Lead oxide (PbO)	0.005	Moisture	6.76
Zinc oxide (ZnO)	0.018		

Note the fact that it contains iodine. We see, therefore, that bone meal is not only important for good teeth but also as an insurance of general bodily health. In our typical modern diet there is no bone. Here is a wonderful way to include it. And we must remember that bone meal is not a medicine. It is a food.

There are ways of taking mineral supplements that you can purchase in a drug store but bone meal is safer because the minerals in bone are diffused in more natural proportions. There is no danger of an overdose.

In connection with the proper mineralization of the skeleton, much medical data exists that vitamin D promotes better absorption of minerals. This vitamin seems to exert some sort of controlling action, especially so in the process of calcification at the ends of growing bones and in the healing of bone fractures. Vitamin D is obtained by being out in the sun, but it should not be overdone in this form. Too much tanning is dangerous. Cod liver oil gives vitamin D. I recommend the combination of D and A made from fish liver oils. This and bone meal are blood-brothers.

In parting on this subject, bear in mind that you will get more minerals if you will consume food that is closest to its natural state. Avoid processed foods as much as possible. Eat your vegetables raw as much as is possible. Do not cook peas, for example. Cooking destroys minerals. Nature has created a delicate balance of minerals in plants and the less you change it the better, with a few exceptions, of course. To cook carrots is a crime against nature. Much of the mineral matter goes down the drain in the cooking waters that are thrown away, and then sugar is substituted to restore the taste. In the raw carrot, the minerals contributed their share toward the taste. Look to your minerals and they will look after you.

CHAPTER 256

Bone Meal Protects against Broken Bones

Broken bones are an alarmingly common occurrence in the United States. Lucky is the child who hasn't missed a summer of fun due to a broken limb, for most everyone can find a history of a bone fracture somewhere in his medical record. Why should such a condition exist? Surely normal play and exercise don't place undue strain on a healthy frame. That's what it is intended for! Yet the bones of modern Americans seem to become more brittle with every generation.

Ribs Broken by a Cough

One of the most incredible medical documents we've seen gives support to this assertion. In the *International Medical Digest* (January, 1958) the author of this article calls fractures of the rib, *due to coughing,* a common form of stress fracture. Other violent contractions, he goes on to say, such as sneezing or vomiting can also produce rib fractures. In a period of 6 years 28 cases of cough fractures of the ribs were seen by the author alone. Is it possible that the normal reflex of coughing could produce such dire results in a well-nourished, normal person's bones? We think not. The answer lies in brittle bones, bones that do not possess an essential resiliency and cohesiveness that lets bones give under stress without breaking. This condition is largely due to a lack of calcium. The importance of calcium is emphasized by James S. McLester, M.D., in his book, *Diet in Health and Diseases.* "Calcium forms 99 per cent of the skeleton. In addition it plays an essential role in many physiological processes . . . as is shown in the studies of Sherman, the diet of Americans is more likely to be faulty in respect to calcium than to any other mineral element."

In the *Annual Review of Biochemistry,* 12, 403-405 (1943), calcium gets another boost from Lanford and Sherman when they say, "Liberal calcium allowances are good for adults of both sexes and at all times . . . A liberal margin of intake above the literal requirements (.75 gram per day) for maintenance thus appears clearly desirable for all . . ."

Calcium Scarce Past Middle Age

It has been shown that older people are most likely to be short on calcium. Dr. Clive McCay, in the Cornell University Agriculture Experimental Station *Bulletin* for January, 1949, reported that studies at Iowa State College showed that older women lost calcium from their bodies faster than they could store it from food. It was further found that, after 60, the body needs as much calcium per day as one gets from a full quart of milk. Even persons who include milk in their diet seldom come near that requirement, and those who are convinced that milk is an undesirable food, as we are, must indeed be careful to include a definite supplementary source of calcium in their diet. There is no richer natural source than bone meal.

A Pioneer in the Use of Bone Meal

Bone meal is the fine dry powder obtained commercially by boiling bones to remove fat and most of the organic material, then drying with hot air and grinding. Of course, the consumption of bones is an innate instinct on the part of many animals, and primitive man followed suit. With the coming of civilization the practice was discontinued, and a valuable source of calcium was almost lost to man. In the mid-nineteenth century an interesting book was published by a German priest, Father Sebastian Kneipp, in which the use of bone was once more recommended as a health measure. Father Kneipp was what would probably be described today as a naturopath. He had worked out many self-cures of his own which he described in his book, *Wasser Kur (Water Cure)*, as well as passing on those traditional natural remedies that he had inherited from his predecessors. No one knows how or why he came to do so, since the facts of calcium and body chemistry were completely unknown at the time, but Father Kneipp had invented a process for making bone meal, and was using it with great effect among his people. He was probably one of the pioneers in bringing the advantages of bone meal to the attention of the civilized world and opening the way for modern methods and experiments. These facts were brought to our attention in a letter which we feel is most appropriate to this discussion. We quote:

"Dear Sir: I was immediately interested in your 'Bone Meal,' because it awakened memories and you may perhaps be interested in what I am going to tell you on that subject, (excuse my rambling!). It goes back to the first decade of the century. Still young, I was already a wreck; sick from top to toe, the chief miseries being excruciating weekly migraines and incessant trouble with chest and lungs. The doctor gave me 2 (two!) years to live and pronounced slow T.B. (in those days called 'Consumption').

"I was living, at the time, with German friends and so got to know all about 'Pastor Kneipp', and his wonderful, famous healing methods. Guided only by his book 'Wasser-Kur', I plunged into his methods, to the great alarm of my friends who were sure it meant premature death for me! And I know that I have to thank him for my slowly—*very* slowly—regaining strength and then health. I am now 79!

"But after reading your leaflet, I feel convinced that water, alone, did not do the trick. You have shown that bone meal is not only a build-up for teeth and bones, but definitely a germ-killer (witness the cure of pimples, rash, warts, etc.). And I used bone meal freely merely because Kneipp recommended it as a general *tonic* for the body. There was, I feel sure, never mention of *disinfecting* the system. But the fact is that in the course of 2 to 3 years, all symptoms of 'Consumption' disappeared—slow work, it may seem, but I was pretty far gone and at 40 I had a health as never before in my life and started—hiking!

"Well—that's all I can tell you but it's enough to make you understand my faith in your bone meal, and at my age, bones *need* new life put into them for they do get very brittle.

"Wishing you great success in your most useful work for health and happiness, I am, dear Sir,

> Faithfully yours,
>
> (Miss) Elizabeth Ryley
> Putney, London, England"

If bone meal did nothing other than give added strength and resistance to breakage to the bones of older people, its use would be well worth the effort. A broken bone in a person of advancing years can mean long immobility, lasting ill effects and even death. Obviously the avoidance of such a calamity is to be pursued devoutly. A daily dose of calcium in the form of bone meal is an easy way to accomplish this goal.

Frequent Falls Among Older Folks

The tendency in older persons to fall is one of the main causes of broken bones in that age bracket. A study of the problem is discussed in *Medical Press* (October 9, 1957) by Dr. Stanley Firth. Dr. Firth prefaces his finding by stating that as one grows older one must come to rely more on care and thought to compensate for slower skeletal or physical response. Should a throw-rug slip out from under foot, a young person's reflexes and muscular coordination are likely to save him from a bad fall, an older person is seldom in possession of such keen powers of recovery. Therefore, nature warns older persons to move more carefully and to attempt to foresee accidents before they happen.

Physical Disabilities Cause Many Falls

Oftentimes some physical problem will afflict an older person, making even the utmost care in walking useless in avoiding falls. One of the most common of these problems is a reduction of adequate blood supply to the brain. This can result in slower mental response, giddiness, blackouts, fainting or a feeling of uncertainty. All of these, of course, increase one's tendency to fall. A number of things can cause this shortage of blood supply in the brain, the most common are vascular disorders due to degeneration of blood vessels, cardiac conditions, nutritional deficiencies (iron deficiency anemia) or faulty metabolism as in cases of diabetes.

Arthritis and other disturbances of the joints can contribute to the likelihood of falls by robbing the older walker of sureness of footing. Muscles of the legs gone weak from decreased activity make lifting the feet more difficult and result in the shuffling gait common to the elderly. It is easy to see that such a gait leaves the walker open to catching his feet in the edges of mats, rugs, stair treads or sidewalk gutters. A fall is often the result. Obesity is another condition which can lead to falls in the elderly by cutting down on what precious mobility a person has, as well as by leading to a number of the other conditions described above.

Finally, defects in sight, so common in persons of long life, contribute mightily to the danger of falls. Poor eyesight, preventing one from perceiving potential hazards, is yet another disadvantage to an older person, already handicapped by slower reflexes.

In the case of hearing loss the problem is twofold: the person is not likely to hear warnings of unsafety, nor can he depend on proper balance, since the body's center of equilibrium lies in the inner ear and can be affected by diseases which affect the hearing itself.

Now the logical thing would be to avoid as much as possible any of the conditions described above. Good diet and proper exercise will do a lot in that direction. However, even elderly people who are well and healthy face the possibility of falling sometimes. Don't let that fall mean prolonged convalescence or worse, due to a broken bone. Make your body ready to withstand hard bumps. Keep replenishing the skeleton's supply of calcium. Don't let your body lose more of this vital mineral than it takes in. The relationship between healthy bones and calcium-rich bone meal is not to be ignored by anyone interested in getting and keeping a healthy skeleton. Add bone meal to your diet today!

CHAPTER 257

What They've Been Doing with Bone Marrow

What is a doctor to do when he has tried all of the conventional methods of treatment and the patient's condition continues to grow worse? Sometimes he gives up and sometimes he puts two and two together and comes up with a new idea that's worth a try. Dr. Thomas Fraser reported in the *British Medical Journal* (June 2, 1894) on his idea of treating anemia, and other doctors might well refer to his finding today.

Anemia is a condition in which the body either does not produce enough blood, or produces blood of such poor quality that it does not permit the body to carry on its proper functions. Dr. Fraser was treating a man, aged 60, who had all of the worst symptoms of anemia—frequent vomiting, diarrhea, swelling of the feet and ankles, fever, dimness of vision, dizziness, hemorrhages of the retina and, finally, complete helplessness. The standard treatment for anemia had been instituted, and the only result was an even further deterioration of the blood.

Bone Marrow Manufactures Blood

Dr. Fraser was aware that the function of bone marrow is to manufacture blood in the body. He reasoned that bone marrow taken by mouth might supply the element missing in his patient's marrow, the factor needed for an adequate supply of good blood. So after 5 weeks of the arsenic-iron treatment, Dr. Fraser began to add 3 ounces of uncooked ox-bone marrow to his patient's diet each day. The marrow was taken by mouth.

A rapid improvement followed: the patient soon recovered his strength and weight. At the end of 4 months the quality of the blood was much improved and could be classed almost as normal. He felt strong and enjoyed doing light manual work. In 8 months he was discharged as fit to return to his job as a laborer.

Dr. I. N. Danforth wrote in the *Chicago Clinical Review* (October, 1894) of a similar experience. His patient also showed every hopeless sign of anemia. After trying every resource of treatment he knew, Dr. Danforth was of the opinion that recovery seemed impossible. He then happened by chance to read of Dr. Fraser's experience with bone marrow. The patient began an intake of one tablespoon of a bone marrow mixture after each meal. In 4 weeks the hemoglobin (the red, oxygen-carrying protein of the blood) had increased from a low reading of 35 per cent to a normal 80 per cent, and the patient presumably recovered. (Editor's note: Both of these cases were mentioned in a clinical lecture delivered at the Post Graduate Medical School by John A. Robinson, M.D.)

Bone Marrow Against Radiation

In recent times a new threat has been posed to the proper formation of healthy blood. That threat is nuclear radiation. Recently it was discovered that the marrow of bones somehow offers some protection from the harmful effects of radiation. The National Cancer Institute in their August, 1951, *Journal* reported that if a few milligrams of bone marrow, from an animal that had not been subjected to radiation, were injected into one that was exposed, within an hour after exposure to X-rays or deadly radioactivity, the exposed animal was protected from damage.

The human extension of these findings occurred in February of 1959. Five Yugoslavians were brought to Curie Hospital in Paris for treatment after an accident in an atomic center in which they worked had resulted in their serious exposures to radiation. There was a shortage of white corpuscles in their blood. It was decided to transfuse bone marrow directly into their bones. This had never before been done successfully because in previous trials the bone marrow was affected adversely by antibodies in the blood. In the case of the Yugoslavs, however, it was believed that the antibodies were affected by the radiation and could not operate against the bone marrow. After the transfusions, says the story in the *New York Herald Tribune* (February 17, 1959) the survivors were able once more to produce the vital white corpuscles in sufficient quantities and were headed toward recovery. From these few indications it would appear that bone marrow is likely to become as potent a weapon against the effects of an atomic war as it is against anemia.

If bone marrow can help in curing anemia and radiation damage, might we not assume that a frequent intake of bone marrow will help to protect us against anemia altogether, and tone down the deadly effects of excessive exposure to radiation, if we should be exposed? In Europe people eat bone marrow pretty regularly. Among their knives and forks is included a special tool for digging the marrow from cooked bones at the dinner table. While we know little about bone marrow's mysterious nutritional reserves, we do know that this is the stuff that produces our red blood cells, and we know that it is used in medicine as a treatment for diseases marked by the blood's incapacity to renew itself. It is obviously, therefore, a valuable addition to the diet. But when was the last time you had some bone marrow to eat? Have you ever had it? Does anybody you know crack the bones, from, say, a roast to scoop out the marrow?

A Perfect Answer in Homogenized Whole Bone

It is almost two years since we came across homogenized whole bone, a product which is pure bone and which has been pulverized into a paste by means of a special process which does not involve exposure to high heat. This means that none of the nutrients contained in bones are lost as they are in most processing. And not only does one get the marrow in homogenized bone, but the complete bone—the minerals that are contained in bone meal and the protein, which is normally lost when bones are made into bone meal. Formerly bones have been subjected to high heat in order to process them for edibility. By a newly discovered process fresh bones of U.S. Government-inspected animals are selected directly from cutting tables and still holding whatever connective tissue is left by the trimmers. By purely physical means these bones are broken down into smaller particles—homogenized—finally reduced to such fineness that they emerge from the process in a form close to jelly. One cannot help but be impressed by the nutritional quality of the final product. Aside from a calcium content equal to 3 dozen quarts of whole milk and a phosphorus content surpassing that of 6 dozen eggs, a pound of homogenized whole bone also offers as much protein as a pound of raw beef and iron equal to that found in 1½ pounds of fresh liver. In that same pound of homogenized whole bone you will find vitamins A, B_1, B_2, niacin, pantothenic acid, a trace of B_6, biotin, vitamin D and a trace of vitamin E. This is not to say that homogenized whole bone is an ideal source of vitamins, for many food supplements are richer in this or that vitamin, but a fabulous source of minerals endowed with a respectable vitamin content as well is a bonus well worth having.

Bone Meal or Whole Bone?

Ever since the first announcement of homogenized whole bone was made, readers have been asking us whether they should abandon bone meal for this new product. The answer is a personal one, for only you know what kind of a diet you eat, and the food supplements you take. The main value of homogenized whole bone is that it is a complete food, offering minerals as well as vitamins and protein. The process which maintains these values is an expensive one, and the cost is reflected in the price of the finished product. It is, therefore, up to you to decide whether you are getting the "extras" offered by homogenized whole bone from other sources, or if you must depend on this new supplementary food for your needs. Are you getting as much protein as you should have from your regular diet and supplements?

Do you take brewer's yeast or wheat germ as a source of B vitamins? If you are already meeting your need for these nutrients, then you can save some by buying bone meal as a source of calcium, phosphorus and other minerals, for bone meal is unsurpassed as a source for minerals alone.

However, if you have trouble getting sufficient protein, or if you must eat foods cooked in such a way that their values are diminished or lost entirely, or if you depend upon the one-a-day, all-in-one type of supplement, homogenized whole bone is for you. The all-in-ones must, of necessity, omit much of the original food which contains the natural vitamins and minerals. You simply couldn't swallow a capsule big enough to have such complete foods including proteins and trace elements in it. Homogenized whole bone has them. It has whatever food value a fresh, unprocessed, uncooked bone has—and that's a good deal. Take stock of your diet and your supplements; homogenized whole bone might be just the thing you need to round out your nutritional program.

CHAPTER 258

An Example Where Bone Meal Was of Help

By J. I. Rodale

On a recent trip to Florida I met Dr. Mathewson, a dentist, and when I mentioned the value of taking bone meal he told me an interesting story. I had him write me a letter describing his case and here it is:

Dear Mr. Rodale,

In November, 1950, I had a severe attack of tetany which made my muscles all over my body other than the legs so sore that I was crippled for 3 days afterward. This attack occurred in a hotel while I was away visiting a friend. When the hotel physician was summoned he injected ¼ grain of morphine sulphate with atropine. This treatment relieved the symptoms and produced relaxation of the affected muscles.

The next morning I was removed to the home of friends and their family physician was called. His tentative diagnosis was paratyphoid infection. Subsequent tests disproved this diagnosis. After 3 days I had sufficiently recovered to return to the University where I was studying Dentistry.

A week later I felt the same pre-tetany symptoms coming over me. I immediately went next door to the hospital and was admitted and put to sleep with a large dose of barbiturate. For three days students, graduates, and members of the faculty gave me a thorough going-over including blood phosphorus and calcium which were both within normal limits. It was inferred that my trouble was more in my mind, than in my body; that I was overly tired (which was true) and I was discharged at my own request.

I was not satisfied with this explanation of things and I consulted a physician who also was a Ph.D. in Physiology. He stated that my trouble was due to a lack of ionizable calcium which would not show up in a blood calcium test. He prescribed calcium lactate. I took this for several months and my troubles ceased. Occasionally, for the past 8 or 10 years I have taken some form of calcium. The organic salts are the only ones that are effective. Dicalcium phosphate is not absorbed and does no good.

In October of 1948 I suffered an acute heart failure. This responded to a digitalis derivative which was discontinued after about 4 weeks. My blood pressure was 264/214. I took mannitol hexinitrate and phenobarbital for 6 weeks and rested in bed. The pressure came down to 180/90. I eliminated coffee, tea, alcohol, tobacco, and physical exercise until the following February when the showers of extra-systoles ceased. I drank about one cup of coffee per day for a month and a half.

In the latter part of March 1949 I suffered an acute tetany attack. I had been taking up to 12 capsules of dicalcium phosphate with viosterol daily. It took 15 cc of calcium levulate intravenously to bring me out of this attack. About the same time I had a strange sensation in my abdomen, like going down a roller coaster. My feet and hands were icy cold, my pressure rose a bit, the minute volume output of my heart increased, and I had a sensation of impending death.

These attacks were repeated at frequent intervals several times daily without the tetany (I was having intravenous calcium) until after a week I was taken to the hospital during a very severe attack. I had a low blood sugar, low blood calcium, high white count, blood in the stool and casts in the urine. Diagnosis: kidney infection, bowel infection, heart OK, pressure 145/90. The roller coaster feeling, etc., diagnosed as vagal attack or vago-vagii syndrome. I was given a complete check up to eliminate the possibilities of adrenal tumor, duodenal ulcer, colitis and nephritis. All were negative. However, I still had the vagal attacks several times daily, and need I say that after the first half hour of that roller coaster feeling all the thrill was worn off.

Streptomycin cleared up the infections and lowered the white count. Glucose solution and vitamins were given intravenously and sucrose by mouth. Everything else healed up, but after the vagal attacks continued, I was discharged from the hospital after a week. I was taking 14 mms of tincture of belladonna 5 times daily to attempt to control the vagal attacks. Their intensity was lessened, but I still had them. After 3 weeks I had another complete gastro-intestinal examination. The only finding was a slight spasm in the duodenum.

Over a year's period I gradually was able to reduce the dosage of belladonna to 3 to 5 drops three times daily. I had 5 or 6 attacks per month, with several dozen light attacks which did not put me in bed.

Finally, I felt that I didn't want to take that drug any more, and I thought the attacks might be related to my faulty absorption of calcium. Accordingly I started on the bone meal, made from raw dehydrated veal bone without heat processing. In a month I had stopped taking belladonna entirely, and had but a dozen or so small attacks, and no big attack. After two months on the bone meal I stopped taking it. Four days later I had a big vagal attack. I was given intravenous calcium, and the attack was arrested immediately. Five times, I deliberately stopped taking bone meal, and each time after a period of 3 or 4 days I had a big attack. By this time (6 months) I didn't even have the little attacks anymore. I have continued to take one or two heaping teaspoons of bone meal daily and two Catalyn tablets and one vitamin F daily. I have had no recurrence of the attacks except on two occasions when I became very upset emotionally. Then I had big attacks. Two vitamin F tablets relieved these attacks in about half an hour.

Since taking bone meal I have a better sense of well-being and pep.

Sincerely, Richard L. Mathewson, D.D.S.
Miami Beach, Florida

CHAPTER 259

Do You Really Need Bone Meal?

The Aquarium at Golden Gate Park, San Francisco, lost two of their prize alligators one day, when they died mysteriously within hours of one another. An autopsy revealed that the alligators' bones were mushy, indicating a lack of calcium. A quick revision in diet was made to save the rest of the alligators. They had been receiving fresh horse meat, cut up without any bones. The new diet consisted of fish and horse meat, stuffed with bone meal and cod liver oil—bone meal for calcium and other minerals, cod liver oil for the vitamin D necessary for calcium assimilation.

A letter from Earl S. Herald, Curator of Aquatic Biology at the Aquarium tells us that bone meal is used as a normal constituent of the Aquarium's prepared food. "This is primarily as a guard against calcium deficiency and seems to be most important in turtles and alligators," says he. An alligator, in his native jungle, gets plenty of calcium, for he eats his meat, bones and all. His river-home is flooded with tropical sunshine all day long. But when he is placed in an aquarium in a northern country and fed a boneless diet, things go from bad to worse for him very rapidly.

A release from the Canadian Press relates an incident in Macleod, Alberta, where a man who had shot a bob cat received a request from a Chinese restaurant proprietor for the animal's bones. He wanted them to prepare a prescription for a rheumatism cure—a very ancient cure handed down in his family, no doubt. Older generations than ours in all countries have known the value of bone minerals in diet.

Can Ample Calcium Prevent Cancer?

The *Chicago Tribune* for March 29, 1952, underlines once again the vital importance of the calcium for a healthy body. Dr. Ralph Jones, Assistant Professor of Medicine at the University of Pennsylvania, told a conference of science writers that his researchers suggest the possibility that cancer cells may spread and scatter to other parts of the body because they lack sufficient calcium. The theory that Dr. Jones then elaborated on is consistent with the efforts of cancer researchers to find a cure for cancer. He indicated that "diet alone will not do the trick" says the article, "for example, more calcium cannot be forced into the cells merely by drinking more milk." Instead he suggested that researchers are investigating the possibility of injecting bone marrow into human beings to make them more resistant to excessive X-ray radiation needed to kill some cancers.

This is, of course, the emphasis that a cancer-cure researcher would place on such a discovery. But where are the researchers who are working on cancer prevention? Why have they not investigated the results of available calcium in the diet from childhood on, *as a preventive of cancer?* The mere suggestion of calcium deficiency as a possible cause of cancer should be enough to start a nation-wide clamor for bone meal, rich in calcium that is easily assimilated, and phosphorus which works in combination with calcium in the body's laboratory.

In *The Healthy Hunzas,* Editor Rodale's book on the healthiest people in the world living in northern India, he describes the diet of the Hunzas: flat bread made of wholemeal wheat flour, lightly smeared with butter, sprouted pulse, fresh raw carrots and cabbage, milk, a small amount of meat with bones once a week and plenty of water. In an experiment conducted by Sir Robert McCarrison, 1,189 rats were put on this same diet with the result that "both clinically and at post mortem examinations this stock has been shown to be remarkably free from disease." The bone meal used was undoubtedly an important factor. The Hunzas would not be the healthy individuals they are without the addition of bone to their weekly diet.

Calcium in Pregnancy

Without sufficient calcium and phosphorus in the diet of a pregnant woman, says Edward Podolsky, M.D., writing in the March, 1952, issue of *Parents* magazine, the baby's bones and teeth will not develop properly. In addition to preserving the mother's teeth during pregnancy and assuring the excellence of the baby's teeth and bones, calcium also helps the blood in clotting—an aid to the mother in childbirth. It improves nerves and muscles, especially the muscles of the heart. The requirement for calcium is more than doubled during pregnancy, so that the expectant mother should make certain she is getting enough. Dr. Podolsky did not advise bone meal. But we predict many doctors will, when they become familiar with its use for human beings.

One of our readers told us about the experience of a friend of hers who wanted desperately to have a baby. She was in good health, but had an allergy to milk. She was afraid she would not be able to bear a healthy baby without drinking any milk at all during her pregnancy. Her friend suggested that she take bone meal instead. She consulted her doctor who agreed that it was worth trying. The last we heard, this mother and her new baby were both happy and well.

The wife of one of our staff members of PREVENTION was concerned about the effect of pregnancy on her teeth. She had always had poor teeth and, though she made a point of eating a good diet, she was afraid that the unborn baby's share of her calcium would result in many more cavities for her. She bought bone meal tablets which she took every day during her pregnancy. The fine baby boy is now six months old. For the first time in her life there was a report of "no cavities" when his mother visited her dentist the other day.

The Calcium-Phosphorus Ratio Is Very Important

An experiment with the diet of minks, reported in the *Journal of Nutrition* for July 10, 1950, demonstrates well just why bone meal brings about such uniformly excellent results. Newly weaned minks were fed a diet deficient in vitamin D and containing .06 per cent calcium and .54 per cent phosphorus. They were confined away from sunshine and, sure enough, bone weaknesses developed. Two weeks of daily sunshine or the addition of one per cent bone meal to their diet produced good healing of the bone condition.

It has been recognized by nutritionists for some time that, for healthy bones and teeth, not only must there be enough calcium and vitamin D (preferably from the sun) but the calcium-phosphorus balance in the body must be maintained at the proper level. How to achieve this balance by diet has not been determined. But, as the experiment with minks demonstrates and as the experiences of many individuals indicate, bone meal in itself supplies the proper proportions. This seems completely reasonable, since bone meal is made from the bones of healthy young cattle. The calcium-phosphorus ratio must have been correctly balanced in these cattle or they would have shown evidence of bone disease.

Calcium and Middle Age

Just one final note on the importance of sufficient calcium. The famous nutritionist, Henry C. Sherman of Columbia University, writing in *Nutrition Reviews* for April, 1952, reports the following comment by Dr. F. J. Stare in 1942, before the Conference on Nutrition in Relation to Public Health: "In speaking of his hospital experience, Dr. Stare stated 'It was a surprise to me to see that the majority of X-ray studies of adults past the age of 45 to 50 years showed considerable demineralization of bone and one wondered if low dietary intake of calcium or of vitamin D over many years might not have been prominent factors in the (cause) of this demineralization'."

What choice do you have, then, for yourself and your children? Well, you can take some synthetic calcium preparation which may do actual harm by disturbing your calcium-phosphorus balance. Or, fretting over the children's cavities, you can have their teeth treated with 'inorganic fluoride (a deadly poison) either in drinking water or by application in a dentist's office, with no assurance that there will be any lasting benefit, let alone no eventual harm.

Or you can take bone meal, a natural product, in which all the mineral elements that constitute healthy bone structure, in nature, are combined exactly as nature combines them, nothing added, nothing substracted. Remember that scientists have not analyzed as yet the entire composition of bone. But bone meal must and does contain it all, known and unknown. You may take it in tablet or capsule form with your meals or in powdered form, on cereal or in baked food. Bone meal is your safest, surest food supplement, for minerals, including the all-important calcium and phosphorus.

CHAPTER 260

Bone Meal—An Essential for You

Of all the various food elements, calcium is the one most widely deficient in American diets, according to most nutrition experts. Says Henry C. Sherman in his book, *Calcium and Phosphorus in Foods and Nutrition,* published by Columbia University Press, "Evidences of calcium deficiency are not usually clear-cut, so probably a great deal of it goes undetected," and "there is much evidence that in the Western world also, calcium deficiencies, while seldom so drastic as to declare themselves unmistakably in the clinic, are frequently present in borderline degree." He goes on to say that a British investigation showed that much of the arthritis of middle-aged and elderly people is the result of long-continued shortage of food calcium.

In the *Canadian Medical Association Journal* for August, 1954, we read of an experiment on the diet of expectant mothers to determine whether or not added calcium might make labor easier. The 100 patients who agreed to take the calcium supplements were eating a regular diet, along with a vitamin-mineral supplement that is given regularly to all expectant mothers at this clinic. Sixty of the women were given additional calcium in the form of calcium gluconate and 40 were given bone meal. It is interesting to note, incidentally, that they were told to take the calcium tablets and bone meal an hour or so before meals, rather than with meals. It seems that calcium has a tendency to combine with fatty foods and make calcium "soaps" that are not digested. So not taking the tablets at meal time probably helped in the assimilation of the calcium.

About 10 per cent of the women who were taking calcium gluconate complained of heartburn and regurgitation and the medication had to be stopped. Of those taking bone meal, only two believed that it was causing heartburn.

When the time came for the babies to be delivered to each of these 100 women, it was found that the additional calcium in the supplement made a considerable difference in the mother's experience. Labor went along much more easily; there was little or no hysteria or panic right through the first stage of labor. The results were consistently better in the patients who had been taking the bone meal preparation. Ten of these did not believe that they were ready for delivery when they were asked to get on the delivery table. Two of them volunteered the statement that they even enjoyed this delivery.

The conclusion of Solomon Gold, M.D., the author of the article, is: "Calcium taken by mouth in the last month of pregnancy . . . in the suggested amounts was found to have a favorable effect on the course of labor in normal cases." In general, the labor was shorter and more regular, and progressed more consistently than in the women who had not taken the calcium or bone meal supplements. Their tolerance for the labor pains was greater. And there were absolutely no ill effects noted.

We are always pleasantly surprised at how readily members of the Canadian medical profession use bone meal when they want their patients to have additional calcium. An article from the *Canadian Medical Association Journal* for June, 1944, by Elizabeth M. Martin, M.D., describes the use of bone meal at a clinic for both mothers and children where excellent results were obtained in relieving cramps, "growing pains", tooth decay, dental neuralgia and so forth. Says Dr. Martin, "We use bone meal in place of any other form of calcium for all evidences of calcium deficiency in our patients." Then, too, we can't help but remind our readers that bone meal is used in all bread baked on ships in the Canadian Navy.

Calcium in the Diets of Senior Citizens

An article, "Current Research in the Science of Nutrition," reviewed in the June, 1953, issue of *Nutrition Reviews,* tells us of the changes that take place as we grow older, so far as the important minerals such as calcium are concerned. Loss of the calcium in bones, known as *osteoporosis,* is quite common. No one knows exactly why this takes place but it has been suggested that there is a certain change in the protein part of bone which prevents the replacement of the bone calcium lost as a part of living.

Others have suggested that just plain not getting enough calcium in food may be responsible. Most figures showing average diets for older people indicate that they are short, very short, on calcium. Take for instance, a study by Dr. N. Vinthur-Paulsen in Denmark, who worked with a group of older folks in an institution. Thirty-three women and 5 men, from 68 to 96 years of age were studied during two 7-day periods. Most of them were suffering from heart disease, senility, nervous system or blood vessel disorders. The calcium they ate in their food daily varied from .2 to 1.1 grams. (The recommended minimum daily allowance for this important mineral is officially .8 grams for adults and it is generally agreed that far higher amounts than this are necessary for the best of health.)

Of the 19 subjects in this study who were getting only 5 grams or less of calcium per day, 74 per cent showed loss of the calcium in their bones. Of those who got more than .5 grams, only 14 per cent showed loss of calcium or osteoporosis. When these folks were tested for phosphorus, about the same results were obtained. So the reasonable conclusion is that more calcium and phosphorus in the diet leads naturally to healthier bones in old age.

According to the March, 1954, issue of *Nutrition Reviews,* not all of the calcium we get in food is used by the body. In fact only about 20 to 30 per cent may be used. Your body will assimilate more calcium if you are eating a diet high in protein than if you eat mostly starches and sweets. And, of course, you must have a sufficient amount of vitamin D in the diet as well, for good assimilation.

[971]

Now in the case of older folks, we know very well that they tend to eat meals high in starches and sweets rather than proteins. The carbohydrate foods are easier to chew; they "go down the hatch" with less trouble. Then, too, many older, retired folks are living on smaller incomes and cannot afford the higher price of animal protein foods in large enough quantity. All this adds up to only one conclusion. Bone meal is the best and least expensive way of obtaining calcium. In addition, it's easy to take. No cooking, no preparing. If you buy powdered bone, sprinkle it over your food or into your soup. If you buy tablets, take them 3 times daily along with your other food supplements.

What About Fluorine in Bone Meal?

The question of the fluorine contained in bone meal has arisen again and again since all the recent hullabaloo about fluoridating water. Several dentists have attacked us for advocating bone meal which contains 400 part per million of fluorine and counselling against water fluoridation which involves only one part per million of fluorine. We figured out the amount of fluorine obtained in two quarts of fluoridated water (the amount most of us drink every day, supposedly) and the amount obtained in a day's ration of bone meal (two grams). There is about 10 times as much fluorine in the two quarts of water.

Quite apart from this mathematics, however, we have this information from the Research and Technical Division of Wilson and Company, who produce bone meal for human consumption and have made extensive studies of everything pertaining to it. They say, "Adequate evidence is available that fluorine in bone meal does not affect people adversely. In 1944 hearings were held in Washington, D. C. before the Administrator of the Federal Security Agency to determine the effect of fluorine when ingested as spray residues on fruit. At the same time testimony regarding fluorine in bone meal was offered. The country's outstanding experts on the pertinent subject testified. Evidence was brought out from experiments using both rats and humans that the ingestion of bone meal in quantities far exceeding any practical amounts was not harmful to man.

"Later Dr. Frank McClure of the National Institute of Health, showed that only 50 per cent of the fluoride in bone is absorbed and passes through the normal metabolic channels. Of such an amount none accumulates in the body as measured by balance experiments . . . Thus, there is no evidence that fluoride in bone meal is deleterious, but there is much good evidence that it does not have an adverse physiological effect." Every time you boil a bone to make soup, of course you get fluorine from the bone in the soup.

Bone Meal and Heart Health

One final thought on the importance of bone meal as a food supplement. We tend to think of calcium (the main ingredient of bone meal) as important mostly to teeth and bones. And so it is, but it has many other functions in the body, too. Not the least of these is the health of the heart. In Editor Rodale's book, *How to Eat for a Healthy Heart,*

(Rodale Press, Emmaus, Pennsylvania, $1.00) the importance of calcium is stressed. He quotes W. T. Lander in the *South Carolina Medical Journal* for January, 1948, who described heart patients of his who remained perfectly healthy and could live completely normal lives, so long as they never neglected to take their calcium every day. Dr. Edward Podolsky in the *Illinois Medical Journal* for August, 1939, tells us that calcium has nothing but a good effect on any symptoms connected with heart or blood vessel disorders—rapid pulse, breathlessness and so forth. Alfred S. Rogen in the *Glasgow Medical Journal*, November, 1940, speaks very highly of results obtained from giving calcium to heart patients. In the case of 26 patients who had heart failure, 20 reacted to calcium by a slowing of the heart rate of from 6 to 78 beats per minute.

To sum up then, bone meal is good for expectant mothers and children, the sailors in the Canadian Navy, heart patients or those who want to avoid heart trouble, old folks whose bones tend to become soft and any of the rest of us who want to stay healthy. It's inexpensive, easy to take and safe. It is a perfectly natural product, giving you in slightly concentrated form all the natural minerals you get when you boil a soup bone to make soup. Is there any reason under the sun why you should not take bone meal and give it to every member of your family?

CHAPTER 261

Desiccated Liver
the Wonder Food

Since the days of earliest history man has been looking for a wonder food—a food that would completely satisfy his needs, keep him young and strong and protect him from disease. We doubt if such a food exists, for we require a wide variety of foods to keep us healthy. But we believe that the closest thing to a wonder food that is available is probably liver, rich in the B vitamins, vitamins A, C, and D, iron, calcium, phosphorus, copper and the extremely important amino acids, which are elements in protein.

Liver has been known as excellent food for many years, but it seems that scientific research has not as yet nearly exhausted the possible findings as to the virtues of this food.

Liver Protects Against Poisons

It is well known among physiologists that the liver is the detoxifying organ of the body. It destroys poisons we take in. For instance, according to an article in the *Journal of Nutrition* for March 10, 1954, whole liver in the diet or even fractions of liver have been found to be very powerful against the effects of massive doses of strychnine, sulfanilimide, promin, atabrine, dinitrophenol, diethylstilbesterol, alpha-estradiol, cortisone acetate and so forth. All of these long names refer to one or another industrial substance or medical drug to which we may be exposed. The liver is constantly on guard to protect us against these products.

According to the article in the *Journal*, there is apparently a protective factor in that part of liver that is insoluble in water. In fact, it seems to be at least two factors which are not part of any of the known nutrients, whose requirements may be increased under conditions of stress, such as poisoning of some kind.

In the experiment described in the *Journal of Nutrition*, the author, Benjamin H. Ershoff of the University of Southern California tested desiccated liver, milk protein and all of the known B vitamins to see which would protect his laboratory animals from the effects of large doses of thiouracil, a drug that interferes with the workings of the thyroid gland. Now, as we know, it may be necessary to take this drug under certain conditions of illness. But physicians who prescribe it understand well that an overdose can have serious effects on the thyroid glands. So they prescribe it with great care. Dr. Ershoff, however, deliberately gave his rats large overdoses to see whether or not he could then protect them against this overdose by feeding them special things.

He found that there was indeed something in certain batches of desiccated liver that protected the rats against the ill effects of the drug. This substance was not present in casein (the milk protein) or in kelp or in any or all of the known B vitamins. Apparently the substance in the liver is thyroid hormone and it occurs in connection with iodine in the liver. Apparently there is a considerable amount of it in some batches of liver, and little or none in others.

Now, of course, none of us is taking harmful doses of this particular drug. But, we know well that liver protects against other poisons to which we are subjected—insecticides, for instance. Testifying before the Committee to Investigate Chemicals in Foods, Bernard Krohn, M.D., of Long Beach, California, described many cases of poisoning from insecticides, which he was treating with injections of liver extract and also large amounts of liver given by mouth. Said he, "Treatment of the disease is largely a matter of repairing damaged tissues. High protein and high vitamin diet, especially the B complex of vitamins, is useful. Injections of crude liver extract speed the process."

Recent articles on insecticides indicate that all of us are exposed to them almost continuously and that it is well nigh impossible to escape from some exposure to DDT, chlordane, lindane and the other new insecticides no matter how careful we individually are to avoid them in our

[974]

homes. Now, if liver is part of the treatment for insecticide poisoning, there is every reason to believe that including plenty of liver in your diet will protect you against the poisoning.

The Liver and the Endocrine Glands

A further testimony to the power of liver in the diet is given in the *Lancet* for February 16, 1952. According to this editorial, the human liver is closely connected with the proper functioning of the endocrine glands. We all know how extremely important these glands are to our welfare. It appears that the liver regulates the functioning of the glands. Two vitamins, riboflavin and thiamin, and one amino acid or form of protein have been named as the absolute essentials for the proper functioning of the sex hormones, for instance. In other words, these food substances are necessary to keep the liver healthy and the liver must be healthy for the sex hormones to do their work.

In a series of 450 cases studied by Morton S. Biskind, M.D. (New York), and reported in *Vitamins and Hormones,* Vol. 4, p. 147, disturbance of sex hormones had resulted in an excess of the female sex hormone—estrogen. In the women patients this brought about various menstrual disorders, painful breasts and acne; in the men, excessive development of the breast, softening of the testes, loss of hair in the armpits and so forth. In both sexes there was infertility. Dr. Biskind treated the patients with desiccated whole liver which resulted in completely healing all their symptoms of vitamin deficiency as well as the sex hormone disturbances.

In another series of cases described in *Archives of Internal Medicine,* Vol. 88, p. 762, R. S. Long and E. E. Simmons tell of similar symptoms in persons who apparently had perfectly healthy livers and were not lacking in any of the vitamins. However, in these cases, too, the disorders of sex hormone functioning were cured by a diet high in protein, low in fat, richly supplemented with the B vitamins and crude liver extract. In the two cases where there was liver disease the effect of the diet was "truly impressive," say these authors.

Suppose you don't like liver for some reason or other and can't eat it. Is there anything you can take instead that will give you the same good results? Apparently not, for literature is full of comparisons of liver with other foods, showing the great superiority of liver and also showing that there are apparently many as yet unidentified substances in liver which are not known vitamins or minerals but which have astonishing characteristics. For instance an article in the *Journal of Nutrition* for January, 1949, shows that there is something in liver which is essential for the growth of laboratory animals. This element is not present in brewer's yeast or wheat germ (for the animals fed these two substances did not respond) and it is not in any of the known vitamins. Could it be vitamin B_{12}, the miracle vitamin used to cure pernicious anemia? Apparently not, for in the June 28, 1952, issue of the *British Medical Journal* appears the account of feeding desiccated liver to a group of children and comparing their growth to that of an evenly matched group of children who did not get the liver. The author, John Mudkin, M.D., of the University of London, tells us that the liver factor which produced this result is not vitamin B_{12}, since vitamin B_{12} given alone does not have this effect. The children who got the liver showed 20 to 40 per cent more gain in growth than those who did not.

Liver Combats Fatigue

B. H. Ershoff, M.D., writing in the *Proceedings of the Society of Experimental Biology and Medicine*, July, 1951, tells of testing for an anti-fatigue diet in his laboratory. He used 3 groups of rats on 3 different diets which he fed for 12 weeks. The first group ate a usual laboratory diet to which were added nine synthetic and two natural vitamins. By this we mean that the synthetic ones were made in a laboratory of the various chemical substances of which the vitamins are made. The natural ones were extracted from foods—brewer's yeast, wheat germ or something like that.

The second group of rats had this same diet, added vitamins and all, with, in addition, a batch of B vitamins added—all the known B vitamins. The third group ate the original diet with 10 per cent desiccated liver added instead of vitamins. Desiccated liver is liver dried at low heat (to conserve vitamins) and powdered.

Now for the test. Each rat was placed in a drum of water from which he could not climb out. He had to keep swimming or drown. So, as you can see, this was a real test of endurance and anti-fatigue. The first group of rats swam for an average of 13.3 minutes before they gave up and indicated that they had no strength left. The second group swam for an average of 13.4 minutes and gave up. The third group—those which had the desiccated liver in their chow—broke all records. Three of them swam for 63, 83 and 87 minutes. The other rats in the group were all swimming vigorously at the end of two hours when the test was ended. Now, notice please, we did not say that Dr. Ershoff gave these super-rats a shot of something, nor did we say that they took liver for a day and then could perform this feat of endurance. We said that Dr. Ershoff fed them liver for a period of 12 weeks, which corresponds to a number of years in human beings, and *then* they were able to swim almost 10 times longer than the ordinary rats, or the ones which had been taking synthetic B vitamins.

Liver Protects Against Cancer

In an experiment which took place at the Sloan-Kettering Institute for Cancer Research over many years, written up in the *Journal of Nutrition* for July 10, 1951, Kanematsu Suguira, who conducted the experiment, tells us that he tried out various food substances to prevent cancer in laboratory animals. As you know, there are certain coal-tar substances which are sure cancer-producers. One of these is butter yellow, which was used in food, but which is today prohibited in food. Mixed with rice, it will produce cancer when it is fed to laboratory rats in given quantity.

A group of rats was put on a diet of butter yellow and rice. Another group was given the same diet plus 10 per cent desiccated liver. After a suitable period of time, the rats were examined for cancer. All 50 of the animals in the group receiving no liver had cancerous livers within 150 days. The rats to whose diet desiccated liver was added were completely protected from the cancer. But when the amount of liver was cut to 2 per cent rather than 10 per cent, the protection was less. It was also found that the liver supplement did not make for permanent protection. After it was stopped, cancer later developed in most of the animals. So it would seem that liver should be a permanent part of a good diet.

Liver, therefore, actually seems to be the "wonder-food" or as near it as we will ever come. Does this mean you should attempt to live entirely on liver? No, although we have heard of people who were at death's door who cured themselves by eating liver 3 times a day—every single meal— for the rest of their lives. Didn't seem to mind it, either!

Growth, regulation of hormones, protection from poisons, protection from cancer and an assurance of strength and endurance—these are the health reasons we have uncovered so far which indicate that liver is an absolute necessity for anyone who would be healthy these days. You and your family should eat liver as often as possible—and surely at least once a week. If you don't like it, you will be amazed at how soon you can come to like it especially if you experiment with different ways of fixing it until you discover which one pleases you most.

Somewhere along the line of American cookery there arose a tradition of soaking liver. *Of course no fresh food should ever be soaked.* But soaking liver is probably the worst crime against good health that you can commit, for most of the vitamins in liver are water-soluble. Many of the unknown factors (such as the anti-fatigue factor) may be water-soluble. This means that they dissolve in water. By soaking liver, you dissolve away—down the drain—all the precious food elements which make liver valuable! Cook liver the very day you get it from the store. Whisk it out of the refrigerator and on to the stove. Cook it at slow heat, for as little time as possible, to preserve vitamins. If you have it sliced thin, it will take less time to cook through.

Statistics in nutrition books indicate that there is a wide-spread vitamin B deficiency in this country, due to the processing all of our foods go through before they reach us. For this reason we advise all readers to take vitamin B as a natural food supplement every day. Brewer's yeast and liver are the two substances richest in all the B vitamins. Desiccated liver is more expensive than brewer's yeast because of the infinite care needed to dry it so that none of the vitamins will be lost. But it does contain food factors not found in yeast, as we have shown above. By all means, take desiccated liver as a food supplement, especially if, for one reason or another, you cannot eat liver at meals at least once a week.

CHAPTER 262

Brewer's Yeast

What is it? Brewer's yeast is a plant product, formerly used only in breweries, now available in purified form as a food supplement.

How is it made? Over the centuries since the days of the early Egyptians, yeast has been used by men for baking and brewing. As more and more information has been accumulated about the nature of yeast plants, the cultivation of them has developed into a major industry. Yeast is the smallest of all cultivated plants—about 1/4000th of an inch in diameter or about the size of a human blood corpuscle. The cultivation and harvesting of the plant is carried on under conditions where the composition of the seedbed and the temperature surrounding growth are controlled. The production of present-day brewer's yeast can be guided very much as plant specialists can guide the production of fruits and vegetables, so that only the best breeds will be used, to produce yeast plants rich in vitamins, proteins and minerals. Manufacturers of yeast can also foretell what the content of the final product will be in protein, vitamins and poundage. The yeast is grown in large vats until it has produced the maximum amount of yeast cells possible. It is then separated from the waste products of this growing process and dried at such a temperature that none of the nutritive value is lost. Then it is pulverized and made into powdered or tablet form.

What does it contain? The yeast plant stores enormous quantities of vitamins for its own use. These are then utilized as a food supplement by human beings, after the yeast plant is dried. Brewer's yeast contains all the elements of the vitamin B complex. It is also a rich source of complete protein—that is, protein containing all the substances necessary for digestion and assimilation. Other foods containing complete protein are meat, fish, milk and milk products, nuts and eggs, but large quantities of these must be eaten to equal the quantity of protein in brewer's yeast. An excess of protein is not harmful, incidentally, and will not be converted into fat in the body, as will an excess of carbohydrates.

Brewer's yeast also contains 16 of the 20 amino acids—forms of protein that are essential for the proper functioning of our bodies, for longevity, for resistance to disease, for rebuilding tissues that disease has harmed.

In comparison with several other foods high in vitamin B, here's how brewer's yeast stands:

Food	Parts of Vitamin B_1 Per 100 Grams	Food	Parts of Vitamin B_2 Per 100 Grams
Brewer's yeast	5,000 to 8,000	Brewer's yeast	2,500 to 4,700
Lean pork	300 to 750	Lean pork	200
Dried lima beans	450 to 600	Kidney	1,700 to 2,200
Liver	300 to 420	Dried lima beans	790
		Liver	1,800 to 2,200

[978]

What conditions is brewer's yeast good for? In present-day America there is a widespread deficiency of the vitamin B complex due partly to our over-refined foods, also to the fact that use of sugar and alcohol use up the body's supplies of vitamin B very rapidly. As our national consumption of both sugar and alcohol has increased enormously in the last 50 years, our national vitamin B deficiency has probably increased in proportion.

A lack of thiamin (vitamin B_1) results in personality changes—irritability, depression, "nerves." Some skin diseases, muscular weaknesses, hives, are signs of too little thiamin.

A lack of riboflavin (vitamin B_2) produces an extreme sensitivity to light, eye fatigue, sores around the mouth, nostrils, ears. An extreme deficiency in niacin produces pellagra—a disease resulting in dementia, painful mouth and tongue symptoms and diarrhea. When the deficiency is a little less, these symptoms may exist to a lesser degree. Choline and inositol are two vitamins of the B complex that combat hardening of the arteries and its associated diseases. Four other members of the B complex are also very important for good health, though not so much is known of their effects as yet.

All these vitamins exist abundantly in brewer's yeast, in the natural proportions which are most important for good results. Because brewer's yeast contains all the B complex, it is a valuable food supplement. A diet poor in one vitamin is usually poor in others, too. And a dose of just one of the B vitamins without the others may result in a deficiency. Brewer's yeast contains them all.

Where is it available? Brewer's yeast is available in tablet or powder form. They are equally good. Tablets should be taken with meals; powder may be sprinkled over various foods or mixed in a liquid. Directions for the quantity to take appear on the bottles in which you buy the yeast.

As a Cancer Preventive

The effect of diet in preventing cancer has now been scientifically established. The experiments involved only cancer of the liver and 10 different kinds of food, but the results are so astonishing that we can surely look forward to far more rapid progress in this field of research.

These remarkable experiments took place at the Sloan-Kettering Institute for Cancer Research over the course of many years. They are described in detail in *Journal of Nutrition* by Kanematsu Sugiura who contributed a major share of the work involved.

Cancer Induced by Butter Yellow

The experiments started in 1937 when scientists found that an artificial coloring substance, a dye known as butter yellow, could produce liver cancer in rats within the dramatically short time of 150 days. Formerly used to color oleomargarine and other butter substitutes with a vegetable origin, this highly poisonous chemical was banned from use in our food

[979]

industry several years ago. Mixed with rice it proved to be a sure-fire producer of liver cancer in rats.

The reason rice was chosen as the basic food for use in the experiments has an interesting scientific explanation. It is, of course, the staple food of the Orient where from 6 to 10 per cent of all cancers are found in the liver. In Japan and Korea in particular liver cancer accounts for 45 per cent of all cancers. In China the proportion is only 10 per cent because other dietary factors offset the low vitamin and protein content of rice. Brown rice contains, for example, only a half a milligram of riboflavin (vitamin B_2) per gram, as against the 70 milligrams found in the same amount of brewer's yeast. And whereas yeast is 49 per cent protein, only 8 per cent is found in rice.

Cancer Prevented by Brewer's Yeast and Dried Liver

To test the effect of brewer's yeast in a cancer-encouraging diet, 3 groups of rats were put on a diet of rice and butter yellow. In addition, one group was given 3 per cent brewer's yeast, the second 6 per cent and the third 15 per cent, while a control group of 50 animals were fed only rice and butter yellow. Reported on in 1941, this test successfully demonstrated that brewer's yeast prevents liver cancer. *All 50 animals in the control group receiving no yeast had cancerous livers within 150 days. All of the rats receiving yeast had smooth and practically normal livers.* But it was found that the 15 per cent ration of yeast was necessary to offset the disease. Thirty per cent of those who received 3 per cent of brewer's yeast had completely healthy livers, but 70 per cent had livers with numerous cancer nodules. Of the animals who received 6 per cent brewer's yeast, 40 per cent of them still had normal livers at the end of the same 150 days, but 30 per cent of them had developed cirrhosis while another 30 per cent had a few cancer nodules. To summarize: this experiment proved that the inclusion of 15 per cent brewer's yeast in the diet will prevent liver cancer in rats.

In a second experiment dried beef liver was substituted for yeast with similar results. Ten per cent of this food saved animals on the cancer-producing diet. When this protection was cut to 2 per cent, cancer appeared in the livers of the test animals. It seems certain, therefore, that both yeast and dried beef liver contain substances which, when included in the diet in sufficient quantity, prevent cancer. But this fact was not enough for the researchers. See preceding chapter.

The Protective Agent in Brewer's Yeast

Knowing that yeast and liver are rich in protein and the vitamins of the B complex, they wanted to discover next whether the protective effect of the yeast and liver was due to the correction of a deficiency in diet, probably of vitamins. When the rats were fed daily with only the small amount of riboflavin (vitamin B_2) and casein sufficient to promote normal growth, there was almost no protection from the liver cancer. However, when the daily consumption was increased, the protective effect was striking.

Then Dr. Sugiura and his co-workers checked other foods for possible protection against liver cancers. Dried kidney, dried spleen, wheat, rye, millet seed, milk, whole beef liver and coconut oil offered no results comparable to the riboflavin-casein diet, the dried beef liver one or the most successful one of all—that containing brewer's yeast.

The other question for which the researchers wanted an answer was this: Is protection against liver cancer by feeding yeast or dried liver temporary or permanent? To solve this problem, experimental rats were kept on the butter yellow-cancer-producing diet supplemented by 15 per cent yeast until their death. Of the animals that died between 150 and 200 days later, 100 per cent had completely normal livers. Of those dying between 280 and 350 days after the start of the tests, 43 per cent had normal livers, 7 per cent showed signs of cirrhosis, while 50 per cent had cancer nodules. Animals dying from 400 to 700 days later showed a proportion of 25 per cent normal to 75 per cent diseased with cancer. Animals still living at the end of 800 days were killed. Of these 15 per cent had normal livers, the other 85 per cent cancerous livers. In the words of Sugiura, "this indicates that only a small percentage of the animals appeared to be permanently protected by the yeast feeding" which means that, for protection, brewer's yeast must be a permanent, every-day part of the diet.

Can Well Developed Cancer Be Cured?

Can brewer's yeast cure liver cancer once the disease has taken hold? To answer this question another group of rats was fed on the cancer-inducing diet for 60 days—long enough to permit the growth of cancer in their livers. Then this diet was replaced by a diet of rice and 15 per cent yeast or dried milk which was fed for another period of 250 days. A small control group of animals was fed on brown rice alone after the cancer-inducing diet was stopped. Of these latter, 22 out of 25 developed cancerous tumors of the liver. Of the rats whose diet included yeast, only 4 out of 25 showed evidence of disease at the end of the test, and of those receiving dried milk, 8 out of 25 had cancer.

Some animals had been fed butter yellow for longer than 85 days and these proved too seriously diseased to be able to recover, even though yeast, liver or milk were fed for long periods after the butter yellow diet was stopped. Dr. Sugiura believes, therefore, on the basis of the experiments that while the addition of 15 per cent brewer's yeast to the diet will not destroy cancerous tumors which have been permitted to develop to any degree, *early stages of cirrhosis can be arrested and treated successfully by this method. And, most important of all, the inclusion of 15 per cent brewer's yeast in the diet will prevent the start of the growth of liver cancer.* Although the experiments described were conducted entirely in the realm of animals, Dr. Sugiura tells us, "These dietary influences may prove to play a very large part in the causation, prevention and treatment of human cancer." Mind you, no X-rays, no radium treatment, no operations —just the simple inclusion in your everyday diet of brewer's yeast which is available in tablet or powder form!

Since, with the exception of butter yellow, we do not yet know the food substances which may cause cancer, a diet fortified daily by ample amounts of brewer's yeast is for the present the only proven preventative of cancer.

In a parlor game some people play, one of the questions asked is: "What do you think you'll die of?" More than 50 per cent usually answer "Cancer." Dread of the disease is so widespread that psychiatrists have a name for it—carcinophobia, "fear of cancer." Yet its final defeat may lie in as simple a prescription as "Eat daily a sufficient quantity of brewer's yeast." We believe there are other nutritional preventatives of cancer. In this test Dr. Sugiura used only brewer's yeast and beef livers, but common-sense should tell us that a healthy body should not get cancerous and that other vitamins and minerals, which were not tested, would greatly aid in the building of bodily health.

CHAPTER 263

Why Brewer's Yeast Is Important

In spite of everything that has been written in recent years about brewer's yeast and its place in our diets as the richest known source of B vitamins, as well as a treasure-house of other valuable food elements, there is still confusion in some people's minds as to just what brewer's yeast is and how it differs from the yeast bakers use to raise bread and cakes.

We receive plenty of letters from readers asking if they can eat yeast cakes or, if not, then how about the dried yeast sold in grocery stores in little packages? Isn't that the same thing as brewer's yeast, they ask. The answer is no. Any yeast which can be used to raise dough in baking should not be eaten raw—that is, it should not be eaten unless it *has* been used in baking. The dry powdered yeast is intended for use in baking. The yeast plants it contains are still alive. They will certainly rob you of B vitamins, if you eat them, for the yeast plant has a voracious appetite for B vitamins. While it is alive, it will absorb great quantities (relatively speaking) of whatever B vitamins are present in its environment.

Do not eat raw, uncooked yeast cakes or dried baker's yeast. They can be harmful. Brewer's yeast is something different.

It is a plant product which has been produced specifically for food. The tiny yeast plants are grown on a food substance called "wort," made of various ingredients depending on what kind of yeast is grown. Cereal grains and hops are the "wort" in a brewery. The yeast cells produced on these foods are washed free of beer and then dried. They are dried in such a way that all the rich nutrients are preserved but the plant itself is no longer alive and cannot be used to raise dough in baking.

The yeast plant is microscopic. It has the ability to reproduce itself (in a process called "budding") at a fantastically rapid rate. That is why this food, so rich in precious protein, vitamins and minerals, can be produced and sold so inexpensively, compared to other high protein foods like meat, eggs and so forth.

Official Statements on Yeast

The United States Dispensatory is an official book describing and defining drugs and medicines and setting official standards for the use of doctors and druggists. Dried yeast is defined in the *Dispensatory* as a yeast which contains not less than 45 per cent protein and in each gram the equivalent of not less than .30 milligrams of niacin, .04 milligrams of riboflavin and .12 milligrams of thiamin. All these are B vitamins.

This gives you an idea of the importance of yeast as a preventive and cure for dietary deficiencies which might involve pellagra or beriberi, serious and often fatal diseases which are caused directly by lack of B vitamins. Here are the official comments on brewer's yeast: "Dried yeast powder is a valuable source of the vitamin B factors and of protein for therapeutic utilization. Although the amount of thiamin and other vitamins which it contains is small, it is sufficiently cheap to be used in large doses as a dietary supplement in institutions and in geographic areas with inadequate supplies of food. In the treatment of cirrhosis of the liver, sprue, pellagra, pernicious anemia, etc., as much as 30 to 90 grams is ingested daily. It may be suspended in milk, fruit, or vegetable juices, soup or coffee, according to the taste; it should preferably be rubbed to a paste with a small amount of liquid and then dispersed in a large volume so that it will not adhere to the utensils employed. . . . Tablets provide a more palatable dosage form. It is to be noted that pellagra has developed in patients receiving many yeast tablets daily; the amount of nicotinic acid (niacin) represented is small and may be inadequate."

Brewer's Yeast High In Nutrient Values

Under "dosage" we find: "The usual dose of dried yeast is 10 grams 4 times daily, the range of dose being 1 to 10 grams. One tablespoon of the yeast weighs about 10 grams and represents approximately 35 calories, 4.6 grams of vegetable protein, .2 grams of fat, 3.7 grams of carbohydrate, 11 milligrams of calcium, 189 milligrams of phosphorus, 1.8 milligrams of iron, 1.2 milligrams of thiamin, .54 milligrams of riboflavin and 3.6 milligrams of nicotinic acid" (niacin).

This gives you some idea of the rich nutrient value of brewer's yeast. Here are some comparisons. The tablespoon of yeast contains as much protein as ¼ cup of wheat germ. It contains as much calcium as ½ cup of orange juice, as much phosphorus as ¼ pound of fillet of haddock, as much iron as 1 cup of cooked spinach, as much thiamin as a cup of wheat germ, as much riboflavin as 4 eggs, as much niacin as ½ cup of brown rice.

If you take 4 tablespoons of yeast a day, as the official dispensatory recommends, multiply these amounts by 4.

Please note the comment above on taking yeast tablets. Here is one instance where we believe it is far more beneficial to use the powdered form. While yeast tablets are more convenient, it takes so many of them to equal a tablespoon of powder that it seems best to use the powder to begin with. Some authorities estimate that one tablespoon of yeast is equal to about 20 tablets.

Why We Recommend Yeast as a Food

Why do we recommend the use of brewer's yeast when we believe in natural foods and counsel against synthetics? There is nothing synthetic about brewer's yeast and nothing unnatural. Yeast has been an item of food since very early times. Its wealth of nutritional riches was discovered only recently, so only in this century has it been dried as an item for food. Careful cultivation is necessary to get exactly the yeast that is wanted, but the same can be said for almost any other plant. As for the processing brewer's yeast undergoes, we believe it is far less than most fruits and vegetables that are available in the average market. Preservatives are unknown in brewer's yeast. There is no possibility of contamination by insecticides.

We are often asked why we always recommend taking food supplements individually rather than in an all-in-one tablet which contains a wide selection of vitamins and minerals. The composition of brewer's yeast is a good answer to this question. Every grain of yeast is food—good food. Compare the volume of 4 tablespoons of this fine food to the volume of an all-in-one tablet. Yeast is all food. There is no waste. So in taking a tablespoon of this very inexpensive food you are getting a far greater volume of nutrients (all in good natural combinations, of course) than you can get in all-in-one supplements.

Can You Get Too Much?

Isn't there a chance that yeast may be "too rich?" Are we safe in taking such large quantities of so concentrated a food? In a booklet, *Yeasts in Feeding,* published in 1948 by the Brewer's Yeast Council and several other groups, we find the following statement from Clive M. McCay, one of the world's greatest experts on nutrition who is with the Department of Animal Nutrition, Cornell University. He says. "Extensive use of yeast has been made in studies in the field of gerontology (the study of old age). Rats have been employed throughout these attempts to determine the interrelationship between diet and aging. In the first studies in which the extreme span of life of the rat was greatly extended, all rats were fed a diet throughout life containing 5 per cent of dried yeast. The oldest rats in this study exceeded 1400 days of age, whereas the average rat lives about 700 days. These data indicate that a substantial level of yeast can be fed during the whole span of life without evidence of injury. This answers one of the common queries concerning the possible injury from the purines

[984]

found in yeast. As far as we are aware, there is no evidence of injury from any constituent of yeast."

Improvements are continually being made in this field as one might expect. We hear now about a yeast that is especially effective for people who need large amounts of thiamin and fear that they may have some block against assimilating it. Thiamin, the B vitamin, is not used in the body in the form of thiamin. It must be transformed first into what is called a co-enzyme named cocarboxylase. This kind of thing happens frequently in the complex chemical factory that is one's body. Carotene, for instance, is the yellow substance which appears in carrots and other vegetables and fruits. It is not used by the body as such, but must be changed into vitamin A by the liver before it is taken up and used for other body functions.

Can't Convert Carotene Into Vitamin A

Just so is thiamin changed into cocarboxylase before the body can use it. We know that, for many people with liver trouble or other disorders of digestion, carotene is not used very well, that is, they could eat quantities of carrots and still be short on vitamin A because they could not convert the carotene into vitamin A. We do not know of any conditions where thiamin cannot be used because of digestive malfunctioning of any part of the body. But, presumably, there might be such conditions and perhaps later investigation may uncover them. At any rate, it seems apparent that getting your thiamin in the form of cocarboxylase would eliminate one step that must be performed by the body and hence make its digestive job easier.

We found, for instance, a reference to cramps in pregnancy, which is a common enough occurrence. Three French researchers reported in *Bulletin de la Société de Gynécologie et d'Obstétrique*, Vol. 4, pp. 230-232, 1952, that injections of cocarboxylase were effective in relieving such cramps. The authors point out that lack of thiamin is believed to be one of the main causes of such cramps. They tell us that furnishing the primary material for the synthesis of cocarboxylase is the main reason for giving thiamin. So why not administer the cocarboxylase directly?

Cramps Disappeared with Treatment

In 60 cases reported, cocarboxylase was given in muscular injections daily for 6 days. In all cases the cramps disappeared during the course of treatment. Generally, with the third injection relief was complete, although some patients required five injections and others only one. The authors point out that they got better results with the cocarboxylase than with thiamin which they had given to other patients, with only 70 per cent success. In 10 other patients treated earlier they had gotten no response at all giving thiamin.

While the cramps were being treated, patients noticed that another complaint was vanishing—parathesia—that is, a numbness or a tingling, "pins and needles" feeling in the legs. So they treated 25 patients who suffered just from this discomfort and got complete relief in all but two!

Such an experiment would certainly suggest that there may be conditions in which thiamin is not used as well as it could be, and cocarboxylase is preferable. At any rate, it is good to know that a considerable amount of cocarboxylase is found in brewer's yeast. It is even more cheering to know that newer yeasts which are being developed have more and more of their thiamin in this enzyme form. For people who fear they may have trouble absorbing vitamin B_1, it would seem to be a wise idea to buy brewer's yeast with as high a content of cocarboxylase as possible.

CHAPTER 264

Protection against Radiation

Crude yeast extract provided a moderate amount of protection against lethal radiation doses in rats injected with yeast autolysate (a yeast substance produced by digesting part of the yeast by enzymes).

Katherine D. Detre and Dr. Stuart C. Finch of the Yale Department of Internal Medicine, Yale University School of Medicine, found that in one group of 27 animals receiving 1 milliliter of the yeast substance, 11 (or 41 per cent) were alive 30 days after irradiation. By contrast, all but one of the animals which had been irradiated but had not received the yeast, were dead by the thirteenth day. The final animal in this group died on the twenty-first day. The report was made in *Science* for September 19, 1958.

The researchers believed that this protection from harm was probably due to a substance called ribonucleic acid which is present in the yeast. So, in another test, they injected *this* into irradiated mice. Nine of 14 mice so protected were alive 30 days after irradiation. This compares with no survival at all in 105 mice who did not receive the protective injection and a survival of 27 per cent in a third group injected with the crude yeast substance.

We probably won't be able to follow through on what happens to this interesting bit of information. It will probably be filed away between the covers of reference books, never to see the light again. Or, if someone does decide to do further research on it, they will set out to produce synthetically whatever substance it is in yeast that protects against radiation. Then a drug company will begin to manufacture and sell this isolated product at great profit.

Protection against radiation has become one of the main concerns of scientists, since we began testing atomic weapons and employing atomic installations for peacetime use. All of us are being submitted to ever-increasing doses of deadly radiation and it looks as though this situation is getting steadily worse rather than better. Yeast apparently contains something powerful against the lethal rays.

And those of us who continue to urge people to take brewer's yeast daily, as a wonderful source of all kinds of protective elements, are called "food faddists."

Who are the food faddists anyway?

CHAPTER 265

Stick to Yeast and Liver

Some recent discoveries emphasize the advantages of natural over synthetic vitamin preparations. The latter may not, for example, contain the entire B complex. Even if they do, they may not be properly balanced as far as concentration goes. But what seems more important is that synthetic vitamin preparations lack *unknown* substances present in natural materials.

No doubt some people will think us strange for being concerned about things that are *unknown*. "After all," they may say, "if you don't know about something, why worry about it?" This attitude has often been expressed by those who take the position "What you don't know won't hurt you."

Well, if we examine this philosophy closely, we see that it's really a sort of negative way of looking at things. First of all, every single vitamin that we now know, and respect, was at one time in the category of the *unknown*. Secondly, even while these substances were still unknown, their vital importance to our health and well-being was recognized. One good example of this is vitamin B_{12}. Not so very long ago, it became increasingly obvious that our bodies required some *unknown* substance in liver. Later on, this turned out to be what we now call B_{12}.

In this and many other instances, it has been precisely things about which we did *not* know enough that harmed us, because we were not getting them in adequate amounts. The obvious moral is that we had better play it safe and give serious consideration to *unknown* materials occurring in natural products but absent from synthetic chemical preparations. Contrary to what some would have us believe, "Ignorance is not bliss." But ignorance about important nutritional factors still causes much illness and suffering.

All this now seems to apply to brewer's yeast and liver once again, as has happened many times in the past. This may startle you if you think we know what's in yeast and liver. As far as vitamins are concerned, we do and we don't. Of course, it is common knowledge that vitamins are present in these materials. But we don't know *all* that brewer's yeast contains, or *everything* to be found in liver. No one, for example, can list every single substance in any given species of yeast, even if he knows how the yeast was produced, including what it grew on.

Coenzyme Q

Recent discoveries of such formerly *unknown* compounds underscore the importance of taking vitamins in the form of yeast rather than as synthetic chemical preparations. These discoveries concern *COENZYME Q*. Enzymes are proteins that carry out chemical reactions by which living things metabolize, e. g., handle food, obtain energy, grow, etc. But many enzymes cannot function alone; that is, the enzyme proteins cannot by themselves do the jobs required of them. They work only in cooperation with other substances called *coenzymes*. This is where vitamins come into the picture, because many vitamins function as coenzymes in enzyme systems. Our bodies manufacture the protein portions of enzymes, but do not always produce the coenzymes, or at least not enough of them. This is why we must obtain vitamins from the food or food supplements we eat. Without enough vitamins, the enzymes do not operate properly.

Coenzyme Q is really a group of compounds, all belonging to the chemical class of substances known as quinones. Vitamin K_1 is also a quinone, but apparently differs from coenzyme Q. So far, coenzyme Q has been isolated from yeast as well as from liver and heart tissue. It is also found in a soil bacterium whose function is to help the soil change nitrogen into a form that plants can use. So it helps maintain soil fertility.

Although we are not yet absolutely certain, there is evidence that coenzyme Q compounds may have vitamin functions. Much of the biochemical machinery which provides our energy is concentrated in tiny particles called *mitochondria*. These mitochondria are the energy-producing factories which keep our batteries charged, so to speak. They are microscopic dynamos located in the cytoplasm which surrounds the nuclei of our cells.

Energy Production

Exactly how does coenzyme Q do its job? To answer this question, let us digress for a moment and consider our rapidly developing atomic energy industry. Now-a-days we hear a lot about efforts to produce *controlled* nuclear reactions. It is necessary to control these processes if we wish to divert their energy to useful ends. Otherwise we may very easily blow ourselves up.

The same thing holds true for the energy that is set free in our bodies. This energy comes primarily from the oxidation of carbohydrates, and is released in a *series of stepwise reactions*. The whole process is carried on by enzymes and coenzymes *inside* our body cells. The important thing to note here is that the energy is made available gradually; that is, at a rate at which our bodies can handle it. If the oxidation were not controlled but happened all at once, we might almost literally burn ourselves up. If the oxidation does not take place rapidly enough, we simply do not get enough energy to keep us going properly.

It is here that coenzyme Q becomes important, for a group of substances functions in the energy-producing machinery of our cells. We now know that coenzyme Q compounds exist, and we know at least something about the role they play in our biochemical processes.

But do our bodies produce enough coenzyme Q, or must we depend on our food for adequate amounts? How much coenzyme Q, if any, do we get from bacteria and other microbes in our intestines? These creatures synthesize vitamins, and we profit from this source of supply. What diseases may result from inadequate amounts of coenzyme Q, and which ones can be treated by coenzyme Q?

Obviously, much information is yet needed to answer these and other questions about coenzyme Q. In the meantime, however, we do know that we get coenzyme Q from brewer's yeast and liver, but not from synthetic vitamin preparations.

CHAPTER 266

Fish Liver Oils Are Food

In the eighteenth century the physicians of England discovered that fish liver oil could cure rickets. Fish liver oil had been eaten in Iceland and Norway for centuries before that. In those days this is how they made oil, because there was no other method known for extracting it from the fish livers. The livers were allowed to putrefy, to rot, until the oil came to the surface and could be skimmed off. The imagination is staggered at the thought of the aroma that must have clung to the walls of the buildings in which this process took place, the clothes worn by the fishermen, the containers in which the fish liver oil was collected.

And yet, hundreds and hundreds of years ago, human beings knew so much about the potency of fish liver oils that determined mothers in northern countries pinned down their squalling youngsters and poured into their protesting gullets quantities of this putrid, offensive oil. And watched them grow tall and straight and healthy as a result. It was not suspected until quite recently why fish liver oil is so important to growth and good health. From the Manchester, England, Infirmary, Dr. Robert Darbey wrote to a friend in 1782: "For several years after I came to the infirmary I observed that many poor patients, who were received into the infirmary for the chronic rheumatism, after several weeks trial of a variety of remedies, were discharged with little or no relief. . . . About 10 years since, an accidental circumstance discovered to us a remedy, which has been used with the greatest success, for the above complaint, but is very little known, in any

[989]

county, except Lancashire; it is the cod, or ling liver oil." Drummond and Wilbraham go on to tell in *The Englishman's Food* that the infirmary doctors were so pleased with the results they obtained that no less than 50 or 60 gallons were prescribed annually in spite of the fact that the smell and taste were so repulsive that many patients could not stomach it.

The New Remedy—Vitamins A and D

In those days almost any disorder of the bones or joints was called "rheumatism" so, of course, rickets, tuberculous joint diseases and so forth were among those cases of "rheumatism" cured by the new remedy. About the middle of the nineteenth century, an incident in the London Zoo confirmed the potency of the new medicine. The curators had always been unable to raise lion and bear cubs, for they developed rickets easily and early and soon died. The animals were fed on a raw meat diet. On the advice of a prominent British physician of the time, crushed bone, milk and cod liver oil were added to the meat. From then on there were no further casualties among the 200 animals. Looking for the reason for such wonderful properties, one investigator of the early nineteenth century decided it was the iodine in the fish liver oil that performed the miracles. And indeed up until the time of Sir Edward Mellanby and his famous experiments with rachitic puppies only about 30 years ago, no one knew that the precious ingredients of fish liver oils are the concentrated vitamin A and D they contain. Nor does anyone know up to the present time why these vitamins occur in such abundance in fish livers. Presumably they are stored there by the fish, but why in such quantity?

"It is not surprising," says Drummond and Wilbraham, "that the possibility of other fish liver oil possessing therapeutic value aroused interest after cod liver oil re-established its reputation in England. The *Lancet* drew attention to the possibilities of using shark liver oil in 1855, but the extraordinary potency of the liver oils of such fish as the halibut and tunny was unsuspected until quite recently. Perhaps this is understandable. Cod liver is exceedingly rich in fat (30-50 per cent), whereas most of the livers which yield the very potent oils contain a much smaller proportion (2.8 per cent). When substitutes for cod liver oil were sought, it was natural to turn to those like the shark, which also have a large amount of oil stored in the liver."

H. C. Sherman, Columbia University's world-famous nutritionist, in his book, *Food Products* (The Macmillan Company, 1941), has this to say about fish liver oils as food: "Hitherto in this country, the fish liver oils have been commonly considered as medicines rather than food. But cod liver oil has been a stable article of food in some fishing communities; moreover its clinical value seems to lie in its contribution of two dietary essentials, vitamin A and vitamin D. For these reasons, there is justification in thinking of these fish liver oils as vitamin-rich foods."

Why Fish Liver Oils Are Important

Let us review for just a moment some important facts on these two important vitamins. Vitamin A can be obtained from animal and vegetable food; whereas vitamin D is available only in animal products and in the ultraviolet rays of the sun—that is, some substance in your skin can manufacture vitamin D from sunlight. And the amount of vitamin D in animal products (cream and butter, for example) is infinitesimal compared with the wealth of vitamin D in fish liver oil.

Vitamin A is necessary for a healthy skin. It is important, too, for the eyes. Its deficiency results in "night blindness" which means inability to adapt to light after darkness, or darkness after light. Research has indicated that vitamin A is important for the prevention of infections, such as colds. It has been found that plenty of vitamin A in the diet helps the condition of people with goiter or other thyroid trouble. Vitamin A deficiency results in inability to store fat. For children the vitamin is an absolute essential if bones and teeth are to be healthy and if the child is to grow strong and tall. Bladder stones are caused in laboratory animals by lack of vitamin A.

Vitamin D is essential for the proper use by the body of calcium and phosphorus—perhaps the two minerals most important for good health. No matter how much of these two minerals you get in your diet, you cannot use them unless you also have plenty of vitamin D. So rickets, a deforming bone disease, can be caused in children by lack of any one or more of these 3—calcium, phosphorus or vitamin D. Animals manufacture their vitamin D from sunlight. And it has been found that hibernating animals do not hibernate when they have been given enough vitamin D. They know, you see, that the sun's rays in wintertime are not strong enough to provide the amount of vitamin D they need. Osteomalacia is the adult disease corresponding to rickets in children, when the bones become decalcified from lack of one of the two important minerals, or vitamin D.

Everyone Should Take Fish Liver Oils

For many years it has been accepted practice to give babies in this country fish liver oil to prevent rickets. And the incidence of rickets has greatly decreased as a result. But why should we stop giving this vitamin-rich food when children reach adolescence? At that time they are growing very rapidly and need all the calcium and phosphorus they can get for making bones and permanent teeth. Calcium is one mineral that, all nutritionists agree, is deficient in the American diet. We do not eat enough leafy green vegetables, eggs and cheese to supply anything like the amount of calcium we need. Why not then, just to be on the safe side, get plenty of vitamin D so that we can use effectively all the calcium we get?

We believe that everyone, children and adults alike, should take fish liver oils to be assured of getting plenty of both vitamin A and vitamin D. In case you live in the South and spend a lot of time out in the sunshine, take one of those oils which is richer in vitamin A and has less vitamin D. If you live in the North, you are well aware how puny and how brief are the rays of the winter sun, especially when they are filtered through the smog and smoke of a large city. Do you think you can afford to take a chance on too little of either of these necessary vitamins?

[991]

How To Take Fish Liver Oils

Here is a table taken from *The Englishman's Food* showing the variety of vitamin D content of the different fish liver oils:

	International Units of Vitamin D per gram
Cod	50-200
Halibut	1,000-4,000
Sea Bass	4,000-5,000
Swordfish	4,000-10,000
Yellow Fin Tunny	13,000-45,000
Striped Tunny	220,000-250,000

Compare this, please, with the vitamin D contained in butter (one unit per gram) or egg yolk (1.5 to 5 units per gram). Halibut liver oil has largely displaced cod liver oil as a food supplement today because it is also extremely rich in vitamin A, so that a small amount of it provides much more vitamin A than cod liver oil does.

Excessive Amounts Are Dangerous

Because of the high concentration of vitamins in fish liver oil, don't make the mistake of deciding that, if a little is good, a lot will be better, for fish liver oil taken in enormous quantities is dangerous. Read the directions on the container in which you get your oil. The minimum daily requirement of vitamin A is 5000 units per day for adults and from 1500 to 6000 units per day for children, according to age. The vitamin D requirements are 400-800 units for children. The National Research Council, which sets these minimums, does not suggest any minimum requirements of vitamin D for adults. More than 400,000 units of vitamin D daily is considered toxic for adults and more than 30,000 units daily is toxic for children. This is easily understandable when you think of the vitamins in terms of food. Eating 5 times as much as you should have of almost any food would be bound to make you sick, no matter how healthful the food may be. So be guided by the suggested daily dose on the container.

Fish Liver Oil and Nothing Else

One word more. There are food supplement manufacturers who do all kinds of things to vitamin preparations. They may use synthetic vitamins —that is, they make up the vitamins in a chemical laboratory putting together the chemical elements (oxygen, hydrogen, nitrogen and so forth) as they occur in the natural vitamin. These are not for you, if you would be healthy. Then some processors take natural fish liver oil and add different substances to it, to increase the potency. These are also not for you. When you buy fish liver oils, for yourself or your children, make certain that they contain nothing—but nothing—except the fish liver oil. The label will tell you what the contents are, and the potency—that is, the label will indicate that one perle contains 5000 units of vitamin A and 200 units of vitamin D or whatever it may happen to be. Take the fish liver oil acccording to the suggested dosage.

And—lucky you!—to be alive today when fish liver oils have been shorn of their taste and smell!

CHAPTER 267

A Rose by Any Other Name Is Vitamin C

That troublesome problem of how to get enough vitamin C keeps cropping up every time we outline a model diet or suggest ideal food supplements everyone should have. Citrus fruits contain vitamin C, but we believe that the consumption of too much citrus juice, especially from commercially-grown citrus (picked when it is green), is not healthy. Green peppers contain vitamin C in abundance. So do water cress and parsley. But, after all, you can't carry around a quart or so of watercress and peppers for all-day nibbling, just to be sure you're getting enough vitamin C. Synthetic vitamin C has been available for a long time, but nutritionists admit that synthetic vitamin C (ascorbic acid) does not have the same healthful effects as the natural vitamin. Other factors are present in natural vitamin C. Food supplements made of natural vitamin C are available, but they're a little more expensive, because they're so difficult to make. Of course, it would be best, too, to get vitamin C in food that contains at least a smattering of other vitamins, as well.

We believe we've found the answer in a fruit you've probably never thought of eating before. It's well known as nourishing food in Europe. It's well known as favorite food among the bird population in our country. It goes by the name of rose hips. For those of you who may not know, rose hips are the fruit of the rose, which mature after the petals of the flower have fallen. Looking back over human history you might well wonder how mankind decided on which plants to eat and which not to eat. Suppose that for generations back, apples were admired only for their blossoms. Perhaps no one would ever have thought of eating the fruit, and today we'd be planting ornamental apple trees, developing larger, more fragrant flowers and having spring shows of apple blossoms in greenhouses. Probably, too, there would be a few "food faddists" who would insist on eating the fruit. Instead of that, we eat the fruit of apples and grow roses as ornamental flowers, with hardly a thought of the possible food value of their fruit.

But all along, the birds have known what delicious food rose hips are. Today many people are growing multiflora rose hedges, to provide food for countless birds next winter. Birds like sunflower seeds and whole grains, too. Perhaps we could do no better than to follow the sensible example of our cardinal, wren and chickadee friends and give ourselves a nutrition treat—rose hips.

They Contain Vitamin A as Well as Vitamin C

Olaf E. Stamberg of the Department of Agricultural Chemistry of the University of Idaho has written in detail about the vitamin content of rose hips in *Food Research* for September-October, 1945. Mr. Stamberg tells us that the garden varieties of rose hips are low in vitamin C, but that some varieties of wild roses contain astonishing amounts not only of vitamin C but also of vitamin A. Rosa Rugosa, for instance, contain from 2275 to 6977 milligrams of vitamin C per hundred grams. Oranges contain only 49 milligrams per hundred grams. Rosa Laxa displays a vitamin C content of 3000 to 4000 milligrams to every hundred grams, compared to 150 milligrams per hundred grams of green peppers.

In preparing the rose fruit for eating. Mr. Stamberg experimented with different methods of preservation. Rose hips packed in sealed mason jars and placed in a freezing locker at a temperature of about 5 degrees below zero were analyzed over a period of 6 months and showed little loss of 'vitamin C in that time. Rose hip jam, made very much as any fruit jam is made, showed a high vitamin C content of which very little was lost over 6 months. But dehydrating the hips caused 80 per cent loss of the vitamin in his experiments. Juice and purée of rose hips kept in a refrigerator for 8 days lost only a small percentage of its vitamin C content.

"The juice of rose hips in various foods, such as fruit soups, juices, jams and jellies should be valuable," says Mr. Stamberg, "owing to their high vitamin C and carotene (vitamin A) content. Investigations into the culinary aspects of preparing rose hips should lead to many new and interesting ways of utilizing them."

Preparing Rose Hips to Eat

Writing in the *Canadian Journal of Research* for December, 1943, J. Tuba, G. Hunter, M. J. Hutchinson and L. L. Kennedy have lots to say about utensils and methods which will help to save the precious vitamin C in preparing rose hips in the kitchen. Care should be taken that they do not come into contact with any copper utensils, as copper destroys vitamin C on contact. Aluminum utensils also cause a considerable loss. Glass or enamelware vessels preserve the most vitamin C, but be sure that the enamel kettles are not cracked, so that the metal underneath shows through. Wooden spoons should be used and stainless steel knives, lest somewhere an edge of copper might touch the hips. These researchers had good luck with drying rose hips at a temperature of 175 degrees Fahrenheit, retaining 80 per cent of the original vitamin C in their dried rose hips. Storing the dried powder, however, resulted in considerable loss.

They also found that the best time to gather the hips is when they are fully ripe, but not overripe. Rose hips are bright scarlet in color when they are ripe, orange when they are unripe and dark red when they are overripe. Altitude and latitude make a difference in vitamin C content, too, with roses farther north showing more vitamin C than those grown farther south . . . perhaps a kindly provision by nature for people and birds whose vitamin C

[994]

is used up during long winters and not sufficiently replenished during short growing seasons.

There's one writer who objects to the taste of rose hip products. H. S. Redgrove tells us in the *Gardener's Chronicle* for October 25, 1941, that he made some rose hip purèe according to directions and found that it tasted like vanilla. There's nothing wrong in this, we guess, except that he had been told it would taste like tomatoes or peaches. He complained of the taste in print and was sent a sample purée prepared by an expert. He admitted that this purée had an aroma and flavor reminiscent of tomatoes, but made into a juice cocktail it lost its flavor and was decidedly unpleasant. Of course, some people who live on drug store lunches and sundaes object to the taste of sunflower seeds! However, Mr. Redgrove agrees that the nutritive value of rose hips should not be wasted and suggests that they be made into food supplements rather than beverages or preserves.

Rose hips have long been a popular delicacy in northern European countries, according to Ivan B. O'Lane writing in the January, 1949, issue of the *Journal of Home Economics*. In Sweden rose hips are carefully gathered and used for soups, tea and puddings. Mr. O'Lane says, "for a soup, the hips are ground and boiled for about 10 minutes, then strained and again brought to a boil, sugared to taste and thickened with 4 level teaspoons of potato flour which has been prepared with 2 cups of cold water. This *nyponsoppa* (soup) is then served hot or cold with cream and almond cookies or oven-toasted bread. Puddings are prepared by adding a greater amount of potato flour. A few almonds added during the boiling enhance the taste."

Vitamin and Mineral Content of Rose Hips

Here are some figures from Sweden showing the vitamin and mineral value of rose hips compared to oranges available in Sweden:

	Rose hips	Oranges
Calories	750 per kilogram	480 per kilogram
Protein	1.2%	0.9%
Carbohydrate	17%	11.2%
Phosphorus	.03%	.02%
Calcium	28% more in rose hips	
Iron	25% more in rose hips	
Vitamin A	5000 International Units	200 International Units
Vitamin C	2000 International Units	50 International Units

The authors of an article on rose hips in *Hippokrates*, No. 6, 1942, the German medical magazine, have as their theme the supreme importance of the relationship of one vitamin to another. For this reason Dr. A. Von Kuhn and Dr. H. Gerhard find that rose hips are superior, for they contain such a wide assortment of vitamins in the natural proportions in which they are found in nature. In speaking of vitamin C requirements, our researchers remind us that what they mean is natural vitamin C the chemical biocatalyst, in its "nature-given harmony with all other biocatalysts and principal nutrients as nature offers it in plant tissue. The effect of each individual vitamin in nutrition is related to the presence of all other vitamins." (A biocatalyst is a substance that brings about chemical reactions in other substances.)

CHAPTER 268

A Message from Norway about Wild Rose Hips

The other day we received a beautifully decorated little pamphlet from Norway, with brightly colored pictures of children rushing from school with baskets in their hands and men and women busily picking something from small bushes. Our knowlege of Norwegian being what it is, we could translate only one word—"Vitamin C." Piecing this together with the pictures, we decided that this was a booklet on rose hips published by a factory in Norway where rose hips are made into a powder sold under the name of C-Nok, which means "Enough C"—that is "enough Vitamin C."

We sent the pamphlet to one of those very generous readers who have offered to translate for us—Mrs. Sterling Slater of Broderick Street, San Francisco. Here, rendered very freely into English, are the contents of the booklet whose plea for good nutrition is all the more moving because it comes from a country where a wide variety of fresh fruits and vegetables is simply not available in winter and early spring.

"The Norwegian people should be strong and healthy," says the booklet, "yet all of us must stay within a reasonable food budget. Any failure in nutrition can have far-reaching and fatal results for a country and its people. Our bodies need vitamins. The name 'vitamin' comes from the Latin, meaning 'life.' Scientists have demonstrated the importance of vitamins for the preservation of life. Vitamin C is widely distributed in the vegetable kingdom. Yet recent researchers at the University Hygienic Institute have shown that the rose hip is our country's most prolific source of vitamin C and is of far more value to us than imported fruit. Rose hip bushes are abundant in our land, but until recently these fruits of the rose bush have been quite ignored and their precious vitamin C has rotted away on the bushes. There are many different kinds of wild roses in Norway. Rose hip literature recognizes 100 varieties. The vitamin C content is not the same in all the different species, but all rose hips contain different vitamin C's in varying amounts, if they are gathered at the proper time.

"It is essential to gather the hips at the right time, but no definite date can be set, for rose hips ripen first in the south. According to scientific research, the hips have a remarkably high content of vitamin C when they become bright red—that is, when they are fully ripe. They should be picked when they are firm and have this high red color. They must not be under-ripe and certainly not overripe, dark red, or mushy, for then they have less vitamin C. After they are picked, the hips should be cleaned from clinging stems and shoots. Pinch these off with your fingers rather than using a knife or scissors which can easily infect the hip with mold where the incision is made. Discard worm-eaten hips with dark spots. Gathering rose hips is fast work and it is fun but it is well to beware of the thorns. Better wear old clothes!"

The booklet goes on to describe how the rose hips are to be delivered to the C-Nok factory and urges everybody—children and adults alike—to go on a rose hip picking campaign. Don't let a single one go to waste!

A Norweigan Doctor Speaks

Dr. Anton Jervel, chief physician of the Vestfold District Hospital then has a few words to say about the importance of vitamin C in the diet. Says Dr. Jervel: "Of late we have revived an interest in regard to food budgets and vitamin content. Meantime our living standard has risen so high and we have such a rich and varied fare that there should be practically no illness caused by lack of vitamins. But in the near future this situation may be quite different and even this year we may have difficulty in nourishing our population. Hence we must see to it that what we eat indeed furnishes us with what we need, so we must make use of all our knowledge about vitamins and the other elements of our food supply, so as to be fortified in the fight to maintain our health.

"It is not our intention here to go deeply into the problem of the diet in its details. This is being worked out from all angles so as to utilize all the food resources of the land. We will touch only on the problem of vitamin C.

"A proper diet is a complicated matter. We can have plenty of food and yet be helpless in the face of illness if our diet lacks some one important item—vitamin C, for instance. One disease to be feared is scurvy, caused by deficiency of vitamin C. In its milder phases it is accompanied by fatigue, lassitude and anemia—in the more serious phases, by skin eruptions and bleeding gums. Vitamin C is the only preventive or cure for scurvy. We should take vitamin C daily.

"As food rations diminish, it is best to know where to obtain the necessary amounts of vitamin C. Milk contains some, but the quantity varies greatly in different samples of milk. The only other sources are in the vegetable kingdom, especially potatoes and the members of the cabbage family. But fresh vegetables are hard to get in winter and early spring. Potatoes and the cabbage family lose a lot of vitamin C in storage. Oranges and other citrus fruits contain a great deal of vitamin C but these fruits are hardly a daily fare. If we had nothing else to depend on, we could justly fear that scurvy, at least in its milder phases, might threaten our population, from lack of vitamin C.

"However we are fortunate because we have rose hips which contain more vitamin C than any other food. Then too, they keep their vitamin content when they are dried and powdered. One teaspoon of rose hip powder a day supplies our daily requirement of vitamin C throughout the year. The thing to do is to gather rose hips! All of us, especially the children and young people, can help. Do not let this valuable fruit rot on the bushes this fall. Each one of us can dry what he requires or else gather the rose hips for those factories that make the powder. This is not difficult and it is one way in which we can serve our country. For our own sake and for our country, it is vastly important to safeguard our health."

We believe you will be touched, as we were, by this message from faraway Norway, where, as the good doctor says, citrus fruits are "hardly daily fare." The Norwegians are steering straight for their goal of perfect health and it is a goal we in this country cannot ignore. For, in spite of the abundance of citrus fruit and fresh vegetables in America, many of us do not get enough vitamin C. Rose hips can supply this vitamin more abundantly than any other food. So take the excellent advice of our cousins across the sea. Gather rose hips this fall!

CHAPTER 269

You Can Prepare Rose Hips

The ascorbic acid—or vitamin C—content of rose hips (the large, berry-like fruit that forms after the rose has blossomed) is from *10 to 100 times greater than in any other food,* including the highly touted citrus fruits. In England, the Scandinavian countries and throughout all Europe, the value of rose hips is well-known. Here are some of the methods for making the most of all the ripe hips you can gather this fall:

Because the elusive vitamin C is difficult to hold through a drying process, rose hips are not easily prepared in powder form. If you grow your own roses or if you have access to roses whose hips you can use, the best idea is to make an extract or purèe of them. This can then be stored with a minimum loss of food value, and used throughout the year by the tablespoonful or in fruit juices, salads, soups, sauces, etc.

Rose Hip Extract

One of the most practical recipes for rose hip extract comes from Adelle Davis' excellent cookbook, *Let's Cook It Right.* Says Miss Davis:

"Gather rose hips; chill. (This is to inactivate the enzymes which might otherwise cause a loss of vitamin C.) Remove blossom ends, stems and leaves; wash quickly. For each cup of rose hips bring to a boil 1½ cups of water. Add one cup of rose hips. Cover utensil and simmer 15 minutes. Let stand in a pottery utensil for 24 hours. Strain off the extract, bring to a rolling boil, add 2 tablespoons lemon juice for each pint, pour into jars and seal. (Remember, don't make the mistake of using copper or aluminum utensils when you are cooking rose hips.)"

That cautioning note at the end of the recipe is there because copper destroys vitamin C on contact, and aluminum cookware also causes a considerable loss. Remember, researchers have found that the best time to gather the hips is when they are fully ripe, but not overripe. Rose hips are bright scarlet when ripe, orange when unripe and dark red when overripe. Location makes a difference in vitamin content, too, with roses farther north showing more vitamin C than those grown farther south.

Regardless of what you're making, follow these few rules:

1. Trim both ends of the rose hips with a pair of scissors before cooking.
2. Use stainless steel knives, wooden spoons, earthenware or china bowls and glass or enamel saucepans.
3. Cook quickly with the lid on so there will not be much loss of vitamin C.
4. After the hips have been cooked the required time, strain out the spines and seeds or break them down by rubbing the cooked pulp through a sieve.

Rose Hip Purèe

Take two pounds of rose hips and two pints of water. Remove the stalk and remnants of the rose from the end of the berries and stew them in a saucepan until tender. This will take about 20 minutes and the lid should be kept on. Then press the mixture through a sieve and the result will be a brownish-tinted purèe of about the same consistency and thickness as jam.

Rose Hip Soup

In Sweden rose hip soup is a popular, healthful dish. It's easy to make: The hips are ground and boiled for 10 minutes, then strained and again brought to a boil and thickened with 4 level teaspoons of potato flour (you can use soybean or whole wheat flour) which has been prepared with two cups of cold water. This soup can be served hot or cold.

No matter how you get your rose hips, you can be sure you're treating yourself to one of nature's greatest treasures of nutrition.

CHAPTER 270

Acerola or Rose Hips for Vitamin C?

A number of years ago, scientific nutrition workers in Puerto Rico were surprised to find that the acerola cherry which grows there in great abundance had an astonishingly high content of vitamin C. Soon acerola trees were planted in school yards and the government encouraged planting them near private homes, so that another source of this important vitamin would be close at hand.

A baby foods company soon began to include acerola juice in its cans of fruit juice for infants. Apple juice, pineapple juice and so forth were fortified with acerola which naturally increased the vitamin C content of the cans. Of course, there was no way whereby one could know how much vitamin C had been added, since this was a drink, not a food supplement.

Eventually there were enough acerola cherries so that they could be used as a source of vitamin C in food supplements. And recently a health foods company has advertised its acerola product as a natural vitamin C food supplement, which, of course, it is.

Many readers, receiving announcements through the mail about this new product, have written us asking whether this is as good a source of vitamin C as rose hips. "Which has the most vitamin C" they ask? Shall we stop taking rose hips and take acerola preparations instead?

Just to refresh our memories, here is a list of foods high in vitamin C:

	Milligrams	Per
Broccoli	90	¾ cup or 100 grams
Cantaloupe	50	½ small cantaloupe or 100 grams
Collards	70	½ cup or 100 grams
Grapefruit	45	½ grapefruit or 100 grams
Guavas	125	1 guava or 100 grams
Honeydew	90	¼ honeydew or 100 grams
Kale	96	¾ cup
Mustard greens	125	½ cup
Orange juice	59	100 grams
Peppers, green	125	1 medium pepper
Peppers, pimento	200	2 medium peppers
Rose hips	500-6000	100 grams
Turnip tops	130	½ cup

Vitamin C Content of the Acerola

An article by Lydia J. Roberts in the *American Journal of Nursing,* September, 1957, tells us that one large acerola (about one inch in diameter) weighs about 8 grams and furnishes 80 milligrams of vitamin C, or the same amount as a medium-sized orange. Two acerolas per day are recommended, she says, to supply liberally the day's requirement of vitamin C.

Using these facts, one would assume that 100 grams of acerola would furnish 1000 milligrams of vitamin C, making acerola an excellent source of this vitamin. Our information on rose hips shows that, depending on variety and the climate in which they are grown, rose hips may contain from 500 to 6000 milligrams of vitamin C per 100 grams.

What does this mean to the reader in terms of adding acerola juice to his diet? When and if acerola juice becomes available, bottled, we would certainly urge readers to buy it, for it will provide a fine practical source of vitamin C. If frozen acerola berries should become available, they, too, would be excellent sources of the vitamin.

The Best Source of Vitamin C

If there were a question of raising rose hips or raising acerola cherries for their vitamin C content, we would, of course, be concerned with which is the richest source of vitamin C. But since not many of us live in climates where the acerola can be grown and since rose hips can be grown very easily in almost any climate, and, in fact, contain more vitamin C the farther north they grow, it seems that few of us will be concerned with making a decision as to which we should plant for a crop rich in vitamin C—acerola or rose hips. Rose hips are more practical.

If there were a question of buying fresh rose hips or fresh acerola cherries at the market, then, too, we should be concerned with which is the better source of vitamin C. We hope that some day both rose hips and acerola will indeed be sold in markets.

But meanwhile the only decision we must make is which supplement to take—one made of rose hips or one made of acerola. A moment's thought will show you that it makes no difference, for food supplements are labeled according to their vitamin content. Let's say we have 4 vitamin C supplements of equal weight per tablet lined up on a table. Each contains 100 milligrams of vitamin C, according to the label. One is made from green peppers, one from lemons, one from rose hips and one from acerola. It doesn't matter at all to you, the consumer, which of these foods originally had the most vitamin C, does it? The manufacturer of the supplement has concentrated the vitamin C, leaving some natural substances from the original food along with it.

So each of the 4 supplements contains exactly the same amount of vitamin C. Depending upon how they are prepared, each also contains some of the other elements that accompany vitamin C in food—the bioflavonoids, vitamin P, minerals and so forth. The question of which original food contained the most vitamin C concerns only the manufacturer of the supplement, not you and not the general public.

You can easily see that it does not matter a bit which of the supplements you decide on. You may like the taste of one better than the other. If you prefer to chew your vitamin C supplements, taste would be important.

The estimated bare minimum amount of vitamin C that will protect an adult from scurvy is about 30 milligrams a day. Considering the fact that vitamin C protects one against many poisonous substances to which we are all exposed daily, we recommend that our readers should get far more vitamin C than this. People who smoke or work in establishments where poisonous substances are used should get even larger doses of vitamin C. Those of us who, for some reason, cannot get very much fresh raw food should pay special attention to taking plenty of vitamin C in food supplements, for it cannot be stored by the body and must be replenished every day.

CHAPTER 271

The Facts on Royal Jelly

For thousands of years honeybees have occupied a unique niche among all the living creatures that have come to live with man. Because of their intricate and fascinating community life, we human beings have always known that there was something special about bees—something not quite comprehensible to mere man. In all parts of the world in times past, and in many agricultural countries even today, the bees share in family celebrations. At Christmas and Easter, for weddings and funerals, special ceremonies must be performed near the beehives. If a disaster or a blessing befalls the family, the bees must be told, first of all.

It is not surprising that men have such reverence for these furious and conscientious little insects. Bees not only organize their community life along the strictest lines, not only do they work at unbelievable speeds and collect incredible amounts of food in the way of nectar and pollen, but they communicate with one another. They have their own system of mathematics, geometry and geography so well worked out that the bee who discovers a cache of honey can describe to the other members of the hive exactly where the honey is located, how much there is and what is the shortest and best route to take to get there. All these facts have been verified by scientists.

Recently another fabulous aspect of bee-life has been getting publicity —royal jelly, the food of the queen bee. We have been reading a lot about royal jelly, *Look* for October 19, 1954, carried a feature story on it. The New York Sunday *Mirror* for June 27, 1954, carried a syndicated feature story. The *News* from Sarasota, Florida, for October 21, 1954, carried a front page story on a beekeeper there who shipped in 20 million bees, in the hope that he can produce royal jelly commercially. We have received clippings on royal jelly from state after state. And many letters from readers asking where they can buy this miracle food.

[1002]

How to Get Royal Jelly

Apparently the answer to this one is—nowhere, for there is a peculiar problem involved in producing royal jelly which will invariably limit its usefulness so far as human consumption is concerned. Royal jelly is the food produced by the worker bees to feed the queen bee. A queen bee is both mother and ruler of an entire hive. During one season she may become the mother of as many as a quarter of a million bees. A queen bee has been known to lay more than 2000 eggs (more than her own weight) in a single day. Of the eggs she lays, the fertile ones may develop into either worker bees or queens. Their development depends entirely on their food. All the eggs are fed royal jelly for the first two or three days after hatching. But the egg destined to be a queen bee, and then the queen bee herself, receives royal jelly throughout her life. So it seems reasonable to assume that the food is solely responsible for the great difference between the queen bee and the workers, for no other circumstances of their growth are different, except for food.

Worker bees grow up in from 21 to 24 days. Queen bees mature in 16 days. Worker bees work furiously and live from two to six months. Queen bees, working just as hard at their egg laying, may live as long as eight years. What a powerful force of longevity and fertility must be contained in royal jelly!

But here is the catch to the whole thing. Worker bees feed royal jelly to create a queen only when they need a queen—that is when the old queen is dying or they have decided to get rid of her, or when, for some other mysterious reason of their own, they want a new queen. To produce royal jelly for experiments, scientists must first remove the reigning queen. The bees know at once that she is gone and they work desperately feeding royal jelly to several more larvae in order to produce a new queen. The experimenters again remove the royal jelly and the bees must frantically produce more.

As more and more royal jelly is removed it seems to us that the frenzy and frustration of the bee colony must become frightening. And which of us can predict what will be the final effect on the well-ordered life of the bee colony after this process has gone on for some time? Can we afford to endanger the whole structure of bee society and possibly do serious damage to the bees in order to procure for ourselves the marvelous royal jelly that has such potency so far as bees are concerned?

What Does Royal Jelly Contain?

Well, then, you might say, let us study the royal jelly, find out what it contains, and manufacture our own! Easier said than done. Royal jelly has so intrigued scientists of recent years that they have conducted extensive researches on it, without finding in it any substance that would explain its marvelous power. They have taken royal jelly apart until they know what all its ingredients are, they think. Then they put these ingredients together in the laboratory and what they get is not royal jelly at all! So apparently there are substances in the jelly with which we are not only unfamiliar, but whose presence we cannot even detect.

Melampy and Jones reported in the *Proceedings of the Society of Experimental Biology and Medicine,* Vol. 41, p. 382, 1939, that they could detect no vitamin A in royal jelly. There was some vitamin B_1 (thiamin). Pearson and Burgin in the same magazine, Vol. 48, p. 415, 1941, reported that royal jelly contains more pantothenic acid than any other known substance—between 2½ and 6 times as much as yeast and liver. Pantothenic acid is another B vitamin.

Other investigators have reported little or no vitamin E in royal jelly, and no detectable amount of vitamin C. Thomas S. Gardner, writing in the *Journal of Gerontology* for January, 1948, tells of experiments involving fruit flies which were fed royal jelly. According to him, the pantothenic acid in royal jelly increased the life span of the flies. He goes on to say that no one knows as yet how much of this valuable B vitamin is needed by the average human being, but it has been estimated that we need about 11 to 15 milligrams a day. In the average American diet most of us obtain only about 5 milligrams a day. However, no one has done any research apparently to find out whether pantothenic acid, either in or out of royal jelly, will increase the life span of human beings.

We Welcome Scientific Material on Royal Jelly

And so the story goes. When we first began to collect clippings about royal jelly, we wrote to some 10 or 15 laboratories where, according to the clippings, research is in progress. None of them could give us any help. They referred us to the information we have given above, but without exception they told us that they know of no research involving human beings. We also wrote to people who sell honey. More than anyone else, beekeepers are respectful when they speak of all the marvels of bee-life and community organization. And they are all sure that royal jelly must be a truly miraculous substance, for they see what happens in their beehives to those individual bees that feed on royal jelly as compared with those which do not. But none of our beekeeper friends had heard of any research involving human beings. And most of them stated that royal jelly is not very tasty. It is a white milky paste with an acid flavor.

Until we have further information, it is our considered opinion that royal jelly, while completely harmless, does not perform the miracles attributed to it—for human beings.

CHAPTER 272

Kelp for Trace Minerals

In the Chinese *Book of Poetry* written in the time of Confucius (between 800 and 600 B. C.) there is a poem about a housewife cooking seaweed. During this period in Chinese history seaweed was considered a delicacy, worthy of being offered to the gods as a sacrificial food. Several kinds of seaweed were used in ancient China. And seaweed still forms an important part of the diet in Eastern countries.

In Japan, we are told, seaweed is used to a far greater extent than in any other country and provides about 25 per cent of the daily diet! The brown seaweeds are incorporated into flour and are used in almost every household as noodles, toasted and served with rice or in soup. Two other kinds of seaweed are used for sweetening and flavoring. Relishes, beverages and cakes are made from them.

In Western countries seaweeds have never been generally accepted as part of daily meals, although in Ireland, Iceland, Denmark, Wales, Scotland and the Faroe Islands, seaweeds have been eaten extensively. The national dish of South Wales is laverbread, which contains seaweed. The Irish eat dulse, a seaweed that is called "sea lettuce" because it is tender, crisp and tasty like the land variety. W. A. P. Black, writing in the *Proceedings of the Nutrition Society* of England, Vol. 12, p. 32, 1953, says that a certain seaweed, porphyra, is eaten in Scotland, grilled on toast. He tells us it looks like spinach and tastes like oysters.

Intestinal Bacteria Digest Seaweed

Dr. Black also tells us that there may be present in the intestinal tracts of the Japanese people a specialized bacterial flora, giving the seaweeds a greater nutritional value. The bacterial flora are the beneficial bacteria which live in the intestines and manufacture certain vitamins there, as well as helping in the digestion of food. Dr. Black says that in digestibility tests with cattle it has been found that when seaweed is first introduced into the diet, it is completely undigested and appears unaltered in the feces. After a few days, however, no seaweed as such is found in the feces. So it seems that the bacteria in the intestines have an important part in the digestion of seaweed. In Japan it appears that children develop the proper intestinal bacteria since they are fed seaweed products from infancy on.

Seaweed—A Valuable Food

Back in 1920, according to *Popular Mechanics,* for July 1952, a man named Philip Park who was touring England was startled to see cattle passing over rich, lush grass so that they could feed on kelp or seaweed. He investigated the food content of this seaweed and went into business to produce it for animal food and human consumption as well. At his nonprofit research organization, experiments are carried on to find out even more about this remarkable plant.

Kelp is harvested by special boats equipped with a great hook which pulls the plant up out of the sea. Special cutters then mow off the tops of the kelp plants which are carried back to the boat on a conveyor belt arrangement. At the processing plant, the kelp is chopped fine, dried, sterilized and shredded. There is no boiling or draining off of water. Everything in the way of minerals remains that was in the original plant. We are told that kelp plants are so vigorous in growth that plants cut to a depth of 4 feet will reach the surface of the sea again within 48 to 60 hours.

We are well acquainted, all of us, with the fact that plants growing on the land form, or should form, a large part of the diet of the healthy individual. What of the plants that grow in the sea? Is there any indication that they may be good for us, too?

Something About Seaweeds

Sea plants go under the collective name of "algae." There are three kinds, depending on color—the green, the brown and the red. In some ways they are like land plants, but in other ways many of them have little in common with what we are accustomed to thinking of as plants. They have no roots. They cling to stones, wharves or pilings with "holdfasts." They do not have stalks and branches in the same sense that land plants do. In many seaweeds there are no special parts of the plant either for support (like the stems of land flowers or the trunks of land trees) or for conducting nourishment from one part of the plant to another. Many seaweeds have structures that look like leaves, but they are not leaves in the same sense that we use for leaves of land plants. They do not manufacture food for the rest of the plant to eat. In seaweeds almost every part of the plant can make its own food. Seaweeds have nothing that looks like flowers, fruit or seeds.

They grow tall, some of the largest kelps stretching up for a hundred feet or more from the floor of the ocean. Because of their simple structure and the fossils in which they have been found, paleontologists (scientists who decide about the age of earthly things) have said that algae probably represent the first form of life that appeared on our planet. The seaweeds you find today have developed considerably since those first primitive times, of course, but even so, they still retain many of the primitive characteristics of early life. They are not nearly so complicated as the land plants which came much later in history.

The Brown Seaweeds

The brown seaweeds are the ones we are going to talk about, for they are the commonest and the ones used most widely for food. Many of them are thick and leathery. Kelp comes in this category. Just as people in far corners of the world have eaten seeds, bones, insects and other foods that seem peculiar to us, just so have many peoples of the world eaten seaweed. And now it seems likely that kelp will become an important part of American diets.

Content of Seaweeds

What do seaweeds contain that might make them valuable as food? First of all, of course, just like other plants, they contain carbohydrates— that is, starches and sugars. The sugar of seaweed is called mannitol. It is not very sweet, has a mild laxative effect in large doses and does not increase the sugar content of the blood. This would be an important factor to diabetics if the seaweed-sugar should ever be used to a wide extent. Fats and proteins also exist in seaweed, the proteins about as useful to human bodies as the protein of land plants— that is, not as useful as protein that comes from animal sources, such as meat and eggs. Seaweed is not a very fatty plant, but it does contain at least one of the unsaturated fatty acids necessary to human health.

In the way of vitamins there seems to be some vitamin A and a certain amount of the B vitamins. Dr. Black of the British Nutrition Society tells us that the vitamin C content of seaweed is comparable with that of many vegetables and fruits. With some Eskimo nations seaweed was at one time used as their chief source of vitamin C. One test showed a vitamin C content of 5 to 140 milligrams of vitamin C per 100 grams of wet seaweed. Oranges contain about 50 milligrams per 100 grams.

The Minerals in Seaweed

However, our main interest in seaweed or kelp as food is not in its protein, carbohydrates or vitamins—although it is good to know the status of any new food in these categories. What interests us mainly about kelp is its mineral content. It seems reasonable, does it not, to expect sea foods to be rich in minerals? Aside from the fact that sea water as such is a veritable treasure trove of minerals, land minerals are constantly washing into the sea, enriching it still further. Every river in the world carrying silt and soil that has washed away or eroded from the land runs eventually to the sea, giving up its minerals into the salty depths.

Plants that grow on land take up minerals from the soil. By testing the amount of minerals in any given plant we can get a good idea of how many minerals were in the soil in which it grew, for vegetables and fruits from mineral-rich land will also be rich in these so-important food elements. The same is true of sea plants. So we can expect seaweed or kelp to be a good source of minerals. How good it is surprised even us. Dr. Black tells us that the ash of seaweed may be from 10 per cent to as high as 50 per cent. This means that if you burn seaweed you may have half the volume of the seaweed left as minerals! Compare this to some other foods. Carrots leave an ash of 1 per cent as minerals. Apples have a mineral ash of .3 per cent, almonds 3.0 per cent, beets 1.1 per cent.

Dr. Black says further, "It can be said that seaweed contains all the elements that have so far been shown to play an important part in the physiological processes of man. In a balanced diet, therefore, they would appear to be an excellent mineral supplement." We know that, of the minerals which are needed in relatively large amounts like calcium, iron, phosphorus, potassium and so forth, the average fruit or vegetable contains an amount approximate to the amounts listed on the tables and charts in nutrition books.

They Supply Trace Minerals

But, as important as these minerals are, perhaps even more important are the trace minerals—iodine, copper, manganese, boron, zinc and so forth. These minerals appear in minute quantities in food. Our bodies need only microscopically small amounts of them. Yet if that tiny amount is not there, the consequences may be fatal. Our land is becoming trace-mineral-poor. Floods and poor farming practices are causing our soil to be washed away. And with it go the trace minerals. Applying commercial fertilizer to the soil does not improve the situation, for this does not, cannot, contain the trace minerals. Only by organic farming—that is, returning to the soil everything that has been taken from it—can we be certain that our food contains all of the precious trace minerals necessary for health. What happens to the trace minerals that wash away from our farmlands? They wash into the ocean and are taken up into seaweeds. So the worse-off we become so far as trace minerals in foods are concerned, the more do we need a substance like kelp as a food supplement. Those of us who farm organically probably need it less than those of us who must buy all our food from a store.

Iodine in Kelp

From the point of view of nutrition the most important single trace mineral in kelp or seaweed is iodine. Why do we say this? How can one be more important than the others? It isn't that iodine is more important, exactly. It's simply that there are whole sections of the world where iodine *is completely lacking* in the soil. No food grown there contains any iodine at all. Many parts of the middle inland section of our country are deficient in iodine so far as soil is concerned. These localities are called "The Goiter Belt." We know that iodine is an absolute essential for the body, for it is the main ingredient of the product of one of our most important glands —the thyroid gland. Goiters are just one of the possible unhealthful results of too little iodine in the diet. There are many others.

Iodine From Iodized Salt

For a long time public health authorities have promoted the use of iodized salt to prevent goiter. This is plain table salt to which potassium iodide has been added by chemists. Our objection to this is our objection to all medicated foods. Table salt (sodium chloride) is a drug—a pure substance denuded of everything that accompanies sodium chloride in nature. To this we add another drug—potassium iodide. Such a product still has no relation to nature, so far as we are concerned. Besides we believe that most of us get far too much salt. So we recommend not using table salt either in cooking or at the table. Where then can someone who lives in the "goiter belt" get the iodine that is so essential for his well-being? Why not from kelp?

In Borden's *Review of Nutrition Research* for July-August, 1955, we are told that to get 100 micrograms of iodine (estimated as the normal daily requirement for human beings) one would have to eat

    10 pounds of fresh vegetables and fruits, or
    8 pounds of cereals, grains and nuts, or
    6 pounds of meat, freshwater fish, fowl, or
    2 pounds of eggs, or
    .3 pounds of marine fish, or
    .2 pounds of shellfish

They go on to state: "The problem of obtaining sufficient iodine from food of non-marine origin may be seen from values shown in this table. Iodine-rich seaweed is an abundant source on a limited scale for some peoples. Kelp contains about 200,000 micrograms per kilogram (about 2 pounds) and the dried kelp meal nearly 10 times as much, or .1 per cent to .2 per cent of iodine. Used as a condiment this would provide 10 times as much iodine as American iodized salt."

Best Source of Iodine and Minerals

Kelp, then, it seems to us is the perfect answer for a mineral supplement for health-conscious folks. It is practically the only reliable food source of iodine, aside from seafood. It is rich in potassium and magnesium. It contains, in addition, all of the trace minerals that have been shown to be important for human nutrition and many more whose purposes we have not yet discovered.

It does contain sodium chloride, true. So does almost everything else that you eat. It contains more sodium chloride than vegetables and meats because it comes from the salty sea. But its content of sodium chloride is not high compared to table salt which is, of course, 100 per cent sodium chloride. We do not believe that the salt in kelp is harmful, because it occurs along with the other minerals as a natural part of the food. We do believe that the other minerals, especially the iodine in kelp, make it one of our most valuable food supplements.

Here is an analysis of an average sample of kelp, neither especially high nor low in minerals. In some cases we have compared the mineral content of kelp with that of some other food especially rich in this same mineral. You will note in every instance how much higher is the mineral content of the kelp.

	Kelp	Other Food	
Iodine	.18%	Clams	1900 parts per billion
Calcium	1.05%	Milk	.001%
Phosphorus	.339%	Wheat Germ	.01%
Iron	.37%	Eggs	.0005%
Copper	.0008%	Eggs	.0000023%
Potassium	11.15%	Almonds	7%
Magnesium	.740%		
Sodium	3.98%		
Chlorine	13.07%		
Manganese	.0015%		
Sulfur	1%		

Trace minerals in kelp, not listed above are: barium, boron, chromium, lithium, nickel, silicon, silver, strontium, titanium, vanadium and zinc.

CHAPTER 273

The Value of Seaweed
in Nutrition

The effectiveness of seaweed as a food for animals should give us some better idea of the worth of this food for human beings. Has seaweed been used to feed animals? If so, with what results? Dr. W. A. P. Black, who seems to be a world authority on the subject has a lot to say about seaweed in animal nutrition in an article in the British magazine, *Agriculture*, Vol. 62, pp. 12-15 and 57-62, 1955.

Says Dr. Black, feeding trials with animals must be carried out for a considerable length of time because it apparently takes some time for the intestines to accustom themselves to this diet, so that the seaweed can be completely digested.

Mineral Content of Seaweed

"Seaweeds have the advantage over land crops in that they grow in an ideal environment, in which the nutrients in sea water are being constantly renewed by nature," says Dr. Black, "whereas on the land modern methods of intensive cultivation lead to complete exhaustion of the soil unless, with a knowledge of the nutritional and other growth requirements of the crops, the deficiencies are replaced by man. Seaweeds, therefore, contain all the elements found in sea water, as well as a rich bacterial microflora which contributes to their composition."

The brown seaweeds (of which kelp is one) contain all the elements present in sea water, says Dr. Black, and can accumulate some of them to *several thousand times* their concentration in the surrounding water. So they must contain all the elements shown to play an important part in animal nutrition. We know full well, Dr. Black goes on, that several of the well-known animal diseases result from not having in the diet enough of one or another of the "trace" minerals—that is, minerals which occur in food in such small amounts that one can say there is only a "trace." One cannot use kelp as the only mineral supplement, he believes, because its calcium and phosphorus content is too low. But if you use also some mineral supplement (such as bone meal, we suggest) which is rich in calcium and phosphorus, seaweed can provide everything else that is needed in the way of mineral supplement.

The Value of Iodine in Seaweed

The iodine in seaweed is in the form of iodine amino acids—in other words it occurs in kelp in just the same form in which it occurs in the thyroid gland. Possibly this is the reason that kelp is so effective. There can be no question about how well its iodine is used by the body—it is in the same form in which it occurs in the thyroid gland where most of the body's iodine is.

Dr. Black tells us that these iodine amino acids make kelp a valuable food supplement for animals, "increasing the milk and butterfat production of dairy cows, for egg production, fattening swine and reviving spermatogenesis in bulls and rams." We are especially interested in the last part of that sentence, for it seems to indicate that trace minerals (is it the iodine or something else?) have a noteworthy effect on fertility.

Doesn't it seem possible that human infertility, too, may result from lack of the important trace minerals which are found so abundantly in kelp? It would seem that just the evidence alone which is presented here by Dr. Black should be enough to send medical researchers scurrying to use kelp in treatment of their patients who are trying to overcome infertility.

Vitamins in Seaweed

Seaweeds are interesting for their vitamins, too, says Dr. Black, most particularly because they contain vitamins like B_{12} which, he thinks, exists in seaweed because of its attached bacteria. The vitamin B_{12} content varies with the kind of seaweed, but several of the green varieties, he says, contain as much vitamin B_{12} as is found in liver—the richest source.

Vitamin E, not so plentiful in present-day foodstuffs, is present in kelp in rather large quantity. Vitamin K is there, too. It is believed by scientists that vitamin D does not occur in vegetable matter. We need vitamin D in order to use calcium properly. Children need it so that they will not get rickets. Fish liver oil and sunlight are the two best sources for vitamin D. No one has ever been able to find vitamin D, as such, in any vegetable product. But now we hear that scientists have kept young chicks from getting rickets by feeding them seaweed. Up to the age of 16 weeks these chicks had seaweed as their only possible source of vitamin D—and they thrived. So there must be vitamin D in seaweed.

Seaweed in Animal Food

As early as 1812 Englishmen were feeding seaweed to their cows in wintertime. It improved their health and increased their milk yield. Since the First World War, many feeding experiments have shown that kelp can take its place among other fodder as a valuable nutritional aid. In one experiment in Ireland it was shown that seaweed meal of one kind has a food value about two and a half times that of potatoes and is about halfway between hay and oats. In addition, because it exerts a very favorable effect on the digestive tract of the animal, it enhances the nutritional value of the original ration fed, for the animal can profit nutritionally from other food much more when seaweed is also fed. Fed to hens, seaweed increases the iodine content of their eggs.

It was found, in feeding seaweed to hens, that one per cent seaweed meal given to the hen each day was enough to supply all the iodine requirement of an adult man eating one of this hen's eggs each day! In many cases studies were made of how much seaweed could profitably be added to the ration. And it was found, in general, that 10 per cent was about the right amount that might be fed with good results.

In many of the trials, says Dr. Black, no beneficial effects have resulted from adding seaweed to the ration. But it must be remembered that in these cases the seaweed has merely replaced an equal amount of a carefully balanced diet which could not possibly be improved by any supplement. (Human beings don't live on diets nearly that good!)

In Eire seaweed meal is added in quantity to many animal foodstuffs. In New Zealand seaweed meal has benefited cattle grazing on mineral-deficient land, by replacing the minerals missing from the soil. In this country great improvement has been noted in the health of cattle and chickens when seaweed was fed. In France 10,000 tons of seaweed meal go annually into cattle foods. In the British Isles the seaweed industry, still in its infancy, sells 7,000 tons per year.

We have a newspaper clipping from Saint John, New Brunswick, Canada (no date available), telling us that dulse, another kind of seaweed, is being processed there. Pills and capsules are being made. Dulse is being added to flour, too, which can be used to enrich biscuits, bread, cake and so forth. Dulse is said to contain 300 times more iodine than whole wheat and 50 times as much iron. In New Brunswick, the clipping tells us, dulse sells for 10 cents a bag in grocery stores.

A Medicinal Use of Seaweed

An unusual comment on a medicinal use of seaweed comes from the *Journal of the Philippine Medical Association* for June, 1946. Several investigators there used a kind of seaweed called *Digenia simplex* as an anti-helmintic—that is, to kill intestinal worms. During the war they were unable to get their usual drugs (which was just as well, we'd say, for they were probably highly toxic preparations) so they tried the powdered seaweed, made into tea. Their conclusions were that the drug, as they call it, is 73 per cent effective; it is nontoxic, can be administered under any conditions without preparing the patient prior to giving it to him. They suggest that further study be given to the matter. We have not been able to find in medical literature any indication that any further research has been done.

Seaweed for Sausage Casings

The *New York Times* for October 23, 1955, published an article about a new sausage casing made of seaweed which is being promoted by the Visking Corporation, largest producers of sausage casings. Up to now, cellulose casings have been used. They have no food value whatsoever. Of course, the seaweed does.

CHAPTER 274

Do You Need Lecithin?

The word "cholesterol" has come to have all the cheerful sound of a funeral bell for those of us who are worried about hardening of the arteries and coronary thrombosis. Cholesterol is the fatty substance that collects on the inside walls of the blood vessels, narrowing them so that the blood has a difficult time getting through. Eventually calcium becomes deposited on the cholesterol and the situation becomes worse and worse. A chunk of cholesterol breaking off and floating around in a blood vessel can, of course, shut off the supply of blood entirely and, if this happens in a main artery, consequences can be fatal.

L. M. Morrison and K. D. Johnson writing in the *American Heart Journal*, Vol. 39, 1950, tell the results of a survey of the cholesterol content of the coronary arteries and blood of a group of patients who died of coronary thrombosis (a blood clot in the coronary artery). It was, in general, 4 times the average of that of normal patients. Hypercholesterolemia (an overabundance of cholesterol) was found in most of the patients who died of coronary thrombosis, so it is reasonable to believe that some disturbance in the way the body handles fatty substances is responsible for hardening of the arteries and also for coronary thrombosis.

T. Leary writing in the *Archives of Pathology*, Vol. 47, 1949, says it is generally accepted these days that cholesterol is constantly present in the disordered blood vessels of a patient with hardening of the arteries. It is also true that cholesterol in the blood vessels appears to increase with advancing age. What is cholesterol? It is a fatty substance that occurs in many foods—among them egg yolk and butter. According to *Bridges' Dietetics for the Clinician*, it is extremely important for good health. It is responsible in part for the semi-solid consistency of living cells. It is important to nerve tissues and it has a vital part to play in preventing destruction of red blood cells. In general, we do not know as yet all of the beneficial things cholesterol does in the body.

Why, then, should we speak the word with dread? If cholesterol is so necessary to health, why not just forget about it and go happily on our way? We can't, it seems, for cholesterol is also the substance chiefly responsible for hardening of the arteries and coronary thrombosis. How can this be— that a substance our bodies need can play such a treacherous trick on us? Apparently the answer is that for some reason some people's bodies cannot use cholesterol properly. Then it collects in blood vessels or it forms gallstones.

How Can You Avoid Cholesterol Deposits?

The treatment for high cholesterol content of the blood has been, among some physicians, to tell their patients to cut out all foods that are

[1013]

high in cholesterol. This would include: brains, egg yolk, fish roe, kidney, liver, sweetbreads and poultry.

Now these are all good foods, containing vitamins and minerals that we need. How can we possibly cure a sick person by taking away the very foods that will give him large amounts of vitamin A, vitamin E and the unsaturated fatty acids, sometimes called vitamin F? The sick person needs these vitamins even more than the well person. So, even though we may reduce the cholesterol content of his blood by removing foods that are high in cholesterol, we may also bring on something far worse if we consistently deprive him of the foods he needs.

A far better point of view, it seems to us, is to study everything about the patient's diet and see if perhaps he is getting too little of something else which is the very thing he needs so that his body can use cholesterol properly and it will not accumulate in his blood vessels or gall bladder. Is there such a substance? A great many medical researchers believe there is and they have done years of hard work to prove their theories.

The substance that apparently protects against accumulations of cholesterol is lecithin. It is pronounced *less-i-thin* with the accent on the first syllable. The word comes from the Greek *Likithos,* meaning *the yolk of an egg,* for lecithin is most abundant in egg yolk. In fact, when it was first studied in Germany towards the end of the last century, the researchers could then obtain lecithin only from egg yolk and this was too expensive a source for use by the general public. So they didn't get very far with their research and it was not until quite recently that another source has been discovered.

Lecithin and Cholesterol in Natural Foods

How does it happen that the lecithin occurs in egg yolk where cholesterol also is plentiful? Doesn't it sound like another of Mother Nature's provisions for good health? Cholesterol without lecithin can be harmful. So they are both included together in this one especially healthful food. Why then should we have any trouble with cholesterol—aren't we all getting enough lecithin in our food?

Apparently not, and the reason is that the processing which our various fats and oils go through before they appear on grocery shelves destroys the lecithin content, but leaves the cholesterol. Hydrogenated fats, for instance, —the shortenings used in pastry and for frying—do not contain lecithin, for it has been destroyed in the hydrogenation process. What happens as a result? The lecithin was put there by nature to act as an emulsifying agent for the cholesterol.

This means simply that when the cholesterol tends to coalesce or lump together, the lecithin breaks it up, mixes with it, and keeps it finely divided so that it can be circulated throughout the body as a perfectly stable "emulsion" that will not solidify or congeal. Once the lecithin is removed, there is nothing to keep the cholesterol moving along through the blood stream—it cakes; it gathers in lumps.

One other aspect of our increasing need for lecithin has been investigated perhaps least of all—that is the incredible amount of synthetic fats that are now being used in foods. You are not aware of these. No one but the food processor has the formula for what amounts of synthetic fats are contained in various foods. At best, their names appear in tiny print at the bottom of a label some place and you are given the impression that they have been used in infinitely small amounts. As a matter of fact they are being used in increasing quantity, even in such daily necessities as bread. They are cheaper and they can be "worked with" better as the food is processed. But very little study has been made of their effect on the body over a long period of time. Can they not have a great deal to do with the deposit of cholesterol in the blood vessels?

Complex and baffling as is the whole subject of fats in human nutrition, very, very little has actually been done in the way of research. We do know, however, a number of things about the relation between lecithin and cholesterol. Here, for instance, are some laboratory experiments and observations on human beings that make very good sense to us.

Experiments With Lecithin Prove Its Healthfulness

H. D. Keston and R. Silbowitz reported in the *Proceedings of the Society of Experimental Biology and Medicine*, Vol. 49, 1942, that feeding lecithin to rabbits who were receiving large amounts of cholesterol kept the cholesterol from collecting in the blood and in the blood vessels and prevented hardening of the arteries in the rabbits. G. L. Duff and T. P. B. Payne wrote in the *Journal of Experimental Medicine*, Vol. 92, 1950, that they had shown in laboratory animals that the amount of cholesterol taken is *not* the important thing in hardening of the arteries—*the important thing is the instability of the cholesterol*. That is, when the cholesterol is not emulsified, it deposits on artery walls. Lecithin, of course, emulsifies it.

D. Adlersburg and H. Sobotka showed in *Gasteroenterology*, Vol. 1, 1943, that lecithin helps greatly in absorbing vitamin A and fats in patients whose diseases make this nearly impossible. A. Scharf and C. A. Slanetz tell us that there is an unknown factor in lecithin which is absolutely essential for the body in order to use vitamin A properly. It also improves the utilization of vitamin E in their laboratory experiments. This information comes from the *Proceedings of the Society of Experimental Biology and Medicine*, Vol. 57, 1944.

In the *Southern Medical Journal* for August, 1950, a researcher named H. W. Dietrich described his results in giving lecithin and vitamin E to patients with diabetes. The insulin requirements of these patients went down considerably and their diabetes improved. This would seem to indicate that the lecithin brought about many beneficial changes in the body, for diabetes is a most complex disease and is not by any manner of means understood fully as yet. P. Gross and B. M. Kesten have given lecithin to several hundred psoriasis patients wtih excellent results. Several other researchers also reported benefits from lecithin in cases of psoriasis.

Dr. Francis Pottenger of Monrovia, California, has contributed much to our knowledge of various nutrition matters. In the April, 1944, issue of the *Southern Medical Journal* Dr. Pottenger discusses the use of lecithin in cases of skin diseases. He says, "The effect of processing cereals with the accompanying loss of minerals and the vitamin B complex has received much attention. However, the loss of the important fats in the processing of our vegetable oils and our cereals has not received due consideration. The removal of the fats would appear to be as deleterious as the removal of the water soluble parts of the germ." He tells us that the best commercial source of lecithin is the solvent-processed soybean lecithin in which no great heat is used for producing the lecithin. In the series of cases he describes, he gave a high protein diet, with raw brain and liver (high in lecithin) as well as soybean lecithin. Of the many cases he describes, there was improvement or complete cure in all. The cases included patients with keratoses (any skin disorder with horny growths), a bronzing of the skin thought to be indicative of fat deficiency, infantile eczema, the more severe types of eczema, scleroderma (another skin disorder involving hard, pigmented patches), senile atrophy of the skin, seborrheas, acne and keloid formation (a tumor-like scar).

Why We Do Not Get Enough Lecithin

So here we have disorders as widely varied as hardening of the arteries, acne, diabetes and psoriasis benefiting from the administration of lecithin. And we have a perfectly sound reason for why these diseases should be increasing daily. Look at the menu the next time you are in a restaurant. A goodly portion of the main dishes are fried in deep fat or prepared with fat. This means prepared with hydrogenated shortening from which the lecithin and vitamins have been removed. Dessert consists of a variety of pastries, pies and cakes, all made with hydrogenated shortening or synthetic fats which also contain no lecithin. Salad dressing is made from refined oil—again no lecithin. Margarine is probably used on vegetables or bread. Margarine goes through a dozen or so processes at high heat, guaranteeing that no vitamins or lecithin will remain in it. In addition, your restaurant meal has included "hidden" fats—the cracker with your tomato juice probably contains synthetic shortening—the bread probably does, too.

So almost everything you eat in a restaurant today brings into your body cholesterol without bringing along with it the lecithin that is necessary to emulsify it and keep it from collecting in lethal amounts on the walls of blood vessels. Is it any wonder that hardening of the arteries kills, either directly or indirectly, more Americans than any other disease?

At home what do you eat? If you use hydrogenated shortenings (that is, the white, solid shortening like Crisco) for any purpose whatsoever, you are inviting disaster. If you use margarine instead of butter, if you use crackers or any other prepared foods made with shortening, if you buy baker's bread, or, in fact, anything from a commercial bakery, chances are you are getting, every day, large amounts of cholesterol and no lecithin to help your body manage the cholesterol properly.

What is left for you to eat in the way of fats? Only completely natural fats that have not been tampered with in any way. This is a difficult assignment, for you have been used to buying all kinds of things you believed were wholesome which you can now no longer buy. Egg yolks are still probably the best food you can eat from the point of view of lecithin content. Although poultry raisers have invented a lot of incredible things to do to the chickens that lay eggs, they have fortunately not as yet discovered any way they can get inside an eggshell and do things to the egg before it reaches you. You will get cholesterol in your egg yolk, yes. But you will also get the lecithin that belongs with it, so the yolk can't do you any harm.

In her fine book, *Let's Eat Right to Keep Fit* (Harcourt Brace and Company, 1954), Adelle Davis tells us of a study in the Alameda County Hospital in which patients were given fat from egg yolks equivalent to 36 eggs daily, and in no case did the blood cholesterol rise above normal. This fat supplied lecithin, cholesterol and the B vitamin that is associated with lecithin—choline.

Take Lecithin as a Food Supplement

Finally, if you are worried about hardening of the arteries—and who of us over the age of 40 is not?—your best bet is to include lecithin in your food supplements, *especially* if you cannot possibly omit from your meals all the processed foods we have mentioned above which will increase your cholesterol without increasing your lecithin.

Lecithin for human consumption is made chiefly from soybeans. In fact, soya-lecithin has come to be the name generally used for lecithin because it is practically always made from soybeans. The way soya-lecithin was discovered is typical of our modern blundering way of doing things. Soybeans have become a profitable crop in this country and the oil they contain is used for all kinds of different products, most of them having nothing to do with food—rubber, petroleum, paint, ink, leather, soap, shaving creams, putty and so forth. So, as the chemists were devising ways and means of using this perfectly splendid food to manufacture these various non-food articles, they found that one substance interfered with many of the processes they wanted to use. So they removed the substance —lecithin. It became a waste product.

Isn't that a typical feat of modern genius—to remove from a food product the main substance that makes it valuable as food and then sit and ponder what to do with it so it won't be wasted! Lecithin is used in some food processing for it is a good emulsifier outside the body as well as inside. But it apparently never occurred to anybody that it was put into soybeans for some nutritional purpose, and certainly it would never occur to anybody to put it *back* into foods so that they would be more nourishing! In our country today the food industry seems bent on making food just something that will last a long time on grocery shelves, will look pretty and will be convenient. And, of course, all of this means that more and more nutritional value must be sacrificed.

Take lecithin—it's convenient, inexpensive and easy to take—if you have the slightest suspicion that you are getting too much cholesterol for your own good. Don't cut down on eggs and liver—but do cut down on the processed foods from which the lecithin has been removed!

CHAPTER 275

Why Do You Need Lecithin?

Our interest in lecithin at this particular moment in history springs almost entirely from our interest in another fatty substance—cholesterol. Because of cholesterol we have come, during the past 10 years, to think of any fat in the diet as being dangerous, even possibly to the point of being actually poisonous to us.

As a result, diets are being prescribed right and left in which fat has been reduced to a minimum. A recent issue of a women's magazine carried a reducing diet which had obviously been worked out with great care to include all the vitamins and minerals for which official daily minimum requirements have been set. We checked it closely and found indeed that vitamins A, B_1 and B_2, vitamin C, calcium and iron were all plentiful in this diet. But most of the other B vitamins, vitamin E and the essential unsaturated fatty acids, sometimes called vitamin F, were practicaly nonexistent in the menus, for the simple reason that the diet was low in fat. No salad dressings were used, foods were prepared without vegetable oils and whole grain cereals (one of our best sources of vitamin-rich fats) were not recommended.

Why this furor over fats? The reason is simple. Not so long ago it was discovered that cholesterol, a fatty substance occurring only in animal fats, may be largely responsible for hardening of the arteries. Investigating the thick chunks of matter that clog hardened arteries, researchers found that it consisted mostly of cholesterol. So right away everybody became panicky about cholesterol. The popular magazines carried frightening articles about it. Fat-free diets became the rage. Fat—any and all kinds of fat—became anathema.

The *American Heart Journal,* Vol. 39, 1950, tells the results of a survey of the cholesterol content of the coronary arteries and blood of a group of patients who died of coronary thrombosis (a blood clot in the coronary artery). It was about 4 times the average of that of normal patients. Since an overabundance of cholesterol was found in patients who died of coronary thrombosis, it seems reasonable to believe that for some reason the bodies of these individuals are not able to handle fatty substances properly.

Another article in *Archives of Pathology,* Vol. 47, 1949, states that cholesterol is constantly present in the disordered blood vessels of a patient with hardening of the arteries. And it seems to be true, too, that the amount of cholesterol in the blood vessels increases with age.

Suppose we delete all food that contains cholesterol. Will we then be free from any menace? No, we won't, because cholesterol is produced in the body at a much faster rate than we could eat it. Apparently it is necessary for many body functions among them the formation of vitamin D, the sex hormones and the adrenal hormones and the bile salts, so important for the proper digestion of all kinds of fats.

It has been shown that, by eating a high-fat diet, approximately 800 milligrams of cholesterol are obtained daily. But the perfectly normal human liver produces 3000 milligrams of cholesterol or more per day, all by itself! So even though you cut out any and all foods containing cholesterol, your body will still continue to manufacture it—and probably will also continue to misuse it so that you will still get deposits of cholesterol where they are not wanted—in the walls of blood vessels and in gallstones.

You see, once you cut out all fatty foods you also cut out all foods that contain lecithin, which is the substance that apparently can control cholesterol, keep it going its helpful way and prevent it from depositing where it is not wanted.

The What and How of Lecithin

Adelle Davis, in her book, *Let's Eat Right to Keep Fit* (Harcourt Brace and Company, New York, New York) has this to say about lecithin. "Another cousin of the fat family, lecithin, is supplied by all natural oils and by the fat of egg yolk, liver and brains. Lecithin is an excellent source of the two B vitamins, choline and inositol; if health is to be maintained, the more fat eaten, the larger must be the intake of these two vitamins. This substance can be made in the intestinal wall provided choline, inositol and essential fatty acids are supplied. Lecithin appears to be a homogenizing agent capable of breaking fat and probably cholesterol into tiny particles which can pass readily into the tissues. There is evidence that the major causes of death, coronary occlusion and coronary thrombosis are associated with deficiencies of linoleic acids (essential unsaturated fatty acids) and the two B vitamins, choline and inositol and perhaps with a lack of lecithin itself. Huge particles of cholesterol get stuck in the walls of the arteries; they might be homogenized into tiny particles if sufficient nutrients were available for the normal production of lecithin. When oils are refined or hydrogenated, lecithin is discarded."

Processing At Fault

So we come back again to the only possible conclusion—we ourselves have created the threat that cholesterol poses—by our arrogant meddling with natural foods. Hardening of the arteries, heart disorders, gallstones—these are the results of our meddling.

Cholesterol appears in foods of animal origin—fat meats, butter, oils from fish, eggs and so forth. So far our brilliant food chemists have not found any way to meddle with these fats. We cook them and if we raise the temperature to an excessively high degree, the fats are bound to be harmful to us. Deep fat frying and browning butter are two cooking processes that should be forbidden by law. But aside from this, fats of animal origin have not been tampered with to any great extent.

What about fats of vegetable and cereal origin, so rich in lecithin, the B vitamins and the essential fatty acids sometimes called vitamin F? We have done everything possible to destroy completely these vitally important fats and not just destroy them but render what remains in the food positively harmful to human cells.

First we remove all the health-giving fats when we refine grains. The germ of the cereal contains the lecithin, the B vitamins, the essential fatty acids and vitamin E. So we throw this exceedingly important part of the grain away (because it spoils easily!) and eat only the starchy remnant, practically vitamin free, which bakes into white, pasty bread with just about the same nutritive value as laundry starch. Your baker will tell you how they have "enriched" this pasty mass by adding some synthetic vitamin B_1 and iron. Ask him how much of the fatty part of the cereal grain has been replaced! This part is used instead for stock feed. Animals thrive on it.

Where Can You Get Lecithin in Your Diet?

And what of other natural sources of lecithin and all its accompanying vitamins? Seeds are rich sources. What seeds does the average American ever eat that have not been tampered with? Nuts are the only ones we can think of at the moment and even these he seems unable to eat unless they have been roasted to nothingness. Primitive peoples eat seeds of all kinds—melon seeds, sunflower seeds, cereal seeds, corn kernels, acorns, millet, whole rice and so forth. We Americans take the perfectly good seeds and other healthful foods Mother Nature gives and press out the oil. So far so good. It we stopped there (cold-pressed olive oil, for instance), all would be well. Such oils are rich in lecithin, vitamin E, the unsaturated fatty acids and the B vitamins. And research seems to prove that in lands where cold-pressed oils are the basic fatty foods, hardening of the arteries, heart disease, gallstones and other diseases involving cholesterol deposits are not common.

Hydrogenation

But our food technologists have developed ways of "improving" our vegetable oils. And you can be certain when that word "improve" comes in the front door, Mother Nature goes out the back. We "improve" oils by hydrogenating them. What does this give us? Hydrogenated shortenings— those lifeless (and, we are firmly convinced, deadly) solid white shortenings you buy in a can and use for making pastry, frying, cake-baking, deep-fat frying and so forth. They don't spoil; they're so economical; they're so much more convenient than messy liquid shortenings. You have all the arguments for them on your television commercials.

But unfortunately for you and me, all the lecithin, the B vitamins, vitamin E and the essential fatty acids have been destroyed in the process of hydrogenation. How is your body going to handle fats such as these without the natural substances that accompany fats in nature? It's an obvious impossibility. And all of the other food substances that depend on fats for their proper absorption—calcium, phosphorus, vitamin A and so forth—all these are going to be used improperly, too.

Consider for a moment all the conscientious mothers who "bake" for their families. To worthless white flour, completely denuded of all its nutritional value, they add white sugar (a drug with no food value but calories). Then, adding insult to injury, they cream into their cake hydrogenated shortening. The women's magazines, supported by advertising for these very products, devote themselves to dreaming up new horrors in the way of cake-making, to persuade the completely unaware housewife and mother that she is not "doing her duty" to her family if she doesn't whip up one of these monstrous pieces of nutritional rubbish this very day.

Is it any wonder we as a nation shudder at the word "cholesterol" and bring children into the world already afflicted with heart disease? What can we do to avoid cholesterol deposits? Stop eating eggs, fish and meat? No, of course not. Stop eating any fat that has been tampered with by food technologists. Read labels looking for the word "hydrogenated" and don't buy any product so labeled. Incidentally, margarine is, of course, hydrogenated vegetable oils. And any packaged foods you buy like crackers are probably made with hydrogenated shortenings. Get completely natural oils from plant sources. If you can, buy and use cold-pressed oils. Olive oil is often available from Italian importers in large cities. Cold-pressed oils are available in many health food stores.

INDEX

A

Abortion
  vitamin E and, 90
  wheat germ oil and, 90-91

Abrahamson, Dr. E. M., 16-19

Acerola
  compared to rose hips, 1001
  vitamin C in, 1000-1001

Acid-alkaline balance, 512, 934

Acne
  chocolate and, 446
  iodized salt and, 302-303
  vegetable oils and, 721-722

Acorn
  flour from, 270, 324
  how American Indians used, 324, 350
  human consumption of, 270, 324-325
  uses of, 324-325

Acute urticaria
  description of, 460
  saccharin and, 460-461

Addison's disease and salt, 283

Adrenal gland and salt, 286

Africa
  dental health in, 629-633, 649
  diet of childbearing in, 649
  native diets, 629-633, 648-649
  way of life in, 648

Agene
  alcoholism and, 50
  discovery of toxicity of, 49, 835
  effect on wheat protein, 836
  in flour bleaching, 49
  skin disease and, 152-153

Agriculture
  beginnings of, 70
  changes due to, 71
  civilization and, 71, 609
  dental caries and, 70-71
  loss of sewage to, 611
  malnutrition and, 70
  methods and food quality, 782-783, 871-872
  methods and plant parasites, 612
  methods and soil fertility, 609-610
  methods of the Hunzans, 785
  problems of, 609
  purpose of fertilization, 610
  trend to planting of crops of lower mineral requirement, 777-778
  See also chemical fertilizers, organic method.

Alcoholism and nutrition, 737-738

Alfalfa
  growth, 945
  human consumption of, 945, 946
  minerals in, 946 (table)
  protein in, 946
  vitamins in, 945

Allergy
  bleached flour and, 49-50
  difficulty in finding cause of, 201
  dysfunction of enzyme systems and, 566-567
  method of determining cause of, 141, 338
  refined sugar and, 404
  to beets, 476
  to citric acid, 201-203
  to fish, 254
  to milk, 140-141, 241
  wheat and, 59

Almonds
  calories in, 272-273
  hydrocyanic acid in bitter, 341-342
  minerals in, 273 (table)
  protein in, 273
  tips on serving, 273
  tree, 272
  vitamins in, 273 (table)

Aluminum cooking utensils
  danger in, 845, 917
  potato salad and, 916-917

American Indians. *See* Indians, American.

Amino acids
  essential. *See* essential amino acids.
  in brewer's yeast, 978
  in honey, 458
  manufactured in the body, 672
  names of, 671-672
  protein and, 316
  synthetic, 674-675
  See also essential amino acids, protein.

Aminotriazole
  carcinogenic properties of, 207
  soil fertility and, 210
  used on cranberry bogs, 207

Anemia
  bananas and, 173
  bone marrow and, 962
  honey and, 458-459
  onions and, 521-522
  protein deficiency and, 672
  tea and, 40

Animal fats
  cholesterol in, 683
  digestibility of, 683

Aniseeds, 325

Antibiotics
  blood clotting and, 139
  effect on meat, 121-122
  forbidden as food preservative, 138
  harm of continued ingestion of, 845
  in baby food, 868
  in cabbage, 479
  increased use in animals, 138-139
  in curing plant blights, 139
  in meats, 241-243
  in milk, 101
  in preserving fish, 263
  reaction to, increasing, 139
  See also penicillin.

Appetite
  bananas for stimulating, 175
  instinct and natural foods, 585-586
  instinct interfered with, 586-587
  nutmeg for stimulating, 231

Apples
  decalcifying effect of, 164
  dieting and, 163
  gums and, 225
  insecticide residues in, 164
  iron absorption and, 163-164
  mineral content, 164 (table)
  poison in seed, 341
  reaction to eating seeds, 341
  seed oil and muscular diseases, 325
  storage of, 164
  sugar in, 163
  therapeutic uses of, 163
  tooth health and, 164, 225
  vitamin C in, 165-166
  vitamins in, 164 (table)

Arsenic
  cancer and, 568, 844
  in cigarette smoke, 568

Arteriosclerosis
  cholesterol and, 702, 1013, 1018
  dietary control of, 771
  factors in, 771
  inositol and, 187

Arthritis
  cherries and, 188-189
  milk and, 119-120

Artificial insemination
  effect on births, 117
  in cows, 117

Asparagus
  flavor of, 471
  minerals in, 471 (table)
  production, 471

selection of, 471
vitamins in, 471 (table)

Australian aborigines, 649

Avidin
  biotin and, 103, 106
  in egg white, 103, 106
  possible function of, 109

B

Bacon
  chemically cured, 261, 262

Baked goods
  artificial coloring and flavoring and,
    55
  metallic decorations danger, 55
  nitric acid in, 55
  See also bread.

Baldness and salt, 296-298

Bananas
  advantages of, 177
  anemia and, 173
  appetite stimulation, 175
  calories in, 169
  celiac disease and, 174-175
  colitis and, 172
  constipation and, 169, 172
  diabetes and, 173-174
  diarrhea and, 176
  dieting and, 177
  digestibility of, 170
  eczema and, 176
  for elderly people, 167, 170
  for infants, 167, 764
  hemoglobin formation and, 173
  in low-sodium diets, 178
  in various diseases, 173
  iron in, 173
  kidney diseases and, 173
  lack seeds, 325-326
  minerals in, 167 (table), 171 (table)
  non-allergenic properties of, 173
  protein in, 169
  ripening of, 167, 168, 170
  satisfy craving for sweets, 168-169
  scurvy and, 175-176
  sodium content of, 170
  ulcers and, 172
  vitamin A in, 169
  vitamin B absorption and, 173
  vitamin B in, 169
  vitamin C in, 169
  vitamins in, 167-168 (table),
    171 (table)
  weight increase in infants and, 175

Barley, 326

Basil, 326

Beans
availability of iron in, 326-327
hemoglobin regeneration and, 326-327
raw, 326

Beans, sprouted
consumption of, 472
cooking, 474
methods of sprouting, 473-474, 538
uses, 472
vitamin increase in, 473

Bees
life cycle of, 1003
man's respect for, 1002
reproduction, 1003
way of life, 1002
See also honey, royal jelly.

Beets
allergy to, 476
cooking, 475, 898
introduction into English diet, 475
minerals in, 476 (table)
minerals in greens, 476 (table)
oxalic acid in greens, 476
sugar in, 475
vitamin loss in cooking, 475-476
vitamins in, 476 (table)
vitamins in greens, 476 (table)

Beriberi
and the discovery of vitamins, 79
white rice and, 78, 79

Berries
descriptions of black poisonous, 180-182
descriptions of edible, 184-186
descriptions of red poisonous, 182-184
identification of, 179-180
seeds, 327

Bible
carob in, 443
chemicals in food in light of, 890-891
food restrictions in, 888, 889, 890

Biotin
avidin and, 103, 106
cancer and, 108
produced by digestive tract micro-organism, 569
symptoms of deficiency, 107-108

Black jelly bean crisis, 209

Blackouts and thiamin, 407

Blackstrap molasses
animal food, 442
food value of, 390, 442-443
in tapering off refined sugar, 443
minerals in, 390 (table), 442

vitamin B in, 390 (table), 442
what it is, 441

Bleeding gums. See pyorrhea.

Blood as food, 648

Blood pressure
coffee and, 12-13
See also hypertension.

Blood sugar
defects in mechanism of, 16
diet for attaining normal, 19
high. See diabetes.
ideal level of, 17
level in coffee addicts, 18
low. See hypoglycemia.

Blueberries, synthetic, 865

Body
main structural defects, 747
result of structural defects, 748
temperature control, 715

Bone marrow
anemia and, 962
function of, 962
homogenized whole bone for, 963
in the diet, 963
radiation and, 963

Bone meal
and fracture prevention, 960, 961
calcium-phosphorus ratio and, 968-969
case demonstrating benefits from, 960, 965-966
childbirth labor and, 970-971
compared to calcium salts, 955
composition of, 957
dental caries and, 947-948
dental caries in pregnancy and, 955-956
discovery of effect on dental caries, 947-950
during pregnancy, 953, 968
experience at an aquarium, 967
fluorine in, 972
for minerals, 957-958
"growing pains" and, 954-955
heart and, 972-973
history of use, 959-960
inexpensive, 954
in health of the sportsman, 87
osteomyelitis and, 953-954
what it is, 946
See also homogenized whole bone.

Bones
brittleness and lack of calcium, 959
composition of, 952
fracture prevention and bone meal, 960, 961
fractures from normal reflexes, 958-959

Botulism
cause of, 815
sausage and, 815

Bread
chemicals and staleness, 53
chemicals in, 52-53
conditioning of dough, 52-53
decline in consumption of, 57-58
harmful effects of, 58-59
poison ivy and, 57
white vs. whole wheat, 56

Bread, white
compared to whole wheat, 56
enriching, 577-578, 769
flavor of, 55
processing of wheat for, 47-52
skin disease and, 152
thiamin in, 769

Bread, whole wheat
amount of chemical preservatives in, 56
compared to white, 56
in food-faddism, 59

Breakfast, light, 750

Brewer's yeast
advantages of, 984
amino acids in, 978
cancer and, 979-982
can you get too much, 984-985
cocarboxylase in, 985, 986
in *The United States Dispensatory*, 983
manufacture of, 978
nutrients in, 978, 984
production of, 982-983
vitamin B in, 978 (table), 979

Broccoli and fallout, 548

Bronchial asthma
allergen testing period, 74
cases demonstrating extent of allergens, 74
cereals and, 72
characteristics of an attack, 73
drugs used for, 74-75
emotions and, 75
incidence, 73
patch tests, 73
pattern of, 73
physiological reasons for, 73
vitamin C and, 74

Brussels sprouts
cooking, 477
minerals in, 477-478 (table)
vitamin C in, 477
vitamins in, 478 (table)

Buckwheat
honey, 327
how to make cakes, 327

rutin in, 327

Butter
harm done by rancid, 97
in merry old England, 97
manufacture of, 97
minerals in, 98 (table)
summer and winter, 98
U. S. consumption, 97
vitamin A in, 98
vitamins in, 98 (table)
whipped, 97

Buttermilk
fat content, 100
manufacture of, 100

C

Cabbage
antibiotic in, 479
fallout and, 548
goiter and, 479
how to prepare, 479
juice and digestive disorders, 548-549
minerals in, 478
ulcers and, 479, 549
vitamins in, 478

Caffeine
compared to morphine, 15-16
effect in body, 7, 10, 11-12, 29
effect on embryo, 15
effect varies in different animals, 15
hyperthyroidism symptoms and, 22
in chocolate, 451
in cocoa, 451
in coffee, 6, 7-8
in cola drinks, 29, 41
in tea, 36, 37, 919
narcotic quality of, 10
ulcers and, 29

Calcium
conditions related to deficiency, 775, 951, 959, 967-968, 971
deficient in American diet, 453, 970
deficient in older people, 971, 972
effect of citric acid on, 195-196
factors affecting absorption of, 142-143, 144, 149-150, 279, 414, 452, 971
honey and retention of, 459
in bones, 717
individual need varies, 735-736
in *Pacaya,* 729
in roselle, 729
in sesame seeds, 342-343, 728
nervousness and, 752
oatmeal and body's supply of, 76
oxalic acid and, 452
past middle age, 959, 969

phosphorus use in the body and, 312
phytate and, 76
sources of, 531-532
sugar and loss of, 876
vitamin C and, 143

Calcium-phosphorus ratio
bone meal and, 968-969
factors affecting, 311-312
ideal, 406, 411-412
measuring stick of disease resistance, 411
refined sugar and, 406, 407, 412

Calories
factors affecting requirements, 753-754
requirements and activity, 753 (table)

Cancer
among American Indians, 637
among Navajo Indians, 408-409, 639, 640, 641
arsenic and, 568, 844
biotin and, 108
brewer's yeast and, 979-982
butter yellow and, 979-980
calcium deficiency and, 967-968
chemical fertilizers and, 620, 621, 638
chemicals causing, 846-853
coffee tars and, 14
cow's milk and, 134-135
deaths from, in U. S., 856
desiccated liver and, 976-977
difficulty in proving insecticides' role in, 820
digestive tract most favorable for, 854
dyes and, 596, 853-854, 856
figs and, 215
garlic and, 506
heated fats and, 687-688
heavy eating and, 758-759
hot foods and gastric, 913-914
injected estrogen and, 848
liver and, 980
natural foods and, 593-594, 595
organic fertilizers and, 620, 621
oxidation-enzyme deficiency and, 594-595
pace and, 641
paraffin and, 812-813
protein and, 46
radiation and, 883-884
refined sugar and, 412-413, 428
salt and, 280-281, 596
stilbestrol and, 211, 242, 845, 860
sulfur-containing amino acids and, 567
trace minerals and, 718-719
vitamin C and, 747-748
vitamin deficiencies and, 595, 845
See also carcinogens.

Candling, 102

Cantaloupe
inositol in, 187
minerals in, 188 (table)
vine-ripened best, 186-187
vitamin C in, 187
vitamins in, 187-188 (table)

Caraway seed, 328

Carbohydrates
become sugar in the body, 394
dental caries and, 615, 790-793
factors affecting absorption, 394
heart disease and, 416-417
periodontal diseases and, 722
premature births and, 722
proper amount in the diet, 615-616
refined, and polio, 504
in various fruits, 392, 681
in various nutritious foods, 682 (table)
in various prepared foods, 681 (table)
in various vegetables, 392, 681

Carbon dioxide
harm done by, 41
in soft drinks, 32

Carbonic acid
effect on eyes, 31-32
in soft drinks, 31-32

Carcinogens
children more susceptible to, 843-844
delayed action of, 846-847, 858
in cattle food, 864
in food, 849-850, 852-853
information on, 850
in processed cheese, 99
testing, 847-848, 851-852
tolerances for, 847
See also cancer.

Carcinophobia, 982

Cardamon, 328

Carob
alkaline reaction of, 447
chocolate substitute, 446
composition, 444
diarrhea and, 444, 446-447, 448, 449-450
history of, 448
infant vomiting and, 446
in the Bible, 443
minerals in, 444 (table), 445
nutrients, 328
sugar in, 447
sugar substitute, 431, 446
uses, 328
vitamins in, 444 (table), 445

Cocoa
  caffeine in, 451
  calcium absorption and, 452
  calories in, 451
  not for children, 454
  oxalic acid in, 452
  popularity in U. S., 451
  processing of, 451
  size of business, 450-451
  theobromine in, 451
  vitamins in, 451-452
  See also chocolate.

Coconut
  minerals in, 328
  therapeutic value of, 329

Coenzyme Q
  function of, 988-989
  sources, 988, 989
  what it is, 988

Coffee
  as a medicine, 9, 10
  as a stimulant, 13
  break, 13-14
  caffeine in, 6, 7-8
  cancer and tars of, 14
  case of addiction to, 18-19
  chemical changes by roasting, 6
  chicory added to, 8
  consumption in U. S., 8
  contents of, 6-8
  decaffeinated, 7
  during pregnancy, 15
  effect on dieting, 18, 39
  harmful effects of, 7, 9-10, 12-13, 14
  history of, 5-6
  how to make good, 7-8
  insomnia and, 5, 7
  low blood sugar and, 17-18
  research on, declined, 9
  roasting, 6
  sterility and, 9
  tannin in, 6-7
  tolerance for, 12
  tree, 5
  ulcers and, 10-12
  vitamin B in, 7
  who should give up, 16

Coffee houses
  early, 5
  reputation of, 5-6

Cogeners, 40

Cola drinks
  acidity of, 29
  caffeine in, 29, 41
  composition of, 41, 837
  teeth and, 29, 30, 32, 837
  See also soft drinks.

Colds
  bread and, 58

reduced food intake and, 759

Colon
  factors affecting, 114
  intestinal bacteria in, 114

Congenital defects
  parental diet and, 652-653
  personality problems and, 654

Constipation
  bananas and, 169, 172
  bread and, 59
  intestinal bacteria and, 114
  wheat and, 340
  yogurt and, 157-158

Cooking
  advantages of, 898-899
  disadvantages of, 899
  enzyme destruction in, 874
  herbs in, 911-912
  meats, 908-910
  methods and mineral retention, 904-905 (table)
  methods and vitamin retention, 905-906 (table)
  methods compared, 906-907, 906 (table)
  methods tested, 903-904
  of protein foods, 908-909
  vitamin loss in, 874, 898

Copper
  iron use and, 716
  nervous system disease of lambs and, 716
  poisoning and soda vending machines, 863

Coriander seeds, 329

Corn
  how American Indians used, 349-350
  how to prepare, 489-490
  Mexican processing of, 877-878
  minerals in, 490 (table)
  niacin deficiency and processed, 489
  pellagra and processed, 489
  processing of, 488
  protein in, 488-489
  raw, 329, 878, 898
  uses of, 488
  value of wet-milled, 878
  vitamins in, 490 (table)

Cornaro, Louis, 758

Corn flakes, 63

Corn oil
  cholesterol level and, 685
  in experiments on fats, 684-685
  sitosterols in, 685

Coronary thrombosis and cholesterol, 1013, 1018

[1029]

[1030]

Diabetes
among Navajo Indians, 639, 640
bananas and, 173-174
blood sugar and, 16
glucose and, 425
lecithin and, 1015
overweight and, 421-422

Diarrhea
bacterial, 507-508
bananas and, 176
carob and, 446-447, 448-449
carrot soup for infant, 481-485
foods which stop, 448
garlic and, 508-509, 510
losses through, 447, 483
mortality in infants, 481

Diet
acid-alkaline balance in, 60
calcium in American, 453
characteristics of modern, 419,
651-652
chemicals in average American,
807-809
childbirth and, 647, 649, 652-653,
657-658
civilized and disease, 409-411
dental health and, 628-636, 643, 644,
645-646, 647, 649
Dr. Hay's, 934-935
Editor Rodale's, 122-123
effect of agriculture upon, 70-71
effect of bread on, 58
effect of soft drinks on, 29
experiments on, 770-771
Eisenhower's, 798-799
evolution of man's, 69-71
experiment on all-meat, 69
factors for optimum health, 772-773
for reducing, 796-798
habits formed in childhood, 64
harm in one-sided, 781-782
high fat vs. high carbohydrate, 754
Hunzan, and health, 770-771
in Loetenschal Valley, 643-644
longevity and, 659-661
need for variety in, 178-179
of African natives, 629-633, 648-649
of American children, 799
of American Indians, 656
of Australian aborigines, 649
of average American family,
726-727, 798
of Eskimos, 646
of Navajo Indians, 639, 641
of northern Canadian Indians,
646-647
of Peruvian Indians, 650
of primitive man, 607-608
of South Pacific Islanders, 647
polio and, 504-505
primitive. See primitive diet.
time to adapt to change in, 71-72

typical English, and health, 771
wheatless, 60

Dieting
apples and, 163
bananas and, 177
danger in crash, 799-800
effect of coffee on, 18, 39
simple diet, 796-798
See also overweight.

Digestion
bread and, 58-59
enzymes in, 713-714
excessive fruit juice and, 190
garlic and, 502
intestinal bacteria in, 113-114
of protein, 933
of starches, 930-931, 933
path of, 113
process of change, 704, 713

Digestive disorders
cabbage juice and, 548-549
fennel seed and, 231
yogurt and, 156

Digestive tract
caffeine and, 11-12
carob and, 448
hot foods and, 913-914
most favorable for cancer, 854
raw food and, 899
refined sugar and strain on, 419-420,
421, 428-429

Digitalis, 345

Dill seed, 329

Disease
chemical fertilizers and, 575-576
chief causes of, 572
cost of, 732-733
definition of, 611
emotions and, 572-573
environment and, 612-613, 617
extent of, in U. S., 732
factors in, 611-612
See also degenerative disease.

Dizziness
insecticides and, 589-592
symptom of many disorders, 589
visionary disturbance and, 590-591

Dried milk, 100

Dropsy and salt, 281

Drugs
for bronchial asthma, 74-75
from poisonous seeds, 345
home remedies as basis of, 353
when to use, 762-763

Dyes
cancer-causing, in foods, 596, 853-

854, 856, 857
declared unsafe, 844-845
in dairy products, 99
in soft drinks, 33
in vitamin preparations, 855
necessity of, 856
toxicity testing of coal tar, 829

Dysentery and garlic, 500-509

Dyspepsia and garlic, 510-511

E

Earthworms
bactericidal enzymes in, 561
human consumption of, 888-889
organic matter in the soil and, 561
paralysis and, 889

Eczema
bananas and, 176
raw potatoes and, 898
unsaturated fatty acids and, 692

Edema and salt, 292-293

Eggplant
insecticides and, 491
minerals in, 492 (table)
unpopular, 490-491
vitamins in, 491 (table)

Eggs
as a seed, 381
as a symbol, 103
avidin in, 103
candling, 102
cholesterol in, 103
choline in, 104
dried, 102
eating raw, 381
essential amino acids in, 676 (table)
fertile vs. non-fertile, 380-381, 579
freshness important, 102
frozen, 102
in heart disease, 381
lecithin in, 1014, 1017
minerals in, 104 (table), 676 (table)
parts of, 102
pores in shells, 103
protein in, 101
raw egg white injury, 103, 106-110
rheumatic fever and, 104-105
sign of diseased, 159
storage, 103
vitamins in, 103-104 (table), 676
(table)

Elderberry seed, 329-330

Electric potential of plants, 379

Emotions
bronchial asthma and, 75

disease and, 572-573
heart disease and, 572
hypoglycemia and, 398

Endurance
desiccated liver and, 87, 976
wheat germ oil and, 66-67, 85

Enzymes
acidity, alkalinity and, 707
consideration in food preparation,
706
destruction of, 708, 874
discovery of, 704-705
effect of cold on, 706
effect of heat on, 706, 714
from raw foods, 708-711
function of, 705-707, 708, 712,
714-715, 988
getting enough, 710-711
in digestion, 713-714
in figs, 215
in garlic, 506-507
in human milk, 137
in saliva, 713
in wheat germ, 67-68
manufacture of, in the body, 708
minerals in, 714
naming of, 707
oxidation, and cancer, 594-595
oxidation, and chlorophyll, 594
oxidation, and vitamin B₁, 595
repeated use of, 713-714
substrate and, 506-507, 988
synthetic, unprotected, 710
synthetic, to restore natural flavor,
863
See also enzyme systems.

Enzyme systems
allergy and dysfunction of, 566-567
nature of, 566
symptoms of dysfunction, 566-567
vitamins in, 707

Epilepsy, 759

Ergotism, 336

Eskimos
canned food brings polio to, 665
dental health of, 646
diet of, 646
effect of cereals on, 71
favorite dishes of, 921
health of, 663, 664
living conditions, 646
meat only nutrient source, 663

Essential amino acids
compared in eggs, meats, soybeans,
676 (table)
from vegetables with proper
combining, 678
importance of, 239, 316, 671
in soybeans, 239, 536-537

names of, 671
why so called, 316
sources of, 671, 673-674, 678
See also amino acids, protein.

Essential fatty acids. *See* unsaturated
fatty acids.

Estrogen and cancer, 848

Eyes
effect of carbonic acid on, 31-32
good nutrition and, 377, 378
soft drinks and, 377-378
sunflower seeds and, 352, 376

F

Fairleigh-Dickinson University
nutrition experiment at, 755-757
organic method at, 755, 756

Fallout
broccoli and, 548
cabbage and, 548

Falls, 960-961

Fatigue and refined sugar, 401

Fats
advice on using, 689-690, 697-698
affinity of insecticides for, 810
animal vs. vegetable, 683, 685-686,
689, 695
cancer and heated, 687-688
classification of, 682
consumption and heart disease, 124
controversy over, 699-700
daily requirement of, 754
differences in human and cow's milk,
137
factors in consumption of, 587
hydrogenated, 688-689
importance of, 682, 687
in American diet, 682
in nuts, 267
in various animals' milk, 133
in various foods, 696-697 (table)
natural, healthful, 701
sunflower seeds for, 702
synthetic, 1014-1015
unsaturated fatty acids in, 694
(table)
unsaturated fatty acids in absorption
of, 693
vitamin destruction in heated, 687
See also animal fats, oils, vegetable
fats.

Fava bean, 345-346

Favoring one side of the body, 356-357

Fennel seed
culinary uses, 330

digestive trouble and, 231
therapeutic uses, 330

Figs
cancer and, 215
drying of, 215
enzyme in, 215
historical uses of, 214
laxative properties of, 214
minerals in, 215 (table)
preparation of, 214
seeds and constipation, 330
uses of, 214
vitamins in, 215 (table)

Fish
advantages of ocean, 252
allergy to, 254
canned, 254-255
cheap protein source, 251
danger in precooked frozen, 892
deterioration of, 253
disadvantages of inland, 252
fluorine in, 253-254
freezing of, 253
history of fish trade, 251-252
iodine in ocean, 255
minerals in, 254, 255 (table)
preserved with antibiotics, 263
protein in, 253
size of industry, 252
vitamins in, 255 (table)
See also shellfish.

Fish liver oils
excessive, dangerous, 992
experience at London Zoo, 990
fish best for, 990
in eighteenth century England,
989-990
purity important, 992
vitamin D in various, 992 (table)
vitamins A and D in, 990
who should take, 991

Fishmeal, 254

Flatulence and yogurt, 158

Flaxseed
lore concerning, 330
oil from, 330
unsaturated fatty acids in, 330
uses, 330

Fleas, 405-406

Flour
bleach and allergy, 49-50
bleach and mental illness, 50
bleach and vitamin E, 749
bleaching of, 48-49, 50
disinfectant used on, 52
economic factors in switch to
white, 88
enriching of, 51
milling, 47-48

white, and degenerative disease, 88-89
white, unfit for human consumption, 577

Fluoridated water
and tea-drinking, 37
value of, questioned, 749-750

Fluorine
dental caries and, 950
in bone meal, 972
in fish, 253-254
in many foods, 369
in raw wheat seeds, 339
in tea, 37

Folic acid in mushrooms, 519-520

Food
criteria applied to, 444
how early man obtained, 69-70, 71
minimal amount for survival, 757
restrictions in the Bible, 888, 889, 890
processed. See processed foods.
raw. See raw foods.
superstitions concerning, 920-921
tampering with, 636-637
trend to ready-mixed, 891

Food combinations
acid-alkaline balance and, 934
Dr. Hay on, 925, 932-935
Dr. Munro on, 925
Dr. Shelton on, 925, 928-932
incompatible, 933
in Nature, 926-927
natural best, 927
natural, easily handled, 930
success of, 925-926

Food processing
cholesterol threat and, 1019-1021
degenerative disease and, 876
example of, in the home, 872-876
primitive, healthful, 877-878, 891-892
types of, 871
See also processed foods.

Food supplements
energy and, 751
in infant feeding, 765-766
protein-rich, 20
vitamin B-containing, 773
why we need, 56-57, 877

Formaldehyde in plastic dishes, 915

Fruit
carbohydrate content of, 681
dental caries and, 225, 793-794, 794 (table)
for dessert, 912
insecticide residues in, 625

peeled by caustic soda, 863
protected from insecticides, 625-626
seedless, 225-226
toxicity of kernels, 181
tree-ripened best, 579
waxed, 811-813

Fruit drinks and tooth erosion, 23-24

Fruit juice
added sugar in canned, 25
digestion and excessive, 190
losses in straining, 26
more damaging than fruit, 196-197
thirst center and, 204-205
tooth erosion and, 25, 191-192
ulcers and, 192-193
unnatural food, 25

G

Galactosemia
cause of, 147
consequences of, 155
meat for victims of, 241
milk substitute for victims of, 151-152
symptoms, 147, 155

Garden cress, 233

Garlic
antibiotic power of, 493, 495, 500-501
cancer and, 506
diarrhea and, 508-509, 510
digestion and, 502, 512-513
dysentery and, 500, 509
dyspepsia and, 510-511
enzyme in, 506-507
grippe and, 515
healing powers of, 492, 499
high blood pressure and, 495-496, 497
historical use of, 492-493
in food preparation, 911
intestinal catarrh and, 500, 503
intestinal disorders and, 495, 508, 509
nutrients in, 497
perles, 493, 498, 505
polio and, 503-504
pre-cancerous lip and, 514
running nose and, 515
sore throat and, 515
tablet form, 499-500
toxemia and, 501-502
tuberculosis and, 493-495
virus and, 515

Gelatin protein, 674

Ginger, 230

Glucose
diabetes and, 425
manufacture, 425
occurrence of, 391

Goiter
cabbage and, 479
milk and, 150

Gout and cherries, 188-189

Grains
decrease of protein in, 46
seeds subject to disease-killing
poison, 46

Grape
drying of, 216
fumigation of, 216
"Grape Cure," 216
minerals in, 216 (table)
seeds, 330
sugar in, 216
U. S. production, 216
vitamins in, 216-217 (table)

Grape juice, 192, 216

Grippe
garlic and, 515

"Growing pains," 954-955

Guano, 651

Guisquil, 729

Gums, bleeding. *See* pyorrhea.

H

Hartootian, Dr. S. G., 948-951

Haughley Experiment, 558

Hay, Dr. William Howard, 925, 932-935

Heart and bone meal, 972-973

Heart disease
among Navajo Indians, 639, 640
carbohydrates and, 416-417
dairy products and, 124
eggs in, 381
emotions and, 572
fat consumption and, 124, 381
nutrition and, 871
salt and, 281-282
thiamin deficiency and, 417-418

Hemlock, 345

Hemoglobin
bananas and, 173
level in American children, 739
regeneration and beans, 326-327

regeneration and leafy vegetables.
326

Herbs
cooking with, 234-235, 431, 911-912
how to grow herbs indoors, 232-233
list of valuable, 233-234
medical use of, 234
medical uses of teas from, 235
salt substitute, 299
scientific basis for therapeutic
properties, 610
teas from, 235-236, 919

High blood pressure. *See* hypertension.

Hizato
diet compared to that of another
village, 660-661
foods eaten in, 659-660
noted for longevity, 659

Hollyhock seed, 331

Homogenization, 145

Homogenized whole bone
nutrients in, 964
processing of, 963-964
who should take, 964

Honey
adulteration of, 457, 466
alkaline reaction of, 459
amino acids in, 458
anemia and, 458-459
calcium retention and, 459
clarifying, 457
consumption in U. S., 456, 457
extracted, 456
history of use, 455-456
insecticides in, 865
minerals in, 458 (table)
naturalness of, 393
nutrients and color, 458
removing from comb, 456
strained, 456
sugar substitute, 438-439, 440, 460
therapeutic uses, 457
vitamin B in, 457 (table)
vitamin C in, 457-458
vitamin K in, 459
wild best, 579
See also royal jelly.

Hormones
body temperature control and, 715
used as weed-killers, 834

Hunza
absence of degenerative disease in,
555-556
a geologist in, 788-789
agricultural methods in, 426, 785
changes in, 786-787
contagious disease in, 785-786
diet in, 770-771, 968

Lettuce
iceberg, 533
insecticides on, 517
losses in soaking, 517
medicinal use of seed, 331
nutrients in, 517
storage of, 516-517
vitamins in, 518 (table)

Leucocytes
cooked food and increase of, 900-902, 907
critical food temperature and, 901-902, 907
function of, 900
illness and increase of, 900

Levin-Day report, 358-359

Life expectancy, 563-565, 746-747

Lima beans
cooking, 518-519
insecticides and, 518
minerals in, 519 (table)
protein in, 518
vitamins in, 519 (table)

Linoleic acid
best sources of, 698
cholesterol and, 224, 538
function of, 703
in safflower oil, 702-703
in soybeans, 538
in various foods, 696-697 (table)
in various oils, 685 (table)
pyridoxine and, 703
vitamin E and 703

Liquids at meal's end, 38-39

Liquor
substance which causes hangover, 40
synthetic around the corner, 40-41

Lithium in soft drinks, 31

Liver
cancer and, 980
disturbances of sex hormones and, 975
endocrine glands and, 975
growth and, 975-976
insecticides and, 974-975
nutrients in, 973
poisons and, 974
soaking, 977
See also desiccated liver.

Loetenschal Valley
diet in, 643-644
health in, 638
way of life in, 643-644

Longevity
diet and, 659-661, 771-772
Japanese village noted for, 659, 661

radiation and, 883
reduced food intake and, 758

Lotus seeds, 331-332

Low blood sugar. See hypoglycemia.

Low salt diet
cirrhosis of the liver and, 303-304
dropsy and, 281
effects of, 289
foods forbidden on, 282-283
getting along on, 286, 289-290
high blood pressure and, 281, 288-289
salt-free dishes, 300
unadvisable in certain diseases, 289

Lust, John B., 26-28

M

Macuy, 728

Magnesium, importance of, 313

Malocclusion
incidence of, 355
pyorrhea and, 355

Maltose
occurrence, 391
uses of, 394

Malva, 728

Maraschino cherry
FDA definition of pure, 886
indestructability of, 892-893

Margarine
chemicals in, 98
hydrogenated oils in, 683
mouth ulcers and, 893
synthetic vitamin A in, 98, 683

McCarrison, Sir Robert, 781-784, 785-786

Meals
light breakfast and efficiency, 750
light midday and efficiency, 750-751
time between, 752

Meats
calories in muscle, 244 (table)
calories in organ, 245 (table)
chemically cured bacon, 261, 262
composition of muscle, 244 (table)
composition of organ, 245 (table)
cooking of, 246, 908-910
danger in precooked, 262
danger in rare beef, 261
danger in raw, 262
danger in tainted, 263
essential amino acids in, 239, 676 (table)

in beets, 476 (table)
in blackstrap molasses, 390 (table), 442
in Brussels sprouts, 477-478 (table)
in butter, 98 (table)
in cabbage, 478
in cantaloupe, 188 (table)
in carob, 444 (table), 445
in carrots, 480 (table)
in celery, 487 (table)
in corn, 490 (table)
in cranberries, 206 (table)
in dates, 213 (table)
in eggplant, 492 (table)
in eggs, 104 (table)
in enzymes, 714
in figs, 215 (table)
in fish, 254, 255 (table)
in grapes, 216 (table)
in green leafy vegetables, 534 (table)
in honey, 458 (table), 459
in kelp, 1009 (table)
in lima beans, 519 (table)
in muscle meats, 244 (table)
in mushrooms, 520 (table)
in nuts, 271 (table)
in oatmeal, 77 (table)
in organ meats, 243 (table), 245 (table)
in peaches, 218 (table)
in peanuts, 275 (table)
in peas, 524 (table)
in peppers, 525 (table)
in pineapple, 220 (table)
in potatoes, 527 (table)
in prunes, 222 (table)
in pumpkins, 530 (table)
in rhubarb, 532 (table)
in rice germ, 81 (table)
in rose hips, 995 (table)
in seaweed, 1007-1008, 1010
in seeds, 315 (table)
in soybeans, 537 (table)
in spinach, 544 (table)
in sprouted mung beans, 474 (table)
in sprouted soybeans, 474 (table)
in strawberries, 546 (table)
in sunflower seeds, 368 (table)
in tomatoes, 548 (table)
in various grasses, 778 (table)
in watermelon, 224 (table)
in wheat germ, 83
lactose and absorption of, 115
loss in soaking, 873-874
retention and cooking method, 904-905 (table)
use and protein, 673
variation in content in vegetables, 720 (table)
vitamin D and absorption of, 958
See also trace minerals.

Mint, 233

Miscarriage
salt and, 293
vitamin E and, 90

Monkshead, 345

Mukojima
diet in, 661
noted for longevity, 661

Multiple sclerosis
absent in China, 603
chemical fertilizers and, 570, 598, 605
deaths from, by state, 599-602 (tables)
incidence of, 599, 603
nature of, 598
precipitating factors in, 598-599
soil depletion and, 598

Mung beans, sprouted
compared to sprouted soybeans, 472-473
minerals in, 474 (table)
vitamins in 472, 474 (table)

Munro, Dr. Daniel C., 925

Mushrooms
folic acid in, 519-520
minerals in, 520 (table)
poisonous, 520
reproduction, 519
vitamins in, 520 (table)

Mustard
nutrients in, 728
therapeutic uses of seed, 332

Mycobahn, 52

Mycorrhiza, 571

N

Nasturtium seeds, 332

Natural foods
appetite instinct and, 385-386, 404-405, 585-586
cancer and, 593-594, 595
difficulty in obtaining, 635
disease and, 576-580
health of people on, 410
reduce desire for sweets, 433
what are, 701
See also organically grown foods, primitive diet.

Navajo Indians
attachment to "mother earth," 639
cancer among, 408-409, 639, 640, 641
diabetes among, 639, 640

diet of, 639, 641-642
heart disease among, 639, 640
living conditions, 639, 640
tuberculosis among, 640

Nearsightedness and soft drinks, 31-32, 377-378

Nervousness
calcium and, 752
empty stomach and, 752

Niacin
deficiency and pellagra, 489
deficiency and processed corn, 489

Night blindness, 481

Nitrogen trichloride, *See* agene.

Nutmeg
appetite stimulant, 231
historical uses of, 333
intoxicating properties of, 231

Nutrition
alcoholism and, 737-738
bone defect responds to good, 761
convincing children of importance of, 87, 463
deficiencies in factory workers, 731-732
deficiency universal, 770
development and, 777
Dr. Cleave's rules of, 587-588
Dr. Stare on, 741
experiment at Fairleigh-Dickinson University, 755-757
fresh foods important in, 727
heart disease and, 871
longevity and, 771-772
mental health and, 761-762
minor aches and pains and, 761
more urgent in illness, 761
psychosomatic illness and, 799
soil fertility and, 774, 779, 783
state of, in U. S., 584, 725-726, 730-732, 742-743
survey demonstrating need for education, 733-734
test of selected children, 738-740
who finances research, 741-742, 743-744
wholeness in, 871

Nuts
advantages of, 267, 272
calories in, 267, 270-271 (table)
composition of, 270-271 (table)
cooking of, 269
definition of, 267
digestibility of, 268, 273
fat in, 267
flour from, 269-270
for dessert, 912
minerals in, 271 (table)
processing of, 268-269

protein in, 268
source of, 269
spoilage, 268
storage of, 270
synthetic, 893
toxic substances in, 267-268, 272
trace minerals in, 267
U. S. consumption of, 269
used by American Indians, 351
vitamins in, 268, 271 (table)
See also acorn, almonds, chestnuts, peanuts.

O

Oatmeal
calcium-robbing substance in, 76
consumption of, 75
minerals in, 77 (table)
processing of, 75-76
vitamins in, 77 (table)

Oils
descriptions of various, 683-684
extraction from vegetable substances, 701-702
linoleic acid in various, 685 (table)
refining of salad, 684
vegetable, and acne, 721-722

Okra seed, 333

Olive oil, 684

Onions and anemia, 521-522

Orange dye, 848-849

Organically grown foods
better drugs from, 339-340
birds choose, 57
cancer and, 620, 621
chicken egg production and, 622
dental caries and, 570, 580-581, 582-583
difficulty in demonstrating value of, 555-556
for trace minerals, 719
growth and, 621-622
Haughley experiment, 558
health and, 556-558, 562, 570, 622-623, 711
nerves and, 620-621
Peckham experiment, 556
protein in, 560
tartar on the teeth and, 581
vitamins in, 560-561, 622, 623
See also natural foods, organic method, primitive diet.

Organic matter
disease bacteria and, 561
earthworms and, 561
growth hormone factors, 560
vitamins in food and, 560-561

Organic method
advantages of, 558
at Fairleigh-Dickinson University, 755, 756
civilization and, 618-619
compared to chemical farming, 620-624
history of, 619
insecticides unnecessary, 822
plant deficiency diseases and, 623-624
provides complete fertilizer, 604-605
rejected by government, 624
soil fertility and, 576, 580
water problems and, 580
what it consists of, 619-620
See also organically grown foods, organic matter.

Osteomyelitis, 953-954

Osteoporosis, 971

Overweight
diabetes and, 421-422
refined sugar and, 415, 421
retained fluids and, 177-178
salt and, 178, 282
simple diet for reducing, 796-798
See also dieting.

Oxalic acid
calcium and, 429-430, 452
effect in the body, 531
in chocolate, 446, 452
in cocoa, 452
in rhubarb, 531
in spinach, 452, 543
in various vegetables, 530-531
refined sugar and formation of, 429

Oxidation
chlorophyll and, 594
energy process, 714-715
enzyme deficiency and cancer, 594-595
enzymes in, 715
method of control, 988
vitamin C in, 595

Oxygenation
as one grows older, 68
improper breathing and, 596
vitamin E and, 68

P

Pacaya, 729

Paraffin
cancer and, 812-813
in milk cartons, 812
in waxing fruits, 812

Parathion banned, 859

Parsley
growing, 233
in food preparation, 912
therapeutic value of, 912
value of seed, 333

Pasteurization
destruction of pathogenic bacteria by, 153-154
effectiveness of, 127
effect on milk, 153-154

Patch tests, 73

Peaches
acids in, 217
bagging for more vitamins, 217
dried, 217-218
history of, 217
insecticides in, 218
minerals in, 218 (table)
preserving, 217
ripening of, 217
storage of, 217
vitamins in, 218

Peanut butter, 272, 276

Peanuts
advantages of, 275-276
flour from, 269
keeping qualities of, 274
minerals in, 275 (table)
nutrients in, 274
oil in, 275
plant, 274
processing of, 276
products from, 274
vitamin B in, 272
vitamins in, 274-275 (table)

Pear seeds, 342

Peas
composition, 524
cooking, 523
detergent in canned, 523
eating raw, 523, 897
freezing, 522-523
freshness important, 522
history as a food, 522
minerals in, 524 (table)
protein in, 523
vitamins in, 523-524 (table)

Peckham experiment, 556

Pellagra
niacin deficiency and, 489
processed corn and, 489

Penicillin
in milk, 140, 146-147, 152, 834
organism produces vitamins, 569
sensitivity to, 139, 146
See also antibiotics.

Peony seeds, 334

diet during, 652-653, 658
interval between, 653

Price, Dr. Weston A., 638, 642-654

Primitive diet and health, 643-650, 652, 662-663, 664-666

Primitive man
diet of, 607-608
health of, compared to modern man, 608-609
quality of his food, 608
senses more acute, 322

Primitive peoples
dental health of, 409, 410
diet before conception, 410
effect of civilized diet on, 409-411, 425-426, 648-650, 657-658, 664-665

Processed foods
adulterants in, 886
consumption of, in U. S., 770
health and, 643-650
mislabeling of, 885-886

Prostate gland
unsaturated fatty acids and, 693
zinc in, 370

Protein
agene and wheat, 836
amount in foods, 670
cancer and, 46
"complete." *See* essential amino acids.
carries life, 772
composition of, 670
cost of foods high in, 251
daily requirement of, 674, 753, 754
decreasing in cereals, 46, 317
deficiency, 244, 672, 679, 721
digestibility of, from various sources, 240, 673
digestion of, 933
factors affecting absorption, 673
food supplements containing, 20
function of, 559, 669-670, 677-678
healing process and, 672-673
hypoproteinosis, 679-680
importance of, 101, 239, 316
in alfalfa, 946
in almonds, 273
in bananas, 169
in corn, 488-489
industrial uses of, 375
in eggs, 101
in fish, 253
in gelatin, 674
in lima beans, 518
in nuts, 268
in organically grown foods, 560
in peas, 523
in potatoes, 527
in sesame seeds, 343

in soybeans, 472-473
in sprouted seeds, 347
in sunflower seed meal, 373-374
in various animals' milk, 133, 137
in various nutritious foods, 682 (table)
in wheat germ, 82
mineral use and, 560, 673
muscles and, 673
seeds for added, 318
vegetable, 316-317, 679
vitamin use and, 673
See also amino acids, essential amino acids.

Prune juice
manufacture of, 221
tooth erosion and, 192

Prunes
acid reaction of, 221
cooking, 221
laxative qualities of, 221
minerals in, 222 (table)
packaging of, 221
processing of, 220-221
vitamins in, 221-222 (table)

Pruritus ani
chocolate and, 454-455
citrus fruit and, 226
citrus juices and, 194

Psyllium seed, 335-336

Pumpkin
minerals in, 530 (table)
nutrients in leaves, 728
shunned as food, 528-529
value of seeds, 529
vitamins in, 530 (table)

Pyorrhea
citrus juices and, 193
complaints accompanying, 402
malocclusion and, 355
refined sugar and, 401-402, 403
sunflower seeds and, 352-353
what it is, 403, 412

Pyridoxine
deficiency and disease, 748
in seeds, 313
linoleic acid and, 703
neuromuscular disorders and, 313
removed from flour, 749
unsaturated fatty acids and, 747

R

Radiation
accumulation of, in the body, 883
bone marrow and, 962
cancer and, 883-884

hazards of, 882
in botanical experiments, 881-882
in fruit ripening, 859
of food, 879-882
problem of waste disposal, 878-879
reproductive cells and, 884
ribonucleic acid and, 986
shortening of life and, 883
yeast and, 986-987

Raisins, 216, 435

Rapeseed, 336

Raw foods
advantages of, 899
disadvantages of, 898-899
leucocyte increase and, 900, 901
stomach ulcers and, 920
tips on using more, 902
vegetables best as, 897-898

Refining
what is lost in, 386
what it means, 386-387

Reproduction
calcium deficiency and, 775
radiation and, 884
vitamin B in, 89
vitamin E and, 89, 578
wheat germ oil and, 67

Restaurants
chemicals in food and, 865-866
nutritional mistakes in, 921
open letter to owners of, 914-920

Rheumatic fever, 104-105

Rhubarb
minerals in, 532 (table)
oxalic acid in, 531
sugar in cooking, 532
vitamins in, 532 (table)

Riboflavin
daily need, 246
sources of, 246

Ribonucleic acid, 986

Rice
advantages of wild, 79
antioxidant in, 867
consumption of, 80
enriching process, 78
losses during milling, 77-78, 80, 577
nutrients in white and brown, 78
rarity of wild, 78-79
types of, 80
white, and beriberi, 78

Rice germ
compared to other germs, 81
nutrients in, 81 (table)
uses of, 80-81

Rickets, 68

Rose hips
compared to acerola, 1001
favorite of birds, 993
in Norway, 996-998
nutrients in, 995 (table)
preservation of, 994
recipes for, 995, 998-999
taste of, 995
tips on preparing, 999
utensils in preparing, 994
vitamin C in, 994
when to pick, 994-995, 996

Roselle, 729

Royal jelly
contents of, 1003-1004
food of queen bee, 1003
pantothenic acid in, 1004
production of, 1003
publicity about, 1002

Running nose, 515

Rye seeds, 340

S

Saccharin
acute urticaria and, 460-461
symptoms of overdose, 461
toxicity of, 461-462
what it is, 461

Safflower oil
cholesterol and, 703
extraction of, 702
linoleic acid in, 702-703

Saffron, 229

Saliva
diluted by water, 931
in starch digestion, 423, 712-713, 930-931
resists tooth erosion, 24-25, 196

Salk vaccine, 504

Salt
Addison's disease and, 283
adrenal gland and, 286
bacteria in, 280
baldness and, 296-298
calcium use and excess, 279
cancer and, 280-281, 596
chemicals in, 280
chemicals which remove, 280
consumption of, 287, 298
deafness and, 282
dropsy and, 281
edema and, 292-293
effect on thirst, 39

fluid retention and, 178, 280, 292
getting along without, 285, 287, 289-290
harmfulness of, 915-916
heart disease and, 281-282
heat and, 283
hidden, 300, 805
high blood pressure and, 281, 287, 288-289
how much should you eat, 279, 290
hyperacidity and excess, 279
in common foods, 291 (table), 295-296 (table)
insomnia and, 298-299
irritating properties of, 279-280
kidneys and, 285-286
labor in childbirth and, 282
miscarriage and, 293
necessity of added, 284-285, 292
overweight and, 178, 282
pregnancy complications and, 292-294
sleepwalking and, 298
refining of, 304-305, 306-307
sausage spoilage and, 815
substitute, 283, 290-291, 299, 308, 886-887
See also, low salt diet; salt, iodized; salt, sea.

Salt, iodized
acne and, 302-303
a drug, 1008
hypersensitivity to iodine and, 301-302
hyperthyroidism and, 301
potassium iodide loss in, 302
reason for, 300

Salt, sea
advantages of kelp over, 308
for trace minerals, 305-306
nutritional benefits of, 307
substitute for refined, 308

Saturated fatty acids in various foods, 696-697 (table)

Sausage
casings and spoilage, 816
difficult to detect spoiled, 816
in botulism outbreaks, 815
manufacture of synthetic casings, 818
seaweed for casings, 1012
testing spoilage of, 815

Scented geraniums, 234

Scurvy
bananas and, 175-176
symptoms of, 194, 997
vitamin C and, 997

Sea salt. See salt, sea.

Sea water
benefits from, 305-306

similar to body fluids, 305, 306

Seaweed
advantages over land crops, 1010
animal food, 1005-1006, 1011-1012
as ice cream filler, 890
description of, 1006
for sausage casings, 1012
human consumption of, 1005
intestinal bacteria digest, 1005
iodine in, 1010-1011
medicinal use of, 1012
minerals in, 1007-1008, 1010
vitamins in, 1011
See also kelp.

Seeds
best food elements in, 319
composition of various, 315 (table)
consistency of quality in, 320
descriptions of poisonous, 345-346
for added protein, 318
for snacks, 318
for strengthening the mind, 322-323
in Biblical times, 322
in diet of more intelligent animals, 321-322
in history, 322-323
iron in, 312
keeping qualities of, 318-319
leafy foods complement, 311
lecithin in, 314
magnesium in, 313
minerals in, 315 (table)
miscellany on various, 324-337
Nature's method of protecting, 344
phosphorus in, 311, 321
poisonous, in drug manufacture, 345
pyridoxine in, 313
unsaturated fatty acids in, 314
value of, 314, 318, 319, 320-321, 380
vitamin B in, 313
vitamins in, 315 (table)

Seeds, sprouted
advantages of, 346-347
best, 348
ideal sprout sizes, 347-348
methods of sprouting, 348
protein in, 347
vitamin B in, 346-347
vitamin C in, 346

Senna seeds, 336

Sesame seeds
calcium in, 342-343, 728
flavor of, 343
lecithin in, 343
milk from, 155, 344
protein in, 343
unsaturated fatty acids in, 343
uses, 336
vitamin B in, 343
vitamin E in, 343

[1048]

incidence and dental caries incidence, 644

more plentiful in staked tomatoes, 547, 549-550
polio and, 504
problem of getting enough, 993, 997
scurvy and, 997
sources of, 941, 1000

Vitamin D
and effect of phytate, 76
daily requirement, 942
importance of, 942, 991
in mushrooms, 520
in fish liver oils, 992 (table)
mineral absorption and, 958
overdose dangerous, 992
sources of, 942

Vitamin E
baseball team's success with, 86
deficiency and disease, 748
destruction of, 749, 942
discovery of, 88
effect on race horses, 86
importance of, 86, 313, 370, 942
in sesame seeds, 343
in sunflower seeds, 370
in sunflower seed oil, 686
in wheat germ, 86
linoleic acid and, 703
menopausal discomfort and, 91
muscles and, 505
occurrence in foods, 93
oxygenation and, 68
reproduction and, 89-90, 578
sources of, 942, 943
spices and, 749
sterility and, 89-90
unsaturated fatty acids and, 747

Vitamin F
See unsaturated fatty acids.

Vitamin K
destruction of, 943
importance of, 943
in carrot greens, 872
in honey, 459
sources of, 943

Vitamin P
importance of, 943
sources of, 943

Vomiting and carob, 446

W

Watermelon
choosing a, 224
history of use, 222-223
kidneys and seed, 337
minerals in, 224 (table)
popularity of, 222, 223

therapeutic value, 223
vitamin C content, 223
vitamins in, 224 (table)

Waxed containers
cancer and, 812-813
wide use of, 813

Waxing produce
added substances in, 812
danger in, 811-812
paraffin in, 812
purpose of, 812

Weed-killers
may kill other crops, 46
necessity for, 46-47

Wheat
allergies and, 59
asthma and, 59
chemicals in flour from, 614
constipating properties of, 340
dental caries and, 59
dysfunctions caused by, 58-59
fattening properties of, 58
grain, 82 (illus.)
losses in processing, 48, 614
poison used to prevent spoilage, 47
seed subjected to poison, 46
steel roller milling process, 47-48
try a diet without, 60

Wheat germ
added to foods, 83-84
cooked, 84
economic reasons for removal, 88
effect on athletes, 85
enzymes in, 67-68
flakes, 84
in breaking cold cereal habit, 65
iron in, 82-83
minerals in, 83
nutrients in, 48
protein in, 82
rickets and, 68
storage of, 83
toasted, 84
value of, 578
vitamin B in, 83
vitamin E in, 86
what it is, 82

Wheat germ oil
abortion and, 90-91
endurance and, 66-67, 85, 751
how it is produced, 84
in the daily diet, 92
iron supplements and, 92
muscular dystrophy and, 67
neuromuscular disorders and, 68
rancid ineffective, 92
reproductive function and, 67, 91-92
seasonal need for, 92

Wheat, raw seeds
complete food, 339
eating, 338
fluorine in, 339
vitamin retention in, 339

Whey
advantages of, 158
constituents of, 100
intestinal tract and, 100
what it is, 158

Whole wheat bread. *See* bread, whole wheat.

Wine as antiseptic, 40

See also brewer's yeast.

Yierbabuena, 728

Yogurt
acidophilus milk added to, 156
advantages over milk, 157
constipation and, 157-158
digestibility of, 157
digestive disorders and, 156
effect on digestion, 157
flatulence and, 158
gastroenteritis and, 158
how to make, 158
qualities of, 156
what it is, 156

Yucca flowers, 728

Y

Yakimochi, 659-660

Yeast
radiation and, 986-987
ribonucleic acid in, 986

Z

Zinc
in various foods, 370 (table)
prostate gland and, 370